The Oxford Russian Minidictionary

Edited by
Della Thompson

OXFORD
UNIVERSITY PRESS

Great Clarendon Street, Oxford OX2 6DP

Oxford University Press is a department of the University of Oxford. It furthers the University's objective of excellence in research, scholarship, and education by publishing worldwide in

Oxford New York

Auckland Bangkok Buenos Aires Cape Town Chennai Dar es Salaam Delhi Hong Kong Istanbul Karachi Kolkata Kuala Lumpur Madrid Melbourne Mexico City Mumbai Nairobi São Paulo Shanghai Taipei Tokyo Toronto

Published in the United States by Oxford University Press Inc., New York

First published 1995
Reissued with corrections 1997
Revised edition 2002

British Library Cataloguing in Publication Data

Data available

Library of Congress Cataloging in Publication Data

The Oxford Russian minidictionary / edited by Della Thompson.—Rev. ed.
p. cm.
1. Russian language—Dictionaries—English. 2. English language—Dictionaries—Russian. I. Thompson, Della.
PG2640.O94 2002 491.73'21—dc21 2002072577

ISBN 0-19-860543-9

10 9 8 7 6 5 4

Printed in Great Britain by
Charles Letts & Co Ltd, Dalkeith, Scotland

OXFORD
UNIVERSITY PRESS

Great Clarendon Street, Oxford OX2 6DP

Oxford University Press is a department of the University of Oxford. It furthers the University's objective of excellence in research, scholarship, and education by publishing worldwide in

Oxford New York

Auckland Bangkok Buenos Aires Cape Town Chennai
Dar es Salaam Delhi Hong Kong Istanbul Karachi Kolkata
Kuala Lumpur Madrid Melbourne Mexico City Mumbai Nairobi
São Paulo Shanghai Taipei Tokyo Toronto

Oxford is a registered trade mark of Oxford University Press in the UK and in certain other countries

Published in the United States
by Oxford University Press Inc., New York

First published 1995
Reissued with corrections 1997
Revised edition 2002

British Library Cataloguing in Publication Data

Data available

Library of Congress Cataloging in Publication Data

The Oxford Russian minidictionary / edited by Della Thompson.—Rev. ed.
p. cm.
1. Russian language—Dictionaries—English. 2. English language—Dictionaries—Russian. I. Thompson, Della.
PG2640.O94 2002 491.73'21—dc21 2002072577

ISBN 0-19-860543-9

10 9 8 7 6 5 4

Printed in Great Britain by
Charles Letts & Co Ltd, Dalkeith, Scotland

The Oxford Russian Minidictionary

Edited by
Della Thompson

Contents

Preface

The Oxford Russian Minidictionary is designed primarily for English-speaking users. It provides a handy yet extremely comprehensive reference work for students of Russian, tourists, and business people.

Particular attention has been given to the provision of inflected forms where these cause difficulty, and to showing the stressed syllable of every Russian word as well as changes in stress where they occur. Perfective and imperfective aspects are distinguished and both are given wherever appropriate.

Thanks are due to Alexander and Nina Levtov for their editorial help and valuable advice on contemporary Russian usage.

D.J.T.

Introduction

In order to save space, related words are often grouped together in paragraphs, as are cross-references and compound entries.

The swung dash (~) and the hyphen are also used to save space. The swung dash represents the headword preceding it in bold, or the preceding Russian word, e.g. **Georgian** *n* грузи́н, ~ка. The hyphen is mainly used, in giving grammatical forms, to stand for part of the preceding, or (less often) following, Russian word, e.g. **приходи́ть** (-ожу́, -о́дишь).

Russian headwords are followed by inflexional information where considered necessary. So-called regular inflexions for the purpose of this dictionary are listed in the Appendices.

Where a noun ending is given but not labelled in the singular, it is the genitive ending; other cases are named; in the plural, where cases are identifiable by their endings, they are not labelled, e.g. **сестра́** (*pl* сёстры, сестёр, сёстрам). The gender of Russian nouns can usually be deduced from their endings and it is indicated only in exceptional cases (e.g. for masculine nouns in **-а, -я,** and **-ь,** neuter nouns in **-мя,** and all indeclinable nouns).

Verbs are labelled *impf* or *pf* to show their aspect. Where a perfective verb is formed by the addition of a prefix to the imperfective, this is shown at the headword by a light vertical stroke, e.g. **про|лепета́ть.** When a verb requires the use of a case other than the accusative, this is indicated, e.g. **маха́ть** *impf*, **махну́ть** *pf* + *instr* wave, brandish.

Both the comma and the ampersand (&) are used to show alternatives, e.g. **хоте́ть** + *gen*, *acc* means that the Russian verb may govern either the genitive or accusative; **сирота́** *m* & *f* orphan means that the Russian noun is treated as masculine or feminine according to the sex of the person denoted; **Cossack** *n* каза́к, -а́чка represents the masculine and feminine translations of Cossack; **dilate** *vt* & *i* расширя́ть(ся) means that the Russian verb forms cover both the transitive and intransitive English verbs.

Stress

The stress of Russian words is shown by an acute accent over the vowel of the stressed syllable. The vowel **ё** has no stress-mark since it is almost always stressed. The presence of two stress-marks indicates that either of the marked syllables may be stressed.

Changes of stress in inflexion are shown, e.g.

i) **предложи́ть** (-жу́, -жишь)

The absence of a stress-mark on the second person singular indicates that the stress is on the preceding syllable and that the rest of the conjugation is stressed in this way.

ii) **нача́ть** (..............; на́чал, -а́, -о)

The final form, на́чало, takes the stress of the first of the two preceding forms when these differ from each other. Forms that are not shown, here на́чали, are stressed like the last form given.

iii) **дождь** (-дя́)

The single form given in brackets is the genitive singular and all other forms have the same stressed syllable.

iv) **душа́** (*acc* -у; *pl* -и)

If only one case-labelled form is given in the singular, it is an exception to the regular paradigm. If only one plural form is given (the nominative), the rest follow this. In other words, in this example, the accusative singular and all the plural forms have initial stress.

v) **скоба́** (*pl* -ы, -а́м)

In the plural, forms that are not shown (here instrumental and prepositional) are stressed like the last form given.

Proprietary terms

This dictionary includes some words which are, or are asserted to be, proprietary names or trade marks. Their inclusion does not imply that they have acquired for legal purposes a non-proprietary or general significance, nor is any other judgement implied concerning their legal status. In cases where the editor has some evidence that a word is used as a proprietary name or trade mark this is indicated by the label *propr,* but no judgement concerning the legal status of such words is made or implied thereby.

Abbreviations used in the Dictionary

abbr	abbreviation	eccl	ecclesiastical
abs	absolute	econ	economics
acc	accusative	electr	electricity
adj, adjs	adjective(s)	electron	electronics
adv, advs	adverb(s)	emph	emphatic
aeron	aeronautics	esp	especially
agric	agriculture	etc.	etcetera
anat	anatomy		
approx	approximate(ly)	f	feminine
archaeol	archaeology	fig	figurative
archit	architecture	fut	future (tense)
astron	astronomy		
attrib	attributive	gen	genitive
aux	auxiliary	geog	geography
		geol	geology
bibl	biblical	geom	geometry
biol	biology	gram	grammar
bot	botany		
		hist	historical
chem	chemistry		
cin	cinema(tography)	imper	imperative
coll	colloquial	impers	impersonal
collect	collective(ly)	impf	imperfective
comb	combination	indecl	indeclinable
comm	commerce	indef	indefinite
comp	comparative	indet	indeterminate
comput	computing	inf	infinitive
conj, conjs	conjunction(s)	instr	instrumental
cul	culinary	int	interjection
		interrog	interrogative
dat	dative		
def	definite	ling	linguistics
derog	derogatory	loc	locative
det	determinate		
dim	diminutive	m	masculine

math	mathematics
med	medicine
meteorol	meteorology
mil	military
mus	music
n	noun
naut	nautical
neg	negative
neut	neuter
nn	nouns
nom	nominative
o.s.	oneself
parl	parliamentary
part	participle
partl	particle
pers	person
pf	perfective
philos	philosophy
phon	phonetics
phot	photography
phys	physics
pl	plural
polit	political
poss	possessive
predic	predicate; predicative
pref	prefix
prep	preposition; prepositional
pres	present (tense)
pron, prons	pronoun(s)

propr	proprietary term
psych	psychology
refl	reflexive
rel	relative
relig	religion; religious
rly	railway
sb	substantive
sg	singular
sl	slang
s.o.	someone
sth	something
superl	superlative
tech	technical
tel	telephony
theat	theatre
theol	theology
univ	university
usu	usually
v	verb
v aux	auxiliary verb
vbl	verbal
vi	intransitive verb
voc	vocative
vt	transitive verb
vulg	vulgar
vv	verbs
zool	zoology

A

а[1] *conj* and, but; **а (не) тó** or else, otherwise.
а[2] *int* oh, ah.
абажýр lampshade.
аббáтство abbey.
аббревиатýра abbreviation.
абзáц indention; paragraph.
абонемéнт subscription, season ticket. **абонéнт** subscriber.
аборигéн aborigine.
абóрт abortion; **дéлать** *impf*, **с~** *pf* **~** have an abortion.
абрикóс apricot.
абсолю́тно *adv* absolutely. **абсолю́тный** absolute.
абстрáктный abstract.
абсýрд absurdity; the absurd. **абсýрдный** absurd.
абсцéсс abscess.
авангáрд advanced guard; vanguard; avant-garde. **авангáрдный** avant-garde. **аванпóст** outpost; forward position.
авáнс advance (*of money*); *pl* advances, overtures. **авáнсом** *adv* in advance, on account.
авансцéна proscenium.
авантю́ра (*derog*) adventure; venture; escapade; shady enterprise. **авантюри́ст** (*derog*) adventurer. **авантюри́стка** (*derog*) adventuress. **авантю́рный** adventurous; adventure.
авари́йный breakdown; emergency. **авáрия** accident, crash; breakdown.
áвгуст August. **áвгустовский** August.
áвиа *abbr* (*of* **авиапóчтой**) by airmail.
авиа- *abbr in comb* (*of* **авиациóнный**) air-, aero-; aircraft; aviation. **авиакомпáния** airline. **~ли́ния** air-route, airway. **~нóсец** (-сца) aircraft carrier. **~пóчта** airmail.
авиациóнный aviation; flying; aircraft. **авиáция** aviation; aircraft; air-force.
авокáдо *neut indecl* avocado (pear).
авóсь *adv* perhaps; **на ~** at random, on the off-chance.
австрали́ец (-и́йца), **австрали́йка** Australian. **австрали́йский** Australian. **Австрáлия** Australia.
австри́ец (-и́йца), **австри́йка** Austrian. **австри́йский** Austrian. **Áвстрия** Austria.
авто- *in comb* self-; auto-; automatic; motor-. **автобáза** motor-transport depot. **~биографи́ческий** autobiographical. **~биогрáфия** autobiography; curriculum vitae. **автóбус** bus. **~вокзáл** bus-station. **автóграф** autograph. **~заправочная стáнция** petrol station. **~крáт** autocrat. **~крати́ческий** autocratic. **~крáтия** autocracy. **~магистрáль** motorway. **~маши́на** motor vehicle. **~моби́ль** *m* car. **~нóмия**

autonomy. **~но́мный** autonomous; self-contained. **~пило́т** automatic pilot. **~портре́т** self-portrait. **~ру́чка** fountain-pen. **~ста́нция** bus-station. **~стра́да** motorway.
автома́т slot-machine; automatic device, weapon, etc.; sub-machine gun; robot; **(телефо́н-)~** public call-box.
автоматиза́ция automation.
автоматизи́ровать *impf* & *pf* automate; make automatic.
автомати́ческий automatic.
а́втор author; composer; inventor; (*fig*) architect.
авторизо́ванный authorized.
авторите́т authority. **авторите́тный** authoritative.
а́вторск|ий author's; **~ий гонора́р** royalty; **~ое пра́во** copyright. **а́вторство** authorship.
ага́ *int* aha; yes.
аге́нт agent. **аге́нтство** agency. **агенту́ра** (network of) agents.
агита́тор agitator, propagandist; canvasser. **агитацио́нный** propaganda. **агита́ция** propaganda, agitation; campaign. **агити́ровать** *impf* (*pf* **с~**) agitate, campaign; (try to) persuade, win over. **агитпу́нкт** *abbr* agitation centre.
аго́ния agony.
агра́рный agrarian.
агрега́т aggregate; unit.
агресси́вный aggressive. **агре́ссия** aggression. **агре́ссор** aggressor.
агроно́м agronomist. **агроно́мия** agriculture.
ад (*loc* -ý) hell.
ада́птер adapter; (*mus*) pick-up.
адвока́т lawyer. **адвокату́ра** legal profession; lawyers.
администрати́вный administrative. **администра́тор** administrator; manager. **администра́ция** administration; management.
адмира́л admiral.
а́дрес (*pl* -á) address. **адреса́т** addressee. **а́дресн|ый** address; **~ая кни́га** directory.
адресова́ть *impf* & *pf* address, send.
а́дский infernal, hellish.
адъюта́нт aide-de-camp; **ста́рший ~** adjutant.
ажу́рн|ый delicate, lacy; **~ая рабо́та** openwork; tracery.
аза́рт heat; excitement; fervour, ardour, passion. **аза́ртн|ый** venturesome; heated; **~ая игра́** game of chance.
а́збука alphabet; ABC.
Азербайджа́н Azerbaijan. **азербайджа́нец** (-нца), **азербайджа́нка** Azerbaijani. **азербайджа́нский** Azerbaijani.
азиа́т, ~ка Asian. **азиа́тский** Asian, Asiatic. **А́зия** Asia.
азо́т nitrogen.
а́ист stork.
ай *int* oh; oo.
а́йсберг iceberg.
акаде́мик academician. **академи́ческий** academic. **акаде́мия** academy.
аквала́нг aqualung.
акваре́ль water-colour.
аква́риум aquarium.
акведу́к aqueduct.
акклиматизи́ровать *impf* & *pf* acclimatize; **~ся** become acclimatized.
аккомпанеме́нт accompaniment; **под ~+*gen*** to the accompaniment of. **аккомпаниа́тор**

accompanist. **аккомпани́ровать** *impf +dat* accompany.
аккóрд chord.
аккордеóн accordion.
аккóрдн|ый by agreement; **~ая рабóта** piece-work.
аккредити́в letter of credit. **аккредитовáть** *impf & pf* accredit.
аккумуля́тор accumulator.
аккурáтный neat, careful; punctual; exact, thorough.
акри́л acrylic. **акри́ловый** acrylic.
акробáт acrobat.
аксессуáр accessory; (stage) props.
аксиóма axiom.
акт act; deed, document; **обвини́тельный ~** indictment.
актёр actor.
акти́в (*comm*) asset(s).
активизáция stirring up, making (more) active. **активизи́ровать** *impf & pf* make (more) active, stir up. **акти́вный** active.
акти́ровать *impf & pf* (*pf also* **с~**) register, record, presence or absence of; (*sl*) write off.
áктовый зал assembly hall.
актри́са actress.
актуáльный topical, urgent.
акýла shark.
акýстика acoustics. **акусти́ческий** acoustic.
акушéр obstetrician. **акушéрка** midwife.
акцéнт accent, stress. **акценти́ровать** *impf & pf* accent; accentuate.
акционéр shareholder. **акционéрный** joint-stock. **áкция**[1] share; *pl* stock. **áкция**[2] action.
áлгебра algebra.
áлиби *neut indecl* alibi.
алимéнты (*pl*; *gen* -ов) (*law*) maintenance.
алкоголи́зм alcoholism. **алкогóлик** alcoholic. **алкогóль** *m* alcohol. **алкогóльный** alcoholic.
аллегóрия allegory.
аллерги́я allergy.
аллéя avenue; path, walk.
аллигáтор alligator.
аллó hello! (*on telephone*).
алмáз diamond.
алтáрь (-я́) *m* altar; chancel, sanctuary.
алфави́т alphabet. **алфави́тный** alphabetical.
áлчный greedy, grasping.
áлый scarlet.
альбóм album; sketch-book.
альманáх literary miscellany; almanac.
альпи́йский Alpine. **альпини́зм** mountaineering. **альпини́ст, альпини́стка** (mountain-)climber.
альт (-á; *pl* -ы́) alto; viola.
альтернати́ва alternative. **альтернати́вный** alternative.
альтруисти́ческий altruistic.
алюми́ний aluminium.
амазóнка Amazon; horsewoman; riding-habit.
амбáр barn; storehouse, warehouse.
амби́ция pride; arrogance.
амбулатóрия out-patients' department; surgery. **амбулатóрный больнóй** *sb* out-patient.
Амéрика America. **америкáнец** (-нца), **америкáнка** American. **америкáнский** American; US.
аминокислотá amino acid.
ами́нь *m* amen.

аммиа́к ammonia.
амни́стия amnesty.
амора́льный amoral; immoral.
амортиза́тор shock-absorber. **амортиза́ция** depreciation; shock-absorption.
ампе́р (*gen pl* ампе́р) ampere.
ампута́ция amputation. **ампути́ровать** *impf* & *pf* amputate.
амфетами́н amphetamine.
амфи́бия amphibian.
амфитеа́тр amphitheatre; circle.
ана́лиз analysis; ~ **кро́ви** blood test. **анализи́ровать** *impf* & *pf* analyse. **анали́тик** analyst. **аналити́ческий** analytic(al).
ана́лог analogue. **аналоги́чный** analogous. **анало́гия** analogy.
анана́с pineapple.
анархи́ст, ~ка anarchist. **анархи́ческий** anarchic. **ана́рхия** anarchy.
анатоми́ческий anatomical. **анато́мия** anatomy.
анахрони́зм anachronism. **анахрони́ческий** anachronistic.
анга́р hangar.
а́нгел angel. **а́нгельский** angelic.
анги́на sore throat.
англи́йск|ий English; **~ая була́вка** safety-pin. **англича́нин** (*pl* -ча́не, -ча́н) Englishman. **англича́нка** Englishwoman. **А́нглия** England, Britain.
анекдо́т anecdote, story; funny thing.
анеми́я anaemia.
анестезио́лог anaesthetist. **анестези́ровать** *impf* & *pf* anaesthetize. **анестези́рующее сре́дство** anaesthetic.
анестези́я anaesthesia.
анке́та questionnaire, form.
аннекси́ровать *impf* & *pf* annex. **анне́ксия** annexation.
аннули́ровать *impf* & *pf* annul; cancel, abolish.
анома́лия anomaly. **анома́льный** anomalous.
анони́мка anonymous letter. **анони́мный** anonymous.
анонси́ровать *impf* & *pf* announce.
анаре́ксия anorexia.
анса́мбль *m* ensemble; company, troupe.
антагони́зм antagonism.
Анта́рктика the Antarctic.
анте́нна antenna; aerial.
антибио́тик antibiotic(s).
антидепресса́нт antidepressant.
антиква́р antiquary; antique-dealer. **антиквариа́т** antique-shop. **антиква́рный** antiquarian; antique.
антило́па antelope.
антипа́тия antipathy.
антисемити́зм anti-Semitism. **антисеми́тский** anti-Semitic.
антисе́птик antiseptic. **антисепти́ческий** antiseptic.
антите́зис (*philos*) antithesis.
антите́ло (*pl* -а́) antibody.
антифри́з antifreeze.
анти́чность antiquity. **анти́чный** ancient, classical.
антоло́гия anthology.
антра́кт interval.
антраци́т anthracite.
антреко́т entrecôte, steak.
антрепренёр impresario.
антресо́ли (*pl*; *gen* -ей) mezzanine; shelf.
антропо́лог anthropologist. **антропологи́ческий** anthropological. **антрополо́гия** anthropology.

анфила́да suite (of rooms). **анчо́ус** anchovy. **аншла́г** 'house full' notice. **апартеи́д** apartheid. **апати́чный** apathetic. **апа́тия** apathy. **апелли́ровать** *impf & pf* appeal. **апелляцио́нный суд** Court of Appeal. **апелля́ция** appeal. **апельси́н** orange; orange-tree. **апельси́нный, апельси́новый** orange. **аплоди́ровать** *impf +dat* applaud. **аплодисме́нты** *m pl* applause. **апло́мб** aplomb. **Апока́липсис** Revelation. **апокалипти́ческий** apocalyptic. **апо́стол** apostle. **апостро́ф** apostrophe. **аппара́т** apparatus; machinery, organs. **аппарату́ра** apparatus, gear; (*comput*) hardware. **аппара́тчик** operator; apparatchik. **аппе́ндикс** appendix. **аппендици́т** appendicitis. **аппети́т** appetite; **прия́тного ~а!** bon appétit! **аппети́тный** appetizing. **апре́ль** *m* April. **апре́льский** April. **апте́ка** chemist's. **апте́карь** *m* chemist. **апте́чка** medicine chest; first-aid kit. **ара́б, ара́бка** Arab. **ара́бский** Arab, Arabic. **арави́йский** Arabian. **аранжи́ровать** *impf & pf* (*mus*) arrange. **аранжиро́вка** (*mus*) arrangement. **ара́хис** peanut. **арби́тр** arbitrator. **арбитра́ж** arbitration. **арбу́з** water-melon. **аргуме́нт** argument. **аргумента́ция** reasoning; arguments. **аргументи́ровать** *impf & pf* argue, (try to) prove. **аре́на** arena, ring. **аре́нда** lease. **аренда́тор** tenant. **аре́ндная пла́та** rent. **арендова́ть** *impf & pf* rent. **аре́ст** arrest. **арестова́ть** *pf*, **аресто́вывать** *impf* arrest; seize, sequestrate. **аристокра́т, ~ка** aristocrat. **аристократи́ческий** aristocratic. **аристокра́тия** aristocracy. **арифме́тика** arithmetic. **арифмети́ческий** arithmetical. **а́рия** aria. **а́рка** arch. **А́рктика** the Arctic. **аркти́ческий** arctic. **армату́ра** fittings; reinforcement; armature. **армату́рщик** fitter. **арме́йский** army. **Арме́ния** Armenia. **а́рмия** army. **армяни́н** (*pl* -я́не, -я́н), **армя́нка** Armenian. **армя́нский** Armenian. **арома́т** scent, aroma. **ароматерапи́я** aromatherapy. **арома́тный** aromatic, fragrant. **арсена́л** arsenal. **арте́рия** artery. **арти́куль** *m* (*gram*) article. **артилле́рия** artillery. **арти́ст, ~ка** artiste, artist; expert. **артисти́ческий** artistic. **артри́т** arthritis. **а́рфа** harp. **архаи́ческий** archaic. **арха́нгел** archangel. **архео́лог** archaeologist. **археологи́ческий** archaeological. **археоло́гия** archaeology. **архи́в** archives. **архиви́ст**

archivist. **архи́вный** archive, archival.

архиепи́скоп archbishop. **архиере́й** bishop.

архипела́г archipelago.

архите́ктор architect. **архитекту́ра** architecture. **архитекту́рный** architectural.

арши́н arshin (*71 cm.*).

асбе́ст asbestos.

асимметри́чный asymmetrical. **асимметри́я** asymmetry.

аске́т ascetic. **аскети́зм** asceticism. **аскети́ческий** ascetic.

асоциа́льный antisocial.

аспира́нт, ~ка post-graduate student. **аспиранту́ра** post-graduate course.

аспири́н aspirin

ассамбле́я assembly.

ассигна́ция banknote.

ассимиля́ция assimilation.

ассисте́нт assistant; junior lecturer, research assistant.

ассортиме́нт assortment.

ассоциа́ция association. **ассоцийровать** *impf* & *pf* associate.

а́стма asthma. **астмати́ческий** asthmatic.

астро́лог astrologer. **астроло́гия** astrology.

астрона́вт astronaut. **астроно́м** astronomer. **астрономи́ческий** astronomical. **астроно́мия** astronomy.

асфа́льт asphalt.

ата́ка attack. **атакова́ть** *impf* & *pf* attack.

атама́н ataman (*Cossack chieftain*); (gang-)leader.

атеи́зм atheism. **атеи́ст** atheist.

ателье́ *neut indecl* studio; atelier.

а́тлас[1] atlas.

атла́с[2] satin. **атла́сный** satin.

атле́т athlete; strong man. **атле́тика** athletics. **атлети́ческий** athletic.

атмосфе́ра atmosphere. **атмосфе́рный** atmospheric.

а́том atom. **а́томный** atomic.

атташе́ *m indecl* attaché.

аттеста́т testimonial; certificate; pedigree. **аттестова́ть** *impf* & *pf* attest; recommend.

аттракцио́н attraction; sideshow; star turn.

ау́ *int* hi, cooee.

аудито́рия auditorium, lecture-room.

аукцио́н auction.

ау́л aul (*Caucasian or Central Asian village*).

аутопсия autopsy.

афе́ра speculation, trickery. **афери́ст** speculator, trickster.

афи́ша placard, poster.

афори́зм aphorism.

А́фрика Africa. **африка́нец** (-нца), **африка́нка** African. **африка́нский** African.

аффе́кт fit of passion; temporary insanity.

ах *int* ah, oh. **а́хать** *impf* (*pf* **а́хнуть**) sigh; exclaim; gasp.

аэро|вокза́л air terminal. **~дина́мика** aerodynamics. **~дро́м** aerodrome, air-field. **~зо́ль** *m* aerosol. **~по́рт** (*loc* -у́) airport.

Б

б *partl*: *see* **бы**

ба́ба (*coll*) (old) woman; **сне́жная ~** snowman.

ба́бочка butterfly.

ба́бушка grandmother; grandma.

бага́ж (-а́) luggage. **бага́жник**

carrier; luggage-rack; boot. **багáжный вагóн** luggage-van.
багóр (-грá) boat-hook.
багрóвый crimson, purple.
бадминтóн badminton.
бáза base; depot; basis; **~ дáнных** database.
базáр market; din.
бáзис base; basis.
байдáрка canoe.
бáйка flannelette.
бак[1] tank, cistern.
бак[2] forecastle.
бакалáвр (*univ*) bachelor.
бакалéйный grocery. **бакалéя** groceries.
бáкен buoy.
бакенбáрды (*pl*; *gen* -бáрд) side-whiskers.
баклажáн (*gen pl* -ов *or* -жáн) aubergine.
бактéрия bacterium.
бал (*loc* -ý; *pl* -ы́) dance, ball.
балагáн farce.
балалáйка balalaika.
балáнс (*econ*) balance.
баланси́ровать *impf* (*pf* **с~**) balance; keep one's balance.
балбéс booby.
балдахи́н canopy.
балери́на ballerina. **балéт** ballet.
бáлка[1] beam, girder.
бáлка[2] gully.
балкóн balcony.
балл mark (*in school*); degree; force; **вéтер в пять ~ов** wind force 5.
баллáда ballad.
баллáст ballast.
баллóн container, carboy, cylinder; balloon tyre.
баллоти́ровать *impf* vote; put to the vote; **~ся** stand, be a candidate (**в** *or* **на**+*acc* for).
баловáть *impf* (*pf* **из~**) spoil, pamper; **~ся** play about, get up to tricks; amuse o.s. **баловствó** spoiling; mischief.
Балти́йское мóре Baltic (Sea).
бальзáм balsam; balm.
балюстрáда balustrade.
бамбýк bamboo.
бáмпер bumper.
банáльность banality; platitude. **банáльный** banal.
банáн banana.
бáнда band, gang.
бандáж (-á) truss; belt, band.
бандерóль wrapper; printed matter, book-post.
бáнджо *neut indecl* banjo.
бандúт bandit; gangster.
банк bank.
бáнка jar; tin.
банкéт banquet.
банки́р banker. **банкнóта** banknote. **банкрóт** bankrupt.
банкрóтство bankruptcy.
бант bow.
бáня bath; bath-house.
бар bar; snack-bar.
барабáн drum. **барабáнить** *impf* drum, thump. **барабáнная перепóнка** ear-drum.
барабáнщик drummer.
барáк wooden barrack, hut.
барáн ram; sheep. **барáнина** mutton; lamb.
барáнка ring-shaped roll; (steering-)wheel.
барахлó old clothes, jumble; odds and ends. **барахóлка** flea market.
барáшек (-шка) young ram; lamb; wing nut; catkin. **барáшковый** lambskin.
бáржá (*gen pl* барж(éй)) barge.
бáрин (*pl* -ре *or* -ры, бар) landowner; sir.
баритóн baritone.

ба́рка barge.
ба́рмен barman.
баро́кко *neut indecl* baroque.
баро́метр barometer.
баро́н baron. **барон́есса** baroness.
баро́чный baroque
баррика́да barricade.
барс snow-leopard.
ба́рский lordly; grand.
барсу́к (-а́) badger.
барха́н dune.
ба́рхат (-у) velvet. **ба́рхатный** velvet.
ба́рыня landowner's wife; madam.
бары́ш (-а́) profit. **бары́шник** dealer; (ticket) speculator.
ба́рышня (*gen pl* -шень) young lady; miss.
барье́р barrier; hurdle.
бас (*pl* -ы́) bass.
баскетбо́л basket-ball.
баснословный mythical, legendary; fabulous. **ба́сня** (*gen pl* -сен) fable; fabrication.
басо́вый bass.
бассе́йн (*geog*) basin; pool; reservoir.
бастова́ть *impf* be on strike.
батальо́н battalion.
батаре́йка, батаре́я battery; radiator.
бато́н long loaf; stick, bar.
ба́тька *m*, **ба́тюшка** *m* father; priest. **ба́тюшки** *int* good gracious!
бах *int* bang!
бахва́льство bragging.
бахрома́ fringe.
бац *int* bang! crack!
баци́лла bacillus. **бациллоноси́тель** *m* carrier.
бачо́к (-чка́) cistern.
башка́ head.
башлы́к (-а́) hood.
башма́к (-а́) shoe; **под ~о́м у**+*gen* under the thumb of.
ба́шня (*gen pl* -шен) tower, turret.
баю́кать *impf* (*pf* **у~**) sing lullabies (to). **ба́юшки-баю́** *int* hushabye!
бая́н accordion.
бде́ние vigil. **бди́тельность** vigilance. **бди́тельный** vigilant.
бег (*loc* -у́; *pl* -а́) run, running; race. **бе́гать** *indet* (*det* **бежа́ть**) *impf* run.
бегемо́т hippopotamus.
бегле́ц (-а́), **бегля́нка** fugitive. **бе́глость** speed, fluency, dexterity. **бе́глый** rapid, fluent; fleeting, cursory; *sb* fugitive, runaway. **беговой** running; race. **бего́м** *adv* running, at the double. **беготня́** running about; bustle. **бе́гство** flight; escape. **бегу́н** (-а́), **бегу́нья** (*gen pl* -ний) runner.
беда́ (*pl* -ы) misfortune; disaster; trouble; **~ в том, что** the trouble is (that). **бедне́ть** *impf* (*pf* **о~**) grow poor. **бе́дность** poverty; the poor. **бе́дный** (-ден, -дна́, -дно) poor. **бедня́га** *m*, **бедня́жка** *m* & *f* poor thing. **бедня́к** (-а́), **бедня́чка** poor peasant; poor man, poor woman.
бедро́ (*pl* бёдра, -дер) thigh; hip.
бе́дственный disastrous. **бе́дствие** disaster. **бе́дствовать** *impf* live in poverty.
бежа́ть (бегу́ *det*; *indet* бе́гать) *impf* (*pf* **по~**) run; flow; fly; boil over; *impf* & *pf* escape. **бе́женец** (-нца), **бе́женка** refugee.
без *prep*+*gen* without; **~ пяти**

(минут) три five (minutes) to three; ~ **четверти** a quarter to.

без-, безъ-, бес- *in comb* in-, un-; non-; -less. **без|алкогольный** non-alcoholic. **~апелляционный** peremptory, categorical. **~божие** atheism. **~божный** godless; shameless, outrageous. **~болезненный** painless. **~брачный** celibate. **~брежный** boundless. **~вестный** unknown; obscure. **~вкусие** lack of taste, bad taste. **~вкусный** tasteless. **~властие** anarchy. **~водный** arid. **~возвратный** irrevocable; irrecoverable. **~возмездный** free, gratis. **~волие** lack of will. **~вольный** weak-willed. **~вредный** harmless. **~временный** untimely. **~выходный** hopeless, desperate; uninterrupted. **~глазый** one-eyed; eyeless. **~грамотный** illiterate. **~граничный** boundless, infinite. **~дарный** untalented. **~действенный** inactive. **~действие** inertia, idleness; negligence. **~действовать** *impf* be idle, be inactive; stand idle.

безделица trifle. **безделушка** knick-knack. **бездельник** idler; ne'er-do-well. **бездельничать** *impf* idle, loaf.

бездна abyss, chasm; a huge number, a multitude.

без-. бездоказательный unsubstantiated. **~домный** homeless. **~донный** bottomless; fathomless. **~дорожье** lack of (good) roads; season when roads are impassable. **~думный** unthinking. **~душный** heartless; inanimate; lifeless. **~жалостный** pitiless, ruthless. **~жизненный** lifeless. **~заботный** carefree; careless. **~заветный** selfless, wholehearted. **~законие** lawlessness; unlawful act. **~законный** illegal; lawless. **~застенчивый** shameless, barefaced. **~защитный** defenceless. **~звучный** silent. **~злобный** good-natured. **~личный** characterless; impersonal. **~людный** uninhabited; sparsely populated; lonely.

безмен steelyard.

без-. безмерный immense; excessive. **~молвие** silence. **~молвный** silent, mute. **~мятежный** serene, placid. **~надёжный** hopeless. **~надзорный** neglected. **~наказанно** *adv* with impunity. **~наказанный** unpunished. **~ногий** legless; one-legged. **~нравственный** immoral.

безо *prep+gen* = **без** (*used before* **весь** *and* **всякий**).

безобразие ugliness; disgrace, scandal. **безобразничать** *impf* make a nuisance of o.s. **безобразный** ugly; disgraceful.

без-. безоговорочный unconditional. **~опасность** safety; security. **~опасный** safe; secure. **~оружный** unarmed. **~основательный** groundless. **~остановочный** unceasing; non-stop. **~ответный** meek, unanswering; dumb. **~ответственный** irresponsible. **~отказно** *adv* without a hitch. **~отказный** trouble-free, smooth-(running). **~отлагательный** urgent. **~относи-**

тельно *adv+к+dat* irrespective of. **~отчётный** unaccountable. **~оши́бочный** unerring; correct. **~рабо́тица** unemployment. **~рабо́тный** unemployed. **~разли́чие** indifference. **~разли́чно** *adv* indifferently; it is all the same. **~разли́чный** indifferent. **~рассу́дный** reckless, imprudent. **~ро́дный** alone in the world; without relatives. **~ро́потный** uncomplaining; meek. **~рука́вка** sleeveless pullover. **~ру́кий** armless; one-armed. **~уда́рный** unstressed. **~у́держный** unrestrained; impetuous. **~укори́зненный** irreproachable.

безу́мец (-мца) madman. **безу́мие** madness. **безу́мный** mad. **безу́мство** madness.

без-. безупре́чный irreproachable, faultless. **~усло́вно** *adv* unconditionally; of course, undoubtedly. **~усло́вный** unconditional, absolute; indisputable. **~успе́шный** unsuccessful. **~уста́нный** tireless. **~уте́шный** inconsolable. **~уча́стие** indifference, apathy. **~уча́стный** indifferent, apathetic. **~ымя́нный** nameless, anonymous; **~ымя́нный па́лец** ring-finger. **~ыску́сный** artless, ingenuous. **~ысхо́дный** irreparable; interminable.

бейсбо́л baseball.

бека́р (*mus*) natural.

бека́с snipe.

беко́н bacon.

Белару́сь Belarus.

беле́ть *impf* (*pf* **по~**) turn white; show white.

белизна́ whiteness. **бели́ла** (*pl*; *gen* -и́л) whitewash; Tippex (*propr*). **бели́ть** (бе́лишь) *impf* (*pf* **вы́~, на~, по~**) whitewash; whiten; bleach.

бе́лка squirrel.

беллетри́ст writer of fiction. **беллетри́стика** fiction.

бело- *in comb* white-, leuco-. **белогварде́ец** (-е́йца) White Guard. **~кро́вие** leukaemia. **~ку́рый** fair, blonde. **~ру́с, ~ру́ска, ~ру́сский** Belorussian. **~сне́жный** snow-white.

белови́к (-а́) fair copy. **белово́й** clean, fair.

бело́к (-лка́) white (*of egg, eye*); protein.

белошве́йка seamstress. **белошве́йный** linen.

белу́га white sturgeon. **белу́ха** white whale.

бе́л|ый (бел, -а́, бе́ло́) white; clean, blank; *sb* white person; **~ая берёза** silver birch; **~ое кале́ние** white heat; **~ый медве́дь** polar bear; **~ые но́чи** white nights, midnight sun.

бельги́ец, -ги́йка Belgian. **бельги́йский** Belgian. **Бе́льгия** Belgium.

бельё linen; bedclothes; underclothes; washing.

бельмо́ (*pl* -а) cataract.

бельэта́ж first floor; dress circle.

бемо́ль *m* (*mus*) flat.

бенефи́с benefit (performance).

бензи́н petrol.

бензо- *in comb* petrol. **бензоба́к** petrol-tank. **~во́з** petrol tanker. **~запра́вочная** *sb* filling-station. **~коло́нка** petrol pump. **~прово́д** petrol pipe, fuel line.

берёг *etc.*: *see* **беречь**
берег (*loc* -ý; *pl* -á) bank, shore; coast; **на ~ý моря** at the seaside. **береговóй** coast; coastal.
бережёшь *etc.*: *see* **беречь.**
бережливый thrifty. **бережный** careful.
берёза birch. **Берёзка** hard-currency shop.
беременеть *impf* (*pf* **за~**) be(come) pregnant. **беременная** pregnant (*+instr* with). **беременность** pregnancy; gestation.
берéт beret.
беречь (-регý, -режёшь; -рёг, -лá) *impf* take care of; keep; cherish; husband; be sparing of; **~ся** take care; beware (*+gen* of).
берлóга den, lair.
берý *etc.*: *see* **брать**
бес devil, demon.
бес-: *see* **без-**
беседа talk, conversation. **беседка** summer-house. **беседовать** *impf* talk, converse.
бесить (бешý, бéсишь) *impf* (*pf* **вз~**) enrage; **~ся** go mad; be furious.
бес-. бесконечность infinity; endlessness. **~конечный** endless. **~корыстие** disinterestedness. **~корыстный** disinterested. **~крáйний** boundless.
бесóвский devilish.
бес-. беспáмятство unconsciousness. **~партийный** non-party **~перспективный** without prospects; hopeless. **~печность** carelessness, unconcern. **~плáтно** *adv* free. **~плáтный** free. **~плóдие** sterility, barrenness. **~плóдность** futility. **~плóдный** sterile, barren; futile. **~поворóтный** irrevocable. **~подóбный** incomparable. **~позвонóчный** invertebrate.
беспокóить *impf* (*pf* **о~, по~**) disturb, bother; trouble; **~ся** worry; trouble. **беспокóйный** anxious; troubled; fidgety. **беспокóйство** anxiety.
бес-. бесполéзный useless. **~пóмощный** helpless; feeble. **~порóдный** mongrel, not thoroughbred. **~порядок** (-дка) disorder; untidy state. **~порядочный** disorderly; untidy. **~посáдочный** non-stop. **~пóчвенный** groundless. **~пóшлинный** duty-free. **~пощáдный** merciless. **~прáвный** without rights. **~предéльный** boundless. **~предмéтный** aimless; abstract. **~препятственный** unhindered; unimpeded. **~прерывный** continuous. **~престáнный** continual.
беспризóрник, -ница waif, homeless child. **беспризóрный** neglected; homeless; *sb* waif, homeless child.
бес-. беспримéрный unparalleled. **~принципный** unscrupulous. **~пристрáстие** impartiality. **~пристрáстный** impartial. **~просвéтный** pitch-dark; hopeless; unrelieved. **~пýтный** dissolute. **~свя́зный** incoherent. **~сердéчный** heartless. **~силие** impotence; feebleness. **~сильный** impotent, powerless. **~слáвный** inglorious. **~слéдно** *adv* without

trace. **~слове́сный** dumb; silent, meek; (*theat*) walk-on. **~сме́нный** permanent, continuous. **~сме́ртие** immortality. **~сме́ртный** immortal. **~смы́сленный** senseless; foolish; meaningless. **~смы́слица** nonsense. **~со́вестный** unscrupulous; shameless. **~созна́тельный** unconscious; involuntary. **~со́нница** insomnia. **~спо́рный** indisputable. **~сро́чный** indefinite; without a time limit. **~стра́стный** impassive. **~стра́шный** fearless. **~сты́дный** shameless. **~та́ктный** tactless.

бестолко́вщина confusion, disorder. **бестолко́вый** muddle-headed, stupid; incoherent.

бес-. бесфо́рменный shapeless. **~хара́ктерный** weak, spineless. **~хи́тростный** artless; unsophisticated. **~хозя́йственный** improvident. **~цве́тный** colourless. **~це́льный** aimless; pointless. **~це́нный** priceless. **~це́нок: за ~це́нок** very cheap, for a song. **~церемо́нный** unceremonious. **~челове́чный** inhuman. **~че́стить** (-е́щу) *impf* (*pf* **о~че́стить**) dishonour. **~че́стный** dishonourable. **~чи́сленный** innumerable, countless.

бесчу́вственный insensible; insensitive. **бесчу́вствие** insensibility; insensitivity.

бес-. бесшу́мный noiseless.

бето́н concrete. **бето́нный** concrete. **бетономеша́лка** concrete-mixer. **бето́нщик** concrete-worker.

бечева́ tow-rope; rope. **бечёвка** cord, string.

бе́шенство rabies; rage. **бе́шеный** rabid; furious.

бешу́ *etc*.: *see* **беси́ть**

библе́йский biblical. **библиографи́ческий** bibliographical. **библиогра́фия** bibliography. **библиоте́ка** library. **библиоте́карь** *m*, **-те́карша** librarian. **би́блия** bible.

бива́к bivouac, camp.

би́вень (-вня) *m* tusk.

бигуди́ *pl indecl* curlers.

бидо́н can; churn.

бие́ние beating; beat.

бижуте́рия costume jewellery.

би́знес business. **бизнесме́н** businessman.

биле́т ticket; card; pass. **биле́тный** ticket.

биллио́н billion.

билья́рд billiards.

бино́кль *m* binoculars.

бинт (-а́) bandage. **бинтова́ть** *impf* (*pf* **за~**) bandage. **бинто́вка** bandaging.

био́граф biographer. **биографи́ческий** biographical. **биогра́фия** biography. **био́лог** biologist. **биологи́ческий** biological. **биоло́гия** biology. **биохи́мия** biochemistry.

би́ржа exchange.

би́рка name-plate; label.

бирюза́ turquoise

бис *int* encore.

би́сер (*no pl*) beads.

бискви́т sponge cake.

бита́ bat.

би́тва battle.

битко́м *adv*: **~ наби́т** packed.

биту́м bitumen.

бить (бью, бьёшь) *impf* (*pf* **за~, по~, про~, уда́рить**) beat; hit; defeat; sound; thump, bang; smash; **~ в цель** hit the target; **~ на**+*acc* strive for; **~ отбо́й** beat a retreat;

~ **по**+*dat* damage, wound; **~ся** fight; beat; struggle; break; +*instr* knock, hit, strike; +**над**+*instr* struggle with, rack one's brains over.
бифштéкс beefsteak.
бич (-á) whip, lash; scourge; homeless person. **бичевáть** (-чýю) *impf* flog; castigate.
блáго good; blessing.
блáго- *in comb* well-, good-. **Благовéщение** Annunciation. **~вúдный** plausible, specious. **~волéние** goodwill; favour. **~воспúтанный** well-brought-up.
благодарúть (-рю́) *impf* (*pf* **по~**) thank. **благодáрность** gratitude; **не стóит благодáрности** don't mention it. **благодáрный** grateful. **благодаря́** *prep+dat* thanks to, owing to.
благо-. благодéтель *m* benefactor. **~дéтельница** benefactress. **~дéтельный** beneficial. **~дýшный** placid; good-humoured. **~желáтель** *m* well-wisher. **~желáтельный** well-disposed; benevolent. **~звýчный** melodious, harmonious. **~надёжный** reliable. **~намéренный** well-intentioned. **~полýчие** well-being; happiness. **~полýчно** *adv* all right, well; happily; safely. **~полýчный** happy, successful; safe. **~прия́тный** favourable. **~прия́тствовать** *impf +dat* favour. **~разýмие** sense; prudence. **~разýмный** sensible. **~рóдие: вáше ~рóдие** Your Honour. **~рóдный** noble. **~рóдство** nobility. **~склóнность** favour, good graces. **~склóнный** favourable; gracious. **~словúть** *pf*, **благословля́ть** *impf* bless. **~состоя́ние** prosperity. **~творúтель** *m*, **-ница** philanthropist. **~творúтельный** charitable, charity. **~твóрный** salutary; beneficial; wholesome. **~устрóенный** well-equipped, well-planned; with all amenities.
блажéнный blissful; simple-minded. **блажéнство** bliss.
бланк form.
блат (*sl*) string-pulling; pull, influence. **блатнóй** criminal; soft, cushy.
бледнéть (-éю) *impf* (*pf* **по~**) (grow) pale. **блéдность** paleness, pallor. **блéдный** (-ден, -днá, -о) pale.
блеск brightness, brilliance, lustre; magnificence.
блеснýть (-нý, -нёшь) *pf* flash, gleam; shine. **блестéть** (-ещý, -стúшь *or* блéщешь) *impf* shine; glitter. **блёстка** sparkle; sequin. **блестя́щий** shining, bright; brilliant.
блéять (-éет) *impf* bleat.
ближáйший nearest, closest; next. **блúже** *comp of* **блúзкий, блúзко. блúжний** near, close; neighbouring; *sb* neighbour. **близ** *prep+gen* near, by.
блúз|кий (-зок, -úзкá, -о) near; close; imminent; **~кие** *sb pl* one's nearest and dearest, close relatives. **блúзко** *adv* near (**от**+*gen* to). **близнéц** (-á) twin; *pl* Gemini. **близорýкий** short-sighted. **блúзость** closeness, proximity.
блик patch of light; highlight.
блин (-á) pancake.
блиндáж (-á) dug-out.
блистáть *impf* shine; sparkle.
блок block, pulley, sheave.

блока́да blockade. **блоки́ровать** *impf* & *pf* blockade; **~ся** form a bloc. **блокно́т** writing-pad, note-book.

блонди́н, блонди́нка blond(e).

блоха́ (*pl* -и, -а́м) flea.

блуд lechery. **блудни́ца** whore.

блужда́ть *impf* roam, wander.

блу́за, блу́зка blouse.

блю́дечко saucer; small dish. **блю́до** dish; course. **блю́дце** saucer.

боб (-а́) bean. **бобо́вый** bean.

бобр (-а́) beaver.

Бог (*voc* **Бо́же**) God; **дай ~** God grant; **~ его́ зна́ет** who knows? **не дай ~** God forbid; **Бо́же (мой)!** my God! good God!; **ра́ди ~а** for God's sake; **сла́ва ~у** thank God.

богате́ть *impf* (*pf* **раз~**) grow rich. **бога́тство** wealth. **бога́тый** rich, wealthy; *sb* rich man. **бога́ч** (-а́) rich man.

богаты́рь (-я́) *m* hero; strong man.

боги́ня goddess. **Богома́терь** Mother of God. **богомо́лец** (-льца), **богомо́лка** devout person; pilgrim. **богомо́лье** pilgrimage. **богомо́льный** religious, devout. **Богоро́дица** the Virgin Mary. **богосло́в** theologian. **богосло́вие** theology. **богослуже́ние** divine service. **боготвори́ть** *impf* idolize; deify. **богоху́льство** blasphemy.

бодри́ть *impf.* stimulate, invigorate; **~ся** try to keep up one's spirits. **бо́дрость** cheerfulness, courage. **бо́дрствовать** be awake; stay awake; keep vigil. **бо́дрый** (бодр, -а́, -о) cheerful, bright.

боеви́к (-а́) smash hit. **боево́й** fighting, battle. **боеголо́вка** warhead. **боеприпа́сы** (*pl*; *gen* -ов) ammunition. **боеспосо́бный** battle-worthy. **бое́ц** (бойца́) soldier; fighter, warrior.

Бо́же: *see* **Бог. бо́жеский** divine; just. **боже́ственный** divine. **божество́** deity; divinity. **бо́ж|ий** God's; **~ья коро́вка** ladybird. **божо́к** (-жка́) idol.

бой (*loc* -ю́; *pl* -и́, -ёв) battle, action, fight; fighting; slaughtering; striking; breakage(s).

бо́йкий (бо́ек, бойка́, -о) smart, sharp; glib; lively.

бойко́т boycott.

бо́йня (*gen pl* бо́ен) slaughter-house; butchery.

бок (*loc* -у́; *pl* -а́) side; flank; **~ о ~** side by side; **на́ ~** to the side; **на ~у́** on one side; **по́д ~ом** near by; **с ~у** from the side, from the flank; **с ~у на́ бок** from side to side.

бока́л glass; goblet.

боково́й side; lateral. **бо́ком** *adv* sideways.

бокс boxing. **боксёр** boxer.

болва́н blockhead. **болва́нка** pig (*of iron etc.*).

болга́рин (*pl* -га́ры), **болга́рка** Bulgarian. **болга́рский** Bulgarian. **Болга́рия** Bulgaria.

бо́лее *adv* more; **~ всего́** most of all; **тем ~, что** especially as.

боле́зненный sickly; unhealthy; painful. **боле́знь** illness, disease; abnormality.

боле́льщик, -щица fan, supporter. **боле́ть**[1] (-е́ю) *impf* be ill, suffer. **боле́ть**[2] (-ли́т) *impf* ache, hurt.

боло́тистый marshy. **боло́то** marsh, bog.

болта́ть[1] *impf* stir; shake; dangle; **~ся** dangle, swing; hang about.

болта́ть[2] *impf* chat, natter. **болтли́вый** talkative; indiscreet. **болтовня́** talk; chatter; gossip. **болту́н** (-а́), **болту́нья** chatterbox.

боль pain; ache. **больни́ца** hospital. **больни́чный** hospital; **~ листо́к** medical certificate. **бо́льно**[1] *adv* painfully, badly; *predic+dat* it hurts. **бо́льно**[2] *adv* very, terribly. **больно́й** (-лен, -льна́) ill, sick; diseased; sore; *sb* patient, invalid.

бо́льше *comp of* **большо́й, мно́го**; bigger, larger; greater; more; **~ не** not any more, no longer; **~ того́** and what is more; *adv* for the most part. **большеви́к** Bolshevik. **бо́льш|ий** greater, larger; **~ей ча́стью** for the most part. **большинство́** majority. **больш|о́й** big, large; great; grown-up; **~а́я бу́ква** capital letter; **~о́й па́лец** thumb; big toe; **~и́е** *sb pl* grown-ups.

бо́мба bomb. **бомбардирова́ть** *impf* bombard; bomb. **бомбардиро́вка** bombardment, bombing. **бомбардиро́вщик** bomber. **бомбёжка** bombing. **бомби́ть** (-блю́) bomb. **бомбоубе́жище** bomb shelter.

бор (*loc* -у́; *pl* -ы́) coniferous forest.

бордо́вый wine-red.

бордю́р border.

боре́ц (-рца́) fighter; wrestler.

бо́рзый swift.

бормаши́на (dentist's) drill.

бормота́ть (-очу́, -о́чешь) *impf* (*pf* **про~**) mutter, mumble.

борода́ (*acc* бо́роду; *pl* бо́роды, -ро́д, -а́м) beard. **борода́вка** wart. **борода́тый** bearded.

борозда́ (*pl* бо́розды, -о́зд, -а́м) furrow. **борозди́ть** (-зжу́) *impf* (*pf* **вз~**) furrow.

борона́ (*acc* бо́рону; *pl* бо́роны, -ро́н, -а́м) harrow. **борони́ть** *impf* (*pf* **вз~**) harrow.

боро́ться (-рю́сь, бо́решься) *impf* wrestle; struggle, fight.

борт (*loc* -у́; *pl* -а́, -о́в) side, ship's side; front; **за ~, за ~ом** overboard; **на ~, на ~у́** on board. **бортпроводни́к** (-а́) air steward. **бортпроводни́ца** air hostess.

борщ (-а́) borshch (*beetroot soup*).

борьба́ wrestling; struggle, fight.

босико́м *adv* barefoot.

босни́ец (-и́йца), **босни́йка** Bosnian. **босни́йский** Bosnian. **Бо́сния** Bosnia.

босо́й (бос, -а́, -о) barefooted.

босоно́жка sandal.

бот, бо́тик small boat.

бота́ник botanist. **бота́ника** botany. **ботани́ческий** botanical.

боти́нок (-нка; *gen pl* -нок) (*ankle-high*) boot.

бо́цман boatswain

бо́чка barrel. **бочо́нок** (-нка) keg, small barrel.

боязли́вый timid, timorous. **боя́знь** fear, dread.

боя́рин (*pl* -я́ре, -я́р) boyar.

боя́рышник hawthorn.

боя́ться (бою́сь) *impf +gen* be afraid of, fear; dislike.

брак[1] marriage.

брак[2] defective goods; flaw. **бракова́ть** *impf* (*pf* **за~**) reject.

браконье́р poacher.
бракоразво́дный divorce.
бракосочета́ние wedding.
брани́ть *impf* (*pf* **вы́~**) scold; abuse, curse; **~ся** (*pf* **по~**) swear, curse; quarrel. **бра́н|ный** abusive; **~ое сло́во** swear-word.
брань bad language; abuse.
брасле́т bracelet.
брасс breast stroke.
брат (*pl* -тья, -тьев) brother; comrade; mate; lay brother, monk. **брата́ться** *impf* (*pf* **по~**) fraternize. **братоуби́йство** fratricide. **бра́тский** brotherly, fraternal. **бра́тство** brotherhood, fraternity.
брать (беру́, -рёшь; брал, -а́, -о) *impf* (*pf* **взять**) take; obtain; hire; seize; demand, require; surmount, clear; work; *+instr* succeed by means of; **~ся** **+за***+acc* touch; seize; get down to; **+за***+acc or inf* undertake; appear, come.
бра́чный marriage; mating.
бреве́нчатый log. **бревно́** (*pl* брёвна, -вен) log, beam.
бред (*loc* -у́) delirium; raving(s). **бре́дить** (-е́жу) *impf* be delirious, rave; *+instr* rave about, be infatuated with. **бредо́вый** delirious; fantastic, nonsensical.
бреду́ *etc.*: *see* **брести́. бре́жу** *etc.*: *see* **бре́дить**
бре́згать *impf* (*pf* **по~**) *+inf or instr* be squeamish about. **брезгли́вый** squeamish.
брезе́нт tarpaulin.
бре́зжить(ся *impf* dawn; gleam faintly, glimmer.
брёл *etc.*: *see* **бре́сти**
брело́к charm, pendant.
бремени́ть *impf* (*pf* **о~**) burden. **бре́мя** (-мени) *neut* burden; load.
бренча́ть (-чу́) *impf* strum; jingle.
брести́ (-еду́, -едёшь; брёл, -а́) *impf* stroll; drag o.s. along.
брете́ль, брете́лька shoulder strap.
брешь breach; gap.
бре́ю *etc.*: *see* **брить**
брига́да brigade; crew, team. **бригади́р** brigadier; team-leader; foreman.
брилли́ант, брилья́нт diamond.
брита́нец (-нца), **брита́нка** Briton. **брита́нск|ий** British; **Б~ие острова́** the British Isles.
бри́тва razor. **бри́твенный** shaving. **бри́тый** shaved; clean-shaven. **брить** (бре́ю) *impf* (*pf* **по~**) shave; **~ся** shave (o.s.).
бровь (*pl* -и, -е́й) (eye)brow.
брод ford.
броди́ть (-ожу́, -о́дишь) *impf* wander, roam, stroll; ferment. **бродя́га** *m* & *f* tramp, vagrant. **бродя́жничество** vagrancy. **бродя́чий** vagrant; wandering. **броже́ние** ferment, fermentation.
бро́кер broker.
броне- *in comb* armoured, armour. **броневи́к** (-а́) armoured car. **~во́й** armoured. **~но́сец** (-сца) battleship; armadillo.
бро́нза bronze; bronzes. **бро́нзовый** bronze; tanned.
брониро́ванный armoured.
брони́ровать *impf* & *pf* (*pf also* **за~**) reserve, book.
бронхи́т bronchitis.
бро́ня[1] reservation; commandeering.
броня́[2] armour.

бросáть *impf*, **брóсить** (-óшу) *pf* throw (down); leave, desert; give up, leave off; **~ся** throw o.s., rush; *+inf* begin; *+instr* squander; pelt one another with; **~ся в глазá** be striking. **брóский** striking; garish, glaring. **бросóк** (-скá) throw; bound, spurt.

брóузер (*comput*) browser.

брóшка, брошь brooch.

брошю́ра pamphlet, brochure.

брус (*pl* -сья, -сьев) squared beam, joist; **(параллéльные) ~ья** parallel bars.

брусни́ка red whortleberry; red whortleberries.

брусóк (-скá) bar; ingot.

брýтто *indecl adj* gross.

брызгать (-зжу *or* -гаю) *impf*, **брызнуть** (-ну) *pf* splash; sprinkle. **брызги** (брызг) *pl* spray, splashes; fragments.

брыкáть *impf*, **брыкнýть** (-нý, -нёшь) *pf* kick.

брюзгá *m* & *f* grumbler. **брюзгли́вый** grumbling. **брюзжáть** (-жý) *impf* grumble.

брю́ква swede.

брю́ки (*pl*; *gen* брюк) trousers.

брюнéт dark-haired man. **брюнéтка** brunette.

брю́хо (*pl* -и) belly; stomach.

брюшнóй abdominal; **~ тиф** typhoid.

бряцáть *impf* rattle; clank, clang.

бýбен (-бна) tambourine. **бубенéц** (-нцá) small bell.

бýбны (*pl*; *gen* -бён, *dat* -бнáм) (*cards*) diamonds. **бубнóвый** diamond.

бугóр (-грá) mound, hillock; bump, lump.

будди́зм Buddhism. **будди́йский** Buddhist. **будди́ст** Buddhist.

бýдет that will do.

буди́льник alarm-clock. **буди́ть** (бужý, бýдишь) *impf* (*pf* **про~, раз~**) wake; arouse.

бýдка box, booth; hut; stall.

бýдни (*pl*; *gen* **-ней**) *pl* weekdays; working days; humdrum existence. **бýдний, бýдничный** weekday; everyday; humdrum.

бýдто *conj* as if, as though; **~ (бы), (как) ~** apparently, ostensibly.

бýду *etc.*: *see* **быть. бýдучи** being. **бýдущ|ий** future; next; **~ее** *sb* future. **бýдущность** future. **бýдь(те):** *see* **быть**

бужý: *see* **буди́ть**

бузинá (*bot*) elder.

буй (*pl* -и́, -ёв) buoy.

бýйвол buffalo.

бýйный (бýен, буйнá, -о) violent, turbulent; luxuriant, lush. **бýйство** unruly behaviour. **бýйствовать** *impf* create an uproar, behave violently.

бук beech.

букáшка small insect.

бýква (*gen pl* букв) letter; **~ в бýкву** literally. **буквáльно** *adv* literally. **буквáльный** literal. **буквáрь** (-я́) *m* ABC.

буквоéд pedant.

букéт bouquet; aroma.

букини́ст second-hand bookseller.

бýкля curl, ringlet.

бýковый beech.

букси́р tug-boat; tow-rope. **букси́ровать** *impf* tow.

буксовáть *impf* spin, slip.

булáвка pin.

бýлка roll; white loaf. **бýлочка** roll, bun. **бýлочная** *sb* baker's. **бýлочник** baker.

булыжник cobble-stone, cobbles.

бульва́р avenue; boulevard.
бульдо́г bulldog.
бульдо́зер bulldozer.
бу́лькать *impf* gurgle.
бульо́н broth.
бум (*sport*) beam.
бума́га cotton; paper; document. **бума́жка** piece of paper; (bank)note. **бума́жник** wallet; paper-maker. **бума́жный** cotton; paper.
бу́нкер bunker.
бунт (*pl* -ы) rebellion; riot; mutiny. **бунта́рь** (-я́) *m* rebel; insurgent. **бунтова́ть(ся** *impf* (*pf* **вз~**) rebel; riot. **бунтовщи́к** (-а́), **-щи́ца** rebel, insurgent.
бур auger.
бура́в (-а́; *pl* -а́) auger; gimlet. **бура́вить** (-влю) *impf* (*pf* **про~**) bore, drill.
бура́н snowstorm.
буреве́стник stormy petrel.
буре́ние boring, drilling.
буржуа́ *m indecl* bourgeois. **буржуази́я** bourgeoisie. **буржуа́зный** bourgeois.
бури́льщик borer, driller. **бури́ть** *impf* (*pf* **про~**) bore, drill.
бурли́ть *impf* seethe.
бу́рный (-рен, -рна́, -о) stormy; rapid; energetic.
буров|о́й boring; **~а́я вы́шка** derrick; **~а́я (сква́жина)** borehole; **~о́й стано́к** drilling rig.
бу́рый (бур, -а́, -о) brown.
бурья́н tall weeds.
бу́ря storm.
бу́сина bead. **бу́сы** (*pl*; *gen* бус) beads.
бутафо́рия (*theat*) props.
бутербро́д open sandwich.
буто́н bud.
бу́тсы (*pl*; *gen* -ов) *pl* football boots.
буты́лка bottle. **буты́ль** large bottle; carboy.
буфе́т snack bar; sideboard; counter. **буфе́тчик** barman. **буфе́тчица** barmaid.
бух *int* bang, plonk. **бу́хать** *impf* (*pf* **бу́хнуть**) thump, bang; bang down; thunder, thud; blurt out.
буха́нка loaf.
бухга́лтер accountant. **бухгалте́рия** accountancy; accounts department.
бу́хнуть (-ну) *impf* swell.
бу́хта bay.
бушева́ть (-шу́ю) *impf* rage, storm.
буя́н rowdy. **буя́нить** *impf* create an uproar.
бы, б *partl* **I.** *+past tense or inf indicates the conditional or subjunctive.* **II. (+ни)** *forms indef prons and conjs.*
быва́лый experienced; former; habitual, familiar. **быва́ть** *impf* be; happen; be inclined to be; **как ни в чём не быва́ло** as if nothing had happened; **быва́ло** *partl* used to, would; **мать быва́ло ча́сто пе́ла э́ту пе́сню** my mother would often sing this song.
бы́вший former, ex-.
бык (-а́) bull, ox; pier.
были́на ancient Russian epic.
бы́ло *partl* nearly, on the point of; (only) just. **был|о́й** past, bygone; **~о́е** *sb* the past. **быль** true story; fact.
быстрота́ speed. **бы́стрый** (быстр, -а́, -о) fast, quick.
быт (*loc* -у́) way of life. **бытие́** being, existence; objective reality; **книга́ Бытия́** Genesis.
бытово́й everyday; social.
быть (*pres 3rd sg* есть, *pl* суть; *fut* бу́ду; *past* был, -а́, -о; *imper*

бу́дь(те)) *impf* be; be situated; happen. **бытьё** way of life.
бычо́к (-чка́) steer.
бью *etc.*: *see* **бить**
бюдже́т budget.
бюллете́нь *m* bulletin; ballot-paper; doctor's certificate.
бюро́ *neut indecl* bureau; office; writing-desk. **бюрокра́т** bureaucrat. **бюрократи́зм** bureaucracy. **бюрократи́ческий** bureaucratic. **бюрокра́тия** bureaucracy; bureaucrats.
бюст bust. **бюстга́льтер** bra.

В

в, во *prep* **I.** *+acc* into, to; on; at; within; through; **быть в** take after; **в два ра́за бо́льше** twice as big; **в на́ши дни** in our day; **войти́ в дом** go into the house; **в понеде́льник** on Monday; **в тече́ние**+*gen* during; **в четы́ре часа́** at four o'clock **высото́й в три ме́тра** three metres high; **игра́ть в ша́хматы** play chess; **пое́хать в Москву́** go to Moscow; **сесть в ваго́н** get into the carriage; **смотре́ть в окно́** look out of the window. **II.** *+prep* in; at; **в двадца́том ве́ке** in the twentieth century; **в теа́тре** at the theatre; **в трёх киломе́трах от го́рода** three kilometres from the town; **в э́том году́** this year; **в январе́** in January.
ваго́н carriage, coach; **~-рестора́н** restaurant car. **ваго́нетка** truck, trolley. **вагоновожа́тый** *sb* tram-driver.
ва́жничать *impf* give o.s. airs; *+instr* plume o.s., pride o.s., on. **ва́жность** importance; pomposity. **ва́жный** (-жен, -жна́, -о) important; weighty; pompous.
ва́за vase, bowl.
вазели́н Vaseline (*propr*).
вака́нсия vacancy. **вака́нтный** vacant.
ва́кса (shoe-)polish.
ва́куум vacuum.
вакци́на vaccine.
вал[1] (*loc* -у́; *pl* -ы́) bank; rampart; billow, roller; barrage.
вал[2] (*loc* -у́; *pl* -ы́) shaft.
ва́ленок (-нка; *gen pl* -нок) felt boot.
вале́т knave, Jack.
ва́лик roller, cylinder.
вали́ть[1] *impf* flock, throng.
вали́ть[2] (-лю́, -лишь) *impf* (*pf* **по~, с~**) throw down, bring down; pile up; **~ся** fall, collapse.
валли́ец (-и́йца) Welshman. **валли́йка** Welshwoman.
валово́й gross; wholesale.
валто́рна French horn.
валу́н (-а́) boulder.
вальс waltz. **вальси́ровать** *impf* waltz.
валю́та currency; foreign currency.
валя́ть *impf* (*pf* **на~, с~**) drag; roll; shape; bungle; **~ дурака́** play the fool; **~ся** lie, lie about; roll, wallow.
вам, ва́ми: *see* **вы**
вампи́р vampire.
ванда́л vandal. **вандали́зм** vandalism.
вани́ль vanilla.
ва́нна bath. **ва́нная** *sb* bathroom.
ва́рвар barbarian. **ва́рварский** barbaric. **ва́рварство** barbarity; vandalism.
ва́режка mitten.

варёный boiled. **варе́нье** jam. **вари́ть** (-рю́, -ришь) *impf* (*pf* **с~**) boil; cook; **~ся** boil; cook.
вариа́нт version; option; scenario.
вас: *see* **вы**
василёк (-лька́) cornflower.
ва́та cotton wool; wadding.
ватерли́ния water-line. **ватерпа́с** (spirit-)level.
вати́н (sheet) wadding. **ва́тник** quilted jacket. **ва́тный** quilted, wadded.
ватру́шка cheese-cake.
ватт (*gen pl* **ватт**) watt.
ва́учер coupon (*exchangeable for government-issued share*).
ва́фля (*gen pl* -фель) wafer; waffle.
ва́хта (*naut*) watch. **вахтёр** janitor, porter.
ваш (-его) *m*, **ва́ша** (-ей) *f*, **ва́ше** (-его) *neut*, **ва́ши** (-их) *pl*, *pron* your, yours.
вбега́ть *impf*, **вбежа́ть** (вбегу́) *pf* run in.
вберу́ *etc.*: *see* **вобра́ть**
вбива́ть *impf of* **вбить**
вбира́ть *impf of* **вобра́ть**
вбить (вобью́, -бьёшь) *pf* (*impf* **вбива́ть**) drive in, hammer in.
вблизи́ *adv* (+**от**+*gen*) close (to), near by.
вбок *adv* sideways, to one side.
вброд *adv*: **переходи́ть ~** ford, wade.
вва́ливать *impf*, **ввали́ть** (-лю́, -лишь) *pf* throw heavily, heave, bundle; **~ся** fall heavily; sink, become sunken; burst in.
введе́ние introduction. **введу́** *etc.*: *see* **ввести́**
ввезти́ (-зу́, -зёшь; ввёз, -ла́) *pf* (*impf* **ввози́ть**) import; bring in.
вве́рить *pf* (*impf* **вверя́ть**) entrust, confide; **~ся** +*dat* trust in, put one's faith in.
вверну́ть (-ну́, -нёшь) *pf*, **ввёртывать** *impf* screw in; insert.
вверх *adv* up, upward(s); **~дном** upside down; **~ (по ле́стнице)** upstairs. **вверху́** *adv* above, overhead.
вверя́ть(ся) *impf of* **вве́рить(ся)**
ввести́ (-еду́, -едёшь; ввёл, -а́) *pf* (*impf* **вводи́ть**) bring in; introduce.
ввиду́ *prep*+*gen* in view of.
ввинти́ть (-нчу́) *pf*, **вви́нчивать** *impf* screw in.
ввод lead-in. **вводи́ть** (-ожу́, -о́дишь) *impf of* **ввести́**. **вво́дный** introductory; parenthetic.
ввожу́ *see* **вводи́ть, ввози́ть**
ввоз importation; import(s). **ввози́ть** (-ожу́, -о́зишь) *impf of* **ввезти́**
вво́лю *adv* to one's heart's content.
ввысь *adv* up, upward(s).
ввяза́ть (-яжу́, -я́жешь) *pf*, **ввя́зывать** *impf* knit in; involve; **~ся** meddle, get or be mixed up (in).
вглубь *adv* & *prep*+*gen* deep (into), into the depths.
вгляде́ться (-яжу́сь) *pf*, **вгля́дываться** *impf* peer, look closely (**в**+*acc* at).
вгоня́ть *impf of* **вогна́ть**.
вдава́ться (вдаю́сь, -ёшься) *impf of* **вда́ться**
вдави́ть (-авлю́, -а́вишь) *pf*, **вда́вливать** *impf* press in.
вдалеке́, вдали́ *adv* in the distance, far away. **вдаль** *adv*

into the distance.
вдáться (-áмся, -áшься, -áстся, -адимся; -áлся, -лáсь) *pf* (*impf* **вдавáться**) jut out; penetrate, go in; (*fig*) get immersed.
вдвóе *adv* twice; double; ~ **бóльше** twice as big, as much, as many. **вдвоём** *adv* (the) two together, both. **вдвойнé** *adv* twice, double; doubly.
вдевáть *impf of* **вдеть**
вдéлать *pf*, **вдéлывать** *impf* set in, fit in.
вдёргивать *impf*, **вдёрнуть** (-ну) *pf* **в**+*acc* thread through, pull through.
вдеть (-éну) *pf* (*impf* **вдевáть**) put in, thread.
вдобáвок *adv* in addition; besides.
вдовá widow. **вдовéц** (-вцá) widower.
вдóволь *adv* enough; in abundance.
вдогóнку *adv* (**за**+*instr*) after, in pursuit (of).
вдоль *adv* lengthwise; ~ **и поперёк** far and wide; in detail; *prep*+*gen or* **по**+*dat* along.
вдох breath. **вдохновéние** inspiration, **вдохновéнный** inspired. **вдохновúть** (-влю) *pf*, **вдохновля́ть** *impf* inspire. **вдохнýть** (-нý, -нёшь) *pf* (*impf* **вдыхáть**) breathe in.
вдрéбезги *adv* to smithereens.
вдруг *adv* suddenly.
вдýматься *pf*, **вдýмываться** *impf* ponder, meditate; +**в**+*acc* think over. **вдýмчивый** thoughtful.
вдыхáние inhalation. **вдыхáть** *impf of* **вдохнýть**
веб (*comput*) the Web. **веб-сáйт** (*comput*) web site.
вегетариáнец (-нца), **-нка** vegetarian. **вегетариáнский** vegetarian.
вéдать *impf* know; +*instr* manage, handle. **вéдение**[1] authority, jurisdiction.
ведéние[2] conducting, conduct; ~ **книг** book-keeping.
вéдомость (*gen pl* -éй) list, register. **вéдомственный** departmental. **вéдомство** department.
ведрó (*pl* вёдра, -дер) bucket; vedro (*approx 12 litres*).
ведý *etc.*: *see* **вестú**. **ведýщий** leading.
ведь *partl* & *conj* you see, you know; isn't it? is it?
вéдьма witch.
вéер (*pl* -á) fan.
вéжливость politeness. **вéжливый** polite.
вездé *adv* everywhere.
везéние luck. **везýчий** lucky.
везтú (-зý, -зёшь; вёз, -лá) *impf* (*pf* **по**~) convey; bring, take; *impers*+*dat* be lucky; **емý не везлó** he had no luck.
век (*loc* -ý; *pl* -á) century; age; life(time). **век** *adv* for ages.
вéко (*pl* -и, век) eyelid.
віковóй ancient, age-old.
вéксель (*pl* -я́, -éй) *m* promissory note, bill (of exchange).
вёл *etc.*: *see* **вестú**
велéть (-лю́) *impf* & *pf* order; **не** ~ forbid.
великáн giant. **велúкий** (велúк, -а *or* -á) great; big, large; too big; ~ **пост** Lent.
велико- *in comb* great. **Великобритáния** Great Britain. **великодýшие** magnanimity. **~дýшный** magnanimous. **~лéпие** splendour. **~лéпный** splendid.
величáвый stately, majestic.
величáйший greatest, supreme. **велúчественный**

majestic, grand. **вели́чество** Majesty. **вели́чие** greatness, grandeur. **величина́** (*pl* -и́ны, -а́м) size; quantity, magnitude; value; great figure.
велосипе́д bicycle. **велосипеди́ст** cyclist.
вельве́т velveteen; **~ в ру́бчик** corduroy.
вельмо́жа *m* grandee.
ве́на vein.
венге́рец (-рца), **венге́рка** Hungarian. **венге́рский** Hungarian. **венгр** Hungarian. **Ве́нгрия** Hungary.
венде́тта vendetta.
венери́ческий venereal.
вене́ц (-нца́) crown; wreath.
ве́ник besom; birch twigs.
вено́к (-нка́) wreath, garland.
ве́нтиль *m* valve.
вентиля́тор ventilator; extractor (fan). **вентиля́ция** ventilation.
венча́ние wedding; coronation. **венча́ть** *impf* (*pf* **об~, по~, у~**) crown; marry; **~ся** be married, marry. **ве́нчик** halo; corolla; rim; ring, bolt.
ве́ра faith, belief.
вера́нда veranda.
ве́рба willow; willow branch. **ве́рбн|ый; ~ое воскресе́нье** Palm Sunday.
верблю́д camel.
вербова́ть *impf* (*pf* **за~**) recruit; win over. **вербо́вка** recruitment.
верёвка rope; string; cord. **верёвочный** rope.
верени́ца row, file, line, string.
ве́реск heather.
веретено́ (*pl* -тёна) spindle.
вереща́ть (-щу́) *impf* squeal; chirp.
ве́рить *impf* (*pf* **по~**) believe, have faith; *+dat or* **в**+*acc* trust (in), believe in.
вермише́ль vermicelli.
верне́е *adv* rather. **ве́рно** *partl* probably, I suppose. **ве́рность** faithfulness, loyalty.
верну́ть (-ну́, -нёшь) *pf* (*impf* **возвраща́ть**) give back, return; **~ся** return.
ве́рный (-рен, -рна́, -о) faithful, loyal; true; correct; reliable.
ве́рование belief. **ве́ровать** *impf* believe. **вероиспове́дание** religion; denomination. **вероло́мный** treacherous, perfidious. **вероотсту́пник** apostate. **веротерпи́мость** (religious) toleration.
вероя́тно *adv* probably. **вероя́тность** probability. **вероя́тный** probable.
ве́рсия version.
верста́ (*pl* вёрсты) verst (*1.06 km.*).
верста́к (-а́) work-bench.
ве́ртел (*pl* -а́) spit, skewer.
верте́ть (-чу́, -тишь) *impf* turn (round); twirl; **~ся** turn (round), spin. **вертля́вый** fidgety; flighty.
вертика́ль vertical line. **вертика́льный** vertical.
вертолёт helicopter.
верту́шка flirt.
ве́рующий *sb* believer.
верфь shipyard.
верх (*loc* -у́; *pl* -и́) top; summit; height; *pl* upper crust, top brass; high notes. **ве́рхний** upper; top. **верхо́вный** supreme. **верхово́й** riding; *sb* rider. **верхо́вье** (*gen pl* -вьев) upper reaches. **верхола́з** steeple-jack. **верхо́м** *adv* on horseback; astride. **верху́шка** top, summit; apex; top brass.

верчу́ *etc.*: *see* **верте́ть**
верши́на top, summit; peak; apex. **верши́ть** *impf +instr* manage, control.
вершо́к vershok (*4.4 cm.*); smattering.
вес (*loc* -у́, *pl* -а́) weight.
весели́ть *impf* (*pf* **раз~**) cheer, gladden; **~ся** enjoy o.s.; amuse o.s. **ве́село** *adv* merrily. **весёлый** (ве́сел, -а́, -о) merry; cheerful. **весе́лье** merriment.
весе́нний spring.
ве́сить (ве́шу) *impf* weigh. **ве́ский** weighty, solid.
весло́ (*pl* вёсла, -сел) oar.
весна́ (*pl* вёсны, -сен) spring. **весно́й** *adv* in (the) spring. **весну́шка** freckle.
вест (*naut*) west; west wind.
вести́ (веду́, -дёшь; вёл, -а́) *impf* (*pf* **по~**) lead, take; conduct; drive; run; keep; **~ себя́** behave, conduct o.s.; **~сь** be the custom.
вестибю́ль *m* (entrance) hall, lobby.
ве́стник herald; bulletin. **весть**[1] (*gen pl* -е́й) news; **бе́з вести** without trace. **весть**[2]: **Бог ~** God knows.
весы́ (*pl*; *gen* -о́в) scales, balance; Libra.
весь (всего́ *m*, **вся**, всей *f*, **всё**, всего́ *neut*, **все**, всех *pl*) *pron* all, the whole of; **всего́ хоро́шего!** all the best!; **всё** everything; **без всего́** without anything; **все** everybody.
весьма́ *adv* very, highly.
ветвь (*gen pl* -е́й) branch; bough.
ве́тер (-тра, *loc* -у́) wind. **ветеро́к** (-рка́) breeze.
ветера́н veteran.
ветерина́р vet.
ве́тка branch; twig.
ве́то *neut indecl* veto.
ве́тошь old clothes, rags.
ве́треный windy; frivolous.
ветров|о́й wind; **~о́е стекло́** windscreen. **ветря́к** (-а́) wind turbine; windmill.
ве́тхий (ветх, -а́, -о) old; dilapidated; **В~ заве́т** Old Testament.
ветчина́ ham.
ветша́ть *impf* (*pf* **об~**) decay; become dilapidated.
ве́ха landmark.
ве́чер (*pl* -а́) evening; party. **вечери́нка** party. **вече́рний** evening. **вече́рня** (*gen pl* -рен) vespers. **ве́чером** *adv* in the evening.
ве́чно *adv* for ever, eternally. **вечнозелёный** evergreen. **ве́чность** eternity; ages. **ве́чный** eternal.
ве́шалка peg, rack; tab, hanger. **ве́шать** *impf* (*pf* **взве́сить, пове́сить, све́шать**) hang; weigh (out); **~ся** hang o.s.; weigh o.s.
ве́шу *etc.*: *see* **ве́сить**
веща́ние broadcasting. **веща́ть** *impf* broadcast.
вещево́й clothing; **~ мешо́к** hold-all, kit-bag. **веще́ственный** substantial, material, real. **вещество́** substance; matter. **вещь** (*gen pl* -е́й) thing.
ве́ялка winnowing-machine. **ве́яние** winnowing; blowing; trend. **ве́ять** (ве́ю) *impf* (*pf* **про~**) winnow; blow; flutter.
взад *adv* backwards; **~ и вперёд** back and forth.
взаи́мность reciprocity. **взаи́мный** mutual, reciprocal.
взаимо- *in comb* inter-. **взаимоде́йствие** interaction; co-

operation. **~действовать** *impf* interact; cooperate. **~отношение** interrelation; *pl* relations. **~помощь** mutual aid. **~понимание** mutual understanding. **~связь** interdependence, correlation.

взаймы *adv*: **взять ~** borrow; **дать ~** lend.

взамен *prep+gen* instead of; in return for.

взаперти *adv* under lock and key; in seclusion.

взбалмошный unbalanced, eccentric.

взбегать *impf*, **взбежать** (-егу) *pf* run up.

взберусь *etc*.: *see* **взобраться.**

вз|бесить(ся (-ешу(сь, -есишь(ся) *pf*. **взбивать** *impf of* **взбить. взбираться** *impf of* **взобраться**

взбитый whipped, beaten. **взбить** (взобью, -бьёшь) *pf* (*impf* **взбивать**) beat (up), whip; shake up.

вз|бороздить (-зжу) *pf*.

вз|бунтоваться *pf*.

взбухать *impf*, **взбухнуть** (-нет; -ух) *pf* swell (out).

взваливать *impf*, **взвалить** (-лю, -лишь) *pf* load; **+на**+*acc* saddle with.

взвесить (-ешу) *pf* (*impf* **вешать, взвешивать**) weigh.

взвести (-еду, -едёшь; -ёл, -á) *pf* (*impf* **взводить**) lead up; raise; cock; **+на**+*acc* impute to.

взвешивать *impf of* **взвесить**

взвивать(ся *impf of* **взвить(ся**

взвизг scream; yelp. **взвизгивать** *impf*, **взвизгнуть** (-ну) *pf* scream; yelp.

взвинтить (-нчу) *pf*, **взвинчивать** *impf* excite, work up; inflate. **взвинченный** worked up; nervy; inflated.

взвить (взовью, -ёшь; -ил, -á, -о) *pf* (*impf* **взвивать**) raise; **~ся** rise, be hoisted; soar.

взвод[1] platoon, troop.

взвод[2] notch. **взводить** (-ожу, -óдишь) *impf of* **взвести**

взволнованный agitated; worried. **вз|волновать(ся** (-ную(сь) *pf*.

взгляд look; glance; opinion. **взглядывать** *impf*, **взглянуть** (-яну, -янешь) *pf* look, glance.

взгорье hillock.

вздёргивать *impf*, **вздёрнуть** (-ну) *pf* hitch up; jerk up; turn up.

вздор nonsense. **вздорный** cantankerous; foolish.

вздорожание rise in price. **вз|дорожать** *pf*.

вздох sigh. **вздохнуть** (-ну, -нёшь) *pf* (*impf* **вздыхать**) sigh.

вздрагивать *impf* (*pf* **вздрогнуть**) shudder, quiver.

вздремнуть *pf* have a nap, doze.

вздрогнуть (-ну) *pf* (*impf* **вздрагивать**) start; wince.

вздувать(ся *impf of* **вздуть**[1]**(ся**

вздумать *pf* take it into one's head; **не вздумай(те)!** don't you dare!

вздутие swelling. **вздутый** swollen. **вздуть**[1] *pf* (*impf* **вздувать**) inflate; **~ся** swell.

вздуть[2] *pf* thrash.

вздыхать *impf* (*pf* **вздохнуть**) breathe; sigh.

взимать *impf* levy, collect.

взламывать *impf of* **взломать. вз|лелеять** *pf*.

взлёт flight; take-off. **взле-**

тать *impf*, **взлететь** (-лечу) *pf* fly (up); take off. **взлётный** take-off; **взлётно-посадочная полоса** runway.
взлом breaking open, breaking in. **взломать** *pf* (*impf* **взламывать**) break open; break up. **взломщик** burglar.
взлохмаченный dishevelled.
взмах stroke, wave, flap. **взмахивать** *impf*, **взмахнуть** (-ну, -нёшь) *pf* +*instr* wave, flap.
взморье seaside; coastal waters.
вз|мутить (-учу, -утишь) *pf*.
взнос payment; fee, dues.
взнуздать *pf*, **взнуздывать** *impf* bridle.
взобраться (взберусь, -ёшься; -ался, -лась, -алось) *pf* (*impf* **взбираться**) climb (up).
взобью *etc.*: *see* **взбить. взовью** *etc.*: *see* **взвить**
взойти (-йду, -йдёшь; -ошёл, -шла) *pf* (*impf* **вос-, всходить**) rise, go up; **на**+*acc* mount.
взор look, glance.
взорвать (-ву, -вёшь; -ал, -а, -о) *pf* (*impf* **взрывать**) blow up; exasperate; **~ся** burst, explode.
взрослый *adj* & *sb* adult.
взрыв explosion; outburst. **взрыватель** *m* fuse. **взрывать** *impf*, **взрыть** (-рою) *pf* (*pf also* **взорвать**) blow up; **~ся** explode. **взрывной** explosive; blasting. **взрывчатка** explosive. **взрывчатый** explosive.
взъерошенный tousled, dishevelled. **взъерошивать** *impf*, **взъерошить** (-шу) *pf* tousle, rumple.
взывать *impf of* **воззвать**
взыскание penalty; exaction.
взыскательный exacting. **взыскать** (-ыщу, -ыщешь) *pf*, **взыскивать** *impf* exact, recover; call to account.
взятие taking, capture. **взятка** bribe. **взяточничество** bribery. **взять(ся** (возьму(сь, -мёшь(ся; -ял(ся, -а(сь, -о(сь) *pf of* **брать(ся**
вибрация vibration. **вибрировать** *impf* vibrate.
вивисекция vivisection.
вид[1] (*loc* -у) look; appearance; shape, form; condition; view; prospect; sight; aspect; **делать вид** pretend; **иметь в ~у** intend; mean; bear in mind.
вид[2] kind; species.
видаться *impf* (*pf* **по~**) meet.
видение[1] sight, vision. **видение**[2] vision, apparition.
видео *neut indecl* video (cassette) recorder; video film; video cassette. **видеоигра** video game.
видеокамера video camera.
видеокассета video cassette.
видеомагнитофон video (cassette) recorder.
видеть (вижу) *impf* (*pf* **у~**) see; **~ во сне** dream (of); **~ся** see one another; appear.
видимо *adv* evidently. **видимость** visibility; appearance.
видимый visible; apparent, evident. **видный** (-ден, -дна, -о) visible; distinguished.
видоизменение modification. **видоизменить** *pf*, **видоизменять** *impf* modify.
видоискатель *m* view-finder.
вижу *see* **видеть**
виза visa.
визг squeal; yelp. **визжать** (-жу) *impf* squeal, yelp, squeak.
визит visit. **визитка** business card.
викторина quiz.

ви́лка fork; plug. **ви́лы** (*pl*; *gen* вил) pitchfork.
вильну́ть (-ну́, -нёшь) *pf*, **виля́ть** *impf* twist and turn; prevaricate; *+instr* wag.
вина́ (*pl* ви́ны) fault, guilt; blame.
винегре́т Russian salad; medley.
вини́тельный accusative. **вини́ть** *impf* accuse; **~ся** (*pf* **по~**) confess.
ви́нный wine; winy. **вино́** (*pl* -а) wine.
винова́тый guilty. **вино́вник** initiator; culprit. **вино́вный** guilty.
виногра́д vine; grapes. **виногра́дина** grape. **виногра́дник** vineyard. **виногра́дный** grape; wine. **виноку́ренный заво́д** distillery.
винт (-а́) screw. **винти́ть** (-нчу́) *impf* screw up. **винто́вка** rifle. **винтово́й** screw; spiral.
виолонче́ль cello.
вира́ж (-а́) turn; bend.
виртуа́льный (*comput*) virtual.
виртуо́з virtuoso. **виртуо́зный** masterly.
ви́рус virus. **ви́русный** virus.
ви́селица gallows. **висе́ть** (вишу́) *impf* hang. **ви́снуть** (-ну; ви́с(нул)) *impf* hang; droop.
ви́ски *neut indecl* whisky.
висо́к (-ска́) (*anat*) temple.
високо́сный год leap-year.
вист whist.
вися́чий hanging; **~ замо́к** padlock; **~ мост** suspension bridge.
витами́н vitamin.
витиева́тый flowery, ornate.
вито́й twisted, spiral. **вито́к** (-тка́) turn, coil.
витра́ж (-а́) stained-glass window. **витри́на** shop-window; showcase.
вить (вью, вьёшь; вил, -а́, -о) *impf* (*pf* **с~**) twist, wind, weave; **~ся** wind, twine; curl; twist; whirl.
вихо́р (-хра́) tuft. **вихра́стый** shaggy.
вихрь *m* whirlwind; vortex; **сне́жный ~** blizzard.
ви́це- *pref* vice-. **ви́це-адмира́л** vice-admiral. **~президе́нт** vice-president.
ВИЧ (*abbr of* **ви́рус иммунодефици́та челове́ка**) HIV.
вишнёвый cherry. **ви́шня** (*gen pl* -шен) cherry, cherries; cherry-tree.
вишу́: *see* **висе́ть**
вишь *partl* look, just look!
вка́лывать *impf* (*sl*) work hard; *impf of* **вколо́ть**
вка́пывать *impf of* **вкопа́ть**
вкати́ть (-ачу́, -а́тишь) *pf*, **вка́тывать** *impf* roll in; administer.
вклад deposit; contribution.
вкла́дка, вкладно́й лист loose leaf, insert. **вкла́дчик** depositor.
вкла́дывать *impf of* **вложи́ть**.
вкле́ивать *impf*, **вкле́ить** *pf* stick in.
вкли́ниваться *impf*, **вкли́ниться** *pf* edge one's way in.
включа́тель *m* switch. **включа́ть** *impf*, **включи́ть** (-чу́) *pf* include; switch on; plug in; **~ся в**+*acc* join in, enter into. **включа́я** including. **включе́ние** inclusion, insertion; switching on. **включи́тельно** *adv* inclusive.
вкола́чивать *impf*, **вколоти́ть** (-очу́, -о́тишь) *pf* hammer in, knock in.

вколо́ть (-олю́, -о́лешь) *pf* (*impf* **вка́лывать**) stick (in).
вкопа́ть *pf* (*impf* **вка́пывать**) dig in.
вкось *adv* obliquely.
вкра́дчивый ingratiating. **вкра́дываться** *impf*, **вкра́сться** (-аду́сь, -адёшься) *pf* creep in; insinuate o.s.
вкра́тце *adv* briefly, succinctly.
вкривь *adv* aslant; wrongly, perversely.
вкруг = **вокру́г**
вкруту́ю *adv* hard(-boiled).
вкус taste. **вкуси́ть** (-ушу́, -у́сишь) *pf*, **вкуша́ть** *impf* taste; partake of. **вку́сный** (-сен, -сна́, -о) tasty, nice.
вла́га moisture.
влага́лище vagina.
владе́лец (-льца), **-лица** owner. **владе́ние** ownership; possession; property. **владе́тель** *m*, **-ница** possessor; sovereign. **владе́ть** (-е́ю) *impf* +*instr* own, possess; control.
влады́ка *m* master, sovereign.
влады́чество dominion, sway.
вла́жность humidity; moisture. **вла́жный** (-жен, -жна́, -о) damp, moist, humid.
вла́мываться *impf of* **вломи́ться**
вла́ствовать *impf* +(**над**+) *instr* rule, hold sway over. **властели́н** ruler; master. **вла́стный** imperious, commanding; empowered, competent. **власть** (*gen pl* -е́й) power; authority.
вле́во *adv* to the left (**от**+*gen* of).
влеза́ть *impf*, **влезть** (-зу; влез) *pf* climb in; get in; fit in.
влёк *etc.*: *see* **влечь**
влета́ть *impf*, **влете́ть** (-ечу́) *pf* fly in; rush in.
влече́ние attraction; inclination. **влечь** (-еку́, -ечёшь; влёк, -ла́) *impf* draw; attract; ~ **за собо́й** involve, entail.
влива́ть *impf*, **влить** (волью́, -ёшь; влил, -а́, -о) *pf* pour in; instil.
влия́ние influence. **влия́тельный** influential. **влия́ть** *impf* (*pf* **по**~) **на**+*acc* influence, affect.
вложе́ние enclosure; investment. **вложи́ть** (-ожу́, -о́жишь) *pf* (*impf* **вкла́дывать**) put in, insert; enclose; invest.
вломи́ться (-млю́сь, -мишься) *pf* (*impf* **вла́мываться**) break in.
влюби́ть (-блю́, -бишь) *pf*, **влюбля́ть** *impf* make fall in love (**в**+*acc* with); ~**ся** fall in love. **влюблённый** (-лён, -а́) in love; *sb* lover.
вма́зать (-а́жу) *pf*, **вма́зывать** *impf* cement, putty in.
вмени́ть *pf*, **вменя́ть** *impf* impute; impose. **вменя́емый** (*law*) responsible; sane.
вме́сте *adv* together; ~ **с тем** at the same time, also.
вмести́лище receptacle. **вмести́мость** capacity; tonnage. **вмести́тельный** capacious. **вмести́ть** (-ещу́) *pf* (*impf* **вмеща́ть**) hold, accommodate; put; ~**ся** go in.
вме́сто *prep*+*gen* instead of.
вмеша́тельство interference; intervention. **вмеша́ть** *pf*, **вме́шивать** *impf* mix in; implicate; ~**ся** interfere, intervene.
вмеща́ть(ся *impf of* **вмести́ть(ся**
вмиг *adv* in an instant.

вминáть *impf*, **вмять** (вомнý, -нёшь) *pf* press in, dent. **вмя́тина** dent.

внаём, внаймы́ *adv* to let; for hire.

вначáле *adv* at first.

вне *prep+gen* outside; ~ **себя́** beside o.s.

вне- *pref* extra-; outside; -less. **внебрáчный** extra-marital; illegitimate. **~врéменный** timeless. **~клáссный** extra-curricular. **~очереднóй** out of turn; extraordinary. **~штáтный** freelance, casual.

внедрéние introduction; inculcation. **внедри́ть** *pf*, **внедря́ть** *impf* inculcate; introduce; **~ся** take root.

внезáпно *adv* suddenly. **внезáпный** sudden.

внéмлю *etc.*: *see* **внимáть**

внесéние bringing in; deposit. **внести́** (-сý, -сёшь; внёс, -лá) *pf* (*impf* **вноси́ть**) bring in; introduce; deposit; insert.

внéшне *adv* outwardly. **внéшний** outer; external; outside; foreign. **внéшность** exterior; appearance.

вниз *adv* down(wards); ~ **по**+*dat* down. **внизý** *adv* below; downstairs.

вникáть *impf*, **вни́кнуть** (-ну; вник) *pf* **+в**+*acc* go carefully into, investigate thoroughly.

внимáние attention. **внимáтельный** attentive. **внимáть** *impf* (*pf* **внять**) listen to; heed.

вничью́ *adv*: **окóнчиться** ~ end in a draw; **сыгрáть** ~ draw.

вновь *adv* anew, again.

вноси́ть (-ошý, -óсишь) *impf of* **внести́**

внук grandson; *pl* grandchildren, descendants.

внýтренний inner; internal. **внýтренность** interior; *pl* entrails; internal organs. **внутри́** *adv* & *prep+gen* inside. **внутрь** *adv* & *prep+gen* inside, in; inwards.

внучáта (*pl*; *gen* -чáт) grandchildren. **внучáтый** second, great-; ~ **брат** second cousin; ~ **племя́нник** great-nephew. **внýчка** grand-daughter.

внушáть *impf*, **внуши́ть** (-шý) *pf* instil; *+dat* inspire with. **внушéние** suggestion; reproof. **внуши́тельный** inspiring; imposing.

вня́тный distinct. **внять** (*no fut*; -ял, -á, -о) *pf of* **внимáть**

во: *see* **в**

вобрáть (вберý, -рёшь; -áл, -á, -о) *pf* (*impf* **вбирáть**) absorb; inhale.

вобью́ *etc.*: *see* **вбить**

вовлекáть *impf*, **вовлéчь** (-екý, -ечёшь; -ёк, -еклá) *pf* draw in, involve.

вóвремя *adv* in time; on time.

вóвсе *adv* quite; ~ **не** not at all.

во-вторы́х *adv* secondly.

вогнáть (вгоню́, -óнишь; -гнáл, -á, -о) *pf* (*impf* **вгоня́ть**) drive in. **вóгнутый** concave. **вогнýть** (-нý, -нёшь) *pf* (*impf* **вгибáть**) bend or curve inwards.

водá (*acc* вóду, *gen* -ы́; *pl* -ы) water; *pl* the waters; spa.

водвори́ть *pf*, **водворя́ть** *impf* settle, install; establish.

води́тель *m* driver. **води́ть** (вожý, вóдишь) *impf* lead; conduct; take; drive; **~ся** be found; associate (with); be the custom.

вóдка vodka. **вóдн|ый** water; **~ые лы́жи** water-skiing; water-skis.

водо- *in comb* water, water-; hydraulic; hydro-. **водобоя́знь** hydrophobia. **~воро́т** whirlpool; maelstrom. **~ём** reservoir. **~измещéние** displacement. **~ка́чка** water-tower, pumping station. **~ла́з** diver. **~лéй** Aquarius. **~непроница́емый** waterproof. **~отво́дный** drainage. **~па́д** waterfall. **~по́й** watering-place. **~прово́д** water-pipe, water-main; water supply. **~прово́дчик** plumber. **~раздéл** watershed. **~ро́д** hydrogen. **во́доросль** water-plant; seaweed. **~снабжéние** water supply. **~сто́к** drain, gutter. **~храни́лище** reservoir.

водружа́ть *impf*, **водрузи́ть** (-ужу́) *pf* hoist; erect.

водяни́стый watery. **водяно́й** water.

воева́ть (вою́ю) *impf* wage war. **воево́да** *m* voivode; commander.

воеди́но *adv* together.

военко́м military commissar.

военно- *in comb* military; war-. **вое́нно-возду́шный** air-, air-force. **вое́нно-морско́й** naval. **~плéнный** *sb* prisoner of war. **вое́нно-полево́й суд** court-martial. **~слу́жащий** *sb* serviceman.

вое́нн|ый military; war; *sb* serviceman; **~ое положéние** martial law; **~ый суд** court-martial.

вожа́к (-á) guide; leader. **вожа́тый** *sb* guide; tram-driver.

вождéлéние desire, lust.

вождь (-я́) *m* leader, chief.

вожжа́ (*pl* -и, -éй) rein.

вожу́ *etc.*: *see* **води́ть, вози́ть**

воз (*loc* -ý; *pl* -ы́) cart; cartload.

возбуди́мый excitable. **возбуди́тель** *m* agent; instigator. **возбуди́ть** (-ужу́) *pf*, **возбужда́ть** *impf* excite, arouse; incite. **возбужда́ющ|ий: ~ее срéдство** stimulant. **возбуждéние** excitement. **возбуждённый** excited.

возвести́ (-еду́, -дёшь; -вёл, -ла́) *pf* (*impf* **возводи́ть**) elevate; erect; level; **+к+***dat* trace to.

возвести́ть (-ещу́) *pf*, **возвеща́ть** *impf* proclaim.

возводи́ть (-ожу́, -о́дишь) *impf of* **возвести́**

возвра́т return; repayment. **возврати́ть** (-ащу́) *pf*, **возвраща́ть** *impf* (*pf also* **верну́ть**) return, give back; **~ся** return; go back, come back. **возвра́тный** return; reflexive. **возвращéние** return.

возвы́сить *pf*, **возвыша́ть** *impf* raise; ennoble; **~ся** rise. **возвышéние** rise; raised place. **возвы́шенность** height; loftiness. **возвы́шенный** high; elevated.

возгла́вить (-влю) *pf*, **возглавля́ть** *impf* head.

во́зглас exclamation. **возгласи́ть** (-ашу́) *pf*, **возглаша́ть** *impf* proclaim.

возгора́емый inflammable. **возгора́ться** *impf*, **возгорéться** (-рю́сь) *pf* flare up; be seized (with).

воздава́ть (-даю́, -даёшь) *impf*, **возда́ть** (-а́м, -а́шь, -а́ст, -ади́м; -а́л, -á, -о) *pf* render.

воздвига́ть *impf*, **воздви́гнуть** (-ну; -дви́г) *pf* raise.

воздéйствие influence. **воздéйствовать** *impf* & *pf* **+на+***acc* influence.

воздéлать *pf*, **воздéлывать**

impf cultivate, till.
воздержáние abstinence; abstention. **воздéржанный** abstemious. **воздержáться** (-жýсь, -жишься) *pf*, **воздéрживаться** *impf* refrain; abstain.
вóздух air. **воздухонепроницáемый** air-tight. **воздýшн|ый** air, aerial; airy; flimsy; **~ый змей** kite; **~ый шар** balloon.
воззвáние appeal. **воззвáть** (-зовý, -вёшь) *pf* (*impf* **взывáть**) appeal (**о**+*prep* for).
воззрéние opinion, outlook.
возúть (вожý, вóзишь) *impf* convey; carry; bring, take; **~ся** romp, play noisily; busy o.s.; potter about.
возлагáть *impf of* **возложúть**
вóзле *adv* & *prep+gen* by, near; near by; past.
возложúть (-жý, -жишь) *pf* (*impf* **возлагáть**) lay; place.
возлю́бленный beloved; *sb* sweetheart.
возмéздие retribution.
возместúть (-ещý) *pf*, **возмещáть** *impf* compensate for; refund. **возмещéние** compensation; refund.
возмóжно *adv* possibly; *+comp* as ... as possible. **возмóжность** possibility; opportunity. **возмóжный** possible.
возмужáлый mature; grown up. **возмужáть** *pf* grow up; gain strength.
возмутúтельный disgraceful. **возмутúть** (-ущý) *pf*, **возмущáть** *impf* disturb; stir up; rouse to indignation; **~ся** be indignant. **возмущéние** indignation. **возмущённый** (-щён, -щенá) indignant.
вознаградúть (-ажý) *pf*, **вознаграждáть** *impf* reward. **вознаграждéние** reward; fee.
возненавúдеть (-úжу) *pf* conceive a hatred for.
вознесéние Ascension. **вознестú** (-несý, -несёшь; -нёс, -лá) *pf* (*impf* **возносúть**) raise, lift up; **~сь** rise; ascend.
возникáть *impf*, **вознúкнуть** (-нет; -нúк) *pf* arise, spring up. **возникновéние** rise, beginning, origin.
вознúца *m* coachman.
возносúть(ся (-ошý(сь, -óсишь(ся) *impf of* **вознестú(сь. возношéние** raising, elevation.
возня́ row, noise; bother.
возобновúть (-влю́) *pf*, **возобновля́ть** *impf* renew; restore; **~ся** begin again. **возобновлéние** renewal; revival.
возражáть *impf*, **возразúть** (-ажý) *pf* object. **возражéние** objection.
вóзраст age. **возрастáние** growth, increase. **возрастáть** *impf*, **возрастú** (-тёт; -рóс, -лá) *pf* grow, increase.
возродúть (-ожý) *pf*, **возрождáть** *impf* revive; **~ся** revive. **возрождéние** revival; Renaissance.
возрóс *etc.*: *see* **возрастú.**
возрóсший increased.
вóзчик carter, carrier.
возьмý *etc.*: *see* **взять**
вóин warrior; soldier. **вóинск|ий** military; **~ая повúнность** conscription. **воúнственный** warlike. **воúнствующий** militant.
вой howl(ing); wail(ing).
войдý *etc.*: *see* **войтú**
вóйлок felt. **вóйлочный** felt.

война́ (*pl* -ы) war.
во́йско (*pl* -а́) army; *pl* troops, forces. **войсково́й** military.
войти́ (-йду́, -йдёшь; вошёл, -шла́) *pf* (*impf* **входи́ть**) go in, come in, enter; get in(to); **~ в систе́му** (*comput*) log on.
вокза́л (railway) station.
во́кмен Walkman (*propr*), personal stereo.
вокру́г *adv* & *prep+gen* round, around.
вол (-а́) ox, bullock.
вола́н flounce; shuttlecock.
волды́рь (-я́) *m* blister; bump.
волево́й strong-willed.
волейбо́л volleyball.
во́лей-нево́лей *adv* willy-nilly.
волк (*pl* -и, -о́в) wolf. **волкода́в** wolf-hound.
волна́ (*pl* -ы, во́лна́м) wave. **волне́ние** choppiness; agitation; emotion. **волни́стый** wavy. **волнова́ть** *impf* (*pf* **вз~**) disturb; agitate; excite; **~ся** be disturbed; worry, be nervous. **волноло́м, волноре́з** breakwater. **волну́ющий** disturbing; exciting.
волоки́та red tape; rigmarole.
волокни́стый fibrous, stringy. **волокно́** (*pl* -а) fibre.
волоку́ *etc.*: *see* **воло́чь**
во́лос (*pl* -ы, -о́с, -а́м); *pl* hair. **волоса́тый** hairy. **волосно́й** capillary.
во́лость (*pl* -и, -е́й) volost (*administrative division*).
волочи́ть (-очу́, -о́чишь) *impf* drag; **~ся** drag, trail; +**за**+*instr* run after, court. **воло́чь** (-оку́, -очёшь; -о́к, -ла́) *impf* drag.
во́лчий wolf's; wolfish. **волчи́ха, волчи́ца** she-wolf.
волчо́к (-чка́) top; gyroscope.
волчо́нок (-нка; *pl* -ча́та, -ча́т) wolf cub.
волше́бник magician; wizard. **волше́бница** enchantress. **волше́бный** magic, magical; enchanting. **волшебство́** magic, enchantment.
вольнонаёмный civilian.
во́льность liberty; license. **во́льный** (-лен, -льна́, -о, во́льны́) free; free-style.
вольт[1] (*gen pl* вольт) volt.
вольт[2] (*loc* -у́) vault.
вольфра́м tungsten.
во́ля will; liberty.
вомну́ *etc.*: *see* **вмять**
вон *adv* out; off, away.
вон *partl* there, over there.
вонза́ть *impf*, **вонзи́ть** (-нжу́) *pf* plunge, thrust.
вонь stench. **вонючий** stinking. **воня́ть** stink.
вообража́емый imaginary. **вообража́ть** *impf*, **вообрази́ть** (-ажу́) *pf* imagine. **воображе́ние** imagination. **вообрази́мый** imaginable.
вообще́ *adv* in general; generally.
воодушеви́ть (-влю́) *pf*, **воодушевля́ть** *impf* inspire. **воодушевле́ние** inspiration; fervour.
вооружа́ть *impf*, **вооружи́ть** (-жу́) *pf* arm, equip; **~ся** arm o.s.; take up arms. **вооруже́ние** arming; arms; equipment. **вооружённый** (-жён, -а́) armed; equipped.
во́очию *adv* with one's own eyes.
во-пе́рвых *adv* first, first of all.
вопи́ть (-плю́) *impf* yell, howl. **вопию́щий** crying; scandalous.
воплоти́ть (-ощу́) *pf*, **воплоща́ть** *impf* embody. **воплоще́ние** embodiment.

вопль *m* cry, wail; howling.
вопреки́ *prep+dat* in spite of.
вопро́с question; problem. **вопроси́тельный** interrogative; questioning; ~ **знак** question-mark.
вор (*pl* -ы, -о́в) thief; criminal.
ворва́ться (-ву́сь, -вёшься; -а́лся, -ла́сь, -а́ло́сь) *pf* (*impf* **врыва́ться**) burst in.
воркотня́ grumbling.
воробе́й sparrow.
ворова́тый thievish; furtive. **ворова́ть** *impf* (*pf* **с~**) steal. **воро́вка** woman thief. **воровски́** *adv* furtively. **воровско́й** thieves'. **воровство́** stealing; theft.
во́рон raven. **воро́на** crow.
воро́нка funnel; crater.
вороно́й black.
во́рот[1] collar; neckband.
во́рот[2] winch; windlass.
воро́та (*pl*; *gen* -ро́т) gate(s); gateway; goal.
вороти́ть (-очу́, -о́тишь) *pf* bring back, get back; turn back; **~ся** return.
воротни́к (-а́) collar.
во́рох (*pl* -а́) heap, pile; heaps.
воро́чать *impf* turn; move; *+instr* have control of; **~ся** move, turn.
ворочу́(сь *etc.*: *see* **вороти́ть(ся**
вороши́ть (-шу́) *impf* stir up; turn (over).
ворс nap, pile.
ворча́ть (-чу́) *impf* grumble; growl. **ворчли́вый** peevish; grumpy.
восвоя́си *adv* home.
восемна́дцатый eighteenth. **восемна́дцать** eighteen.
во́семь (-сьми́, *instr* -сьмью́ *or* -семью́) eight. **во́семьдесят** (-сьми́десяти, -сьмью́десятью) eighty. **восемьсо́т** (-сьмисо́т, -ста́ми) eight hundred. **во́семью** *adv* eight times.
воск wax, beeswax.
воскли́кнуть (-ну) *pf*, **восклица́ть** *impf* exclaim. **восклица́ние** exclamation. **восклица́тельный** exclamatory; ~ **знак** exclamation mark.
восково́й wax; waxy; waxed.
воскреса́ть *impf*, **воскре́снуть** (-ну; -е́с) *pf* rise from the dead; revive. **воскресе́ние** resurrection. **воскресе́нье** Sunday. **воскреси́ть** (-ешу́) *pf*, **воскреша́ть** *impf* resurrect; revive. **воскреше́ние** resurrection; revival.
воспале́ние inflammation. **воспалённый** (-лён, -а́) inflamed. **воспали́ть** *pf*, **воспаля́ть** *impf* inflame; **~ся** become inflamed.
воспита́ние upbringing, education. **воспи́танник, -ница** pupil. **воспи́танный** well-brought-up. **воспита́тель** *m* tutor; educator. **воспита́тельный** educational. **воспита́ть** *pf*, **воспи́тывать** *impf* bring up; foster; educate.
воспламени́ть *pf*, **воспламеня́ть** *impf* ignite; fire; **~ся** ignite; flare up. **воспламеня́емый** inflammable.
вос|по́льзоваться *pf*.
воспомина́ние recollection, memory; *pl* memoirs; reminiscences.
вос|препя́тствовать *pf*.
воспрети́ть (-ещу́) *pf*, **воспреща́ть** *impf* forbid. **воспреще́ние** prohibition. **воспрещённый** (-щён, -а́) prohibited.
восприи́мчивый impressionable; susceptible. **восприни-**

мáть *impf*, **восприня́ть** (-иму́, -и́мешь; -и́нял, -á, -o) *pf* perceive; grasp. **восприя́тие** perception.

воспроизведéние reproduction. **воспроизвести́** (-еду́, -едёшь; -вёл, -á) *pf*, **воспроизводи́ть** (-ожу́, -óдишь) *impf* reproduce. **воспроизводи́тельный** reproductive.

вос|проти́виться (-влюсь) *pf*.

воссоединéние reunification. **воссоедини́ть** *pf*, **воссоединя́ть** *impf* reunite.

восставáть (-таю́, -таёшь) *impf of* **восстáть**.

восстáние insurrection, uprising.

восстанови́ть (-влю́, -вишь) *pf* (*impf* **восстанáвливать**) restore; reinstate; recall; ~ **прóтив**+*gen* set against. **восстановлéние** restoration.

восстáть (-áну) *pf* (*impf* **восставáть**) rise (up).

востóк east.

востóрг delight, rapture. **восторгáться**+*instr* be delighted with, go into raptures over. **востóрженный** enthusiastic.

востóчный east, eastern; easterly; oriental.

вострéбование: до вострéбования to be called for, poste restante.

восхвали́ть (-лю́, -лишь) *pf*, **восхваля́ть** *impf* praise, extol.

восхити́тельный entrancing; delightful. **восхити́ть** (-хищу́) *pf*, **восхищáть** *impf* enrapture; **~ся** +*instr* be enraptured by. **восхищéние** delight; admiration.

восхóд rising. **восходи́ть** (-ожу́, -óдишь) *impf of* **взойти́**; ~ **к**+*dat* go back to, date from. **восхождéние** ascent. **восходя́щий** rising.

восшéствие accession.

восьмáя *sb* eighth; octave.

восьмёрка eight; figure eight; No. 8; figure of eight.

восьми- *in comb* eight-; octo-. **восьмигрáнник** octahedron. **~деся́тый** eightieth. **~лéтний** eight-year; eight-year-old. **~сóтый** eight-hundredth. **~угóльник** octagon. **~угóльный** octagonal.

восьмóй eighth.

вот *partl* here (is), there (is); this (is); ~ **и всё** and that's all; ~ **как!** no! really? ~ **тáк!** that's right!; ~ **что!** no! not really? **вот-вóт** *adv* just, on the point of; *partl* that's right!

воткну́ть (-ну́, -нёшь) *pf* (*impf* **втыкáть**) stick in, drive in.

вотру́ *etc.*: *see* **втерéть**

воцари́ться *pf*, **воцаря́ться** *impf* come to the throne; set in.

вошёл *etc.*: *see* **войти́**

вошь (вши; *gen pl* вшей) louse.

вошью́ *etc.*: *see* **вшить**

вóю *etc.*: *see* **выть**

вою́ю *etc.*: *see* **воевáть**

впадáть *impf*, **впасть** (-аду́) *pf* flow; lapse; fall in; +**в**+*acc* verge on, approximate to. **впадéние** confluence, (river-)mouth. **впáдина** cavity, hollow; socket. **впáлый** sunken.

впервы́е *adv* for the first time.

вперёд *adv* forward(s), ahead; in future; in advance; **идти́** ~ (*of clock*) be fast. **впереди́** *adv* in front, ahead; in (the) future; *prep*+*gen* in front of, before.

впечатлéние impression. **впечатли́тельный** impressionable.

вписа́ть (-ишу́, -и́шешь) *pf*, **впи́сывать** *impf* enter, insert; **~ся** be enrolled, join.

впита́ть *pf*, **впи́тывать** *impf* absorb, take in; **~ся** soak.

впи́хивать *impf*, **впи́хнуть** (-ну́, -нёшь) *pf* cram in; shove.

вплавь *adv* (by) swimming.

вплести́ (-ету́, -етёшь; -ёл, -á) *pf*, **вплета́ть** *impf* plait in, intertwine; involve.

вплотну́ю *adv* close; in earnest.

вплоть *adv*; **~ до**+*gen* (right) up to.

вполго́лоса *adv* under one's breath.

вполне́ *adv* fully, entirely; quite.

впопыха́х *adv* hastily; in one's haste.

впо́ру *adv* at the right time; just right, exactly.

впосле́дствии *adv* subsequently.

впотьма́х *adv* in the dark.

впра́ве *adv*: **быть ~** have a right.

впра́во *adv* to the right (**от**+*gen* of).

впредь *adv* in (the) future; **~ до**+*gen* until.

впро́голодь *adv* half starving.

впро́чем *conj* however, but; though.

впры́скивание injection. **впры́скивать** *impf*, **впры́снуть** (-ну) *pf* inject.

впряга́ть *impf* **впрячь** (-ягу́, -яжёшь; -яг, -ла́) *pf* harness.

впуск admittance. **впуска́ть** *impf*, **впусти́ть** (-ущу́, -у́стишь) *pf* admit, let in.

впусту́ю *adv* to no purpose, in vain.

впущу́ *etc.*: *see* **впусти́ть**

враг (-á) enemy. **вражда́** enmity. **вражде́бный** hostile. **враждова́ть** be at enmity.

вра́жеский enemy.

вразбро́д *adv* separately, disunitedly.

вразре́з *adv*: **идти́ ~ с**+*instr* go against.

вразуми́тельный intelligible, clear; persuasive.

врасплóх *adv* unawares.

враста́ть *impf*, **врасти́** (-тёт; врос, -ла́) *pf* grow in; take root.

врата́рь (-я́) *m* goalkeeper.

врать (вру, врёшь; -ал, -á, -о) *impf* (*pf* **на~**, **со~**) lie, tell lies; talk nonsense.

врач (-á) doctor. **враче́бный** medical.

враща́ть *impf* rotate, revolve; **~ся** revolve, rotate. **враще́ние** rotation, revolution.

вред (-á) harm; damage.

вреди́тель *m* pest; wrecker; *pl* vermin. **вреди́тельство** wrecking, (act of) sabotage.

вреди́ть (-ежу́) *impf* (*pf* **по~**) +*dat* harm; damage. **вре́дный** (-ден, -дна́, -о) harmful.

вре́зать (-е́жу) *pf*, **вреза́ть** *impf* cut in; set in; (*sl*) +*dat* hit; **~ся** cut (into); run (into); be engraved; fall in love.

времена́ми *adv* at times. **вре́менно** *adv* temporarily. **временно́й** temporal. **вре́менный** temporary; provisional.

вре́мя (-мени; *pl* -мена́, -мён, -а́м) *neut* time; tense; **~ го́да** season; **~ от вре́мени** at times, from time to time; **на ~** for a time; **ско́лько вре́мени?** what is the time?; **тем вре́менем** meanwhile.

вро́вень *adv* level, on a level.

вро́де *prep*+*gen* like; *partl* such as, like; apparently.

врождённый (-дён, -á) innate.

врознь, врозь *adv* separately, apart.

врос *etc.*: *see* **врасти. вру** *etc.*: *see* **врать**
врун (-á), **врýнья** liar.
вручáть *impf*, **вручи́ть** (-чý) *pf* hand, deliver; entrust.
вручнýю *adv* by hand.
врывáть(ся *impf of* **ворвáться**
вряд (ли) *adv* it's not likely; hardly, scarcely.
всади́ть (-ажý, -áдишь) *pf*, **всáживать** *impf* thrust in; sink in. **всáдник** rider, horseman. **всáдница** rider, horsewoman.
всáсывать *impf of* **всосáть**
всё, все *pron*: *see* **весь. всё** *adv* always, all the time; ~ **(ещё)** still; *conj* however, nevertheless; ~ **же** all the same.
все- *in comb* all-, omni-. **всевозмóжный** of every kind; all possible. **~дозвóленность** permissiveness. **~мéрный** of every kind. **~ми́рный** world, world-wide. **~могýщий** omnipotent. **~нарóдно** *adv* publicly. **~нарóдный** national; nation-wide. **~объéмлющий** comprehensive, all-embracing. **~росси́йский** All-Russian. **~си́льный** omnipotent. **~сторóнний** all-round; comprehensive.
всегдá always.
всегó *adv* in all, all told; only.
вселéнная *sb* universe.
всели́ть *pf*, **вселя́ть** *impf* install, lodge; inspire; **~ся** move in, install o.s.; be implanted.
всéнощная *sb* night service.
всеóбщий general, universal.
всерьёз *adv* seriously, in earnest.
всё-таки *conj & partl* all the same, still. **всецéло** *adv* completely.
вскáкивать *impf of* **вскочи́ть**
вскачь *adv* at a gallop.
вскипáть *impf*, **вс|кипéть** (-плю́) *pf* boil up; flare up.
вс|кипяти́ть(ся (-ячý(сь) *pf*.
всколыхнýть (-нý, -нёшь) *pf* stir; stir up.
вскользь *adv* slightly; in passing.
вскóре *adv* soon, shortly after.
вскочи́ть (-очý, -óчишь) *pf* (*impf* **вскáкивать**) jump up.
вскри́кивать *impf*, **вскри́кнуть** (-ну) *pf* shriek, scream.
вскричáть (-чý) *pf* exclaim.
вскрывáть *impf*, **вскрыть** (-рóю) *pf* open; reveal; dissect. **вскры́тие** opening; revelation; post-mortem.
вслед *adv & prep+dat* after; ~ **за**+*instr* after, following.
вслéдствие *prep+gen* in consequence of.
вслепýю *adv* blindly; blindfold.
вслух *adv* aloud.
вслýшаться *pf*, **вслýшиваться** *impf* listen attentively.
всмáтриваться *impf*, **всмотрéться** (-рюсь, -ришься) *pf* look closely.
всмя́тку *adv* soft(-boiled).
всóвывать *impf of* **всýнуть**
всосáть (-сý, -сёшь) *pf* (*impf* **всáсывать**) suck in; absorb; imbibe.
вс|пахáть (-ашý, -áшешь) *pf*, **вспáхивать** *impf* plough up. **вспáшка** ploughing.
вс|пéниться *pf*.
всплеск splash. **всплёскивать** *impf*, **всплеснýть** (-нý, -нёшь) *pf* splash; ~ **рукáми** throw up one's hands.
всплывáть *impf*, **всплыть**

(-ывý, -ывёшь; -ыл, -á, -о) *pf* rise to the surface; come to light.

вспоминáть *impf*, **вспóмнить** *pf* remember; **~ся** *impers* +*dat*: **мне вспóмнилось** I remembered.

вспомогáтельный auxiliary.

вс|потéть *pf*.

вспрыгивать *impf*, **вспрыгнуть** (-ну) *pf* jump up.

вспухáть *impf*, **вс|пýхнуть** (-нет; -ух) *pf* swell up.

вспылúть *pf* flare up. **вспы́льчивый** hot-tempered.

вспы́хивать *impf*, **вспы́хнуть** (-ну) *pf* blaze up; flare up. **вспы́шка** flash; outburst; outbreak.

вставáть (-таю, -таёшь) *impf of* **встать**

встáвить (-влю) *pf*, **вставля́ть** *impf* put in, insert. **встáвка** insertion; framing, mounting; inset. **вставн|óй** inserted; set in; **~ы́е зýбы** false teeth.

встать (-áну) *pf* (*impf* **вставáть**) get up; stand up.

встревóженный *adj* anxious.

вс|тревóжить (-жу) *pf*.

встрепенýться (-нýсь, -нёшься) *pf* rouse o.s.; start (up); beat faster.

встрéтить (-éчу) *pf*, **встречáть** *impf* meet (with); **~ся** meet; be found. **встрéча** meeting. **встрéчный** coming to meet; contrary, head; counter; *sb* person met with; **пéрвый ~** the first person you meet, anybody.

встря́ска shaking; shock. **встря́хивать** *impf*, **встряхнýть** (-нý, -нёшь) *pf* shake (up); rouse; **~ся** shake o.s.; rouse o.s.

вступáть *impf*, **вступúть** (-плю, -пишь) *pf* +**в**+*acc* enter (into); join (in); +**на**+*acc* go up, mount; **~ся** intervene; +**за**+*acc* stand up for. **вступúтельный** introductory; entrance. **вступлéние** entry, joining; introduction.

всýнуть (-ну) *pf* (*impf* **всóвывать**) put in, stick in.

всхлúпнуть (-ну) *pf*, **всхлúпывать** *impf* sob.

всходúть (-ожý, -óдишь) *impf of* **взойтú. всхóды** (*pl*; *gen* -ов) (corn-)shoots.

всю: *see* **весь**

всюду *adv* everywhere.

вся: *see* **весь**

вся́к|ий any; every, all kinds of; **~ом слýчае** in any case; **на ~ий слýчай** just in case; *pron* anyone. **вся́чески** *adv* in every possible way.

втáйне *adv* secretly.

втáлкивать *impf of* **втолкнýть. втáптывать** *impf of* **втоптáть. втáскивать** *impf*, **втащúть** (-щý, -щишь) *pf* drag in.

втерéть (вотрý, вотрёшь; втёр) *pf* (*impf* **втирáть**) rub in; **~ся** insinuate o.s., worm o.s.

втирáть(ся *impf of* **втерéть(ся**

втúскивать *impf*, **втúснуть** (-ну) *pf* squeeze in; **~ся** squeeze (o.s.) in.

втихомóлку *adv* surreptitiously.

втолкнýть (-нý, -нёшь) *pf* (*impf* **втáлкивать**) push in.

втоптáть (-пчý, -пчешь) *pf* (*impf* **втáптывать**) trample (in).

вторгáться *impf*, **вторгнуться** (-нусь; вторгся, -лась)

pf invade; intrude. **вторже́ние** invasion; intrusion.
вто́рить *impf* play or sing second part; *+dat* repeat, echo. **втори́чный** second, secondary. **вто́рник** Tuesday. **втор|о́й** second; **~о́е** *sb* second course. **второстепе́нный** secondary, minor.
второпя́х *adv* in haste.
в-тре́тьих *adv* thirdly. **втро́е** *adv* three times. **втроём** *adv* three (together). **втройне́** *adv* three times as much.
вту́лка plug.
втыка́ть *impf of* **воткну́ть**
втя́гивать *impf*, **втяну́ть** (-ну́, -нешь) *pf* draw in; **~ся** +**в**+*acc* enter; get used to.
вуа́ль veil.
вуз *abbr* (*of* **вы́сшее учёбное заведе́ние**) higher educational establishment; college.
вулка́н volcano.
вульга́рный vulgar.
вундерки́нд infant prodigy.
вход entrance; entry. **входи́ть** (-ожу́, -о́дишь) *impf of* **войти́**. **входно́й** entrance.
вхолосту́ю *adv* idle, free.
вцепи́ться (-плю́сь, -пишься) *pf*, **вцепля́ться** *impf* +**в**+*acc* clutch, catch hold of.
вчера́ *adv* yesterday. **вчера́шний** yesterday's.
вчерне́ in rough.
вче́тверо *adv* four times. **вчетверо́м** *adv* four (together).
вши *etc.*: *see* **вошь**
вшива́ть *impf of* **вшить**
вши́вый lousy.
вширь *adv* in breadth; widely.
вшить (вошью́, -ьёшь) *pf* (*impf* **вшива́ть**) sew in.
въе́дливый corrosive; caustic.
въезд entry; entrance. **въезжа́ть** *impf*, **въе́хать** (-е́ду, -е́дешь) *pf* (+**в**+*acc*) ride in(to); drive in(to); crash into.
вы (вас, вам, ва́ми, вас) *pron* you.
выбега́ть *impf*, **вы́бежать** (-егу, -ежишь) *pf* run out.
вы́|белить *pf*.
вы́беру *etc.*: *see* **вы́брать**.
выбива́ть(ся *impf of* **вы́бить(ся**. **выбира́ть(ся** *impf of* **вы́брать(ся**
вы́бить (-бью) *pf* (*impf* **выбива́ть**) knock out; dislodge; **~ся** get out; break loose; come out; **~ся из сил** exhaust o.s.
вы́бор choice; selection; *pl* election(s). **вы́борный** elective; electoral. **вы́борочный** selective.
вы́|бранить *pf*. **выбра́сывать(ся** *impf of* **вы́бросить(ся**
вы́брать (-беру) *pf* (*impf* **выбира́ть**) choose; elect; take out; **~ся** get out.
выбрива́ть *impf*, **вы́брить** (-рею) *pf* shave.
вы́бросить (-ошу) *pf* (*impf* **выбра́сывать**) throw out; throw away; **~ся** throw o.s. out, leap out.
выбыва́ть *impf*, **вы́быть** (-буду) *pf* **из**+*gen* leave, quit.
выва́ливать *impf*, **вы́валить** *pf* throw out; pour out; **~ся** tumble out.
вы́везти (-зу; -ез) *pf* (*impf* **вывози́ть**) take, bring, out; export; rescue.
вы́верить *pf* (*impf* **выверя́ть**) adjust, regulate.
вы́вернуть (-ну) *pf*, **вывёртывать** *impf* turn inside out; unscrew; wrench.
выверя́ть *impf of* **вы́верить**

вы́весить (-ешу) *pf* (*impf* **вывéшивать**) weigh; hang out. **вы́веска** sign; pretext.

вы́вести (-еду; -ел) *pf* (*impf* **выводи́ть**) lead, bring, take, out; drive out; remove; exterminate; deduce; hatch; grow, breed; erect; depict; draw; **~сь** go out of use; become extinct; come out; hatch out.

выве́тривание airing.

выве́шивать *impf of* **вы́весить**

вы́вих dislocation. **выви́хивать** *impf*, **вы́вихнуть** (-ну) *pf* dislocate.

вы́вод conclusion; withdrawal. **выводи́ть(ся** (-ожу́(сь, -о́дишь(ся) *impf of* **вы́вести(сь. вы́водок** (-дка) brood; litter.

вывожу́ *see* **выводи́ть, вывози́ть**

вы́воз export; removal. **вывози́ть** (-ожу́, -о́зишь) *impf of* **вы́везти. вывозно́й** export.

вы́гадать *pf*, **выга́дывать** *impf* gain, save.

вы́гиб curve. **выгиба́ть** *impf of* **вы́гнуть**

вы|гладить (-ажу) *pf*.

вы́глядеть (-яжу) *impf* look, look like. **выгля́дывать** *impf*, **вы́глянуть** (-ну) *pf* look out; peep out.

вы́гнать (-гоню) *pf* (*impf* **выгоня́ть**) drive out; distil.

вы́гнутый curved, convex. **вы́гнуть** (-ну) *pf* (*impf* **выгиба́ть**) bend, arch.

выгова́ривать *impf*, **вы́говорить** *pf* pronounce, speak; *+dat* reprimand; **~ся** speak out. **вы́говор** pronunciation; reprimand.

вы́года advantage; gain. **вы́годный** advantageous; profitable.

вы́гон pasture; common. **выгоня́ть** *impf of* **вы́гнать**

выгора́ть *impf*, **вы́гореть** (-рит) *pf* burn down; fade.

вы́|гравировать *pf*.

выгружа́ть *impf*, **вы́грузить** (-ужу) *pf* unload; disembark. **вы́грузка** unloading; disembarkation.

выдава́ть (-даю́, -даёшь) *impf*, **вы́дать** (-ам, -ашь, -аст, -адим) *pf* give (out), issue; betray; extradite; **+за**+*acc* pass off as; **~ся** protrude; stand out; present itself. **вы́дача** issue; payment; extradition. **выдаю́щийся** prominent.

выдвига́ть *impf*, **вы́двинуть** (-ну) *pf* move out; pull out; put forward, nominate; **~ся** move forward, move out; come out; get on (in the world). **выдвиже́ние** nomination; promotion.

выделе́ние secretion; excretion; isolation; apportionment. **вы́делить** *pf*, **выделя́ть** *impf* pick out; detach; allot; secrete; excrete; isolate; **~ курси́вом** italicize; **~ся** stand out, be noted (*+instr* for).

выдёргивать *impf of* **вы́дернуть**

вы́держанный consistent; self-possessed; firm; matured, seasoned. **вы́держать** (-жу) *pf*, **выде́рживать** *impf* bear; endure; contain o.s.; pass (*exam*); sustain. **вы́держка**[1] endurance; self-possession; exposure.

вы́держка[2] excerpt.

вы́дернуть *pf* (*impf* **выдёргивать**) pull out.

вы́дохнуть (-ну) *pf* (*impf* **выдыха́ть**) breathe out; **~ся**

have lost fragrance or smell; be past one's best.

вы́дра otter.

вы́|драть (-деру) *pf.* **вы́|дрессировать** *pf.*

выдува́ть *impf of* **вы́дуть**

вы́думанный made-up, fabricated. **вы́думать** *pf*, **выду́мывать** *impf* invent; fabricate. **вы́думка** invention; device; inventiveness.

вы́дуть *pf* (*impf* **выдува́ть**) blow; blow out.

выдыха́ние exhalation. **выдыха́ть(ся** *impf of* **вы́дохнуть(ся**

вы́езд departure; exit. **вы́ездн|о́й** exit; **~ая се́ссия суда́** assizes. **выезжа́ть** *impf of* **вы́ехать**

вы́емка taking out; excavation; hollow.

вы́ехать (-еду) *pf* (*impf* **выезжа́ть**) go out, depart; drive out, ride out; move (house).

вы́жать (-жму, -жмешь) *pf* (*impf* **выжима́ть**) squeeze out; wring out.

вы́жечь (-жгу) *pf* (*impf* **выжига́ть**) burn out; cauterize.

выжива́ние survival. **выжива́ть** *impf of* **вы́жить**

выжига́ть *impf of* **вы́жечь**

выжида́тельный waiting; temporizing.

выжима́ть *impf of* **вы́жать**

вы́жить (-иву) *pf* (*impf* **выжива́ть**) survive; hound out; **~ из ума́** become senile.

вы́звать (-зову) *pf* (*impf* **вызыва́ть**) call (out); send for; challenge; provoke; **~ся** volunteer.

выздора́вливать *impf*, **вы́здороветь** (-ею) *pf* recover. **выздоровле́ние** recovery; convalescence.

вы́зов call; summons; challenge.

вы́золоченный gilt.

вызу́бривать *impf*, **вы́|зубрить** *pf* learn by heart.

вызыва́ть(ся *impf of* **вы́звать(ся. вызыва́ющий** defiant; provocative.

вы́играть *pf*, **выи́грывать** *impf* win; gain. **вы́игрыш** win; gain; prize. **вы́игрышный** winning; advantageous.

вы́йти (-йду; -шел, -шла) *pf* (*impf* **выходи́ть**) go out; come out; get out; appear; turn out; be used up; have expired; **~ в свет** appear; **~ за́муж (за+***acc*) marry; **~ из себя́** lose one's temper; **~ из систе́мы** (*comput*) log off.

выка́лывать *impf of* **вы́колоть. выка́пывать** *impf of* **вы́копать**

вырка́рмливать *impf of* **вы́кормить**

вы́качать *pf*, **выка́чивать** *impf* pump out.

выки́дывать *impf*, **вы́кинуть** *pf* throw out, reject; put out; miscarry, abort; **~ флаг** hoist a flag. **вы́кидыш** miscarriage, abortion.

вы́кладка laying out; lay-out; facing; kit; computation, calculation. **выкла́дывать** *impf of* **вы́ложить**

выключа́тель *m* switch. **выключа́ть** *impf*, **вы́ключить** (-чу) *pf* turn off, switch off; remove, exclude.

выкола́чивать *impf*, **вы́колотить** (-лочу) *pf* knock out, beat out; beat; extort, wring out.

вы́колоть (-лю) *pf* (*impf* **выка́лывать**) put out; gouge out; tattoo.

вы́|копать *pf* (*impf also* **вы-ка́пывать**) dig; dig up, dig out; exhume; unearth.
вы́кормить (-млю) *pf* (*impf* **выка́рмливать**) rear, bring up.
вы́корчевать (-чую) *pf*, **вы-корчёвывать** *impf* uproot, root out; eradicate.
выкра́ивать *impf of* **вы́кро-ить**
вы́|красить (-ашу) *pf*, **вы-кра́шивать** *impf* paint; dye.
выкри́кивать *impf*, **вы́крик-нуть** (-ну) *pf* cry out; yell.
вы́кроить *pf* (*impf* **выкра́-ивать**) cut out; find (*time etc.*). **вы́кройка** pattern.
вы́крутить (-учу) *pf*, **выкру́-чивать** *impf* unscrew; twist; **~ся** extricate o.s.
вы́куп ransom; redemption.
вы́|купать¹**(ся** *pf*.
выкупа́ть² *impf*, **вы́купить** (-плю) *pf* ransom, redeem.
вы́лазка sally, sortie; excursion.
выла́мывать *impf of* **вы́ло-мать**
вылеза́ть *impf*, **вы́лезти** (-зу; -лез) *pf* climb out; come out.
вы́|лепить (-плю) *pf*.
вы́лет flight; take-off. **выле-та́ть** *impf*, **вы́лететь** (-ечу) *pf* fly out; take off.
выле́чивать *impf*, **вы́ле-чить** (-чу) *pf* cure; **~ся** recover, be cured.
вылива́ть(ся *pf of* **вы́лить-(ся**
вы́|линять *pf*.
вы́лить (-лью) *pf* (*impf* **вы-лива́ть**) pour out; cast, found; **~ся** flow (out); be expressed.
вы́ложить (-жу) *pf* (*impf* **выкла́дывать**) lay out.
вы́ломать *pf*, **вы́ломить** (-млю) *pf* (*impf* **выла́мы-вать**) break open.
вы́лупиться (-плюсь) *pf*, **вы-лупля́ться** *impf* hatch (out).
вы́лью *etc.*: *see* **вы́лить**
вы́|мазать (-мажу) *pf*, **выма́-зывать** *impf* smear, dirty.
выма́нивать *impf*, **вы́манить** *pf* entice, lure.
вы́мереть (-мрет; -мер) *pf* (*impf* **вымира́ть**) die out; become extinct. **вы́мерший** extinct.
вы́мести (-ету) *pf*, **вы́метать** *impf* sweep (out).
вымога́тельство blackmail, extortion. **вымога́ть** *impf* extort.
вымока́ть *impf*, **вы́мокнуть** (-ну; -ок) *pf* be drenched; soak; rot.
вы́молвить (-влю) *pf* say, utter.
вы́|мостить (-ощу) *pf*. **вы́-мою** *etc.*: *see* **вы́мыть**
вы́мпел pennant.
вы́мрет *see* **вы́мереть**. **вы-мыва́ть(ся** *impf of* **вы́-мыть(ся**
вы́мысел (-сла) invention, fabrication; fantasy.
вы́|мыть (-мою) *pf* (*impf also* **вымыва́ть**) wash; wash out, off; wash away; **~ся** wash o.s.
вы́мышленный fictitious.
вы́мя (-мени) *neut* udder.
вына́шивать *impf of* **вы́но-сить**²
вы́нести (-су; -нес) *pf* (*impf* **выноси́ть**¹) carry out, take out; carry away; endure.
вынима́ть (*impf of* **вы́-нуть**
вы́нос carrying out. **выно-си́ть**¹ (-ошу́, -о́сишь) *impf of* **вы́нести**. **вы́носить**² *pf* (*impf* **вына́шивать**) bear; nurture.
вы́носка carrying out; re-

moval; footnote. **выно́сливость** endurance; hardiness.
вы́нудить (-ужу) *pf*, **вынужда́ть** *impf* force, compel. **вы́нужденный** forced.
вы́нуть (-ну) *pf* (*impf* **вынима́ть**) take out.
вы́пад attack; lunge. **выпада́ть** *impf of* **вы́пасть**
выпа́лывать *impf of* **вы́полоть**
выпа́ривать *impf*, **вы́парить** evaporate; steam.
выпа́рывать *impf of* **вы́пороть**[2]
вы́пасть (-аду; -ал) *pf* (*impf* **выпада́ть**) fall out; fall; occur, turn out; lunge.
выпека́ть *impf*, **вы́печь** (-еку; -ек) *pf* bake.
выпива́ть *impf of* **вы́пить**; enjoy a drink. **вы́пивка** drinking bout; drinks.
выпи́ливать *impf*, **вы́пилить** *pf* saw, cut out.
вы́писать (-ишу) *pf*, **выпи́сывать** *impf* copy out; write out; order; subscribe to; send for; discharge, release; **~ся** be discharged; check out. **вы́писка** writing out; extract; ordering, subscription; discharge.
вы́|пить (-пью) *pf* (*impf also* **выпива́ть**) drink; drink up.
вы́плавить (-влю) *pf*, **выплавля́ть** *impf* smelt. **вы́плавка** smelting; smelted metal.
вы́плата payment. **вы́платить** (-ачу) *pf*, **выпла́чивать** *impf* pay (out); pay off.
выплёвывать *impf of* **вы́плюнуть**
выплыва́ть *impf*, **вы́плыть** (-ыву) *pf* swim out, sail out; emerge; crop up.
вы́плюнуть (-ну) *pf* (*impf* **выплёвывать**) spit out.
выполза́ть *impf*, **вы́ползти** (-зу; -олз) *pf* crawl out.
выполне́ние execution, carrying out; fulfilment. **вы́полнить** *pf*, **выполня́ть** *impf* execute, carry out; fulfil.
вы́|полоскать (-ощу) *pf*.
вы́|полоть (-лю) *pf* (*impf also* **выпа́лывать**) weed out; weed.
вы́|пороть[1] (-рю) *pf*.
вы́пороть[2] (-рю) *pf* (*impf* **выпа́рывать**) rip out, rip up.
вы́|потрошить (-шу) *pf*.
вы́правка bearing; correction.
выпра́шивать *impf of* **вы́просить**; solicit.
выпрова́живать *impf*, **вы́проводить** (-ожу) *pf* send packing.
вы́просить (-ошу) *pf* (*impf* **выпра́шивать**) (ask for and) get.
выпряга́ть *impf of* **вы́прячь**
вы́прямить (-млю) *pf*, **выпрямля́ть** *impf* straighten (out); rectify; **~ся** become straight; draw o.s. up.
вы́прячь (-ягу; -яг) *pf* (*impf* **выпряга́ть**) unharness.
вы́пуклый protuberant; bulging; convex.
вы́пуск output; issue; discharge; part, instalment; final-year students; omission. **выпуска́ть** *impf*, **вы́пустить** (-ущу) *pf* let out; issue; produce; omit. **выпускни́к** (-а́), **-и́ца** final-year student. **выпускн|о́й** discharge; exhaust; **~о́й экза́мен** finals, final examination.
вы́путать *pf*, **выпу́тывать** *impf* disentangle; **~ся** extricate o.s.
вы́пью *etc.*: *see* **вы́пить**

вырабáтывать *impf*, **вы́работать** *pf* work out; work up; draw up; produce, make; earn. **вы́работка** manufacture; production; working out; drawing up; output; make.

вырáвнивать(ся *impf of* **вы́ровнять(ся**

выражáть *impf*, **вы́разить** (-ажу) *pf* express; **~ся** express o.s. **выражéние** expression. **вырази́тельный** expressive.

вырастáть *impf*, **вы́расти** (-ту; -рос) *pf* grow, grow up. **вы́растить** (-ащу) *pf*, **вырáщивать** *impf* bring up; breed; cultivate.

вы́рвать[1] (-ву) *pf* (*impf* **вырывáть**[2]) pull out, tear out; extort; **~ся** break loose, break free; escape; shoot.

вы́|рвать[2] (-ву) *pf*.

вы́рез cut; décolletage. **вы́резать** (-ежу) *pf*, **вырезáть** *impf*, **вырéзывать** *impf* cut (out); engrave. **вы́резка** cutting out, excision; cutting; fillet.

вы́ровнять *pf* (*impf* **вырáвнивать**) level; straighten (out); draw up; **~ся** become level; equalize; catch up.

вы́родиться *pf*, **вырождáться** *impf* degenerate. **вы́родок** (-дка) degenerate; black sheep. **вырождéние** degeneration.

вы́ронить *pf* drop.

вы́рос *etc.*: *see* **вы́расти**

вы́рою *etc.*: *see* **вы́рыть**

вырубáть *impf*, **вы́рубить** (-блю) *pf* cut down; cut (out); carve (out). **вы́рубка** cutting down; hewing out.

вы́|ругать(ся *pf*.

выру́ливать *impf*, **вы́|рулить** *pf* taxi.

выручáть *impf*, **вы́ручить** (-чу) *pf* rescue; help out; gain; make. **вы́ручка** rescue; gain; proceeds; earnings.

вырывáть[1] *impf*, **вы́|рыть** (-рою) *pf* dig up, unearth.

вырывáть[2]**(ся** *impf of* **вы́рвать(ся**

вы́садить (-ажу) *pf*, **высáживать** *impf* set down; put ashore; transplant; smash; **~ся** alight; disembark. **вы́садка** disembarkation; landing; transplanting.

высáсывать *impf of* **вы́сосать**

вы́свободить (-божу) *pf*, **высвобождáть** *impf* free; release.

высекáть *impf of* **вы́сечь**[2]

выселéние eviction. **вы́селить** *pf*, **выселя́ть** *impf* evict; evacuate, move; **~ся** move, remove.

вы́|сечь[1] (-еку; -сек) *pf*. **вы́сечь**[2] (-еку; -сек) (*impf* **высекáть**) cut (out); carve.

вы́сидеть (-ижу) *pf*, **выси́живать** *impf* sit out; stay; hatch.

вы́ситься *impf* rise, tower.

выскáбливать *impf of* **вы́скоблить**

вы́сказать (-кажу) *pf*, **выскáзывать** *impf* express; state; **~ся** speak out. **выскáзывание** utterance; pronouncement.

выскáкивать *impf of* **вы́скочить**

вы́скоблить *pf* (*impf* **выскáбливать**) scrape out; erase; remove.

вы́скочить (-чу) *pf* (*impf* **выскáкивать**) jump out; spring out; **~ с**+*instr* come out with. **вы́скочка** upstart.

вы́слать (вы́шлю) *pf* (*impf*

высыла́ть) send (out); exile; deport.

вы́следить (-ежу) *pf*, **выслеж́ивать** *impf* trace; shadow.

выслу́живать *impf*, **вы́служить** (-жу) *pf* qualify for; serve (out); **~ся** gain promotion; curry favour.

вы́слушать *pf*, **выслу́шивать** *impf* hear out; sound; listen to.

высме́ивать *impf*, **вы́смеять** (-ею) *pf* ridicule.

вы́|сморкать(ся *pf*. **высо́вывать(ся** *impf of* **вы́сунуть(ся**

высо́кий (-о́к, -а́, -о́ко́) high; tall; lofty; elevated.

высоко- *in comb* high-, highly. **высокоблагоро́дие** (your) Honour, Worship. **~во́льтный** high-tension. **~го́рный** mountain. **~ка́чественный** high-quality. **~квалифици́рованный** highly qualified. **~ме́рие** haughtiness. **~ме́рный** haughty. **~па́рный** high-flown; bombastic. **~часто́тный** high-frequency.

вы́сосать (-осу) *pf* (*impf* **выса́сывать**) suck out.

высота́ (*pl* -ы) height, altitude. **высо́тный** high-altitude; high-rise.

вы́|сохнуть (-ну; -ох) *pf* (*impf also* **высыха́ть**) dry (out); dry up; wither (away).

вы́спаться (-плюсь, -пишься) *pf* (*impf* **высыпа́ться**[2]) have a good sleep.

вы́ставить (-влю) *pf*, **выставля́ть** *impf* display, exhibit; post; put forward; set down; take out; *+instr* represent as; **~ся** show off. **вы́ставка** exhibition.

выста́ивать *impf of* **вы́стоять**

вы́|стегать *pf*. **вы́|стирать** *pf*.

вы́стоять (-ою) *pf* (*impf* **выста́ивать**) stand; stand one's ground.

вы́страдать *pf* suffer; gain through suffering.

выстра́ивать(ся *impf of* **вы́строить(ся**

вы́стрел shot; report. **вы́стрелить** *pf* shoot, fire.

вы́|строгать *pf*.

вы́строить *pf* (*impf* **выстра́ивать**) build; draw up, order, arrange; form up. **~ся** form up.

вы́ступ protuberance, projection. **выступа́ть** *impf*, **вы́ступить** (-плю) *pf* come forward; come out; perform; speak; *+***из***+gen* go beyond. **выступле́ние** appearance, performance; speech; setting out.

вы́сунуть (-ну) *pf* (*impf* **высо́вывать**) put out, thrust out; **~ся** show o.s., thrust o.s. forward.

вы́|сушить(ся (-шу(сь) *pf*.

вы́сший highest; high; higher.

высыла́ть *impf of* **вы́слать.** **вы́сылка** sending, dispatch; expulsion, exile.

вы́сыпать (-плю) *pf*, **высыпа́ть** *impf* pour out; spill; **~ся**[1] pour out; spill.

высыпа́ться[2] *impf of* **вы́спаться**

высыха́ть *impf of* **вы́сохнуть**

высь height; summit.

выта́лкивать *impf of* **вы́толкать, вы́толкнуть.** **выта́скивать** *impf of* **вы́тащить.** **выта́чивать** *impf of* **вы́точить**

вы́|тащить (-щу) *pf* (*impf also* **выта́скивать**) drag out; pull out.

вы́|твердить (-ржу) *pf*.

вытека́ть *impf* (*pf* **вы́течь**); ~ **из**+*gen* flow from, out of; result from.

вы́тереть (-тру; -тер) *pf* (*impf* **вытира́ть**) wipe (up); dry; wear out.

вы́терпеть (-плю) *pf* endure.

вы́тертый threadbare.

вы́теснить *pf*, **вытесня́ть** *impf* force out; oust; displace.

вы́течь (-чет; -ек) *pf* (*impf* **вытека́ть**) flow out, run out.

вытира́ть *impf of* **вы́тереть**

вы́толкать *pf*, **вы́толкнуть** (-ну) *pf* (*impf* **выта́лкивать**) throw out; push out.

вы́точенный turned. **вы́|точить** (-чу) *pf* (*impf also* **выта́чивать**) turn; sharpen; gnaw through.

вы́|травить (-влю) *pf*, **вытра́вливать** *impf*, **вытравля́ть** *impf* exterminate, destroy; remove; etch; trample down, damage.

вытрезви́тель *m* detoxification centre. **вы́трезвить(ся** (-влю(сь) *pf*, **вытрезвля́ть(ся** *impf* sober up.

вы́тру *etc.*: *see* **вы́тереть**

вы́|трясти (-су; -яс) *pf* shake out.

вытря́хивать *impf*, **вы́тряхнуть** (-ну) *pf* shake out.

выть (во́ю) *impf* howl; wail.

вытя́гивать *impf*, **вы́тянуть** (-ну) *pf* stretch (out); extend; extract; endure; **~ся** stretch, stretch out, stretch o.s.; shoot up; draw o.s. up. **вы́тяжка** drawing out, extraction; extract.

вы́|утюжить (-жу) *pf*.

выу́чивать *impf*, **вы́|учить** (-чу) *pf* learn; teach; **~ся** +*dat or inf* learn.

выха́живать *impf of* **вы́ходить**[2]

вы́хватить (-ачу) *pf*, **выхва́тывать** *impf* snatch out, up, away; pull out.

вы́хлоп exhaust. **выхлопно́й** exhaust, discharge.

вы́ход going out; departure; way out, exit; vent; appearance; yield; ~ **за́муж** marriage. **вы́ходец** (-дца) emigrant; immigrant. **выходи́ть**[1] (-ожу́, -о́дишь) *impf of* **вы́йти; +на**+*acc* look out on.

вы́ходить[2] (-ожу) *pf* (*impf* **выха́живать**) nurse; rear, bring up.

вы́ходка trick; prank.

выходн|о́й exit; going-out, outgoing; discharge; **~о́й день** day off; **~о́й** *sb* person off duty; day off. **выхожу́** *etc.*: *see* **выходи́ть**[1]. **вы́хожу** *etc.*: *see* **вы́ходить**[2]

вы́цвести (-ветет) *pf*, **выцвета́ть** *impf* fade. **вы́цветший** faded.

вычёркивать *impf*, **вы́черкнуть** (-ну) *pf* cross out.

вы́черпать *pf*, **выче́рпывать** *impf* bale out.

вы́честь (-чту; -чел, -чла) *pf* (*impf* **вычита́ть**) subtract. **вы́чет** deduction.

вычисле́ние calculation. **вычисли́тель** *m* calculator. **вычисли́тельн|ый** calculating, computing; **~ая маши́на** computer; **~ая те́хника** computers. **вы́числить** *pf*, **вычисля́ть** *impf* calculate, compute.

вы́|чистить (-ищу) *pf* (*impf also* **вычища́ть**) clean, clean up.

вычита́ние subtraction. **вычита́ть** *impf of* **вы́честь**

вычища́ть *impf of* **вы́чистить**. **вы́чту** *etc.*: *see* **вы́честь**

вы́швырнуть (-ну) *pf*, **вы-**

швы́ривать *impf* chuck out. **вы́ше** higher, taller; *prep+gen* beyond; over; *adv* above. **выше-** *in comb* above-, afore-. **вышеизло́женный** foregoing. **~на́званный** aforenamed. **~ска́занный, ~ука́занный** aforesaid. **~упомя́нутый** afore-mentioned.
вы́шел *etc.*: *see* **вы́йти**
вышиба́ла *m* chucker-out. **вышиба́ть** *impf*, **вы́шибить** (-бу; -иб) *pf* knock out; chuck out.
вышива́ние embroidery, needlework. **вышива́ть** *impf of* **вы́шить. вы́шивка** embroidery.
вышина́ height.
вы́шить (-шью) *pf* (*impf* **вышива́ть**) embroider. **вы́шитый** embroidered.
вы́шка tower; **(бурова́я) ~** derrick.
вы́шлю *etc.*: *see* **вы́слать.**
вы́шью *etc.*: *see* **вы́шить**
вы́явить (-влю) *pf*, **выявля́ть** *impf* reveal; make known; expose; **~ся** come to light, be revealed.
выясне́ние elucidation; explanation. **вы́яснить** *pf*, **выясня́ть** *impf* elucidate; explain; **~ся** become clear; turn out.
Вьетна́м Vietnam. **вьетна́мец, -мка** Vietnamese. **вьетна́мский** Vietnamese.
вью *etc.*: *see* **вить**
вью́га snow-storm, blizzard.
вьюно́к (-нка́) bindweed.
вью́чн|ый pack; **~ое живо́тное** beast of burden.
вью́щийся climbing; curly.
вяжу́ *etc.*: **вяза́ть. вя́жущий** binding; astringent.
вяз elm.
вяза́ние knitting, crocheting; binding, tying. **вя́занка**[1] knitted garment. **вяза́нка**[2] bundle. **вя́заный** knitted, crocheted. **вяза́нье** knitting; crochet(-work). **вяза́ть** (вяжу́, вя́жешь) *impf* (*pf* **с~**) tie, bind; knit, crochet; be astringent; **~ся** accord; tally. **вя́зка** tying; knitting, crocheting; bunch.
вя́зкий (-зок, -зка́, -о) viscous; sticky; boggy. **вя́знуть** (-ну; вя́з(нул), -зла) *impf* (*pf* **за~, у~**) stick, get stuck.
вя́зовый elm.
вязь ligature; arabesque.
вя́леный dried; sun-cured.
вя́лый limp; sluggish; slack.
вя́нуть (-ну; вял) *impf* (*pf* **за~, у~**) fade, wither; flag.

Г

г. *abbr* (*of* **год**) year; (*of* **го́род**) city; (*of* **господи́н**) Mr.
г *abbr* (*of* **грамм**) gram.
га *abbr* (*of* **гекта́р**) hectare.
га́вань harbour.
гага́чий пух eiderdown.
гад reptile; repulsive person; *pl.* vermin.
гада́лка fortune-teller. **гада́ние** fortune-telling; guesswork. **гада́ть** *impf* (*pf* **по~**) tell fortunes; guess.
га́дина reptile; repulsive person; *pl* vermin. **га́дить** (га́жу) *impf* (*pf* **на~**) **+в**+*prep*, **на**+*acc*, *prep* foul, dirty, defile. **га́дкий** (-док, -дка́, -о) nasty, vile repulsive. **га́дость** filth, muck; dirty trick; *pl* filthy expressions. **гадю́ка** adder, viper; repulsive person.
га́ечный ключ spanner, wrench.
газ[1] gauze.

газ[2] gas; wind; **дать ~** step on the gas; **сба́вить ~** reduce speed.
газе́та newspaper. **газе́тчик** journalist; newspaper-seller.
газиро́ванный aerated. **га́зовый** gas.
газо́н lawn. **газонокоси́лка** lawn-mower.
газопрово́д gas pipeline; gas-main.
га́йка nut; female screw.
гала́ктика galaxy.
галантере́йный магази́н haberdasher's. **галантере́я** haberdashery.
гала́нтный gallant.
галере́я gallery. **галёрка** gallery, gods.
галифе́ *indecl pl* riding-breeches.
га́лка jackdaw.
галлюцина́ция hallucination.
гало́п gallop.
га́лочка tick.
га́лстук tie; neckerchief.
галу́шка dumpling.
га́лька pebble; pebbles, shingle.
гам din, uproar.
гама́к (-а́) hammock.
га́мма scale; gamut; range.
гангре́на gangrene.
га́нгстер gangster.
ганте́ль dumb-bell.
гара́ж (-а́) garage.
гаранти́ровать *impf & pf* guarantee. **гара́нтия** guarantee.
гардеро́б wardrobe; cloakroom. **гардеро́бщик, -щица** cloakroom attendant.
гарди́на curtain.
гармонизи́ровать *impf & pf* harmonize.
гармо́ника accordion, concertina. **гармони́ческий, гармони́чный** harmonious. **гармо́ния** harmony; concord. **гармо́нь** accordion, concertina.
гарнизо́н garrison.
гарни́р garnish; vegetables.
гарниту́р set; suite.
гарь burning; cinders.
гаси́тель *m* extinguisher; suppressor. **гаси́ть** (гашу́, га́сишь) *impf* (*pf* **за~, по~**) extinguish; suppress. **га́снуть** (-ну; гас) *impf* (*pf* **за~, по~, у~**) be extinguished, go out; grow feeble.
гастро́ли *f pl* tour; guest-appearance, performance. **гастроли́ровать** *impf* (be on) tour.
гастроно́м gourmet; provision shop. **гастрономи́ческий** gastronomic; provision. **гастроно́мия** gastronomy; provisions; delicatessen.
гауптва́хта guardroom.
гаши́ш hashish.
гварде́ец (-е́йца) guardsman.
гварде́йский guards'. **гва́рдия** Guards.
гво́здик tack. **гвозди́ка** pink(s), carnation(s); cloves.
гво́здики (-ов) *pl* stilettos.
гвоздь (-я́; *pl* -и, -е́й) *m* nail; tack; crux; highlight, hit.
гг. *abbr* (*of* **го́ды**) years.
где *adv* where; **~ бы ни** wherever. **где́-либо** *adv* anywhere.
где́-нибудь *adv* somewhere; anywhere. **где́-то** *adv* somewhere.
гекта́р hectare.
ге́лий helium.
гемоглоби́н haemoglobin.
геморро́й haemorrhoids. **гемофили́я** haemophilia.
ген gene.
ге́незис origin, genesis.
генера́л general. **генера́льн|ый** general; **~ая репети́ция** dress rehearsal.

генера́тор generator.

гене́тик geneticist. **гене́тика** genetics. **генети́ческий** genetic.

гениа́льный brilliant. **ге́ний** genius.

гено́м genome.

гео- *in comb* geo-. **гео́граф** geographer. **~графи́ческий** geographical. **~гра́фия** geography. **гео́лог** geologist. **~логи́ческий** geological. **~ло́гия** geology. **~метри́ческий** geometric. **~ме́трия** geometry.

георги́н dahlia.

геофи́зика geophysics.

гепа́рд cheetah.

гепати́т hepatitis.

гера́нь geranium.

герб arms, coat of arms. **ге́рбов|ый** heraldic; **~ая печа́ть** official stamp.

геркуле́с Hercules; rolled oats.

герма́нец (-нца) ancient German. **Герма́ния** Germany. **герма́нский** Germanic.

гермафроди́т hermaphrodite.

гермети́чный hermetic; hermetically sealed; air-tight.

герои́зм heroism. **герои́ня** heroine. **герои́ческий** heroic. **геро́й** hero. **геро́йский** heroic.

герц (*gen pl* **герц**) hertz.

ге́рцог duke. **герцоги́ня** duchess.

г-жа *abbr* (*of* **госпожа́**) Mrs.; Miss.

гиаци́нт hyacinth.

ги́бель death; destruction, ruin; loss; wreck; downfall. **ги́бельный** disastrous, fatal.

ги́бкий (-бок, -бка́, -бко) flexible, adaptable, versatile; supple. **ги́бкость** flexibility; suppleness.

ги́бнуть (-ну; ги́б(нул)) *impf* (*pf* **по~**) perish.

гибри́д hybrid.

гига́нт giant. **гига́нтский** gigantic.

гигие́на hygiene. **гигиени́ческий, -и́чный** hygienic, sanitary.

гид guide.

гидравли́ческий hydraulic.

гидро- *pref* hydro-. **~электроста́нция** hydro-electric power-station.

гие́на hyena.

ги́льза cartridge-case; sleeve; (cigarette-)wrapper.

гимн hymn.

гимна́зия grammar school, high school.

гимна́ст gymnast. **гимна́стика** gymnastics. **гимнасти́ческий** gymnastic.

гинеко́лог gynaecologist. **гинеколо́гия** gynaecology.

гипе́рбола hyperbole.

гипно́з hypnosis. **гипнотизёр** hypnotist. **гипнотизи́ровать** *impf* (*pf* **за~**) hypnotize. **гипноти́ческий** hypnotic.

гипо́теза hypothesis. **гипотети́ческий** hypothetical.

гиппопота́м hippopotamus.

гипс gypsum, plaster (of Paris); plaster cast. **ги́псовый** plaster.

гирля́нда garland.

ги́ря weight.

гистерэктоми́я hysterectomy.

гита́ра guitar.

гл. *abbr* (*of* **глава́**) chapter.

глав- *abbr in comb* head, chief, main.

глава́ (*pl* -ы) head; chief; chapter; cupola. **глава́рь** (-я́) *m* leader, ring-leader. **главк** central directorate. **главнокома́ндующий** *sb* commander-in-chief. **гла́вн|ый** chief, main;

~ым о́бразом chiefly, mainly, for the most part; **~ое** *sb* the main thing; the essentials.
глаго́л verb.
гла́дить (-а́жу) *impf* (*pf* **вы~, по~**) stroke; iron. **гла́дкий** smooth; plain. **гла́дко** *adv* smoothly. **гладь** smooth surface.
глаз (*loc* -у́; *pl* -а́, глаз) eye; **в ~а́** to one's face; **за ~а́**+*gen* behind the back of; **смотре́ть во все ~а́** be all eyes.
глазиро́ванный glazed; glossy; iced; glacé.
глазни́ца eye-socket. **глазно́й** eye; optic; **~ врач** oculist. **глазо́к** (-зка́) peephole.
глазу́нья fried eggs.
глазу́рь glaze; syrup; icing.
гла́нды (гланд) *pl* tonsils.
гла́сность publicity; glasnost, openness. **гла́сный** public; vowel; *sb* vowel.
гли́на clay. **гли́нистый** clayey. **гли́няный** clay; clayey.
гли́ссер speed-boat.
глист (*intestinal*) worm.
глицери́н glycerine.
глоба́льный global; extensive.
гло́бус globe.
глота́ть *impf* swallow. **гло́тка** gullet; throat. **глото́к** (-тка́) gulp; mouthful.
гло́хнуть (-ну; глох) *impf* (*pf* **за~, о~**) become deaf; die away, subside; grow wild.
глубина́ (*pl* -ы) depth; heart, interior. **глубо́кий** (-о́к, -а́, -о́ко́) deep; profound; late, advanced, extreme. **глубокомы́слие** profundity. **глубокоуважа́емый** (*in formal letters*) dear.
глуми́ться (-млю́сь) *impf* mock, jeer (**над**+*instr* at). **глумле́ние** mockery.
глупе́ть (-е́ю) *impf* (*pf* **по~**) grow stupid. **глупе́ц** (-пца́) fool. **глу́пость** stupidity. **глу́пый** (глуп, -а́, -о) stupid.
глуха́рь (-я́) *m* capercaillie.
глух|о́й (глух, -а́, -о) deaf; muffled; obscure, vague; dense; wild; remote; deserted; sealed; blank; **~о́й, ~а́я** *sb* deaf man, woman. **глухонемо́й** deaf and dumb; *sb* deaf mute. **глухота́** deafness. **глуши́тель** *m* silencer. **глуши́ть** (-шу́) *impf* (*pf* **за~, о~**) stun; muffle; dull; jam; extinguish; stifle; suppress. **глушь** backwoods.
глы́ба clod; lump, block.
глюко́за glucose.
гляде́ть (-яжу́) *impf* (*pf* **по~, гля́нуть**) look, gaze, peer; **~ в о́ба** be on one's guard; **(того́ и) гляди́** it looks as if; I'm afraid; **гля́дя по**+*dat* depending on.
гля́нец (-нца) gloss, lustre; polish.
гля́нуть (-ну) *pf* (*impf* **гляде́ть**) glance.
гм *int* hm!
г-н *abbr* (*of* **господи́н**) Mr.
гнать (гоню́, го́нишь; гнал, -а́, -о) *impf* drive; urge (on); hunt, chase; persecute; distil; **~ся за**+*instr* pursue.
гнев anger, rage. **гне́ваться** *impf* (*pf* **раз~**) be angry. **гне́вный** angry.
гнедо́й bay.
гнездо́ (*pl* гнёзда) nest.
гнёт weight; oppression. **гнету́щий** oppressive.
гни́да nit.
гние́ние decay, putrefaction, rot. **гнило́й** (-ил, -а́, -о) rotten; muggy. **гнить** (-ию́, -иёшь; -ил, -а́, -о) *impf* (*pf* **с~**) rot. **гное́ние** suppuration. **гнои́ться** *impf* (*pf* **с~**) suppu-

rate, discharge matter. **гной** pus. **гнойни́к** abscess; ulcer. **гно́йный** purulent.

гну́сный (-сен, -сна́, -о) vile.

гнуть (гну, гнёшь) *impf* (*pf* **со~**) bend; aim at; **~ся** bend; stoop.

гнуша́ться *impf* (*pf* **по~**) disdain; *+gen or instr* shun; abhor.

гобеле́н tapestry.

гобо́й oboe.

гове́ть (-е́ю) *impf* fast.

говно́ (*vulg*) shit.

говори́ть *impf* (*pf* **по~, сказа́ть**) speak, talk; say; tell; **~ся: как говори́тся** as they say.

говя́дина beef. **говя́жий** beef.

го́гот cackle; loud laughter. **гогота́ть** (-очу́, -о́чешь) *impf* cackle; roar with laughter.

год (*loc* -у́; *pl* -ы *or* -а́, *gen* -о́в *or* лет) year. **года́ми** *adv* for years (on end).

годи́ться, (-жу́сь) *impf* be fit, suitable; serve.

годи́чный a year's; annual.

го́дный (-ден, -дна́, -о, -ы *or* -ы́) fit, suitable; valid.

годова́лый one-year-old. **годово́й** annual. **годовщи́на** anniversary.

гожу́сь *etc.*: *see* **годи́ться**

гол goal.

голени́ще (boot-)top. **го́лень** shin.

голла́ндец (-дца) Dutchman. **Голла́ндия** Holland. **голла́ндка** Dutchwoman; tiled stove. **голла́ндский** Dutch.

голова́ (*acc* го́лову; *pl* го́ловы, -о́в, -а́м) head. **голова́стик** tadpole. **голо́вка** head; cap, nose, tip. **головн|о́й** head; leading; **~а́я боль** headache; **~о́й мозг** brain, cerebrum; **~о́й убо́р** headgear, headdress. **головокруже́ние** giddiness, dizziness. **головоло́мка** puzzle. **головоре́з** cut-throat; rascal.

го́лод hunger; famine; acute shortage. **голода́ние** starvation; fasting. **голода́ть** *impf* go hungry, starve; fast. **голо́дный** (го́лоден, -дна́, -о, -ы *or* -ы́) hungry. **голодо́вка** hunger-strike.

гололёд, гололе́дица (period of) black ice.

го́лос (*pl* -а́) voice; part; vote. **голоси́ть** (-ошу́) *impf* sing loudly; cry; wail.

голосло́вный unsubstantiated, unfounded.

голосова́ние voting; poll. **голосова́ть** *impf* (*pf* **про~**) vote; vote on.

голу́бка pigeon; (my) dear, darling. **голубо́й** light blue. **голу́бчик** my dear (fellow); darling. **го́лубь** *m* pigeon, dove. **голубя́тня** (*gen pl* -тен) dovecot, pigeon-loft.

го́лый (гол, -ла́, -ло) naked, bare.

гольф golf.

гомоге́нный homogeneous.

го́мон hubbub.

гомосексуали́ст homosexual. **гомосексуа́льный** homosexual.

гондо́ла gondola.

гоне́ние persecution. **го́нка** race; dashing; haste.

гонора́р fee.

го́ночный racing.

гонча́р (-а́) potter.

го́нщик racing driver *or* cyclist.

гоню́ *etc.*: *see* **гнать. гоня́ть** *impf* drive; send on errands; **~ся** *+за+instr* chase, hunt.

гора́ (*acc* го́ру; *pl* го́ры, -а́м) mountain; hill; **в го́ру** uphill; **под гору** downhill.

гора́здо *adv* much, far, by far. **горб** (-á, *loc* -ý) hump; bulge. **горба́тый** hunchbacked. **го́рбить** (-блю) *impf* (*pf* **с~**) arch, hunch; **~ся** stoop. **горбу́н** (-á) *m*, **горбу́нья** (*gen pl* -ний) hunchback. **горбу́шка** (*gen pl* -шек) crust (*of loaf*).

горди́ться (-ржýсь) *impf* put on airs; *+instr* be proud of. **го́рдость** pride. **го́рдый** (горд, -á, -о, го́рды́) proud. **горды́ня** arrogance.

го́ре grief, sorrow; trouble. **горева́ть** (-рю́ю) *impf* grieve.

горе́лка burner. **горе́лый** burnt. **горе́ние** burning, combustion; enthusiasm.

го́рестный sad; mournful. **го́ресть** sorrow; *pl* misfortunes.

горе́ть (-рю́) *impf* burn; be on fire.

го́рец (-рца) mountain-dweller.

го́речь bitterness; bitter taste.

горизо́нт horizon. **горизонта́ль** horizontal. **горизонта́льный** horizontal.

гори́стый mountainous, hilly. **го́рка** hill; hillock; steep climb.

го́рло throat; neck. **горлово́й** throat; guttural; raucous. **го́рлышко** neck.

гормо́н hormone.

горн[1] furnace, forge.

горн[2] bugle.

го́рничная *sb* maid, chambermaid.

горнорабо́чий *sb* miner.

горноста́й ermine.

го́рный mountain; mountainous; mineral; mining. **горня́к** (-á) miner.

го́род (*pl* -á) town; city. **городо́к** (-дкá) small town. **городско́й** urban; city; municipal. **горожа́нин** (*pl* -áне, -áн) *m*, **-жа́нка** town-dweller.

гороско́п horoscope.

горо́х pea, peas. **горо́шек** (-шка) spots, spotted pattern; **души́стый ~** sweet peas; **зелёный ~** green peas. **горо́шина** pea.

горсове́т *abbr* (*of* **городско́й сове́т**) city soviet, town soviet.

горсть (*gen pl* -е́й) handful.

горта́нный guttural. **горта́нь** larynx.

горчи́ца mustard. **горчи́чник** mustard plaster.

горшо́к (-шкá) flowerpot; pot; potty; chamber-pot.

го́рький (-рек, -рькá, -о) bitter.

горю́ч|ий combustible; **~ее** *sb* fuel. **горя́чий** (-ря́ч, -á) hot; passionate; ardent.

горячи́ться (-чýсь) *impf* (*pf* **раз~**) get excited. **горя́чка** fever; feverish haste. **горя́чность** zeal.

гос- *abbr in comb* (*of* **госуда́рственный**) state.

го́спиталь *m* (military) hospital.

го́споди *int* good heavens! **господи́н** (*pl* -одá, -óд, -áм) master; gentleman; Mr; *pl* ladies and gentlemen. **госпо́дство** supremacy. **госпо́дствовать** *impf* hold sway; prevail. **Госпо́дь** (Го́спода, *voc* Го́споди) *m* God, the Lord. **госпожа́** lady; Mrs.

гостеприи́мный hospitable. **гостеприи́мство** hospitality. **гости́ная** *sb* sitting-room, living-room, drawing-room. **гости́ница** hotel. **гости́ть** (гощý) *impf* stay, be on a visit. **гость** (*gen pl* -е́й) *m*, **го́стья** (*gen pl* -ий) guest, visitor.

госуда́рственный State, public. **госуда́рство** State. **госуда́рыня, госуда́рь** *m* sovereign; Your Majesty.
готи́ческий Gothic.
гото́вить (-влю) *impf* (*pf* **с~**) prepare; **~ся** prepare (o.s.); be at hand. **гото́вность** readiness, willingness. **гото́вый** ready.
гофриро́ванный corrugated; waved; pleated.
грабёж robbery; pillage. **граби́тель** *m* robber. **граби́тельский** predatory; exorbitant. **гра́бить** (-блю) *impf* (*pf* **о~**) rob, pillage.
гра́бли (-бель *or* -блей) *pl* rake.
гравёр, гравиро́вщик engraver.
гра́вий gravel. **гравирова́ть** *impf* (*pf* **вы́~**) engrave; etch. **гравиро́вка** engraving.
гравитацио́нный gravitational.
гравю́ра engraving, print; etching.
град[1] city, town.
град[2] hail; volley. **гра́дина** hailstone.
гра́дус degree. **гра́дусник** thermometer.
граждани́н (*pl* гра́ждане, -дан), **гражда́нка** citizen. **гражда́нский** civil; civic; civilian. **гражда́нство** citizenship.
грамза́пись (gramophone) recording.
грамм gram.
грамма́тика grammar. **граммати́ческий** grammatical.
гра́мота reading and writing; official document; deed. **гра́мотность** literacy. **гра́мотный** literate; competent.
грампласти́нка (gramophone) record.
грана́т pomegranate; garnet.
грана́та shell, grenade.
грандио́зный grandiose.
гранёный cut, faceted; cut-glass.
грани́т granite.
грани́ца border; boundary, limit; **за грани́цей, за грани́цу** abroad. **грани́чить** *impf* border.
грань border, verge; side, facet.
граф count; earl.
графа́ column. **гра́фик** graph; chart; schedule; graphic artist. **гра́фика** drawing; graphics; script.
графи́н carafe; decanter.
графи́ня countess.
графи́т graphite.
графи́ческий graphic.
графлёный ruled.
гра́фство county.
грацио́зный graceful. **гра́ция** grace.
грач (-а́) rook.
гребёнка comb. **гре́бень** (-бня) *m* comb; crest. **гребе́ц** (-бца́) rower, oarsman. **гребно́й** rowing. **гребу́** *etc.*: *see* **грести́**
грёза day-dream, dream. **гре́зить** (-е́жу) *impf* dream.
грек Greek.
гре́лка hot-water bottle.
греме́ть *impf* (*pf* **про~**) thunder, roar; rattle; resound. **гриму́чая змея́** rattlesnake.
грести́ (-ебу́, -ебёшь; грёб, -бла́) *impf* row; rake.
греть (-е́ю) *impf* warm, heat; **~ся** warm o.s., bask.
грех (-а́) sin. **грехо́вный** sinful. **грехопаде́ние** the Fall; fall.
Гре́ция Greece. **гре́цкий оре́х** walnut. **греча́нка** Greek. **гре́ческий** Greek, Grecian.

гречи́ха buckwheat. **гре́чневый** buckwheat.
греши́ть (-шу́) *impf* (*pf* **по~**, **со~**) sin. **гре́шник, -ница** sinner. **гре́шный** (-шен, -шна́, -о) sinful.
гриб (-а́) mushroom. **грибно́й** mushroom.
гри́ва mane.
гри́венник ten-copeck piece.
грим make-up; grease-paint.
гримирова́ть *impf* (*pf* **за~**) make up; *+instr* make up as.
грипп flu.
гриф neck (*of violin etc.*).
гри́фель *m* pencil lead.
гроб (*loc* -у́; *pl* -ы́ *or* -а́) coffin; grave. **гробни́ца** tomb. **гробово́й** coffin; deathly. **гробовщи́к** (-а́) coffin-maker; undertaker.
гроза́ (*pl* -ы) (thunder-)storm.
гроздь (*pl* -ди *or* -дья, -де́й *or* -дьев) cluster, bunch.
грози́ть(ся (-ожу́(сь) *impf* (*pf* **по~, при~**) threaten. **гро́зный** (-зен, -зна́, -о) menacing; terrible; severe.
гром (*pl* -ы, -о́в) thunder.
грома́да mass; bulk, pile. **грома́дный** huge, colossal.
громи́ть (-млю́) *impf* destroy; smash, rout.
гро́мкий (-мок, -мка́, -о) loud; famous; notorious; fine-sounding. **гро́мко** *adv* loud(ly); aloud. **громкоговори́тель** *m* loud-speaker. **громово́й** thunder; thunderous; crushing. **громогла́сный** loud; public.
громозди́ть (-зжу́) *impf* (*pf* **на~**) pile up; **~ся** tower; clamber up. **громо́здкий** cumbersome.
гро́мче *comp of* **гро́мкий, гро́мко**
гроссме́йстер grand master.
гроте́скный grotesque.
гро́хот crash, din.
грохота́ть (-очу́, -о́чешь) *impf* (*pf* **про~**) crash; rumble; roar.
грош (-а́) half-copeck piece; farthing. **гроШо́вый** cheap; trifling.
грубе́ть (-е́ю) *impf* (*pf* **за~, о~, по~**) grow coarse. **груби́ть** (-блю́) *impf* (*pf* **на~**) be rude. **грубия́н** boor. **гру́бость** rudeness; coarseness; rude remark. **гру́бый** (груб, -а́, -о) coarse; rude.
гру́да heap, pile.
груди́на breastbone. **груди́нка** brisket; breast. **грудно́й** breast, chest; pectoral. **грудь** (-и́ *or* -и, *instr* -ю, *loc* -и́; *pl* -и, -е́й) breast; chest.
груз load; burden.
грузи́н (*gen pl* -и́н), **грузи́нка** Georgian. **грузи́нский** Georgian.
грузи́ть (-ужу́, -у́зишь) *impf* (*pf* **за~, на~, по~**) load; **~ся** load, take on cargo.
Гру́зия Georgia.
гру́зный (-зен, -зна́, -о) weighty; bulky. **грузови́к** (*gen* -а́) lorry, truck. **грузово́й** goods, cargo. **гру́зчик** stevedore; loader.
грунт ground, soil; priming. **грунтова́ть** *impf* (*pf* **за~**) prime. **грунтово́й** soil, earth; priming.
гру́ппа group. **группирова́ть** *impf* (*pf* **с~**) group; **~ся** group, form groups. **группиро́вка** grouping. **группово́й** group; team.
грусти́ть (-ущу́) *impf* grieve, mourn; **+по**+*dat* pine for. **гру́стный** (-тен, -тна́, -о) sad. **грусть** sadness.

гру́ша pear.
гры́жа hernia, rupture.
грызть (-зу́, -зёшь; грыз) *impf* (*pf* **раз~**) gnaw; nag; **~ся** fight; squabble. **грызу́н** (-а́) rodent.
гряда́ (*pl* -ы, -а́м) ridge; bed; row, series; bank. **гря́дка** (flower-)bed.
гряду́щий approaching; future.
гря́зный (-зен, -зна́, -о) muddy; dirty. **грязь** (*loc* -и́) mud; dirt, filth; *pl* mud-cure.
гря́нуть (-ну) *pf* ring out, crash out; strike up.
губа́ (*pl* -ы, -а́м) lip; *pl* pincers.
губерна́тор governor. **губе́рния** province. **губе́рнский** provincial.
губи́тельный ruinous; pernicious. **губи́ть** (-блю́, -бишь) *impf* (*pf* **по~**) ruin; spoil.
гу́бка sponge.
губна́я пома́да lipstick.
гу́бчатый porous, spongy.
гуверна́нтка governess. **гувернёр** tutor.
гуде́ть (гужу́) *impf* (*pf* **про~**) hum; drone; buzz; hoot. **гудо́к** (-дка́) hooter, siren, horn, whistle; hoot.
гудро́н tar. **гудро́нный** tar, tarred.
гул rumble. **гу́лкий** (-лок, -лка́, -о) resonant; booming.
гуля́нье (*gen pl* -ний) walk; fête; outdoor party. **гуля́ть** *impf* (*pf* **по~**) stroll; go for a walk; have a good time.
гуманита́рный of the humanities; humane. **гума́нный** humane.
гумно́ (*pl* -а, -мен *or* -мён, -ам) threshing-floor; barn.
гурт (-а́) herd; flock. **гуртовщи́к** (-а́) herdsman. **гурто́м** *adv* wholesale; en masse.
гуса́к (-а́) gander.
гу́сеница caterpillar; (caterpillar) track. **гу́сеничный** caterpillar.
гусёнок (-нка; *pl* -ся́та, -ся́т) gosling. **гуси́н|ый** goose; **~ая ко́жа** goose-flesh.
густе́ть (-е́ет) *impf* (*pf* **за~**) thicken. **густо́й** (густ, -а́, -о) thick, dense; rich. **густота́** thickness, density; richness.
гусы́ня goose. **гусь** (*pl* -и, -е́й) *m* goose. **гусько́м** *adv* in single file.
гутали́н shoe-polish.
гу́ща grounds, sediment; thicket; thick. **гу́ще** *comp of* **густо́й**.
ГЭС *abbr* (*of* **гидроэлектроста́нция**) hydro-electric power station.

Д

д. *abbr* (*of* **дере́вня**) village; (*of* **дом**) house.
да *conj* and; but.
да *partl* yes; really? well; *+3rd pers of v*, may, let; **да здра́вствует...!** long live ..!
дава́ть (даю́, -ёшь) *impf of* **дать**; **дава́й(те)** let us, let's; come on; **~ся** yield; come easy.
дави́ть (-влю́, -вишь) *impf* (*pf* **за~, по~, раз~, у~**) press; squeeze; crush; oppress; **~ся** choke; hang o.s. **да́вка** crushing; crush. **давле́ние** pressure.
да́вний ancient; of long standing. **давно́** *adv* long ago; for a long time. **да́вность** antiquity; remoteness; long standing. **давны́м-давно́** *adv* long long ago.

дади́м *etc.*: *see* **дать. даю́** *etc.*: *see* **дава́ть**
да́же *adv* even.
да́лее *adv* further; **и так ~** and so on, etc. **далёкий** (-ёк, -á, -ёкó) distant, remote; far (-away). **далекó** *adv* far; far off; by a long way; **~ за** long after; **~ не** far from. **даль** (*loc* -и́) distance. **дальне́йший** further. **да́льний** distant, remote; long; **~ Востóк** the Far East. **дальнозóркий** long-sighted. **да́льность** distance; range. **да́льше** *adv* further; then, next; longer.
дам *etc.*: *see* **дать**
да́ма lady; partner; queen.
да́мба dike; dam.
да́мский ladies'.
Да́ния Denmark.
да́нные *sb pl* data; facts. **да́нный** given, present. **дань** tribute; debt.
данти́ст dentist.
дар (*pl* -ы́) gift. **дари́ть** (-рю́, -ришь) *impf* (*pf* **по~**) *+dat* give, make a present.
дарова́ние talent. **дарова́ть** *impf* & *pf* grant, confer. **дарови́тый** gifted. **даровóй** free (of charge). **да́ром** *adv* free, gratis; in vain.
да́та date.
да́тельный dative.
дати́ровать *impf* & *pf* date.
да́тский Danish. **датча́нин** (*pl* -áне, -áн), **датча́нка** Dane.
дать (дам, дашь, даст, дади́м; дал, -á, дáлó) *pf* (*impf* **дава́ть**) give; grant; let; **~ взаймы́** lend; **~ся** *pf of* **дава́ться**
да́ча dacha; **на да́че** in the country. **да́чник** (holiday) visitor.
два *m* & *neut*, **две** *f* (двух, -ум, -умя́, -ух) two. **двадцатиле́тний** twenty-year; twenty-year-old. **двадца́т|ый** twentieth; **~ые гóды** the twenties. **два́дцать** (-и́, *instr* -ью́) twenty. **два́жды** *adv* twice; double. **двена́дцатый** twelfth. **двена́дцать** twelve.
дверь (*loc* -и́; *pl* -и, -éй, *instr* -я́ми *or* -ьми́) door.
двéсти (двухсóт, -умстáм, -умястáми, -ухстáх) two hundred.
дви́гатель *m* engine, motor; motive force. **дви́гать** (-аю *or* -и́жу) *impf*, **дви́нуть** (-ну) *pf* move; set in motion; advance; **~ся** move; advance; get started. **движе́ние** movement; motion; exercise; traffic. **дви́жимость** chattels; personal property. **дви́жимый** movable; moved. **дви́жущий** motive.
двóе (-и́х) two; two pairs.
двое- *in comb* two-; double(-). **двоебóрье** biathlon. **~же́нец** (-нца) bigamist. **~жёнство** bigamy. **~тóчие** colon.
двои́ться *impf* divide in two; appear double; **у негó двои́лось в глаза́х** he saw double. **двои́чный** binary. **двóйка** two; figure 2; No. 2. **двойни́к** (-á) double. **двойнóй** double, twofold; binary. **двóйня** (*gen pl* -óен) twins. **двóйственный** two-faced; dual.
двор (-á) yard; courtyard; homestead; court. **дворе́ц** (-рцá) palace. **двóрник** yard caretaker; windscreen-wiper. **двóрня** servants. **дворóвый** yard, courtyard; *sb* house-serf. **дворяни́н** (*pl* -я́не, -я́н), **дворя́нка** member of the nobility or gentry. **дворя́нство**

nobility, gentry.
двою́родн|ый; **~ый брат**, **~ая сестра́** (first) cousin; **~ый дя́дя**, **~ая тётка** first cousin once removed. **двоя́кий** double; two-fold.
дву-, двух- *in comb* two-; bi-; double. **двубо́ртный** double-breasted. **~ли́чный** two-faced. **~но́гий** two-legged. **~ру́чный** two-handed; two-handled. **~ру́шник** double-dealer. **~смы́сленный** ambiguous. **~(х)спа́льный** double. **~сторо́нний** double-sided; two-way; bilateral. **~хгоди́чный** two-year. **~хле́тний** two-year; two-year-old; biennial. **~хме́стный** two-seater; two-berth. **~хмото́рный** twin-engined. **~хсотле́тие** bicentenary. **~хсо́тый** two-hundredth. **~хта́ктный** two-stroke. **~хэта́жный** two-storey. **~язы́чный** bilingual.
деба́ты (-ов) *pl* debate.
де́бет debit. **дебетова́ть** *impf* & *pf* debit.
деби́т yield, output.
де́бри (-ей) *pl* jungle; thickets; the wilds.
дебю́т début.
де́ва maid, maiden; Virgo.
девальва́ция devaluation.
дева́ться *impf of* **де́ться**
деви́з motto; device.
деви́ца spinster; girl. **де́вич|ий** girlish, maidenly; **~ья фами́лия** maiden name. **де́вка** wench, lass; tart. **де́вочка** (little) girl. **де́вственник, -ица** virgin. **де́вственный** virgin; innocent. **де́вушка** girl. **девчо́нка** girl.
девяно́сто ninety. **девяно́стый** ninetieth. **девя́тка** nine; figure 9; No. 9. **девятна́дцатый** nineteenth. **девятна́дцать** nineteen. **девя́тый** ninth. **де́вять** (-и́, *instr* -ью́) nine. **девятьсо́т** (-тисо́т, -тиста́м, -тьюста́ми, -тиста́х) nine hundred.
дегенери́ровать *impf* & *pf* degenerate.
дёготь (-гтя) tar.
дегуста́ция tasting.
дед grandfather; grandad. **де́душка** grandfather; grandad.
дееприча́стие adverbial participle.
дежу́рить *impf* be on duty. **дежу́рный** duty; on duty; *sb* person on duty. **дежу́рство** (being on) duty.
дезерти́р deserter. **дезерти́ровать** *impf* & *pf* desert.
дезинфе́кция disinfection. **дезинфици́ровать** *impf* & *pf* disinfect.
дезодора́нт deodorant; air-freshener.
дезориента́ция disorientation. **дезориенти́ровать** *impf* & *pf* disorient; **~ся** lose one's bearings.
де́йственный efficacious; effective. **де́йствие** action; operation; effect; act. **действи́тельно** *adv* really; indeed. **действи́тельность** reality; validity; efficacy. **действи́тельный** actual; valid; efficacious; active. **де́йствовать** *impf* (*pf* **по~**) affect, have an effect; act; work. **де́йствующ|ий** active; in force; working; **~ее лицо́** character; **~ие ли́ца** cast.
декабри́ст Decembrist. **дека́брь** (-я́) *m* December. **дека́брьский** December.
дека́да ten-day period *or* festival.

декáн dean. **деканáт** office of dean.
декламáция recitation, declamation. **декламúровать** *impf* (*pf* **про~**) recite, declaim.
декларáция declaration.
декоратúвный decorative. **декорáтор** scene-painter. **декорáция** scenery.
декрéт decree; maternity leave. **декрéтный óтпуск** maternity leave.
дéланный artificial, affected. **дéлать** *impf* (*pf* **с~**) make; do; **~ вид** pretend; **~ся** become; happen.
делегáт delegate. **делегáция** delegation; group.
делёж (-á), **делёжка** sharing; partition. **делéние** division; point (*on a scale*).
делéц (-льцá) smart operator.
деликáтный delicate.
делúмое *sb* dividend. **делúмость** divisibility. **делúтель** *m* divisor. **делúть** (-лю́, -лишь) *impf* (*pf* **по~, раз~**) divide; share; **~ шесть нá три** divide six by three; **~ся** divide; be divisible; *+instr* share.
дéло (*pl* -á) business; affair; matter; deed; thing; case; **в сáмом дéле** really, indeed; **~ в том** the point is; **как (вáши) делá?** how are things?; **на сáмом дéле** in actual fact; **по дéлу, по делáм** on business. **деловúтый** business-like, efficient. **деловóй** business; business-like. **дéльный** efficient; sensible.
дéльта delta.
дельфúн dolphin.
демагóг demagogue.
демобилизáция demobilization. **демобилизовáть** *impf* & *pf* demobilize.
демокрáт democrat. **демократизáция** democratization. **демократизúровать** *impf* & *pf* democratize. **демократúческий** democratic. **демокрáтия** democracy.
дéмон demon.
демонстрáция demonstration. **демонстрúровать** *impf* & *pf* demonstrate.
дéнежный monetary; money; **~ перевóд** money order.
дéнусь *etc.*: *see* **дéться**
день (дня) *m* day; afternoon; **днём** in the afternoon; **на днях** the other day; one of these days; **чéрез ~** every other day.
дéньги (-нег, -ьгáм) *pl* money.
департáмент department.
депó *neut indecl* depot.
депортáция deportation. **депортúровать** *impf* & *pf* deport.
депутáт (*parl*) deputy; delegate.
дёргать *impf* (*pf* **дёрнуть**) pull, tug; pester; **~ся** twitch; jerk.
деревéнский village; rural. **дерéвня** (*pl* -и, -вéнь, -вням) village; the country. **дéрево** (*pl* -éвья, -ьев) tree; wood. **деревя́нный** wood; wooden.
держáва power. **держáть** (-жу́, -жишь) *impf* hold; support; keep; **~ парú** bet; **~ себя́** behave; **~ся** *+за+acc* hold on to; be held up; hold o.s.; hold out; *+gen* keep to.
дерзáние daring. **дерзáть** *impf*, **дерзнýть** (-ну́, -нёшь) *pf* dare. **дéрзкий** impudent; daring. **дéрзость** impertinence; daring.
дёрн turf.
дёрнуть(ся (-ну(сь) *pf of* **дёргать(ся**

дерý *etc.*: *see* **драть**
десáнт landing; landing force.
десéрт dessert.
дéскать *partl indicating reported speech.*
деснá (*pl* дёсны, -сен) gum.
дéспот despot.
десятилéтие decade; tenth anniversary. **десятилéтка** ten-year (*secondary*) school. **десятилéтний** ten-year; ten-year-old. **десятúчный** decimal. **десятка** ten; figure 10; No. 10; tenner (*10-rouble note*). **десяток** (-тка) ten; decade. **десятый** tenth. **дéсять** (-й, *instr* -ью) ten.
детáль detail; part, component. **детáльный** detailed; minute.
детдóм (*pl* -á) children's home.
детектúв detective story.
детёныш young animal; *pl* young. **дéти** (-тéй, -тям, -тьмú, -тях) *pl* children. **детсáд** (*pl* -ы́) kindergarten.
дéтская *sb* nursery. **дéтский** children's; childish. **дéтство** childhood.
дéться (дéнусь) *pf* (*impf* **девáться**) get to, disappear to.
дефéкт defect.
дефúс hyphen.
дефицúт deficit; shortage. **дефицúтный** scarce.
дешевéть (-éет) *impf* (*pf* **по~**) fall in price. **дешéвле** *comp of* **дёшево, дешёвый. дёшево** *adv* cheap, cheaply. **дешёвый** (дёшев, -á, -о) cheap.
дéятель *m*: **государственный ~** statesman; **общéственный ~** public figure. **дéятельность** activity; work. **дéятельный** active, energetic.
джаз jazz.
джéмпер pullover.
джентльмéн gentleman.
джинсóвый denim. **джúнсы** (-ов) *pl* jeans.
джóйстик joystick.
джýнгли (-ей) *pl* jungle.
диабéт diabetes. **диабéтик** diabetic.
диáгноз diagnosis.
диагонáль diagonal
диагрáмма diagram.
диалéкт dialect. **диалéктика** dialectics.
диалóг dialogue.
диáметр diameter.
диапазóн range; band.
диапозитúв slide.
диафрáгма diaphragm.
диван sofa; divan.
диверсáнт saboteur. **дивéрсия** sabotage.
дивúзия division.
дúвный marvellous. **дúво** wonder, marvel.
дидáктика didactics.
диéз (*mus*) sharp.
диéта diet. **диетúческий** dietetic.
дизáйн design. **дизáйнер** designer.
дúзель *m* diesel; diesel engine. **дúзельный** diesel.
дизентерúя dysentery.
дикáрь (-я́) *m*, **дикáрка** savage. **дúкий** wild; savage; queer; preposterous. **дикобрáз** porcupine. **дикорастýщий** wild. **дúкость** wildness, savagery; absurdity.
диктáнт dictation. **диктáтор** dictator. **диктатýра** dictatorship.
диктовáть *impf* (*pf* **про~**) dictate. **дúктор** announcer. **дúкция** diction.
дилéмма dilemma.
дилетáнт dilettante.

дина́мика dynamics.
динами́т dynamite.
динами́ческий dynamic.
дина́стия dynasty.
диноза́вр dinosaur.
дипло́м diploma; degree; degree work. **диплома́т** diplomat. **дипломати́ческий** diplomatic.
директи́ва instructions; directives. **дире́ктор** (*pl* ~а́) director; principal. **дире́кция** management.
дирижа́бль *m* airship, dirigible.
дирижёр conductor. **дирижи́ровать** *impf +instr* conduct.
диск disc, disk; dial; discus.
ди́скант treble.
дисково́д disk drive.
дискоте́ка discotheque.
дискре́тный discrete.
дискримина́ция discrimination.
диску́ссия discussion, debate.
диспансе́р clinic.
диспе́тчер controller.
ди́спут public debate.
диссерта́ция dissertation, thesis.
дистанцио́нный distance, distant, remote; remote-control. **диста́нция** distance; range; region.
дисципли́на discipline.
дитя́ (дитя́ти; *pl* де́ти, -е́й) *neut* child; baby.
дифтери́т diptheria.
дифто́нг diphthong.
диффама́ция libel.
дичь game.
длина́ length. **дли́нный** (-нен, -нна́, -о) long. **дли́тельность** duration. **дли́тельный** long, protracted. **дли́ться** *impf* (*pf* **про~**) last.
для *prep+gen* for; for the sake of; ~ **того́, что́бы...** in order to.
днева́льный *sb* (*mil*) orderly.
дневни́к (-а́) diary, journal.
дневно́й day; daily. **днём** *adv* in the day time; in the afternoon. **дни** *etc.*: *see* **день**
дни́ще bottom.
ДНК *abbr* (*of* **дезоксирибонуклеи́новая кислота́**) DNA.
дно (дна; *pl* до́нья, -ьев) bottom.
до *prep+gen* (up) to; as far as; until; before; to the point of; **до на́шей э́ры** BC; **до сих пор** till now; **до тех пор** till then, before; **до того́, как** before; **до того́, что** to such an extent that, to the point where: **мне не до** I'm not in the mood for.
доба́вить (-влю) *pf*, **добавля́ть** *impf* (*+acc or gen*) add. **доба́вка** addition; second helping. **добавле́ние** addition; supplement; extra. **доба́вочный** additional.
добега́ть *impf*, **добежа́ть** (-егу́) *pf* +**до**+*gen* run to, as far as; reach.
добива́ть *impf*, **доби́ть** (-бью́, -бьёшь) *pf* finish (off); **~ся** *+gen* get, obtain; **~ся своего́** get one's way.
добира́ться *impf of* **добра́ться**
до́блесть valour.
добра́ться (-беру́сь, -ёшься; -а́лся, -ла́сь, -а́ло́сь) *pf* (*impf* **добира́ться**) +**до**+*gen* get to, reach.
добро́ good; **э́то не к добру́** it is a bad sign.
добро- *in comb* good-, well-. **доброво́лец** (-льца) volunteer. **~во́льно** *adv* voluntarily. **~во́льный** voluntary. **~де́тель** virtue. **~де́тель-**

ный virtuous. **~ду́шие** good nature. **~ду́шный** good-natured. **~жела́тельный** benevolent. **~ка́чественный** of good quality; benign. **~со́вестный** conscientious.

доброта́ goodness, kindness.

добро́тный of good quality.

до́брый (добр, -á, -о, до́бры) good; kind; **бу́дьте добры́** +*imper* please; would you be kind enough to.

добыва́ть *impf*, **добы́ть** (-бу́ду; до́был, -á, -о) *pf* get, obtain, procure; mine. **добы́ча** output; mining; booty.

добью́ *etc.*: *see* **доби́ть. доведу́** *etc.*: *see* **довести́**

довезти́ (-езу́, -езёшь; -вёз, -ла́) *pf* (*impf* **довози́ть**) take (to), carry (to), drive (to).

дове́ренность warrant; power of attorney. **дове́ренный** trusted; *sb* agent, proxy. **дове́рие** trust, confidence. **дове́рить** *pf* (*impf* **доверя́ть**) entrust; **~ся** +*dat* trust in; confide in.

до́верху *adv* to the top.

дове́рчивый trustful, credulous. **доверя́ть** *impf* *of* **дове́рить**; (+*dat*) to trust.

дове́сок (-ска) makeweight.

довести́ (-еду́, -едёшь; -вёл, -á) *pf*, **доводи́ть** (-ожу́, -о́дишь) *impf* lead, take (to); bring, drive (to). **до́вод** argument, reason.

довое́нный pre-war.

довози́ть (-ожу́, -о́зишь) *impf* *of* **довезти́**

дово́льно *adv* enough; quite, fairly. **дово́льный** satisfied; pleased. **дово́льство** contentment. **дово́льствоваться** *impf* (*pf* **у~**) be content.

догада́ться *pf*, **дога́дываться** *impf* guess; suspect. **дога́дка** surmise, conjecture. **дога́дливый** quick-witted.

до́гма dogma.

догна́ть (-гоню́, -го́нишь; -гна́л, -á, -о) *pf* (*impf* **догоня́ть**) catch up (with).

догова́риваться *impf*, **договори́ться** *pf* come to an agreement; arrange. **до́гово́р** (*pl* -ы *or* -á, -о́в) agreement; contract; treaty. **догово́рный** contractual; agreed.

догоня́ть *impf* *of* **догна́ть**

догора́ть *impf*, **догоре́ть** (-ри́т) *pf* burn out, burn down.

дое́ду *etc.*: *see* **дое́хать. доезжа́ть** *impf* *of* **дое́хать**

дое́хать (-е́ду) *pf* (*impf* **доезжа́ть**) +**до**+*gen* reach, arrive at.

дожда́ться (-ду́сь, -дёшься; -а́лся, -ла́сь, -а́ло́сь) *pf* +*gen* wait for, wait until.

дождеви́к (-á) raincoat. **дождево́й** rain(y). **дождли́вый** rainy. **дождь** (-я́) *m* rain; ~ **идёт** it is raining.

дожива́ть *impf*, **дожи́ть** (-иву́, -ивёшь; до́жил, -á, -о) *pf* live out; spend.

дожида́ться *impf* +*gen* wait for.

до́за dose.

дозво́лить *pf*, **дозволя́ть** *impf* permit.

дозвони́ться *pf* get through, reach by telephone.

дозо́р patrol.

дозрева́ть *impf*, **дозре́ть** (-е́ет) *pf* ripen.

доистори́ческий prehistoric.

дои́ть *impf* (*pf* **по~**) milk.

дойти́ (дойду́, -дёшь; дошёл, -шла́) *pf* (*impf* **доходи́ть**) +**до**+*gen* reach; get through to.

док dock.

доказа́тельный conclusive. **доказа́тельство** proof, evidence. **доказа́ть** (-ажу́, -а́жешь) *pf*, **дока́зывать** *impf* demonstrate, prove.

докати́ться (-ачу́сь, -а́тишься) *pf*, **дока́тываться** *impf* roll; boom; +**до**+*gen* sink into.

докла́д report; lecture. **докладна́я (запи́ска)** report; memo. **докла́дчик** speaker, lecturer. **докла́дывать** *impf of* **доложи́ть**

до́красна́ *adv* to red heat; to redness.

до́ктор (*pl* -а́) doctor. **до́кторский** doctoral. **до́кторша** woman doctor; doctor's wife.

доктри́на doctrine.

докуме́нт document; deed. **документа́льный** documentary. **документа́ция** documentation; documents.

долби́ть (-блю́) *impf* hollow; chisel; repeat; swot up.

долг (*loc* -у́; *pl* -и́) duty; debt; **взять в ~** borrow; **дать в ~** lend.

до́лгий (до́лог, -лга́, -о) long. **до́лго** *adv* long, (for) a long time. **долгове́чный** lasting; durable. **долгожда́нный** long-awaited. **долгоигра́ющая пласти́нка** LP.

долголе́тие longevity. **долголе́тний** of many years; long-standing. **долгосро́чный** long-term.

долгота́ (*pl* -ы) length; longitude.

долево́й lengthwise. **до́лее** *adv* longer.

должа́ть *impf* (*pf* **за~**) borrow.

до́лжен (-жна́) *predic*+*dat* in debt to; +*inf* obliged, bound; likely; must, have to, ought to; **должно́ быть** probably. **должни́к** (-а́), **-ни́ца** debtor. **до́лжное** *sb* due. **должностно́й** official. **до́лжность** (*gen pl* -е́й) post, office; duties. **до́лжный** due, fitting.

доли́на valley.

до́ллар dollar.

доложи́ть[1] (-ожу́, -о́жишь) *pf* (*impf* **докла́дывать**) add.

доложи́ть[2] (-ожу́, -о́жишь) *pf* (*impf* **докла́дывать**) +*acc or* **о**+*prep* report; announce.

доло́й *adv* away, off; +*acc* down with!

долото́ (*pl* -а) chisel.

до́лька segment; clove.

до́льше *adv* longer.

до́ля (*gen pl* -е́й) portion; share; lot, fate.

дом (*pl* -а́) house; home. **до́ма** *adv* at home. **дома́шн|ий** house; home; domestic; home-made; **~яя хозя́йка** housewife.

до́менн|ый blast-furnace; **~ая печь** blast-furnace.

домини́ровать *impf* dominate, predominate.

домкра́т jack.

до́мна blast-furnace.

домовладе́лец (-льца), **-лица** house-owner; landlord. **домово́дство** housekeeping; domestic science. **домо́вый** house; household; housing.

домога́тельство solicitation; bid. **домога́ться** *impf* +*gen* solicit, bid for.

домо́й *adv* home, homewards.

домохозя́йка housewife. **домрабо́тница** domestic servant, maid. **домофо́н** entryphone (*propr*).

доне́льзя *adv* in the extreme.

донесе́ние dispatch, report. **донести́** (-су́, -сёшь; -нёс, -сла́) *pf* (*impf* **доноси́ть**) report, announce; *+dat* inform; **+на**+*acc* inform against; **~сь** be heard; **+до**+*gen* reach.

до́низу *adv* to the bottom; **све́рху ~** from top to bottom.

до́нор donor.

доно́с denunciation, information. **доноси́ть(ся** (-ношу́(сь, -но́сишь(ся) *impf of* **донести́(сь**

доно́счик informer.

донско́й Don.

доны́не *adv* hitherto.

до́нья *etc.*: *see* **дно**

до н.э. *abbr* (*of* **до на́шей э́ры**) BC.

допла́та additional payment, excess fare. **доплати́ть** (-ачу́, -а́тишь) *pf*, **допла́чивать** *impf* pay in addition; pay the rest.

допо́длинно *adv* for certain. **допо́длинный** authentic, genuine.

дополне́ние supplement, addition; (*gram*) object. **дополни́тельно** *adv* in addition. **дополни́тельный** supplementary, additional. **допо́лнить** *pf*, **дополня́ть** *impf* supplement.

допра́шивать *impf*, **допроси́ть** (-ошу́, -о́сишь) *pf* interrogate. **допро́с** interrogation.

до́пуск right of entry, admittance. **допуска́ть** *impf*, **допусти́ть** (-ущу́, -у́стишь) *pf* admit; permit; tolerate; suppose. **допусти́мый** permissible, acceptable. **допуще́ние** assumption.

дореволюцио́нный pre-revolutionary.

доро́га road; way; journey; route; **по доро́ге** on the way.

до́рого *adv* dear, dearly. **дорогови́зна** high prices.

дорого́й (до́рог, -а́, -о) dear.

доро́дный portly.

дорожа́ть *impf* (*pf* **вз~, по~**) rise in price, go up. **доро́же** *comp of* **до́рого, дорого́й.**

дорожи́ть (-жу́) *impf* *+instr* value.

доро́жка path; track; lane; runway; strip, runner, stair-carpet. **доро́жный** road; highway; travelling.

доса́да annoyance. **досади́ть** (-ажу́) *pf*, **досажда́ть** *impf* *+dat* annoy. **доса́дный** annoying. **доса́довать** be annoyed (**на**+*acc* with).

доска́ (*acc* до́ску; *pl* -и, -со́к, -ска́м) board; slab; plaque.

досло́вный literal; word-for-word.

досмо́тр inspection.

доспе́хи *pl* armour.

досро́чный ahead of time, early.

достава́ть(ся (-таю́(сь, -ёшь(ся) *impf of* **доста́ть(ся**

доста́вить (-влю) *pf*, **доставля́ть** *impf* deliver; supply; cause, give. **доста́вка** delivery.

доста́ну *etc.*: *see* **доста́ть**

доста́ток (-тка) sufficiency; prosperity. **доста́точно** *adv* enough, sufficiently. **доста́точный** sufficient; adequate.

доста́ть (-а́ну) *pf* (*impf* **достава́ть**) take (out); get, obtain; *+gen or* **до**+*gen* touch; reach; *impers* suffice; **~ся** *+dat* be inherited by; fall to the lot of; **ему́ доста́нется** he'll catch it.

достига́ть *impf*, **дости́гнуть, дости́чь** (-и́гну; -сти́г) *pf* *+gen* reach, achieve; *+gen or* **до**+*gen* reach. **достиже́ние** achievement.

достове́рный reliable, trustworthy; authentic.

досто́инство dignity; merit; value. **досто́йный** deserved; suitable; worthy; *+gen* worthy of.

достопримеча́тельность sight, notable place.

достоя́ние property.

до́ступ access. **досту́пный** accessible; approachable; reasonable; available.

досу́г leisure, (spare) time. **досу́жий** leisure; idle.

до́сыта *adv* to satiety.

досье́ *neut indecl* dossier.

досяга́емый attainable.

дота́ция grant, subsidy.

дотла́ utterly; to the ground.

дотра́гиваться *impf*, **дотро́нуться** (-нусь) *pf* **+до**+*gen* touch.

дотя́гивать *impf*, **дотяну́ть** (-яну́, -я́нешь) *pf* draw, drag, stretch out; hold out; live; put off; **~ся** stretch, reach; drag on.

до́хлый dead; sickly. **до́хнуть**[1] (-нет; дох) (*pf* **из~, по~, с~**) die; kick the bucket.

дохну́ть[2] (-ну́, -нёшь) *pf* draw a breath.

дохо́д income; revenue. **доходи́ть** (-ожу́, -о́дишь) *impf of* **дойти́. дохо́дный** profitable. **дохо́дчивый** intelligible.

доце́нт reader, senior lecturer.

до́чиста *adv* clean; completely.

до́чка daughter. **дочь** (-чери, *instr* -черью; *pl* -чери, -черей, *instr* -черьми́) daughter.

дошёл *etc.*: *see* **дойти́**

дошко́льник, -ница child under school age. **дошко́льный** pre-school.

доща́тый plank, board. **доще́чка** small plank, board; plaque.

доя́рка milkmaid.

драгоце́нность jewel; treasure; *pl* jewellery; valuables. **драгоце́нный** precious.

дразни́ть (-ню́, -нишь) *impf* tease.

дра́ка fight.

драко́н dragon.

дра́ма drama. **драмати́ческий** dramatic. **драмату́рг** playwright. **драматурги́я** dramatic art; plays.

драп thick woollen cloth.

драпиро́вка draping; curtain; hangings. **драпиро́вщик** upholsterer.

драть (деру́, -рёшь; драл, -а́, -о) *impf* (*pf* **вы́~, за~, со~**) tear (up); irritate; make off; flog; **~ся** fight.

дре́безги *pl*; **в ~** to smithereens. **дребезжа́ть** (-жи́т) *impf* jingle, tinkle.

древеси́на wood; timber. **древе́сный** wood; **~ у́голь** charcoal.

дре́вко (*pl* -и, -ов) pole, staff; shaft.

древнегре́ческий ancient Greek. **древнеевре́йский** Hebrew. **древнеру́сский** Old Russian. **дре́вний** ancient; aged. **дре́вность** antiquity.

дрейф drift; leeway. **дрейфова́ть** *impf* drift.

дрема́ть (-млю́, -млешь) *impf* doze; slumber. **дремо́та** drowsiness.

дрему́чий dense.

дрессиро́ванный trained; performing. **дрессирова́ть** *impf* (*pf* **вы́~**) train; school. **дрессиро́вка** training. **дрессиро́вщик** trainer.

дроби́ть (-блю́) *impf* (*pf* **раз~**) break up, smash; crush;

~ся break to pieces, smash. **дробови́к** (-á) shot-gun. **дробь** (small) shot; drumming; fraction. **дро́бный** fractional.
дрова́ (дров) *pl* firewood.
дро́гнуть (-ну) *pf*, **дрожа́ть** (-жу́) *impf* tremble; shiver; quiver.
дро́жжи (-е́й) *pl* yeast.
дрожь shivering, trembling.
дрозд (-á) thrush.
дро́ссель *m* throttle, choke.
дро́тик javelin, dart.
друг[1] (*pl* -узья́, -зе́й) friend.
друг[2]: **~ дру́га (дру́гу)** each other, one another. **друго́й** other, another; different; **на ~ день** (the) next day. **дру́жба** friendship. **дружелю́бный, дру́жеский, дру́жественный** friendly. **дружи́ть** (-жу́, -у́жишь) *impf* be friends; **~ся** (*pf* **по~ся**) make friends. **дру́жный** (-жен, -жна́, -о) amicable; harmonious; simultaneous, concerted.
дря́блый (дрябл, -á, -о) flabby.
дря́зги (-зг) *pl* squabbles.
дрянно́й worthless; good-for-nothing. **дрянь** rubbish.
дряхле́ть (-е́ю) *impf* (*pf* **о~**) become decrepit. **дря́хлый** (-хл, -ла́, -о) decrepit, senile.
дуб (*pl* -ы́) oak; blockhead. **дуби́на** club, cudgel; blockhead. **дуби́нка** truncheon, baton.
дублёнка sheepskin coat.
дублёр understudy. **дублика́т** duplicate. **дубли́ровать** duplicate; understudy; dub.
дубо́вый oak; coarse; clumsy.
дуга́ (*pl* -и) arc; arch.
ду́дка pipe, fife.
ду́ло muzzle; barrel.
ду́ма thought; Duma; council.
ду́мать *impf* (*pf* **по~**) think; *+inf* think of, intend. **ду́маться** *impf* (*impers +dat*) seem.
дунове́ние puff, breath. **ду́нуть** (-ну) *pf of* **дуть**
дупло́ (*pl* -а, -пел) hollow; hole; cavity.
ду́ра, дура́к (-á) fool. **дура́чить** (-чу) *impf* (*pf* **о~**) fool, dupe; **~ся** play the fool.
дуре́ть (-е́ю) *impf* (*pf* **о~**) grow stupid.
дурма́н narcotic; intoxicant. **дурма́нить** *impf* (*pf* **о~**) stupefy.
дурно́й (-рен, -рна́, -о) bad, evil; ugly; **мне ду́рно** I feel faint, sick. **дурнота́** faintness; nausea.
ду́тый hollow; inflated. **дуть** (ду́ю) *impf* (*pf* **вы́~, по~, ду́нуть**) blow; **ду́ет** there is a draught. **дутьё** glass-blowing. **ду́ться** (ду́юсь) *impf* pout; sulk.
дух spirit; spirits; heart; mind; breath; ghost; smell; **в ~е** in a good mood; **не в моём ~е** not to my taste; **ни слу́ху ни ~у** no news, not a word. **духи́** (-о́в) *pl* scent, perfume. **Ду́хов день** Whit Monday. **духове́нство** clergy. **духови́дец** (-дца) clairvoyant; medium. **духо́вка** oven. **духо́вный** spiritual; ecclesiastical. **духово́й** wind. **духота́** stuffiness, closeness.
душ shower(-bath).
душа́ (*acc* -у; *pl* -и) soul; heart; feeling; spirit; inspiration; **в душе́** inwardly; at heart; **от всей души́** with all one's heart.
душева́я *sb* shower-room.
душевнобольно́й mentally ill, insane; *sb* mental patient;

lunatic. **душевный** mental; sincere, cordial.

душистый fragrant; ~ **горошек** sweet pea(s).

душить (-шу, -шишь) *impf* (*pf* **за~**) strangle; stifle, smother.

душиться (-шусь, -шишься) *impf* (*pf* **на~**) use, put on, perfume.

душный (-шен, -шна, -о) stuffy, close.

дуэль duel.

дуэт duet.

дыбом *adv* on end; **у меня волосы встали** ~ my hair stood on end. **дыбы: становиться на** ~ rear; resist.

дым (*loc* -у; *pl* -ы) smoke. **дымить** (-млю) *impf* (*pf* **на~**) smoke; **~ся** smoke; billow. **дымка** haze. **дымный** smoky. **дымов|ой**: **~ая труба** flue, chimney. **дымок** (-мка) puff of smoke. **дымоход** flue.

дыня melon.

дыра (*pl* -ы), **дырка** (*gen pl* -рок) hole; gap.

дыхание breathing; breath. **дыхательн|ый** respiratory; breathing; **~ое горло** windpipe. **дышать** (-шу, -шишь) *impf* breathe.

дьявол devil. **дьявольский** devilish, diabolical.

дьякон (*pl* -а) deacon.

дюжина dozen.

дюйм inch.

дюна dune.

дядя (*gen pl* -ей) *m* uncle.

дятел (-тла) woodpecker.

Е

евангелие gospel; the Gospels. **евангелический** evangelical.

еврей, еврейка Jew; Hebrew. **еврейский** Jewish.

евро *neut indecl* euro. **Европа** Europe. **европеец** (-ейца) European. **европейский** European.

Египет Egypt. **египетский** Egyptian. **египтянин** (*pl* -яне, -ян), **египтянка** Egyptian.

его *see* **он, оно**; *pron* his; its.

еда food; meal.

едва *adv* & *conj* hardly; just; scarcely; ~ **ли** hardly; ~ **(ли) не** almost, all but.

един *etc.*: *see* **есть**[1]

единение unity. **единица** (figure) one; unity; unit; individual. **единичный** single; individual.

едино- *in comb* mono-, uni-; one; co-. **единобрачие** monogamy. **~властие** autocracy. **~временно** *adv* only once; simultaneously. **~гласие, ~душие** unanimity. **~гласный, ~душный** unanimous. **~кровный брат** half-brother. **~мыслие** like-mindedness; agreement. **~мышленник** like-minded person. **~утробный брат** half-brother.

единственно *adv* only, solely. **единственный** only, sole. **единство** unity. **единый** one; single; united.

едкий (едок, едка, -о) caustic; pungent.

едок (-а) mouth, head; eater.

еду *etc.*: *see* **ехать**

её *see* **она**; *pron* her, hers; its.

ёж (ежа) hedgehog.

еже- *in comb* every; -ly. **ежегодник** annual, year-book. **~годный** annual. **~дневный** daily. **~месячник, ~месячный** monthly. **~недельник, ~недельный** weekly.

ежевика (*no pl*; *usu collect*)

blackberry; blackberries; blackberry bush.

ёжели *conj* if.

ёжиться (ёжусь) *impf* (*pf* **съ~**) huddle up; shrink away.

езда́ ride, riding; drive, driving; journey. **е́здить** (е́зжу) *impf* go; ride, drive; **~ верхо́м** ride. **ездо́к** (-а́) rider.

ей *see* **она́**

ей-бо́гу *int* really! truly!

ел *etc.*: *see* **есть**[1]

е́ле *adv* scarcely; only just. **е́ле-е́ле** *emphatic variant of* **е́ле**

ёлка fir-tree, spruce; Christmas tree. **ёлочка** herring-bone pattern. **ёлочный** Christmas-tree. **ель** fir-tree; spruce.

ем *etc.*: *see* **есть**[1]

ёмкий capacious. **ёмкость** capacity.

ему́ *see* **он, оно́**

епи́скоп bishop.

е́ресь heresy. **ерети́к** (-а́) heretic. **ерети́ческий** heretical.

ёрзать *impf* fidget.

еро́шить (-шу) *impf* (*pf* **взъ~**) ruffle, rumple.

ерунда́ nonsense.

е́сли *conj* if; **~ бы** if only; **~ бы не** but for, if it were not for; **~ не** unless.

ест *see* **есть**[1]

есте́ственно *adv* naturally. **есте́ственный** natural. **естество́** nature; essence. **естествозна́ние** (natural) science.

есть[1] (ем, ешь, ест, еди́м; ел) *impf* (*pf* **съ~**) eat; corrode, eat away.

есть[2] *see* **быть**; is, are; there is, there are; **у меня́ ~** I have.

ефре́йтор lance-corporal.

е́хать (е́ду) *impf* (*pf* **по~**) go; ride, drive; travel; **~ верхо́м** ride.

ехи́дный malicious, spiteful.

ешь *see* **есть**[1]

ещё *adv* still; yet; (some) more; any more; yet, further; again; *+comp* still, yet even; **всё ~** still; **~ бы!** of course! oh yes! can you ask?; **~ не, нет ~** not yet; **~ раз** once more, again; **пока́ ~** for the present, for the time being.

е́ю *see* **она́**

Ж

ж *conj*: *see* **же**

жа́ба toad.

жа́бра (*gen pl* -бр) gill.

жа́воронок (-нка) lark.

жа́дничать *impf* be greedy; be mean. **жа́дность** greed; meanness. **жа́дный** (-ден, -дна́, -о) greedy; avid; mean.

жа́жда thirst; *+gen* thirst, craving for. **жа́ждать** (-ду) *impf* thirst, yearn.

жаке́т, жаке́тка jacket.

жале́ть (-е́ю) *impf* (*pf* **по~**) pity, feel sorry for; regret; *+acc or gen* grudge.

жа́лить *impf* (*pf* **у~**) sting, bite.

жа́лкий (-лок, -лка́, -о) pitiful. **жа́лко** *predic*: *see* **жаль**

жа́ло sting.

жа́лоба complaint. **жа́лобный** plaintive.

жа́лованье salary. **жа́ловать** *impf* (*pf* **по~**) *+acc or dat of person, instr or acc of thing* grant, bestow on; **~ся** complain (**на***+acc* of, about).

жа́лостливый compassionate. **жа́лостный** piteous; compassionate. **жа́лость** pity.

жаль, жа́лко *predic, impers* (it is) a pity; *+dat* it grieves;

+*gen* grudge; **как ~** what a pity; **мне ~ его́** I'm sorry for him.

жалюзи́ *neut indecl* Venetian blind.

жанр genre.

жар (*loc* -у́) heat; heat of the day; fever; (high) temperature; ardour. **жара́** heat; hot weather.

жарго́н slang.

жа́реный roast; grilled; fried. **жа́рить** *impf* (*pf* **за~, из~**) roast; grill; fry; scorch, burn; **~ся** roast, fry. **жа́рк|ий** (-рок, -рка́, -о) hot; passionate; **-ое** *sb* roast (meat). **жаро́вня** (*gen pl* -вен) brazier. **жар-пти́ца** Firebird. **жа́рче** *comp of* **жа́ркий**

жа́тва harvest. **жать**[1] (жну, жнёшь) *impf* (*pf* **с~**) reap, cut.

жать[2] (жму, жмёшь) *impf* press, squeeze; pinch; oppress.

жва́чка chewing, rumination; cud; chewing-gum. **жва́чн|ый** ruminant; **~ое** *sb* ruminant.

жгу *etc.*: *see* **жечь**

жгут (-а́) plait; tourniquet.

жгу́чий burning. **жёг** *etc.*: *see* **жечь**

ждать (жду, ждёшь; -ал, -а́, -о) *impf* +*gen* wait (for); expect.

же, ж *conj* but; and; however; also; *partl* giving emphasis or expressing identity; **мне же ка́жется** it seems to me, however; **сего́дня же** this very day; **что же ты де́лаешь?** what on earth are you doing?

жева́тельная рези́нка chewing-gum. **жева́ть** (жую́, жуёшь) *impf* chew; ruminate.

жезл (-а́) rod; staff.

жела́ние wish, desire. **жела́нный** longed-for; beloved. **жела́тельный** desirable; advisable. **жела́ть** *impf* (*pf* **по~**) +*gen* wish for, desire; want.

желе́ *neut indecl* jelly.

железа́ (*pl* же́лезы, -лёз, -за́м) gland; *pl* tonsils.

железнодоро́жник railwayman. **железнодоро́жный** railway. **желе́зн|ый** iron; **~ая доро́га** railway. **желе́зо** iron.

железобето́н reinforced concrete.

жёлоб (*pl* -а́) gutter. **жело-бо́к** (-бка́) groove, channel, flute.

желте́ть (-е́ю) *impf* (*pf* **по~**) turn yellow; be yellow. **жел-то́к** (-тка́) yolk. **желту́ха** jaundice. **жёлтый** (жёлт, -а́, жёлто́) yellow.

желу́док (-дка) stomach. **желу́дочный** stomach; gastric.

жёлудь (*gen pl* -е́й) *m* acorn.

жёлчный bilious; gall; irritable. **жёлчь** bile, gall.

жема́ниться *impf* mince, put on airs. **жема́нный** mincing, affected. **жема́нство** affectedness.

же́мчуг (*pl* -а́) pearl(s). **жемчу́жина** pearl. **жемчу́жный** pear(ly).

жена́ (*pl* жёны) wife. **жена́тый** married.

жени́ть (-ню́, -нишь) *impf & pf* (*pf also* **по~**) marry. **женить-ба** marriage. **жени́ться** (-ню́сь, -нишься) *impf & pf* (+**на**+*prep*) marry, get married (to). **жени́х** (-а́) fiancé; bridegroom.

же́нский woman's; feminine; female. **же́нственный** womanly, feminine. **же́нщина** woman.

жердь (*gen pl* -е́й) pole; stake.

жеребёнок (-нка; *pl* -бя́та,

-бя́т) foal. **жеребе́ц** (-бца́) stallion.
жеребьёвка casting of lots.
жерло́ (*pl* -а) muzzle; crater.
жёрнов (*pl* -а́, -о́в) millstone.
же́ртва sacrifice; victim. **же́ртвенный** sacrificial. **же́ртвовать** *impf* (*pf* **по~**) present, make a donation (of); *+instr* sacrifice.
жест gesture. **жестикули́ровать** *impf* gesticulate.
жёсткий (-ток, -тка́, -о) hard, tough; rigid, strict.
жесто́кий (-то́к, -а́, -о) cruel; severe. **жесто́кость** cruelty.
жесть tin(-plate). **жестяно́й** tin.
жето́н medal; counter; token.
жечь (жгу, жжёшь; жёг, жгла) *impf* (*pf* **с~**) burn; **~ся** burn, sting; burn o.s.
живи́тельный invigorating.
жи́вность poultry, fowl. **жив|о́й** (жив, -а́, -о) living, alive; lively; vivid; brisk; animated; poignant; bright; **на ~у́ю ни́тку** hastily, anyhow; **шить на ~у́ю ни́тку** tack. **живопи́сец** (-сца) painter. **живопи́сный** picturesque. **жи́вопись** painting. **жи́вость** liveliness.
живо́т (-а́) abdomen; stomach.
животново́дство animal husbandry. **живо́тное** *sb* animal. **живо́тный** animal.
живу́ *etc.*: *see* **жить. живу́чий** hardy. **живьём** *adv* alive.
жи́дк|ий (-док, -дка́, -о) liquid; watery; weak; sparse; **~ий криста́лл** liquid crystal.
жи́дкость liquid, fluid; wateriness, weakness. **жи́жа** sludge; slush; liquid. **жи́же** *comp of* **жи́дкий**
жи́зненный life, of life; vital; living; **~ у́ровень** standard of living. **жизнеописа́ние** biography. **жизнера́достный** cheerful. **жизнеспосо́бный** capable of living; viable. **жизнь** life.
жи́ла vein; tendon, sinew.
жиле́т, жиле́тка waistcoat.
жиле́ц (-льца́), **жили́ца** lodger; tenant; inhabitant.
жили́ще dwelling, abode. **жили́щный** housing; living.
жи́лка vein; fibre; streak.
жил|о́й dwelling; habitable; **~о́й дом** dwelling house; block of flats; **~а́я пло́щадь, жилпло́щадь** floor-space; housing, accommodation. **жильё** habitation; dwelling.
жир (*loc* -у́; *pl* -ы́) fat; grease.
жире́ть (-ре́ю) *impf* (*pf* **о~, раз~**) grow fat. **жи́рный** (-рен, -рна́, -о) fatty; greasy; rich.
жирово́й fatty; fat.
жира́ф giraffe.
жите́йский worldly; everyday. **жи́тель** *m* inhabitant; dweller. **жи́тельство** residence. **жи́тница** granary.
жи́то corn, cereal. **жить** (живу́, -вёшь; жил, -а́, -о) *impf* live. **житьё** life; existence; habitation.
жму *etc.*: *see* **жать**[2]
жму́риться *impf* (*pf* **за~**) screw up one's eyes, frown.
жнивьё (*pl* -ья, -ьев) stubble (-field). **жну** *etc.*: *see* **жать**[1]
жоке́й jockey.
жонглёр juggler.
жрать (жру, жрёшь; -ал, -а́, -о) guzzle.
жре́бий lot; fate, destiny; **~ бро́шен** the die is cast.
жрец priest. **жри́ца** priestess.
жужжа́ть (-жжу́) hum, buzz, drone; whiz(z).

жук (-а́) beetle.

жу́лик petty thief; cheat. **жу́льничать** *impf* (*pf* **с~**) cheat.

жура́вль (-я́) *m* crane.

жури́ть *impf* reprove.

журна́л magazine, periodical. **журнали́ст** journalist. **журнали́стика** journalism.

журча́ние babble; murmur. **журча́ть** (-чи́т) *impf* babble, murmur.

жу́ткий (-ток, -тка́, -о) uncanny; terrible, terrifying. **жу́тко** *adv* terrifyingly; terribly, awfully.

жую́ *etc.*: *see* **жева́ть**

жюри́ *neut indecl* judges.

З

за *prep* **I.** *+acc* (*indicating motion or action*) *or instr* (*indicating rest or state*) behind; beyond; across, the other side of; at; to; **за́ го́род, за́ го́родом** out of town; **за рубежо́м** abroad; **сесть за роя́ль** sit down at the piano; **сиде́ть за роя́лем** be at the piano; **за́ у́гол, за угло́м** round the corner. **II.** *+acc* after; over; during, in the space of; by; for; to; **за ва́ше здоро́вье!** your health!; **вести́ за́ руку** lead by the hand; **далеко́ за́ по́лночь** long after midnight; **за два дня до**+*gen* two days before; **за́ три киломе́тра от дере́вни** three kilometres from the village; **плати́ть за биле́т** pay for a ticket; **за после́днее вре́мя** lately. **III.** *+instr* after; for; because of; at, during; **год за го́дом** year after year; **идти́ за молоко́м** go for milk; **за обе́дом** at dinner.

заба́ва amusement; game; fun. **забавля́ть** *impf* amuse; **~ся** amuse o.s. **заба́вный** amusing, funny.

забастова́ть *pf* strike; go on strike. **забасто́вка** strike. **забасто́вщик** striker.

забве́ние oblivion.

забе́г heat, race. **забега́ть** *impf*, **забежа́ть** (-егу́) *pf* run up; **+к**+*dat* drop in on; **~ вперёд** run ahead; anticipate.

за|бере́менеть (-ею) *pf* become pregnant.

заберу́ *etc.*: *see* **забра́ть**

забива́ние jamming. **забива́ть(ся** *impf of* **заби́ть(ся**[1]

забинтова́ть *pf*, **забинто́вывать** *impf* bandage.

забира́ть(ся *impf of* **забра́ть(ся**

заби́тый downtrodden. **заби́ть**[1] (-бью́, -бьёшь) *pf* (*impf* **забива́ть**) drive in, hammer in; score; seal, block up; obstruct; choke; jam; cram; beat up; beat; **~ся** hide, take refuge; become cluttered *or* clogged; **+в**+*acc* get into, penetrate. **за|би́ть(ся**[2] *pf* begin to beat. **забия́ка** *m & f* squabbler; bully.

заблаговре́менно *adv* in good time; well in advance. **заблаговре́менный** timely.

заблесте́ть (-ещу́, -ести́шь *or* -е́щешь) *pf* begin to shine, glitter, glow.

заблуди́ться (-ужу́сь, -у́дишься) *pf* get lost. **заблу́дший** lost, stray. **заблужда́ться** *impf* be mistaken. **заблужде́ние** error; delusion.

забо́й (pit-)face.

заболева́емость sickness

rate. **заболева́ние** sickness, illness; falling ill. **заболева́ть**[1] *impf*, **заболе́ть**[1] (-е́ю) *pf* fall ill; *+instr* go down with. **заболева́ть**[2] *impf*, **заболе́ть**[2] (-ли́т) *pf* (begin to) ache, hurt.

забо́р[1] fence.

забо́р[2] taking away; obtaining on credit.

забо́та concern; care; trouble(s). **забо́тить** (-о́чу) *impf* (*pf* **о~**) trouble, worry; **~ся** *impf* (*pf* **по~**) worry; take care (**о**+*prep* of); take trouble; care. **забо́тливый** solicitous, thoughtful.

за|бракова́ть *pf.*

забра́сывать *impf of* **заброса́ть, забро́сить**

забра́ть (-беру́, -берёшь; -а́л, -а́, -о) *pf* (*impf* **забира́ть**) take; take away; seize; appropriate; **~ся** climb; get to, into.

забреда́ть *impf*, **забрести́** (-еду́, -едёшь; -ёл, -а́) *pf* stray, wander; drop in.

за|брони́ровать *pf.*

заброса́ть *pf* (*impf* **забра́сывать**) fill up; bespatter, deluge. **забро́сить** (-о́шу) *pf* (*impf* **забра́сывать**) throw; abandon; neglect. **забро́шенный** neglected; deserted.

забры́згать *pf*, **забры́згивать** *impf* splash, bespatter.

забыва́ть *impf*, **забы́ть** (-бу́ду) *pf* forget; **~ся** doze off; lose consciousness; forget o.s. **забы́вчивый** forgetful. **забытьё** oblivion; drowsiness.

забью́ *etc.*: *see* **заби́ть**

зава́ливать *impf*, **завали́ть** (-лю́, -лишь) *pf* block up; pile; cram; overload; knock down; make a mess of; **~ся** fall; collapse; tip up.

зава́ривать *impf*, **завари́ть** (-арю́, -а́ришь) *pf* make; brew; weld. **зава́рка** brewing; brew; welding.

заведе́ние establishment. **заве́довать** *impf +instr* manage.

заве́домо *adv* wittingly. **заве́домый** notorious, undoubted.

заведу́ *etc.*: *see* **завести́**

заве́дующий *sb* (*+instr*) manager; head.

завезти́ (-зу́, -зёшь; -ёз, -ла́) *pf* (*impf* **завози́ть**) convey, deliver.

за|вербова́ть *pf.*

завери́тель *m* witness. **заве́рить** *pf* (*impf* **заверя́ть**) assure; certify; witness.

заверну́ть (-ну́, -нёшь) *pf* (*impf* **завёртывать, завора́чивать**) wrap, wrap up; roll up; screw tight, screw up; turn (off); drop in, call in.

заверте́ться (-рчу́сь, -ртишься) *pf* begin to turn *or* spin; lose one's head.

завёртывать *impf of* **заверну́ть**

заверша́ть *impf*, **заверши́ть** (-шу́) *pf* complete, conclude. **заверше́ние** completion; end.

заверя́ть *impf of* **заве́рить**

заве́са veil, screen. **заве́сить** (-е́шу) *pf* (*impf* **заве́шивать**) curtain (off).

завести́ (-еду́, -ёшь; -вёл, -а́) *pf* (*impf* **заводи́ть**) take, bring; drop off; start up; acquire; introduce; wind (up), crank; **~сь** be; appear; be established; start.

заве́т behest, bidding, ordinance; Testament. **заве́тный** cherished; secret.

заве́шивать *impf of* **заве́сить**

завеща́ние will, testament.

завеща́ть bequeath.
завя́тый inveterate, out-and-out.
завива́ть(ся *impf of* **зави́ть(ся**. **зави́вка** waving; curling; wave.
зави́дно *impers+dat*: **мне** ~ I feel envious. **зави́дный** enviable. **зави́довать** *impf* (*pf* **по**~) *+dat* envy.
завинти́ть (-нчу́) *pf*, **зави́нчивать** *impf* screw up.
зави́сеть (-и́шу) *impf +***от***+gen* depend on. **зави́симость** dependence; **в зави́симости от** depending on, subject to. **зави́симый** dependent.
зави́стливый envious. **за́висть** envy.
завито́й (за́вит, -а́, -о) curled, waved. **завито́к** (-тка́) curl, lock; flourish. **зави́ть** (-вью́, -вьёшь; -и́л, -а́, -о) *pf* (*impf* **завива́ть**) curl, wave; **~ся** curl, wave, twine; have one's hair curled.
завладева́ть *impf*, **завладе́ть** (-е́ю) *pf +instr* take possession of; seize.
завлека́тельный alluring; fascinating. **завлека́ть** *impf*, **завле́чь** (-еку́, -ечёшь; -лёк, -ла́) *pf* lure; fascinate.
заво́д[1] factory; works; stud-farm.
заво́д[2] winding mechanism.
заводи́ть(ся (-ожу́(сь, -о́дишь(ся) *impf of* **завести́(сь**. **заводно́й** clockwork; winding, cranking.
заводско́й factory; *sb* factory worker. **заво́дчик** factory owner.
за́водь backwater.
завоева́ние winning; conquest; achievement. **завоева́тель** *m* conqueror. **завоева́ть** (-ою́ю) *pf*, **завоёвывать** *impf* conquer; win, gain; try to get.
завожу́ *etc.*: *see* **заводи́ть, завози́ть**
заво́з delivery; carriage. **завози́ть** (-ожу́, -о́зишь) *impf of* **завезти́**
завора́чивать *impf of* **заверну́ть**. **заворо́т** turn, turning; sharp bend.
заво́ю *etc.*: *see* **завы́ть**
завсегда́ *adv* always. **завсегда́тай** habitué, frequenter.
за́втра tomorrow. **за́втрак** breakfast; lunch. **за́втракать** *impf* (*pf* **по**~) have breakfast; have lunch. **за́втрашний** tomorrow's; ~ **день** tomorrow.
завыва́ть *impf*, **завы́ть** (-во́ю) *pf* (begin to) howl.
завяза́ть (-яжу́, -я́жешь) *pf* (*impf* **завя́зывать**) tie, tie up; start; **~ся** start; arise; (*of fruit*) set. **завя́зка** string, lace; start; opening.
за|вя́знуть (-ну; -я́з) *pf*. **завя́зывать(ся** *impf of* **завяза́ть(ся**
за|вя́нуть (-ну; -я́л) *pf*.
загада́ть *pf*, **зага́дывать** *impf* think of; plan ahead; guess at the future; ~ **зага́дку** ask a riddle. **зага́дка** riddle; enigma. **зага́дочный** enigmatic, mysterious.
зага́р sunburn, tan.
за|гаси́ть (-ашу́, -а́сишь) *pf*.
за|га́снуть (-ну) *pf*.
загво́здка snag; difficulty.
заги́б fold; exaggeration. **загиба́ть** *impf of* **загну́ть**
за|гипнотизи́ровать *pf*.
загла́вие title; heading. **загла́вн|ый** title; **~ая бу́ква** capital letter.
загла́дить (-а́жу) *pf*, **загла́-**

живать *impf* iron, iron out; make up for; expiate; **~ся** iron out, become smooth; fade.
за|гло́хнуть (-ну; -гло́х) *pf.*
заглуша́ть *impf*, **за|глуши́ть** (-шу́) *pf* drown, muffle; jam; suppress, stifle; alleviate.
загляде́нье lovely sight. **загляде́ться** (-яжу́сь) *pf*, **загля́дываться** *impf* **на**+*acc* stare at; be lost in admiration of. **загля́дывать** *impf*, **загляну́ть** (-ну́, -нешь) *pf* peep; drop in.
загна́ть (-гоню́, -го́нишь; -а́л, -а́, -о) *pf* (*impf* **загоня́ть**) drive in, drive home; drive; exhaust.
загнива́ние decay; suppuration. **загнива́ть** *impf*, **загни́ть** (-ию́, -иёшь; -и́л, -а́, -о) *pf* rot; decay; fester.
загну́ть (-ну́, -нёшь) *pf* (*impf* **загиба́ть**) turn up, turn down; bend.
загова́ривать *impf*, **заговори́ть** *pf* begin to speak; tire out with talk; cast a spell over; protect with a charm (**от**+*gen* against). **за́говор** plot; spell. **загово́рщик** conspirator.
заголо́вок (-вка) title; heading; headline.
заго́н enclosure, pen; driving in. **загоня́ть**[1] *impf of* **загна́ть**. **загоня́ть**[2] *pf* tire out; work to death.
загора́живать *impf of* **загороди́ть**
загора́ть *impf*, **загоре́ть** (-рю́) *pf* become sunburnt; **~ся** catch fire; blaze; *impers*+*dat* want very much. **загоре́лый** sunburnt.
загороди́ть (-рожу́, -ро́дишь) *pf* (*impf* **загора́живать**) enclose, fence in; obstruct. **загоро́дка** fence, enclosure.
за́городный suburban; country.
загота́вливать *impf*, **заготовля́ть** *impf*, **загото́вить** (-влю) *pf* lay in (a stock of); store; prepare. **загото́вка** (State) procurement; laying in.
загради́ть (-ажу́) *pf*, **загражда́ть** *impf* block, obstruct; bar. **загражде́ние** obstruction; barrier.
грани́ца abroad, foreign parts. **грани́чный** foreign.
загреба́ть *impf*, **загрести́** (-ебу́, -ебёшь; -ёб, -ла́) *pf* rake up, gather; rake in.
загри́вок (-вка) withers; nape (of the neck).
за|гримирова́ть *pf.*
загроможда́ть *impf*, **загромозди́ть** (-зжу́) *pf* block up, encumber; cram.
загружа́ть *impf*, **за|грузи́ть** (-ужу́, -у́зи́шь) *pf* load; feed; (*comput*) boot; load; download; **~ся** +*instr* load up with, take on. **загру́зка** loading, feeding; charge, load, capacity.
за|грунтова́ть *pf.*
загрусти́ть (-ущу́) *pf* grow sad.
загрязне́ние pollution. **за|грязни́ть** *pf*, **загрязня́ть** *impf* soil; pollute; **~ся** become dirty.
загс *abbr* (*of* **(отде́л) за́писи а́ктов гражда́нского состоя́ния**) registry office.
загуби́ть (-блю́, -бишь) *pf* ruin; squander, waste.
загуля́ть *pf*, **загу́ливать** *impf* take to drink.
за|густе́ть *pf.*
зад (*loc* -у́; *pl* -ы́) back; hindquarters; buttocks; **~ом наперёд** back to front.
задава́ть(ся (-даю́(сь) *impf of* **зада́ть(ся**

задави́ть (-влю́, -вишь) *pf* crush; run over.
зададим *etc.*, **задам** *etc.*: *see* **зада́ть**
зада́ние task, job.
зада́тки (-тков) *pl* abilities, promise.
зада́ток (-тка) deposit, advance.
зада́ть (-а́м, -а́шь, -а́ст, -адим; за́дал, -а́, -о) *pf* (*impf* **задава́ть**) set; give; ~ **вопро́с** ask a question; ~**ся** turn out well; succeed; ~**ся мы́слью, це́лью** make up one's mind. **зада́ча** problem; task.
задвига́ть *impf*, **задви́нуть** (-ну) *pf* bolt; bar; push; ~**ся** shut; slide. **задви́жка** bolt; catch.
задво́рки (-рок) *pl* back yard; backwoods.
задева́ть *impf of* **заде́ть**
заде́лать *pf*, **заде́лывать** *impf* do up; block up, close up.
заде́ну *etc.*: *see* **заде́ть. задёргивать** *impf of* **задёрнуть**
задержа́ние detention. **задержа́ть** (-жу́, -жишь) *pf*, **заде́рживать** *impf* delay; withhold; arrest; ~**ся** stay too long; be delayed. **заде́ржка** delay.
задёрнуть (-ну) *pf* (*impf* **задёргивать**) pull; draw.
задеру́ *etc.*: *see* **задра́ть**
заде́ть (-е́ну) *pf* (*impf* **задева́ть**) brush (against), graze; offend; catch (against).
задира *m* & *f* bully; troublemaker. **задира́ть** *impf of* **задра́ть**
за́дн|ий back, rear; **дать** ~**ий ход** reverse; ~**яя мысль** ulterior motive; ~**ий план** background; ~**ий прохо́д** anus.
за́дник back; backdrop.
задо́лго *adv* +**до**+*gen* long before.
за|должа́ть *pf*. **задо́лженность** debts.
задо́р fervour. **задо́рный** provocative; fervent.
задохну́ться (-ну́сь, -нёшься; -о́хся *or* -у́лся) *pf* (*impf* **задыха́ться**) suffocate; choke; pant.
за|дра́ть (-деру́, -дерёшь; -а́л, -а́, -о) *pf* (*impf also* **задира́ть**) tear to pieces, kill; lift up; break; provoke, insult.
задрема́ть (-млю́, -млешь) *pf* doze off.
задрожа́ть (-жу́) *pf* begin to tremble.
задува́ть *impf of* **заду́ть**
заду́мать *pf*, **заду́мывать** *impf* plan; intend; think of; ~**ся** become thoughtful; meditate. **заду́мчивость** reverie. **заду́мчивый** pensive.
заду́ть (-у́ю) *pf* (*impf* **задува́ть**) blow out; begin to blow.
задуше́вный sincere; intimate.
за|души́ть (-ушу́, -у́шишь) *pf*.
задыха́ться *impf of* **задохну́ться**
заеда́ть *impf of* **зае́сть**
зае́зд calling in; lap, heat. **зае́здить** (-зжу) *pf* override; wear out. **заезжа́ть** *impf of* **зае́хать. зае́зженный** hackneyed; worn out. **зае́зжий** visiting.
заём (за́йма) loan.
зае́сть (-е́м, -е́шь, -е́ст, -еди́м) *pf* (*impf* **заеда́ть**) torment; jam; entangle.
зае́хать (-е́ду) *pf* (*impf* **заезжа́ть**) call in; enter, ride in, drive in; reach; +**за**+*acc* go past; +**за**+*instr* call for, fetch.
за|жа́рить(ся *pf*.
зажа́ть (-жму́, -жмёшь) *pf*

(*impf* **зажима́ть**) squeeze; grip; suppress.
заже́чь (-жгу́, -жжёшь; -жёг, -жгла́) *pf* (*impf* **зажига́ть**) set fire to; kindle; light; **~ся** catch fire.
зажива́ть *impf of* **зажи́ть. заживи́ть** (-влю́) *pf*, **заживля́ть** *impf* heal. **за́живо** *adv* alive.
зажига́лка lighter. **зажига́ние** ignition. **зажига́тельный** inflammatory; incendiary. **зажига́ть(ся** *impf of* **заже́чь(ся**
зажи́м clamp; terminal; suppression. **зажима́ть** *impf of* **зажа́ть. зажимно́й** tight-fisted.
зажи́точный prosperous. **зажи́ть** (-иву́, -ивёшь; -ил, -а́, -о) *pf* (*impf* **зажива́ть**) heal; begin to live.
зажму́ *etc.*: *see* **зажа́ть. за|жму́риться** *pf.*
зазвене́ть (-и́т) *pf* begin to ring.
зазелене́ть (-е́ет) *pf* turn green.
заземле́ние earthing; earth. **заземли́ть** *pf*, **заземля́ть** *impf* earth.
зазнава́ться (-наю́сь, -наёшься) *impf*, **зазна́ться** *pf* give o.s. airs.
зазу́брина notch.
за|зубри́ть (-рю́, -у́бри́шь) *pf.*
заи́грывать *impf* flirt.
за́ика *m & f* stammerer. **заика́ние** stammer. **заика́ться** *impf*, **заикну́ться** (-ну́сь, -нёшься) *pf* stammer, stutter; **+о**+*prep* mention.
заи́мствование borrowing. **заи́мствовать** *impf & pf* (*pf also* **по~**) borrow.
заинтересо́ванный interested. **заинтересова́ть** *pf*, **заинтересо́вывать** *impf* interest; **~ся** +*instr* become interested in.
заи́скивать *impf* ingratiate o.s.
зайду́ *etc.*: *see* **зайти́. займу́** *etc.*: *see* **заня́ть**
зайти́ (-йду́, -йдёшь; зашёл, -шла́) *pf* (*impf* **заходи́ть**) call; drop in; set; **+в**+*acc* reach; **+за**+*acc* go behind, turn; **+за** +*instr* call for, fetch.
за́йчик little hare (*esp. as endearment*); reflection of sunlight. **зайчи́ха** doe hare.
закабали́ть *pf*, **закабаля́ть** *impf* enslave.
закады́чный intimate, bosom.
зака́з order; **на ~** to order. **заказа́ть** (-ажу́, -а́жешь) *pf*, **зака́зывать** *impf* order; book. **заказн|о́й** made to order; **~о́е (письмо́)** registered letter. **зака́зчик** customer, client.
зака́л temper; cast. **зака́ливать** *impf*, **закали́ть** (-лю́) *pf* (*impf also* **закаля́ть**) temper; harden. **зака́лка** tempering, hardening.
зака́лывать *impf of* **заколо́ть. закаля́ть** *impf of* **закали́ть. зака́нчивать(ся** *impf of* **зако́нчить(ся**
зака́пать *pf*, **зака́пывать**[1] *impf* begin to drip; rain; spot.
зака́пывать[2] *impf of* **закопа́ть**
зака́т sunset. **заката́ть** *pf*, **зака́тывать**[1] *impf* begin to roll; roll up; roll out. **закати́ть** (-ачу́, -а́тишь) *pf*, **зака́тывать**[2] *impf* roll; **~ся** roll; set.
заква́ска ferment; leaven.
закида́ть *pf*, **заки́дывать**[1] *impf* shower; bespatter.
заки́дывать[2] *impf*, **заки́нуть** (-ну) *pf* throw (out, away).

закипа́ть *impf*, **закипе́ть** (-пи́т) *pf* begin to boil.
закиса́ть *impf*, **заки́снуть** (-ну; -и́с, -ла) *pf* turn sour; become apathetic. **за́кись** oxide.
закла́д pawn; pledge; bet; **би́ться об ~** bet; **в ~е** in pawn. **закла́дка** laying; bookmark. **закладно́й** pawn. **закла́дывать** *impf of* **заложи́ть**
закле́ивать *impf*, **закле́ить** *pf* glue up.
за|клейми́ть (-млю́) *pf*.
заклепа́ть *pf*, **заклёпывать** *impf* rivet. **заклёпка** rivet; riveting.
заклина́ние incantation; spell. **заклина́ть** *impf* invoke; entreat.
заключа́ть *impf*, **заключи́ть** (-чу́) *pf* conclude; enter into; contain; confine. **заключа́ться** consist; lie, be. **заключе́ние** conclusion; decision; confinement. **заключённый** *sb* prisoner. **заключи́тельный** final, concluding.
закля́тие pledge. **закля́тый** sworn.
закова́ть (-кую́, -куёшь) *pf*, **зако́вывать** *impf* chain; shackle.
закола́чивать *impf of* **заколоти́ть**
заколдо́ванный bewitched; **~ круг** vicious circle. **заколдова́ть** *pf* bewitch; lay a spell on.
зако́лка hair-grip; hair-slide.
заколоти́ть (-лочу́, -ло́тишь) *pf* (*impf* **закола́чивать**) board up; knock in; knock insensible.
за|коло́ть (-олю́, -о́лешь) *pf* (*impf also* **зака́лывать**) stab; pin up; (*impers*) **у меня́ заколо́ло в боку́** I have a stitch.
зако́н law. **законнорождённый** legitimate. **зако́нность** legality. **зако́нный** legal; legitimate.
зако́но- *in comb* law, legal. **законове́дение** law, jurisprudence. **~да́тельный** legislative. **~да́тельство** legislation. **~ме́рность** regularity, normality. **~ме́рный** regular, natural. **~прое́кт** bill.
за|консерви́ровать *pf*. **за|конспекти́ровать** *pf*.
зако́нченность completeness. **зако́нченный** finished; accomplished. **зако́нчить** (-чу) *pf* (*impf* **зака́нчивать**) end, finish; **~ся** end, finish.
закопа́ть *pf* (*impf* **зака́пывать**[2]) begin to dig; bury.
закопте́лый sooty, smutty. **за|копте́ть** (-ти́т) *pf*. **за|копти́ть** (-пчу́) *pf*.
закорене́лый deep-rooted; inveterate.
закосне́лый incorrigible.
закоу́лок (-лка) alley; nook.
закочене́лый numb with cold. **за|кочене́ть** (-е́ю) *pf*.
закра́дываться *impf of* **закра́сться**
закра́сить (-а́шу) *pf* (*impf* **закра́шивать**) paint over.
закра́сться (-аду́сь, -адёшься) *pf* (*impf* **закра́дываться**) steal in, creep in.
закра́шивать *impf of* **закра́сить**
закрепи́тель *m* fixative. **закрепи́ть** (-плю́) *pf*, **закрепля́ть** *impf* fasten; fix; consolidate; +**за**+*instr* assign to; **~ за собо́й** secure.
закрепости́ть (-ощу́) *pf*, **закрепоща́ть** *impf* enslave.

закрепощéние enslavement; slavery, serfdom.

закричáть (-чý) *pf* cry out; begin to shout.

закрóйщик cutter.

закрóю *etc.*: *see* **закры́ть**

закруглéние rounding; curve. **закругли́ть** (-лю́) *pf*, **закругля́ть** *impf* make round; round off; **~ся** become round; round off.

закружи́ться (-ужу́сь, -у́жишься) *pf* begin to whirl *or* go round.

за|крути́ть (-учу́, -у́тишь) *pf*, **закру́чивать** *impf* twist, twirl; wind round; turn; screw in; turn the head of; **~ся** twist, twirl, whirl; wind round.

закрывáть *impf*, **закры́ть** (-рóю) *pf* close, shut; turn off; close down; cover; **~ся** close, shut; end; close down; cover o.s.; shelter. **закры́тие** closing; shutting; closing down; shelter. **закры́тый** closed, shut; private.

закули́сный behind the scenes; backstage.

закупáть *impf*, **закупи́ть** (-плю́, -пишь) *pf* buy up; stock up with. **закýпка** purchase.

закýпоривать *impf*, **закýпорить** *pf* cork; stop up; coop up. **закýпорка** corking; thrombosis.

закýпочный purchase. **закýпщик** buyer.

закýривать *impf*, **закури́ть** (-рю́, -ришь) *pf* light up; begin to smoke.

закуси́ть (-ушý, -ýсишь) *pf*, **закýсывать** *impf* have a snack; bite. **закýска** hors-d'oeuvre; snack. **закýсочная** *sb* snack-bar.

за|кýтать *pf*, **закýтывать** *impf* wrap up; **~ся** wrap o.s. up.

зал hall; **~ ожидáния** waiting-room.

залегáть *impf of* **залéчь**

за|леденéть (-éю) *pf*.

залежáлый stale, long unused. **залежáться** (-жýсь) *pf*, **залёживаться** *impf* lie too long; find no market; become stale. **зáлежь** deposit, seam; stale goods.

залезáть *impf*, **залéзть** (-зу; -éз) *pf* climb, climb up; get in; creep in.

за|лепи́ть (-плю́, -пишь) *pf*, **залепля́ть** *impf* paste over; glue up.

залетáть *impf*, **залетéть** (-ечý) *pf* fly; **+в+***acc* fly into.

залéчивать *impf*, **залечи́ть** (-чý, -чишь) *pf* heal, cure; **~ся** heal (up).

залéчь (-ля́гу, -ля́жешь; залёг, -лá) *pf* (*impf* **залегáть**) lie down; lie low; lie, be deposited.

зали́в bay; gulf. **заливáть** *impf*, **зали́ть** (-лью́, -льёшь; зáлил, -á, -о) *pf* flood, inundate; spill on; extinguish; spread; **~ся** be flooded; pour, spill; *+instr* break into.

залóг deposit; pledge; security, mortgage; token; voice. **заложи́ть** (-жý, -жишь) *pf* (*impf* **заклáдывать**) lay; put; mislay; pile up; pawn, mortgage; harness; lay in. **залóжник** hostage.

залп volley, salvo; **~ом** without pausing for breath.

залью́ *etc.*: *see* **зали́ть. заля́гу** *etc.*: *see* **залéчь**

зам *abbr* (*of* **замести́тель**) assistant, deputy. **зам-** *abbr in comb* (*of* **замести́тель**) assistant, deputy, vice-.

за|мáзать (-áжу) *pf*, **замáзывать** *impf* paint over; putty;

smear; soil; **~ся** get dirty. **зама́зка** putty; puttying.

зама́лчивать *impf of* **замолча́ть**

зама́нивать *impf*, **замани́ть** (-ню́, -нишь) *pf* entice; decoy. **зама́нчивый** tempting.

за|маринова́ть *pf.*

за|маскирова́ть *pf*, **замаскиро́вывать** *impf* mask; disguise; **~ся** disguise o.s.

зама́хиваться *impf*, **замахну́ться** (-ну́сь, -нёшься) *pf +instr* raise threateningly.

зама́чивать *impf of* **замочи́ть**

замедле́ние slowing down, deceleration; delay. **заме́длить** *pf*, **замедля́ть** *impf* slow down; slacken; delay; **~ся** slow down.

замёл *etc.*: *see* **замести́**

заме́на substitution; substitute. **замени́мый** replaceable. **замени́тель** *m* (*+gen*) substitute (for). **замени́ть** (-ню́, -нишь) *pf*, **заменя́ть** *impf* replace; be a substitute for.

замере́ть (-мру́, -мрёшь; за́мер, -ла́, -о) *pf* (*impf* **замира́ть**) stand still; freeze; die away.

замерза́ние freezing. **замерза́ть** *impf*, **за|мёрзнуть** (-ну; замёрз) *pf* freeze (up); freeze to death.

заме́рить *pf* (*impf* **замеря́ть**) measure, gauge.

замеси́ть (-ешу́, -е́сишь) *pf* (*impf* **заме́шивать**[2]) knead.

замести́ (-ету́, -етёшь; -мёл, -а́) *pf* (*impf* **замета́ть**) sweep up; cover.

замести́тель *m* substitute; assistant, deputy, vice-. **замести́ть** (-ещу́) *pf* (*impf* **замеща́ть**) replace; deputize for.

замета́ть *impf of* **замести́**

заме́тить (-е́чу) *pf* (*impf* **замеча́ть**) notice; note; remark. **заме́тка** mark; note. **заме́тный** noticeable; outstanding.

замеча́ние remark; reprimand. **замеча́тельный** remarkable; splendid. **замеча́ть** *impf of* **заме́тить**

замеша́тельство confusion; embarrassment. **замеша́ть** *pf*, **заме́шивать**[1] *impf* mix up, entangle. **заме́шивать**[2] *impf of* **замеси́ть**

замеща́ть *impf of* **замести́ть.** **замеще́ние** substitution; filling.

зами́нка hitch; hesitation.

замира́ть *impf of* **замере́ть**

за́мкнутый reserved; closed, exclusive. **замкну́ть** (-ну́, -нёшь) *pf* (*impf* **замыка́ть**) lock; close; **~ся** close; shut o.s. up; become reserved.

за́мок[1] (-мка) castle.

замо́к[2] (-мка́) lock; padlock; clasp.

замолка́ть *impf*, **замо́лкнуть** (-ну; -мо́лк) *pf* fall silent; stop.

замолча́ть (-чу́) *pf* (*impf* **зама́лчивать**) fall silent; cease corresponding; hush up.

замора́живать *impf*, **заморо́зить** (-ро́жу) *pf* freeze. **заморо́женный** frozen; iced. **за́морозки** (-ов) *pl* (slight) frosts.

замо́рский overseas.

за|мочи́ть (-чу́, -чишь) *pf* (*impf also* **зама́чивать**) wet; soak; ret.

замо́чная сква́жина keyhole.

замру́ *etc.*: *see* **замере́ть**

за́муж *adv*: **вы́йти ~** (**за**+*acc*) marry. **за́мужем** *adv* married (**за**+*instr* to).

за|му́чить (-чу) *pf* torment; wear out; bore to tears. **за|му́читься** (-чусь) *pf.*

за́мша suede.
замыка́ние locking; short circuit. **замыка́ть(ся** *impf of* **замкну́ть(ся**
за́мысел (-сла) project, plan. **замы́слить** *pf*, **замышля́ть** *impf* plan; contemplate.
за́навес, занаве́ска curtain.
занести́ (-су́, -сёшь; -ёс, -ла́) *pf* (*impf* **заноси́ть**) bring; note down; (*impers*) cover with snow etc.; (*impers*) skid.
занима́ть *impf* (*pf* **заня́ть**) occupy; interest; engage; borrow; **~ся** *+instr* be occupied with; work at; study.
зано́за splinter. **занози́ть** (-ожу́) *pf* get a splinter in.
зано́с snow-drift; skid. **заноси́ть** (-ошу́, -о́сишь) *impf of* **занести́**. **зано́счивый** arrogant.
заня́тие occupation; *pl* studies.
занято́й busy. **за́нятый** (-нят, -а́, -о) occupied; taken; engaged. **заня́ть(ся** (займу́(сь, -мёшь(ся; за́нял(ся, -а́(сь, -о(сь) *pf of* **занима́ть(ся**
заодно́ *adv* in concert; at one; at the same time.
заостри́ть *pf*, **заостря́ть** *impf* sharpen; emphasize.
зао́чник, -ница student taking correspondence course; external student. **зао́чно** *adv* in one's absence; by correspondence course. **зао́чный курс** correspondence course.
за́пад west. **за́падный** west, western; westerly.
западня́ (*gen pl* -не́й) trap; pitfall, snare.
за|пакова́ть *pf*, **запако́вывать** *impf* pack; wrap up.
запа́л ignition; fuse. **запа́льная свеча́** (spark-)plug.
запа́с reserve; supply; hem.
запаса́ть *impf*, **запасти́** (-су́, -сёшь; -а́с, -ла́) *pf* lay in a stock of; **~ся** *+instr* stock up with. **запасно́й, запа́сный** spare; reserve; **~ вы́ход** emergency exit.
за́пах smell.
запа́хивать *impf*, **запахну́ть**[2] (-ну́, -нёшь) *pf* wrap up.
запа́хнуть[1] (-ну; -а́х) *pf* begin to smell.
за|па́чкать *pf*.
запева́ть *impf of* **запе́ть**; lead the singing.
запека́ть(ся *impf of* **запе́чь(ся**. **запеку́** *etc.*: *see* **запе́чь**
за|пелена́ть *pf*.
запере́ть (-пру́, -прёшь; за́пер, -ла́, -ло) *pf* (*impf* **запира́ть**) lock; lock in; bar; **~ся** lock o.s. in.
запе́ть (-пою́, -поёшь) *pf* (*impf* **запева́ть**) begin to sing.
запеча́тать *pf*, **запеча́тывать** *impf* seal. **запечатлева́ть** *impf*, **запечатле́ть** (-е́ю) *pf* imprint, engrave.
запе́чь (-еку́, -ечёшь; -пёк, -ла́) *pf* (*impf* **запека́ть**) bake; **~ся** bake; become parched; clot, coagulate.
запива́ть *impf of* **запи́ть**
запина́ться *impf of* **запну́ться**. **запи́нка** hesitation.
запира́ть(ся *impf of* **запере́ть(ся**
записа́ть (-ишу́, -и́шешь) *pf*, **запи́сывать** *impf* note; take down; record; enter; enrol; **~ся** register, enrol (**в**+*acc* at, in). **запи́ска** note. **записн|о́й** note; inveterate; **~а́я кни́жка** notebook. **за́пись** recording; registration; record.
запи́ть (-пью́, -пьёшь; за́пил, -а́, -о) *pf* (*impf* **запива́ть**) begin drinking; wash down (with).

запихáть *pf*, **запи́хивать** *impf*, **запихнýть** (-нý, -нёшь) *pf* push in, cram in.
запишý *etc.*: *see* **записáть**
заплáкать (-áчу) *pf* begin to cry.
за|плани́ровать *pf.*
заплáта patch.
за|плати́ть (-ачý, -áтишь) *pf* pay (**за**+*acc* for).
заплáчу *etc.*: *see* **заплáкать.**
заплачý *see* **заплати́ть**
заплести́ (-етý, -етёшь; -ёл, -á) *pf*, **заплетáть** *impf* plait.
за|пломбировáть *pf.*
заплы́в heat, round. **заплывáть** *impf*, **заплы́ть** (-ывý, -ывёшь; -ы́л, -á, -о) *pf* swim in, sail in; swim out, sail out; be bloated.
запнýться (-нусь, -нёшься) *pf* (*impf* **запинáться**) hesitate; stumble.
заповéдник reserve; preserve; **госудáрственный** ~ national park. **заповéдный** prohibited. **зáповедь** precept; commandment.
заподáзривать *impf*, **заподóзрить** *pf* suspect (**в**+*prep* of).
запоздáлый belated; delayed. **запоздáть** *pf* (*impf* **запáздывать**) be late.
запóй hard drinking.
заползáть *impf*, **заползти́** *pf* (-зý, -зёшь; -óлз, -злá) creep, crawl.
запóлнить *pf*, **заполня́ть** *impf* fill (in, up).
запоминáть *impf*, **запóмнить** *pf* remember; memorize; **~ся** stay in one's mind.
зáпонка cuff-link; stud.
запóр bolt; lock; constipation.
за|потéть (-éет) *pf* mist over.
запою́ *etc.*: *see* **запéть**
заправить (-влю) *pf*, **заправля́ть** *impf* tuck in; prepare; refuel; season, dress; mix in; **~ся** refuel. **запрáвка** refuelling; seasoning, dressing.
запрáшивать *impf of* **запроси́ть**
запрéт prohibition, ban. **запрети́ть** (-ещý) *pf*, **запрещáть** *impf* prohibit, ban. **запрéтный** forbidden. **запрещéние** prohibition.
за|программи́ровать *pf.*
запрóс inquiry; overcharging; *pl* needs. **запроси́ть** (-ошý, -óсишь) *pf* (*impf* **запрáшивать**) inquire.
зáпросто *adv* without ceremony.
запрошý *etc.*: *see* **запроси́ть.**
запрý *etc.*: *see* **заперéть**
запрýда dam, weir; mill-pond.
запрягáть *impf*, **запря́чь** (-ягý, -яжёшь; -я́г, -лá) *pf* harness; yoke.
запугáть *pf*, **запýгивать** *impf* cow, intimidate.
зáпуск launching. **запускáть** *impf*, **запусти́ть** (-ущý, -ýстишь) *pf* thrust (in); start; launch; (+*acc or instr*) fling; neglect. **запустéлый** neglected; desolate. **запустéние** neglect; desolation.
за|пýтать *pf*, **запýтывать** *impf* tangle; confuse; **~ся** get tangled; get involved.
запущý *etc.*: *see* **запусти́ть**
запчáсть (*gen pl* -éй) *abbr* (*of* **запаснáя часть**) spare part.
запыхáться *pf* be out of breath.
запью́ *etc.*: *see* **запи́ть**
запя́стье wrist.
запятáя *sb* comma.
за|пятнáть *pf.*
зарабáтывать *impf*, **зарабóтать** *pf* earn; start (up). **зáра-**

ботн|ый: ~ая пла́та wages; pay. **за́работок** (-тка) earnings.
заража́ть *impf*, **зарази́ть** (-ажу́) *pf* infect; **~ся** *+instr* be infected with, catch. **зара́за** infection. **зарази́тельный** infectious. **зара́зный** infectious.
зара́нее *adv* in good time; in advance.
зараста́ть *impf*, **зарасти́** (-ту́, -тёшь; -ро́с, -ла́) *pf* be overgrown; heal.
за́рево glow.
за|регистри́ровать(ся *pf*.
за|ре́зать (-е́жу) *pf* kill, knife; slaughter.
зарека́ться *impf of* **заре́чься**
зарекомендова́ть *pf*: **~ себя́** *+instr* show o.s. to be.
заре́чься (-еку́сь, -ечёшься; -ёкся, -екла́сь) *pf* (*impf* **зарека́ться**) *+inf* renounce.
за|ржаве́ть (-е́ет) *pf*.
зарисо́вка sketching; sketch.
зароди́ть (-ожу́) *pf*, **зарожда́ть** *impf* generate; **~ся** be born; arise. **заро́дыш** foetus; embryo. **зарожде́ние** conception; origin.
заро́к vow, pledge.
заро́с *etc.*: *see* **зарасти́**
заро́ю *etc.*: *see* **зары́ть**
зарпла́та *abbr* (*of* **за́работная пла́та**) wages; pay.
заруба́ть *impf of* **заруби́ть**
зарубе́жный foreign.
заруби́ть (-блю́, -бишь) *pf* (*impf* **заруба́ть**) kill, cut down; notch. **зару́бка** notch.
заруча́ться *impf*, **заручи́ться** (-учу́сь) *pf* *+instr* secure.
зарыва́ть *impf*, **зары́ть** (-ро́ю) *pf* bury.
заря́ (*pl* зо́ри, зорь) dawn; sunset.
заря́д charge; supply. **заряди́ть** (-яжу́, -я́дишь) *pf*, **заряжа́ть** *impf* load; charge; stoke; **~ся** be loaded; be charged. **заря́дка** loading; charging; exercises.
заса́да ambush. **засади́ть** (-ажу́, -а́дишь) *pf*, **заса́живать** *impf* plant; drive; set (**за**+*acc* to); **~ (в тюрьму́)** put in prison. **заса́живаться** *impf of* **засе́сть**
заса́ливать *impf of* **засоли́ть**
засвети́ть (-ечу́, -е́тишь) *pf* light; **~ся** light up.
за|свиде́тельствовать *pf*.
засе́в sowing; seed; sown area.
засева́ть *impf of* **засе́ять**
заседа́ние meeting; session. **заседа́ть** *impf* sit, be in session.
засе́ивать *impf of* **засе́ять.**
засе́к *etc.*: *see* **засе́чь. засека́ть** *impf of* **засе́чь**
засекре́тить (-ре́чу) *pf*, **засекре́чивать** *impf* classify as secret; clear, give access to secret material.
засеку́ *etc.*: *see* **засе́чь. засе́л** *etc.*: *see* **засе́сть**
заселе́ние settlement. **засели́ть** *pf*, **заселя́ть** *impf* settle; colonize; populate.
засе́сть (-ся́ду; -се́л) *pf* (*impf* **заса́живаться**) sit down; sit tight; settle; lodge in.
засе́чь (-еку́, -ечёшь; -ёк, -ла́) *pf* (*impf* **засека́ть**) flog to death; notch.
засе́ять (-е́ю) *pf* (*impf* **засева́ть, засе́ивать**) sow.
заси́лье dominance, sway.
заслони́ть *pf*, **заслоня́ть** *impf* cover, screen; push into the background. **засло́нка** (*furnace, oven*) door.
заслу́га merit, desert; service.

заслу́женный deserved, merited; Honoured; time-honoured. **заслу́живать** *impf*, **заслужи́ть** (-ужу́, -у́жишь) *pf* deserve; earn; +*gen* be worthy of.
засмея́ться (-ею́сь, -еёшься) begin to laugh.
заснима́ть *impf of* **засня́ть**
засну́ть (-ну́, -нёшь) *pf* (*impf* **засыпа́ть**) fall asleep.
засня́ть (-ниму́, -и́мешь; -я́л, -а́, -о) *pf* (*impf* **заснима́ть**) photograph.
засо́в bolt, bar.
засо́вывать *impf of* **засу́нуть**
засо́л salting, pickling. **засоли́ть** (-олю́, -о́ли́шь) *pf* (*impf* **заса́ливать**) salt, pickle.
засоре́ние littering; contamination; obstruction. **засори́ть** *pf*, **засоря́ть** *impf* litter; get dirt into; clog.
за|со́хнуть (-ну; -со́х) *pf* (*impf also* **засыха́ть**) dry (up); wither.
заста́ва gate; outpost.
застава́ть (-таю́, -таёшь) *impf of* **заста́ть**
заста́вить (-влю) *pf*, **заставля́ть** *impf* make; compel.
заста́иваться *impf of* **засто́яться.** **заста́ну** *etc.*: *see* **заста́ть**
заста́ть (-а́ну) *pf* (*impf* **застава́ть**) find; catch.
застёгивать *impf*, **застегну́ть** (-ну́, -нёшь) *pf* fasten, do up. **застёжка** fastening; clasp, buckle; **~-мо́лния** zip.
застекли́ть *pf*, **застекля́ть** *impf* glaze.
засте́нок (-нка) torture chamber.
засте́нчивый shy.
застига́ть *impf*, **засти́гнуть**, **засти́чь** (-и́гну; -сти́г) *pf* catch; take unawares.
засти́чь *see* **засти́гнуть**
засто́й stagnation. **засто́йный** stagnant.
за|сто́пориться *pf*.
засто́яться (-и́тся) *pf* (*impf* **заста́иваться**) stagnate; stand too long.
застра́ивать *impf of* **застро́ить**
застрахо́ванный insured. **за|страхова́ть** *pf*, **застрахо́вывать** *impf* insure.
застрева́ть *impf of* **застря́ть**
застрели́ть (-елю́, -е́лишь) *pf* shoot (dead); **~ся** shoot o.s.
застро́ить (-о́ю) *pf* (*impf* **застра́ивать**) build over, on, up. **застро́йка** building.
застря́ть (-я́ну) *pf* (*impf* **застрева́ть**) stick; get stuck.
засту́п spade.
заступа́ться *impf*, **заступи́ться** (-плю́сь, -пишься) *pf* +**за**+*acc* stand up for. **засту́пник** defender. **засту́пничество** protection; intercession.
застыва́ть *impf*, **засты́ть** (-ы́ну) *pf* harden, set; become stiff; freeze; be petrified.
засу́нуть (-ну) *pf* (*impf* **засо́вывать**) thrust in, push in.
за́суха drought.
засы́пать[1] (-плю) *pf*, **засыпа́ть** *impf* fill up; strew.
засыпа́ть[2] *impf of* **засну́ть**
засыха́ть *impf of* **засо́хнуть.**
зася́ду *etc.*: *see* **засе́сть**
затаённый (-ён, -ена́) secret; repressed. **зата́ивать** *impf*, **затаи́ть** *pf* suppress; conceal; harbour; **~ дыха́ние** hold one's breath.
зата́пливать *impf of* **затопи́ть.** **зата́птывать** *impf of* **затопта́ть**
зата́скивать *impf*, **затащи́ть** (-щу́, -щишь) *pf* drag in; drag off; drag away.

затвердева́ть *impf*, **за|тверде́ть** (-е́ет) *pf* become hard; set. **затверде́ние** hardening; callus.

затво́р bolt; lock; shutter; flood-gate. **затвори́ть** (-рю́, -ришь) *pf*, **затворя́ть** *impf* shut, close; **~ся** shut o.s. up, lock o.s. in. **затво́рник** hermit, recluse.

затева́ть *impf of* **зате́ять**

затёк *etc*.: *see* **зате́чь. затека́ть** *impf of* **зате́чь**

зате́м *adv* then, next; ~ **что** because.

затемне́ние darkening, obscuring; blacking out; blackout. **затемни́ть** *pf*, **затемня́ть** *impf* darken, obscure; black out.

зате́ривать *impf*, **затеря́ть** *pf* lose, mislay; **~ся** be lost; be mislaid; be forgotten.

зате́чь (-ечёт, -еку́т; -тёк, -кла́) *pf* (*impf* **затека́ть**) pour, flow; swell up; become numb.

зате́я undertaking, venture; escapade; joke. **зате́ять** *pf* (*impf* **затева́ть**) undertake, venture.

затиха́ть *impf*, **зати́хнуть** (-ну; -ти́х) *pf* die down, abate; fade. **зати́шье** calm; lull.

заткну́ть (-ну́, -нёшь) *pf* (*impf* **затыка́ть**) stop up; stick, thrust.

затмева́ть *impf*, **затми́ть** (-ми́шь) *pf* darken; eclipse; overshadow. **затме́ние** eclipse.

зато́ *conj* but then, but on the other hand.

затону́ть (-о́нет) *pf* sink, be submerged.

затопи́ть[1] (-плю́, -пишь) *pf* (*impf* **зата́пливать**) light; turn on the heating.

затопи́ть[2] (-плю́, -пишь) *pf*, **затопля́ть** *impf* flood, submerge; sink.

затопта́ть (-пчу́, -пчешь) *pf* (*impf* **зата́птывать**) trample (down).

зато́р obstruction, jam; congestion.

за|тормози́ть (-ожу́) *pf*.

заточа́ть *impf*, **заточи́ть** (-чу́) *pf* incarcerate. **заточе́ние** incarceration.

затра́гивать *impf of* **затро́нуть**

затра́та expense; outlay. **затра́тить** (-а́чу) *pf*, **затра́чивать** *impf* spend.

затре́бовать *pf* request, require; ask for.

затро́нуть (-ну) *pf* (*impf* **затра́гивать**) affect; touch (on).

затрудне́ние difficulty. **затрудни́тельный** difficult.

затрудни́ть *pf*, **затрудня́ть** *impf* trouble; make difficult; hamper; **~ся** *+inf or instr* find difficulty in.

за|тупи́ться (-пится) *pf*.

за|туши́ть (-шу́, -шишь) *pf* extinguish; suppress.

за́тхлый musty, mouldy; stuffy.

затыка́ть *impf of* **заткну́ть**

заты́лок (-лка) back of the head; scrag-end.

затя́гивать *impf*, **затяну́ть** (-ну́, -нешь) *pf* tighten; cover; close, heal; spin out; **~ся** be covered; close; be delayed; drag on; inhale. **затя́жка** inhaling; prolongation; delaying, putting off; lagging. **затяжно́й** long-drawn-out.

зауря́дный ordinary; mediocre.

зау́треня morning service.

зау́чивать *impf*, **заучи́ть** (-чу́, -чишь) *pf* learn by heart.

за|фаршировать *pf.* **за|фиксировать** *pf.* **за|фрахтовать** *pf.*

захват seizure, capture. **захватить** (-ачу, -атишь) *pf,* **захватывать** *impf* take; seize; thrill. **захватнический** aggressive. **захватчик** aggressor. **захватывающий** gripping.

захлебнуться (-нусь, -нёшься) *pf,* **захлёбываться** *impf* choke (**от**+*gen* with).

захлестнуть (-ну, -нёшь) *pf,* **захлёстывать** *impf* flow over, swamp, overwhelm.

захлопнуть (-ну) *pf,* **захлопывать** *impf* slam, bang; **~ся** slam (to).

заход sunset; calling in. **заходить** (-ожу, -одишь) *impf of* **зайти**

захолустный remote, provincial. **захолустье** backwoods.

за|хоронить (-ню, -нишь) *pf.* **за|хотеть(ся** (-очу(сь, -очешь(ся, -отим(ся) *pf.*

зацвести (-етёт; -вёл, -а) *pf,* **зацветать** *impf* come into bloom.

зацепить (-плю, -пишь) *pf,* **зацеплять** *impf* hook; engage; sting; catch (**за**+*acc* on); **~ся за**+*acc* catch on; catch hold of.

зачастую *adv* often.

зачатие conception. **зачаток** (-тка) embryo; rudiment; germ. **зачаточный** rudimentary. **зачать** (-чну, -чнёшь; -чал, -а, -о) *pf* (*impf* **зачинать**) conceive.

зачёл *etc.*: *see* **зачесть**

зачем *adv* why; what for. **зачем-то** *adv* for some reason.

зачёркивать *impf,* **зачеркнуть** (-ну, -нёшь) *pf* cross out.

зачерпнуть (-ну, -нёшь) *pf,* **зачерпывать** *impf* scoop up; draw up.

за|черстветь (-еет) *pf.*

зачесть (-чту, -чтёшь; -чёл, -чла) *pf* (*impf* **зачитывать**) take into account, reckon as credit. **зачёт** test; **получить, сдать ~ по**+*dat* pass a test in; **поставить ~ по**+*dat* pass in. **зачётная книжка** (student's) record book.

зачинать *impf of* **зачать.**

зачинщик instigator.

зачислить *pf,* **зачислять** *impf* include; enter; enlist; **~ся** join, enter.

зачитывать *impf of* **зачесть.**

зачту *etc.*: *see* **зачесть. зашёл** *etc.*: *see* **зайти**

зашивать *impf,* **зашить** (-шью, -шьёшь) *pf* sew up.

за|шифровать *pf,* **зашифровывать** *impf* encipher, encode.

за|шнуровать *pf,* **зашнуровывать** *impf* lace up.

за|шпаклевать (-люю) *pf.* **за|штопать** *pf.* **за|штриховать** *pf.* **зашью** *etc.*: *see* **зашить**

защита defence; protection. **защитить** (-ищу) *pf,* **защищать** *impf* defend, protect. **защитник** defender. **защитный** protective.

заявить (-влю, -вишь) *pf,* **заявлять** *impf* announce, declare; **~ся** turn up. **заявка** claim; demand. **заявление** statement; application.

заяц (зайца) hare; stowaway; **ехать зайцем** travel without a ticket.

звание rank; title. **званый** invited; **~ обед** banquet, dinner.

зва́тельный vocative. **звать** (зову́, -вёшь; звал, -а́, -о) *impf* (*pf* **по~**) call; ask, invite; **как вас зову́т?** what is your name?; **~ся** be called.
звезда́ (*pl* звёзды) star. **звёздный** star; starry; starlit; stellar. **звёздочка** little star; asterisk.
звене́ть (-ню́) *impf* ring; *+instr* jingle, clink.
звено́ (*pl* зве́нья, -ьев) link; team, section; unit; component. **звеньево́й** *sb* section leader.
звери́нец (-нца) menagerie.
зверово́дство fur farming.
зве́рский brutal; terrific.
зве́рство atrocity. **зве́рствовать** *impf* commit atrocities. **зверь** (*pl* -и, -е́й) *m* wild animal.
звон ringing (sound); peal, chink, clink. **звони́ть** *impf* (*pf* **по~**) ring; ring up; **~ кому́-нибу́дь (по телефо́ну)** ring s.o. up. **зво́нкий** (-нок, -нка́, -о) ringing, clear. **звоно́к** (-нка́) bell; (*telephone*) call.
звук sound.
звуко- *in comb* sound. **звукоза́пись** (sound) recording. **~изоля́ция** sound-proofing. **~непроница́емый** soundproof. **~снима́тель** *m* pick-up.
звуково́й sound; audio; acoustic. **звуча́ние** sound(ing); vibration. **звуча́ть** (-чи́т) *impf* (*pf* **про~**) be heard; sound. **зву́чный** (-чен, -чна́, -о) sonorous.
зда́ние building.
здесь *adv* here. **зде́шний** local; **не ~** a stranger here.
здоро́ваться *impf* (*pf* **по~**) exchange greetings. **здо́рово** *adv* splendidly; very (much); well done!; great! **здоро́вый** healthy, strong; well; wholesome, sound. **здоро́вье** health; **за ва́ше ~!** your health! **как ва́ше ~?** how are you? **здра́вница** sanatorium.
здравомы́слящий sensible, judicious. **здравоохране́ние** public health.
здра́вствовать *impf* be healthy; prosper. **здра́вствуй(те)** how do you do?; hello! **да здра́вствует!** long live! **здра́вый** sensible; **~ смысл** common sense.
зе́бра zebra.
зева́ть *impf*, **зевну́ть** (-ну́, -нёшь) *pf* yawn; gape; (*pf also* **про~**) miss, let slip, lose.
зево́к (-вка́), **зево́та** yawn.
зелене́ть (-е́ет) *impf* (*pf* **по~**) turn green; show green.
зелёный (зе́лен, -а́, -о) green; **~ лук** spring onions. **зе́лень** green; greenery; greens.
земе́льный land.
земле- *in comb* land; earth. **землевладе́лец** (-льца) landowner. **~де́лец** (-льца) farmer, **~де́лие** farming, agriculture. **~де́льческий** agricultural. **~ко́п** navvy. **~ро́йный** excavating. **~трясе́ние** earthquake.
земля́ (*acc* -ю; *pl* -и, земе́ль, -ям) earth; ground; land; soil.
земля́к (-а́) fellow-countryman. **земляни́ка** (*no pl*; *usu collect*) wild strawberry; wild strawberries. **земля́нка** dugout; mud hut. **земляно́й** earthen; earth. **земля́чка** country-woman. **земно́й** earthly; terrestrial; ground; mundane; **~ шар** the globe.
зени́т zenith. **зени́тный** zenith; anti-aircraft.

зе́ркало (*pl* -а́) mirror. **зерка́льный** mirror; smooth; plate-glass.
зерни́стый grainy. **зерно́** (*pl* зёрна, зёрен) grain; seed; kernel, core; **ко́фе в зёрнах** coffee beans. **зерново́й** grain. **зерновы́е** *sb pl* cereals. **зернохрани́лище** granary.
зигза́г zigzag.
зима́ (*acc* -у; *pl* -ы) winter. **зи́мний** winter, wintry. **зимова́ть** *impf* (*pf* **пере~, про~**) spend the winter; hibernate. **зимо́вка** wintering; hibernation. **зимо́вье** winter quarters. **зимо́й** *adv* in winter.
зия́ть *impf* gape, yawn.
злак grass; cereal.
злить (злю) *impf* (*pf* **обо~, о~, разо~**) anger; irritate; **~ся** be angry, be in a bad temper; rage. **зло** (*gen pl* зол) evil; harm; misfortune; malice.
зло- *in comb* evil, harm, malice. **злове́щий** ominous. **~во́ние** stink. **~во́нный** stinking. **~ка́чественный** malignant; pernicious. **~па́мятный** rancorous, unforgiving. **~ра́дный** malevolent, gloating. **~сло́вие** malicious gossip. **~умы́шленник** malefactor; plotter. **~язы́чный** slanderous.
зло́ба spite; anger; **~ дня** topic of the day, latest news. **зло́бный** malicious. **злободне́вный** topical. **злоде́й** villain. **злоде́йский** villainous. **злоде́йство** villainy; crime, evil deed. **злодея́ние** crime, evil deed. **злой** (зол, зла) evil; wicked; malicious; vicious; bad-tempered; severe. **зло́стный** malicious; intentional. **злость** malice; fury.
злоупотреби́ть (-блю́) *pf*, **злоупотребля́ть** *impf* +*instr* abuse. **злоупотребле́ние** +*instr* abuse of.
зме́йный snake; cunning. **змей** snake; dragon; kite. **змея́** (*pl* -и) snake.
знак sign; mark; symbol.
знако́мить (-млю) *impf* (*pf* **о~, по~**) acquaint; introduce; **~ся** become acquainted; get to know; **+с**+*instr* meet, make the acquaintance of. **знако́мство** acquaintance; (circle of) acquaintances. **знако́м|ый** familiar; **быть ~ым с**+*instr* be acquainted with, know; **~ый, ~ая** *sb* acquaintance.
знамена́тель *m* denominator. **знамена́тельный** significant. **зна́мение** sign. **знамени́тость** celebrity. **знамени́тый** celebrated, famous. **зна́мя** (-мени; *pl* -мёна) *neut* banner; flag.
зна́ние knowledge.
зна́тный (-тен, -тна́, -о) distinguished; aristocratic; splendid.
знато́к (-а́) expert; connoisseur. **знать** *impf* know; **дать ~** inform, let know.
значе́ние meaning; significance; importance. **зна́чит** so then; that means. **значи́тельный** considerable; important; significant. **зна́чить** (-чу) *impf* mean; signify; be of importance; **~ся** be; be mentioned, appear. **значо́к** (-чка́) badge; mark.
зна́ющий expert; learned.
зноби́ть *impf*, *impers*+*acc*: **меня́**, *etc.*, **зноби́т** I feel shivery.

зной intense heat. **зно́йный** hot; burning.
зов call, summons. **зову́** *etc.*: *see* **звать**
зо́дчество architecture. **зо́дчий** *sb* architect.
зол *see* **зло, злой**
зола́ ashes, cinders.
золо́вка sister-in-law (*husband's sister*).
золоти́стый golden. **зо́лото** gold. **золото́й** gold; golden.
золочёный gilt, gilded.
зо́на zone; region.
зонд probe. **зонди́ровать** *impf* sound, probe.
зонт (-а́), **зо́нтик** umbrella.
зоо́лог zoologist. **зоологи́ческий** zoological. **зооло́гия** zoology. **зоопа́рк** zoo. **зооте́хник** livestock specialist.
зо́ри *etc.*: *see* **заря́**
зо́ркий (-рок, -рка́, -о) sharp-sighted; perspicacious.
зрачо́к (-чка́) pupil (*of the eye*).
зре́лище sight; spectacle.
зре́лость ripeness; maturity; **аттеста́т зре́лости** school-leaving certificate. **зре́лый** (зрел, -а́, -о) ripe, mature.
зре́ние (eye)sight, vision; **то́чка зре́ния** point of view.
зреть (-е́ю) *impf* (*pf* **со~**) ripen; mature.
зри́мый visible.
зри́тель *m* spectator, observer; *pl* audience. **зри́тельный** visual; optic; **~ зал** hall, auditorium.
зря *adv* in vain.
зуб (*pl* -ы *or* -бья, -о́в *or* -бьев) tooth; cog. **зуби́ло** chisel. **зубно́й** dental; tooth; **~ врач** dentist. **зубовраче́бный** dentists', dental; **~ кабине́т** dental surgery. **зубочи́стка** toothpick.
зубр (European) bison; die-hard.
зубри́ть (-рю́, зу́бри́шь) *impf* (*pf* **вы́~, за~**) cram.
зубча́тый toothed; serrated.
зуд itch. **зуде́ть** (-и́т) itch.
зы́бкий (-бок, -бка́, -о) unsteady, shaky; vacillating. **зыбь** (*gen pl* -е́й) ripple, rippling.
зюйд (*naut*) south; south wind.
зя́блик chaffinch.
зя́бнуть (-ну; зяб) *impf* suffer from cold, feel the cold.
зябь land ploughed in autumn for spring sowing.
зять (*pl* -тья́, -тьёв) son-in-law; brother-in-law (*sister's husband or husband's sister's husband*).

И, Й

и *conj* and; even; too; (*with neg*) either; **и... и** both ... and.
и́бо *conj* for.
и́ва willow.
игла́ (*pl* -ы) needle; thorn; spine; quill. **иглоука́лывание** acupuncture.
игнори́ровать *impf & pf* ignore.
и́го yoke.
иго́лка needle.
иго́рный gaming, gambling.
игра́ (*pl* -ы) play, playing; game; hand; turn; **~ слов** pun. **игра́льн|ый** playing; **~ые ко́сти** dice. **игра́ть** *impf* (*pf* **сыгра́ть**) play; act; **~ в**+*acc* play (*game*); **~ на**+*prep* play (*an instrument*). **игри́вый** playful. **игро́к** (-а́) player; gambler. **игру́шка** toy.
идеа́л ideal. **идеали́зм** idealism. **идеа́льный** ideal.

идейный high-principled; acting on principle; ideological. **идеологический** ideological. **идеология** ideology.
идёт *etc.*: *see* **идти**
идея idea; concept.
идиллия idyll.
идиот idiot.
идол idol.
идти (иду, идёшь; шёл, шла) *impf* (*pf* **пойти**) go; come; run, work; pass; go on, be in progress; be on; fall; +(к+)*dat* suit.
иерей priest.
иждивенец (-нца), **-венка** dependant. **иждивение** maintenance; **на иждивении** at the expense of.
из, изо *prep+gen* from, out of, of.
изба (*pl* -ы) izba (*hut*).
избавить (-влю) *pf*, **избавлять** *impf* save, deliver; **~ся** be saved, escape; **~ся от** get rid of; get out of.
избалованный spoilt. **из|баловать** *pf*.
избегать *impf*, **избегнуть** (-ну; -бег(нул)) *pf*, **избежать** (-егу) *pf +gen or inf* avoid; escape.
изберу *etc.*: *see* **избрать**
избивать *impf of* **избить. избиение** slaughter, massacre; beating, beating-up.
избиратель *m*, **~ница** elector, voter. **избирательный** electoral; election. **избирать** *impf of* **избрать**
избитый trite, hackneyed. **избить** (изобью, -бьёшь) *pf* (*impf* **избивать**) beat unmercifully, beat up; massacre.
избранн|ый selected; select; **~ые** *sb pl* the élite. **избрать** (-беру, -берёшь; -ал, -а, -о) *pf* (*impf* **избирать**) elect; choose.
избыток (-тка) surplus; abundance. **избыточный** surplus; abundant.
изверг monster. **извержение** eruption; expulsion; excretion.
извернуться (-нусь, -нёшься) *pf* (*impf* **изворачиваться**) dodge, be evasive.
известие news; information; *pl* proceedings. **известить** (-ещу) *pf* (*impf* **извещать**) inform, notify.
извёстка lime.
известно it is (well) known; of course, certainly. **известность** fame, reputation. **известный** known; well-known, famous; notorious; certain.
известняк (-а) limestone. **известь** lime.
извещать *impf of* **известить. извещение** notification; advice.
извиваться *impf* coil; writhe; twist, wind; meander. **извилина** bend, twist. **извилистый** winding; meandering.
извинение excuse; apology. **извинить** *pf*, **извинять** *impf* excuse; **извините (меня)** excuse me, (I'm) sorry; **~ся** apologize; excuse o.s.
извиться (изовьюсь, -вьёшься; -ился, -ась, -ось) *pf* coil; writhe.
извлекать *impf*, **извлечь** (-еку, -ечёшь; -ёк, -ла) *pf* extract; derive, elicit.
извне *adv* from outside.
извозчик cabman; carrier.
изворачиваться *impf of* **извернуться. изворот** bend, twist; *pl* tricks, wiles. **изворотливый** resourceful; shrewd.
извратить (-ащу) *pf*, **извращать** *impf* distort; pervert. **извращение** perversion; distortion. **извращённый** perverted, unnatural.

изги́б bend, twist. **изгиба́ть(ся** *impf of* **изогну́ть(ся**

изгна́ние banishment; exile. **изгна́нник** exile. **изгна́ть** (-гоню́, -го́нишь; -а́л, -а́, -о) *pf* (*impf* **изгоня́ть**) banish; exile.

изголо́вье bed-head.

изголода́ться be famished, starve; +**по**+*dat* yearn for.

изгоню́ *etc.*: *see* **изгна́ть. изгоня́ть** *impf of* **изгна́ть**

и́згородь fence, hedge.

изгота́вливать *impf*, **изгото́вить** (-влю) *pf*, **изготовля́ть** *impf* make, manufacture; **~ся** get ready. **изготовле́ние** making, manufacture.

издава́ть (-даю́, -даёшь) *impf of* **изда́ть**

и́здавна *adv* from time immemorial; for a very long time.

издади́м *etc.*: *see* **изда́ть**

издалека́, и́здали *advs* from afar.

изда́ние publication; edition; promulgation. **изда́тель** *m* publisher. **изда́тельство** publishing house. **изда́ть** (-а́м, -а́шь, -а́ст, -ади́м; -а́л, -а́, -о) *pf* (*impf* **издава́ть**) publish; promulgate; produce; emit; **~ся** be published.

издева́тельство mockery; taunt. **издева́ться** *impf* (+**над**+*instr*) mock (at).

изде́лие work; make; article; *pl* wares.

изде́ржки (-жек) *pl* expenses; costs; cost.

из|до́хнуть *pf*.

из|жа́рить(ся *pf*.

изжо́га heartburn.

из-за *prep*+*gen* from behind; because of.

излага́ть *impf of* **изложи́ть**

излече́ние treatment; recovery; cure. **излечи́ть** (-чу́, -чишь) cure; **~ся** be cured; +**от**+*gen* rid o.s. of.

изли́шек (-шка) surplus; excess. **изли́шество** excess; over-indulgence. **изли́шний** (-шен, -шня) superfluous.

изложе́ние exposition; account. **изложи́ть** (-жу́, -жишь) *pf* (*impf* **излага́ть**) expound; set forth; word.

изло́м break, fracture; sharp bend. **излома́ть** *pf* break; smash; wear out; warp.

излуча́ть *impf* radiate, emit. **излуче́ние** radiation; emanation.

из|ма́зать (-а́жу) *pf* dirty, smear all over; use up; **~ся** get dirty, smear o.s. all over.

изме́на betrayal; treason; infidelity.

измене́ние change, alteration; inflection. **измени́ть**[1] (-ню́, -нишь) *pf* (*impf* **изменя́ть**[1]) change, alter; **~ся** change.

измени́ть[2] (-ню́, -нишь) *pf* (*impf* **изменя́ть**[2]) +*dat* betray; be unfaithful to. **изме́нник, -ица** traitor.

изменя́емый variable. **изменя́ть**[1,2]**(ся** *impf of* **измени́ть**[1,2]**(ся**

измере́ние measurement, measuring. **изме́рить** *pf*, **измеря́ть** *impf* measure, gauge.

измождённый (-ён, -а́) worn out.

из|му́чить (-чу) *pf* torment; tire out, exhaust; **~ся** be exhausted. **изму́ченный** worn out.

измышле́ние fabrication, invention.

измя́тый crumpled, creased; haggard, jaded. **из|мя́ть(ся** (изомну́(сь, -нёшь(ся) *pf*.

изна́нка wrong side; seamy side.
из|наси́ловать *pf* rape, assault.
изна́шивание wear (and tear). **изна́шивать(ся** *impf of* **износи́ть(ся**
изне́женный pampered; delicate; effeminate.
изнемога́ть *impf*, **изнемо́чь** (-огу́, -о́жешь; -о́г, -ла́) *pf* be exhausted. **изнеможе́ние** exhaustion.
изно́с wear; wear and tear; deterioration. **износи́ть** (-ошу́, -о́сишь) *pf* (*impf* **изна́шивать**) wear out; **~ся** wear out; be used up. **изно́шенный** worn out; threadbare.
изнуре́ние exhaustion. **изнурённый** (-ён, -ена́) exhausted, worn out; jaded. **изнури́тельный** exhausting.
изнутри́ *adv* from inside, from within.
изо *see* **из**
изоби́лие abundance, plenty. **изоби́ловать** *impf* +*instr* abound in, be rich in. **изоби́льный** abundant.
изоблича́ть *impf*, **изобличи́ть** (-чу́) *pf* expose; show. **изобличе́ние** exposure; conviction.
изобража́ть *impf*, **изобрази́ть** (-ажу́) *pf* represent, depict, portray (+*instr* as); **~ из себя́**+*acc* make o.s. out to be. **изображе́ние** image; representation; portrayal. **изобрази́тельн|ый** graphic; decorative; **~ые иску́сства** fine arts.
изобрести́ (-ету́, -етёшь; -ёл, -а́) *pf*, **изобрета́ть** *impf* invent; devise. **изобрета́тель** *m* inventor. **изобрета́тельный** inventive. **изобрете́ние** invention.
изобью́ *etc.*: *see* **изби́ть**. **изовью́сь** *etc.*: *see* **изви́ться**
изо́гнутый bent, curved; winding. **изогну́ть(ся** (-ну́(сь, -нёшь(ся) *pf* (*impf* **изгиба́ть(ся)** bend, curve.
изоли́ровать *impf* & *pf* isolate; insulate. **изоля́тор** insulator; isolation ward; solitary confinement cell. **изоля́ция** isolation; quarantine; insulation.
изомну́(сь *etc.*: *see* **измя́ть**
изо́рванный tattered, torn. **изорва́ть** (-ву́, -вёшь; -а́л, -а́, -о) *pf* tear, tear to pieces; **~ся** be in tatters.
изощрённый (-рён, -а́) refined; keen. **изощри́ться** *pf*, **изощря́ться** *impf* acquire refinement; excel.
из-под *prep*+*gen* from under.
Изра́иль *m* Israel. **изра́ильский** Israeli.
из|расхо́довать(ся *pf*.
и́зредка *adv* now and then.
изре́зать (-е́жу) *pf* cut up.
изрече́ние dictum, saying.
изры́ть (-ро́ю) *pf* dig up, plough up. **изры́тый** pitted.
изря́дно *adv* fairly, pretty. **изря́дный** fair, handsome; fairly large.
изуве́чить (-чу) *pf* maim, mutilate.
изуми́тельный amazing. **изуми́ть** (-млю́) *pf*, **изумля́ть** *impf* amaze; **~ся** be amazed. **изумле́ние** amazement.
изумру́д emerald.
изуро́дованный maimed; disfigured. **из|уро́довать** *pf*.
изуча́ть *impf*, **изучи́ть** (-чу́, -чишь) *pf* learn, study. **изуче́ние** study.
изъе́здить (-зжу) *pf* travel all

over; wear out.
изъяви́ть (-влю́, -вишь) *pf*, **изъявля́ть** *impf* express.
изъя́н defect, flaw.
изъя́тие withdrawal; removal; exception. **изъя́ть** (изыму́, -мешь) *pf*. **изыма́ть** *impf* withdraw.
изыска́ние investigation, research; prospecting; survey. **изы́сканный** refined. **изыска́ть** (-ыщу́, -ы́щешь) *pf*, **изы́скивать** *impf* search out; (try to) find.
изю́м raisins.
изя́щество elegance, grace. **изя́щный** elegant, graceful.
ика́ть *impf*, **икну́ть** (-ну́, -нёшь) *pf* hiccup.
ико́на icon.
ико́та hiccup, hiccups.
икра́[1] (hard) roe; caviare.
икра́[2] (*pl* -ы) calf (*of leg*).
ил silt; sludge.
и́ли *conj* or; **~... ~** either ... or.
и́листый muddy, silty.
иллюзиони́ст conjurer. **иллю́зия** illusion.
иллюмина́тор porthole. **иллюмина́ция** illumination.
иллюстра́ция illustration. **иллюстри́ровать** *impf* & *pf* illustrate.
им *see* **он, они́, оно́**
им. *abbr* (*of* **и́мени**) named after.
и́мени *etc.*: *see* **и́мя**
име́ние estate.
имени́ны (-и́н) *pl* name-day (party). **имени́тельный** nominative. **и́менно** *adv* namely; exactly, precisely; **вот ~!** exactly!
име́ть (-е́ю) *impf* have; **~ де́ло с**+*instr* have dealings with; **~ ме́сто** take place; **~ся** be; be available.
и́ми *see* **они́**
имита́ция imitation. **імити́ровать** *impf* imitate.
иммигра́нт, ~ка immigrant. **иммигра́ция** immigration.
импера́тор emperor. **импера́торский** imperial. **императри́ца** empress. **империали́зм** imperialism. **империали́ст** imperialist. **империалисти́ческий** imperialist(ic). **импе́рия** empire.
и́мпорт import. **импорти́ровать** *impf* & *pf* import. **и́мпортный** import(ed).
импровиза́ция improvisation. **импровизи́ровать** *impf* & *pf* improvise.
и́мпульс impulse.
иму́щество property.
и́мя (и́мени; *pl* имена́, -ён) *neut* name; first name; noun; **~ прилага́тельное** adjective; **~ существи́тельное** noun; **~ числи́тельное** numeral.
и́на́че *adv* differently, otherwise; **так и́ли ~** in any event; *conj* otherwise, or else.
инвали́д disabled person; invalid. **инвали́дность** disablement, disability.
инвента́рь (-я́) *m* stock; equipment; inventory.
инде́ец (-е́йца) (American) Indian. **инде́йка** (*gen pl* -е́ек) turkey(-hen). **инде́йский** (American) Indian.
и́ндекс index; code.
индиа́нка Indian; American Indian. **инди́ец** (-и́йца) Indian.
индивидуали́зм individualism. **индивидуа́льность** individuality. **индивидуа́льный** individual. **индиви́дуум** individual.

инди́йский Indian. **И́ндия** India. **инду́с, инду́ска** Hindu.
индустриализа́ция industrialization. **индустриализи́ровать** *impf* & *pf* industrialize. **индустриа́льный** industrial. **инду́стрия** industry.
индю́к, индю́шка turkey.
и́ней hoar-frost.
ине́ртность inertia; sluggishness. **ине́рция** inertia.
инжене́р engineer; **~-меха́ник** mechanical engineer; **~-строи́тель** *m* civil engineer.
инжи́р fig.
инициа́л initial.
инициати́ва initiative. **инициа́тор** initiator.
инквизи́ция inquisition.
инкруста́ция inlaid work, inlay.
инкуба́тор incubator.
ино- *in comb* other, different; hetero-. **иногоро́дний** of, from, another town. **~ро́дный** foreign. **~сказа́тельный** allegorical. **~стра́нец** (-нца), **~стра́нка** (*gen pl* -нок) foreigner. **~стра́нный** foreign. **~язы́чный** foreign.
иногда́ *adv* sometimes.
ино́й different; other; some; **~ раз** sometimes.
и́нок monk. **и́нокиня** nun.
инотде́л foreign department.
инсектици́д insecticide.
инспе́ктор inspector. **инспе́кция** inspection; inspectorate.
инста́нция instance.
инсти́нкт instinct. **инстинкти́вный** instinctive.
институ́т institute.
инстру́ктор instructor. **инстру́кция** instructions.
инструме́нт instrument; tool.
инсули́н insulin.
инсцениро́вка dramatization, adaptation; pretence.
интегра́ция integration.
интелле́кт intellect. **интеллектуа́льный** intellectual.
интеллиге́нт intellectual. **интеллиге́нтный** cultured, educated. **интеллиге́нция** intelligentsia.
интенси́вность intensity. **интенси́вный** intensive.
интеракти́вный interactive.
интерва́л interval.
интерве́нция intervention.
интервью́ *neut indecl* interview.
интере́с interest. **интере́сный** interesting. **интересова́ть** *impf* interest; **~ся** be interested (+*instr* in).
интерна́т boarding-school.
интернациона́льный international.
Интерне́т the Internet; **в ~е** on the Internet.
интерни́ровать *impf* & *pf* intern.
интерпрета́ция interpretation. **интерпрети́ровать** *impf* & *pf* interpret.
интерье́р interior.
инти́мный intimate.
интона́ция intonation.
интри́га intrigue; plot. **интригова́ть** *impf*, (*pf* **за~**) intrigue.
интуи́ция intuition.
инфа́ркт infarct; coronary (thrombosis), heart attack.
инфекцио́нный infectious. **инфе́кция** infection.
инфля́ция inflation.
информа́тика IT.
информа́ция information.
инфракра́сный infra-red.
ио́д *etc.*: *see* **йод**
ио́н ion.
ипохо́ндрик hypochondriac. **ипохо́ндрия** hypochondria.
ипподро́м racecourse.

Ира́к Iraq. **ира́кец** (-кца) Iraqi. **ира́кский** Iraqi.
Ира́н Iran. **ира́нец** (-нца), **ира́нка** Iranian. **ира́нский** Iranian.
ирла́ндец (-дца) Irishman. **Ирла́ндия** Ireland. **ирла́ндка** Irishwoman. **ирла́ндский** Irish.
ирони́ческий ironic. **иро́ния** irony.
ирригáция irrigation.
иск suit, action.
искажа́ть *impf*, **искази́ть** (-ажу́) *pf* distort, pervert; misrepresent. **искаже́ние** distortion, perversion.
искале́ченный crippled, maimed. **искале́чить** (-чу́) *pf* cripple, maim; break.
иска́ть (ищу́, и́щешь) *impf* (+*acc or gen*) seek, look for.
исключа́ть *impf*, **исключи́ть** (-чу́) *pf* exclude; eliminate; expel. **исключа́я** *prep*+*gen* except. **исключе́ние** exception; exclusion; expulsion; elimination; **за исключе́нием** +*gen* with the exception of. **исключи́тельно** *adv* exceptionally; exclusively. **исключи́тельный** exceptional; exclusive.
иско́нный primordial.
ископа́емое *sb* mineral; fossil. **ископа́емый** fossilized, fossil.
искорени́ть *pf*, **искореня́ть** *impf* eradicate.
и́скоса *adv* askance; sidelong.
и́скра spark.
и́скренний sincere. **и́скренность** sincerity.
искривле́ние bend; distortion, warping.
ис|купа́ть[1]**(ся** *pf*.
искупа́ть[2] *impf*, **искупи́ть** (-плю́, -пишь) *pf* atone for; make up for. **искупле́ние** redemption, atonement.
искуси́ть (-ушу́) *pf of* **искуша́ть**
иску́сный skilful; expert.
иску́сственный artificial; feigned. **иску́сство** art; skill.
искусствове́д art historian.
искуша́ть *impf* (*pf* **искуси́ть**) tempt; seduce. **искуше́ние** temptation, seduction.
испа́нец (-нца) Spaniard. **Испа́ния** Spain. **испа́нка** Spanish woman. **испа́нский** Spanish.
испаре́ние evaporation; *pl* fumes. **испари́ться** *pf*, **испаря́ться** *impf* evaporate.
ис|па́чкать *pf*. **ис|пе́чь** (-еку́, -ечёшь) *pf*.
испове́довать *impf* & *pf* confess; profess; **~ся** confess; make one's confession; **+в+***prep* unburden o.s. of. **и́споведь** confession.
исподтишка́ *adv* in an underhand way; on the quiet.
исполи́н giant. **исполи́нский** gigantic.
исполко́м *abbr* (*of* **исполни́тельный комите́т**) executive committee.
исполне́ние fulfilment, execution. **исполни́тель** *m*, **~ница** executor; performer. **исполни́тельный** executive. **испо́лнить** *pf*, **исполня́ть** *impf* carry out, execute; fulfil; perform; **~ся** be fulfilled.
испо́льзование utilization. **испо́льзовать** *impf* & *pf* make (good) use of, utilize.
ис|по́ртить(ся (-рчу(сь) *pf*. **испо́рченный** depraved; spoiled; rotten.

исправи́тельный correctional; corrective. **испра́вить** (-влю) *pf*, **исправля́ть** *impf* rectify, correct; mend; reform; **~ся** improve, reform. **исправле́ние** repairing; improvement; correction. **испра́вленный** improved, corrected; revised; reformed. **испра́вный** in good order; punctual; meticulous.

ис|про́бовать *pf.*

испу́г fright. **ис|пуга́ть(ся** *pf.*

испуска́ть *impf*, **испусти́ть** (-ущу́, -у́стишь) *pf* emit, let out.

испыта́ние test, trial; ordeal. **испыта́ть** *pf*, **испы́тывать** *impf* test; try; experience.

иссле́дование investigation; research. **иссле́дователь** *m* researcher; investigator. **иссле́довательский** research. **иссле́довать** *impf* & *pf* investigate, examine; research into.

истаска́ться *pf*, **иста́скиваться** *impf* wear out; be worn out.

истека́ть *impf of* **исте́чь**. **исте́кший** past.

исте́рика hysterics. **истери́ческий** hysterical. **истери́я** hysteria.

истече́ние outflow; expiry. **исте́чь** (-ечёт; -тёк, -ла́) *pf* (*impf* **истека́ть**) elapse; expire.

и́стина truth. **и́стинный** true.

истлева́ть *impf*, **истле́ть** (-е́ю) *pf* rot, decay; be reduced to ashes.

исто́к source.

истолкова́ть *pf*, **истолко́вывать** *impf* interpret; comment on.

ис|толо́чь (-лку́, -лчёшь; -ло́к, -лкла́) *pf.*

исто́ма languor.

исторга́ть *impf*, **исто́ргнуть** (-ну; -о́рг) *pf* throw out.

исто́рик historian. **истори́ческий** historical; historic. **исто́рия** history; story; incident.

исто́чник spring; source.

истоща́ть *impf*, **истощи́ть** (-щу́) *pf* exhaust; emaciate. **истоще́ние** emaciation; exhaustion.

ис|тра́тить (-а́чу) *pf.*

истреби́тель *m* destroyer; fighter. **истреби́ть** (-блю́) *pf*, **истребля́ть** *impf* destroy; exterminate.

ис|тупи́тся (-пится) *pf.*

истяза́ние torture. **истяза́ть** *impf* torture.

исхо́д outcome; end; Exodus. **исходи́ть** (-ожу́, -о́дишь) *impf* (+**из** *or* **от**+*gen*) issue (from), come (from); proceed (from). **исхо́дный** initial; departure.

исхуда́лый undernourished, emaciated.

исцеле́ние healing; recovery. **исцели́ть** *pf*, **исцеля́ть** *impf* heal, cure.

исчеза́ть *impf*, **исчё́знуть** (-ну; -е́з) *pf* disappear, vanish. **исчезнове́ние** disappearance.

исче́рпать *pf*, **исче́рпывать** *impf* exhaust; conclude. **исче́рпывающий** exhaustive.

исчисле́ние calculation; calculus.

ита́к *conj* thus; so then.

Ита́лия Italy. **италья́нец** (-нца), **италья́нка** Italian. **италья́нский** Italian.

ИТАР-ТА́СС *abbr* (*of* **Информацио́нное телегра́фное аге́нтство Росси́и**; *see* **ТАСС**) ITAR-Tass.

и т.д. *abbr* (*of* **и так да́лее**) etc., and so on.

ито́г sum; total; result. **итого́**

adv in all, altogether.
и т.п. *abbr* (*of* **и тому́ подо́бное**) etc., and so on.
иуде́й, иуде́йка Jew. **иуде́йский** Judaic.
их their, theirs; *see* **они́**.
иша́к (-а́) donkey.
ище́йка bloodhound; police dog.
ищу́ *etc.*: *see* **иска́ть**
ию́ль *m* July. **ию́льский** July.
ию́нь *m* June. **ию́ньский** June.
йо́га yoga.
йод iodine.
йо́та iota.

К

к, ко *prep+dat* to, towards; by; for; on; on the occasion of; **к пе́рвому января́** by the first of January; **к тому́ вре́мени** by then; **к тому́ же** besides, moreover; **к чему́?** what for?
-ка *partl modifying force of imper or expressing decision or intention*; **да́йте-ка пройти́** let me pass, please; **скажи́-ка мне** do tell me.
каба́к (-а́) tavern.
кабала́ servitude.
каба́н (-а́) wild boar.
кабаре́ *neut indecl* cabaret.
кабачо́к (-чка́) marrow.
ка́бель *m* cable. **ка́бельтов** cable, hawser.
каби́на cabin; booth; cockpit; cubicle; cab. **кабине́т** study; surgery; room; office; Cabinet.
каблу́к (-а́) heel.
кабота́ж coastal shipping. **кабота́жный** coastal.
кабы if.
кавале́р knight; partner, gentleman. **кавалери́йский** cavalry. **кавалери́ст** cavalryman.
кавале́рия cavalry.
ка́верзный tricky.
Кавка́з the Caucasus. **кавка́зец** (-зца́), **кавка́зка** Caucasian. **кавка́зский** Caucasian.
кавы́чки (-чек) *pl* inverted commas, quotation marks.
каде́т cadet. **каде́тский ко́рпус** military school.
ка́дка tub, vat.
кадр frame, still; close-up; cadre; *pl* establishment; staff; personnel; specialists. **ка́дровый** (*mil*) regular; skilled, trained.
кады́к (-а́) Adam's apple.
каждодне́вный daily, everyday. **ка́ждый** each, every; *sb* everybody.
ка́жется *etc.*: *see* **каза́ться**
каза́к (-а́; *pl* -аки́, -ако́в), **каза́чка** Cossack.
каза́рма barracks.
каза́ться (кажу́сь, ка́жешься) *impf* (*pf* **по~**) seem, appear; *impers* **ка́жется, каза́лось** apparently; **каза́лось бы** it would seem; *+dat*: **мне ка́жется** it seems to me; I think.
Казахста́н Kazakhstan. **каза́чий** Cossack.
казема́т casemate.
казённый State; government; fiscal; public; formal; banal, conventional. **казна́** Exchequer, Treasury; public purse; the State. **казначе́й** treasurer, bursar; paymaster.
казино́ *neut indecl* casino.
казни́ть *impf* & *pf* executè; punish; castigate. **казнь** execution.
каймá (*gen pl* каём) border, edging.
как *adv* how; what; **вот ~!** you don't say!; **~ вы ду́маете?**

what do you think?; ~ **его зовут?** what is his name?; ~ **же** naturally, of course; ~ **же так?** how is that?; ~ **ни** however. **как** *conj* as; like; when; since; *+neg* but, except, than; **в то время** ~ while, whereas; ~ **можно,** ~ **нельзя**+*comp* as ... as possible; ~ **можно скорее** as soon as possible; ~ **нельзя лучше** as well as possible; ~ **только** as soon as, when; **между тем,** ~ while, whereas. **как будто** *conj* as if; *partl* apparently. **как бы** how; as if; **как бы... не** what if, supposing; **как бы... ни** however. **как-либо** *adv* somehow. **как-нибудь** *adv* somehow; anyhow. **как раз** *adv* just, exactly. **как-то** *adv* somehow; once.

какао *neut indecl* cocoa.

каков (-á, -ó, -ы́) *pron* what, what sort (of); ~ **он?** what is he like?; ~ **он собой?** what does he look like?; **погода-то какова!** what weather! **каково** *adv* how. **какой** *pron* what; (such) as; which; ~... **ни** whatever, whichever. **какой-либо, какой-нибудь** *prons* some; any; only. **какой-то** *pron* some; a; a kind of.

как раз, как-то *see* **как**

кактус cactus.

кал faeces, excrement.

каламбур pun.

калека *m* & *f* cripple.

календарь (-я́) *m* calendar.

каление incandescence.

калечить (-чу) *impf* (*pf* **ис~, по~**) cripple, maim; **~ся** become a cripple.

калибр calibre; bore; gauge.

калий potassium.

калитка (wicket-)gate.

каллиграфия calligraphy.

калория calorie.

калоша galosh.

калька tracing-paper; tracing.

калькуляция calculation.

кальсоны (-н) *pl* long johns.

кальций calcium.

камбала flat-fish; plaice; flounder.

каменистый stony, rocky.

каменноугольный coal; ~ **бассейн** coal-field. **каменный** stone; rock; stony; hard, immovable; ~ **век** Stone Age; ~ **уголь** coal. **каменоломня** (*gen pl* -мен) quarry. **каменщик** (stone)mason; bricklayer. **камень** (-мня; *pl* -мни, -мне́й) *m* stone.

камера chamber; cell; camera; inner tube, (football) bladder; ~ **хранения** cloak-room, left-luggage office. **камерный** chamber. **камертон** tuning-fork.

камин fireplace; fire.

камкордер camcorder.

каморка closet, very small room.

кампания campaign; cruise.

камыш (-á) reed, rush; cane.

канава ditch; gutter.

Канада Canada. **канадец** (-дца), **канадка** Canadian. **канадский** Canadian.

канал canal; channel. **канализация** sewerage (system).

канарейка canary.

канат rope; cable.

канва canvas; groundwork; outline, design.

кандалы (-о́в) *pl* shackles.

кандидат candidate; ~ **наук** person with higher degree. **кандидатура** candidature.

каникулы (-ул) *pl* vacation; holidays.

кани́стра can, canister.
канони́ческий canon(ical).
кано́э *neut indecl* canoe.
кант edging; mount. **кантова́ть** *impf*; «**не** ~» 'this way up'.
кану́н eve.
ка́нуть (-ну) *pf* drop, sink; **как в во́ду** ~ vanish into thin air.
канцеля́рия office. **канцеля́рский** office; clerical. **канцеля́рщина** red-tape.
ка́нцлер chancellor.
ка́пать (-аю *or* -плю) *impf* (*pf* **ка́пнуть, на**~) drip, drop; trickle; +*instr* spill.
капе́лла choir; chapel.
ка́пелька small drop; a little; ~ **росы́** dew-drop.
капельме́йстер conductor; bandmaster.
капилля́р capillary.
капита́л capital. **капитали́зм** capitalism. **капитали́ст** capitalist. **капиталисти́ческий** capitalist. **капита́льный** capital; main, fundamental; major.
капита́н captain; skipper.
капитули́ровать *impf* & *pf* capitulate. **капитуля́ция** capitulation.
капка́н trap.
ка́пля (*gen pl* -пель) drop; bit, scrap. **ка́пнуть** (-ну) *pf of* **ка́пать**
капо́т hood, cowl, cowling; bonnet; house-coat.
капри́з caprice. **капри́зничать** *impf* play up. **капри́зный** capricious.
капу́ста cabbage.
капюшо́н hood.
ка́ра punishment.
кара́бкаться *impf* (*pf* **вс**~) clamber.
карава́н caravan; convoy.
кара́кули *f pl* scribble.
караме́ль caramel; caramels.
каранда́ш (-а́) pencil.
каранти́н quarantine.
кара́т carat.
кара́тельный punitive. **кара́ть** *impf* (*pf* **по**~) punish.
карау́л guard; watch; ~! help! **карау́лить** *impf* guard; lie in wait for. **карау́льный** guard; *sb* sentry, sentinel, guard.
карбюра́тор carburettor.
каре́та carriage, coach.
ка́рий brown; hazel.
карикату́ра caricature; cartoon.
карка́с frame; framework.
ка́ркать *impf*, **ка́ркнуть** (-ну) *pf* caw, croak.
ка́рлик, ка́рлица dwarf; pygmy. **ка́рликовый** dwarf; pygmy.
карма́н pocket. **карма́нник** pickpocket. **карма́нный** *adj* pocket.
карни́з cornice; ledge.
карп carp.
ка́рта map; (playing-)card.
карта́вить (-влю) *impf* burr.
картёжник gambler.
карте́чь case-shot, grape-shot.
карти́на picture; scene. **карти́нка** picture; illustration. **карти́нный** picturesque; picture.
карто́н cardboard. **карто́нка** cardboard box.
картоте́ка card-index.
карто́фель *m* potatoes; potato(-plant). **карто́фельн|ый** potato; ~**ое пюре́** mashed potatoes.
ка́рточка card; season ticket; photo. **ка́рточный** card.
карто́шка potatoes; potato.
карусе́ль merry-go-round.
ка́рцер cell, lock-up.
карье́р[1] full gallop.

карье́р[2] quarry; sand-pit.
карье́ра career. **карьери́ст** careerist.
каса́ние contact. **каса́тельная** *sb* tangent. **каса́ться** *impf* (*pf* **косну́ться**) *+gen or* **до**+*gen* touch; touch on; concern; **что каса́ется** as regards.
ка́ска helmet.
каска́д cascade.
каспи́йский Caspian.
ка́сса till; cash-box; booking-office; box-office; cash-desk; cash.
кассе́та cassette. **кассе́тный магнитофо́н** cassette recorder.
касси́р, касси́рша cashier.
кастра́т eunuch. **кастра́ция** castration. **кастри́ровать** *impf* & *pf* castrate, geld.
кастрю́ля saucepan.
катало́г catalogue.
ката́ние rolling; driving; ~ **верхо́м** riding; ~ **на конька́х** skating.
катапу́льта catapult. **катапульти́ровать(ся** *impf* & *pf* catapult.
ката́р catarrh.
катара́кта cataract.
катастро́фа catastrophe. **катастрофи́ческий** catastrophic.
ката́ть *impf* roll; (take for a) drive; **~ся** (*pf* **по~**) roll, roll about; go for a drive; **~ся верхо́м** ride, go riding; **~ся на конька́х** skate, go skating.
категори́ческий categorical.
катего́рия category.
ка́тер (*pl* -á) cutter; launch.
кати́ть (-ачу́, -а́тишь) *impf* bowl along, rip, tear; **~ся** rush, tear; flow, stream, roll; **кати́сь, кати́тесь** get out! clear off! **като́к** (-тка́) skating-rink; roller.
като́лик, католи́чка Catholic. **католи́ческий** Catholic.
ка́торга penal servitude, hard labour. **ка́торжник** convict.
ка́торжн|ый penal; **~ые рабо́ты** hard labour; drudgery.
кату́шка reel, bobbin; spool; coil.
каучу́к rubber.
кафе́ *neut indecl* café.
ка́федра pulpit; rostrum; chair; department.
ка́фель *m* Dutch tile.
кача́лка rocking-chair. **кача́ние** rocking, swinging; pumping. **кача́ть** *impf* (*pf* **качну́ть**) *+acc or instr* rock, swing; shake; **~ся** rock, swing; roll; reel. **каче́ли** (-ей) *pl* swing.
ка́чественный qualitative; high-quality. **ка́чество** quality; **в ка́честве**+*gen* as, in the capacity of.
ка́чка rocking; tossing.
качну́ть(ся (-ну́(сь, -нёшь(ся) *pf of* **кача́ть(ся. качу́** *etc.*: *see* **кати́ть**
ка́ша gruel, porridge; **завари́ть ка́шу** stir up trouble.
ка́шель (-шля) cough. **ка́шлянуть** (-ну) *pf*, **ка́шлять** *impf* (have a) cough.
кашта́н chestnut. **кашта́новый** chestnut.
каю́та cabin, stateroom.
ка́ющийся penitent. **ка́яться** (ка́юсь) *impf* (*pf* **по~, рас~**) repent; confess; **ка́юсь** I (must) confess.
кв. *abbr* (*of* **квадра́тный**) square; (*of* **кварти́ра**) flat.
квадра́т square; quad; **в квадра́те** squared; **возвести́ в** ~ square. **квадра́тный** square; quadratic.
ква́кать *impf*, **ква́кнуть** (-ну) *pf* croak.

квалифика́ция qualification. **квалифици́рованный** qualified, skilled.
квант, ква́нта quantum. **ква́нтовый** quantum.
кварта́л block; quarter. **кварта́льный** quarterly.
кварте́т quartet.
кварти́ра flat; apartment(s); quarters. **квартира́нт, -ра́нтка** lodger; tenant. **кварти́рная пла́та, квартпла́та** rent.
кварц quartz.
квас (*pl* ~ы́) kvass. **ква́сить** (-а́шу) *impf* sour; pickle. **ква́шеная капу́ста** sauerkraut.
кве́рху *adv* up, upwards.
квит, кви́ты quits.
квита́нция receipt. **квито́к** (-тка́) ticket, check.
КГБ *abbr* (*of* **Комите́т госуда́рственной безопа́сности**) KGB.
ке́гля skittle.
кедр cedar.
ке́ды (-ов) *pl* trainers.
кекс (fruit-)cake.
ке́лья (*gen pl* -лий) cell.
кем *see* **кто**
ке́мпинг campsite.
кенгуру́ *m indecl* kangaroo.
ке́пка cloth cap.
кера́мика ceramics.
керога́з stove. **кероси́н** paraffin. **кероси́нка** paraffin stove.
ке́та Siberian salmon. **ке́тов|ый: ~ая икра́** red caviare.
кефи́р kefir, yoghurt.
киберне́тика cybernetics.
кива́ть *impf*, **кивну́ть** (-ну́, -нёшь) *pf* (**голово́й**) nod (one's head); (+**на**+*acc*) motion (to). **киво́к** (-вка́) nod.
кида́ть *impf* (*pf* **ки́нуть**) throw, fling; **~ся** fling o.s.; rush; +*instr* throw.
кий (-я́; *pl* -и́, -ёв) (*billiard*) cue.
килев|о́й keel; **~а́я ка́чка** pitching.
кило́ *neut indecl* kilo. **килова́тт** kilowatt. **килогра́мм** kilogram. **киломе́тр** kilometre.
киль *m* keel; fin. **кильва́тер** wake.
ки́лька sprat.
кинжа́л dagger.
кино́ *neut indecl* cinema.
кино- *in comb* film-, cine-. **киноаппара́т** cinecamera. **~арти́ст, ~арти́стка** film actor, actress. **~журна́л** newsreel. **~за́л** cinema; auditorium. **~звезда́** film-star. **~зри́тель** *m* film-goer. **~карти́на** film. **~опера́тор** camera-man. **~плёнка** film. **~режиссёр** film director. **~теа́тр** cinema. **~хро́ника** news-reel.
ки́нуть(ся (-ну(сь) *pf of* **кида́ть(ся**
кио́ск kiosk, stall.
ки́па pile, stack; bale.
кипари́с cypress.
кипе́ние boiling. **кипе́ть** (-плю́) *impf* (*pf* **вс~**) boil, seethe.
кипу́чий boiling, seething; ebullient. **кипяти́льник** kettle, boiler. **кипяти́ть** (-ячу́) *impf* (*pf* **вс~**) boil; **~ся** boil; get excited. **кипято́к** (-тка́) boiling water. **кипячёный** boiled.
Кирги́зия Kirghizia.
кирка́ pick(axe).
кирпи́ч (-а́) brick; bricks. **кирпи́чный** brick; brick-red.
кисе́ль *m* kissel, blancmange.
кисе́т tobacco-pouch.
кисея́ muslin.
кислоро́д oxygen. **кислота́**

(*pl* -ы) acid; acidity. **кисло́тный** acid. **ки́слый** sour; acid. **ки́снуть** (-ну; кис) *impf* (*pf* **про~**) turn sour.

ки́сточка brush; tassel. **кисть** (*gen pl* -е́й) cluster, bunch; brush; tassel; hand.

кит (-а́) whale.

кита́ец (-а́йца; *pl* -цы, -цев) Chinese. **Кита́й** China. **кита́йский** Chinese. **китая́нка** Chinese (woman).

китобо́й whaler. **кито́вый** whale.

кичи́ться (-чу́сь) *impf* plume o.s.; strut. **кичли́вость** conceit. **кичли́вый** conceited.

кише́ть (-ши́т) *impf* swarm, teem.

кише́чник bowels, intestines. **кише́чный** intestinal. **кишка́** gut, intestine; hose.

клавеси́н harpsichord. **клавиату́ра** keyboard. **кла́виша** key. **кла́вишный**: ~ **инструме́нт** keyboard instrument.

клад treasure.

кла́дбище cemetery, graveyard.

кла́дка laying; masonry. **кладова́я** *sb* pantry; store-room. **кладовщи́к** (-а́) storeman. **кладу́** *etc.*: *see* **класть**

кла́няться *impf* (*pf* **поклони́ться**) +*dat* bow to; greet.

кла́пан valve; vent.

кларне́т clarinet.

класс class; class-room. **кла́ссик** classic. **кла́ссика** the classics. **классифици́ровать** *impf & pf* classify. **класси́ческий** classical. **кла́ссный** class; first-class. **кла́ссовый** class.

класть (-аду́, -адёшь; -ал) *impf* (*pf* **положи́ть, сложи́ть**) lay; put.

клева́ть (клюю́, клюёшь) *impf* (*pf* **клю́нуть**) peck; bite.

кле́вер (*pl* -а́) clover.

клевета́ slander; libel. **клевета́ть** (-ещу́, -е́щешь) *impf* (*pf* **на~**) +**на**+*acc* slander; libel. **клеветни́к** (-а́), **-ни́ца** slanderer. **клеветни́ческий** slanderous; libellous.

клеёнка oilcloth. **кле́ить** *impf* (*pf* **с~**) glue; stick; **~ся** stick; become sticky. **клей** (*loc* -ю́; *pl* -и́) glue, adhesive. **кле́йкий** sticky.

клейми́ть (-млю́) *impf* (*pf* **за~**) brand; stamp; stigmatize. **клеймо́** (*pl* -а) brand; stamp; mark.

кле́йстер paste.

клён maple.

клепа́ть *impf* rivet.

кле́тка cage; check; cell. **кле́точка** cellule. **кле́точный** cellular. **клетча́тка** cellulose. **кле́тчатый** checked.

клёш flare.

клешня́ (*gen pl* -е́й) claw.

кле́щи (-е́й) *pl* pincers, tongs.

клие́нт client. **клиенту́ра** clientèle.

кли́зма enema.

клик cry, call. **кли́кать** (-и́чу) *impf*, **кли́кнуть** (-ну) *pf* call.

кли́макс menopause.

кли́мат climate. **климати́ческий** climatic.

клин (*pl* -нья, -ньев) wedge. **клино́к** (-нка́) blade.

кли́ника clinic. **клини́ческий** clinical.

клипс clip-on ear-ring.

клич call. **кли́чка** name; nickname. **кли́чу** *etc.*: *see* **кли́кать**

клок (-а́; *pl* -о́чья, -ьев *or* -и́, -о́в) rag, shred; tuft.

кло́кот bubbling; gurgling.

клокота́ть (-о́чет) *impf* bubble; gurgle; boil up.
клон clone.
клони́ть (-ню́, -нишь) *impf* bend; incline; **+к**+*dat* drive at; **~ся** bow, bend; **+к**+*dat* near, approach.
клоп (-а́) bug.
кло́ун clown.
клочо́к (-чка́) scrap, shred. **кло́чья** *etc.*: *see* **клок**
клуб[1] club.
клуб[2] (*pl* -ы́) puff; cloud.
клу́бень (-бня) *m* tuber.
клуби́ться *impf* swirl; curl.
клубни́ка (*no pl*; *usu collect*) strawberry; strawberries.
клубо́к (-бка́) ball; tangle.
клу́мба (flower-)bed.
клык (-а́) fang; tusk; canine (*tooth*).
клюв beak.
клю́ква cranberry; cranberries.
клю́нуть (-ну) *pf of* **клева́ть**
ключ[1] (-а́) key; clue; keystone; clef; wrench, spanner.
ключ[2] (-а́) spring; source.
ключево́й key. **ключи́ца** collarbone.
клю́шка (hockey) stick; (golf-) club.
клюю́ *etc.*: *see* **клева́ть**
кля́кса blot, smudge.
кляну́ *etc.*: *see* **клясть**
кля́нчить (-чу́) *impf* (*pf* **вы́~**) beg.
кляп gag.
клясть (-яну́, -янёшь; -ял, -а́, -о) *impf* curse; **~ся** (*pf* **по~ся**) swear, vow. **кля́тва** oath, vow. **кля́твенный** on oath.
кни́га book.
книго- *in comb* book, biblio-. **книгове́дение**[1] bibliography. **~ве́дение**[2] book-keeping. **~изда́тель** *m* publisher. **~люб** bibliophile. **~храни́лище** library; book-stack.
кни́жечка booklet. **кни́жка** book; note-book; bank-book. **кни́жный** book; bookish.
книзу *adv* downwards.
кно́пка drawing-pin; press-stud; (push-)button, knob.
кнут (-а́) whip.
княги́ня princess. **кня́жество** principality. **княжна́** (*gen pl* -жо́н) princess. **кня́зь** (*pl* -зья́, -зе́й) *m* prince.
ко *see* **к** *prep*.
коали́ция coalition.
кобура́ holster.
кобы́ла mare; (vaulting-)horse.
ко́ваный forged; wrought; terse.
кова́рный insidious, crafty; perfidious. **кова́рство** insidiousness, craftiness; perfidy.
кова́ть (кую́, -ёшь) *impf* (*pf* **под~**) forge; hammer; shoe.
ковёр (-вра́) carpet; rug; mat.
кове́ркать *impf* (*pf* **ис~**) distort, mangle, ruin.
ко́вка forging; shoeing.
коври́жка honeycake, gingerbread.
ко́врик rug; mat.
ковче́г ark.
ковш (-а́) scoop, ladle.
ковы́ль *m* feather-grass.
ковыля́ть *impf* hobble.
ковырну́ть (-ну́, -нёшь) *pf*, **ковыря́ть** *impf* dig into; tinker; **+в**+*prep* pick (at); **~ся** rummage; tinker.
когда́ *adv* when; **~ (бы) ни** whenever; *conj* when; while, as; if. **когда́-либо, когда́-нибудь** *advs* some time; ever. **когда́-то** *adv* once; formerly; some time.
кого́ *see* **кто**
ко́готь (-гтя; *pl* -гти, -гте́й) *m* claw; talon.

код code.
кодеи́н codeine.
ко́декс code.
ко́е-где́ *adv* here and there. **ко́е-ка́к** *adv* anyhow; somehow (or other). **ко́е-како́й** *pron* some. **ко́е-кто́** *pron* somebody; some people. **ко́е-что́** (-чего́) *pron* something; a little.
ко́жа skin; leather; peel. **ко́жанка** leather jacket. **ко́жаный** leather. **коже́венный** leather; tanning. **ко́жный** skin. **кожура́** rind, peel, skin.
коза́ (*pl* -ы) goat, nanny-goat. **козёл** (-зла́) billy-goat. **козеро́г** ibex; Capricorn. **ко́зий** goat; ~ **пух** angora. **козлёнок** (-нка; *pl* -ля́та, -ля́т) kid.
ко́злы (-зел) *pl* coach driver's seat; trestle(s); saw-horse.
ко́зни (-ей) *pl* machinations.
козырёк (-рька́) peak.
козырно́й trump. **козырну́ть** (-ну́, -нёшь) *pf*, **козыря́ть** *impf* lead trumps; trump; play one's trump card; salute. **ко́зырь** (*pl* -и, -е́й) *m* trump.
ко́йка (*gen pl* ко́ек) berth, bunk; bed.
кокаи́н cocaine .
ко́ка-ко́ла Coca-Cola (*propr*).
коке́тка coquette. **коке́тство** coquetry.
коклю́ш whooping-cough.
ко́кон cocoon.
коко́с coconut.
кокс coke.
кокте́йль *m* cocktail.
кол (-а́; *pl* -лья, -ьев) stake, picket.
ко́лба retort.
колбаса́ (*pl* -ы) sausage.
колго́тки (-ток) *pl* tights.
колдова́ть *impf* practise witchcraft. **колдовство́** sorcery. **колду́н** (-а́) sorcerer, wizard. **колду́нья** (*gen pl* -ний) witch, sorceress.
колеба́ние oscillation; variation; hesitation. **колеба́ть** (-е́блю) *impf* (*pf* **по~**) shake; **~ся** oscillate; fluctuate; hesitate.
коле́но (*pl* -и, -ей, -ям) knee; (*in pl*) lap. **коле́нчатый** crank, cranked; bent; ~ **вал** crankshaft.
колесни́ца chariot. **колесо́** (*pl* -ёса) wheel.
колея́ rut; track, gauge.
ко́лика (*usu pl*) colic; stitch.
коли́чественн|ый quantitative; **~ое числи́тельное** cardinal number. **коли́чество** quantity; number.
колле́га *m* & *f* colleague. **колле́гия** board; college.
коллекти́в collective. **коллективиза́ция** collectivization. **коллекти́вный** collective. **коллекционе́р** collector. **колле́кция** collection.
колли́зия clash, conflict.
коло́да block; pack (*of cards*).
коло́дец (-дца) well.
ко́локол (*pl* -а́, -о́в) bell. **коло́кольный** bell. **колоко́льня** bell-tower. **колоко́льчик** small bell; bluebell.
колониали́зм colonialism. **колониа́льный** colonial. **колониза́тор** colonizer. **колониза́ция** colonization. **колонизова́ть** *impf* & *pf* colonize. **коло́ния** colony.
коло́нка geyser; (*street*) water fountain; stand-pipe; column; **бензи́новая ~** petrol pump.
коло́нна column.
колори́т colouring, colour. **колори́тный** colourful, graphic.
ко́лос (-о́сья, -ьев) ear. **колоси́ться** *impf* form ears.

колосса́льный huge; terrific. **колоти́ть** (-очу́, -о́тишь) *impf* (*pf* **по~**) beat; pound; thrash; smash; **~ся** pound, thump; shake.

коло́ть[1] (-лю́, -лешь) *impf* (*pf* **рас~**) break, chop.

коло́ть[2] (-лю́, -лешь) *impf* (*pf* **за~, кольну́ть**) prick; stab; sting; slaughter; **~ся** prick.

колпа́к (-а́) cap; hood, cowl.

колхо́з *abbr* (*of* **коллекти́вное хозя́йство**) kolkhoz, collective farm. **колхо́зник, ~ица** kolkhoz member. **колхо́зный** kolkhoz.

колыбе́ль cradle.

колыха́ть (-ы́шу) *impf*, **колыхну́ть** (-ну́, -нёшь) *pf* sway, rock; **~ся** sway; flutter.

кольну́ть (-ну́, -нёшь) *pf of* **коло́ть**

кольцо́ (*pl* -а, -ле́ц, -льцам) ring.

колю́ч|ий prickly; sharp; **~ая про́волока** barbed wire. **колю́чка** prickle; thorn.

коля́ска carriage; pram; sidecar.

ком (*pl* -мья, -мьев) lump; ball.

ком *see* **кто**

кома́нда command; order; detachment; crew; team. **команди́р** commander. **командирова́ть** *impf* & *pf* post, send on a mission. **командиро́вка** posting; mission, business trip. **командиро́вочные** *sb pl* travelling expenses. **кома́ндование** command. **кома́ндовать** *impf* (*pf* **с~**) give orders; be in command; *+instr* command. **кома́ндующий** *sb* commander.

кома́р (-а́) mosquito.

комба́йн combine harvester.

комбина́т industrial complex.

комбина́ция combination; manoeuvre; slip. **комбинезо́н** overalls, boiler suit; dungarees. **комбини́ровать** *impf* (*pf* **с~**) combine.

коме́дия comedy.

коменда́нт commandant; manager; warden. **комендату́ра** commandant's office.

коме́та comet.

ко́мик comic actor; comedian.

ко́микс comic, comic strip.

комисса́р commissar.

комиссионе́р (commission-) agent, broker. **комиссио́нн|ый** commission; **~ый магази́н** second-hand shop; **~ые** *sb pl* commission. **коми́ссия** commission; committee.

комите́т committee.

коми́ческий comic; comical. **коми́чный** comical, funny.

ко́мкать *impf* (*pf* **с~**) crumple.

коммента́рий commentary; *pl* comment. **коммента́тор** commentator. **комменти́ровать** *impf* & *pf* comment (on).

коммерса́нт merchant; businessman **комме́рция** commerce. **комме́рческий** commercial.

коммивояжёр commercial traveller.

комму́на commune. **коммуна́льный** communal; municipal. **коммуни́зм** communism.

коммуника́ция communication.

коммуни́ст, ~ка communist. **коммунисти́ческий** communist.

коммута́тор switchboard.

коммюнике́ *neut indecl* communiqué.

ко́мната room. **ко́мнатный** room; indoor.

комо́д chest of drawers.

комóк (-мкá) lump.

компáкт-дúск compact disc; ~ ПЗУ CD-ROM. **компáктный** compact.

компáния company. **компаньóн, ~ка** companion; partner.

компáртия Communist Party.

кóмпас compass.

компенсáция compensation. **компенсúровать** *impf* & *pf* compensate.

кóмплекс complex. **кóмплексный** complex, composite; combined. **комплéкт** (complete) set; complement; kit. **комплектовáть** *impf* (*pf* с~, у~) complete; bring up to strength. **комплéкция** build; constitution.

комплимéнт compliment.

композúтор composer. **композúция** composition.

компонéнт component.

компóст compost.

компóстер punch. **компостúровать** *impf* (*pf* про~) punch.

компóт stewed fruit.

компрéссор compressor.

компрометúровать *impf* (*pf* с~) compromise. **компромúсс** compromise.

компьютер computer.

комсомóл Komsomol. **комсомóлец** (-льца), **-лка** Komsomol member. **комсомóльский** Komsomol.

комý *see* **кто**

комфóрт comfort.

конвéйер conveyor.

конвéрт envelope; sleeve.

конвóир escort. **конвоúровать** *impf* escort. **конвóй** escort, convoy.

конгрéсс congress.

конденсáтор condenser.

кондúтерская *sb* confectioner's, cake shop.

кондиционéр air-conditioner. **кондициóнный** air-conditioning.

кондýктор (*pl* -á), **-торша** conductor; guard.

коневóдство horse-breeding.

конёк (-нькá) *dim of* **конь**; hobby(-horse).

конéц (-нцá) end; **в концé концóв** in the end, after all.

конéчно *adv* of course. **конéчность** extremity. **конéчный** final, last; ultimate; finite.

конúческий conic, conical.

конкрéтный concrete.

конкурéнт competitor. **конкурéнция** competition. **конкурúровать** *impf* compete. **кóнкурс** competition; contest.

кóнница cavalry. **кóнный** horse; mounted; equestrian; ~ **завóд** stud.

коноплá hemp.

консервативный conservative. **консервáтор** Conservative.

консерватóрия conservatoire.

консервúровать *impf* & *pf* (*pf also* **за~**) preserve; can, bottle. **консéрвн|ый** preserving; **~ая бáнка** tin; **~ый нож** tin-opener. **консéрвооткрывáтель** *m* tin-opener. **консéрвы** (-ов) *pl* tinned goods.

консúлиум consultation.

конспéкт synopsis, summary. **конспектúровать** *impf* (*pf* **за~, про~**) make an abstract of.

конспиратúвный secret, clandestine. **конспирáция** security.

констатáция ascertaining; establishment. **констатúровать**

impf & *pf* ascertain; establish. **конституцио́нный** constitutional. **конститу́ция** constitution.

конструи́ровать *impf* & *pf* (*pf also* **с~**) construct; design. **конструкти́вный** structural; constructional; constructive. **констру́ктор** designer, constructor. **констру́кция** construction; design.

ко́нсул consul. **ко́нсульство** consulate.

консульта́ция consultation; advice; clinic; tutorial. **консульти́ровать** *impf* (*pf* **про~**) advise; +**с**+*instr* consult; **~ся** obtain advice; +**с**+*instr* consult.

конта́кт contact. **конта́ктные ли́нзы** *f pl* contact lenses.

конте́йнер container.

конте́кст context.

контине́нт continent.

конто́ра office. **конто́рский** office.

контраба́нда contraband. **контрабанди́ст** smuggler.

контраба́с double-bass.

контра́кт contract.

контра́льто *neut/fem indecl* contralto (*voice/person*).

контрама́рка complimentary ticket.

контрапу́нкт counterpoint.

контра́ст contrast.

контрибу́ция indemnity.

контрнаступле́ние counter-offensive.

контролёр inspector; ticket-collector. **контроли́ровать** *impf* (*pf* **про~**) check; inspect. **контро́ль** *m* control; check; inspection. **контро́льн|ый** control; **~ая рабо́та** test.

контрразве́дка counter-intelligence; security service. **контрреволю́ция** counter-revolution.

конту́зия bruising; shell-shock.

ко́нтур contour, outline; circuit.

конура́ kennel.

ко́нус cone.

конфедера́ция confederation.

конфере́нция conference.

конфе́та sweet.

конфискова́ть *impf* & *pf* confiscate.

конфли́кт conflict.

конфо́рка ring (*on stove*).

конфу́з discomforture, embarrassment. **конфу́зить** (-у́жу) *impf* (*pf* **с~**) confuse, embarrass; **~ся** feel embarrassed.

концентра́т concentrate. **концентрацио́нный** concentration. **концентра́ция** concentration. **концентри́ровать(ся** *impf* (*pf* **с~**) concentrate.

конце́пция conception.

конце́рт concert; concerto. **концертме́йстер** leader. **конце́ртный** concert.

концла́герь *abbr* (*of* **концентрацио́нный ла́герь**) concentration camp.

конча́ть *impf*, **ко́нчить** *pf* finish; end; +*inf* stop; **~ся** end, finish; expire. **ко́нчик** tip. **кончи́на** decease.

конь (-я́; *pl* -и, -е́й) *m* horse; knight. **коньки́** (-о́в) *pl* skates; **~ на ро́ликах** roller skates. **конькобе́жец** (-жца) skater.

конья́к (-а́) cognac.

ко́нюх groom, stable-boy. **коню́шня** (*gen pl* -шен) stable.

кооперати́в cooperative. **кооперати́вный** cooperative. **коопера́ция** cooperation.

координа́та coordinate. **координа́ция** coordination.

копа́ть *impf* (*pf* **копну́ть, вы́~**) dig; dig up, dig out; **~ся** rummage.
копе́йка copeck.
ко́пи (-ей) *pl* mines.
копи́лка money-box.
копи́рка carbon paper. **копирова́льный** copying. **копи́ровать** *impf* (*pf* **с~**) copy; imitate.
копи́ть (-плю́, -пишь) *impf* (*pf* **на~**) save (up); accumulate; **~ся** accumulate.
ко́пия copy.
копна́ (*pl* -ы, -пён) shock, stook.
копну́ть (-ну́, -нёшь) *pf of* **копа́ть**
ко́поть soot.
копте́ть (-пчу́) *impf* swot; vegetate. **копти́ть** (-пчу́) *impf* (*pf* **за~, на~**) smoke, cure; blacken with smoke. **копче́ние** smoking; smoked foods. **копчёный** smoked.
копы́то hoof.
копьё (*pl* -я, -пий) spear, lance.
кора́ bark; cortex; crust.
корабе́льный ship; naval. **кораблевожде́ние** navigation. **кораблекруше́ние** shipwreck. **кораблестрое́ние** shipbuilding. **кора́бль** (-я́) *m* ship, vessel; nave.
кора́лл coral.
коре́йский Korean. **Коре́я** Korea.
корена́стый thickset. **корени́ться** *impf* be rooted. **коренно́й** radical, fundamental; native. **ко́рень** (-рня; *pl* -и, -е́й) *m* root. **корешо́к** (-шка́) root(let); spine; counterfoil.
корзи́на, корзи́нка basket.
коридо́р corridor.
кори́ца cinnamon.
кори́чневый brown.
ко́рка crust; rind, peel.
корм (*loc* -у́; *pl* -а́) fodder.
корма́ stern.
корми́лец (-льца) bread-winner. **корми́ть** (-млю́, -мишь) *impf* (*pf* **на~, по~, про~**) feed; **~ся** feed; *+instr* live on, make a living by. **кормле́ние** feeding. **кормово́й**[1] fodder.
кормово́й[2] stern.
корнево́й root; radical. **корнеплоды** (-ов) root-crops.
коро́бить (-блю) *impf* (*pf* **по~**) warp; jar upon; **~ся** (*pf also* **с~ся**) warp.
коро́бка box.
коро́ва cow.
короле́ва queen. **короле́вский** royal. **короле́вство** kingdom. **коро́ль** (-я́) *m* king.
коромы́сло yoke; beam; rocking shaft.
коро́на crown.
коронаротромбо́з coronary (thrombosis).
коро́нка crown. **короно́вать** *impf* & *pf* crown.
коро́ткий (ко́роток, -тка́, ко́ротко́, ко́ротки́) short; intimate. **ко́ротко** *adv* briefly; intimately. **коротково́лновый** short-wave. **коро́че** *comp of* **коро́ткий, ко́ротко**
корпора́ция corporation.
ко́рпус (*pl* -ы, -ов *or* -а́, -о́в) corps; services; building; hull; housing, case; body.
корректи́ровать *impf* (*pf* **про~, с~**) correct, edit. **корре́ктный** correct, proper. **корре́ктор** (*pl* -а́) proofreader. **корректу́ра** proofreading; proof.
корреспонде́нт correspondent. **корреспонде́нция** correspondence.
корро́зия corrosion.

корру́пция corruption.
корт (tennis-)court.
корте́ж cortège; motorcade.
ко́ртик dirk.
ко́рточки (-чек) *pl*; **сиде́ть на ко́рточках** squat.
корчева́ть (-чу́ю) *impf* root out.
ко́рчить (-чу) *impf* (*pf* **с~**) contort; *impers* convulse; **~ из себя́** pose as; **~ся** writhe.
ко́ршун kite.
коры́стный mercenary. **коры́сть** avarice; profit.
коры́то trough; wash-tub.
корь measles.
коса́[1] (*acc* -у; *pl* -ы) plait, tress.
коса́[2] (*acc* ко́су́; *pl* -ы) spit.
коса́[3] (*acc* ко́су́; *pl* -ы) scythe.
ко́свенный indirect.
коси́лка mowing-machine, mower. **коси́ть**[1] (кошу́, ко́сишь) *impf* (*pf* **с~**) cut; mow (down).
коси́ть[2] (кошу́) *impf* (*pf* **по~**, **с~**) squint; be crooked; **~ся** slant; look sideways; look askance.
косме́тика cosmetics, make-up.
косми́ческий cosmic; space. **космодро́м** spacecraft launching-site. **космона́вт, -на́втка** cosmonaut, astronaut. **ко́смос** cosmos; (outer) space.
косноязы́чный tongue-tied.
косну́ться (-ну́сь, -нёшься) *pf of* **каса́ться**
косогла́зие squint. **косо́й** (кос, -á, -о) slanting; oblique; sidelong; squinting, cross-eyed.
костёр (-тра́) bonfire; camp-fire.
костля́вый bony. **ко́стный** bone. **ко́сточка** (small) bone; stone.
косты́ль (-я́) *m* crutch.
кость (*loc* -и́; *pl* -и, -е́й) bone; die.
костю́м clothes; suit. **костюми́рованный** fancy-dress.
костяно́й bone; ivory.
косы́нка (*triangular*) head-scarf, shawl.
кот (-á) tom-cat.
котёл (-тла́) boiler; copper, cauldron. **котело́к** (-лка́) pot; mess-tin; bowler (hat). **коте́льная** *sb* boiler-room, -house.
котёнок (-нка; *pl* -тя́та, -тя́т) kitten. **ко́тик** fur-seal; sealskin.
котле́та rissole; burger; **отбивна́я ~** chop.
котлова́н foundation pit, trench.
кото́мка knapsack.
кото́рый *pron* which, what; who; that; **~ час?** what time is it?
котя́та *etc.*: *see* **котёнок**
ко́фе *m indecl* coffee. **кофева́рка** percolator. **кофеи́н** caffeine.
ко́фта, ко́фточка blouse, top.
коча́н (-á *or* -чна́) (cabbage-) head.
кочева́ть (-чу́ю) *impf* be a nomad; wander; migrate. **коче́вник** nomad. **кочево́й** nomadic.
кочега́р stoker, fireman. **кочега́рка** stokehold, stokehole.
кочене́ть *impf* (*pf* **за~**, **о~**) grow numb.
кочерга́ (*gen pl* -рёг) poker.
ко́чка hummock.
кошелёк (-лька́) purse.
ко́шка cat.
кошма́р nightmare. **кошма́рный** nightmarish.
кошу́ *etc.*: *see* **коси́ть**
кощу́нство blasphemy.
коэффицие́нт coefficient.
КП *abbr* (*of* **Коммунисти́ческая па́ртия**) Communist

Party. **КПСС** *abbr* (*of* **Коммунистическая партия Советского Союза**) Communist Party of the Soviet Union, CPSU.
краб crab.
краденый stolen. **краду** *etc.*: *see* **красть**
кража theft; ~ **со взломом** burglary.
край (*loc* -ю; *pl* -я, -ёв) edge; brink; land; region. **крайне** *adv* extremely. **крайний** extreme; last; outside, wing; **по крайней мере** at least. **крайность** extreme; extremity.
крал *etc.*: *see* **красть**
кран tap; crane.
крапива nettle.
красавец (-вца) handsome man. **красавица** beauty. **красивый** beautiful; handsome.
краситель *m* dye. **красить** (-ашу) *impf* (*pf* **вы~**, **о~**, **по~**) paint; colour; dye; stain; **~ся** (*pf* **на~**) make-up.
краска paint, dye; colour.
краснеть (-ею) *impf* (*pf* **по~**) blush; redden; show red.
красноармеец (-ейца) Red Army man. **красноармейский** Red Army. **красноречивый** eloquent.
краснота redness. **краснуха** German measles. **красн|ый** (-сен, -сна, -о) red; beautiful; fine; **~ое дерево** mahogany; **~ая смородина** (*no pl*; *usu collect*) redcurrant; redcurrants; **~ая строка** (first line of) new paragraph.
красоваться *impf* impress by one's beauty; show off. **красота** (*pl* -ы) beauty. **красочный** paint; ink; colourful.
красть (-аду, -адёшь; крал) *impf* (*pf* **у~**) steal; **~ся** creep.
кратер crater.
краткий (-ток, -тка, -о) short; brief. **кратковременный** brief; transitory. **краткосрочный** short-term.
кратное *sb* multiple.
кратчайший *superl of* **краткий**. **кратче** *comp of* **краткий, кратко**
крах crash; failure.
крахмал starch. **крахмалить** *impf* (*pf* **на~**) starch.
краше *comp of* **красивый, красиво**
крашеный painted; coloured; dyed; made up. **крашу** *etc.*: *see* **красить**
креветка shrimp; prawn.
кредит credit. **кредитный** credit. **кредитоспособный** solvent.
крейсер (*pl* -а, -ов) cruiser.
крем cream.
крематорий crematorium.
кремень (-мня) *m* flint.
кремль (-я) *m* citadel; Kremlin.
кремний silicon.
кремовый cream.
крен list, heel; bank. **крениться** *impf* (*pf* **на~**) heel over, list; bank.
крепить (-плю) *impf* strengthen; support; make fast; constipate; **~ся** hold out. **крепк|ий** (-пок, -пка, -о) strong; firm; **~ие напитки** spirits. **крепление** strengthening; fastening.
крепнуть (-ну; -еп) *impf* (*pf* **о~**) get stronger.
крепостничество serfdom.
крепостн|ой serf; **~ое право** serfdom; **~ой** *sb* serf.
крепость fortress; strength.
крепче *comp of* **крепкий, крепко**

кре́сло (*gen pl* -сел) armchair; stall.

крест (-а́) cross. **крести́ны** (-и́н) *pl* christening. **крести́ть** (крещу́, -е́стишь) *impf* & *pf* (*pf also* **о~, пере~**) christen; make sign of the cross over; **~ся** cross o.s.; be christened. **крест-на́крест** *adv* crosswise. **кре́стник, кре́стница** god-child. **крёстн|ый**; **~ая (мать)** godmother; **~ый оте́ц** godfather. **кресто́вый похо́д** crusade. **крестоно́сец** (-сца) crusader.

крестья́нин (*pl* -я́не, -я́н), **крестья́нка** peasant. **крестья́нский** peasant. **крестья́нство** peasantry.

креще́ние christening; Epiphany. **крещён|ый** (-ён, -ена́) baptized; *sb* Christian. **крещу́** *etc.*: *see* **крести́ть**

крива́я *sb* curve. **кривизна́** crookedness; curvature. **криви́ть** (-влю́) *impf* (*pf* **по~, с~**) bend, distort; **~ душо́й** go against one's conscience; **~ся** become crooked or bent; make a wry face. **кривля́ться** *impf* give o.s. airs.

криво́й (крив, -а́, -о) crooked; curved; one-eyed.

кри́зис crisis.

крик cry, shout.

кри́кет cricket.

кри́кнуть (-ну) *pf of* **крича́ть**

кримина́льный criminal.

криста́лл crystal. **кристалли́ческий** crystal.

крите́рий criterion.

кри́тик critic. **кри́тика** criticism; critique. **критикова́ть** *impf* criticize. **крити́ческий** critical.

крича́ть (-чу́) *impf* (*pf* **кри́кнуть**) cry, shout.

кров roof; shelter.

крова́вый bloody.

крова́тка, крова́ть bed.

кровено́сный blood-; circulatory.

кро́вля (*gen pl* -вель) roof.

кро́вный blood; thoroughbred; vital, intimate.

крово- *in comb* blood. **кровожа́дный** bloodthirsty. **~излия́ние** haemorrhage. **~обраще́ние** circulation. **~проли́тие** bloodshed. **~проли́тный** bloody. **~смеше́ние** incest. **~тече́ние** bleeding; haemorrhage. **~точи́ть** (-чи́т) *impf* bleed.

кровь (*loc* -и́) blood. **кровяно́й** blood.

крои́ть (крою́) *impf* (*pf* **с~**) cut (out). **кро́йка** cutting out.

крокоди́л crocodile.

кро́лик rabbit.

кроль *m* crawl(-stroke).

крольчи́ха she-rabbit, doe.

кро́ме *prep+gen* except; besides; **~ того́** besides, moreover.

кро́мка edge.

кро́на crown; top.

кронште́йн bracket; corbel.

кропотли́вый. painstaking; laborious.

кросс cross-country race.

кроссво́рд crossword (puzzle).

крот (-а́) mole.

кро́ткий (-ток, -тка́, -тко) meek, gentle. **кро́тость** gentleness; mildness.

кро́хотный, кро́шечный tiny. **кро́шка** crumb; a bit.

круг (*loc* -у́, *pl* -и́) circle; circuit; sphere. **круглосу́точный** round-the-clock. **кру́глый** (кругл, -а́, -о) round; complete; **~ год** all the year round. **кругово́й** circular;

all-round. **кругозо́р** prospect; outlook. **круго́м** *adv* around; *prep+gen* round. **кругосве́тный** round-the-world.

кружевно́й lace; lacy. **кру́жево** (*pl* -а́, -ев, -а́м) lace.

кружи́ть (-ужу́, -у́жи́шь) *impf* whirl, spin round; **~ся** whirl, spin round.

кру́жка mug.

кружо́к (-жка́) circle, group.

круи́з cruise.

крупа́ (*pl* -ы) groats; sleet. **крупи́ца** grain.

кру́пный large, big; great; coarse; **~ый план** close-up.

крутизна́ steepness.

крути́ть (-учу́, -у́тишь) *impf* (*pf* **за~, с~**) twist, twirl; roll; turn, wind; **~ся** turn, spin; whirl.

круто́й (крут, -а́, -о) steep; sudden; sharp; severe; drastic. **кру́ча** steep slope. **кру́че** *comp of* **круто́й, кру́то**

кручу́ *etc.*: *see* **крути́ть**

круше́ние crash; ruin; collapse.

крыжо́вник gooseberries; gooseberry bush.

крыла́тый winged. **крыло́** (*pl* -лья, -льев) wing; vane; mudguard.

крыльцо́ (*pl* -а, -ле́ц, -ца́м) porch; (front, back) steps.

Кры́м the Crimea. **кры́мский** Crimean.

кры́са rat.

крыть (кро́ю) *impf* cover; roof; trump; **~ся** be, lie; be concealed. **кры́ша** roof. **кры́шка** lid.

крюк (-а́; *pl* -ки́, -ко́в *or* -ю́чья, -чьев) hook; detour. **крючо́к** (-чка́) hook.

кря́ду *adv* in succession.

кряж ridge.

кря́кать *impf*, **кря́кнуть** (-ну) *pf* quack.

кряхте́ть (-хчу́) *impf* groan.

кста́ти *adv* to the point; opportunely; at the same time; by the way.

кто (кого́, кому́, кем, ком) *pron* who; anyone; **~ (бы) ни** whoever. **кто́-либо, кто́-нибудь** *prons* anyone; someone. **кто́-то** *pron* someone.

куб (*pl* -ы́) cube; boiler; **в ~е** cubed.

ку́бик brick, block.

куби́нский Cuban.

куби́ческий cubic; cube.

ку́бок (-бка) goblet; cup.

кубоме́тр cubic metre.

кувши́н jug; pitcher. **кувши́нка** water-lily.

кувырка́ться *impf*, **кувыркну́ться** (-ну́сь) *pf* turn somersaults. **кувырко́м** *adv* head over heels; topsy-turvy.

куда́ *adv* where (to); what for; *+comp* much, far; **~ (бы) ни** wherever. **куда́-либо, куда́-нибудь** *adv* anywhere, somewhere. **куда́-то** *adv* somewhere.

ку́дри (-е́й) *pl* curls. **кудря́вый** curly; florid.

кузне́ц (-а́) blacksmith. **кузне́чик** grasshopper. **ку́зница** forge, smithy.

ку́зов (*pl* -а́) basket; body.

ку́кла doll; puppet. **ку́колка** dolly; chrysalis. **ку́кольный** doll's; puppet.

кукуру́за maize.

куку́шка cuckoo.

кула́к (-а́) fist; kulak. **кула́цкий** kulak. **кула́чный** fist.

кулёк (-лька́) bag.

кули́к (-а́) sandpiper.

кулина́рия cookery. **кулина́рный** culinary.

кули́сы (-и́с) wings; **за кули́сами** behind the scenes.

кули́ч (-á) Easter cake.
кулуа́ры (-ов) *pl* lobby.
кульмина́ция culmination.
культ cult. **культиви́ровать** *impf* cultivate.
культу́ра culture; standard; cultivation. **культури́зм** body-building. **культу́рно** *adv* in a civilized manner. **культу́рный** cultured; cultivated; cultural.
куми́р idol.
кумы́с koumiss (*fermented mare's milk*).
куни́ца marten.
купа́льный bathing. **купа́льня** bathing-place. **купа́ть** *impf* (*pf* **вы**~, **ис**~) bathe; bath; ~**ся** bathe; take a bath.
купе́ *neut indecl* compartment.
купе́ц (-пцá) merchant. **купе́ческий** merchant. **купи́ть** (-плю́, -пишь) *pf* (*impf* **покупа́ть**) buy.
ку́пол (*pl* -á) cupola, dome.
купо́н coupon.
купчи́ха merchant's wife; female merchant.
кура́нты (-ов) *pl* chiming clock; chimes.
курга́н barrow; tumulus.
куре́ние smoking. **кури́льщик, -щица** smoker.
кури́ный hen's; chicken's.
кури́ть (-рю́, -ришь) *impf* (*pf* **по**~) smoke; ~**ся** burn; smoke.
ку́рица (*pl* ку́ры, кур) hen, chicken.
куро́к (-ркá) cocking-piece; **взвести́** ~ cock a gun; **спусти́ть** ~ pull the trigger.
куропа́тка partridge.
куро́рт health-resort; spa.
курс course; policy; year; exchange rate. **курса́нт** student.
курси́в italics.
курси́ровать *impf* ply.
курсо́р (*comput*) cursor.
ку́ртка jacket.
курча́вый curly(-headed).
ку́ры *etc.*: *see* **ку́рица**
курьёз a funny thing. **курьёзный** curious.
курье́р messenger; courier. **курье́рский** express.
куря́тник hen-house.
куря́щий *sb* smoker.
куса́ть *impf* bite; sting; ~**ся** bite.
кусо́к (-скá) piece; lump. **кусо́чек** (-чка) piece.
куст (-á) bush, shrub. **куста́рник** bush(es), shrub(s).
куста́рн|ый hand-made; handicrafts; primitive; ~**ая промы́шленность** cottage industry.
куста́рь (-я́) *m* craftsman.
ку́тать *impf* (*pf* **за**~) wrap up; ~**ся** muffle o.s. up.
кути́ть (кучу́, ку́тишь) *impf*, **кутну́ть** (-ну́, -нёшь) *pf* carouse; go on a binge.
куха́рка cook. **ку́хня** (*gen pl* -хонь) kitchen; cuisine. **ку́хонный** kitchen.
ку́ча heap; heaps.
ку́чер (*pl* -á) coachman.
ку́чка small heap *or* group.
кучу́ *see* **кути́ть**
куша́к (-á) sash; girdle.
ку́шанье food; dish. **ку́шать** *impf* (*pf* **по**~, **с**~) eat.
куше́тка couch.
кую́ *etc.*: *see* **кова́ть**

Л

лабора́нт, -а́нтка laboratory assistant. **лаборато́рия** laboratory.
ла́ва lava.
лави́на avalanche.
ла́вка bench; shop. **ла́вочка**

small shop.
лавр bay tree, laurel.
лáгерный camp. **лáгерь** (*pl* -я́ *or* -и, -éй *or* -ей) *m* camp; campsite.
лад (*loc* -ý; *pl* -ы́, -óв) harmony; manner, way; stop, fret.
лáдан incense.
лáдить (лáжу) *impf* get on, be on good terms. **лáдно** *adv* all right; very well! **лáдный** fine, excellent; harmonious.
ладóнь palm.
ладья́ rook, castle; boat.
лáжу *etc.*: *see* **лáдить, лáзить**
лазарéт field hospital; sick-bay.
лáзать *see* **лáзить. лазéйка** hole; loop-hole.
лáзер laser.
лáзить (лáжу), **лáзать** *impf* climb, clamber.
лазýрный sky-blue, azure.
лазýрь azure.
лазýтчик scout; spy.
лай bark, barking. **лáйка**[1] (Siberian) husky, laika.
лáйка[2] kid. **лáйковый** kid; kidskin.
лáйнер liner; airliner.
лак varnish, lacquer.
лакáть *impf* (*pf* **вы~**) lap.
лакéй footman, man-servant; lackey.
лакировáть *impf* (*pf* **от~**) varnish; lacquer.
лáкмус litmus.
лáковый varnished, lacquered.
лáкомиться (-млюсь) *impf* (*pf* **по~**) +*instr* treat o.s. to. **лáкомка** *m* & *f* gourmand. **лáкомство** delicacy. **лáкомый** dainty, tasty; +**до** fond of.
лакони́чный laconic.
лáмпа lamp; valve, tube. **лампáда** icon-lamp. **лáмпочка** lamp; bulb.
ландшáфт landscape.
лáндыш lily of the valley.
лань fallow deer; doe.
лáпа paw; tenon.
лáпоть (-птя; *pl* -и, -éй) *m* bast shoe.
лáпочка pet, sweetie.
лапшá noodles; noodle soup.
ларёк (-рькá) stall. **ларь** (-я́) *m* chest; bin.
лáска[1] caress.
лáска[2] weasel.
ласкáть *impf* caress, fondle; **~ся** +**к**+*dat* make up to; fawn upon. **лáсковый** affectionate, tender.
лáсточка swallow.
латви́ец (-и́йца), **-и́йка** Latvian. **латви́йский** Latvian.
Лáтвия Latvia.
лати́нский Latin.
латýнь brass.
лáты (лат) *pl* armour.
латы́нь Latin.
латы́ш, латы́шка Latvian, Lett. **латы́шский** Latvian, Lettish.
лауреáт prize-winner.
лáцкан lapel.
лачýга hovel, shack.
лáять (лáю) *impf* bark.
лба *etc.*: *see* **лоб**
лгать (лгу, лжёшь; лгал, -á, -о) *impf* (*pf* **на~, со~**) lie; tell lies; +**на**+*acc* slander. **лгун** (-á), **лгýнья** liar.
лебеди́ный swan. **лебёдка** swan, pen; winch. **лéбедь** (*pl* -и, -éй) *m* swan, cob.
лев (льва) lion.
левобережный left-bank.
левшá (*gen pl* -éй) *m* & *f* left-hander. **лéвый** *adj* left; left-hand; left-wing.
лёг *etc.*: *see* **лечь**
легáльный legal.

леге́нда legend. **легенда́рный** legendary.

лёгк|ий (-гок, -гка́, лёгки́) light; easy; slight, mild; **~ая атле́тика** field and track events. **легко́** *adv* easily, lightly, slightly.

легко- *in comb* light; easy, easily. **легкове́рный** credulous. **~ве́с** light-weight. **~мы́сленный** thoughtless; flippant, frivolous, superficial. **~мы́слие** flippancy, frivolity.

легков|о́й: ~а́я маши́на (private) car. **лёгкое** *sb* lung. **лёгкость** lightness; easiness. **ле́гче** *comp of* **лёгкий, легко́**

лёд (льда, *loc* -у) ice. **ледене́ть** (-е́ю) *impf* (*pf* **за~, о~**) freeze; grow numb with cold. **ледене́ц** (-нца́) fruit-drop. **леденя́щий** chilling, icy.

ле́ди *f indecl* lady.

ле́дник[1] ice-box; refrigerator van. **ледни́к**[2] (-а́) glacier. **леднико́вый** glacial; **~ пери́од** Ice Age. **ледо́вый** ice. **ледоко́л** ice-breaker. **ледяно́й** ice; icy.

лежа́ть (-жу́) *impf* lie; be, be situated. **лежа́чий** lying (down).

ле́звие (cutting) edge; razorblade.

лезть (-зу; лез) *impf* (*pf* **по~**) climb; clamber, crawl; get, go; fall out.

лейбори́ст Labourite.

ле́йка watering-can.

лейтена́нт lieutenant.

лека́рство medicine.

ле́ксика vocabulary. **лексико́н** lexicon; vocabulary.

ле́ктор lecturer. **ле́кция** lecture.

леле́ять (-е́ю) *impf* (*pf* **вз~**) cherish, foster.

лён (льна) flax.

лени́вый lazy.

ленингра́дский (of) Leningrad. **ле́нинский** (of) Lenin; Leninist.

лени́ться (-ню́сь, -нишься) *impf* (*pf* **по~**) be lazy; *+inf* be too lazy to.

ле́нта ribbon; band; tape.

лентя́й, -я́йка lazy-bones. **лень** laziness.

лепесто́к (-тка́) petal.

ле́пет babble; prattle. **лепета́ть** (-ечу́, -е́чешь) *impf* (*pf* **про~**) babble, prattle.

лепёшка scone; tablet, pastille.

лепи́ть (-плю́, -пишь) *impf* (*pf* **вы́~, за~, с~**) model, fashion; mould; **~ся** cling; crawl. **ле́пка** modelling. **лепно́й** modelled, moulded.

лес (*loc* -у́; *pl* -а́) forest, wood; *pl* scaffolding.

ле́са́ (*pl* ле́сы) fishing-line.

лесни́к (-а́) forester. **лесни́чий** *sb* forestry officer; forest warden. **лесно́й** forest.

лесо- *in comb* forest, forestry; timber wood. **лесово́дство** forestry. **~загото́вка** logging. **~пи́лка, ~пи́льня** (*gen pl* -лен) sawmill. **~ру́б** woodcutter.

ле́стница stairs, staircase; ladder.

ле́стный flattering. **лесть** flattery.

лёт (*loc* -у́) flight, flying.

лета́ (лет) *pl* years; age; **ско́лько вам лет?** how old are you?

лета́тельный flying. **лета́ть** *impf*, **лете́ть** (лечу́) *impf* (*pf* **полете́ть**) fly; rush; fall.

ле́тний summer.

лётный flying, flight.
лéто (*pl* -á) summer; *pl* years. **лéтом** *adv* in summer.
лéтопись chronicle.
летосчислéние chronology.
летýч|ий flying; passing; brief; volatile; **~ая мышь** bat.
лётчик, -чица pilot.
лечéбница clinic. **лечéбный** medical; medicinal. **лечéние** (medical) treatment. **лечи́ть** (-чý, -чишь) *impf* treat (**от** for); **~ся** be given, have treatment (**от** for).
лечý *etc.*: *see* **летéть, лечи́ть**
лечь (ля́гу, ля́жешь; лёг, -лá) *pf* (*impf* **ложи́ться**) lie, lie down; go to bed.
лещ (-á) bream.
лжесвидéтельство false witness.
лжец (-á) liar. **лжи́вый** lying; deceitful.
ли, ль *interrog partl & conj* whether, if; **ли,... ли** whether ... or; **рáно ли, пóздно ли** sooner or later.
либерáл liberal. **либерáльный** liberal.
ли́бо *conj* or; **~... ~** either ... or.
ли́вень (-вня) *m* heavy shower, downpour.
ливрéя livery.
ли́га league.
ли́дер leader. **лиди́ровать** *impf & pf* be in the lead.
лизáть (лижý, -ешь) *impf*, **лизнýть** (-нý, -нёшь) *pf* lick.
ликвидáция liquidation; abolition. **ликвиди́ровать** *impf & pf* liquidate; abolish.
ликёр liqueur.
ликовáние rejoicing. **ликовáть** *impf* rejoice.
ли́лия lily.
лилóвый lilac, violet.
лимáн estuary.
лими́т limit.
лимóн lemon. **лимонáд** lemonade; squash. **лимóнный** lemon.
ли́мфа lymph.
лингви́ст linguist. **лингви́стика** linguistics. **лингвисти́ческий** linguistic.
линéйка ruler; line. **линéйный** linear; **~ корáбль** battleship.
ли́нза lens.
ли́ния line.
линóлеум lino(leum).
линя́ть *impf* (*pf* **вы́~, по~, с~**) fade; moult.
ли́па lime tree.
ли́пкий (-пок, -пкá, -о) sticky. **ли́пнуть** (-ну; лип) *impf* stick.
ли́повый lime.
ли́ра lyre. **ли́рик** lyric poet. **ли́рика** lyric poetry. **лири́ческий** lyric; lyrical.
лисá (*pl* -ы), **-си́ца** fox.
лист (-á; *pl* -ы́ *or* -ья, -óв *or* -ьев) leaf; sheet; page; form; **игрáть с ~á** play at sight. **листáть** *impf* leaf through. **листвá** foliage. **ли́ственница** larch **ли́ственный** deciduous. **листóвка** leaflet. **листовóй** sheet, plate; leaf. **листóк** (-ткá) *dim of* **лист**; leaflet; form, pro-forma.
Литвá Lithuania.
литéйный founding, casting.
литерáтор man of letters. **литератýра** literature. **литератýрный** literary.
литóвец (-вца), **литóвка** Lithuanian. **литóвский** Lithuanian.
литóй cast.
литр litre.
лить (лью, льёшь; лил, -á, -о) *impf* (*pf* **с~**) pour; shed; cast,

mould. **литьё** founding, casting, moulding; castings, mouldings. **ли́ться** (льётся; ли́лся, -áсь, ли́лóсь) *impf* flow; pour.
лиф bodice. **ли́фчик** bra.
лифт lift.
лихóй[1] (лих, -á, -о) dashing, spirited.
лихóй[2] (лих, -á, -о, ли́хи́) evil.
лихорáдка fever. **лихорáдочный** feverish.
лицевóй facial; exterior; front.
лицемéр hypocrite. **лицемéрие** hypocrisy. **лицемéрный** hypocritical.
лицó (*pl* -а) face; exterior; right side; person; **быть к лицý** *+dat* suit, befit. **личи́нка** larva, grub; maggot. **ли́чно** *adv* personally, in person. **ли́чность** personality; person. **ли́чный** personal; private; ~ **состáв** staff, personnel.
лишáй lichen; herpes; shingles. **лишáйник** lichen.
лишáть(ся *impf of* **лиши́ть(ся**
лишéние deprivation; privation. **лишённый** (-ён, -енá) *+gen* lacking in, devoid of. **лиши́ть** (-шý) *pf* (*impf* **лишáть**) *+gen* deprive of; **~ся** *+gen* lose, be deprived of. **ли́шн|ий** superfluous; unnecessary; spare; ~ **раз** once more; **с ~им** odd, and more.
лишь *adv* only; *conj* as soon as; ~ **бы** if only, provided that.
лоб (лба, *loc* лбу) forehead.
лóбзик fret-saw.
лови́ть (-влю́, -вишь) *impf* (*pf* **поймáть**) catch, try to catch.
лóвкий (-вок, -вкá, -о) adroit; cunning. **лóвкость** adroitness; cunning.
лóвля (*gen pl* -вель) catching, hunting; fishing-ground. **ловýшка** trap.
лóвче *comp of* **лóвкий**
логари́фм logarithm.
лóгика logic. **логи́ческий, логи́чный** logical.
лóговище, лóгово den, lair.
лóдка boat.
лóдырничать *impf* loaf, idle about. **лóдырь** *m* loafer, idler.
лóжа box; (masonic) lodge.
ложби́на hollow.
лóже couch; bed.
ложи́ться (-жýсь) *impf of* **лечь**
лóжка spoon.
лóжный false. **ложь** (лжи) lie, falsehood.
лозá (*pl* -ы) vine.
лóзунг slogan, catchword.
локáтор radar *or* sonar apparatus.
локомоти́в locomotive.
лóкон lock, curl.
лóкоть (-ктя; *pl* -и, -éй) *m* elbow.
лом (*pl* -ы, -óв) crowbar; scrap, waste. **лóманый** broken. **ломáть** *impf* (*pf* **по~, с~**) break; cause to ache; **~ся** break; crack; put on airs; be obstinate.
ломбáрд pawnshop.
лóмберный стол card-table.
ломи́ть (лóмит) *impf* break; break through, rush; *impers* cause to ache; **~ся** be (near to) breaking. **лóмка** breaking; *pl* quarry. **лóмкий** (-мок, -мкá, -о) fragile, brittle.
ломóть (-мтя́; *pl* -мти́) *m* large slice; hunk; chunk. **лóмтик** slice.
лóно bosom, lap.
лóпасть (*pl* -и, -éй) blade; fan, vane; paddle.
лопáта spade; shovel. **лопáтка** shoulder-blade; shovel; trowel.

ло́паться *impf*, **ло́пнуть** (-ну) *pf* burst; split; break; fail; crash.

лопу́х (-á) burdock.

лорд lord.

лоси́на elk-skin, chamois leather; elk-meat.

лоск lustre, shine.

лоску́т (-á; *pl* -ы́ *or* -ья, -о́в *or* -ьев) rag, shred, scrap.

лосни́ться *impf* be glossy, shine.

ло́со́сь *m* salmon.

лось (*pl* -и, -е́й) *m* elk.

лосьо́н lotion; aftershave; cream.

лот lead, plummet.

лотере́я lottery, raffle.

лото́к (-тка́) hawker's stand *or* tray; chute; gutter; trough.

лохма́тый shaggy; dishevelled.

лохмо́тья (-ьев) *pl* rags.

ло́цман pilot.

лошади́ный horse; equine. **ло́шадь** (*pl* -и, -е́й, *instr* -дьми́ *or* -дя́ми) horse.

лощёный glossy, polished.

лощи́на hollow, depression.

лоя́льный fair, honest; loyal.

лубо́к (-бка́) splint; popular print.

луг (*loc* -у́; *pl* -á) meadow.

лу́жа puddle.

лужа́йка lawn, glade.

лужёный tin-plated.

лук[1] onions.

лук[2] bow.

лука́вить (-влю) *impf* (*pf* с~) be cunning. **лука́вство** craftiness. **лука́вый** crafty, cunning.

лу́ковица onion; bulb

луна́ (*pl* -ы) moon. **луна́тик** sleep-walker.

лу́нка hole; socket.

лу́нный moon; lunar.

лу́па magnifying-glass.

лупи́ть (-плю́, -пишь) *impf* (*pf* от~) flog.

луч (-á) ray; beam. **лучево́й** ray, beam; radial; radiation. **лучеза́рный** radiant.

лучи́на splinter.

лу́чше better; ~ **всего́**, ~ **всех** best of all. **лу́чш|ий** better; best; **в ~ем слу́чае** at best; **всего́ ~его!** all the best!

лы́жа ski. **лы́жник** skier. **лы́жный спорт** skiing. **лыжня́** ski-track.

лы́ко bast.

лысе́ть (-е́ю) *impf* (*pf* **об~, по~**) grow bald. **лы́сина** bald spot; blaze. **лы́сый** (лыс, -á, -о) bald.

ль *see* **ли**

льва *etc.*: *see* **лев. льви́ный** lion, lion's. **льви́ца** lioness.

льго́та privilege; advantage. **льго́тный** privileged; favourable.

льда *etc.*: *see* **лёд. льди́на** block of ice; ice-floe.

льна *etc.*: *see* **лён. льново́дство** flax-growing.

льнуть (-ну, -нёшь) *impf* (*pf* **при~**) +**к**+*dat* cling to; have a weakness for; make up to.

льняно́й flax, flaxen; linen; linseed.

льсте́ц (-á) flatterer. **льсти́вый** flattering; smooth-tongued. **льстить** (льщу) *impf* (*pf* **по~**) +*dat* flatter.

лью *etc.*: *see* **лить**

любе́зность courtesy; kindness; compliment. **любе́зн|ый** courteous; obliging; kind; **бу́дьте ~ы** be so kind (as to).

люби́мец (-мца), **-мица** pet, favourite. **люби́мый** beloved; favourite. **люби́тель** *m*, **-ница** lover; amateur. **люби́тельский** amateur. **люби́ть** (-блю́, -бишь) *impf* love; like.

любова́ться *impf* (*pf* **по~**) *+instr or* **на***+acc* admire.

любо́вник lover. **любо́вница** mistress. **любо́вный** love-; loving. **любо́вь** (-бви́, *instr* -бо́вью) love.

любозна́тельный inquisitive.

любо́й any; either; *sb* anyone.

любопы́тный curious; inquisitive. **любопы́тство** curiosity.

лю́бящий loving.

лю́ди (-е́й, -ям, -дьми́, -ях) *pl* people. **лю́дный** populous; crowded. **людое́д** cannibal; ogre. **людско́й** human.

люк hatch(way); trap; manhole.

лю́лька cradle.

люминесце́нтный luminescent. **люминесце́нция** luminescence.

лю́стра chandelier.

лю́тня (*gen pl* -тен) lute.

лю́тый (лют, -á, -о) ferocious.

ляга́ть *impf*, **лягну́ть** (-ну́, -нёшь) *pf* kick; **~ся** kick.

ля́гу *etc.*: *see* **лечь**

лягу́шка frog.

ля́жка thigh, haunch.

ля́згать *impf* clank; *+instr* rattle.

ля́мка strap; **тяну́ть ля́мку** toil.

М

мавзоле́й mausoleum.

мавр, маврита́нка Moor. **маврита́нский** Moorish.

магази́н shop.

маги́стр (holder of) master's degree.

магистра́ль main; main line, main road.

маги́ческий magic(al). **ма́гия** magic.

магнети́зм magnetism.

ма́гний magnesium.

магни́т magnet. **магни́тный** magnetic. **магнитофо́н** tape-recorder.

мада́м *f indecl* madam, madame.

мажо́р major (key); cheerful mood. **мажо́рный** major; cheerful.

ма́зать (ма́жу) *impf* (*pf* **вы́~, за~, из~, на~, по~, про~**) oil, grease; smear, spread; soil; **~ся** get dirty; make up. **мазо́к** (-зка́) touch, dab; smear. **мазу́т** fuel oil. **мазь** ointment; grease.

маи́с maize.

май May. **ма́йский** May.

ма́йка T-shirt.

майо́р major.

мак poppy, poppy-seeds.

макаро́ны (-н) *pl* macaroni.

мака́ть *impf* (*pf* **макну́ть**) dip.

маке́т model; dummy.

макну́ть (-ну́, -нёшь) *pf of* **мака́ть**

макре́ль mackerel.

максима́льный maximum.

ма́ксимум maximum; at most.

макулату́ра waste paper; pulp literature.

маку́шка top; crown.

мал *etc.*: *see* **ма́лый**

малахи́т malachite.

мале́йший least, slightest. **ма́ленький** little; small.

мали́на (*no pl*; *usu collect*) raspberry; raspberries; raspberry-bush. **мали́новый** raspberry.

ма́ло *adv* little, few; not enough; **~ того́** moreover; **~ того́ что...** not only ....

мало- *in comb* (too) little. **малова́жный** of little importance. **~вероя́тный** unlikely. **~гра́мотный** semi-literate;

crude. **~ду́шный** faint-hearted. **~иму́щий** needy. **~кро́вие** anaemia. **~ле́тний** young; juvenile; minor. **~о́пытный** inexperienced. **~чи́сленный** small (in number), few.

мало-ма́льски *adv* in the slightest degree; at all. **малопома́лу** *adv* little by little.

ма́л|ый (мал, -á) little, (too) small; **са́мое ~ое** at the least; *sb* fellow; lad. **малы́ш** (-á) kiddy; little boy. **ма́льчик** boy. **мальчи́шка** *m* urchin, boy. **мальчуга́н** little boy. **малю́тка** *m* & *f* baby.

маля́р (-á) painter, decorator.

маляри́я malaria.

ма́ма mother, mummy. **ма́маша** mummy. **ма́мин** mother's.

ма́монт mammoth.

мандари́н mandarin, tangerine.

манда́т warrant; mandate.

манёвр manoeuvre; shunting. **маневри́ровать** *impf* (*pf* **с~**) manoeuvre; shunt; *+instr* make good use of.

мане́ж riding-school.

манеке́н dummy; mannequin. **манеке́нщик, -щица** model.

мане́ра manner; style. **мане́рный** affected.

манже́та cuff.

маникю́р manicure.

манипули́ровать *impf* manipulate. **манипуля́ция** manipulation; machination.

мани́ть (-ню́, -нишь) *impf* (*pf* **по~**) beckon; attract; lure.

манифе́ст manifesto. **манифеста́ция** demonstration.

мани́шка (false) shirt-front.

ма́ния mania; **~ величи́я** megalomania.

ма́нная ка́ша semolina.

мано́метр pressure-gauge.

ма́нтия cloak; robe, gown.

мануфакту́ра manufacture; textiles.

манья́к maniac.

марафо́нский бег marathon.

ма́рганец (-нца) manganese.

маргари́н margarine.

маргари́тка daisy.

марино́ванный pickled. **маринова́ть** *impf* (*pf* **за~**) pickle; put off.

марионе́тка puppet.

ма́рка stamp; counter; brand; trade-mark; grade; reputation.

ма́ркетинг marketing.

ма́ркий easily soiled.

маркси́зм Marxism. **маркси́ст** Marxist. **маркси́стский** Marxist.

ма́рлевый gauze. **ма́рля** gauze; cheesecloth.

мармела́д fruit jellies.

ма́рочный high-quality.

Марс Mars.

март March. **ма́ртовский** March.

марты́шка marmoset; monkey.

марш march.

ма́ршал marshal.

маршировáть *impf* march.

маршру́т route, itinerary.

ма́ска mask. **маскара́д** masked ball; masquerade. **маскирова́ть** *impf* (*pf* **за~**) disguise; camouflage. **маскиро́вка** disguise; camouflage.

Ма́сленица Shrovetide. **маслёнка** butter-dish; oil-can. **масли́на** olive. **ма́сло** (*pl* -á, ма́сел, -сла́м) butter; oil; oil paints. **маслобо́йка** churn. **маслобо́йня** (*gen pl* -óен), **маслозаво́д** dairy. **масляни́стый** oily. **ма́сляный** oil.

ма́сса mass; a lot, lots.

масса́ж massage. **массирова́ть** *impf* & *pf* massage.

масси́в massif; expanse, tract. **масси́вный** massive.

ма́ссовый mass.

ма́стер (*pl* -а́), **мастери́ца** foreman, forewoman; (master) craftsman; expert. **мастери́ть** *impf* (*pf* с~) make, build. **мастерска́я** *sb* workshop. **мастерско́й** masterly. **мастерство́** craft; skill.

масти́ка mastic; putty; floor-polish.

масти́тый venerable.

масть (*pl* -и, -е́й) colour; suit.

масшта́б scale.

мат[1] checkmate.

мат[2] mat.

мат[3] foul language.

матема́тик mathematician. **матема́тика** mathematics. **математи́ческий** mathematical.

материа́л material. **материали́зм** materialism. **материалисти́ческий** materialist. **материа́льный** material.

матери́к (-а́) continent; mainland. **материко́вый** continental.

матери́нский maternal, motherly. **матери́нство** maternity.

мате́рия material; pus; topic.

ма́тка womb; female.

ма́товый matt; frosted.

матра́с, матра́ц mattress.

матрёшка Russian doll.

ма́трица matrix; die, mould.

матро́с sailor, seaman.

матч match.

мать (ма́тери, *instr* -рью; *pl* -тери, -ре́й) mother.

ма́фия Mafia.

мах swing, stroke. **маха́ть** (машу́, ма́шешь) *impf*, **махну́ть** (-ну́, -нёшь) *pf* +*instr* wave; brandish; wag; flap; go; rush.

махина́ция machinations.

махови́к (-а́) fly-wheel.

махро́вый dyed-in-the-wool; terry.

ма́чеха stepmother.

ма́чта mast.

маши́на machine; car. **машина́льный** mechanical. **машини́ст** operator; engine-driver; scene-shifter. **машини́стка** typist; ~-**стенографи́стка** shorthand-typist. **маши́нка** machine; typewriter; sewing-machine. **машинопи́сный** typewritten. **маши́нопись** typing; typescript. **машинострое́ние** mechanical engineering.

мая́к (-а́) lighthouse; beacon.

ма́ятник pendulum. **ма́яться** *impf* toil; suffer; languish.

мгла haze; gloom.

мгнове́ние instant, moment. **мгнове́нный** instantaneous, momentary.

ме́бель furniture. **меблиро́ванный** furnished. **меблиро́вка** furnishing; furniture.

мегава́тт (*gen pl* -а́тт) megawatt. **мего́м** megohm. **мегато́нна** megaton.

мёд (*loc* -у́; *pl* -ы́) honey.

меда́ль medal. **медальо́н** medallion.

медве́дица she-bear. **медве́дь** *m* bear. **медве́жий** bear('s). **медвежо́нок** (-нка; *pl* -жа́та, -жа́т) bear cub.

ме́дик medical student; doctor. **медикаме́нты** (-ов) *pl* medicines.

медици́на medicine. **медици́нский** medical.

ме́дленный slow. **медли́тельный** sluggish; slow. **ме́длить** *impf* linger; be slow.

ме́дный copper; brass.

медо́вый honey; ~ **ме́сяц** honeymoon.
медосмо́тр medical examination, check-up. **медпу́нкт** first aid post. **медсестра́** (*pl* -сёстры, -сестёр, -сёстрам) nurse.
меду́за jellyfish.
медь copper.
меж *prep+instr* between.
меж- *in comb* inter-.
межа́ (*pl* -и, меж, -а́м) boundary.
междоме́тие interjection.
ме́жду *prep+instr* between; among; ~ **про́чим** incidentally, by the way; ~ **тем** meanwhile; ~ **тем, как** while.
между- *in comb* inter-. **междугоро́дный** inter-city. **~наро́дный** international.
межконтинента́льный intercontinental. **межплане́тный** interplanetary.
мезони́н attic (storey); mezzanine (floor).
Ме́ксика Mexico.
мел (*loc* -у́) chalk.
мёл *etc.*: *see* **мести́**
меланхо́лия melancholy.
меле́ть (-е́ет) *impf* (*pf* **об~**) grow shallow.
мелиора́ция land improvement.
ме́лкий (-лок, -лка́, -о) small; shallow; fine; petty. **ме́лко** *adv* fine, small. **мелкобуржуа́зный** petty bourgeois. **мелково́дный** shallow.
мелоди́чный melodious, melodic. **мело́дия** melody.
ме́лочный petty. **ме́лочь** (*pl* -и, -е́й) small items; (small) change; *pl* trifles, trivialities.
мель (*loc* -и́) shoal; bank; **на мели́** aground.
мелька́ть *impf*, **мелькну́ть** (-ну́, -нёшь) *pf* be glimpsed fleetingly. **ме́льком** *adv* in passing; fleetingly.
ме́льник miller. **ме́льница** mill.
мельча́йший *superl of* **ме́лкий**. **ме́льче** *comp of* **ме́лкий**, **ме́лко**. **мелюзга́** small fry.
мелю́ *etc.*: *see* **моло́ть**
мембра́на membrane; diaphragm.
мемора́ндум memorandum.
мемуа́ры (-ов) *pl* memoirs.
ме́на exchange, barter.
ме́неджер manager.
ме́нее *adv* less; **тем не** ~ none the less.
мензу́рка measuring-glass.
менково́й exchange; barter.
менуэ́т minuet.
ме́ньше smaller; less. **меньшеви́к** (-а́) Menshevik. **ме́ньший** lesser, smaller; younger. **меньшинство́** minority.
меню́ *neut indecl* menu.
меня́ *see* **я** *pron*
меня́ть *impf* (*pf* **об~**, **по~**) change; exchange; **~ся** change; *+instr* exchange.
ме́ра measure.
мере́щиться (-щусь) *impf* (*pf* **по~**) seem, appear.
мерза́вец (-вца) swine, bastard. **ме́рзкий** (-зок, -зка́, -о) disgusting.
мерзлота́: **ве́чная** ~ permafrost. **мёрзнуть** (-ну; мёрз) *impf* (*pf* **за~**) freeze.
ме́рзость vileness; abomination.
меридиа́н meridian.
мери́ло standard, criterion.
ме́рин gelding.
ме́рить *impf* (*pf* **по~**, **с~**) measure; try on. **ме́рка** measure.
ме́рный measured; rhythmi-

cal. **мероприя́тие** measure.

мертве́ть (-е́ю) *impf* (*pf* **о~, по~**) grow numb; be benumbed. **мертве́ц** (-а́) corpse, dead man. **мёртвый** (мёртв, -а́, мёртво́) dead.

мерца́ть *impf* twinkle; flicker.

меси́ть (мешу́, ме́сишь) *impf* (*pf* **с~**) knead.

ме́сса Mass.

места́ми *adv* here and there.

месте́чко (*pl* -и, -чек) small town.

мести́ (мету́, -тёшь; мёл, -а́) *impf* sweep; whirl.

ме́стность locality; area. **ме́стный** local; locative. **-ме́стный** *in comb* -berth, -seater.

ме́сто (*pl* -а́) place; site; seat; room; job. **местожи́тельство** (place of) residence. **местоиме́ние** pronoun. **местонахожде́ние** location, whereabouts. **месторожде́ние** deposit; layer.

месть vengeance, revenge.

ме́сяц month; moon. **ме́сячный** monthly; *sb pl* period.

мета́лл metal. **металли́ческий** metal, metallic. **металлу́ргия** metallurgy.

мета́н methane.

мета́ние throwing, flinging. **мета́ть**[1] (мечу́, ме́чешь) *impf* (*pf* **метну́ть**) throw, fling; **~ся** rush about; toss (and turn).

мета́ть[2] *impf* (*pf* **на~, с~**) tack.

метафи́зика metaphysics.

мета́фора metaphor.

метёлка panicle.

мете́ль snow-storm.

метео́р meteor. **метеори́т** meteorite. **метеоро́лог** meteorologist. **метеорологи́ческий** meteorological. **метеороло́гия** meteorology.

метеосво́дка weather report.

метеоста́нция weather-station.

ме́тить[1] (ме́чу) *impf* (*pf* **на~, по~**) mark.

ме́тить[2] (ме́чу) *impf* (*pf* **на~**) aim; mean.

ме́тка marking, mark.

ме́ткий (-ток, -тка́, -о) well-aimed, accurate.

метла́ (*pl* мётлы, -тел) broom.

метну́ть (-ну́, -нёшь) *pf of* **мета́ть**[1]

ме́тод method. **мето́дика** method(s); methodology. **методи́чный** methodical. **методо́логия** methodology.

метр metre.

ме́трика birth certificate. **метри́ческ|ий**[1]: **~ое свиде́тельство** birth certificate.

метри́ческий[2] metric; metrical.

метро́ *neut indecl*, **метрополите́н** Metro; underground.

мету́ *etc.*: *see* **мести́**

мех[1] (*loc* -у́; *pl* -а́) fur.

мех[2] (*pl* -и́) wine-skin, water-skin; *pl* bellows.

механиза́ция mechanization.

механи́зм mechanism; gear(ing). **меха́ник** mechanic. **меха́ника** mechanics; trick; knack. **механи́ческий** mechanical; mechanistic.

мехово́й fur.

меч (-а́) sword.

ме́ченый marked.

мече́ть mosque.

мечта́ (day-)dream. **мечта́тельный** dreamy. **мечта́ть** *impf* dream.

ме́чу *etc.*: *see* **ме́тить. мечу́** *etc.*: *see* **мета́ть**

меша́лка mixer.

меша́ть[1] *impf* (*pf* **по~**) +*dat* hinder; prevent; disturb.

меша́ть[2] *impf* (*pf* **по~, с~**)

stir; mix; mix up; **~ся** (в+*acc*) interfere (in), meddle (with).
мешо́к (-шка́) bag; sack. **мешкови́на** sacking, hessian.
мещани́н (*pl* -а́не, -а́н) petty bourgeois; Philistine. **мещა́нский** bourgeois, narrow-minded; Philistine. **меща́нство** petty bourgeoisie; philistinism, narrow-mindedness.
миг moment, instant.
мига́ть *impf*, **мигну́ть** (-ну́, -нёшь) *pf* blink; wink, twinkle.
ми́гом *adv* in a flash.
мигра́ция migration.
мигре́нь migraine. .
мизантро́п misanthrope.
мизи́нец (-нца) little finger; little toe.
микро́б microbe.
микроволно́вая печь microwave oven.
микро́н micron.
микрооргани́зм micro-organism.
микроско́п microscope. **микроскопи́ческий** microscopic.
микросхе́ма microchip.
микрофо́н (*gen pl* -н) microphone.
ми́ксер (*cul*) mixer, blender.
миксту́ра medicine, mixture.
ми́ленький pretty; sweet; dear.
милитари́зм militarism.
милиционе́р militiaman, policeman. **мили́ция** militia, police force.
миллиа́рд billion, a thousand million. **миллиме́тр** millimetre. **миллио́н** million. **миллионе́р** millionaire.
милосе́рдие mercy, charity. **милосе́рдный** merciful, charitable.
ми́лостивый gracious, kind. **ми́лостыня** alms. **ми́лость** favour, grace. **ми́лый** (мил, -а́, -о) nice; kind; sweet; dear.
ми́ля mile.
ми́мика (facial) expression; mimicry.
ми́мо *adv* & *prep* +*gen* by, past. **мимолётный** fleeting. **мимохо́дом** *adv* in passing.
ми́на[1] mine; bomb.
ми́на[2] expression, mien.
минда́ль (-я́) *m* almond(-tree); almonds.
минера́л mineral. **минерало́гия** mineralogy. **минера́льный** mineral.
миниатю́ра miniature. **миниатю́рный** miniature; tiny.
миниди́ск minidisc.
минима́льный minimum.
ми́нимум minimum.
министе́рство ministry. **мини́стр** minister.
минова́ть *impf* & *pf* pass; *impers+dat* escape.
миномёт mortar. **миноно́сец** (-сца) torpedo-boat.
мино́р minor (key).
мину́вш|ий past; **~ее** *sb* the past.
ми́нус minus.
мину́та minute. **мину́тный** minute; momentary.
мину́ть (-нешь; ми́ну́л) *pf* pass.
мир[1] (*pl* -ы́) world.
мир[2] peace.
мира́ж mirage.
мири́ть *impf* (*pf* **по~, при~**) reconcile; **~ся** be reconciled.
ми́рный peace; peaceful.
мировоззре́ние (world-)outlook; philosophy. **мирово́й** world. **мирозда́ние** universe.
миролюби́вый peace-loving.
ми́ска basin, bowl.
мисс *f indecl* Miss.
миссионе́р missionary.
ми́ссис *f indecl* Mrs.

ми́ссия mission.
ми́стер Mr.
ми́стика mysticism.
мистифика́ция hoax.
ми́тинг mass meeting; rally.
митропол́ит metropolitan.
миф myth. **мифи́ческий** mythical. **мифологи́ческий** mythological. **мифоло́гия** mythology.
ми́чман warrant officer.
мише́нь target.
ми́шка (Teddy) bear.
младе́нец (-нца) baby; infant. **мла́дший** younger; youngest; junior.
млекопита́ющие *sb pl* mammals. **Мле́чный Путь** Milky Way.
мне *see* **я** *pron*
мне́ние opinion.
мни́мый imaginary; sham. **мни́тельный** hypochondriac; mistrustful. **мнить** (мню) *impf* think.
мно́гие *sb pl* many (people); **~ое** *sb* much, a great deal. **мно́го** *adv+gen* much; many; **на ~** by far.
много- *in comb* many-, poly-, multi-, multiple-. **многобо́рье** combined event. **~гра́нный** polyhedral; many-sided. **~де́тный** having many children. **~жёнство** polygamy. **~значи́тельный** significant. **~кра́тный** repeated; frequentative. **~ле́тний** lasting, living, many years; of many years' standing; perennial. **~лю́дный** crowded. **~национа́льный** multi-national. **~обеща́ющий** promising. **~обра́зие** diversity. **~сло́вный** verbose. **~сторо́нний** multi-lateral; many-sided, versatile. **~то́чие** dots, omission points. **~уважа́емый** respected; Dear. **~уго́льный** polygonal. **~цве́тный** multi-coloured; multiflorous. **~чи́сленный** numerous. **~эта́жный** many-storeyed. **~язы́чный** polyglot.
мно́жественный plural. **мно́жество** great number. **мно́жить** (-жу) *impf* (*pf* **у~**) multiply; increase.
мной *etc.*: *see* **я** *pron.* **мну** *etc.*: *see* **мять**
мобилиза́ция mobilization. **мобилизова́ть** *impf* & *pf* mobilize.
мог *etc.*: *see* **мочь**
моги́ла grave. **моги́льный** (of the) grave; sepulchral.
могу́ *etc.*: *see* **мочь. могу́чий** mighty. **могу́щественный** powerful. **могу́щество** power, might.
мо́да fashion.
модели́ровать *impf* & *pf* design. **моде́ль** model; pattern. **моделье́р** fashion designer. **моде́льный** model; fashionable.
мо́де́м (*comput*) modem.
модернизи́ровать *impf* & *pf* modernize.
моди́стка milliner.
модифика́ция modification. **модифици́ровать** *impf* & *pf* modify.
мо́дный (-ден, -дна́, -о) fashionable; fashion.
мо́жет *see* **мочь**
можжеве́льник juniper.
мо́жно one may, one can; it is permissible; it is possible; **как ~**+*comp* as ... as possible; **как ~ скоре́е** as soon as possible.
моза́ика mosaic; jigsaw.
мозг (*loc* -у́, *pl* -и́) brain; marrow. **мозгово́й** cerebral.
мозо́ль corn; callus.

мой (моего́) *m*, **моя́** (мое́й) *f*, **моё** (моего́) *neut*, **мои́** (-и́х) *pl pron* my; mine; **по-мо́ему** in my opinion; in my way.

мо́йка washing.

мо́кнуть (-ну; мок) *impf* get wet; soak. **мокро́та** phlegm. **мо́крый** wet, damp.

мол (*loc* -у́) mole, pier.

молва́ rumour, talk.

моле́бен (-бна) church service.

моле́кула molecule. **молекуля́рный** molecular.

моли́тва prayer. **моли́ть** (-лю́, -лишь) *impf* pray; beg; **~ся** (*pf* **по~ся**) pray.

моллю́ск mollusc.

молниено́сный lightning. **мо́лния** lightning; zip(-fastener).

молодёжь youth, young people. **молоде́ть** (-е́ю) *impf* (*pf* **по~**) get younger, look younger. **молоде́ц** (-дца́) fine fellow *or* girl; ~! well done! **молодожёны** (-ов) *pl* newly-weds. **молодо́й** (мо́лод, -а́, -о) young. **мо́лодость** youth. **моло́же** *comp of* **молодо́й**

молоко́ milk.

мо́лот hammer. **молоти́ть** (-очу́, -о́тишь) *impf* (*pf* **с~**) thresh; hammer. **молото́к** (-тка́) hammer. **мо́лотый** ground. **моло́ть** (мелю́, ме́лешь) *impf* (*pf* **с~**) grind, mill.

моло́чная *sb* dairy. **моло́чный** milk; dairy; milky.

мо́лча *adv* silently, in silence. **молчали́вый** silent, taciturn; tacit. **молча́ние** silence. **молча́ть** (-чу́) *impf* be *or* keep silent.

моль moth.

мольба́ entreaty.

мольбе́рт easel.

моме́нт moment; feature. **момента́льно** *adv* instantly. **момента́льный** instantaneous.

мона́рх monarch. **монархи́ст** monarchist.

монасты́рь (-я́) *m* monastery; convent. **мона́х** monk. **мона́хиня** nun.

монго́л, ~ка Mongol.

моне́та coin.

моногра́фия monograph.

моноли́тный monolithic.

моноло́г monologue.

монопо́лия monopoly.

моното́нный monotonous.

монта́ж (-а́) assembling, mounting; editing. **монта́жник** rigger, fitter. **монтёр** fitter, mechanic. **монтировать** *impf* (*pf* **с~**) mount; install, fit; edit.

монуме́нт monument. **монумента́льный** monumental.

мора́ль moral; morals, ethics. **мора́льный** moral; ethical.

морг morgue.

морга́ть *impf*, **моргну́ть** (-ну́, -нёшь) *pf* blink; wink.

мо́рда snout, muzzle; (ugly) mug.

мо́ре (*pl* -я́, -е́й) sea.

морепла́вание navigation. **морепла́ватель** *m* seafarer. **морехо́дный** nautical.

морж (-а́), **моржи́ха** walrus.

Мо́рзе *indecl* Morse; **а́збука ~** Morse code.

мори́ть *impf* (*pf* **у~**) exhaust; **~ го́лодом** starve.

морко́вка carrot. **морко́вь** carrots.

моро́женое *sb* ice-cream. **моро́женый** frozen, chilled. **моро́з** frost; *pl* intensely cold weather. **морози́лка** freezer compartment; freezer. **морози́льник** deep-freeze.

моро́зить (-о́жу) freeze. **моро́зный** frosty.
мороси́ть *impf* drizzle.
морск|о́й sea; maritime; marine, nautical; **~а́я сви́нка** guinea-pig; **~о́й флот** navy, fleet.
мо́рфий morphine.
морщи́на wrinkle; crease. **мо́рщить** (-щу) *impf* (*pf* **на~, по~, с~**) wrinkle; pucker; **~ся** knit one's brow; wince; crease, wrinkle.
моря́к (-а́) sailor, seaman.
москви́ч (-а́), **~ка** Muscovite. **моско́вский** (of) Moscow.
мост (мо́ста́, *loc* -у́; *pl* -ы́) bridge. **мо́стик** bridge. **мости́ть** (-ощу́) *impf* (*pf* **вы́~**) pave. **мостки́** (-о́в) *pl* planked footway. **мостова́я** *sb* roadway; pavement. **мостово́й** bridge.
мота́ть[1] *impf* (*pf* **мотну́ть, на~**) wind, reel.
мота́ть[2] *impf* (*pf* **про~**) squander.
мота́ться *impf* dangle; wander; rush about.
моти́в motive; reason; tune; motif. **мотиви́ровать** *impf* & *pf* give reasons for, justify. **мотивиро́вка** reason(s); justification.
мотну́ть (-ну́, -нёшь) *pf of* **мота́ть**
мото- *in comb* motor-, engine-. **мотого́нки** (-нок) *pl* motorcycle races. **~пе́д** moped. **~пехо́та** motorized infantry. **~ро́ллер** (motor-)scooter. **~ци́кл** motor cycle.
мото́к (-тка́) skein, hank.
мото́р motor, engine. **мотори́ст** motor-mechanic. **мото́рный** motor; engine.
моты́га hoe, mattock.
мотылёк (-лька́) butterfly, moth.
мох (мха *or* мо́ха, *loc* мху; *pl* мхи, мхов) moss. **мохна́тый** hairy, shaggy.
моча́ urine.
моча́лка loofah.
мочево́й пузы́рь bladder. **мочи́ть** (-чу́, -чишь) *impf* (*pf* **за~, на~**) wet, moisten; soak; **~ся** (*pf* **по~ся**) urinate.
мо́чка ear lobe.
мочь (могу́, мо́жешь; мог, -ла́) *impf* (*pf* **с~**) be able; **мо́жет (быть)** perhaps.
моше́нник rogue. **моше́нничать** *impf* (*pf* **с~**) cheat, swindle. **моше́ннический** rascally.
мо́шка midge. **мошкара́** (swarm of) midges.
мо́щность power; capacity. **мо́щный** (-щен, -щна́, -о) powerful.
мощу́ *etc.*: *see* **мости́ть**
мощь power.
мо́ю *etc.*: *see* **мыть. мо́ющий** washing; detergent.
мрак darkness, gloom. **мракобе́с** obscurantist.
мра́мор marble. **мра́морный** marble.
мра́чный dark; gloomy.
мсти́тельный vindictive. **мстить** (мщу) *impf* (*pf* **ото~**) take vengeance on; **+за**+*acc* avenge.
мудре́ц (-а́) sage, wise man. **му́дрость** wisdom. **му́дрый** (-др, -а́, -о) wise, sage.
муж (*pl* -жья́ *or* -и́) husband. **мужа́ть** *impf* grow up; mature; **~ся** take courage. **мужеподо́бный** mannish; masculine. **му́жественный** manly, steadfast. **му́жество** courage.

мужи́к (-á) peasant; fellow.
мужско́й masculine; male. **мужчи́на** *m* man.
му́за muse.
музе́й museum.
му́зыка music. **музыка́льный** musical. **музыка́нт** musician.
му́ка[1] torment.
мука́[2] flour.
мультипликá́ция, мульт-фи́льм cartoon film.
му́мия mummy.
мунди́р (full-dress) uniform.
мундшту́к (-á) mouthpiece; cigarette-holder.
муниципа́льный municipal.
мураве́й (-вья́) ant. **мураве́йник** ant-hill.
мурлы́кать (-ы́чу *or* -каю) *impf* purr.
муска́т nutmeg.
му́скул muscle. **му́скульный** muscular.
му́сор refuse; rubbish. **му́сорный я́щик** dustbin.
мусульма́нин (*pl* -ма́не, -ма́н), **-а́нка** Muslim.
мути́ть (мучу́, му́тишь) *impf* (*pf* **вз~**) make muddy; stir up, upset. **му́тный** (-тен, -тна́, -о) turbid, troubled; dull. **муть** sediment; murk.
му́ха fly.
муче́ние torment, torture. **му́ченик, му́ченица** martyr. **мучи́тельный** agonizing. **му́чить** (-чу) *impf* (*pf* **за~, из~**) torment; harass; **~ся** torment o.s.; suffer agonies.
мучно́й flour, meal; starchy.
мха *etc.*: *see* **мох**
мчать (мчу) *impf* rush along, whirl along; **~ся** rush.
мщу *etc.*: *see* **мстить**
мы (нас, нам, на́ми, нас) *pron* we; **мы с ва́ми** you and I.
мы́лить *impf* (*pf* **на~**) soap; **~ся** wash o.s. **мы́ло** (*pl* -á) soap. **мы́льница** soap-dish. **мы́льный** soap, soapy.
мыс cape, promontory.
мы́сленный mental. **мысли́мый** conceivable. **мысли́тель** *m* thinker. **мы́слить** *impf* think; conceive. **мысль** thought; idea. **мы́слящий** thinking.
мыть (мо́ю) *impf* (*pf* **вы́~, по~**) wash; **~ся** wash (o.s.).
мыча́ть (-чу́) *impf* (*pf* **про~**) low, moo; bellow; mumble.
мышело́вка mousetrap.
мы́шечный muscular.
мышле́ние thinking, thought.
мы́шца muscle.
мышь (*gen pl* -е́й) mouse.
мэр mayor. **мэ́рия** town hall.
мя́гкий (-гок, -гка́, -о) soft; mild; **~ знак** soft sign, the letter **ь**. **мя́гче** *comp of* **мя́гкий, мя́гко. мя́коть** fleshy part, flesh; pulp.
мяси́стый fleshy; meaty. **мясни́к** (-á) butcher. **мясно́й** meat. **мя́со** meat; flesh. **мясору́бка** mincer.
мя́та mint; peppermint.
мяте́ж (-á) mutiny, revolt. **мяте́жник** mutineer, rebel. **мяте́жный** rebellious; restless.
мя́тный mint, peppermint.
мять (мну, мнёшь) *impf* (*pf* **из~, раз~, с~**) work up; knead; crumple; **~ся** become crumpled; crush (easily).
мяу́кать *impf* miaow.
мяч (-á), **мя́чик** ball.

Н

на[1] *prep* **I.** *+acc* on; on to, to, into; at; till, until; for; by. **II.** *+prep* on, upon; in; at.

на[2] *partl* here; here you are.
наба́вить (-влю) *pf*, **набавля́ть** *impf* add (to), increase.
наба́т alarm-bell.
набе́г raid, foray.
набекре́нь *adv* aslant.
на|бели́ть (-е́ли́шь) *pf*. **на́бело** *adv* without corrections.
на́бережная *sb* embankment, quay.
наберу́ *etc.*: *see* **набра́ть**
набива́ть(ся *impf of* **наби́ть(ся**. **наби́вка** stuffing, padding; (textile) printing.
набира́ть(ся *impf of* **набра́ть(ся**
наби́тый packed, stuffed; crowded. **наби́ть** (-бью́, -бьёшь) *pf* (*impf* **набива́ть**) stuff, pack, fill; smash; print; hammer, drive; **~ся** crowd in.
наблюда́тель *m* observer. **наблюда́тельный** observant; observation. **наблюда́ть** *impf* observe,watch; +**за**+*instr* look after; supervise. **наблюде́ние** observation; supervision.
на́божный devout, pious.
на́бок *adv* on one side, crooked.
наболе́вший sore, painful.
набо́р recruiting; collection, set; type-setting.
набра́сывать(ся *impf of* **наброса́ть, набро́сить(ся**
набра́ть (-беру́, -берёшь; -а́л, -а́, -о) *pf* (*impf* **набира́ть**) gather; enlist; compose, set up; **~ но́мер** dial a number; **~ся** assemble, collect; +*gen* find, acquire, pick up; **~ся сме́лости** pluck up courage.
набрести́ (-еду́, -дёшь; -ёл, -ела́) *pf* +**на**+*acc* come across.
наброса́ть *pf* (*impf* **набра́сывать**) throw (down); sketch; jot down. **набро́сить** (-о́шу) *pf* (*impf* **набра́сывать**) throw; **~ся** throw o.s.; **~ся на** attack.
набро́сок (-ска) sketch, draft.
набуха́ть *impf*, **набу́хнуть** (-нет; -у́х) *pf* swell.
набью́ *etc.*: *see* **наби́ть**
наважде́ние delusion.
нава́ливать *impf*, **навали́ть** (-лю́, -лишь) *pf* heap, pile up; load; **~ся** lean; +**на**+*acc* fall (up)on.
наведе́ние laying (on); placing.
наведу́ *etc.*: *see* **навести́**
наве́к, наве́ки *adv* for ever.
навёл *etc.*: *see* **навести́**
наве́рно, наве́рное *adv* probably. **наверняка́** *adv* certainly, for sure.
наверста́ть *pf*, **навёрстывать** *impf* make up for.
наве́рх *adv* up(wards); upstairs. **наверху́** *adv* above; upstairs.
наве́с awning.
наве́сить (-е́шу) *pf* (*impf* **наве́шивать**) hang (up). **навесно́й** hanging.
навести́ (-еду́, -едёшь; -вёл, -а́) *pf* (*impf* **наводи́ть**) direct; aim; cover (with), spread; introduce, bring; make.
навести́ть (-ещу́) *pf* (*impf* **навеща́ть**) visit.
наве́шать *pf*, **наве́шивать**[1] *impf* hang (out); weigh out.
наве́шивать[2] *impf of* **наве́сить**. **навеща́ть** *impf of* **навести́ть**
на́взничь *adv* backwards, on one's back.
навзры́д *adv*: **пла́кать ~** sob.
навига́ция navigation.
нависа́ть *impf*, **нави́снуть** (-нет; -ви́с) *pf* overhang, hang (over); threaten. **нави́сший** beetling.

навлека́ть *impf*, **навле́чь** (-еку́, -ечёшь; -ёк, -ла́) *pf* bring, draw; incur.
наводи́ть (-ожу́, -о́дишь) *impf of* **навести́; наводя́щий вопро́с** leading question. **наво́дка** aiming; applying.
наводне́ние flood. **наводни́ть** *pf*, **наводня́ть** *impf* flood; inundate.
наво́з dung, manure.
на́волочка pillowcase.
на|вра́ть (-ру́, -рёшь; -а́л, -а́, -о) *pf* tell lies, romance; talk nonsense; +в+*prep* make mistake(s) in.
навреди́ть (-ежу́) *pf* +*dat* harm.
навсегда́ *adv* for ever.
навстре́чу *adv* to meet; **идти́** ~ go to meet; meet halfway.
навы́ворот *adv* inside out; back to front.
на́вык experience, skill.
навы́нос *adv* to take away.
навы́пуск *adv* worn outside.
навью́чивать *impf*, **на|вью́чить** (-чу) *pf* load.
навяза́ть (-яжу́, -я́жешь) *pf*, **навя́зывать** *impf* tie, fasten; thrust, foist; **~ся** thrust o.s. **навя́зчивый** importunate; obsessive.
на|га́дить (-а́жу) *pf*.
нага́н revolver.
нагиба́ть(ся *impf of* **нагну́ть(ся**
нагишо́м *adv* stark naked.
нагле́ц (-а́) impudent fellow. **на́глость** impudence. **на́глый** (нагл, -а́, -о) impudent.
нагля́дный clear, graphic; visual.
нагна́ть (-гоню́, -го́нишь; -а́л, -а́, -о) *pf* (*impf* **нагоня́ть**) overtake, catch up (with); inspire, arouse.
нагнести́ (-ету́, -етёшь) *pf*, **нагнета́ть** *impf* compress; supercharge.
нагное́ние suppuration. **нагнои́ться** *pf* suppurate.
нагну́ть (-ну́, -нёшь) *pf* (*impf* **нагиба́ть**) bend; **~ся** bend, stoop.
нагова́ривать *impf*, **наговори́ть** *pf* slander; talk a lot (of); record.
наго́й (наг, -а́, -о) naked, bare.
на́голо́ *adv* naked, bare.
нагоня́ть *impf of* **нагна́ть**
нагора́ть *impf*, **нагоре́ть** (-ри́т) *pf* be consumed; *impers*+*dat* be scolded.
наго́рный upland, mountain; mountainous.
нагота́ nakedness, nudity.
награ́бить (-блю) *pf* amass by dishonest means.
награ́да reward; decoration; prize. **награди́ть** (-ажу́) *pf*, **награжда́ть** *impf* reward; decorate; award prize to.
нагрева́тельный heating. **нагрева́ть** *impf*, **нагре́ть** (-е́ю) *pf* warm, heat; **~ся** get hot, warm up.
нагроможда́ть *impf*, **на|громозди́ть** (-зжу́) *pf* heap up, pile up. **нагроможде́ние** heaping up; conglomeration.
на|груби́ть (-блю́) *pf*.
нагружа́ть *impf*, **на|грузи́ть** (-ужу́, -у́зишь) *pf* load; **~ся** load o.s. **нагру́зка** loading; load; work; commitments.
нагря́нуть (-ну) *pf* appear unexpectedly.
над, надо *prep*+*instr* over, above; on, at.
надави́ть (-влю́, -вишь) *pf*, **нада́вливать** *impf* press; squeeze out; crush.
надба́вка addition, increase.
надвига́ть *impf*, **надви́нуть**

(-ну) *pf* move, pull, push; **~ся** approach.
на́двое *adv* in two.
надгро́бие epitaph. **надгро́бный** (*on or over a*) grave.
надева́ть *impf of* **наде́ть**
наде́жда hope. **надёжность** reliability. **надёжный** reliable.
наде́л allotment.
наде́лать *pf* make; cause; do.
надели́ть (-лю́, -ли́шь) *pf*, **наделя́ть** *impf* endow, provide.
наде́ть (-е́ну) *pf* (*impf* **надева́ть**) put on.
наде́яться (-е́юсь) *impf* (*pf* **по~**) hope; rely.
надзира́тель *m* overseer, supervisor. **надзира́ть** *impf* +**за**+*instr* supervise, oversee.
надзо́р supervision; surveillance.
надла́мывать(ся *impf of* **надломи́ть(ся**
надлежа́щий fitting, proper, appropriate. **надлежи́т** (-жа́ло) *impers* (+*dat*) it is necessary, required.
надло́м break; crack; breakdown. **надломи́ть** (-млю́, -мишь) *pf* (*impf* **надла́мывать**) break; crack; breakdown; **~ся** break, crack, breakdown.
надло́мленный broken.
надме́нный haughty, arrogant.
на́до[1] (+*dat*) it is necessary; I (*etc.*) must, ought to; I (*etc.*) need. **на́добность** necessity, need.
надо[2]: *see* **над**.
надоеда́ть *impf*, **надое́сть** (-е́м, -е́шь, -е́ст, -еди́м) *pf* +*dat* bore, pester. **надое́дливый** boring, tiresome.
надо́лго *adv* for a long time.
надорва́ть (-ву́, -вёшь; -а́л, -а́, -о) *pf* (*impf* **надрыва́ть**) tear; strain; **~ся** tear; overstrain o.s.
на́дпись inscription.
надре́з cut, incision. **надре́зать** (-е́жу) *pf*, **надреза́ть** *impf*, **надре́зывать** *impf* make an incision in.
надруга́тельство outrage.
надруга́ться *pf* +**над**+*instr* outrage, insult.
надры́в tear; strain; breakdown; outburst. **надрыва́ть(ся** *impf of* **надорва́ть(ся**.
надры́вный hysterical; heartrending.
надста́вить (-влю) *pf*, **надставля́ть** *impf* lengthen.
надстра́ивать *impf*, **надстро́ить** (-о́ю) *pf* build on top; extend upwards. **надстро́йка** building upwards; superstructure.
надува́тельство swindle. **надува́ть(ся** *impf. of* **наду́ть(ся**. **надувно́й** pneumatic, inflatable.
наду́манный far-fetched.
наду́тый swollen; haughty; sulky. **наду́ть** (-у́ю) *pf* (*impf* **надува́ть**) inflate; swindle; **~ся** swell out; sulk.
на|души́ть(ся (-шу́(сь, -шишь(ся) *pf*.
наеда́ться *impf of* **нае́сться**
наедине́ *adv* privately, alone.
нае́зд flying visit; raid. **нае́здник, -ица** rider. **наезжа́ть** *impf of* **нае́здить, нае́хать**; pay occasional visits.
наём (на́йма) hire; renting; **взять в ~** rent; **сдать в ~** let. **наёмник** hireling; mercenary. **наёмный** hired, rented.
нае́сться (-е́мся, -е́шься, -е́стся, -еди́мся) *pf* (*impf* **наеда́ться**) eat one's fill; stuff o.s.
нае́хать (-е́ду) *pf* (*impf* **наезжа́ть**) arrive unexpectedly;

+**на**+*acc* run into, collide with. **нажа́ть** (-жму́, -жмёшь) *pf* (*impf* **нажима́ть**) press; put pressure (on).
нажда́к (-а́) emery. **нажда́чная бума́га** emery paper.
нажи́ва profit, gain.
нажива́ть(ся *impf of* **нажи́ть-(ся**
нажи́м pressure; clamp. **нажима́ть** *impf of* **нажа́ть**.
нажи́ть (-иву́, -ивёшь; на́жил, -а́, -о) *pf* (*impf* **нажива́ть**) acquire; contract, incur; **~ся** (-жи́лся, -а́сь) get rich.
нажму́ *etc.*: *see* **нажа́ть**
наза́втра *adv* (the) next day.
наза́д *adv* back(wards); **(тому́) ~** ago.
назва́ние name; title. **назва́ть** (-зову́, -зовёшь; -а́л, -а́, -о) *pf* (*impf* **называ́ть**) call, name; **~ся** be called.
назе́мный ground, surface.
на́зло́ *adv* out of spite; to spite.
назнача́ть *impf*, **назна́чить** (-чу) *pf* appoint; fix, set; prescribe. **назначе́ние** appointment; fixing, setting; prescription.
назову́ *etc.*: *see* **назва́ть**
назо́йливый importunate.
назрева́ть *impf*, **назре́ть** (-е́ет) *pf* ripen, mature; become imminent.
называ́емый: так ~ so-called. **называ́ть(ся** *impf of* **назва́ть(ся**.
наибо́лее *adv* (the) most. **наибо́льший** greatest, biggest.
наи́вный naive.
наивы́сший highest.
наигра́ть *pf*, **наи́грывать** *impf* win; play, pick out.
наизна́нку *adv* inside out.
наизу́сть *adv* by heart.
наилу́чший best.
наименова́ние name; title.
на́искось *adv* obliquely.
найму́ *etc.*: *see* **наня́ть**
найти́ (-йду́, -йдёшь; нашёл, -шла́, -шло́) *pf* (*impf* **находи́ть**) find; **~сь** be found; be, be situated.
наказа́ние punishment. **наказа́ть** (-ажу́, -а́жешь) *pf*, **нака́зывать** *impf* punish.
нака́л incandescence. **нака́ливать** *impf*, **накали́ть** *pf*, **накаля́ть** *impf* heat; make red-hot; strain, make tense; **~ся** glow, become incandescent; become strained.
нака́лывать(ся *impf of* **наколо́ть(ся**
накану́не *adv* the day before.
нака́пливать(ся *impf of* **накопи́ть(ся**
накача́ть *pf*, **нака́чивать** *impf* pump (up).
наки́дка cloak, cape; extra charge. **наки́нуть** (-ну) *pf*, **наки́дывать** *impf* throw; throw on; **~ся** throw o.s.; **~ся на** attack.
на́кипь scum; scale.
накладна́я *sb* invoice. **накладн|о́й** laid on; false; **~ы́е расхо́ды** overheads. **накла́дывать** *impf of* **наложи́ть**
на|клевета́ть (-ещу́, -е́щешь) *pf*.
накле́ивать *impf*, **накле́ить** *pf* stick on. **накле́йка** sticking (on, up); label.
накло́н slope, incline. **наклоне́ние** inclination; mood. **наклони́ть** (-ню́, -нишь) *pf*, **наклоня́ть** *impf* incline, bend; **~ся** stoop, bend. **накло́нный** inclined, sloping.
нако́лка pinning; (*pinned-on*) ornament for hair; tattoo.
наколо́ть[1] (-лю́, -лешь) *pf*

(*impf* **нака́лывать**) prick; pin; **~ся** prick o.s.
наколо́ть[2] (-лю́, -лешь) *pf* (*impf* **нака́лывать**) chop.
наконе́ц *adv* at last. **наконе́чник** tip, point.
на|копи́ть (-плю́, -пишь) *pf*, **накопля́ть** *impf* (*impf also* **нака́пливать**) accumulate; **~ся** accumulate. **накопле́ние** accumulation.
на|копти́ть (-пчу́) *pf*. **на|корми́ть** (-млю́, -мишь) *pf*.
накра́сить (-а́шу) *pf* paint; make up. **на|кра́ситься** (-а́шусь) *pf*.
на|крахма́лить *pf*.
на|крени́ть *pf*. **накрени́ться** (-ни́тся) *pf*, **накреня́ться** *impf* tilt; list.
накрича́ть (-чу́) *pf* (+**на**+*acc*) shout (at).
накро́ю *etc.*: *see* **накры́ть**
накрыва́ть *impf*, **накры́ть** (-ро́ю) *pf* cover; catch; ~ **(на) стол** lay the table; **~ся** cover o.s.
накури́ть (-рю́, -ришь) *pf* fill with smoke.
налага́ть *impf of* **наложи́ть**
нала́дить (-а́жу) *pf*, **нала́живать** *impf* regulate, adjust; repair; organize; **~ся** come right; get going.
на|лга́ть (-лгу́, -лжёшь; -а́л, -а́, -о) *pf*.
нале́во *adv* to the left.
налёг *etc.*: *see* **нале́чь**. **налега́ть** *impf of* **нале́чь**
налегке́ *adv* lightly dressed; without luggage.
налёт raid; flight; thin coating. **налета́ть**[1] *pf* have flown. **налета́ть**[2] *impf*, **налете́ть** (-лечу́) *pf* swoop down; come flying; spring up.
нале́чь (-ля́гу, -ля́жешь; -лёг, -ла́) *pf* (*impf* **налега́ть**) lean, apply one's weight, lie; apply o.s.
налжёшь *etc.*: *see* **налга́ть**
налива́ть(ся *impf of* **нали́ть(ся**. **нали́вка** fruit liqueur.
нали́ть (-лью́, -льёшь; на́лил, -а́, -о) *pf* (*impf* **налива́ть**) pour (out), fill; **~ся** (-и́лся́, -а́сь, -и́ло́сь) pour in; ripen.
налицо́ *adv* present; available.
нали́чие presence. **нали́чн|ый** on hand; cash; **~ые (де́ньги)** ready money.
нало́г tax. **налогоплате́льщик** taxpayer. **нало́женн|ый**: **~ым платежо́м** C.O.D. **наложи́ть** (-жу́, -жишь) *pf* (*impf* **накла́дывать**, **налага́ть**) lay (in, on), put (in, on); apply; impose.
налью́ *etc.*: *see* **нали́ть**
наля́гу *etc.*: *see* **нале́чь**
нам *etc.*: *see* **мы**
на|ма́зать (-а́жу) *pf*, **нама́зывать** *impf* oil, grease; smear, spread.
нама́тывать *impf of* **намота́ть**. **нама́чивать** *impf of* **намочи́ть**
намёк hint. **намека́ть** *impf*, **намекну́ть** (-ну́, -нёшь) *pf* hint.
намерева́ться *impf* +*inf* intend to. **наме́рен** *predic*: **я** ~**(а)**+*inf* I intend to. **наме́рение** intention. **наме́ренный** intentional.
на|мета́ть *pf*. **на|ме́тить**[1] (-е́чу) *pf*.
наме́тить[2] (-е́чу) *pf* (*impf* **намеча́ть**) plan; outline; nominate; **~ся** be outlined, take shape.
намно́го *adv* much, far.
намока́ть *impf*, **намо́кнуть** (-ну) *pf* get wet.

намо́рдник muzzle.
на|мо́рщить(ся (-щу(сь) *pf*.
на|мота́ть *pf* (*impf also* **на-ма́тывать**) wind, reel.
на|мочи́ть (-очу́, -о́чишь) *pf* (*impf also* **нама́чивать**) wet; soak; splash, spill.
намы́ливать *impf*, **на|мы́лить** *pf* soap.
нанести́ (-су́, -сёшь; -ёс, -ла́) *pf* (*impf* **наноси́ть**) carry, bring; draw, plot; inflict.
на|низа́ть (-ижу́, -и́жешь) *pf*, **нани́зывать** *impf* string, thread.
нанима́тель *m* tenant; employer. **нанима́ть(ся** *impf of* **наня́ть(ся**
наноси́ть (-ошу́, -о́сишь) *impf of* **нанести́**
наня́ть (найму́, -мёшь; на́нял, -а́, -о) *pf* (*impf* **нанима́ть**) hire; rent; **~ся** get a job.
наоборо́т *adv* on the contrary; back to front; the other, the wrong, way (round); vice versa.
нао́тмашь *adv* violently.
наотре́з *adv* flatly, point-blank.
напада́ть *impf of* **напа́сть**. **напада́ющий** *sb* forward. **нападе́ние** attack; forwards.
напа́рник co-driver, (work)-mate.
напа́сть (-аду́, -адёшь; -а́л) *pf* (*impf* **напада́ть**) **на**+*acc* attack; descend on; seize; come upon. **напа́сть** misfortune.
напе́в tune. **напева́ть** *impf of* **напе́ть**
наперебо́й *adv* interrupting, vying with, one another.
напере́д *adv* in advance.
напереко́р *adv*+*dat* in defiance of, counter to.
напёрсток (-тка) thimble.
напе́ть (-пою́, -поёшь) *pf* (*impf* **напева́ть**) sing; hum, croon.
на|печа́тать(ся *pf*. **напива́ться** *impf of* **напи́ться**
напи́льник file.
на|писа́ть (-ишу́, -и́шешь) *pf*.
напи́ток (-тка) drink. **напи́ться** (-пью́сь, -пьёшься; -и́лся, -а́сь, -и́ло́сь) *pf* (*impf* **напива́ться**) quench one's thirst, drink; get drunk.
напиха́ть *pf*, **напи́хивать** *impf* cram, stuff.
на|плева́ть (-плюю́, -плюёшь) *pf*; **~!** to hell with it! who cares?
наплы́в influx; accumulation; canker.
наплюю́ *etc*.: *see* **наплева́ть**
напова́л outright.
наподо́бие *prep*+*gen* like, not unlike.
на|пои́ть (-ою́, -о́ишь) *pf*.
напока́з *adv* for show.
наполни́тель *m* filler. **напо́лнить(ся** *pf*, **наполня́ть(ся** *impf* fill.
наполови́ну *adv* half.
напомина́ние reminder. **напомина́ть** *impf*, **напо́мнить** *pf* (+*dat*) remind.
напо́р pressure. **напо́ристый** energetic, pushing.
напосле́док *adv* in the end; after all.
напою́ *etc*.: *see* **напе́ть, напои́ть**
напр. *abbr* (*of* **наприме́р**) e.g., for example.
напра́вить (-влю) *pf*, **направля́ть** *impf* direct; send; sharpen; **~ся** make (for), go (towards). **направле́ние** direction; trend; warrant; order.
напра́вленный purposeful.
напра́во *adv* to the right.
напра́сно *adv* in vain, for nothing; unjustly, mistakenly.
напра́шиваться *impf of* **напроси́ться**

наприме́р for example.
на|прока́зничать *pf.*
напрока́т *adv* for, on, hire.
напролёт *adv* through, without a break.
напроло́м *adv* straight, regardless of obstacles.
напроси́ться (-ошу́сь, -о́сишься) *pf* (*impf* **напра́шиваться**) thrust o.s.; suggest itself; **~ на** ask for, invite.
напро́тив *adv* opposite; on the contrary. **напро́тив** *prep+gen* opposite.
напряга́ть(ся *impf of* **напря́чь(ся. напряже́ние** tension; exertion; voltage. **напряжённый** tense; intense; intensive.
напрями́к *adv* straight (out).
напря́чь (-ягу́, -яжёшь; -я́г, -ла́) *pf* (*impf* **напряга́ть**) strain; **~ся** strain o.s.
на|пуга́ть(ся *pf.* **на|пу́дриться** *pf.*
напуска́ть *impf*, **напусти́ть** (-ущу́, -у́стишь) *pf* let in; let loose; **~ся +на+***acc* fly at, go for.
напу́тать *pf* **+в+***prep* make a mess of.
на|пыли́ть *pf.*
напью́сь *etc.*: *see* **напи́ться**
наравне́ *adv* level; equally.
нараспа́шку *adv* unbuttoned.
нараста́ние growth, accumulation. **нараста́ть** *impf*, **нарасти́** (-тёт; -ро́с, -ла́) *pf* grow; increase.
нарасхва́т *adv* very quickly, like hot cakes.
нарва́ть[1] (-рву́, -рвёшь; -а́л, -а́, -о) *pf* (*impf* **нарыва́ть**) pick; tear up.
нарва́ть[2] (-вёт; -а́л, -а́, -о) *pf* (*impf* **нарыва́ть**) gather.
нарва́ться (-ву́сь, -вёшься; -а́лся, -ала́сь, -а́ло́сь) *pf* (*impf* **нарыва́ться**) **+на+***acc* run into, run up against.
наре́зать (-е́жу) *pf*, **нареза́ть** *impf* cut (up), slice, carve; thread, rifle.
наре́чие[1] dialect.
наре́чие[2] adverb.
на|рисова́ть *pf.*
нарко́з narcosis. **нарко́ма́н, -ма́нка** drug addict. **наркома́ния** drug addiction. **нарко́тик** narcotic.
наро́д people. **наро́дность** nationality; national character. **наро́дный** national; folk; popular; people's.
наро́с *etc.*: *see* **нарасти́**
наро́чно *adv* on purpose, deliberately. **на́рочный** *sb* courier.
нару́жность exterior. **нару́жный** external, outward.
нару́жу *adv* outside.
нару́чник handcuff. **нару́чный** wrist.
наруше́ние breach; infringement. **наруши́тель** *m* transgressor. **нару́шить** (-шу) *pf*, **наруша́ть** *impf* break; disturb, infringe, violate.
нарци́сс narcissus; daffodil.
на́ры (нар) *pl* plank-bed.
нары́в abscess, boil. **нарыва́ть(ся** *impf of* **нарва́ть(ся**
наря́д[1] order, warrant.
наря́д[2] attire; dress. **наряди́ть** (-яжу́) *pf* (*impf* **наряжа́ть**) dress (up); **~ся** dress up. **наря́дный** well-dressed.
наряду́ *adv* alike, equally; side by side.
наряжа́ть(ся *impf of* **наряди́ть(ся. нас** *see* **мы**
насади́ть (-ажу́, -а́дишь) *pf*, **насажда́ть** *impf* (*impf also* **наса́живать**) plant; propa-

gate; implant. **наса́дка** setting, fixing. **насажде́ние** planting; plantation; propagation. **наса́живать** *impf of* **насади́ть**
насеко́мое *sb* insect.
населе́ние population. **населённость** density of population. **населённый** populated; ~ **пункт** settlement; built-up area. **насели́ть** *pf*, **населя́ть** *impf* settle, people.
наси́лие violence, force. **наси́ловать** *impf* (*pf* **из**~) coerce; rape. **наси́лу** *adv* with difficulty. **наси́льник** aggressor; rapist; violator. **наси́льно** *adv* by force. **наси́льственный** violent, forcible.
наска́кивать *impf of* **наскочи́ть**
наскво́зь *adv* through, throughout.
наско́лько *adv* how much?, how far?; as far as.
на́скоро *adv* hastily.
наскочи́ть (-очу́, -о́чишь) *pf* (*impf* **наска́кивать**) +**на**+*acc* run into, collide with; fly at.
наску́чить (-чу) *pf* bore.
наслади́ться (-ажу́сь) *pf*, **наслажда́ться** *impf* (+*instr*) enjoy, take pleasure. **наслажде́ние** pleasure, enjoyment.
насле́дие legacy; heritage.
на|следи́ть (-ежу́) *pf*. **насле́дник** heir; successor. **насле́дница** heiress. **насле́дный** next in succession. **насле́довать** *impf* & *pf* (*pf also* **у**~) inherit, succeed to. **насле́дственность** heredity. **насле́дственный** hereditary, inherited. **насле́дство** inheritance; heritage.
на́смерть *adv* to (the) death.
на|смеши́ть (-шу́) *pf* **насме́шка** mockery; gibe. **насме́шливый** mocking.
на́сморк runny nose; cold.
на|сори́ть *pf*.
насо́с pump.
на́спех *adv* hastily.
на|спле́тничать *pf*. **настава́ть** (-таёт) *impf of* **наста́ть**
наставле́ние exhortation; directions, manual.
наста́вник tutor, mentor.
наста́ивать[1] *impf of* **настоя́ть**[1]. **наста́ивать**[2](**ся** *impf of* **настоя́ть**[2](**ся**
наста́ть (-а́нет) *pf* (*impf* **настава́ть**) come, begin, set in.
на́стежь *adv* wide (open).
настелю́ *etc.*: *see* **настла́ть**
настига́ть *impf*, **насти́гнуть**, **насти́чь** (-и́гну; -и́г) *pf* catch up with, overtake.
насти́л flooring, planking. **настила́ть** *impf of* **настла́ть**
насти́чь *see* **настига́ть**
настла́ть (-телю́, -те́лешь) *pf* (*impf* **настила́ть**) lay, spread.
насто́йка liqueur, cordial.
насто́йчивый persistent; urgent.
насто́лько *adv* so, so much.
насто́льный table, desk; reference.
насторáживать *impf*, **насторожи́ть** (-жу́) *pf* set; prick up; ~**ся** prick up one's ears. **насторо́женный** (-ен, -енна) guarded; alert.
настоя́тельный insistent; urgent. **настоя́ть**[1] (-ою́) *pf* (*impf* **наста́ивать**[1]) insist.
настоя́ть[2] (-ою́) *pf* (*impf* **наста́ивать**[2]) brew; ~**ся** draw, stand.
настоя́щее *sb* the present. **настоя́щий** (the) present, this; real, genuine.
настра́ивать(ся *impf of* **настро́ить(ся**

настри́чь (-игу́, -ижёшь; -и́г) *pf* shear, clip.
настрое́ние mood. **настро́ить** (-о́ю) *pf* (*impf* **настра́ивать**) tune (in); dispose; **~ся** dispose o.s. **настро́йка** tuning. **настро́йщик** tuner.
на|строчи́ть (-чу́) *pf*.
наступа́тельный offensive.
наступа́ть[1] *impf of* **наступи́ть**[1]
наступа́ть[2] *impf of* **наступи́ть**[2]. **наступа́ющий**[1] coming.
наступа́ющий[2] *sb* attacker.
наступи́ть[1] (-плю́, -пишь) *pf* (*impf* **наступа́ть**[1]) tread; attack; advance.
наступи́ть[2] (-у́пит) *pf* (*impf* **наступа́ть**[2]) come, set in. **наступле́ние**[1] coming.
наступле́ние[2] offensive, attack.
насу́питься (-плюсь) *pf*, **насу́пливаться** *impf* frown.
на́сухо *adv* dry. **насуши́ть** (-шу́, -шишь) *pf* dry.
насу́щный urgent, vital; **хлеб ~** daily bread.
насчёт *prep+gen* about, concerning; as regards. **насчита́ть** *pf*, **насчи́тывать** *impf* count; hold; **~ся** *+gen* number.
насы́пать (-плю) *pf*, **насыпа́ть** *impf* pour in, on; fill; spread; heap up. **на́сыпь** embankment.
насы́тить (-ы́щу) *pf*, **насыща́ть** *impf* satiate; saturate; **~ся** be full; be saturated.
ната́лкивать(ся *impf of* **натолкну́ть(ся**. **ната́пливать** *impf of* **натопи́ть**
натаска́ть *pf*, **ната́скивать** *impf* train; coach, cram; bring in, lay in.
натвори́ть *pf* do, get up to.
натере́ть (-тру́, -трёшь; -тёр) *pf* (*impf* **натира́ть**) rub on, in; polish; chafe; grate; **~ся** rub o.s.
на́тиск onslaught.
наткну́ться (-ну́сь, -нёшься) *pf* (*impf* **натыка́ться**) **+на**+*acc* run into; strike, stumble on.
натолкну́ть (-ну́, -нёшь) *pf* (*impf* **ната́лкивать**) push; lead; **~ся** run against, across.
натопи́ть (-плю́, -пишь) *pf* (*impf* **ната́пливать**) heat (up); stoke up; melt.
на|точи́ть (-чу́, -чишь) *pf*.
натоща́к *adv* on an empty stomach.
натрави́ть (-влю́, -вишь) *pf*, **натра́вливать** *impf*, **натравля́ть** *impf* set (on); stir up.
на|тренирова́ть(ся *pf*.
на́трий sodium.
нату́ра nature. **натура́льный** natural; genuine. **нату́рщик, -щица** artist's model.
натыка́ть(ся *impf of* **наткну́ть(ся**
натюрмо́рт still life.
натя́гивать *impf*, **натяну́ть** (-ну́, -нешь) *pf* stretch; draw; pull (on); **~ся** stretch. **натя́нутость** tension. **натя́нутый** tight; strained.
наугáд *adv* at random.
нау́ка science; learning.
нау́тро *adv* (the) next morning.
на|учи́ть(ся (-чу́(сь, -чишь(ся) *pf*.
нау́чн|ый scientific; **~ая фанта́стика** science fiction.
нау́шник ear-flap; ear-phone.
нафтали́н naphthalene.
наха́л, -ха́лка impudent creature. **наха́льный** impudent. **наха́льство** impudence.
нахвата́ть *pf*, **нахва́тывать**

impf pick up, get hold of; ~**ся** *+gen* pick up.
нахле́бник hanger-on.
нахлы́нуть (-нет) *pf* well up; surge; gush.
на|хму́рить(ся *pf.*
находи́ть(ся (-ожу́(сь, -о́дишь(ся) *impf of* **найти́(сь. нахо́дка** find. **нахо́дчивый** resourceful, quick-witted.
наце́ливать *impf*, **на|це́лить** *pf* aim; ~**ся** (take) aim.
наце́нка surcharge, mark-up.
нацизм Nazism. **национализа́ция** nationalization. **национализи́ровать** *impf & pf* nationalize. **национали́зм** nationalism. **националисти́ческий** nationalist(ic). **национа́льность** nationality; ethnic group. **национа́льный** national. **наци́ст, -и́стка** Nazi. **наци́стский** Nazi. **на́ция** nation. **нацме́н, -ме́нка** *abbr* member of national minority.
нача́ло beginning; origin; principle, basis. **нача́льник** head, chief; boss. **нача́льный** initial; primary. **нача́льство** the authorities; command.
нача́ть (-чну́, -чнёшь; на́чал, -á, -о) *pf* (*impf* **начина́ть**) begin; ~**ся** begin.
начерта́ть *pf* trace, inscribe.
на|черти́ть (-рчу́, -ртишь) *pf.*
начина́ние undertaking. **начина́ть(ся** *impf of* **нача́ть(ся. начина́ющий** *sb* beginner.
начини́ть *pf*, **начиня́ть** *impf* stuff, fill. **начи́нка** stuffing, filling.
начи́стить (-и́щу) *pf* (*impf* **начища́ть**) clean. **на́чисто** *adv* clean; flatly, decidedly; openly, frankly. **начистоту́** *adv* openly, frankly.
начи́танность learning; wide reading. **начи́танный** well-read.
начища́ть *impf of* **начи́стить**
наш (-его) *m*, **на́ша** (-ей) *f*, **на́ше** (-его) *neut*, **на́ши** (-их) *pl*, *pron* our, ours.
нашаты́рный спирт ammonia. **нашаты́рь** (-я́) *m* sal-ammoniac; ammonia.
нашёл *etc.*: *see* **найти́**
наше́ствие invasion.
нашива́ть *impf*, **наши́ть** (-шью́, -шьёшь) *pf* sew on. **наши́вка** stripe, chevron; tab.
нашлёпать *impf* slap.
нашуме́ть (-млю́) *pf* make a din; cause a sensation.
нашью́ *etc.*: *see* **наши́ть**
нащу́пать *pf*, **нащу́пывать** *impf* grope for.
на|электризова́ть *pf.*
наяву́ *adv* awake; in reality.
не *partl* not.
не- *pref* un-, in-, non-, mis-, dis-; -less; not. **неаккура́тный** careless; untidy; unpunctual. **небезразли́чный** not indifferent. **небезызве́стный** not unknown; notorious; well-known.
небеса́ *etc.*: *see* **не́бо**[2]. **небе́сный** heavenly; celestial.
не-. неблагода́рный ungrateful; thankless. **неблагонадёжный** unreliable. **неблагополу́чный** unsuccessful, bad, unfavourable. **неблагоприя́тный** unfavourable. **неблагоразу́мный** imprudent. **неблагоро́дный** ignoble, base.
нёбо[1] palate.
не́бо[2] (*pl* -беса́, -бе́с) sky; heaven.
не-. небога́тый of modest

means, modest. **небольшóй** small, not great; **с небольшúм** a little over.

небосвóд firmament. **небосклóн** horizon. **небоскрёб** skyscraper.

небóсь *adv* I dare say; probably.

не-. небрéжный careless. **небывáлый** unprecedented; fantastic. **небылúца** fable, cock-and-bull story. **небытиé** non-existence. **небьющийся** unbreakable. **невáжно** *adv* not too well, indifferently. **невáжный** unimportant; indifferent. **невдалекé** *adv* not far away. **невéдение** ignorance. **невéдомый** unknown; mysterious. **невéжа** *m & f* boor, lout. **невéжда** *m & f* ignoramus. **невéжественный** ignorant. **невéжество** ignorance. **невéжливый** rude. **невелúкий** (-úк, -á, -úкó) small. **невéрие** unbelief, atheism; scepticism. **невéрный** (-рен, -рнá, -о) incorrect, wrong; inaccurate, unsteady; unfaithful. **невероятный** improbable; incredible. **невéрующий** unbelieving; *sb* atheist. **невесёлый** joyless, sad. **невесóмый** weightless; imponderable.

невéста fiancée; bride. **невéстка** daughter-in-law; brother's wife, sister-in-law.

не-. невзгóда adversity. **невзирáя на** *prep+acc* regardless of. **невзначáй** *adv* by chance. **невзрáчный** unattractive, plain. **невúданный** unprecedented, unheard-of. **невúдимый** invisible. **невúнность** innocence. **невúнный, невинóвный** innocent. **невменяемый** irresponsible. **невмешáтельство** non-intervention; non-interference. **невмоготý, невмóчь** *advs* unbearable, too much (for). **невнимáтельный** inattentive, thoughtless.

нéвод seine(-net).

не-. невозвратúмый, невозврáтный irrevocable, irrecoverable. **невозмóжный** impossible. **невозмутúмый** imperturbable.

невóльник, -ница slave. **невóльный** involuntary; unintentional; forced. **невóля** captivity; necessity.

не-. невообразúмый unimaginable, inconceivable. **невооружённ|ый** unarmed; **~ным глáзом** with the naked eye. **невоспúтанный** ill-bred, bad-mannered. **невоспламеняющийся** non-flammable. **невосприúмчивый** unreceptive; immune.

невралгúя neuralgia.

невредúмый safe, unharmed.

неврóз neurosis. **неврологúческий** neurological. **невротúческий** neurotic.

не-. невы́годный disadvantageous; unprofitable. **невы́держанный** lacking self-control; unmatured. **невыносúмый** unbearable. **невыполнúмый** impracticable. **невысóкий** (-сóк, -á, -óкó) low; short.

нéга luxury; bliss.

негатúвный negative.

нéгде *adv* (there is) nowhere.

не-. негúбкий (-бок, -бкá, -о) inflexible, stiff. **неглáсный** secret. **неглубóкий** (-óк, -á, -о) shallow. **неглýпый** (-ýп, -á, -о) sensible, quite intelligent. **негóдный** (-ден, -днá, -о) unfit, unsuitable; worthless. **негодовáние** indignation. **негодовáть** *impf* be indignant. **негодя́й** scoundrel. **негостеприи́мный** inhospitable.

негр Negro, black man.

негрáмотность illiteracy. **негрáмотный** illiterate.

негритя́нка Negress, black woman. **негритя́нский** Negro.

не-. негрóмкий (-мок, -мкá, -о) quiet. **недáвний** recent. **недáвно** *adv* recently. **недалёкий** (-ёк, -á, -ёкó) near; short; not bright, dull-witted. **недалёкó** *adv* not far, near. **недáром** *adv* not for nothing, not without reason. **недви́жимость** real estate. **недви́жимый** immovable. **недвусмы́сленный** unequivocal. **недействи́тельный** ineffective; invalid. **недели́мый** indivisible.

недéльный of a week, week's.

недéля week.

не-. недёшево *adv* dear(ly). **недоброжелáтель** *m* ill-wisher. **недоброжелáтельность** hostility. **недоброкáчественный** of poor quality. **недобросóвестный** unscrupulous; careless. **недóбрый** (-óбр, -брá, -о) unkind; bad. **недовéрие** distrust. **недовéрчивый** distrustful **недовóльный** dissatisfied. **недовóльство** dissatisfaction. **недоедáние** malnutrition. **недоедáть** *impf* be undernourished.

не-. недóлгий (-лог, -лгá, -о) short, brief. **недóлго** *adv* not long. **недолговéчный** short-lived. **недомогáние** indisposition. **недомогáть** *impf* be unwell. **недомы́слие** thoughtlessness. **недонóшенный** premature. **недооцéнивать** *impf*, **недооцени́ть** (-ню́, -нишь) *pf* underestimate; underrate. **недооцéнка** underestimation. **недопусти́мый** inadmissible, intolerable. **недоразумéние** misunderstanding. **недорогóй** (-дóрог, -á, -о) inexpensive. **недосмотрéть** (-рю́, -ришь) *pf* overlook. **недоспáть** (-плю́; -áл, -á, -о) *pf* (*impf* **недосыпáть**) not have enough sleep.

недоставáть (-таёт) *impf*, **недостáть** (-áнет) *pf impers* be missing, be lacking. **недостáток** (-тка) shortage, deficiency. **недостáточный** insufficient, inadequate. **недостáча** lack, shortage.

не-. недостижи́мый unattainable. **недостóйный** unworthy, **недостýпный** inaccessible. **недосчитáться** *pf*, **недосчи́тываться** *impf* miss, find missing, be short (of). **недосыпáть** *impf of* **недоспáть. недосягáемый** unattainable.

недоумевáть *impf* be at a loss, be bewildered. **недоумéние** bewilderment.

не-. недоýчка *m* & *f* half-educated person. **недочёт** deficit; defect.

нéдра (недр) *pl* depths, heart, bowels.

не-. нéдруг enemy. **недружелю́бный** unfriendly.

недýг illness, disease.

недурнóй not bad; not bad-looking.

не-. неестéственный unnatural. **неждáнный** unexpected. **нежелáние** unwill-

ingness. **нежела́тельный** undesirable.
не́жели than.
неженáтый unmarried.
не́женка *m & f* mollycoddle.
нежило́й uninhabited; uninhabitable.
не́житься (-жусь) *impf* luxuriate, bask. **не́жность** tenderness; *pl* endearments. **не́жный** tender; affectionate.
не-. незабве́нный unforgettable. **незабу́дка** forget-me-not. **незабыва́емый** unforgettable. **незави́симость** independence. **незави́симый** independent. **незадо́лго** *adv* not long. **незаконнорождённый** illegitimate. **незако́нный** illegal, illicit; illegitimate. **незако́нченный** unfinished. **незамени́мый** irreplaceable. **незамерза́ющий** ice-free; anti-freeze. **незаме́тный** imperceptible. **незаму́жняя** unmarried. **незапа́мятный** immemorial. **незаслу́женный** unmerited. **незауря́дный** uncommon, outstanding.
не́зачем *adv* there is no need.
не-. незащищённый unprotected. **незва́ный** uninvited. **нездоро́виться** *impf, impers* +dat: **мне нездоро́вится** I don't feel well. **нездоро́вый** unhealthy. **нездоро́вье** ill health. **незнако́мец** (-мца), **незнако́мка** stranger. **незнако́мый** unknown, unfamiliar. **незна́ние** ignorance. **незначи́тельный** insignificant. **незре́лый** unripe, immature. **незри́мый** invisible. **незы́блемый** unshakable, firm. **неизбе́жность** inevitability. **неизбе́жный** inevitable. **неизве́данный** unknown. **неизве́стность** uncertainty; ignorance; obscurity. **неизве́стный** unknown; *sb* stranger.
не-. неизлечи́мый incurable. **неизме́нный** unchanged, unchanging; devoted. **неизменя́емый** unalterable. **неизмери́мый** immeasurable, immense. **неизу́ченный** unstudied; unexplored. **неиму́щий** poor. **неинтере́сный** uninteresting. **неи́скренний** insincere. **неискушённый** inexperienced, unsophisticated. **неисполни́мый** impracticable. **неисправи́мый** incorrigible; irreparable. **неиспра́вный** out of order, defective; careless. **неиссле́дованный** unexplored. **неисяка́емый** inexhaustible. **не́истовство** fury, frenzy; atrocity. **не́истовый** furious, frenzied, uncontrolled. **неистощи́мый, неисчерпа́емый** inexhaustible. **неисчисли́мый** innumerable.
нейло́н, нейло́новый nylon.
нейро́н neuron.
нейтрализа́ция neutralization. **нейтрализова́ть** *impf & pf* neutralize. **нейтралите́т** neutrality. **нейтра́льный** neutral. **нейтро́н** neutron.
неквалифици́рованный unskilled.
не́кий *pron* a certain, some.
не́когда[1] *adv* once, formerly.
не́когда[2] *adv* there is no time; **мне ~** I have no time.
не́кого (не́кому, не́кем, не́ о ком) *pron* there is nobody.
некомпете́нтный not competent, unqualified.

не́котор|ый *pron* some; **~ые** *sb pl* some (people).
некраси́вый plain, ugly; not nice.
некроло́г obituary.
некста́ти *adv* at the wrong time, out of place.
не́кто *pron* somebody; a certain.
не́куда *adv* there is nowhere.
не-. некульту́рный uncivilized, uncultured. **некуря́щий** *sb* non-smoker. **нела́дный** wrong. **нелега́льный** illegal. **нелёгкий** not easy; heavy. **неле́пость** absurdity, nonsense. **неле́пый** absurd. **нело́вкий** awkward. **нело́вкость** awkwardness.
нельзя́ *adv* it is impossible; it is not allowed.
не-. нелюби́мый unloved. **нелюди́мый** unsociable. **нема́ло** *adv* quite a lot (of). **нема́лый** considerable. **неме́дленно** *adv* immediately. **неме́дленный** immediate.
неме́ть (-е́ю) *impf* (*pf* **о~**) become dumb. **не́мец** (-мца) German. **неме́цкий** German.
немину́емый inevitable.
не́мка German woman.
немно́гие *sb pl* (a) few. **немно́го** *adv* a little; some; a few. **немно́жко** *adv* a little.
немо́й (нем, -á, -о) dumb, mute, silent. **немота́** dumbness.
не́мощный feeble.
немы́слимый unthinkable.
ненави́деть (-и́жу) *impf* hate. **ненави́стный** hated; hateful. **не́нависть** hatred.
не-. ненагля́дный beloved. **ненадёжный** unreliable. **ненадо́лго** *adv* for a short time. **нена́стье** bad weather. **ненасы́тный** insatiable. **ненорма́льный** abnormal. **нену́жный** unnecessary, unneeded. **необду́манный** thoughtless, hasty. **необеспе́ченный** without means, unprovided for. **необита́емый** uninhabited. **необозри́мый** boundless, immense. **необосно́ванный** unfounded, groundless. **необрабо́танный** uncultivated; crude; unpolished. **необразо́ванный** uneducated.
необходи́мость necessity. **необходи́мый** necessary.
не-. необъясни́мый inexplicable. **необъя́тный** immense. **необыкнове́нный** unusual. **необыча́йный** extraordinary. **необы́чный** unusual. **необяза́тельный** optional. **неограни́ченный** unlimited. **неоднокра́тный** repeated. **неодобри́тельный** disapproving. **неодушевлённый** inanimate.
неожи́данность unexpectedness. **неожи́данный** unexpected, sudden.
неоклассици́зм neoclassicism.
не-. неоко́нченный unfinished. **неопла́ченный** unpaid. **неопра́вданный** unjustified. **неопределённый** indefinite; infinitive; vague. **неопровержи́мый** irrefutable. **неопублико́ванный** unpublished. **нео́пытный** inexperienced. **неоргани́ческий** inorganic. **неоспори́мый** incontestable. **неосторо́жный** careless. **неосуществи́мый** impracticable. **неотврати́мый** inevitable.
не́откуда *adv* there is nowhere.
не-. неотло́жный urgent. **неотрази́мый** irresistible. **неот-**

сту́пный persistent. **неотъе́млемый** inalienable. **неофициа́льный** unofficial. **неохо́та** reluctance. **неохо́тно** *adv* reluctantly. **неоцени́мый** inestimable, invaluable. **непарти́йный** non-party; unbefitting a member of the (Communist) Party. **непереводи́мый** untranslatable. **неперехо́дный** intransitive. **неплатёжеспосо́бный** insolvent.

не-. непло́хо *adv* not badly, quite well. **неплохо́й** not bad, quite good. **непобеди́мый** invincible. **неповинове́ние** insubordination. **неповоро́тливый** clumsy. **неповтори́мый** inimitable, unique. **непого́да** bad weather. **непогреши́мый** infallible. **непода лёку** *adv* not far (away). **неподви́жный** motionless, immovable; fixed. **неподде́льный** genuine; sincere. **неподку́пный** incorruptible. **неподража́емый** inimitable. **неподходя́щий** unsuitable, inappropriate. **непоколеби́мый** unshakable, steadfast. **непоко́рный** recalcitrant, unruly.

не-. непола́дки (-док) *pl* defects. **неполноце́нность; ко́мплекс неполноце́нности** inferiority complex. **неполноце́нный** defective; inadequate. **непо́лный** incomplete; not (a) full. **непоме́рный** excessive. **непонима́ние** incomprehension, lack of understanding. **непоня́тный** incomprehensible. **непоправи́мый** irreparable. **непоря́док** (-дка) disorder. **непоря́дочный** dishonourable. **непосе́да** *m & f* fidget. **непоси́льный** beyond one's strength. **непосле́довательный** inconsistent. **непослуша́ние** disobedience. **непослу́шный** disobedient. **непосре́дственный** immediate; spontaneous. **непостижи́мый** incomprehensible. **непостоя́нный** inconstant, changeable. **непохо́жий** unlike; different.

не-. непра́вда untruth. **неправдоподо́бный** improbable. **непра́вильно** *adv* wrong. **непра́вильный** irregular; wrong. **непра́вый** wrong. **непракти́чный** unpractical. **непревзойдённый** unsurpassed. **непредви́денный** unforeseen. **непредубеждённый** unprejudiced. **непредусмо́тренный** unforeseen. **непредусмотри́тельный** short-sighted. **непреклóнный** inflexible; adamant. **непрело́жный** immutable.

не-. непреме́нно *adv* without fail. **непреме́нный** indispensable. **непреодоли́мый** insuperable. **непререка́емый** unquestionable. **непреры́вно** *adv* continuously. **непреры́вный** continuous. **непреста́нный** incessant. **неприве́тливый** unfriendly; bleak. **непривлека́тельный** unattractive. **непривы́чный** unaccustomed. **непригля́дный** unattractive. **неприго́дный** unfit, useless. **неприе́млемый** unacceptable. **неприкоснове́нность** inviolability, immunity. **неприкоснове́нный** inviolable; reserve. **неприли́чный** indecent. **непримири́мый** irreconcilable.

непринуждённый unconstrained; relaxed. **неприспосо́бленный** unadapted; maladjusted. **непристо́йный** obscene. **непристу́пный** inaccessible. **непритяза́тельный, неприхотли́вый** unpretentious, simple. **неприя́зненный** hostile, inimical. **неприя́знь** hostility. **неприя́тель** *m* enemy. **неприя́тельский** enemy. **неприя́тность** unpleasantness; trouble. **неприя́тный** unpleasant.

не-. непрове́ренный unverified. **непрогля́дный** pitch-dark. **непрое́зжий** impassable. **непрозра́чный** opaque. **непроизводи́тельный** unproductive. **непроизво́льный** involuntary. **непромока́емый** waterproof. **непроница́емый** impenetrable. **непрости́тельный** unforgivable. **непроходи́мый** impassable. **непро́чный** (-чен, -чна́, -о) fragile, flimsy.

не прочь *predic* not averse.

не-. непро́шеный uninvited, unsolicited. **неработоспосо́бный** disabled. **нерабо́чий: ~ день** day off. **нера́венство** inequality. **неравноме́рный** uneven. **нера́вный** unequal. **неради́вый** lackadaisical. **неразбери́ха** muddle. **неразбо́рчивый** not fastidious; illegible. **неразвито́й** (-ра́звит, -а́, -о) undeveloped; backward. **неразгово́рчивый** taciturn. **неразделённый: ~ая любо́вь** unrequited love. **неразличи́мый** indistinguishable. **неразлу́чный** inseparable. **неразрешённый** unsolved; forbidden. **неразреши́мый** insoluble. **неразры́вный** indissoluble. **неразу́мный** unwise; unreasonable. **нерастворимый** insoluble.

нерв nerve. **не́рвничать** *impf* fret, be nervous. **нервнобольно́й** *sb* neurotic. **не́рвный** (-вен, -вна́, -о) nervous; nerve; irritable. **нерво́зный** nervy, irritable.

не-. нереа́льный unreal; unrealistic. **нере́дкий** (-док, -дка́, -о) not infrequent, not uncommon. **нереши́тельность** indecision. **нереши́тельный** indecisive, irresolute. **нержаве́ющая сталь** stainless steel. **неро́вный** (-вен, -вна́, -о) uneven, rough; irregular. **неруши́мый** inviolable.

неря́ха *m* & *f* sloven. **неря́шливый** slovenly.

не-. несбы́точный unrealizable. **несваре́ние желу́дка** indigestion. **несве́жий** (-е́ж, -а́) not fresh; tainted; weary. **несвоевре́менный** ill-timed; overdue. **несво́йственный** not characteristic. **несгора́емый** fireproof. **несерьёзный** not serious.

несессе́р case.

несимметри́чный asymmetrical.

нескла́дный incoherent; awkward.

несклоня́емый indeclinable.

не́сколько (-их) *pron* some, several; *adv* somewhat.

не-. нескончаемый interminable. **нескро́мный** (-мен, -мна́, -о) immodest; indiscreet. **несло́жный** simple. **неслы́ханный** unprecedented. **неслы́шный** inaudible. **несме́тный** countless, incalculable. **несмолка́емый** ceaseless.

несмотря́ на *prep+acc* in spite of.

не-. несно́сный intolerable. **несоблюде́ние** non-observance. **несовершенноле́тний** under-age; *sb* minor. **несоверше́нный** imperfect, incomplete; imperfective. **несоверше́нство** imperfection. **несовмести́мый** incompatible. **несогла́сие** disagreement. **несогласо́ванный** uncoordinated. **несозна́тельный** irresponsible. **несоизмери́мый** incommensurable. **несокруши́мый** indestructible. **несомне́нный** undoubted, unquestionable. **несообра́зный** incongruous. **несоотве́тствие** disparity. **несостоя́тельный** insolvent; of modest means; untenable. **неспе́лый** unripe. **неспоко́йный** restless; uneasy. **неспосо́бный** not bright; incapable. **несправедли́вость** injustice. **несправедли́вый** unjust, unfair; incorrect. **несравне́нный** (-е́нен, -е́нна) incomparable. **несравни́мый** incomparable. **нестерпи́мый** unbearable.

нести́ (-су́, -сёшь; нёс, -ла́) *impf* (*pf* **по~, с~**) carry; bear; bring, take; suffer; incur; lay; **~сь** rush, fly; float, be carried.

не-. несто́йкий unstable. **несуще́ственный** immaterial, inessential.

несу́ *etc.*: *see* **нести́**

несхо́дный unlike, dissimilar.

несчастли́вый unfortunate, unlucky; unhappy. **несча́стный** unhappy, unfortunate; **~ слу́чай** accident. **несча́стье** misfortune; **к несча́стью** unfortunately.

несчётный innumerable.

нет *partl* no, not; nothing. **нет, не́ту** there is not, there are not.

не-. нетакти́чный tactless. **нетвёрдый** (-ёрд, -а́, -о) unsteady, shaky. **нетерпели́вый** impatient. **нетерпе́ние** impatience. **нетерпи́мый** intolerable, intolerant. **нетороопли́вый** leisurely. **нето́чный** (-чен, -чна́, -о) inaccurate, inexact. **нетре́звый** drunk. **нетро́нутый** untouched; chaste, virginal. **нетрудово́й дохо́д** unearned income. **нетрудоспосо́бность** disability.

не́тто *indecl adj & adv* net(t).

не́ту *see* **нет**

не-. неубеди́тельный unconvincing. **неуваже́ние** disrespect. **неуве́ренность** uncertainty. **неуве́ренный** uncertain. **неувяда́емый, неувяда́ющий** unfading. **неугомо́нный** indefatigable. **неуда́ча** failure. **неуда́чливый** unlucky. **неуда́чник, -ница** unlucky person, failure. **неуда́чный** unsuccessful, unfortunate. **неудержи́мый** irrepressible. **неудо́бный** uncomfortable; inconvenient; embarrassing. **неудо́бство** discomfort; inconvenience; embarrassment. **неудовлетворе́ние** dissatisfaction. **неудовлетворённый** dissatisfied. **неудовлетвори́тельный** unsatisfactory. **неудово́льствие** displeasure.

неуже́ли? *partl* really?

не-. неузнава́емый unrecognizable. **неукло́нный** steady; undeviating. **неуклю́жий**

clumsy. **неуловимый** elusive; subtle. **неуме́лый** inept; clumsy. **неуме́ренный** immoderate. **неуме́стный** inappropriate; irrelevant. **неумоли́мый** implacable, inexorable. **неумы́шленный** unintentional.

не-. неупла́та non-payment. **неуравнове́шенный** unbalanced. **неурожа́й** bad harvest. **неуро́чный** untimely, inopportune. **неуря́дица** disorder, mess. **неуспева́емость** poor progress. **неусто́йка** forfeit. **неусто́йчивый** unstable; unsteady. **неусту́пчивый** unyielding. **неуте́шный** inconsolable. **неутоли́мый** unquenchable. **неутоми́мый** tireless. **не́уч** ignoramus. **неучти́вый** discourteous. **неуязви́мый** invulnerable.

нефри́т jade.

нефте- *in comb* oil, petroleum. **нефтено́сный** oil-bearing. **~перего́нный заво́д** oil refinery. **~прово́д** (oil) pipeline. **~проду́кты** (-ов) *pl* petroleum products.

нефть oil, petroleum. **нефтяно́й** oil, petroleum.

не-. нехва́тка shortage. **нехорошо́** *adv* badly. **нехоро́ш\|ий** (-óш, -á) bad; **~о́** it is bad, it is wrong. **не́хотя** *adv* unwillingly; unintentionally. **нецелесообра́зный** inexpedient; pointless. **нецензу́рный** unprintable. **нечая́нный** unexpected; accidental.

не́чего (не́чему, -чем, не́ о чем) *pron* (*with separable pref*) (there is) nothing.

нечелове́ческий inhuman, superhuman.

нече́стный dishonest, unfair.

нечётный odd.

нечистопло́тный dirty; slovenly; unscrupulous. **нечистота́** (*pl* -о́ты, -о́т) dirtiness, filth; *pl* sewage. **нечи́стый** (-и́ст, -á, -о) dirty, unclean; impure; unclear. **не́чисть** evil spirits; scum.

нечленоразде́льный inarticulate.

не́что *pron* something.

не-. неэконо́мный uneconomical. **неэффекти́вный** ineffective; inefficient. **нея́вка** failure to appear. **нея́ркий** dim, faint; dull, subdued. **нея́сный** (-сен, -сна́, -о) not clear; vague.

ни *partl* not a; **ни оди́н (одна́, одно́)** not a single; (*with prons and pronominal advs*) -ever; **кто... ни** whoever. **ни** *conj*: **ни... ни** neither ... nor; **ни то ни сё** neither one thing nor the other.

ни́ва cornfield, field.

нивели́р level.

нигде́ *adv* nowhere.

нидерла́ндец (-дца; *gen pl* -дцев) Dutchman. **нидерла́ндка** Dutchwoman. **нидерла́ндский** Dutch. **Нидерла́нды** (-ов) *pl* the Netherlands.

ни́же *adj* lower, humbler; *adv* below; *prep+gen* below, beneath. **нижесле́дующий** following. **ни́жн\|ий** lower, under-; **~ее бельё** underclothes; **~ий эта́ж** ground floor. **низ** (*loc* -ý; *pl* -ы́) bottom; *pl* lower classes; low notes.

низа́ть (нижу́, ни́жешь) *impf* (*pf* на~) string, thread.

низверга́ть *impf*, **низве́рг-**

нуть (-ну; -ёрг) *pf* throw down, overthrow; **~ся** crash down; be overthrown. **низверже́ние** overthrow.

низи́на low-lying place. **ни́зкий** (-зок, -зка́, -о) low; base. **низкопокло́нство** servility. **низкопро́бный** low-grade. **низкоро́слый** undersized. **низкосо́ртный** low-grade.

ни́зменность lowland; baseness. **ни́зменный** low-lying; base.

низо́вье (*gen pl* -ьев) the lower reaches. **ни́зость** baseness, meanness. **ни́зш|ий** lower, lowest; **~ее образова́ние** primary education.

ника́к *adv* in no way. **никако́й** *pron* no; no ... whatever

ни́кель *m* nickel.

нике́м *see* **никто́. никогда́** *adv* never. **никто́** (-кого́, -кому́, -ке́м, ни о ко́м) *pron* (*with separable pref*) nobody, no one. **никуда́** nowhere. **никчёмный** useless. **нима́ло** *adv* not in the least.

нимб halo, nimbus.

ни́мфа nymph; pupa.

ниотку́да *adv* from nowhere.

нипочём *adv* it is nothing; dirt cheap; in no circumstances.

нисколько *adv* not at all.

ниспроверга́ть *impf*, **ниспрове́ргнуть** (-ну; -ёрг) *pf* overthrow. **ниспроверже́ние** overthrow.

нисходя́щий descending.

ни́тка thread; string; **до ни́тки** to the skin; **на живу́ю ни́тку** hastily, anyhow. **ни́точка** thread. **нить** thread; filament.

ничего́ *etc.*: *see* **ничто́. ничего́** *adv* all right; it doesn't matter, never mind; *as indecl adj* not bad, pretty good. **ниче́й** (-чья́, -чьё) *pron* nobody's; **ничья́ земля́** no man's land. **ничья́** *sb* draw; tie.

ничко́м *adv* face down, prone.

ничто́ (-чего́, -чему́, -чём, ни о чём) *pron* (*with separable pref*) nothing. **ничто́жество** nonentity, nobody. **ничто́жный** insignificant; worthless.

ничу́ть *adv* not a bit.

ничьё, ничья́: *see* **ниче́й**

ни́ша niche, recess.

ни́щенка beggar-woman. **ни́щенский** beggarly. **нищета́** poverty. **ни́щий** (нищ, -á, -е) destitute, poor; *sb* beggar.

но *conj* but; still.

нова́тор innovator. **нова́торский** innovative. **нова́торство** innovation.

Но́вая Зела́ндия New Zealand.

нове́йший newest, latest.

нове́лла short story.

но́венький brand-new.

новизна́ novelty; newness. **нови́нка** novelty. **новичо́к** (-чка́) novice.

ново- *in comb* new(ly). **новобра́нец** (-нца) new recruit. **~бра́чный** *sb* newly-wed. **~введе́ние** innovation. **~го́дний** new year's. **~зела́ндец** (-дца; *gen pl* -дцев), **~зела́ндка** New-Zealander. **~зела́ндский** New Zealand. **~лу́ние** new moon. **~прибы́вший** newly-arrived; *sb* newcomer. **~рождённый** newborn. **~сёл** new settler. **~се́лье** new home; house-warming. **новостро́йка** new building.

но́вость (*gen pl* -е́й) news; novelty. **но́вшество** innovation, novelty. **но́вый** (нов, -á, -о)

нóвый (нов, -á, -о) new; modern; ~ **год** New Year's Day. **ногá** (*acc* нóгу; *pl* нóги, ног, ногáм) foot, leg. **нóготь** (-гтя; *pl* -и) *m* finger-nail, toe-nail. **нож** (-á) knife. **нóжка** small foot or leg; leg; stem, stalk. **нóжницы** (-иц) *pl* scissors, shears. **нóжны** (-жен) *pl* sheath, scabbard. **ножóвка** saw, hacksaw. **ноздря́** (*pl* -и, -éй) nostril. **нокáут** knock-out. **нокаути́ровать** *impf* & *pf* knock out. **нолевóй, нулевóй** zero. **ноль** (-я́), **нуль** (-я́) *m* nought, zero, nil. **номенклатýра** nomenclature; top positions in government. **нóмер** (*pl* -á) number; size; (hotel-)room; item; trick. **номерóк** (-ркá) tag; label, ticket. **номинáл** face value. **номинáльный** nominal. **норá** (*pl* -ы) burrow, hole. **Норвéгия** Norway. **норвéжец** (-жца), **норвéжка** Norwegian. **норвéжский** Norwegian. **норд** (*naut*) north; north wind. **нóрка** mink. **нóрма** standard, norm; rate. **нормализáция** standardization. **нормáльно** all right, OK. **нормáльный** normal; standard. **нормировáние, нормирóвка** regulation; rate-fixing; rationing. **нормировáть** *impf* & *pf* regulate, standardize; ration. **нос** (*loc* -ý; *pl* -ы́) nose; beak; bow, prow. **нóсик** (*small*) nose; spout.

носи́лки (-лок) *pl* stretcher; litter. **носи́льщик** porter. **носи́тель** *m*, **~ница** (*fig*) bearer; (*med*) carrier. **носи́ть** (-ошý, -óсишь) *impf* carry, bear; wear; **~ся** rush, tear along, fly; float, be carried; wear. **нóска** carrying, wearing. **нóский** hard-wearing. **носовóй** nose; nasal; ~ **платóк** (pocket) handkerchief. **носóк** (-скá) little nose; toe; sock. **носорóг** rhinoceros. **нóта** note; *pl* music. **нотáция** notation; lecture, reprimand. **нотáриус** notary. **ночевáть** (-чýю) *impf* (*pf* **пере~**) spend the night. **ночёвка** spending the night. **ночлéг** place to spend the night; passing the night. **ночлéжка** doss-house. **ночни́к** (-á) night-light. **ночн|óй** night, nocturnal; **~áя рубáшка** nightdress; **~óй горшóк** potty; chamber-pot. **ночь** (*loc* -и́; *gen pl* -éй) night. **нóчью** *adv* at night. **нóша** burden. **нóшеный** worn; second-hand. **нóю** *etc.*: *see* **ныть** **ноя́брь** (-я́) *m* November. **ноя́брьский** November. **нрав** disposition, temper; *pl* customs, ways. **нрáвиться** (-влюсь) *impf* (*pf* **по~**) +*dat* please; **мне нрáвится** I like. **нрáвственность** morality, morals. **нрáвственный** moral. **ну** *int* & *partl* well, well then. **нýдный** tedious. **нуждá** (*pl* -ы) need. **нуждáться** *impf* be in need; +**в**+*prep* need, require. **нýжн|ый** (-жен, -жнá, -о, нýжны́) necessary; **~о** it is necessary; +*dat* I, *etc.*, must, ought to, need.

нулевóй, нуль *see* **нолевóй, ноль**
нумерáция numeration; numbering. **нумеровáть** *impf* (*pf* **про~**) number.
нутрó inside, interior; instinct(s).
ны́не *adv* now; today. **ны́нешний** present; today's. **ны́нче** *adv* today; now.
нырну́ть (-ну́, -нёшь) *pf*, **ныря́ть** *impf* dive.
ныть (нóю) *impf* ache; whine. **нытьё** whining.
н.э. *abbr* (*of* **нáшей э́ры**) AD.
нюх scent; flair. **ню́хать** *impf* (*pf* **по~**) smell, sniff.
ня́нчить (-чу) *impf* nurse, look after; **~ся с**+*instr* nurse; fuss over. **ня́нька** nanny. **ня́ня** (*children's*) nurse, nanny.

О

о, об, обо *prep* **I.** +*prep* of, about, concerning. **II.** +*acc* against; on, upon.
о *int* oh!
оáзис oasis.
об *see* **о** *prep.*
óба (обóих) *m* & *neut*, **óбе** (обéих) *f* both.
обалдевáть *impf*, **обалдéть** (-éю) *pf* go crazy; become dulled; be stunned.
обанкрóтиться (-óчусь) *pf* go bankrupt.
обая́ние fascination, charm. **обая́тельный** fascinating, charming.
обвáл fall(ing); crumbling; collapse; caving-in; landslide; **(снéжный) ~** avalanche. **обвали́ть** (-лю́, -лишь) *pf* (*impf* **обвáливать**) cause to fall *or* collapse; crumble; heap round; **~ся** collapse, cave in; crumble.
обваля́ть *pf* (*impf* **обвáливать**) roll.
обвáривать *impf*, **обвари́ть** (-рю́, -ришь) *pf* pour boiling water over; scald; **~ся** scald o.s.
обведу́ *etc.*: *see* **обвести́. обвёл** *etc.*: *see* **обвести́. об|венчáть(ся** *pf.*
оберну́ть (-ну́, -нёшь) *pf*, **обвёртывать** *impf* wrap, wrap up.
обвéс short weight. **обвéсить** (-éшу) *pf* (*impf* **обвéшивать**) cheat in weighing.
обвести́ (-еду́, -едёшь; -ёл, -елá) *pf* (*impf* **обводи́ть**) lead round, take round; encircle; surround; outline; dodge.
обвéтренный weather-beaten.
обветшáлый decrepit. **об|ветшáть** *pf.*
обвéшивать *impf of* **обвéсить. обвивáть(ся** *impf of* **обви́ть(ся**
обвинéние charge, accusation; prosecution. **обвини́тель** *m* accuser; prosecutor. **обвини́тельный** accusatory; **~ акт** indictment; **~ пригово́р** verdict of guilty. **обвини́ть** *pf*, **обвиня́ть** *impf* prosecute, indict; **+в**+*prep* accuse of, charge with. **обвиня́емый** *sb* the accused; defendant.
обви́ть (обовью́, обовьёшь; обви́л, -á, -о) *pf* (*impf* **обвивáть**) wind round; **~ся** wind round.
обводи́ть (-ожу́, -óдишь) *impf of* **обвести́**
обворáживать *impf*, **обворожи́ть** (-жу́) *pf* charm, enchant. **обворожи́тельный** charming, enchanting.

обвязáть (-яжý, -я́жешь) *pf*, **обвя́зывать** *impf* tie round; **~ся** *+instr* tie round o.s.

обгóн passing. **обгоня́ть** *impf of* **обогнáть**

обгорáть *impf*, **обгорéть** (-рю́) *pf* be burnt, be scorched. **обгорéлый** burnt, charred, scorched.

обдéлать *pf* (*impf* **обдéлывать**) finish; polish, set; manage, arrange.

обделúть (-лю́, -лишь) *pf* (*impf* **обделя́ть**) *+instr* do out of one's (fair) share of.

обдéлывать *impf of* **обдéлать**. **обделя́ть** *impf of* **обделúть**

обдерý *etc.*: *see* **ободрáть**. **обдирáть** *impf of* **ободрáть**

обдýманный deliberate, well-considered. **обдýмать** *pf*, **обдýмывать** *impf* consider, think over.

óбе: *see* **óба**. **обегáть** *impf of* **обежáть**. **обегý** *etc.*: *see* **обежáть**

обéд dinner, lunch. **обéдать** *impf* (*pf* **по~**) have dinner, dine. **обéденный** dinner.

обеднéвший impoverished. **обеднéние** impoverishment. **о|беднéть** (-éю) *pf*.

обéдня (*gen pl* -ден) mass.

обежáть (-егý) *pf* (*impf* **обегáть**) run round; run past; outrun.

обезбóливание anaesthetization. **обезбóливать** *impf*, **обезбóлить** *pf* anaesthetize.

обезврéдить (-éжу) *pf*, **обезврéживать** *impf* render harmless.

обездóленный unfortunate, hapless.

обеззарáживающий disinfectant.

обезлúченный depersonalized; robbed of individuality.

обезобрáживать *impf*, **о|безобрáзить** (-áжу) *pf* disfigure.

обезопáсить (-áшу) *pf* secure.

обезорýживать *impf*, **обезорýжить** (-жу) *pf* disarm.

обезýметь (-ею) *pf* lose one's senses, lose one's head.

обезья́на monkey; ape.

обелúть *pf*, **обеля́ть** *impf* vindicate; clear of blame.

оберегáть *impf*, **оберéчь** (-егý, -ежёшь; -рёг, -лá) *pf* guard; protect.

обернýть (-нý, -нёшь) *pf*, **обёртывать** *impf* (*impf also* **оборáчивать**) twist, wrap up, turn; **~ся** turn (round); turn out; *+instr or* **в**+*acc* turn into.

обёртка wrapper; (dust-) jacket, cover. **обёрточный** wrapping.

оберý *etc.*: *see* **обобрáть**

обескурáживать *impf*, **обескурáжить** (-жу) *pf* discourage; dishearten.

обескрóвить (-влю) *pf*, **обескрóвливать** *impf* drain of blood, bleed white; render lifeless.

обеспéчение securing, guaranteeing; ensuring; provision; guarantee; security. **обеспéченность** security; *+instr* provision of. **обеспéченный** well-to-do; well provided for. **обеспéчивать** *impf*, **обеспéчить** (-чу) *pf* provide for; secure; ensure; protect; *+instr* provide with.

о|беспокóить(ся *pf*.

обессúлеть (-ею) *pf* grow weak, lose one's strength. **обессúливать** *impf*, **обес-**

сúлить *pf* weaken.
о|бесслáвить (-влю) *pf.*
обессмéртить (-рчу) *pf* immortalize.
обесценéние depreciation.
обесцéнивать *impf,* **обесцéнить** *pf* depreciate; cheapen; **~ся** depreciate.
о|бесчéстить (-éщу) *pf.*
обéт vow, promise. **обетовáнный** promised. **обещáние** promise. **обещáть** *impf* & *pf* (*pf also* **по~**) promise.
обжáлование appeal. **обжáловать** *pf* appeal against.
обжéчь (обожгý, обожжёшь; обжёг, обожглá) *pf,* **обжигáть** *impf* burn; scorch; bake; **~ся** burn o.s.; burn one's fingers.
обжóра *m* & *f* glutton. **обжóрство** gluttony.
обзавестúсь (-едýсь, -едёшься; -вёлся, -лáсь) *pf,* **обзаводúться** (-ожýсь, -óдишься) *impf* +*instr* provide o.s. with; acquire.
обзовý *etc.*: *see* **обозвáть**
обзóр survey, review.
обзывáть *impf of* **обозвáть**
обивáть *impf of* **обúть. обúвка** upholstering; upholstery.
обúда offence, insult; nuisance. **обúдеть** (-úжу) *pf,* **обижáть** *impf* offend; hurt, wound; **~ся** take offence; feel hurt. **обúдный** offensive; annoying. **обúдчивый** touchy. **обúженный** offended.
обúлие abundance. **обúльный** abundant.
обирáть *impf of* **обобрáть**
обитáемый inhabited. **обитáтель** *m* inhabitant. **обитáть** *impf* live.
обúть (обобью, -ьёшь) *pf* (*impf* **обивáть**) upholster; knock off.
обихóд custom, (general) use, practice. **обихóдный** everyday.
обклáдывать(ся *impf of* **обложúть(ся**
обкрáдывать *impf of* **обокрáсть**
облáва raid; cordon, cordoning off.
облагáемый taxable. **облагáть(ся** *impf of* **обложúть(ся: ~ся налóгом** be liable to tax.
обладáние possession. **облaдáтель** *m* possessor. **обладáть** *impf* +*instr* possess.
óблако (*pl* -á, -óв) cloud.
облáмывать(ся *impf of* **обломáть(ся, обломúться**
областнóй regional. **óбласть** (*gen pl* -éй) region; field, sphere.
óблачность cloudiness. **óблачный** cloudy.
облёг *etc.*: *see* **облéчь. облегáть** *impf of* **облéчь**
облегчáть *impf,* **облегчúть** (-чý) *pf* lighten; relieve; alleviate; facilitate. **облегчéние** relief.
обледенéлый ice-covered. **обледенéние** icing over. **обледенéть** (-éет) *pf* become covered with ice.
облéзлый shabby; mangy.
облекáть(ся *impf of* **облéчь[2](ся. облекý** *etc.*: *see* **облéчь[2]**
облепúть (-плю, -пишь) *pf,* **облеплять** *impf* stick to, cling to; throng round; plaster.
облетáть *impf,* **облетéть** (-лечý) fly (round); spread (all over); fall.
облéчь[1] (-ляжет; -лёг, -лá) *pf* (*impf* **облегáть**) cover, envelop; fit tightly.

обле́чь[2] (-еку́, -ечёшь; -ёк, -кла́) *pf* (*impf* **облека́ть**) clothe, invest; **~ся** clothe o.s.; *+gen* take the form of.

облива́ть(ся *impf of* **обли́ть(ся**

облига́ция bond.

облиза́ть (-ижу́, -и́жешь) *pf*, **обли́зывать** *impf* lick (all over); **~ся** smack one's lips.

о́блик look, appearance.

о́бли́тый (о́бли́т, -а́, -о) covered, enveloped. **обли́ть** (оболью́, -льёшь; о́бли́л, -ила́, -о) *pf* (*impf* **облива́ть**) pour, sluice, spill; **~ся** sponge down, take a shower; pour over o.s.

облицева́ть (-цу́ю) *pf*, **облицо́вывать** *impf* face. **облицо́вка** facing; lining.

облича́ть *impf*, **обличи́ть** (-чу́) *pf* expose; reveal; point to. **обличе́ние** exposure, denunciation. **обличи́тельный** denunciatory.

обложе́ние taxation; assessment. **обложи́ть** (-жу́, -жишь) *pf* (*impf* **обкла́дывать, облага́ть**) edge; face; cover; surround; assess; **круго́м обложи́ло (не́бо)** the sky is completely overcast; **~ нало́гом** tax; **~ся** *+instr* surround o.s. with. **обло́жка** (dust-)cover; folder.

облока́чиваться *impf*, **облокоти́ться** (-очу́сь, -о́ти́шься) *pf* **на**+*acc* lean one's elbows on.

облома́ть *pf* (*impf* **обла́мывать**) break off; **~ся** break off. **обломи́ться** (-ло́мится) *pf* (*impf* **обла́мываться**) break off. **обло́мок** (-мка) fragment.

облу́пленный chipped.

облучи́ть (-чу́) *pf*, **облуча́ть** *impf* irradiate. **облуче́ние** irradiation.

об|лысе́ть (-е́ю) *pf*.

обля́жет *etc.*: *see* **обле́чь**[1]

обма́зать (-а́жу) *pf*, **обма́зывать** *impf* coat; putty; besmear; **~ся** *+instr* get covered with.

обма́кивать *impf*, **обмакну́ть** (-ну́, -нёшь) *pf* dip.

обма́н deceit; illusion; **~ зре́ния** optical illusion. **обма́нный** deceitful. **обману́ть** (-ну́, -нешь) *pf*, **обма́нывать** *impf* deceive; cheat; **~ся** be deceived. **обма́нчивый** deceptive. **обма́нщик** deceiver; fraud.

обма́тывать(ся *impf of* **обмота́ть(ся**

обма́хивать *impf*, **обмахну́ть** (-ну́, -нёшь) *pf* brush off; fan; **~ся** fan o.s.

обмёл *etc.*: *see* **обмести́**

обмеле́ние shallowing. **об|меле́ть** (-е́ет) *pf* become shallow.

обме́н exchange; barter; **в ~ за**+*acc* in exchange for; **~ веще́ств** metabolism. **обме́нивать** *impf*, **обменя́ть** (-ню́, -нишь) *pf*, **об|меня́ть** *pf* exchange; **~ся** *+instr* exchange. **обме́нный** exchange.

обме́р measurement; false measure.

обмере́ть (обомру́, -рёшь; о́бмер, -ла́, -ло) *pf* (*impf* **обмира́ть**) faint; **~ от у́жаса** be horror-struck.

обме́ривать *impf*, **обме́рить** *pf* measure; cheat in measuring.

обмести́ (-ету́, -етёшь; -мёл, -а́) *pf*, **обмета́ть**[1] *impf* sweep off, dust.

обмета́ть[2] (-ечу́ *or* -а́ю, -е́чешь

or -а́ешь) *pf* (*impf* **обмётывать**) oversew.
обмету́ *etc.*: *see* **обмести́. обмётывать** *impf of* **обмета́ть.**
обмира́ть *impf of* **обмере́ть**
обмо́лвиться (-влюсь) *pf* make a slip of the tongue; *+instr* say, utter. **обмо́лвка** slip of the tongue.
обморо́женный frost-bitten.
о́бморок fainting-fit, swoon.
обмота́ть *pf* (*impf* **обма́тывать**) wind round; **~ся** *+instr* wrap o.s. in. **обмо́тка** winding; *pl* puttees.
обмо́ю *etc.*: *see* **обмы́ть**
обмундирова́ние fitting out (with uniform); uniform. **обмундирова́ть** *pf*, **обмундиро́вывать** *impf* fit out (with uniform).
обмыва́ть *impf*, **обмы́ть** (-мо́ю) *pf* bathe, wash; **~ся** wash, bathe.
обмяка́ть *impf*, **обмя́кнуть** (-ну; -мя́к) *pf* become soft *or* flabby.
обнадёживать *impf*, **обнадёжить** (-жу) *pf* reassure.
обнажа́ть *impf*, **обнажи́ть** (-жу́) *pf* bare, uncover; reveal.
обнажённый (-ён, -ена́) naked, bare; nude.
обнаро́довать *impf & pf* promulgate.
обнару́же́ние revealing; discovery; detection. **обнару́живать** *impf*, **обнару́жить** (-жу) *pf* display; reveal; discover; **~ся** come to light.
обнести́ (-су́, -сёшь; -нёс, -ла́) *pf* (*impf* **обноси́ть**) enclose; *+instr* serve round; pass over, leave out.
обнима́ть(ся *impf of* **обня́ть(ся. обниму́** *etc.*: *see* **обня́ть**
обнища́ние impoverishment.
обнови́ть (-влю́) *pf*, **обновля́ть** *impf* renovate; renew. **обно́вка** new acquisition; new garment. **обновле́ние** renovation, renewal.
обноси́ть (-ошу́, -о́сишь) *impf of* **обнести́; ~ся** *pf* have worn out one's clothes.
обня́ть (-ниму́, -ни́мешь; о́бнял, -а́, -о) *pf* (*impf* **обнима́ть**) embrace; clasp; **~ся** embrace; hug one another.
обо *see* **о** *prep.*
обобра́ть (оберу́, -рёшь; обо́бра́л, -а́, -о) *pf* (*impf* **обира́ть**) rob; pick.
обобща́ть *impf*, **обобщи́ть** (-щу́) *pf* generalize. **обобще́ние** generalization. **обобществи́ть** (-влю́) *pf*, **обобществля́ть** *impf* socialize; collectivize. **обобществле́ние** socialization; collectivization.
обобью́ *etc.*: *see* **оби́ть. обовью́** *etc.*: *see* **обви́ть**
обогати́ть (-ащу́) *pf*, **обогаща́ть** *impf* enrich; **~ся** become rich; enrich o.s. **обогаще́ние** enrichment.
обогна́ть (обгоню́, -о́нишь; обогна́л, -а́, -о) *pf* (*impf* **обгоня́ть**) pass; outstrip.
обогну́ть (-ну́, -нёшь) *pf* (*impf* **огиба́ть**) round, skirt; bend round.
обогрева́тель *m* heater.
обогрева́ть *impf*, **обогре́ть** (-е́ю) *pf* heat, warm; **~ся** warm up.
о́бод (*pl* -о́дья, -ьев) rim. **ободо́к** (-дка́) thin rim, narrow border.
обо́дранный ragged. **ободра́ть** (обдеру́, -рёшь; -а́л, -а́, -о) *pf* (*impf* **обдира́ть**) skin, flay; peel; fleece.

ободре́ние encouragement, reassurance. **ободри́тельный** encouraging, reassuring. **ободри́ть** *pf*, **ободря́ть** *impf* encourage, reassure; **~ся** cheer up, take heart.

обожа́ть *impf* adore.

обожгу́ *etc.*: *see* **обже́чь**

обожестви́ть (-влю́) *pf*, **обожествля́ть** *impf* deify.

обожжённый (-ён, -ена́) burnt, scorched.

обо́з string of vehicles; transport.

обозва́ть (обзову́, -вёшь; -а́л, -а́, -о) *pf* (*impf* **обзыва́ть**) call; call names.

обозлённый (-ён, -а́) angered; embittered. **обо|зли́ть** *pf*, **о|зли́ть** *pf* anger; embitter; **~ся** get angry.

обозна́ться *pf* mistake s.o. for s.o. else.

обознача́ть *impf*, **обозна́чить** (-чу) *pf* mean; mark; **~ся** appear, reveal o.s. **обозначе́ние** sign, symbol.

обозрева́тель *m* reviewer; columnist. **обозрева́ть** *impf*, **обозре́ть** (-рю́) *pf* survey. **обозре́ние** survey; review; revue. **обозри́мый** visible.

обо́и (-ев) *pl* wallpaper.

обо́йма (*gen pl* **-о́йм**) cartridge clip.

обойти́ (-йду́, -йдёшь; -ошёл, -ошла́) *pf* (*impf* **обходи́ть**) go round; pass; avoid; pass over; **~сь** manage, make do; **+с+*instr*** treat.

обокра́сть (обкраду́, -дёшь) *pf* (*impf* **обкра́дывать**) rob.

оболо́чка casing; membrane; cover, envelope, jacket; shell.

обольсти́тель *m* seducer. **обольсти́тельный** seductive. **обольсти́ть** (-льщу́) *pf*, **обольща́ть** *impf* seduce. **обольще́ние** seduction; delusion.

оболью́ *etc.*: *see* **обли́ть**

обомру́ *etc.*: *see* **обмере́ть**

обоня́ние (sense of) smell. **обоня́тельный** olfactory.

обопру́ *etc.*: *see* **опере́ть**

обора́чивать(ся *impf of* **оберну́ть(ся, обороти́ть(ся**

обо́рванный torn, ragged. **оборва́ть** (-ву́, -вёшь; -а́л, -а́, -о) *pf* (*impf* **обрыва́ть**) tear off; break; snap; cut short; **~ся** break; snap; fall; stop suddenly.

обо́рка frill, flounce.

оборо́на defence. **обороны́тельный** defensive. **оборони́ть** *pf*, **обороня́ть** *impf* defend; **~ся** defend o.s. **оборо́нный** defence, defensive.

оборо́т turn; revolution; circulation; turnover; back; **~ ре́чи** (turn of) phrase; **смотри́ на ~е** P.T.O. **обороти́ть** (-рочу́, -ро́тишь) *pf* (*impf* **обора́чивать**) turn; **~ся** turn (round); *+instr or* **в**+*acc* turn into. **оборо́тный** circulating; reverse; **~ капита́л** working capital.

обору́дование equipping; equipment. **обору́довать** *impf* & *pf* equip.

обоснова́ние basing; basis, ground. **обосно́ванный** well-founded. **обоснова́ть** *pf*, **обосно́вывать** *impf* ground, base; substantiate; **~ся** settle down.

обосо́бленный isolated, solitary.

обостре́ние aggravation. **обострённый** keen; strained; sharp, pointed. **обостри́ть** *pf*, **обостря́ть** *impf* sharpen;

strain; aggravate; **~ся** become strained; be aggravated; become acute.
оботру́ *etc.*: *see* **обтере́ть**
обо́чина verge; shoulder, edge.
обошёл *etc.*: *see* **обойти́. обошью́** *etc.*: *see* **обши́ть**
обою́дный mutual, reciprocal.
обраба́тывать *impf*, **обрабо́тать** *pf* till, cultivate; work, work up; treat, process. **обрабо́тка** working (up); processing; cultivation.
об|ра́довать(ся *pf*.
о́браз shape, form; image; manner; way; icon; **гла́вным ~ом** mainly; **таки́м ~ом** thus.
образе́ц (-зца́) model; pattern; sample. **о́бразный** graphic; figurative. **образова́ние** formation; education.
образо́ванный educated.
образова́тельный educational. **образова́ть** *impf* & *pf*, **образо́вывать** *impf* form; **~ся** form; arise; turn out well.
образу́мить (-млю) *pf* bring to reason; **~ся** see reason.
образцо́вый model. **обра́зчик** specimen, sample.
обра́мить (-млю) *pf*, **обрамля́ть** *impf* frame.
обраста́ть *impf*, **обрасти́** (-ту́, -тёшь; -ро́с, -ла́) *pf* be overgrown.
обрати́мый reversible, convertible. **обрати́ть** (-ащу́) *pf*, **обраща́ть** *impf* turn; convert; **~ внима́ние на**+*acc* pay *or* draw attention to; **~ся** turn; appeal; apply; address; **+в**+*acc* turn into; **+с**+*instr* treat; handle. **обра́тно** *adv* back; backwards; conversely; **~ пропорциона́льный** inversely proportional. **обра́тный** reverse; return; opposite; inverse. **обраще́ние** appeal, address; conversion; (**+с**+*instr*) treatment (of); handling (of); use (of).
обре́з edge; sawn-off gun; **в ~**+*gen* only just enough. **обре́зать** (-е́жу) *pf*, **обреза́ть** *impf* cut (off); clip, trim; pare; prune; circumcise; **~ся** cut o.s. **обре́зок** (-зка) scrap; *pl* ends; clippings.
обрека́ть *impf of* **обре́чь. обреку́** *etc.*: *see* **обре́чь. обрёл** *etc.*: *see* **обрести́**
обремени́тельный onerous.
о|бремени́ть *pf*, **обременя́ть** *impf* burden.
обрести́ (-ету́, -етёшь; -рёл, -а́) *pf*, **обрета́ть** *impf* find.
обрече́ние doom. **обречённый** doomed. **обре́чь** (-еку́, -ечёшь; -ёк, -ла́) *pf* (*impf* **обрека́ть**) doom.
обрисова́ть *pf*, **обрисо́вывать** *impf* outline, depict; **~ся** appear (in outline).
оброни́ть (-ню́, -нишь) *pf* drop; let drop.
обро́с *etc.*: *see* **обрасти́**.
обруба́ть *impf*, **обруби́ть** (-блю́, -бишь) *pf* chop off; cut off. **обру́бок** (-бка) stump.
об|руга́ть *pf*.
о́бруч (*pl* -и, -е́й) hoop. **обруча́льн|ый** engagement; **~ое кольцо́** betrothal ring, wedding ring. **обруча́ть** *impf*, **обручи́ть** (-чу́) betroth; **~ся +с**+*instr* become engaged to.
обруче́ние engagement.
обру́шивать *impf*, **об|ру́шить** (-шу) *pf* bring down; **~ся** come down, collapse.
обры́в precipice. **обрыва́ть(ся** *impf of* **оборва́ть(ся. обры́вок** (-вка) scrap; snatch.

обры́згать *pf*, **обры́згивать** *impf* splash; sprinkle.
обрю́зглый flabby.
обря́д rite, ceremony.
обсервато́рия observatory.
обсле́дование inspection. **обсле́дователь** *m* inspector. **обсле́довать** *impf* & *pf* inspect.
обслу́живание service; maintenance. **обслу́живать** *impf*, **обслужи́ть** (-жу́, -жишь) *pf* serve; operate.
обсо́хнуть (-ну; -о́х) *pf* (*impf* **обсыха́ть**) dry (off).
обста́вить (-влю) *pf*, **обставля́ть** *impf* surround; furnish; arrange. **обстано́вка** furniture; situation, conditions; set.
обстоя́тельный thorough, reliable; detailed. **обстоя́тельство** circumstance. **обстоя́ть** (-ои́т) *impf* be; go; **как обстои́т де́ло?** how is it going?
обстре́л firing, fire; **под ~ом** under fire. **обстре́ливать** *impf*, **обстреля́ть** *pf* fire at; bombard.
обступа́ть *impf*, **обступи́ть** (-у́пит) *pf* surround.
обсуди́ть (-ужу́, -у́дишь) *pf*, **обсужда́ть** *impf* discuss. **обсужде́ние** discussion.
обсчита́ть *pf*, **обсчи́тывать** *impf* shortchange; **~ся** miscount, miscalculate.
обсы́пать (-плю) *pf*, **обсыпа́ть** *impf* strew; sprinkle.
обсыха́ть *impf of* **обсо́хнуть**.
обта́чивать *impf of* **обточи́ть**
обтека́емый streamlined.
обтере́ть (оботру́, -трёшь; обтёр) *pf* (*impf* **обтира́ть**) wipe; rub; **~ся** dry o.s.; sponge down.
о(б)теса́ть (-ешу́, -е́шешь) *pf*, **о(б)тёсывать** *impf* rough-hew; teach good manners to; trim.
обтира́ние sponge-down. **обтира́ть(ся** *pf of* **обтере́ть(ся**
обточи́ть (-чу́, -чишь) *pf* (*impf* **обта́чивать**) grind; machine.
обтрёпанный frayed; shabby.
обтя́гивать *impf*, **обтяну́ть** (-ну́, -нешь) *pf* cover; fit close. **обтя́жка** cover; skin; **в обтя́жку** close-fitting.
обува́ть(ся *impf of* **обу́ть(ся**.
о́бувь footwear; boots, shoes.
обу́гливать *impf*, **обу́глить** *pf* char; carbonize; **~ся** char, become charred.
обу́за burden.
обузда́ть *pf*, **обу́здывать** *impf* bridle, curb.
обурева́ть *impf* grip; possess.
обусло́вить (-влю) *pf*, **обусло́вливать** *impf* cause; *+instr* make conditional on; **~ся** *+instr* be conditional on; depend on.
обу́тый shod. **обу́ть** (-у́ю) *pf* (*impf* **обува́ть**) put shoes on; **~ся** put on one's shoes.
о́бух butt, back.
обуча́ть *impf*, **об|учи́ть** (-чу́, -чишь) *pf* teach; train; **~ся** *+dat or inf* learn. **обуче́ние** teaching; training.
обхва́т girth; **в ~е** in circumference. **обхвати́ть** (-ачу́, -а́тишь) *pf*, **обхва́тывать** *impf* embrace; clasp.
обхо́д round(s); roundabout way; bypass. **обходи́тельный** courteous; pleasant. **обходи́ть(ся** (-ожу́(сь, -о́дишь(ся) *impf of* **обойти́(сь**. **обхо́дный** roundabout.
обша́ривать *impf*, **обша́рить** *pf* rummage through, ransack.

обшивáть *impf of* **обши́ть.** **обши́вка** edging; trimming; boarding, panelling; plating.
обши́рный extensive; vast.
обши́ть (обошью́, -шьёшь) *pf* (*impf* **обшивáть**) edge; trim; make outfit(s) for; plank.
обшлáг (-á; *pl* -á, -óв) cuff.
общáться *impf* associate.
обще- *in comb* common(ly), general(ly). **общедосту́пный** moderate in price; popular. **~жи́тие** hostel. **~извéстный** generally known. **~нарóдный** national, public. **~образовáтельный** of general education. **~при́нятый** generally accepted. **~сою́зный** All-Union. **~человéческий** common to all mankind; universal.
общéние contact; social intercourse. **общéственность** (the) public; public opinion; community. **общéственный** social, public; voluntary. **óбщество** society; company.
óбщ|ий general; common; **в ~ем** on the whole, in general. **óбщи́на** community; commune.
об|щипáть (-плю́, -плешь) *pf.*
общи́тельный sociable. **óбщность** community.
объедáть(ся *impf of* **объéсть(ся**
объединéние unification; merger; union, association. **объединённый** (-ён, -á) united. **объедини́тельный** unifying. **объедини́ть** *pf*, **объединя́ть** *impf* unite; join; combine; **~ся** unite.
объéдки (-ов) *pl* leftovers, scraps.
объéзд riding round; detour.
объéздить (-зжу, -здишь) *pf* (*impf* **объезжáть**) travel over; break in.
объезжáть *impf of* **объéздить, объéхать**
объéкт object; objective; establishment, works. **объекти́в** lens. **объекти́вность** objectivity. **объекти́вный** objective.
объём volume; scope. **объёмный** by volume, volumetric.
объéсть (-éм, -éшь, -éст, -еди́м) *pf* (*impf* **объедáть**) gnaw (round), nibble; **~ся** overeat.
объéхать (-éду) *pf* (*impf* **объезжáть**) drive *or* go round; go past; travel over.
объяви́ть (-влю́, -вишь) *pf*, **объявля́ть** *impf* declare, announce; **~ся** turn up; *+instr* declare o.s. **объявлéние** declaration, announcement; advertisement.
объяснéние explanation. **объясни́мый** explainable. **объясни́ть** *pf*, **объясня́ть** *impf* explain; **~ся** be explained; make o.s. understood; **+с**+*instr* have it out with.
объя́тие embrace.
обывáтель *m* Philistine. **обывáтельский** narrow-minded.
обыгрáть *pf*, **обы́грывать** *impf* beat (*in a game*).
обы́денный ordinary; everyday.
обыкновéние habit. **обыкновéнно** *adv* usually. **обыкновéнный** usual; ordinary.
óбыск search. **обыскáть** (-ыщу́, -ы́щешь) *pf*, **обы́скивать** *impf* search.
обы́чай custom; usage. **обы́чно** *adv* usually. **обы́чный** usual.
обя́занность duty; responsibility. **обя́занный** (*+inf*)

obliged; *+dat* indebted to (*+instr* for). **обяза́тельно** *adv* without fail. **обяза́тельный** obligatory. **обяза́тельство** obligation; commitment. **обяза́ть** (-яжу́, -я́жешь) *pf*, **обя́зывать** *impf* bind; commit; oblige; **~ся** pledge o.s., undertake.

ова́л oval. **ова́льный** oval.

ова́ция ovation.

овдове́ть (-е́ю) *pf* become a widow, widower.

овёс (овса́) oats.

ове́чка *dim of* **овца́**; harmless person.

овладева́ть *impf*, **овладе́ть** (-е́ю) *pf +instr* seize; capture; master.

о́вод (*pl* -ы *or* -а́) gadfly.

о́вощ (*pl* -и, -е́й) vegetable. **овощно́й** vegetable.

овра́г ravine, gully.

овся́нка oatmeal; porridge. **овся́ный** oat, oatmeal.

овца́ (*pl* -ы, ове́ц, о́вцам) sheep; ewe. **овча́рка** sheep-dog. **овчи́на** sheepskin.

ога́рок (-рка) candle-end.

огиба́ть *impf of* **обогну́ть**

оглавле́ние table of contents.

огласи́ть (-ашу́) *pf*, **оглаша́ть** *impf* announce; fill (with sound); **~ся** resound. **огла́ска** publicity. **оглаше́ние** publication.

огло́бля (*gen pl* -бель) shaft.

о|гло́хнуть (-ну; -о́х) *pf*.

оглуша́ть *impf*, **о|глуши́ть** (-шу́) *pf* deafen; stun. **оглуши́тельный** deafening.

огляде́ть (-яжу́) *pf*, **огля́дывать** *impf*, **огляну́ть** (-ну́, -нешь) *pf* look round; look over; **~ся** look round; look back. **огля́дка** looking back.

огнево́й fire; fiery. **о́гненный** fiery. **огнеопа́сный** inflammable. **огнеприпа́сы** (-ов) *pl* ammunition. **огнесто́йкий** fire-proof. **огнестре́льн|ый**: **~ое ору́жие** firearm(s). **огнетуши́тель** *m* fire-extinguisher. **огнеупо́рный** fire-resistant.

ого́ *int* oho!

огова́ривать *impf*, **оговори́ть** *pf* slander; stipulate (for); **~ся** make a proviso; make a slip (of the tongue). **огово́р** slander. **огово́рка** reservation, proviso; slip of the tongue.

оголённый bare, nude. **оголи́ть** *pf* (*impf* **оголя́ть**) bare; strip; **~ся** strip o.s.; become exposed.

оголя́ть(ся *impf of* **оголи́ть(ся**

огонёк (-нька́) (*small*) light; zest. **ого́нь** (огня́) *m* fire; light.

огора́живать *impf*, **огороди́ть** (-рожу́, -ро́дишь) *pf* fence in, enclose; **~ся** fence o.s. in. **огоро́д** kitchen-garden. **огоро́дный** kitchen-garden.

огорча́ть *impf*, **огорчи́ть** (-чу́) *pf* grieve, pain; **~ся** grieve, be distressed. **огорче́ние** grief; chagrin.

о|гра́бить (-блю) *pf*. **ограбле́ние** robbery; burglary.

огра́да fence. **огради́ть** (-ажу́) *pf*, **огражда́ть** *impf* guard, protect.

ограниче́ние limitation, restriction. **ограни́ченный** limited. **ограни́чивать** *impf*, **ограни́чить** (-чу) *pf* limit, restrict; **~ся** *+instr* limit *or* confine o.s. to; be limited to.

огро́мный huge; enormous.

о|грубе́ть (-е́ю) *pf*.

огры́зок (-зка) bit, end; stub.
огуре́ц (-рца́) cucumber.
ода́лживать *impf of* **одолжи́ть**
одарённый gifted. **ода́ривать** *impf*, **одари́ть** *pf*, **одаря́ть** *impf* give presents (to); *+instr* endow with.
одева́ть(ся *impf of* **оде́ть(ся**
оде́жда clothes; clothing.
одеколо́н eau-de-Cologne.
одели́ть *pf*, **оделя́ть** *impf* (*+instr*) present (with); endow (with).
оде́ну *etc.*: *see* **оде́ть. одёргивать** *impf of* **одёрнуть**
о|деревене́ть (-е́ю) *pf*.
одержа́ть (-жу́, -жишь) *pf*, **оде́рживать** *impf* gain. **одержи́мый** possessed.
одёрнуть (-ну) *pf* (*impf* **одёргивать**) pull down, straighten.
оде́тый dressed; clothed. **оде́ть** (-е́ну) *pf* (*impf* **одева́ть**) dress; clothe; **~ся** dress (o.s.). **одея́ло** blanket. **одея́ние** garb, attire.
оди́н (одного́), **одна́** (одно́й), **одно́** (одного́); *pl* **одни́** (одни́х) one; a, an; a certain; alone; only; nothing but; same; **одно́ и то же** the same thing; **оди́н на оди́н** in private; **оди́н раз** once; **одни́м сло́вом** in a word; **по одному́** one by one.
одина́ковый identical, the same, equal.
оди́ннадцатый eleventh. **оди́ннадцать** eleven.
одино́кий solitary; lonely; single. **одино́чество** solitude; loneliness. **одино́чка** *m & f* (one) person alone. **одино́чн|ый** individual; one-man; single; **~ое заключе́ние** solitary confinement.
одича́лый wild.
одна́жды *adv* once; one day; once upon a time.
одна́ко *conj* however.
одно- *in comb* single, one; uni-, mono-, homo-. **однобо́кий** one-sided. **~вре́ме́нно** *adv* simultaneously, at the same time. **~вре́ме́нный** simultaneous. **~зву́чный** monotonous. **~зна́чащий** synonymous. **~зна́чный** synonymous; one-digit. **~имённый** of the same name. **~кла́ссник** classmate. **~клёточный** unicellular. **~кра́тный** single. **~ле́тний** one-year; annual. **~ме́стный** single-seater. **~обра́зие, ~обра́зность** monotony. **~обра́зный** monotonous. **~ро́дность** homogeneity, uniformity. **~ро́дный** homogeneous; similar. **~сторо́нний** one-sided; unilateral; one-way. **~фами́лец** (-льца) person of the same surname. **~цве́тный** one-colour; monochrome. **~эта́жный** one-storeyed.
одобре́ние approval. **одобри́тельный** approving. **одо́брить** *pf*, **одобря́ть** *impf* approve (of).
одолева́ть *impf*, **одоле́ть** (-е́ю) *pf* overcome.
одолжа́ть *impf*, **одолжи́ть** (-жу́) *pf* lend; **+у**+*gen* borrow from. **одолже́ние** favour.
о|дряхле́ть (-е́ю) *pf*.
одува́нчик dandelion.
оду́маться *pf*, **оду́мываться** *impf* change one's mind.
одуре́лый stupid. **о|дуре́ть** (-е́ю) *pf*.
одурма́нивать *impf*, **о|дурма́нить** *pf* stupefy. **одуря́ть** *impf* stupefy.

одухотворённый inspired; spiritual. **одухотвори́ть** *pf*, **одухотворя́ть** *impf* inspire.
одушеви́ть (-влю́) *pf*, **одушевля́ть** *impf* animate. **одушевле́ние** animation.
оды́шка shortness of breath.
ожере́лье necklace.
ожесточа́ть *impf*, **ожесточи́ть** (-чу́) *pf* embitter, harden. **ожесточе́ние** bitterness. **ожесточённый** bitter; hard.
ожива́ть *impf of* **ожи́ть**
оживи́ть (-влю́) *pf*, **оживля́ть** *impf* revive; enliven; **~ся** become animated. **оживле́ние** animation; reviving; enlivening. **оживлённый** animated, lively.
ожида́ние expectation; waiting. **ожида́ть** *impf + gen or acc* wait for; expect.
ожире́ние obesity. **о|жире́ть** (-е́ю) *pf*.
ожи́ть (-иву́, -ивёшь; о́жил, -á, -о) *pf* (*impf* **ожива́ть**) come to life, revive.
ожо́г burn, scald.
озабо́ченность preoccupation; anxiety. **озабо́ченный** preoccupied; anxious.
озагла́вить (-лю) *pf*, **озагла́вливать** *impf* entitle; head.
озада́чивать *impf*, **озада́чить** (-чу) *pf* perplex, puzzle.
озари́ть *pf*, **озаря́ть** *impf* light up, illuminate; **~ся** light up.
оздорови́тельный бег jogging. **оздоровле́ние** sanitation.
озелени́ть *pf*, **озеленя́ть** *impf* plant (*with trees etc.*).
о́зеро (*pl* озёра) lake.
ози́мые *sb* winter crops. **ози́мый** winter. **о́зимь** winter crop.
озира́ться *impf* look round; look back.
о|зли́ть(ся: *see* **обозли́ть(ся**
озло́бить (-блю) *pf*, **озлобля́ть** *impf* embitter; **~ся** grow bitter. **озлобле́ние** bitterness, animosity. **озло́бленный** embittered.
о|знако́мить (-млю) *pf*, **ознакомля́ть** *impf* **с**+*instr* acquaint with; **~ся с**+*instr* familiarize o.s. with.
ознаменова́ть *pf*, **ознамено́вывать** *impf* mark; celebrate.
означа́ть *impf* mean, signify.
озно́б shivering, chill.
озо́н ozone.
озорни́к (-á) mischief-maker. **озорно́й** naughty, mischievous. **озорство́** mischief.
озя́бнуть (-ну; озя́б) *pf* be cold, be freezing.
ой *int* oh.
оказа́ть (-ажу́, -а́жешь) *pf* (*impf* **ока́зывать**) render, provide, show; **~ся** turn out, prove; find o.s., be found.
ока́зия unexpected event, funny thing.
ока́зывать(ся *impf of* **оказа́ть(ся**
окамене́лость fossil. **окамене́лый** fossilized; petrified. **о|камене́ть** (-е́ю) *pf*.
оканто́вка mount.
ока́нчивать(ся *impf of* **око́нчить(ся**. **ока́пывать(ся** *impf of* **окопа́ть(ся**
окая́нный damned, cursed.
океа́н ocean. **океа́нский** ocean; oceanic.
оки́дывать *impf*, **оки́нуть** (-ну) *pf*; **~ взгля́дом** take in at a glance, glance over.
о́кисел (-сла) oxide. **окисле́ние** oxidation. **о́кись** oxide.

оккупа́нт invader. **оккупа́ция** occupation. **оккупи́ровать** *impf & pf* occupy.
окла́д salary scale; (basic) pay.
оклевета́ть (-ещу́, -е́щешь) *pf* slander.
окле́ивать *impf*, **окле́ить** *pf* cover; paste over; ~ **обо́ями** paper.
окно́ (*pl* о́кна) window.
о́ко (*pl* о́чи, оче́й) eye.
око́вы (око́в) *pl* fetters.
околдова́ть *pf*, **околдо́вывать** *impf* bewitch.
о́коло *adv & prep+gen* by; close (to), near; around; about.
око́льный roundabout.
око́нный window.
оконча́ние end; conclusion, termination; ending. **оконча́тельный** final. **око́нчить** (-чу) *pf* (*impf* **ока́нчивать**) finish, end; **~ся** finish, end.
око́п trench. **окопа́ть** *pf* (*impf* **ока́пывать**) dig round; **~ся** entrench o.s., dig in. **око́пный** trench.
о́корок (*pl* -а́, -о́в) ham, gammon.
окочене́лый stiff with cold. **о|кочене́ть** (-е́ю) *pf.*
око́шечко, око́шко (*small*) window.
окра́ина outskirts, outlying districts.
о|кра́сить (-а́шу) *pf*, **окра́шивать** *impf* paint, colour; dye. **окра́ска** painting; colouring; dyeing; colouration.
о|кре́пнуть (-ну) *pf.* **о|крести́ть(ся** (-ещу́(сь, -е́стишь(ся) *pf.*
окре́стность environs. **окре́стный** neighbouring.
о́крик hail; shout. **окри́кивать** *impf*, **окри́кнуть** (-ну) *pf* hail, call, shout to.
окрова́вленный blood-stained.
о́круг (*pl* ~а́) district. **окру́га** neighbourhood. **округли́ть** *pf*, **округля́ть** *impf* round; round off. **окру́глый** rounded.
окружа́ть *impf*, **окружи́ть** (-жу́) *pf* surround; encircle. **окружа́ющ|ий** surrounding; **~ее** *sb* environment; **~ие** *sb pl* associates. **окруже́ние** encirclement; environment. **окружно́й** district. **окру́жность** circumference.
окрыли́ть *pf*, **окрыля́ть** *impf* inspire, encourage.
окта́ва octave.
окта́н octane.
октя́брь (-я́) *m* October. **октя́брьский** October.
окули́ст oculist.
окуна́ть *impf*, **окуну́ть** (-ну́, -нёшь) *pf* dip; **~ся** dip; plunge; become absorbed.
о́кунь (*pl* -и, -е́й) *m* perch.
окупа́ть *impf*, **окупи́ть** (-плю́, -пишь) *pf* compensate, repay; **~ся** be repaid, pay for itself.
оку́рок (-рка) cigarette-end.
оку́тать *pf*, **оку́тывать** *impf* wrap up; shroud, cloak.
оку́чивать *impf*, **оку́чить** (-чу) *pf* earth up.
ола́дья (*gen pl* -ий) fritter; drop-scone.
оледене́лый frozen. **о|ледене́ть** (-е́ю) *pf.*
оле́ний deer, deer's; reindeer. **оле́нина** venison. **оле́нь** *m* deer; reindeer.
оли́ва olive. **оли́вковый** olive; olive-coloured.
олига́рхия oligarchy.
олимпиа́да olympiad; Olympics. **олимпи́йск|ий** Olympic; Olympian; **~ие игры** Olympic games.

олифа drying oil (*e.g. linseed oil*).
олицетворение personification; embodiment. **олицетворить** *pf*, **олицетворять** *impf* personify, embody.
олово tin. **оловянный** tin.
ом ohm.
омар lobster.
омерзение loathing. **омерзительный** loathsome.
омертвелый stiff, numb; necrotic. **о|мертветь** (-ею) *pf.*
омлет omelette.
омоложение rejuvenation.
омоним homonym.
омою *etc.*: *see* **омыть**
омрачать *impf*, **омрачить** (-чу) *pf* darken, cloud.
омут whirlpool; maelstrom.
омывать *impf*, **омыть** (омою) *pf* wash; **~ся** be washed.
он (его, ему, им, о нём) *pron* he. **она** (её, ей, ей (ею), о ней) *pron* she.
ондатра musk-rat.
онемелый numb. **о|неметь** (-ею) *pf.*
они (их, им, ими, о них) *pron* they. **оно** (его, ему, им, о нём) *pron* it; this, that.
опадать *impf of* **опасть**.
опаздывать *impf of* **опоздать**
опала disgrace.
о|палить *pf.*
опаловый opal.
опалубка casing.
опасаться *impf +gen* fear; avoid, keep off. **опасение** fear; apprehension.
опасность danger; peril. **опасный** dangerous.
опасть (-адёт) *pf* (*impf* **опадать**) fall, fall off; subside.
опека guardianship; trusteeship.
опекаемый *sb* ward. **опекать** *impf* be guardian of; take care of. **опекун** (-а), **-унша** guardian; tutor; trustee.
опера opera.
оперативный efficient; operative, surgical; operation(s), operational. **оператор** operator; cameraman. **операционн|ый** operating; **~ая** *sb* operating theatre. **операция** operation.
опередить (-режу) *pf*, **опережать** *impf* outstrip, leave behind.
оперение plumage.
оперетта, -етка operetta.
опереть (обопру, -прёшь; опёр, -ла) *pf* (*impf* **опирать**) **+о+***acc* lean against; **~ся на** *or* **о+***acc* lean on, lean against.
оперировать *impf* & *pf* operate on; operate, act; *+instr* use.
оперный opera; operatic.
о|печалить(ся *pf.*
опечатать *pf* (*impf* **опечатывать**) seal up.
опечатка misprint.
опечатывать *impf of* **опечатать**
опешить (-шу) *pf* be taken aback.
опилки (-лок) *pl* sawdust; filings.
опирать(ся *impf of* **опереть(ся**
описание description. **описательный** descriptive. **описать** (-ишу, -ишешь) *pf*, **описывать** *impf* describe; **~ся** make a slip of the pen. **описка** slip of the pen. **опись** inventory.
опиум opium.
оплакать (-ачу) *pf*, **оплакивать** *impf* mourn for; bewail.
оплата payment. **оплатить** (-ачу, -атишь) *pf*, **оплачи-**

вать *impf* pay (for).
опла́чу *etc.*: *see* **опла́кать.** **оплачу́** *etc.*: *see* **оплати́ть**
оплеу́ха slap in the face.
оплодотвори́ть *pf*, **оплодотворя́ть** *impf* impregnate; fertilize.
о|пломбирова́ть *pf*.
опло́т stronghold, bulwark.
опло́шность blunder, mistake.
оповести́ть (-ещу́) *pf*, **оповеща́ть** *impf* notify. **оповеще́ние** notification.
опозда́вший *sb* late-comer. **опозда́ние** lateness; delay. **опозда́ть** *pf* (*impf* **опа́здывать**) be late; +**на**+*acc* miss.
опознава́тельный distinguishing; ~ **знак** landmark. **опознава́ть** (-наю́, -наёшь) *impf*, **опозна́ть** *pf* identify. **опозна́ние** identification.
о|позо́рить(ся *pf*.
оползать *impf*, **оползти́** (-зёт; -о́лз, -ла́) *pf* slip, slide. **о́ползень** (-зня) *m* landslide.
ополче́ние militia.
опо́мниться *pf* come to one's senses.
опо́р: во весь ~ at full speed.
опо́ра support; pier; **то́чка опо́ры** fulcrum, foothold.
опора́жнивать *impf of* **опорожни́ть**
опо́рный support, supporting, supported; bearing.
опоро́жни́ть *pf*, **опорожня́ть** *impf* (*impf also* **опора́жнивать**) empty.
о|поро́чить (-чу) *pf*.
опохмели́ться *pf*, **опохмеля́ться** *impf* take a hair of the dog that bit you.
опо́шлить *pf*, **опошля́ть** *impf* vulgarize, debase.
опоя́сать (-я́шу) *pf*, **опоя́сывать** *impf* gird; girdle.
оппозицио́нный opposition.
оппози́ция opposition.
оппортуни́зм opportunism.
опра́ва setting, mounting; spectacle frames.
оправда́ние justification; excuse; acquittal. **оправда́тельный пригово́р** verdict of not guilty. **оправда́ть** *pf*, **опра́вдывать** *impf* justify; excuse; acquit; **~ся** justify o.s.; be justified.
опра́вить (-влю) *pf*, **оправля́ть** *impf* set right, adjust; mount; **~ся** put one's dress in order; recover; +**от**+*gen* get over.
опра́шивать *impf of* **опроси́ть**
определе́ние definition; determination; decision. **определённый** definite; certain. **определи́мый** definable. **определи́ть** *pf*, **определя́ть** *impf* define; determine; appoint; **~ся** be formed; be determined; find one's position.
опроверга́ть *impf*, **опрове́ргнуть** (-ну; -ве́рг) *pf* refute, disprove. **опроверже́ние** refutation; denial.
опроки́дывать *impf*, **опроки́нуть** (-ну) *pf* overturn; topple; **~ся** overturn; capsize.
опроме́тчивый rash, hasty.
опро́с (cross-)examination; (opinion) poll. **опроси́ть** (-ошу́, -о́сишь) *pf* (*impf* **опра́шивать**) question; (cross-)examine. **опро́сный лист** questionnaire.
опры́скать *pf*, **опры́скивать** *impf* sprinkle; spray.
опря́тный neat, tidy.
о́птик optician. **о́птика** op-

tics. **опти́ческий** optic, optical.

оптима́льный optimal. **оптими́зм** optimism. **оптими́ст** optimist. **оптимисти́ческий** optimistic.

опто́вый wholesale. **о́птом** *adv* wholesale.

опубликова́ние publication; promulgation. **о|публикова́ть** *pf*, **опублико́вывать** *impf* publish; promulgate.

опуска́ть(ся *impf of* **опусти́ть(ся**

опусте́лый deserted. **о|пусте́ть** (-е́ет) *pf*.

опусти́ть (-ущу́, -у́стишь) *pf* (*impf* **опуска́ть**) lower; let down; turn down; omit; post; **~ся** lower o.s.; sink; fall; go down; go to pieces.

опустоша́ть *impf*, **опустоши́ть** (-шу́) *pf* devastate. **опустоше́ние** devastation. **опустоши́тельный** devastating.

опу́тать *pf*, **опу́тывать** *impf* entangle; ensnare.

опуха́ть *impf*, **о|пу́хнуть** (-ну; опу́х) *pf* swell, swell up. **о́пухоль** swelling; tumour.

опу́шка edge of a forest; trimming.

опущу́ *etc.*: *see* **опусти́ть**

опыле́ние pollination. **опыли́ть** *pf*, **опыля́ть** *impf* pollinate.

о́пыт experience; experiment. **о́пытный** experienced; experimental.

опьяне́ние intoxication. **о|пьяне́ть** (-е́ю) *pf*, **о|пьяни́ть** *pf*, **опьяня́ть** *impf* intoxicate, make drunk.

опя́ть *adv* again.

ора́ва crowd, horde.

ора́кул oracle.

орангута́нг orangutan.

ора́нжевый orange. **оранжере́я** greenhouse, conservatory.

ора́тор orator. **орато́рия** oratorio.

ора́ть (ору́, орёшь) *impf* yell.

орби́та orbit; (eye-)socket.

о́рган[1] organ; body. **орга́н**[2] (*mus*) organ. **организа́тор** organizer. **организацио́нный** organization(al). **организа́ция** organization. **органи́зм** organism. **организо́ванный** organized. **организова́ть** *impf* & *pf* (*pf also* с~) organize; **~ся** be organized; organize. **органи́ческий** organic.

о́ргия orgy.

орда́ (*pl* -ы) horde.

о́рден (*pl* -а́) order.

о́рдер (*pl* -а́) order; warrant; writ.

ордина́та ordinate.

ордина́тор house-surgeon.

орёл (орла́) eagle; **~ или ре́шка?** heads or tails?

орео́л halo.

оре́х nut, nuts; walnut. **оре́ховый** nut; walnut. **оре́шник** hazel; hazel-thicket.

оригина́л original; eccentric. **оригина́льный** original.

ориента́ция orientation. **ориенти́р** landmark; reference point. **ориенти́роваться** *impf* & *pf* orient o.s.; **+на**+*acc* head for; aim at. **ориентиро́вка** orientation. **ориентиро́вочный** reference; tentative; approximate.

орке́стр orchestra.

орли́ный eagle; aquiline.

орна́мент ornament; ornamental design.

о|робе́ть (-е́ю) *pf*.

ороси́тельный irrigation.

оросúть (-ошý) *pf*, **орошáть** *impf* irrigate. **орошéние** irrigation; **поля́ орошéния** sewage farm.
орý *etc.*: *see* **орáть**
орýдие instrument; tool; gun. **орудúйный** gun. **орýдовать** *impf +instr* handle; run. **оружéйный** arms; gun. **орýжие** arm, arms; weapons.
орфографúческий orthographic(al). **орфогрáфия** orthography, spelling.
осá (*pl* -ы) wasp.
осáда siege. **осадúть**[1] (-ажý) *pf* (*impf* **осаждáть**) besiege.
осадúть[2] (-ажý, -áдишь) *pf* (*impf* **осáживать**) check; force back; rein in; take down a peg.
осáдный siege.
осáдок (-дка) sediment; fall-out; after-taste; *pl* precipitation, fall-out. **осáдочный** sedimentary.
осаждáть *impf of* **осадúть**[1]
осáживать *impf of* **осадúть**[2].
осажý *see* **осадúть**[1,2]
осáнка carriage, bearing.
освáивать(ся *impf of* **освóить(ся**
осведомúтельный informative; information. **освéдомить** (-млю) *pf*, **осведомля́ть** *impf* inform; **~ся** о+*prep* inquire about, ask after. **осведомлéние** notification. **осведомлённый** well-informed, knowledgeable.
освежáть *impf*, **освежúть** (-жý) *pf* refresh; air. **освежúтельный** refreshing.
осветúтельный illuminating. **осветúть** (-ещý) *pf*, **освещáть** *pf* light up; illuminate; throw light on; **~ся** light up. **освещéние** lighting, illumination. **освещённый** (-ён, -á) lit.
о|свидéтельствовать *pf*.
освистáть (-ищý, -úщешь) *pf*, **освúстывать** *impf* hiss (off); boo.
освободúтель *m* liberator. **освободúтельный** liberation, emancipation. **освободúть** (-ожý) *pf*, **освобождáть** *impf* liberate; emancipate; dismiss; vacate; empty; **~ся** free o.s.; become free. **освобождéние** liberation; release; emancipation; vacation. **освобождённый** (-ён, -á) freed, free; exempt.
освоéние mastery; opening up. **освóить** *pf* (*impf* **осваúвать**) master; become familiar with; **~ся** familiarize o.s.
освящённый (-ён, -енá) consecrated; sanctified; **~ векáми** time-honoured.
оседáть *impf of* **осéсть**
о|седлáть *pf*, **осёдлывать** *impf* saddle.
осéдлый settled.
осекáться *impf of* **осéчься**
осёл (-слá) donkey; ass.
оселóк (-лкá) touchstone; whetstone.
осенúть *pf* (*impf* **осеня́ть**) overshadow; dawn upon.
осéнний autumn(al). **óсень** autumn. **óсенью** *adv* in autumn.
осеня́ть *impf of* **осенúть**
осéсть (ося́ду; осéл) *pf* (*impf* **оседáть**) settle; subside.
осётр (-á) sturgeon. **осетрúна** sturgeon.
осéчка misfire. **осéчься** (-екýсь, -ечёшься; -ёкся, -еклáсь) *pf* (*impf* **осекáться**) stop short.
осúливать *impf*, **осúлить** *pf* overpower; master.

оси́на aspen.

о|си́пнуть (-ну; оси́п) get hoarse.

осироте́лый orphaned. **осироте́ть** (-е́ю) *pf* be orphaned.

оска́ливать *impf*, **о|ска́лить** *pf*; ~ **зу́бы**, **~ся** bare one's teeth.

о|сканда́лить(ся *pf*.

оскверни́ть *pf*, **оскверня́ть** *impf* profane; defile.

оско́лок (-лка) splinter; fragment.

оско́мина bitter taste (in the mouth); **наби́ть оско́мину** set the teeth on edge.

оскорби́тельный insulting, abusive. **оскорби́ть** (-блю́) *pf*, **оскорбля́ть** *impf* insult; offend; **~ся** take offence. **оскорбле́ние** insult. **оскорблённый** (-ён, -á) insulted.

ослабева́ть *impf*, **о|слабе́ть** (-е́ю) *pf* weaken; slacken. **осла́бить** (-блю) *pf*, **ослабля́ть** *impf* weaken; slacken. **ослабле́ние** weakening; slackening, relaxation.

ослепи́тельный blinding, dazzling. **ослепи́ть** (-плю́) *pf*, **ослепля́ть** *impf* blind, dazzle. **ослепле́ние** blinding, dazzling; blindness. **о|сле́пнуть** (-ну; -е́п) *pf*.

осли́ный donkey; asinine. **осли́ца** she-ass.

осложне́ние complication. **осложни́ть** *pf*, **осложня́ть** *impf* complicate; **~ся** become complicated.

ослы́шаться (-шусь) *pf* mishear.

осма́тривать(ся *impf of* **осмотре́ть(ся**. **осме́ивать** *impf of* **осмея́ть**

о|смеле́ть (-е́ю) *pf*. **осме́ливаться** *impf*, **осме́литься** *pf* dare; venture.

осмея́ть (-ею́, -еёшь) *pf* (*impf* **осме́ивать**) ridicule.

осмо́тр examination, inspection. **осмотре́ть** (-рю́, -ришь) *pf* (*impf* **осма́тривать**) examine, inspect; look round; **~ся** look round. **осмотри́тельный** circumspect.

осмы́сленный sensible, intelligent. **осмы́сливать** *impf*, **осмы́слить** *pf*, **осмысля́ть** *impf* interpret; comprehend.

оснасти́ть (-ащу́) *pf*, **оснаща́ть** *impf* fit out, equip. **осна́стка** rigging. **оснаще́ние** fitting out; equipment.

осно́ва base, basis, foundation; *pl* fundamentals; stem (*of a word*). **основа́ние** founding, foundation; base; basis; reason; **на како́м основа́нии?** on what grounds? **основа́тель** *m* founder. **основа́тельный** well-founded; solid; thorough. **основа́ть** (-ную́, -нуёшь) *pf*, **осно́вывать** *impf* found; base; **~ся** settle; be founded, be based. **основно́й** fundamental, basic; main; **в основно́м** in the main, on the whole. **основополо́жник** founder.

осо́ба person. **осо́бенно** *adv* especially. **осо́бенность** peculiarity; **в осо́бенности** in particular. **осо́бенный** special, particular, peculiar. **особня́к** (-á) private residence; detached house. **особняко́м** *adv* by o.s. **осо́бо** *adv* apart; especially. **осо́бый** special; particular.

осознава́ть (-наю́, -наёшь) *impf*, **осозна́ть** *pf* realize.

осо́ка sedge.

óспа smallpox; pock-marks.

оспа́ривать *impf*, **оспо́рить** *pf* dispute; contest.
о|срами́ть(ся (-млю(сь) *pf*.
остава́ться (-таю́сь, -таёшься) *impf of* **оста́ться**
ост (*naut*) east; east wind.
оста́вить (-влю) *pf*, **оставля́ть** *impf* leave; abandon; reserve.
остальн|о́й the rest of; **~о́е** *sb* the rest; **~ы́е** *sb pl* the others.
остана́вливать(ся *impf of* **останови́ть(ся**
оста́нки (-ов) *pl* remains.
останови́ть (-влю́, -вишь) *pf* (*impf* **остана́вливать**) stop; restrain; **~ся** stop, halt; stay; +**на**+*prep* dwell on; settle on. **остано́вка** stop.
оста́ток (-тка) remainder; rest; residue; *pl* remains; leftovers. **оста́ться** (-а́нусь) *pf* (*impf* **остава́ться**) remain; stay; *impers* it remains, it is necessary; **нам не остаётся ничего́ друго́го, как** we have no choice but.
остекли́ть *pf*, **остекля́ть** *impf* glaze.
остервене́ть *pf* become enraged.
остерега́ть *impf*, **остере́чь** (-регу́, -режёшь; -рёг, -ла́) *pf* warn; **~ся** (+*gen*) beware (of).
о́стов frame, framework; skeleton.
о|столбене́ть (-е́ю) *pf*.
осторо́жно *adv* carefully; **~!** look out! **осторо́жность** care, caution. **осторо́жный** careful, cautious.
острига́ть(ся *impf of* **остри́чь(ся**
остриё point; spike; (cutting) edge. **остри́ть**[1] *impf* sharpen.
остри́ть[2] *impf* (*pf* **с~**) be witty.
о|стри́чь (-игу́, -ижёшь; -и́г) *pf* (*impf also* **острига́ть**) cut, clip; **~ся** have one's hair cut.
о́стров (*pl* -а́) island. **острово́к** (-вка́) islet; **~ безопа́сности** (traffic) island.
остро́та[1] witticism, joke.
острота́[2] sharpness; keenness; pungency.
остроу́мие wit. **остроу́мный** witty.
о́стрый (остр, -а́, -о) sharp; pointed; acute; keen. **остря́к** (-а́) wit.
о|студи́ть (-ужу́, -у́дишь) *pf*, **остужа́ть** *impf* cool.
оступа́ться *impf*, **оступи́ться** (-плю́сь, -пишься) *pf* stumble.
остыва́ть *impf*, **осты́ть** (-ы́ну) *pf* get cold; cool down.
осуди́ть (-ужу́, -у́дишь) *pf*, **осужда́ть** *impf* condemn; convict. **осужде́ние** condemnation; conviction. **осуждённый** (-ён, -а́) condemned, convicted; *sb* convict.
осу́нуться (-нусь) *pf* grow thin, become drawn.
осуша́ть *impf*, **осуши́ть** (-шу́, -шишь) *pf* drain; dry. **осуше́ние** drainage.
осуществи́мый feasible. **осуществи́ть** (-влю́) *pf*, **осуществля́ть** *impf* realize, bring about; accomplish; **~ся** be fulfilled, come true. **осуществле́ние** realization; accomplishment.
осчастли́вить (-влю) *pf*, **осчастли́вливать** *impf* make happy.
осы́пать (-плю) *pf*, **осыпа́ть** *impf* strew; shower; **~ся** crumble; fall. **о́сыпь** scree.
ось (*gen pl* -е́й) axis; axle.

осьминóг octopus.
осяду *etc.*: *see* **осéсть**
осязáемый tangible. **осязáние** touch. **осязáтельный** tactile; tangible. **осязáть** *impf* feel.
от, ото *prep+gen* from; of; against.
отáпливать *impf of* **отопúть**
отáра flock (*of sheep*).
отбáвить (-влю) *pf*, **отбавлять** *impf* pour off; **хоть отбавляй** more than enough.
отбегáть *impf*, **отбежáть** (-егý) *pf* run off.
отберý *etc.*: *see* **отобрáть**
отбивáть(ся *impf of* **отбúть(ся**
отбивнáя котлéта cutlet, chop.
отбирáть *impf of* **отобрáть**
отбúть (отобью, -ёшь) *pf* (*impf* **отбивáть**) beat (off), repel; win over; break off; **~ся** break off; drop behind; **+от**+*gen* defend o.s. against.
óтблеск reflection.
отбóй repelling; retreat; ringing off; **бить ~** beat a retreat; **дать ~** ring off.
отбóйный молотóк (-ткá) pneumatic drill.
отбóр selection. **отбóрный** choice, select(ed).
отбрáсывать *impf*, **отбрóсить** (-óшу) *pf* throw off *or* away; hurl back; reject; **~ тень** cast a shadow. **отбрóсы** (-ов) *pl* garbage.
отбывáть *impf*, **отбы́ть** (-бýду; óтбыл, -á, -о) *pf* depart; serve (*a sentence*).
отвáга courage, bravery.
отвáживаться *impf*, **отвáжиться** (-жусь) *pf* dare. **отвáжный** courageous.
отвáл dump, slag-heap; casting off; **до ~а** to satiety.
отвáливать *impf*, **отвалúть** (-лю, -лишь) *pf* push aside; cast off; fork out.
отвáр broth; decoction. **отвáривать** *impf*, **отварúть** (-рю, -ришь) *pf* boil. **отварнóй** boiled.
отвéдать *pf* (*impf* **отвéдывать**) taste, try.
отведý *etc.*: *see* **отвестú**
отвéдывать *impf of* **отвéдать**
отвезтú (-зý, -зёшь; -вёз, -лá) *pf* (*impf* **отвозúть**) take *or* cart away.
отвёл *etc.*: *see* **отвестú**
отвергáть *impf*, **отвéргнуть** (-ну; -вéрг) *pf* reject; repudiate.
отвéрженный outcast.
отвернýть (-нý, -нёшь) *pf* (*impf* **отвёртывать, отворáчивать**) turn aside; turn down; turn on; unscrew; screw off; **~ся** turn away; come unscrewed.
отвéрстие opening; hole.
отвертéть (-рчý, -ртишь) *pf* (*impf* **отвёртывать**) unscrew; twist off; **~ся** come unscrewed; get off. **отвёртка** screwdriver.
отвёртывать(ся *impf of* **отвернýть(ся, отвертéть(ся**
отвéс plumb; vertical slope.
отвéсить (-éшу) *pf* (*impf* **отвéшивать**) weigh out. **отвéсный** perpendicular, sheer.
отвестú (-едý, -едёшь; -вёл, -á) *pf* (*impf* **отводúть**) lead, take; draw *or* take aside; deflect; draw off; reject; allot.
отвéт answer.
ответвúться *pf*, **ответвляться** *impf* branch off. **ответвлéние** branch, offshoot.

отве́тить (-е́чу) *pf*, **отвеча́ть** *impf* answer; +**на**+*acc* reply to; +**за**+*acc* answer for. **отве́тный** in reply, return. **отве́тственность** responsibility. **отве́тственный** responsible. **отве́тчик** defendant.

отве́шивать *impf of* **отве́сить. отве́шу** *etc.*: *see* **отве́сить**

отвинти́ть (-нчу́) *pf*, **отви́нчивать** *impf* unscrew.

отвиса́ть *impf*, **отви́снуть** (-нет; -и́с) *pf* hang down, sag. **отви́слый** hanging, baggy.

отвлека́ть *impf*, **отвле́чь** (-еку́, -ечёшь; -влёк, -ла́) *pf* distract, divert; **~ся** be distracted. **отвлечённый** abstract.

отво́д taking aside; diversion; leading, taking; rejection; allotment. **отводи́ть** (-ожу́, -о́дишь) *impf of* **отвести́**.

отвоева́ть (-ою́ю) *pf*, **отвоёвывать** *impf* win back; spend in fighting.

отвози́ть (-ожу́, -о́зишь) *impf of* **отвезти́. отвора́чивать(ся** *impf of* **отверну́ть(ся**

отвори́ть (-рю́, -ришь) *pf* (*impf* **отворя́ть**) open; **~ся** open.

отворя́ть(ся *impf of* **отвори́ть(ся. отво́ю** *etc.*: *see* **отвоева́ть**

отврати́тельный disgusting. **отвраще́ние** disgust, repugnance.

отвыка́ть *impf*, **отвы́кнуть** (-ну; -вы́к) *pf* +**от** *or inf* lose the habit of; grow out of.

отвяза́ть (-яжу́, -я́жешь) *pf*, **отвя́зывать** *impf* untie, unfasten; **~ся** come untied, come loose; +**от**+*gen* get rid of; leave alone.

отгада́ть *pf*, **отга́дывать** *impf* guess. **отга́дка** answer.

отгиба́ть(ся *impf of* **отогну́ть(ся**

отгла́дить (-а́жу) *pf*, **отгла́живать** *impf* iron (out).

отгова́ривать *impf*, **отговори́ть** *pf* dissuade; **~ся** +*instr* plead. **отгово́рка** excuse, pretext.

отголо́сок (-ска) echo.

отгоня́ть *impf of* **отогна́ть**

отгора́живать *impf*, **отгороди́ть** (-ожу́, -о́дишь) *pf* fence off; partition off; **~ся** shut o.s. off.

отдава́ть[1]**(ся** (-даю́(сь) *impf of* **отда́ть(ся. отдава́ть**[2] (-аёт) *impf impers*+*instr* taste of; smell of; smack of; **от него́ отдаёт во́дкой** he reeks of vodka.

отдале́ние removal; distance. **отдалённый** remote. **отдали́ть** *pf*, **отдаля́ть** *impf* remove; estrange; postpone; **~ся** move away; digress.

отда́ть (-а́м, -а́шь, -а́ст, -ади́м; о́тдал, -а́, -о) *pf* (*impf* **отдава́ть**[1]) give back, return; give; give up; give away; recoil; cast off; **~ся** give o.s. (up); resound. **отда́ча** return; payment; casting off; efficiency; output; recoil.

отде́л department; section.

отде́лать *pf* (*impf* **отде́лывать**) finish, put the finishing touches to; trim; **~ся** +**от**+*gen* get rid of; +*instr* get off with.

отделе́ние separation; department; compartment; section. **отдели́ть** (-елю́, -е́лишь) *pf* (*impf* **отделя́ть**) separate; detach; **~ся** separate; detach o.s.; get detached.

отде́лка finishing; finish,

decoration. **отдéлывать(ся** *impf of* **отдéлать(ся**

отдéльно separately; apart. **отдéльный** separate. **отделя́ть(ся** *impf of* **отдели́ть(ся**

отдёргивать *impf*, **отдёрнуть** (-ну) *pf* draw *or* pull aside *or* back.

отдеру́ *etc.*: *see* **отодрáть**. **отдирáть** *impf of* **отодрáть**

отдохну́ть (-ну́, -нёшь) *pf* (*impf* **отдыхáть**) rest.

отду́шина air-hole, vent.

óтдых rest. **отдыхáть** *impf* (*pf* **отдохну́ть**) rest; be on holiday.

отдышáться (-шу́сь, -шишься) *pf* recover one's breath.

отекáть *impf of* **отéчь**. **о|тели́ться** (-éлится) *pf*.

отéль *m* hotel.

отесáть *etc.*: *see* **обтесáть**

отéц (отцá) father. **отéческий** fatherly, paternal. **отéчественный** home, native. **отéчество** native land, fatherland.

отéчь (-еку́, -ечёшь; отёк, -лá) *pf* (*impf* **отекáть**) swell (up).

отживáть *impf*, **отжи́ть** (-иву́, -ивёшь; óтжил, -á, -о) *pf* become obsolete *or* outmoded. **отжи́вший** obsolete; outmoded.

óтзвук echo.

óтзыв[1] opinion; reference; review; response. **отзы́в**[2] recall. **отзывáть(ся** *impf of* **отозвáть(ся**. **отзы́вчивый** responsive.

откáз refusal; repudiation; failure; natural. **отказáть** (-ажу́, -áжешь) *pf*, **откáзывать** *impf* break down; (*+dat* **в**+*prep*) refuse, deny (*s.o. sth*); **~ся** (**+от**+*gen or +inf*) refuse; turn down; renounce, give up.

откáлывать(ся *impf of* **отколóть(ся**. **откáпывать** *impf of* **откопáть**. **откáрмливать** *impf of* **откорми́ть**

откати́ть (-ачу́, -áтишь) *pf*, **откáтывать** *impf* roll away; **~ся** roll away *or* back; be forced back.

откачáть *pf*, **откáчивать** *impf* pump out; give artificial respiration to.

откáшливаться *impf*, **откáшляться** *pf* clear one's throat.

откидно́й folding, collapsible. **отки́дывать** *impf*, **отки́нуть** (-ну) *pf* fold back; throw aside.

отклáдывать *impf of* **отложи́ть**

откле́ивать *impf*, **откле́ить** (-éю) *pf* unstick; **~ся** come unstuck.

óтклик response; comment; echo. **откликáться** *impf*, **откли́кнуться** (-нусь) *pf* answer, respond.

отклонéние deviation; declining, refusal; deflection. **отклони́ть** (-ню́, -нишь) *pf*, **отклоня́ть** *impf* deflect; decline; **~ся** deviate; diverge.

отключáть *impf*, **отключи́ть** (-чу́) *pf* cut off, disconnect.

отколоти́ть (-очу́, -óтишь) *pf* knock off; beat up.

отколóть (-лю́, -лешь) *pf* (*impf* **откáлывать**) break off; chop off; unpin; **~ся** break off; come unpinned; break away.

откопáть *pf* (*impf* **откáпывать**) dig up; exhume.

откорми́ть (-млю́, -мишь) *pf* (*impf* **откáрмливать**) fatten.

откóс slope.

открепи́ть (-плю́) *pf*, **откреплять** *impf* unfasten; **~ся**

become unfastened.
открове́ние revelation. **откровéнный** frank; outspoken; unconcealed. **открóю** *etc.: see* **откры́ть**
открути́ть (-учý, -ýтишь) *pf*, **открýчивать** *impf* untwist, unscrew.
открыва́ть *impf*, **откры́ть** (-рóю) *pf* open; reveal; discover; turn on; **~ся** open; come to light, be revealed. **откры́тие** discovery; revelation; opening. **откры́тка** postcard, card. **откры́то** openly. **откры́тый** open.
откýда *adv* from where; from which; how; **~ ни возьми́сь** from out of nowhere. **откýда-либо, -нибудь** from somewhere or other. **откýда-то** from somewhere.
откýпоривать *impf*, **откýпорить** *pf* uncork.
откуси́ть (-ушý, -ýсишь) *pf*, **откýсывать** *impf* bite off.
отлага́тельство delay. **отлага́ть** *impf of* **отложи́ть**
от|лакирова́ть *pf*. **отла́мывать** *impf of* **отлома́ть, отломи́ть**
отлепи́ть (-плю́, -пишь) *pf* unstick, take off; **~ся** come unstuck, come off.
отлёт flying away; departure. **отлета́ть** *impf*, **отлете́ть** (-лечý) *pf*, fly, fly away, fly off; rebound.
отли́в ebb, ebb-tide; tint; play of colours. **отлива́ть** *impf*, **отли́ть** (отолью́; óтли́л, -á, -о) *pf* pour off; pump out; cast, found; (*no pf*) *+instr* be shot with. **отли́вка** casting; moulding.
отлича́ть *impf*, **отличи́ть** (-чý) *pf* distinguish; **~ся** distinguish o.s.; differ; *+instr* be notable for. **отли́чие** difference; distinction; **знак отли́чия** order, decoration; **с отли́чием** with honours. **отли́чник** outstanding student, worker, etc. **отличи́тельный** distinctive; distinguishing. **отли́чный** different; excellent.
отлóгий sloping.
отложе́ние sediment; deposit. **отложи́ть** (-ожý, -óжишь) *pf* (*impf* **откла́дывать, отлага́ть**) put aside; postpone; deposit.
отлома́ть, отломи́ть (-млю́, -мишь) *pf* (*impf* **отла́мывать**) break off.
от|лупи́ть *pf*.
отлуча́ть *impf*, **отлучи́ть** (-чý) *pf* **(от це́ркви)** excommunicate; **~ся** absent o.s. **отлýчка** absence.
отлы́нивать *impf* *+***от***+gen* shirk.
отма́хиваться *impf*, **отмахнýться** (-нýсь, -нёшься) *pf* **от***+gen* brush off; brush aside.
отмежева́ться (-жýюсь) *pf*, **отмежёвываться** *impf* **от***+gen* dissociate o.s. from.
óтмель (sand-)bank.
отмéна abolition; cancellation. **отмени́ть** (-ню́, -нишь) *pf*, **отменя́ть** *impf* repeal; abolish; cancel.
отмере́ть (отомрёт; óтмер, -лá, -ло) *pf* (*impf* **отмира́ть**) die off; die out.
отмéривать *impf*, **отмéрить** *pf*, **отмеря́ть** *impf* measure off.
отмести́ (-етý, -етёшь; -ёл, -á) *pf* (*impf* **отмета́ть**) sweep aside.
отмета́ть *impf of* **отмести́**
отмéтить (-éчу) *pf*, **отмеча́ть**

impf mark, note; celebrate; **~ся** sign one's name; sign out. **отме́тка** note; mark.
отмира́ть *impf of* **отмере́ть**
отмора́живать *impf*, **отморо́зить** (-о́жу) *pf* injure by frost-bite. **отмороже́ние** frost-bite. **отморо́женный** frost-bitten.
отмо́ю *etc.*: *see* **отмы́ть**
отмыва́ть *impf*, **отмы́ть** (-мо́ю) *pf* wash clean; wash off; **~ся** wash o.s. clean; come out.
отмыка́ть *impf of* **отомкну́ть**
отмы́чка master key.
отнести́ (-су́, -сёшь; -нёс, -ла́) *pf* (*impf* **относи́ть**) take; carry away; ascribe, attribute; **~сь к**+*dat* treat; regard; apply to; concern, have to do with.
отнима́ть(ся *impf of* **отня́ть(ся**
относи́тельно *adv* relatively; *prep+gen* concerning. **относи́тельность** relativity. **относи́тельный** relative. **относи́ть(ся** (-ошу́(сь, -о́сишь(ся) *impf of* **отнести́(сь. отноше́ние** attitude; relation; respect; ratio; **в отноше́нии**+*gen*, **по отноше́нию к**+*dat* with regard to; **в прямо́м (обра́тном) отноше́нии** in direct (inverse) ratio.
отны́не *adv* henceforth.
отню́дь not at all.
отня́тие taking away; amputation. **отня́ть** (-ниму́, -ни́мешь; о́тнял, -а́, -о) *pf* (*impf* **отнима́ть**) take (away); amputate; **~ от груди́** wean; **~ся** be paralysed.
ото: *see* **от**
отобража́ть *impf*, **отобрази́ть** (-ажу́) *pf* reflect; represent. **отображе́ние** reflection; representation.
отобра́ть (отберу́, -рёшь; отобра́л, -а́, -о) *pf* (*impf* **отбира́ть**) take (away); select.
отобью́ *etc.*: *see* **отби́ть**
отовсю́ду *adv* from everywhere.
отогна́ть (отгоню́, -о́нишь; отогна́л, -а́, -о) *pf* (*impf* **отгоня́ть**) drive away, off.
отогну́ть (-ну́, -нёшь) *pf* (*impf* **отгиба́ть**) bend back; **~ся** bend.
отогрева́ть *impf*, **отогре́ть** (-е́ю) *pf* warm.
отодвига́ть *impf*, **отодви́нуть** (-ну) *pf* move aside; put off.
отодра́ть (отдеру́, -рёшь; отодра́л, -а́, -о) *pf* (*impf* **отдира́ть**) tear off, rip off.
отож(д)естви́ть (-влю́) *pf*, **отож(д)ествля́ть** *impf* identify.
отозва́ть (отзову́, -вёшь; отозва́л, -а́, -о)*pf* (*impf* **отзыва́ть**) take aside; recall; **~ся на**+*acc* answer; **на**+*acc or prep* tell on; have an affect on.
отойти́ (-йду́, -йдёшь; отошёл, -шла́) *pf* (*impf* **отходи́ть**) move away; depart; withdraw; digress; come out; recover.
отолью́ *etc.*: *see* **отли́ть. отомрёт** *etc.*: *see* **отмере́ть.**
ото|мсти́ть (-мщу́) *pf.*
отомкну́ть (-ну́, -нёшь) *pf* (*impf* **отмыка́ть**) unlock, unbolt.
отопи́тельный heating. **отопи́ть** (-плю́, -пишь) *pf* (*impf* **ота́пливать**) heat. **отопле́ние** heating.
отопру́ *etc.*: *see* **отпере́ть.**
отопью́ *etc.*: *see* **отпи́ть**
ото́рванный cut off, isolated.
оторва́ть (-ву́, -вёшь) *pf*

(*impf* **отрыва́ть**) tear off; tear away; **~ся** come off, be torn off; be cut off, lose touch; break away; tear o.s. away; **~ся от земли́** take off.

оторопе́ть (-е́ю) *pf* be struck dumb.

отосла́ть (-ошлю́, -ошлёшь) *pf* (*impf* **отсыла́ть**) send (off); send back; **+к**+*dat* refer to.

отоспа́ться (-сплю́сь; -а́лся, -ала́сь, -ось) *pf* (*impf* **отсыпа́ться**) catch up on one's sleep.

отошёл *etc.*: *see* **отойти́**. **отошлю́** *etc.*: *see* **отосла́ть**

отпада́ть *impf of* **отпа́сть**.

от|пари́ровать *pf*. **отпа́рывать** *impf of* **отпоро́ть**

отпа́сть (-адёт) *pf* (*impf* **отпада́ть**) fall off; fall away; pass.

отпева́ние funeral service.

отпере́ть (отопру́, -прёшь; о́тпер, -ла́, -ло) *pf* (*impf* **отпира́ть**) unlock; **~ся** open; **+от**+*gen* deny; disown.

от|печа́тать *pf*, **отпеча́тывать** *impf* print (off); type (out); imprint. **отпеча́ток** (-тка) imprint, print.

отпива́ть *impf of* **отпи́ть**

отпи́ливать *impf*, **отпили́ть** (-лю́, -лишь) *pf* saw off.

от|пира́тельство denial. **отпира́ть(ся** *impf of* **отпере́ть(ся**

отпи́ть (отопью́, -пьёшь; о́тпи́л, -а́, -о) *pf* (*impf* **отпива́ть**) take a sip of.

отпи́хивать *impf*, **отпихну́ть** (-ну́, -нёшь) *pf* push off; shove aside.

отплати́ть (-ачу́, -а́тишь) *pf*, **отпла́чивать** *impf* **+***dat* pay back.

отплыва́ть *impf*, **отплы́ть** (-ыву́, -ывёшь; -ы́л, -а́, -о) *pf* (set) sail; swim off. **отплы́тие** sailing, departure.

о́тповедь rebuke.

отполза́ть *impf*, **отползти́** (-зу́, -зёшь; -о́лз, -ла́) *pf* crawl away.

от|полирова́ть *pf*. **от|полоска́ть** (-ощу́) *pf*.

отпо́р repulse; rebuff.

отпоро́ть (-рю́, -решь) *pf* (*impf* **отпа́рывать**) rip off.

отправи́тель *m* sender. **отпра́вить** (-влю) *pf*, **отправля́ть** *impf* send, dispatch; **~ся** set off, start. **отпра́вка** dispatch. **отправле́ние** sending; departure; performance.

отправн|о́й: **~о́й пункт**, **~а́я то́чка** starting-point.

от|пра́здновать *pf*.

отпра́шиваться *impf*, **отпроси́ться** (-ошу́сь, -о́сишься) *pf* ask for leave, get leave.

отпры́гивать *impf*, **отпры́гнуть** (-ну) *pf* jump *or* spring back *or* aside.

о́тпрыск offshoot, scion.

отпряга́ть *impf of* **отпря́чь**

отпря́нуть (-ну) *pf* recoil, start back.

отпря́чь (-ягу́, -яжёшь; -я́г, -ла́) *pf* (*impf* **отпряга́ть**) unharness.

отпу́гивать *impf*, **отпугну́ть** (-ну́, -нёшь) *pf* frighten off.

о́тпуск (*pl* -а́) leave, holiday(s). **отпуска́ть** *impf*, **отпусти́ть** (-ущу́, -у́стишь) *pf* let go, let off; set free; release; slacken; (let) grow; allot; remit. **отпускни́к** (-а́) person on leave. **отпускно́й** holiday; leave. **отпуще́ние** remission; **козёл отпуще́ния** scapegoat.

отраба́тывать *impf*, **отрабо́тать** *pf* work off; master.

отрабо́танный worked out; waste, spent, exhaust.
отра́ва poison. **отрави́ть** (-влю́, -вишь) *pf*, **отравля́ть** *impf* poison.
отра́да joy, delight. **отра́дный** gratifying, pleasing.
отража́тель *m* reflector; scanner. **отража́ть** *impf*, **отрази́ть** (-ажу́) *pf* reflect; repulse; **~ся** be reflected; **+на**+*prep* affect. **отраже́ние** reflection; repulse.
о́трасль branch.
отраста́ть *impf*, **отрасти́** (-тёт; отро́с, -ла́) *pf* grow. **отрасти́ть** (-ащу́) *pf*, **отра́щивать** *impf* (let) grow.
от|реаги́ровать *pf*. **от|регули́ровать** *pf*. **от|редакти́ровать** *pf*.
отре́з cut; length. **отре́зать** (-е́жу) *pf*, **отреза́ть** *impf* cut off; snap.
о|трезве́ть (-е́ю) *pf*. **отрезви́ть** (-влю́, -ви́шь) *pf*, **отрезвля́ть** *impf* sober; **~ся** sober up.
отре́зок (-зка) piece; section; segment.
отрека́ться *impf of* **отре́чься**
от|рекомендова́ть(ся *pf*.
отрёкся *etc*.: *see* **отре́чься**.
от|ремонти́ровать *pf*. **от|репети́ровать** *pf*.
отре́пье, отре́пья (-ьев) *pl* rags.
от|реставри́ровать *pf*.
отрече́ние renunciation; **~ от престо́ла** abdication. **отре́чься** (-еку́сь, -ечёшься) *pf* (*impf* **отрека́ться**) renounce.
отреша́ться *impf*, **отреши́ться** (-шу́сь) *pf* renounce; get rid of.
отрица́ние denial; negation. **отрица́тельный** negative. **отрица́ть** *impf* deny.
отро́с *etc*.: *see* **отрасти́**. **отро́сток** (-тка) shoot, sprout; appendix.
о́трочество adolescence.
отруба́ть *impf of* **отруби́ть**
о́труби (-ей) *pl* bran.
отруби́ть (-блю́, -бишь) *pf* (*impf* **отруба́ть**) chop off; snap back.
от|руга́ть *pf*.
отры́в tearing off; alienation, isolation; **в ~е от**+*gen* out of touch with; **~ (от земли́)** take-off. **отрыва́ть(ся** *impf of* **оторва́ть(ся**. **отры́вистый** staccato; disjointed. **отрывно́й** tear-off. **отры́вок** (-вка) fragment, excerpt. **отры́вочный** fragmentary, scrappy.
отры́жка belch; throw-back.
от|ры́ть (-ро́ю) *pf*.
отря́д detachment; order.
отря́хивать *impf*, **отряхну́ть** (-ну́, -нёшь) *pf* shake down *or* off.
от|салютова́ть *pf*.
отса́сывание suction. **отса́сывать** *impf of* **отсоса́ть**
отсве́чивать *impf* be reflected; *+instr* shine with.
отсе́в sifting, selection; dropping out. **отсева́ть(ся, отсе́ивать(ся** *impf of* **отсе́ять(ся**
отсе́к compartment. **отсека́ть** *impf*, **отсе́чь** (-еку́, -ечёшь; -сёк, -ла́) *pf* chop off.
отсе́ять (-е́ю) *pf* (*impf* **отсева́ть, отсе́ивать**) sift, screen; eliminate; **~ся** drop out.
отсиде́ть (-ижу́) *pf*, **отси́живать** *impf* make numb by sitting; sit through; serve out.
отска́кивать *impf*, **отскочи́ть** (-чу́, -чишь) *pf* jump aside *or* away; rebound; come off.

отслу́живать *impf*, **отслужи́ть** (-жу́, -жишь) *pf* serve one's time; be worn out.
отсоса́ть (-осу́, -осёшь) *pf* (*impf* **отса́сывать**) suck off, draw off.
отсо́хнуть (-ну) *pf* (*impf* **отсыха́ть**) wither.
отсро́чивать *impf*, **отсро́чить** *pf* postpone, defer. **отсро́чка** postponement, deferment.
отстава́ние lag; lagging behind. **отстава́ть** (-таю́, -аёшь) *impf of* **отста́ть**
отста́вить (-влю) *pf*, **отставля́ть** *impf* set *or* put aside. **отста́вка** resignation; retirement; **в отста́вке** retired; **вы́йти в отста́вку** resign, retire. **отставно́й** retired.
отста́ивать(ся *impf of* **отстоя́ть(ся**
отста́лость backwardness. **отста́лый** backward. **отста́ть** (-а́ну) *pf* (*impf* **отстава́ть**) fall behind; lag behind; become detached; lose touch; break (off); be slow. **отстаю́щий** *sb* backward pupil.
от|стега́ть *pf*.
отстёгивать *impf*, **отстегну́ть** (-ну́, -нёшь) *pf* unfasten, undo; **~ся** come unfastened *or* undone.
отстоя́ть[1] (-ою́) *pf* (*impf* **отста́ивать**) defend; stand up for. **отстоя́ть**[2] (-ои́т) *impf* **на**+*acc* be ... distant (**от**+*gen* from). **отстоя́ться** *pf* (*impf* **отста́иваться**) settle; become stabilized.
отстра́ивать(ся *impf of* **отстро́ить(ся**
отстране́ние pushing aside; dismissal. **отстрани́ть** *pf*, **отстраня́ть** *impf* push aside; remove; suspend; **~ся** move away; keep aloof; **~ся от** dodge.
отстре́ливаться *impf*, **отстреля́ться** *pf* fire back.
отстрига́ть *impf*, **отстри́чь** (-игу́, -ижёшь; -ри́г) *pf* cut off.
отстро́ить *pf* (*impf* **отстра́ивать**) finish building; build up.
отступа́ть *impf*, **отступи́ть** (-плю́, -пишь) *pf* step back; recede; retreat; back down; **~ от**+*gen* give up; deviate from; **~ся от**+*gen* give up; go back on. **отступле́ние** retreat; deviation; digression. **отступн|о́й: ~ы́е де́ньги, ~о́е** *sb* indemnity, compensation. **отступя́** *adv* (farther) off, away (**от**+*gen* from).
отсу́тствие absence; lack. **отсу́тствовать** *impf* be absent. **отсу́тствующий** absent; *sb* absentee.
отсчита́ть *pf*, **отсчи́тывать** *impf* count off.
отсыла́ть *impf of* **отосла́ть**
отсы́пать (-плю) *pf*, **отсыпа́ть** *impf* pour out; measure off.
отсыпа́ться *impf of* **отоспа́ться**
отсыре́лый damp. **от|сыре́ть** (-е́ет) *pf*.
отсыха́ть *impf of* **отсо́хнуть**
отсю́да *adv* from here; hence.
отта́ивать *impf of* **отта́ять**
отта́лкивать *impf of* **оттолкну́ть. отта́лкивающий** repulsive, repellent.
отта́чивать *impf of* **отточи́ть**
отта́ять (-а́ю) *pf* (*impf* **отта́ивать**) thaw out.
отте́нок (-нка) shade, nuance; tint.
о́ттепель thaw.
оттесни́ть *pf*, **оттесня́ть**

impf drive back; push aside. **о́ттиск** impression; off-print, reprint. **оттого́** *adv* that is why; **~, что** because. **оттолкну́ть** (-ну́, -нёшь) *pf* (*impf* **отта́лкивать**) push away; antagonize; **~ся** push off. **оттопы́ренный** protruding. **оттопы́ривать** *impf*, **оттопы́рить** *pf* stick out; **~ся** protrude; bulge. **отточи́ть** (-чу́, -чишь) *pf* (*impf* **отта́чивать**) sharpen. **отту́да** *adv* from there. **оття́гивать** *impf*, **оттяну́ть** (-ну́, -нешь) *pf* draw out; draw off; delay. **оття́жка** delay. **отупе́ние** stupefaction. **о|тупе́ть** (-е́ю) *pf* sink into torpor. **от|утю́жить** (-жу) *pf*. **отуча́ть** *impf*, **отучи́ть** (-чу́, -чишь) *pf* break (of); **~ся** break o.s. (of). **отха́ркать** *pf*, **отха́ркивать** *impf* expectorate. **отхвати́ть** (-чу́, -тишь) *pf*, **отхва́тывать** *impf* snip *or* chop off. **отхлебну́ть** (-ну́, -нёшь) *pf*, **отхлёбывать** *impf* sip, take a sip of. **отхлы́нуть** (-нет) *pf* flood *or* rush back. **отхо́д** departure; withdrawal. **отходи́ть** (-ожу́, -о́дишь) *impf of* **отойти́**. **отхо́ды** (-ов) *pl* waste. **отцвести́** (-ету́, -етёшь; -ёл, -а́) *pf*, **отцвета́ть** *impf* finish blossoming, fade. **отцепи́ть** (-плю́, -пишь) *pf*, **отцепля́ть** *impf* unhook; uncouple. **отцо́вский** father's; paternal. **отча́иваться** *impf of* **отча́яться**

отча́ливать *impf*, **отча́лить** *pf* cast off. **отча́сти** *adv* partly. **отча́яние** despair. **отча́янный** desperate. **отча́яться** (-а́юсь) *pf* (*impf* **отча́иваться**) despair. **отчего́** *adv* why. **отчего́-либо, -нибудь** *adv* for some reason or other. **отчего́-то** *adv* for some reason. **от|чека́нить** *pf*. **о́тчество** patronymic. **отчёт** account; **отда́ть себе́ ~ в**+*prep* be aware of, realize. **отчётливый** distinct; clear. **отчётность** book-keeping; accounts. **отчётный** *adj*: **~ год** financial year, current year; **~ докла́д** report. **отчи́зна** native land. **о́тчий** paternal. **о́тчим** step-father. **отчисле́ние** deduction; dismissal. **отчи́слить** *pf*, **отчисля́ть** *impf* deduct; dismiss. **отчита́ть** *pf*, **отчи́тывать** *impf* tell off; **~ся** report back. **отчужде́ние** alienation; estrangement. **отшатну́ться** (-ну́сь, -нёшься) *pf*, **отша́тываться** *impf* start back, recoil; **+от**+*gen* give up, forsake. **отшвы́ривать** *impf*, **отшвырну́ть** (-ну́, -нёшь) *pf* fling away; throw off. **отше́льник** hermit; recluse. **отшлёпать** *pf* spank. **от|шлифова́ть** *pf*. **от|штукату́рить** *pf*. **отщепе́нец** (-нца) renegade. **отъе́зд** departure. **отъезжа́ть** *impf*, **отъе́хать** (-е́ду) *pf* drive off, go off. **отъя́вленный** inveterate. **отыгра́ть** *pf*, **оты́грывать** *impf* win back; **~ся** win back what one has lost.

отыска́ть (-ыщу́, -ы́щешь) *pf*, **оты́скивать** *impf* find; look for; ~**ся** turn up, appear.
отяготи́ть (-ощу́) *pf*, **отягоща́ть** *impf* burden.
офице́р officer. **офице́рский** officer's, officers'.
официа́льный official.
официа́нт waiter. **официа́нтка** waitress.
официо́з semi-official organ. **официо́зный** semi-official.
оформи́тель *m* designer; stage-painter. **офо́рмить** (-млю) *pf*, **оформля́ть** *impf* design; put into shape; make official; process; ~**ся** take shape; go through the formalities. **оформле́ние** design; mounting, staging; processing.
ох *int* oh! ah!
оха́пка armful.
о|характеризова́ть *pf*.
о́хать *impf* (*pf* **о́хнуть**) moan; sigh.
охва́т scope; inclusion; outflanking. **охвати́ть** (-ачу́, -а́тишь) *pf*, **охва́тывать** *impf* envelop; seize; comprehend.
охладева́ть *impf*, **охладе́ть** (-е́ю) *pf* grow cold. **охлади́ть** (-ажу́) *pf*, **охлажда́ть** *impf* cool; ~**ся** become cool, cool down. **охлажде́ние** cooling; coolness.
о|хмеле́ть (-е́ю) *pf*. **о́хнуть** (-ну) *pf of* **о́хать**
охо́та[1] hunt, hunting; chase.
охо́та[2] wish, desire.
охо́титься (-о́чусь) *impf* hunt. **охо́тник**[1] hunter.
охо́тник[2] volunteer; enthusiast.
охо́тничий hunting.
охо́тно *adv* willingly, gladly.
о́хра ochre.
охра́на guarding; protection; guard. **охрани́ть** *pf*, **охраня́ть** *impf* guard, protect.
охри́плый, охри́пший hoarse. **о|хри́пнуть** (-ну; охри́п) *pf* become hoarse.
о|цара́пать(ся *pf*.
оце́нивать *impf*, **оцени́ть** (-ню́, -нишь) *pf* estimate; appraise. **оце́нка** estimation; appraisal; estimate. **оце́нщик** valuer.
о|цепене́ть (-е́ю) *pf*.
оцепи́ть (-плю́, -пишь) *pf*, **оцепля́ть** *impf* surround; cordon off.
оча́г (-а́) hearth; centre; breeding ground; hotbed.
очарова́ние charm, fascination. **очарова́тельный** charming. **очарова́ть** *pf*, **очаро́вывать** *impf* charm, fascinate.
очеви́дец (-дца) eye-witness. **очеви́дно** *adv* obviously, evidently. **очеви́дный** obvious.
о́чень *adv* very; very much.
очередно́й next in turn; usual, regular; routine. **о́чередь** (*gen pl* -е́й) turn; queue.
о́черк essay, sketch.
о|черни́ть *pf*.
о|черстве́ть (-е́ю) *pf*.
очерта́ние outline(s), contour(s). **очерти́ть** (-рчу́, -ртишь) *pf*, **оче́рчивать** *impf* outline.
о́чи *etc.*: *see* **о́ко**
очисти́тельный cleansing. **о|чи́стить** (-и́щу) *pf*, **очища́ть** *impf* clean; refine; clear; peel; ~**ся** clear o.s.; become clear (**от**+*gen* of). **очи́стка** cleaning; purification; clearance. **очи́стки** (-ов) *pl* peelings. **очище́ние** cleansing; purification.
очки́ (-о́в) *pl* spectacles. **очко́** (*gen pl* -о́в) pip; point. **очко́вая змея́** cobra.
очну́ться (-ну́сь, -нёшься) *pf* wake up; regain consciousness.

о́чн|ый: ~ое обуче́ние classroom instruction; **~ая ста́вка** confrontation.
очути́ться (-у́тишься) *pf* find o.s.
оше́йник collar.
ошеломи́тельный stunning. **ошеломи́ть** (-млю́) *pf*, **ошеломля́ть** *impf* stun.
ошиба́ться *impf*, **ошиби́ться** (-бу́сь, -бёшься; -и́бся) *pf* be mistaken, make a mistake; be wrong. **оши́бка** mistake; error. **оши́бочный** erroneous.
ошпа́ривать *impf*, **о|шпа́рить** *pf* scald.
о|штрафова́ть *pf*. **о|штукату́рить** *pf*.
ощети́ниваться *impf*, **о|щети́ниться** *pf* bristle (up).
о|щипа́ть (-плю́, -плешь) *pf*, **щи́пывать** *impf* pluck.
ощу́пать *pf*, **ощу́пывать** *impf* feel; grope about. **о́щупь: на ~** to the touch; by touch. **о́щупью** *adv* gropingly; by touch.
ощути́мый, ощути́тельный perceptible; appreciable. **ощути́ть** (-ущу́) *pf*, **ощуща́ть** *impf* feel, sense. **ощуще́ние** sensation; feeling.

П

па *neut indecl* dance step.
павильо́н pavilion; film studio.
павли́н peacock.
па́водок (-дка) (sudden) flood.
па́вший fallen.
па́губный pernicious, ruinous.
па́даль carrion.
па́дать *impf* (*pf* **пасть, упа́сть**) fall; **~ ду́хом** lose heart. **паде́ж** (-а́) case. **паде́ние** fall; degradation; incidence. **па́дкий на**+*acc or* **до**+*gen* having a weakness for.
па́дчерица step-daughter.
паёк (пайка́) ration.
па́зуха bosom; sinus; axil.
пай (*pl* -и́, -ёв) share. **па́йщик** shareholder.
паке́т package; packet; paper bag.
Пакиста́н Pakistan. **пакиста́нец** (-нца), **-а́нка** Pakistani. **пакиста́нский** Pakistani.
па́кля tow; oakum.
пакова́ть *impf* (*pf* **за~, у~**) pack.
па́костный dirty, mean. **па́кость** dirty trick; obscenity.
пакт pact.
пала́та chamber, house. **пала́тка** tent; stall, booth.
пала́ч (-а́) executioner.
па́лец (-льца) finger; toe.
палиса́дник (*small*) front garden.
палиса́ндр rosewood.
пали́тра palette.
пали́ть[1] *impf* (*pf* **о~, с~**) burn; scorch.
пали́ть[2] *impf* (*pf* **вы~, пальну́ть**) fire, shoot.
па́лка stick; walking-stick.
пало́мник pilgrim. **пало́мничество** pilgrimage.
па́лочка stick; bacillus; wand; baton.
па́луба deck.
пальба́ fire.
па́льма palm(-tree). **па́льмовый** palm.
пальну́ть (-ну́, -нёшь) *pf of* **пали́ть**
пальто́ *neut indecl* (over)coat.
паля́щий burning, scorching.
па́мятник monument; memorial. **па́мятный** memorable; memorial. **па́мять** memory; consciousness; **на ~** as a keepsake.

панацéя panacea.
панéль footpath; panel(ling), wainscot(ing). **панéльный** panelling.
пáника panic. **паникёр** alarmist.
панихúда requiem.
панúческий panic; panicky.
паннó *neut indecl* panel.
панорáма panorama.
пансиóн boarding-house; board and lodging. **пансионáт** holiday hotel. **пансионéр** boarder; guest.
панталóны (-óн) *pl* knickers.
пантéра panther.
пантомúма mime.
пáнцирь *m* armour, coat of mail.
пáпа[1] *m* pope.
пáпа[2] *m*, **папáша** *m* daddy.
папáха tall fur cap.
папирóса (*Russian*) cigarette.
пáпка file; folder.
пáпоротник fern.
пар[1] (*loc* -ý; *pl* -ы́) steam.
пар[2] (*loc* -ý, *pl* -ы́) fallow.
пáра pair; couple; (two-piece) suit.
парáграф paragraph.
парáд parade; review. **парáдн|ый** parade; gala; main, front; **~ая фóрма** full dress (uniform).
парадóкс paradox. **парадоксáльный** paradoxical.
паразúт parasite.
парализовáть *impf* & *pf* paralyse. **паралúч** (-á) paralysis.
параллéль parallel. **параллéльный** parallel.
парáметр parameter.
паранóйя paranoia.
парашю́т parachute.
парéние soaring.
пáрень (-рня; *gen pl* -рнéй) *m* lad; fellow.
парú *neut indecl* bet; **держáть ~** bet, lay a bet.
парúк (-á) wig. **парикмáхер** hairdresser. **парикмáхерская** *sb* hairdresser's.
парúровать *impf* & *pf* (*pf also* **от~**) parry, counter.
паритéт parity.
парúть[1] *impf* soar, hover.
пáрить[2] *impf* steam; stew; *impers* **пáрит** it is sultry; **~ся** (*pf* **по~ся**) steam, sweat; stew.
парк park; depot; stock.
паркéт parquet.
парлáмент parliament. **парламентáрный** parliamentarian. **парламентёр** envoy; bearer of flag of truce. **парлáментский** parliamentary; **~ закóн** Act of Parliament.
парнúк (-á) hotbed; seed-bed.
парникóв|ый *adj*: **~ые растéния** hothouse plants.
парнúшка *m* boy, lad.
парнóй fresh; steamy.
пáрный (forming a) pair; twin.
паро- *in comb* steam-. **паровóз** (steam-)engine, locomotive. **~обрáзный** vaporous. **~хóд** steamer; steamship. **~хóдство** steamship-line.
паровóй steam; steamed.
парóдия parody.
парóль *m* password.
парóм ferry(-boat).
парт- *abbr in comb* Party. **партбилéт** Party (membership) card. **~кóм** Party committee. **~организáция** Party organization.
пáрта (*school*) desk.
партéр stalls; pit.
партизáн (*gen pl* -áн) partisan; guerilla. **партизáнский** partisan, guerilla; unplanned.
партúйный party; Party; *sb* Party member.

партитýра (*mus*) score.
пáртия party; group; batch; game, set; part.
партнёр partner.
пáрус (*pl* -á, -óв) sail. **парусúна** canvas. **пáрусник** sailing vessel. **пáрусный** sail; ~ **спорт** sailing.
парфюмéрия perfumes.
парчá (*gen pl* -éй) brocade.
пáсека apiary, beehive.
пасётся *see* **пастúсь**
пáсквиль *m* lampoon; libel.
пáсмурный overcast; gloomy.
пáспорт (*pl* -á) passport.
пассáж passage; arcade.
пассажúр passenger.
пассúвный passive.
пáста paste.
пáстбище pasture.
пáства flock.
пастéль pastel.
пастернáк parsnip.
пастú (-сý, -сёшь; пас, -лá) *impf* graze; tend.
пастúсь (-сётся; пáсся, -лáсь) *impf* graze. **пастýх** (-á) shepherd. **пáстырь** *m* pastor.
пасть[1] mouth; jaws.
пасть[2] (падý, -дёшь; пал) *pf of* **пáдать**
Пáсха Easter; Passover.
пáсынок (-нка) stepson, stepchild.
пат stalemate.
патéнт patent.
патетúческий passionate.
пáтока treacle; syrup.
патолóгия pathology.
патриáрх patriarch.
патриóт, ~ка patriot. **патриотúзм** patriotism. **патриотúческий** patriotic.
патрóн cartridge; chuck; lamp-socket.
патрýль (-я́) *m* patrol.
пáуза pause; (*also mus*) rest.
паýк (-á) spider. **паутúна** cobweb; gossamer; web.
пáфос zeal, enthusiasm.
пах (*loc* -ý) groin.
пáхарь *m* ploughman. **пахáть** (пашý, пáшешь) *impf* (*pf* **вс~**) plough.
пáхнуть[1] (-ну; пах) *impf* smell (+*instr* of).
пахнýть[2] (-нёт) *pf* puff, blow.
пáхота ploughing. **пáхотный** arable.
пахýчий odorous, strong-smelling.
пациéнт, ~ка patient.
пацифúзм pacificism. **пацифúст** pacifist.
пáчка bundle; packet, pack; tutu.
пáчкать *impf* (*pf* **за~, ис~**) dirty, soil, stain.
пашý *etc.*: *see* **пахáть. пáшня** (*gen pl* -шен) ploughed field.
паштéт pâté.
пая́льная лáмпа blow-lamp. **пая́льник** soldering iron.
пая́ть (-я́ю) *impf* solder.
пая́ц clown, buffoon.
певéц (-вцá), **певúца** singer. **певýчий** melodious. **пéвчий** singing; *sb* chorister.
пéгий piebald.
педагóг teacher; pedagogue. **педагóгика** pedagogy. **педагогúческий** pedagogical; educational; ~ **инститýт** (teachers') training college.
педáль pedal.
педиáтр paediatrician. **педиатрúческий** paediatric.
педикю́р chiropody.
пейзáж landscape; scenery.
пёк *see* **печь. пекáрный** baking. **пекáрня** (*gen pl* -рен) bakery. **пéкарь** (*pl* -я́, -éй) *m* baker. **пéкло** scorching heat; hell-fire. **пекý** *etc.*: *see* **печь**

пелена́ (*gen pl* -лён) shroud. **пелена́ть** *impf* (*pf* **за~**) swaddle; put a nappy on.

пе́ленг bearing. **пеленгова́ть** *impf* & *pf* take the bearings of.

пелёнка nappy.

пельме́нь *m* meat dumpling.

пе́на foam; scum; froth.

пена́л pencil-case.

пе́ние singing.

пе́нистый foamy; frothy. **пе́ниться** *impf* (*pf* **вс~**) foam.

пе́нка skin. **пенопла́ст** plastic foam.

пеницилли́н penicillin.

пенсионе́р, пенсионе́рка pensioner. **пенсио́нный** pensionable. **пе́нсия** pension.

пень (пня) *m* stump, stub.

пенька́ hemp.

пе́пел (-пла) ash, ashes. **пе́пельница** ashtray.

перве́йший the first; first-class. **пе́рвенец** (-нца) first-born. **пе́рвенство** first place; championship. **пе́рвенствовать** *impf* take first place; take priority. **перви́чный** primary.

перво- *in comb* first; prime. **первобы́тный** primitive; primeval. **~исто́чник** source; origin. **~кла́ссный** first-class. **~ку́рсник** first-year student. **~нача́льный** original; primary. **~со́ртный** best-quality; first-class. **~степе́нный** paramount.

пе́рвое *sb* first course. **пе́рвый** first; former.

перга́мент parchment.

перебега́ть *impf*, **перебежа́ть** (-бегу́) *pf* cross, run across; desert. **перебе́жчик** deserter; turncoat.

переберу́ *etc.*: *see* **перебра́ть**

перебива́ть(ся *impf of* **перебить(ся**

перебира́ть(ся *impf of* **перебра́ть(ся**

переби́ть (-бью́, -бьёшь) *pf* (*impf* **перебива́ть**) interrupt; slaughter; beat; break; re-upholster; **~ся** break; make ends meet. **перебо́й** interruption; stoppage; irregularity.

перебо́рка sorting out; partition; bulkhead.

переборо́ть (-рю́, -решь) *pf* overcome.

переборщи́ть (-щу́) *pf* go too far; overdo it.

перебра́сывать(ся *impf of* **перебро́сить(ся**

перебра́ть (-беру́, -берёшь; -а́л, -а́, -о) *pf* (*impf* **перебира́ть**) sort out; look through; turn over in one's mind; finger; **~ся** get over, cross; move.

перебро́сить (-о́шу) *pf* (*impf* **перебра́сывать**) throw over; transfer; **~ся** fling o.s.; spread. **перебро́ска** transfer.

перебью́ *etc.*: *see* **переби́ть**

перева́л crossing; pass. **перева́ливать** *impf*, **перевали́ть** (-лю́, -лишь) *pf* transfer, shift; cross, pass.

перева́ривать *impf*, **перевари́ть** (-рю́, -ришь) *pf* reheat; overcook; digest; tolerate.

переведу́ *etc.*: *see* **перевести́**

перевезти́ (-зу́, -зёшь; -вёз, -ла́) *pf* (*impf* **перевози́ть**) take across; transport; (re)move.

переверну́ть (-ну́, -нёшь) *pf*, **перевёртывать** *impf* (*impf also* **перевора́чивать**) turn (over); upset; turn inside out; **~ся** turn (over).

переве́с preponderance; advantage. **переве́сить** (-е́шу) *pf* (*impf* **переве́шивать**) reweigh; outweigh; tip the scales; hang elsewhere.

перевести́ (-веду́, -ведёшь; -вёл, -а́) *pf* (*impf* **переводи́ть**) take across; transfer, move, shift; translate; convert; **~сь** be transferred; run out; become extinct.

переве́шивать *impf of* **переве́сить. перевира́ть** *impf of* **перевра́ть**

перево́д transfer, move, shift; translation; conversion; waste. **переводи́ть(ся** (-ожу́(сь, -о́дишь(ся) *impf of* **перевести́(сь. переводн|о́й**: **~а́я бума́га** carbon paper; **~а́я карти́нка** transfer. **перево́дный** transfer; translated. **перево́дчик, ~ица** translator; interpreter.

перево́з transporting; ferry. **перевози́ть** (-ожу́, -о́зишь) *impf of* **перевезти́. перево́зка** conveyance. **перево́зчик** ferryman; removal man.

перевооружа́ть *impf*, **перевооружи́ть** (-жу́) *pf* rearm; **~ся** rearm. **перевооруже́ние** rearmament.

перевоплоти́ть (-лощу́) *pf*, **перевоплоща́ть** *impf* reincarnate; **~ся** be reincarnated. **перевоплоще́ние** reincarnation.

перевора́чивать(ся *impf of* **переверну́ть(ся. переворо́т** revolution; overturn; cataclysm; **госуда́рственный ~** coup d'état.

перевоспита́ние re-education. **перевоспита́ть** *pf*, **перевоспи́тывать** *impf* reeducate.

перевра́ть (-ру́, -рёшь; -а́л, -а́, -о) *pf* (*impf* **перевира́ть**) garble; misquote.

перевыполне́ние overfulfilment. **перевы́полнить** *pf*, **перевыполня́ть** *impf* over-fulfil.

перевяза́ть (-яжу́, -я́жешь) *pf*, **перевя́зывать** *impf* bandage; tie up; re-tie. **перевя́зка** dressing, bandage.

переги́б bend; excess, extreme. **перегиба́ть(ся** *impf of* **перегну́ть(ся**

перегля́дываться *impf*, **перегляну́ться** (-ну́сь, -нешься) *pf* exchange glances.

перегна́ть (-гоню́, -го́нишь; -а́л, -а́, -о) *pf* (*impf* **перегоня́ть**) outdistance; surpass; drive; distil.

перегно́й humus.

перегну́ть (-ну́, -нёшь) *pf* (*impf* **перегиба́ть**) bend; **~ па́лку** go too far; **~ся** bend; lean over.

перегова́ривать *impf*, **переговори́ть** *pf* talk; out-talk; **~ся** (**с**+*instr*) exchange remarks (with). **перегово́ры** (-ов) *pl* negotiations, parley. **перегово́рный** *adj*: **~ пункт** public call-boxes; trunk-call office.

перего́н driving; stage. **перего́нка** distillation. **перего́нный** distilling, distillation. **перегоню́** *etc.*: *see* **перегна́ть.**

перегоня́ть *impf of* **перегна́ть**

перегора́живать *impf of* **перегороди́ть**

перегора́ть *impf*, **перегоре́ть** (-ри́т) *pf* burn out, fuse.

перегороди́ть (-рожу́, -ро́дишь) *pf* (*impf* **перегора́живать**) partition off; block. **перегоро́дка** partition.

перегре́в overheating. **перегрева́ть** *impf*, **перегре́ть** (-е́ю) *pf* overheat; **~ся** overheat.

перегружа́ть *impf*, **перегрузи́ть** (-ужу́, -у́зишь) *pf* overload; transfer. **перегру́зка** overload; transfer.

перегрыза́ть *impf*, **перегры́зть** (-зу́, -зёшь; -гры́з) *pf* gnaw through.

пе́ред, пе́редо, пред, пре́до *prep+instr* before; in front of; compared to. **перёд** (пе́реда; *pl* -а́) front, forepart.

передава́ть (-даю́, -даёшь) *impf*, **переда́ть** (-а́м, -а́шь, -а́ст, -ади́м; пе́редал, -а́, -о) *pf* pass, hand, hand over; transfer; hand down; make over; tell; communicate; convey; give too much; **~ся** pass; be transmitted; be communicated; be inherited. **переда́тчик** transmitter. **переда́ча** passing; transmission; communication; transfer; broadcast; drive; gear, gearing.

передвига́ть *impf*, **передви́нуть** (-ну) *pf* move, shift; **~ся** move, shift. **передвиже́ние** movement; transportation. **передви́жка** movement; *in comb* travelling; itinerant. **передвижно́й** movable, mobile.

переде́лать *pf*, **переде́лывать** *impf* alter; refashion. **переде́лка** alteration.

передёргивать(ся *impf of* **передёрнуть(ся**

передержа́ть (-жу́, -жишь) *pf*, **переде́рживать** *impf* overdo; overcook; overexpose.

передёрнуть (-ну) *pf* (*impf* **передёргивать**) pull aside *or* across; cheat; distort; **~ся** wince.

пере́дний front; **~ план** foreground. **пере́дник** apron. **пере́дняя** *sb* (entrance) hall, lobby. **пе́редо:** *see* **пе́ред.** **передови́к** (-а́) exemplary worker. **передови́ца** leading article. **передово́й** advanced; foremost; leading.

передохну́ть (-ну́, -нёшь) *pf* pause for breath.

передра́знивать *impf*, **передразни́ть** (-ню́, -нишь) *pf* mimic.

переду́мать *pf*, **переду́мывать** *impf* change one's mind.

переды́шка respite.

перее́зд crossing; move. **переезжа́ть** *impf*, **перее́хать** (-е́ду) *pf* cross; run over, knock down; move (house).

пережа́ривать *impf*, **пережа́рить** *pf* overdo, overcook.

пережда́ть (-жду́, -ждёшь; -а́л, -а́, -о) *pf* (*impf* **пережида́ть**) wait for the end of.

пережёвывать *impf* chew; repeat over and over again.

пережива́ние experience. **пережива́ть** *impf of* **пережи́ть**

пережида́ть *impf of* **пережда́ть**

пережито́е *sb* the past. **пережи́ток** (-тка) survival; vestige. **пережи́ть** (-иву́, -ивёшь; пе́режил, -а́, -о) *pf* (*impf* **пережива́ть**) experience; go through; endure; outlive.

перезаряди́ть (-яжу́, -я́ди́шь) *pf*, **перезаряжа́ть** *impf* recharge, reload.

перезва́нивать *impf*, **перезвони́ть** *pf +dat* ring back.

пере|зимова́ть *pf.*

перезре́лый overripe.

переигра́ть *pf*, **переи́гры-**

вать *impf* play again; overact.

переизбира́ть *impf*, **переизбра́ть** (-беру́, -берёшь; -бра́л, -á, -о) *pf* re-elect. **переизбра́ние** re-election.

переиздава́ть (-даю́, -даёшь) *impf*, **переизда́ть** (-а́м, -а́шь, -а́ст, -ади́м; -а́л, -á, -о) *pf* republish, reprint. **переизда́ние** republication; new edition.

переименова́ть *pf*, **переимено́вывать** *impf* rename.

переймý *etc.*: *see* **переня́ть**

перейти́ (-йдý, -йдёшь; перешёл, -шла́) *pf* (*impf* **переходи́ть**) cross; go, walk, pass; move, change, switch; turn (**в**+*acc* to, into).

перека́пывать *impf of* **перекопа́ть**

перекати́ть (-чý, -тишь) *pf*, **перека́тывать** *impf* roll; **~ся** roll.

перекача́ть *pf*, **перека́чивать** *impf* pump (across).

переквалифици́роваться *impf* & *pf* retrain.

переки́дывать *impf*, **переки́нуть** (-ну) *pf* throw over; **~ся** leap.

пе́рекись peroxide.

перекла́дина cross-beam; joist; horizontal bar.

перекла́дывать *impf of* **переложи́ть**

перекли́чка roll-call.

переключа́тель *m* switch. **переключа́ть** *impf*, **переключи́ть** (-чý) *pf* switch (over); **~ся** switch (over) (**на**+*acc* to).

перекова́ть (-кую́, -куёшь) *pf*, **переко́вывать** *impf* re-shoe; re-forge.

перекопа́ть *pf* (*impf* **перека́пывать**) dig (all of); dig again.

перекоси́ть (-ошý, -о́сишь) *pf* warp; distort; **~ся** warp; become distorted.

перекочева́ть (-чу́ю) *pf*, **перекочёвывать** *impf* migrate.

переко́шенный distorted, twisted.

перекра́ивать *impf of* **перекрои́ть**

перекра́сить (-а́шу) *pf*, **перекра́шивать** *impf* (re-)paint; (re-)dye; **~ся** change colour; turn one's coat.

пере|крести́ть (-ещý, -е́стишь) *pf*, **перекре́щивать** *impf* cross; **~ся** cross, intersect; cross o.s. **перекрёстн|ый** cross; **~ый вопро́с** cross examination; **~ый ого́нь** cross-fire; **~ая ссы́лка** cross-reference. **перекрёсток** (-тка) cross-roads, crossing.

перекри́кивать *impf*, **перекрича́ть** (-чý) *pf* shout down.

перекрои́ть (-ою́) *pf* (*impf* **перекра́ивать**) cut out again; reshape.

перекрыва́ть *impf*, **перекры́ть** (-ро́ю) *pf* re-cover; exceed. **перекры́тие** ceiling.

перекую́ *etc.*: *see* **перекова́ть**

перекупа́ть *impf*, **перекупи́ть** (-плю́, -пишь) *pf* buy up; buy by outbidding s.o. **переку́пщик** second-hand dealer.

перекуси́ть (-ушý, -у́сишь) *pf*, **переку́сывать** *impf* bite through; have a snack.

перелага́ть *impf of* **переложи́ть**

перела́мывать *impf of* **переломи́ть**

перелеза́ть *impf*, **переле́зть** (-зу; -е́з) *pf* climb over.

переле́сок (-ска) copse.

перелёт migration; flight.

перелетáть *impf*, **перелетéть** (-лечý) *pf* fly over. **перелётный** migratory.

переливáние decanting; transfusion. **переливáть** *impf of* **перелить. переливáться** *impf of* **перелиться;** gleam; modulate.

перелистáть *pf*, **перелистывать** *impf* leaf through.

перелить (-лью, -льёшь; -йл, -á, -о) *pf* (*impf* **переливáть**) pour; decant; let overflow; transfuse. **перелиться** (-льётся; -лился, -лилáсь, -лилóсь) *pf* (*impf* **переливáться**) flow; overflow.

перелицевáть (-цýю) *pf*, **перелицóвывать** *impf* turn; have turned.

переложéние arrangement. **переложить** (-жý, -жишь) *pf* (*impf* **перекладывать, перелагáть**) put elsewhere; shift; transfer; interlay; put in too much; set; arrange; transpose.

перелóм breaking; fracture; turning-point, crisis; sudden change. **переломáть** *pf* break; **~ся** break, be broken. **переломить** (-млю, -мишь) *pf* (*impf* **перелáмывать**) break in two; master. **перелóмный** critical.

перелью *etc.*: *see* **перелить**

перемáнивать *impf*, **переманить** (-ню, -нишь) *pf* win over; entice.

перемежáться *impf* alternate.

перемéна change; break. **переменить** (-ню, -нишь) *pf*, **переменять** *impf* change; **~ся** change. **перемéнный** variable; **~ ток** alternating current. **перемéнчивый** changeable.

переместить (-мещý) *pf* (*impf* **перемещáть**) move; transfer; **~ся** move.

перемешáть *pf*, **перемéшивать** *impf* mix; mix up; shuffle; **~ся** get mixed (up).

перемещáть(ся *impf of* **переместить(ся. перемещéние** transference; displacement. **перемещённ|ый** displaced; **~ые лица** displaced persons.

перемирие armistice, truce.

перемывáть *impf*, **перемыть** (-мóю) *pf* wash (up) again.

перенапрягáть *impf*, **перенапрячь** (-ягý, -яжёшь: -яг, -лá) *pf* overstrain.

перенаселéние overpopulation. **перенаселённый** (-лён, -á) overpopulated; overcrowded.

перенести (-сý, -сёшь; -нёс, -лá) *pf* (*impf* **переносить**) carry, move, take; transfer; take over; postpone; endure, bear; **~сь** be carried; be carried away.

перенимáть *impf of* **перенять**

перенóс transfer; word division; **знак ~а** end-of-line hyphen. **переносимый** endurable. **переносить(ся** (-ошý(сь, -óсишь(ся) *impf of* **перенести(сь**

перенóсица bridge (*of the nose*).

перенóска carrying over; transporting; carriage. **перенóсный** portable; figurative. **перенóсчик** carrier.

пере|ночевáть (-чýю) *pf*.

переношý *etc.*: *see* **переносить**

перенять (-еймý, -еймёшь; пéренял, -á, -о) *pf* (*impf* **перенимáть**) imitate; adopt.

переоборýдовать *impf* & *pf* re-equip.

переобувáться *impf*, **переобýться** (-ýюсь, -ýешься) *pf* change one's shoes.

переодевáться *impf*, **переодéться** (-éнусь) *pf* change (one's clothes).

переосвидéтельствовать *impf* & *pf* re-examine.

переоцéнивать *impf*, **переоценúть** (-ню́, -нишь) *pf* overestimate; revalue. **переоцéнка** overestimation; revaluation.

перепáчкать *pf* make dirty; **~ся** get dirty.

пéрепел (*pl* -á) quail.

перепеленáть *pf* change (*a baby*).

перепечáтать *pf*, **перепечáтывать** *impf* reprint. **перепечáтка** reprint.

перепúливать *impf*, **перепилúть** (-лю́, -лишь) *pf* saw in two.

переписáть (-ишý, -úшешь) *pf*, **перепúсывать** *impf* copy; rewrite; make a list of. **перепúска** copying; correspondence. **перепúсываться** *impf* correspond. **пéрепись** census.

переплáвить (-влю) *pf*, **переплавля́ть** *impf* smelt.

переплатúть (-ачý, -áтишь) *pf*, **переплáчивать** *impf* overpay.

переплестú (-летý, -летёшь; -лёл, -á) *pf*, **переплетáть** *impf* bind; interlace, intertwine; re-plait; **~ся** interlace, interweave; get mixed up. **переплёт** binding. **переплётчик** bookbinder.

переплывáть *impf*, **переплы́ть** (-ывý, -ывёшь; -ы́л, -á, -о) *pf* swim *or* sail across.

переподготóвка further training; refresher course.

переползáть *impf*, **переползтú** (-зý, -зёшь; -óлз, -лá) *pf* crawl *or* creep across.

переполнéние overfilling; overcrowding. **перепóлненный** overcrowded; too full.

перепóлнить *pf*, **переполня́ть** *impf* overfill; overcrowd.

переполóх commotion.

перепóнка membrane; web.

переправа crossing; ford.

переправить (-влю) *pf*, **переправля́ть** *impf* convey; take across; forward; **~ся** cross, get across.

перепродавáть (-даю́, -даёшь) *impf*, **перепродáть** (-áм, -áшь, -áст, -адúм; -прóдáл, -á, -о) *pf* re-sell. **перепродáжа** re-sale.

перепроизвóдство overproduction.

перепры́гивать *impf*, **перепры́гнуть** (-ну) *pf* jump (over).

перепугáть *pf* frighten, scare; **~ся** get a fright.

пере|пýтать *pf*, **перепýтывать** *impf* tangle; confuse, mix up.

перепýтье cross-roads.

перерабáтывать *impf*, **перерабóтать** *pf* convert; treat; re-make; re-cast; process; work overtime; overwork; **~ся** overwork. **перерабóтка** processing; reworking; overtime work.

перераспределéние redistribution. **перераспределúть** *pf*, **перераспределя́ть** *impf* redistribute.

перерастáние outgrowing; escalation; development (into).

перерастáть *impf*, **пере-**

расти́ (-ту́, -тёшь; -ро́с, -ла́) *pf* outgrow; develop.
перерасхо́д over-expenditure; overdraft. **перерасхо́довать** *impf* & *pf* expend too much of.
перерасчёт recalculation.
перерва́ть (-ву́, -вёшь; -а́л, -а́, -о) *pf* (*impf* **перерыва́ть**) break, tear asunder; **~ся** break, come apart.
перере́зать (-е́жу) *pf*, **перереза́ть** *impf*, **перере́зывать** *impf* cut; cut off; kill.
перероди́ть (-ожу́) *pf*, **перерожда́ть** *impf* regenerate; **~ся** be reborn; be regenerated; degenerate. **перерожде́ние** regeneration; degeneration.
переро́с *etc.*: *see* **перерасти́**.
переро́ю *etc.*: *see* **перерыть**
перерубáть *impf*, **перерубить** (-блю́, -бишь) *pf* chop in two.
переры́в break; interruption; interval.
перерыва́ть[1](**ся** *impf of* **перерва́ть**(**ся**
перерыва́ть[2] *impf*, **перерыть** (-ро́ю) *pf* dig up; rummage through.
пересади́ть (-ажу́, -а́дишь) *pf*, **переса́живать** *impf* transplant; graft; seat somewhere else. **переса́дка** transplantation; grafting; change.
переса́живаться *impf of* **пересе́сть**. **переса́ливать** *impf of* **пересоли́ть**
пересдава́ть (-даю́сь) *impf*, **пересда́ть** (-а́м, -а́шь, -а́ст, -адим; -да́л, -а́, -о) *pf* sublet; re-sit.
пересека́ть(**ся** *impf of* **пересе́чь**(**ся**
пересе́ленец (-нца) settler; immigrant. **переселе́ние** migration; immigration, resettlement; moving. **пересели́ть** *pf*, **переселя́ть** *impf* move; **~ся** move; migrate.
пересе́сть (-ся́ду) *pf* (*impf* **переса́живаться**) change one's seat; change (*trains etc.*).
пересече́ние crossing, intersection. **пересе́чь** (-секу́, -сечёшь; -се́к, -ла́) *pf* (*impf* **пересека́ть**) cross; intersect; **~ся** cross, intersect.
переси́ливать *impf*, **переси́лить** *pf* overpower.
переска́з (re)telling; exposition.
пересказа́ть (-ажу́, -а́жешь) *pf*, **переска́зывать** *impf* retell.
переска́кивать *impf*, **перескочи́ть** (-чу́, -чишь) *pf* jump *or* skip (over).
пересла́ть (-ешлю́, -шлёшь) *pf* (*impf* **пересыла́ть**) send; forward.
пересма́тривать *impf*, **пересмотре́ть** (-трю́, -тришь) *pf* look over; reconsider. **пересмо́тр** revision; reconsideration; review.
пересоли́ть (-олю́, -о́ли́шь) *pf* (*impf* **переса́ливать**) oversalt; overdo it.
пересо́хнуть (-нет; -о́х) *pf* (*impf* **пересыха́ть**) dry up, become parched.
переспа́ть (-плю́; -а́л, -а́, -о) *pf* oversleep; spend the night.
переспе́лый overripe.
переспра́шивать *impf*, **переспроси́ть** (-ошу́, -о́сишь) *pf* ask again.
перестава́ть (-таю́, -таёшь) *impf of* **переста́ть**
переста́вить (-влю) *pf*, **переставля́ть** *impf* move; rearrange; transpose. **переста-**

нóвка rearrangement; transposition.

перестáть (-áну) *pf* (*impf* **переставáть**) stop, cease.

перестрадáть *pf* have suffered.

перестрáивать(ся *impf of* **перестрóить(ся**

перестрахóвка re-insurance; overcautiousness.

перестрéлка exchange of fire. **перестрелять** *pf* shoot (down).

перестрóить *pf* (*impf* **перестрáивать**) rebuild; reorganize; retune; **~ся** re-form; reorganize o.s.; switch over (**на**+*acc* to). **перестрóйка** reconstruction; reorganization; retuning; perestroika.

переступáть *impf*, **переступи́ть** (-плю́, -пишь) *pf* step over; cross; overstep.

пересчитáть *pf*, **пересчи́тывать** *impf* (*pf also* **перечéсть**) re-count; count.

пересылáть *impf of* **переслáть. пересы́лка** sending, forwarding.

пересыпáть *impf*, **пересы́пать** (-плю, -плешь) *pf* pour; sprinkle; pour too much.

пересыхáть *impf of* **пересóхнуть. пересяду** *etc.*: *see* **пересéсть. перетáпливать** *impf of* **перетопи́ть**

перетáскивать *impf*, **перетащи́ть** (-щу́, -щишь) *pf* drag (over, through); move.

перетерéть (-тру́, -трёшь; -тёр) *pf*, **перетирáть** *impf* wear out, wear down; grind; wipe; **~ся** wear out *or* through.

перетопи́ть (-плю́, -пишь) *pf* (*impf* **перетáпливать**) melt.

перетру́ *etc.*: *see* **перетерéть**

перéть (пру, прёшь; пёр, -ла) *impf* go; make *or* force one's way; haul; come out.

перетя́гивать *impf*, **перетяну́ть** (-ну́, -нешь) *pf* pull, draw; win over; outweigh.

переубеди́ть *pf*, **переубеждáть** *impf* make change one's mind.

переу́лок (-лка) side street, alley, lane.

переустрóйство reconstruction, reorganization.

переутоми́ть (-млю́) *pf*, **переутомля́ть** *impf* overtire; **~ся** overtire o.s. **переутомлéние** overwork.

переучёт stock-taking.

переу́чивать *impf*, **переучи́ть** (-чу́, -чишь) *pf* teach again.

перефрази́ровать *impf* & *pf* paraphrase.

перехвати́ть (-ачу́, -áтишь) *pf*, **перехвáтывать** *impf* intercept; snatch a bite (of); borrow.

перехитри́ть *pf* outwit.

перехóд transition; crossing; conversion. **переходи́ть** (-ожу́, -óдишь) *impf of* **перейти́. перехóдный** transitional; transitive. **переходя́щий** transient; intermittent; brought forward.

пéрец (-рца) pepper.

перечёл *etc.*: *see* **перечéсть**

пéречень (-чня) *m* list, enumeration.

перечёркивать *impf*, **перечеркну́ть** (-ну́, -нёшь) *pf* cross out, cancel.

перечéсть (-чту́, -чтёшь; -чёл, -члá) *pf*: *see* **пересчитáть, перечитáть**

перечислéние enumeration; transfer. **перечи́слить** *pf*, **перечисля́ть** *impf* enumerate; transfer.

перечитáть *pf*, **перечи́тывать** *impf* (*pf also* **перечéсть**) re-read.
перéчить (-чу) *impf* contradict; cross, go against.
пéречница pepper-pot.
перечтý *etc.*: *see* **перечéсть.**
перéчу *etc.*: *see* **перéчить**
перешáгивать *impf*, **перешагнýть** (-нý, -нёшь) *pf* step over.
перешéек (-éйка) isthmus, neck.
перешёл *etc.*: *see* **перейти́**
перешивáть *impf*, **переши́ть** (-шью́, -шьёшь) *pf* alter; have altered.
перешлю́ *etc.*: *see* **переслáть**
переэкзаменовáть *pf.*, **переэкзаменóвывать** *impf* re-examine; **~ся** retake an exam.
пери́ла (-и́л) *pl* railing(s); banisters.
пери́на feather-bed.
пери́од period. **периóдика** periodicals. **периоди́ческий** periodical; recurring.
пéристый feathery; cirrus.
перифери́я periphery.
перламýтр mother-of-pearl. **перламýтровый** mother-of-pearl. **перлóв|ый: ~ая крупá** pearl barley.
перманéнт perm. **перманéнтный** permanent.
пернáтый feathered. **пернáтые** *sb pl* birds. **перó** (*pl* пéрья, -ьев) feather; nib. **перочи́нный нож, нóжик** penknife.
перпендикуля́рный perpendicular.
перрóн platform.
перс Persian. **перси́дский** Persian.
пéрсик peach.
персия́нка Persian woman.
персóна person; **сóбственной персóной** in person. **персонáж** character; personage. **персонáл** personnel, staff. **персонáльный** personal.
перспекти́ва perspective; vista; prospect. **перспекти́вный** perspective; long-term; promising.
пéрстень (-тня) *m* ring.
перфокáрта punched card.
пéрхоть dandruff.
перчáтка glove.
пéрчить (-чу) *impf* (*pf* **по~**) pepper.
пёс (пса) dog.
пéсенник song-book; (choral) singer; song-writer. **пéсенный** song; of songs.
песéц (-сцá) (polar) fox.
песнь (*gen pl* -ей) song; canto.
пéсня (*gen pl* -сен) song.
песóк (-скá) sand. **песóчный** sand; sandy.
пессими́зм pessimism. **пессими́ст** pessimist. **пессимисти́ческий** pessimistic.
пестротá diversity of colours; diversity. **пёстрый** variegated; diverse; colourful.
песчáник sandstone. **песчáный** sandy. **песчи́нка** grain of sand.
петербýргский (of) St Petersburg.
пети́ция petition.
петли́ца buttonhole; tab. **пéтля** (*gen pl* -тель) loop; noose; buttonhole; stitch; hinge.
петрýшка[1] parsley.
петрýшка[2] *m* Punch; *f* Punch-and-Judy show.
петýх (-á) cock. **петушóк** (-шкá) cockerel.
петь (пою́, поёшь) *impf* (*pf* **про~, с~**) sing.

пехóта infantry, foot. **пехотúнец** (-нца) infantryman. **пехóтный** infantry.
печáлить *impf* (*pf* **о~**) sadden; **~ся** grieve, be sad. **печáль** sorrow. **печáльный** sad.
печáтать *impf* (*pf* **на~, от~**) print; **~ся** write, be published; be at the printer's. **печáтн|ый** printing; printer's; printed; **~ые бýквы** block capitals; **~ый станóк** printing-press. **печáть** seal, stamp; print; printing; press.
печéние baking.
печёнка liver.
печёный baked.
пéчень liver.
печéнье pastry; biscuit. **пéчка** stove. **печнóй** stove; oven; kiln. **печь** (*loc* -ú; *gen pl* -éй) stove; oven; kiln. **печь** (пекý, -чёшь; пёк, -лá) *impf* (*pf* **ис~**) bake; **~ся** bake.
пешехóд pedestrian. **пешехóдный** pedestrian; foot-. **пéший** pedestrian; foot. **пéшка** pawn. **пешкóм** *adv* on foot.
пещéра cave. **пещéрный** cave; **~ человéк** cave-dweller.
пианúно *neut indecl* (upright) piano. **пианúст, ~ка** pianist.
пивнáя *sb* pub. **пивнóй** beer.
пúво beer. **пивовáр** brewer.
пигмéй pygmy.
пиджáк (-á) jacket.
пижáма pyjamas.
пижóн dandy.
пик peak; **часы́ пик** rush-hour.
пúка lance.
пикáнтный piquant; spicy.
пикáп pick-up (van).
пикé *neut indecl* dive.
пикéт picket. **пикéтчик** picket.
пúки (пик) *pl* (*cards*) spades.
пикúровать *impf* & *pf* (*pf also* **с~**) dive.
пикирóвщик, пикúрующий бомбардирóвщик dive-bomber.
пикнúк (-á) picnic.
пúкнуть (-ну) *pf* squeak; make a sound.
пúковый of spades.
пилá (*pl* -ы) saw; nagger. **пилёный** sawed, sawn. **пилúть** (-лю́, -лишь) *impf* saw; nag (at). **пúлка** sawing; fret-saw; nail-file.
пилóт pilot.
пилóтка forage-cap.
пилотúровать *impf* pilot.
пилю́ля pill.
пинáть *impf* (*pf* пнуть) kick. **пинóк** (-нкá) kick.
пингвúн penguin.
пинцéт tweezers.
пиóн peony.
пионéр pioneer. **пионéрский** pioneer.
пипéтка pipette.
пир (*loc* -ý; *pl* -ы́) feast, banquet. **пировáть** *impf* feast.
пирамúда pyramid.
пирáт pirate.
пирóг (-á) pie. **пирóжное** *sb* cake, pastry. **пирожóк** (-жкá) pasty.
пирс pier.
пиру́эт pirouette.
пúршество feast; celebration.
пúсаный handwritten. **пúсарь** (*pl* -я́) *m* clerk. **писáтель** *m*, **писáтельница** writer, author. **писáть** (пишý, пúшешь) *impf* (*pf* **на~**) write; paint; **~ мáслом** paint in oils; **~ся** be spelt.
писк squeak, chirp. **писклúвый** squeaky. **пúскнуть** (-ну) *pf of* **пищáть**
пистолéт pistol; gun; **~-пулемёт** sub-machine gun.
пистóн (percussion-)cap; piston.

писчебума́жный stationery. **пи́счая бума́га** writing paper. **пи́сьменно** *adv* in writing. **пи́сьменность** literature. **пи́сьменный** writing, written. **письмо́** (*pl* -а, -сем) letter.

пита́ние nourishment; feeding. **пита́тельный** nutritious; alimentary; feed. **пита́ть** *impf* feed; nourish; supply; **~ся** feed; eat; live; +*instr* feed on.

пито́мец (-мца) charge; pupil; alumnus. **пито́мник** nursery.

пить (пью, пьёшь; пил, -á, -о) *impf* (*pf* **вы́~**) drink. **питьево́й** drinkable; drinking.

пиха́ть *impf*, **пихну́ть** (-ну́, -нёшь) *pf* push, shove.

пи́хта (silver) fir.

пи́чкать *impf* (*pf* **на~**) stuff.

пи́шущ|ий writing; **~ая маши́нка** typewriter.

пи́ща food.

пища́ть (-щу́) *impf* (*pf* **пи́скнуть**) squeak; cheep.

пищеваре́ние digestion. **пищево́д** oesophagus, gullet. **пищево́й** food.

пия́вка leech.

ПК *abbr* (*of* **персона́льный компью́тер**) PC (*personal computer*).

пла́вание swimming; sailing; voyage. **пла́вательный** swimming; ~ **бассе́йн** swimming-pool. **пла́вать** *impf* swim; float; sail. **плавба́за** depot ship, factory ship.

плави́льный melting, smelting. **плави́льня** foundry. **пла́вить** (-влю) *impf* (*pf* **рас~**) melt, smelt; **~ся** melt. **пла́вка** fusing; melting.

пла́вки (-вок) *pl* bathing trunks.

пла́вкий fusible; fuse. **плавле́ние** melting.

плавни́к (-á) fin; flipper.

пла́вный smooth, flowing; liquid. **плаву́чий** floating.

плагиа́т plagiarism. **плагиа́тор** plagiarist.

пла́зма plasma.

плака́т poster; placard.

пла́кать (-áчу) *impf* cry, weep; **~ся** complain, lament; +**на**+*acc* complain of; bemoan.

пла́кса cry-baby. **плакси́вый** whining. **плаку́чий** weeping.

пла́менный flaming; ardent. **пла́мя** (-мени) *neut* flame; blaze.

план plan

планёр glider. **планери́зм** gliding. **планери́ст** glider-pilot.

плане́та planet. **плане́тный** planetary.

плани́рование[1] planning.

плани́рование[2] gliding; glide.

плани́ровать[1] *impf* (*pf* **за~**) plan.

плани́ровать[2] *impf* (*pf* **с~**) glide (down).

пла́нка lath, slat.

пла́новый planned, systematic; planning. **планоме́рный** systematic, planned.

планта́ция plantation.

пласт (-á) layer; stratum. **пласти́на** plate. **пласти́нка** plate; (*gramophone*) record.

пласти́ческий, пласти́чный plastic. **пластма́сса** plastic. **пластма́ссовый** plastic.

пла́стырь *m* plaster.

пла́та pay; charge; fee. **платёж** (-á) payment. **платёжеспосо́бный** solvent. **платёжный** pay.

пла́тина platinum.

плати́ть (-ачу́, -áтишь) *impf* (*pf* **за~, у~**) pay; **~ся** (*pf*

по~ся) **за**+*acc* pay for. **пла́тный** paid; requiring payment.

плато́к (-тка́) shawl; head-scarf; handkerchief.

платони́ческий platonic.

платфо́рма platform; truck.

пла́тье (*gen pl* -ьев) clothes, clothing; dress; gown. **платяно́й** clothes.

плафо́н ceiling; lamp shade.

плацда́рм bridgehead, beach-head; base; springboard.

плацка́рта reserved-seat ticket.

плач weeping. **плаче́вный** lamentable. **пла́чу** *etc.*: *see* **пла́кать**

плачу́ *etc.*: *see* **плати́ть**

плашмя́ *adv* flat, prone.

плащ (-а́) cloak; raincoat.

плебе́й plebeian.

плева́тельница spittoon.

плева́ть (плюю́, плюёшь) *impf* (*pf* **на~**, **плю́нуть**) spit; *inf*+*dat*: **мне ~** I don't give a damn (**на**+*acc* about); **~ся** spit. **плево́к** (-вка́) spit, spittle.

плеври́т pleurisy.

плед rug; plaid.

плёл *etc.*: *see* **плести́**

племенно́й tribal; pedigree. **пле́мя** (-мени; *pl* -мена́, -мён) *neut* tribe. **племя́нник** nephew. **племя́нница** niece.

плен (*loc* -у́) captivity.

плена́рный plenary.

плени́тельный captivating. **плени́ть** *pf* (*impf* **пленя́ть**) captivate; **~ся** be captivated.

плёнка film; tape; pellicle.

пле́нник prisoner. **пле́нный** captive.

пле́нум plenary session.

пленя́ть(ся *impf of* **плени́ть(ся**

пле́сень mould.

плеск splash, lapping. **плеска́ть** (-ещу́, -е́щешь) *impf* (*pf* **плесну́ть**) splash; lap; **~ся** splash; lap.

пле́сневеть (-еет) *impf* (*pf* **за~**) go mouldy, grow musty.

плесну́ть (-ну́, -нёшь) *pf of* **плеска́ть**

плести́ (-ету́, -етёшь; плёл, -а́) *impf* (*pf* **с~**) plait; weave; **~сь** trudge along. **плете́ние** plaiting; wickerwork. **плетёный** wattled; wicker. **плете́нь** (-тня́) *m* wattle fencing.

плётка, плеть (*gen pl* -е́й) lash.

пле́чико (*pl* -и, -ов) shoulder-strap; *pl* coat-hanger. **плечи́стый** broad-shouldered. **плечо́** (*pl* -и, -а́м) shoulder.

плеши́вый bald. **плеши́на**, **плешь** bald patch.

плещу́ *etc.*: *see* **плеска́ть**

пли́нтус plinth; skirting-board.

плис velveteen.

плиссирова́ть *impf* pleat.

плита́ (*pl* -ы) slab; flag(stone); stove, cooker; **моги́льная ~** gravestone. **пли́тка** tile; (thin) slab; stove, cooker; **~ шокола́да** bar of chocolate. **пли́точный** tiled.

плове́ц (-вца́), **пловчи́ха** swimmer. **плову́чий** floating; buoyant.

плод (-а́) fruit. **плоди́ть** (-ожу́) *impf* (*pf* **рас~**) produce, procreate; **~ся** propagate.

плодо- *in comb* fruit-. **плодови́тый** fruitful, prolific; fertile. **~во́дство** fruit-growing. **~но́сный** fruit-bearing, fruitful. **~овощно́й** fruit and vegetable. **~ро́дный** fertile. **~тво́рный** fruitful.

пло́мба seal; filling. **пломбирова́ть** *impf* (*pf* **за~**, **о~**) fill; seal.

плóский (-сок, -скá, -о) flat; trivial.
плоско- *in comb* flat. **плоскогóрье** plateau. **~гýбцы** (-ев) *pl* pliers. **~дóнный** flat-bottomed.
плóскость (*gen pl* -éй) flatness; plane; platitude.
плот (-á) raft.
плотúна dam; weir; dyke.
плóтник carpenter.
плóтность solidity; density. **плóтный** (-тен, -тнá, -о) thick; compact; dense; solid, strong; hearty.
плотоя́дный carnivorous.
плоть flesh.
плохóй bad; poor.
площáдка area, (sports) ground, court, playground; site; landing; platform. **плóщадь** (*gen pl* -éй) area; space; square.
плуг (*pl* -и́) plough.
плут (-á) cheat, swindler; rogue. **плутовáтый** cunning. **плутовскóй** roguish; picaresque.
плутóний plutonium.
плыть (-ывý, -ывёшь; плыл, -á, -о) *impf* swim; float; sail.
плю́нуть (-ну) *pf of* **плевáть**
плюс plus; advantage.
плюш plush.
плющ (-á) ivy.
плюю́ *etc.*: *see* **плевáть**
пляж beach.
плясáть (-яшý, -я́шешь) *impf* (*pf* **с~**) dance. **пля́ска** dance; dancing.
пневматúческий pneumatic.
пневмонúя pneumonia.
пнуть (пну, пнёшь) *pf of* **пинáть**
пня *etc.*: *see* **пень**
по *prep* **I.** *+dat* on; along; round, about; by; over; according to; in accordance with; for; in; at; by (reason of); on account of; from; **по понедéльникам** on Mondays; **по профéссии** by profession; **по рáдио** over the radio. **II.** *+dat or acc of cardinal number, forms distributive number*: **пó два, пó двое** in twos, two by two; **по пять рублéй штýка** at five roubles each. **III.** *+acc* to, up to; for, to get; **идтú по вóду** go to get water; **по пéрвое сентября́** up to (and including) 1st September. **IV.** *+prep* on, (immediately) after; **по прибы́тии** on arrival.
по- *pref* **I.** *in comb +dat of adjs, or with advs in* **-и**, *indicates manner, use of a named language, or accordance with the opinion or wish of*: **говорúть по-рýсски** speak Russian; **жить по-стáрому** live in the old style; **по-мóему** in my opinion. **II.** *in comb with adjs and nn, indicates situation along or near a thing*: **помóрье** seaboard, coastal region. **III.** *in comb with comp of adjs indicates a smaller degree of comparison*: **помéньше** a little less.
побáиваться *impf* be rather afraid.
побéг[1] flight; escape.
побéг[2] shoot; sucker.
побегýшки: быть на побегýшках run errands.
побéда victory. **победúтель** *m* victor; winner. **победúть** *pf* (*impf* **побеждáть**) conquer; win. **побéдный, победонóсный** victorious, triumphant.
по|бежáть *pf.*
побеждáть *impf of* **победúть**
по|белéть (-éю) *pf.* **по|белúть** *pf.* **побéлка** whitewashing.

побере́жный coastal. **побере́жье** (sea-)coast.
по|беспоко́ить(ся *pf.*
побира́ться *impf* beg; live by begging.
по|би́ть(ся (-бью́(сь, -бьёшь(ся) *pf.* **по|благодари́ть** *pf.*
побла́жка indulgence.
по|бледне́ть (-е́ю) *pf.*
поблёскивать *impf* gleam.
побли́зости *adv* nearby.
побо́и (-ев) *pl* beating. **побо́ище** slaughter; bloody battle.
побо́рник champion, advocate. **поборо́ть** (-рю́, -решь) *pf* overcome.
побо́чный secondary; done on the side; ~ **проду́кт** by-product.
по|брани́ться *pf.*
по|брата́ться *pf.* **побрати́м** twin town.
по|бре́згать *pf.* **по|бри́ть(ся** (-бре́ю(сь) *pf.*
побуди́тельный stimulating. **побуди́ть** (-ужу́) *pf*, **побужда́ть** *impf* induce, prompt. **побужде́ние** motive; inducement.
побыва́ть *pf* have been, have visited; look in, visit. **побы́вка** leave. **побы́ть** (-бу́ду, -дешь; по́был, -а́, -о) *pf* stay (for a short time).
побью́(сь *etc.*: *see* **поби́ть(ся**
пова́диться (-а́жусь) get into the habit (of). **пова́дка** habit.
по|вали́ть(ся (-лю́(сь, -лишь(ся) *pf.*
пова́льно *adv* without exception. **пова́льный** general, mass.
по́вар (*pl* -а́) cook, chef. **пова́ренный** culinary; cookery, cooking.
по-ва́шему *adv* in your opinion.
пове́дать *pf* disclose; relate.
поведе́ние behaviour.
поведу́ *etc.*: *see* **повести́.**
по|везти́ (-зу́, -зёшь; -вёз, -ла́) *pf.* **повёл** *etc.*: *see* **повести́**
повелева́ть *impf* +*instr* rule (over); +*dat* command. **повеле́ние** command. **повели́тельный** imperious; imperative.
по|венча́ть(ся *pf.*
поверга́ть *impf*, **пове́ргнуть** (-ну; -ве́рг) *pf* throw down; plunge.
пове́ренная *sb* confidante. **пове́ренный** *sb* attorney; confidant; ~ **в дела́х** chargé d'affaires. **по|ве́рить**[1]. **пове́рить**[2] *pf* (*impf* **поверя́ть**) check; confide. **пове́рка** check; roll-call.
поверну́ть (-ну́, -нёшь) *pf*, **повёртывать** *impf* (*impf also* **повора́чивать**) turn; **~ся** turn.
пове́рх *prep*+*gen* over. **пове́рхностный** surface, superficial. **пове́рхность** surface.
пове́рье (*gen pl* -ий) popular belief, superstition. **поверя́ть** *impf of* **пове́рить**[2]
пове́са playboy.
по|весели́ть (-е́ю) *pf.*
повесели́ть *pf* cheer (up), amuse; **~ся** have fun.
пове́сить(ся (-ве́шу(сь) *pf of* **ве́шать(ся**
повествова́ние narrative, narration. **повествова́тельный** narrative. **повествова́ть** *impf* +**о**+*prep* narrate, relate.
по|вести́ (-еду́, -едёшь; -вёл, -а́) *pf* (*impf* **поводи́ть**) +*instr* move.
пове́стка notice; summons; ~ **(дня)** agenda.

по́весть (*gen pl* -е́й) story, tale. **пове́трие** epidemic; craze. **пове́шу** *etc.*: *see* **пове́сить.** **по|вздо́рить** *pf.* **повзросле́ть** (-е́ю) *pf* grow up. **по|вида́ть(ся** *pf.* **по-ви́димому** apparently. **пови́дло** jam. **по|вини́ться** *pf.* **пови́нность** duty, obligation; **во́инская ~** conscription. **пови́нный** guilty. **повинова́ться** *impf* & *pf* obey. **повинове́ние** obedience. **повиса́ть** *impf*, **по|ви́снуть** (-ну; -ви́с) *pf* hang (on); hang down, droop. **повле́чь** (-еку́, -ечёшь; -ёк, -ла́) *pf* **(за собо́й)** entail, bring in its train. **по|влия́ть** *pf.* **по́вод**[1] occasion, cause; **по ~у**+*gen* as regards, concerning. **по́вод**[2] (*loc* -у́; *pl* -о́дья, -ьев) rein; **быть на ~у́ у**+*gen* be under the thumb of. **поводи́ть** (-ожу́, -о́дишь) *impf of* **повести́. поводо́к** (-дка́) leash. **поводы́рь** (-я́) *m* guide. **пово́зка** cart; vehicle. **повора́чивать(ся** *impf of* **поверну́ть(ся, повороти́ть(ся; повора́чивайся, -айтесь!** get a move on! **поворо́т** turn, turning; bend; turning-point. **повороти́ть(ся** (-рочу́(сь, -ро́тишь(ся) *pf* (*impf* **повора́чивать(ся)** turn. **поворо́тливый** agile, nimble; manoeuvrable. **поворо́тный** turning; rotary; revolving. **по|вреди́ть** (-ежу́) *pf*, **повреждáть** *impf* damage; injure; **~ся** be damaged; be injured. **поврежде́ние** damage, injury. **повремени́ть** *pf* wait a little; **+с+***instr* delay over. **повседне́вный** daily; everyday. **повсеме́стно** *adv* everywhere. **повсеме́стный** universal, general. **повста́нец** (-нца) rebel, insurgent. **повста́нческий** rebel; insurgent. **повсю́ду** *adv* everywhere. **повторе́ние** repetition. **повтори́ть** *pf*, **повторя́ть** *impf* repeat; **~ся** repeat o.s.; be repeated; recur. **повто́рный** repeated. **повы́сить** (-ы́шу) *pf*, **повыша́ть** *impf* raise, heighten; **~ся** rise. **повыше́ние** rise; promotion. **повы́шенный** heightened, high. **повяза́ть** (-яжу́, -я́жешь) *pf*, **повя́зывать** *impf* tie. **повя́зка** band; bandage. **по|гада́ть** *pf.* **пога́нка** toadstool. **пога́ный** foul; unclean. **погаса́ть** *impf*, **по|га́снуть** (-ну) *pf* go out, be extinguished. **по|гаси́ть** (-ашу́, -а́сишь) *pf.* **погаша́ть** *impf* liquidate, cancel. **пога́шенный** used, cancelled, cashed. **погиба́ть** *impf*, **по|ги́бнуть** (-ну; -ги́б) *pf* perish; be lost. **поги́бель** ruin. **поги́бший** lost; ruined; killed. **по|гла́дить** (-а́жу) *pf.* **поглоти́ть** (-ощу́, -о́тишь) *pf*, **поглоща́ть** *impf* swallow up; absorb. **поглоще́ние** absorption. **по|глупе́ть** (-е́ю) *pf.* **по|гляде́ть** (-яжу́) *pf.* **погля́дывать** *impf* glance (from time to time); **+за+***instr* keep an eye on.

погна́ть (-гоню́, -го́нишь; -гна́л, -а́, -о) *pf* drive; **~ся за**+*instr* run after; start in pursuit of.

по|гну́ть(ся (-ну́(сь, -нёшь(ся) *pf*. **по|гнуша́ться** *pf*.

поговори́ть *pf* have a talk.

погово́рка saying, proverb.

пого́да weather.

погоди́ть (-ожу́) *pf* wait a little; **немно́го погодя́** a little later.

поголо́вно *adv* one and all. **поголо́вный** general; capitation. **поголо́вье** number.

пого́н (*gen pl* -о́н) shoulder-strap.

пого́нщик driver. **погоню́** *etc*.: *see* **погна́ть. пого́ня** pursuit, chase. **погоня́ть** *impf* urge on, drive.

погорячи́ться (-чу́сь) *pf* get worked up.

пого́ст graveyard.

пограни́чник frontier guard. **пограни́чный** frontier.

по́греб (*pl* -а́) cellar. **погреба́льный** funeral. **погреба́ть** *impf of* **погрести́. погребе́ние** burial.

погрему́шка rattle.

погрести́[1] (-ебу́, -ебёшь; -рёб, -ла́) *pf* (*impf* **погреба́ть**) bury.

погрести́[2] (-ебу́, -ебёшь; -рёб, -ла́) *pf* row for a while.

погре́ть (-е́ю) *pf* warm; **~ся** warm o.s.

по|греши́ть (-шу́) *pf* sin; err. **погре́шность** error, mistake.

по|грози́ть(ся (-ожу́(сь) *pf*. **по|грубе́ть** (-е́ю) *pf*.

погружа́ть *impf*, **по|грузи́ть** (-ужу́, -у́зи́шь) *pf* load; ship; dip, plunge, immerse; **~ся** sink, plunge; dive; be plunged, absorbed. **погруже́ние** submergence; immersion; dive. **погру́зка** loading; shipment.

погряза́ть *impf*, **по|гря́знуть** (-ну; -я́з) *pf* be bogged down; wallow.

по|губи́ть (-блю́, -бишь) *pf*. **по|гуля́ть** *pf*.

под, подо *prep* **I.** +*acc or instr* under; near, close to; **взять по́д руку**+*acc* take the arm of; **~ ви́дом**+*gen* under the guise of; **по́д гору** downhill; **~ Москво́й** in the environs of Moscow. **II.** +*instr* occupied by, used as; (meant, implied) by; in, with; **говя́дина ~ хре́ном** beef with horse-radish. **III.** +*acc* towards; to (the accompaniment of); in imitation of; on; for, to serve as; **ему́ ~ пятьдеся́т (лет)** he is getting on for fifty.

подава́ть(ся (-даю́(сь, -даёшь(ся) *impf of* **пода́ть(ся**

подави́ть (-влю́, -вишь) *pf*, **подавля́ть** *impf* suppress; depress; overwhelm. **по|дави́ться** (-влю́сь, -вишься) *pf*. **подавле́ние** suppression; repression. **пода́вленность** depression. **пода́вленный** suppressed; depressed. **подавля́ющий** overwhelming.

пода́вно *adv* all the more.

пода́гра gout.

пода́льше *adv* a little further.

по|дари́ть (-рю́, -ришь) *pf*. **пода́рок** (-рка) present.

пода́тливый pliant, pliable.

по́дать (*gen pl* -е́й) tax. **пода́ть** (-а́м, -а́шь, -а́ст, -ади́м; по́дал, -а́, -о) *pf* (*impf* **подава́ть**) serve; give; put, move, turn; put forward, present, hand in; **~ся** move; give way; yield; **+на**+*acc* set out for. **пода́ча** giving, presenting; serve; feed, supply. **пода́чка** handout, crumb. **подаю́** *etc*.:

see **подава́ть. подая́ние** alms.
подбега́ть *impf*, **подбежа́ть** (-егу́) *pf* come running (up).
подбива́ть *impf of* **подби́ть**
подберу́ *etc.*: *see* **подобра́ть.**
подбира́ть(ся *impf of* **подобра́ть(ся**
подби́ть (-добью́, -добьёшь) *pf* (*impf* **подбива́ть**) line; re-sole; bruise; put out of action; incite.
подбодри́ть *pf*, **подбодря́ть** *impf* cheer up, encourage; **~ся** cheer up, take heart.
подбо́р selection, assortment.
подборо́док (-дка) chin.
подбоче́нившись *adv* with hands on hips.
подбра́сывать *impf*, **подбро́сить** (-ро́шу) *pf* throw up.
подва́л cellar; basement. **подва́льный** basement, cellar.
подведу́ *etc.*: *see* **подвести́**
подвезти́ (-зу́, -зёшь; -вёз, -ла́) *pf* (*impf* **подвози́ть**) bring, take; give a lift.
подвене́чный wedding.
подверга́ть *impf*, **подве́ргнуть** (-ну; -ве́рг) *pf* subject; expose; **~ся** *+dat* undergo. **подве́рженный** subject, liable.
подверну́ть (-ну́, -нёшь) *pf*, **подвёртывать** *impf* turn up; tuck under; sprain; tighten; **~ся** be sprained; be turned up; be tucked under.
подве́сить (-е́шу) *pf* (*impf* **подве́шивать**) hang up, suspend. **подвесно́й** hanging, suspended.
подвести́ (-еду́, -едёшь; -вёл, -а́) *pf* (*impf* **подводи́ть**) lead up, bring up; place (under); bring under, subsume; let down; **~ ито́ги** reckon up; sum up.
подве́шивать *impf of* **подве́сить**
по́двиг exploit, feat.
подвига́ть(ся *impf of* **подви́нуть(ся**
подви́жник religious ascetic; champion.
подвижно́й mobile; **~ соста́в** rolling-stock. **подви́жность** mobility. **подви́жный** mobile; lively; agile.
подвиза́ться *impf* (**в** *or* **на**+*prep*) work (in).
подви́нуть (-ну) *pf* (*impf* **подвига́ть**) move; push; advance; **~ся** move; advance.
подвла́стный *+dat* subject to; under the control of.
подво́да cart. **подводи́ть** (-ожу́, -о́дишь) *impf of* **подвести́**
подво́дн|ый submarine; underwater; **~ая скала́** reef.
подво́з transport; supply. **подвози́ть** (-ожу́, -о́зишь) *impf of* **подвезти́**
подворо́тня (*gen pl* -тен) gateway.
подво́х trick.
подвы́пивший tipsy.
подвяза́ть (-яжу́, -я́жешь) *pf*, **подвя́зывать** *impf* tie up. **подвя́зка** garter; suspender.
подгиба́ть *impf of* **подогну́ть**
подгляде́ть (-яжу́) *pf*, **подгля́дывать** *impf* peep; spy.
подгова́ривать *impf*, **подговори́ть** *pf* incite.
подгоню́ *etc.*: *see* **подогна́ть.**
подгоня́ть *impf of* **подогна́ть**
подгора́ть *impf*, **подгоре́ть** (-ри́т) *pf* get a bit burnt. **подгоре́лый** slightly burnt.
подготови́тельный preparatory. **подгото́вить** (-влю) *pf*, **подгота́вливать** *impf* prepare; **~ся** prepare, get ready.
подгото́вка preparation, training.

поддава́ться (-даю́сь, -даёшься) *impf of* **подда́ться**
подда́кивать *impf* agree, assent.
по́дданный *sb* subject; citizen. **по́дданство** citizenship.
подда́ться (-а́мся, -а́шься, -а́стся, -ади́мся; -а́лся, -ла́сь) *pf* (*impf* **поддава́ться**) yield, give way.
подде́лать *pf*, **подде́лывать** *impf* counterfeit; forge. **подде́лка** falsification; forgery; imitation. **подде́льный** false, counterfeit.
поддержа́ть (-жу́, -жишь) *pf*, **подде́рживать** *impf* support; maintain. **подде́ржка** support.
по|де́йствовать *pf*.
поде́лать *pf* do; **ничего́ не поде́лаешь** it can't be helped.
по|дели́ть(ся (-лю́(сь, -лишь(ся) *pf*.
поде́лка *pl* small (handmade) articles.
подело́м *adv*: ~ **ему́** (*etc.*) it serves him (*etc.*) right.
подённый by the day. **подёнщик, -ица** day-labourer.
подёргиваться *impf* twitch.
поде́ржанный second-hand.
подёрнуть (-нет) *pf* cover.
подеру́ *etc.*: *see* **подра́ть.**
по|дешеве́ть (-е́ет) *pf*.
поджа́ривать(ся *impf*, **поджа́рить(ся** *pf* fry, roast, grill; toast. **поджа́ристый** brown(ed).
поджа́рый lean, wiry.
поджа́ть (-дожму́, -дожмёшь) *pf* (*impf* **поджима́ть**) draw in, draw under; ~ **гу́бы** purse one's lips.
подже́чь (-дожгу́, -ожжёшь; -жёг, -дожгла́) *pf*, **поджига́ть** *impf* set fire to; burn. **поджига́тель** *m* arsonist; instigator.
поджида́ть *impf* (+*gen*) wait (for).
поджима́ть *impf of* **поджа́ть**
поджо́г arson.
подзаголо́вок (-вка) subtitle, sub-heading.
подзащи́тный *sb* client.
подземе́лье (*gen pl* -лий) cave; dungeon. **подзе́мный** underground.
подзову́ *etc.*: *see* **подозва́ть**
подзо́рная труба́ telescope.
подзыва́ть *impf of* **подозва́ть**
по|диви́ться (-влю́сь) *pf*.
подка́пывать(ся *impf of* **подкопа́ть(ся**
подкарау́ливать *impf*, **подкарау́лить** *pf* be on the watch (for).
подкати́ть (-ачу́, -а́тишь) *pf*, **подка́тывать** *impf* roll up, drive up; roll.
подка́шивать(ся *impf of* **подкоси́ть(ся**
подки́дывать *impf*, **подки́нуть** (-ну) *pf* throw up. **подки́дыш** foundling.
подкла́дка lining. **подкла́дывать** *impf of* **подложи́ть**
подкле́ивать *impf*, **подкле́ить** *pf* glue (up); mend.
подко́ва (horse-)shoe. **под|кова́ть** (-кую́, -ёшь) *pf*, **подко́вывать** *impf* shoe.
подко́жный hypodermic.
подкоми́ссия, подкомите́т sub-committee.
подко́п undermining; underground passage. **подкопа́ть** *pf* (*impf* **подка́пывать**) undermine; ~**ся под**+*acc* undermine; burrow under.
подкоси́ть (-ошу́, -о́сишь) *pf* (*impf* **подка́шивать**) cut down; ~**ся** give way.

подкра́дываться *impf of* **подкра́сться**
подкра́сить (-а́шу) *pf* (*impf* **подкра́шивать**) touch up; **~ся** make up lightly.
подкра́сться (-аду́сь, -адёшься) *pf* (*impf* **подкра́дываться**) sneak up.
подкра́шивать(ся *impf of* **подкра́сить(ся. подкра́шу** *etc.*: *see* **подкра́сить**
подкрепи́ть (-плю́) *pf*, **подкрепля́ть** *impf* reinforce; support; corroborate; fortify; **~ся** fortify o.s. **подкрепле́ние** confirmation; sustenance; reinforcement.
подкрути́ть (-учу́, -у́тишь) *pf* (*impf* **подкру́чивать**) tighten up.
по́дкуп bribery. **подкупа́ть** *impf*, **подкупи́ть** (-плю́, -пишь) *pf* bribe; win over.
подла́диться (-а́жусь) *pf*, **подла́живаться** *impf* +к+*dat* adapt o.s. to; make up to.
подла́мываться *impf of* **подломи́ться**
по́дле *prep*+*gen* by the side of, beside.
подлежа́ть (-жу́) *impf* +*dat* be subject to; **не подлежи́т сомне́нию** it is beyond doubt. **подлежа́щее** *sb* subject. **подлежа́щий**+*dat* subject to.
подлеза́ть *impf*, **подле́зть** (-зу; -е́з) *pf* crawl (under).
подле́сок (-ска) undergrowth.
подле́ц (-а́) scoundrel.
подлива́ть *impf of* **подли́ть. подли́вка** sauce, dressing; gravy.
подли́за *m* & *f* toady. **подлиза́ться** (-ижу́сь, -и́жешься) *pf*, **подли́зываться** *impf* +к+*dat* suck up to.
по́длинник original. **по́длинно** *adv* really. **по́длинный** genuine; authentic; original; real.
подли́ть (-долью́, -дольёшь; по́дли́л, -а́, -о) *pf* (*impf* **подлива́ть**) pour; add.
подло́г forgery.
подло́дка submarine.
подложи́ть (-жу́, -жишь) *pf* (*impf* **подкла́дывать**) add; +**под**+*acc* lay under; line.
подло́жный false, spurious; counterfeit, forged.
подлоко́тник arm (*of chair*).
подломи́ться (-о́мится) *pf* (*impf* **подла́мываться**) break; give way.
по́длость meanness, baseness; mean trick. **по́длый** (подл, -а́, -о) mean, base.
подма́зать (-а́жу) *pf*, **подма́зывать** *impf* grease; bribe.
подмасте́рье (*gen pl* -ьев) *m* apprentice.
подме́н, подме́на replacement. **подме́нивать** *impf*, **подмени́ть** (-ню́, -нишь) *pf*, **подменя́ть** *impf* replace.
подмести́ (-ету́, -етёшь; -мёл, -а́) *pf*, **подмета́ть**[1] *impf* sweep.
подмета́ть[2] *pf* (*impf* **подмётывать**) tack.
подме́тить (-е́чу) *pf* (*impf* **подмеча́ть**) notice.
подмётка sole.
подмётывать *impf of* **подмета́ть**[2]. **подмеча́ть** *impf of* **подме́тить**
подмеша́ть *pf*, **подме́шивать** *impf* mix in, stir in.
подми́гивать *impf*, **подмигну́ть** (-ну́, -нёшь) *pf* +*dat* wink at.
подмо́га help.
подмока́ть *impf*, **подмо́кнуть** (-нет; -мо́к) *pf* get damp, get wet.

подмора́живать *impf*, **подморо́зить** *pf* freeze.
подмоско́вный (situated) near Moscow.
подмо́стки (-ов) *pl* scaffolding; stage.
подмо́ченный damp; tarnished.
подмыва́ть *impf*, **подмы́ть** (-о́ю) *pf* wash; wash away; **его́ так и подмыва́ет** he feels an urge (to).
подмы́шка armpit.
поднево́льный dependent; forced.
поднести́ (-су́, -сёшь; -ёс, -ла́) *pf* (*impf* **подноси́ть**) present; take, bring.
поднима́ть(ся *impf of* **подня́ть(ся**
обнови́ть (-влю́) *pf*, **подновля́ть** *impf* renew, renovate.
подного́тная *sb* ins and outs.
подно́жие foot; pedestal. **подно́жка** running-board. **подно́жный корм** pasture.
подно́с tray. **подноси́ть** (-ошу́, -о́сишь) *impf of* **поднести́**. **подноше́ние** giving; present.
подня́тие raising. **подня́ть** (-ниму́, -ни́мешь; по́днял, -а́, -о) *pf* (*impf* **поднима́ть, подыма́ть**) raise; lift (up); rouse; **~ся** rise; go up.
подо *see* **под**
подоба́ть *impf* befit, become. **подоба́ющий** proper.
подо́бие likeness; similarity. **подо́бн|ый** like, similar; **и тому́ ~ое** and so on, and such like; **ничего́ ~ого!** nothing of the sort!
подобостра́стие servility. **подобостра́стный** servile.
подобра́ть (-дберу́, -дберёшь; -бра́л, -а́, -о) *pf* (*impf* **подбира́ть**) pick up; tuck up, put up; pick; **~ся** steal up.
подобью́ *etc.*: *see* **подби́ть**
подогна́ть (-дгоню́, -дго́нишь; -а́л, -а́, -о) *pf* (*impf* **подгоня́ть**) drive; urge on; adjust.
подогну́ть (-ну́, -нёшь) *pf* (*impf* **подгиба́ть**) tuck in; bend under.
подогрева́ть *impf*, **подогре́ть** (-е́ю) *pf* warm up.
пододвига́ть *impf*, **пододви́нуть** (-ну) *pf* move up.
пододея́льник blanket cover; top sheet.
подожгу́ *etc.*: *see* **подже́чь**
подожда́ть (-ду́, -дёшь; -а́л, -а́, -о) *pf* wait (*+gen or acc* for).
подожму́ *etc.*: *see* **поджа́ть**
подозва́ть (-дзову́, -дзовёшь; -а́л, -а́, -о) *pf* (*impf* **подзыва́ть**) call to; beckon.
подозрева́емый suspected; suspect. **подозрева́ть** *impf* suspect. **подозре́ние** suspicion. **подозри́тельный** suspicious.
по|дои́ть (-ою́, -о́ишь) *pf.*
подойти́ (-йду́, -йдёшь; -ошёл, -шла́) *pf* (*impf* **подходи́ть**) approach; come up; *+dat* suit, fit.
подоко́нник window-sill.
подо́л hem.
подо́лгу *adv* for ages; for hours (*etc.*) on end.
подолью́ *etc.*: *see* **подли́ть**
подо́нки (-ов) *pl* dregs; scum.
подоплёка underlying cause.
подопру́ *etc.*: *see* **подпере́ть**
подо́пытный experimental.
подорва́ть (-рву́, -рвёшь; -а́л, -а́, -о) *pf* (*impf* **подрыва́ть**) undermine; blow up.
по|дорожа́ть *pf.*
подоро́жник plantain. **подоро́жный** roadside.

подосла́ть (-ошлю́, -ошлёшь) *pf* (*impf* **подсыла́ть**) send (secretly).
подоспева́ть *impf*, **подоспе́ть** (-е́ю) *pf* arrive, appear (in time).
подостла́ть (-дстелю́, -дсте́лешь) *pf* (*impf* **подстила́ть**) lay under.
подотде́л section, subdivision.
подотру́ *etc.*: *see* **подтере́ть**
подотчётный accountable.
по|до́хнуть (-ну) *pf* (*impf also* **подыха́ть**).
подохо́дный нало́г income-tax.
подо́шва sole; foot.
подошёл *etc.*: *see* **подойти́.** **подошлю́** *etc.*: *see* **подосла́ть** **подошью́** *etc.*: *see* **подши́ть.**
подпада́ть *impf*, **подпа́сть** (-аду́, -адёшь; -а́л) *pf* **под**+*acc* fall under.
подпева́ть *impf* (+*dat*) sing along (with).
подпере́ть (-допру́; -пёр) *pf* (*impf* **подпира́ть**) prop up.
подпи́ливать *impf*, **подпили́ть** (-лю́, -лишь) *pf* saw; saw a little off.
подпира́ть *impf of* **подпере́ть**
подписа́ние signing. **подписа́ть** (-ишу́, -и́шешь) *pf*, **подпи́сывать** *impf* sign; **~ся** sign; subscribe. **подпи́ска** subscription. **подписно́й** subscription. **подпи́счик** subscriber. **по́дпись** signature.
подплыва́ть *impf*, **подплы́ть** (-ыву́, -ывёшь; -плы́л, -а́, -о) *pf* **к**+*dat* swim *or* sail up to.
подполза́ть *impf*, **подползти́** (-зу́, -зёшь; -по́лз, -ла́) *pf* creep up (**к**+*dat* to); +**под**+*acc* crawl under.
подполко́вник lieutenant-colonel.
подпо́лье cellar; underground. **подпо́льный** underfloor; underground.
подпо́ра, подпо́рка prop, support.
подпо́чва subsoil.
подпра́вить (-влю) *pf*, **подправля́ть** *impf* touch up, adjust.
подпры́гивать *impf*, **подпры́гнуть** (-ну) *pf* jump up (and down).
подпуска́ть *impf*, **подпусти́ть** (-ущу́, -у́стишь) *pf* allow to approach.
подраба́тывать *impf*, **подрабо́тать** *pf* earn on the side; work up.
подра́внивать *impf of* **подровня́ть**
подража́ние imitation. **подража́ть** *impf* imitate.
подразделе́ние subdivision. **подраздели́ть** *pf*, **подразделя́ть** *impf* subdivide.
подразумева́ть *impf* imply, mean; **~ся** be meant, be understood.
подраста́ть *impf*, **подрасти́** (-ту́, -тёшь; -ро́с, -ла́) *pf* grow.
по|дра́ть(ся (-деру́(сь, -дерёшь(ся, -а́л(ся, -ла́(сь, -о́(сь *or* -о(сь) *pf*.
подре́зать (-е́жу) *pf*, **подреза́ть** *impf* cut; clip, trim.
подро́бно *adv* in detail. **подро́бность** detail. **подро́бный** detailed.
подровня́ть *pf* (*impf* **подра́внивать**) level, even; trim.
подро́с *etc.*: *see* **подрасти́.** **подро́сток** (-тка) adolescent; youth.
подро́ю *etc.*: *see* **подры́ть**

подрубáть[1] *impf*, **подрубúть** (-блю́, -бишь) *pf* chop down; cut short(er).

подрубáть[2] *impf*, **подрубúть** (-блю́, -бишь) *pf* hem.

подрýга friend; girlfriend. **подрýжески** *adv* in a friendly way. **подружúться** (-жýсь) *pf* make friends.

по-другóму *adv* differently.

подрýчный at hand; improvised; *sb* assistant.

подры́в undermining; injury.

подрывáть[1] *impf of* **подорвáть**

подрывáть[2] *impf*, **подры́ть** (-рóю) *pf* undermine, sap. **подрывнóй** blasting, demolition; subversive.

подря́д[1] *adv* in succession.

подря́д[2] contract. **подря́дчик** contractor.

подсáживаться *impf of* **подсéсть**

подсáливать *impf of* **подсолúть**

подсвéчник candlestick.

подсéсть (-ся́ду; -сéл) *pf* (*impf* **подсáживаться**) sit down (**к**+*dat* near).

подсказáть (-ажý, -áжешь) *pf*, **подскáзывать** *impf* prompt; suggest. **подскáзка** prompting.

подскáкивать *impf*, **подскочúть** (-чý, -чишь) *pf* jump (up); soar; come running.

подсластúть (-ащý) *pf*, **подслáщивать** *impf* sweeten.

подслéдственный under investigation.

подслýшать *pf*, **подслýшивать** *impf* overhear; eavesdrop, listen.

подсмáтривать *impf*, **подсмотрéть** (-рю́, -ришь) *pf* spy (on).

подснéжник snowdrop.

подсóбный subsidiary; auxiliary.

подсóвывать *impf of* **подсýнуть**

подсознáние subconscious (mind). **подсознáтельный** subconscious.

подсолúть (-сóлишь) *pf* (*impf* **подсáливать**) add salt to.

подсóлнечник sunflower. **подсóлнечный** sunflower.

подсóхнуть (-ну) *pf* (*impf* **подсыхáть**) dry out a little.

подспóрье help.

подстáвить (-влю) *pf*, **подставля́ть** *impf* put (under); bring up; expose; ~ **нóжку** +*dat* trip up. **подстáвка** stand; support. **подставнóй** false.

подстакáнник glass-holder.

подстелю́ *etc.*: *see* **подостлáть**

подстерегáть *impf*, **подстерéчь** (-егý, -ежёшь; -рёг, -лá) *pf* lie in wait for.

подстилáть *impf of* **подостлáть**. **подстúлка** litter.

подстрáивать *impf of* **подстрóить**

подстрекáтель *m* instigator. **подстрекáтельство** instigation. **подстрекáть** *impf*, **подстрекнýть** (-нý, -нёшь) *pf* instigate, incite.

подстрéливать *impf*, **подстрелúть** (-лю́, -лишь) *pf* wound.

подстригáть *impf*, **подстрúчь** (-игý, -ижёшь; -úг) *pf* cut; clip, trim; **~ся** have a hair-cut.

подстрóить *pf* (*impf* **подстрáивать**) build on; cook up.

подстрóчн|ый literal; **~ое примечáние** footnote.

по́дступ approach. **подступа́ть** *impf*, **подступи́ть** (-плю́, -пишь) *pf* approach; **~ся к**+*dat* approach.

подсуди́мый *sb* defendant; the accused. **подсу́дный**+*dat* under the jurisdiction of.

подсу́нуть (-ну) *pf* (*impf* **подсо́вывать**) put, shove; palm off.

подсчёт calculation; count. **подсчита́ть** *pf*, **подсчи́тывать** count (up); calculate.

подсыла́ть *impf of* **подосла́ть**. **подсыха́ть** *impf of* **подсо́хнуть**. **подся́ду** *etc.*: *see* **подсе́сть**. **подта́лкивать** *impf of* **подтолкну́ть**

подта́скивать *impf of* **подтащи́ть**

подтасова́ть *pf*, **подтасо́вывать** *impf* shuffle unfairly; juggle with.

подта́чивать *impf of* **подточи́ть**

подтащи́ть (-щу́, -щишь) *pf* (*impf* **подта́скивать**) drag up.

подтверди́ть (-ржу́) *pf*, **подтвержда́ть** *impf* confirm; corroborate. **подтвержде́ние** confirmation, corroboration.

подтёк bruise. **подтека́ть** *impf of* **подте́чь**; leak.

подтере́ть (-дотру́, -дотрёшь; подтёр) *pf* (*impf* **подтира́ть**) wipe (up).

подте́чь (-ечёт; -тёк, -ла́) *pf* (*impf* **подтека́ть**) **под**+*acc* flow under.

подтира́ть *impf of* **подтере́ть**

подтолкну́ть (-ну́, -нёшь) *pf* (*impf* **подта́лкивать**) push; urge on.

подточи́ть (-чу́, -чишь) *pf* (*impf* **подта́чивать**) sharpen; eat away; undermine.

подтру́нивать *impf*, **подтруни́ть** *pf* **над**+*instr* tease.

подтя́гивать *impf*, **подтяну́ть** (-ну́, -нешь) *pf* tighten; pull up; move up; **~ся** tighten one's belt *etc.*; move up; pull o.s. together. **подтя́жки** (-жек) *pl* braces, suspenders. **подтя́нутый** smart.

по|ду́мать *pf* think (for a while). **поду́мывать** *impf*+*inf or* **о**+*prep* think about.

по|ду́ть (-у́ю) *pf*.

поду́шка pillow; cushion.

подхали́м *m* toady. **подхали́мство** grovelling.

подхвати́ть (-ачу́, -а́тишь) *pf*, **подхва́тывать** *impf* catch (up), pick up, take up.

подхлестну́ть (-ну́, -нёшь) *pf*, **подхлёстывать** *impf* whip up.

подхо́д approach. **подходи́ть** (-ожу́, -о́дишь) *impf of* **подойти́**. **подходя́щий** suitable.

подцепи́ть (-плю́, -пишь) *pf*, **подцепля́ть** *impf* hook on; pick up.

подча́с *adv* sometimes.

подчёркивать *impf*, **подчеркну́ть** (-ну́, -нёшь) *pf* underline; emphasize.

подчине́ние subordination; submission. **подчинённый** subordinate. **подчини́ть** *pf*, **подчиня́ть** *impf* subordinate, subject; **~ся** +*dat* submit to.

подшива́ть *impf of* **подши́ть**. **подши́вка** hemming; lining; soling.

подши́пник bearing.

подши́ть (-дошью́, -дошьёшь) *pf* (*impf* **подшива́ть**) hem, line; sole.

подшути́ть (-учу́, -у́тишь) *pf*,

подшу́чивать *impf* **над**+*instr* mock; play a trick on.
подъе́ду *etc.*: *see* **подъе́хать**
подъе́зд entrance, doorway; approach. **подъезжа́ть** *impf of* **подъе́хать**
подъём lifting; raising; ascent; climb; enthusiasm; instep; reveille. **подъёмник** lift, elevator, hoist. **подъёмный** lifting; ~ **кран** crane; ~ **мост** drawbridge.
подъе́хать (-е́ду) *pf* (*impf* **подъезжа́ть**) drive up.
подыма́ть(ся *impf of* **подня́ть(ся**
подыска́ть (-ыщу́, -ы́щешь) *pf*, **поды́скивать** *impf* seek (out).
подыто́живать *impf*, **подыто́жить** (-жу) *pf* sum up.
подыха́ть *impf of* **подо́хнуть**
подыша́ть (-шу́, -шишь) *pf* breathe.
поеда́ть *impf of* **пое́сть**
поеди́нок (-нка) duel.
по́езд (*pl* -а́) train. **пое́здка** trip.
пое́сть (-е́м, -е́шь, -е́ст, -еди́м; -е́л) *pf* (*impf* **поеда́ть**) eat, eat up; have a bite to eat.
по|е́хать (-е́ду) *pf* go; set off.
по|жале́ть (-е́ю) *pf.*
по|жа́ловать(ся *pf.* **пожа́луй** *adv* perhaps. **пожа́луйста** *partl* please; you're welcome.
пожа́р fire. **пожа́рище** scene of a fire. **пожа́рник, пожа́рный** *sb* fireman. **пожа́рн|ый** fire; ~**ая кома́нда** fire-brigade; ~**ая ле́стница** fire-escape; ~**ая маши́на** fire-engine.
пожа́тие handshake. **пожа́ть**[1] (-жму́, -жмёшь) *pf* (*impf* **пожима́ть**) press; ~ **ру́ку**+*dat* shake hands with; ~ **плеча́ми** shrug one's shoulders.
пожа́ть[2] (-жну́, -жнёшь) *pf* (*impf* **пожина́ть**) reap.
пожела́ние wish, desire. **по|жела́ть** *pf.*
по|желте́ть (-е́ю) *pf.*
по|жени́ть (-ню́, -нишь) *pf.* **пожени́ться** (-же́нимся) *pf* get married.
поже́ртвование donation. **по|же́ртвовать** *pf.*
пожива́ть *impf* live; **как (вы) пожива́ете?** how are you (getting on)? **пожи́зненный** life(long). **пожило́й** elderly.
пожима́ть *impf of* **пожа́ть**[1].
пожина́ть *impf of* **пожа́ть**[2].
пожира́ть *impf of* **пожра́ть**
пожи́тки (-ов) *pl* belongings.
пожи́ть (-иву́, -ивёшь; по́жил, -а́, -о) *pf.* live for a while; stay.
пожму́ *etc.*: *see* **пожа́ть**[1].
пожну́ *etc.*: *see* **пожа́ть**[2]
пожра́ть (-ру́, -рёшь; -а́л, -а́, -о) *pf* (*impf* **пожира́ть**) devour.
по́за pose.
по|забо́титься (-о́чусь) *pf.*
позабыва́ть *impf*, **позабы́ть** (-у́ду) *pf* forget all about.
по|зави́довать *pf.* **по|за́втракать** *pf.*
позавчера́ *adv* the day before yesterday.
позади́ *adv* & *prep*+*gen* behind.
по|заи́мствовать *pf.*
позапро́шлый before last.
по|зва́ть (-зову́, -зовёшь; -а́л, -а́, -о) *pf.*
позволе́ние permission. **позволи́тельный** permissible. **позво́лить** *pf*, **позволя́ть** *impf* + *dat* allow, permit; **позво́ль(те)** allow me; excuse me.

по|звони́ть *pf.*
позвоно́к (-нка́) vertebra. **позвоно́чник** spine. **позвоно́чн|ый** spinal; vertebrate; **~ые** *sb pl* vertebrates.
поздне́е *adv* later. **по́здний** late; **по́здно** it is late.
по|здоро́ваться *pf.* **поздра́вить** (-влю) *pf,* **поздравля́ть** *impf* **с**+*instr* congratulate on. **поздравле́ние** congratulation.
по|зелене́ть (-е́ет) *pf.*
по́зже *adv* later (on).
пози́ровать *impf* pose.
позити́в positive. **позити́вный** positive.
пози́ция position.
познава́тельный cognitive.
познава́ть (-наю́, -наёшь) *impf of* **позна́ть**
по|знако́мить(ся (-млю(сь) *pf.*
позна́ние cognition. **позна́ть** *pf* (*impf* **познава́ть**) get to know.
позоло́та gilding. **по|золоти́ть** (-лочу́) *pf.*
позо́р shame, disgrace. **позо́рить** *impf* (*pf* **о~**) disgrace; **~ся** disgrace o.s. **позо́рный** shameful.
поигра́ть *pf* play (for a while).
поимённо *adv* by name.
поимка capture.
поинтересова́ться *pf* be curious.
поиска́ть (-ищу́, -и́щешь) *pf* look for. **по́иски** (-ов) *pl* search.
поистине *adv* indeed.
пои́ть (пою́, по́ишь) *impf* (*pf* **на~**) give something to drink; water.
пойду́ *etc.*: *see* **пойти́**
по́йло swill.
пойма́ть *pf of* **лови́ть. пойму́** *etc.*: *see* **поня́ть**
пойти́ (-йду́, -йдёшь; *пошёл,* -шла́) *pf of* **идти́, ходи́ть**; go, walk; begin to walk; +*inf* begin; **пошёл!** off you go! I'm off; **пошёл вон!** be off!
пока́ *adv* for the present; cheerio; **~ что** in the meanwhile.
пока́ *conj* while; **~ не** until.
пока́з showing, demonstration. **показа́ние** testimony, evidence; reading. **показа́тель** *m* index. **показа́тельный** significant; model; demonstration. **показа́ть** (-ажу́, -а́жешь) *pf,* **пока́зывать** *impf* show. **по|каза́ться** (-ажу́сь, -а́жешься) *pf,* **пока́зываться** *impf* show o.s.; appear.
показно́й for show; ostentatious. **показу́ха** show.
по|кале́чить(ся (-чу(сь) *pf.*
пока́мест *adv & conj* for the present; while; meanwhile.
по|кара́ть *pf.*
по|ката́ться *pf.*
покати́ть (-чу́, -тишь) *pf* start (rolling); **~ся** start rolling.
пока́тый sloping; slanting.
покача́ть *pf* rock, swing; **~ голово́й** shake one's head.
пока́чивать rock slightly; **~ся** rock; stagger. **покачну́ть** (-ну́, -нёшь) shake; rock; **~ся** sway, totter, lurch.
пока́шливать *impf* have a slight cough.
покая́ние confession; repentance. **по|ка́яться** *pf.*
поквита́ться *pf* be quits; get even.
покида́ть *impf,* **поки́нуть** (-ну) *pf* leave; abandon. **поки́нутый** deserted.
поклада́я: не ~ рук untiringly.
покла́дистый complaisant, obliging.

покло́н bow; greeting; regards. **поклоне́ние** worship. **поклони́ться** (-ню́сь, -ни́шься) *pf of* **кла́няться. покло́нник** admirer; worshipper. **поклоня́ться** *impf +dat* worship.

по|кля́сться (-яну́сь, -нёшься; -я́лся, -ла́сь) *pf.*

поко́иться *impf* rest, repose. **поко́й** rest, peace; room. **поко́йник, -ица** the deceased. **поко́йный** calm, quiet; deceased.

по|колеба́ть(ся (-е́блю(сь) *pf.*

поколе́ние generation.

по|колоти́ть(ся (-очу́(сь, -о́тишь(ся) *pf.*

поко́нчить (-чу) *pf* **с**+*instr* finish; put an end to; ~ **с собо́й** commit suicide.

покоре́ние conquest. **покори́ть** *pf* (*impf* **покоря́ть**) subdue; conquer; **~ся** submit.

по|корми́ть(ся (-млю́(сь, -мишь(ся) *pf.*

поко́рный humble; submissive, obedient.

по|коро́бить(ся (-блю(сь) *pf.*

покоря́ть(ся *impf of* **покори́ть(ся**

поко́с mowing; meadow(-land).

покоси́вшийся rickety, ramshackle. **по|коси́ть(ся** (-ошу́(сь) *pf.*

по|кра́сить (-а́шу) *pf.* **покра́ска** painting, colouring.

по|красне́ть (-е́ю) *pf.* **по|криви́ть(ся** (-влю(сь) *pf.*

покро́в cover. **покрови́тель** *m*, **покрови́тельница** patron; sponsor. **покрови́тельственный** protective; patronizing. **покрови́тельство** protection, patronage. **покрови́тельствовать** *impf +dat* protect, patronize.

покро́й cut.

покроши́ть (-шу́, -шишь) *pf* crumble; chop.

покрути́ть (-учу́, -у́тишь) *pf* twist.

покрыва́ло cover; bedspread; veil. **покрыва́ть** *impf*, **по|кры́ть** (-ро́ю) *pf* cover; **~ся** cover o.s.; get covered. **покры́тие** covering; surfacing; payment. **покры́шка** cover; tyre.

покупа́тель *m* buyer; customer. **покупа́ть** *impf of* **купи́ть. поку́пка** purchase. **покупно́й** bought, purchased; purchase.

по|кури́ть (-рю́, -ришь) *pf* have a smoke.

по|ку́шать *pf.*

покуше́ние **+на**+*acc* attempted assassination of.

пол[1] (*loc* -у́; *pl* -ы́) floor.

пол[2] sex.

пол- *in comb with n in gen, in oblique cases usu* **полу-**, half.

пола́ (*pl* -ы) flap; **из-под полы́** on the sly.

полага́ть *impf* suppose, think. **полага́ться** *impf of* **положи́ться; полага́ется** *impers* one is supposed to; *+dat* it is due to.

по|ла́комить(ся (-млю(сь) *pf.*

полго́да (полуго́да) *m* half a year.

по́лдень (-дня *or* -лу́дня) *m* noon. **полдне́вный** *adj.*

по́ле (*pl* -я́, -е́й) field; ground; margin; brim. **полев|о́й** field; **~ы́е цветы́** wild flowers.

полежа́ть (-жу́) *pf* lie down for a while.

поле́зн|ый useful; helpful; good, wholesome; **~ая нагру́зка** payload.

по|ле́зть (-зу; -ле́з) *pf.*

полемизи́ровать *impf* debate, engage in controversy. **поле́мика** controversy; polemics. **полеми́ческий** polemical.

по|лени́ться (-ню́сь, -ни́шься) *pf.*

поле́но (*pl* -е́нья, -ьев) log.

полёт flight. **по|лете́ть** (-лечу́) *pf.*

по́лзать *indet impf*, **ползти́** (-зу́, -зёшь; полз, -ла́) *det impf* crawl, creep; ooze; fray. **ползу́чий** creeping.

поли- *in comb* poly-.

полива́ть(ся *impf of* **поли́ть(ся. поли́вка** watering.

полига́мия polygamy.

полигло́т polyglot.

полиграфи́ческий printing. **полиграфи́я** printing.

полиго́н range.

поликли́ника polyclinic.

полиме́р polymer.

полиня́лый faded. **по|линя́ть** *pf.*

полиомиели́т poliomyelitis

полирова́ть *impf* (*pf* **от~**) polish. **полиро́вка** polishing; polish.

полит- *abbr in comb* (*of* **полити́ческий**) political. **политбюро́** *neut indecl* Politburo. **~заключённый** *sb* political prisoner.

политехни́ческий polytechnic.

поли́тик politician. **поли́тика** policy; politics. **полити́ческий** political; **полити́чески корре́ктный** politically correct.

поли́ть (-лью́, -льёшь; по́лил, -á, -о) *pf* (*impf* **полива́ть**) pour over; water; **~ся** *+instr* pour over o.s.

полице́йский police; *sb* policeman. **поли́ция** police.

поли́чн|ое *sb*: **с ~ым** red-handed.

полк (-á, *loc* -у́) regiment.

по́лка shelf; berth.

полко́вник colonel. **полково́дец** (-дца) commander; general. **полково́й** regimental.

пол-ли́тра half a litre.

полне́ть (-е́ю) *impf* (*pf* **по~**) put on weight.

по́лно *adv* that's enough! stop it!

полно- *in comb* full; completely. **полнолу́ние** full moon. **~метра́жный** full-length. **~пра́вный** enjoying full rights; competent. **~це́нный** of full value.

полномо́чие (*usu pl*) authority, power. **полномо́чный** plenipotentiary.

по́лностью *adv* in full; completely. **полнота́** completeness; corpulence.

по́лночь (-л(у́)ночи) midnight.

по́лный (-лон, -лна́, по́лно́) full; complete; plump.

полови́к (-á) mat, matting.

полови́на half; **два с полови́ной** two and a half; **~ шесто́го** half-past five. **полови́нка** half.

полови́ца floor-board.

полово́дье high water.

полово́й[1] floor.

полово́й[2] sexual.

поло́гий gently sloping.

положе́ние position; situation; status; regulations; thesis; provisions. **поло́женный** agreed; determined. **поло́жим** let us assume; suppose. **положи́тельный** positive. **положи́ть** (-жу́, -жишь) *pf* (*impf* **класть**) put; lay (down); **~ся** (*impf* **полага́ться**) rely.

по́лоз (*pl* -о́зья, -ьев) runner.
по|лома́ть(ся *pf.* **поло́мка** breakage.
полоса́ (*acc* по́лосу́; *pl* по́лосы, -ло́с, -а́м) stripe; strip; band; region; belt; period. **полоса́тый** striped.
полоска́ть (-ощу́, -о́щешь) *impf* (*pf* **вы́~**, **от~**, **про~**) rinse; **~ го́рло** gargle; **~ся** paddle; flap.
по́лость[1] (*gen pl* -е́й) cavity.
по́лость[2] (*gen pl* -е́й) travelling rug.
полоте́нце (*gen pl* -нец) towel.
полотёр floor-polisher.
поло́тнище width; panel. **полотно́** (*pl* -а, -тен) linen; canvas. **полотня́ный** linen.
поло́ть (-лю́, -лешь) *impf* (*pf* **вы́~**) weed.
полощу́ *etc.*: *see* **полоска́ть**
полти́нник fifty copecks.
полтора́ (-лу́тора) *m & neut*, **полторы́** (-лу́тора) *f* one and a half. **полтора́ста** (полу́т-) a hundred and fifty.
полу-[1] *see* **пол-**
полу-[2] *in comb* half-, semi-, demi-. **полуботи́нок** (-нка; *gen pl* -нок) shoe. **~го́дие** half a year. **~годи́чный** six months', lasting six months. **~година́лый** six-month-old. **~годово́й** half-yearly, six-monthly. **~гра́мотный** semi-literate. **~защи́тник** half-back. **~кру́г** semicircle. **~кру́глый** semicircular. **~ме́сяц** crescent (moon). **~мра́к** semi-darkness. **~но́чный** mid-night. **~о́стров** peninsula. **~откры́тый** ajar. **~проводни́к** (-а́) semi-conductor, transistor. **~ста́нок** (-нка) halt. **~тьма́** semi-darkness. **~фабрика́т** semi-finished product, convenience food. **~фина́л** semi-final. **~часово́й** half-hourly. **~ша́рие** hemisphere. **~шу́бок** (-бка) sheepskin coat.
полу́денный midday.
получа́тель *m* recipient. **получа́ть** *impf*, **получи́ть** (-чу́, -чишь) *pf* get, receive, obtain; **~ся** come, turn up; turn out; **из э́того ничего́ не получи́лось** nothing came of it. **получе́ние** receipt. **получ́ка** receipt; pay(-packet).
полу́чше *adv* a little better.
полчаса́ (получа́са) *m* half an hour.
по́лчище horde.
по́лый hollow; flood.
по|лысе́ть (-е́ю) *pf.*
по́льза use; benefit, profit; **в по́льзу**+*gen* in favour of, on behalf of. **по́льзование** use. **по́льзоваться** *impf* (*pf* **вос~**) +*instr* make use of, utilize; profit by; enjoy.
по́лька Pole; polka. **по́льский** Polish; *sb* polonaise.
по|льсти́ть(ся (-льщу́(сь) *pf.*
полью́ *etc. see* **поли́ть**
По́льша Poland.
полюби́ть (-блю́, -бишь) *pf* come to like; fall in love with.
по|любова́ться (-бу́юсь) *pf.*
полюбо́вный amicable.
по|любопы́тствовать *pf.*
по́люс pole.
поля́к Pole.
поля́на glade, clearing.
поляриза́ция polarization.
поля́рник polar explorer. **поля́рн|ый** polar; **~ая звезда́** pole-star.
пом- *abbr in comb* (*of* **помо́щник**) assistant. **~на́ч** assistant chief, assistant head.
пома́да pomade; lipstick.

помазáние anointment. **по|мáзать(ся** (-áжу(сь) *pf.* **помазóк** (-зкá) small brush.
помалéньку *adv* gradually; gently; modestly; so-so.
помáлкивать *impf* hold one's tongue.
по|манúть (-ню́, -нишь) *pf.*
помáрка blot; pencil mark; correction.
по|мáслить *pf.*
помахáть (-машу́, -мáшешь) *pf*, **помáхивать** *impf +instr* wave; wag.
помéдлить *pf +с+instr* delay.
помéньше a little smaller; a little less.
по|менять(ся *pf.*
померéть (-мру́, -мрёшь; -мер, -лá, -ло) *pf* (*impf* **помирáть**) die.
по|мерéщиться (-щусь) *pf.*
по|мéрить *pf.*
помертвéлый deathly pale.
по|мертвéть (-éю) *pf.*
поместúть (-ещу́) *pf* (*impf* **помещáть**) accommodate; place, locate; invest; **~ся** lodge; find room. **помéстье** (*gen pl* -тий, -тьям) estate.
пóмесь cross(-breed), hybrid.
помёт dung; droppings; litter, brood.
помéта, помéтка mark, note.
по|мéтить (-éчу) *pf* (*impf also* **помечáть**) mark; date; **~ гáлочкой** tick.
помéха hindrance; obstacle; *pl* interference.
помечáть *impf of* **помéтить**
помéшанный mad; *sb* lunatic. **помешáтелство** madness; craze. **по|мешáть** *pf.* **помешáться** *pf* go mad.
помещáть *impf of* **поместúть.**
помещáться *impf of* **поместúться**; be (situated); be accommodated, find room. **помещéние** premises; apartment, room, lodging; location; investment. **помéщик** landowner.
помидóр tomato.
помúлование forgiveness. **помúловать** *pf* forgive.
помúмо *prep+gen* apart from; besides; without the knowledge of.
поминáть *impf of* **помянýть; не ~ лúхом** remember kindly.
помúнки (-нок) *pl* funeral repast.
помирáть *impf of* **померéть**
по|мирúть(ся *pf.*
пóмнить *impf* remember.
помогáть *impf of* **помóчь**
по-мóему *adv* in my opinion.
помóи (-ев) *pl* slops. **помóйка** (*gen pl* -óек) rubbish dump. **помóйный** slop.
помóл grinding.
помóлвка betrothal.
по|молúться (-лю́сь, -лишься) *pf.* **по|молодéть** (-éю) *pf.*
помолчáть (-чу́) *pf* be silent for a time.
помóрье: *see* **по- II.**
по|мóрщиться (-щу́сь) *pf.*
помóст dais; rostrum.
по|мочúться (-чу́сь, -чишься) *pf.*
помóчь (-огу́, -óжешь; -óг, -лá) *pf* (*impf* **помогáть**) (*+dat*) help. **помóщник, помóщница** assistant. **пóмощь** help; **на ~!** help!
помóю *etc.*: *see* **помы́ть**
пóмпа pump.
помутнéние dimness, clouding.
помчáться (-чу́сь) *pf* rush; dart off.
помыкáть *impf +instr* order about.

по́мысел (-сла) intention; thought.
по|мы́ть(ся (-мо́ю(сь) *pf.*
помяну́ть (-ну́, -нешь) *pf* (*impf* **помина́ть**) mention; pray for.
помя́тый crumpled. **по|мя́ться** (-мнётся) *pf.*
по|наде́яться (-е́юсь) *pf* count, rely.
пона́добиться (-блюсь) *pf* be *or* become necessary; **е́сли пона́добится** if necessary.
понапра́сну *adv* in vain.
понаслы́шке *adv* by hearsay.
по-настоя́щему *adv* properly, truly.
поонача́лу *adv* at first.
понево́ле *adv* willynilly; against one's will.
понеде́льник Monday.
понемно́гу, понемно́жку *adv* little by little.
по|нести́(сь (-су́(сь, -сёшь(ся; -нёс(ся, -ла́(сь) *pf.*
понижа́ть *impf*, **пони́зить** (-ни́жу) *pf* lower; reduce; **~ся** fall, drop, go down. **пониже́ние** fall; lowering; reduction.
поника́ть *impf*, **по|ни́кнуть** (-ну; -ни́к) *pf* droop, wilt.
понима́ние understanding.
понима́ть *impf of* **поня́ть**
по-но́вому *adv* in a new fashion.
поно́с diarrhoea.
поноси́ть[1] (-ошу́, -о́сишь) *pf* carry; wear.
поноси́ть[2] (-ошу́, -о́сишь) *impf* abuse (*verbally*).
поно́шенный worn; threadbare.
по|нра́виться (-влюсь) *pf.*
понто́н pontoon.
пону́дить (-у́жу) *pf*, **понужда́ть** *impf* compel.
понука́ть *impf* urge on.
пону́рить *pf*: **~ го́лову** hang one's head. **пону́рый** downcast.
по|ню́хать *pf.* **понюшка: ~ табаку́** pinch of snuff.
поня́тие concept; notion, idea.
поня́тливый bright, quick.
поня́тн|ый understandable, comprehensible; clear; **~о** naturally; **~о?** (do you) see?
поня́ть (пойму́, -мёшь; по́нял, -а́, -о) *pf* (*impf* **понима́ть**) understand; realize.
по|обе́дать *pf.* **по|обеща́ть** *pf.*
по́одаль *adv* at some distance.
поодино́чке *adv* one by one.
поочерёдно *adv* in turn.
поощре́ние encouragement.
поощри́ть *pf*, **поощря́ть** *impf* encourage.
поп (-а́) priest.
попада́ние hit. **попада́ть(ся** *impf of* **попа́сть(ся**
попадья́ priest's wife.
попа́ло: *see* **попа́сть. по|па́риться** *pf.*
попа́рно *adv* in pairs, two by two.
попа́сть (-аду́, -адёшь; -а́л) *pf* (*impf* **попада́ть**) +**в**+*acc* hit; get (in)to, find o.s. in; +**на**+*acc* hit upon, come on; **не туда́ ~** get the wrong number; **~ся** be caught; find o.s.; turn up; **что попадётся** anything. **попа́ло** *with prons & advs*: **где ~** anywhere; **как ~** anyhow; **что ~** the first thing to hand.
поперёк *adv* & *prep+gen* across.
попереме́нно *adv* in turns.
попере́чник diameter. **попере́чн|ый** transverse, diametrical, cross; **~ый разре́з, ~ое сече́ние** cross-section.

поперхну́ться (-ну́сь, -нёшься) *pf* choke.

по|пе́рчить (-чу́) *pf*.

попече́ние care; charge; **на попече́нии**+*gen* in the care of. **попечи́тель** *m* guardian, trustee.

попира́ть *impf* (*pf* **попра́ть**) trample on; flout.

попи́ть (-пью́, -пьёшь; по́пил, -ла́, по́пило) *pf* have a drink.

поплаво́к (-вка́) float.

popла́кать (-а́чу) *pf* cry a little.

по|плати́ться (-чу́сь, -тишься) *pf*.

поплы́ть (-ыву́, -ывёшь; -ы́л, -ыла́, -о) *pf*. start swimming.

попо́йка drinking-bout.

попола́м *adv* in two, in half; half-and-half.

поползнове́ние half a mind; pretension(s).

пополне́ние replenishment; reinforcement. **по|полне́ть** (-е́ю) *pf*. **попо́лнить** *pf*, **пополня́ть** *impf* replenish; restock; reinforce.

пополу́дни *adv* in the afternoon; p.m.

попо́на horse-cloth.

по|по́тчевать (-чую) *pf*.

поправи́мый rectifiable. **попра́вить** (-влю) *pf*, **поправля́ть** *impf* repair; correct, put right; set straight; **~ся** correct o.s.; get better, recover; improve. **попра́вка** correction; repair; adjustment; recovery.

попра́ть *pf of* **попира́ть**

по-пре́жнему *adv* as before.

попрёк reproach. **попрека́ть** *impf*, **попрекну́ть** (-ну́, -нёшь) *pf* reproach.

по́прище field; walk of life.

по|про́бовать *pf*. **по|проси́ть(ся** (-ошу́(сь, -о́сишь(ся) *pf*.

по́просту *adv* simply; without ceremony.

попроша́йка *m* & *f* cadger. **попроша́йничать** *impf* cadge.

попроща́ться *pf* (+**с**+*instr*) say goodbye (to).

попры́гать *pf* jump, hop.

попуга́й parrot.

популя́рность popularity. **популя́рный** popular.

попусти́тельство connivance.

по-пусто́му, по́пусту *adv* in vain.

попу́тно *adv* at the same time; in passing. **попу́тный** passing. **попу́тчик** fellow-traveller.

по|пыта́ться *pf*. **попы́тка** attempt.

по|пя́титься (-я́чусь) *pf*. **попя́тный** backward; **идти́ на ~** go back on one's word.

по́ра[1] pore.

пора́[2] (*acc* -у; *pl* -ы, пор, -а́м) time; it is time; **до каки́х пор?** till when?; **до сих пор** till now; **с каки́х пор?** since when?

порабо́тать *pf* do some work.

поработи́ть (-ощу́) *pf*, **порабоща́ть** *impf* enslave. **порабоще́ние** enslavement.

поравня́ться *pf* come alongside.

по|ра́довать(ся *pf*.

поража́ть *impf*, **по|рази́ть** (-ажу́) *pf* hit; strike; defeat; affect; astonish; **~ся** be astounded. **пораже́ние** defeat. **порази́тельный** striking; astonishing.

по-ра́зному *adv* differently.

пора́нить *pf* wound; injure.

порва́ть (-ву́, -вёшь; -ва́л, -а́, -о) *pf* (*impf* **порыва́ть**) tear (up); break, break off; **~ся** tear; break (off).

по|реде́ть (-е́ет) *pf*.

поре́з cut. **поре́зать** (-е́жу) *pf* cut; **~ся** cut o.s.

поре́й leek.

по|рекомендова́ть *pf.*

по|ржаве́ть (-е́ет) *pf.*

по́ристый porous.

порица́ние reprimand. **порица́ть** *impf* reprimand.

по́рка flogging.

по́ровну *adv* equally.

поро́г threshold; rapids.

поро́да breed, race, species; (*also* **го́рная поро́да**) rock. **поро́дистый** thoroughbred. **породи́ть** (-ожу́) *pf* (*impf* **порожда́ть**) give birth to; give rise to.

по|ródни́ть(ся *pf.* **поро́дный** pedigree

порожда́ть *impf of* **породи́ть**

по́рознь *adv* separately, apart.

поро́й, поро́ю *adv* at times.

поро́к vice; defect.

поросёнок (-нка; *pl* -ся́та, -ся́т) piglet.

по́росль shoots; young wood.

поро́ть[1] (-рю́, -решь) *impf* (*pf* **вы~**) thrash; whip.

поро́ть[2] (-рю́, -решь) *impf* (*pf* **рас~**) undo, unpick; **~ся** come unstitched.

по́рох (*pl* **~а́**) gunpowder, powder. **порохово́й** powder.

поро́чить (-чу) *impf* (*pf* **о~**) discredit; smear. **поро́чный** vicious, depraved; faulty.

пороши́ть (-ши́т) *impf* snow slightly.

порошо́к (-шка́) powder.

порт (*loc* -у́; *pl* -ы, -о́в) port.

портати́вный portable; **~ компью́тер** laptop; **~ телефо́н** mobile phone.

портве́йн port (wine).

по́ртить (-чу) *impf* (*pf* **ис~**) spoil; corrupt; **~ся** deteriorate; go bad.

портни́ха dressmaker. **портно́вский** tailor's. **портно́й** *sb* tailor.

порто́вый port.

портре́т portrait.

портсига́р cigarette-case.

португа́лец (-льца), **-лка** Portuguese. **Португа́лия** Portugal. **португа́льский** Portuguese.

портфе́ль *m* brief-case; portfolio.

портье́ра curtain(s), portière.

портя́нка foot-binding; puttee.

поруга́ние desecration.

пору́ганный desecrated; outraged. **поруга́ть** *pf* scold, swear at; **~ся** swear; fall out.

пору́ка bail; guarantee; surety; **на пору́ки** on bail.

по-ру́сски *adv* (in) Russian.

поруча́ть *impf of* **поручи́ть.** **поруче́ние** assignment; errand; message.

по́ручень (-чня) *m* handrail.

поручи́тельство guarantee; bail.

поручи́ть (-чу́, -чишь) *pf* (*impf* **поруча́ть**) entrust; instruct.

поручи́ться (-чу́сь, -чишься) *pf of* **руча́ться**

порха́ть *impf*, **порхну́ть** (-ну́, -нёшь) *pf* flutter, flit.

по́рция portion; helping.

по́рча spoiling; damage; curse.

по́ршень (-шня) *m* piston.

поры́в[1] gust; rush; fit

поры́в[2] breaking. **порыва́ть(ся**[1] *impf of* **порва́ть(ся**

порыва́ться[2] *impf* make jerky movements; endeavour. **поры́вистый** gusty; jerky; impetuous; fitful.

поря́дковый ordinal. **поря́док** (-дка) order; sequence; manner, way; procedure; **всё в поря́дке** everything is alright; ~ **дня** agenda, order of the day. **порядочный** decent; honest; respectable; fair, considerable.

посадить (-ажу́, -а́дишь) *pf of* **садить, сажать. посадка** planting; embarkation; boarding; landing. **посадочный** planting; landing.

посажу *etc.*: *see* **посадить.**

по|сватать(ся *pf.* **по|свежеть** (-еет) *pf.* **по|светить** (-ечу́, -е́тишь) *pf.* **по|светлеть** (-еет) *pf.*

посвистывать *impf* whistle.

по-своему *adv* (in) one's own way.

посвятить (-ящу́) *pf,* **посвящать** *impf* devote; dedicate; let in; ordain. **посвящение** dedication; initiation; ordination.

посев sowing; crops. **посевн|ой** sowing; **~ая площадь** area under crops.

по|седеть (-е́ю) *pf.*

поселенец (-нца) settler; exile. **поселение** settlement; exile. **по|селить** *pf,* **поселять** *impf* settle; lodge; arouse; **~ся** settle, take up residence. **посёлок** (-лка) settlement; housing estate.

посеребрённый (-рён, -а́) silver-plated. **по|серебрить** *pf.*

посередине *adv* & *prep+gen* in the middle (of).

посетитель *m* visitor. **посетить** (-ещу́) *pf* (*impf* **посещать**) visit; attend.

по|сетовать *pf.*

посещаемость attendance.

посещать *impf of* **посетить. посещение** visit.

по|сеять (-е́ю) *pf.*

посидеть (-ижу́) *pf* sit (for a while).

посильный within one's powers; feasible.

посинелый gone blue. **по|синеть** (-е́ю) *pf.*

по|скакать (-ачу́, -а́чешь) *pf.*

поскользнуться (-ну́сь, -нёшься) *pf* slip.

поскольку *conj* as far as, (in) so far as.

по|скромничать *pf.* **по|скупиться** (-плю́сь) *pf.*

посланец (-нца) messenger, envoy. **послание** message; epistle. **посланник** envoy, minister.

послать (-шлю́, -шлёшь) *pf* (*impf* **посылать**) send.

после *adv* & *prep+gen* after; afterwards.

после- *in comb* post-; after-. **послевоенный** post-war. **~завтра** *adv* the day after tomorrow. **~родовой** post-natal. **~словие** epilogue; concluding remarks.

последний last; recent; latest; latter. **последователь** *m* follower. **последовательность** sequence; consistency. **последовательный** consecutive; consistent. **по|следовать** *pf.*

последствие consequence.

последующий subsequent; consequent.

пословица proverb, saying.

по|служить (-жу́, -жишь) *pf.*

послужной service.

послушание obedience.

по|слушать(ся *pf.* **послушный** obedient.

по|слышаться (-шится) *pf.*

посматривать *impf* look from time to time.

посмеиваться *impf* chuckle.

посмертный posthumous.

по|сметь (-е́ю) *pf.*

посмеяние ridicule. **посмеяться** (-ею́сь, -еёшься) *pf*

laugh; +**над**+*instr* laugh at.
по|смотре́ть(ся (-рю́(сь, -ришь-(ся) *pf*.
посо́бие aid; allowance, benefit; textbook. **посо́бник** accomplice.
по|сове́товать(ся *pf*. **по|соде́йствовать** *pf*.
посо́л (-сла́) ambassador.
по|соли́ть (-олю́, -о́ли́шь) *pf*.
посо́льство embassy.
поспа́ть (-сплю́; -а́л, -а́, -о) *pf* sleep; have a nap.
поспева́ть[1] *impf*, **по|спе́ть**[1] (-е́ет) *pf* ripen.
поспева́ть[2] *impf*, **поспе́ть**[2] (-е́ю) *pf* have time; be in time (**к**+*dat*, **на**+*acc* for); +**за**+*instr* keep up with.
по|спеши́ть (-шу́) *pf*. **поспе́шный** hasty, hurried.
по|спо́рить *pf*. **по|спосо́бствовать** *pf*.
посрами́ть (-млю́) *pf*, **посрамля́ть** *impf* disgrace.
посреди́, посреди́не *adv* & *prep+gen* in the middle (of).
посре́дник mediator. **посре́дничество** mediation. **посре́дственный** mediocre. **посре́дством** *prep+gen* by means of.
по|ссо́рить(ся *pf*.
пост[1] (-а́, *loc* -у́) post.
пост[2] (-а́, *loc* -у́) fast(ing).
по|ста́вить[1] (-влю) *pf*.
поста́вить[2] (-влю) *pf*, **поставля́ть** *impf* supply. **поста́вка** delivery. **поставщи́к** (-а́) supplier.
постаме́нт pedestal.
постанови́ть (-влю́, -вишь) *pf* (*impf* **постановля́ть**) decree; decide.
постано́вка production; arrangement; putting, placing.
постановле́ние decree; decision. **постановля́ть** *impf of* **постанови́ть**
постано́вщик producer; (film) director.
по|стара́ться *pf*.
по|старе́ть (-е́ю) *pf*. **по-ста́рому** *adv* as before.
посте́ль bed. **постелю́** *etc*.: *see* **постла́ть**
постепе́нный gradual.
по|стесня́ться *pf*.
постига́ть *impf of* **пости́чь.**
пости́гнуть: *see* **пости́чь.**
постиже́ние comprehension, grasp. **постижи́мый** comprehensible.
постила́ть *impf of* **постла́ть**
постира́ть *pf* do some washing.
пости́ться (-щу́сь) *impf* fast.
пости́чь, пости́гнуть (-и́гну; -и́г(нул)) *pf* (*impf* **постига́ть**) comprehend, grasp; befall.
по|стла́ть (-стелю́, -сте́лешь) *pf* (*impf also* **постила́ть**) spread; make (*bed*).
по́стн|ый lenten; lean; glum; **~ое ма́сло** vegetable oil.
постово́й on point duty.
посто́й billeting.
посто́льку: **~, поско́льку** *conj* to that extent, insofar as.
по|сторони́ться (-ню́сь, -нишься) *pf*. **посторо́нний** strange; foreign; extraneous, outside; *sb* stranger, outsider.
постоя́нный permanent; constant; continual; **~ый ток** direct current. **постоя́нство** constancy.
по|стоя́ть (-ою́) *pf* stand (for a while); +**за**+*acc* stand up for.
пострада́вший *sb* victim.
по|страда́ть *pf*.
пострига́ться *impf*, **постри́чься** (-игу́сь, -ижёшься; -и́гся) *pf* take monastic vows; get one's hair cut.

построéние construction; building; formation. **по|стрóить(ся** (-рóю(сь) *pf.* **пострóйка** building.
постскрúптум postscript.
постулúровать *impf & pf* postulate.
поступáтельный forward. **поступáть** *impf*, **поступúть** (-плю́, -пишь) *pf* act; do; be received; +**в** *or* **на**+*acc* enter, join; +**с**+*instr* treat; **~ся** +*instr* waive, forgo. **поступлéние** entering, joining; receipt. **постýпок** (-пка) act, deed. **пóступь** gait; step.
по|стучáть(ся (-чý(сь) *pf.*
по|стыдúться (-ыжýсь) *pf.* **постьíдный** shameful.
посýда crockery; dishes. **посýдный** china; dish.
по|сулúть *pf.*
посчастлúвиться *pf impers* (+*dat*) be lucky; **ей посчастлúвилось** +*inf* she had the luck to.
посчитáть *pf* count (up). **по|считáться** *pf.*
посылáть *impf of* **послáть**. **посьíлка** sending; parcel; errand; premise. **посьíльный** *sb* messenger.
посьíпать (-плю, -плешь) *pf*, **посыпáть** *impf* strew. **посыпаться** (-плется) *pf* begin to fall; rain down.
посягáтельство encroachment; infringement. **посягáть** *impf*, **посягнýть** (-нý, -нёшь) *pf* encroach, infringe.
пот (*loc* -ý; *pl* -ы́) sweat.
потайнóй secret.
потакáть *impf* +*dat* indulge.
потасóвка brawl.
потáш (-á) potash.
по-твóему *adv* in your opinion.
потвóрствовать *impf* (+*dat*) be indulgent (towards), pander (to).
потёк damp patch.
потёмки (-мок) *pl* darkness.
по|темнéть (-éет) *pf.*
потенциáл potential. **потенциáльный** potential.
по|теплéть (-éет) *pf.*
потерпéвший *sb* victim. **по|терпéть** (-плю́, -пишь) *pf.*
потéря loss; waste; *pl* casualties. **по|терять(ся** *pf.*
по|теснúть *pf.* **по|теснúться** *pf* sit closer, squeeze up.
потéть (-éю) *impf* (*pf* **вс~**, **за~**) sweat; mist over.
потéха fun. **по|тéшить(ся** (-шу(сь) *pf.* **потéшный** amusing.
потéчь (-чёт, -тёк, -лá) *pf* begin to flow.
потирáть *impf* rub.
потихóньку *adv* softly; secretly; slowly.
пóтный (-тен, -тнá, -тно) sweaty.
потóк stream; torrent; flood.
потолóк (-лкá) ceiling.
по|толстéть (-éю) *pf.*
потóм *adv* later (on); then. **потóмок** (-мка) descendant. **потóмство** posterity.
потомý *adv* that is why; **~ что** *conj* because.
по|тонýть (-нý, -нешь) *pf.* **потóп** flood, deluge. **по|топúть** (-плю́, -пишь) *pf*, **потоплять** *impf* sink.
по|топтáть (-пчý, -пчешь) *pf.* **по|торопúть(ся** (-плю́(сь, -пишь(ся) *pf.*
потóчный continuous; production-line.
по|трáтить (-áчу) *pf.*
потребúтель *m* consumer, user. **потребúтельский** consumer; consumers'. **потребúть** (-блю́) *pf*, **потреблять**

impf consume. **потреблéние** consumption. **потрéбность** need, requirement. **по|трéбовать(ся** *pf.*
по|тревóжить(ся (-жу(сь) *pf.*
потрёпанный shabby; tattered. **по|трепáть(ся** (-плю́(сь, -плешь(ся) *pf.*
по|трéскаться *pf.* **потрéскивать** *impf* crackle.
потрóгать *pf* touch, feel, finger.
потрохá (-óв) *pl* giblets. **потрошúть** (-шý) *impf* (*pf* **вы́~**) disembowel, clean.
потрудúться (-ужýсь, -ýдишься) *pf* do some work; take the trouble.
потрясáть *impf*, **потрястú** (-сý, -сёшь; -я́с, -лá) *pf* shake; rock; stagger; *+acc or instr* brandish, shake. **потрясáющий** staggering, tremendous. **потрясéние** shock.
потýги *f pl* vain attempts; **родовы́е ~** labour.
потýпить (-плю) *pf*, **потупля́ть** *impf* lower; **~ся** look down.
по|тускнéть (-éет) *pf.*
потусторóний мир the next world.
потухáть *impf*, **по|тýхнуть** (-нет, -ýх) *pf* go out; die out. **потýхший** extinct; lifeless.
по|тушúть (-шý, -шишь) *pf.*
пóтчевать (-чую) *impf* (*pf* **по~**) *+instr* treat to.
потя́гиваться *impf*, **по|тянýться** (-нýсь, -нешься) *pf* stretch o.s. **по|тянýть** (-нý, -нешь) *pf.*
по|ýжинать *pf.* **по|умнéть** (-éю) *pf.*
поучáть *impf* preach at.
поучúтельный instructive.
похáбный obscene.
похвалá praise. **по|хвалúть(ся** (-лю́(сь, -лишь(ся) *pf.* **похвáльный** laudable; laudatory.
по|хвáстать(ся *pf.*
похитúтель *m* kidnapper; abductor; thief. **похúтить** (-хúщу) *pf*, **похищáть** *impf* kidnap; abduct; steal. **похищéние** theft; kidnapping; abduction.
похлёбка broth, soup.
похлóпать *pf* slap; clap.
по|хлопотáть (-очý, -óчешь) *pf.*
похмéлье hangover.
похóд campaign; march; hike; excursion.
по|ходáтайствовать *pf.*
походúть (-ожý, -óдишь) *impf* **на**+*acc* resemble.
похóдка gait, walk. **похóдный** mobile, field; marching.
похождéние adventure.
похóжий alike; **~ на** like.
похолодáние drop in temperature.
по|хоронúть (-ню́, -нишь) *pf.*
похорóнный funeral. **пóхороны** (-рóн, -ронáм) *pl* funeral.
по|хорошéть (-éю) *pf.*
пóхоть lust.
по|худéть (-éю) *pf.*
по|целовáть(ся *pf.* **поцелýй** kiss.
початóк (-тка) ear; (corn) cob.
пóчва soil; ground; basis. **пóчвенный** soil; **~ покрóв** topsoil.
почём *adv* how much; how; **~ знать?** who can tell?; **~ я знáю?** how should I know?
почемý *adv* why. **почемý-либо, -нибудь** *advs* for some reason or other. **почемý-то** *adv* for some reason.
пóчерк hand(writing).
почернéлый blackened, darkened. **по|чернéть** (-éю) *pf.*
почерпнýть (-нý, -нёшь) *pf*

draw, scoop up; glean.
по|черстве́ть (-е́ю) *pf.* **по|чеса́ть(ся** (-ешу́(сь, -е́шешь(ся) *pf.*
по́честь honour. **почёт** honour; respect. **почётный** of honour; honourable; honorary.
по́чечный renal; kidney.
почива́ть *impf of* **почи́ть**
почи́н initiative.
по|чини́ть (-ню́, -нишь) *pf*, **починя́ть** *impf* repair, mend. **почи́нка** repair.
по|чи́стить(ся (-и́щу(сь) *pf.*
почита́ть[1] *impf* honour; revere.
почита́ть[2] *pf* read for a while.
почи́ть (-и́ю, -и́ешь) *pf* (*impf* **почива́ть**) rest; pass away; ~ **на ла́врах** rest on one's laurels.
по́чка[1] bud.
по́чка[2] kidney.
по́чта post, mail; post-office. **почтальо́н** postman. **почта́мт** (*main*) post-office.
почте́ние respect. **почте́нный** venerable; considerable.
почти́ *adv* almost.
почти́тельный respectful. **почти́ть** (-чту́) *pf* honour.
почто́в|ый postal; ~**ая ка́рточка** postcard; ~**ый перево́д** postal order; ~**ый я́щик** letter-box.
по|чу́вствовать *pf.*
по|чу́диться (-ишься) *pf.*
пошатну́ть (-ну́, -нёшь) *pf* shake; ~**ся** shake; stagger.
по|шевели́ть(ся (-елю́(сь, -е́ли́шь(ся) *pf.* **пошёл** *etc.*: *see* **пойти́**
поши́вочный sewing.
по́шлина duty.
по́шлость vulgarity; banality. **по́шлый** vulgar; banal.
поштучный by the piece.
по|шути́ть (-учу́, -у́тишь) *pf.*
поща́да mercy. **по|щади́ть** (-ажу́) *pf.*
по|щекота́ть (-очу́, -о́чешь) *pf.*
пощёчина slap in the face.
по|щу́пать *pf.*
поэ́зия poetry. **поэ́ма** poem. **поэ́т** poet. **поэти́ческий** poetic.
поэ́тому *adv* therefore.
пою́ *etc.*: *see* **петь, пои́ть**
появи́ться (-влю́сь, -вишься) *pf*, **появля́ться** *impf* appear. **появле́ние** appearance.
по́яс (*pl* -á) belt; girdle; waistband; waist; zone.
поясне́ние explanation. **поясни́тельный** explanatory. **поясни́ть** *pf* (*impf* **поясня́ть**) explain, elucidate.
поясни́ца small of the back. **поясно́й** waist; to the waist; zonal.
поясня́ть *impf of* **поясни́ть**
пра- *pref* first; great-. **праба́бушка** great-grandmother.
пра́вда (the) truth. **правди́вый** true; truthful. **правдоподо́бный** likely; plausible.
пра́ведный righteous; just.
пра́вило rule; principle.
пра́вильн|ый right, correct; regular; ~**о!** that's right!
прави́тель *m* ruler. **прави́тельственный** government(al). **прави́тельство** government. **пра́вить**[1] (-влю) +*instr* rule, govern; drive.
пра́вить[2] (-влю) *impf* correct. **пра́вка** correcting.
правле́ние board; administration; government.
пра́|внук, ~**внучка** great-grandson, -granddaughter.
пра́во[1] (*pl* -á) law; right; (**води́тельские**) **права́** driving licence; **на права́х**+*gen* in the

capacity of, as.

пра́во[2] *adv* really.

право-[1] *in comb* law; right. **праве́рный** orthodox. **~ме́рный** lawful, rightful. **~мо́чный** competent. **~наруше́ние** infringement of the law, offence. **~наруши́тель** *m* offender, delinquent. **~писа́ние** spelling, orthography. **~сла́вный** orthodox; *sb* member of the Orthodox Church. **~су́дие** justice.

право-[2] *in comb* right, right-hand. **правосторо́нний** right; right-hand.

правово́й legal.

правота́ rightness; innocence.

пра́вый[1] right; right-hand; right-wing.

пра́вый[2] (прав, -á, -о) right, correct; just.

пра́вящий ruling.

пра́дед great-grandfather; *pl* ancestors. **праде́душка** *m* great-grandfather.

пра́здник (public) holiday. **пра́здничный** festive. **пра́зднование** celebration. **пра́здновать** *impf* (*pf* **от~**) celebrate. **пра́здность** idleness. **пра́здный** idle; useless.

пра́ктика practice; practical work. **практикова́ть** *impf* practise; **~ся** (*pf* **на~ся**) be practised; **+в+***prep* practise. **практи́ческий, практи́чный** practical.

пра́отец (-тца) forefather.

пра́порщик ensign.

прапра́дед great-great-grandfather. **прароди́тель** *m* forefather.

прах dust; remains.

пра́чечная *sb* laundry. **пра́чка** laundress.

пребыва́ние stay. **пребыва́ть** *impf* be; reside.

превзойти́ (-йду́, -йдёшь; -ошёл, -шла́) *pf* (*impf* **превосходи́ть**) surpass; excel.

превозмога́ть *impf*, **превозмо́чь** (-огу́, -о́жешь; -о́г, -ла́) *pf* overcome.

превознести́ (-су́, -сёшь; -ёс, -ла́) *pf*, **превозноси́ть** (-ошу́, -о́сишь) *impf* extol, praise.

превосходи́тельство Excellency. **превосходи́ть** (-ожу́, -о́дишь) *impf of* **превзойти́**. **превосхо́дный** superlative; superb, excellent. **превосхо́дство** superiority. **превосходя́щий** superior.

превратить (-ащу́) *pf*, **превраща́ть** *impf* convert, turn, reduce; **~ся** turn, change. **превра́тный** wrong; changeful. **превраще́ние** transformation.

превы́сить (-ы́шу) *pf*, **превыша́ть** *impf* exceed. **превыше́ние** exceeding, excess.

прегра́да obstacle; barrier. **прегради́ть** (-ажу́) *pf*, **прегражда́ть** *impf* bar, block.

пред *prep+instr*: *see* **пе́ред**

предава́ть(ся (-даю́(сь, -даёшь(ся) *impf of* **преда́ть(ся**

преда́ние legend; tradition; handing over, committal. **пре́данность** devotion. **пре́данный** devoted. **преда́тель** *m*, **~ница** betrayer, traitor. **преда́тельский** treacherous. **преда́тельство** treachery.

преда́ть (-а́м, -а́шь, -а́ст, -ади́м; пре́дал, -á, -о) *pf* (*impf* **предава́ть**) hand over, commit; betray; **~ся** abandon o.s.; give way, indulge.

предаю́ *etc.*: *see* **предава́ть**

предвари́тельный preliminary; prior. **предвари́ть** *pf*,

предваря́ть *impf* forestall, anticipate.

предве́стник forerunner; harbinger. **предвеща́ть** *impf* portend; augur.

предвзя́тый preconceived; biased.

предви́деть (-и́жу) *impf* foresee.

предвкуси́ть (-ушу́, -у́сишь) *pf*, **предвкуша́ть** *impf* look forward to.

предводи́тель *m* leader. **предводи́тельствовать** *impf +instr* lead.

предвое́нный pre-war.

предвосхи́тить (-и́щу) *pf*, **предвосхища́ть** *impf* anticipate.

предвы́борный (pre-)election.

предго́рье foothills.

преддве́рие threshold.

преде́л limit; bound. **преде́льный** boundary; maximum; utmost.

предзнаменова́ние omen, augury.

предисло́вие preface.

предлага́ть *impf of* **предложи́ть. предло́г**[1] pretext.

предло́г[2] preposition.

предложе́ние[1] sentence; clause.

предложе́ние[2] offer; proposition; proposal; motion; suggestion; supply. **предложи́ть** (-жу́, -жишь) *pf* (*impf* **предлага́ть**) offer; propose; suggest; order.

предло́жный prepositional.

предме́стье suburb.

предме́т object; subject.

предназнача́ть *impf*, **предназна́чить** (-чу) *pf* destine, intend; earmark.

преднаме́ренный premeditated.

пре́до: *see* **пе́ред**

пре́док (-дка) ancestor.

предопределе́ние predetermination. **предопредели́ть** *pf*, **предопределя́ть** *impf* predetermine, predestine.

предоста́вить (-влю) *pf*, **предоставля́ть** *impf* grant; leave; give.

предостерега́ть *impf*, **предостере́чь** (-егу́, -ежёшь; -ёг, -ла́) *pf* warn. **предостереже́ние** warning. **предосторо́жность** precaution.

предосуди́тельный reprehensible.

предотврати́ть (-ащу́) *pf*, **предотвраща́ть** *impf* avert, prevent.

предохране́ние protection; preservation. **предохрани́тель** *m* guard; safety device, safety-catch; fuse. **предохрани́тельный** preservative; preventive; safety. **предохрани́ть** *pf*, **предохраня́ть** *impf* preserve, protect.

предписа́ние order; *pl* directions, instructions. **предписа́ть** (-ишу́, -и́шешь) *pf*, **предпи́сывать** *impf* order, direct; prescribe.

предпле́чье forearm.

предполага́емый supposed. **предполага́ется** *impers* it is proposed. **предполага́ть** *impf*, **предположи́ть** (-жу́, -о́жишь) *pf* suppose, assume. **предположе́ние** supposition, assumption. **предположи́тельный** conjectural; hypothetical.

предпосле́дний penultimate, last-but-one.

предпосы́лка precondition; premise.

предпоче́сть (-чту́, -чтёшь; -чёл,

-чла́) *pf*, **предпочита́ть** *impf* prefer. **предпочте́ние** preference. **предпочти́тельный** preferable.

предприи́мчивый enterprising.

предпринима́тель *m* owner; entrepreneur; employer. **предпринима́тельство**: **свобо́дное** ~ free enterprise. **предпринима́ть** *impf*, **предприня́ть** (-иму́, -и́мешь; -и́нял, -а́, -о) *pf* undertake. **предприя́тие** undertaking, enterprise.

предрасположе́ние predisposition.

предрассу́док (-дка) prejudice.

предрека́ть *impf*, **предре́чь** (-еку́, -ечёшь; -рёк, -ла́) *pf* foretell.

предреша́ть *impf*, **предреши́ть** (-шу́) *pf* decide beforehand; predetermine.

председа́тель *m* chairman.

предсказа́ние prediction. **предсказа́ть** (-ажу́, -а́жешь) *pf*, **предска́зывать** *impf* predict; prophesy.

предсме́ртный dying.

представа́ть (-таю́, -таёшь) *impf of* **предста́ть**

представи́тель *m* representative. **представи́тельный** representative; imposing. **представи́тельство** representation; representatives.

предста́вить (-влю) *pf*, **представля́ть** *impf* present; submit; introduce; represent; ~ **себе́** imagine; **представля́ть собо́й** represent, be; **~ся** present itself, occur; seem; introduce o.s.; *+instr* pretend to be. **представле́ние** presentation; performance; idea, notion.

предста́ть (-а́ну) *pf* (*impf* **представа́ть**) appear.

предстоя́ть (-ои́т) *impf* be in prospect, lie ahead. **предстоя́щий** forthcoming; imminent.

предте́ча *m* & *f* forerunner, precursor.

предубежде́ние prejudice.

предугада́ть *pf*, **предуга́дывать** *impf* guess; foresee.

предупреди́тельный preventive; warning; courteous, obliging. **предупреди́ть** (-ежу́) *pf*, **предупрежда́ть** *impf* warn; give notice; prevent; anticipate. **предупрежде́ние** notice; warning; prevention.

предусма́тривать *impf*, **предусмотре́ть** (-рю́, -ришь) *pf* envisage, foresee; provide for. **предусмотри́тельный** prudent; far-sighted.

предчу́вствие presentiment; foreboding. **предчу́вствовать** *impf* have a presentiment (about).

предше́ственник predecessor. **предше́ствовать** *impf* *+dat* precede.

предъяви́тель *m* bearer. **предъяви́ть** (-влю́, -вишь) *pf*, **предъявля́ть** *impf* show, produce; bring (*lawsuit*); ~ **пра́во на**+*acc* lay claim to.

преды́дущий previous.

прее́мник successor. **прее́мственность** succession; continuity.

пре́жде *adv* first; formerly; *prep+gen* before; ~ **всего́** first of all; first and foremost; ~ **чем** *conj* before. **преждевре́менный** premature.

пре́жний previous, former.

презервати́в condom.

президе́нт president. **президе́нтский** presidential. **прези́диум** presidium.

презира́ть *impf* despise. **презре́ние** contempt. **презре́нный** contemptible. **презри́тельный** scornful.

преиму́щественно *adv* mainly, chiefly, principally. **преиму́щественный** main, primary; preferential. **преиму́щество** advantage; preference; **по преиму́ществу** for the most part.

преиспо́дняя *sb* the underworld.

прейскура́нт price list, catalogue.

преклоне́ние admiration. **преклони́ть** *pf*, **преклоня́ть** *impf* bow, bend; **~ся** bow down; *+dat or* **перед***+instr* admire, worship. **прекло́нный**: **~ во́зраст** old age.

прекра́сный beautiful; fine; excellent.

прекрати́ть (-ащу́) *pf*, **прекраща́ть** *impf* stop, discontinue; **~ся** cease, end. **прекраще́ние** halt; cessation.

преле́стный delightful. **пре́лесть** charm, delight.

преломи́ть (-млю́, -мишь) *pf*, **преломля́ть** *impf* refract. **преломле́ние** refraction.

прельсти́ть (-льщу́) *pf*, **прельща́ть** *impf* attract; entice; **~ся** be attracted; fall (*+instr* for).

прелюбодея́ние adultery.

прелю́дия prelude.

преми́нуть (-ну) *pf with neg* not fail.

премирова́ть *impf & pf* award a prize to; give a bonus. **пре́мия** prize; bonus; premium.

премье́р prime minister; lead(-ing actor). **премье́ра** première. **премье́р-мини́стр** prime minister. **премье́рша** leading lady.

пренебрега́ть *impf*, **пренебре́чь** (-егу́, -ежёшь; -ёг, -ла́) *pf +instr* scorn; neglect. **пренебреже́ние** scorn; neglect. **пренебрежи́тельный** scornful.

пре́ния (-ий) *pl* debate.

преоблада́ние predominance. **преоблада́ть** *impf* predominate; prevail.

преобража́ть *impf*, **преобрази́ть** (-ажу́) *pf* transform. **преображе́ние** transformation; Transfiguration. **преобразова́ние** transformation; reform. **преобразова́ть** *pf*, **преобразо́вывать** *impf* transform; reform, reorganize.

преодолева́ть *impf*, **преодоле́ть** (-е́ю) *pf* overcome.

препара́т preparation.

препина́ние: **зна́ки препина́ния** punctuation marks.

препира́тельство altercation, wrangling.

преподава́ние teaching. **преподава́тель** *m*, **~ница** teacher. **преподава́тельский** teaching. **преподава́ть** (-даю́, -даёшь) *impf* teach.

преподнести́ (-су́, -сёшь; -ёс, -ла́) *pf*, **преподноси́ть** (-ошу́, -о́сишь) present with, give.

препроводи́ть (-вожу́, -во́дишь) *pf*, **препровожда́ть** *impf* send, forward.

препя́тствие obstacle; hurdle. **препя́тствовать** *impf* (*pf* **вос~**) *+dat* hinder.

прерва́ть (-ву́, -вёшь; -а́л, -а́, -о) *pf* (*impf* **прерыва́ть**) interrupt; break off; **~ся** be interrupted; break.

пререка́ние argument. **пререка́ться** *impf* argue.

прерыва́ть(ся *impf of* **прерва́ть(ся**

пресекáть *impf*, **пресéчь** (-екý, -ечёшь; -ёк, -еклá) *pf* stop; put an end to; **~ся** stop; break.

преслéдование pursuit; persecution; prosecution. **преслéдовать** *impf* pursue; haunt; persecute; prosecute.

пресловýтый notorious.

пресмыкáться *impf* grovel. **пресмыкáющееся** *sb* reptile.

пресновóдный freshwater. **прéсный** fresh; unleavened; insipid; bland.

пресс press. **прéсса** the press. **пресс-конферéнция** press-conference.

престарéлый aged.

престúж prestige.

престóл throne.

преступлéние crime. **престýпник** criminal. **престýпность** criminality; crime, delinquency. **престýпный** criminal.

пресы́титься (-ы́щусь) *pf*, **пресыщáться** *impf* be satiated. **пресыщéние** surfeit, satiety.

претвори́ть *pf*, **претворя́ть** *impf* (**в**+*acc*) turn, change, convert; **~ в жизнь** realize, carry out.

претендéнт claimant; candidate; pretender. **претендовáть** *impf* **на**+*acc* lay claim to; have pretensions to. **претéнзия** claim; pretension; **быть в претéнзии на**+*acc* have a grudge, a grievance, against.

претерпевáть *impf*, **претерпéть** (-плю́, -пишь) *pf* undergo; suffer.

прéть (прéет) *impf* (*pf* **со~**) rot.

преувеличéние exaggeration. **преувели́чивать** *impf*, **преувели́чить** (-чу) *pf* exaggerate.

преуменьшáть *impf*, **преумéньшить** (-éньшу) *pf* underestimate; understate.

преуспевáть *impf*, **преуспéть** (-éю) *pf* be successful; thrive.

преходя́щий transient.

прецедéнт precedent.

при *prep* +*prep* by, at; in the presence of; attached to, affiliated to; with; about; on; in the time of; under; during; when, in case of; **~ всём том** for all that.

прибáвить (-влю) *pf*, **прибавля́ть** add; increase; **~ся** increase; rise; wax; **день прибáвился** the days are getting longer. **прибáвка** addition; increase. **прибавлéние** addition; supplement, appendix. **прибáвочный** additional; surplus.

Прибáлтика the Baltic States.

прибаýтка humorous saying.

прибегáть[1] *impf of* **прибежáть**

прибегáть[2] *impf*, **прибéгнуть** (-ну; -бéг) *pf* **+к**+*dat* resort to.

прибежáть (-егý) *pf* (*impf* **прибегáть**) come running.

прибéжище refuge.

приберегáть *impf*, **приберéчь** (-егý, -ежёшь; -ёг, -лá) *pf* save (up), reserve.

приберý *etc.*: *see* **прибрáть.**

прибивáть *impf of* **приби́ть.**

прибирáть *impf of* **прибрáть**

приби́ть (-бью́, -бьёшь) *pf* (*impf* **прибивáть**) nail; flatten; drive.

приближáть *impf*, **прибли́зить** (-и́жу) *pf* bring *or* move nearer; **~ся** approach; draw nearer. **приближéние** approach. **приблизи́тельный**

approximate.
прибо́й surf, breakers.
прибо́р instrument, device, apparatus; set. **прибо́рная доска́** instrument panel; dashboard.
прибра́ть (-беру́, -берёшь; -а́л, -а́, -о) *pf* (*impf* **прибира́ть**) tidy (up); put away.
прибре́жный coastal; offshore.
прибыва́ть *impf*, **прибы́ть** (-бу́ду; при́был, -а́, -о) *pf* arrive; increase, grow; rise; wax. **при́быль** profit, gain; increase, rise. **при́быльный** profitable. **прибы́тие** arrival.
прибью́ *etc.*: *see* **приби́ть**
прива́л halt.
прива́ривать *impf*, **привари́ть** (-рю́, -ришь) *pf* weld on.
приватиза́ция privatization. **приватизи́ровать** *impf* & *pf* privatize.
приведу́ *etc.*: *see* **привести́**
привезти́ (-зу́, -зёшь; -ёз, -ла́) (*impf* **привози́ть**) bring.
привере́дливый pernickety.
приве́рженец (-нца) adherent. **приве́рженный** devoted.
приве́сить (-е́шу) *pf* (*impf* **приве́шивать**) hang up, suspend.
привести́ (-еду́, -едёшь; -ёл, -а́) *pf* (*impf* **приводи́ть**) bring; lead; take; reduce; cite; put in(to), set.
приве́т greeting(s); regards; hi! **приве́тливый** friendly; affable. **приве́тствие** greeting; speech of welcome. **приве́тствовать** *impf* & *pf* greet, salute; welcome.
приве́шивать *impf of* **приве́сить**
привива́ть(ся *impf of* **приви́ть(ся**. **приви́вка** inoculation.
привиде́ние ghost; apparition. **при|ви́деться** (-дится) *pf*.
привилегиро́ванный privileged. **привиле́гия** privilege.
привинти́ть (-нчу́) *pf*, **приви́нчивать** *impf* screw on.
приви́ть (-вью́, -вьёшь; -и́л, -а́, -о) *pf* (*impf* **привива́ть**) inoculate; graft; inculcate; foster; **~ся** take; become established.
при́вкус after-taste; smack.
привлека́тельный attractive. **привлека́ть** *impf*, **привле́чь** (-еку́, -ечёшь; -ёк, -ла́) *pf* attract; draw; draw in, win over; (*law*) have up; **~ к суду́** sue. **привлече́ние** attraction.
приво́д drive, gear. **приводи́ть** (-ожу́, -о́дишь) *impf of* **привести́**. **приводно́й** driving.
привожу́ *etc.*: *see* **приводи́ть, привози́ть**
приво́з bringing; importation; load. **привози́ть** (-ожу́, -о́зишь) *impf of* **привезти́**. **привозно́й, приво́зный** imported.
приво́льный free.
привстава́ть (-таю́, -таёшь) *impf*, **привста́ть** (-а́ну) *pf* half-rise; rise.
привыка́ть *impf*, **привы́кнуть** (-ну; -ы́к) *pf* get accustomed. **привы́чка** habit. **привы́чный** habitual, usual.
привью́ *etc.*: *see* **приви́ть**
привя́занность attachment; affection. **привяза́ть** (-яжу́, -я́жешь) *pf*, **привя́зывать** *impf* attach; tie, bind; **~ся** become attached; attach o.s.; +**к**+*dat* pester. **привя́зчивый** annoying; affectionate. **при́вязь** tie; lead, leash; tether.

пригиба́ть *impf of* **пригну́ть**
пригласи́ть (-ашу́) *pf*, **приглаша́ть** *impf* invite. **приглаше́ние** invitation.
пригляде́ться (-яжу́сь) *pf*, **пригля́дываться** *impf* look closely; +к+*dat* scrutinize; get used to.
пригна́ть (-гоню́, -го́нишь; -а́л, -а́, -о) *pf* (*impf* **пригоня́ть**) bring in; fit, adjust.
пригну́ть (-ну́, -нёшь) *pf* (*impf* **пригиба́ть**) bend down.
пригова́ривать[1] *impf* keep saying.
пригова́ривать[2] *impf*, **приговори́ть** *pf* sentence, condemn. **пригово́р** verdict, sentence.
пригоди́ться (-ожу́сь) *pf* prove useful. **приго́дный** fit, suitable.
пригоня́ть *impf of* **пригна́ть**
пригора́ть *impf*, **пригоре́ть** (-ри́т) *pf* be burnt.
при́город suburb. **при́городный** suburban.
пригоро́к (-рка) hillock.
при́горшня (*gen pl* -ей) handful.
приготови́тельный preparatory. **пригото́вить** (-влю) *pf*, **приготовля́ть** *impf* prepare; ~**ся** prepare. **приготовле́ние** preparation.
пригрева́ть *impf*, **пригре́ть** (-е́ю) *pf* warm; cherish.
при|грози́ть (-ожу́) *pf*.
придава́ть (-даю́, -даёшь) *impf*, **прида́ть** (-а́м, -а́шь, -а́ст, -ади́м; при́дал, -а́, -о) *pf* add; give; attach. **прида́ча** adding; addition; **в прида́чу** into the bargain.
придави́ть (-влю́, -вишь) *pf*, **прида́вливать** *impf* press (down).
прида́ное *sb* dowry. **прида́ток** (-тка) appendage.
придвига́ть *impf*, **придви́нуть** (-ну) *pf* move up, draw up; ~**ся** move up, draw near.
придво́рный court.
приде́лать *pf*, **приде́лывать** *impf* attach.
приде́рживаться *impf* hold on, hold; +*gen* keep to.
придеру́сь *etc.*: *see* **придра́ться. придира́ться** *impf of* **придра́ться. приди́рка** quibble; fault-finding. **приди́рчивый** fault-finding.
придоро́жный roadside.
придра́ться (-деру́сь, -дерёшься; -а́лся, -а́сь, -а́ло́сь) *pf* (*impf* **придира́ться**) find fault.
приду́ *etc.*: *see* **прийти́**
приду́мать *pf*, **приду́мывать** *impf* think up, invent.
прие́ду *etc.*: *see* **прие́хать. прие́зд** arrival. **приезжа́ть** *impf of* **прие́хать. прие́зжий** newly arrived; *sb* newcomer.
приём receiving; reception; surgery; welcome; admittance; dose; go; movement; method, way; trick. **прие́млемый** acceptable. **приёмная** *sb* waiting-room; reception room. **приёмник** (radio) receiver. **приёмный** receiving; reception; entrance; foster, adopted.
прие́хать (-е́ду) *pf* (*impf* **приезжа́ть**) arrive, come.
прижа́ть (-жму́, -жмёшь) *pf* (*impf* **прижима́ть**) press; clasp; ~**ся** nestle up.
прижéчь (-жгу́, -жжёшь; -жёг, -жгла́) *pf* (*impf* **прижига́ть**) cauterize.
прижива́ться *impf of* **прижи́ться**
прижига́ние cauterization. **прижига́ть** *impf of* **прижéчь**
прижима́ть(ся *impf of*

прижа́ть(ся
прижи́ться (-иву́сь, -ивёшься; -жи́лся, -а́сь) *pf* (*impf* **прижива́ться**) become acclimatized.
прижму́ *etc.*: *see* **прижа́ть**
приз (*pl* -ы́) prize.
призва́ние vocation. **призва́ть** (-зову́, -зовёшь; -а́л, -а́, -о) *pf* (*impf* **призыва́ть**) call; call upon; call up.
призе́мистый stocky, squat.
приземле́ние landing. **приземли́ться** *pf*, **приземля́ться** *impf* land.
призёр prizewinner.
при́зма prism.
признава́ть (-наю́, -наёшь) *impf*, **призна́ть** *pf* recognize; admit; **~ся** confess. **при́знак** sign, symptom; indication. **призна́ние** confession, declaration; acknowledgement; recognition. **при́знанный** acknowledged, recognized. **призна́тельный** grateful.
призову́ *etc.*: *see* **призва́ть**
при́зрак spectre, ghost. **при́зрачный** ghostly; illusory, imagined.
призы́в call, appeal; slogan; call-up. **призыва́ть** *impf of* **призва́ть. призывно́й** conscription.
при́иск mine.
прийти́ (приду́, -дёшь; пришёл, -шла́) *pf* (*impf* **приходи́ть**) come; arrive; **~ в себя́** regain consciousness; **~сь +по**+*dat* fit; suit; **+на**+*acc* fall on; *impers*+*dat* have to; happen (to), fall to the lot (of).
прика́з order, command. **приказа́ние** order, command. **приказа́ть** (-ажу́, -а́жешь) *pf*, **прика́зывать** *impf* order, command.
прика́лывать *impf of* **приколо́ть. прикаса́ться** *impf of* **прикосну́ться**
прика́нчивать *impf of* **прико́нчить**
прикати́ть (-ачу́, -а́тишь) *pf*, **прика́тывать** *impf* roll up.
прики́дывать *impf*, **прики́нуть** (-ну) *pf* throw in, add; weigh; estimate; **~ся** +*instr* pretend (to be).
прикла́д[1] butt.
прикла́д[2] trimmings. **прикладно́й** applied. **прикла́дывать(ся** *impf of* **приложи́ть(ся**
прикле́ивать *impf*, **прикле́ить** *pf* stick; glue.
приключа́ться *impf*, **приключи́ться** *pf* happen, occur. **приключе́ние** adventure. **приключе́нческий** adventure.
прикова́ть (-кую́, -куёшь) *pf*, **прико́вывать** *impf* chain; rivet.
прикола́чивать *impf*, **приколоти́ть** (-очу́, -о́тишь) *pf* nail.
приколо́ть (-лю́, -лешь) *pf* (*impf* **прика́лывать**) pin; stab.
прикомандирова́ть *pf*, **прикомандиро́вывать** *impf* attach.
прико́нчить (-чу) *pf* (*impf* **прика́нчивать**) use up; finish off.
прикоснове́ние touch; concern. **прикосну́ться** (-ну́сь, -нёшься) *pf* (*impf* **прикаса́ться**) **к**+*dat* touch.
прикрепи́ть (-плю́) *pf*, **прикрепля́ть** *impf* fasten, attach. **прикрепле́ние** fastening; registration.
прикрыва́ть *impf*, **прикры́ть** (-ро́ю) *pf* cover; screen; shelter. **прикры́тие** cover; escort.
прику́ривать *impf*, **прику-**

рить (-рю, -ришь) *pf* get a light.
прикусить (-ушу, -усишь) *pf*, **прикусывать** *impf* bite.
прилавок (-вка) counter.
прилагательное *sb* adjective. **прилагать** *impf of* **приложить**
приладить (-ажу) *pf*, **прилаживать** *impf* fit, adjust.
приласкать *pf* caress, pet; **~ся** snuggle up.
прилегать *impf* (*pf* **прилечь**) к+*dat* fit; adjoin. **прилегающий** close-fitting; adjoining, adjacent.
прилежный diligent.
прилепить(ся (-плю(сь, -пишь(ся) *pf*, **прилеплять(ся** *impf* stick.
прилёт arrival. **прилетать** *impf*, **прилететь** (-ечу) *pf* arrive, fly in; come flying.
прилечь (-лягу, -ляжешь; -ёг, -гла) *pf* (*impf* **прилегать**) lie down.
прилив flow, flood; rising tide; surge. **приливать** *impf of* **прилить**. **приливный** tidal.
прилипать *impf*, **прилипнуть** (-нет; -лип) *pf* stick.
прилить (-льёт; -ил, -а, -о) *pf* (*impf* **приливать**) flow; rush.
приличие decency. **приличный** decent.
приложение application; enclosure; supplement; appendix.
приложить (-жу, -жишь) *pf* (*impf* **прикладывать, прилагать**) put; apply; affix; add; enclose; **~ся** take aim; +*instr* put, apply; +к+*dat* kiss.
прильёт *etc.*: *see* **прилить**.
при|льнуть (-ну, -нёшь) *pf*.
прилягу *etc.*: *see* **прилечь**
приманивать *impf*, **приманить** (-ню, -нишь) *pf* lure; entice. **приманка** bait, lure.
применение application; use.
применить (-ню, -нишь) *pf*, **применять** *impf* apply; use; **~ся** adapt o.s., conform.
пример example.
при|мерить *pf* (*impf also* **примерять**) try on. **примерка** fitting.
примерно *adv* approximately.
примерный exemplary; approximate.
примерять *impf of* **примерить**
примесь admixture.
примета sign, token. **приметный** perceptible; conspicuous.
примечание note, footnote; *pl* comments. **примечательный** notable.
примешать *pf*, **примешивать** *impf* add, mix in.
приминать *impf of* **примять**
примирение reconciliation.
примирительный conciliatory. **при|мирить** *pf*, **примирять** *impf* reconcile; conciliate; **~ся** be reconciled.
примитивный primitive.
примкнуть (-ну, -нёшь) *pf* (*impf* **примыкать**) join; fix, attach.
примну *etc.*: *see* **примять**
приморский seaside; maritime. **приморье** seaside.
примочка wash, lotion.
приму *etc.*: *see* **принять**
примчаться (-чусь) *pf* come tearing along.
примыкать *impf of* **примкнуть**; +к+*dat* adjoin. **примыкающий** affiliated.
примять (-мну, -мнёшь) *pf* (*impf* **приминать**) crush; trample down.
принадлежать (-жу) *impf* belong. **принадлежность** belonging; membership; *pl* ac-

cessories; equipment.
принести́ (-су́, -сёшь; -нёс, -ла́) *pf* (*impf* **приноси́ть**) bring; fetch.
принижа́ть *impf*, **прини́зить** (-и́жу) *pf* humiliate; belittle.
принима́ть(ся *impf of* **приня́ть(ся**
приноси́ть (-ошу́, -о́сишь) *impf of* **принести́**. **приноше́ние** gift, offering.
при́нтер (*comput*) printer.
принуди́тельный compulsory. **прину́дить** (-у́жу) *pf*, **принужда́ть** *impf* compel. **принужде́ние** compulsion, coercion. **принуждённый** constrained, forced.
принц prince. **принце́сса** princess.
при́нцип principle. **принципиа́льно** *adv* on principle; in principle. **принципиа́льный** of principle; general.
приня́тие taking; acceptance; admission. **при́нято** it is accepted, it is usual; **не** ~ it is not done. **приня́ть** (-иму́, -и́мешь; при́нял, -а́, -о) *pf* (*impf* **принима́ть**) take; accept; take over; receive; +**за**+*acc* take for; ~ **уча́стие** take part; ~**ся** begin; take; take root; ~ **за рабо́ту** set to work.
приободри́ть *pf*, **приободря́ть** *impf* cheer up; ~**ся** cheer up.
приобрести́ (-ету́, -етёшь; -рёл, -а́) *pf*, **приобрета́ть** *impf* acquire. **приобрете́ние** acquisition.
приобща́ть *impf*, **приобщи́ть** (-щу́) *pf* join, attach, unite; ~**ся к**+*dat* join in.
приорите́т priority.
приостана́вливать *impf*, **приостанови́ть** (-влю́, -вишь) *pf* stop, suspend; ~**ся** stop. **приостано́вка** halt, suspension.
приоткрыва́ть *impf*, **приоткры́ть** (-ро́ю) *pf* open slightly.
припа́док (-дка) fit; attack.
припа́сы (-ов) *pl* supplies.
припе́в refrain.
приписа́ть (-ишу́, -и́шешь) *pf*, **припи́сывать** *impf* add; attribute. **припи́ска** postscript; codicil.
припло́д offspring; increase.
приплыва́ть *impf*, **приплы́ть** (-ыву́, -ывёшь; -ы́л, -а́, -о) *pf* swim up; sail up.
приплю́снуть (-ну) *pf*, **приплю́щивать** *impf* flatten.
приподнима́ть *impf*, **приподня́ть** (-ниму́, -ни́мешь; -о́днял, -а́, -о) *pf* raise (a little); ~**ся** raise o.s. (a little).
припо́й solder.
приполза́ть *impf*, **приползти́** (-зу́, -зёшь; -полз, -ла́) *pf* creep up, crawl up.
припомина́ть *impf*, **припо́мнить** *pf* recollect.
припра́ва seasoning, flavouring. **припра́вить** (-влю) *pf*, **приправля́ть** *impf* season, flavour.
припря́тать (-я́чу) *pf*, **припря́тывать** *impf* secrete, put by.
припу́гивать *impf*, **припугну́ть** (-ну́, -нёшь) *pf* scare.
прираба́тывать *impf*, **прирабо́тать** *pf* earn ... extra. **при́работок** (-тка) additional earnings.
прира́внивать *impf*, **приравня́ть** *pf* equate (with **к**+*dat*).
прираста́ть *impf*, **прирасти́** (-тёт; -ро́с, -ла́) *pf* adhere; take; increase; accrue.

приро́да nature. **приро́дный** natural; by birth; innate. **прирождённый** innate; born.

прирос́ *etc.*: *see* **прирасти́**.

приро́ст increase.

приуча́ть *impf*, **приучи́ть** (-чу́) *pf* tame; domesticate.

приса́живаться *impf of* **присе́сть**

присва́ивать *impf*, **присво́ить** *pf* appropriate; award.

приседа́ть *impf*, **присе́сть** (-ся́ду) *pf* (*impf also* **приса́живаться**) sit down, take a seat.

прискака́ть (-ачу́, -а́чешь) *pf* come galloping.

прискорбный sorrowful.

присла́ть (-ишлю́, -ишлёшь) *pf* (*impf* **присыла́ть**) send.

прислони́ть(ся (-оню́(сь, -о́нишь-(ся) *pf*, **прислоня́ть(ся** *impf* lean, rest.

прислу́га servant; crew. **прислу́живать** *impf* (**к**+*dat*) wait (on), attend.

прислу́шаться *pf*, **прислу́шиваться** *impf* listen; +**к**+*dat* listen to; heed.

присма́тривать *impf*, **присмотре́ть** (-рю́, -ришь) *pf* +**за**+*instr* look after, keep an eye on; **~ся** (**к**+*dat*) look closely (at). **присмо́тр** supervision.

при|сни́ться *pf*.

присоедине́ние joining; addition; annexation. **присоедини́ть** *pf*, **присоединя́ть** *impf* join; add; annex; **~ся** **к**+*dat* join; subscribe to (*an opinion*).

приспосо́бить (-блю) *pf*, **приспособля́ть** *impf* fit, adjust, adapt; **~ся** adapt o.s. **приспособле́ние** adaptation; device; appliance. **приспособля́емость** adaptability.

пристава́ть (-таю́, -таёшь) *impf of* **приста́ть**

приста́вить (-влю) *pf* (*impf* **приставля́ть**) **к**+*dat* place, set, *or* lean against; add; appoint to look after.

приста́вка prefix.

приставля́ть *impf of* **приста́вить**

при́стальный intent.

приста́нище refuge, shelter.

при́стань (*gen pl* -е́й) landing-stage; pier; wharf.

приста́ть (-а́ну) *pf* (*impf* **пристава́ть**) stick, adhere (**к**+*dat* to); pester.

пристёгивать *impf*, **пристегну́ть** (-ну́, -нёшь) *pf* fasten.

присто́йный decent, proper.

пристра́ивать(ся *impf of* **пристро́ить(ся**

пристра́стие predilection, passion; bias. **пристра́стный** biased.

пристре́ливать *impf*, **пристрели́ть** *pf* shoot (down).

пристро́ить (-о́ю) *pf* (*impf* **пристра́ивать**) add, build on; fix up; **~ся** be fixed up, get a place. **пристро́йка** annexe, extension.

при́ступ assault; fit, attack.

приступа́ть *impf*, **приступи́ть** (-плю́, -пишь) *pf* **к**+*dat* set about, start.

при|стыди́ть (-ыжу́) *pf*.

при|стыкова́ться *pf*.

присуди́ть (-ужу́, -у́дишь) *pf*, **присужда́ть** *impf* sentence, condemn; award; confer. **присужде́ние** awarding; conferment.

прису́тствие presence. **прису́тствовать** *impf* be present, attend. **прису́тствующие** *sb pl* those present.

прису́щий inherent; characteristic.

присыла́ть *impf of* **присла́ть**
прися́га oath. **присяга́ть** *impf*, **присягну́ть** (-ну́, -нёшь) *pf* swear.
прися́ду *etc.*: *see* **присе́сть**
прися́жный *sb* juror.
прита́иться *pf* hide.
прита́птывать *impf of* **притопта́ть**
прита́скивать *impf*, **притащи́ть** (-ащу́, -а́щишь) *pf* bring, drag, haul; **~ся** drag o.s.
притвори́ться *pf*, **притворя́ться** *impf +instr* pretend to be. **притво́рный** pretended, feigned. **притво́рство** pretence, sham. **притво́рщик** sham; hypocrite.
притека́ть *impf of* **прите́чь**
притесне́ние oppression. **притесни́ть** *pf*, **притесня́ть** *impf* oppress.
прите́чь (-ечёт, -еку́т; -ёк, -ла́) *pf* (*impf* **притека́ть**) pour in.
притиха́ть *impf*, **прити́хнуть** (-ну; -и́х) *pf* quiet down.
прито́к tributary; influx.
при́толока lintel.
прито́м *conj* (and) besides.
прито́н den, haunt.
притопта́ть (-пчу́, -пчешь) *pf* (*impf* **прита́птывать**) trample down.
при́торный sickly-sweet, luscious, cloying.
притра́гиваться *impf*, **притро́нуться** (-нусь) *pf* touch.
притупи́ть (-плю́, -пишь) *pf*, **притупля́ть** *impf* blunt, dull; deaden; **~ся** become blunt *or* dull.
при́тча parable.
притяга́тельный attractive, magnetic. **притя́гивать** *impf of* **притяну́ть**
притяжа́тельный possessive.
притяже́ние attraction.
притяза́ние claim, pretension. **притяза́тельный** demanding.
притя́нутый far-fetched. **притяну́ть** (-ну́, -нешь) *pf* (*impf* **притя́гивать**) attract; drag (up).
приуро́чивать *impf*, **приуро́чить** (-чу) *pf* к+*dat* time for.
приуса́дебный: ~ уча́сток individual plot (*in kolkhoz*).
приуча́ть *impf*, **приучи́ть** (-чу́, -чишь) *pf* train, school.
прихлеба́тель *m* sponger.
прихо́д coming, arrival; receipts; parish. **приходи́ть(ся** (-ожу́(сь, -о́дишь(ся) *impf of* **прийти́(сь. прихо́дный** receipt. **приходя́щий** non-resident; **~ больно́й** outpatient. **прихожа́нин** (*pl* -а́не, -а́н), **-а́нка** parishioner.
прихо́жая *sb* hall, lobby.
прихотли́вый capricious; fanciful, intricate. **при́хоть** whim, caprice.
прихра́мывать limp (slightly).
прице́л sight; aiming. **прице́ливаться** *impf*, **прице́литься** *pf* take aim.
прице́ниваться *impf*, **прицени́ться** (-ню́сь, -нишься) *pf* (к+*dat*) ask the price (of).
прице́п trailer. **прицепи́ть** (-плю́, -пишь) *pf*, **прицепля́ть** *impf* hitch, hook on; **~ся** к+*dat* stick to, cling to. **прице́пка** hitching, hooking on; quibble. **прицепно́й: ~ ваго́н** trailer.
прича́л mooring; mooring line. **прича́ливать** *impf*, **прича́лить** *pf* moor.
прича́стие[1] participle. **прича́стие**[2] communion. **причасти́ть** (-ащу́) *pf* (*impf* **причаща́ть**) give communion to; **~ся** receive communion.
прича́стный[1] participial. **при-**

чáстный[2] concerned; privy.
причащáть *impf of* **причастúть**
причём *conj* moreover, and.
причесáть (-ешý, -éшешь) *pf*, **причёсывать** *impf* comb; do the hair (of); **~ся** do one's hair, have one's hair done. **причёска** hair-do; haircut.
причúна cause; reason. **причинúть** *pf*, **причинять** *impf* cause.
причúслить *pf*, **причислять** *impf* number, rank (**к**+*dat* among); add on.
причитáние lamentation. **причитáть** *impf* lament.
причитáться *impf* be due.
причмóкивать *impf*, **причмóкнуть** (-ну) *pf* smack one's lips.
причýда caprice, whim.
при|чýдиться *pf*.
причýдливый odd; fantastic; whimsical.
при|швартовáть *pf*. **пришёл** *etc.*: *see* **прийтú**
пришéлец (-ьца) newcomer.
пришéствие coming; advent.
пришивáть *impf*, **пришúть** (-шью, -шьёшь) *pf* sew on.
пришлю *etc.*: *see* **прислáть**
пришпúливать *impf*, **пришпúлить** *pf* pin on.
пришпóривать *impf*, **пришпóрить** *pf* spur (on).
прищемúть (-млю) *pf*, **прищемлять** *impf* pinch.
прищéпка clothes-peg.
прищýриваться *impf*, **прищýриться** *pf* screw up one's eyes.
приют shelter, refuge. **приютúть** (-ючý) *pf* shelter; **~ся** take shelter.
приятель *m*, **приятельница** friend. **приятельский** friendly. **приятный** nice, pleasant.
про *prep+acc* about; for; **~ себя** to o.s.
про|анализúровать *pf*.
прóба test; hallmark; sample.
пробéг run; race. **пробегáть** *impf*, **пробежáть** (-егý) *pf* run; cover; run past. **пробéжка** run.
пробéл blank, gap; flaw.
проберý *etc.*: *see* **пробрáть**.
пробивáть(ся *impf of* **пробúть(ся**. **пробирáть(ся** *impf of* **пробрáть(ся**
пробúрка test-tube. **пробúровать** *impf* test, assay.
про|бúть (-бью, -бьёшь) *pf* (*impf also* **пробивáть**) make a hole in; pierce; punch; **~ся** force, make, one's way.
прóбка cork; stopper; fuse; (traffic) jam, congestion. **прóбковый** cork.
проблéма problem.
прóблеск flash; gleam, ray.
прóбный trial, test; **~ кáмень** touchstone. **прóбовать** *impf* (*pf* **ис~**, **по~**) try; attempt.
пробóина hole.
пробóр parting.
про|бормотáть (-очý, -óчешь) *pf*.
пробрáть (-берý, -берёшь; -áл, -á, -о) *pf* (*impf* **пробирáть**) penetrate; scold; **~ся** make *or* force one's way.
пробýду *etc.*: *see* **пробыть**
про|будúть (-ужý, -ýдишь) *pf*, **пробуждáть** *impf* wake (up); arouse; **~ся** wake up. **пробуждéние** awakening.
про|бурáвить (-влю) *pf*, **пробурáвливать** *impf* bore (through), drill.
про|бурúть *pf*.
пробыть (-бýду; прóбыл, -á, -о) *pf* stay; be.
пробью *etc.*: *see* **пробúть**

прова́л failure; downfall; gap. **прова́ливать** *impf*, **провали́ть** (-лю́, -лишь) *pf* bring down; ruin; reject, fail; **~ся** collapse; fall in; fail; disappear.

прове́дать *pf*, **прове́дывать** *impf* call on; learn.

проведе́ние conducting; construction; installation.

провезти́ (-зу́, -зёшь; -ёз, -ла́) *pf* (*impf* **провози́ть**) convey, transport.

прове́рить *pf*, **проверя́ть** *impf* check; test. **прове́рка** checking, check; testing.

про|вести́ (-еду́, -едёшь; -ёл, -а́) *pf* (*impf also* **проводи́ть**) lead, take; build; install; carry out; conduct; pass; draw; spend; +*instr* pass over.

прове́тривать *impf*, **прове́трить** *pf* air.

про|ве́ять (-е́ю) *pf*.

провиде́ние Providence.

прови́зия provisions.

провини́ться *pf* be guilty; do wrong.

провинциа́льный provincial. **прови́нция** province; the provinces.

про́вод (*pl* -а́) wire, lead, line. **проводи́мость** conductivity. **проводи́ть**[1] (-ожу́, -о́дишь) *impf of* **провести́**; conduct.

проводи́ть[2] (-ожу́, -о́дишь) *pf* (*impf* **провожа́ть**) accompany; see off.

прово́дка leading, taking; building; installation; wiring, wires.

проводни́к[1] (-а́) guide; conductor.

проводни́к[2] (-а́) conductor; bearer; transmitter.

про́воды (-ов) *pl* send-off. **провожа́тый** *sb* guide, escort. **провожа́ть** *impf of* **проводи́ть**

прово́з conveyance, transport.

провозгласи́ть (-ашу́) *pf*, **провозглаша́ть** *impf* proclaim; propose. **провозглаше́ние** proclamation.

провози́ть (-ожу́, -о́зишь) *impf of* **провезти́**

провока́тор agent provocateur. **провока́ция** provocation.

про́волока wire. **про́волочный** wire.

прово́рный quick; agile. **прово́рство** quickness; agility.

провоци́ровать *impf* & *pf* (*pf* **с~**) provoke.

прогада́ть *pf*, **прога́дывать** *impf* miscalculate.

прога́лина glade; space.

прогиба́ть(ся *impf of* **прогну́ть(ся**

прогла́тывать *impf*, **проглоти́ть** (-очу́, -о́тишь) *pf* swallow.

прогляде́ть (-яжу́) *pf*, **прогля́дывать**[1] *impf* overlook; look through. **прогляну́ть** (-я́нет) *pf*, **прогля́дывать**[2] *impf* show, peep through, appear.

прогна́ть (-гоню́, -го́нишь; -а́л, -а́, -о) *pf* (*impf* **прогоня́ть**) drive away; banish; drive; sack.

прогнива́ть *impf*, **прогни́ть** (-ниёт; -и́л, -а́, -о) *pf* rot through.

прогно́з prognosis; (weather) forecast.

прогну́ть (-ну́, -нёшь) *pf* (*impf* **прогиба́ть**) cause to sag; **~ся** sag, bend.

прогова́ривать *impf*, **проговори́ть** *pf* say, utter; talk; **~ся** let the cat out of the bag.

проголода́ться *pf* get hungry.

про|голосова́ть *pf*.

прого́н purlin; girder; stairwell.

прогоня́ть *impf of* **прогна́ть**
прогора́ть *impf*, **прогоре́ть** (-рю́) *pf* burn (through); burn out; go bankrupt.
прого́рклый rancid, rank.
програ́мма programme; syllabus. **программи́ровать** *impf* (*pf* **за~**) programme. **программи́ст** (computer) programmer.
прогрева́ть *impf*, **прогре́ть** (-е́ю) *pf* heat; warm up; **~ся** warm up.
про|греме́ть (-млю́) *pf.* **про|грохота́ть** (-очу́, -о́чешь) *pf.*
прогре́сс progress. **прогресси́вный** progressive. **прогресси́ровать** *impf* progress.
прогрыза́ть *impf*, **прогры́зть** (-зу́, -зёшь; -ы́з) *pf* gnaw through.
про|гуде́ть (-гужу́) *pf.*
прогу́л truancy; absenteeism. **прогу́ливать** *impf*, **прогуля́ть** *pf* play truant, be absent, (from); miss; take for a walk; **~ся** take a walk. **прогу́лка** walk, stroll; outing. **прогу́льщик** absentee, truant.
продава́ть (-даю́, -даёшь) *impf*, **прода́ть** (-а́м, -а́шь, -а́ст, -ади́м; про́дал, -а́, -о) *pf* sell. **продава́ться** (-даётся) *impf* be for sale; sell. **продаве́ц** (-вца́) seller, vendor; salesman. **продавщи́ца** seller, vendor; saleswoman. **прода́жа** sale. **прода́жный** for sale; corrupt.
продвига́ть *impf*, **продви́нуть** (-ну) *pf* move on, push forward; advance; **~ся** advance; move forward; push on. **продвиже́ние** advancement.
продева́ть *impf of* **проде́ть**
про|деклами́ровать *pf.*
проде́лать *pf*, **проде́лывать** *impf* do, perform, make. **проде́лка** trick; prank.
продемонстри́ровать *pf* demonstrate, show.
продёргивать *impf of* **продёрнуть**
продержа́ть (-жу́, -жишь) *pf* hold; keep; **~ся** hold out.
продёрнуть (-ну, -нешь) *pf* (*impf* **продёргивать**) pass, run; criticize severely.
проде́ть (-е́ну) *pf* (*impf* **продева́ть**) pass; **~ ни́тку в иго́лку** thread a needle.
продешеви́ть (-влю́) *pf* sell too cheap.
про|диктова́ть *pf.*
продлева́ть *impf*, **продли́ть** *pf* prolong. **продле́ние** extension. **про|дли́ться** *pf.*
продма́г grocery. **продово́льственный** food. **продово́льствие** food; provisions.
продолгова́тый oblong.
продолжа́тель *m* continuer. **продолжа́ть** *impf*, **продо́лжить** (-жу) *pf* continue; prolong; **~ся** continue, last, go on. **продолже́ние** continuation; sequel; **в ~+gen** in the course of. **продолжи́тельность** duration. **продолжи́тельный** long; prolonged.
продо́льный longitudinal.
продро́гнуть (-ну; -о́г) *pf* be chilled to the bone.
продтова́ры (-ов) *pl* food products.
продува́ть *impf* **проду́ть**
проду́кт product; *pl* food-stuffs. **продукти́вность** productivity. **продукти́вный** productive. **продукто́вый** food. **проду́кция** production.
проду́манный well thought-out. **проду́мать** *pf*, **проду́мывать** *impf* think over; think out.
проду́ть (-у́ю, -у́ешь) *pf* (*impf* **продува́ть**) blow through.

продыря́вить (-влю) *pf* make a hole in.

проеда́ть *impf of* **прое́сть.**

прое́ду *etc.*: *see* **прое́хать**

прое́зд passage, thoroughfare; trip. **прое́здить** (-зжу) *pf* (*impf* **проезжа́ть**) spend travelling. **проездн|о́й** travelling; **~о́й биле́т** ticket; **~а́я пла́та** fare; **~ы́е** *sb pl* travelling expenses. **проезжа́ть** *impf of* **прое́здить, прое́хать.** **прое́зжий** passing (by); *sb* passer-by.

прое́кт project, plan, design; draft. **проекти́ровать** *impf* (*pf* **с~**) project; plan. **прое́ктный** planning; planned. **прое́ктор** projector.

проекцио́нный фона́рь projector. **прое́кция** projection.

прое́сть (-е́м, -е́шь, -е́ст, -еди́м; -е́л) *pf* (*impf* **проеда́ть**) eat through, corrode; spend on food.

прое́хать (-е́ду) *pf* (*impf* **проезжа́ть**) pass, ride, drive (by, through); cover.

прожа́ренный (*cul*) well-done.

прожева́ть (-жую́, -жуёшь) *pf*, **прожёвывать** *impf* chew well.

проже́ктор (*pl* -ы *or* -а́) searchlight.

проже́чь (-жгу́, -жжёшь; -жёг, -жгла́) *pf* (*impf* **прожига́ть**) burn (through).

прожива́ть *impf of* **прожи́ть.**

прожига́ть *impf of* **проже́чь**

прожи́точный ми́нимум living wage. **прожи́ть** (-иву́, -ивёшь; -о́жил, -а́, -о) *pf* (*impf* **прожива́ть**) live; spend.

прожо́рливый gluttonous.

про́за prose. **прозаи́ческий** prose; prosaic.

прозва́ние, про́звище nickname. **прозва́ть** (-зову́, -зовёшь; -а́л, -а́, -о) *pf* (*impf* **прозыва́ть**) nickname, name.

про|звуча́ть *pf.*

про|зева́ть *pf.* **про|зимова́ть** *pf.* **прозову́** *etc.*: *see* **прозва́ть**

прозорли́вый perspicacious.

прозра́чный transparent.

прозрева́ть *impf*, **прозре́ть** *pf* regain one's sight; see clearly. **прозре́ние** recovery of sight; insight.

прозыва́ть *impf of* **прозва́ть**

прозяба́ние vegetation. **прозяба́ть** *impf* vegetate.

проигра́ть *pf*, **прои́грывать** *impf* lose; play; **~ся** gamble away all one's money. **прои́грыватель** *m* record-player. **про́игрыш** loss.

произведе́ние work; production; product. **произвести́** (-еду́, -едёшь; -ёл, -а́) *pf*, **производи́ть** (-ожу́, -о́дишь) *impf* make; carry out; produce; **+в**+*acc/nom pl* promote to (the rank of). **производи́тель** *m* producer. **производи́тельность** productivity. **производи́тельный** productive. **произво́дный** derivative. **произво́дственный** industrial; production. **произво́дство** production.

произво́л arbitrariness; arbitrary rule. **произво́льный** arbitrary.

произнести́ (-су́, -сёшь; -ёс, -ла́) *pf*, **произноси́ть** (-ошу́, -о́сишь) *impf* pronounce; utter. **произноше́ние** pronunciation.

произойти́ (-ойдёт; -ошёл, -шла́) *pf* (*impf* **происходи́ть**) happen, occur; result; be descended.

произраста́ть *impf*, **произрасти́** (-ту́; -тёшь; -рос, -ла́) *pf* sprout; grow.

про́иски (-ов) *pl* intrigues.

проистека́ть *impf*, **происте́чь** (-ечёт; -ёк, -ла́) *pf* spring, result.

происходи́ть (-ожу́, -о́дишь) *impf of* **произойти́. происхожде́ние** origin; birth.

происше́ствие event, incident.

пройдо́ха *m & f* sly person.

пройти́ (-йду́, -йдёшь; -ошёл, -шла́) *pf* (*impf* **проходи́ть**) pass; go; go past; cover; study; get through; **~сь** (*impf* **прохáживаться**) take a stroll.

прок use, benefit.

прокажённый *sb* leper. **прока́за**[1] leprosy.

прока́за[2] mischief, prank. **прока́зничать** *impf* (*pf* **на~**) be up to mischief. **прока́зник** prankster.

прока́лывать *impf of* **проколо́ть**

прока́пывать *impf of* **прокопа́ть**

прока́т hire.

прокати́ться (-ачу́сь, -а́тишься) *pf* roll; go for a drive.

прока́тный rolling; rolled.

прокипяти́ть (-ячу́) *pf* boil (thoroughly).

прокиса́ть *impf*, **про|ки́снуть** (-нет) *pf* turn (sour).

прокла́дка laying; construction; washer; packing. **прокла́дывать** *impf of* **проложи́ть**

проклама́ция leaflet.

проклина́ть *impf*, **прокля́сть** (-яну́, -янёшь; -о́клял, -а́, -о) *pf* curse, damn. **прокля́тие** curse; damnation. **прокля́тый** (-я́т, -а́, -о) damned.

проко́л puncture.

проколо́ть (-лю́, -лешь) *pf* (*impf* **прока́лывать**) prick, pierce.

прокомменти́ровать *pf* comment (upon).

про|компости́ровать *pf*.

про|конспекти́ровать *pf*.

про|консульти́ровать(ся *pf*. **про|контроли́ровать** *pf*.

прокопа́ть *pf* (*impf* **прока́пывать**) dig, dig through.

прoко́рм nourishment, sustenance. **про|корми́ть(ся** (-млю́(сь, -мишь(ся) *pf*.

про|корректи́ровать *pf*.

прокра́дываться *impf*, **прокра́сться** (-аду́сь, -адёшься) *pf* steal in.

прокурату́ра office of public prosecutor. **прокуро́р** public prosecutor.

прокуси́ть (-ушу́, -у́сишь) *pf*, **проку́сывать** *impf* bite through.

прокути́ть (-учу́, -у́тишь) *pf*, **проку́чивать** *impf* squander; go on a binge.

пролага́ть *impf of* **проложи́ть**

прола́мывать *impf of* **пролома́ть**

пролега́ть *impf* lie, run.

пролеза́ть *impf*, **проле́зть** (-зу; -ле́з) *pf* get through, climb through.

про|лепета́ть (-ечу́, -е́чешь) *pf*.

пролёт span; stairwell; bay.

пролетариа́т proletariat. **пролета́рий** proletarian. **пролета́рский** proletarian.

пролета́ть *impf*, **пролете́ть** (-ечу́) *pf* fly; cover; fly by, past, through.

проли́в strait. **пролива́ть** *impf*, **проли́ть** (-лью́, -льёшь; -о́лил, -а́, -о) *pf* spill, shed; **~ся** be spilt.

проло́г prologue.

проложи́ть (-жу́, -жишь) *pf* (*impf* **прокла́дывать, прола-**

га́ть) lay; build; interlay.
проло́м breach, break. **пролома́ть, проломи́ть** (-млю́, -ми́шь) *pf* (*impf* **прола́мывать**) break (through).
пролью́ *etc.*: *see* **проли́ть**
про|ма́зать (-а́жу) *pf.* **прома́тывать(ся** *impf of* **промота́ть(ся**
про́мах miss; slip, blunder. **прома́хиваться** *impf*, **промахну́ться** (-ну́сь, -нёшься) *pf* miss; make a blunder.
прома́чивать *impf of* **промочи́ть**
промедле́ние delay. **проме́длить** *pf* delay; procrastinate.
промежу́ток (-тка) interval; space. **промежу́точный** intermediate
промелькну́ть (-ну́, -нёшь) *pf* flash (past, by).
проме́нивать *impf*, **променя́ть** *pf* exchange.
промерза́ть *impf*, **промёрзнуть** (-ну; -ёрз) *pf* freeze through. **промёрзлый** frozen.
промока́ть *impf*, **промо́кнуть** (-ну; -мо́к) *pf* get soaked; let water in.
промо́лвить (-влю) *pf* say, utter.
промолча́ть (-чу́) *pf* keep silent.
про|мота́ть *pf* (*impf also* **прома́тывать**) squander.
промочи́ть (-чу́, -чишь) *pf* (*impf* **прома́чивать**) soak, drench.
промо́ю *etc.*: *see* **промы́ть**
промтова́ры (-ов) *pl* manufactured goods.
промча́ться (-чу́сь) *pf* rush by.
промыва́ть *impf of* **промы́ть**
про́мысел (-сла) trade, business; *pl* works. **промысло́вый** producers'; business; game.
промы́ть (-мо́ю) *pf* (*impf* **промыва́ть**) wash (thoroughly); bathe; ~ **мозги́**+*dat* brain-wash.
про|мыча́ть (-чу́) *pf.*
промы́шленник industrialist. **промы́шленность** industry. **промы́шленный** industrial.
пронести́ (-су́, -сёшь; -ёс, -ла́) *pf* (*impf* **проноси́ть**) carry (past, through); pass (over); **~сь** rush past, through; scud (past); fly; spread.
пронза́ть *impf*, **пронзи́ть** (-нжу́) *pf* pierce, transfix. **пронзи́тельный** piercing.
прониза́ть (-ижу́, -и́жешь) *pf*, **прони́зывать** *impf* pierce; permeate.
проника́ть *impf*, **прони́кнуть** (-ну; -и́к) *pf* penetrate; percolate; **~ся** be imbued.
проникнове́ние penetration; feeling. **проникнове́нный** heartfelt.
проница́емый permeable. **проница́тельный** perspicacious.
проноси́ть(ся (-ошу́(сь, -о́сишь(ся) *impf of* **пронести́(сь.**
про|нумерова́ть *pf.*
пронюхать *pf*, **пронюхивать** *impf* smell out, get wind of.
прообраз prototype.
пропага́нда propaganda. **пропаганди́ст** propagandist.
пропада́ть *impf of* **пропа́сть.**
пропа́жа loss.
пропа́лывать *impf of* **прополо́ть**
про́пасть precipice; abyss; lots of.
пропа́сть (-аду́, -адёшь) *pf* (*impf* **пропада́ть**) be missing; be lost; disappear; be done for, die; be wasted. **пропа́щий** lost; hopeless.
пропека́ть(ся *impf of* **пропе́чь(ся.** **про|пе́ть** (-пою́, -поёшь) *pf.*

пропе́чь (-еку́, -ечёшь; -ёк, -ла́) *pf* (*impf* **пропека́ть**) bake thoroughly; **~ся** get baked through.
пропива́ть *impf of* **пропи́ть**
прописа́ть (-ишу́, -и́шешь) *pf*, **прописывать** *impf* prescribe; register; **~ся** register. **прописка** registration; residence permit. **прописн|о́й:** **~а́я бу́ква** capital letter; **~а́я и́стина** truism. **про́писью** *adv* in words.
пропита́ние subsistence, sustenance. **пропита́ть** *pf*, **пропи́тывать** *impf* impregnate, saturate.
пропи́ть (-пью́, -пьёшь; -о́пи́л, -а́, -о) *pf* (*impf* **пропива́ть**) spend on drink.
проплыва́ть *impf*, **проплы́ть** (-ыву́, -ывёшь; -ы́л, -а́, -о) *pf* swim, sail, *or* float past *or* through.
пропове́дник preacher; advocate. **пропове́довать** *impf* preach; advocate. **про́поведь** sermon; advocacy.
прополза́ть *impf*, **проползти́** (-зу́, -зёшь; -по́лз, -ла́) *pf* crawl, creep.
пропо́лка weeding. **прополо́ть** (-лю́, -лешь) *pf* (*impf* **пропа́лывать**) weed.
про|полоска́ть (-ощу́, -о́щешь) *pf*.
пропорциона́льный proportional, proportionate. **пропо́рция** proportion.
про́пуск (*pl* -а́ *or* -и, -о́в *or* -ов) pass, permit; password; admission; omission; non-attendance; blank, gap. **пропуска́ть** *impf*, **пропусти́ть** (-ущу́, -у́стишь) *pf* let pass; let in; pass; leave out; miss. **пропускно́й** admission.
про|пылесо́сить *pf*.
пропью́ *etc.*: *see* **пропи́ть**
прора́б works superintendent.
праба́тывать *impf*, **прорабо́тать** *pf* work (through, at); study; pick holes in.
прораста́ние germination; sprouting. **прораста́ть** *impf*, **прорасти́** (-тёт; -ро́с, -ла́) *pf* germinate, sprout.
прорва́ть (-ву́, -вёшь; -а́л, -а́, -о) *pf* (*impf* **прорыва́ть**) break through; **~ся** burst open; break through.
про|реаги́ровать *pf*.
прореди́ть (-ежу́) *pf*, **проре́живать** *impf* thin out.
проре́з cut; slit, notch. **про|ре́зать** (-е́жу) *pf*, **прореза́ть** *impf* (*impf also* **проре́зывать**) cut through; **~ся** be cut, come through.
проре́зывать(ся *impf of* **проре́зать(ся**. **про|репети́ровать** *pf*.
проре́ха tear, slit; flies; deficiency.
про|рецензи́ровать *pf*.
проро́к prophet.
пророни́ть *pf* utter.
проро́с *etc.*: *see* **прорасти́**
проро́ческий prophetic. **проро́чество** prophecy.
проро́ю *etc.*: *see* **проры́ть**
проруба́ть *impf*, **прораби́ть** (-блю́, -бишь) *pf* cut *or* hack through. **про́рубь** ice-hole.
проры́в break; break-through; hitch. **прорыва́ть**[1]**(ся** *impf of* **прорва́ть(ся**
прорыва́ть[2] *impf*, **проры́ть** (-ро́ю) *pf* dig through; **~ся** dig one's way through.
проса́чиваться *impf of* **просочи́ться**
просве́рливать *impf*, **просверли́ть** *pf* drill, bore;

perforate.

просвéт (clear) space; shaft of light; ray of hope; opening. **просветúтельный** educational. **просветúть**[1] (-ещý) *pf* (*impf* **просвещáть**) enlighten.

просветúть[2] (-ечý, -éтишь) *pf* (*impf* **просвéчивать**) X-ray.

просветлéние brightening (up); lucidity. **про|светлéть** (-éет) *pf.*

просвéчивание radioscopy. **просвéчивать** *impf of* **просветúть**; be translucent; be visible.

просвещáть *impf of* **просветúть. просвещéние** enlightenment.

просвúра communion bread.

прóседь streak(s) of grey.

просéивать *impf of* **просéять**

прóсека cutting, ride.

просёлок (-лка) country road.

просéять (-éю) *pf* (*impf* **просéивать**) sift.

про|сигнализúровать *pf.*

просидéть (-ижý) *pf*, **просúживать** *impf* sit.

просúтельный pleading. **просúть** (-ошý, -óсишь) *impf* (*pf* **по~**) ask; beg; invite; **~ся** ask; apply.

проскáкивать *impf of* **проскочúть**

проскáльзывать *impf*, **проскользнýть** (-нý, -нёшь) *pf* slip, creep.

проскочúть (-чý, -чишь) *pf* (*impf* **проскáкивать**) rush by; slip through; creep in.

прослáвить (-влю) *pf*, **прославлять** *impf* glorify; make famous; **~ся** become famous. **прослáвленный** renowned.

проследúть (-ежý) *pf*, **прослéживать** *impf* track (down); trace.

прослезúться (-ежýсь) *pf* shed a few tears.

прослóйка layer, stratum.

прослужúть (-жý, -жишь) *pf* serve (for a certain time).

про|слýшать *pf*, **прослýшивать** *impf* hear; listen to; miss, not catch.

про|слы́ть (-ывý, -ывёшь; -ы́л, -á, -о) *pf.*

просмáтривать *impf*, **просмотрéть** (-рю́, -ришь) *pf* look over; overlook. **просмóтр** survey; view, viewing; examination.

проснýться (-нýсь, -нёшься) *pf* (*impf* **просыпáться**) wake up.

прóсо millet.

просóвывать(ся *impf of* **просýнуть(ся**

про|сóхнуть (-ну; -óх) *pf* (*impf also* **просыхáть**) dry out.

просочúться (-úтся) *pf* (*impf* **просáчиваться**) percolate; seep (out); leak (out).

проспáть (-плю́; -áл, -á, -о) *pf* (*impf* **просыпáть**) sleep (through); oversleep.

проспéкт avenue.

про|спрягáть *pf.*

просрóченный overdue; expired. **просрóчить** (-чу) *pf* allow to run out; be behind with; overstay. **просрóчка** delay; expiry of time limit.

простáивать *impf of* **простоя́ть**

простáк (-á) simpleton.

простéнок (-нка) pier (*between windows*).

простерéться (-трётся; -тёрся) *pf*, **простирáться** *impf* extend.

простúтельный pardonable, excusable. **простúть** (-ощý) *pf* (*impf* **прощáть**) forgive;

excuse; **~ся** (**с**+*instr*) say goodbye (to).

проститу́тка prostitute. **проститу́ция** prostitution.

про́сто *adv* simply.

простоволо́сый bare-headed.

простоду́шный simple-hearted; ingenuous.

просто́й[1] downtime.

прост|о́й[2] simple; plain; mere; **~ы́м гла́зом** with the naked eye; **~о́е число́** prime number.

простокваша thick sour milk.

про́сто-на́просто *adv* simply.

простонаро́дный of the common people.

просто́р spaciousness; space. **просто́рный** spacious.

простора́чие popular speech.

простосерде́чный simple-hearted.

простота́ simplicity.

просто|я́ть (-ою́) *pf* (*impf* **проста́ивать**) stand (idle).

простра́нный extensive, vast. **простра́нственный** spatial. **простра́нство** space.

простре́л lumbago. **простре́ливать** *impf*, **прострели́ть** (-лю́, -лишь) *pf* shoot through.

про|строчи́ть (-очу́, -о́чи́шь) *pf*.

просту́да cold. **простуди́ться** (-ужу́сь, -у́дишься) *pf*, **простужа́ться** *impf* catch (a) cold.

проступа́ть *impf*, **проступи́ть** (-ит) *pf* appear.

просту́пок (-пка) misdemeanour.

простыня́ (*pl* про́стыни, -ы́нь, -ня́м) sheet.

просты́ть (-ы́ну) *pf* get cold.

просу́нуть (-ну) *pf* (*impf* **просо́вывать**) push, thrust.

просу́шивать *impf*, **просуши́ть** (-шу́, -шишь) *pf* dry out; **~ся** (get) dry.

просуществова́ть *pf* exist; endure.

просчёт error. **просчита́ться** *pf*, **просчи́тываться** *impf* miscalculate.

просы́пать (-плю) *pf*, **просыпа́ть**[1] *impf* spill; **~ся** get spilt.

просыпа́ть[2] *impf of* **проспа́ть**. **просыпа́ться** *impf of* **просну́ться**. **просыха́ть** *impf of* **просо́хнуть**

про́сьба request.

прота́лкивать(ся *impf of* **протолкну́ть(ся**. **прота́пливать** *impf of* **протопи́ть**

прота́птывать *impf of* **протопта́ть**

прота́скивать *impf*, **протащи́ть** (-щу́, -щишь) *pf* drag, push (through).

проте́з artificial limb, prosthesis; **зубно́й ~** denture.

протеи́н protein.

протека́ть *impf of* **проте́чь**

проте́кция patronage.

протере́ть (-тру́, -трёшь; -тёр) *pf* (*impf* **протира́ть**) wipe (over); wear (through).

проте́ст protest. **протеста́нт, ~ка** Protestant. **протестова́ть** *impf* & *pf* protest.

проте́чь (-ечёт; -тёк, -ла́) *pf* (*impf* **протека́ть**) flow; leak; seep; pass; take its course.

про́тив *prep*+*gen* against; opposite; contrary to, as against.

про́тивень (-вня) *m* baking-tray; meat-pan.

проти́виться (-влюсь) *impf* (*pf* **вос~**) +*dat* oppose; resist. **проти́вник** opponent; the enemy. **проти́вный**[1] opposite; contrary. **проти́вный**[2] nasty, disgusting.

противо- *in comb* anti-, contra-,

counter-. **противовéс** counterbalance. **~воздýшный** anti-aircraft. **~гáз** gas-mask. **~дéйствие** opposition. **~дéйствовать** *impf +dat* oppose, counteract. **~естéственный** unnatural. **~закóнный** illegal. **~зачáточный** contraceptive. **~полóжность** opposite; opposition, contrast. **~полóжный** opposite; contrary. **~постáвить** (-влю) *pf*, **~поставлять** *impf* oppose; contrast. **~речи́вый** contradictory; conflicting. **~рéчие** contradiction. **~рéчить** (-чу) *impf +dat* contradict. **~стоя́ть** (-ою́) *impf +dat* resist, withstand. **~тáнковый** anti-tank. **~я́дие** antidote.

протирáть *impf of* **протерéть**

проти́скивать *impf*, **проти́снуть** (-ну) *pf* force, squeeze (through, into).

проткнýть (-нý, -нёшь) *pf* (*impf* **протыкáть**) pierce.

протокóл minutes; report; protocol.

протолкнýть (-нý, -нёшь) *pf* (*impf* **протáлкивать**) push through; **~ся** push one's way through.

протóн proton.

протопи́ть (-плю́, -пишь) *pf* (*impf* **протáпливать**) heat (thoroughly).

протоптáть (-пчý, -пчешь) *pf* (*impf* **протáптывать**) tread; wear out.

проторённый beaten, well-trodden.

прототи́п prototype.

протóчный flowing, running.

про|трáлить *pf*. **протрý** *etc*.: *see* **протерéть**. **про|труби́ть** (-блю́) *pf*.

протрезви́ться (-влю́сь) *pf*, **протрезвля́ться** *impf* sober up.

протухáть *impf*, **протýхнуть** (-нет; -ýх) *pf* become rotten; go bad.

протыкáть *impf of* **проткнýть**

протя́гивать *impf*, **протянýть** (-нý, -нешь) *pf* stretch; extend; hold out; **~ся** stretch out; extend; last. **протяжéние** extent, stretch; period. **протя́жный** long-drawn-out; drawling.

проýчивать *impf*, **проучи́ть** (-чý, -чишь) *pf* study; teach a lesson.

профáн ignoramus.

профанáция profanation.

профессионáл professional.

профессионáльный professional; occupational. **профéссия** profession. **профéссор** (*pl* -á) professor.

профилáктика prophylaxis; preventive measures.

прóфиль *m* profile; type.

про|фильтровáть *pf*.

профсою́з trade-union.

прохáживаться *impf of* **пройти́сь**

прохвóст scoundrel.

прохлáда coolness. **прохладительный** refreshing, cooling. **прохлáдный** cool, chilly.

прохóд passage; gangway, aisle; duct. **проходи́мец** (-мца) rogue. **проходи́мый** passable. **проходи́ть** (-ожý, -óдишь) *impf of* **пройти́**. **проходнóй** entrance; communicating. **проходя́щий** passing. **прохóжий** passing, in transit; *sb* passer-by.

процветáние prosperity. **процветáть** *impf* prosper, flourish.

процеди́ть (-ежу́, -е́дишь) *pf* (*impf* **проце́живать**) filter, strain.

процеду́ра procedure; (*usu in pl*) treatment.

проце́живать *pf of* **процеди́ть**

проце́нт percentage; per cent; interest.

проце́сс process; trial; legal proceedings. **проце́ссия** procession.

про|цити́ровать *pf*.

прочёска screening; combing.

проче́сть (-чту́, -чтёшь; -чёл, -чла́) *pf of* **чита́ть**

про́чий other.

прочи́стить (-ищу) *pf* (*impf* **прочища́ть**) clean; clear.

про|чита́ть *pf*, **прочи́тывать** *impf* read (through).

прочища́ть *impf of* **прочи́стить**

про́чность firmness, stability, durability. **про́чный** (-чен, -чна́, -о) firm, sound, solid; durable.

прочте́ние reading. **прочту́** *etc.*: *see* **проче́сть**

прочу́вствовать *pf* feel deeply; experience, go through.

прочь *adv* away, off; averse to.

проше́дший past; last. **прошёл** *etc.*: *see* **пройти́**

проше́ние application, petition.

прошепта́ть (-пчу́, -пчешь) *pf* whisper.

проше́ствие: по проше́ствии +*gen* after.

прошива́ть *impf*, **проши́ть** (-шью́, -шьёшь) *pf* sew, stitch.

прошлого́дний last year's.

про́шл|ый past; last; **~ое** *sb* the past.

про|шнурова́ть *pf*. **про|штуди́ровать** *pf*. **прошью́** *etc.*: *see* **проши́ть**

проща́й(те) goodbye. **проща́льный** parting; farewell. **проща́ние** farewell; parting.

проща́ть(ся *impf of* **прости́ть(ся**

про́ще simpler, plainer.

проще́ние forgiveness, pardon.

прощу́пать *pf*, **прощу́пывать** *impf* feel.

про|экзаменова́ть *pf*.

прояви́тель *m* developer. **прояви́ть** (-влю́, -вишь) *pf*, **проявля́ть** *impf* show, display; develop; **~ся** reveal itself. **проявле́ние** display; manifestation; developing.

проясни́ться *pf*, **проясня́ться** *impf* clear, clear up.

пруд (-а́, *loc* -у́) pond. **пруди́ть** (-ужу́, -у́дишь) *impf* (*pf* **за~**) dam.

пружи́на spring. **пружи́нистый** springy. **пружи́нный** spring.

пру́сский Prussian.

прут (-а *or* -а́; *pl* -тья) twig.

пры́гать *impf*, **пры́гнуть** (-ну) *pf* jump, leap; bounce; **~ с шесто́м** pole-vault. **прыгу́н** (-а́), **прыгу́нья** (*gen pl* -ний) jumper. **прыжо́к** (-жка́) jump; leap; **прыжки́** jumping; **прыжки́ в во́ду** diving; **~ в высоту́** high jump; **~ в длину́** long jump.

пры́скать *impf*, **пры́снуть** (-ну) *pf* spurt; sprinkle; burst out laughing.

прыть speed; energy.

прыщ (-а́), **пры́щик** pimple.

пряди́льный spinning. **пряди́льня** (*gen pl* -лен) (spinning-)mill. **пряди́льщик** spinner. **пряду́** *etc.*: *see* **прясть.**

прядь lock; strand. **пря́жа** yarn, thread.

пря́жка buckle, clasp.
пря́лка distaff; spinning-wheel.
пряма́я *sb* straight line. **пря́мо** *adv* straight; straight on; frankly; really.
прямоду́шие directness, straightforwardness. **~ду́шный** direct, straightforward.
прямо́й (-ям, -á, -о) straight; upright, erect; through; direct; straightforward; real.
прямолине́йный rectilinear; straightforward. **прямоуго́льник** rectangle. **прямоуго́льный** rectangular.
пря́ник spice cake. **пря́ность** spice. **пря́ный** spicy; heady.
прясть (-яду́, -ядёшь; -ял, -ялá, -о) *impf* (*pf* **с~**) spin.
пря́тать (-я́чу) *impf* (*pf* **с~**) hide; **~ся** hide. **пря́тки** (-ток) *pl* hide-and-seek.
пса *etc.*: *see* **пёс**
псало́м (-лмá) psalm. **псалты́рь** Psalter.
псевдони́м pseudonym.
псих madman, lunatic. **психиатри́я** psychiatry. **пси́хика** psyche; psychology. **психи́ческий** mental, psychical.
психоана́лиз psychoanalysis. **психо́з** psychosis. **психо́лог** psychologist. **психологи́ческий** psychological. **психоло́гия** psychology. **психопа́т** psychopath. **психопати́ческий** psychopathic. **психосомати́ческий** psychosomatic. **психотерапе́вт** psychotherapist. **психотерапи́я** psychotherapy. **психоти́ческий** psychotic.
птене́ц (-нцá) nestling; fledgeling. **пти́ца** bird. **птицефе́рма** poultry-farm. **пти́чий** bird, bird's, poultry. **пти́чка** bird; tick.
пу́блика public; audience. **публика́ция** publication; notice, advertisement. **публикова́ть** *impf* (*pf* **о~**) publish. **публици́стика** writing on current affairs. **публи́чность** publicity. **публи́чный** public; **~ дом** brothel.
пу́гало scarecrow. **пуга́ть** *impf* (*pf* **ис~, на~**) frighten, scare; **~ся** (+*gen*) be frightened (of). **пуга́ч** (-á) toy pistol. **пугли́вый** fearful.
пу́говица button.
пуд (*pl* -ы́) pood (= *16.38 kg*). **пудово́й, пудо́вый** one pood in weight.
пу́дель *m* poodle.
пу́динг blancmange.
пу́дра powder. **пу́дреница** powder compact. **пу́дреный** powdered. **пу́дриться** *impf* (*pf* **на~**) powder one's face.
пуза́тый pot-bellied.
пузырёк (-рькá) vial; bubble. **пузы́рь** (-я́) *m* bubble; blister; bladder.
пук (*pl* -и́) bunch, bundle; tuft.
пу́кать *impf*, **пу́кнуть** *pf* fart.
пулемёт machine-gun. **пулемётчик** machine-gunner. **пуленепробива́емый** bulletproof.
пульвериза́тор atomizer; spray.
пульс pulse. **пульса́р** pulsar. **пульси́ровать** *impf* pulsate.
пульт desk, stand; control panel.
пу́ля bullet.
пункт point; spot; post; item. **пункти́р** dotted line. **пункти́рный** dotted, broken.
пунктуа́льный punctual.
пунктуа́ция punctuation.
пунцо́вый crimson.
пуп (-á) navel. **пупови́на** um-

bilical cord. **пупóк** (-пкá) navel; gizzard.
пургá blizzard.
пуритáнин (*pl* -тáне, -тáн), **-áнка** Puritan.
пýрпур purple, crimson. **пурпýр|ный, ~овый** purple.
пуск starting (up). **пускáй** *see* **пусть. пускáть(ся** *impf of* **пустúть(ся. пусковóй** starting.
пустéть (-éет) *impf* (*pf* **о~**) empty; become deserted.
пустúть (пущý, пýстишь) *pf* (*impf* **пускáть**) let go; let in; let; start; send; set in motion; throw; put forth; **~ся** set out; start.
пустовáть *impf* be *or* stand empty. **пустóй** (-ст, -á, -о) empty; uninhabited; idle; shallow. **пустотá** (*pl* -ы) emptiness; void; vacuum; futility. **пустотéлый** hollow.
пустынный uninhabited; deserted; desert. **пустыня** desert. **пустырь** (-я́) *m* waste land; vacant plot.
пустышка blank; hollow object; dummy.
пусть, пускáй *partl* let; all right; though, even if.
пустя́к (-á) trifle. **пустякóвый** trivial.
пýтаница muddle, confusion. **пýтаный** muddled, confused. **пýтать** *impf* (*pf* **за~, пере~, с~**) tangle; confuse; mix up; **~ся** get confused *or* mixed up.
путёвка pass; place on a group tour. **путеводúтель** *m* guide, guide-book. **путевóй** travelling; road. **путём** *prep+gen* by means of. **путешéственник** traveller. **путешéствие** journey; voyage. **путешéствовать** *impf* travel; voyage.
пýты (пут) *pl* shackles.
путь (-й, *instr* -ём, *prep* -й) way; track; path; course; journey; voyage; means; **в путú** en route, on one's way.
пух (*loc* -ý) down; fluff.
пýхлый (-хл, -á, -о) plump.
пýхнуть (-ну; пух) *impf* (*pf* **вс~, о~**) swell.
пуховúк (-á) feather-bed. **пухóвка** powder-puff. **пухóвый** downy.
пучúна abyss; the deep.
пучóк (-чкá) bunch, bundle.
пýшечный gun, cannon.
пушúнка bit of fluff. **пушúстый** fluffy.
пýшка gun, cannon.
пушнúна furs, pelts. **пушнóй** fur; fur-bearing.
пýще *adv* more; **~ всегó** most of all.
пущý *etc.*: *see* **пустúть**
пчелá (*pl* -ёлы) bee. **пчелúный** bee, bees'. **пчеловóд** bee-keeper. **пчéльник** apiary.
пшенúца wheat. **пшенúчный** wheat(en).
пшённый millet. **пшенó** millet.
пыл (*loc* -ý) heat, ardour. **пылáть** *impf* blaze; burn.
пылесóс vacuum cleaner. **пылесóсить** *impf* (*pf* **про~**) vacuum(-clean). **пылúнка** speck of dust. **пылúть** *impf* (*pf* **за~, на~**) raise a dust; cover with dust; **~ся** get dusty.
пылкий ardent; fervent.
пыль (*loc* -й) dust. **пыльный** (-лен, -льнá, -о) dusty. **пыльцá** pollen.
пырéй couch grass.
пырнýть (-нý, -нёшь) *pf* jab.
пытáть *impf* torture. **пытáться** *impf* (*pf* **по~**) try. **пытка** torture, torment. **пытлúвый** inquisitive.

пыхтéть (-хчý) *impf* puff, pant.
пы́шка bun.
пы́шность splendour. **пы́шный** (-шен, -шнá, -шно) splendid; lush.
пьедестáл pedestal.
пьéса play; piece.
пью *etc.*: *see* **пить**
пьянéть (-éю) *impf* (*pf* **о~**) get drunk. **пьяни́ть** *impf* (*pf* **о~**) intoxicate, make drunk. **пья́ница** *m* & *f* drunkard. **пья́нство** drunkenness. **пья́нствовать** *impf* drink heavily. **пья́ный** drunk.
пюпи́тр lectern; stand.
пюрé *neut indecl* purée.
пядь (*gen pl* -éй) span; **ни пя́ди** not an inch.
пя́льцы (-лец) *pl* embroidery frame.
пятá (*pl* -ы, -áм) heel.
пятáк (-á), **пятачóк** (-чкá) five-copeck piece. **пятёрка** five; figure 5; No. 5; fiver (5-*rouble note*).
пяти- *in comb* five; penta-. **пятибóрье** pentathlon. **~десятилéтие** fifty years; fiftieth anniversary, birthday. **П~деся́тница** Pentecost. **~деся́тый** fiftieth; **~деся́тые гóды** the fifties. **~конéчный** five-pointed. **~лéтие** five years; fifth anniversary. **~лéтка** five-year plan. **~сóтый** five-hundredth. **~угóльник** pentagon. **~угóльный** pentagonal.
пя́титься (пя́чусь) *impf* (*pf* **по~**) move backwards; back.
пя́тка heel.
пятнáдцатый fifteenth. **пятнáдцать** fifteen.
пятнáть *impf* (*pf* **за~**) spot, stain. **пятнáшки** (-шек) *pl* tag. **пятни́стый** spotted.
пя́тница Friday.
пятнó (*pl* -а, -тен) stain; spot; blot; **роди́мое ~** birth-mark.
пя́тый fifth. **пять** (-и́, *instr* -ью) five. **пятьдеся́т** (-и́десяти, *instr* -ью́десятью) fifty. **пятьсóт** (-тисóт, -тистáм) five hundred. **пя́тью** *adv* five times.

Р

раб (-á), **рабá** slave. **рабовладéлец** (-льца) slave-owner. **раболéпие** servility. **раболéпный** servile. **раболéпствовать** cringe, fawn.
рабóта work; job; functioning. **рабóтать** *impf* work; function; be open; **~ над**+*instr* work on. **рабóтник, -ица** worker. **работоспосóбность** capacity for work, efficiency. **работоспосóбный** able-bodied, hardworking. **работя́щий** hardworking. **рабóчий** *sb* worker. **рабóч\|ий** worker's; working; **~ая си́ла** manpower.
рáбский slave; servile. **рáбство** slavery. **рабы́ня** female slave.
равви́н rabbi.
рáвенство equality. **равнéние** alignment. **равни́на** plain.
равнó *adv* alike; equally; **~ как** as well as. **равнó** *predic*: *see* **рáвный**
равно- *in comb* equi-, iso-. **равнобéдренный** isosceles. **~вéсие** equilibrium; balance. **~дéнствие** equinox. **~дýшие** indifference. **~дýшный** indifferent. **~мéрный** even; uniform. **~прáвие** equality of rights. **~прáвный** having equal rights. **~си́льный** of

equal strength; equal, equivalent, tantamount. **~сторо́нний** equilateral. **~це́нный** of equal value; equivalent.
ра́вный (-вен, -вна́) equal. **равно́** *predic* make(s), equals; **всё ~о́** (it is) all the same. **равня́ть** *impf* (*pf* **с~**) make even; treat equally; **+с+***instr* compare with, treat as equal to; **~ся** compete, compare; be equal; be tantamount.
рад (-а, -о) *predic* glad.
рада́р radar.
ра́ди *prep+gen* for the sake of.
радиа́тор radiator. **радиа́ция** radiation.
ра́дий radium.
радика́льный radical.
ра́дио *neut indecl* radio.
радио- *in comb* radio-; radioactive. **радиоакти́вный** radioactive. **~веща́ние** broadcasting. **~волна́** radio-wave. **~гра́мма** radio-telegram. **радио́лог** radiologist. **~ло́гия** radiology. **~лока́тор** radar (set). **~люби́тель** *m* radio amateur, ham. **~мая́к** (-а́) radio beacon. **~переда́тчик** transmitter. **~переда́ча** broadcast. **~приёмник** radio (set). **~свя́зь** radio communication. **~слу́шатель** *m* listener. **~ста́нция** radio station. **~электро́ника** radio-electronics.
радио́ла radiogram.
ради́ровать *impf* & *pf* radio.
ради́ст radio operator.
ра́диус radius.
ра́довать *impf* (*pf* **об~, по~**) gladden, make happy; **~ся** be glad, rejoice. **ра́достный** joyful. **ра́дость** gladness, joy.
ра́дуга rainbow. **ра́дужн|ый** iridescent; cheerful; **~ая обо́лочка** iris.
раду́шие cordiality. **раду́шный** cordial.
ражу́ *etc.*: *see* **рази́ть**
раз (*pl* -ы́, раз) time, occasion; one; **ещё ~** (once) again; **как ~** just, exactly; **не ~** more than once; **ни ~у** not once. **раз** *adv* once, one day. **раз** *conj* if; since.
разба́вить (-влю) *pf*, **разбавля́ть** *impf* dilute.
разбаза́ривать *impf*, **разбаза́рить** *pf* squander.
разба́лтывать(ся *impf of* **разболта́ть(ся**
разбе́г running start. **разбега́ться** *impf*, **разбежа́ться** (-бегусь) *pf* take a run, run up; scatter.
разберу́ *etc.*: *see* **разобра́ть**
разбива́ть(ся *impf of* **разби́ть(ся. разби́вка** laying out; spacing (out).
разбинтова́ть *pf*, **разбинто́вывать** *impf* unbandage.
разбира́тельство investigation. **разбира́ть** *impf of* **разобра́ть**; **~ся** *impf of* **разобра́ться**
разби́ть (-зобью, -зобьёшь) *pf* (*impf* **разбива́ть**) break; smash; divide (up); damage; defeat; mark out; space (out); **~ся** break, get broken; hurt o.s. **разби́тый** broken; jaded.
раз|богате́ть (-е́ю) *pf*.
разбо́й robbery. **разбо́йник** robber. **разбо́йничий** robber.
разболе́ться[1] (-ли́тся) *pf* begin to ache badly.
разболе́ться[2] (-е́юсь) *pf* become ill.
разболта́ть[1] *pf* (*impf* **разба́лтывать**) divulge, give away.
разболта́ть[2] *pf* (*impf* **раз-**

ба́лтывать) shake up; loosen; **~ся** work loose; get out of hand.

разбомби́ть (-блю́) *pf* bomb, destroy by bombing.

разбо́р analysis; critique; discrimination; investigation. **разбо́рка** sorting out; dismantling. **разбо́рный** collapsible. **разбо́рчивый** legible; discriminating.

разбра́сывать *impf of* **разброса́ть**

разбреда́ться *impf*, **разбрести́сь** (-едётся; -ёлся, -ла́сь) *pf* disperse; straggle. **разбро́д** disorder.

разбро́санный scattered; disconnected, incoherent. **разброса́ть** *pf* (*impf* **разбра́сывать**) throw about; scatter.

раз|буди́ть (-ужу́, -у́дишь) *pf*.

разбуха́ть *impf*, **разбу́хнуть** (-нет; -бу́х) *pf* swell.

разбушева́ться (-шу́юсь) *pf* fly into a rage; blow up; rage.

разва́л breakdown, collapse. **разва́ливать** *impf*, **развали́ть** (-лю́, -лишь) *pf* pull down; mess up; **~ся** collapse; go to pieces; tumble down; sprawl. **разва́лина** ruin; wreck.

ра́зве *partl* really?; **~** (**то́лько**), **~** (**что**) except that, only.

развева́ться *impf* fly, flutter.

разве́дать *pf* (*impf* **разве́дывать**) find out; reconnoitre.

разведе́ние breeding; cultivation.

разведённ|ый divorced; **~ый, ~ая** *sb* divorcee.

разве́дка intelligence (service); reconnaissance; prospecting. **разве́дочный** prospecting, exploratory.

разведу́ *etc.*: *see* **развести́**

разве́дчик intelligence officer; scout; prospector. **разве́дывать** *impf of* **разве́дать**

развезти́ (-зу́, -зёшь; -ёз, -ла́) *pf* (*impf* **развози́ть**) convey, transport; deliver.

разве́ивать(ся *impf of* **разве́ять(ся**. **развёл** *etc.*: *see* **развести́**

развенча́ть *pf*, **разве́нчивать** *impf* dethrone; debunk.

развёрнутый extensive, all-out; detailed. **разверну́ть** (-ну́, -нёшь) *pf* (*impf* **развёртывать, развора́чивать**) unfold, unwrap; unroll; unfurl; deploy; expand; develop; turn; scan; display; **~ся** unfold, unroll, come unwrapped; deploy; develop; spread; turn.

развёрстка allotment, apportionment.

развёртывать(ся *impf of* **разверну́ть(ся**

раз|весели́ть *pf* cheer up, amuse; **~ся** cheer up.

разве́сить[1] (-е́шу) *pf* (*impf* **разве́шивать**) spread; hang (out).

разве́сить[2] (-е́шу) *pf* (*impf* **разве́шивать**) weigh out. **разве́ска** weighing. **развесно́й** sold by weight.

развести́ (-еду́, -едёшь; -ёл, -а́) *pf* (*impf* **разводи́ть**) take; separate; divorce; dilute; dissolve; start; breed; cultivate; **~сь** get divorced; breed, multiply.

разветви́ться (-ви́тся) *pf*, **разветвля́ться** *impf* branch; fork. **разветвле́ние** branching, forking; branch; fork.

разве́шать *pf*, **разве́шивать** *impf* hang.

развéшивать *impf of* **развéсить, развéшать. развéшу** *etc.*: *see* **развéсить**
развéять (-éю) *pf* (*impf* **развéивать**) scatter, disperse; dispel; **~ся** disperse; be dispelled.
развивáть(ся *impf of* **развить(ся**
развилка fork.
развинтить (-нчý) *pf*, **развинчивать** *impf* unscrew.
развитие development. **развитóй** (рáзвит, -á, -о) developed; mature. **развить** (-зовью; -зовьёшь; -ил, -á, -о) *pf* (*impf* **развивáть**) develop; unwind; **~ся** develop.
развлекáть *impf*, **развлéчь** (-екý, -ечёшь; -ёк, -лá) *pf* entertain, amuse; **~ся** have a good time; amuse o.s. **развлечéние** entertainment, amusement.
развóд divorce. **разводить(ся** (-ожý(сь, -óдишь(ся) *impf of* **развести(сь. развóдка** separation. **разводнóй: ~ ключ** adjustable spanner; **~ мост** drawbridge.
развозить (-ожý, -óзишь) *impf of* **развезти**
разволновáть(ся *pf* get excited, be agitated.
разворáчивать(ся *impf of* **развернýть(ся**
разворовáть *pf*, **разворóвывать** *impf* loot; steal.
разворóт U-turn; turn; development.
разврáт depravity, corruption. **развратить** (-ащý) *pf*. **развращáть** *impf* corrupt; deprave. **разврáтничать** *impf* lead a depraved life. **разврáтный** debauched, corrupt. **развращённый** (-ён, -á) corrupt.
развязáть (-яжý, -яжешь) *pf*, **развязывать** *impf* untie; unleash; **~ся** come untied; **~ся** с+*instr* rid o.s. of. **развязка** dénouement; outcome. **развязный** overfamiliar.
разгадáть *pf*, **разгáдывать** *impf* solve, guess, interpret. **разгáдка** solution.
разгáр height, climax.
разгибáть(ся *impf of* **разогнýть(ся**
разглагóльствовать *impf* hold forth.
разглáдить (-áжу) *pf*, **разглáживать** *impf* smooth out; iron (out).
разгласить (-ашý) *pf*, **разглашáть** *impf* divulge; +о+*prep* trumpet. **разглашéние** disclosure.
разглядéть (-яжý) *pf*, **разглядывать** *impf* make out, discern.
разгнéвать *pf* anger. **раз|гнéваться** *pf*.
разговáривать *impf* talk, converse. **разговóр** conversation. **разговóрник** phrase-book. **разговóрный** colloquial. **разговóрчивый** talkative.
разгóн dispersal; running start; distance. **разгонять(ся** *impf of* **разогнáть(ся**
разгорáживать *impf of* **разгородить**
разгорáться *impf*, **разгорéться** (-рюсь) *pf* flare up.
разгородить (-ожý, -óдишь) *pf* (*impf* **разгорáживать**) partition off.
раз|горячить(ся (-чý(сь) *pf*.
разгрáбить (-блю) *pf* plunder, loot. **разграблéние** plunder, looting.
разграничéние demarcation; differentiation. **разграни-**

чивать *impf*, **разгранúчить** (-чу) *pf* delimit; differentiate.
разгребáть *impf*, **разгрестú** (-ебý, -ебёшь; -ёб, -лá) *pf* rake *or* shovel (away).
разгрóм crushing defeat; devastation; havoc. **разгромúть** (-млю) *pf* rout, defeat.
разгружáть *impf*, **разгрузúть** (-ужý, -ýзишь) *pf* unload; relieve; **~ся** unload; be relieved. **разгрýзка** unloading; relief.
разгрызáть *impf*, **раз|грызть** (-зý, -зёшь; -ыз) *pf* crack.
разгýл revelry; outburst. **разгýливать** *impf* stroll about. **разгýливаться** *impf*, **разгуля́ться** *pf* spread o.s.; become wide awake; clear up. **разгýльный** wild, rakish.
раздавáть(ся (-даю(сь, -даёшь(ся) *impf of* **раздáть(ся**
раз|давúть (-влю, -вишь) *pf*, **раздáвливать** *impf* crush; run over.
раздáть (-áм, -áшь, -áст, -адúм; рóз- *or* раздáл, -á, -о) *pf* (*impf* **раздавáть**) distribute, give out; **~ся** be heard; resound; ring out; make way; expand; put on weight. **раздáча** distribution. **раздаю** *etc.*: *see* **раздавáть**
раздвáивать(ся *impf of* **раздвоúть(ся**
раздвигáть *impf*, **раздвúнуть** (-ну) *pf* move apart; **~ся** move apart. **раздвижнóй** expanding; sliding.
раздвоéние division; split; **~ лúчности** split personality. **раздвóенный** forked; cloven; split. **раздвоúть** *pf* (*impf* **раздвáивать**) divide into two; bisect; **~ся** fork; split.
раздевáлка cloakroom. **раздевáть(ся** *impf of* **раздéть(ся**
раздéл division; section.
раздéлаться *pf* +с+*instr* finish with; settle accounts with.
разделéние division. **разделúмый** divisible. **раз|делúть** (-лю, -лишь) *pf*, **разделя́ть** *impf* divide; separate; share; **~ся** divide; be divided; be divisible; separate. **раздéльный** separate.
раздéну *etc.*: *see* **раздéть.**
раздерý *etc.*: *see* **разодрáть**
раздéть (-дéну) *pf* (*impf* **раздевáть**) undress; **~ся** undress; take off one's coat.
раздирáть *impf of* **разодрáть**
раздобывáть *impf*, **раздобы́ть** (-бýду) *pf* get, get hold of.
раздóлье expanse; liberty. **раздóльный** free.
раздóр discord.
раздосáдовать *pf* vex.
раздражáть *impf*, **раздражúть** (-жý) *pf* irritate; annoy; **~ся** get annoyed. **раздражéние** irritation. **раздражúтельный** irritable.
раз|дробúть (-блю) *pf*, **раздробля́ть** *impf* break; smash to pieces.
раздувáть(ся *impf of* **раздýть(ся**
раздýмать *pf*, **раздýмывать** *impf* change one's mind; ponder. **раздýмье** meditation; thought.
раздýть (-ýю) *pf* (*impf* **раздувáть**) blow; fan; exaggerate; whip up; swell; **~ся** swell.
разевáть *impf of* **разúнуть**
разжáлобить (-блю) *pf* move (to pity).
разжáловать *pf* demote.
разжáть (-зожмý, -мёшь) *pf*

(*impf* **разжима́ть**) unclasp, open; release.

разжева́ть (-жую́, -жуёшь) *pf*, **разжёвывать** *impf* chew.

разже́чь (-зожгу́, -зожжёшь; -жёг, -зожгла́) *pf*, **разжига́ть** *impf* kindle; rouse.

разжима́ть *impf of* **разжа́ть**.

раз|жире́ть (-е́ю) *pf*.

рази́нуть (-ну) *pf* (*impf* **разева́ть**) open; ~ **рот** gape. **рази́ня** *m & f* scatter-brain.

рази́тельный striking. **рази́ть** (ражу́) *impf* (*pf* **по~**) strike.

разлага́ть(ся *impf of* **разложи́ть(ся**

разла́д discord; disorder.

разла́мывать(ся *impf of* **разлома́ть(ся, разломи́ть(ся**

разлёгся *etc.*: *see* **разле́чься**

разлеза́ться *impf*, **разле́зться** (-зется; -ле́зся) *pf* come to pieces; fall apart.

разлета́ться *impf*, **разлете́ться** (-лечу́сь) *pf* fly away; scatter; shatter; rush.

разле́чься (-ля́гусь; -лёгся, -гла́сь) *pf* stretch out.

разли́в bottling; flood; overflow. **разлива́ть** *impf*, **разли́ть** (-золью́, -зольёшь; -и́л, -а́, -о) *pf* pour out; spill; flood (with); **~ся** spill; overflow; spread. **разливно́й** draught.

различа́ть *impf*, **различи́ть** (-чу́) *pf* distinguish; discern; **~ся** differ. **разли́чие** distinction; difference. **различи́тельный** distinctive, distinguishing. **разли́чный** different.

разложе́ние decomposition; decay; disintegration. **разложи́ть** (-жу́, -жишь) *pf* (*impf* **разлага́ть, раскла́дывать**) put away; spread (out); distribute; break down; decompose; resolve; corrupt; **~ся** decompose; become demoralized; be corrupted; disintegrate, go to pieces.

разло́м breaking; break. **разлома́ть, разломи́ть** (-млю́, -мишь) *pf* (*impf* **разла́мывать**) break to pieces; pull down; **~ся** break to pieces.

разлу́ка separation. **разлуча́ть** *impf*, **разлучи́ть** (-чу́) *pf* separate, part; **~ся** separate, part.

разлюби́ть (-блю́, -бишь) *pf* stop loving *or* liking.

разля́гусь *etc.*: *see* **разле́чься**

разма́зать (-а́жу) *pf*, **разма́зывать** *impf* spread, smear.

разма́лывать *impf of* **размоло́ть**

разма́тывать *impf of* **размота́ть**

разма́х sweep; swing; span; scope. **разма́хивать** *impf* +*instr* swing; brandish. **разма́хиваться** *impf*, **размахну́ться** (-ну́сь, -нёшься) *pf* swing one's arm. **разма́шистый** sweeping.

размежева́ние demarcation, delimitation. **размежева́ть** (-жу́ю) *pf*, **размежёвывать** *impf* delimit.

размёл *etc.*: *see* **размести́**

размельча́ть *impf*, **раз|мельчи́ть** (-чу́) *pf* crush, pulverize.

размелю́ *etc.*: *see* **размоло́ть**

разме́н exchange. **разме́нивать** *impf*, **разменя́ть** *pf* change; **~ся** +*instr* exchange; dissipate. **разме́нная моне́та** (small) change.

разме́р size; measurement; amount; scale, extent; *pl* proportions. **разме́ренный** measured. **разме́рить** *pf*, **размеря́ть** *impf* measure.

разместѝ (-ету́, -етёшь; -мёл, -а́) *pf* (*impf* **размета́ть**) sweep clear; sweep away.
размести́ть (-ещу́) *pf* (*impf* **размеща́ть**) place, accommodate; distribute; **~ся** take one's seat.
размета́ть *impf of* **разместѝ**
разме́тить (-е́чу) *pf*, **размеча́ть** *impf* mark.
размеша́ть *pf*, **разме́шивать** *impf* stir (in).
размеща́ть(ся *impf of* **размести́ть(ся. размеще́ние** placing; accommodation; distribution. **размещу́** *etc.*: *see* **размести́ть**
размина́ть(ся *impf of* **размя́ть(ся**
разми́нка limbering up.
размину́ться (-ну́сь, -нёшься) *pf* pass; +**с**+*instr* pass; miss.
размножа́ть *impf*, **размно́жить** (-жу) *pf* multiply, duplicate; breed; **~ся** multiply; breed.
размозжи́ть (-жу́) *pf* smash.
размо́лвка tiff.
размоло́ть (-мелю́, -ме́лешь) *pf* (*impf* **размалывать**) grind.
размора́живать *impf*, **размо́розить** (-о́жу) *pf* unfreeze, defrost; **~ся** unfreeze; defrost.
размота́ть *pf* (*impf* **разма́тывать**) unwind.
размыва́ть *impf*, **размы́ть** (-о́ет) *pf* wash away; erode.
размыка́ть *impf of* **разомкну́ть**
размышле́ние reflection; meditation. **размышля́ть** *impf* reflect, ponder.
размягча́ть *impf*, **размягчи́ть** (-чу́) *pf* soften; **~ся** soften.
размяка́ть *impf*, **размя́кнуть** (-ну; -мя́к) *pf* soften.
раз|мя́ть (-зомну́, -зомнёшь) *pf* (*impf also* **размина́ть**) knead; mash; **~ся** stretch one's legs; limber up.
разна́шивать *impf of* **разноси́ть**
разнестѝ (-су́, -сёшь; -ёс, -ла́) *pf* (*impf* **разноси́ть**) carry; deliver; spread; note down; smash; scold; scatter; *impers* make puffy, swell.
разнима́ть *impf of* **разня́ть**
ра́зниться *impf* differ. **ра́зница** difference.
разно- *in comb* different, vari-, hetero-. **разнобо́й** lack of coordination; difference. **~ви́дность** variety. **~гла́сие** disagreement; discrepancy. **~обра́зие** variety, diversity. **~обра́зный** various, diverse. **~речи́вый** contradictory. **~ро́дный** heterogeneous. **~сторо́нний** many-sided; versatile. **~цве́тный** variegated. **~шёрстный** of different colours; ill-assorted.
разноси́ть[1] (-ошу́, -о́сишь) *pf* (*impf* **разна́шивать**) wear in.
разноси́ть[2] (-ошу́, -о́сишь) *impf of* **разнестѝ. разно́ска** delivery.
ра́зность difference.
разно́счик pedlar.
разношу́ *etc.*: *see* **разноси́ть**
разну́зданный unbridled.
ра́зн|ый different; various; **~ое** *sb* various things.
разню́хать *pf*, **разню́хивать** *impf* smell out.
разня́ть (-ниму́, -ни́мешь; ро́з- *or* разня́л, -а́, -о) *pf* (*impf* **разнима́ть**) take to pieces; separate.
разоблача́ть *impf*, **разоблачи́ть** (-чу́) *pf* expose.

разоблаче́ние exposure. **разобра́ть** (-зберу́, -рёшь; -а́л, -а́, -о) *pf* (*impf* **разбира́ть**) take to pieces; buy up; sort out; investigate; analyse; understand; **~ся** sort things out; **+в+***prep* investigate, look into; understand.

разобща́ть *impf*, **разобщи́ть** (-щу́) *pf* separate; estrange, alienate.

разобью́ *etc.*: *see* **разби́ть**. **разовью́** *etc.*: *see* **разви́ть**

ра́зовый single.

разогна́ть (-згоню́, -о́нишь; -гна́л, -а́, -о) *pf* (*impf* **разгоня́ть**) scatter; disperse; dispel; drive fast; **~ся** gather speed.

разогну́ть (-ну́, -нёшь) *pf* (*impf* **разгиба́ть**) unbend, straighten; **~ся** straighten up.

разогрева́ть *impf*, **разогре́ть** (-е́ю) *pf* warm up.

разоде́ть(ся (-е́ну(сь) *pf* dress up.

разодра́ть (-здеру́, -рёшь; -а́л, -а́, -о) *pf* (*impf* **раздира́ть**) tear (up); lacerate.

разожгу́ *etc.*: *see* **разже́чь**. **разожму́** *etc.*: *see* **разжа́ть**

разо|зли́ть *pf*.

разойти́сь (-йду́сь, -йдёшься; -ошёлся, -ошла́сь) *pf* (*impf* **расходи́ться**) disperse; diverge; radiate; differ; conflict; part; be spent; be sold out.

разолью́ *etc.*: *see* **разли́ть**

ра́зом *adv* at once, at one go.

разомкну́ть (-ну, -нёшь) *pf* (*impf* **размыка́ть**) open; break.

разомну́ *etc.*: *see* **размя́ть**

разорва́ть (-ву́, -вёшь; -а́л, -а́, -о) *pf* (*impf* **разрыва́ть**) tear; break (off); blow up; **~ся** tear; break; explode.

разоре́ние ruin; destruction.

разори́тельный ruinous; wasteful. **разори́ть** *pf* (*impf* **разоря́ть**) ruin; destroy; **~ся** ruin o.s.

разоружа́ть *impf*, **разоружи́ть** (-жу́) *pf* disarm; **~ся** disarm. **разоруже́ние** disarmament.

разоря́ть(ся *impf of* **разори́ть(ся**

разосла́ть (-ошлю́, -ошлёшь) *pf* (*impf* **рассыла́ть**) distribute, circulate.

разостла́ть, расстели́ть (-сстелю́, -те́лешь) *pf* (*impf* **расстила́ть**) spread (out); lay; **~ся** spread.

разотру́ *etc.*: *see* **растере́ть**

разочарова́ние disappointment.

разочарова́ть *pf*, **разочаро́вывать** *impf* disappoint; **~ся** be disappointed.

разочту́ *etc.*: *see* **расче́сть**. **разошёлся** *etc.*: *see* **разойти́сь**. **разошлю́** *etc.*: *see* **разосла́ть**. **разошью́** *etc.*: *see* **расши́ть**

разраба́тывать *impf*, **разрабо́тать** *pf* cultivate; work, exploit; work out; develop. **разрабо́тка** cultivation; exploitation; working out; mining; quarry.

разража́ться *impf*, **разрази́ться** (-ажу́сь) *pf* break out; burst out.

разраста́ться *impf*, **разрасти́сь** (-тётся; -ро́сся, -ла́сь) *pf* grow; spread.

разрежённый (-ён, -а́) rarefied.

разре́з cut; section; point of view. **разре́зать** (-е́жу) *pf*, **разреза́ть** *impf* cut; slit.

разреша́ть *impf*, **разреши́ть** (-шу́) *pf* (+*dat*) allow; solve;

settle; **~ся** be allowed; be solved; be settled. **разреше́ние** permission; permit; solution; settlement. **разреши́мый** solvable.
разро́зненный uncoordinated; odd; incomplete.
разро́сся *etc.*: *see* **разрасти́сь. разро́ю** *etc.*: *see* **разры́ть**
разруба́ть *impf*, **разруби́ть** (-блю́, -бишь) *pf* cut; chop up.
разру́ха ruin, collapse. **разруша́ть** *impf*, **разру́шить** (-шу) *pf* destroy; demolish; ruin; **~ся** go to ruin, collapse. **разруше́ние** destruction. **разруши́тельный** destructive.
разры́в break; gap; rupture; burst. **разрыва́ть**[1]**(ся** *impf of* **разорва́ть(ся**
разрыва́ть[2] *impf of* **разры́ть**
разрывно́й explosive.
разрыда́ться *pf* burst into tears.
разры́ть (-ро́ю) *pf* (*impf* **разрыва́ть**) dig (up).
раз|рыхли́ть *pf*, **разрыхля́ть** *impf* loosen; hoe.
разря́д[1] category; class.
разря́д[2] discharge. **разряди́ть** (-яжу́, -я́дишь) *pf* (*impf* **разряжа́ть**) unload; discharge; space out; **~ся** run down; clear, ease. **разря́дка** spacing (out); discharging; unloading; relieving.
разряжа́ть(ся *impf of* **разряди́ть(ся**
разубеди́ть (-ежу́) *pf*, **разубежда́ть** *impf* dissuade; **~ся** change one's mind.
разува́ться *impf of* **разу́ться**
разуве́рить *pf*, **разуверя́ть** *impf* dissuade, undeceive; **~ся** (**в**+*prep*) lose faith (in).
разузнава́ть (-наю́, -наёшь) *impf*, **разузна́ть** *pf* (try to) find out.
разукра́сить (-а́шу) *pf*, **разукра́шивать** *impf* adorn, embellish.
ра́зум reason; intellect. **разуме́ться** (-е́ется) *impf* be understood, be meant; **(само́ собо́й) разуме́ется** of course; it goes without saying. **разу́мный** rational, intelligent; sensible; reasonable; wise.
разу́ться (-у́юсь) *pf* (*impf* **разува́ться**) take off one's shoes.
разу́чивать *impf*, **разучи́ть** (-чу́, -чишь) *pf* learn (up).
разу́чиваться *impf*, **разучи́ться** (-чу́сь, -чишься) *pf* forget (how to).
разъеда́ть *impf of* **разъе́сть**
разъедини́ть *pf*, **разъединя́ть** *impf* separate; disconnect.
разъе́дусь *etc.*: *see* **разъе́хаться**
разъе́зд departure; siding (track); mounted patrol; *pl* travel; journeys. **разъездно́й** travelling. **разъезжа́ть** *impf* drive *or* ride about; travel; **~ся** *impf of* **разъе́хаться**
разъе́сть (-е́ст, -едя́т; -е́л) *pf* (*impf* **разъеда́ть**) eat away; corrode.
разъе́хаться (-е́дусь) *pf* (*impf* **разъезжа́ться**) depart; separate; pass (one another); miss one another.
разъярённый (-ён, -а́) furious. **разъяри́ть** *pf*, **разъяря́ть** *impf* infuriate; **~ся** get furious.
разъясне́ние explanation; interpretation. **разъясни́тельный** explanatory.
разъясни́ть *pf*, **разъясня́ть** *impf* explain; interpret; **~ся**

…ome clear, be cleared up. …**ыгрáть** *pf*, **разы́грывать** …*npf* perform; draw; raffle; play a trick on; **~ся** get up; run high.

разыскáть (-ыщу́, -ы́щешь) *pf* find. **разы́скивать** *impf* search for.

рай (*loc* -ю́) paradise; garden of Eden.

райкóм district committee.

райóн region. **райóнный** district.

рáйский heavenly.

рак crayfish; cancer; Cancer.

ракéта[1], **ракéтка** racket.

ракéта[2] rocket; missile; flare.

рáковина shell; sink.

рáковый cancer; cancerous.

раку́шка cockle-shell, mussel.

рáма frame. **рáмка** frame; *pl* framework.

рáмпа footlights.

рáна wound. **ранéние** wounding; wound. **рáненый** wounded; injured.

ранг rank.

рáнец (-нца) knapsack; satchel.

рáнить *impf* & *pf* wound; injure.

рáнний early. **рáно** *adv* early. **рáньше** *adv* earlier; before; formerly.

рапи́ра foil.

рáпорт report. **рапортовáть** *impf* & *pf* report.

рáса race. **раси́зм**, racism. **раси́стский** racist.

раскáиваться *impf of* **раскáяться**

раскалённый (-ён, -á) scorching; incandescent. **раскали́ть** *pf* (*impf* **раскаля́ть**) make red-hot; **~ся** become red-hot. **раскáлывать(ся** *impf of* **расколóть(ся**. **раскаля́ть(ся** *impf of* **раскали́ть(ся**. **раскáпывать** *impf of* **раскопáть**

раскáт roll, peal. **раскатáть** *pf*, **раскáтывать** *impf* roll (out), smooth out, level; drive *or* ride (about). **раскáтистый** rolling, booming. **раскати́ться** (-ачу́сь, -áтишься) *pf*, **раскáтываться** *impf* gather speed; roll away; peal, boom.

раскачáть *pf*, **раскáчивать** *impf* swing; rock; **~ся** swing, rock.

раскáяние repentance. **рас|кáяться** *pf* (*impf also* **раскáиваться**) repent.

расквитáться *pf* settle accounts.

раски́дывать *impf*, **раски́нуть** (-ну) *pf* stretch (out); spread; pitch; **~ся** spread out; sprawl.

раскладнóй folding. **раскладу́шка** camp-bed. **расклáдывать** *impf of* **разложи́ть**

расклáняться *pf* bow; take leave.

расклéивать *impf*, **расклéить** *pf* unstick; stick (up); **~ся** come unstuck.

раскóл split; schism. **рас|колóть** (-лю́, -лешь) *pf* (*impf also* **раскáлывать**) split; break; disrupt; **~ся** split. **раскóльник** dissenter.

раскопáть *pf* (*impf* **раскáпывать**) dig up, unearth, excavate. **раскóпки** (-пок) *pl* excavations.

раскóсый slanting.

раскрáивать *impf of* **раскрои́ть**

раскрáсить (-áшу) *pf*, *impf* **раскрáшивать** paint, colour.

раскрепости́ть (-ощу́) *pf*, **раскрепощáть** *impf* liberate. **раскрепощéние** emancipation.

раскритиковáть *pf* criticize harshly.
раскроить *pf* (*impf* **раскрáивать**) cut out.
раскрóю *etc.*: *see* **раскрыть**
раскрутить (-учý, -ýтишь) *pf*, **раскрýчивать** *impf* untwist; **~ся** come untwisted.
раскрывáть *impf*, **раскрыть** (-óю) *pf* open; expose; reveal; discover; **~ся** open; uncover o.s.; come to light.
раскупáть *impf*, **раскупить** (-ýпит) *pf* buy up.
раскýпоривать *impf*, **раскýпорить** *pf* uncork, open.
раскусить (-ушý, -ýсишь) *pf*, **раскýсывать** *impf* bite through; see through.
рáсовый racial.
распáд disintegration; collapse. **распадáться** *impf of* **распáсться**
распаковáть *pf*, **распакóвывать** *impf* unpack.
распáрывать(ся *impf of* **распорóть(ся**
распáсться (-адётся) *pf* (*impf* **распадáться**) disintegrate, fall to pieces.
распахáть (-ашý, -áшешь) *pf*, **распáхивать**[1] *impf* plough up.
распáхивать[2] *impf*, **распахнýть** (-нý, -нёшь) *pf* throw open; **~ся** fly open, swing open.
распашóнка baby's vest.
распевáть *impf* sing.
распечáтать *pf*, **распечáтывать** *impf* open; unseal.
распиливать *impf*, **распилить** (-лю, -лишь) *pf* saw up.
распинáть *impf of* **распять**
расписáние time-table. **расписáть** (-ишý, -ишешь) *pf*, **расписывать** *impf* enter; assign; paint; **~ся** sign; register one's marriage; **+в**+*prep* sign for; acknowledge. **расписка** receipt. **расписнóй** painted, decorated.
распихáть *pf*, **распихивать** *impf* push, shove, stuff.
рас|плáвить (-влю) *pf*, **расплавлять** *impf* melt, fuse. **расплáвленный** molten.
расплáкаться (-áчусь) *pf* burst into tears.
распластáть *pf*, **распластывать** *impf* spread; flatten; split; **~ся** sprawl.
расплáта payment; retribution. **расплатиться** (-ачýсь, -áтишься) *pf*, **расплáчиваться** *impf* (+**с**+*instr*) pay off; get even; +**за**+*acc* pay for.
расплескáть(ся (-ещý(сь, -éщешь(ся) *pf*, **расплёскивать(ся** *impf* spill.
расплести (-етý, -етёшь; -ёл, -á) *pf*, **расплетáть** *impf* unplait; untwist.
рас|плодить(ся (-ожý(сь) *pf*.
расплывáться *impf*, **расплыться** (-ывётся; -ылся, -áсь) *pf* run. **расплывчатый** indistinct; vague.
расплющивать *impf*, **расплющить** (-щу) *pf* flatten out, hammer out.
распнý *etc.*: *see* **распять**
распознавáть (-наю, -наёшь) *impf*, **распознáть** *pf* recognize, identify; diagnose.
располагáть *impf* +*instr* have at one's disposal. **располагáться** *impf of* **расположиться**
расползáться *impf*, **расползтись** (-зётся; -óлзся, -злáсь) *pf* crawl (away); give at the seams.
расположéние disposition; arrangement; situation; ten-

dency; liking; mood. **располо́женный** disposed, inclined. **расположи́ть** (-жу́, -жишь) *pf* (*impf* **располага́ть**) dispose; set out; win over; **~ся** settle down.

распо́рка cross-bar, strut.

рас|поро́ть (-рю́, -решь) *pf* (*impf also* **распа́рывать**) unpick, rip; **~ся** rip, come undone.

распоряди́тель *m* manager. **распоряди́тельный** capable; efficient. **распоряди́ться** (-яжу́сь) *pf*, **распоряжа́ться** *impf* order, give orders; see; *+instr* manage, deal with. **распоря́док** (-дка) order; routine. **распоряже́ние** order; instruction; disposal, command.

распра́ва violence; reprisal.

распра́вить (-влю) *pf*, **расправля́ть** *impf* straighten; smooth out; spread.

распра́виться (-влюсь) *pf*, **расправля́ться** *impf* **с**+*instr* deal with severely; make short work of.

распределе́ние distribution; allocation. **распредели́тель** *m* distributor. **распредели́тельный** distributive, distributing; **~ щит** switchboard. **распредели́ть** *pf*, **распределя́ть** *impf* distribute; allocate.

распродава́ть (-даю́, -даёшь) *impf*, **распрода́ть** (-а́м, -а́шь, -а́ст, -ади́м; -о́дал, -а́, -о) *pf* sell off; sell out of. **распрода́жа** (clearance) sale.

распростёртый outstretched; prostrate.

распростране́ние spreading; dissemination. **распространённый** (-ён, -а́) widespread, prevalent. **распространи́ть** *pf*, **распространя́ть** *impf* spread; **~ся** spread.

ра́спря (*gen pl* -ей) quarrel.

распряга́ть *impf*, **распря́чь** (-ягу́, -яжёшь; -я́г, -ла́) *pf* unharness.

распрями́ться *pf*, **распрямля́ться** *impf* straighten up.

распуска́ть *impf*, **распусти́ть** (-ущу́, -у́стишь) *pf* dismiss; dissolve; let out; relax; let get out of hand; melt; spread; **~ся** open; come loose; dissolve; melt; get out of hand; let o.s. go.

распу́тать *pf* (*impf* **распу́тывать**) untangle; unravel.

распу́тица season of bad roads.

распу́тный dissolute. **распу́тство** debauchery.

распу́тывать *impf of* **распу́тать**

распу́тье crossroads.

распуха́ть *impf*, **распу́хнуть** (-ну; -у́х) *pf* swell (up).

распу́щенный undisciplined; spoilt; dissolute.

распыли́тель *m* spray, atomizer. **распыли́ть** *pf*, **распыля́ть** *impf* spray; pulverize; disperse.

распя́тие crucifixion; crucifix.

распя́ть (-пну́, -пнёшь) *pf* (*impf* **распина́ть**) crucify.

расса́да seedlings. **рассади́ть** (-ажу́, -а́дишь) *pf*, **расса́живать** *impf* plant out; seat; separate, seat separately.

расса́живаться *impf of* **рассе́сться**. **расса́сываться** *impf of* **рассоса́ться**

рассвести́ (-етёт; -ело́) *pf*, **рассвета́ть** *impf* dawn. **рассве́т** dawn.

рас|свирепе́ть (-е́ю) *pf*.

расседлáть *pf* unsaddle.
рассéивание dispersal, scattering. **рассéивать(ся** *impf of* **рассéять(ся**
рассекáть *impf of* **рассéчь**
расселéние settling, resettlement; separation.
рассéлина cleft, fissure.
расселúть *pf*, **расселя́ть** *impf* settle, resettle; separate.
рас|сердúть(ся (-жу́(сь, -рдишь-(ся) *pf*.
рассéсться (-ся́дусь) *pf* (*impf* **рассáживаться**) take seats.
рассéчь (-еку́, -ечёшь; -ёк, -лá) *pf* (*impf* **рассекáть**) cut (through); cleave.
рассéянность absent-mindedness; dispersion. **рассéянный** absent-minded; diffused; scattered. **рассéять** (-éю) *pf* (*impf* **рассéивать**) disperse, scatter; dispel; **~ся** disperse, scatter; clear; divert o.s.
расскáз story; account. **рассказáть** (-ажу́, -áжешь) *pf*, **расскáзывать** *impf* tell, recount. **расскáзчик** storyteller, narrator.
расслáбить (-блю) *pf*, **расслабля́ть** *impf* weaken; **~ся** relax.
расслáивать(ся *impf of* **расслоúть(ся**
расслéдование investigation, examination; inquiry; **произвестú** *~+gen* hold an inquiry into. **расслéдовать** *impf* & *pf* investigate, look into, hold an inquiry into.
расслоúть *pf* (*impf* **расслáивать**) divide into layers; **~ся** become stratified; flake off.
расслы́шать (-шу) *pf* catch.
рассмáтривать *impf of* **рассмотрéть**; examine; consider.
рас|смешúть (-шу́) *pf*.
рассмея́ться (-ею́сь, -еёшься) *pf* burst out laughing.
рассмотрéние examination; consideration. **рассмотрéть** (-рю́, -ришь) *pf* (*impf* **рассмáтривать**) examine, consider; discern, make out.
рассовáть (-сую́, -суёшь) *pf*, **рассóвывать** *impf* **по**+*dat* shove into.
рассóл brine; pickle.
рассóриться *pf* **с**+*instr* fall out with.
рас|сортировáть *pf*, **рассортирóвывать** *impf* sort out.
рассосáться (-сётся) *pf* (*impf* **рассáсываться**) resolve.
рассóхнуться (-нется; -óхся) *pf* (*impf* **рассыхáться**) crack.
расспрáшивать *impf*, **расспросúть** (-ошу́, -óсишь) *pf* question; make inquiries of.
рассрóчить (-чу) *pf* spread (over a period). **рассрóчка** instalment.
расставáние parting. **расставáться** (-таю́сь, -таёшься) *impf of* **расстáться**
расстáвить (-влю) *pf*, **расставля́ть** *impf* place, arrange; move apart. **расстанóвка** arrangement; pause.
расстáться (-áнусь) *pf* (*impf* **расставáться**) part, separate.
расстёгивать *impf*, **расстегну́ть** (-ну́, -нёшь) *pf* undo, unfasten; **~ся** come undone; undo one's coat.
расстелúть(ся, *etc.*: *see* **разостлáть(ся. расстилáть(ся**, **-áю(сь** *impf of* **разостлáть(ся**
расстоя́ние distance.
расстрáивать(ся *impf of* **расстрóить(ся**
расстрéл execution by firing squad. **расстрéливать** *impf*,

расстреля́ть *pf* shoot.
расстро́енный disordered; upset; out of tune. **расстро́ить** *pf* (*impf* **расстра́ивать**) upset; thwart; disturb; throw into confusion; put out of tune; **~ся** be upset; get out of tune; fall into confusion; fall through. **расстро́йство** upset; disarray; confusion; frustration.
расступа́ться *impf*, **расступи́ться** (-у́пится) *pf* part, make way.
рассуди́тельный reasonable; sensible. **рассуди́ть** (-ужу́, -у́дишь) *pf* judge; think; decide. **рассу́док** (-дка) reason; intellect. **рассужда́ть** *impf* reason; +**о**+*prep* discuss. **рассужде́ние** reasoning; discussion; argument.
рассую́ *etc.*: *see* **рассова́ть**
рассчи́танный deliberate; intended. **рассчита́ть** *pf*, **рассчи́тывать** *impf*, **расче́сть** (разочту́, -тёшь; расчёл, разочла́) *pf* calculate; count; depend; **~ся** settle accounts.
рассыла́ть *impf of* **разосла́ть. рассы́лка** distribution. **рассы́льный** *sb* delivery man.
рассы́пать (-плю) *pf*, **рассыпа́ть** *impf* spill; scatter; **~ся** spill, scatter; spread out; crumble. **рассы́пчатый** friable; crumbly.
рассыха́ться *impf of* **рассо́хнуться. расся́дусь** *etc.*: *see* **рассе́сться. раста́лкивать** *impf of* **растолка́ть. раста́пливать(ся** *impf of* **растопи́ть(ся**
растаска́ть *pf*, **раста́скивать** *impf*, **растащи́ть** (-щу́, -щишь) *pf* pilfer, filch.
растащи́ть *see* **растаска́ть.**
рас|та́ять (-а́ю) *pf.*
раство́р[2] opening, span. **раство́р**[1] solution; mortar. **раствори́мый** soluble. **раствори́тель** *m* solvent. **раствори́ть**[1] *pf* (*impf* **растворя́ть**) dissolve; **~ся** dissolve.
раствори́ть[2] (-рю́, -ришь) *pf* (*impf* **растворя́ть**) open; **~ся** open.
растворя́ть(ся *impf of* **раствори́ть(ся. растека́ться** *impf of* **растéчься**
расте́ние plant.
растере́ть (разотру́, -трёшь; растёр) *pf* (*impf* **растира́ть**) grind; spread; rub; massage.
растерза́ть *pf*, **растёрзывать** *impf* tear to pieces.
растéрянность confusion, dismay. **растéрянный** confused, dismayed. **растеря́ть** *pf* lose; **~ся** get lost; lose one's head.
расте́чься (-ечётся, -еку́тся; -тёкся, -ла́сь) *pf* (*impf* **растека́ться**) run; spread.
расти́ (-ту́, -тёшь; рос, -ла́) *impf* grow; grow up.
растира́ние grinding; rubbing, massage. **растира́ть(ся** *impf of* **растере́ть(ся**
расти́тельность vegetation; hair. **расти́тельный** vegetable. **расти́ть** (ращу́) *impf* bring up; train; grow.
растлева́ть *impf*, **растли́ть** *pf* seduce; corrupt.
растолка́ть *pf* (*impf* **раста́лкивать**) push apart; shake.
растолкова́ть *pf*, **растолко́вывать** *impf* explain.
рас|толо́чь (-лку́, -лчёшь; -ло́к, -лкла́) *pf.*
растолсте́ть (-е́ю) *pf* put on weight.
растопи́ть[1] (-плю́, -пишь) *pf*

(*impf* **растáпливать**) melt; thaw; **~ся** melt.
растопи́ть[2] (-плю́, -пишь) *pf* (*impf* **растáпливать**) light, kindle; **~ся** begin to burn.
растоптáть (-пчу́, -пчешь) *pf* trample, stamp on.
расторгáть *impf*, **растóргнуть** (-ну; -óрг) *pf* annul, dissolve. **расторжéние** annulment, dissolution.
растορόпный quick; efficient.
расточáть *impf*, **расточи́ть** (-чу́) *pf* squander, dissipate. **расточи́тельный** extravagant, wasteful.
растрави́ть (-влю́, -вишь) *pf*, **растравля́ть** *impf* irritate.
растрáта spending; waste; embezzlement. **растрáтить** (-áчу) *pf*, **растрáчивать** *impf* spend; waste; embezzle.
растрёпанный dishevelled; tattered. **рас|трепáть** (-плю́, -плешь) *pf* disarrange; tatter.
растрéскаться *pf*, **растрéскиваться** *impf* crack, chap.
растрóгать *pf* move, touch; **~ся** be moved.
растýщий growing.
растя́гивать *impf*, **растяну́ть** (-ну́, -нешь) *pf* stretch (out); strain, sprain; drag out; **~ся** stretch; drag on; sprawl. **растяжéние** tension; strain, sprain. **растяжи́мый** tensile; stretchable. **растя́нутый** stretched; long-winded.
рас|фасовáть *pf*.
расформировáть *pf*, **расформирóвывать** *impf* break up; disband.
расхáживать *impf* walk about; pace up and down.
расхвáливать *impf*, **расхвали́ть** (-лю́, -лишь) *pf* lavish praises on.
расхватáть *pf*, **расхвáтывать** *impf* seize on, buy up.
расхити́тель *m* embezzler.
расхи́тить (-и́щу) *pf*, **расхищáть** *impf* steal, misappropriate. **расхищéние** misappropriation.
расхля́банный loose; lax.
расхóд expenditure; consumption; *pl* expenses, outlay.
расходи́ться (-ожу́сь, -óдишься) *impf of* **разойти́сь. расхóдование** expense, expenditure. **расхóдовать** *impf* (*pf* **из~**) spend; consume. **расхождéние** divergence.
расхолáживать *impf*, **расхолоди́ть** (-ожу́) *pf* damp the ardour of.
расхотéть (-очу́, -óчешь, -оти́м) *pf* no longer want.
расхохотáться (-очу́сь, -óчешься) *pf* burst out laughing.
расцарáпать *pf* scratch (all over).
расцвести́ (-ету́, -етёшь; -ёл, -á) *pf*, **расцветáть** *impf* blossom; flourish. **расцвéт** blossoming (out); flowering, heyday.
расцвéтка colours; colouring.
расцéнивать *impf*, **расцени́ть** (-ню́, -нишь) *pf* estimate, value; consider. **расцéнка** valuation; price; (wage-)rate.
расцепи́ть (-плю́, -пишь) *pf*, **расцепля́ть** *impf* uncouple, unhook.
расчесáть (-ешу́, -éшешь) *pf* (*impf* **расчёсывать**) comb; scratch. **расчёска** comb.
расчéсть *etc.*: *see* **рассчитáть.**
расчёсывать *impf of* **расчесáть**
расчёт[1] calculation; estimate; gain; settlement. **расчётливый** thrifty; careful. **расчёт-**

ный calculation; pay; accounts; calculated.
расчи́стить (-и́щу) *pf*, **расчища́ть** *impf* clear; **~ся** clear. **расчи́стка** clearing.
рас|членить *pf*, **расчленя́ть** *impf* dismember; divide.
расшата́ть *pf*, **расша́тывать** *impf* shake loose, make rickety; impair.
расшевели́ть (-лю́, -е́ли́шь) *pf* stir; rouse.
расшиба́ть *impf*, **расшиби́ть** (-бу́, -бёшь; -и́б) *pf* smash to pieces; hurt; stub; **~ся** hurt o.s.
расшива́ть *impf of* **расши́ть**
расшире́ние widening; expansion; dilation, dilatation. **расши́рить** *pf*, **расширя́ть** *impf* widen; enlarge; expand; **~ся** broaden, widen; expand, dilate.
расши́ть (разошью́, -шьёшь) *pf* (*impf* **расшива́ть**) embroider; unpick.
расшифрова́ть *pf*, **расшифро́вывать** *impf* decipher.
расшнурова́ть *pf*, **расшнуро́вывать** *impf* unlace.
расще́лина crevice.
расщепи́ть (-плю́) *pf*, **расщепля́ть** *impf* split; **~ся** split. **расщепле́ние** splitting; fission.
ратифици́ровать *impf* & *pf* ratify.
рать army, battle.
ра́унд round.
рафини́рованный refined.
рацио́н ration.
рационализа́ция rationalization. **рационализи́ровать** *impf* & *pf* rationalize. **рациона́льный** rational; efficient.
ра́ция walkie-talkie.
рвану́ться (-ну́сь, -нёшься) *pf* dart, dash.
рва́ный torn; lacerated. **рвать**[1] (рву, рвёшь; рвал, -а́, -о) *impf* tear (out); pull out; pick; blow up; break off; **~ся** break; tear; burst, explode; be bursting.
рвать[2] (рвёт; рва́ло) *impf* (*pf* **вы́~**) *impers+acc* vomit.
рвач (-а́) self-seeker.
рве́ние zeal.
рво́та vomiting.
реабилита́ция rehabilitation. **реабилити́ровать** *impf* & *pf* rehabilitate.
реаги́ровать *impf* (*pf* **от~**, **про~**) react.
реакти́в reagent. **реакти́вный** reactive; jet-propelled.
реа́ктор reactor.
реакционе́р reactionary. **реакцио́нный** reactionary. **реа́кция** reaction.
реализа́ция realization. **реали́зм** realism. **реализова́ть** *impf* & *pf* realize. **реали́ст** realist. **реалисти́ческий** realistic.
реа́льность reality; practicability. **реа́льный** real; practicable.
ребёнок (-нка; *pl* ребя́та, -я́т *and* де́ти, -е́й) child; infant.
ребро́ (*pl* рёбра, -бер) rib; edge.
ребя́та (-я́т) *pl* children; guys; lads. **ребя́ческий** child's; childish. **ребя́чество** childishness. **ребя́читься** (-чусь) *impf* be childish.
рёв roar; howl.
рева́нш revenge; return match.
релера́нс curtsey.
реве́ть (-ву́, -вёшь) *impf* roar; bellow; howl.
ревизио́нный inspection; auditing. **реви́зия** inspection; audit; revision. **ревизо́р** inspector.

ревмати́зм rheumatism.
ревни́вый jealous. **ревнова́ть** *impf* (*pf* **при~**) be jealous. **ре́вностный** zealous. **ре́вность** jealousy.
револьве́р revolver.
революционе́р revolutionary. **революцио́нный** revolutionary. **револю́ция** revolution.
рега́та regatta.
ре́гби *neut indecl* rugby.
ре́гент regent.
регио́н region. **региона́льный** regional.
регистра́тор registrar. **регистрату́ра** registry. **регистра́ция** registration. **регистри́ровать** *impf* & *pf* (*pf also* **за~**) register, record; **~ся** register; register one's marriage.
регла́мент standing orders; time-limit. **регламента́ция** regulation. **регламенти́ровать** *impf* & *pf* regulate.
регресси́ровать *impf* regress.
регули́ровать *impf* (*pf* **от~, у~**) regulate; adjust. **регули́ровщик** traffic controller. **регуля́рный** regular. **регуля́тор** regulator.
редакти́ровать *impf* (*pf* **от~**) edit. **реда́ктор** editor. **реда́кторский** editorial. **редакцио́нный** editorial, editing. **реда́кция** editorial staff; editorial office; editing.
реде́ть (-е́ет) *impf* (*pf* **по~**) thin (out).
реди́с radishes. **реди́ска** radish.
ре́дкий (-док, -дка́, -о) thin; sparse; rare. **ре́дко** *adv* sparsely; rarely, seldom. **ре́дкость** rarity.
редколле́гия editorial board.
рее́стр register.
режи́м régime; routine; procedure; regimen; conditions.
режиссёр-(постано́вщик) producer; director.
ре́жущий cutting, sharp.
ре́зать (ре́жу) *impf* (*pf* **за~, про~, с~**) cut; engrave; kill, slaughter.
резви́ться (-влю́сь) *impf* gambol, play. **ре́звый** frisky, playful.
резе́рв reserve. **резе́рвный** reserve; back-up.
резервуа́р reservoir.
резе́ц (-зца́) cutter; chisel; incisor.
резиде́нция residence.
рези́на rubber. **рези́нка** rubber; elastic band. **рези́новый** rubber.
ре́зкий sharp; harsh; abrupt; shrill. **резно́й** carved. **резня́** carnage.
резолю́ция resolution.
резона́нс resonance; response.
результа́т result.
резьба́ carving, fretwork.
резюме́ *neut indecl* résumé.
рейд[1] roads, roadstead.
рейд[2] raid.
ре́йка lath, rod.
рейс trip; voyage; flight.
рейту́зы (-у́з) *pl* leggings; riding breeches.
река́ (*acc* ре́ку́; *pl* -и, ре́ка́м) river.
ре́квием requiem.
реквизи́т props.
рекла́ма advertising, advertisement. **реклами́ровать** *impf* & *pf* advertise. **рекла́мный** publicity.
рекоменда́тельный of recommendation. **рекоменда́ция** recommendation; refer-

ence. **рекомендова́ть** *impf* & *pf* (*pf also* **от~, по~**) recommend; **~ся** introduce o.s.; be advisable.

реконструи́ровать *impf* & *pf* reconstruct. **реконстру́кция** reconstruction.

реко́рд record. **реко́рдный** record, record-breaking. **рекордсме́н, -е́нка** record-holder.

ре́ктор principal (*of university*).

реле́ (*electr*) *neut indecl* relay.

религио́зный religious. **рели́гия** religion.

рели́квия relic.

релье́ф relief. **релье́фный** relief; raised, bold.

рельс rail.

рема́рка stage direction.

реме́нь (-мня́) *m* strap; belt.

реме́сленник artisan, craftsman. **реме́сленный** handicraft; mechanical. **ремесло́** (*pl* -ёсла, -ёсел) craft; trade.

ремо́нт repair(s); maintenance. **ремонти́ровать** *impf* & *pf* (*pf also* **от~**) repair; recondition. **ремо́нтный** repair.

ре́нта rent; income. **рента́бельный** paying, profitable.

рентге́н X-rays. **рентге́новский** X-ray. **рентгено́лог** radiologist. **рентгеноло́гия** radiology.

реорганиза́ция reorganization. **реорганизова́ть** *impf* & *pf* reorganize.

ре́па turnip.

репатрии́ровать *impf* & *pf* repatriate.

репертуа́р repertoire.

репети́ровать *impf* (*pf* **от~, про~, с~**) rehearse; coach. **репети́тор** coach. **репети́ция** rehearsal.

ре́плика retort; cue.

репорта́ж report; reporting.

репортёр reporter.

репре́ссия repression.

репроду́ктор loud-speaker.

репроду́кция reproduction.

репута́ция reputation.

ресни́ца eyelash.

респу́блика republic. **республика́нский** republican.

рессо́ра spring.

реставра́ция restoration.

реставри́ровать *impf* & *pf* (*pf also* **от~**) restore.

рестора́н restaurant.

ресу́рс resort; *pl* resources.

ретрансля́тор (radio-)relay.

рефера́т synopsis, abstract; paper, essay.

рефере́ндум referendum.

рефле́кс reflex. **рефле́ктор** reflector.

рефо́рма reform. **реформи́ровать** *impf* & *pf* reform.

рефрижера́тор refrigerator.

рецензи́ровать *impf* (*pf* **про~**) review. **реце́нзия** review.

реце́пт prescription; recipe.

рециди́в relapse. **рециди́вист** recidivist.

речево́й speech; vocal.

ре́чка river. **речно́й** river.

речь (*gen pl* -е́й) speech.

реша́ть(ся *impf of* **реши́ть(ся. реша́ющий** decisive, deciding. **реше́ние** decision; solution.

решётка grating; grille, railing; lattice; trellis; fender, (fire)guard; (fire-)grate; tail.

решето́ (*pl* -ёта) sieve. **решётчатый** lattice, latticed.

реши́мость resoluteness; resolve. **реши́тельно** *adv* resolutely; definitely; absolutely. **реши́тельность** determination. **реши́тельный** definite;

decisive. **реши́ть** (-шу́) *pf* (*impf* **реша́ть**) decide; solve; **~ся** make up one's mind.
ржаве́ть (-е́ет) *impf* (*pf* **за~, по~**) rust. **ржа́вчина** rust. **ржа́вый** rusty.
ржано́й rye.
ржать (ржу, ржёшь) *impf* neigh.
ри́млянин (*pl* -яне, -ян), **ри́млянка** Roman. **ри́мский** Roman.
ринг boxing ring.
ри́нуться (-нусь) *pf* rush, dart.
рис rice.
риск risk. **риско́ванный** risky; risqué. **рискова́ть** *impf*, **рискну́ть** *pf* run risks; *+instr or inf* risk.
рисова́ние drawing. **рисова́ть** *impf* (*pf* **на~**) draw; paint, depict; **~ся** be silhouetted; appear; pose.
ри́совый rice.
рису́нок (-нка) drawing; figure; pattern, design.
ритм rhythm. **ритми́ческий, ритми́чный** rhythmic.
ритуа́л ritual.
риф reef.
ри́фма rhyme. **рифмова́ть** *impf* rhyme; **~ся** rhyme.
робе́ть (-е́ю) *impf* (*pf* **о~**) be timid. **ро́бкий** (-бок, -бка́, -о) timid, shy. **ро́бость** shyness.
ро́бот robot.
ров (рва, *loc* -у) ditch.
рове́сник coeval. **ро́вно** *adv* evenly; exactly; absolutely. **ро́вный** flat; even; level; equable; exact; equal. **ровня́ть** *impf* (*pf* **с~**) even, level.
рог (*pl* -а́, -о́в) horn; antler. **рога́тка** catapult. **рога́тый** horned. **рогови́ца** cornea. **рогово́й** horn; horny; horn-rimmed.
род (*loc* -у́; *pl* -ы́) family, kin, clan; birth, origin, stock; generation; genus; sort, kind. **роди́льный** maternity. **ро́дина** native land; homeland. **ро́динка** birth-mark. **роди́тели** (-ей) *pl* parents. **роди́тельный** genitive. **роди́тельский** parental. **роди́ть** (рожу́, -и́л, -ила́, -о) *impf* & *pf* (*impf also* **рожа́ть, рожда́ть**) give birth to; **~ся** be born.
родни́к (-а́) spring.
родни́ть *impf* (*pf* **по~**) make related, link; **~ся** become related. **родн|о́й** own; native; home; **~о́й брат** brother; **~ы́е** *sb pl* relatives. **родня́** relative(s); kinsfolk. **родово́й** tribal; ancestral; generic; gender. **родонача́льник** ancestor; father. **родосло́вн|ый** genealogical; **~ая** *sb* genealogy, pedigree. **ро́дственник** relative. **ро́дственный** related. **родство́** relationship, kinship. **ро́ды** (-ов) *pl* childbirth; labour.
ро́жа (ugly) mug.
рожа́ть, рожда́ть(ся *impf of* **роди́ть(ся. рожда́емость** birth-rate. **рожде́ние** birth. **рожде́ственский** Christmas. **Рождество́** Christmas.
рожь (ржи) rye.
ро́за rose.
ро́зга (*gen pl* -зог) birch.
ро́здал *etc.*: *see* **разда́ть**
розе́тка electric socket, power point; rosette.
ро́зница retail; **в ~у** retail. **ро́зничный** retail. **рознь** difference; dissension.
ро́знял *etc.*: *see* **разня́ть**
ро́зовый pink.
ро́зыгрыш draw; drawn game.

ро́зыск search; inquiry.

рои́ться swarm. **рой** (*loc* -ю́; *pl* -и́, -ёв) swarm.

рок fate.

рокиро́вка castling.

рок-му́зыка rock music.

роково́й fateful; fatal.

ро́кот roar, rumble. **рокота́ть** (-о́чет) *impf* roar, rumble.

ро́лик roller; castor; *pl* roller skates.

роль (*gen pl* -е́й) role.

ром rum.

рома́н novel; romance. **романи́ст** novelist.

рома́нс (*mus*) romance.

рома́нтик romantic. **рома́нтика** romance. **романти́ческий, романти́чный** romantic.

рома́шка camomile.

ромб rhombus.

роня́ть *impf* (*pf* **урони́ть**) drop.

ро́пот murmur, grumble. **ропта́ть** (-пщу́, -пщешь) *impf* murmur, grumble.

рос *etc.*: *see* **расти́**

роса́ (*pl* -ы) dew. **роси́стый** dewy.

роско́шный luxurious; luxuriant. **ро́скошь** luxury; luxuriance.

ро́слый strapping.

ро́спись painting(s), mural(s).

ро́спуск dismissal; disbandment.

росси́йский Russian. **Росси́я** Russia.

ро́ссыпи *f pl* deposit.

рост growth; increase; height, stature.

ро́стбиф roast beef.

ростовщи́к (-а́) usurer, money-lender.

ро́сто́к (-тка́) sprout, shoot.

ро́счерк flourish.

рот (рта, *loc* рту) mouth.

ро́та company.

рота́тор duplicator.

ро́тный company; *sb* company commander.

ротозе́й, -зе́йка gaper, rubberneck; scatter-brain.

ро́ща grove.

ро́ю *etc.*: *see* **рыть**

роя́ль *m* (grand) piano.

ртуть mercury.

руба́нок (-нка) plane.

руба́ха, руба́шка shirt.

рубе́ж (-а́) boundary, border(line); line; **за ~о́м** abroad.

рубе́ц (-бца́) scar; weal; hem; tripe.

руби́н ruby. **руби́новый** ruby; ruby-coloured.

руби́ть (-блю́, -бишь) *impf* (*pf* **с~**) fell; hew, chop; mince; build (of logs).

ру́бище rags.

ру́бка[1] felling; chopping; mincing.

ру́бка[2] deck house; **боева́я ~** conning-tower; **рулева́я ~** wheelhouse.

рублёвка one-rouble note. **рублёвый** (one-)rouble.

ру́бленый minced, chopped; of logs.

рубль (-я́) *m* rouble.

ру́брика rubric, heading.

ру́бчатый ribbed. **ру́бчик** scar; rib.

ру́гань abuse, swearing. **руга́тельный** abusive. **руга́тельство** oath, swear-word. **руга́ть** *impf* (*pf* **вы́~, об~, от~**) curse, swear at; abuse; **~ся** curse, swear; swear at one another.

руда́ (*pl* -ы) ore. **рудни́к** (-а́) mine, pit. **рудни́чный** mine, pit; **~ газ** fire-damp. **рудоко́п** miner.

руже́йный rifle, gun. **ружьё** (*pl* -ья, -жей, -ьям) gun, rifle.

руи́на *usu pl* ruin.
рука́ (*acc* -у, *pl* -и, рук, -а́м) hand; arm; **идти́ по́д руку с**+*instr* walk arm in arm with; **под руко́й** at hand; **руко́й пода́ть** a stone's throw away; **э́то мне на́ руку** that suits me.
рука́в (-а́; *pl* -а́, -о́в) sleeve. **рукави́ца** mitten; gauntlet.
руководи́тель *m* leader; manager; instructor; guide. **руководи́ть** (-ожу́) *impf* +*instr* lead; guide; direct, manage. **руково́дство** leadership; guidance; direction; guide; handbook, manual; leaders. **руково́дствоваться**+*instr* follow; be guided by. **руководя́щий** leading; guiding.
рукоде́лие needlework.
рукомо́йник washstand.
рукопа́шный hand-to-hand.
рукопи́сный manuscript. **ру́копись** manuscript.
рукоплеска́ние applause. **рукоплеска́ть** (-ещу́, -е́щешь) *impf* +*dat* applaud.
рукопожа́тие handshake.
рукоя́тка handle.
рулево́й steering; *sb* helmsman.
руле́тка tape-measure; roulette.
рули́ть *impf* (*pf* **вы́~**) taxi.
руль (-я́) *m* rudder; helm; (steering-)wheel; handlebar.
румы́н (*gen pl* -ы́н), **~ка** Romanian. **Румы́ния** Romania. **румы́нский** Romanian.
румя́на (-я́н) *pl* rouge. **румя́нец** (-нца) (high) colour; flush; blush. **румя́ный** rosy, ruddy.
ру́пор megaphone; mouthpiece.
руса́к (-а́) hare.
руса́лка mermaid.
русифици́ровать *impf & pf* Russify.
ру́сло river-bed; course.
ру́сский Russian; *sb* Russian.
ру́сый light brown.
Русь (*hist*)Russia.
рути́на routine.
ру́хлядь junk.
ру́хнуть (-ну) *pf* crash down.
руча́тельство guarantee. **руча́ться** *impf* (*pf* **поручи́ться**) +**за**+*acc* vouch for, guarantee.
руче́й (-чья́) brook.
ру́чка handle; (door-)knob; (chair-)arm; pen. **ручн|о́й** hand; arm; manual; tame; **~ы́е часы́** wrist-watch.
ру́шить (-у) *impf* (*pf* **об~**) pull down; **~ся** collapse.
РФ *abbr* (*of* **Росси́йская Федера́ция**) Russian Federation.
ры́ба fish. **рыба́к** (-а́) fisherman. **рыба́лка** fishing. **рыба́цкий, рыба́чий** fishing. **ры́бий** fish; fishy; **~ жир** cod-liver oil. **ры́бный** fish.
рыболо́в fisherman. **рыболо́вный** fishing.
рыво́к (-вка́) jerk.
рыда́ние sobbing. **рыда́ть** *impf* sob.
ры́жий (рыж, -а́, -е) red, red-haired; chestnut.
ры́ло snout; mug.
ры́нок (-нка) market; market-place. **ры́ночный** market.
рыса́к (-а́) trotter.
рысь[1] (*loc* -и́) trot; **~ю, на рыся́х** at a trot.
рысь[2] lynx.
ры́твина rut, groove. **ры́ть(ся** (ро́ю(сь) *impf* (*pf* **вы́~, от~**) dig; rummage.
рыхли́ть *impf* (*pf* **вз~, раз~**) loosen. **ры́хлый** (-л, -а́, -о) friable; loose.
ры́царский chivalrous. **ры́царь** *m* knight.
рыча́г (-а́) lever.
рыча́ть (-чу́) *impf* growl, snarl.

рья́ный zealous.
рюкза́к (*gen* -а́) rucksack.
рю́мка wineglass.
ряби́на[1] rowan, mountain ash.
ряби́на[2] pit, pock. **ряби́ть** (-и́т) *impf* ripple; *impers*: **у меня́ ряби́т в глаза́х** I am dazzled. **рябо́й** pock-marked. **ря́бчик** hazel hen, hazel grouse. **рябь** ripples; dazzle.
ря́вкать *impf*, **ря́вкнуть** (-ну) *pf* bellow, roar.
ряд (*loc* -у́; *pl* -ы́) row; line; file, rank; series; number. **рядово́й** ordinary; common; ~ **соста́в** rank and file; *sb* private. **ря́дом** *adv* alongside; close by; +**с**+*instr* next to.
ря́са cassock.

С

с, со *prep* I. +*gen* from; since; off; for, with; on; by; **с ра́дости** for joy; **с утра́** since morning. II. +*acc* about; the size of; **с неде́лю** for about a week. III. +*instr* with; and; **мы с ва́ми** you and I; **что с ва́ми?** what is the matter?
са́бля (*gen pl* -бель) sabre.
сабота́ж sabotage. **саботи́ровать** *impf* & *pf* sabotage.
са́ван shroud; blanket.
с|агити́ровать *pf*.
сад (*loc* -у́; *pl* -ы́) garden. **сади́ть** (сажу́, са́дишь) *impf* (*pf* **по~**) plant. **сади́ться** (сажу́сь) *impf of* **сесть**. **садо́вник, -ница** gardener. **садово́дство** gardening; horticulture. **садо́вый** garden; cultivated.
сади́зм sadism. **сади́ст** sadist. **сади́стский** sadistic.
са́жа soot.
сажа́ть *impf* (*pf* **посади́ть**) plant; seat; set, put. **са́женец** (-нца) seedling; sapling.
са́же́нь (*pl* -и, -жен *or* -же́не́й) sazhen (*2.13 metres*).
сажу́ *etc.*: *see* **сади́ть**
са́йка roll.
саксофо́н saxophone.
с|акти́ровать *pf*.
сала́зки (-зок) *pl* toboggan.
сала́т lettuce; salad.
са́ло fat, lard; suet; tallow.
сало́н salon; saloon.
салфе́тка napkin.
са́льный greasy; tallow; obscene.
салю́т salute. **салютова́ть** *impf* & *pf* (*pf also* **от~**) +*dat* salute.
сам (-ого́) *m*, **сама́** (-о́й *acc* -оё) *f*, **само́** (-ого́) *neut*, **са́ми** (-и́х) *pl*, *pron* -self, -selves; myself, *etc.*, ourselves, *etc.*; ~ **по себе́** in itself; by o.s.; ~ **собо́й** of itself, of its own accord; **~о́ собо́й (разуме́ется)** of course; it goes without saying.
са́мбо *neut indecl abbr* (*of* **самозащи́та без ору́жия**) unarmed combat.
саме́ц (-мца́) male. **са́мка** female.
само- *in comb* self-, auto-. **самобы́тный** original, distinctive. **~возгора́ние** spontaneous combustion. **~во́льный** wilful; unauthorized. **~де́льный** home-made. **~держа́вие** autocracy. **~держа́вный** autocratic. **~де́ятельность** amateur work, amateur performance; initiative. **~дово́льный** self-satisfied. **~ду́р** petty tyrant. **~ду́рство** high-handedness. **~забве́ние** selflessness. **~забве́нный** selfless. **~защи́та** self-defence. **~зва́нец** (-нца) impostor,

pretender. **~ка́т** scooter. **~кри́тика** self-criticism. **~люби́вый** proud; touchy. **~любие** pride, self-esteem. **~мне́ние** conceit, self-importance. **~надéянный** presumptuous. **~облада́ние** self-control. **~обма́н** self-deception. **~оборо́на** self-defence. **~образова́ние** self-education. **~обслу́живание** self-service. **~определе́ние** self-determination. **~отве́рженность** selflessness. **~отве́рженный** selfless. **~поже́ртвование** self-sacrifice. **~ро́док** (-дка) nugget; person with natural talent. **~сва́л** tip-up lorry. **~созна́ние** (self-)consciousness. **~сохране́ние** self-preservation. **~стоя́тельность** independence. **~стоя́тельный** independent. **~су́д** lynch law, mob law. **~тёк** drift. **~тёком** *adv* by gravity; of its own accord. **~уби́йственный** suicidal. **~уби́йство** suicide. **~уби́йца** *m* & *f* suicide. **~уваже́ние** self-respect. **~уве́ренность** self-confidence. **~уве́ренный** self-confident. **~униже́ние** self-abasement. **~управле́ние** self-government. **~управля́ющийся** self-governing. **~упра́вный** arbitrary. **~учи́тель** *m* self-instructor, manual. **~у́чка** *m* & *f* self-taught person. **~хо́дный** self-propelled. **~чу́вствие** general state; **как ва́ше ~чу́вствие?** how do you feel?

самова́р samovar.

самого́н home-made vodka.

самолёт aeroplane.

самоцве́т semi-precious stone.

са́мый *pron* (the) very, (the) right; (the) same; (the) most.

сан dignity, office.

санато́рий sanatorium.

санда́лия sandal.

са́ни (-е́й) *pl* sledge, sleigh.

санита́р medical orderly; stretcher-bearer. **санитари́я** sanitation. **санита́рка** nurse.

санита́рн|ый medical; health; sanitary; **~ая маши́на** ambulance; **~ый у́зел = сану́зел.**

са́нки (-нок) *pl* sledge; toboggan.

санкциони́ровать *impf* & *pf* sanction. **са́нкция** sanction.

сано́вник dignitary.

санпу́нкт medical centre.

санскри́т Sanskrit.

санте́хник plumber.

сантиме́тр centimetre; tape-measure.

сану́зел (-зла́) sanitary arrangements; WC.

санча́сть (*gen pl* -е́й) medical unit.

сапёр sapper.

сапо́г(-а́; *gen pl* -о́г) boot. **сапо́жник** shoemaker; cobbler. **сапо́жный** shoe.

сапфи́р sapphire.

сара́й shed; barn.

саранча́ locust(s).

сарафа́н sarafan; pinafore dress.

сарде́лька small fat sausage.

сарди́на sardine.

сарка́зм sarcasm. **саркасти́ческий** sarcastic.

сатана́ *m* Satan. **сатани́нский** satanic.

сателли́т satellite.

сати́н sateen.

сати́ра satire. **сати́рик** satirist. **сатири́ческий** satirical.

Сау́довская Ара́вия Saudi Arabia.

сафья́н morocco. **сафья́новый** morocco.

са́хар sugar. **сахари́н** saccharine. **са́харистый** sugary. **са́харница** sugar-basin. **са́харн|ый** sugar; sugary; **~ый заво́д** sugar-refinery; **~ый песо́к** granulated sugar; **~ая пу́дра** castor sugar; **~ая свёкла** sugar-beet.
сачо́к (-чка́) net.
сба́вить (-влю) *pf*, **сбавля́ть** *impf* take off; reduce.
с|баланси́ровать *pf*.
сбе́гать[1] *pf* run; **+за**+*instr* run for. **сбега́ть**[2] *impf*, **сбежа́ть** (-егу́) *pf* run down (from); run away; disappear; **~ся** come running.
сберега́тельная ка́сса savings bank. **сберега́ть** *impf*, **сбере́чь** (-егу́, -ежёшь; -ёг, -ла́) *pf* save; save up; preserve. **сбереже́ние** economy; saving; savings. **сберка́сса** savings bank.
сбива́ть *impf*, **с|бить** (собью́, -бьёшь) *pf* bring down, knock down; knock off; distract; wear down; knock together; churn; whip, whisk; **~ся** be dislodged; slip; go wrong; be confused; **~ся с пути́** lose one's way; **~ся с ног** be run off one's feet. **сби́вчивый** confused; inconsistent.
сближа́ть *impf*, **сбли́зить** (-и́жу) *pf* bring (closer) together, draw together; **~ся** draw together; become good friends. **сближе́ние** rapprochement; closing in.
сбо́ку *adv* from one side; on one side.
сбор collection; duty; fee, toll; takings; gathering. **сбо́рище** crowd, mob. **сбо́рка** assembling, assembly; gather. **сбо́рник** collection. **сбо́рный** assembly; mixed, combined; prefabricated; detachable. **сбо́рочный** assembly. **сбо́рщик** collector; assembler.
сбра́сывать(ся *impf of* **сбро́сить(ся**
сбрива́ть *impf*, **сбрить** (сбре́ю) *pf* shave off.
сброд riff-raff.
сброс fault, break. **сбро́сить** (-о́шу) *pf* (*impf* **сбра́сывать**) throw down, drop; throw off; shed; discard.
сбру́я (*collect*) (riding) tack.
сбыва́ть *impf*, **сбыть** (сбу́ду; сбыл, -а́, -о) *pf* sell, market; get rid of; **~ся** come true, be realized. **сбыт** (*no pl*) sale; market.
св. *abbr* (*of* **свято́й**) Saint.
сва́дебный wedding. **сва́дьба** (*gen pl* -деб) wedding.
сва́ливать *impf*, **с|вали́ть** (-лю́, -лишь) *pf* throw down; overthrow; pile up; **~ся** fall (down), collapse. **сва́лка** dump; scuffle.
с|валя́ть *pf*.
сва́ривать *impf*, **с|вари́ть** (-рю́, -ришь) *pf* boil; cook; weld. **сва́рка** welding.
сварли́вый cantankerous.
сварно́й welded. **сва́рочный** welding. **сва́рщик** welder.
сва́стика swastika.
сва́тать *impf* (*pf* **по~**, **со~**) propose as a husband or wife; propose to; **~ся к**+*dat or* **за**+*acc* propose to.
сва́я pile.
све́дение piece of information; knowledge; *pl* information, intelligence; knowledge. **све́дущий** knowledgeable; versed.
сведу́ *etc.*: *see* **свести́**
свежезаморо́женный fresh-frozen; chilled. **све́жесть**

freshness. **свеже́ть** (-е́ет) *impf* (*pf* **по~**) become cooler; freshen. **све́жий** (-еж, -á, -ó, -и) fresh; new.
свезти́ (-зу́, -зёшь; свёз, -ла́) *pf* (*impf* **свози́ть**) take; bring *or* take down *or* away.
свёкла beet, beetroot.
свёкор (-кра) father-in-law. **свекро́вь** mother-in-law.
свёл *etc.*: *see* **свести́**
сверга́ть *impf*, **све́ргнуть** (-ну; сверг) *pf* throw down, overthrow. **сверже́ние** overthrow.
све́рить *pf* (*impf* **сверя́ть**) collate.
сверка́ть *impf* sparkle, twinkle; glitter; gleam. **сверкну́ть** (-ну́, -нёшь) *pf* flash.
сверли́льный drill, drilling; boring. **сверли́ть** *impf* (*pf* **про~**) drill; bore (through); nag. **сверло́** drill. **сверля́щий** gnawing, piercing.
сверну́ть (-ну́, -нёшь) *pf* (*impf* **свёртывать, свора́чивать**) roll (up); turn; curtail, cut down; **~ ше́ю**+*dat* wring the neck of; **~ся** roll up, curl up; curdle, coagulate; contract.
све́рстник contemporary.
свёрток (-тка) package, bundle. **свёртывание** rolling (up); curdling; coagulation; curtailment, cuts. **свёртывать(ся** *impf of* **сверну́ть(ся**
сверх *prep*+*gen* over, above, on top of; beyond; in addition to; **~ того́** moreover.
сверх- *in comb* super-, over-, hyper-. **сверхзвуково́й** supersonic. **~пла́новый** over and above the plan. **~при́быль** excess profit. **~проводни́к** (-á) superconductor. **~секре́тный** top secret. **~уро́чный** overtime. **~уро́чные** *sb pl* overtime. **~челове́к** superman. **~челове́ческий** superhuman. **~ъесте́ственный** supernatural.
све́рху *adv* from above; **~ до́низу** from top to bottom.
сверчо́к (-чка́) cricket.
сверше́ние achievement.
сверя́ть *impf of* **све́рить**
све́сить (-е́шу) *pf* (*impf* **све́шивать**) let down, lower; **~ся** hang over, lean over.
свести́ (-еду́, -едёшь; -ёл, -á) *pf* (*impf* **своди́ть**) take; take down; take away; remove; bring together; reduce, bring; cramp.
свет[1] light; daybreak.
свет[2] world; society.
света́ть *impf impers* dawn. **свети́ло** luminary. **свети́ть** (-ечу́, -е́тишь) *impf* (*pf* **по~**) shine; +*dat* light; light the way for; **~ся** shine, gleam. **светле́ть** (-е́ет) *impf* (*pf* **по~, про~**) brighten (up); grow lighter. **све́тлость** brightness; Grace. **све́тлый** light; bright; joyous. **светлячо́к** (-чка́) glow-worm.
свето- *in comb* light, photo-. **светонепроница́емый** lightproof. **~фи́льтр** light filter. **~фо́р** traffic light(s).
светово́й light; luminous; **~ день** daylight hours.
светопреставле́ние end of the world.
све́тский fashionable; refined; secular.
светя́щийся luminous, fluorescent. **свеча́** (*pl* -и, -е́й) candle; (spark-)plug. **свече́ние** luminescence, fluorescence. **све́чка** candle. **свечу́** *etc.*: *see* **свети́ть**

с|вéшать *pf.* **свéшивать(ся** *impf of* **свéсить(ся. свивáть** *impf of* **свить**

свидáние meeting; appointment; **до свидáния!** goodbye!

свидéтель *m*, **-ница** witness. **свидéтельство** evidence; testimony; certificate. **свидéтельствовать** *impf* (*pf* **за~, о~**) give evidence, testify; be evidence (of); witness.

свинáрник pigsty.

свинéц (-нцá) lead.

свинúна pork. **свúнка** mumps. **свинóй** pig; pork. **свúнство** despicable act; outrage; squalor.

свинцóвый lead; leaden.

свинья́ (*pl* -ньи, -нéй, -ньям) pig, swine.

свирéль (reed-)pipe.

свирепéть (-éю) *impf* (*pf* **рас~**) grow savage; become violent. **свирéпствовать** *impf* rage; be rife. **свирéпый** fierce, ferocious.

свисáть *impf*, **свúснуть** (-ну; -ис) *pf* hang down, dangle; trail.

свист whistle; whistling. **свистáть** (-ищý, -úщешь) *impf* whistle. **свистéть** (-ищý) *impf*, **свúстнуть** (-ну) *pf* whistle; hiss. **свистóк** (-ткá) whistle.

свúта suite; retinue.

свúтер sweater.

свúток (-тка) roll, scroll.

с|вить (совью, совьёшь; -ил, -á, -о) *pf* (*impf also* **свивáть**) twist, wind; **~ся** roll up.

свихнýться (-нýсь, -нёшься) *impf* go mad; go astray.

свищ (-á) flaw; (knot-)hole; fistula.

свищý *etc.*: *see* **свистáть, свистéть**

свобóда freedom. **свобóдно** *adv* freely; easily; fluently; loose(ly). **свобóдный** free; easy; vacant; spare; loose; flowing. **свободолюбúвый** freedom-loving. **свободомы́слие** free-thinking.

свод code; collection; arch, vault.

сводúть (-ожý, -óдишь) *impf of* **свестú**

свóдка summary; report.

свóдный composite; step-.

свóдчатый arched, vaulted.

своевóлие self-will, wilfulness. **своевóльный** wilful.

своеврéменно *adv* in good time; opportunely. **своеврéменный** timely, opportune.

своенрáвие capriciousness. **своенрáвный** wilful, capricious.

своеобрáзие originality; peculiarity. **своеобрáзный** original; peculiar.

свожý *etc.*: *see* **сводúть, свозúть. свозúть** (-ожý, -óзишь) *impf of* **свезтú**

свой (своегó) *m*, **своя́** (своéй) *f*, **своё** (своегó) *neut*, **свои́** (свои́х) *pl*, *pron* one's (own); my, his, her, its; our, your, their.

свóйственный peculiar, characteristic. **свóйство** property, attribute, characteristic.

свóлочь swine; riff-raff.

свóра leash; pack.

сворáчивать *impf of* **свернýть, своротúть. с|воровáть** *pf.*

своротúть (-очý, -óтишь) *pf* (*impf* **сворáчивать**) dislodge, shift; turn; twist.

свояк brother-in-law (*husband of wife's sister*). **свояченица** sister-in-law (*wife's sister*).

свыкáться *impf*, **сы́кнуть-**

ся (-нусь; -ыкся) *pf* get used. **свысока́** *adv* haughtily. **свы́ше** *adv* from above. **свы́ше** *prep+gen* over; beyond.

свя́занный constrained; combined; bound; coupled. **с|вяза́ть** (-яжу́, -я́жешь) *pf*, **свя́зывать** *impf* tie, bind; connect; **~ся** get in touch; get involved. **связи́ст, -и́стка** signaller; worker in communication services. **свя́зка** sheaf, bundle; ligament. **свя́зный** connected, coherent. **связь** (*loc* -и́) connection; link, bond; liaison; communication(s).

святи́лище sanctuary. **свя́тки** (-ток) *pl* Christmas-tide. **свя́то** *adv* piously; religiously. **свят|о́й** (-ят, -á, -о) holy; **~о́й, ~а́я** *sb* saint. **святы́ня** sacred object *or* place. **свяще́нник** priest. **свяще́нный** sacred.

сгиб bend. **сгиба́ть** *impf of* **согну́ть**

сгла́дить (-а́жу) *pf*, **сгла́живать** *impf* smooth out; smooth over, soften.

сгла́зить (-а́жу) *pf* put the evil eye on.

сгнива́ть *impf*, **с|гнить** (-ию́, -иёшь; -ил, -á, -о) *pf* rot.

с|гнои́ться *pf*.

сгова́риваться *impf*, **сговори́ться** *pf* come to an arrangement; arrange. **сго́вор** agreement. **сгово́рчивый** compliant.

сгоня́ть *impf of* **согна́ть**

сгора́ние combustion; **двига́тель вну́треннего сгора́ния** internal-combustion engine. **сгора́ть** *impf of* **сгоре́ть**

с|го́рбить(ся (-блю(сь) *pf*.

с|горе́ть (-рю́) *pf* (*impf also* **сгора́ть**) burn down; be burnt down; be used up; burn; burn o.s. out. **сгоряча́** *adv* in the heat of the moment.

с|гото́вить(ся (-влю(сь) *pf*.

сгреба́ть *impf*, **сгрести́** (-ебу́, -ебёшь; -ёб, -ла́) *pf* rake up, rake together.

сгружа́ть *impf*, **сгрузи́ть** (-ужу́, -у́зишь) *pf* unload.

с|группирова́ть(ся *pf*.

сгусти́ть (-ущу́) *pf*, **сгуща́ть** *impf* thicken; condense; **~ся** thicken; condense; clot. **сгу́сток** (-тка) clot. **сгуще́ние** thickening, condensation; clotting.

сдава́ть (сдаю́, сдаёшь) *impf of* **сдать; ~ экза́мен** take an examination; **~ся** *impf of* **сда́ться**

сдави́ть (-влю́, -вишь) *pf*, **сда́вливать** *impf* squeeze.

сдать (-ам, -ашь, -аст, -ади́м; -ал, -á, -о) *pf* (*impf* **сдава́ть**) hand over; pass; let, hire out; surrender, give up; deal; **~ся** surrender, yield. **сда́ча** handing over; hiring out; surrender; change; deal.

сдвиг displacement; fault; change, improvement. **сдвига́ть** *impf*, **сдви́нуть** (-ну) *pf* shift, move; move together; **~ся** move, budge; come together.

с|де́лать(ся *pf*. **сде́лка** transaction; deal, bargain. **сде́льн|ый** piece-work; **~ая рабо́та** piece-work. **сде́льщина** piecework.

сдёргивать *impf of* **сдёрнуть**

сде́ржанный restrained, reserved. **сдержа́ть** (-жу́, -жишь) *pf*, **сде́рживать** *impf* hold back; restrain; keep.

сдёрнуть (-ну) *pf* (*impf* **сдёргивать**) pull off.

сдеру́ *etc.*: *see* **содра́ть.** **сдира́ть** *impf of* **содра́ть**

сдо́ба shortening; fancy bread, bun(s). **сдо́бный** (-бен, -бна́, -о) rich, short.

с|до́хнуть (-нет; сдох) *pf* die; kick the bucket.

сдружи́ться (-жу́сь) *pf* become friends.

сдува́ть *impf*, **сду́нуть** (-ну) *pf*, **сдуть** (-у́ю) *pf* blow away *or* off.

сеа́нс performance; showing; sitting.

себесто́имость prime cost; cost (price).

себя́ (*dat* & *prep* себе́, *instr* собо́й *or* собо́ю) *refl pron* oneself; myself, yourself, himself, *etc.*; **ничего́ себе́** not bad; **собо́й** -looking, in appearance.

себялю́бие selfishness.

сев sowing.

се́вер north. **се́верный** north, northern; northerly. **се́веро-восто́к** north-east **се́веро-восто́чный** north-east(ern). **се́веро-за́пад** north-west. **се́веро-за́падный** north-west(ern). **северя́нин** (*pl* -я́не, -я́н) northerner.

севооборо́т crop rotation.

сего́ *see* **сей. сего́дня** *adv* today. **сего́дняшний** of today, today's.

седе́ть (-е́ю) *impf* (*pf* **по~**) turn grey. **седина́** (*pl* -ы) grey hair(s).

седла́ть *impf* (*pf* **о~**) saddle. **седло́** (*pl* сёдла, -дел) saddle.

седоборо́дый grey-bearded. **седоволо́сый** grey-haired. **седо́й** (сед, -á, -о) grey(-haired).

седо́к (-á) passenger; rider.

седьмо́й seventh.

сезо́н season. **сезо́нный** seasonal.

сей (сего́) *m*, **сия́** (сей) *f*, **сие́** (сего́) *neut*, **сии́** (сих) *pl*, *pron* this; these; **сию́ мину́ту** at once, instantly.

сейсми́ческий seismic.

сейф safe.

сейча́с *adv* (just) now; soon; immediately.

сёк *etc.*: *see* **сечь**

секре́т secret.

секретариа́т secretariat.

секрета́рский secretarial. **секрета́рша, секрета́рь** (-я́) *m* secretary.

секре́тный secret.

секс sex. **сексуа́льный** sexual; sexy.

сексте́т sextet.

се́кта sect. **секта́нт** sectarian.

се́ктор sector.

секу́ *etc.*: *see* **сечь**

секуляриза́ция secularization.

секу́нда second. **секунда́нт** second. **секу́ндный** second. **секундоме́р** stop-watch.

секцио́нный sectional. **се́кция** section.

селёдка herring.

селезёнка spleen.

се́лезень (-зня) *m* drake.

селе́кция breeding.

селе́ние settlement, village.

сели́тра saltpetre, nitre.

сели́ть(ся *impf* (*pf* **по~**) settle. **село́** (*pl* сёла) village.

сельдере́й celery.

сельдь (*pl* -и, -е́й) herring.

се́льск|ий rural; village; **~ое хозя́йство** agriculture. **сельскохозя́йственный** agricultural.

сельсове́т village soviet.

сема́нтика semantics. **семанти́ческий** semantic.

семафо́р semaphore; signal.

сёмга (smoked) salmon.

семе́йный family; domestic.

семе́йство family.
се́мени *etc.*: *see* **се́мя**
семени́ть *impf* mince.
семени́ться *impf* seed. **семенни́к** (-а́) testicle; seed-vessel. **семенно́й** seed; seminal.
семёрка seven; figure 7; No. 7. **се́меро** (-ы́х) seven.
семе́стр term, semester.
се́мечко (*pl* -и) seed; *pl* sunflower seeds.
семидесятиле́тие seventy years; seventieth anniversary, birthday. **семидеся́т|ый** seventieth; **~ые го́ды** the seventies. **семиле́тка** seven-year school. **семиле́тний** seven-year; seven-year-old.
семина́р seminar. **семина́рия** seminary.
семисо́тый seven-hundredth. **семна́дцатый** seventeenth. **семна́дцать** seventeen. **семь** (-ми́, -мью́) seven. **се́мьдесят** (-ми́десяти, -мью́десятью) seventy. **семьсо́т** (-мисо́т, *instr* -мьюста́ми) seven hundred. **се́мью** *adv* seven times.
семья́ (*pl* -мьи, -ме́й, -мьям) family. **семьяни́н** family man.
се́мя (-мени; *pl* -мена́, -мя́н, -мена́м) seed; semen, sperm.
сена́т senate. **сена́тор** senator.
се́ни (-е́й) *pl* (entrance-)hall.
се́но hay. **сенова́л** hayloft. **сеноко́с** haymaking; hayfield.
сенсацио́нный sensational. **сенса́ция** sensation.
сенте́нция maxim.
сентимента́льный sentimental.
сентя́брь (-я́) *m* September. **сентя́брьский** September.
се́псис sepsis.
се́ра sulphur; ear-wax.
серб, ~ка Serb. **Се́рбия** Serbia. **се́рбский** Serb(ian). **сербскохорва́тский** Serbo-Croat(ian).
серва́нт sideboard.
се́рвер (*comput*) server.
серви́з service, set. **сервирова́ть** *impf & pf* serve; lay (a table). **сервиро́вка** laying; table lay-out.
серде́чник core. **серде́чность** cordiality; warmth. **серде́чный** heart; cardiac; cordial; warm(-hearted). **серди́тый** angry. **серди́ть** (-ржу́, -рдишь) *impf* (*pf* **рас~**) anger; **~ся** be angry. **сердобо́льный** tender-hearted.
се́рдце (*pl* -а́, -де́ц) heart; **в сердца́х** in anger; **от всего́ се́рдца** from the bottom of one's heart. **сердцебие́ние** palpitation. **сердцеви́дный** heart-shaped. **сердцеви́на** core, pith, heart.
серебрёный silver-plated. **серебри́стый** silvery. **серебри́ть** *impf* (*pf* **по~**) silver, silver-plate; **~ся** become silvery. **серебро́** silver. **сере́бряный** silver.
середи́на middle.
серёжка earring; catkin.
серена́да serenade.
се́ренький grey; dull.
сержа́нт sergeant.
сери́йный serial; mass. **се́рия** series; part.
се́рный sulphur; sulphuric.
серогла́зый grey-eyed.
се́рость uncouthness; ignorance.
серп (-а́) sickle; **~ луны́** crescent moon.
серпанти́н streamer.
сертифика́т certificate.
се́рый (сер, -а́, -о) grey; dull; uneducated.

серьгá (*pl* -и, -рёг) earring. **серьёзность** seriousness. **серьёзный** serious.
сéссия session.
сестрá (*pl* сёстры, сестёр, сёстрам) sister.
сесть (сяду) *pf* (*impf* **садиться**) sit down; land; set; shrink; +**на**+*acc* board, get on.
сéтка net, netting; (luggage-) rack; string bag; grid.
сéтовать *impf* (*pf* **по~**) complain.
сетчáтка retina. **сеть** (*loc* -и́; *pl* -и, -éй) net; network.
сечéние section. **сечь** (секу́, сечёшь; сёк) *impf* (*pf* **вы́~**) cut to pieces; flog; **~ся** split.
сéялка seed drill. **сéять** (сéю) *impf* (*pf* **по~**) sow.
сжáлиться *pf* take pity (**над**+*instr*) on.
сжáтие pressure; grasp, grip; compression. **сжáтый** compressed; compact; concise.
с|жать[1] (сожну́, -нёшь) *pf*.
сжать[2] (сожму́, -мёшь) *pf* (*impf* **сжимáть**) squeeze; compress; grip; clench; **~ся** tighten, clench; shrink, contract.
с|жечь (сожгу́, сожжёшь; сжёг, сожглá) *pf* (*impf* **сжигáть**) burn (down); cremate.
сживáться *impf of* **сжи́ться**
сжигáть *impf of* **сжечь**
сжимáть(ся *impf of* **сжáть**[2]**(ся**
сжи́ться (-иву́сь, -ивёшься; -и́лся, -áсь) *pf* (*impf* **сживáться**) **с**+*instr* get used to.
с|жу́льничать *pf*.
сзáди *adv* from behind; behind. **сзáди** *prep+gen* behind.
сзывáть *impf of* **созвáть**
сиби́рский Siberian. **Сиби́рь** Siberia. **сибиря́к** (-á), **сибиря́чка** Siberian.
сигáра cigar. **сигарéта** cigarette.
сигнáл signal. **сигнализáция** signalling. **сигнализи́ровать** *impf* & *pf* (*pf also* **про~**) signal. **сигнáльный** signal. **сигнáльщик** signalman.
сидéлка sick-nurse. **сидéние** sitting. **сидéнье** seat. **сидéть** (-ижу́) *impf* sit; be; fit.
сидя́чий sitting; sedentary.
сие́ *etc.*: *see* **сей**
си́зый (сиз, -á, -о) (blue-)grey.
сий *see* **сей**
си́ла strength; force; power; **в си́лу** *+gen* on the strength of, because of; **не по ~ам** beyond one's powers; **си́лой** by force.
силáч (-á) strong man. **си́литься** *impf* try, make efforts. **силово́й** power; of force.
сило́к (-лкá) noose, snare.
си́лос silo; silage.
силуэ́т silhouette.
си́льно *adv* strongly, violently; very much, greatly. **си́льный** (-лен *or* -лён, -льнá, -о) strong; powerful; intense, hard.
симбио́з symbiosis.
си́мвол symbol. **символизи́ровать** *impf* symbolize. **символи́зм** symbolism. **символи́ческий** symbolic.
симметри́я symmetry.
симпатизи́ровать *impf* +*dat* like, sympathize with. **симпати́чный** likeable, nice. **симпáтия** liking; sympathy.
симпо́зиум symposium.
симпто́м symptom.
симули́ровать *impf* & *pf* simulate, feign. **симуля́нт** malingerer, sham. **симуля́ция** simulation, pretence.
симфо́ния symphony.
синаго́га synagogue.
синевá blue. **синевáтый** bluish. **синеглáзый** blue-eyed.

сине́ть (-е́ю) *impf* (*pf* **по~**) turn blue; show blue. **си́ний** (синь, -ня́, -не) (dark) blue.

сини́ца titmouse.

сино́д synod. **сино́ним** synonym. **си́нтаксис** syntax.

си́нтез synthesis. **синтези́ровать** *impf* & *pf* synthesize. **синтети́ческий** synthetic.

си́нус sine; sinus.

синхронизи́ровать *impf* & *pf* synchronize.

синь[1] blue. **синь**[2] *see* **си́ний.**

си́нька blueing; blue-print.

синя́к (-а́) bruise.

сиони́зм Zionism.

си́плый hoarse, husky. **си́пнуть** (-ну; сип) *impf* (*pf* **о~**) become hoarse, husky.

сире́на siren; hooter.

сире́невый lilac(-coloured). **сире́нь** lilac.

Си́рия Syria.

сиро́п syrup.

сирота́ (*pl* -ы) *m* & *f* orphan. **сиротли́вый** lonely.

систе́ма system. **систематизи́ровать** *impf* & *pf* systematize. **систематиче́ский, системати́чный** systematic.

си́тец (-тца) (printed) cotton; chintz.

си́то sieve.

ситуа́ция situation.

си́тцевый print, chintz.

си́филис syphilis.

сифо́н siphon.

сия *see* **сей**

сия́ние radiance. **сия́ть** *impf* shine, beam.

сказ tale. **сказа́ние** story, legend. **сказа́ть** (-ажу́, -а́жешь) *pf* (*impf* **говори́ть**) say; speak; tell. **сказа́ться** (-ажу́сь, -а́жешься) *pf*, **ска́зываться** *impf* tell (on); declare o.s. **сказа́тель** *m* story-teller. **ска́зка** (fairy-)tale; fib. **ска́зочный** fairy-tale; fantastic. **сказу́емое** *sb* predicate.

скака́лка skipping-rope. **скака́ть** (-ачу́, -а́чешь) *impf* (*pf* **по~**) skip, jump; gallop. **скаково́й** race, racing.

скала́ (*pl* -ы) rock; cliff. **скали́стый** rocky.

ска́лить *impf* (*pf* **о~**); **~ зу́бы** bare one's teeth; grin; **~ся** bare one's teeth.

ска́лка rolling-pin.

скалола́з rock-climber.

ска́лывать *impf of* **сколо́ть**

скальп scalp.

ска́льпель *m* scalpel.

скаме́ечка footstool; small bench. **скаме́йка** bench. **скамья́** (*pl* ска́мьи, -е́й) bench; **~ подсуди́мых** dock.

сканда́л scandal; brawl, rowdy scene. **скандали́ст** troublemaker. **сканда́литься** *impf* (*pf* **о~**) disgrace o.s. **сканда́льный** scandalous.

скандина́вский Scandinavian.

сканди́ровать *impf* & *pf* declaim.

ска́нер (*comput*, *med*) scanner.

ска́пливать(ся *impf of* **скопи́ть(ся**

скарб goods and chattels.

ска́редный stingy.

скарлати́на scarlet fever.

скат slope; pitch.

ската́ть *pf* (*impf* **ска́тывать**) roll (up).

ска́терть (*pl* -и, -е́й) tablecloth.

скати́ть (-ачу́, -а́тишь) *pf*, **ска́тывать**[1] *impf* roll down; **~ся** roll down; slip, slide. **ска́тывать**[2] *impf of* **ската́ть**

скафа́ндр diving-suit; spacesuit.

ска́чка gallop, galloping. **ска́чки** (-чек) *pl* horse-race; races.

скачóк (-чкá) jump, leap.
скáшивать *impf of* **скосúть**
сквáжина slit, chink; well.
сквер public garden.
сквéрно badly; bad. **сквернослóвить** (-влю) *impf* use foul language. **сквéрный** foul; bad.
сквозúть *impf* be transparent; show through; **сквозúт** *impers* there is a draught. **сквознóй** through; transparent. **сквознЯк** (-á) draught. **сквозь** *prep+acc* through.
скворéц (-рцá) starling.
скелéт skeleton.
скéптик sceptic. **скептицúзм** scepticism. **скептúческий** sceptical.
скетч sketch.
скúдка reduction. **скúдывать** *impf*, **скúнуть** (-ну) *pf* throw off *or* down; knock off.
скúпетр sceptre.
скипидáр turpentine.
скирд (-á; *pl* -ы́), **скирдá** (*pl* -ы, -áм) stack, rick.
скисáть *impf*, **скúснуть** (-ну; скис) *pf* go sour.
скитáлец (-льца) wanderer. **скитáться** *impf* wander.
скиф Scythian.
склад[1] depot; store.
склад[2] mould; turn; logical connection; ~ **умá** mentality.
склáдка fold; pleat; crease; wrinkle.
склáдно *adv* smoothly.
складнóй folding, collapsible.
склáдный (-ден, -дна, -о) well-knit, well-built; smooth, coherent.
склáдчина: в склáдчину by clubbing together. **склáдывать(ся** *impf of* **сложúть(ся**
склéивать *impf*, **с|клéить** *pf* stick together; **~ся** stick together.
склеп (burial) vault, crypt.
склепáть *pf*, **склёпывать** *impf* rivet. **склёпка** riveting.
склерóз sclerosis.
склóка squabble.
склон slope; **на ~е лет** in one's declining years. **склонéние** inclination; declension. **склонúть** (-ню́, -нишь) *pf*, **склонЯть** *impf* incline; bow; win over; decline; **~ся** bend, bow; yield; be declined. **склóнность** inclination; tendency. **склóнный** (-нен, -ннá, -нно) inclined, disposed. **склонЯемый** declinable.
склЯнка phial; bottle; (*naut*) bell.
скобá (*pl* -ы, -áм) cramp, clamp; staple.
скóбка *dim of* **скобá**; bracket; *pl* parenthesis, parentheses.
скоблúть (-облю́, -óблишь) *impf* scrape, plane.
скóванность constraint. **скóванный** constrained; bound. **сковáть** (скую́, скуёшь) *pf* (*impf* **скóвывать**) forge; chain; fetter; pin down, hold, contain.
сковородá (*pl* скóвороды, -рóд, -áм), **сковорóдка** frying-pan.
скóвывать *impf of* **сковáть**
скалáчивать *impf*, **сколотúть** (-очу́, -óтишь) *pf* knock together.
сколóть (-лю́, -лешь) *pf* (*impf* **скáлывать**) chop off; pin together.
скольжéние sliding, slipping; glide. **скользúть** (-льжу́) *impf*, **скользнýть** (-ну́, -нёшь) *pf* slide; slip; glide. **скóльзкий** (-зок, -зкá, -о) slippery. **скользЯщий** sliding.
скóлько *adv* how much; how many; as far as.
с|комáндовать *pf*. **с|комби-**

ни́ровать *pf.* **с|ко́мкать** *pf.* **с|комплектова́ть** *pf.* **с|компромети́ровать** *pf.* **с|конструи́ровать** *pf.*
сконфу́женный embarrassed, confused, disconcerted. **с|конфу́зить(ся** (-у́жу(сь) *pf.*
с|концентри́ровать *pf.*
сконча́ться *pf* pass away, die.
с|копи́ровать *pf.*
скопи́ть (-плю́, -пишь) *pf* (*impf* **ска́пливать**) save (up); amass; **~ся** accumulate. **скопле́ние** accumulation; crowd.
ско́пом *adv* in a crowd, en masse.
скорбе́ть (-блю́) *impf* grieve. **ско́рбный** sorrowful. **скорбь** (*pl* -и, -е́й) sorrow.
скоре́е, скоре́й *comp of* **ско́ро, ско́рый**; *adv* rather, sooner; **как мо́жно ~** as soon as possible; **~ всего́** most likely.
скорлупа́ (*pl* -ы) shell.
скорня́к (-а́) furrier.
ско́ро *adv* quickly; soon.
скоро- *in comb* quick-, fast-. **скорова́рка** pressure-cooker. **~гово́рка** patter; tongue-twister. **ско́ропись** cursive; shorthand. **~по́ртящийся** perishable. **~пости́жный** sudden. **~спе́лый** early; fast-ripening; premature; hasty. **~сшива́тель** *m* binder, file. **~те́чный** transient, short-lived.
скоростно́й high-speed. **ско́рость** (*gen pl* -е́й) speed; gear.
скорпио́н scorpion; Scorpio.
с|корректи́ровать *pf.* **с|ко́рчить(ся** (-чу(сь) *pf.*
ско́р|ый (скор, -а́, -о) quick, fast; near; forthcoming; **~ая по́мощь** first-aid; ambulance.
с|коси́ть[1] (-ошу́, -о́сишь) *pf* (*impf also* **ска́шивать**) mow.
с|коси́ть[2] (-ошу́) *pf* (*impf also* **ска́шивать**) squint; cut on the cross.
скот (-а́), **скоти́на** cattle; live-stock; beast. **ско́тный** cattle.
ското- *in comb* cattle. **скотобо́йня** (*gen pl* -о́ен) slaughter-house. **~во́д** cattle-breeder. **~во́дство** cattle-raising.
ско́тский cattle; brutish. **ско́тство** brutish condition; brutality.
скра́сить (-а́шу) *pf*, **скра́шивать** *impf* smooth over; relieve.
скребо́к (-бка́) scraper. **скребу́** *etc.*: *see* **скрести́**
скре́жет grating; gnashing. **скрежета́ть** (-ещу́, -е́щешь) *impf* grate; *+instr* gnash.
скре́па clamp, brace; counter-signature.
скрепи́ть (-плю́) *pf*, **скрепля́ть** *impf* fasten (together), make fast; clamp; countersign, ratify; **скрепя́ се́рдце** reluctantly. **скре́пка** paper-clip. **скрепле́ние** fastening; clamping; tie, clamp.
скрести́ (-ебу́, -ебёшь; -ёб, -ла́) *impf* scrape; scratch; **~сь** scratch.
скрести́ть (-ещу́) *pf*, **скре́щивать** *impf* cross; inter-breed. **скреще́ние** crossing. **скре́щивание** crossing; inter-breeding.
с|криви́ть(ся (-влю́(сь) *pf.*
скрип squeak, creak. **скрипа́ч** (-а́) violinist. **скрипе́ть** (-плю́) *impf*, **скри́пнуть** (-ну) *pf* squeak, creak; scratch. **скрипи́чный** violin; **~ ключ** treble clef. **скри́пка** violin. **скрипу́чий** squeaky, creaking.

с|кройть *pf.*
скро́мничать *impf* (*pf* **по~**) be (too) modest. **скро́мность** modesty. **скро́мный** (-мен, -мна́, -о) modest.
скро́ю *etc.*: *see* **скрыть.**
скрою́ *etc.*: *see* **скрои́ть**
скрупулёзный scrupulous.
с|крути́ть (-учу́, -у́тишь) *pf*, **скру́чивать** *impf* twist; roll; tie up.
скрыва́ть *impf*, **скрыть** (-о́ю) *pf* hide, conceal; **~ся** hide, go into hiding, be hidden; steal away; disappear. **скры́тничать** *impf* be secretive. **скры́тный** secretive. **скры́тый** secret, hidden; latent.
скря́га *m* & *f* miser.
ску́дный (-ден, -дна́, -о) scanty; meagre. **ску́дость** scarcity, paucity.
ску́ка boredom.
скула́ (*pl* -ы) cheek-bone. **скула́стый** with high cheek-bones.
скули́ть *impf* whine, whimper.
ску́льптор sculptor. **скульпту́ра** sculpture.
ску́мбрия mackerel.
скунс skunk.
скупа́ть *impf of* **скупи́ть**
скупе́ц (-пца́) miser.
скупи́ть (-плю́, -пишь) *pf* (*impf* **скупа́ть**) buy (up).
скупи́ться (-плю́сь) *impf* (*pf* **по~**) be stingy; skimp; be sparing (of +**на**+*acc*).
ску́пка buying (up).
ску́по *adv* sparingly. **скупо́й** (-п, -а́, -о) stingy, meagre. **ску́пость** stinginess.
ску́пщик buyer(-up).
ску́тер (*pl* -а́) outboard speed-boat.
скуча́ть *impf* be bored; **+по** +*dat* miss, yearn for.
ску́ченность density, overcrowding. **ску́ченный** dense, overcrowded. **ску́чить** (-чу) *pf* crowd (together); **~ся** cluster; crowd together.
ску́чный (-чен, -чна́, -о) boring; **мне ску́чно** I'm bored.
с|ку́шать *pf*. **скую́** *etc.*: *see* **скова́ть**
слабе́ть (-е́ю) *impf* (*pf* **о~**) weaken, grow weak. **слаби́тельн|ый** laxative; **~ое** *sb* laxative. **сла́бить** *impf impers*: **его́ сла́бит** he has diarrhoea.
слабо- *in comb* weak, feeble, slight. **слабово́лие** weakness of will. **~во́льный** weak-willed. **~не́рвный** nervy, nervous. **~ра́звитый** underdeveloped. **~у́мие** feeble-mindedness. **~у́мный** feeble-minded.
сла́бость weakness. **сла́бый** (-б, -а́, -о) weak.
сла́ва glory; fame; **на сла́ву** wonderfully well. **сла́вить** (-влю) *impf* celebrate, sing the praises of; **~ся** (*+instr*) be famous (for). **сла́вный** glorious, renowned; nice.
славяни́н (*pl* -я́не, -я́н), **славя́нка** Slav. **славянофи́л** Slavophil(e). **славя́нский** Slav, Slavonic.
слага́емое *sb* component, term, member. **слага́ть** *impf of* **сложи́ть**
сла́дить (-а́жу) *pf* **с**+*instr* cope with, handle; arrange.
сла́дк|ий (-док, -дка́, -о) sweet; **~ое** *sb* sweet course.
сладостра́стник voluptuary. **сладостра́стный** voluptuous. **сла́дость** joy; sweetness; *pl* sweets.
сла́женность harmony. **сла́женный** co-ordinated, harmonious.

сла́мывать *impf of* **слома́ть**

сла́нец (-нца) shale, slate.

сластёна *m & f* person with a sweet tooth. **сласть** (*pl* -и, -е́й) delight; *pl* sweets, sweet things.

слать (шлю, шлёшь) *impf* send.

слаща́вый sugary, sickly-sweet. **сла́ще** *comp of* **сла́дкий**

сле́ва *adv* to *or* on the left; ~ **напра́во** from left to right.

слёг *etc.*: *see* **слечь**

слегка́ *adv* slightly; lightly.

след (следа́, *dat* -у, *loc* -у́; *pl* -ы́) track; footprint; trace. **следи́ть**[1] (-ежу́) *impf* +**за**+*instr* watch; follow; keep up with; look after; keep an eye on. **следи́ть**[2] (-ежу́) *impf* (*pf* **на**~) leave footprints. **сле́дование** movement. **сле́дователь** *m* investigator. **сле́довательно** *adv* consequently. **сле́довать** *impf* (*pf* **по**~) **I.** +*dat or* **за**+*instr* follow; go, be bound; **II.** *impers* (+*dat*) ought; be owing, be owed; **вам сле́дует** +*inf* you ought to; **как сле́дует** properly; as it should be; **ско́лько с меня́ сле́дует?** how much do I owe (you)? **сле́дом** *adv* (**за**+*instr*) immediately after, close behind. **сле́дственный** investigation, inquiry. **сле́дствие**[1] consequence. **сле́дствие**[2] investigation. **сле́дующий** following, next. **сле́жка** shadowing.

слеза́ (*pl* -ёзы, -а́м) tear.

слеза́ть *impf of* **слезть**

слези́ться (-и́тся) *impf* water. **слезли́вый** tearful. **слёзный** tear; tearful. **слезоточи́вый** watering; ~ **газ** tear-gas.

слезть (-зу; слез) *pf* (*impf* **слеза́ть**) climb *or* get down; dismount; get off; come off.

слепе́нь (-пня́) *m* horse-fly.

слепе́ц (-пца́) blind man. **слепи́ть**[1] *impf* blind; dazzle.

с|лепи́ть[2] (-плю́, -пишь) *pf* stick together.

сле́пнуть (-ну; слеп) *impf* (*pf* **о**~) go blind. **сле́по** *adv* blindly. **слеп|о́й** (-п, -а́, -о) blind; ~**ы́е** *sb pl* the blind.

сле́пок (-пка) cast.

слепота́ blindness.

сле́сарь (*pl* -я́ *or* -и) *m* metalworker; locksmith.

слёт gathering; rally. **слета́ть** *impf*, **слете́ть** (-ечу́) *pf* fly down *or* away; fall down *or* off; ~**ся** fly together; congregate.

слечь (сля́гу, -я́жешь; слёг, -ла́) *pf* take to one's bed.

сли́ва plum; plum-tree.

слива́ть(ся *impf of* **сли́ть(ся.**

сли́вки (-вок) *pl* cream. **сли́вочн|ый** cream; creamy; ~**ое ма́сло** butter; ~**ое моро́женое** dairy ice-cream.

сли́зистый slimy. **слизня́к** (-а́) slug. **слизь** mucus; slime.

с|линя́ть *pf.*

слипа́ться *impf*, **сли́пнуться** (-нется; -и́пся) *pf* stick together.

сли́тно together, as one word. **сли́ток** (-тка) ingot, bar.

с|лить (солью́, -ьёшь; -ил, -а́, -о) *pf* (*impf also* **слива́ть**) pour, pour out *or* off; fuse, amalgamate; ~**ся** flow together; blend; merge.

слича́ть *impf*, **сличи́ть** (-чу́) *pf* collate; check. **сличе́ние** collation, checking.

сли́шком *adv* too; too much.

слия́ние confluence; merging; merger.

слова́к, -а́чка Slovak. **слова́цкий** Slovak.
слова́рный lexical; dictionary. **слова́рь** (-я́) *m* dictionary; vocabulary. **слове́сность** literature; philology. **слове́сный** verbal, oral. **сло́вно** *conj* as if; like, as. **сло́во** (*pl* -á) word; **одни́м ~м** in a word. **сло́вом** *adv* in a word. **словообразова́ние** word-formation. **словоохо́тливый** talkative. **словосочета́ние** word combination, phrase. **словоупотребле́ние** usage.
слог[1] style.
слог[2] (*pl* -и, -о́в) syllable.
слоёный flaky.
сложе́ние composition; addition; build, constitution. **сложи́ть** (-жу́, -жишь) *pf* (*impf* **класть, скла́дывать, слага́ть**) put *or* lay (together); pile, stack; add, add up; fold (up); compose; take off, put down; lay down; **~ся** turn out; take shape; arise; club together. **сло́жность** complication; complexity. **сло́жный** (-жен, -жна́, -о) complicated; complex; compound.
слои́стый stratified; flaky.
слой (*pl* -и́, -ёв) layer; stratum.
слом demolition, pulling down. **с|лома́ть(ся** *pf.* **сломи́ть** (-млю́, -мишь) *pf* (*impf* **сла́мывать**) break (off); overcome; **сломя́ го́лову** at breakneck speed; **~ся** break.
слон (-á) elephant; bishop. **слони́ха** she-elephant. **слоно́в|ый** elephant; **~ая кость** ivory.
слоня́ться *impf* loiter, mooch (about).
слуга́ (*pl* -и) *m* (man) servant. **служа́нка** servant, maid. **слу́жащий** *sb* employee. **слу́жба** service; work. **служе́бный** office; official; auxiliary; secondary. **служе́ние** service, serving. **служи́ть** (-жу́, -жишь) *impf* (*pf* **по~**) serve; work.
с|лука́вить (-влю) *pf.*
слух hearing; ear; rumour; **по ~у** by ear. **слухов|о́й** acoustic, auditory, aural; **~о́й аппара́т** hearing aid; **~о́е окно́** dormer (window).
слу́чай incident, event; case; opportunity; chance; **ни в ко́ем слу́чае** in no circumstances. **случа́йно** *adv* by chance, accidentally; by any chance. **случа́йность** chance. **случа́йный** accidental; chance; incidental. **случа́ться** *impf*, **случи́ться** *pf* happen.
слу́шание listening; hearing. **слу́шатель** *m* listener; student; *pl* audience. **слу́шать** *impf* (*pf* **по~, про~**) listen (to); hear; attend lectures on; **(я) слу́шаю!** hello!; very well; **~ся** *+acc* obey, *+gen* heed.
слыть (-ыву́, -ывёшь; -ыл, -á, -о) *impf* (*pf* **про~**) have the reputation (*+instr or* **за***+acc* for).
слыха́ть *impf*, **слы́шать** (-шу) *impf* (*pf* **у~**) hear; sense. **слы́шаться** (-шится) *impf* (*pf* **по~**) be heard. **слы́шимость** audibility. **слы́шимый** audible. **слы́шный** (-шен, -шна́, -шно) audible.
слюда́ mica.
слюна́ (*pl* -и, -е́й) saliva; spit; *pl* spittle. **слюня́вый** dribbling.
сля́гу *etc.*: *see* **слечь**
сля́коть slush.

см. *abbr* (*of* **смотри́**) see, *vide*.
сма́зать (-а́жу) *pf*, **сма́зывать** *impf* lubricate; grease; slur over. **сма́зка** lubrication; greasing; grease. **сма́зочный** lubricating.
смак relish. **смакова́ть** *impf* relish; savour.
с|маневри́ровать *pf*.
сма́нивать *impf*, **смани́ть** (-ню́, -нишь) *pf* entice.
с|мастери́ть *pf*. **сма́тывать** *impf of* **смота́ть**
сма́хивать *impf*, **смахну́ть** (-ну́, -нёшь) *pf* brush away *or* off.
сма́чивать *impf of* **смочи́ть**
сме́жный adjacent.
смека́лка native wit.
смёл *etc*.: *see* **смести́**
смеле́ть (-е́ю) *impf* (*pf* **о~**) grow bolder. **сме́лость** boldness, courage. **сме́лый** (-л, -ла́, -ло) bold, courageous. **смельча́к** (-а́) daredevil.
смелю́ *etc*.: *see* **смоло́ть**
сме́на changing; change; replacement(s); relief; shift. **смени́ть** (-ню́, -нишь) *pf*, **сменя́ть**[1] *impf* change; replace; relieve; **~ся** hand over; be relieved; take turns; *+instr* give place to. **сме́нный** shift; changeable. **сме́нщик** relief; *pl* new shift. **сменя́ть**[2] *pf* exchange.
с|ме́рить *pf*.
смерка́ться *impf*, **сме́ркнуться** (-нется) *pf* get dark.
смерте́льный mortal, fatal, death; extreme. **сме́ртность** mortality. **сме́ртный** mortal; death; deadly, extreme. **смерть** (*gen pl* -е́й) death.
смерч whirlwind; waterspout.
смеси́тельный mixing. **с|меси́ть** (-ешу́, -е́сишь) *pf*.
смести́ (-ету́, -етёшь; -ёл, -а́) *pf* (*impf* **смета́ть**) sweep off, away.
смести́ть (-ещу́) *pf* (*impf* **смеща́ть**) displace; remove.
смесь mixture; medley.
сме́та estimate.
смета́на sour cream.
с|мета́ть[1] *pf* (*impf also* **смётывать**) tack (together).
смета́ть[2] *impf of* **смести́**
сме́тливый quick, sharp.
смету́ *etc*.: *see* **смести́**. **смётывать** *impf of* **смета́ть**
сметь (-е́ю) *impf* (*pf* **по~**) dare.
смех laughter; laugh. **смехотво́рный** laughable.
сме́шанный mixed; combined. **с|меша́ть** *pf*, **сме́шивать** *impf* mix, blend; confuse; **~ся** mix, (inter)blend; get mixed up. **смеше́ние** mixture; mixing up.
смеши́ть (-шу́) *impf* (*pf* **на~**, **рас~**) make laugh. **смешли́вый** given to laughing. **смешно́й** (-шо́н, -шна́) funny; ridiculous.
смешу́ *etc*.: *see* **смеси́ть**, **смеши́ть**
смеща́ть(ся *impf of* **смести́ть(ся**. **смеще́ние** displacement, removal. **смещу́** *etc*.: *see* **смести́ть**
сме́яться (-ею́сь, -еёшься) *impf* laugh (at **+над**+*instr*).
смире́ние humility, meekness. **смире́нный** humble, meek. **смири́тельн|ый**: **~ая руба́шка** straitjacket. **смири́ть** *pf*, **смиря́ть** *impf* restrain, subdue; **~ся** submit; resign o.s. **сми́рно** *adv* quietly; **~!** attention! **сми́рный** quiet; submissive.
смогу́ *etc*.: *see* **смочь**

смола́ (*pl* -ы) resin; pitch, tar; rosin. **смоли́стый** resinous.
смолка́ть *impf*, **смо́лкнуть** (-ну; -олк) *pf* fall silent.
смо́лоду *adv* from one's youth.
с|молоти́ть (-очу́, -о́тишь) *pf*.
с|моло́ть (смелю́, сме́лешь) *pf*.
смоляно́й pitch, tar, resin.
с|монти́ровать *pf*.
сморка́ть *impf* (*pf* **вы́~**) blow; **~ся** blow one's nose.
сморо́дина (*no pl*; *usu collect*) currant; currants; currant-bush.
смо́рщенный wrinkled.
с|мо́рщить(ся (-щу(сь) *pf*.
смота́ть *pf* (*impf* **сма́тывать**) wind, reel.
смотр (*loc* -у́; *pl* -о́тры́) review, inspection. **смотре́ть** (-рю́, -ришь) *impf* (*pf* **по~**) look (at **на**+*acc*); see; watch; look through; examine; +**за**+*instr* look after; +**в**+*acc*, **на**+*acc* look on to; +*instr* look (like); **смотри́(те)!** take care!; **смотря́** it depends; **смотря́ по**+*dat* depending on; **~ся** look at o.s. **смотрово́й** observation, inspection.
смочи́ть (-чу́, -чишь) *pf* (*impf* **сма́чивать**) moisten.
с|мочь (-огу́, -о́жешь; смог, -ла́) *pf*.
с|моше́нничать *pf*. **смо́ю** *etc.*: *see* **смы́ть**
смрад stench. **смра́дный** stinking.
сму́глый (-гл, -а́, -о) dark-complexioned, swarthy.
смути́ть (-ущу́) *pf*, **смуща́ть** *impf* embarrass, confuse; **~ся** be embarrassed, be confused. **сму́тный** vague; dim; troubled. **смуще́ние** embarrassment, confusion. **смущённый** (-ён, -а́) embarrassed, confused.
смыва́ть *impf of* **смыть**
смыка́ть(ся *impf of* **сомкну́ть(ся**
смысл sense; meaning. **смы́слить** *impf* understand. **смыслово́й** semantic.
смыть (смо́ю) *pf* (*impf* **смыва́ть**) wash off, away.
смычо́к (-чка́) bow.
смышлёный clever.
смягча́ть *impf*, **смягчи́ть** (-чу́) *pf* soften; alleviate; **~ся** soften; relent; grow mild.
смяте́ние confusion; commotion. **с|мять(ся** (сомну́(сь, -нёшь(ся) *pf*.
снабди́ть (-бжу́) *pf*, **снабжа́ть** *impf* +*instr* supply with. **снабже́ние** supply, supplying.
сна́йпер sniper.
снару́жи *adv* on *or* from (the) outside.
снаря́д projectile, missile; shell; contrivance; tackle, gear. **снаряди́ть** (-яжу́) *pf*, **снаряжа́ть** *impf* equip, fit out. **снаряже́ние** equipment, outfit.
снасть (*gen pl* -е́й) tackle; *pl* rigging.
снача́ла *adv* at first; all over again.
сна́шивать *impf of* **сноси́ть**
СНГ *abbr* (*of* **Содру́жество незави́симых госуда́рств**) CIS.
снег (*loc* -у́; *pl* -а́) snow.
снеги́рь (-я́) bullfinch.
снегово́й snow. **снегопа́д** snowfall. **Снегу́рочка** Snow Maiden. **снежи́нка** snowflake. **сне́жн|ый** snow(y); **~ая ба́ба** snowman. **снежо́к** (-жка́) light snow; snowball.
снести́[1] (-су́, -сёшь; -ёс, -ла́) *pf* (*impf* **сноси́ть**) take; bring

together; bring *or* fetch down; carry away; blow off; demolish; endure; **~сь** communicate (**с**+*instr* with).

с|нести́²(сь (-су́(сь, -сёшь(ся; снёс(ся, -сла́(сь) *pf*.

снижа́ть *impf*, **сни́зить** (-и́жу) *pf* lower; bring down; reduce; **~ся** come down; fall. **сниже́ние** lowering; loss of height.

снизойти́ (-йду́, -йдёшь; -ошёл, -шла́) *pf* (*impf* **снисходи́ть**) condescend.

сни́зу *adv* from below.

снима́ть(ся *impf of* **снять(ся**.

сни́мок (-мка) photograph.

сниму́ *etc*.: *see* **снять**

сниска́ть (-ищу́, -и́щешь) *pf*, **сни́скивать** *impf* gain, win.

снисходи́тельность condescension; leniency. **снисходи́тельный** condescending; lenient. **снисходи́ть** (-ожу́, -о́дишь) *impf of* **снизойти́**. **снисхожде́ние** indulgence, leniency.

сни́ться *impf* (*pf* **при~**) *impers+dat* dream.

сноби́зм snobbery.

сно́ва *adv* again, anew.

снова́ть (сную́, снуёшь) *impf* rush about.

сновиде́ние dream.

сноп (-а́) sheaf.

сноро́вка knack, skill.

снос demolition; drift; wear.

сноси́ть¹ (-ошу́, -о́сишь) *pf* (*impf* **сна́шивать**) wear out.

сноси́ть²(ся (-ошу́(сь, -о́сишь(ся) *impf of* **снести́(сь**.

сно́ска footnote. **сно́сно** *adv* tolerably, so-so. **сно́сный** tolerable; fair.

снотво́рный soporific.

снoха́ (*pl* -и) daughter-in-law.

сноше́ние intercourse; relations, dealings.

сношу́ *etc*.: *see* **сноси́ть**

сня́тие taking down; removal; making. **снять** (сниму́, -и́мешь; -ял, -а́, -о) *pf* (*impf* **снима́ть**) take off; take down; gather in; remove; rent; take; make; photograph; **~ся** come off; move off; be photographed.

со *see* **с** *prep*.

со- *pref* co-, joint. **соа́втор** co-author.

соба́ка dog. **соба́чий** dog's; canine. **соба́чка** little dog; trigger.

соберу́ *etc*.: *see* **собра́ть**

собе́с *abbr* (*of* **социа́льное обеспе́чение**) social security (department).

собесе́дник interlocutor, companion. **собесе́дование** conversation.

собира́тель *m* collector. **собира́ть(ся** *impf of* **собра́ть(ся**

собла́зн temptation. **соблазни́тель** *m*, **~ница** tempter; seducer. **соблазни́тельный** tempting; seductive. **соблазни́ть** *pf*, **соблазня́ть** *impf* tempt; seduce.

соблюда́ть *impf*, **со|блюсти́** (-юду́, -дёшь; -юл, -а́) *pf* observe; keep (to). **соблюде́ние** observance; maintenance.

собо́й, собо́ю *see* **себя́**

соболе́знование sympathy, condolence(s). **соболе́зновать** *impf* +*dat* sympathize *or* commiserate with.

со́боль (*pl* -и *or* -я́) *m* sable.

собо́р cathedral; council, synod. **собо́рный** cathedral.

собра́ние meeting; assembly; collection. **со́бранный** collected; concentrated.

собра́т (*pl* -ья, -ьев) colleague.

собрáть (-берý, -берёшь; -áл, -á, -о) *pf* (*impf* **собирáть**) gather; collect; **~ся** gather; prepare; intend, be going; +**с**+*instr* collect.
сóбственник owner, proprietor. **сóбственнический** proprietary; proprietorial. **сóбственно** *adv*: ~ **(говоря́)** strictly speaking, as a matter of fact.
собственнорýчно *adv* personally, with one's own hand.
сóбственность property; ownership. **сóбственн|ый** (one's) own; proper; true; **имя ~ое** proper name; **~ой персóной** in person.
событие event.
собью *etc.*: *see* **сбить**
совá (*pl* -ы) owl.
совáть (сую, -ёшь) *impf* (*pf* **сýнуть**) thrust, shove; **~ся** push, push in; butt in.
совершáть *impf*, **совершить** (-шý) *pf* accomplish; carry out; commit; complete; **~ся** happen; be accomplished. **совершéние** accomplishment; perpetration. **совершéнно** *adv* perfectly; absolutely, completely. **совершеннолéтие** majority. **совершеннолéтний** of age. **совершéнный**[1] perfect; absolute, complete. **совершéнный**[2] perfective. **совершéнство** perfection. **совершéнствование** perfecting; improvement. **совершéнствовать** *impf* (*pf* **у~**) perfect; improve; **~ся в**+*instr* perfect o.s. in; improve.
сóвестливый conscientious. **сóвестно** *impers*+*dat* be ashamed. **сóвесть** conscience.
совéт advice, counsel; opinion; council; soviet, Soviet. **совéтник** adviser. **совéтовать** *impf* (*pf* **по~**) advise; **~ся с**+*instr* consult, ask advice of. **совéтолог** Kremlinologist. **совéтск|ий** Soviet; **~ая власть** the Soviet regime; **~ий Союз** the Soviet Union. **совéтчик** adviser.
совещáние conference. **совещáтельный** consultative, deliberative. **совещáться** *impf* deliberate; consult.
совладáть *pf* **с**+*instr* control, cope with.
совместимый compatible.
совместитель *m* person holding more than one office.
совместить (-ещý) *pf*, **совмещáть** *impf* combine; **~ся** coincide; be combined, combine. **совмéстно** jointly. **совмéстный** joint, combined.
совóк (-вкá) shovel; scoop; dust-pan.
совокупиться (-плюсь) *pf*, **совокупля́ться** *impf* copulate. **совокуплéние** copulation. **совокýпно** *adv* jointly.
совокýпность aggregate, sum total.
совпадáть *impf*, **совпáсть** (-адёт) *pf* coincide; agree, tally.
совпадéние coincidence.
совратить (-ащý) *pf* (*impf* **совращáть**) pervert, seduce.
со|врáть (-врý, -врёшь; -áл, -á, -о) *pf*.
совращáть(ся *impf of* **совратить(ся**. **совращéние** perverting, seduction.
соврéменник contemporary.
соврéменность the present (time); contemporaneity. **соврéменный** contemporary; modern.
соврý *etc.*: *see* **соврáть**
совсéм *adv* quite; entirely.
совхóз State farm.

совью́ *etc.*: *see* **свить**

согла́сие consent; assent; agreement; harmony. **согласи́ться** (-ашу́сь) *pf* (*impf* **соглаша́ться**) consent; agree. **согла́сно** *adv* in accord, in harmony; *prep+dat* in accordance with. **согла́сн|ый**[1] agreeable (to); in agreement; harmonious. **согла́сный**[2] consonant(al); *sb* consonant.

согласова́ние co-ordination; agreement. **согласо́ванность** co-ordination. **согласова́ть** *pf*, **согласо́вывать** *impf* co-ordinate; make agree; **~ся** conform; agree.

соглаша́ться *impf of* **согласи́ться. соглаше́ние** agreement. **соглашу́** *etc.*: *see* **согласи́ть**

согна́ть (сгоню́, сго́нишь; -а́л, -а́, -о) *pf* (*impf* **сгоня́ть**) drive away; drive together.

со|гну́ть (-ну́, -нёшь) *pf* (*impf also* **сгиба́ть**) bend, curve; **~ся** bend (down).

согрева́ть *impf*, **согре́ть** (-е́ю) *pf* warm, heat; **~ся** get warm; warm o.s.

со|греши́ть (-шу́) *pf.*

со́да soda.

соде́йствие assistance. **соде́йствовать** *impf* & *pf* (*pf also* **по~**) *+dat* assist; promote; contribute to.

содержа́ние maintenance, upkeep; content(s); pay. **содержа́тельный** rich in content; pithy. **содержа́ть** (-жу́, -жишь) *impf* keep; maintain; contain; **~ся** be kept; be maintained; be; be contained. **содержи́мое** *sb* contents.

со|дра́ть (сдеру́, -рёшь; -а́л, -а́, -о) *pf* (*impf also* **сдира́ть**) tear off, strip off; fleece.

содрога́ние shudder. **содрога́ться** *impf*, **содрогну́ться** (-ну́сь, -нёшься) *pf* shudder.

содру́жество concord; commonwealth.

соедине́ние joining, combination; joint; compound; formation. **Соединённое Короле́вство** United Kingdom. **Соединённые Шта́ты (Аме́рики)** *m pl* United States (of America). **соединённый** (-ён, -а́) united, joint. **соедини́тельный** connective, connecting. **соедини́ть** *pf*, **соединя́ть** *impf* join, unite; connect; combine; **~ся** join, unite; combine.

сожале́ние regret; pity; **к сожале́нию** unfortunately. **сожале́ть** (-е́ю) *impf* regret, deplore.

сожгу́ *etc.*: *see* **сжечь. сожже́ние** burning; cremation.

сожи́тель *m*, **~ница** roommate, flat-mate; lover. **сожи́тельство** co-habitation.

сожму́ *etc.*: *see* **сжать**[2]. **сожну́** *etc.*: *see* **сжать**[1]. **созва́ниваться** *impf of* **созвони́ться**

созва́ть (-зову́, -зовёшь; -а́л, -а́, -о) *pf* (*impf* **сзыва́ть, созыва́ть**) call together; call; invite.

созве́здие constellation.

созвони́ться *pf* (*impf* **созва́ниваться**) ring up; speak on the telephone.

созву́чие accord; assonance. **созву́чный** harmonious; *+dat* in keeping with.

создава́ть (-даю́, -даёшь) *impf*, **созда́ть** (-а́м, -а́шь, -а́ст, -адим; со́здал, -а́, -о) *pf* create; establish; **~ся** be created; arise, spring up. **созда́ние** creation; work; creature. **созда́тель** *m* creator; originator.

созерца́ние contemplation. **созерца́тельный** contemplative. **созерца́ть** *impf* contemplate.
созида́ние creation. **созида́тельный** creative.
сознава́ть (-наю́, -наёшь) *impf*, **созна́ть** *pf* be conscious of, realize; acknowledge; **~ся** confess. **созна́ние** consciousness; acknowledgement; confession. **созна́тельность** awareness, consciousness. **созна́тельный** conscious; deliberate.
созову́ *etc.*: *see* **созва́ть**
созрева́ть *impf*, **со|зре́ть** (-е́ю) *pf* ripen, mature.
созы́в summoning, calling. **созыва́ть** *impf of* **созва́ть**
соизмери́мый commensurable.
соиска́ние competition. **соиска́тель** *m*, **~ница** competitor, candidate.
сойти́ (-йду́, -йдёшь; сошёл, -шла́) *pf* (*impf* **сходи́ть**) go *or* come down; get off; leave; come off; pass, go off; **~ с ума́** go mad, go out of one's mind; **~сь** meet; gather; become friends; become intimate; agree.
сок (*loc* -у́) juice.
со́кол falcon.
сократи́ть (-ащу́) *pf*, **сокраща́ть** *impf* shorten; abbreviate; reduce; **~ся** grow shorter; decrease; contract. **сокраще́ние** shortening; abridgement; abbreviation; reduction.
сокрове́нный secret; innermost. **сокро́вище** treasure. **сокро́вищница** treasure-house.
сокруша́ть *impf*, **сокруши́ть** (-шу́) *pf* shatter; smash; distress; **~ся** grieve, be distressed. **сокруше́ние** smashing; grief. **сокрушённый** (-ён, -а́) grief-stricken. **сокруши́тельный** shattering.
сокры́тие concealment.
со|лга́ть (-лгу́, -лжёшь; -а́л, -а́, -о) *pf*.
солда́т (*gen pl* -а́т) soldier. **солда́тский** soldier's.
соле́ние salting; pickling. **солёный** (со́лон, -а́, -о) salt(y); salted; pickled. **соле́нье** salted food(s); pickles.
солида́рность solidarity. **соли́дный** solid; strong; reliable; respectable; sizeable.
соли́ст, соли́стка soloist.
соли́ть (-лю́, со́ли́шь) *impf* (*pf* **по~**) salt; pickle.
со́лнечный sun; solar; sunny; **~ свет** sunlight; sunshine; **~ уда́р** sunstroke. **со́лнце** sun.
солнцепёк: на ~е in the sun.
солнцестоя́ние solstice.
со́ло *neut indecl* solo; *adv* solo.
солове́й (-вья́) nightingale.
со́лод malt.
солодко́вый liquorice.
соло́ма straw; thatch. **соло́менный** straw; thatch. **соло́минка** straw.
со́лон *etc.*: *see* **солёный**. **солони́на** corned beef. **соло́нка** salt-cellar. **солонча́к** (-а́) saline soil; *pl* salt marshes.
соль (*pl* -и, -е́й) salt.
со́льный solo.
солью́ *etc.*: *see* **слить**
соляно́й, соля́ный salt, saline; **соля́ная кислота́** hydrochloric acid.
со́мкнутый close. **сомкну́ть** (-ну́, -нёшь) *pf* (*impf* **смыка́ть**) close; **~ся** close.
сомнева́ться *impf* doubt, have doubts. **сомне́ние** doubt. **сомни́тельный** doubtful.

сомну́ *etc.*: *see* **смять**
сон (сна) sleep; dream. **сонли́вость** sleepiness; somnolence. **сонли́вый** sleepy. **со́нный** sleepy; sleeping.
сона́та sonata.
соне́т sonnet.
сообража́ть *impf*, **сообрази́ть** (-ажу́) *pf* consider, think out; weigh; understand. **соображе́ние** consideration; understanding; notion. **сообрази́тельный** quick-witted.
сообра́зный с+*instr* conforming to, in keeping with.
сообща́ *adv* together. **сообща́ть** *impf*, **сообщи́ть** (-щу́) *pf* communicate, report, announce; impart; +*dat* inform. **сообще́ние** communication, report; announcement. **соо́бщество** association. **соо́бщник** accomplice.
соорути́ть (-ужу́) *pf*, **сооружа́ть** *impf* build, erect. **сооруже́ние** building; structure.
соотве́тственно *adv* accordingly, correspondingly; *prep* +*dat* according to, in accordance with. **соотве́тственный** corresponding. **соотве́тствие** accordance, correspondence. **соотве́тствовать** *impf* correspond, conform. **соотве́тствующий** corresponding; suitable.
сооте́чественник fellow-countryman.
соотноше́ние correlation.
сопе́рник rival. **сопе́рничать** *impf* compete, vie. **сопе́рничество** rivalry.
сопе́ть (-плю́) *impf* wheeze; snuffle.
со́пка hill, mound.
сопли́вый snotty.
сопоста́вить (-влю) *pf*, **сопоставля́ть** *impf* compare. **сопоставле́ние** comparison.
сопреде́льный contiguous.
со|пре́ть *pf*.
соприкаса́ться *impf*, **соприкосну́ться** (-ну́сь, -нёшься) *pf* adjoin; come into contact. **соприкоснове́ние** contact.
сопроводи́тельный accompanying. **сопроводи́ть** (-ожу́) *pf*, **сопровожда́ть** *impf* accompany; escort. **сопровожде́ние** accompaniment; escort.
сопротивле́ние resistance. **сопротивля́ться** *impf* +*dat* resist, oppose.
сопу́тствовать *impf* +*dat* accompany.
сопью́сь *etc.*: *see* **спи́ться**
сор litter, rubbish.
соразме́рить *pf*, **соразмеря́ть** *impf* balance, match. **соразме́рный** proportionate, commensurate.
сора́тник comrade-in-arms.
сорва́ть (-ву́, -вёшь; -а́л, -а́, -о) *pf* (*impf* **срыва́ть**) tear off, away, down; break off; pick; get; break; ruin, spoil; vent; **~ся** break away, break loose; fall, come down; fall through.
с|организова́ть *pf*.
соревнова́ние competition; contest. **соревнова́ться** *impf* compete.
сори́ть *impf* (*pf* **на~**) +*acc or instr* litter; throw about.
со́рн|ый rubbish, refuse; **~ая трава́** weed(s). **сорня́к** (-а́) weed.
со́рок (-а́) forty.
соро́ка magpie.
сороков|о́й fortieth; **~ы́е го́ды** the forties.
соро́чка shirt; blouse; shift.

сорт (*pl* -á) grade, quality; sort. **сортировáть** *impf* (*pf* **рас~**) sort, grade. **сортирóвка** sorting. **сортирóвочн|ый** sorting; **~ая** *sb* marshalling-yard. **сортирóвщик** sorter. **сóртный** high quality.

сосáть (-сý, -сёшь) *impf* suck.

со|свáтать *pf*.

сосéд (*pl* -и, -ей, -ям), **сосéдка** neighbour. **сосéдний** neighbouring; adjacent, next. **сосéдский** neighbours'. **сосéдство** neighbourhood. **сосúска** frankfurter, sausage.

сóска (*baby's*) dummy.

соскáкивать *impf of* **соскочúть**

соскáльзывать *impf*, **соскользнýть** (-нý, -нёшь) *pf* slide down, slide off.

соскочúть (-чý, -чишь) *pf* (*impf* **соскáкивать**) jump off *or* down; come off.

соскýчиться (-чусь) *pf* get bored; ~ **по**+*dat* miss.

сослагáтельный subjunctive.

сослáть (сошлю, -лёшь) *pf* (*impf* **ссылáть**) exile, deport; **~ся на**+*acc* refer to; cite; plead, allege.

сослóвие estate; class.

сослужúвец (-вца) colleague.

соснá (*pl* -ы, -сен) pine(-tree). **соснóвый** pine; deal.

сосóк (-скá) nipple, teat.

сосредотóченный concentrated. **сосредотóчивать** *impf*, **сосредотóчить** (-чу) *pf* concentrate; focus; **~ся** concentrate.

состáв composition; structure; compound; staff; strength; train; **в ~е** +*gen* consisting of. **составúтель** *m* compiler. **состáвить** (-влю) *pf*, **составлять** *impf* put together; make (up); draw up; compile; be, constitute; total; **~ся** form, be formed. **составнóй** compound; component, constituent.

со|стáрить(ся *pf*.

состоя́ние state, condition; fortune. **состоя́тельный** well-to-do; well-grounded. **состоя́ть** (-ою́) *impf* be; +**из**+*gen* consist of; +**в**+*prep* consist in, be. **состоя́ться** (-оится) *pf* take place.

сострадáние compassion. **сострадáтельный** compassionate.

с|острúть *pf*. **со|стряпать** *pf*.

со|стыковáть *pf*, **состыкóвывать** *impf* dock; **~ся** dock.

состязáние competition, contest. **состязáться** *impf* compete.

сосýд vessel.

сосýлька icicle.

сосуществовáние co-existence.

со|считáть *pf*. **сот** *see* **сто**.

сотворéние creation. **со|творúть** *pf*.

со|ткáть (-кý, -кёшь; -áл, -алá, -о) *pf*.

сóтня (*gen pl* -тен) a hundred.

сотрý *etc*.: *see* **стерéть**

сотрýдник collaborator; colleague; employee. **сотрýдничать** *impf* collaborate; +**в**+*prep* contribute to. **сотрýдничество** collaboration.

сотрясáть *impf*, **сотрястú** (-сý, -сёшь; -я́с, -лá) *pf* shake; **~ся** tremble. **сотрясéние** shaking; concussion.

сóты (-ов) *pl* honeycomb.

сóтый hundredth.

соумы́шленник accomplice.

сóус sauce; gravy; dressing.

соучáстие participation; com-

plicity. **соуча́стник** participant; accomplice.
софа́ (*pl* -ы) sofa.
соха́ (*pl* -и) (*wooden*) plough.
со́хнуть (-ну; сох) *impf* (*pf* **вы́~, за~, про~**) (get) dry; wither.
сохране́ние preservation; conservation; (safe)keeping; retention. **сохрани́ть** *pf*, **сохраня́ть** *impf* preserve, keep; **~ся** remain (intact); last out; be well preserved. **сохра́нный** safe.
социа́л-демокра́т Social Democrat. **социа́л-демократи́ческий** Social Democratic. **социали́зм** socialism. **социали́ст** socialist. **социалисти́ческий** socialist. **социа́льн|ый** social; **~ое обеспече́ние** social security. **социо́лог** sociologist. **социоло́гия** sociology.
соцреали́зм socialist realism.
сочета́ние combination. **сочета́ть** *impf* & *pf* combine; **~ся** combine; harmonize; match.
сочине́ние composition; work. **сочини́ть** *pf*, **сочиня́ть** *impf* compose; write; make up.
сочи́ться (-и́тся) *impf* ooze (out), trickle; **~ кро́вью** bleed.
со́чный (-чен, -чна́, -о) juicy; rich.
сочту́ *etc.*: *see* **счесть**
сочу́вствие sympathy. **сочу́вствовать** *impf +dat* sympathize with.
сошёл *etc.*: *see* **сойти́. сошлю́** *etc.*: *see* **сосла́ть. сошью́** *etc.*: *see* **сшить**
сощу́ривать *impf*, **со|щу́рить** *pf* screw up, narrow; **~ся** screw up one's eyes; narrow.
сою́з[1] union; alliance; league.
сою́з[2] conjunction. **сою́зник** ally. **сою́зный** allied; Union.
спад recession; abatement.
спада́ть *impf of* **спасть**
спазм spasm.
спа́ивать *impf of* **спая́ть, спои́ть**
спа́йка soldered joint; solidarity, unity.
с|пали́ть *pf*.
спа́льн|ый sleeping; **~ый ваго́н** sleeping car; **~ое ме́сто** berth. **спа́льня** (*gen pl* -лен) bedroom.
спа́ржа asparagus.
спартакиа́да sports meeting.
спаса́тельный rescue; **~ жиле́т** life jacket; **~ круг** lifebuoy; **~ по́яс** lifebelt. **спаса́ть(ся** *impf of* **спасти́(сь. спасе́ние** rescue, escape; salvation. **спаси́бо** thank you. **спаси́тель** *m* rescuer; saviour. **спаси́тельный** saving; salutary.
спасти́ (-су́, -сёшь; спас, -ла́) *pf* (*impf* **спаса́ть**) save; rescue; **~сь** escape; be saved.
спасть (-адёт) *pf* (*impf* **спада́ть**) fall (down); abate.
спать (сплю; -ал, -а́, -о) *impf* sleep; **лечь ~** go to bed.
спа́янность cohesion, unity. **спа́янный** united. **спая́ть** *pf* (*impf* **спа́ивать**) solder, weld; unite.
спекта́кль *m* performance; show.
спектр spectrum.
спекули́ровать *impf* speculate. **спекуля́нт** speculator, profiteer. **спекуля́ция** speculation; profiteering.
спе́лый ripe.
сперва́ *adv* at first; first.
спе́реди *adv* in front, from the front; *prep+gen* (from) in front of.
спёртый close, stuffy.

спеси́вый arrogant, haughty. **спесь** arrogance, haughtiness.

спеть[1] (-е́ет) *impf* (*pf* **по~**) ripen.

с|петь[2] (спою́, споёшь) *pf.*

спец- *abbr in comb* (*of* **специа́льный**) special. **спецко́р** special correspondent. **~оде́жда** protective clothing; overalls.

специализа́ция specialization. **специализи́роваться** *impf & pf* specialize. **специали́ст, ~ка** specialist, expert. **специа́льность** speciality; profession. **специа́льный** special; specialist.

специ́фика specific character. **специфи́ческий** specific.

спе́ция spice.

спецо́вка protective clothing; overall(s).

спеши́ть (-шу́) *impf* (*pf* **по~**) hurry, be in a hurry; be fast.

спе́шка hurry, haste. **спе́шный** urgent.

спива́ться *impf of* **спи́ться**

СПИД *abbr* (*of* **синдро́м приобретённого иммýнного дефици́та**) Aids.

с|пики́ровать *pf.*

спи́ливать *impf*, **спили́ть** (-лю́, -лишь) *pf* saw down, off.

спина́ (*acc* -у; *pl* -ы) back. **спи́нка** back. **спинно́й** spinal; **~ мозг** spinal cord.

спира́ль spiral.

спирт alcohol, spirit(s). **спиртн|о́й** alcoholic; **~о́е** *sb* alcohol. **спирто́вка** spirit-stove. **спиртово́й** spirit, alcoholic.

списа́ть (-ишу́, -и́шешь) *pf*, **спи́сывать** *impf* copy; **~ся** exchange letters. **спи́сок** (-ска) list; record.

спи́ться (сопью́сь, -ьёшься; -и́лся, -а́сь) *pf* (*impf* **спива́ться**) take to drink.

спи́хивать *impf*, **спихну́ть** (-ну́, -нёшь) *pf* push aside, down.

спи́ца knitting-needle; spoke.

спи́чечн|ый match; **~ая коро́бка** match-box. **спи́чка** match.

спишу́ *etc.*: *see* **списа́ть**

сплав[1] floating. **сплав**[2] alloy. **спла́вить**[1] (-влю) *pf*, **сплавля́ть**[1] *impf* float; raft; get rid of. **спла́вить**[2] (-влю) *pf*, **сплавля́ть**[2] *impf* alloy; **~ся** fuse.

с|плани́ровать *pf.* **спла́чивать(ся** *impf of* **сплоти́ть(ся.**

сплёвывать *impf of* **сплю́нуть**

с|плести́ (-ету́, -етёшь; -ёл, -а́) *pf*, **сплета́ть** *impf* weave, plait; interlace. **сплете́ние** interlacing; plexus.

сплéтник, -ница gossip, scandalmonger. **спле́тничать** *impf* (*pf* **на~**) gossip. **спле́тня** (*gen pl* -тен) gossip, scandal.

сплоти́ть (-очу́) *pf* (*impf* **спла́чивать**) join; unite, rally; **~ся** unite, rally; close ranks. **сплоче́ние** uniting. **сплочённость** cohesion, unity. **сплочённый** (-ён, -а́) united; firm; unbroken.

сплошно́й solid; complete; continuous; utter. **сплошь** *adv* all over; completely; **~ да ря́дом** pretty often.

сплю *see* **спать**

сплю́нуть (-ну) *pf* (*impf* **сплёвывать**) spit; spit out.

сплю́щивать *impf*, **сплю́щить** (-щу) *pf* flatten; **~ся** become flat.

с|пляса́ть (-яшу́, -я́шешь) *pf.*

сподви́жник comrade-in-arms.

споить (-ою́, -о́ишь) *pf* (*impf* **спа́ивать**) make a drunkard of.

споко́йн|ый quiet; calm; **~ой**

ночи good night! **спокойствие** quiet; calm, serenity.

споласкивать *impf of* **сполоснуть**

сползать *impf*, **сползти** (-зу́, -зёшь; -олз, -ла́) *pf* climb down; slip (down); fall away.

сполна́ *adv* in full.

сполосну́ть (-ну́, -нёшь) *pf* (*impf* **спола́скивать**) rinse.

спо́нсор sponsor, backer.

спор argument; controversy; dispute. **спо́рить** *impf* (*pf* **по~**) argue; dispute; debate. **спо́рный** debatable, questionable; disputed; moot.

спо́ра spore.

спорт sport. **спорти́вный** sports; ~ **зал** gymnasium. **спортсме́н, ~ка** athlete, player.

спо́соб way, method; **таки́м ~ом** in this way. **спосо́бность** ability, aptitude; capacity. **спосо́бный** able; clever; capable. **спосо́бствовать** *impf* (*pf* **по~**) *+dat* assist; further.

споткну́ться (-ну́сь, -нёшься) *pf*, **спотыка́ться** *impf* stumble.

спохвати́ться (-ачу́сь, -а́тишься) *pf*, **спохва́тываться** *impf* remember suddenly.

спою *etc.*: *see* **спеть, спои́ть**

спра́ва *adv* to *or* on the right.

справедли́вость justice; fairness; truth. **справедли́вый** just; fair; justified.

спра́вить (-влю) *pf*, **справля́ть** *impf* celebrate. **спра́виться**[1] (-влюсь) *pf*, **справля́ться** *impf* **с**+*instr* cope with, manage. **спра́виться**[2] (-влюсь) *pf*, **справля́ться** *impf* inquire; +**в**+*prep* consult. **спра́вка** information; reference; certificate; **наводи́ть спра́вку** make inquiries. **спра́вочник** reference-book, directory. **спра́вочный** inquiry, information, reference.

спра́шивать(ся *impf of* **спроси́ть(ся**

спринт sprint. **спри́нтер** sprinter.

с|провоци́ровать *pf*. **с|проекти́ровать** *pf*.

спрос demand; asking; **без ~у** without permission. **спроси́ть** (-ошу́, -о́сишь) *pf* (*impf* **спра́шивать**) ask (for); inquire; **~ся** ask permission.

спрут octopus.

спры́гивать *impf*, **спры́гнуть** (-ну) *pf* jump off, jump down.

спры́скивать *impf*, **спры́снуть** (-ну) *pf* sprinkle.

спряга́ть *impf* (*pf* **про~**) conjugate. **спряже́ние** conjugation.

с|прясть (-яду́, -ядёшь; -ял, -яла́, -о) *pf*. **с|пря́тать(ся** (-я́чу(сь) *pf*.

спу́гивать *impf*, **спугну́ть** (-ну́, -нёшь) *pf* frighten off.

спуск lowering; descent; slope. **спуска́ть** *impf*, **спусти́ть** (-ущу́, -у́стишь) *pf* let down, lower; release; let out; send out; go down; forgive; squander; ~ **кора́бль** launch a ship; ~ **куро́к** pull the trigger; ~ **пе́тлю** drop a stitch; **~ся** go down, descend. **спускно́й** drain. **спусково́й** trigger.

спустя́ *prep+acc* after; *adv* later.

с|пу́тать(ся *pf*.

спу́тник satellite, sputnik; (travelling) companion.

спущу́ *etc.*: *see* **спусти́ть**

спя́чка hibernation; sleepiness.

ср. *abbr* (*of* **сравни́**) cf.
сраба́тывать *impf*, **срабо́тать** *pf* make; work, operate.
сравне́ние comparison; simile. **сра́внивать** *impf of* **сравни́ть, сравня́ть. сравни́мый** comparable. **сравни́тельно** *adv* comparatively. **сравни́тельный** comparative. **сравни́ть** *pf* (*impf* **сра́внивать**) compare; **~ся с**+*instr* compare with. **с|равня́ть** *pf* (*impf also* **сра́внивать**) make even, equal; level.
сража́ть *impf*, **срази́ть** (-ажу́) *pf* strike down; overwhelm, crush; **~ся** fight. **сраже́ние** battle.
сра́зу *adv* at once.
срам shame. **срами́ть** (-млю́) *impf* (*pf* **о~**) shame; **~ся** cover o.s. with shame. **срамота́** shame.
сраста́ние growing together. **сраста́ться** *impf*, **срасти́сь** (-тётся; сро́сся, -ла́сь) *pf* grow together; knit.
среда́[1] (*pl* -ы) environment, surroundings; medium. **среда́**[2] (*acc* -у; *pl* -ы, -а́м *or* -ам) Wednesday. **среди́** *prep+gen* among; in the middle of; **~ бе́ла дня** in broad daylight. **средиземномо́рский** Mediterranean. **сре́дне** *adv* so-so. **средневеко́вый** medieval. **средневеко́вье** the Middle Ages. **сре́дний** middle; medium; mean; average; middling; secondary; neuter; **~ее** *sb* mean, average. **средото́чие** focus. **сре́дство** means; remedy.
срез cut; section; slice. **с|ре́зать** (-е́жу) *pf*. **среза́ть** *impf* cut off; slice; fail; **~ся** fail.
с|репети́ровать *pf*.
срисова́ть *pf*, **срисо́вывать** *impf* copy.
с|ровня́ть *pf*.
сродство́ affinity.
срок date; term; time, period; **в ~, к ~у** in time, to time.
сро́сся *etc*.: *see* **срасти́сь**
сро́чно *adv* urgently. **сро́чность** urgency. **сро́чный** urgent; for a fixed period.
сро́ю *etc*.: *see* **срыть**
сруб felling; framework. **сруба́ть** *impf*, **с|руби́ть** (-блю́, -бишь) *pf* cut down; build (*of logs*).
срыв disruption; breakdown; ruining. **срыва́ть**[1](**ся** *impf of* **сорва́ть(ся**
срыва́ть[2] *impf*, **срыть** (сро́ю) *pf* raze to the ground.
сря́ду *adv* running.
ссади́на scratch. **ссади́ть** (-ажу́, -а́дишь) *pf*, **сса́живать** *impf* set down; help down; turn off.
ссо́ра quarrel. **ссо́рить** *impf* (*pf* **по~**) cause to quarrel; **~ся** quarrel.
СССР *abbr* (*of* **Сою́з Сове́тских Социалисти́ческих Респу́блик**) USSR.
ссу́да loan. **ссуди́ть** (-ужу́, -у́дишь) *pf*, **ссужа́ть** *impf* lend, loan.
ссыла́ть(ся *impf of* **сосла́ть(ся. ссы́лка**[1] exile. **ссы́лка**[2] reference. **ссы́льный, ссы́льная** *sb* exile.
ссы́пать (-плю) *pf*, **ссыпа́ть** *impf* pour.
стабилиза́тор stabilizer; tailplane. **стабилизи́ровать(ся** *impf & pf* stabilize. **стаби́льность** stability. **стаби́льный** stable, firm.
ста́вень (-вня; *gen pl* -вней) *m*, **ста́вня** (*gen pl* -вен) shutter.

ста́вить (-влю) *impf* (*pf* **по~**) put, place, set; stand; station; erect; install; apply; present, stage. **ста́вка**[1] rate; stake. **ста́вка**[2] headquarters.
ста́вня *see* **ста́вень**
стадио́н stadium.
ста́дия stage.
ста́дность herd instinct. **ста́дный** gregarious. **ста́до** (*pl* -а́) herd, flock.
стаж length of service; probation. **стажёр** probationer; student on a special non-degree course. **стажиро́вка** period of training.
стака́н glass.
сталелите́йный steel-founding; ~ **заво́д** steel foundry. **сталеплави́льный** steel-making; ~ **заво́д** steel works. **сталепрока́тный** (steel-)rolling; ~ **стан** rolling-mill.
ста́лкивать(ся *impf of* **столкну́ть(ся**
ста́ло быть *conj* consequently.
сталь steel. **стально́й** steel.
стаме́ска chisel.
стан[1] figure, torso.
стан[2] camp.
стан[3] mill.
станда́рт standard. **станда́ртный** standard.
стани́ца Cossack village.
станкострое́ние machine-tool engineering.
станови́ться (-влю́сь, -вишься) *impf of* **стать**[1]
стано́к (-нка́) machine tool, machine.
ста́ну *etc.*: *see* **стать**[2]
станцио́нный station. **ста́нция** station.
ста́пель (*pl* -я́) *m* stocks.
ста́птывать(ся *impf of* **стопта́ть(ся**
стара́ние effort. **стара́тельность** diligence. **стара́тельный** diligent. **стара́ться** *impf* (*pf* **по~**) try.
старе́ть *impf* (*pf* **по~, у~**) grow old. **ста́рец** (-рца) elder, (*venerable*) old man. **стари́к** (-а́) old man. **старина́** antiquity, olden times; antique(s); old fellow. **стари́нный** ancient; old; antique. **ста́рить** *impf* (*pf* **со~**) age, make old; **~ся** age, grow old.
старо- *in comb* old. **старове́р** Old Believer. **~жи́л** old resident. **~мо́дный** old-fashioned. **~славя́нский** Old Slavonic.
ста́роста head; monitor; churchwarden. **ста́рость** old age.
старт start; **на ~!** on your marks! **ста́ртёр** starter.
стартова́ть *impf* & *pf* start.
ста́ртовый starting.
стару́ха, стару́шка old woman. **ста́рческий** old man's; senile. **ста́рше** *comp of* **ста́рый. ста́рш|ий** oldest, eldest; older, elder; senior; head; **~ие** *sb pl* (one's) elders; **~ий** *sb* chief; man in charge. **старшина́** *m* sergeant-major; petty officer; leader. **ста́рый** (-ар, -а́, -о) old. **старьё** old things, junk.
ста́скивать *impf of* **стащи́ть**
с|тасова́ть *pf.*
стати́ст extra.
стати́стика statistics. **статисти́ческий** statistical.
ста́тный stately.
ста́тский civil, civilian.
ста́тус status. **ста́тус-кво́** *neut indecl* status quo.
статуэ́тка statuette.
ста́туя statue.

стать[1] (-а́ну) *pf* (*impf* **станови́ться**) stand; take up position; stop; cost; begin; *+instr* become; **+с**+*instr* become of; **не ~** *impers+gen* cease to be; disappear; **его́ не ста́ло** he is no more; **~ на коле́ни** kneel.
стать[2] physique, build.
ста́ться (-а́нется) *pf* happen.
статья́ (*gen pl* -е́й) article; clause; item; matter.
стациона́р permanent establishment; hospital. **стациона́рный** stationary; permanent; **~ больно́й** in-patient.
ста́чечник striker. **ста́чка** strike.
с|тащи́ть (-щу́, -щишь) *pf* (*impf also* **ста́скивать**) drag off pull off.
ста́я flock; school, shoal; pack.
ствол (-а́) trunk; barrel.
ство́рка leaf, fold.
сте́бель (-бля; *gen pl* -бле́й) *m* stem, stalk.
стёган|ый quilted; **~ое одея́ло** quilt, duvet. **стега́ть**[1] *impf* (*pf* **вы́~**) quilt.
стега́ть[2] *impf*, **стегну́ть** (-ну́) *pf* (*pf also* **от~**) whip, lash.
стежо́к (-жка́) stitch.
стезя́ path, way.
стёк *etc.*: *see* **стечь. стека́ть(ся** *impf of* **сте́чь(ся**
стекло́ (*pl* -ёкла, -кол) glass; lens; (window-)pane.
стекло- *in comb* glass. **стекловолокно́** glass fibre. **~очисти́тель** *m* windscreen-wiper. **~ре́з** glass-cutter. **~тка́нь** fibreglass.
стекля́нный glass; glassy. **стеко́льщик** glazier.
стели́ть *see* **стлать**
стелла́ж (-а́) shelves, shelving.
сте́лька insole.
стелю́ *etc.*: *see* **стлать**
с|темне́ть (-е́ет) *pf*.
стена́ (*acc* -у; *pl* -ы, -а́м) wall. **стенгазе́та** wall newspaper.
стенд stand.
сте́нка wall; side. **стенно́й** wall.
стеногра́мма shorthand record. **стено́граф, стенографи́ст, ~ка** stenographer. **стенографи́ровать** *impf* & *pf* take down in shorthand. **стенографи́ческий** shorthand. **стеногра́фия** shorthand.
стенокарди́я angina.
степе́нный staid; middle-aged.
сте́пень (*gen pl* -е́й) degree; extent; power.
степно́й steppe. **степь** (*loc* -и́; *gen pl* -е́й) steppe.
стервя́тник vulture.
стерегу́ *etc.*: *see* **стере́чь**
сте́рео *indecl adj* stereo. **стерео-** *in comb* stereo. **стереоти́п** stereotype. **стереоти́пный** stereotype(d). **стереофони́ческий** stereo(phonic). **~фо́ния** stereo(phony).
стере́ть (сотру́, сотрёшь; стёр) *pf* (*impf* **стира́ть**[1]) wipe off; rub out, rub sore; **~ся** rub off; wear down; be effaced.
стере́чь (-регу́, -режёшь; -ёг, -ла́) *impf* guard; watch for.
сте́ржень (-жня) *m* pivot; rod; core.
стерилизова́ть *impf* & *pf* sterilize. **стери́льный** sterile.
сте́рлинг sterling.
сте́рлядь (*gen pl* -е́й) sterlet.
стерпе́ть (-плю́, -пишь) *pf* bear, endure.
стёртый worn, effaced.
стесне́ние constraint. **стесни́тельный** shy; inconvenient.
с|тесни́ть *pf*, **стесня́ть** *impf* constrain; hamper; inhibit.

с|теснúться *pf*, **стеснять-ся** *impf* (*pf also* **по~**) *+inf* feel too shy (to), be ashamed to.
стечéние confluence; gathering; combination. **стечь** (-чёт; -ёк, -лá) *pf* (*impf* **стекáть**) flow down; **~ся** flow together; gather.
стилистúческий stylistic.
стиль *m* style. **стúльный** stylish; period.
стúмул stimulus, incentive.
стимулúровать *impf* & *pf* stimulate.
стипéндия grant.
стирáльный washing.
стирáть[1](**ся** *impf of* **стерéть(ся**
стирáть[2] *impf* (*pf* **вы́~**) wash, launder; **~ся** wash. **стúрка** washing, wash, laundering.
стúскивать *impf*, **стúснуть** (-ну) *pf* squeeze; clench; hug.
стих (-á) verse; line; *pl* poetry.
стихáть *impf of* **стúхнуть**
стихúйный elemental; spontaneous. **стихúя** element.
стúхнуть (-ну; стих) *pf* (*impf* **стихáть**) subside; calm down.
стихотворéние poem. **стихотвóрный** in verse form.
стлать, стелúть (стелю, стéлешь) *impf* (*pf* **по~**) spread; **~ постéль** make a bed; **~ся** spread; creep.
сто (ста; *gen pl* сот) a hundred.
стог (*loc* -е & -ý; *pl* -á) stack, rick.
стóимость cost; value. **стóить** *impf* cost; be worth(while); deserve.
стой *see* **стоять**
стóйка counter, bar; prop; upright; strut. **стóйкий** firm; stable; steadfast. **стóйкость** firmness, stability; steadfastness. **стóйло** stall. **стоймя́** *adv* upright.
сток flow; drainage; drain, gutter; sewer.
стол (-á) table; desk; cuisine.
столб (-á) post, pole, pillar, column. **столбенéть** (-éю) *impf* (*pf* **о~**) be rooted to the ground. **столбня́к** (-á) stupor; tetanus.
столéтие century; centenary. **столéтний** hundred-year-old; of a hundred years.
столúца capital; metropolis. **столúчный** (of the) capital.
столкновéние collision; clash.
столкнýть (-нý, -нёшь) *pf* (*impf* **стáлкивать**) push off, away; cause to collide; bring together; **~ся** collide, clash; +**с**+*instr* run into.
столóвая *sb* dining-room; canteen. **столóвый** table.
столп (-á) pillar.
столпúться *pf* crowd.
столь *adv* so. **стóлько** *adv* so much, so many.
столя́р (-á) joiner, carpenter.
столя́рный joiner's.
стоматóлог dentist.
стометрóвка (the) hundred metres.
стон groan. **стонáть** (-нý, -нешь) *impf* groan.
стоп! *int* stop!
стопá[1] foot.
стопá[2] (*pl* -ы) ream; pile.
стóпка[1] pile.
стóпка[2] small glass.
стóпор stop, catch. **стóпориться** *impf* (*pf* **за~**) come to a stop.
стопроцéнтный hundred-per-cent.
стоп-сигнáл brake-light.
стоптáть (-пчý, -пчешь) *pf* (*impf* **стáптывать**) wear down; **~ся** wear down.

с|торговáть(ся *pf.*
стóрож (*pl* -á) watchman, guard. **сторожевóй** watch; patrol-. **сторожи́ть** (-жý) *impf* guard, watch (over).
сторонá (*acc* стóрону; *pl* стóроны, -рóн, -áм) side; direction; hand; feature; part; land; **в стóрону** aside; **с моéй стороны́** for my part; **с однóй стороны́** on the one hand. **сторони́ться** (-ню́сь, -нишься) *impf* (*pf* **по~**) stand aside; *+gen* avoid. **сторóнник** supporter, advocate.
стóчный sewage, drainage.
стоя́нка stop; parking; stopping place, parking space; stand; rank. **стоя́ть** (-ою́) *impf* (*pf* **по~**) stand; be; stay; stop; have stopped; **+за**+*acc* stand up for; ~ **на колéнях** kneel. **стоя́чий** standing; upright; stagnant.
стóящий deserving; worthwhile.
стр. *abbr* (*of* **страни́ца**) page.
страдá (*pl* -ды) (hard work at) harvest time.
страдáлец (-льца) sufferer. **страдáние** suffering. **страдáтельный** passive. **страдáть** (-áю *or* -рáжду) *impf* (*pf* **по~**) suffer; ~ **за** *+gen* feel for.
стрáжа guard, watch; **под стрáжей** under arrest, in custody; **стоя́ть на стрáже** *+gen* guard.
странá (*pl* -ы) country; land; ~ **свéта** cardinal point.
страни́ца page.
стрáнник, стрáнница wanderer.
стрáнно *adv* strangely. **стрáнность** strangeness; eccentricity. **стрáнн|ый** (-áнен, -аннá, -о) strange.
стрáнствие wandering. **стрáнствовать** *impf* wander.
Страстн|óй of Holy Week; **~áя пя́тница** Good Friday.
стрáстный (-тен, -тнá, -о) passionate. **страсть**[1] (*gen pl* -éй) passion. **страсть**[2] *adv* awfully, frightfully.
стратеги́ческий strategic(al).
стратéгия strategy.
стратосфéра stratosphere.
стрáус ostrich.
страх fear.
страховáние insurance; ~ **жи́зни** life insurance. **страховáть** *impf* (*pf* **за~**) insure (**от**+*gen* against); **~ся** insure o.s. **страхóвка** insurance.
страши́ться (-шу́сь) *impf* *+gen* be afraid of. **стрáшно** *adv* awfully. **стрáшный** (-шен, -шнá, -о) terrible, awful.
стрекозá (*pl* -ы) dragonfly.
стрекотáть (-очу́, -óчешь) *impf* chirr.
стрелá (*pl* -ы) arrow; boom. **стрелéц** (-льцá) Sagittarius. **стрéлка** pointer; hand; needle; arrow; spit; points. **стрелкóвый** rifle; shooting; infantry. **стрелóк** (-лкá) shot; rifleman, gunner. **стрéлочник** pointsman. **стрельбá** (*pl* -ы) shooting, firing. **стрéльчатый** lancet; arched. **стреля́ть** *impf* shoot; fire; **~ся** shoot o.s.; fight a duel.
стремглáв *adv* headlong.
стреми́тельный swift; impetuous. **стреми́ться** (-млю́сь) *impf* strive. **стремлéние** striving, aspiration. **стремни́на** rapid(s).
стрéмя (-мени; *pl* -менá, -мя́н, -áм) *neut* stirrup. **стремя́нка** step-ladder.
стресс stress. **стрéссовый** stressful, stressed.

стри́женый short; short-haired, cropped; shorn. **стри́жка** hair-cut; shearing. **стричь** (-игу́, -ижёшь; -иг) *impf* (*pf* **о~**) cut, clip; cut the hair of; shear; **~ся** have one's hair cut.

строга́ть *impf* (*pf* **вы́~**) plane, shave.

стро́гий strict; severe. **стро́гость** strictness.

строево́й combatant; line; drill. **строе́ние** building; structure; composition.

строжа́йший, стро́же *superl & comp of* **стро́гий**

строи́тель *m* builder. **строи́тельный** building, construction. **строи́тельство** building, construction; building site. **стро́ить** *impf* (*pf* **по~**) build; construct; make; base; draw up; **~ся** be built, be under construction; draw up; **стро́йся!** fall in! **строй** (*loc* -ю́; *pl* -и *or* -и́, -ев *or* -ёв) system; régime; structure; pitch; formation. **стро́йка** building; building-site. **стро́йность** proportion; harmony; balance, order. **стро́йный** (-о́ен, -ойна́, -о) harmonious, orderly, well-proportioned, shapely.

строка́ (acc -о́ку́; pl -и, -а́м) line; **кра́сная ~** new paragraph.

строп, стро́па sling; shroud line.

стропи́ло rafter, beam.

строптúвый refractory.

строфа́ (*pl* -ы, -а́м) stanza.

строчи́ть (-чу́, -о́чишь) *impf* (*pf* **на~, про~**) stitch; scribble, dash off. **стро́чка** stitch; line.

стро́ю *etc.*: *see* **стро́ить**

струга́ть *impf* (*pf* **вы́~**) plane. **стру́жка** shaving.

струи́ться *impf* stream.

структу́ра structure.

струна́ (*pl* -ы) string. **стру́нный** stringed.

струп (*pl* -пья, -пьев) scab.

с|тру́сить (-у́шу) *pf.*

стручо́к (-чка́) pod.

струя́ (*pl* -и, -у́й) jet, spurt, stream.

стря́пать *impf* (*pf* **со~**) cook; concoct. **стряпня́** cooking.

стря́хивать *impf*, **стряхну́ть** (-ну́, -нёшь) *pf* shake off.

студени́стый jelly-like.

студе́нт, студе́нтка student. **студе́нческий** student.

сту́день (-дня) *m* jelly; aspic.

студи́ть (-ужу́, -у́дишь) *impf* (*pf* **о~**) cool.

сту́дия studio.

сту́жа severe cold, hard frost.

стук knock; clatter. **сту́кать** *impf*, **сту́кнуть** (-ну) *pf* knock; bang; strike; **~ся** knock (o.s.), bang. **стука́ч** (-а́) informer.

стул (*pl* -лья, -льев) chair. **стульча́к** (-а́) (*lavatory*) seat. **сту́льчик** stool.

сту́па mortar.

ступа́ть *impf*, **ступи́ть** (-плю́, -пишь) *pf* step; tread. **ступе́нчатый** stepped, graded. **ступе́нь** (*gen pl* -е́не́й) step, rung; stage, grade. **ступе́нька** step. **ступня́** foot; sole.

стуча́ть (-чу́) *impf* (*pf* **по~**) knock; chatter; pound; **~ся в**+*acc* knock at.

стушева́ться (-шу́юсь) *pf*, **стушёвываться** *impf* efface o.s.

с|туши́ть (-шу́, -шишь) *pf.*

стыд (-а́) shame. **стыди́ть** (-ыжу́) *impf* (*pf* **при~**) put to shame; **~ся** (*pf* **по~ся**) be ashamed. **стыдли́вый** bashful. **сты́дн|ый** shameful; **~о!** shame! **~о** *impers*+*dat* **ему́**

~о he is ashamed; **как тебé не ~о!** you ought to be ashamed of yourself!
стык joint; junction. **стыковáть** *impf* (*pf* **со~**) join end to end; **~ся** (*pf* **при~ся**) dock. **стыкóвка** docking.
сты́нуть, стыть (-ы́ну; стыл) *impf* cool; get cold.
сты́чка skirmish; squabble.
стюардécca stewardess.
стя́гивать *impf*, **стянýть** (-нý, -нешь) *pf* tighten; pull together; assemble; pull off; steal; **~ся** tighten; assemble.
стяжáтель (-я) *m* money-grubber. **стяжáть** *impf* & *pf* gain, win.
суббóта Saturday.
субсиди́ровать *impf* & *pf* subsidize. **субси́дия** subsidy.
субъéкт subject; ego; person; character, type. **субъекти́вный** subjective.
сувени́р souvenir.
суверенитéт sovereignty. **суверéнный** sovereign.
сугли́нок (-нка) loam.
сугрóб snowdrift.
сугýбо *adv* especially.
суд (-á) court; trial; verdict.
судá *etc.*: *see* **суд, сýдно**[1]
судáк (-á) pike-perch.
судéбный judicial; legal; forensic. **судéйский** judge's; referee's, umpire's. **суди́мость** previous convictions.
суди́ть (сужý, сýдишь) *impf* judge; try; referee, umpire; foreordain; **~ся** go to law.
сýдно[1] (*pl* -дá, -óв) vessel, craft.
сýдно[2] (*gen pl* -ден) bed-pan.
судовóй ship's; marine.
судомóйка kitchen-maid; scullery.
судопроизвóдство legal proceedings.
сýдорога cramp, convulsion. **сýдорожный** convulsive.
судостроéние shipbuilding. **судострои́тельный** shipbuilding. **судохóдный** navigable; shipping.
судьбá (*pl* -ы, -деб) fate, destiny.
судья́ (*pl* -дьи, -дéй, -дьям) *m* judge; referee; umpire.
суевéрие superstition. **суевéрный** superstitious.
сусетá bustle, fuss. **суети́ться** (-ечýсь) *impf* bustle, fuss. **суетли́вый** fussy, bustling.
суждéние opinion; judgement.
сужéние narrowing; constriction. **сýживать** *impf*, **сýзить** (-ýжу) *pf* narrow, contract; **~ся** narrow; taper.
сук (-á, *loc* -ý; *pl* сýчья, -ьев *or* -и́, -óв) bough.
сýка bitch. **сýкин** *adj*: **~ сын** son of a bitch.
сукнó (*pl* -a, -кон) cloth; **положи́ть под ~** shelve. **сукóнный** cloth; clumsy, crude.
сули́ть *impf* (*pf* **по~**) promise.
султáн plume.
сумасбрóд, сумасбрóдка nutcase. **сумасбрóдный** wild, mad. **сумасбрóдство** wild behaviour. **сумасшéдш|ий** mad; **~ий** *sb*, **~ая** *sb* lunatic. **сумасшéствие** madness.
суматóха turmoil; bustle.
сумбýр confusion. **сумбýрный** confused.
сýмеречный twilight. **сýмерки** (-рек) *pl* twilight, dusk.
сумéть (-éю) *pf* +*inf* be able to, manage to.
сýмка bag.
сýмма sum. **суммáрный** summary; total. **сумми́ровать** *impf* & *pf* add up; summarize.

су́мрак twilight; murk. **су́мрачный** gloomy.
су́мчатый marsupial.
сунду́к (-á) trunk, chest.
су́нуть(ся (-ну(сь) *pf of* **сова́ть(ся**
суп (*pl* -ы́) soup.
суперма́ркет supermarket.
суперобло́жка dust-jacket.
супру́г husband, spouse; *pl* husband and wife, (*married*) couple. **супру́га** wife, spouse.
супру́жеский conjugal. **супру́жество** matrimony.
сургу́ч (-á) sealing-wax.
сурди́нка mute; **под сурди́нку** on the sly.
суро́вость severity, sternness. **суро́вый** severe, stern; bleak; unbleached.
суро́к (-рка́) marmot.
суррога́т substitute.
су́слик ground-squirrel.
суста́в joint, articulation.
су́тки (-ток) *pl* twenty-four hours; a day.
су́толока commotion.
су́точн|ый daily; round-the-clock; **~ые** *sb pl* per diem allowance.
суту́литься *impf* stoop. **суту́лый** round-shouldered.
суть essence, main point.
суфлёр prompter. **суфли́ровать** *impf +dat* prompt.
су́ффикс suffix.
суха́рь (-я́) *m* rusk; *pl* breadcrumbs. **су́хо** *adv* drily; coldly.
сухожи́лие tendon.
сухо́й (сух, -á, -о) dry; cold. **сухопу́тный** land. **су́хость** dryness; coldness. **сухоща́вый** lean, skinny.
сучкова́тый knotty; gnarled. **сучо́к** (-чка́) twig; knot.
су́ша (dry) land. **су́ше** *comp of* **сухо́й**. **сушёный** dried.
суши́лка dryer; drying-room.
суши́ть (-шу́, -шишь) *impf* (*pf* **вы́~**) dry, dry out, up; **~ся** (get) dry.
суще́ственный essential, vital. **существи́тельное** *sb* noun. **существо́** being, creature; essence. **существова́ние** existence. **существова́ть** *impf* exist. **су́щий** absolute, downright. **су́щность** essence.
сую́ *etc.*: *see* **сова́ть**. **с|фабрикова́ть** *pf.* **с|фальши́вить** (-влю) *pf.*
с|фантази́ровать *pf.*
сфе́ра sphere. **сфери́ческий** spherical.
сфинкс sphinx.
с|формирова́ть(ся *pf.* **с|формова́ть** *pf.* **с|формули́ровать** *pf.* **с|фотографи́ровать(ся** *pf.*
схвати́ть (-ачу́, -а́тишь) *pf*, **схва́тывать** *impf* (*impf also* **хвата́ть**) seize; catch; grasp; **~ся** snatch, catch; grapple. **схва́тка** skirmish; *pl* contractions.
схе́ма diagram; outline, plan; circuit. **схемати́ческий** schematic; sketchy. **схемати́чный** sketchy.
с|хитри́ть *pf.*
схлы́нуть (-нет) *pf* (break and) flow back; subside.
сход coming off; descent; gathering. **сходи́ть**[1]**(ся** (-ожу́(сь, -о́дишь(ся) *impf of* **сойти́(сь**. **сходи́ть**[2] (-ожу́, -о́дишь) *pf* go; **+за**+*instr* go to fetch. **схо́дка** gathering, meeting. **схо́дный** (-ден, -дна́, -о) similar; reasonable. **схо́дня** (*gen pl* -ей) (*usu pl*) gang-plank. **схо́дство** similarity.
с|хорони́ть(ся (-ню́(сь, -нишь(ся) *pf.*

сцеди́ть (-ежу́, -е́дишь) *pf*, **сце́живать** *impf* strain off, decant.

сце́на stage; scene. **сцена́рий** scenario; script. **сценари́ст** script-writer. **сцени́ческий** stage.

сцепи́ть (-плю́, -пишь) *pf*, **сцепля́ть** *impf* couple; **~ся** be coupled; grapple. **сце́пка** coupling. **сцепле́ние** coupling; clutch.

счастли́вец (-вца), **счастли́вчик** lucky man. **счастли́вица** lucky woman. **счастли́в|ый** (сча́стли́в) happy; lucky; **~o!** all the best!; **~ого пути́** bon voyage. **сча́стье** happiness; good fortune.

сче́сть(ся (сочту́(сь, -тёшь(ся; счёл(ся, сочла́(сь) *pf of* **счита́ть(ся. счёт** (*loc* -у́; *pl* -а́) bill; account; counting, calculation; score; expense. **счётный** calculating; accounts. **счетово́д** book-keeper, accountant. **счётчик** counter; meter. **счёты** (-ов) *pl* abacus.

счи́стить (-и́щу) *pf* (*impf* **счища́ть**) clean off; clear away.

счита́ть *impf* (*pf* **со~, сче́сть**) count; reckon; consider; **~ся** (*pf also* **по~ся**) settle accounts; be considered; +**с**+*instr* take into consideration; reckon with.

счища́ть *impf of* **счи́стить**

США *pl indecl abbr* (*of* **Соединённые Шта́ты Аме́рики**) USA.

сшиба́ть *impf*, **сшиби́ть** (-бу́, -бёшь; сшиб) *pf* strike, hit, knock (off); **~ с ног** knock down; **~ся** collide; come to blows.

сшива́ть *impf*, **с|шить** (сошью́, -ьёшь) *pf* sew (together).

съеда́ть *impf of* **съесть. съедо́бный** edible; nice.

съе́ду *etc.*: *see* **съе́хать**

съёживаться *impf*, **съ|ёжиться** (-жусь) *pf* shrivel, shrink.

съезд congress; conference; arrival. **съе́здить** (-зжу) *pf* go, drive, travel.

съезжа́ть(ся *impf of* **съе́хать(ся. съел** *etc.*: *see* **съесть**

съёмка removal; survey, surveying; shooting. **съёмный** detachable, removable. **съёмщик, съёмщица** tenant; surveyor.

съестно́й food; **~о́е** *sb* food (supplies). **съ|есть** (-ем, -ешь, -ест, -еди́м; съел) *pf* (*impf also* **съеда́ть**)

съе́хать (-е́ду) *pf* (*impf* **съезжа́ть**) go down; come down; move; **~ся** meet; assemble.

съ|язви́ть (-влю́) *pf*.

сы́воротка whey; serum.

сыгра́ть *pf of* **игра́ть; ~ся** play (well) together.

сын (*pl* сыновья́, -ве́й, -вья́м *or* -ы́, -о́в) son. **сыно́вний** filial. **сыно́к** (-нка́) little son; sonny.

сы́пать (-плю) *impf* pour; pour forth; **~ся** fall; pour out; rain down; fray. **сыпно́й тиф** typhus. **сыпу́чий** friable; free-flowing; shifting. **сыпь** rash, eruption.

сыр (*loc* -у́; *pl* -ы́) cheese.

сыре́ть (-е́ю) *impf* (*pf* **от~**) become damp.

сыре́ц (-рца́) raw product.

сыр|о́й (сыр, -а́, -о) damp; raw; uncooked; unboiled; unfinished; unripe. **сы́рость** dampness. **сырьё** raw material(s).

сыска́ть (сыщу́, сы́щешь) *pf* find.

сы́тный (-тен, -тна́, -о) filling. **сы́тость** satiety. **сы́тый** (сыт, -а́, -о) full.

сыч (-á) little owl.
сы́щик detective.
с|эконо́мить (-млю) *pf.*
сэр sir.
сюда́ *adv* here, hither.
сюже́т subject; plot; topic. **сюже́тный** subject; having a theme.
сюи́та suite.
сюрпри́з surprise.
сюрреали́зм surrealism. **сюрреалисти́ческий** surrealist.
сюрту́к (-á) frock-coat.
сяк *adv*: *see* **так.** **сям** *adv*: *see* **там**

Т

та *see* **тот**
таба́к (-á) tobacco. **табаке́рка** snuff-box. **таба́чный** tobacco.
та́бель (-я; *pl* -и, -ей *or* -я́, -е́й) *m* table, list. **та́бельный** table; time.
табле́тка tablet.
табли́ца table; ~ **умноже́ния** multiplication table.
та́бор (gipsy) camp.
табу́н (-á) herd.
табуре́т, табуре́тка stool.
тавро́ (*pl* -а, -áм) brand.
тавтоло́гия tautology.
таджик, -и́чка Tadzhik.
Таджикиста́н Tadzhikistan.
таёжный taiga.
таз (*loc* -ý; *pl* -ы́) basin; pelvis. **тазобе́дренный** hip. **та́зовый** pelvic.
таи́нственный mysterious; secret. **таи́ть** *impf* hide, harbour; **~ся** hide; lurk.
Тайва́нь *m* Taiwan.
тайга́ taiga.
тайко́м *adv* secretly, surreptitiously; ~ **от**+*gen* behind the back of.
тайм half; period of play.
та́йна secret; mystery. **тайни́к** (-á) hiding-place; *pl* recesses. **та́йный** secret; privy.
тайфу́н typhoon.
так *adv* so; like this; as it should be; just like that; **и** ~ even so; as it is; **и** ~ **да́лее** and so on; ~ **и сяк** this way and that; **не** ~ wrong; ~ **же** in the same way; ~ **же... как** as ... as; ~ **и есть** I thought so!; ~ **ему́ и на́до** serves him right; ~ **и́ли ина́че** one way or another; ~ **себе́** so-so. **так** *conj* then; so; ~ **как** as, since; ~ **что** so.
такела́ж rigging.
та́кже *adv* also, too, as well.
тако́в *m* (-á *f*, -ó *neut*, -ы́ *pl*) *pron* such.
так|о́й *pron* such (a); **в ~о́м слу́чае** in that case; **кто он ~о́й?** who is he?; **~о́й же** the same; **~и́м о́бразом** in this way; **что э́то ~о́е?** what is this? **тако́й-то** *pron* so-and-so; such-and-such.
та́кса fixed rate; tariff.
таксёр taxi-driver. **такси́** *neut indecl* taxi. **таксúст** taxi-driver. **таксопа́рк** taxi depot.
такт time; bar; beat; tact.
та́к-таки after all, really.
та́ктика tactics. **такти́ческий** tactical.
такти́чность tact. **такти́чный** tactful.
та́ктов|ый time, timing; **~ая черта́** bar-line.
тала́нт talent. **тала́нтливый** talented.
талисма́н talisman.
та́лия waist.
тало́н, тало́нчик coupon.
та́лый thawed, melted.

тальк talc; talcum powder.
там *adv* there; ~ **и сям** here and there; ~ **же** in the same place; ibid.
тамада́ *m* toast-master.
та́мбур[1] tambour; lobby; platform. **та́мбур**[2] chain-stitch.
тамо́женник customs official. **тамо́женный** customs. **тамо́жня** custom-house.
та́мошний of that place, local.
тампо́н tampon.
та́нгенс tangent.
та́нго *neut indecl* tango.
та́нец (-нца) dance; dancing.
тани́н tannin.
танк tank. **та́нкер** tanker. **танки́ст** member of a tank crew. **та́нковый** tank, armoured.
танцева́льный dancing; ~ **ве́чер** dance. **танцева́ть** (-цу́ю) *impf* dance. **танцо́вщик, танцо́вщица** (ballet) dancer. **танцо́р, танцо́рка** dancer.
та́пка, та́почка slipper.
та́ра packing; tare.
育тарака́н cockroach.
тара́н battering-ram.
тара́нтул tarantula.
таре́лка plate; cymbal; satellite dish.
тари́ф tariff.
таска́ть *impf* drag, lug; carry; pull; take; pull out; swipe; wear; **~ся** drag; hang about.
тасова́ть *impf* (*pf* **с~**) shuffle.
ТАСС *abbr* (*of* **Телегра́фное аге́нтство Сове́тского Сою́за**) Tass (Telegraph Agency of the Soviet Union).
тата́рин, тата́рка Tatar.
татуиро́вка tattooing, tattoo.
тафта́ taffeta.
тахта́ ottoman.
та́чка wheelbarrow.
тащи́ть (-щу́, -щишь) *impf* (*pf* **вы́~, с~**) pull; drag, lug; carry; take; pull out; swipe; **~ся** drag o.s. along; drag.
та́ять (та́ю) *impf* (*pf* **рас~**) melt; thaw; dwindle.
тварь creature(s); wretch.
тверде́ть (-е́ет) *impf* (*pf* **за~**) harden, become hard. **тверди́ть** (-ржу́) *impf* (*pf* **вы́~**) repeat, say again and again; memorize. **твёрдо** *adv* hard; firmly, firm. **твердоло́бый** thick-skulled; diehard. **твёрдый** hard; firm; solid; steadfast; ~ **знак** hard sign, ъ; **~ое те́ло** solid. **тверды́ня** stronghold.
твой (-его́) *m*, **твоя́** (-е́й) *f*, **твоё** (-его́) *neut*, **твои́** (-и́х) *pl* your, yours.
творе́ние creation, work; creature. **творе́ц** (-рца́) creator. **твори́тельный** instrumental. **твори́ть** *impf* (*pf* **со~**) create; do; make; **~ся** happen.
творо́г (-а́) curds; cottage cheese.
тво́рческий creative. **тво́рчество** creation; creative work; works.
те *see* **тот**
т.е. *abbr* (*of* **то есть**) that is, i.e.
теа́тр theatre. **театра́льный** theatre; theatrical.
тебя́ *etc.*: *see* **ты**
те́зис thesis.
тёзка *m & f* namesake.
тёк *see* **течь**
текст text; libretto, lyrics.
тексти́ль *m* textiles. **тексти́льный** textile.
тексту́ра texture.
теку́чий fluid; unstable. **теку́щий** current; routine.
теле- *in comb* tele-; television. **телеателье́** *neut indecl* television maintenance workshop.

~вúдение television. **~визиóнный** television. **~вúзор** television (set). **~грáмма** telegram. **~грáф** telegraph (office). **~графúровать** *impf* & *pf* telegraph. **~грáфный** telegraph(ic). **~зрúтель** *m* (television) viewer. **~объектúв** telephoto lens. **~патúческий** telepathic. **~пáтия** telepathy. **~скóп** telescope. **~стáнция** television station. **~стýдия** television studio. **~фóн** telephone; (telephone) number; **(по)звонúть по ~фóну** *+dat* ring up. **~фон-автомáт** public telephone, call-box. **~фонúст, -úстка** (telephone) operator. **~фóнный** telephone; **~фóнная кнúга** telephone directory; **~фóнная стáнция** telephone exchange; **~фóнная трýбка** receiver. **~фон-ответчик** answering machine. **~цéнтр** television centre.

телéга cart, wagon. **телéжка** small cart; trolley.

тéлекс telex.

телёнок (-нка; *pl* -ята, -ят) calf.

телéсн|ый bodily; corporal; **~ого цвéта** flesh-coloured.

Телéц (-льцá) Taurus.

телúться *impf* (*pf* **о~**) calve.

тёлка heifer.

тéло (*pl* -á) body. **телогрéйка** padded jacket. **телосложéние** build. **телохранúтель** *m* bodyguard.

телята *etc.*: *see* **телёнок. телятина** veal. **телячий** calf; veal.

тем *conj* (so much) the; **~ лýчше** so much the better; **~ не мéнее** nevertheless.

тем *see* **тот, тьма**

тéма subject; theme. **темáтика** subject-matter; themes. **темати́ческий** subject; thematic.

тембр timbre.

темнéть (-éет) *impf* (*pf* **по~, с~**) become dark. **темнúца** dungeon. **темнó** *predic* it is dark. **темнокóжий** dark-skinned, swarthy. **тёмно-сúний** dark blue. **темнотá** darkness. **тёмный** dark.

темп tempo; rate.

темперáмент temperament. **темперáментный** temperamental.

температýра temperature.

тéмя (-мени) *neut* crown, top of the head.

тендéнция tendency; bias.

теневóй, тенúстый shady.

тéннис tennis. **теннисúст, -úстка** tennis-player. **тéннисн|ый** tennis; **~ая площáдка** tennis-court.

тéнор (*pl* -á) tenor.

тент awning.

тень (*loc* -ú; *pl* -и, -éй) shade; shadow; phantom; ghost; particle, vestige, atom; suspicion; **тéни для век** *pl* eyeshadow.

теóлог theologian. **теологúческий** theological. **теолóгия** theology.

теорéма theorem. **теорéтик** theoretician. **теоретúческий** theoretical. **теóрия** theory.

тепéрешн|ий present. **тепéрь** *adv* now; today.

теплéть (-éет) *impf* (*pf* **по~**) get warm. **тéплиться** (-ится) *impf* flicker; glimmer. **теплúца** greenhouse, conservatory. **теплúчный** hothouse. **теплó** heat; warmth. **теплó** *adv* warmly; *predic* it is warm.

тепло- *in comb* heat; thermal;

thermo-. **тепловóз** diesel locomotive. **~крóвный** warm-blooded. **~обмéн** heat exchange. **~провóдный** heat-conducting. **~стóйкий** heat-resistant. **~хóд** motor ship. **~централь** heat and power station.

тепловóй heat; thermal. **теплотá** heat; warmth. **тёплый** (-пел, -плá, тёплó) warm.

терáкт terrorist act.

терапéвт therapeutist. **терапия** therapy.

теребить (-блю) *impf* pull (at); pester.

терéть (тру, трёшь; тёр) *impf* rub; grate; **~ся** rub o.s.; **~ся óколо**+*gen* hang about, hang around; **~ся средú** +*gen* mix with.

терзáть *impf* tear to pieces; torment; **~ся** +*instr* suffer; be a prey to.

тёрка grater.

тéрмин term. **терминолóгия** terminology.

терми́ческий thermic, thermal. **термóметр** thermometer. **тéрмос** thermos (flask). **термостáт** thermostat. **термоя́дерный** thermonuclear.

тернóвник sloe, blackthorn. **терни́стый** thorny.

терпели́вый patient. **терпéние** patience. **терпéть** (-плю, -пишь) *impf* (*pf* **по~**) suffer; bear, endure. **терпéться** (-пится) *impf impers+dat*: **емý не тéрпится** +*inf* he is impatient to. **терпи́мость** tolerance. **терпи́мый** tolerant; tolerable.

тéрпкий (-пок, -пкá, -о) astringent; tart.

террáса terrace.

территориáльный territorial.

террито́рия territory.

террóр terror. **терроризи́ровать** *impf & pf* terrorize. **террори́ст** terrorist.

тёртый grated; experienced.

терьéр terrier.

теря́ть *impf* (*pf* **по~, у~**) lose; shed; **~ся** get lost; disappear; fail, decline; become flustered.

тёс boards, planks. **тесáть** (тешý, тéшешь) *impf* cut, hew.

тесёмка ribbon, braid.

тесни́ть *impf* (*pf* **по~, с~**) crowd; squeeze, constrict; be too tight; **~ся** press through; move up; crowd, jostle. **теснотá** crowded state; crush. **тéсн|ый** crowded; (too) tight; close; compact; **~о** it is crowded.

тесóвый board, plank.

тест test.

тéсто dough; pastry.

тесть *m* father-in-law.

тесьмá ribbon, braid.

тéтерев (*pl* -á) black grouse. **тетёрка** grey hen.

тётка aunt.

тетрáдка, тетрáдь exercise book.

тётя (*gen pl* -ей) aunt.

тех- *abbr in comb* (*of* **техни́ческий**) technical.

тéхник technician. **тéхника** technical equipment; technology; technique. **тéхникум** technical college. **техни́ческ|ий** technical; **~ие услóвия** specifications. **технóлог** technologist. **технологи́ческий** technological. **технолóгия** technology. **техперсонáл** technical personnel.

течéние flow; course; current, stream; trend.

течь[1] (-чёт; тёк, -лá) *impf* flow; stream; leak. **течь**[2] leak.

тéшить (**-шу**) *impf* (*pf* **по~**)

amuse; gratify; **~ся** (*+instr*) amuse o.s. (with).

тешу́ *etc.*: *see* **теса́ть**

тёща mother-in-law.

тигр tiger. **тигри́ца** tigress.

тик¹ tic.

тик² teak.

ти́на slime, mud.

тип type. **типи́чный** typical. **типово́й** standard; model. **типогра́фия** printing-house, press. **типогра́фский** typographical.

тир shooting-range, -gallery. **тира́ж** (-а́) draw; circulation; edition.

тира́н tyrant. **тира́нить** *impf* tyrannize. **тирани́ческий** tyrannical. **тирани́я** tyranny.

тире́ *neut indecl* dash.

ти́скать *impf*, **ти́снуть** (-ну) *pf* press, squeeze. **тиски́** (-о́в) *pl* vice; **в тиска́х** *+gen* in the grip of. **тисне́ние** stamping; imprint; design. **тиснёный** stamped.

тита́н¹ titanian.

тита́н² boiler.

тита́н³ titan.

титр title, sub-title.

ти́тул title; title-page. **ти́тульный** title.

тиф (*loc* -у́) typhus.

ти́хий (тих, -а́, -о) quiet; silent; calm; slow. **тихоокеа́нский** Pacific. **ти́ше** *comp of* **ти́хий, ти́хо; ти́ше!** quiet! **тишина́** quiet, silence.

т. к. *abbr* (*of* **так как**) as, since.

тка́ный woven. **ткань** fabric, cloth; tissue. **ткать** (тку, ткёшь; -ал, -а́ла́, -о) *impf* (*pf* **со~**) weave. **тка́цкий** weaving; **~ стано́к** loom. **ткач, ткачи́ха** weaver.

ткну́ть(ся (-у(сь, -ёшь(ся) *pf of* **ты́кать(ся**

тле́ние decay; smouldering. **тлеть** (-е́ет) *impf* rot, decay; smoulder; **~ся** smoulder.

тля aphis.

тмин caraway(-seeds).

то *pron* that; **а не то́** or else, otherwise; **(да) и то́** and even then, and that; **то́ есть** that is (to say); **то и де́ло** every now and then. **то** *conj* then; **не то..., не то** either ... or; half ..., half; **то..., то** now ..., now; **то ли..., то ли** whether ... or.

-то *partl* just, exactly; **в то́м-то и де́ло** that's just it.

тобо́й *see* **ты**

това́р goods; commodity.

това́рищ comrade; friend; colleague. **това́рищеский** comradely; friendly.

това́рищество comradeship; company; association.

това́рный goods; commodity.

товаро- *in comb* commodity; goods. **товарообме́н** barter. **~оборо́т** (sales) turnover. **~отправи́тель** *m* consignor. **~получа́тель** *m* consignee.

тогда́ *adv* then; **~ как** whereas. **тогда́шний** of that time.

того́ *see* **тот**

тожде́ственный identical. **то́ждество** identity.

то́же *adv* also, too.

ток (*pl* -и) current.

тока́рный turning; **~ стано́к** lathe. **то́карь** (*pl* -я́, -е́й *or* -и, -ей) *m* turner, lathe operator.

токси́ческий toxic.

толк sense; use; **бе́з ~у** senselessly; **знать ~ в**+*prep* know well; **сбить с ~у** confuse; **с ~ом** intelligently.

толка́ть *impf* (*pf* **толкну́ть**) push, shove; jog; **~ся** jostle.

то́лки (-ов) *pl* rumours, gossip.

толкну́ть(ся (-ну́(сь, -нёшь(ся) *pf of* **толка́ть(ся**

толкова́ние interpretation; *pl* commentary. **толкова́ть** *impf* interpret; explain; talk. **толко́вый** intelligent; clear; **~ слова́рь** defining dictionary. **то́лком** *adv* plainly; seriously.

толкотня́ crush, squash.

толку́ *etc.*: *see* **толо́чь**

толку́чка crush, squash; second-hand market.

толокно́ oatmeal.

толо́чь (-лку́, -лчёшь; -ло́к, -лкла́) *impf* (*pf* **ис~, рас~**) pound, crush.

толпа́ (*pl* -ы) crowd. **толпи́ться** *impf* crowd; throng.

толсте́ть (-е́ю) *impf* (*pf* **по~**) grow fat; put on weight. **толстоко́жий** thick-skinned; pachydermatous. **то́лстый** (-а́, -о) fat; thick. **толстя́к** (-а́) fat man *or* boy.

толчёный crushed; ground.

толчёт *etc.*: *see* **толо́чь**

толчея́ crush, squash.

толчо́к (-чка́) push, shove; (*sport*) put; jolt; shock, tremor.

то́лща thickness; thick. **то́лще** *comp of* **то́лстый. толщина́** thickness; fatness.

толь *m* roofing felt.

то́лько *adv* only, merely; **~ что** (only) just; *conj* only, but; **(как) ~, (лишь) ~** as soon as; **~ бы** if only.

том (*pl* **~а́**) volume. **то́мик** small volume.

тома́т tomato. **тома́тный** tomato.

томи́тельный tedious, wearing; agonizing. **томи́ть** (**-млю́**) *impf* (*pf* **ис~**) tire; torment; **~ся** languish; be tormented.

томле́ние languor. **то́мный** (-мен, -мна́, -о) languid, languorous.

тон (*pl* -а́ *or* -ы, -о́в) tone; note; shade; form. **тона́льность** key.

то́ненький thin; slim. **то́нкий** (-нок, -нка́, -о) thin; slim; fine; refined; subtle; keen. **то́нкость** thinness; slimness; fineness; subtlety.

то́нна ton.

тонне́ль *see* **тунне́ль**

то́нус tone.

тону́ть (-ну́, -нешь) *impf* (*pf* **по~, у~**) sink; drown.

то́ньше *comp of* **то́нкий**

то́пать *impf* (*pf* **то́пнуть**) stamp.

топи́ть[1] (-плю́, -пишь) *impf* (*pf* **по~, у~**) sink; drown; ruin; **~ся** drown o.s.

топи́ть[2] (-плю́, -пишь) *impf* stoke; heat; melt (down); **~ся** burn; melt. **то́пка** stoking; heating; melting (down); furnace.

то́пкий boggy, marshy.

то́пливный fuel. **то́пливо** fuel.

то́пнуть (-ну) *pf of* **то́пать**

топографи́ческий topographical. **топогра́фия** topography.

то́поль (*pl* -я́ *or* -и) *m* poplar.

топо́р (-а́) axe. **топо́рик** hatchet. **топори́ще** axe-handle. **топо́рный** axe; clumsy, crude.

то́пот tramp; clatter. **топта́ть** (-пчу́, -пчешь) *impf* (*pf* **по~**) trample (down); **~ся** stamp; **~ся на ме́сте** mark time.

топча́н (-а́) trestle-bed.

топь bog, marsh.

торг (*loc* -у́, *pl* -и́) trading; bargaining; *pl* auction. **торгова́ть** *impf* (*pf* **с~**) trade; **~ся** bargain, haggle. **торго́вец** (-вца) merchant; tradesman. **торго́вка** market-

woman; stall-holder. **торго́вля** trade. **торго́вый** trade, commercial; merchant. **торгпре́д** *abbr* trade representative.
торе́ц (-рца́) butt-end; wooden paving-block.
торже́ственный solemn; ceremonial. **торжество́** celebration; triumph. **торжествова́ть** *impf* celebrate; triumph.
торможе́ние braking. **то́рмоз** (*pl* -а́ *or* -ы) brake. **тормози́ть** (-ожу́) *impf* (*pf* **за~**) brake; hamper.
тормоши́ть (-шу́) *impf* pester; bother.
торопи́ть (-плю́, -пишь) *impf* (*pf* **по~**) hurry; hasten; **~ся** hurry. **торопли́вый** hasty.
торпе́да torpedo.
торс torso.
торт cake.
торф peat. **торфяно́й** peat.
торча́ть (-чу́) *impf* stick out; protrude; hang about.
торше́р standard lamp.
тоска́ melancholy; boredom; nostalgia; **~ по**+*dat* longing for. **тоскли́вый** melancholy; depressed; dreary. **тоскова́ть** *impf* be melancholy, depressed; long; **~ по**+*dat* miss.
тост toast.
тот *m* (та *f*, то *neut*, те *pl*) *pron* that; the former; the other; the one; the same; the right; **и ~ и друго́й** both; **к тому́ же** moreover; **не ~** the wrong; **ни ~ ни друго́й** neither; **тот, кто** the one who, the person who. **то́тчас** *adv* immediately.
тоталитари́зм totalitarianism. **тоталита́рный** totalitarian.
тота́льный total.
точи́лка sharpener; pencil-sharpener. **точи́ло** whetstone, grindstone. **точи́льный** grinding, sharpening; **~ ка́мень** whetstone, grindstone. **точи́льщик** (knife-)grinder. **точи́ть** (-чу́, -чишь) *impf* (*pf* **вы́~, на~**) sharpen; hone; turn; eat away; gnaw at.
то́чка spot; dot; full stop; point; **~ зре́ния** point of view; **~ с запято́й** semicolon. **то́чно**[1] *adv* exactly, precisely; punctually. **то́чно**[2] *conj* as though, as if. **то́чность** punctuality; precision; accuracy; **в то́чности** exactly, precisely. **то́чный** (-чен, -чна́, -о) exact, precise; accurate; punctual. **то́чь-в-то́чь** *adv* exactly; word for word.
тошни́ть *impf impers*: **меня́ тошни́т** I feel sick. **тошнота́** nausea. **тошнотво́рный** sickening, nauseating.
то́щий (тощ, -а́, -е) gaunt, emaciated; skinny; empty; poor.
трава́ (*pl* -ы) grass; herb. **тра́ви́нка** blade of grass.
трави́ть (-влю́, -вишь) *impf* (*pf* **вы́~, за~**) poison; exterminate, destroy; etch; hunt; torment; badger. **травле́ние** extermination; etching. **тра́вля** hunting; persecution; badgering.
тра́вма trauma, injury.
травоя́дный herbivorous. **травяни́стый, травяно́й** grass; herbaceous; grassy.
траге́дия tragedy. **тра́гик** tragedian. **траги́ческий, траги́чный** tragic.
традицио́нный traditional. **тради́ция** tradition.
траекто́рия trajectory.
тракта́т treatise; treaty.
тракти́р inn, tavern.
трактова́ть *impf* interpret; treat, discuss. **тракто́вка**

treatment; interpretation.

тра́ктор tractor. **тракто́рист** tractor driver.

трал trawl. **тра́лить** *impf* (*pf* **про~**) trawl; sweep. **тра́льщик** trawler; mine-sweeper.

трамбова́ть *impf* (*pf* **у~**) ram, tamp.

трамва́й tram. **трамва́йный** tram.

трампли́н spring-board; ski-jump.

транзи́стор transistor; transistor radio.

транзи́тный transit.

транс trance.

трансатланти́ческий transatlantic.

трансли́ровать *impf & pf* broadcast, transmit. **трансляцио́нный** transmission; broadcasting. **трансля́ция** broadcast, transmission.

тра́нспорт transport; consignment. **транспортёр** conveyor. **транспорти́р** protractor. **транспорти́ровать** *impf & pf* transport. **тра́нспортный** transport.

трансформа́тор transformer.

транше́я trench.

трап ladder.

тра́пеза meal.

трапе́ция trapezium; trapeze.

тра́сса line, course, direction; route, road.

тра́та expenditure; waste. **тра́тить** (-а́чу) *impf* (*pf* **ис~**, **по~**) spend, expend; waste.

тра́улер trawler.

тра́ур mourning. **тра́урный** mourning; funeral; mournful.

трафаре́т stencil; stereotype; cliché. **трафаре́тный** stencilled; conventional, stereotyped.

тра́чу *etc.*: *see* **тра́тить**

тре́бование demand; request; requirement; requisition, order; *pl* needs. **тре́бовательный** demanding. **тре́бовать** *impf* (*pf* **по~**) summon; *+gen* demand, require; need; **~ся** be needed, be required.

трево́га alarm; anxiety. **трево́жить** (-жу) *impf* (*pf* **вс~**, **по~**) alarm; disturb; worry; **~ся** worry, be anxious; trouble o.s. **трево́жный** worried, anxious; alarming; alarm.

тре́звенник teetotaller. **трезве́ть** (-е́ю) *impf* (*pf* **о~**) sober up.

трезво́н peal (*of bells*); rumours; row.

тре́звость sobriety. **тре́звый** (-зв, -а́, -о) sober; teetotal.

тре́йлер trailer.

трель trill; warble.

тре́нер trainer, coach.

тре́ние friction.

тренирова́ть *impf* (*pf* **на~**) train, coach; **~ся** be in training. **трениро́вка** training, coaching. **трениро́вочный** training.

трепа́ть (-плю́, -плешь) *impf* (*pf* **ис~**, **по~**, **рас~**) blow about; dishevel; wear out; pat; **~ся** fray; wear out; flutter.

тре́пет trembling; trepidation.

трепета́ть (-ещу́, -е́щешь) *impf* tremble; flicker; palpitate. **тре́петный** trembling; flickering; palpitating; timid.

треск crack; crackle; fuss.

треска́ cod.

тре́скаться[1] *impf* (*pf* **по~**) crack; chap.

тре́скаться[2] *impf of* **тре́снуться**

тре́снуть (-нет) *pf* snap, crackle; crack; chap; bang; **~ся** (*impf* **тре́скаться**) *+instr* bang.

трест trust.

тре́т|ий (-ья, -ье) third; **~ье** *sb* sweet (course).

трети́ровать *impf* slight.

треть (*gen pl* -е́й) third.

тре́тье *etc.*: *see* **тре́тий**.

треуго́льник triangle. **треуго́льный** triangular.

тре́фы (треф) *pl* clubs.

трёх- *in comb* three-, tri-. **трёхгоди́чный** three-year. **~голо́сный** three-part. **~гра́нный** three-edged; trihedral. **~колёсный** three-wheeled. **~ле́тний** three-year; three-year old. **~ме́рный** three-dimensional. **~ме́сячный** three-month; quarterly; three-month-old. **~по́лье** three-field system. **~со́тый** three-hundredth. **~сторо́нний** three-sided; trilateral; tripartite. **~эта́жный** three-storeyed.

треща́ть (-щу́) *impf* crack; crackle; creak; chirr; crack up; chatter. **тре́щина** crack, split; fissure; chap.

три (трёх, -ём, -емя́, -ёх) three.

трибу́на platform, rostrum; stand. **трибуна́л** tribunal.

тригономе́трия trigonometry.

тридцатиле́тний thirty-year; thirty-year old. **тридца́тый** thirtieth. **три́дцать** (-и́, *instr* -ью́) thirty. **три́жды** *adv* three times; thrice.

трико́ *neut indecl* tricot; tights; knickers. **трикота́ж** knitted fabric; knitwear. **трикота́жный** jersey, tricot; knitted.

трина́дцатый thirteenth. **трина́дцать** thirteen. **трио́ль** triplet.

три́ппер gonorrhoea.

три́ста (трёхсо́т, -ёмста́м, -емяста́ми, -ёхста́х) three hundred.

трито́н *zool* triton.

триу́мф triumph.

тро́гательный touching, moving. **тро́гать(ся** *impf of* **тро́нуть(ся**

тро́е (-и́х) *pl* three. **троебо́рье** triathlon. **троекра́тный** thrice-repeated. **Тро́ица** Trinity; **тро́ица** trio. **Тро́ицын день** Whit Sunday. **тро́йка** three; figure 3; troika; No. 3; three-piece suit. **тройно́й** triple, treble; three-ply. **тро́йственный** triple; tripartite.

тролле́йбус trolley-bus.

тромб blood clot.

тромбо́н trombone.

трон throne.

тро́нуть (-ну) *pf* (*impf* **тро́гать**) touch; disturb; affect; **~ся** start, set out; be touched; be affected.

тропа́ path.

тро́пик tropic.

тропи́нка path.

тропи́ческий tropical.

трос rope, cable.

тростни́к (-а́) reed, rush. **тро́сточка, трость** (*gen pl* ~е́й) cane, walking-stick.

тротуа́р pavement.

трофе́й trophy; *pl* spoils (*of war*), booty.

троюродн|ый: ~ый брат, ~ая сестра́ second cousin.

тру *etc.*: *see* **тере́ть**

труба́ (*pl* -ы) pipe; chimney; funnel; trumpet; tube. **труба́ч** (-а́) trumpeter; trumpet-player. **труби́ть** (-блю́) *impf* (*pf* **про~**) blow, sound; blare. **тру́бка** tube; pipe; (*telephone*) receiver. **трубопрово́д** pipe-line; piping; manifold. **трубочи́ст** chimney-sweep. **тру́бочный** pipe. **тру́бчатый** tubular.

труд (-á) labour; work; effort; **с ~óм** with difficulty. **труди́ться** (-ужу́сь, -у́дишься) *impf* toil, labour, work; trouble. **тру́дно** *predic* it is difficult. **тру́дность** difficulty. **тру́дный** (-ден, -днá, -о) difficult; hard.

трудо- *in comb* labour, work. **трудоде́нь** (-дня́) *m* workday (*unit*). **~ёмкий** labour-intensive. **~люби́вый** industrious. **~лю́бие** industry. **~спосо́бность** ability to work. **~спосо́бный** able-bodied; capable of working.

трудово́й work; working; earned; hard-earned. **трудя́щ|ийся** working; **~иеся** *sb pl* the workers. **тру́женик, тру́женица** toiler.

труп corpse; carcass.

тру́ппа troupe, company.

трус coward.

тру́сики (-ов) *pl* shorts; trunks; pants.

труси́ть[1] (-ушу́) *impf* trot, jog along.

тру́сить[2] (-у́шу) *impf* (*pf* **с~**) be a coward; lose one's nerve; be afraid. **труси́ха** coward. **трусли́вый** cowardly. **тру́сость** cowardice.

трусы́ (-о́в) *pl* shorts; trunks; pants.

трухá dust; trash.

трушу́ *etc.*: *see* **труси́ть**[1], **тру́сить**[2]

трущо́ба slum; godforsaken hole.

трюк stunt; trick.

трюм hold.

трюмо́ *neut indecl* pier-glass.

трю́фель (*gen pl* -ле́й) *m* truffle.

тря́пка rag; spineless creature; *pl* clothes. **тряпьё** rags; clothes.

тряси́на quagmire. **тря́ска** shaking, jolting. **трясти́** (-су́, -сёшь; -яс, -лá) *impf*, **тряхну́ть** (-ну́, -нёшь) *pf* (*pf also* **вы~**) shake; shake out; jolt; **~сь** shake; tremble, shiver; jolt.

тсс *int* sh! hush!

туале́т dress; toilet. **туале́тный** toilet.

туберкулёз tuberculosis.

ту́го *adv* tight(ly), taut; with difficulty. **туго́й** (туг, -á, -о) tight; taut; tightly filled; difficult.

тудá *adv* there, thither; that way; to the right place; **ни ~ ни сюдá** neither one way nor the other; **~ и обрáтно** there and back.

ту́же *comp of* **ту́го, туго́й**

тужу́рка (double-breasted) jacket.

туз (-á, *acc* -á) ace; bigwig.

тузе́мец (-мца), **-мка** native.

ту́ловище trunk; torso.

тулу́п sheepskin coat.

тумáн fog; mist; haze. **тумáнить** *impf* (*pf* **за~**) dim, cloud, obscure; **~ся** grow misty; be befogged. **тумáнность** fog, mist; nebula; obscurity. **тумáнный** foggy; misty; hazy; obscure, vague.

ту́мба post; bollard; pedestal. **ту́мбочка** bedside table.

ту́ндра tundra.

тунея́дец (-дца) sponger.

туни́ка tunic.

тунне́ль *m*, **тонне́ль** *m* tunnel.

тупе́ть (-е́ю) *impf* (*pf* **о~**) become blunt; grow dull. **тупи́к** (-á) cul-de-sac, dead end; impasse; **постáвить в ~** stump, nonplus. **тупи́ться** (-пится) *impf* (*pf* **за~, ис~**) become blunt. **тупи́ца** *m* & *f* blockhead, dimwit. **тупо́й** (туп, -á, -о) blunt; obtuse; dull; vacant, stupid. **ту́пость** bluntness; vacancy; dullness, slowness.

тур turn; round.

тура́ rook, castle.

турба́за holiday village, campsite.

турби́на turbine.

туре́цкий Turkish; ~ **бараба́н** bass drum.

тури́зм tourism. **тури́ст, -и́стка** tourist. **тури́ст(и́че)ский** tourist.

туркме́н (*gen pl* **-ме́н**), ~**ка** Turkmen. **Туркмениста́н** Turkmenistan.

турне́ *neut indecl* tour.

турне́пс swede.

турни́р tournament.

ту́рок (-рка) Turk. **турча́нка** Turkish woman. **Ту́рция** Turkey.

ту́склый dim, dull; lacklustre. **тускне́ть** (-е́ет) *impf* (*pf* **по~**) grow dim.

тут *adv* here; now; ~ **же** there and then.

ту́фля shoe.

ту́хлый (-хл, -á, -о) rotten, bad. **ту́хнуть**[1] (-нет; тух) go bad.

ту́хнуть[2] (-нет; тух) *impf* (*pf* **по~**) go out.

ту́ча cloud; storm-cloud.

ту́чный (-чен, -чна́, -чно) fat; rich, fertile.

туш flourish.

ту́ша carcass.

тушева́ть (-шу́ю) *impf* (*pf* **за~**) shade.

тушёный stewed. **туши́ть**[1] (-шу́, -шишь) *impf* (*pf* **с~**) stew.

туши́ть[2] (-шу́, -шишь) *impf* (*pf* **за~, по~**) extinguish.

тушу́ю *etc.*: *see* **тушева́ть**. **тушь** Indian ink; ~ **(для ресни́ц)** mascara.

тща́тельность care. **тща́телный** careful; painstaking.

тщеду́шный feeble, frail.

тщесла́вие vanity, vainglory. **тщесла́вный** vain. **тщета́** vanity. **тще́тный** vain, futile.

ты (тебя́, тебе́, тобо́й, тебе́) you; thou; **быть на ты с**+*instr* be on intimate terms with.

ты́кать (ты́чу) *impf* (*pf* **ткнуть**) poke; prod; stick.

ты́ква pumpkin; gourd.

тыл (*loc* -у́; *pl* -ы́) back; rear. **ты́льный** back; rear.

тын paling; palisade.

ты́сяча (*instr* -ей *or* -ью) thousand. **тысячеле́тие** millennium; thousandth anniversary. **ты́сячный** thousandth; of (many) thousands.

тычи́нка stamen.

тьма[1] dark, darkness.

тьма[2] host, multitude.

тюбете́йка skull-cap.

тю́бик tube.

тюк (-á) bale, package.

тюле́нь *m* seal.

тюльпа́н tulip.

тюре́мный prison. **тюре́мщик** gaoler. **тюрьма́** (*pl* -ы, -рем) prison, gaol.

тюфя́к (-á) mattress.

тя́га traction; thrust; draught; attraction; craving. **тяга́ться** *impf* vie, contend. **тяга́ч** (-á) tractor.

тя́гостный burdensome; painful. **тя́гость** burden. **тяготе́ние** gravity, gravitation; bent, inclination. **тяготе́ть** (-е́ю) *impf* gravitate; be attracted; ~ **над** hang over. **тяготи́ть** (-ощу́) *impf* be a burden on; oppress.

тягу́чий malleable, ductile; viscous; slow.

тя́жба lawsuit; competition.

тяжело́ *adv* heavily; seriously. **тяжело́** *predic* it is hard; it is painful. **тяжелоатле́т** weight-lifter. **тяжелове́с** heavyweight. **тяжелове́сный** heavy; ponderous. **тяжёлый** (-ёл, -á) heavy; hard; serious; painful. **тя́жесть** gravity; weight; heaviness; severity. **тя́жкий** heavy; severe; grave.

тяну́ть (-ну́, -нешь) *impf* (*pf* **по~**) pull; draw; drag; drag out; weigh; *impers* attract; be tight; **~ся** stretch; extend; stretch out; stretch o.s.; drag on; crawl; drift; move along one after another; last out; reach.

тяну́чка toffee.

У

у *prep+gen* by; at; with; from, of; belonging to; **у меня́ (есть)** I have; **у нас** at our place; in our country.

уба́вить (-влю) *pf*, **убавля́ть** *impf* reduce, diminish.

у|баю́кать *pf*, **убаю́кивать** *impf* lull (to sleep).

убега́ть *impf of* **убежа́ть**

убеди́тельный convincing; earnest. **убеди́ть** (-и́шь) *pf* (*impf* **убежда́ть**) convince; persuade; **~ся** be convinced; make certain.

убежа́ть (-егу́) *pf* (*impf* **убега́ть**) run away; escape; boil over.

убежда́ть(ся *impf of* **убеди́ть(ся. убежде́ние** persuasion; conviction, belief. **убеждённость** conviction. **убеждённый** (-ён, -á) convinced; staunch.

убе́жище refuge, asylum; shelter.

уберега́ть *impf*, **убере́чь** (-регу́, -режёшь; -рёг, -гла́) *pf* protect, preserve; **~ся от**+*gen* protect o.s. against.

уберу́ *etc.*: *see* **убра́ть**

убива́ть(ся *impf of* **уби́ть(ся. уби́йственный** deadly; murderous; killing. **уби́йство** murder. **уби́йца** *m* & *f* murderer.

убира́ть(ся *impf of* **убра́ть(ся; убира́йся!** clear off!

уби́тый killed; crushed; *sb* dead man. **уби́ть** (убью́, -ьёшь) *pf* (*impf* **убива́ть**) kill; murder; **~ся** hurt o.s.

убо́гий wretched. **убо́жество** poverty; squalor.

убо́й slaughter.

убо́р dress, attire.

убо́рка harvesting; clearing up. **убо́рная** *sb* lavatory; dressing-room. **убо́рочн|ый** harvesting; **~ая маши́на** harvester. **убо́рщик, убо́рщица** cleaner. **убра́нство** furniture. **убра́ть** (уберу́, -рёшь; -áл, -á, -о) *pf* (*impf* **убира́ть**) remove; take away; put away; harvest; clear up; decorate; **~ посте́ль** make a bed; **~ со стола́** clear the table; **~ся** tidy up, clean up; clear off.

убыва́ть *impf*, **убы́ть** (убу́ду; у́был, -á, -о) *pf* diminish; subside; wane; leave. **у́быль** diminution; casualties. **убы́ток** (-тка) loss; *pl* damages. **убы́точный** unprofitable.

убью́ *etc.*: *see* **уби́ть**

уважа́емый respected; dear. **уважа́ть** *impf* respect. **уваже́ние** respect; **с ~м** yours sincerely. **уважи́тельный** valid; respectful.

уве́домить (-млю) *pf*, **уведомля́ть** *impf* inform. **уведомле́ние** notification.

уведу́ *etc.*: *see* **увести́**
увезти́ (-зу́, -зёшь; увёз, -ла́) *pf* (*impf* **увози́ть**) take (away); steal; abduct.
увекове́чивать *impf*, **увекове́чить** (-чу) *pf* immortalize; perpetuate.
увёл *etc.*: *see* **увести́**
увеличе́ние increase; magnification; enlargement. **увели́чивать** *impf*, **увели́чить** (-чу) *pf* increase; magnify; enlarge; **~ся** increase, grow. **увеличи́тель** *m* enlarger. **увеличи́тельн|ый** magnifying; enlarging; **~ое стекло́** magnifying glass.
у|венча́ть *pf*, **уве́нчивать** *impf* crown; **~ся** be crowned.
уве́ренность confidence; certainty. **уве́ренный** confident; sure; certain. **уве́рить** *pf* (*impf* **уверя́ть**) assure; convince; **~ся** satisfy o.s.; be convinced.
уверну́ться (-ну́сь, -нёшься) *pf*, **увёртываться** *impf* **от**+*gen* evade. **увёртка** dodge, evasion; subterfuge; *pl* wiles. **увёртливый** evasive, shifty.
увертю́ра overture.
уверя́ть(ся *impf of* **уве́рить(ся**
увеселе́ние amusement, entertainment. **увесели́тельный** entertainment; pleasure. **увеселя́ть** *impf* amuse, entertain.
уве́систый weighty.
увести́ (-еду́, -едёшь; -ёл, -а́) *pf* (*impf* **уводи́ть**) take (away); walk off with.
уве́чить (-чу) *impf* maim, cripple. **уве́чный** maimed, crippled; *sb* cripple. **уве́чье** maiming; injury.
уве́шать *pf*, **уве́шивать** *impf* hang (+*instr* with).
увеща́ть *impf*, **увещева́ть** *impf* exhort, admonish.
у|вида́ть *pf* see. **у|ви́деть(ся** (-и́жу(сь) *pf*.
уви́ливать *impf*, **увильну́ть** (-ну́, -нёшь) *pf* **от**+*gen* dodge; evade.
увлажни́ть *pf*, **увлажня́ть** *impf* moisten.
увлека́тельный fascinating. **увлека́ть** *impf*, **увле́чь** (-еку́, -ечёшь; -ёк, -ла́) *pf* carry away; fascinate; **~ся** be carried away; become mad (+*instr* about). **увлече́ние** animation; passion; crush.
уво́д withdrawal; stealing. **уводи́ть** (-ожу́, -о́дишь) *impf of* **увести́**
увози́ть (-ожу́, -о́дишь) *impf of* **увезти́**
уво́лить *pf*, **увольня́ть** *impf* discharge, dismiss; retire; **~ся** be discharged, retire. **увольне́ние** discharge, dismissal.
увы́ *int* alas!
увяда́ть *impf of* **увя́нуть**. **увя́дший** withered.
увяза́ть[1] *impf of* **увя́знуть**
увяза́ть[2] (-яжу́, -я́жешь) *pf* (*impf* **увя́зывать**) tie up; pack up; co-ordinate; **~ся** pack; tag along. **увя́зка** tying up; co-ordination.
у|вя́знуть (-ну; -я́з) *pf* (*impf also* **увяза́ть**) get bogged down.
увя́зывать(ся *impf of* **увяза́ть(ся**
у|вя́нуть (-ну) *pf* (*impf also* **увяда́ть**) fade, wither.
угада́ть *pf*, **уга́дывать** *impf* guess.
уга́р carbon monoxide (poisoning); ecstasy. **уга́рный газ** carbon monoxide.
угаса́ть *impf*, **у|га́снуть** (-нет;

-áс) *pf* go out; die down.

угле- *in comb* coal; charcoal; carbon. **углевóд** carbohydrate. **~водорóд** hydrocarbon. **~добы́ча** coal extraction. **~кислотá** carbonic acid; carbon dioxide. **~ки́слый** carbonate (of). **~рóд** carbon.

угловóй corner; angular.

углуби́ть (-блю́) *pf*, **углубля́ть** *impf* deepen; **~ся** deepen; delve deeply; become absorbed. **углублéние** depression, dip; deepening. **углублённый** deepened; profound; absorbed.

угнáть (угоню́, -óнишь; -áл, -á, -о) *pf* (*impf* **угоня́ть**) drive away; despatch; steal; **~ся за**+*instr* keep pace with.

угнетáтель *m* oppressor. **угнетáть** *impf* oppress; depress. **угнетéние** oppression; depression. **угнетённый** oppressed; depressed.

уговáривать *impf*, **уговори́ть** *pf* persuade; **~ся** arrange, agree. **уговóр** persuasion; agreement.

угóда: **в угóду** +*dat* to please. **угоди́ть** (-ожу́) *pf*, **угождáть** *impf* fall, get; bang; (+*dat*) hit; +*dat or* **на**+*acc* please. **угóдливый** obsequious. **угóдно** *predic*+*dat*: **как вам ~** as you wish; **что вам ~?** what would you like?; *partl* **кто ~** anyone (you like); **что ~** anything (you like).

угóдье (*gen pl* -ий) land.

ýгол (углá, *loc* -ý) corner; angle.

уголóвник criminal. **уголóвный** criminal.

уголóк (-лкá, *loc* -ý) corner.

ýголь (ýгля; *pl* ýгли, -ей *or* -éй) *m* coal; charcoal.

угóльник set square.

ýгольный coal; carbon(ic).

угомони́ть *pf* calm down; **~ся** calm down.

угóн driving away; stealing. **угоня́ть** *impf of* **угнáть**

угорáть *impf*, **угорéть** (-рю́) *pf* get carbon monoxide poisoning; be mad. **угорéлый** mad; possessed.

ýгорь[1] (угря́) *m* eel.

ýгорь[2] (угря́) *m* blackhead.

угости́ть (-ощу́) *pf*, **угощáть** *impf* entertain; treat. **угощéние** entertaining, treating; refreshments.

угрожáть *impf* threaten. **угрóза** threat, menace.

угрóзыск *abbr* criminal investigation department.

угрызéние pangs.

угрю́мый sullen, morose.

удавáться (удаётся) *impf of* **удáться**

у|дави́ть(ся (-влю́(сь, -вишь(ся) *pf*. **удáвка** running-knot, half hitch.

удалéние removal; sending away; moving off. **удали́ть** *pf* (*impf* **удаля́ть**) remove; send away; move away; **~ся** move off, away; retire.

удалóй, удáлый (-áл, -á, -о) daring, bold. **ýдаль, удальствó** daring, boldness.

удаля́ть(ся *impf of* **удали́ть(ся**

удáр blow; stroke; attack; kick; thrust; seizure; bolt. **ударéние** accent; stress; emphasis. **удáрить** *pf*, **ударя́ть** *impf* (*impf also* **бить**) strike; hit; beat; **~ся** strike, hit; +**в**+*acc* break into; burst into. **удáрник, -ница** shock-worker. **удáрный** percussion; shock; stressed; urgent.

удáться (-áстся, -адýтся; -áлся, -лáсь) *pf* (*impf* **удавáться**) succeed, be a success; *impers* +*dat* +*inf* succeed, manage; **мне удалóсь найтú рабóту** I managed to find a job. **удáча** good luck; success. **удáчный** successful; felicitous.

удвáивать *impf*, **удвóить** (-óю) *pf* double, redouble. **удвоéние** (re)doubling.

удéл lot, destiny.

уделúть *pf* (*impf* **уделя́ть**) spare, give.

уделя́ть *impf of* **уделúть**

удержáние deduction; retention, keeping. **удержáть** (-жý, -жишь) *pf*, **удéрживать** *impf* hold (on to); retain; restrain; suppress; deduct; **~ся** hold out; stand firm; refrain (from).

удерý *etc.*: *see* **удрáть**

удешевúть (-влю́) *pf*, **удешевля́ть** *impf* reduce the price of.

удивúтельный surprising, amazing; wonderful. **удивúть** (-влю́) *pf*, **удивля́ть** *impf* surprise, amaze; **~ся** be surprised, be amazed. **удивлéние** surprise, amazement.

удилá (-úл) *pl* bit.

удúлище fishing-rod.

удирáть *impf of* **удрáть**

удúть (ужý, ýдишь) *impf* fish for; **~ рыбу** fish; **~ся** bite.

удлинéние lengthening; extension. **удлинúть** *pf*, **удлиня́ть** *impf* lengthen; extend; **~ся** become longer; be extended.

удóбно *adv* comfortably; conveniently. **удóбный** comfortable; convenient.

удобоварúмый digestible.

удобрéние fertilization; fertilizer. **удóбрить** *pf*, **удобря́ть** *impf* fertilize.

удóбство comfort; convenience.

удовлетворéние satisfaction; gratification. **удовлетворённый** (-рён, -á) satisfied. **удовлетворúтельный** satisfactory. **удовлетворúть** *pf*, **удовлетворя́ть** *impf* satisfy; +*dat* meet; +*instr* supply with; **~ся** be satisfied.

удовóльствие pleasure. **у|довóльствоваться** *pf.*

удóй milk-yield; milking.

удостáивать(ся *impf of* **удостóить(ся**

удостоверéние certification; certificate; **~ лúчности** identity card. **удостовéрить** *pf*, **удостоверя́ть** *impf* certify, witness; **~ся** make sure (**в**+*prep* of), assure o.s.

удостóить *pf* (*impf* **удостáивать**) make an award to; +*gen* award; +*instr* favour with; **~ся** +*gen* be awarded; be favoured with.

ýдочка (fishing-)rod.

удрáть (удерý, -ёшь; удрáл, -á, -о) *pf* (*impf* **удирáть**) make off.

удручáть *impf*, **удручúть** (-чý) *pf* depress. **удручённый** (-чён, -á) depressed.

удушáть *impf*, **удушúть** (-шý, -шишь) *pf* stifle, suffocate. **удушéние** suffocation. **удýшливый** stifling. **удýшье** asthma; asphyxia.

уединéние solitude; seclusion. **уединённый** secluded; lonely. **уединúться** *pf*, **уединя́ться** *impf* seclude o.s.

уéзд uyezd, District.

уезжáть *impf*, **уéхать** (уéду) *pf* go away, depart.

уж[1] (-á) grass-snake.

уж[2]: *see* **ужé**[2]. **уж**[3], **ужé**[3] *partl* indeed; really.

у|жа́лить *pf.*
у́жас horror, terror; *predic* it is awful. **ужаса́ть** *impf*, **ужасну́ть** (-ну́, -нёшь) *pf* horrify; **~ся** be horrified, be terrified. **ужа́сно** *adv* terribly; awfully. **ужа́сный** awful, terrible.
у́же[1] *comp of* **у́зкий**
уже́[2], **уж**[2] *adv* already; **~ не** no longer. **уже́**[3]: *see* **уж**[3]
уже́ние fishing.
ужива́ться *impf of* **ужи́ться.** **ужи́вчивый** easy to get on with.
ужи́мка grimace.
у́жин supper. **у́жинать** *impf* (*pf* **по~**) have supper.
ужи́ться (-иву́сь, -ивёшься; -и́лся, -ла́сь) *pf* (*impf* **ужива́ться**) get on.
ужу́ *see* **уди́ть**
узако́нивать *impf*, **узако́нить** *pf* legalize.
узбе́к, -е́чка Uzbek. **Узбекиста́н** Uzbekistan.
узда́ (*pl* -ы) bridle.
у́зел (узла́) knot; junction; centre; node; bundle.
у́зкий (у́зок, узка́, -о) narrow; tight; narrow-minded. **узкоколе́йка** narrow-gauge railway.
узлова́тый knotty. **узлов|о́й** junction; main, key; **~а́я ста́нция** junction.
узнава́ть (-наю́, -наёшь) *impf*, **узна́ть** *pf* recognize; get to know; find out.
у́зник, у́зница prisoner.
узо́р pattern, design. **узо́рчатый** patterned.
у́зость narrowness; tightness.
узурпа́тор usurper. **узурпи́ровать** *impf & pf* usurp.
у́зы (уз) *pl* bonds, ties.
уйду́ *etc.*: *see* **уйти́.**
у́йма lots (of).
уйму́ *etc.*: *see* **уня́ть**
уйти́ (уйду́, -дёшь; ушёл, ушла́) *pf* (*impf* **уходи́ть**) go away, leave, depart; escape; retire; bury o.s.; be used up; pass away.
ука́з decree; edict. **указа́ние** indication; instruction. **ука́занный** appointed, stated.
указа́тель *m* indicator; gauge; index; directory. **указа́тельный** indicating; demonstrative; **~ па́лец** index finger.
указа́ть (-ажу́, -а́жешь) *pf*, **ука́зывать** *impf* show; indicate; point; point out. **ука́зка** pointer; orders.
ука́лывать *impf of* **уколо́ть**
ukата́ть *pf*, **ука́тывать**[1] *impf* roll; flatten; wear out. **ukати́ть** (-ачу́, -а́тишь) *pf*, **ука́тывать**[2] *impf* roll away; drive off; **~ся** roll away.
укача́ть *pf*, **ука́чивать** *impf* rock to sleep; make sick.
укла́д structure; style; organization. **укла́дка** packing; stacking; laying; setting.
укла́дчик packer; layer.
укла́дывать(ся[1] *impf of* **уложи́ть(ся**
укла́дываться[2] *impf of* **уле́чься**
укло́н slope; incline; gradient; bias; deviation. **уклоне́ние** deviation; digression. **уклони́ться** *pf*, **уклоня́ться** *impf* deviate; *+***от***+gen* turn (off, aside); avoid; evade. **укло́нчивый** evasive.
уклю́чина rowlock.
уко́л prick; injection; thrust.
уколо́ть (-лю́, -лешь) *pf* (*impf* **ука́лывать**) prick; wound.
у|комплектова́ть *pf*, **укомплекто́вывать** *impf* complete; bring up to (full) strength; man; *+instr* equip with.

укóр reproach.
укорáчивать *impf of* **укоротúть**
укоренúть *pf*, **укоренять** *impf* implant, inculcate; **~ся** take root.
укорúзна reproach. **укорúзненный** reproachful. **укорúть** *pf* (*impf* **укорять**) reproach (**в**+*prep* with).
укоротúть (-очý) *pf* (*impf* **укорáчивать**) shorten.
укорять *impf of* **укорúть**
укóс (hay-)crop.
укрáдкой *adv* stealthily. **украдý** *etc.*: *see* **укрáсть**
Украúна Ukraine. **украúнец** (-нца), **украúнка** Ukrainian. **украúнский** Ukrainian.
укрáсить (-áшу) *pf* (*impf* **украшáть**) adorn, decorate; **~ся** be decorated; adorn o.s.
у|крáсть (-адý, -дёшь) *pf*.
украшáть(ся *impf of* **укрáсить(ся. украшéние** decoration; adornment.
укрепúть (-плю) *pf*, **укреплять** *impf* strengthen; fix; fortify; **~ся** become stronger; fortify one's position. **укреплéние** strengthening; reinforcement; fortification.
укрóмный secluded, cosy.
укрóп dill.
укротúтель *m* (animal-)tamer. **укротúть** (-ощý) *pf*, **укрощáть** *impf* tame; curb; **~ся** become tame; calm down. **укрощéние** taming.
укрóю *etc.*: *see* **укрыть**
укрупнéние enlargement; amalgamation. **укрупнúть** *pf*, **укрупнять** *impf* enlarge; amalgamate.
укрывáтель *m* harbourer. **укрывáтельство** harbouring; receiving. **укрывáть** *impf*, **укрыть** (-рóю) *pf* cover; conceal, harbour; shelter; receive; **~ся** cover o.s.; take cover. **укрытие** cover; shelter.
ýксус vinegar.
укýс bite; sting. **укусúть** (-ушý, -ýсишь) *pf* bite; sting.
укýтать *pf*, **укýтывать** *impf* wrap up; **~ся** wrap o.s. up.
укушý *etc.*: *see* **укусúть**
ул. *abbr* (*of* **ýлица**) street, road.
улáвливать *impf of* **уловúть**
улáдить (-áжу) *pf*, **улáживать** *impf* settle, arrange.
ýлей (ýлья) (bee)hive.
улетáть *impf*, **улетéть** (улечý) *pf* fly (away). **улетýчиваться**, *impf*, **улетýчиться** (-чусь) *pf* evaporate; vanish.
улéчься (улягусь, -яжешься; улёгся, -глáсь) *pf* (*impf* **уклáдываться**) lie down; settle; subside.
улúка clue; evidence.
улúтка snail.
ýлица street; **на ýлице** in the street; outside.
уличáть *impf*, **уличúть** (-чý) *pf* establish the guilt of.
ýличный street.
улóв catch. **уловúмый** perceptible; audible. **уловúть** (-влю, -вишь) *pf* (*impf* **улáвливать**) catch; seize. **улóвка** trick, ruse.
уложéние code. **уложúть** (-жý, -жишь) *pf* (*impf* **уклáдывать**) lay; pack; pile; **~ спать** put to bed; **~ся** pack (up); fit in.
улучáть *impf*, **улучúть** (-чý) *pf* find, seize.
улучшáть *impf*, **улýчшить** (-шу) *pf* improve; better; **~ся** improve; get better. **улучшéние** improvement.
улыбáться *impf*, **улыбнýть-**

ся (-ну́сь, -нёшься) *pf* smile. **улы́бка** smile.
ультима́тум ultimatum.
ультра- *in comb* ultra-. **ультразвуково́й** supersonic. **~фиоле́товый** ultra-violet.
уля́гусь *etc.*: *see* **уле́чься**
ум (-а́) mind, intellect; head; **сойти́ с ~а́** go mad.
умали́ть *pf* (*impf* **умаля́ть**) belittle.
умалишённый mad; *sb* lunatic.
ума́лчивать *impf of* **умолча́ть**
умаля́ть *impf of* **умали́ть**
уме́лец (-льца) skilled craftsman. **уме́лый** able, skilful. **уме́ние** ability, skill.
уменьша́ть *impf*, **уме́ньшить** (-шу) *pf* reduce, diminish, decrease; **~ся** diminish, decrease; abate. **уменьше́ние** decrease, reduction; abatement. **уменьши́тельный** diminutive.
уме́ренность moderation. **уме́ренный** moderate; temperate.
умере́ть (умру́, -рёшь; у́мер, -ла́, -о) *pf* (*impf* **умира́ть**) die.
уме́рить *pf* (*impf* **умеря́ть**) moderate; restrain.
умертви́ть (-рщвлю́, -ртви́шь) *pf*, **умерщвля́ть** *impf* kill, destroy; mortify. **у́мерший** dead; *sb* the deceased. **умерщвле́ние** killing, destruction; mortification.
умеря́ть *impf of* **уме́рить**
умести́ть (-ещу́) *pf* (*impf* **умеща́ть**) fit in, find room for; **~ся** fit in. **уме́стный** appropriate; pertinent; timely.
уме́ть (-е́ю) *impf* be able, know how.
умеща́ть(ся *impf of* **умести́ть(ся**
умиле́ние tenderness; emotion. **умили́ть** *pf*, **умиля́ть** *impf* move, touch; **~ся** be moved.
умира́ние dying. **умира́ть** *impf of* **умере́ть. умира́ющий** dying; *sb* dying person.
умиротворе́ние pacification; appeasement. **умиротвори́ть** *pf*, **умиротворя́ть** *impf* pacify; appease.
умне́ть (-е́ю) *impf* (*pf* **по~**) grow wiser. **у́мница** good girl; *m & f* clever person.
умножа́ть *impf*, **у|мно́жить** (-жу) *pf* multiply; increase; **~ся** increase, multiply. **умноже́ние** multiplication; increase. **умножи́тель** *m* multiplier.
у́мный (умён, умна́, у́мно́) clever, wise, intelligent. **умозаключе́ние** deduction; conclusion.
умоли́ть *pf* (*impf* **умоля́ть**) move by entreaties.
умолка́ть *impf*, **умо́лкнуть** (-ну; -о́лк) *pf* fall silent; stop. **умолча́ть** (-чу́) *pf* (*impf* **ума́лчивать**) fail to mention; hush up.
умоля́ть *impf of* **умоли́ть**; beg, entreat.
умопомеша́тельство derangement.
умори́тельный incredibly funny, killing. **у|мори́ть** *pf* kill; exhaust.
умо́ю *etc.*: *see* **умы́ть. умру́** *etc.*: *see* **умере́ть**
у́мственный mental, intellectual.
умудри́ть *pf*, **умудря́ть** *impf* make wiser; **~ся** contrive.
умыва́льная *sb* wash-room. **умыва́льник** wash-stand, wash-basin. **умыва́ть(ся** *impf of* **умы́ть(ся**

у́мысел (-сла) design, intention.
умы́ть (умо́ю) *pf* (*impf* **умыва́ть**) wash; **~ся** wash (o.s.).
умы́шленный intentional.
у|насле́довать *pf*.
унести́ (-су́, -сёшь; -ёс, -ла́) *pf* (*impf* **уноси́ть**) take away; carry off, make off with; **~сь** speed away; fly by; be carried (away).
универма́г *abbr* department store. **универса́льн|ый** universal; all-round; versatile; all-purpose; **~ магази́н** department store; **~ое сре́дство** panacea. **универса́м** *abbr* supermarket.
университе́т university. **университе́тский** university.
унижа́ть *impf*, **уни́зить** (-и́жу) *pf* humiliate; **~ся** humble o.s.; stoop. **униже́ние** humiliation. **уни́женный** humble. **унизи́тельный** humiliating.
уника́льный unique.
унима́ть(ся *impf of* **уня́ть(ся**
унисо́н unison.
унита́з lavatory pan.
унифици́ровать *impf & pf* standardize.
уничижи́тельный pejorative.
уничтожа́ть *impf*, **уничто́жить** (-жу) *pf* destroy, annihilate; abolish; do away with. **уничтоже́ние** destruction, annihilation; abolition.
уноси́ть(ся (-ошу́(сь, -о́сишь(ся) *impf of* **унести́(сь**
у́нция ounce.
унsocва́ть *impf* be dejected. **уны́лый** dejected; doleful, cheerless. **уны́ние** dejection, despondency.
уня́ть (уйму́, -мёшь; -я́л, -а́, -о) *pf* (*impf* **унима́ть**) calm, soothe; **~ся** calm down.
упа́док (-дка) decline; decay; **~ ду́ха** depression. **упа́дочнический** decadent. **упа́дочный** depressive; decadent.
упаду́ *etc.*: *see* **упа́сть**
у|пакова́ть *pf*, **упако́вывать** *impf* pack (up). **упако́вка** packing; wrapping. **упако́вщик** packer.
упа́сть (-аду́, -адёшь) *pf of* **па́дать**
упере́ть (упру́, -рёшь; -ёр) *pf*, **упира́ть** *impf* rest, lean; **~ на**+*acc* stress; **~ся** rest, lean; resist; **+в**+*acc* come up against.
упи́танный well-fed; fattened.
упла́та payment. **у|плати́ть** (-ачу́, -а́тишь) *pf*, **упла́чивать** *impf* pay.
уплотне́ние compression; condensation; consolidation; sealing. **уплотни́ть** *pf*, **уплотня́ть** *impf* condense; compress; pack more into.
уплыва́ть *impf*, **уплы́ть** (-ыву́, -ывёшь; -ы́л, -а́, -о) *pf* swim *or* sail away; pass.
упова́ть *impf* **+на**+*acc* put one's trust in.
уподо́биться (-блюсь) *pf*, **уподобля́ться** *impf* +*dat* become like.
упое́ние ecstasy, rapture. **упои́тельный** intoxicating, ravishing.
уполза́ть *impf*, **уползти́** (-зу́, -зёшь; -о́лз, -зла́) *pf* creep away, crawl away.
уполномо́ченный *sb* (authorized) agent, representative; proxy. **уполнома́чивать, уполномо́чивать** *impf*, **уполномо́чить** (-чу) *pf* authorize, empower.
упомина́ние mention. **упомина́ть** *impf*, **упомяну́ть** (-ну́, -нешь) *pf* mention, refer to.

упóр prop, support; **в ~** point-blank; **сдéлать ~ на**+*acc or prep* lay stress on. **упóрный** stubborn; persistent. **упóрство** stubbornness; persistence. **упóрствовать** *impf* be stubborn; persist (**в**+*prep* in).

упоря́дочивать *impf*, **упоря́дочить** (-чу) *pf* regulate, put in order.

употреби́тельный (widely-) used; common. **употреби́ть** (-блю́) *pf*, **употребля́ть** *impf* use. **употреблéние** use; usage.

упрáва justice.

управдóм *abbr* manager (*of block of flats*). **упрáвиться** (-влюсь) *pf*, **управля́ться** *impf* cope, manage; **+с**+*instr* deal with. **управлéние** management; administration; direction; control; driving, steering; government. **управля́емый снаря́д** guided missile. **управля́ть** *impf* +*instr* manage, direct, run; govern; be in charge of; operate; drive. **управля́ющий** *sb* manager.

упражнéние exercise. **упражня́ть** *impf* exercise, train; **~ся** practise, train.

упраздни́ть *pf*, **упраздня́ть** *impf* abolish.

упрáшивать *impf of* **упроси́ть**

упрёк reproach. **упрекáть** *impf*, **упрекну́ть** (-ну́, -нёшь) *pf* reproach.

упроси́ть (-ошу́, -óсишь) *pf* (*impf* **упрáшивать**) entreat; prevail upon.

упрости́ть (-ощу́) *pf* (*impf* **упрощáть**) (over-)simplify.

упрóчивать *impf*, **упрóчить** (-чу) *pf* strengthen, consolidate; **~ся** be firmly established.

упрошу́ *etc.*: *see* **упроси́ть**

упрощáть *impf of* **упрости́ть.** **упрощённый** (-щён, -á) (over-)simplified.

упру́ *etc.*: *see* **уперéть**

упру́гий elastic; springy. **упру́гость** elasticity; spring. **упру́же** *comp of* **упру́гий**

упря́жка harness; team. **упряжнóй** draught. **у́пряжь** harness.

упря́миться (-млюсь) *impf* be obstinate; persist. **упря́мство** obstinacy. **упря́мый** obstinate; persistent.

упускáть *impf*, **упусти́ть** (-ущу́, -у́стишь) *pf* let go, let slip; miss. **упущéние** omission; slip; negligence.

урá *int* hurrah!

уравнéние equalization; equation. **урáвнивать** *impf*, **уравня́ть** *pf* equalize. **уравни́тельный** equalizing, levelling. **уравновéсить** (-éшу) *pf*, **уравновéшивать** *impf* balance; counterbalance. **уравновéшенность** composure. **уравновéшенный** balanced, composed.

урагáн hurricane; storm.

урáльский Ural.

урáн uranium; Uranus. **урáновый** uranium.

урвáть (-ву́, -вёшь; -áл, -á, -о) *pf* (*impf* **урывáть**) snatch.

урегули́рование regulation; settlement. **у|регули́ровать** *pf*.

урéзать (-éжу) *pf*, **урезáть**, **урéзывать** *impf* cut off; shorten; reduce.

у́рка *m* & *f* (*sl*) lag, convict.

у́рна urn; litter-bin.

у́ровень (-вня) *m* level; standard.

урóд freak, monster.

уроди́ться (-ожу́сь) *pf* ripen; grow.

уро́дливость deformity; ugliness. **уро́дливый** deformed; ugly; bad. **уро́довать** *impf* (*pf* **из~**) disfigure; distort. **уро́дство** disfigurement; ugliness.

урожа́й harvest; crop; abundance. **урожа́йность** yield; productivity. **урожа́йный** productive, high-yield.

урождённый née. **уроже́нец** (-нца), **уроже́нка** native. **урожу́сь** *see* **уроди́ться**

уро́к lesson.

уро́н losses; damage. **урони́ть** (-ню́, -нишь) *pf of* **роня́ть**

урча́ть (-чу́) *impf* rumble.

урыва́ть *impf of* **урва́ть**. **уры́вками** *adv* in snatches, by fits and starts.

ус (*pl* -ы́) whisker; tendril; *pl* moustache.

усади́ть (-ажу́, -а́дишь) *pf*, **уса́живать** *impf* seat, offer a seat; plant. **уса́дьба** (*gen pl* -деб *or* -дьб) country estate; farmstead. **уса́живаться** *impf of* **усе́сться**

уса́тый moustached; whiskered.

усва́ивать *impf*, **усво́ить** *pf* master; assimilate; adopt. **усвое́ние** mastering; assimilation; adoption.

усе́рдие zeal; diligence. **усе́рдный** zealous; diligent.

усе́сться (уся́дусь; -е́лся) *pf* (*impf* **уса́живаться**) take a seat; settle down (to).

усиде́ть (-ижу́) *pf* remain seated; hold down a job. **уси́дчивый** assiduous.

у́сик tendril; runner; antenna; *pl* small moustache.

усиле́ние strengthening; reinforcement; intensification; amplification. **уси́ленный** intensified, increased; earnest. **усили́вать** *impf*, **уси́лить** *pf* intensify, increase; amplify; strengthen, reinforce; **~ся** increase, intensify; become stronger. **уси́лие** effort. **усили́тель** *m* amplifier; booster.

ускака́ть (-ачу́, -а́чешь) *pf* skip off; gallop off.

ускольза́ть *impf*, **ускользну́ть** (-ну́, -нёшь) *pf* slip off; steal away; escape.

ускоре́ние acceleration. **ускоре́нный** accelerated; rapid; crash. **ускори́тель** accelerator. **уско́рить** *pf*, **ускоря́ть** *impf* quicken; accelerate; hasten; **~ся** accelerate, be accelerated; quicken.

усло́вие condition. **усло́виться** (-влюсь) *pf*, **усло́вливаться, усла́вливаться** *impf* agree; arrange. **усло́вленный** agreed, fixed. **усло́вность** convention. **усло́вный** conditional; conditioned; conventional; agreed; relative.

усложне́ние complication. **усложни́ть** *pf*, **усложня́ть** *impf* complicate; **~ся** become complicated.

услу́га service; good turn. **услу́жливый** obliging.

услыха́ть (-ы́шу) *pf*, **у|слы́шать** (-ы́шу) *pf* hear; sense; scent.

усма́тривать *impf of* **усмотре́ть**

усмеха́ться *impf*, **усмехну́ться** (-ну́сь, -нёшься) *pf* smile; grin; smirk. **усме́шка** smile; grin; sneer.

усмире́ние pacification; suppression. **усмири́ть** *pf*, **усмиря́ть** *impf* pacify; calm; suppress.

усмотре́ние discretion, judgement. **усмотре́ть** (-рю́, -ришь) *pf* (*impf* **усма́тривать**) perceive; see; regard; **+за**+*instr* keep an eye on.
усну́ть (-ну́, -нёшь) *pf* go to sleep.
усоверше́нствование advanced studies; improvement, refinement. **у|соверше́нствовать(ся** *pf.*
усомни́ться *pf* doubt.
успева́емость progress. **успева́ть** *impf*, **успе́ть** (-е́ю) *pf* have time; manage; succeed. **успе́х** success; progress. **успе́шный** successful.
успока́ивать *impf*, **успоко́ить** *pf* calm, quiet, soothe; **~ся** calm down; abate. **успока́ивающий** calming, sedative. **успокое́ние** calming, soothing; calm; peace. **успоко́ительн|ый** calming; reassuring; **~ое** *sb* sedative, tranquillizer.
уста́ (-т, -та́м) *pl* mouth.
уста́в regulations, statutes; charter.
устава́ть (-таю́, -ёшь) *impf of* **уста́ть**; **не устава́я** incessantly.
уста́вить (-влю) *pf*, **уставля́ть** *impf* set, arrange; cover, fill; direct; **~ся** find room, go in; stare.
уста́лость tiredness. **уста́лый** tired.
устана́вливать *impf*, **установи́ть** (-влю́, -вишь) *pf* put, set up; install; set; establish; fix; **~ся** dispose o.s.; be established; set in. **устано́вка** putting, setting up; installation; setting; plant, unit; directions. **установле́ние** establishment. **устано́вленный** established, prescribed.
уста́ну *etc.*: *see* **уста́ть**
устарева́ть *impf*, **у|старе́ть** (-е́ю) *pf* become obsolete; become antiquated. **устаре́лый** obsolete; antiquated, out-of-date.
уста́ть (-а́ну) *pf* (*impf* **устава́ть**) get tired.
устила́ть *impf*, **устла́ть** (-телю́, -те́лешь) *pf* cover; pave.
у́стный oral, verbal.
усто́й abutment; foundation, support. **усто́йчивость** stability, steadiness. **усто́йчивый** stable, steady. **устоя́ть** (-ою́) *pf* keep one's balance; stand firm; **~ся** settle; become fixed.
устра́ивать(ся *impf of* **устро́ить(ся**
устране́ние removal, elimination. **устрани́ть** *pf*, **устраня́ть** *impf* remove; eliminate; **~ся** resign, retire.
устраша́ть *impf*, **устраши́ть** (-шу́) *pf* frighten; **~ся** be frightened.
устреми́ть (-млю́) *pf*, **устремля́ть** *impf* direct, fix; **~ся** rush; be directed; concentrate. **устремле́ние** rush; aspiration.
у́стрица oyster.
устро́итель *m*, **~ница** organizer. **устро́ить** *pf* (*impf* **устра́ивать**) arrange, organize; make; cause; settle, put in order; place, fix up; get; suit; **~ся** work out; manage; settle down; be found, get fixed up. **устро́йство** arrangement; construction; mechanism, device; system.
усту́п shelf, ledge. **уступа́ть** *impf*, **уступи́ть** (-плю́, -пишь) *pf* yield; give up; **~ доро́гу**

make way. **усту́пка** concession. **усту́пчивый** pliable; compliant.

устыди́ться (-ыжу́сь) *pf* (+*gen*) be ashamed (of).

у́стье (*gen pl* -ьев) mouth; estuary.

усугу́бить (-у́блю) *pf*, **усугубля́ть** *impf* increase; aggravate.

усы́ *see* **ус**

усынови́ть (-влю́) *pf*, **усыновля́ть** *impf* adopt. **усыновле́ние** adoption.

усы́пать (-плю) *pf*, **усыпа́ть** *impf* strew, scatter.

усыпи́тельный soporific. **усыпи́ть** (-плю́) *pf*, **усыпля́ть** *impf* put to sleep; lull; weaken.

уся́дусь *etc.*: *see* **усе́сться**

ута́ивать *impf*, **утаи́ть** *pf* conceal; keep secret.

ута́птывать *impf of* **утопта́ть**

ута́скивать *impf*, **утащи́ть** (-щу́, -щишь) *pf* drag off.

у́тварь utensils.

утверди́тельный affirmative. **утверди́ть** (-ржу́) *pf*, **утвержда́ть** *impf* confirm; approve; ratify; establish; assert; **~ся** gain a foothold; become established; be confirmed. **утвержде́ние** approval; confirmation; ratification; assertion; establishment.

утека́ть *impf of* **уте́чь**

утёнок (-нка; *pl* утя́та, -я́т) duckling.

утепли́ть *pf*, **утепля́ть** *impf* warm.

утере́ть (утру́, -рёшь; утёр) *pf* (*impf* **утира́ть**) wipe (off, dry).

утерпе́ть (-плю́, -пишь) *pf* restrain o.s.

утёс cliff, crag.

уте́чка leak, leakage; escape; loss. **уте́чь** (-еку́, -ечёшь; утёк, -ла́) *pf* (*impf* **утека́ть**) leak, escape; pass.

утеша́ть *impf*, **уте́шить** (-шу) *pf* console; **~ся** console o.s. **утеше́ние** consolation. **утеши́тельный** comforting.

утилизи́ровать *impf* & *pf* utilize.

ути́ль *m*, **утильсырьё** scrap.

ути́ный duck, duck's.

утира́ть(ся *impf of* **утере́ть(ся**

утиха́ть *impf*, **ути́хнуть** (-ну; -и́х) *pf* abate, subside; calm down.

у́тка duck; canard.

уткну́ть (-ну́, -нёшь) *pf* bury; fix; **~ся** bury o.s.

утоли́ть *pf* (*impf* **утоля́ть**) quench; satisfy; relieve.

утолще́ние thickening; bulge.

утоля́ть *impf of* **утоли́ть**

утоми́тельный tedious; tiring. **утоми́ть** (-млю́) *pf*, **утомля́ть** *impf* tire, fatigue; **~ся** get tired. **утомле́ние** weariness. **утомлённый** weary.

у|тону́ть (-ну́, -нешь) *pf* drown, be drowned; sink.

утончённый refined.

у|топи́ть(ся (-плю́(сь, -пишь(ся) *pf*. **уто́пленник** drowned man.

утопи́ческий utopian. **уто́пия** Utopia.

утопта́ть (-пчу́, -пчешь) *pf* (*impf* **ута́птывать**) trample down.

уточне́ние more precise definition; amplification. **уточни́ть** *pf*, **уточня́ть** *impf* define more precisely; amplify.

утра́ивать *impf of* **утро́ить**

у|трамбова́ть *pf*, **утрамбо́вывать** *impf* ram, tamp; **~ся** become flat.

утрáта loss. **утрáтить** (-áчу) *pf*, **утрáчивать** *impf* lose.
у́тренний morning. **у́тренник** morning performance; early-morning frost.
утри́ровать *impf* & *pf* exaggerate.
у́тро (-а *or* -á, -у *or* -у́; *pl* -а, -ам *or* -áм) morning.
утрóба womb; belly.
утрóить *pf* (*impf* **утрáивать**) triple, treble.
утру́ *etc.*: *see* **утерéть, у́тро**
утруждáть *impf* trouble, tire.
утю́г (-á) iron. **утю́жить** (-жу) *impf* (*pf* **вы́~, от~**) iron.
ух *int* oh, ooh, ah.
ухá fish soup.
ухáб pot-hole. **ухáбистый** bumpy.
ухáживать *impf* **за**+*instr* tend; look after; court.
ухвати́ть (-ачу́, -áтишь) *pf*, **ухвáтывать** *impf* seize; grasp; **~ся за**+*acc* grasp, lay hold of; set to; seize; jump at. **ухвáтка** grip; skill; trick; manner.
ухитри́ться *pf*, **ухитря́ться** *impf* manage, contrive. **ухищрéние** device, trick.
ухмы́лка smirk. **ухмыльну́ться** (-ну́сь, -нёшься) *pf*, **ухмыля́ться** *impf* smirk.
у́хо (*pl* у́ши, ушéй) ear; ear-flap.
ухóд[1] **+за**+*instr* care of; tending, looking after.
ухóд[2] leaving, departure. **уходи́ть** (-ожу́, -óдишь) *impf of* **уйти́**
ухудшáть *impf*, **уху́дшить** (-шу) *pf* make worse; **~ся** get worse. **ухудшéние** deterioration.
уцелéть (-éю) *pf* remain intact; survive.
уцéнивать *impf*, **уцени́ть** (-ню́, -нишь) *pf* reduce the price of.
уцепи́ть (-плю́, -пишь) *pf* catch hold of, seize; **~ся за**+*acc* catch hold of, seize; jump at.
учáствовать *impf* take part; hold shares. **учáствующий** *sb* participant. **учáстие** participation; share; sympathy.
участи́ть (-ащу́) *pf* (*impf* **учащáть**) make more frequent; **~ся** become more frequent, quicken.
учáстливый sympathetic. **учáстник** participant. **учáсток** (-тка) plot; part, section; sector; district; field, sphere.
у́часть lot, fate.
учащáть(ся *impf of* **участи́ть(ся**
учáщийся *sb* student; pupil.
учёба studies; course; training. **учéбник** text-book.
учéбный educational; school; training. **учéние** learning; studies; apprenticeship; teaching; doctrine; exercise.
учени́к (-á), **учени́ца** pupil; apprentice; disciple. **учени́ческий** pupil'(s); apprentice('s); unskilled; crude.
учёность learning, erudition.
учён|ый learned; scholarly; academic; scientific; **~ая стéпень** (*university*) degree; **~ый** *sb* scholar; scientist.
учéсть (учту́, -тёшь; учёл, учлá) *pf* (*impf* **учи́тывать**) take stock of; take into account; discount. **учёт** stock-taking; calculation; taking into account; registration; discount; **без ~а** *+gen* disregarding; **взять на ~** register. **учётный** registration; discount.
учи́лище (*specialist*) school.

у|чини́ть *pf*, **учиня́ть** *impf* make; carry out; commit.

учи́тель (*pl* -я́) *m*, **учи́тельница** teacher. **учи́тельск|ий** teacher's, teachers'; **~ая** *sb* staff-room.

учи́тывать *impf of* **уче́сть**

учи́ть (учу́, у́чишь) *impf* (*pf* **вы́~**, **на~**, **об~**) teach; be a teacher; learn; **~ся** be a student; *+dat or inf* learn, study.

учреди́тельный constituent.

учреди́ть (-ежу́) *pf*, **учрежда́ть** *impf* found, establish. **учрежде́ние** founding; establishment; institution.

учти́вый civil, courteous.

учту́ *etc.*: *see* **уче́сть**

уша́нка hat with ear-flaps.

ушёл *etc.*: *see* **уйти́**. **у́ши** *etc.*: *see* **у́хо**

уши́б injury; bruise. **ушиба́ть** *impf*, **ушиби́ть** (-бу́, -бёшь; уши́б) *pf* injure; bruise; hurt; **~ся** hurt o.s.

ушко́ (*pl* -и́, -о́в) eye; tab.

ушно́й ear, aural.

уще́лье ravine, gorge, canyon.

ущеми́ть (-млю́) *pf*, **ущемля́ть** *impf* pinch, jam; limit; encroach on; hurt. **ущемле́ние** pinching, jamming; limitation; hurting.

уще́рб detriment; loss; damage; prejudice. **уще́рбный** waning.

ущипну́ть (-ну́, -нёшь) *pf of* **щипа́ть**

Уэ́льс Wales. **уэ́льский** Welsh.

ую́т cosiness, comfort. **ую́тный** cosy, comfortable.

уязви́мый vulnerable. **уязви́ть** (-влю́) *pf*, **уязвля́ть** *impf* wound, hurt.

уясни́ть *pf*, **уясня́ть** *impf* understand, make out.

Ф

фа́брика factory. **фабрика́нт** manufacturer. **фабрика́т** finished product, manufactured product. **фабрикова́ть** *impf* (*pf* **с~**) fabricate, forge. **фабри́чн|ый** factory; manufacturing; factory-made; **~ая ма́рка**, **~ое клеймо́** trade-mark.

фа́була plot, story.

фаго́т bassoon.

фа́за phase; stage.

фаза́н pheasant.

фа́зис phase.

файл (*comput*) file.

фа́кел torch, flare.

факс fax.

факси́миле *neut indecl* facsimile.

факт fact; **соверши́вшийся ~** fait accompli. **факти́чески** *adv* in fact; virtually. **факти́ческий** actual; real; virtual.

фа́ктор factor.

факту́ра texture; style, execution.

факультати́вный optional. **факульте́т** faculty, department.

фа́лда tail (*of coat*).

фальсифика́тор falsifier, forger. **фальсифика́ция** falsification; adulteration; forgery. **фальсифици́ровать** *impf* & *pf* falsify; forge; adulterate.

фальши́вить (-влю) *impf* (*pf* **с~**) be a hypocrite; sing *or* play out of tune. **фальши́вка** forged document. **фальши́вый** false; spurious; forged; artificial; out of tune. **фальшь** deception; falseness.

фами́лия surname. **фамилья́рничать** be over-familiar. **фамилья́рность** (over-)familiarity. **фамилья́рный** (over-) familiar; unceremonious.

фанати́зм fanaticism. **фана́тик** fanatic.

фане́ра veneer; plywood.

фантазёр dreamer, visionary. **фантази́ровать** *impf* (*pf* **с**~) dream; make up, dream up; improvise. **фанта́зия** fantasy; fancy; imagination; whim. **фанта́стика** fiction, fantasy. **фантасти́ческий, фантасти́чный** fantastic.

фа́ра headlight.

фарао́н pharaoh; faro.

фарва́тер fairway, channel.

фармазо́н freemason.

фармаце́вт pharmacist.

фарс farce.

фа́ртук apron.

фарфо́р china; porcelain. **фарфо́ровый** china.

фарцо́вщик currency speculator.

фарш stuffing; minced meat. **фарширова́ть** *impf* (*pf* **за**~) stuff.

фаса́д façade.

фасова́ть *impf* (*pf* **рас**~) package.

фасо́ль kidney bean(s), French bean(s); haricot beans.

фасо́н cut; fashion; style; manner. **фасо́нный** shaped.

фата́ veil.

фатали́зм fatalism. **фата́льный** fatal.

фаши́зм Fascism. **фаши́ст** Fascist. **фаши́стский** Fascist.

фая́нс faience, pottery.

февра́ль (-я́) *m* February. **февра́льский** February.

федера́льный federal. **федера́ция** federation.

феери́ческий fairy-tale.

фейерве́рк firework(s).

фе́льдшер (*pl* -а́), **-шери́ца** (*partly-qualified*) medical assistant.

фельето́н feuilleton, feature.

феми́ни́зм feminism. **феминисти́ческий, фемини́стский** feminist.

фен (hair-)dryer.

фено́мен phenomenon. **фенomена́льный** phenomenal.

феода́л feudal lord. **феодали́зм** feudalism. **феода́льный** feudal.

ферзь (-я́) *m* queen.

фе́рма[1] farm.

фе́рма[2] girder, truss.

ферма́та (*mus*) pause.

ферме́нт ferment.

фе́рмер farmer.

фестива́ль *m* festival.

фетр felt. **фе́тровый** felt.

фехтова́льщик, -щица fencer. **фехтова́ние** fencing. **фехтова́ть** *impf* fence.

фе́я fairy.

фиа́лка violet.

фиа́ско *neut indecl* fiasco.

фи́бра fibre.

фигля́р buffoon.

фигу́ра figure; court-card; (chess-)piece. **фигура́льный** figurative, metaphorical. **фигури́ровать** *impf* figure, appear. **фигури́ст, -и́стка** figure-skater. **фигу́рка** figurine, statuette; figure. **фигу́рн|ый** figured; ~**ое ката́ние** figure-skating.

фи́зик physicist. **фи́зика** physics. **физио́лог** physiologist. **физиологи́ческий** physiological. **физиоло́гия** physiology. **физионо́мия** physiognomy; face, expression. **физиотерапе́вт** physiotherapist. **физи́ческий** physical; physics. **физкульту́ра** *abbr* P.E., gym-

nastics. **физкульту́рный** *abbr* gymnastic; athletic; ~ **зал** gymnasium.
фикса́ж fixer. **фикса́ция** fixing. **фикси́ровать** *impf & pf* (*pf also* **за~**) fix; record.
фикти́вный fictitious. ~ **брак** marriage of convenience. **фи́кция** fiction.
филантро́п philanthropist. **филантро́пия** philanthropy.
филармо́ния philharmonic society; concert hall.
филатели́ст philatelist.
филе́ *neut indecl* sirloin; fillet.
филиа́л branch.
фили́стер philistine.
фило́лог philologist. **филологи́ческий** philological. **филоло́гия** philology.
фило́соф philosopher. **филосо́фия** philosophy. **филосо́фский** philosophical.
фильм film. **фильмоско́п** projector.
фильтр filter. **фильтрова́ть** *impf* (*pf* **про~**) filter.
фина́л finale; final. **фина́льный** final.
финанси́ровать *impf & pf* finance. **фина́нсовый** financial. **фина́нсы** (-ов) *pl* finance, finances.
фи́ник date.
фи́ниш finish; finishing post.
фи́нка Finn. **Финля́ндия** Finland. **финля́ндский** Finnish. **финн** Finn. **фи́нский** Finnish.
фиоле́товый violet.
фи́рма firm; company. **фи́рменное блю́до** speciality of the house.
фисгармо́ния harmonium.
фити́ль (-я́) *m* wick; fuse.
флаг flag. **фла́гман** flagship.
флако́н bottle, flask.
фланг flank; wing.
флане́ль flannel.
флегмати́чный phlegmatic.
фле́йта flute.
фле́ксия inflexion. **флекти́вный** inflected.
фли́гель (*pl* -я́) *m* wing; annexe.
флирт flirtation. **флиртова́ть** *impf* flirt.
флома́стер felt-tip pen.
фло́ра flora.
флот fleet. **фло́тский** naval.
флю́гер (*pl* -а́) weather-vane.
флюоресце́нтный fluorescent.
флюс[1] gumboil, abscess.
флюс[2] (*pl* -ы́) flux.
фля́га flask; churn. **фля́жка** flask.
фойе́ *neut indecl* foyer.
фо́кус[1] trick.
фо́кус[2] focus. **фокуси́ровать** *impf* focus.
фо́кусник conjurer, juggler.
фолиа́нт folio.
фольга́ foil.
фолькло́р folklore.
фон background.
фона́рик small lamp; torch. **фона́рный** lamp; ~ **столб** lamp-post. **фона́рь** (-я́) *m* lantern; lamp; light.
фонд fund; stock; reserves.
фоне́тика phonetics. **фонети́ческий** phonetic.
фонта́н fountain.
форе́ль trout.
фо́рма form; shape; mould, cast; uniform. **форма́льность** formality. **форма́льный** formal. **форма́т** format. **форма́ция** structure; stage; formation; mentality. **фо́рменный** uniform; proper, regular. **формирова́ние** forming; unit, formation. **формирова́ть** *impf* (*pf* **с~**) form; organize; **~ся** form, develop. **формова́ть** *impf* (*pf* **с~**)

form, shape; mould, cast.
фо́рмула formula. **формули́ровать** *impf & pf* (*pf also* **с~**) formulate. **формулиро́вка** formulation; wording; formula. **формуля́р** log-book; library card.
форси́ровать *impf & pf* force; speed up.
форсу́нка sprayer; injector.
фортепья́но *neut indecl* piano.
фо́рточка small hinged (window-)pane.
форту́на fortune.
фо́рум forum
фо́сфор phosphorus.
фо́то *neut indecl* photo(graph).
фото- *in comb* photo-, photoelectric. **фотоаппара́т** camera. **~бума́га** photographic paper. **~гени́чный** photogenic. **фото́граф** photographer. **~графи́ровать** *impf* (*pf* **с~**) photograph. **~графи́роваться** be photographed, have one's photograph taken. **~графи́ческий** photographic. **~гра́фия** photography; photograph; photographer's studio. **~ко́пия** photocopy. **~люби́тель** *m* amateur photographer. **~объекти́в** (camera) lens. **~репортёр** press photographer. **~хро́ника** news in pictures. **~элеме́нт** photoelectric cell.
фрагме́нт fragment.
фра́за sentence; phrase. **фразеоло́гия** phraseology.
фрак tail-coat, tails.
фракцио́нный fractional; factional. **фра́кция** fraction; faction.
франк franc.
франкмасо́н Freemason.
франт dandy.
Фра́нция France. **францу́женка** Frenchwoman. **францу́з** Frenchman. **францу́зский** French.
фрахт freight. **фрахтова́ть** *impf* (*pf* **за~**) charter.
фрега́т frigate.
фрезеро́вщик milling machine operator.
фре́ска fresco.
фронт (*pl* -ы, -о́в) front. **фронтови́к** (-а́) front-line soldier. **фронтово́й** front(-line).
фронто́н pediment.
фрукт fruit. **фрукто́вый** fruit; **~ сад** orchard.
ФСБ *abbr* (*of* **федера́льная слу́жба безопа́сности**) Federal Security Service.
фтор fluorine. **фто́ристый** fluorine; fluoride. **~ ка́льций** calcium fluoride.
фу *int* ugh! oh!
фуга́нок (-нка) smoothing-plane.
фуга́с landmine. **фуга́сный** high-explosive.
фунда́мент foundation. **фундамента́льный** solid, sound; main; basic.
функциона́льный functional. **функциони́ровать** *impf* function. **фу́нкция** function.
фунт pound.
фура́ж (-а́) forage, fodder. **фура́жка** peaked cap, forage-cap.
фурго́н van; caravan.
фут foot; foot-rule. **футбо́л** football. **футболи́ст** footballer. **футбо́лка** T-shirt, sports shirt. **футбо́льный** football; **~ мяч** football.
футля́р case, container.
футури́зм futurism.
фуфа́йка jersey; sweater.
фы́ркать *impf*, **фы́ркнуть** (-ну) *pf* snort.
фюзеля́ж fuselage.

X

хала́т dressing-gown. **хала́тный** careless, negligent.
халту́ра pot-boiler; hackwork; money made on the side. **халту́рщик** hack.
хам boor, lout. **ха́мский** boorish, loutish. **ха́мство** boorishness, loutishness.
хамелео́н chameleon.
хан khan.
хандра́ depression. **хандри́ть** *impf* be depressed.
ханжа́ hypocrite. **ха́нжеский** sanctimonious, hypocritical.
хао́с chaos. **хаоти́чный** chaotic.
хара́ктер character. **характеризова́ть** *impf & pf* (*pf also* **о~**) describe; characterize; **~ся** be characterized. **характери́стика** reference; description. **характе́рный** characteristic; distinctive; character.
ха́ркать *impf*, **ха́ркнуть** (-ну) *pf* spit.
ха́ртия charter.
ха́та peasant hut.
хвала́ praise. **хвале́бный** laudatory. **хвалёный** highly-praised. **хвали́ть** (-лю́, -лишь) *impf* (*pf* **по~**) praise; **~ся** boast.
хва́стать(ся *impf* (*pf* **по~**) boast. **хвастли́вый** boastful. **хвастовство́** boasting. **хвасту́н** (-а́) boaster.
хвата́ть[1] *impf*, **хвати́ть** (-ачу́, -а́тишь) *pf* (*pf also* **схвати́ть**) snatch, seize; grab; **~ся** remember; *+gen* realize the absence of; **+за**+*acc* snatch at, clutch at; take up.
хвата́ть[2] *impf*, **хвати́ть** (-а́тит) *pf*, *impers* (*+gen*) suffice, be enough; last out; **вре́мени не хвата́ло** there was not enough time; **у нас не хвата́ет де́нег** we haven't enough money; **хва́тит!** that will do!; **э́того ещё не хвата́ло!** that's all we needed! **хва́тка** grasp, grip; method; skill.
хво́йн|ый coniferous; **~ые** *sb pl* conifers.
хвора́ть *impf* be ill.
хво́рост brushwood; (*pastry*) straws. **хворости́на** stick, switch.
хвост (-а́) tail; tail-end. **хво́стик** tail. **хвостово́й** tail.
хво́я needle(s); (*coniferous*) branch(es).
херуви́м cherub.
хиба́р(к)а shack, hovel.
хи́жина shack, hut.
хи́лый (-л, -а́, -о) sickly.
химе́ра chimera.
хи́мик chemist. **химика́т** chemical. **хими́ческий** chemical. **хи́мия** chemistry.
химчи́стка dry-cleaning; dry-cleaner's.
хи́на, хини́н quinine.
хиру́рг surgeon. **хирурги́ческий** surgical. **хирурги́я** surgery.
хитре́ц (-а́) cunning person. **хитри́ть** *impf* (*pf* **с~**) use cunning, be crafty. **хи́трость** cunning; ruse; skill; intricacy. **хи́трый** cunning; skilful; intricate.
хихи́кать *impf*, **хихи́кнуть** (-ну) *pf* giggle, snigger.
хище́ние theft; embezzlement. **хи́щник** predator, bird *or* beast of prey. **хи́щнический** predatory. **хи́щн|ый** predatory; rapacious; **~ые пти́цы** birds of prey.
хладнокро́вие coolness, composure. **хладнокро́вный** cool, composed.

хлам rubbish.
хлеб (*pl* -ы, -ов *or* -á, -óв) bread; loaf; grain. **хлеба́ть** *impf*, **хлебну́ть** (-ну́, -нёшь) *pf* gulp down. **хле́бный** bread; baker's; grain. **хлебозаво́д** bakery. **хлебопека́рня** (*gen pl* -рен) bakery.
хлев (*loc* -ý; *pl* -á) cow-shed.
хлеста́ть (-ещу́, -е́щешь) *impf*, **хлестну́ть** (-ну́, -нёшь) *pf* lash; whip.
хлоп *int* bang! **хло́пать** *impf* (*pf* **хло́пнуть**) bang; slap; ~ (**в ладо́ши**) clap.
хлопково́дство cotton-growing. **хло́пковый** cotton.
хло́пнуть (-ну) *pf of* **хло́пать**
хлопо́к[1] (-пка́) clap.
хло́пок[2] (-пка) cotton.
хлопота́ть (-очу́, -о́чешь) *impf* (*pf* **по~**) busy o.s.; bustle about; take trouble; +**о**+*prep* *or* **за**+*acc* petition for. **хлопотли́вый** troublesome; exacting; busy, bustling. **хло́поты** (-о́т) *pl* trouble; efforts.
хлопчатобума́жный cotton.
хло́пья (-ьев) *pl* flakes.
хлор chlorine. **хло́ристый**, **хло́рный** chlorine; chloride. **хло́рка** bleach. **хлорофи́лл** chlorophyll. **хлорофо́рм** chloroform.
хлы́нуть (-нет) *pf* gush, pour.
хлыст (-á) whip, switch.
хмеле́ть (-е́ю) *impf* (*pf* **за~**, **о~**) get tipsy. **хмель** (*loc* -ю́) *m* hop, hops; drunkenness; **во хмелю́** tipsy. **хмельно́й** (-лён, -льна́) drunk; intoxicating.
хму́рить *impf* (*pf* **на~**): ~ **бро́ви** knit one's brows; **~ся** frown; become gloomy; be overcast. **хму́рый** gloomy; overcast.
хны́кать (-ы́чу *or* -аю) *impf* whimper, snivel.
хо́бби *neut indecl* hobby.
хо́бот trunk. **хобото́к** (-тка́) proboscis.
ход (*loc* -ý; *pl* -ы, -ов *or* -ы́ *or* -á, -óв) motion; going; speed; course; operation; stroke; move; manoeuvre; entrance; passage; **в ~ý** in demand; **дать за́дний ~** reverse; **дать ~** set in motion; **на ~ý** in transit, on the move; in motion; in operation; **по́лным ~ом** at full speed; **пусти́ть в ~** start, set in motion; **три часа́ ~у** three hours' journey.
хода́тайство petitioning; application. **хода́тайствовать** *impf* (*pf* **по~**) petition, apply.
ходи́ть (хожу́, хо́дишь) *impf* walk; go; run; pass, go round; lead, play; move; +**в**+*prep* wear; +**за**+*instr* look after.
хо́дкий (-док, -дка́, -о) fast; marketable; popular. **ходьба́** walking; walk. **ходя́чий** walking; able to walk; popular; current.
хозрасчёт *abbr* (*of* **хозя́йственный расчёт**) self-financing system.
хозя́ин (*pl* -я́ева, -я́ев) owner, proprietor; master; boss; landlord; host; **хозя́ева по́ля** home team. **хозя́йка** owner; mistress; hostess; landlady. **хозя́йничать** *impf* keep house; be in charge; lord it. **хозя́йственник** financial manager. **хозя́йственный** economic; household; economical. **хозя́йство** economy; housekeeping; equipment; farm; **дома́шнее ~** housekeeping; **се́льское ~** agriculture.
хокке́ист (ice-)hockey-player. **хокке́й** hockey, ice-hockey.
холе́ра cholera.
холестери́н cholesterol.

холл hall, vestibule.
холм (-á) hill. **холмистый** hilly.
хóлод (*pl* -á, -óв) cold; coldness; cold weather. **холодильник** refrigerator. **хóлодно** *adv* coldly. **холóдн|ый** (хóлоден, -днá, -о) cold; inadequate, thin; **~ое орýжие** cold steel.
холóп serf.
холостóй (хóлост, -á) unmarried, single; bachelor; idle; blank. **холостя́к** (-á) bachelor.
холст (-á) canvas; linen.
холу́й (-луя́) *m* lackey.
хому́т (-á) (horse-)collar; burden.
хомя́к (-á) hamster.
хор (*pl* хóры) choir; chorus.
хорвáт, ~ка Croat. **Хорвáтия** Croatia. **хорвáтский** Croatian.
хорёк (-рькá) polecat.
хореографи́ческий choreographic. **хореогрáфия** choreography.
хори́ст member of a choir or chorus.
хорони́ть (-ню́, -ни́шь) *impf* (*pf* **за~, по~, с~**) bury.
хорóшенький pretty; nice. **хорошéнько** *adv* properly, thoroughly. **хорошéть** (-éю) *impf* (*pf* **по~**) grow prettier. **хорóший** (-óш, -á, -ó) good; nice; pretty, nice-looking; **хорошó** *predic* it is good; it is nice. **хорошó** *adv* well; nicely; all right! good.
хóры (хор *or* -ов) *pl* gallery.
хотéть (хочу́, хóчешь, хоти́м) *impf* (*pf* **за~**) wish; *+gen, acc* want; **~ пить** be thirsty; **~ сказáть** mean; **~ся** *impers +dat* want; **мне хотéлось бы** I should like; **мне хóчется** I want.
хоть *conj* although; even if; *partl* at least, if only; for example; **~ бы** if only. **хотя́** *conj* although; **~ бы** even if; if only.
хóхот loud laugh(ter). **хохотáть** (-очу́, -óчешь) *impf* laugh loudly.
хочу́ *etc.*: *see* **хотéть**
храбрéц (-á) brave man. **храбри́ться** make a show of bravery; pluck up courage. **хрáбрость** bravery. **хрáбрый** brave.
храм temple, church.
хранéние keeping; storage; **кáмера хранéния** cloakroom, left-luggage office. **храни́лище** storehouse, depository. **храни́тель** *m* keeper, custodian; curator. **храни́ть** *impf* keep; preserve; **~ся** be, be kept.
храпéть (-плю́) *impf* snore; snort.
хребéт (-бтá) spine; (mountain) range; ridge.
хрен horseradish.
хрестомáтия reader.
хрип wheeze. **хрипéть** (-плю́) *impf* wheeze. **хри́плый** (-пл, -á, -о) hoarse. **хри́пнуть** (-ну; хрип) *impf* (*pf* **о~**) become hoarse. **хрипотá** hoarseness.
христиани́н (*pl* -áне, -áн), **христиáнка** Christian. **христиáнский** Christian. **христиáнство** Christianity. **Христóс** (-истá) Christ.
хром chromium; chrome.
хромати́ческий chromatic.
хромáть *impf* limp; be poor. **хромóй** (хром, -á, -о) lame; *sb* lame person.
хромосóма chromosome.
хромотá lameness.
хрóник chronic invalid. **хрóника** chronicle; news items; news-

reel. **хрони́ческий** chronic.

хронологи́ческий chronological. **хроноло́гия** chronology.

хру́пкий (-пок, -пка́, -о) fragile; frail. **хру́пкость** fragility; frailness.

хруст crunch; crackle.

хруста́ль (-я́) *m* cut glass; crystal. **хруста́льный** cut-glass; crystal; crystal-clear.

хрусте́ть (-ущу́) *impf*, **хру́стнуть** (-ну) *pf* crunch; crackle.

хрю́кать *impf*, **хрю́кнуть** (-ну) *pf* grunt.

хрящ (-а́) cartilage, gristle. **хряще́во́й** cartilaginous, gristly.

худе́ть (-е́ю) *impf* (*pf* **по~**) grow thin.

ху́до harm; evil. **ху́до** *adv* ill, badly.

худоба́ thinness.

худо́жественный art, arts; artistic; ~ **фильм** feature film. **худо́жник** artist.

худо́й[1] (худ, -а́, -о) thin, lean.

худо́й[2] (худ, -а́, -о) bad; full of holes; worn; **ему́ ху́до** he feels bad.

худоща́вый thin, lean.

ху́дший *superl of* **худо́й, плохо́й** (the) worst. **ху́же** *comp of* **худо́й, ху́до, плохо́й, пло́хо** worse.

хула́ abuse, criticism.

хулига́н hooligan. **хулига́нить** *impf* behave like a hooligan. **хулига́нство** hooliganism.

ху́нта junta.

ху́тор (*pl* -а́) farm; small village.

Ц

ца́пля (*gen pl* -пель) heron.

цара́пать *impf*, **цара́пнуть** (-ну) *pf* (*pf also* **на~, о~**) scratch; scribble; **~ся** scratch; scratch one another. **цара́пина** scratch.

цари́зм tsarism. **цари́ть** *impf* reign, prevail. **цари́ца** tsarina; queen. **ца́рский** tsar's; royal; tsarist; regal. **ца́рство** kingdom, realm; reign. **ца́рствование** reign. **ца́рствовать** *impf* reign. **царь** (-я́) *m* tsar; king.

цвести́ (-ету́, -етёшь; -ёл, -а́) *impf* flower, blossom; flourish.

цвет[1] (*pl* -а́) colour; ~ **лица́** complexion.

цвет[2] (*loc* -у́; *pl* -ы́) flower; prime; **в цвету́** in blossom.

цветни́к (-а́) flower-bed, flower-garden.

цветн|о́й coloured; colour; non-ferrous; **~а́я капу́ста** cauliflower; **~о́е стекло́** stained glass.

цветов|о́й colour; **~а́я слепота́** colour-blindness.

цвето́к (-тка́; *pl* цветы́ *or* цветки́, -о́в) flower. **цвето́чный** flower. **цвету́щий** flowering; prosperous.

цеди́ть (цежу́, це́дишь) *impf* strain, filter.

целе́бный curative, healing.

целево́й earmarked for a specific purpose. **целенапра́вленный** purposeful. **целесообра́зный** expedient. **целеустремлённый** (-ён, -ённа *or* -ена́) purposeful.

целико́м *adv* whole; entirely.

целина́ virgin lands, virgin soil. **цели́нн|ый** virgin; **~ые зе́мли** virgin lands.

цели́тельный healing, medicinal.

це́лить(ся *impf* (*pf* **на~**) aim, take aim.

целлофа́н cellophane.

целова́ть *impf* (*pf* **по~**) kiss; **~ся** kiss.

це́лое *sb* whole; integer. **целому́дренный** chaste. **цело-**

мýдрие chastity. **цéлостность** integrity. **цéлый** (цел, -á, -о) whole; safe, intact.
цель target; aim, object, goal.
цéльный (-лен, -льнá, -о) of one piece, solid; whole; integral; single. **цéльность** wholeness.
цемéнт cement. **цементúровать** *impf* & *pf* cement. **цемéнтный** cement.
ценá (*acc* -у; *pl* -ы) price, cost; worth.
ценз qualification. **цéнзор** censor. **цензýра** censorship.
ценúтель *m* judge, connoisseur. **ценúть** (-ню́, -нишь) *impf* value; appreciate. **цéнность** value; price; *pl* valuables; values. **цéнный** valuable.
цент cent. **цéнтнер** centner (*100kg*).
центр centre. **централизáция** centralization. **централизовáть** *impf* & *pf* centralize. **центрáльный** central. **центробéжный** centrifugal.
цепенéть (-éю) *impf* (*pf* **о~**) freeze; become rigid. **цéпкий** tenacious; prehensile; sticky; obstinate. **цéпкость** tenacity. **цеплáться** *impf* **за**+*acc* clutch at; cling to.
цепнóй chain. **цепóчка** chain; file. **цепь** (*loc* -ú; *gen pl* -éй) chain; series; circuit.
церемóниться *impf* (*pf* **по~**) stand on ceremony. **церемóния** ceremony.
церковнославя́нский Church Slavonic. **церкóвный** church; ecclesiastical. **цéрковь** (-кви; *pl* -и, -éй, -áм) church.
цех (*loc* -ý; *pl* -и *or* -á) shop; section; guild.
цивилизáция civilization. **цивилизóванный** civilized. **цивилизовáть** *impf* & *pf* civilize.
цигéйка beaver lamb.
цикл cycle.
цикóрий chicory.
цилúндр cylinder; top hat. **цилиндрúческий** cylindrical.
цимбáлы (-áл) *pl* cymbals.
цингá scurvy.
цинúзм cynicism. **цúник** cynic. **цинúчный** cynical.
цинк zinc. **цúнковый** zinc.
цинóвка mat.
цирк circus.
циркулúровать *impf* circulate. **цúркуль** *m* (pair of) compasses; dividers. **циркуля́р** circular. **циркуля́ция** circulation.
цистéрна cistern, tank.
цитадéль citadel.
цитáта quotation. **цитúровать** *impf* (*pf* **про~**) quote.
цúтрус citrus. **цúтрусов|ый** citrous; **~ые** *sb pl* citrus plants.
циферблáт dial, face.
цúфра figure; number, numeral. **цифровóй** numerical, digital.
цóколь *m* socle, plinth.
цыгáн (*pl* -е, -áн *or* -ы, -ов), **цыгáнка** gipsy. **цыгáнский** gipsy.
цыплёнок (-нка *pl* -пя́та, -пя́т) chicken; chick.
цы́почки: на ~, на цы́почках on tip-toe.

Ч

чабáн (-á) shepherd.
чад (*loc* -ý) fumes, smoke.
чадрá yashmak.
чай (*pl* -ú, -ёв) tea. **чаевы́е** (-ы́х) *sb pl* tip.
чáйка (*gen pl* чáек) (sea-)gull.
чáйная *sb* tea-shop. **чáйник** teapot; kettle. **чáйный** tea.
чайхáнá tea-house.

чалма́ turban.
чан (*loc* -ý; *pl* -ы́) vat, tub.
чарова́ть *impf* bewitch; charm.
час (*with numerals* -á, *loc* -ý, *pl* -ы́) hour; *pl* guard-duty; **кото́рый час?** what's the time?; ~ one o'clock; **в два ~а́** at two o'clock; **стоя́ть на ~а́х** stand guard; **~ы́ пик** rush-hour. **часо́вня** (*gen pl* -вен) chapel. **часово́й** *sb* sentry. **часово́й** clock, watch; of one hour, hour-long. **часовщи́к** (-á) watchmaker.
части́ца small part; particle. **части́чно** *adv* partly, partially. **части́чный** partial.
ча́стник private trader.
ча́стность detail; **в ча́стности** in particular. **ча́стный** private; personal; particular, individual.
ча́сто *adv* often; close, thickly. **частоко́л** paling, palisade. **частота́** (*pl* -ы) frequency. **часто́тный** frequency. **часту́шка** ditty. **ча́стый** (част, -á, -о) frequent; close (together); dense; close-woven; rapid.
часть (*gen pl* -е́й) part; department; field; unit.
часы́ (-о́в) *pl* clock, watch.
ча́хлый stunted; sickly, puny. **чахо́тка** consumption.
ча́ша bowl; chalice; ~ **весо́в** scale, pan. **ча́шка** cup; scale, pan.
ча́ща thicket.
ча́ще *comp of* **ча́сто, ча́стый**; ~ **всего́** most often, mostly.
ча́яние expectation; hope. **ча́ять** (ча́ю) *impf* hope, expect.
чва́нство conceit, arrogance.
чего́ *see* **что**
чей *m*, **чья** *f*, **чьё** *neut*, **чьи** *pl* *pron* whose. **че́й-либо, че́й-нибудь** anyone's. **че́й-то** someone's.
чек cheque; bill; receipt.
чека́нить *impf* (*pf* **вы́~, от~**) mint, coin; stamp, engrave; enunciate. **чека́нка** coinage, minting. **чека́нный** stamping, engraving; stamped, engraved; precise, expressive.
чёлка fringe; forelock.
чёлн (-á; *pl* чёлны́) dug-out (canoe); boat. **челно́к** (-á) dug-out (canoe); shuttle.
челове́к (*pl* лю́ди; with numerals, *gen* -ве́к, -ам) man, person.
человеко- *in comb* man-, anthropo-. **человеколюби́вый** philanthropic. **~лю́бие** philanthropy. **~ненави́стнический** misanthropic. **челове́ко-ча́с** (*pl* -ы́) man-hour.
челове́чек (-чка) little man. **челове́ческий** human; humane. **челове́чество** mankind. **челове́чность** humaneness. **челове́чный** humane.
че́люсть jaw(-bone); dentures, false teeth.
чем, чём *see* **что. чем** *conj* than; **~..., тем...**+*comp* the more ..., the more.
чемода́н suitcase.
чемпио́н, ~ка champion, titleholder. **чемпиона́т** championship.
чему́ *see* **что**
чепуха́ nonsense; trifle.
че́пчик cap; bonnet.
че́рви (-е́й), **че́рвы** (черв) *pl* hearts. **черво́нн|ый** of hearts; **~ое зо́лото** pure gold.
червь (-я́; *pl* -и, -е́й) *m* worm; bug. **червя́к** (-á) worm.
черда́к (-á) attic, loft.
черёд (-á, *loc* -ý) turn; **идти́**

своим ~óм take its course. **чередовáние** alternation. **чередовáть** *impf* alternate; **~ся** alternate, take turns.

чéрез, чрез *prep+acc* across; over; through; via; in; after; every other.

черёмуха bird cherry.

черенóк (-нкá) handle; graft, cutting.

чéреп (*pl* -á) skull.

черепáха tortoise; turtle; tortoiseshell. **черепáховый** tortoise; turtle; tortoiseshell. **черепáший** tortoise, turtle; very slow.

черепи́ца tile. **черепи́чный** tile; tiled.

черепóк (-пкá) potsherd, fragment of pottery.

чересчýр *adv* too; too much.

черéшневый cherry. **черéшня** (*gen pl* -шен) cherry(-tree).

черкéс, черкéшенка Circassian.

черкнýть (-нý, -нёшь) *pf* scrape; leave a mark on; scribble.

чернéть (-éю) *impf* (*pf* **по~**) turn black; show black. **черни́ка** (*no pl*; *usu collect*) bilberry; bilberries. **черни́ла** (-и́л) *pl* ink. **черни́льный** ink. **черни́ть** *impf* (*pf* **о~**) blacken; slander.

черно- *in comb* black; unskilled; rough. **чёрно-бéлый** black-and-white. **~бýрый** dark-brown; **~бýрая лисá** silver fox. **~волóсый** black-haired. **~глáзый** black-eyed. **~зём** chernozem, black earth. **~кóжий** black; *sb* black. **~мóрский** Black-Sea. **~рабóчий** *sb* unskilled worker, labourer. **~сли́в** prunes. **~сморóдинный** blackcurrant.

чернови́к (-á) rough copy, draft. **черновóй** rough; draft. **чернотá** blackness; darkness.

чёрн|ый (-рен, -рнá) black; back; unskilled; ferrous; gloomy; *sb* (*derog*) black person; **~ая сморóдина** (*no pl*; *usu collect*) blackcurrant(s).

черпáк (-á) scoop. **чéрпать** *impf*, **черпнýть** (-нý, -нёшь) *pf* draw; scoop; extract.

черствéть (-éю) *impf* (*pf* **за~, о~, по~**) get stale; become hardened. **чёрствый** (чёрств, -á, -о) stale; hard.

чёрт (*pl* чéрти, -éй) devil.

чертá line; boundary; trait, characteristic. **чертёж** (-á) drawing; blueprint, plan. **чертёжник** draughtsman. **чертёжный** drawing. **черти́ть** (-рчý, -ртишь) *impf* (*pf* **на~**) draw.

чёртов *adj* devil's; devilish. **чертóвский** devilish.

чертополóх thistle.

чёрточка line; hyphen. **черчéние** drawing. **черчý** *etc.*: *see* **черти́ть**

чесáть (чешý, -шешь) *impf* (*pf* **по~**) scratch; comb; card; **~ся** scratch o.s.; itch; comb one's hair.

чеснóк (-á) garlic.

чéствование celebration. **чéствовать** *impf* celebrate; honour. **чéстность** honesty. **чéстный** (-тен, -тнá, -о) honest. **честолюби́вый** ambitious. **честолю́бие** ambition. **честь** (*loc* -и́) honour; **отдáть ~** *+dat* salute.

четá pair, couple.

четвéрг (-á) Thursday. **четверéньки: на ~, на четверéньках** on hands and knees. **четвёрка** four; figure 4; No. 4. **чéтверо** (-ы́х) four. **четвероно́г|ий** four-legged; **~ое** *sb* quadruped. **четверости́шие** quatrain. **четвёр-**

тый fourth. **четверть** (*gen pl* -ей) quarter; quarter of an hour; **без четверти час** a quarter to one. **четвертьфинал** quarter-final.
чёткий (-ток, -тка, -о) precise; clear-cut; clear; distinct. **чёткость** precision; clarity.
чётный even.
четыре (-рёх, -рьмя, -рёх) four. **четыреста** (-рёхсот, -ьмястами, -ёхстах) four hundred.
четырёх- *in comb* four-, tetra-. **четырёхкратный** fourfold. **~местный** four-seater. **~сотый** four-hundredth. **~угольник** quadrangle. **~угольный** quadrangular.
четырнадцатый fourteenth. **четырнадцать** fourteen.
чех Czech.
чехол (-хла) cover, case.
чечевица lentil; lens.
чешка Czech. **чешский** Czech.
чешу *etc.*: *see* **чесать**
чешуйка scale. **чешуя** scales.
чибис lapwing.
чиж (-а) siskin.
чин (*pl* -ы) rank.
чинить[1] (-ню, -нишь) *impf* (*pf* **по~**) repair, mend.
чинить[2] *impf* (*pf* **у~**) carry out; cause; **~ препятствия** *+dat* put obstacles in the way of.
чиновник civil servant; official.
чип (micro)chip.
чипсы (-ов) *pl* (potato) crisps.
чирикать *impf*, **чирикнуть** (-ну) *pf* chirp.
чиркать *impf*, **чиркнуть** (-ну) *pf +instr* strike.
численность numbers; strength. **численный** numerical. **числитель** *m* numerator. **числительное** *sb* numeral. **числить** *impf* count, reckon; **~ся** be; *+instr* be reckoned. **число** (*pl* -а, -сел) number; date, day; **в числе** *+gen* among; **в том числе** including; **единственное ~** singular; **множественное ~** plural. **числовой** numerical.
чистилище purgatory.
чистильщик cleaner. **чистить** (чищу) *impf* (*pf* **вы~, о~, по~**) clean; peel; clear. **чистка** cleaning; purge. **чисто** *adv* cleanly, clean; purely; completely. **чистовой** fair, clean. **чистокровный** thoroughbred. **чистописание** calligraphy. **чистоплотный** clean; neat; decent. **чистосердечный** frank, sincere. **чистота** cleanness; neatness; purity. **чистый** clean; neat; pure; complete.
читаемый widely-read, popular. **читальный** reading. **читатель** *m* reader. **читать** *impf* (*pf* **про~, прочесть**) read; recite; **~ лекции** lecture; **~ся** be legible; be discernible. **читка** reading.
чихать *impf*, **чихнуть** (-ну, -нёшь) *pf* sneeze.
чище *comp of* **чисто, чистый**
чищу *etc.*: *see* **чистить**
член member; limb; term; part; article. **членить** *impf* (*pf* **рас~**) divide; articulate. **член-корреспондент** corresponding member, associate. **членораздельный** articulate. **членский** membership. **членство** membership.
чмокать *impf*, **чмокнуть** (-ну) *pf* smack; squelch; kiss noisily; **~ губами** smack one's lips.
чокаться *impf*, **чокнуться** (-нусь) *pf* clink glasses.
чопорный prim; stand-offish.
чреватый *+instr* fraught with.
чрево belly, womb. **чревовещатель** *m* ventriloquist.

чрез *see* **чéрез. чрезвычáйн|ый** extraordinary; extreme; **~ое положéние** state of emergency. **чрезмéрный** excessive.
чтéние reading. **чтец** (-á) reader; reciter.
чтить (чту) *impf* honour.
что, чегó, чемý, чем, о чём *pron* what?; how?; why?; how much?; which, what, who; anything; **в чём дéло?** what is the matter? **для чегó?** what ... for? why?; **~ емý до э́того?** what does it matter to him?; **~ с тобóй?** what's the matter (with you)?; **~ за** what? what sort of?; what (a) ..!; **что** *conj* that. **что (бы) ни** *pron* whatever, no matter what.
чтоб, чтóбы *conj* in order (to), so as; that; to. **чтó-либо, чтó-нибудь** *prons* anything. **чтó-то**[1] *pron* something. **чтó-то**[2] *adv* somewhat, slightly; somehow, for some reason.
чýвственность sensuality. **чувстви́тельность** sensitivity; perceptibility; sentimentality. **чувстви́тельный** sensitive; perceptible; sentimental. **чýвство** feeling; sense; senses; **прийти́ в ~** come round. **чýвствовать** *impf* (*pf* **по~**) feel; realize; appreciate; **~ себя́** *+adv or instr* feel a certain way; **~ся** be perceptible; make itself felt.
чугýн (-á) cast iron. **чугýнный** cast-iron.
чудáк (-á), **чудáчка** eccentric, crank. **чудáчество** eccentricity.
чудесá *etc.*: *see* **чýдо. чудéсный** miraculous; wonderful.
чýдиться (-ишься) *impf* (*pf* **по~, при~**) seem.
чýдно *adv* wonderfully; wonderful! **чуднóй** (-дён, -днá) odd, strange. **чýдный** wonderful; magical. **чýдо** (*pl* -десá) miracle; wonder. **чудóвище** monster. **чудóвищный** monstrous. **чудодéйственный** miracle-working; miraculous. **чýдом** *adv* miraculously. **чудотвóрный** miraculous, miracle-working.
чужби́на foreign land. **чуждáться** *impf +gen* avoid; stand aloof from. **чýждый** (-жд, -á, -о) alien (to); *+gen* free from, devoid of. **чужезéмец** (-мца), **-зéмка** foreigner. **чужезéмный** foreign.
чужóй someone else's, others'; strange, alien; foreign.
чулáн store-room; larder.
чулóк (-лкá; *gen pl* -лóк) stocking.
чумá plague.
чумáзый dirty.
чурбáн block. **чýрка** block, lump.
чýткий (-ток, -ткá, -о) keen; sensitive; sympathetic; delicate. **чýткость** keenness; delicacy.
чýточка: ни чýточки not in the least; **чýточку** a little (bit).
чýтче *comp of* **чýткий**
чуть *adv* hardly; just; very slightly; **~ не** almost; **~-чуть** a tiny bit.
чутьё scent; flair.
чýчело stuffed animal, stuffed bird; scarecrow.
чушь nonsense.
чýять (чýю) *impf* scent; sense.
чьё *etc.*: *see* **чей**

Ш

шáбаш sabbath.
шаблóн template; mould, stencil; cliché. **шаблóнный** stencil; trite; stereotyped.

шаг (with numerals -а́, *loc* -у́; *pl* -и́) step; footstep; pace. **шага́ть** *impf*, **шагну́ть** (-ну́, -нёшь) *pf* step; stride; pace; make progress. **ша́гом** *adv* at walking pace.
ша́йба washer; puck.
ша́йка[1] tub.
ша́йка[2] gang, band.
шака́л jackal.
шала́ш (-а́) cabin, hut.
шали́ть *impf* be naughty; play up. **шаловли́вый** mischievous, playful. **ша́лость** prank; *pl* mischief. **шалу́н** (-а́), **шалу́нья** (*gen pl* -ний) naughty child.
шаль shawl.
шально́й mad, crazy.
ша́мкать *impf* mumble.
шампа́нское *sb* champagne.
шампиньо́н field mushroom.
шампу́нь *m* shampoo.
шанс chance.
шанта́ж (-а́) blackmail. **шантажи́ровать** *impf* blackmail.
ша́пка hat; banner headline. **ша́почка** hat.
шар (with numerals -а́; *pl* -ы́) sphere; ball; balloon.
шара́хать *impf*, **шара́хнуть** (-ну) hit; **~ся** dash; shy.
шарж caricature.
ша́рик ball; corpuscle. **ша́рико́в|ый: ~ая (авто)ру́чка** ballpoint pen; **~ый подши́пник** ball-bearing. **шарикоподши́пник** ball-bearing.
ша́рить *impf* grope; sweep.
ша́ркать *impf*, **ша́ркнуть** (-ну) *pf* shuffle; scrape.
шарлата́н charlatan.
шарма́нка barrel-organ. **шарма́нщик** organ-grinder.
шарни́р hinge, joint.
шарова́ры (-а́р) *pl* (*wide*) trousers.
шарови́дный spherical. **шарово́й** ball; globular. **шарообра́зный** spherical.
шарф scarf.
шасси́ *neut indecl* chassis.
шата́ть *impf* rock, shake; *impers +acc* **его́ шата́ет** he is reeling; **~ся** sway; reel, stagger; come loose, be loose; be unsteady; loaf about.
шатёр (-тра́) tent; marquee.
ша́ткий unsteady; shaky.
шату́н (-а́) connecting-rod.
ша́фер (*pl* -а́) best man.
шах check; **~ и мат** checkmate. **шахмати́ст** chess-player. **ша́хматы** (-ат) *pl* chess; chessmen.
ша́хта mine, pit; shaft. **шахтёр** miner. **шахтёрский** miner's; mining.
ша́шка[1] draught; *pl* draughts.
ша́шка[2] sabre.
шашлы́к (-а́) kebab; barbecue.
шва *etc.*: *see* **шов**
шва́бра mop.
шваль rubbish; riff-raff.
шварто́в mooring-line; *pl* moorings. **швартова́ть** *impf* (*pf* **при~**) moor; **~ся** moor.
швед, ~ка Swede. **шве́дский** Swedish.
шве́йн|ый sewing; **~ая маши́на** sewing-machine.
швейца́р porter, doorman.
швейца́рец (-рца), **-ца́рка** Swiss. **Швейца́рия** Switzerland. **швейца́рский** Swiss.
Шве́ция Sweden.
швея́ seamstress.
швырну́ть (-ну́, -нёшь) *pf*, **швыря́ть** *impf* throw, fling; **~ся** *+instr* throw (about); treat carelessly.
шевели́ть (-елю́, -е́ли́шь) *impf*, **шевельну́ть** (-ну́, -нёшь) *pf* (*pf also* **по~**) (*+instr*) move, stir; **~ся** move, stir.
шеде́вр masterpiece.
ше́йка (*gen pl* ше́ек) neck.

шёл *see* **идти́**
ше́лест rustle. **шелесте́ть** (-сти́шь) *impf* rustle.
шёлк (*loc* -ý; *pl* -á) silk. **шелкови́стый** silky. **шелкови́ца** mulberry(-tree). **шелкови́чный** mulberry; ~ **червь** silk-worm. **шёлковый** silk.
шелохну́ть (-нý, -нёшь) *pf* stir, agitate; ~**ся** stir, move.
шелуха́ skin; peelings; pod. **шелуши́ть** (-шý) peel; shell; ~**ся** peel (off), flake off.
шепеля́вить (-влю) *impf* lisp. **шепеля́вый** lisping.
шепну́ть (-нý, -нёшь) *pf*, **шепта́ть** (-пчý, -пчешь) *impf* whisper; ~**ся** whisper (together). **шёпот** whisper. **шёпотом** *adv* in a whisper.
шере́нга rank; file.
шерохова́тый rough; uneven.
шерсть wool; hair, coat. **шерстяно́й** wool(len).
шерша́вый rough.
шест (-á) pole; staff.
ше́ствие procession. **ше́ствовать** process; march.
шестёрка six; figure 6; No. 6.
шестерня́ (*gen pl* -рён) gear-wheel, cogwheel.
ше́стеро (-ы́х) six.
шести- *in comb* six-, hexa-, sex(i)-. **шестигра́нник** hexahedron. ~**дне́вка** six-day (*working*) week. ~**деся́тый** sixtieth. ~**ме́сячный** six-month; six-month-old. ~**со́тый** six-hundredth. ~**уго́льник** hexagon.
шестнадцатиле́тний sixteen-year; sixteen-year-old. **шестна́дцатый** sixteenth. **шестна́дцать** sixteen. **шесто́й** sixth. **шесть** (-и́, *instr* -ью́) six. **шестьдеся́т** (-и́десяти, *instr* -ью́десятью) sixty. **шестьсо́т** (-исо́т, -иста́м, -ьюста́ми, -иста́х) six hundred. **ше́стью** *adv* six times.
шеф boss, chief; patron, sponsor. **шеф-по́вар** chef. **ше́фство** patronage, adoption. **ше́фствовать** *impf* +**над**+ *instr* adopt; sponsor.
ше́я neck.
ши́ворот collar.
шика́рный chic, smart; splendid.
ши́ло (*pl* -ья, -ьев) awl.
шимпанзе́ *m indecl* chimpanzee.
ши́на tyre; splint.
шине́ль overcoat.
шинкова́ть *impf* shred, chop.
ши́нный tyre.
шип (-á) thorn, spike, crampon; pin; tenon.
шипе́ние hissing; sizzling. **шипе́ть** (-плю́) *impf* hiss; sizzle; fizz.
шипо́вник dog-rose.
шипу́чий sparkling; fizzy. **шипу́чка** fizzy drink. **шипя́щий** sibilant.
ши́ре *comp of* **широ́кий, широ́ко́. ширина́** width; gauge. **ши́рить** *impf* extend, expand; ~**ся** spread, extend.
ши́рма screen.
широ́к|ий (-óк, -á, -óкó) wide, broad; **това́ры** ~**ого потребле́ния** consumer goods. **широ́ко́** *adv* wide, widely, broadly.
широко- *in comb* wide-, broad-. **широковеща́ние** broadcasting. ~**веща́тельный** broadcasting. ~**экра́нный** wide-screen.
широта́ (*pl* -ы) width, breadth; latitude. **широ́тный** of latitude; latitudinal. **широча́йший** *superl of* **широ́кий. ширпотре́б** *abbr* consumption; consumer goods. **ширь**

(wide) expanse.
шить (шью, шьёшь) *impf* (*pf* **с~**) sew; make; embroider. **шитьё** sewing; embroidery.
ши́фер slate.
шифр cipher, code; shelf mark. **шифро́ванный** coded. **шифрова́ть** *impf* (*pf* **за~**) encipher. **шифро́вка** enciphering; coded communication
ши́шка cone; bump; lump; (*sl*) big shot.
шкала́ (*pl* -ы) scale; dial.
шкату́лка box, casket, case.
шкаф (*loc* -у́; *pl* -ы́) cupboard; wardrobe. **шка́фчик** cupboard, locker.
шквал squall.
шкив (*pl* -ы́) pulley.
шко́ла school. **шко́льник** schoolboy. **шко́льница** schoolgirl. **шко́льный** school.
шку́ра skin, hide, pelt. **шку́рка** skin; rind; sandpaper.
шла *see* **идти́**
шлагба́ум barrier.
шлак slag; dross; clinker. **шлакобло́к** breeze-block.
шланг hose.
шлейф train.
шлем helmet.
шлёпать *impf*, **шлёпнуть** (-ну) *pf* smack, spank; shuffle; tramp; **~ся** fall flat, plop down.
шли *see* **идти́**
шлифова́льный polishing; grinding. **шлифова́ть** *impf* (*pf* **от~**) polish; grind. **шлифо́вка** polishing.
шло *see* **идти́. шлю** *etc.*: *see* **слать**
шлюз lock, sluice.
шлю́пка boat.
шля́па hat. **шля́пка** hat; head.
шмель (-я́) *m* bumble-bee.
шмон *sl* search, frisking.
шмы́гать *impf*, **шмыгну́ть** (-ы́гну́, -ы́гнёшь) *pf* dart, rush; +*instr* rub, brush; **~ но́сом** sniff.
шни́цель *m* schnitzel.
шнур (-а́) cord; lace; flex, cable. **шнурова́ть** *impf* (*pf* **за~, про~**) lace up; tie. **шнуро́к** (-рка́) lace.
шов (шва) seam; stitch; joint.
шовини́зм chauvinism. **шовини́ст** chauvinist. **шовинисти́ческий** chauvinistic.
шок shock. **шоки́ровать** *impf* shock.
шокола́д chocolate. **шокола́дка** chocolate, bar of chocolate. **шокола́дный** chocolate.
шо́рох rustle.
шо́рты (шорт) *pl* shorts.
шо́ры (шор) *pl* blinkers.
шоссе́ *neut indecl* highway.
шотла́ндец (-дца) Scotsman, Scot. **Шотла́ндия** Scotland. **шотла́ндка**[1] Scotswoman. **шотла́ндка**[2] tartan. **шотла́ндский** Scottish, Scots.
шо́у *neut indecl* show; **~-би́знес** show business.
шофёр driver; chauffeur. **шофёрский** driver's; driving.
шпа́га sword.
шпага́т cord; twine; string; splits.
шпаклева́ть (-лю́ю) *impf* (*pf* **за~**) caulk; fill, putty. **шпаклёвка** filling, puttying; putty.
шпа́ла sleeper.
шпана́ (*sl*) hooligan(s); riff-raff.
шпарга́лка crib.
шпа́рить *impf* (*pf* **о~**) scald.
шпат spar.
шпиль *m* spire; capstan. **шпи́лька** hairpin; hat-pin; tack; stiletto heel.
шпина́т spinach.
шпингале́т (vertical) bolt; catch, latch.
шпио́н spy. **шпиона́ж** espionage. **шпио́нить** *impf* spy

(**за**+*instr* on). **шпиóнский** spy's; espionage.
шпóра spur.
шприц syringe.
шпрóта sprat.
шпýлька spool, bobbin.
шрам scar.
шрапнéль shrapnel.
шрифт (*pl* -ы́) type, print.
шт. *abbr* (*of* **штýка**) item, piece.
штаб (*pl* -ы́) staff; headquarters.
штáбель (*pl* -я́) *m* stack.
штабнóй staff; headquarters.
штамп die, punch; stamp; cliché. **штампóванный** punched, stamped, pressed; trite; stock.
штáнга bar, rod, beam; weight. **штанги́ст** weight-lifter.
штани́шки (-шек) *pl* (*child's*) shorts. **штаны́** (-óв) trousers.
штат[1] State.
штат[2], **штáты** (-ов) *pl* staff, establishment.
штати́в tripod, base, stand.
штáтный staff; established.
штáтск|ий civilian; **~ое (плáтье)** civilian clothes; **~ий** *sb* civilian.
штéмпель (*pl* -я́) *m* stamp; **почтóвый ~** postmark.
штéпсель (*pl* -я́) *m* plug, socket.
штиль *m* calm.
штифт (-á) pin, dowel.
штóльня (*gen pl* -лен) gallery.
штóпать *impf* (*pf* **за~**) darn. **штóпка** darning; darning wool.
штóпор corkscrew; spin.
штóра blind.
шторм gale.
штраф fine. **штрафнóй** penal; penalty. **штрафовáть** *impf* (*pf* **о~**) fine.
штрих (-á) stroke; feature. **штриховáть** *impf* (*pf* **за~**) shade, hatch.
штуди́ровать *impf* (*pf* **про~**) study.
штýка item, one; piece; trick.
штукатýр plasterer. **штукатýрить** *impf* (*pf* **от~, о~**) plaster. **штукатýрка** plastering; plaster.
штурвáл (steering-)wheel, helm.
штурм storm, assault.
штýрман (*pl* -ы *or* -á) navigator.
штурмовáть *impf* storm, assault. **штурмов|óй** assault; storming; **~áя авиáция** ground-attack aircraft. **штурмовщи́на** rushed work.
штýчный piece, by the piece.
штык (-á) bayonet.
штырь (-я́) *m* pintle, pin.
шýба fur coat.
шýлер (*pl* -á) card-sharper.
шум noise; uproar, racket; stir.
шумéть (-млю́) *impf* make a noise; row; make a fuss. **шýмный** (-мен, -мнá, -о) noisy; loud; sensational.
шумов|óй sound; **~ы́е эффéкты** sound effects. **шумóк** (-мкá) noise; **под ~** on the quiet.
шýрин brother-in-law (*wife's brother*).
шурф prospecting shaft.
шуршáть (-шý) *impf* rustle.
шýстрый (-тёр, -трá, -о) smart, bright, sharp.
шут (-á) fool; jester. **шути́ть** (-чý, -тишь) *impf* (*pf* **по~**) joke; play, trifle; **+над**+*instr* make fun of. **шýтка** joke, jest. **шутли́вый** humorous; joking, light-hearted. **шýточный** comic; joking. **шутя́** *adv* for fun, in jest; easily.
шушýкаться *impf* whisper together.
шхýна schooner.
шью *etc.*: *see* **шить**

Щ

щаве́ль (-я́) *m* sorrel.

щади́ть (щажу́) *impf* (*pf* **по~**) spare.

щебёнка, ще́бень (-бня) *m* crushed stone, ballast; road-metal.

ще́бет twitter, chirp. **щебета́ть** (-ечу́, -е́чешь) *impf* twitter, chirp.

щего́л (-гла́) goldfinch.

щёголь *m* dandy, fop. **щегольну́ть** (-ну́, -нёшь) *pf*, **щеголя́ть** *impf* dress fashionably; strut about; *+instr* show off, flaunt. **щегольско́й** foppish.

ще́дрость generosity. **ще́дрый** (-др, -а́, -о) generous; liberal.

щека́ (*acc* щёку; *pl* щёки, -а́м) cheek.

щеко́лда latch, catch.

щекота́ть (-очу́, -о́чешь) *impf* (*pf* **по~**) tickle. **щеко́тка** tickling, tickle. **щекотли́вый** ticklish, delicate.

щёлкать *impf*, **щёлкнуть** (-ну) *pf* crack; flick; trill; *+instr* click, snap, pop.

щёлок bleach. **щелочно́й** alkaline. **щёлочь** (*gen pl* -е́й) alkali.

щелчо́к (-чка́) flick; slight; blow.

щель (*gen pl* -е́й) crack; chink; slit; crevice; slit trench.

щеми́ть (-млю́) *impf* constrict; ache; oppress.

щено́к (-нка́; *pl* -нки́, -о́в *or* -ня́та, -я́т) pup; cub.

щепа́ (*pl* -ы, -а́м), **ще́пка** splinter, chip; kindling.

щепети́льный punctilious.

ще́пка *see* **щепа́**

щепо́тка, щёпо́ть pinch.

щети́на bristle; stubble. **щети́нистый** bristly. **щети́ниться** *impf* (*pf* **о~**) bristle. **щётка** brush; fetlock.

щи (щей *or* щец, щам, ща́ми) *pl* shchi, cabbage soup.

щи́колотка ankle.

щипа́ть (-плю́, -плешь) *impf*, **щипну́ть** (-ну́, -нёшь) *pf* (*pf also* **об~, о~, ущипну́ть**) pinch, nip; sting, bite; burn; pluck; nibble; **~ся** pinch. **щипко́м** *adv* pizzicato. **щипо́к** (-пка́) pinch, nip. **щипцы́** (-о́в) *pl* tongs, pincers, pliers; forceps.

щит (-а́) shield; screen; sluice-gate; (tortoise-)shell; board; panel. **щитови́дный** thyroid. **щито́к** (-тка́) dashboard.

щу́ка pike.

щуп probe. **щу́пальце** (*gen pl* -лец) tentacle; antenna. **щу́пать** *impf* (*pf* **по~**) feel, touch.

щу́плый (-пл, -а́, -о) weak, puny.

щу́рить *impf* (*pf* **со~**) screw up, narrow; **~ся** screw up one's eyes; narrow.

Э

эбе́новый ebony.

эвакуа́ция evacuation. **эвакуи́рованный** *sb* evacuee. **эвакуи́ровать** *impf & pf* evacuate.

эвкали́пт eucalyptus.

эволюциони́ровать *impf & pf* evolve. **эволюцио́нный** evolutionary. **эволю́ция** evolution.

эги́да aegis.

эгои́зм egoism, selfishness. **эгои́ст, ~ка** egoist. **эгоисти́ческий, эгоисти́чный** egoistic, selfish.

эй *int* hi! hey!

эйфори́я euphoria.
эква́тор equator.
эквивале́нт equivalent.
экзальта́ция exaltation.
экза́мен examination; **вы́держать, сдать** ~ pass an examination. **экзамена́тор** examiner. **экзаменова́ть** *impf* (*pf* **про**~) examine; **~ся** take an examination.
экзеку́ция (corporal) punishment.
экзе́ма eczema.
экземпля́р specimen; copy.
экзистенциали́зм existentialism.
экзоти́ческий exotic.
э́кий what (a).
экипа́ж[1] carriage.
экипа́ж[2] crew. **экипирова́ть** *impf* & *pf* equip. **экипиро́вка** equipping; equipment.
эклекти́зм eclecticism.
экле́р éclair.
экологи́ческий ecological. **эколо́гия** ecology.
эконо́мика economics; economy. **экономи́ст** economist. **эконо́мить** (-млю) *impf* (*pf* **с**~) use sparingly; save; economize. **экономи́ческий** economic; economical. **экономи́чный** economical. **эконо́мия** economy; saving. **эконо́мка** housekeeper. **эконо́мный** economical; thrifty.
экра́н screen. **экраниза́ция** filming; film version.
экскава́тор excavator.
эксклюзи́вный exclusive.
экскурса́нт tourist. **экскурсио́нный** excursion. **экску́рсия** (conducted) tour; excursion. **экскурсово́д** guide.
экспанси́вный effusive.
экспатриа́нт expatriate.
экспеди́тор shipping agent.
экспеди́ция expedition; dispatch; forwarding office.
экспериме́нт experiment. **эксперимента́льный** experimental. **экспериментирова́ть** *impf* experiment.
экспе́рт expert. **эксперти́за** (expert) examination; commission of experts.
эксплуата́тор exploiter. **эксплуатацио́нный** operating. **эксплуата́ция** exploitation; operation. **эксплуати́ровать** *impf* exploit; operate, run.
экспози́ция lay-out; exposition; exposure. **экспона́т** exhibit. **экспоно́метр** exposure meter.
э́кспорт export. **экспорти́ровать** *impf* & *pf* export. **э́кспортный** export.
экспре́сс express (*train etc.*).
экспро́мт impromptu. **экспро́мтом** *adv* impromptu.
экспроприа́ция expropriation. **экспроприи́ровать** *impf* & *pf* expropriate.
экста́з ectasy.
экстрава́гантный eccentric, bizarre.
экстра́кт extract.
экстреми́ст extremist. **экстреми́стский** extremist.
э́кстренный urgent; emergency; special.
эксцентри́чный eccentric.
эксце́сс excess.
эласти́чный elastic; supple.
элева́тор grain elevator; hoist.
элега́нтный elegant, smart.
эле́гия elegy.
электризова́ть *impf* (*pf* **на**~) electrify. **эле́ктрик** electrician. **электрифика́ция** electrification. **электрифици́ровать** *impf* & *pf* electrify. **электри́ческий** electric(al). **электри́чество** electricity. **электри́чка** electric train.

электро- *in comb* electro-, electric, electrical. **электробытово́й** electrical. **~во́з** electric locomotive. **электро́лиз** electrolysis. **~магни́тный** electromagnetic. **~монтёр** electrician. **~одея́ло** electric blanket. **~по́езд** electric train. **~прибо́р** electrical appliance. **~про́вод** (*pl* -á) electric cable. **~прово́дка** electric wiring. **~ста́нция** power-station. **~те́хник** electrical engineer. **~те́хника** electrical engineering. **~шо́к** electric shock, electric-shock treatment. **~эне́ргия** electrical energy.

электро́д electrode.

электро́д electrode.

электро́н electron. **электро́ника** electronics.

электро́нн|ый electron; electronic; **~ый а́дрес** email address; **~ое письмо́** email (letter); **~ая по́чта** email.

элеме́нт element; cell; character. **элемента́рный** elementary.

эли́та élite.

э́ллипс elipse.

эма́левый enamel. **эмалирова́ть** *impf* enamel. **эма́ль** enamel.

эмансипа́ция emancipation.

эмба́рго *neut indecl* embargo.

эмбле́ма emblem.

эмбрио́н embryo.

эмигра́нт emigrant, émigré. **эмигра́ция** emigration. **эмигри́ровать** *impf & pf* emigrate.

эмоциона́льный emotional. **эмо́ция** emotion.

эмпири́ческий empirical.

эму́льсия emulsion.

э́ндшпиль *m* end-game.

энерге́тика power engineering. **энергети́ческий** energy. **энерги́чный** energetic.

эне́ргия energy.

энтомоло́гия entomology.

энтузиа́зм enthusiasm. **энтузиа́ст** enthusiast.

энциклопеди́ческий encyclopaedic. **энциклопе́дия** encyclopaedia.

эпигра́мма epigram. **эпи́граф** epigraph.

эпиде́мия epidemic.

эпизо́д episode. **эпизоди́ческий** episodic; sporadic.

эпиле́псия epilepsy. **эпиле́птик** epileptic.

эпило́г epilogue. **эпита́фия** epitaph. **эпи́тет** epithet. **эпице́нтр** epicentre.

эпопе́я epic.

эпо́ха epoch, era.

э́ра era, **до на́шей э́ры** BC, **на́шей э́ры** AD.

эре́кция erection.

эро́зия erosion.

эроти́зм eroticism. **эро́тика** sensuality. **эроти́ческий, эроти́чный** erotic, sensual.

эруди́ция erudition.

эска́дра (*naut*) squadron. **эскадри́лья** (*gen pl* -лий) (*aeron*) squadron. **эскадро́н** (*mil*) squadron.

эскала́тор escalator. **эскала́ция** escalation.

эски́з sketch; draft. **эски́зный** sketch; draft.

эскимо́с, эскимо́ска Eskimo.

эско́рт escort.

эсми́нец (-нца) *abbr* (*of* **эска́дренный миноно́сец**) destroyer.

эссе́нция essence.

эстака́да trestle bridge; overpass; pier, boom.

эста́мп print, engraving, plate.

эстафе́та relay race; baton.

эсте́тика aesthetics. **эстети́ческий** aesthetic.

эсто́нец (-нца), **эсто́нка** Es-

tonian. **Эсто́ния** Estonia. **эсто́нский** Estonian.
эстра́да stage, platform; variety. **эстра́дный** stage; variety; ~ **конце́рт** variety show.
эта́ж (-а́) storey, floor. **этаже́рка** shelves.
э́так *adv* so, thus; about. **э́такий** such (a), what (a).
эта́ло́н standard.
эта́п stage; halting-place.
э́тика ethics.
этике́т etiquette.
этике́тка label.
эти́л ethyl.
этимоло́гия etymology.
эти́ческий, эти́чный ethical.
этни́ческий ethnic. **этногра́фия** ethnography.
э́то *partl* this (is), that (is), it (is). **э́тот** *m*, **э́та** *f*, **э́то** *neut*, **э́ти** *pl pron* this, these.
этю́д study, sketch; étude.
эфеме́рный ephemeral.
эфио́п, ~ка Ethiopian. **эфио́пский** Ethiopian.
эфи́р ether; air. **эфи́рный** ethereal; ether, ester.
эффе́кт effect. **эффекти́вность** effectiveness. **эффекти́вный** effective. **эффе́ктный** effective; striking.
эх *int* eh! oh!
э́хо echo.
эшафо́т scaffold.
эшело́н echelon; special train.

Ю

юбиле́й anniversary; jubilee. **юбиле́йный** jubilee.
ю́бка skirt. **ю́бочка** short skirt.
ювели́р jeweller. **ювели́рный** jeweller's, jewellery; fine, intricate.
юг south; **на ~е** in the south. **юго-восто́к** south-east. **юго-за́пад** south-west. **югосла́в, ~ка** Yugoslav. **Югосла́вия** Yugoslavia. **югосла́вский** Yugoslav.
юдофо́б anti-Semite. **юдофо́бство** anti-Semitism.
южа́нин (*pl* -а́не, -а́н), **южа́нка** southerner. **ю́жный** south, southern; southerly.
юла́ top; fidget. **юли́ть** *impf* fidget.
ю́мор humour. **юмори́ст** humourist. **юмористи́ческий** humorous.
ю́ность youth. **ю́ноша** (*gen pl* -шей) *m* youth. **ю́ношеский** youthful. **ю́ношество** youth; young people. **ю́ный** (юн, -а́, -о) young; youthful.
юпи́тер floodlight.
юриди́ческий legal, juridical. **юриско́нсульт** legal adviser. **юри́ст** lawyer.
ю́ркий (-рок, -рка́, -рко) quick-moving, brisk; smart.
юро́дивый crazy.
ю́рта yurt, nomad's tent.
юсти́ция justice.
юти́ться (ючу́сь) *impf* huddle (together).

Я

я (меня́, мне, мной (-о́ю), (обо) мне) *pron* I.
я́беда *m & f*, tell-tale; informer.
я́блоко (*pl* -и, -ок) apple; **глазно́е ~** eyeball. **я́блоневый, я́блочный** apple. **я́блоня** apple-tree.
яви́ться (явлю́сь, я́вишься) *pf*, **явля́ться** *impf* appear; arise; *+instr* be, serve as. **я́вка** appearance, attendance; secret rendez-vous. **явле́ние** phenomenon; appearance; oc-

currence; scene. **я́вный** obvious; overt. **я́вственный** clear. **я́вствовать** be clear, be obvious.

ягнёнок (-нка; *pl* -ня́та, -я́т) lamb.

я́года berry; berries.

я́годица buttock(s).

ягуа́р jaguar.

яд poison; venom.

я́дерный nuclear.

ядови́тый poisonous; venomous.

ядрёный healthy; bracing; juicy. **ядро́** (*pl* -а, я́дер) kernel, core; nucleus; (cannon-) ball; shot.

я́зва ulcer, sore. **я́звенн|ый** ulcerous; **~ая боле́знь** ulcers. **язви́тельный** caustic, sarcastic. **язви́ть** (-влю́) *impf* (*pf* **съ~**) be sarcastic.

язы́к (-а́) tongue; clapper; language. **языкове́д** linguist. **языкове́дение, языкозна́ние** linguistics. **языково́й** linguistic. **языко́вый** tongue; lingual. **язычко́вый** reed. **язы́чник** heathen, pagan. **язычо́к** (-чка́) tongue; reed; catch.

яи́чко (*pl* -и, -чек) egg; testicle. **яи́чник** ovary. **яи́чница** fried eggs. **яйцо́** (*pl* я́йца, яи́ц) egg; ovum.

я́кобы *conj* as if; *partl* supposedly.

я́корн|ый anchor; **~ая стоя́нка** anchorage. **я́корь** (*pl* -я́) *m* anchor.

я́лик skiff.

я́ма pit, hole.

ямщи́к (-а́) coachman.

янва́рский January. **янва́рь** (-я́) *m* January.

янта́рный amber. **янта́рь** (-я́) *m* amber.

япо́нец (-нца), **япо́нка** Japanese. **Япо́ния** Japan. **япо́нский** Japanese.

ярд yard.

я́ркий (я́рок, ярка́, -о) bright; colourful, striking.

ярлы́к (-а́) label; tag.

я́рмарка fair.

ярмо́ (*pl* -а) yoke.

яровой spring.

я́ростный furious, fierce. **я́рость** fury.

я́рус circle; tier; layer.

я́рче *comp of* **я́ркий**

я́рый fervent; furious; violent.

я́сень *m* ash(-tree).

я́сли (-ей) *pl* manger; crèche, day nursery.

ясне́ть (-е́ет) *impf* become clear, clear. **я́сно** *adv* clearly. **ясновиде́ние** clairvoyance. **ясновидец** (-дца), **ясновидица** clairvoyant. **я́сность** clarity; clearness. **я́сный** (я́сен, ясна́, -о) clear; bright; fine.

я́ства (яств) *pl* victuals.

я́стреб (*pl* -а́) hawk.

я́хта yacht.

яче́йка cell.

ячме́нь[1] (-я́) *m* barley.

ячме́нь[2] (-я́) *m* stye.

я́щерица lizard.

я́щик box; drawer.

я́щур foot-and-mouth (disease).

A

a, an *indef article, not usu translated*; **twice a week** два ра́за в неде́лю.
aback *adv*: **take ~** озада́чивать *impf*, озада́чить *pf*.
abacus *n* счёты *m pl*.
abandon *vt* покида́ть *impf*, поки́нуть *pf*; (*give up*) отка́зываться *impf*, отказа́ться *pf* от+*gen*; **~ o.s. to** предава́ться *impf*, преда́ться *pf* +*dat*. **abandoned** *adj* поки́нутый; (*profligate*) распу́тный.
abase *vt* унижа́ть *impf*, уни́зить *pf*. **abasement** *n* униже́ние.
abate *vi* затиха́ть *impf*, зати́хнуть *pf*.
abattoir *n* скотобо́йня.
abbey *n* абба́тство.
abbreviate *vt* сокраща́ть *impf*, сократи́ть *pf*. **abbreviation** *n* сокраще́ние.
abdicate *vi* отрека́ться *impf*, отре́чься *pf* от престо́ла. **abdication** *n* отрече́ние (от престо́ла).
abdomen *n* брюшна́я по́лость. **abdominal** *adj* брюшно́й.
abduct *vt* похища́ть *impf*, похити́ть *pf*. **abduction** *n* похище́ние.
aberration *n* (*mental*) помутне́ние рассу́дка.
abet *vt* подстрека́ть *impf*, подстрекну́ть *pf* (к соверше́нию преступле́ния *etc.*).
abhor *vt* ненави́деть *impf*. **abhorrence** *n* отвраще́ние.
abhorrent *adj* отврати́тельный.
abide *vt* (*tolerate*) выноси́ть *impf*, вы́нести *pf*; **~ by** (*rules etc.*) сле́довать *impf*, по~ *pf*.
ability *n* спосо́бность.
abject *adj* (*wretched*) жа́лкий; (*humble*) уни́женный; **~ poverty** кра́йняя нищета́.
ablaze *predic* охва́ченный огнём.
able *adj* спосо́бный, уме́лый; **be ~ to** мочь *impf*, с~ *pf*; (*know how to*) уме́ть *impf*, с~ *pf*.
abnormal *adj* ненорма́льный. **abnormality** *n* ненорма́льность.
aboard *adv* на борт(у́); (*train*) в по́езд(е).
abode *n* жили́ще; **of no fixed ~** без постоя́нного местожи́тельства.
abolish *vt* отменя́ть *impf*, отмени́ть *pf*. **abolition** *n* отме́на.
abominable *adj* отврати́тельный. **abomination** *n* ме́рзость.
aboriginal *adj* коренно́й; *n* абориге́н, коренно́й жи́тель *m*. **aborigine** *n* абориге́н, коренно́й жи́тель *m*.
abort *vi* (*med*) выки́дывать *impf*, вы́кинуть *pf*; *vt* (*terminate*) прекраща́ть *impf*, прекрати́ть *pf*. **abortion** *n* або́рт; **have an ~** де́лать *impf*, с~ *pf* або́рт. **abortive**

adj безуспе́шный.
abound *vi* быть в изоби́лии; ~ **in** изоби́ловать *impf* +*instr*.
about *adv* & *prep* (*approximately*) о́коло+*gen*; (*concerning*) о+*prep*, насчёт+*gen*; (*up and down*) по+*dat*; (*in the vicinity*) круго́м; **be** ~ **to** собира́ться *impf*, собра́ться *pf* +*inf*.
above *adv* наверху́; (*higher up*) вы́ше; **from** ~ све́рху; свы́ше; *prep* над+*instr*; (*more than*) свы́ше+*gen*. **aboveboard** *adj* че́стный. **abovementioned** *adj* вышеупомя́нутый.
abrasion *n* истира́ние; (*wound*) сса́дина. **abrasive** *adj* абрази́вный; (*manner*) колю́чий; *n* абрази́вный материа́л.
abreast *adv* в ряд; **keep** ~ **of** идти́ в но́гу с+*instr*.
abridge *vt* сокраща́ть *impf*, сократи́ть *pf*. **abridgement** *n* сокраще́ние.
abroad *adv* за грани́цей, за грани́цу; **from** ~ из-за грани́цы.
abrupt *adj* (*steep*) круто́й; (*sudden*) внеза́пный; (*curt*) ре́зкий.
abscess *n* абсце́сс.
abscond *vi* скрыва́ться *impf*, скры́ться *pf*.
absence *n* отсу́тствие. **absent** *adj* отсу́тствующий; **be** ~ отсу́тствовать *impf*; *vt*: ~ **o.s.** отлуча́ться *impf*, отлучи́ться *pf*. **absentee** *n* отсу́тствующий *sb*. **absenteeism** *n* прогу́л. **absent-minded** *adj* рассе́янный.
absolute *adj* абсолю́тный; (*complete*) по́лный, соверше́нный.
absolution *n* отпуще́ние грехо́в. **absolve** *vt* проща́ть *impf*, прости́ть *pf*.
absorb *vt* впи́тывать *impf*, впита́ть *pf*. **absorbed** *adj* поглощённый. **absorbent** *adj* вса́сывающий. **absorption** *n* впи́тывание; (*mental*) погружённость.
abstain *vi* возде́рживаться *impf*, воздержа́ться *pf* (**from** от+*gen*). **abstemious** *adj* возде́ржанный. **abstention** *n* воздержа́ние; (*person*) воздержа́вшийся *sb*. **abstinence** *n* воздержа́ние.
abstract *adj* абстра́ктный, отвлечённый; *n* рефера́т.
absurd *adj* абсу́рдный. **absurdity** *n* абсу́рд.
abundance *n* оби́лие. **abundant** *adj* оби́льный.
abuse *vt* (*insult*) руга́ть *impf*, вы́~, об~, от~ *pf*; (*misuse*) злоупотребля́ть *impf*, злоупотреби́ть *pf*; *n* (*curses*) ру́гань, руга́тельства *neut pl*; (*misuse*) злоупотребле́ние. **abusive** *adj* оскорби́тельный, руга́тельный.
abut *vi* примыка́ть *impf* (**on** к+*dat*).
abysmal *adj* (*extreme*) безграни́чный; (*bad*) ужа́сный.
abyss *n* бе́здна.
academic *adj* академи́ческий. **academician** *n* акаде́мик. **academy** *n* акаде́мия.
accede *vi* вступа́ть *impf*, вступи́ть *pf* (**to** в, на+*acc*); (*assent*) соглаша́ться *impf*, согласи́ться *pf*.
accelerate *vt* & *i* ускоря́ть(ся) *impf*, уско́рить(ся) *pf*; (*motoring*) дава́ть *impf*, дать *pf* газ. **acceleration** *n* ускоре́ние. **accelerator** *n* ускори́тель *m*; (*pedal*) акселера́тор.

accent *n* акце́нт; (*stress*) ударе́ние; *vt* де́лать *impf*, с~ *pf* ударе́ние на+*acc*. **accentuate** *vt* акценти́ровать *impf* & *pf*.

accept *vt* принима́ть *impf*, приня́ть *pf*. **acceptable** *adj* прие́млемый. **acceptance** *n* приня́тие.

access *n* до́ступ. **accessible** *adj* досту́пный. **accession** *n* вступле́ние (на престо́л). **accessories** *n* принадле́жности *f pl*. **accessory** *n* (*accomplice*) соуча́стник, -ица.

accident *n* (*chance*) случа́йность; (*mishap*) несча́стный слу́чай; (*crash*) ава́рия; **by ~** случа́йно. **accidental** *adj* случа́йный.

acclaim *vt* (*praise*) восхваля́ть *impf*, восхвали́ть *pf*; *n* восхвале́ние.

acclimatization *n* акклимати́за́ция. **acclimatize** *vt* акклиматизи́ровать *impf* & *pf*.

accommodate *vt* помеща́ть *impf*, помести́ть *pf*; (*hold*) вмеща́ть *impf*, вмести́ть *pf*. **accommodating** *adj* услу́жливый. **accommodation** *n* (*hotel*) но́мер; (*home*) жильё.

accompaniment *n* сопровожде́ние; (*mus*) аккомпане́мент. **accompanist** *n* аккомпаниа́тор. **accompany** *vt* сопровожда́ть *impf*, сопроводи́ть *pf*; (*escort*) провожа́ть *impf*, проводи́ть *pf*; (*mus*) аккомпани́ровать *impf* +*dat*.

accomplice *n* соуча́стник, -ица.

accomplish *vt* соверша́ть *impf*, соверши́ть *pf*. **accomplished** *adj* зако́нченный. **accomplishment** *n* выполне́ние; (*skill*) соверше́нство.

accord *n* согла́сие; **of one's own ~** доброво́льно; **of its own ~** сам собо́й, сам по себе́. **accordance** *n*: **in ~ with** в соотве́тствии с+*instr*, согла́сно+*dat*. **according** *adv*: **~ to** по+*dat*, **~ to him** по его́ слова́м. **accordingly** *adv* соотве́тственно.

accordion *n* аккордео́н.

accost *vt* пристава́ть *impf*, приста́ть *pf* к+*dat*.

account *n* (*comm*) счёт; (*report*) отчёт; (*description*) описа́ние; **on no ~** ни в ко́ем слу́чае; **on ~** в счёт причита́ющейся су́ммы; **on ~ of** из-за+*gen*, по причи́не+*gen*; **take into ~** принима́ть *impf*, приня́ть *pf* в расчёт; *vi*: **~ for** объясня́ть *impf*, объясни́ть *pf*. **accountable** *adj* отве́тственный.

accountancy *n* бухгалте́рия. **accountant** *n* бухга́лтер.

accrue *vi* нараста́ть *impf*, нарасти́ *pf*.

accumulate *vt* & *i* нака́пливать(ся) *impf*, копи́ть(ся) *impf*, на~ *pf*. **accumulation** *n* накопле́ние. **accumulator** *n* аккумуля́тор.

accuracy *n* то́чность. **accurate** *adj* то́чный.

accusation *n* обвине́ние. **accusative** *adj* (*n*) вини́тельный (паде́ж). **accuse** *vt* обвиня́ть *impf*, обвини́ть *pf* (**of** в+*prep*); **the ~d** обвиня́емый *sb*.

accustom *vt* приуча́ть *impf*, приучи́ть *pf* (**to** к+*dat*). **accustomed** *adj* привы́чный; **be, get ~** привыка́ть *impf*, привы́кнуть *pf* (**to** к+*dat*).

ace *n* туз; (*pilot*) ас.

ache *n* боль; *vi* боле́ть *impf*.

achieve *vt* достига́ть *impf*,

достичь & достигнуть *pf* +*gen*. **achievement** *n* достижение.

acid *n* кислота; *adj* кислый; ~ **rain** кислотный дождь. **acidity** *n* кислота.

acknowledge *vt* признавать *impf*, признать *pf*; (~ *receipt of*) подтверждать *impf*, подтвердить *pf* получение+*gen*. **acknowledgement** *n* признание; подтверждение.

acne *n* прыщи *m pl*.

acorn *n* жёлудь *m*.

acoustic *adj* акустический. **acoustics** *n pl* акустика.

acquaint *vt* знакомить *impf*, по~ *pf*. **acquaintance** *n* знакомство; (*person*) знакомый *sb*. **acquainted** *adj* знакомый.

acquiesce *vi* соглашаться *impf*, согласиться *pf*. **acquiescence** *n* согласие.

acquire *vt* приобретать *impf*, приобрести *pf*. **acquisition** *n* приобретение. **acquisitive** *adj* стяжательский.

acquit *vt* оправдывать *impf*, оправдать *pf*; ~ **o.s.** вести *impf* себя. **acquittal** *n* оправдание.

acre *n* акр.

acrid *adj* едкий.

acrimonious *adj* язвительный.

acrobat *n* акробат. **acrobatic** *adj* акробатический.

across *adv* & *prep* через+*acc*; (*athwart*) поперёк (+*gen*); (*to, on, other side*) на ту сторону (+*gen*), на той стороне (+*gen*); (*crosswise*) крест-накрест.

acrylic *n* акрил; *adj* акриловый.

act *n* (*deed*) акт, поступок; (*law*) акт, закон; (*of play*) действие; (*item*) номер; *vi* поступать *impf*, поступить *pf*; действовать *impf*, по~ *pf*; *vt* играть *impf*, сыграть *pf*. **acting** *n* игра; (*profession*) актёрство; *adj* исполняющий обязанности+*gen*. **action** *n* действие, поступок; (*law*) иск, процесс; (*battle*) бой; ~ **replay** повтор; **be out of** ~ не работать *impf*. **activate** *vt* приводить *impf*, привести *pf* в действие. **active** *adj* активный; ~ **service** действительная служба; ~ **voice** действительный залог. **activity** *n* деятельность. **actor** *n* актёр. **actress** *n* актриса.

actual *adj* действительный. **actuality** *n* действительность. **actually** *adv* на самом деле, фактически.

acumen *n* проницательность.

acupuncture *n* иглоукалывание.

acute *adj* острый.

AD *abbr* н.э. (нашей эры).

adamant *adj* непреклонный.

adapt *vt* приспособлять *impf*, приспособить *pf*; (*theat*) инсценировать *impf* & *pf*; ~ **o.s.** приспособляться *impf*, приспособиться *pf*. **adaptable** *adj* приспособляющийся. **adaptation** *n* приспособление; (*theat*) инсценировка. **adapter** *n* адаптер.

add *vt* прибавлять *impf*, прибавить *pf*; (*say*) добавлять *impf*, добавить *pf*; ~ **together** складывать *impf*, сложить *pf*; ~ **up** суммировать *impf* & *pf*; ~ **up to** составлять *impf*, составить *pf*; (*fig*) сводиться *impf*, свестись *pf* к+*dat*. **addenda** *n* приложения *pl*.

adder *n* гадюка.

addict *n* наркома́н, ~ка. **addicted** *adj*: **be ~ to** быть рабо́м+*gen*; **become ~ to** пристрасти́ться *pf* к+*dat*. **addiction** *n* (*passion*) пристра́стие; (*to drugs*) наркома́ния.

addition *n* прибавле́ние; дополне́ние; (*math*) сложе́ние; **in ~** вдоба́вок, кро́ме того́. **additional** *adj* доба́вочный. **additive** *n* доба́вка.

address *n* а́дрес; (*speech*) речь; **~ book** записна́я кни́жка; *vt* адресова́ть *impf* & *pf*; (*speak to*) обраща́ться *impf*, обрати́ться *pf* к+*dat*; **~ a meeting** выступа́ть *impf*, вы́ступить *pf* на собра́нии. **addressee** *n* адреса́т.

adept *adj* све́дущий; *n* ма́стер.

adequate *adj* доста́точный.

adhere *vi* прилипа́ть *impf*, прили́пнуть *pf* (**to** к+*dat*); (*fig*) приде́рживаться *impf* +*gen*. **adherence** *n* приве́рженность. **adherent** *n* приве́рженец. **adhesive** *adj* ли́пкий; *n* кле́йкое вещество́.

ad hoc *adj* специа́льный.

ad infinitum *adv* до бесконе́чности.

adjacent *adj* сме́жный.

adjective *n* (и́мя) прилага́тельное.

adjoin *vt* прилега́ть *impf* к+*dat*.

adjourn *vt* откла́дывать *impf*, отложи́ть *pf*; *vi* объявля́ть *impf*, объяви́ть *pf* переры́в; (*move*) переходи́ть *impf*, перейти́ *pf*.

adjudicate *vi* выноси́ть *impf*, вы́нести *pf* реше́ние (**in** по+*dat*); суди́ть *impf*.

adjust *vt* & *i* приспособля́ть(ся) *impf*, приспосо́бить(ся) *pf*; *vt* пригоня́ть *impf*, пригна́ть *pf*; (*regulate*) регули́ровать *impf*, от~ *pf*. **adjustable** *adj* регули́руемый. **adjustment** *n* регули́рование, подго́нка.

ad lib *vt* & *i* импровизи́ровать *impf*, сымпровизи́ровать *pf*.

administer *vt* (*manage*) управля́ть *impf* +*instr*; (*give*) дава́ть *impf*, дать *pf*. **administration** *n* управле́ние; (*government*) прави́тельство. **administrative** *adj* администрати́вный. **administrator** *n* администра́тор.

admirable *adj* похва́льный.

admiral *n* адмира́л.

admiration *n* восхище́ние. **admire** *vt* (*look at*) любова́ться *impf*, по~ *pf* +*instr*, на+*acc*; (*respect*) восхища́ться *impf*, восхити́ться *pf* +*instr*. **admirer** *n* покло́нник.

admissible *adj* допусти́мый. **admission** *n* (*access*) до́ступ; (*entry*) вход; (*confession*) призна́ние. **admit** *vt* (*allow in*) впуска́ть *impf*, впусти́ть *pf*; (*confess*) признава́ть *impf*, призна́ть *pf*. **admittance** *n* до́ступ. **admittedly** *adv* призна́ться.

admixture *n* при́месь.

adolescence *n* о́трочество. **adolescent** *adj* подро́стковый; *n* подро́сток.

adopt *vt* (*child*) усыновля́ть *impf*, усынови́ть *pf*; (*thing*) усва́ивать *impf*, усво́ить *pf*; (*accept*) принима́ть *impf*, приня́ть *pf*. **adoptive** *adj* приёмный. **adoption** *n* усыновле́ние; приня́тие.

adorable *adj* преле́стный. **adoration** *n* обожа́ние. **adore** *vt* обожа́ть *impf*.

adorn *vt* украша́ть *impf*, укра́сить *pf*. **adornment** *n* украше́ние.

adrenalin *n* адренали́н.

adroit *adj* ло́вкий.

adulation *n* преклоне́ние.

adult *adj* & *n* взро́слый (*sb*).

adulterate *vt* фальсифици́ровать *impf* & *pf*.

adultery *n* супру́жеская изме́на.

advance *n* (*going forward*) продвиже́ние (вперёд); (*progress*) прогре́сс; (*mil*) наступле́ние; (*of pay etc.*) ава́нс; **in** ~ зара́нее; *pl* (*overtures*) ава́нсы *m pl*; *vi* (*go forward*) продвига́ться *impf*, продви́нуться *pf* вперёд; идти́ *impf* вперёд; (*mil*) наступа́ть *impf*; *vt* продвига́ть *impf*, продви́нуть *pf*; (*put forward*) выдвига́ть *impf*, вы́двинуть *pf*. **advanced** *adj* (*modern*) передово́й. **advancement** *n* продвиже́ние.

advantage *n* преиму́щество; (*profit*) вы́года, по́льза; **take** ~ **of** по́льзоваться *impf*, вос~ *pf* +*instr*. **advantageous** *adj* вы́годный.

adventure *n* приключе́ние. **adventurer** *n* иска́тель *m* приключе́ний. **adventurous** *adj* предприи́мчивый.

adverb *n* наре́чие.

adversary *n* проти́вник. **adverse** *adj* неблагоприя́тный. **adversity** *n* несча́стье.

advertise *vt* (*publicize*) реклами́ровать *impf* & *pf*; *vt* & *i* (~ *for*) дава́ть *impf*, дать *pf* объявле́ние о+*prep*. **advertisement** *n* объявле́ние, рекла́ма.

advice *n* сове́т. **advisable** *adj* жела́тельный. **advise** *vt* сове́товать *impf*, по~ *pf* +*dat* & *inf*; (*notify*) уведомля́ть *impf*, уве́домить *pf*. **advisedly** *adv* наме́ренно. **adviser** *n* сове́тник. **advisory** *adj* совеща́тельный.

advocate *n* (*supporter*) сторо́нник; *vt* выступа́ть *impf*, вы́ступить *pf* за+*acc*; (*advise*) сове́товать *impf*, по~ *pf*.

aegis *n* эги́да.

aerial *n* анте́нна; *adj* возду́шный.

aerobics *n* аэро́бика.

aerodrome *n* аэродро́м. **aerodynamics** *n* аэродина́мика. **aeroplane** *n* самолёт. **aerosol** *n* аэрозо́ль *m*.

aesthetic *adj* эстети́ческий. **aesthetics** *n pl* эсте́тика.

afar *adv*: **from** ~ издалека́.

affable *adj* приве́тливый.

affair *n* (*business*) де́ло; (*love*) рома́н.

affect *vt* влия́ть *impf*, по~ *pf* на+*acc*; (*touch*) тро́гать *impf*, тро́нуть *pf*; (*concern*) затра́гивать *impf*, затро́нуть *pf*; **affectation** *n* жема́нство. **affected** *adj* жема́нный. **affection** *n* привя́занность. **affectionate** *adj* не́жный.

affiliated *adj* свя́занный (**to** с+*instr*).

affinity *n* (*relationship*) родство́; (*resemblance*) схо́дство; (*attraction*) влече́ние.

affirm *vt* утвержда́ть *impf*. **affirmation** *n* утвержде́ние. **affirmative** *adj* утверди́тельный.

affix *vt* прикрепля́ть *impf*, прикрепи́ть *pf*.

afflict *vt* постига́ть *impf*, пости́чь *pf*; **be afflicted with** страда́ть *impf* +*instr*. **affliction** *n* боле́знь.

affluence *n* богáтство. **affluent** *adj* богáтый.
afford *vt* позволя́ть *impf*, позвóлить *pf* себé; (*supply*) предоставля́ть *impf*, предостáвить *pf*.
affront *n* оскорблéние; *vt* оскорбля́ть *impf*, оскорби́ть *pf*.
afield *adv*: **far** ~ далекó; **farther** ~ дáльше.
afloat *adv* & *predic* на водé.
afoot *predic*: **be** ~ готóвиться *impf*.
aforesaid *adj* вышеупомя́нутый.
afraid *predic*: **be** ~ боя́ться *impf*.
afresh *adv* снóва.
Africa *n* Áфрика. **African** *n* африкáнец, -кáнка; *adj* африкáнский.
after *adv* потóм; *prep* пóсле +*gen*; (*time*) чéрез+*acc*; (*behind*) за+*acc*, *instr*; ~ **all** в концé концóв; *conj* пóсле тогó, как.
aftermath *n* послéдствия *neut pl*. **afternoon** *n* вторáя половúна дня; **in the** ~ днём. **aftershave** *n* лосьóн пóсле бритья́. **afterthought** *n* запоздáлая мысль.
afterwards *adv* потóм.
again *adv* опя́ть; (*once more*) ещё раз; (*anew*) снóва.
against *prep* (*opposing*) прóтив+*gen*; (*touching*) к+*dat*; (*hitting*) о+*acc*.
age *n* вóзраст; (*era*) век, эпóха; *vt* стáрить *impf*, со~ *pf*; *vi* старéть *impf*, по~ *pf*. **aged** *adj* престарéлый.
agency *n* агéнтство. **agenda** *n* повéстка дня. **agent** *n* агéнт.
aggravate *vt* ухудшáть *impf*, ухýдшить *pf*; (*annoy*) раздражáть *impf*, раздражи́ть *pf*.
aggregate *adj* совокýпный; *n* совокýпность.
aggression *n* агрéссия. **aggressive** *adj* агресси́вный. **aggressor** *n* агрéссор.
aggrieved *adj* оби́женный.
aghast *predic* в ýжасе (**at** от +*gen*).
agile *adj* проворный. **agility** *n* провóрство.
agitate *vt* волновáть *impf*, вз~ *pf*; *vi* агити́ровать *impf*. **agitation** *n* волнéние; агитáция.
agnostic *n* агнóстик. **agnosticism** *n* агностици́зм.
ago *adv* (томý) назáд; **long** ~ давнó.
agonize *vi* мýчиться *impf*. **agonizing** *adj* мучи́тельный. **agony** *n* агóния.
agrarian *adj* агрáрный.
agree *vi* соглашáться *impf*, согласи́ться *pf*; (*arrange*) договáриваться *impf*, договори́ться *pf*. **agreeable** *adj* (*pleasant*) прия́тный. **agreement** *n* соглáсие; (*treaty*) соглашéние; **in** ~ соглáсен (-сна).
agricultural *adj* сельскохозя́йственный. **agriculture** *n* сéльское хозя́йство.
aground *predic* на мели́; *adv*: **run** ~ сади́ться *impf*, сесть *pf* на мель.
ahead *adv* (*forward*) вперёд; (*in front*) впереди́; ~ **of time** досрóчно.
aid *vt* помогáть *impf*, помóчь *pf* +*dat*; *n* пóмощь; (*teaching*) пособие; **in** ~ **of** в пóльзу +*gen*.
Aids *n* СПИД.
ailing *adj* (*ill*) больнóй.
ailment *n* недýг.

aim *n* цель, наме́рение; **take ~** прице́ливаться *impf*, прице́литься *pf* (**at** в+*acc*); *vi* цели́ться *impf*, на~ *pf* (**at** в+*acc*); (*also fig*) ме́тить *impf*, на~ *pf* (**at** в+*acc*); *vt* наце́ливать *impf*, наце́лить *pf*; (*also fig*) наводи́ть *impf*, навести́ *pf*. **aimless** *adj* бесце́льный.

air *n* во́здух; (*look*) вид; **by ~** самолётом; **on the ~** в эфи́ре; *attrib* возду́шный; *vt* (*ventilate*) прове́тривать *impf*, прове́трить *pf*; (*make known*) выставля́ть *impf*, вы́ставить *pf* напока́з. **air-conditioning** *n* кондициони́рование во́здуха. **aircraft** *n* самолёт. **aircraft-carrier** *n* авиано́сец. **airfield** *n* аэродро́м. **air force** *n* ВВС (вое́нно-возду́шные си́лы) *f pl*. **air hostess** *n* стюарде́сса. **airless** *adj* ду́шный. **airlift** *n* возду́шные перево́зки *f pl*; *vt* перевози́ть *impf*, перевезти́ *pf* по во́здуху. **airline** *n* авиакомпа́ния. **airlock** *n* возду́шная про́бка. **airmail** *n* а́виа(по́чта). **airman** *n* лётчик. **airport** *n* аэропо́рт. **air raid** *n* возду́шный налёт. **airship** *n* дирижа́бль *m*. **airstrip** *n* взлётно-поса́дочная полоса́. **airtight** *adj* гермети́чный. **air traffic controller** *n* диспе́тчер. **airwaves** *n pl* радиово́лны *f pl*.

aisle *n* бокова́й неф; (*passage*) прохо́д.

ajar *predic* приоткры́тый.

akin *predic* (*similar*) похо́жий; **be ~ to** быть сродни́ к+*dat*.

alabaster *n* алеба́стр.

alacrity *n* быстрота́.

alarm *n* трево́га; *vt* трево́жить *impf*, вс~ *pf*; **~ clock** буди́льник. **alarming** *adj* трево́жный. **alarmist** *n* паникёр; *adj* паникёрский.

alas *int* увы́!

album *n* альбо́м.

alcohol *n* алкого́ль *m*, спирт; спиртны́е напи́тки *m pl*. **alcoholic** *adj* алкого́льный; *n* алкого́лик, -и́чка.

alcove *n* алько́в.

alert *adj* бди́тельный; *n* трево́га; *vt* предупрежда́ть *impf*, предупреди́ть *pf*.

algebra *n* а́лгебра.

alias *adv* ина́че (называ́емый); *n* кли́чка, вы́мышленное и́мя *neut*.

alibi *n* а́либи *neut indecl*.

alien *n* иностра́нец, -нка; *adj* иностра́нный; **~ to** чу́ждый +*dat*. **alienate** *vt* отчужда́ть *impf*. **alienation** *n* отчужде́ние.

alight[1] *vi* сходи́ть *impf*, сойти́ *pf*; (*bird*) сади́ться *impf*, сесть *pf*.

alight[2] *predic*: **be ~** горе́ть *impf*; (*shine*) сия́ть *impf*.

align *vt* выра́внивать *impf*, вы́ровнять *pf*. **alignment** *n* выра́внивание.

alike *predic* похо́ж; *adv* одина́ково.

alimentary *adj*: **~ canal** пищевари́тельный кана́л.

alimony *n* алиме́нты *m pl*.

alive *predic* жив, в живы́х.

alkali *n* щёлочь. **alkaline** *adj* щелочно́й.

all *adj* весь; *n* всё, *pl* все; *adv* совсе́м, соверше́нно; **~ along** всё вре́мя; **~ right** хорошо́, ла́дно; (*not bad*) та́к себе; непло́хо; **~ the same** всё равно́; **in ~** всего́; **two ~** по́ два; **not at ~** ниско́лько.

allay *vt* успока́ивать *impf*,

успоко́ить *pf.*
allegation *n* утвержде́ние. **allege** *vt* утвержда́ть *impf.* **allegedly** *adv* я́кобы.
allegiance *adv* ве́рность.
allegorical *adj* аллегори́ческий. **allegory** *n* аллего́рия.
allergic *adj* аллерги́ческий; **be ~ to** име́ть аллерги́ю к+*dat.* **allergy** *n* аллерги́я.
alleviate *vt* облегча́ть *impf*, облегчи́ть *pf.* **alleviation** *n* облегче́ние.
alley *n* переу́лок.
alliance *n* сою́з. **allied** *adj* сою́зный.
alligator *n* аллига́тор.
allocate *vt* (*distribute*) распределя́ть *impf*, распредели́ть *pf*; (*allot*) выделя́ть *impf*, вы́делить *pf.* **allocation** *n* распределе́ние; выделе́ние.
allot *vt* выделя́ть *impf*, вы́делить *pf*; (*distribute*) распределя́ть *impf*, распредели́ть *pf.* **allotment** *n* выделе́ние; (*land*) уча́сток.
allow *vt* разреша́ть *impf*, разреши́ть *pf*; (*let happen*; *concede*) допуска́ть *impf*, допусти́ть *pf*; **~ for** учи́тывать *impf*, уче́сть *pf.* **allowance** *n* (*financial*) посо́бие; (*deduction*, *also fig*) ски́дка; **make ~(s) for** учи́тывать *impf*, уче́сть *pf.*
alloy *n* сплав.
all-round *adj* разносторо́нний.
allude *vi* ссыла́ться *impf*, сосла́ться *pf* (**to** на+*acc*).
allure *vt* зама́нивать *impf*, замани́ть *pf.* **allure(ment)** *n* прима́нка. **alluring** *adj* зама́нчивый.
allusion *n* ссы́лка.
ally *n* сою́зник; *vt* соединя́ть *impf*, соедини́ть *pf*; **~ oneself with** вступа́ть *impf*, вступи́ть *pf* в сою́з с+*instr.*
almighty *adj* всемогу́щий.
almond *n* (*tree*; *pl collect*) минда́ль *m*; (*nut*) минда́льный оре́х.
almost *adv* почти́, едва́ не.
alms *n pl* ми́лостыня.
aloft *adv* наве́рх(-у́).
alone *predic* оди́н; (*lonely*) одино́к; *adv* то́лько; **leave ~** оставля́ть *impf*, оста́вить *pf* в поко́е; **let ~** не говоря́ уже́ о+*prep.*
along *prep* по+*dat*, (*position*) вдоль+*gen*; *adv* (*onward*) да́льше; **all ~** всё вре́мя; **~ with** вме́сте с+*instr.* **alongside** *adv* & *prep* ря́дом (с +*instr*).
aloof *predic* & *adv* (*distant*) сде́ржанный; (*apart*) в стороне́.
aloud *adv* вслух.
alphabet *n* алфави́т. **alphabetical** *adj* алфави́тный.
alpine *adj* альпи́йский.
already *adv* уже́.
also *adv* та́кже, то́же.
altar *n* алта́рь *m.*
alter *vt* (*modify*) переде́лывать *impf*, переде́лать *pf*; *vt* & *i* (*change*) изменя́ть(ся) *impf*, измени́ть(ся) *pf.* **alteration** *n* переде́лка; измене́ние.
alternate *adj* череду́ющийся; *vt* & *i* чередова́ть(ся) *impf*; **alternating current** переме́нный ток; **on ~ days** че́рез день. **alternation** *n* чередова́ние. **alternative** *n* альтернати́ва; *adj* альтернати́вный.
although *conj* хотя́.
altitude *n* высота́.
alto *n* альт.
altogether *adv* (*fully*) совсе́м;

(*in total*) всего́.
altruistic *adj* альтруисти́ческий.
aluminium *n* алюми́ний.
always *adv* всегда́; (*constantly*) постоя́нно.
Alzheimer's disease *n* боле́знь Альцге́ймера.
a.m. *abbr* (*morning*) утра́; (*night*) но́чи.
amalgamate *vt* & *i* слива́ть(ся) *impf*, сли́ть(ся) *pf*; (*chem*) амальгами́ровать(ся) *impf* & *pf*. **amalgamation** *n* слия́ние; (*chem*) амальгами́рование.
amass *vt* копи́ть *impf*, на~ *pf*.
amateur *n* люби́тель *m*, ~ница; *adj* люби́тельский. **amateurish** *adj* дилета́нтский.
amaze *vt* изумля́ть *impf*, изуми́ть *pf*. **amazement** *n* изумле́ние. **amazing** *adj* изуми́тельный.
ambassador *n* посо́л.
amber *n* янта́рь *m*.
ambience *n* среда́; атмосфе́ра.
ambiguity *n* двусмы́сленность. **ambiguous** *adj* двусмы́сленный.
ambition *n* (*quality*) честолю́бие; (*aim*) мечта́. **ambitious** *adj* честолюби́вый.
amble *vi* ходи́ть *indet*, идти́ *det* неторопли́вым ша́гом.
ambulance *n* маши́на ско́рой по́мощи.
ambush *n* заса́да; *vt* напада́ть *impf*, напа́сть *pf* из заса́ды на+*acc*.
ameliorate *vt* & *i* улучша́ть(ся) *impf*, улу́чшить(ся) *pf*. **amelioration** *n* улучше́ние.
amen *int* ами́нь!
amenable *adj* сгово́рчивый (**to** +*dat*)
amend *vt* (*correct*) исправля́ть *impf*, испра́вить *pf*; (*change*) вноси́ть *impf*, внести́ *pf* попра́вки в+*acc*. **amendment** *n* попра́вка, исправле́ние. **amends** *n pl*: **make ~ for** загла́живать *impf*, загла́дить *pf*.
amenities *n pl* удо́бства *neut pl*.
America *n* Аме́рика: **American** *adj* америка́нский; *n* америка́нец, -нка. **Americanism** *n* американи́зм.
amiable *adj* любе́зный. **amicable** *adj* дружелю́бный.
amid(st) *prep* среди́+*gen*.
amino acid *n* аминокислота́.
amiss *adv* нела́дный; **take ~** обижа́ться *impf*, оби́деться *pf* на+*acc*.
ammonia *n* аммиа́к; (*liquid* ~) нашаты́рный спирт.
ammunition *n* боеприпа́сы *m pl*.
amnesia *n* амнези́я.
amnesty *n* амни́стия.
among(st) *prep* (*amidst*) среди́+*gen*, (*between*) ме́жду+*instr*.
amoral *adj* амора́льный.
amorous *adj* влю́бчивый.
amorphous *adj* бесфо́рменный.
amortization *n* амортиза́ция.
amount *n* коли́чество; *vi*: ~ **to** составля́ть *impf*, соста́вить *pf*; (*be equivalent to*) быть равноси́льным+*dat*.
ampere *n* ампе́р.
amphetamine *n* амфетами́н.
amphibian *n* амфи́бия. **amphibious** *adj* земново́дный; (*mil*) пла́вающий.
amphitheatre *n* амфитеа́тр.
ample *adj* доста́точный. **amplification** *n* усиле́ние. **am-**

plifier *n* усили́тель *m*. **amplify** *vt* уси́ливать *impf*, уси́лить *pf*. **amply** *adv* доста́точно.
amputate *vt* ампути́ровать *impf* & *pf*. **amputation** *n* ампута́ция.
amuse *vt* забавля́ть *impf*; развлека́ть *impf*, развле́чь *pf*. **amusement** *n* заба́ва, развлече́ние; *pl* аттракцио́ны *m pl*. **amusing** *adj* заба́вный; (*funny*) смешно́й.
anachronism *n* анахрони́зм. **anachronistic** *adj* анахрони́ческий.
anaemia *n* анеми́я. **anaemic** *adj* анеми́чный.
anaesthesia *n* анестези́я. **anaesthetic** *n* обезбо́ливающее сре́дство. **anaesthetist** *n* анестезио́лог. **anaesthetize** *vt* анестези́ровать *impf* & *pf*.
anagram *n* анагра́мма.
analogous *adj* аналоги́чный. **analogue** *n* ана́лог. **analogy** *n* анало́гия.
analyse *vt* анализи́ровать *impf* & *pf*. **analysis** *n* ана́лиз. **analyst** *n* анали́тик; психоанали́тик. **analytical** *adj* аналити́ческий.
anarchic *adj* анархи́ческий. **anarchist** *n* анархи́ст, ~ка; *adj* анархи́стский. **anarchy** *n* ана́рхия.
anathema *n* ана́фема.
anatomical *adj* анатоми́ческий. **anatomy** *n* анато́мия.
ancestor *n* пре́док. **ancestry** *n* происхожде́ние.
anchor *n* я́корь *m*; *vt* ста́вить *impf*, по~ *pf* на я́корь; *vi* станови́ться *impf*, стать *pf* на я́корь. **anchorage** *n* я́корная стоя́нка.
anchovy *n* анчо́ус.
ancient *adj* дре́вний, стари́нный.
and *conj* и, (*but*) а; с+*instr*; **you ~ I** мы с ва́ми; **my wife ~ I** мы с жено́й.
anecdote *n* анекдо́т.
anew *adv* сно́ва.
angel *n* а́нгел. **angelic** *adj* а́нгельский.
anger *n* гнев; *vt* серди́ть *impf*, рас~ *pf*.
angina *n* стенокарди́я.
angle[1] *n* у́гол; (*fig*) то́чка зре́ния.
angle[2] *vi* уди́ть *impf* ры́бу. **angler** *n* рыболо́в.
angry *adj* серди́тый.
anguish *n* страда́ние, му́ка. **anguished** *adj* отча́янный.
angular *adj* углово́й; (*sharp*) углова́тый.
animal *n* живо́тное *sb*; *adj* живо́тный. **animate** *adj* живо́й. **animated** *adj* оживлённый; **~ cartoon** мультфи́льм. **animation** *n* оживле́ние.
animosity *n* вражде́бность.
ankle *n* лоды́жка.
annals *n pl* ле́топись.
annex *vt* аннекси́ровать *impf* & *pf*. **annexation** *n* анне́ксия. **annexe** *n* пристро́йка.
annihilate *vt* уничтожа́ть *impf*, уничто́жить *pf*. **annihilation** *n* уничтоже́ние.
anniversary *n* годовщи́на.
annotate *vt* комменти́ровать *impf* & *pf*. **annotated** *adj* снабжённый коммента́риями. **annotation** *n* аннота́ция.
announce *vt* объявля́ть *impf*, объяви́ть *pf*; заявля́ть *impf*, заяви́ть *pf*; (*radio*) сообща́ть *impf*, сообщи́ть *pf*. **announcement** *n* объявле́ние; сообще́-

ние. **announcer** *n* ди́ктор.
annoy *vt* досажда́ть *impf*, досади́ть *pf*; раздража́ть *impf*, раздражи́ть *pf*. **annoyance** *n* доса́да. **annoying** *adj* доса́дный.
annual *adj* ежего́дный, (*of a given year*) годово́й; *n* (*book*) ежего́дник; (*bot*) одноле́тник. **annually** *adv* ежего́дно. **annuity** *n* (ежего́дная) ре́нта.
annul *vt* аннули́ровать *impf* & *pf*. **annulment** *n* аннули́рование.
anoint *vt* пома́зывать *impf*, пома́зать *pf*.
anomalous *adj* анома́льный. **anomaly** *n* анома́лия.
anonymous *adj* анони́мный. **anonymity** *n* анони́мность.
anorak *n* ку́ртка.
anorexia *n* анаре́ксия.
another *adj*, *pron* друго́й; ~ **one** ещё (оди́н); **in ~ ten years** ещё че́рез де́сять лет.
answer *n* отве́т; *vt* отвеча́ть *impf*, отве́тить *pf* (*person*) +*dat*, (*question*) на+*acc*; ~ **the door** отворя́ть *impf*, отвори́ть *pf* дверь; ~ **the phone** подходи́ть *impf*, подойти́ *pf* к телефо́ну. **answerable** *adj* отве́тственный. **answering machine** *n* телефо́н-отве́тчик.
ant *n* мураве́й.
antagonism *n* антагони́зм. **antagonistic** *adj* антагонисти́ческий. **antagonize** *vt* настра́ивать *impf*, настро́ить *pf* про́тив себя́.
Antarctic *n* Анта́рктика.
antelope *n* антило́па.
antenna *n* у́сик; (*also radio*) анте́нна.
anthem *n* гимн.
anthology *n* антоло́гия.
anthracite *n* антраци́т.
anthropological *adj* антропологи́ческий. **anthropologist** *n* антропо́лог. **anthropology** антрополо́гия.
anti-aircraft *adj* зени́тный. **antibiotic** *n* антибио́тик. **antibody** *n* антите́ло. **anticlimax** *n* разочарова́ние. **anticlockwise** *adj* & *adv* про́тив часово́й стре́лки. **antidepressant** *n* антидепресса́нт. **antidote** *n* противоя́дие. **antifreeze** *n* антифри́з.
antipathy *n* антипа́тия. **anti-Semitic** *adj* антисеми́тский. **anti-Semitism** *n* антисемити́зм. **antiseptic** *adj* антисепти́ческий; *n* антисе́птик. **antisocial** *adj* асоциа́льный. **anti-tank** *adj* противота́нковый. **antithesis** *n* противополо́жность; (*philos*) антите́зис.
anticipate *vt* ожида́ть *impf* +*gen*; (*with pleasure*) предвкуша́ть *impf*, предвкуси́ть *pf*; (*forestall*) предупрежда́ть *impf*, предупреди́ть *pf*. **anticipation** *n* ожида́ние; предвкуше́ние; предупрежде́ние.
antics *n* вы́ходки *f pl*.
antiquarian *adj* антиква́рный. **antiquated** *adj* устаре́лый. **antique** *adj* стари́нный; *n* антиква́рная вещь; ~ **shop** антиква́рный магази́н. **antiquity** *n* дре́вность.
antler *n* оле́ний рог.
anus *n* за́дний прохо́д.
anvil *n* накова́льня.
anxiety *n* беспоко́йство. **anxious** *adj* беспоко́йный; **be ~** беспоко́иться *impf*; трево́житься *impf*.
any *adj*, *pron* (*some*) како́й-

нибудь; скóлько-нибудь; (*every*) вся́кий, любóй; (*anybody*) ктó-нибудь, (*anything*) чтó-нибудь; (*with neg*) никакóй, ни оди́н; нискóлько; никтó, ничтó; *adv* скóлько-нибудь; (*with neg*) нискóлько, ничу́ть. **anybody, anyone** *pron* ктó-нибудь; (*everybody*) вся́кий, любóй; (*with neg*) никтó. **anyhow** *adv* кáк-нибудь; кóе-как; (*with neg*) никáк; *conj* во вся́ком слу́чае; всё равнó. **anyone** *see* **anybody. anything** *pron* чтó-нибудь; всё (что угóдно); (*with neg*) ничегó. **anyway** *adv* во вся́ком слу́чае; как бы то ни́ было. **anywhere** *adv* где/кудá угóдно; (*with neg, interrog*) гдé-нибудь, кудá-нибудь.

apart *adv* (*aside*) в сторонé, в стóрону; (*separately*) врозь; (*distant*) друг от дру́га; (*into pieces*) на чáсти; ~ **from** крóме+*gen*.

apartheid *n* апартеи́д.

apartment *n* (*flat*) кварти́ра.

apathetic *adj* апати́чный. **apathy** *n* апáтия.

ape *n* обезья́на; *vt* обезья́нничать *impf*, с~ *pf* с+*gen*.

aperture *n* отвéрстие.

apex *n* верши́на.

aphorism *n* афори́зм.

apiece *adv* (*per person*) на кáждого; (*per thing*) за штýку; (*amount*) по+*dat or acc with numbers*.

aplomb *n* аплóмб.

Apocalypse *n* Апокáлипсис. **apocalyptic** *adj* апокалипти́ческий.

apologetic *adj* извиня́ющийся; **be** ~ извиня́ться *impf*. **apologize** *vi* извиня́ться *impf*, извини́ться *pf* (**to** пéред +*instr*; **for** за+*acc*). **apology** *n* извинéние.

apostle *n* апóстол.

apostrophe *n* апострóф.

appal *vi* ужасáть *impf*, ужасну́ть *pf*. **appalling** *adj* ужáсный.

apparatus аппарáт; прибóр; (*gymnastic*) гимнасти́ческие снаря́ды *m pl*.

apparel *n* одея́ние.

apparent *adj* (*seeming*) ви́димый; (*manifest*) очеви́дный. **apparently** *adv* кáжется, по-ви́димому.

apparition *n* видéние.

appeal *n* (*request*) призы́в, обращéние; (*law*) апелля́ция, обжáлование; (*attraction*) привлекáтельность; ~ **court** апелляциóнный суд; *vi* (*request*) взывáть *impf*, воззвáть *pf* (**to** к+*dat*; **for** о+*prep*); обращáться *impf*, обрати́ться *pf* (с призы́вом); (*law*) апелли́ровать *impf* & *pf*; ~ **to** (*attract*) привлекáть *impf*, привлéчь *pf*.

appear *vi* появля́ться *impf*, появи́ться *pf*; (*in public*) выступáть *impf*, вы́ступить *pf*; (*seem*) казáться *impf*, по~ *pf*. **appearance** *n* появлéние; выступлéние; (*aspect*) вид.

appease *vt* умиротворя́ть *impf*, умиротвори́ть *pf*.

append *vt* прилагáть *impf*, приложи́ть *pf*. **appendicitis** *n* аппендици́т. **appendix** *n* приложéние; (*anat*) аппенди́кс.

appertain *vi*: ~ **to** относи́ться *impf* +*dat*.

appetite *n* аппети́т. **appetizing** *adj* аппети́тный.

applaud *vt* аплоди́ровать *impf* +*dat*. **applause** *n* апло-

дисме́нты *m pl*.
apple *n* я́блоко; *adj* я́блочный; ~ **tree** я́блоня.
appliance *n* прибо́р. **applicable** *adj* примени́мый. **applicant** *n* кандида́т. **application** *n* (*use*) примене́ние; (*putting on*) наложе́ние; (*request*) заявле́ние. **applied** *adj* прикладно́й. **apply** *vt* (*use*) применя́ть *impf*, примени́ть *pf*; (*put on*) накла́дывать *impf*, наложи́ть *pf*; *vi* (*request*) обраща́ться *impf*, обрати́ться *pf* (**to** к+*dat*; **for** за +*acc*); ~ **for** (*job*) подава́ть *impf*, пода́ть *pf* заявле́ние на+*acc*; ~ **to** относи́ться *impf* к+*dat*.
appoint *vt* назнача́ть *impf*, назна́чить *pf*. **appointment** *n* назначе́ние; (*job*) до́лжность; (*meeting*) свида́ние.
apposite *adj* уме́стный.
appraise *vt* оце́нивать *impf*, оцени́ть *pf*.
appreciable *adj* заме́тный; (*considerable*) значи́тельный. **appreciate** *vt* цени́ть *impf*; (*understand*) понима́ть *impf*, поня́ть *pf*; *vi* повыша́ться *impf*, повы́ситься *pf* в цене́. **appreciation** *n* (*estimation*) оце́нка; (*gratitude*) призна́тельность; (*rise in value*) повыше́ние цены́. **appreciative** *adj* призна́тельный (**of** за+*acc*).
apprehension *n* (*fear*) опасе́ние. **apprehensive** *adj* опаса́ющийся.
apprentice *n* учени́к; *vt* отдава́ть *impf*, отда́ть *pf* в уче́ние. **apprenticeship** *n* учени́чество.
approach *vt* & *i* подходи́ть *impf*, подойти́ *pf* (к+*dat*); приближа́ться *impf*, прибли́зиться *pf* (к+*dat*); *vt* (*apply to*) обраща́ться *impf*, обрати́ться *pf* к+*dat*; *n* приближе́ние; подхо́д; подъе́зд; (*access*) по́дступ.
approbation *n* одобре́ние.
appropriate *adj* подходя́щий; *vt* присва́ивать *impf*, присво́ить *pf*. **appropriation** *n* присвое́ние.
approval *n* одобре́ние; **on** ~ на про́бу. **approve** *vt* утвержда́ть *impf*, утверди́ть *pf*; *vt* & *i* (~ **of**) одобря́ть *impf*, одо́брить *pf*.
approximate *adj* приблизи́тельный; *vi* приближа́ться *impf* (**to** к+*dat*). **approximation** *n* приближе́ние.
apricot *n* абрико́с.
April *n* апре́ль *m*; *adj* апре́льский.
apron *n* пере́дник.
apropos *adv*: ~ **of** по по́воду+*gen*.
apt *adj* (*suitable*) уда́чный; (*inclined*) скло́нный. **aptitude** *n* спосо́бность.
aqualung *n* аквала́нг. **aquarium** *n* аква́риум. **Aquarius** *n* Водоле́й. **aquatic** *adj* водяно́й; (*of sport*) во́дный. **aqueduct** *n* акведу́к.
aquiline *adj* орли́ный.
Arab *n* ара́б, ~ка; *adj* ара́бский. **Arabian** *adj* арави́йский. **Arabic** *adj* ара́бский.
arable *adj* па́хотный.
arbitrary *adj* произво́льный. **arbitrate** *vi* де́йствовать *impf* в ка́честве трете́йского судьи́. **arbitration** *n* арбитра́ж, трете́йское реше́ние. **arbitrator** *n* арби́тр, трете́йский судья́ *m*.
arc *n* дуга́. **arcade** *n* арка́да, (*shops*) пасса́ж.

arch[1] *n* а́рка, свод; (*of foot*) свод стопы́; *vt* & *i* выгиба́ть(ся) *impf*, вы́гнуть(ся) *pf*.
arch[2] *adj* игри́вый.
archaeological *adj* археологи́ческий. **archaeologist** *n* архео́лог. **archaeology** *n* археоло́гия.
archaic *adj* архаи́ческий.
archangel *n* арха́нгел.
archbishop *n* архиепи́скоп.
arched *adj* сво́дчатый.
arch-enemy *n* закля́тый враг.
archer *n* стрело́к из лу́ка. **archery** *n* стрельба́ из лу́ка.
archipelago *n* архипела́г.
architect *n* архите́ктор. **architectural** *adj* архитекту́рный. **architecture** *n* архитекту́ра.
archive(s) *n* архи́в.
archway *n* сво́дчатый прохо́д.
Arctic *adj* аркти́ческий; *n* А́рктика.
ardent *adj* горя́чий. **ardour** *n* пыл.
arduous *adj* тру́дный.
area *n* (*extent*) пло́щадь; (*region*) райо́н; (*sphere*) о́бласть.
arena *n* аре́на.
argue *vt* (*maintain*) утвержда́ть *impf*; дока́зывать *impf*; *vi* спо́рить *impf*, по~ *pf*. **argument** *n* (*dispute*) спор; (*reason*) до́вод. **argumentative** *adj* лю́бящий спо́рить.
aria *n* а́рия.
arid *adj* сухо́й.
Aries *n*Ове́н.
arise *vi* возника́ть *impf*, возни́кнуть *pf*.
aristocracy *n* аристокра́тия. **aristocrat** *n* аристокра́т, ~ка. **aristocratic** *adj* аристократи́ческий.
arithmetic *n* арифме́тика. **arithmetical** *adj* арифмети́ческий.
ark *n* (Но́ев) ковче́г.
arm[1] *n* (*of body*) рука́; (*of chair*) ру́чка; **~ in ~** по́д руку; **at ~'s length** (*fig*) на почти́тельном расстоя́нии; **with open ~s** с распростёртыми объя́тиями.
arm[2] *n pl* (*weapons*) ору́жие; *vt* вооружа́ть *impf*, вооружи́ть *pf*. **armanents** *n pl* вооруже́ние.
armchair *n* кре́сло.
Armenia *n* Арме́ния. **Armenian** *n* армяни́н, армя́нка; *adj* армя́нский.
armistice *n* переми́рие.
armour *n* (*for body*) доспе́хи *m pl*; (*for vehicles*; *fig*) броня́. **armoured** *adj* брониро́ванный; (*vehicles etc.*) бронета́нковый, броне-; **~ car** броневи́к. **armoury** *n* арсена́л.
armpit *n* подмы́шка.
army *n* а́рмия; *adj* арме́йский.
aroma *n* арома́т. **aromatherapy** *n* ароматерапи́я. **aromatic** *adj* арома́ти́чный.
around *adv* круго́м; *prep* вокру́г+*gen*; **all ~** повсю́ду.
arouse *vt* (*wake up*) буди́ть *impf*, раз~ *pf*; (*stimulate*) возбужда́ть *impf*, возбуди́ть *pf*.
arrange *vt* расставля́ть *impf*, расста́вить *pf*; (*plan*) устра́ивать *impf*, устро́ить *pf*; (*mus*) аранжи́ровать *impf* & *pf*; *vi*: **~ to** догова́риваться *impf*, договори́ться *pf* +*inf*. **arrangement** *n* расположе́ние; устро́йство; (*agreement*) соглаше́ние; (*mus*) аранжиро́вка; *pl* приготовле́ния *neut pl*.
array *vt* выставля́ть *impf*, вы́ставить *pf*; *n* (*dress*) на-

ря́д; (*display*) колле́кция.
arrears *n pl* задо́лженность.
arrest *vt* аресто́вывать *impf*, арестова́ть *pf*; *n* аре́ст.
arrival *n* прибы́тие, прие́зд; (*new* ~) вновь прибы́вший *sb*. **arrive** *vi* прибыва́ть *impf*, прибы́ть *pf*; приезжа́ть *impf*, прие́хать *pf*.
arrogance *n* высокоме́рие. **arrogant** *adj* высокоме́рный.
arrow *n* стрела́; (*pointer*) стре́лка.
arsenal *n* арсена́л.
arsenic *n* мышья́к.
arson *n* поджо́г.
art *n* иску́сство; *pl* гуманита́рные нау́ки *f pl*; *adj* худо́жественный.
arterial *adj*: ~ **road** магистра́ль. **artery** *n* арте́рия.
artful *adj* хи́трый.
arthritis *n* артри́т.
article *n* (*literary*) статья́; (*clause*) пункт; (*thing*) предме́т; (*gram*) арти́кль *m*.
articulate *vt* произноси́ть *impf*, произнести́ *pf*; (*express*) выража́ть *impf*, вы́разить *pf*; *adj* (*of speech*) членоразде́льный; **be** ~ чётко выража́ть *impf* свои́ мы́сли. **articulated lorry** *n* грузово́й автомоби́ль с прице́пом.
artifice *n* хи́трость. **artificial** *adj* иску́сственный.
artillery *n* артилле́рия.
artisan *n* реме́сленник.
artist *n* худо́жник. **artiste** *n* арти́ст, ~ка. **artistic** *adj* худо́жественный.
artless *adj* простоду́шный.
as *adv* как; *conj* (*when*) когда́; в то вре́мя как; (*because*) так как; (*manner*) как; (*though*, *however*) как ни; *rel pron* како́й; кото́рый; что; **as ... as** так (же)... как; **as for, to** относи́тельно+*gen*; что каса́ется+*gen*; **as if** как бу́дто; **as it were** ка́к бы; так сказа́ть; **as soon as** как то́лько; **as well** та́кже; то́же.
asbestos *n* асбе́ст.
ascend *vt* (*go up*) поднима́ться *impf*, подня́ться *pf* по+*dat*; (*throne*) всходи́ть *impf*, взойти́ *pf* на+*acc*; *vi* возноси́ться *impf*, вознести́сь *pf*. **ascendancy** *n* власть. **Ascension** *n* (*eccl*) Вознесе́ние. **ascent** *n* восхожде́ние (**of** на+*acc*).
ascertain *vt* устана́вливать *impf*, установи́ть *pf*.
ascetic *adj* аскети́ческий; *n* аске́т. **asceticism** *n* аскети́зм.
ascribe *vt* припи́сывать *impf*, приписа́ть *pf* (**to** +*dat*).
ash[1] *n* (*tree*) я́сень *m*.
ash[2], **ashes** *n* зола́, пе́пел; (*human remains*) прах. **ashtray** *n* пе́пельница.
ashamed *predic*: **he is** ~ ему́ сты́дно; **be, feel,** ~ **of** стыди́ться *impf*, по~ *pf* +*gen*.
ashen *adj* (*pale*) ме́ртвенно-бле́дный.
ashore *adv* на бе́рег(у́).
Asia *n* А́зия. **Asian, Asiatic** *adj* азиа́тский; *n* азиа́т, ~ка.
aside *adv* в сто́рону.
ask *vt & i* (*enquire of*) спра́шивать *impf*, спроси́ть *pf*; (*request*) проси́ть *impf*, по~ *pf* (**for** *acc*, *gen*, о+*prep*); (*invite*) приглаша́ть *impf*, пригласи́ть *pf*; (*demand*) тре́бовать *impf* +*gen* (**of** от+*gen*); ~ **after** осведомля́ться *impf*, осве́домиться *pf* о+*prep*; ~ **a question** задава́ть *impf*,

задать *pf* вопрос.
askance *adv* косо.
askew *adv* криво.
asleep *predic & adv*: **be ~** спать *impf*; **fall ~** засыпать *impf*, заснуть *pf*.
asparagus *n* спаржа.
aspect *n* вид; (*side*) сторона.
aspersion *n* клевета.
asphalt *n* асфальт.
asphyxiate *vt* удушать *impf*, удушить.
aspiration *n* стремление. **aspire** *vi* стремиться *impf* (**to** к+*dat*).
aspirin *n* аспирин; (*tablet*) таблетка аспирина.
ass *n* осёл.
assail *vt* нападать *impf*, напасть *pf* на+*acc*; (*with questions*) забрасывать *impf*, забросать *pf* вопросами. **assailant** *n* нападающий *sb*.
assassin *n* убийца *m & f*. **assassinate** *vt* убивать *impf*, убить *pf*. **assassination** *n* убийство.
assault *n* нападение; (*mil*) штурм; **~ and battery** оскорбление действием; *vt* нападать *impf*, напасть *pf* на+*acc*.
assemblage *n* сборка. **assemble** *vt & i* собирать(ся) *impf*, собрать(ся) *pf*. **assembly** *n* собрание; (*of machine*) сборка.
assent *vi* соглашаться *impf*, согласиться *pf* (**to** на+*acc*); *n* согласие.
assert *vt* утверждать *impf*; **~ o.s.** отстаивать *impf*, отстоять *pf* свои права. **assertion** *n* утверждение. **assertive** *adj* настойчивый.
assess *vt* (*amount*) определять *impf*, определить *pf*; (*value*) оценивать *impf*, оценить *pf*. **assessment** *n* определение; оценка.
asset *n* ценное качество; (*comm*; *also pl*) актив.
assiduous *adj* прилежный.
assign *vt* (*appoint*) назначать *impf*, назначить *pf*; (*allot*) отводить *impf*, отвести *pf*.
assignation *n* свидание. **assignment** *n* (*task*) задание; (*mission*) командировка.
assimilate *vt* усваивать *impf*, усвоить *pf*. **assimilation** *n* усвоение.
assist *vt* помогать *impf*, помочь *pf* +*dat*. **assistance** *n* помощь. **assistant** *n* помощник, ассистент.
associate *vt* ассоциировать *impf & pf*; *vi* общаться *impf* (**with** с+*instr*); *n* коллега *m & f*. **association** *n* общество, ассоциация.
assorted *adj* разный. **assortment** *n* ассортимент.
assuage *vt* (*calm*) успокаивать *impf*, успокоить *pf*; (*alleviate*) смягчать *impf*, смягчить *pf*.
assume *vt* (*take on*) принимать *impf*, принять *pf*; (*suppose*) предпологать *impf*, предположить *pf*; **~d name** вымышленное имя *neut*; **let us ~** допустим. **assumption** *n* (*taking on*) принятие на себе; (*supposition*) предположение.
assurance *n* заверение; (*self-~*) самоуверенность; (*insurance*) страхование. **assure** *vt* уверять *impf*, уверить *pf*.
asterisk *n* звёздочка.
asthma *n* астма. **asthmatic** *adj* астматический.
astonish *vt* удивлять *impf*, удивить *pf*. **astonishing** *adj*

удиви́тельный. **astonishment** *n* удивле́ние.
astound *vt* изумля́ть *impf*, изуми́ть *pf*. **astounding** *adj* изуми́тельный.
astray *adv*: **go ~** сбива́ться *impf*, сби́ться *pf* с пути́; **lead ~** сбива́ть *impf*, сбить *pf* с пути́.
astride *prep* верхо́м на+*prep*.
astringent *adj* вя́жущий; те́рпкий.
astrologer *n* астро́лог. **astrology** *n* астроло́гия. **astronaut** *n* астрона́вт. **astronomer** *n* астроно́м. **astronomical** *adj* астрономи́ческий. **astronomy** *n* астроно́мия.
astute *adj* проница́тельный.
asunder *adv* (*apart*) врозь; (*in pieces*) на ча́сти.
asylum *n* сумасше́дший дом; (*refuge*) убе́жище.
asymmetrical *adj* асимметри́чный. **asymmetry** *n* асимметри́я.
at *prep* (*position*) на+*prep*, в+*prep*, у+*gen*: **at a concert** на конце́рте; **at the cinema** в кино́; **at the window** у окна́; (*time*) в+*acc*: **at two o'clock** в два часа́; на+*acc*: **at Easter** на Па́сху; (*price*) по+*dat*: **at 5p a pound** по пяти́ пе́нсов за фунт; (*speed*): **at 60 mph** со ско́ростью шестьдеся́т миль в час; **~ first** снача́ла, сперва́; **~ home** до́ма; **~ last** наконе́ц; **~ least** по кра́йней ме́ре; **~ that** на том; (*moreover*) к тому́ же.
atheism *n* атеи́зм. **atheist** *n* атеи́ст, **~**ка.
athlete *n* спортсме́н, **~**ка. **athletic** *adj* атлети́ческий. **athletics** *n* (лёгкая) атле́тика.
atlas *n* а́тлас.
atmosphere *n* атмосфе́ра. **atmospheric** *adj* атмосфе́рный.
atom *n* а́том; **~ bomb** а́томная бо́мба. **atomic** *adj* а́томный.
atone *vi* искупа́ть *impf*, искупи́ть *pf* (**for** *+acc*). **atonement** *n* искупле́ние.
atrocious *adj* ужа́сный. **atrocity** *n* зве́рство.
attach *vt* (*fasten*) прикрепля́ть *impf*, прикрепи́ть *pf*; (*append*) прилага́ть *impf*, приложи́ть *pf*; (*attribute*) придава́ть *impf*, прида́ть *pf*; **attached to** (*devoted*) привя́занный к+*dat*. **attaché** *n* атташе́ *m indecl*. **attachment** *n* прикрепле́ние; привя́занность; (*tech*) принадле́жность.
attack *vt* напада́ть *impf*, напа́сть *pf* на+*acc*; *n* нападе́ние; (*of illness*) припа́док.
attain *vt* достига́ть *impf*, дости́чь & дости́гнуть *pf* +*gen*. **attainment** *n* достиже́ние.
attempt *vt* пыта́ться *impf*, по~ *pf* +*inf*; *n* попы́тка.
attend *vt* & *i* (*be present at*) прису́тствовать *impf* (на+*prep*); *vt* (*accompany*) сопровожда́ть *impf*, сопроводи́ть *pf*; (*go to regularly*) посеща́ть *impf*, посети́ть *pf*; **~ to** занима́ться *impf*, заня́ться *pf*. **attendance** *n* (*presence*) прису́тствие; (*number*) посеща́емость. **attendant** *adj* сопровожда́ющий; *n* дежу́рный *sb*; (*escort*) провожа́тый *sb*.
attention *n* внима́ние; **pay ~** обраща́ть *impf*, обрати́ть *pf* внима́ние (**to** на+*acc*); *int* (*mil*) сми́рно! **attentive** *adj*

внима́тельный; (*solicitous*) забо́тливый.

attest *vt* & *i* (*also* ~ **to**) заверя́ть *impf*, заве́рить *pf*; свиде́тельствовать *impf*, за~ *pf* (о+*prep*).

attic *n* черда́к.

attire *vt* наряжа́ть *impf*, наряди́ть *pf*; *n* наря́д.

attitude *n* (*posture*) по́за; (*opinion*) отноше́ние (**towards** к+*dat*).

attorney *n* пове́ренный *sb*; **power of** ~ дове́ренность.

attract *vt* привлека́ть *impf*, привле́чь *pf*. **attraction** *n* привлека́тельность; (*entertainment*) аттракцио́н. **attractive** *adj* привлека́тельный.

attribute *vt* припи́сывать *impf*, приписа́ть *pf*; *n* (*quality*) сво́йство. **attribution** *n* припи́сывание. **attributive** *adj* атрибути́вный.

attrition *n*: **war of** ~ война́ на истоще́ние.

aubergine *n* баклажа́н.

auburn *adj* тёмно-ры́жий.

auction *n* аукцио́н; *vt* продава́ть *impf*, прода́ть *pf* с аукцио́на. **auctioneer** *n* аукциони́ст.

audacious *adj* (*bold*) сме́лый; (*impudent*) де́рзкий. **audacity** *n* сме́лость; де́рзость.

audible *adj* слы́шный. **audience** *n* пу́блика, аудито́рия; (*listeners*) слу́шатели *m pl*, (*viewers, spectators*) зри́тели *m pl*; (*interview*) аудие́нция.

audit *n* прове́рка счето́в, реви́зия; *vt* проверя́ть *impf*, прове́рить *pf* (счета́+*gen*). **audition** *n* про́ба; *vt* устра́ивать *impf*, устро́ить *pf* про́бу +*gen*. **auditor** *n* ревизо́р. **auditorium** *n* зри́тельный зал.

augment *n* увели́чивать *impf*, увели́чить *pf*.

augur *vt* & *i* предвеща́ть *impf*.

August *n* а́вгуст; *adj* а́вгустовский. **august** *adj* вели́чественный.

aunt *n* тётя, тётка.

au pair *n* домрабо́тница иностра́нного происхожде́ния.

aura *n* орео́л.

auspices *n pl* покрови́тельство. **auspicious** *adj* благоприя́тный.

austere *adj* стро́гий. **austerity** *n* стро́гость.

Australia *n* Австра́лия. **Australian** *n* австрали́ец, -и́йка; *adj* австрали́йский.

Austria *n* А́встрия. **Austrian** *n* австри́ец, -и́йка; *adj* австри́йский.

authentic *adj* по́длинный. **authenticate** *vt* устана́вливать *impf*, установи́ть *pf* по́длинность+*gen*. **authenticity** *n* по́длинность.

author, authoress *n* а́втор.

authoritarian *adj* авторита́рный. **authoritative** *adj* авторите́тный. **authority** *n* (*power*) власть, полномо́чие; (*weight; expert*) авторите́т; (*source*) авторите́тный исто́чник. **authorization** *n* уполномо́чивание; (*permission*) разреше́ние. **authorize** *vt* (*action*) разреша́ть *impf*, разреши́ть *pf*; (*person*) уполномо́чивать *impf*, уполномо́чить *pf*.

authorship *n* а́вторство.

autobiographical автобиографи́ческий. **autobiography** *n* автобиогра́фия. **autocracy** *n* автокра́тия. **autocrat** *n* автокра́т. **autocratic** *adj* автократи́ческий. **autograph** *n* авто́граф. **automatic** *adj* автомати́ческий. **automation** *n* автоматиза́ция. **automaton** *n* автома́т. **automobile** *n* автомоби́ль *m*. **autonomous** *adj* автоно́мный. **autonomy** *n* автоно́мия. **autopilot** *n* автопило́т. **autopsy** *n* вскры́тие; ауто́псия.

autumn *n* о́сень. **autumn(al)** *adj* осе́нний.

auxiliary *adj* вспомога́тельный; *n* помо́щник, -ица.

avail *n*: **to no ~** напра́сно; *vt*: **~ o.s. of** по́льзоваться *impf*, вос~ *pf* +*instr*. **available** *adj* досту́пный, нали́чный.

avalanche *n* лави́на.

avant-garde *n* аванга́рд; *adj* аванга́рдный.

avarice *n* жа́дность. **avaricious** *adj* жа́дный.

avenge *vt* мстить *impf*, ото~ *pf* за+*acc*. **avenger** *n* мсти́тель *m*.

avenue *n* (*of trees*) алле́я; (*wide street*) проспе́кт; (*means*) путь *m*.

average *n* сре́днее число́, сре́днее *sb*; **on ~** в сре́днем; *adj* сре́дний; *vt* де́лать *impf* в сре́днем; *vt & i*: **~ (out at)** составля́ть *impf*, соста́вить *pf* в сре́днем.

averse *adj*: **not ~ to** не прочь +*inf*, не про́тив+*gen*. **aversion** *n* отвраще́ние. **avert** *vt* (*ward off*) предотвраща́ть *impf*, предотврати́ть *pf*; (*turn away*) отводи́ть *impf*, отвести́ *pf*.

aviary *n* пти́чник.

aviation *n* авиа́ция.

avid *adj* жа́дный; (*keen*) стра́стный.

avocado *n* авока́до *neut indecl*.

avoid *vt* избега́ть *impf*, избежа́ть *pf* +*gen*; (*evade*) уклоня́ться *impf*, уклони́ться *pf* от+*gen*. **avoidance** *n* избежа́ние, уклоне́ние.

avowal *n* призна́ние. **avowed** *adj* при́знанный.

await *vt* ждать *impf* +*gen*.

awake *predic*: **be ~** не спать *impf*. **awake(n)** *vt* пробужда́ть *impf*, пробуди́ть *pf*; *vi* просыпа́ться *impf*, просну́ться *pf*.

award *vt* присужда́ть *impf*, присуди́ть *pf* (*person dat*, *thing acc*); награжда́ть *impf*, награди́ть *pf* (*person acc*, *thing instr*); *n* награ́да.

aware *predic*: **be ~ of** сознава́ть *impf*; знать *impf*. **awareness** *n* созна́ние.

away *adv* прочь; **be ~** отсу́тствовать *impf*; **far ~** (*from*) далеко́ (от+*gen*); **5 miles ~** в пяти́ ми́лях отсю́да; **~ game** игра́ на чужо́м по́ле.

awe *n* благогове́йный страх. **awful** *adj* ужа́сный. **awfully** *adv* ужа́сно.

awhile *adv* не́которое вре́мя.

awkward *adj* нело́вкий. **awkwardness** *n* нело́вкость.

awning *n* наве́с, тент.

awry *adv* ко́со.

axe *n* топо́р; *vt* уре́зывать, уреза́ть *impf*, уре́зать *pf*.

axiom *n* аксио́ма. **axiomatic** *adj* аксиомати́ческий.

axis, axle *n* ось.

ay *int* да!; *n* (*in vote*) го́лос „за".

Azerbaijan *n* Азербайджа́н. **Azerbaijani** *n* азербайджа́нец (-нца), -а́нка; *adj* азербайджа́нский.

azure *n* лазу́рь; *adj* лазу́рный.

B

BA *abbr* (*univ*) бакала́вр.
babble *n* (*voices*) болтовня́; (*water*) журча́ние; *vi* болта́ть *impf*; (*water*) журча́ть *impf*.
baboon *n* павиа́н.
baby *n* ребёнок; **~-sit** присма́тривать за детьми́ в отсу́тствие роди́телей; **~-sitter** приходя́щая ня́ня.
babyish *adj* ребя́ческий.
bachelor *n* холостя́к; (*univ*) бакала́вр.
bacillus *n* баци́лла.
back *n* (*of body*) спина́; (*rear*) за́дняя часть; (*reverse*) оборо́т; (*of seat*) спи́нка; (*sport*) защи́тник; *adj* за́дний; *vt* (*support*) подде́рживать *impf*, поддержа́ть *pf*; (*car*) отодвига́ть *impf*, отодви́нуть *pf*; (*horse*) ста́вить *impf*, по~ *pf* на+*acc*; (*finance*) финанси́ровать *impf* & *pf*; *vi* отодвига́ться *impf*, отодви́нуться *pf* наза́д; **backed out of the garage** вы́ехал за́дом из гара́жа; **~ down** уступа́ть *impf*, уступи́ть *pf*; **~ out** уклоня́ться *impf*, уклони́ться *pf* (**of** от+*gen*); **~ up** (*support*) подде́рживать *impf*, поддержа́ть *pf*; (*confirm*) подкрепля́ть *impf*, подкрепи́ть *pf*. **backbiting** *n* сплётня. **backbone** *n* позвоно́чник; (*support*) гла́вная опо́ра; (*firmness*) твёрдость хара́ктера. **backcloth, backdrop** *n* за́дник; (*fig*) фон. **backer** *n* спо́нсор; (*supporter*) сторо́нник. **backfire** *vi* дава́ть *impf*, дать *pf* отсе́чку. **background** *n* фон, за́дний план; (*person's*) происхожде́ние. **backhand(er)** *n* уда́р сле́ва. **backhanded** *adj* (*fig*) сомни́тельный. **backhander** *n* (*bribe*) взя́тка. **backing** *n* подде́ржка. **backlash** *n* реа́кция. **backlog** *n* задо́лженность. **backside** *n* зад. **backstage** *adv* за кули́сами; *adj* закули́сный. **backstroke** *n* пла́вание на спине́. **back-up** *n* подде́ржка; (*copy*) резе́рвная ко́пия; *adj* вспомога́тельный. **backward** *adj* отста́лый. **backward(s)** *adv* наза́д. **backwater** *n* за́водь. **back yard** *n* за́дний двор.
bacon *n* беко́н.
bacterium *n* бакте́рия.
bad *adj* плохо́й; (*food etc.*) испо́рченный; (*language*) гру́бый; **~-mannered** невоспи́танный; **~ taste** безвку́сица; **~-tempered** раздражи́тельный.
badge *n* значо́к.
badger *n* барсу́к; *vt* трави́ть *impf*, за~ *pf*.
badly *adv* пло́хо; (*very much*) о́чень.
badminton *n* бадминто́н.
baffle *vt* озада́чивать *impf*, озада́чить *pf*.
bag *n* (*handbag*) су́мка; (*plastic ~, sack, under eyes*) мешо́к; (*paper ~*) бума́жный паке́т; *pl* (*luggage*) бага́ж.
baggage *n* бага́ж.
baggy *adj* мешкова́тый.
bagpipe *n* волы́нка.
bail[1] *n* (*security*) поручи́тельство; **release on ~** отпуска́ть *impf*, отпусти́ть *pf* на пору́ки; *vt* (**~ out**) брать *impf*, взять *pf* на пору́ки; (*help*) выруча́ть *impf*, вы́ручить *pf*.

bail[2], **bale**[2] *vt* вычéрпывать *impf*, вы́черпнуть *pf* (вóду из+*gen*); ~ **out** *vi* выбрáсываться *impf*, вы́броситься *pf* с парашю́том.
bailiff *n* судéбный исполни́тель.
bait *n* нажи́вка; примáнка (*also fig*); *vt* (*torment*) трави́ть *impf*, за~ *pf*.
bake *vt* & *i* пéчь(ся) *impf*, ис~ *pf*. **baker** *n* пéкарь *m*, бу́лочник. **bakery** *n* пекáрня; (*shop*) бу́лочная *sb*.
balalaika *n* балалáйка.
balance *n* (*scales*) весы́ *m pl*; (*equilibrium*) равновéсие; (*econ*) балáнс; (*remainder*) остáток; ~ **sheet** балáнс; *vt* (*make equal*) уравновéшивать *impf*, уравновéсить *pf*; *vt* & *i* (*econ*; *hold steady*) баланси́ровать *impf*, с~ *pf*.
balcony *n* балкóн.
bald *adj* лы́сый; ~ **patch** лы́сина. **balding** *adj* лысéющий. **baldness** *n* плеши́вость.
bale[1] *n* (*bundle*) ки́па.
bale[2] *see* **bail**[2]
balk *vi* артáчиться *impf*, за~ *pf*; **she balked at the price** ценá её испугáла.
ball[1] *n* (*in games*) мяч; (*sphere*; *billiards*) шар; (*wool*) клубóк; ~**-bearing** шарикоподши́пник; ~**-point (pen)** шáриковая ру́чка.
ball[2] *n* (*dance*) бал.
ballad *n* баллáда.
ballast *n* балла́ст.
ballerina *n* балери́на.
ballet *n* балéт. **ballet-dancer** *n* арти́ст, ~ка, балéта.
balloon *n* возду́шный шар.
ballot *n* голосовáние. **ballot-paper** *n* избирáтельный бюллетéнь *m*; *vt* держáть *impf* голосовáние между́+*instr*.
balm *n* бальзáм. **balmy** *adj* (*soft*) мя́гкий.
Baltic *n* Балти́йское мóре; ~ **States** прибалти́йские госудáрства, Прибáлтика.
balustrade *n* балюстрáда.
bamboo *n* бамбу́к.
bamboozle *vt* надувáть *impf*, наду́ть *pf*.
ban *n* запрéт; *vt* запрещáть *impf*, запрети́ть *pf*.
banal *adj* банáльный. **banality** *n* банáльность.
banana *n* банáн.
band *n* (*stripe*, *strip*) полосá; (*braid*, *tape*) тесьмá; (*category*) категóрия; (*of people*) гру́ппа; (*gang*) бáнда; (*mus*) оркéстр; (*radio*) диапазóн; *vi*: ~ **together** объединя́ться *impf*, объедини́ться *pf*.
bandage *n* бинт; *vt* бинтовáть *impf*, за~ *pf*.
bandit *n* банди́т.
bandstand *n* эстрáда для оркéстра.
bandwagon *n*: **jump on the** ~ пóльзоваться *impf*, вос~ *pf* благоприя́тными обстоя́тельствами.
bandy-legged *adj* кривонóгий.
bane *n* отрáва.
bang *n* (*blow*) удáр; (*noise*) стук; (*of gun*) вы́стрел; *vt* (*strike*) ударя́ть *impf*, удáрить *pf*; *vi* хлóпать *impf*, хлóпнуть *pf*; (*slam shut*) захлóпываться *impf*, захлóпнуться *pf*; ~ **one's head** ударя́ться *impf*, удáриться *pf* головóй; ~ **the door** хлóпать *impf*, хлóпнуть *pf* двéрью.
bangle *n* браслéт.

banish *vt* изгоня́ть *impf*, изгна́ть *pf*.

banister *n* пери́ла *neut pl*.

banjo *n* ба́нджо *neut indecl*.

bank[1] *n* (*of river*) бе́рег; (*of earth*) вал; *vt* сгреба́ть *impf*, сгрести́ *pf* в ку́чу; *vi* (*aeron*) накреня́ться *impf*, накрени́ться *pf*.

bank[2] *n* (*econ*) банк; **~ account** счёт в ба́нке; **~ holiday** устано́вленный пра́здник; *vi* (*keep money*) держа́ть *impf* де́ньги (в ба́нке); *vt* (*put in ~*) класть *impf*, положи́ть *pf* в банк; **~ on** полага́ться *impf*, положи́ться *pf* на+*acc*. **banker** *n* банки́р. **banknote** *n* банкно́та.

bankrupt *n* банкро́т; *adj* обанкро́тившийся; *vt* доводи́ть *impf*, довести́ *pf* до банкро́тства. **bankruptcy** *n* банкро́тство.

banner *n* зна́мя *neut*.

banquet *n* банке́т, пир.

banter *n* подшу́чивание.

baptism *n* креще́ние. **baptize** *vt* крести́ть *impf*, о~ *pf*.

bar *n* (*beam*) брус; (*of cage*) решётка; (*of chocolate*) пли́тка; (*of soap*) кусо́к; (*barrier*) прегра́да; (*law*) адвокату́ра; (*counter*) сто́йка; (*room*) бар; (*mus*) такт; *vt* (*obstruct*) преграждать *impf*, прегради́ть *pf*; (*prohibit*) запреща́ть *impf*, запрети́ть *pf*.

barbarian *n* ва́рвар. **barbaric**, **barbarous** *adj* ва́рварский.

barbecue *n* (*party*) шашлы́к; *vt* жа́рить *impf*, за~ *pf* на ве́ртеле.

barbed wire *n* колю́чая про́волока.

barber *n* парикма́хер; **~'s shop** парикма́херская *sb*.

bar code *n* маркиро́вка.

bard *n* бард.

bare *adj* (*naked*) го́лый; (*empty*) пусто́й; (*small*) минима́льный; *vt* обнажа́ть *impf*, обнажи́ть *pf*; **~ one's teeth** ска́лить *impf*, о~ *pf* зу́бы. **barefaced** *adj* на́глый. **barefoot** *adj* босо́й. **barely** *adv* едва́.

bargain *n* (*deal*) сде́лка; (*good buy*) вы́годная сде́лка; *vi* торгова́ться *impf*, с~ *pf*; **~ for, on** (*expect*) ожида́ть *impf* +*gen*.

barge *n* ба́ржа́; *vi*: **~ into** (*room etc.*) врыва́ться *impf*, ворва́ться *pf* в+*acc*.

baritone *n* барито́н.

bark[1] *n* (*of dog*) лай; *vi* ла́ять *impf*.

bark[2] *n* (*of tree*) кора́.

barley *n* ячме́нь *m*.

barmaid *n* буфе́тчица. **barman** *n* буфе́тчик.

barmy *adj* тро́нутый.

barn *n* амба́р.

barometer *n* баро́метр.

baron *n* баро́н. **baroness** *n* барон́есса.

baroque *n* баро́кко *neut indecl*; *adj* баро́чный.

barrack[1] *n* каза́рма.

barrack[2] *vt* осви́стывать *impf*, освиста́ть *pf*.

barrage *n* (*in river*) запру́да; (*gunfire*) огнево́й вал; (*fig*) град.

barrel *n* бо́чка; (*of gun*) ду́ло.

barren *adj* беспло́дный.

barricade *n* баррика́да; *vt* баррикади́ровать *impf*, за~ *pf*.

barrier *n* барье́р.

barring *prep* исключа́я.

barrister *n* адвока́т.

barrow *n* теле́жка.

barter *n* бáртер, товарообмéн; *vi* обмéниваться *impf*, обменя́ться *pf* товáрами.

base[1] *adj* ни́зкий; (*metal*) неблагорóдный.

base[2] *n* оснóва; (*also mil*) бáза; *vt* оснóвывать *impf*, основáть *pf*. **baseball** *n* бейсбóл. **baseless** *adj* необоснóванный. **basement** *n* подвáл.

bash *vt* трéснуть *pf*; *n*: **have a ~!** попрóбуй(те)!

bashful *adj* застéнчивый.

basic *adj* основнóй. **basically** *adv* в основнóм.

basin *n* таз; (*geog*) бассéйн.

basis *n* оснóва, бáзис.

bask *vi* грéться *impf*; (*fig*) наслаждáться *impf*, наслади́ться *pf* (**in** *+instr*).

basket *n* корзи́на. **basketball** *n* баскетбóл.

bass *n* бас; *adj* басóвый.

bassoon *n* фагóт.

bastard *n* (*sl*) негодя́й.

baste *vt* (*cul*) поливáть *impf*, поли́ть *pf* жи́ром.

bastion *n* бастиóн.

bat[1] *n* (*zool*) летýчая мышь.

bat[2] *n* (*sport*) битá; *vi* бить *impf*, по~ *pf* по мячý.

bat[3] *vt*: **he didn't ~ an eyelid** он и глáзом не моргнýл.

batch *n* пáчка; (*of loaves*) вы́печка.

bated *adj*: **with ~ breath** затаи́в дыхáние.

bath *n* (*vessel*) вáнна; *pl* плáвательный бассéйн; **have a bath** принимáть *impf*, приня́ть *pf* вáнну; *vt* купáть *impf*, вы́~, ис~ *pf*. **bathe** *vi* купáться *impf*, вы́~, ис~ *pf*; *vt* омывáть *impf*, омы́ть *pf*. **bather** *n* купáльщик, -ица. **bath-house** *n* бáня. **bathing** *n*: **~ cap** купáльная шáпочка; **~ costume** купáльный костю́м. **bathroom** *n* вáнная *sb*.

baton *n* (*staff of office*) жезл; (*sport*) эстафéта; (*mus*) (дирижёрская) пáлочка.

battalion *n* батальóн.

batten *n* рéйка.

batter *n* взби́тое тéсто; *vt* колоти́ть *impf*, по~ *pf*.

battery *n* батарéя.

battle *n* би́тва; (*fig*) борьбá; *vi* борóться *impf*. **battlefield** *n* пóле бóя. **battlement** *n* зубчáтая стенá. **battleship** *n* линéйный корáбль *m*.

bawdy *adj* непристóйный.

bawl *vi* орáть *impf*.

bay[1] *n* (*bot*) лáвр; *adj* лаврóвый.

bay[2] *n* (*geog*) зали́в.

bay[3] *n* (*recess*) пролёт; **~ window** фонáрь *m*.

bay[4] *vi* (*bark*) лáять *impf*; (*howl*) выть *impf*.

bay[5] *adj* (*colour*) гнедóй.

bayonet *n* штык.

bazaar *n* базáр.

BC *abbr* до н.э. (до нáшей э́ры).

be[1] *v* **1.** быть: *usually omitted in pres*: **he is a teacher** он учи́тель. **2.** (*exist*) существовáть *impf*. **3.** (*frequentative*) бывáть *impf*. **4.** (*~ situated*) находи́ться *impf*; (*stand*) стоя́ть *impf*; (*lie*) лежáть *impf*. **5.** (*in general definitions*) явля́ться *impf +instr*: **Moscow is the capital of Russia** столи́цей Росси́и явля́ется гóрод Москвá. **6.: there is, are** имéется, имéются; (*emph*) есть.

be[2] *v aux* **1.** *be+inf*, *expressing duty*, *plan*: дóлжен*+inf*. **2.** *be+past participle passive*, *expressing passive*: быть*+past* *participle passive in short form*: **it was done** было сделано; *impers construction of 3 pl+acc*: **I was beaten** меня били; *reflexive construction*: **music was heard** слышалась музыка. **3.** *be+pres participle active, expressing continuous tenses*: *imperfective aspect*: **I am reading** я читаю.

beach *n* пляж.

beacon *n* маяк, сигнальный огонь *m*.

bead *n* бусина; (*drop*) капля; *pl* бусы *f pl*.

beak *n* клюв.

beaker *n* (*child's*) чашка с носиком; (*chem*) мензурка.

beam *n* балка; (*ray*) луч; *vi* (*shine*) сиять *impf*.

bean *n* фасоль, боб.

bear[1] *n* медведь *m*.

bear[2] *vt* (*carry*) носить *indet*, нести *det*, по~ *pf*; (*endure*) терпеть *impf*; (*child*) родить *impf* & *pf*; ~ **out** подтверждать *impf*, подтвердить *pf*; ~ **up** держаться *impf*. **bearable** *adj* терпимый.

beard *n* борода. **bearded** *adj* бородатый.

bearer *n* носитель *m*; (*of cheque*) предъявитель *m*; (*of letter*) податель *m*.

bearing *n* (*deportment*) осанка; (*relation*) отношение; (*position*) пеленг; (*tech*) подшипник; **get one's ~s** ориентироваться *impf* & *pf*; **lose one's ~s** потерять *pf* ориентировку.

beast *n* животное *sb*; (*fig*) скотина *m* & *f*. **beastly** *adj* (*coll*) противный.

beat *n* бой; (*round*) обход; (*mus*) такт; *vt* бить *impf*, по~ *pf*; (*sport*) выигривать *impf*, выиграть *pf* у+*gen*; (*cul*) взбивать *impf*, взбить *pf*; *vi* биться *impf*, ~ **off** отбивать *impf*, отбить *pf*; ~ **up** избивать *impf*, избить *pf*. **beating** *n* битьё; (*defeat*) поражение; (*of heart*) биение.

beautiful *adj* красивый. **beautify** *vt* украшать *impf* украсить *pf*. **beauty** *n* красота; (*person*) красавица.

beaver *n* бобр.

because *conj* потому, что; так как; *adv*: ~ **of** из-за+*gen*.

beckon *vt* манить *impf*, по~ *pf* к себе.

become *vi* становиться *impf*, стать *pf* +*instr*; ~ **of** статься *pf* с+*instr*. **becoming** *adj* (*dress*) идущий к лицу+*dat*.

bed *n* кровать, постель; (*garden*) грядка; (*sea*) дно; (*river*) русло; (*geol*) пласт; **go to ~** ложиться *impf*, лечь *pf* спать; **make the ~** стелить *impf*, по~ *pf* постель. **bed and breakfast** *n* (*hotel*) маленькая гостиница. **bedclothes** *n pl*, **bedding** *n* постельное бельё. **bedridden** *adj* прикованный к постели. **bedroom** *n* спальня. **bedside table** *n* тумбочка. **bedsitter** *n* однокомнатная квартира. **bedspread** *n* покрывало. **bedtime** *n* время *neut* ложиться спать.

bedlam *n* бедлам.

bedraggled *adj* растрёпанный.

bee *n* пчела. **beehive** *n* улей.

beech *n* бук.

beef *n* говядина. **beefburger** *n* котлета.

beer *n* пиво.

beetle *n* жук.

beetroot *n* свёкла.

befall *vt & i* случа́ться *impf*, случи́ться *pf* (+*dat*).
befit *vt* подходи́ть *impf*, подойти́ *pf* +*dat*.
before *adv* ра́ньше; *prep* пе́ред+*instr*, до+*gen*; *conj* до того́ как; пре́жде чем; (*rather than*) скоре́е чем; **the day ~ yesterday** позавчера́. **beforehand** *adv* зара́нее.
befriend *vt* дружи́ться *impf*, по~ *pf* с+*instr*.
beg *vt* (*ask*) о́чень проси́ть *impf*, по~ *pf* (*person*+*acc*; *thing*+*acc* or *gen*); *vi* ни́щенствовать *impf*; (*of dog*) служи́ть *impf*; **~ for** проси́ть *impf*, по~ *pf* +*acc or gen*; **~ pardon** проси́ть *impf* проще́ние.
beggar *n* ни́щий *sb*.
begin *vt* (& *i*) начина́ть(ся) *impf*, нача́ть(ся) *pf*. **beginner** *n* начина́ющий *sb*. **beginning** *n* нача́ло.
begrudge *vt* (*give reluctantly*) жале́ть *impf*, со~ *pf* о+*prep*.
beguile *vt* (*charm*) очаро́вывать *impf*, очарова́ть *pf*; (*seduce, delude*) обольща́ть *impf*, обольсти́ть *pf*.
behalf *n*: **on ~ of** от и́мени +*gen*; (*in interest of*) в по́льзу +*gen*.
behave *vi* вести́ *impf* себя́. **behaviour** *n* поведе́ние.
behest *n* заве́т.
behind *adv*, *prep* сза́ди (+*gen*), позади́ (+*gen*), за (+*acc*, *instr*); *n* зад; **be, fall, ~** отстава́ть *impf*, отста́ть *pf*.
behold *vt* смотре́ть *impf*, по~ *pf*. **beholden** *predic*: **~ to** обя́зан+*dat*.
beige *adj* бе́жевый.
being *n* (*existence*) бытие́; (*creature*) существо́.
Belarus *n* Белару́сь.
belated *adj* запозда́лый.
belch *vi* рыга́ть *impf*, рыгну́ть *pf*; *vt* изверга́ть *impf*, изве́ргнуть *pf*.
beleaguer *vt* осажда́ть *impf*, осади́ть *pf*.
belfry *n* колоко́льня.
Belgian *n* бельги́ец, -ги́йка; *adj* бельги́йский. **Belgium** *n* Бе́льгия.
belie *vt* противоре́чить *impf* +*dat*.
belief *n* (*faith*) ве́ра; (*confidence*) убежде́ние. **believable** *adj* правдоподо́бный. **believe** *vt* ве́рить *impf*, по~ *pf* +*dat*; **~ in** ве́рить *impf* в+*acc*. **believer** *n* ве́рующий *sb*.
belittle *vt* умаля́ть *impf*, умали́ть *pf*.
bell *n* ко́локол; (*doorbell*) звоно́к; **~ tower** колоко́льня.
bellicose *adj* вои́нственный. **belligerence** *n* вои́нственность. **belligerent** *adj* вою́ющий; (*aggressive*) вои́нственный.
bellow *vt & i* реве́ть *impf*.
bellows *n pl* мехи́ *m pl*.
belly *n* живо́т.
belong *vi* принадлежа́ть *impf* (**to** (к)+*dat*). **belongings** *n pl* пожи́тки (-ков) *pl*.
Belorussian *n* белору́с, ~ка; *adj* белору́сский.
beloved *adj & sb* возлю́бленный.
below *adv* (*position*) внизу́; *prep* (*position*) под+*instr*; (*less than*) ни́же+*gen*.
belt *n* (*strap*) по́яс, (*also tech*) реме́нь; (*zone*) зо́на, полоса́.
bench *n* скаме́йка; (*for work*) стано́к.
bend *n* изги́б; *vt* (& *i*, *also* **~ down**) сгиба́ть(ся) *impf*, со-

гну́ть(ся) *pf*; ~ **over** склоня́ться *impf*, склони́ться *pf* над+*instr*.

beneath *prep* под+*instr*.

benediction *n* благослове́ние.

benefactor *n* благоде́тель *m*. **benefactress** *n* благоде́тельница

beneficial *adj* поле́зный. **beneficiary** *n* получа́тель *m*; (*law*) насле́дник. **benefit** *n* по́льза; (*allowance*) посо́бие; (*theat*) бенефи́с; *vt* приноси́ть *impf*, принести́ *pf* по́льзу +*dat*; *vi* извлека́ть *impf*, извле́чь *pf* вы́году.

benevolence *n* благожела́тельность. **benevolent** *adj* благожела́тельный.

benign *adj* до́брый, мя́гкий; (*tumour*) доброка́чественный.

bent *n* скло́нность.

bequeath *vt* завеща́ть *impf* & *pf* (**to**+*dat*). **bequest** *n* посме́ртный дар.

berate *vt* руга́ть *impf*, вы́~ *pf*.

bereave *vt* лиша́ть *impf*, лиши́ть *pf* (**of** +*gen*). **bereavement** *n* тяжёлая утра́та.

berry *n* я́года.

berserk *adj*: **go** ~ взбе́ситься *pf*.

berth *n* (*bunk*) ко́йка; (*naut*) стоя́нка; *vi* прича́ливать *impf*, прича́лить *pf*.

beseech *vt* умоля́ть *impf*, умоли́ть *pf*.

beset *vt* осажда́ть *impf*, осади́ть *pf*.

beside *prep* о́коло+*gen*, ря́дом с+*instr*; ~ **the point** некста́ти; ~ **o.s.** вне себя́. **besides** *adv* кро́ме того́; *prep* кро́ме+*gen*.

besiege *vt* осажда́ть *impf*, осади́ть *pf*.

besotted *adj* одурма́ненный.

bespoke *adj* сде́ланный на зака́з.

best *adj* лу́чший, са́мый лу́чший; *adv* лу́чше всего́, бо́льше всего́; **all the** ~! всего́ наилу́чшего! **at** ~ в лу́чшем слу́чае; **do one's** ~ де́лать *impf*, с~ *pf* всё возмо́жное; ~ **man** ша́фер.

bestial *adj* зве́рский. **bestiality** *n* зве́рство.

bestow *vt* дарова́ть *impf* & *pf*.

bestseller *n* бестсе́ллер.

bet *n* пари́ *neut indecl*; (*stake*) ста́вка; *vi* держа́ть *impf* пари́ (**on** на+*acc*); *vt* (*stake*) ста́вить *impf*, по~ *pf*; **he bet me £5** он поспо́рил со мной на 5 фу́нтов.

betray *vt* изменя́ть *impf*, измени́ть *pf*+*dat*. **betrayal** *n* изме́на.

better *adj* лу́чший; *adv* лу́чше; (*more*) бо́льше; *vt* улучша́ть *impf*, улу́чшить *pf*; **all the** ~ тем лу́чше; ~ **off** бо́лее состоя́тельный; ~ **o.s.** выдвига́ться *impf*, вы́двинуться *pf*; **get** ~ (*health*) поправля́ться *impf*, попра́виться *pf*; **get the** ~ **of** брать *impf*, взять *pf* верх над+*instr*; **had** ~: **you had** ~ **go** вам (*dat*) лу́чше бы пойти́; **think** ~ **of** переду́мывать *impf*, переду́мать *pf*. **betterment** *n* улучше́ние.

between *prep* ме́жду+*instr*.

bevel *vt* ска́шивать *impf*, скоси́ть *pf*.

beverage *n* напи́ток.

bevy *n* ста́йка.

beware *vi* остерега́ться *impf*, остере́чься *pf* (**of** +*gen*).

bewilder *vt* сбива́ть *impf*, сбить *pf* с то́лку. **bewildered** *adj* озада́ченный. **bewilder-**

ment *n* замеша́тельство.
bewitch *vt* заколдо́вывать *impf*, заколдова́ть *pf*; (*fig*) очаро́вывать *impf*, очарова́ть *pf*. **bewitching** *adj* очарова́тельный.
beyond *prep* за+*acc* & *instr*; по ту сто́рону+*gen*; (*above*) сверх+*gen*; (*outside*) вне+*gen*; **the back of** ~ край све́та.
bias *n* (*inclination*) укло́н; (*prejudice*) предубежде́ние. **biased** *adj* предубеждённый.
bib *n* нагру́дник.
Bible *n* Би́блия. **biblical** *adj* библе́йский.
bibliographical *n* библиографи́ческий. **bibliography** *n* библиогра́фия.
bicarbonate (of soda) *n* питьева́я со́да.
biceps *n* би́цепс.
bicker *vi* препира́ться *impf*.
bicycle *n* велосипе́д.
bid *n* предложе́ние цены́; (*attempt*) попы́тка; *vt* & *i* предлага́ть *impf*, предложи́ть *pf* (це́ну) (**for** за+*acc*); *vt* (*command*) прика́зывать *impf*, приказа́ть *pf* +*dat*. **bidding** *n* предложе́ние цены́; (*command*) приказа́ние.
bide *vt*: ~ **one's time** ожида́ть *impf* благоприя́тного слу́чая.
biennial *adj* двухле́тний; *n* двухле́тник.
bier *n* катафа́лк.
bifocals *n pl* бифока́льные очки́ *pl*.
big *adj* большо́й; (*also important*) кру́пный.
bigamist *n* (*man*) двоеже́нец; (*woman*) двуму́жница. **bigamy** *n* двубра́чие.
bigwig *n* ши́шка.
bike *n* велосипе́д. **biker** *n* мотоцикли́ст.
bikini *n* бики́ни *neut indecl*.
bilateral *adj* двусторо́нний.
bilberry *n* черни́ка (*no pl*; *usu collect*).
bile *n* жёлчь. **bilious** *adj* жёлчный.
bilingual *adj* двуязы́чный.
bill[1] *n* счёт; (*parl*) законопрое́кт; (~ *of exchange*) ве́ксель; (*poster*) афи́ша; *vt* (*announce*) объявля́ть *impf*, объяви́ть *pf* в афи́шах; (*charge*) присыла́ть *impf*, присла́ть *pf* счёт+*dat*.
bill[2] *n* (*beak*) клюв.
billet *vt* расквартиро́вывать *impf*, расквартирова́ть *pf*.
billiards *n* билья́рд.
billion *n* биллио́н.
billow *n* вал; *vi* вздыма́ться *impf*.
bin *n* му́сорное ведро́; (*corn*) за́кром.
bind *vt* (*tie*) свя́зывать *impf*, связа́ть *pf*; (*oblige*) обя́зывать *impf*, обяза́ть *pf*; (*book*) переплета́ть *impf*, переплести́ *pf*. **binder** *n* (*person*) переплётчик; (*agric*) вяза́льщик; (*for papers*) па́пка. **binding** *n* переплёт.
binge *n* кутёж.
binoculars *n pl* бино́кль *m*.
biochemistry *n* биохи́мия. **biographer** *n* био́граф. **biographical** *adj* биографи́ческий. **biography** *n* биогра́фия. **biological** *adj* биологи́ческий. **biologist** *n* био́лог. **biology** *n* биоло́гия.
bipartisan *adj* двухпарти́йный.
birch *n* берёза; (*rod*) ро́зга.
bird *n* пти́ца; ~ **of prey** хи́щная пти́ца.
birth *n* рожде́ние; (*descent*)

происхожде́ние; ~ **certificate** ме́трика; ~ **control** противозача́точные ме́ры *f pl.* **birthday** *n* день *m* рожде́ния; **fourth** ~ четырёхле́тие. **birthplace** *n* ме́сто рожде́ния. **birthright** *n* пра́во по рожде́нию.

biscuit *n* пече́нье.

bisect *vt* разреза́ть *impf*, разре́зать *pf* попола́м.

bisexual *adj* бисексуа́льный.

bishop *n* епи́скоп; (*chess*) слон.

bit[1] *n* (*piece*) кусо́чек; **a** ~ немно́го; **not a** ~ ничу́ть.

bit[2] *n* (*tech*) сверло́; (*bridle*) удила́ (-л) *pl.*

bitch *n* (*coll*) сте́рва. **bitchy** *adj* стерво́зный.

bite *n* уку́с; (*snack*) заку́ска; (*fishing*) клёв; *vt* куса́ть *impf*, укуси́ть *pf*; *vi* (*fish*) клева́ть *impf*, клю́нуть *pf.*

biting *adj* е́дкий.

bitter *adj* го́рький. **bitterness** *n* го́речь.

bitumen *n* биту́м.

bivouac *n* бива́к.

bizarre *adj* стра́нный.

black *adj* чёрный; ~ **eye** подби́тый глаз; ~ **market** чёрный ры́нок; *v*: ~ **out** (*vt*) затемня́ть *impf*, затемни́ть *pf*; (*vi*) теря́ть *impf*, по~ *pf* созна́ние; *n* (*colour*) чёрный цвет; (~ *person*) негр, ~итя́нка; (*mourning*) тра́ур. **blackberry** *n* ежеви́ка (*no pl*; *usu collect*). **blackbird** *n* чёрный дрозд. **blackboard** *n* доска́. **blackcurrant** *n* чёрная сморо́дина (*no pl*; *usu collect*). **blacken** *vt* (*fig*) черни́ть *impf*, о~ *pf.* **blackleg** *n* штрейкбре́хер. **blacklist** *n* вноси́ть *impf*, внести́ *pf* в чёрный спи́сок. **blackmail** *n* шанта́ж; *vt* шантажи́ровать *impf.* **blackout** *n* затемне́ние; (*faint*) поте́ря созна́ния. **blacksmith** *n* кузне́ц.

bladder *n* пузы́рь *m.*

blade *n* (*knife*) ле́звие; (*oar*) ло́пасть; (*grass*) были́нка.

blame *n* вина́, порица́ние; *vt* вини́ть *impf* (**for** в+*prep*); **be to** ~ быть винова́тым. **blameless** *adj* безупре́чный.

blanch *vt* (*vegetables*) ошпа́ривать *impf*, ошпа́рить *pf*; *vi* бледне́ть *impf*, по~ *pf.*

bland *adj* мя́гкий; (*dull*) пре́сный.

blandishments *n pl* лесть.

blank *adj* (*look*) отсу́тствующий; (*paper*) чи́стый; *n* (*space*) про́пуск; (*form*) бланк; (*cartridge*) холосто́й патро́н; ~ **cheque** незапо́лненный чек.

blanket *n* одея́ло.

blare *vi* труби́ть *impf*, про~ *pf.*

blasé *adj* пресы́щенный.

blasphemous *adj* богоху́льный. **blasphemy** *n* богоху́льство.

blast *n* (*wind*) поры́в ве́тра; (*explosion*) взрыв; *vt* взрыва́ть *impf*, взорва́ть *pf*; ~ **off** стартова́ть *impf* & *pf.* **blast-furnace** *n* до́мна.

blatant *adj* я́вный.

blaze *n* (*flame*) пла́мя *neut*; (*fire*) пожа́р; *vi* пыла́ть *impf.*

blazer *n* лёгкий пиджа́к.

bleach *n* хло́рка, отбе́ливатель *m*; *vt* отбе́ливать *impf*, отбели́ть *pf.*

bleak *adj* пусты́нный; (*dreary*) уны́лый.

bleary-eyed *adj* с затума́ненными глаза́ми.

bleat *vi* бле́ять *impf.*

bleed *vi* кровоточи́ть *impf.*

bleeper *n* персона́льный сигнализа́тор.

blemish *n* пятно́.

blend *n* смесь; *vt* сме́шивать *impf*, смеша́ть *pf*; *vi* гармони́ровать *impf.* **blender** *n* ми́ксер.

bless *vt* благословля́ть *impf*, благослови́ть *pf.* **blessed** *adj* благослове́нный. **blessing** *n* (*action*) благослове́ние; (*object*) бла́го.

blight *vt* губи́ть *impf*, по~ *pf.*

blind *adj* слепо́й; ~ **alley** тупи́к; *n* што́ра; *vt* ослепля́ть *impf*, ослепи́ть *pf.* **blindfold** *vt* завя́зывать *impf*, завяза́ть *pf* глаза́+*dat.* **blindness** *n* слепота́.

blink *vi* мига́ть *impf*, мигну́ть *pf.* **blinkers** *n pl* шо́ры (-р) *pl.*

bliss *n* блаже́нство. **blissful** *adj* блаже́нный.

blister *n* пузы́рь *m*, волды́рь *m.*

blithe *adj* весёлый; (*carefree*) беспе́чный.

blitz *n* бомбёжка.

blizzard *n* мете́ль.

bloated *adj* взду́тый.

blob *n* (*liquid*) ка́пля; (*colour*) кля́кса.

bloc *n* блок.

block *n* (*wood*) чурба́н; (*stone*) глы́ба; (*flats*) жило́й дом; *vt* прегражда́ть *impf*, прегради́ть *pf*; ~ **up** забива́ть *impf*, заби́ть *pf.*

blockade *n* блока́да; *vt* блоки́ровать *impf & pf.*

blockage *n* зато́р.

bloke *n* па́рень *m.*

blond *n* блонди́н, ~ка; *adj* белоку́рый.

blood *n* кровь; ~ **donor** до́нор; ~**-poisoning** *n* зараже́ние кро́ви; ~ **pressure** кровяно́е давле́ние; ~ **relation** бли́зкий ро́дственник, -ая ро́дственница; ~ **transfusion** перелива́ние кро́ви. **bloodhound** *n* ище́йка. **bloodshed** *n* кровопроли́тие. **bloodshot** *adj* нали́тый кро́вью. **bloodthirsty** *adj* кровожа́дный. **bloody** *adj* крова́вый.

bloom *n* расцве́т; *vi* цвести́ *pf.*

blossom *n* цвет; **in** ~ в цвету́.

blot *n* кля́кса; пятно́; *vt* (*dry*) промока́ть *impf*, промокну́ть *pf*; (*smudge*) па́чкать *impf*, за~ *pf.*

blotch *n* пятно́.

blotting-paper *n* промока́тельная бума́га.

blouse *n* ко́фточка, блу́зка.

blow[1] *n* уда́р.

blow[2] *vt & i* дуть *impf*, по~ *pf*; ~ **away** сноси́ть *impf*, снести́ *pf*; ~ **down** вали́ть *impf*, по~ *pf*; ~ **one's nose** сморка́ться *impf*, сморкну́ться *pf*; ~ **out** задува́ть *impf*, заду́ть *pf*; ~ **over** (*fig*) проходи́ть *impf*, пройти́ *pf*; ~ **up** взрыва́ть *impf*, взорва́ть *pf*; (*inflate*) надува́ть *impf*, наду́ть *pf.* **blow-lamp** *n* паяльная ла́мпа.

blubber[1] *n* во́рвань.

blubber[2] *vi* реве́ть *impf.*

bludgeon *vt* (*compel*) вынужда́ть *impf*, вы́нудить *pf.*

blue *adj* (*dark*) си́ний; (*light*) голубо́й; *n* си́ний, голубо́й, цвет. **bluebell** *n* колоко́льчик. **bluebottle** *n* си́няя му́ха. **blueprint** *n* си́нька, светоко́пия; (*fig*) прое́кт.

bluff *n* блеф; *vi* блефова́ть *impf.*

blunder *n* оплó́шность; *vi* оплоша́ть *pf.*

blunt *adj* тупо́й; (*person*) прямо́й; *vt* тупи́ть *impf*, за~, ис~ *pf*.

blur *vt* затума́нивать *impf*, затума́нить *pf*. **blurred** *adj* расплы́вчатый.

blurt *vt*: ~ **out** выба́лтывать *impf*, вы́болтать *pf*.

blush *vi* красне́ть *impf*, по~ *pf*.

bluster *vi* бушева́ть *impf*; *n* пусты́е слова́ *neut pl*.

boar *n* бо́ров; (*wild*) каба́н.

board *n* доска́; (*committee*) правле́ние, сове́т; **on** ~ на борт(у́); *vt* сади́ться *impf*, се́сть *pf* (на кора́бль, в по́езд и т.д.); ~ **up** забива́ть *impf*, заби́ть *pf*. **boarder** *n* пансионе́р. **boarding-house** *n* пансио́н. **boarding-school** *n* интерна́т.

boast *vi* хва́статься *impf*, по~ *pf*; *vt* горди́ться *impf* +*instr*. **boaster** *n* хвасту́н. **boastful** *adj* хвастли́вый.

boat *n* (*small*) ло́дка; (*large*) кора́бль *m*.

bob *vi* подпры́гивать *impf*, подпры́гнуть *pf*.

bobbin *n* кату́шка.

bobsleigh *n* бобсле́й.

bode *vt*: ~**well/ill** предвеща́ть *impf* хоро́шее/недо́брое.

bodice *n* лиф, корса́ж.

bodily *adv* целико́м; *adj* теле́сный.

body *n* те́ло, ту́ловище; (*corpse*) труп; (*group*) о́рган; (*main part*) основна́я часть. **bodyguard** *n* телохрани́тель *m*. **bodywork** *n* ку́зов.

bog *n* боло́та; **get** ~**ged down** увяза́ть *impf*, увя́знуть *pf*. **boggy** *adj* боло́тистый.

bogus *adj* подде́льный.

boil[1] *n* (*med*) фуру́нкул.

boil[2] *vi* кипе́ть *impf*, вс~ *pf*; *vt* кипяти́ть *impf*, вс~ *pf*; (*cook*) вари́ть *impf*, с~ *pf*; ~ **down to** сходи́ться *impf*, сойти́сь *pf* к тому́, что; ~ **over** выкипа́ть *impf*, вы́кипеть *pf*; *n* кипе́ние; **bring to the** ~ доводи́ть *impf*, довести́ *pf* до кипе́ния. **boiled** *adj* варёный. **boiler** *n* котёл; ~ **suit** комбинезо́н. **boiling** *adj* кипя́щий; ~ **point** то́чка кипе́ния; ~ **water** кипято́к.

boisterous *adj* шумли́вый.

bold *adj* сме́лый; (*type*) жи́рный.

bollard *n* (*in road*) столб; (*on quay*) пал.

bolster *n* ва́лик; *vt*: ~ **up** подпира́ть *impf*, подпере́ть *pf*.

bolt *n* засо́в; (*tech*) болт; *vt* запира́ть *impf*, запере́ть *pf* на засо́в; скрепля́ть *impf*, скрепи́ть *pf* болта́ми; *vi* (*flee*) удира́ть *impf*, удра́ть *pf*; (*horse*) понести́ *pf*.

bomb *n* бо́мба; *vt* бомби́ть *impf*. **bombard** *vt* бомбарди́ровать *impf*. **bombardment** *n* бомбардиро́вка. **bomber** *n* бомбардиро́вщик.

bombastic *adj* напы́щенный.

bond *n* (*econ*) облига́ция; (*link*) связь; *pl* око́вы (-в) *pl*, (*fig*) у́зы (уз) *pl*.

bone *n* кость.

bonfire *n* костёр.

bonnet *n* ка́пор; (*car*) капо́т.

bonus *n* пре́мия.

bony *adj* кости́стый.

boo *vt* осви́стывать *impf*, освиста́ть *pf*; *vi* улюлю́кать *impf*.

booby trap *n* лову́шка.

book *n* кни́га; *vt* (*order*) зака́зывать *impf*, заказа́ть *pf*;

(*reserve*) брони́ровать *impf*, за~ *pf*. **bookbinder** *n* переплётчик. **bookcase** *n* кни́жный шкаф. **booking** *n* зака́з; ~ **office** ка́сса. **bookkeeper** *n* бухга́лтер. **bookmaker** *n* букме́кер. **bookshop** *n* кни́жный магази́н.

boom[1] *n* (*barrier*) бон.

boom[2] *n* (*sound*) гул; (*econ*) бум; *vi* гуде́ть *impf*; (*fig*) процвета́ть *impf*.

boorish *adj* ха́мский.

boost *n* соде́йствие; *vt* увели́чивать *impf*, увели́чить *pf*.

boot *n* боти́нок; (*high*) сапо́г; (*football*) бу́тса; (*car*) бага́жник.

booth *n* кио́ск, бу́дка; (*polling*) каби́на.

booty *n* добы́ча.

booze *n* вы́пивка; *vi* выпива́ть *impf*.

border *n* (*frontier*) грани́ца; (*trim*) кайма́; (*gardening*) бордю́р; *vi* грани́чить *impf* (**on** с +*instr*). **borderline** *n* грани́ца.

bore[1] *n* (*calibre*) кана́л (ствола́); *vt* сверли́ть *impf*, про~ *pf*.

bore[2] *n* (*thing*) ску́ка; (*person*) ску́чный челове́к; *vt* надоеда́ть *impf*, надое́сть *pf* + *dat*. **bored** *impers* + *dat* + ску́чно: **I'm** ~ мне ску́чно; **we were** ~ нам бы́ло ску́чно. **boredom** *n* ску́ка. **boring** *adj* ску́чный.

born *adj* прирождённый; **be** ~ роди́ться *impf* & *pf*.

borough *n* райо́н.

borrow *vt* одолжа́ть *impf*, одолжи́ть *pf* (**from** у+*gen*).

Bosnia *n* Бо́сния. **Bosnian** *n* босни́ец, -и́йка; *adj* босни́йский.

bosom *n* грудь.

boss *n* нача́льник; *vt* кома́ндовать *impf*, с~ *pf* +*instr*. **bossy** *adj* команди́рский.

botanical *adj* ботани́ческий. **botanist** *n* бота́ник. **botany** *n* бота́ника.

botch *vt* зала́тывать *impf*, зала́тать *pf*.

both *adj* & *pron* о́ба *m* & *neut*, о́бе *f*; ~ ... **and** и... и.

bother *n* доса́да; *vt* беспоко́ить *impf*.

bottle *n* буты́лка; *vt* разлива́ть *impf*, разли́ть *pf* по буты́лкам; ~ **up** сде́рживать *impf*, сдержа́ть *pf*.

bottom *n* (*of river, container, etc.*) дно; (*of mountain*) подно́жие; (*buttocks*) зад; **at the** ~ **of** (*stairs, page*) внизу́ +*gen*; **get to the** ~ **of** добира́ться *impf*, добра́ться *pf* до су́ти +*gen*; *adj* ни́жний. **bottomless** *adj* бездо́нный.

bough *n* сук.

boulder *n* валу́н.

bounce *vi* подпры́гивать *impf*, подпры́гнуть *pf*; (*cheque*) верну́ться *pf*.

bound[1] *n* (*limit*) преде́л; *vt* ограни́чивать *impf*, ограни́чить *pf*.

bound[2] *n* (*spring*) прыжо́к; *vi* пры́гать *impf*, пры́гнуть *pf*.

bound[3] *adj*: **he is** ~ **to be there** он обяза́тельно там бу́дет.

bound[4] *adj*: **to be** ~ **for** направля́ться *impf* в+*acc*.

boundary *n* грани́ца.

boundless *adj* безграни́чный.

bountiful *adj* (*generous*) ще́дрый; (*ample*) оби́льный. **bounty** *n* ще́дрость; (*reward*) пре́мия.

bouquet *n* буке́т.

bourgeois *adj* буржуа́зный.

bourgeoisie *n* буржуази́я.
bout *n* (*med*) при́ступ; (*sport*) схва́тка.
bow[1] *n* (*weapon*) лук; (*knot*) бант; (*mus*) смычо́к.
bow[2] *n* (*obeisance*) покло́н; *vi* кла́няться *impf*, поклони́ться *pf*; *vt* склоня́ть *impf*, склони́ть *pf*.
bow[3] *n* (*naut*) нос.
bowel *n* кишка́; (*depths*) не́дра (-р) *pl*.
bowl[1] *n* ми́ска.
bowl[2] *n* (*ball*) шар; *vi* подава́ть *impf*, пода́ть *pf* мяч. **bowler** *n* подаю́щий *sb* мяч; (*hat*) котело́к. **bowling-alley** *n* кегельба́н. **bowls** *n* игра́ в шары́.
box[1] *n* коро́бка, я́щик; (*theat*) ло́жа; ~ **office** ка́сса.
box[2] *vi* бокси́ровать *impf*. **boxer** *n* боксёр. **boxing** *n* бокс. **Boxing Day** *n* второ́й день Рождества́.
boy *n* ма́льчик. **boyfriend** *n* друг, молодо́й челове́к. **boyhood** *n* о́трочество. **boyish** *adj* мальчи́шеский.
boycott *n* бойко́т; *vt* бойкоти́ровать *impf* & *pf*.
bra *n* ли́фчик.
brace *n* (*clamp*) скре́па; *pl* подтя́жки *f pl*; (*dental*) ши́на; *vt* скрепля́ть *impf*, скрепи́ть *pf*; ~ **o.s.** собира́ться *impf*, собра́ться *pf* с си́лами.
bracelet *n* брасле́т.
bracing *adj* бодря́щий.
bracket *n* (*support*) кронште́йн; *pl* ско́бки *f pl*; (*category*) катего́рия.
brag *vi* хва́статься *impf*, по~ *pf*.
braid *n* тесьма́.
braille *n* шрифт Бра́йля.
brain *n* мозг. **brainstorm** *n* припа́док безу́мия. **brainwash** *vt* промыва́ть *impf*, промы́ть *pf* мозги́+*dat*. **brainwave** *n* блестя́щая иде́я.
braise *vt* туши́ть *impf*, с~ *pf*.
brake *n* то́рмоз; *vt* тормози́ть *impf*, за~ *pf*.
bramble *n* ежеви́ка.
bran *n* о́труби (-бе́й) *pl*.
branch *n* ве́тка; (*fig*) о́трасль; (*comm*) филиа́л; *vi* разветвля́ться *impf*, разветви́ться *pf*; ~ **out** (*fig*) расширя́ть *impf*, расши́рить *pf* де́ятельность.
brand *n* (*mark*) клеймо́; (*make*) ма́рка; (*sort*) сорт; *vt* клейми́ть *impf*, за~ *pf*.
brandish *vt* разма́хивать *impf* +*instr*.
brandy *n* конья́к.
brash *adj* наха́льный.
brass *n* лату́нь, жёлтая медь; (*mus*) ме́дные инструме́нты *m pl*; *adj* лату́нный, ме́дный; ~ **band** ме́дный духово́й орке́стр; **top** ~ вы́сшее нача́льство.
brassière *n* бюстга́лтер.
brat *n* чертёнок.
bravado *n* брава́да.
brave *adj* хра́брый; *vt* покоря́ть *impf*, покори́ть *pf*. **bravery** *n* хра́брость.
bravo *int* бра́во.
brawl *n* сканда́л; *vi* дра́ться *impf*, по~ *pf*.
brawny *adj* му́скулистый.
bray *n* крик осла́; *vi* крича́ть *impf*.
brazen *adj* бессты́дный.
brazier *n* жаро́вня.
breach *n* наруше́ние; (*break*) проло́м; (*mil*) брешь; *vt* прорыва́ть *impf*, прорва́ть *pf*; (*rule*) наруша́ть *impf*, нару́шить *pf*.

bread *n* хлеб; (*white*) бу́лка. **breadcrumb** *n* кро́шка. **breadwinner** *n* корми́лец.

breadth *n* ширина́; (*fig*) широта́.

break *n* проло́м, разры́в; (*pause*) переры́в, па́уза; *vt* (& *i*) лома́ть(ся) *impf*, с~ *pf*; разбива́ть(ся) *impf*, разби́ть(ся) *pf*; *vt* (*violate*) наруша́ть *impf*, нару́шить *pf*; ~ **away** вырыва́ться *impf*, вы́рваться *pf*; ~ **down** (*vi*) (*tech*) лома́ться *impf*, с~ *pf*; (*talks*) срыва́ться *impf*, сорва́ться *pf*; (*vt*) (*door*) выла́мывать *impf*, вы́ломать *pf*; ~ **in(to)** вла́мываться *impf*, вломи́ться *pf* в+*acc*; ~ **off** (*vi* & *i*) отла́мывать(ся) *impf*, отломи́ть(ся) *pf*; (*vi*) (*speaking*) замолча́ть *pf*; (*vt*) (*relations*) порыва́ть *impf*, порва́ть *pf*; ~ **out** вырыва́ться *impf*, вы́рваться *pf*; (*fire*, *war*) вспы́хнуть *pf*; ~ **through** пробива́ться *impf*, проби́ться *pf*; ~ **up** (*vi*) (*marriage*) распада́ться *impf*, распа́сться *pf*; (*meeting*) прерыва́ться *impf*, прерва́ться *pf*; (*vt*) (*disperse*) разгоня́ть *impf*, разогна́ть *pf*; (*vt* & *i*) разбива́ть(ся) *impf*, разби́ть(ся) *pf*; ~ **with** порыва́ть *impf*, порва́ть *pf* с+*instr*. **breakage** *n* поло́мка. **breakdown** *n* поло́мка; (*med*) не́рвный срыв. **breaker** *n* буру́н. **breakfast** *n* за́втрак; *vi* за́втракать *impf*, по~ *pf*. **breakneck** *adj*: **at ~ speed** сломя́ го́лову. **breakthrough** *n* проры́в. **breakwater** *n* волноре́з.

breast *n* грудь; **~-feeding** *n* кормле́ние гру́дью; ~ **stroke** *n* брасс.

breath *n* дыха́ние; **be out of ~** запыха́ться *impf* & *pf*. **breathe** *vi* дыша́ть *impf*; ~ **in** вдыха́ть *impf*, вдохну́ть *pf*; ~ **out** выдыха́ть *impf*, вы́дохнуть *pf*. **breather** *n* переды́шка. **breathless** *adj* запыха́вшийся.

breeches *n pl* бри́джи (-жей) *pl*.

breed *n* поро́да; *vi* размножа́ться *impf*, размно́житься *pf*; *vt* разводи́ть *impf*, развести́ *pf*. **breeder** *n* -во́д: **cattle ~** скотово́д. **breeding** *n* разведе́ние, -во́дство; (*upbringing*) воспи́танность.

breeze *n* ветеро́к; (*naut*) бриз. **breezy** *adj* све́жий.

brevity *n* кра́ткость.

brew *vt* (*beer*) вари́ть *impf*, с~ *pf*; (*tea*) зава́ривать *impf*, завари́ть *pf*; (*beer*) ва́рка; (*tea*) зава́рка. **brewer** *n* пивова́р. **brewery** *n* пивова́ренный заво́д.

bribe *n* взя́тка; *vt* подкупа́ть *impf*, подкупи́ть *pf*. **bribery** *n* по́дкуп.

brick *n* кирпи́ч; *adj* кирпи́чный. **bricklayer** *n* ка́менщик.

bridal *adj* сва́дебный. **bride** *n* неве́ста. **bridegroom** *n* жени́х. **bridesmaid** *n* подру́жка неве́сты.

bridge[1] *n* мост; (*of nose*) перено́сица; *vt* (*gap*) заполня́ть *impf*, запо́лнить *pf*; (*overcome*) преодолева́ть *impf*, преодоле́ть *pf*.

bridge[2] *n* (*game*) бридж.

bridle *n* узда́; *vi* возмуща́ться *impf*, возмути́ться *pf*.

brief *adj* недо́лгий; (*concise*) кра́ткий; *n* инстру́кция; *vt* инструкти́ровать *impf* & *pf*.

briefcase *n* портфе́ль *m*. **briefing** *n* инструкта́ж. **briefly** *adv* кра́тко. **briefs** *n pl* трусы́ (-со́в) *pl*.

brigade *n* брига́да. **brigadier** *n* генера́л-майо́р.

bright *adj* я́ркий. **brighten** (*also* ~ **up**) *vi* проясня́ться *impf*, проясни́ться *pf*; *vt* оживля́ть *impf*, оживи́ть *pf*. **brightness** *n* я́ркость.

brilliant *adj* блестя́щий.

brim *n* край; (*hat*) поля́ (-ле́й) *pl*.

brine *n* рассо́л.

bring *vt* (*carry*) приноси́ть *impf*, принести́ *pf*; (*lead*) приводи́ть *impf*, привести́ *pf*; (*transport*) привози́ть *impf*, привезти́ *pf*; ~ **about** приноси́ть *impf*, принести́ *pf*; ~ **back** возвраща́ть *impf*, возврати́ть *pf*; ~ **down** сва́ливать *impf*, свали́ть *pf*; ~ **round** (*unconscious person*) приводи́ть *impf*, привести́ *pf* в себя́; (*deliver*) привози́ть *impf*, привезти́ *pf*; ~ **up** (*educate*) воспи́тывать *impf*, воспита́ть *pf*; (*question*) поднима́ть *impf*, подня́ть *pf*.

brink *n* край.

brisk *adj* (*lively*) оживлённый; (*air etc.*) све́жий; (*quick*) бы́стрый.

bristle *n* щети́на; *vi* щети́ниться *impf*, о~ *pf*.

Britain *n* Великобрита́ния, А́нглия. **British** *adj* брита́нский, англи́йский; ~ **Isles** Брита́нские острова́ *m pl*. **Briton** *n* брита́нец, -нка; англича́нин, -а́нка.

brittle *adj* хру́пкий.

broach *vt* затра́гивать *impf*, затро́нуть *pf*.

broad *adj* широ́кий; **in ~ daylight** средь бе́ла дня; **in ~ outline** в о́бщих черта́х. **broad-minded** *adj* с широ́кими взгля́дами. **broadly** *adv*: ~ **speaking** вообще́ говоря́.

broadcast *n* переда́ча; *vt* передава́ть *impf*, переда́ть *pf* по ра́дио, по телеви́дению; (*seed*) се́ять *impf*, по~ *pf* вразбро́с. **broadcaster** *n* ди́ктор. **broadcasting** *n* радио-, теле-, веща́ние.

brocade *n* парча́.

broccoli *n* бро́кколи *neut indecl*.

brochure *n* брошю́ра.

broke *predic* без гроша́. **broken** *adj* сло́манный; **~-hearted** с разби́тым се́рдцем.

broker *n* бро́кер, ма́клер.

bronchitis *n* бронхи́т.

bronze *n* бро́нза; *adj* бро́нзовый.

brooch *n* брошь, бро́шка.

brood *n* вы́водок; *vi* мра́чно размышля́ть *impf*.

brook[1] *n* руче́й.

brook[2] *vt* терпе́ть *impf*.

broom *n* метла́. **broomstick** *n* (*witches'*) помело́.

broth *n* бульо́н.

brothel *n* публи́чный дом.

brother *n* брат; **~-in-law** *n* (*sister's husband*) зять; (*husband's brother*) де́верь; (*wife's brother*) шу́рин; (*wife's sister's husband*) своя́к. **brotherhood** *n* бра́тство. **brotherly** *adj* бра́тский.

brow *n* (*eyebrow*) бровь; (*forehead*) лоб; (*of hill*) гре́бень *m*. **browbeaten** *adj* запу́ганный.

brown *adj* кори́чневый; (*eyes*) ка́рий; *n* кори́чневый цвет; *vt* (*cul*) подрумя́нивать *impf*, подрумя́нить *pf*.

browse *vi* (*look around*) осма́триваться *impf*, осмотре́ться *pf*; (*in book*) просма́тривать *impf* просмотре́ть *pf* кни́гу. **browser** *n* (*comput*) бро́узер.

bruise *n* синя́к; *vt* ушиба́ть *impf*, ушиби́ть *pf*.

brunette *n* брюне́тка.

brunt *n* основна́я тя́жесть.

brush *n* щётка; (*paint*) кисть; *vt* (*clean*) чи́стить *impf*, вы́~, по~ *pf* (щёткой); (*touch*) легко́ каса́ться *impf*, косну́ться *pf* +*gen*; (*hair*) расчёсывать *impf*, расчеса́ть *pf* щёткой; ~ **aside, off** отма́хиваться *impf*, отмахну́ться *pf* от+*gen*; ~ **up** смета́ть *impf*, смести́ *pf*; (*renew*) подчища́ть *impf*, подчи́стить *pf*.

brushwood *n* хво́рост.

Brussels sprouts *n pl* брюссе́льская капу́ста.

brutal *adj* жесто́кий. **brutality** *n* жесто́кость. **brutalize** *vt* ожесточа́ть *impf*, ожесточи́ть *pf*. **brute** *n* живо́тное *sb*; (*person*) скоти́на. **brutish** *adj* ха́мский.

B.Sc. *abbr* бакала́вр нау́к.

bubble *n* пузы́рь *m*; *vi* пузы́риться *impf*; кипе́ть *impf*, вс~ *pf*.

buck *n* саме́ц оле́ня, кро́лика *etc.*; *vi* брыка́ться *impf*.

bucket *n* ведро́.

buckle *n* пря́жка; *vt* застёгивать *impf*, застегну́ть *pf* (пря́жкой); *vi* (*warp*) коро́биться *impf*, по~, с~ *pf*.

bud *n* по́чка.

Buddhism *n* будди́зм. **Buddhist** *n* будди́ст; *adj* будди́йский.

budge *vt & i* шевели́ть(ся) *impf*, по~ *pf*.

budget *n* бюдже́т; *vi*: ~ **for** предусма́тривать *impf*, предусмотре́ть *pf* в бюдже́те.

buff *adj* све́тло-кори́чневый.

buffalo *n* бу́йвол.

buffet[1] *n* буфе́т.

buffet[2] *vt* броса́ть *impf* (*impers*).

buffoon *n* шут.

bug *n* (*insect*) бука́шка; (*germ*) инфе́кция; (*comput*) оши́бка в програ́мме; (*microphone*) потайно́й микрофо́н; *vt* (*install* ~) устана́вливать *impf*, установи́ть *pf* аппарату́ру для подслу́шивания в+*prep*; (*listen*) подслу́шивать *impf*.

bugle *n* горн.

build *n* (*of person*) телосложе́ние; *vt* стро́ить *impf*, по~ *pf*; ~ **on** пристра́ивать *impf*, пристро́ить *pf* (**to** к+*dat*); ~ **up** (*vt*) создава́ть *impf*, созда́ть *pf*; (*vi*) накопля́ться *impf*; накопи́ться *pf*. **builder** *n* строи́тель *m*. **building** *n* (*edifice*) зда́ние; (*action*) строи́тельство; ~ **site** стро́йка; ~ **society** жили́щно-строи́тельный кооперати́в.

built-up area *n* застро́енный райо́н.

bulb *n* лу́ковица; (*electric*) ла́мпочка. **bulbous** *adj* лу́ковичный.

Bulgaria *n* Болга́рия. **Bulgarian** *n* болга́рин, -га́рка; *adj* болга́рский.

bulge *n* вы́пуклость; *vi* выпя́чиваться *impf*; выпира́ть *impf*. **bulging** *adj* разбу́хший, оттопы́ривающийся.

bulk *n* (*size*) объём; (*greater part*) бо́льшая часть; **in** ~ гурто́м. **bulky** *adj* громо́здкий.

bull *n* бык; (*male*) саме́ц. **bulldog** *n* бульдо́г. **bulldoze**

vt расчища́ть *impf*, расчи́стить *pf* бульдо́зером. **bulldozer** *n* бульдо́зер. **bullfinch** *n* снеги́рь *m*. **bullock** *n* вол. **bull's-eye** *n* я́блоко.
bullet *n* пу́ля. **bullet-proof** *adj* пулесто́йкий.
bulletin *n* бюллете́нь *m*.
bullion *n*: **gold** ~ зо́лото в сли́тках.
bully *n* зади́ра *m* & *f*; *vt* запу́гивать *impf*, запуга́ть *pf*.
bum *n* зад.
bumble-bee *n* шмель *m*.
bump *n* (*blow*) уда́р, толчо́к; (*swelling*) ши́шка; (*in road*) уха́б; *vi* ударя́ться *impf*, уда́риться *pf*; ~ **into**ната́лкиваться *impf*, натолкну́ться *pf* на+*acc*. **bumper** *n* ба́мпер.
bumpkin *n* дереве́нщина *m* & *f*.
bumptious *adj* самоуве́ренный.
bumpy *adj* уха́бистый.
bun *n* сдо́бная бу́лка; (*hair*) пучо́к.
bunch *n* (*of flowers*) буке́т; (*grapes*) гроздь; (*keys*) свя́зка.
bundle *n* у́зел; *vt* свя́зывать *impf*, связа́ть *pf* в у́зел; ~ **off** спрова́живать *impf*, спрова́дить *pf*.
bungalow *n* бу́нгало *neut indecl*.
bungle *vt* по́ртить *impf*, ис~ *pf*.
bunk *n* ко́йка.
bunker *n* бу́нкер.
buoy *n* буй. **buoyancy** *n* плаву́честь; (*fig*) бо́дрость. **buoyant** *adj* плаву́чий; (*fig*) бо́дрый.
burden *n* бре́мя *neut*; *vt* обременя́ть *impf*, обремени́ть *pf*.
bureau *n* бюро́ *neut indecl*. **bureaucracy** *n* бюрокра́тия. **bureaucrat** *n* бюрокра́т. **bureaucratic** *adj* бюрократи́ческий.
burger *n* котле́та.
burglar *n* взло́мщик. **burglary** *n* кра́жа со взло́мом. **burgle** *vt* гра́бить *impf*, о~ *pf*.
burial *n* погребе́ние.
burly *adj* здорове́нный.
burn *vt* жечь *impf*, с~ *pf*; *vt* & *i* (*injure*) обжига́ть(ся) *impf*, обже́чь(ся) *pf*; *vi* горе́ть *impf*, с~ *pf*; (*by sun*) загора́ть *impf*, загоре́ть *pf*; *n* ожо́г. **burner** *n* горе́лка.
burnish *vt* полирова́ть *impf*, от~ *pf*.
burp *vi* рыга́ть *impf*, рыгну́ть *pf*.
burrow *n* нора́; *vi* рыть *impf*, вы́~ *pf* нору́; (*fig*) ры́ться *impf*.
bursar *n* казначе́й. **bursary** *n* стипе́ндия.
burst *n* разры́в, вспы́шка; *vi* разрыва́ться *impf*, разорва́ться *pf*; (*bubble*) ло́паться *impf*, ло́пнуть *pf*; *vt* разрыва́ть *impf*, разорва́ть *pf*; ~ **into tears** распла́каться *pf*.
bury *vt* (*dead*) хорони́ть *impf*, по~ *pf*; (*hide*) зарыва́ть *impf*, зары́ть *pf*.
bus *n* авто́бус; ~ **stop** авто́бусная остано́вка.
bush *n* куст. **bushy** *adj* густо́й.
busily *adv* энерги́чно.
business *n* (*affair, dealings*) де́ло; (*firm*) предприя́тие; **mind your own** ~ не ва́ше де́ло; **on** ~ по де́лу. **businesslike** *adj* делово́й. **businessman** *n* бизнесме́н.

busker *n* ýличный музыкáнт. **bust** *n* бюст; (*bosom*) грудь. **bustle** *n* суетá; *vi* суетиться *impf*. **busy** *adj* занятóй; *vt*: ~ **o.s.** занимáться *impf*, занятьcя *pf* (**with** +*instr*). **busybody** *n* назóйливый человéк. **but** *conj* но, а; ~ **then** затó; *prep* крóме+*gen*. **butcher** *n* мясник; *vt* рéзать *impf*, за~ *pf*; ~**'s shop** мяснáя *sb*. **butler** *n* дворéцкий *sb*. **butt**[1] *n* (*cask*) бóчка. **butt**[2] *n* (*of gun*) приклáд; (*cigarette*) окýрок. **butt**[3] *n* (*target*) мишéнь. **butt**[4] *vt* бодáть *impf*, за[illegible] *pf*, ~ **in** вмéшиваться *impf*, вмешáться *pf*. **butter** *n* (сли́вочное) мáсло; *vt* намáзывать *impf*, намáзать *pf* мáслом; ~ **up** льстить *impf*, по~ *pf*. **buttercup** *n* лю́тик. **butterfly** *n* бáбочка. **buttock** *n* я́годица. **button** *n* пýговица; (*knob*) кнóпка; *vt* застёгивать *impf*, застегнýть *pf*. **buttonhole** *n* пéтля. **buttress** *n* контрфóрс; *vt* подпирáть *impf*, подперéть *pf*. **buxom** *adj* полногрýдая. **buy** *n* покýпка; *vt* покупáть *impf*, купи́ть *pf*. **buyer** *n* покупáтель *m*. **buzz** *n* жужжáние; *vi* жужжáть *impf*. **buzzard** *n* каню́к. **buzzer** *n* зýммер. **by** *adv* ми́мо; *prep* (*near*) óколо+*gen*, у+*gen*; (*beside*) ря́дом с+*instr*; (*past*) ми́мо+*gen*; (*time*) к+*dat*; (*means*) *instr without prep*; ~ **and large** в цéлом. **bye** *int* покá! **by-election** *n* дополни́тельные вы́боры *m pl*. **Byelorussian** *see* **Belorussian** **bygone** *adj* минýвший; **let** ~**s be** ~**s** что прошлó, то прошлó. **by-law** *n* постановлéние. **bypass** *n* обхóд; *vt* обходи́ть *impf*, обойти́ *pf*. **by-product** *n* побóчный продýкт. **byroad** *n* небольшáя дорóга. **bystander** *n* свидéтель *m*. **byway** *n* просёлочная дорóга. **byword** *n* олицетворéние (**for** +*gen*). **Byzantine** *adj* византи́йский.

C

cab *n* (*taxi*) такси́ *neut indecl*; (*of lorry*) каби́на. **cabaret** *n* кабарé *neut indecl*. **cabbage** *n* капýста. **cabin** *n* (*hut*) хи́жина; (*aeron*) каби́на; (*naut*) каю́та. **cabinet** *n* шкаф; (*Cabinet*) кабинéт; ~**-maker** краснодерéвец; ~**-minister** мини́стр-член кабинéта. **cable** *n* (*rope*) канáт; (*electric*) кáбель *m*; (*cablegram*) телегрáмма; *vt* & *i* телеграфи́ровать *impf* & *pf*. **cache** *n* потайнóй склад. **cackle** *vi* гоготáть *impf*. **cactus** *n* кáктус. **caddy** *n* (*box*) чáйница. **cadet** *n* новобрáнец. **cadge** *vt* стреля́ть *impf*, стрельнýть *pf*. **cadres** *n pl* кáдры *m pl*. **Caesarean (section)** *n* кéсарево сечéние. **cafe** *n* кафé *neut indecl*. **cafeteria** *n* кафетéрий. **caffeine** *n* кофеи́н. **cage** *n* клéтка.

cajole *vt* зада́бривать *impf*, задо́брить *pf*.
cake *n* (*large*) торт, (*small*) пиро́жное *sb*; (*fruit-*~) кекс; *vt*: ~**d** обле́пленный (**in** +*instr*).
calamitous *adj* бе́дственный. **calamity** *n* бе́дствие.
calcium *n* ка́льций.
calculate *vt* вычисля́ть *impf*, вы́числить *pf*; *vi* рассчи́тывать *impf*, рассчита́ть *pf* (**on** на+*acc*). **calculation** *n* вычисле́ние, расчёт. **calculator** *n* калькуля́тор.
calendar *n* календа́рь *m*.
calf[1] *n* (*cow*) телёнок.
calf[2] *n* (*leg*) икра́.
calibrate *vt* калиброва́ть *impf*. **calibre** *n* кали́бр.
call *v* звать *impf*, по~ *pf*; (*name*) называ́ть *impf*, назва́ть *pf*; (*cry*) крича́ть *impf*, кри́кнуть *pf*; (*wake*) буди́ть *impf*, раз~ *pf*; (*visit*) заходи́ть *impf*, зайти́ *pf* (**on** к+*dat*; **at** в+*acc*); (*stop at*) остана́вливаться *impf*, останови́ться *pf* (**at** в, на, +*prep*); (*summon*) вызыва́ть *impf*, вы́звать *pf*; (*ring up*) звони́ть *impf*, по~ *pf* +*dat*; ~ **for** (*require*) тре́бовать *impf*, по~ *pf* +*gen*; (*fetch*) заходи́ть *impf*, зайти́ *pf* за+*instr*; ~ **off** отменя́ть *impf*, отмени́ть *pf*; ~ **out** вскри́кивать *impf*, вскри́кнуть *pf*; ~ **up** призыва́ть *impf*, призва́ть *pf*; *n* (*cry*) крик; (*summons*) зов, призы́в; (*telephone*) (телефо́нный) вы́зов, разгово́р; (*visit*) визи́т; (*signal*) сигна́л; ~**-box** телефо́н-автома́т; ~**-up** призы́в. **caller** *n* посети́тель *m*, ~ница; (*tel*) позвони́вший *sb*. **calling** *n* (*vocation*) призва́ние.
callous *adj* (*person*) чёрствый.
callus *n* мозо́ль.
calm *adj* споко́йный; *n* споко́йствие; *vt* & *i* (~ *down*) успока́ивать(ся) *impf*, успоко́ить(ся) *pf*.
calorie *n* кало́рия.
camber *n* скат.
camcorder *n* камко́рдер.
camel *n* верблю́д.
camera *n* фотоаппара́т. **cameraman** *n* кинооперáтор.
camouflage *n* камуфля́ж; *vt* маскирова́ть *impf*, за~ *pf*.
camp *n* ла́герь *m*; *vi* (*set up* ~) располага́ться *impf*, расположи́ться *pf* ла́герем; (*go camping*) жить *impf* в пала́тках; ~**-bed** раскладу́шка; ~**-fire** костёр.
campaign *n* кампа́ния; *vi* проводи́ть *impf*, провести́ *pf* кампа́нию.
campsite *n* ла́герь *m*, ке́мпинг.
campus *n* университе́тский городо́к.
can[1] *n* ба́нка; *vt* консерви́ровать *impf*, за~ *pf*.
can[2] *v aux* (*be able*) мочь *impf*, с~ *pf* +*inf*; (*know how*) уме́ть *impf*, с~ *pf* +*inf*.
Canada *n* Кана́да. **Canadian** *n* кана́дец, -дка; *adj* кана́дский.
canal *n* кана́л.
canary *n* канаре́йка.
cancel *vt* (*make void*) аннули́ровать *impf* & *pf*; (*call off*) отменя́ть *impf*, отмени́ть *pf*; (*stamp*) гаси́ть *impf*, по~ *pf*. **cancellation** *n* аннули́рование; отме́на.
cancer *n* рак; (**C**~) Рак. **cancerous** *adj* ра́ковый.
candelabrum *n* канделя́бр.

candid *adj* открове́нный.
candidate *n* кандида́т.
candied *adj* заса́харенный.
candle *n* свеча́. **candlestick** *n* подсве́чник.
candour *n* открове́нность.
candy *n* сла́дости *f pl*.
cane *n* (*plant*) тростни́к; (*stick*) трость, па́лка; *vt* бить *impf*, по~ *pf* па́лкой.
canine *adj* соба́чий; *n* (*tooth*) клык.
canister *n* ба́нка, коро́бка.
canker *n* рак.
cannabis *n* гаши́ш.
cannibal *n* людое́д. **cannibalism** *n* людое́дство.
cannon *n* пу́шка; **~-ball** пу́шечное ядро́.
canoe *n* кано́э *neut indecl*; *vi* пла́вать *indet*, плыть *det* на кано́э.
canon *n* кано́н; (*person*) кано́ник. **canonize** *vt* канонизова́ть *impf* & *pf*.
canopy *n* балдахи́н.
cant *n* (*hypocrisy*) ха́нжество; (*jargon*) жарго́н.
cantankerous *adj* сварли́вый.
cantata *n* канта́та.
canteen *n* столо́вая *sb*.
canter *n* лёгкий гало́п; *vi* (*rider*) е́здить *indet*, е́хать *det* лёгким гало́пом; (*horse*) ходи́ть *indet*, идти́ *det* лёгким гало́пом.
canvas *n* (*art*) холст; (*naut*) паруси́на; (*tent material*) брезе́нт.
canvass *vi* агити́ровать *impf*, с~ *pf* (**for** за+*acc*); *n* собира́ние голосо́в; агита́ция. **canvasser** *n* собира́тель *m* голосо́в.
canyon *n* каньо́н.
cap *n* (*of uniform*) фура́жка; (*cloth*) ке́пка; (*woman's*) че́пец; (*lid*) кры́шка; *vt* превосходи́ть *impf*, превзойти́ *pf*.
capability *n* спосо́бность. **capable** *adj* спосо́бный (**of** на+*acc*).
capacious *adj* вмести́тельный. **capacity** *n* ёмкость; (*ability*) спосо́бность; **in the ~ of** в ка́честве +*gen*.
cape[1] *n* (*geog*) мыс.
cape[2] *n* (*cloak*) наки́дка.
caper *vi* скака́ть *impf*.
capers[1] *n pl* (*cul*) ка́персы *m pl*.
capillary *adj* капилля́рный.
capital *adj* (*letter*) прописно́й; **~ punishment** сме́ртная казнь; *n* (*town*) столи́ца; (*letter*) прописна́я бу́ква; (*econ*) капита́л. **capitalism** *n* капитали́зм. **capitalist** *n* капитали́ст; *adj* капиталисти́ческий. **capitalize** *vt* извлека́ть *impf*, извле́чь *pf* вы́году (**on** из+*gen*).
capitulate *vi* капитули́ровать *impf* & *pf*. **capitulation** *n* капитуля́ция.
caprice *n* капри́з. **capricious** *adj* капри́зный.
Capricorn *n* Козеро́г.
capsize *vt* & *i* опроки́дывать(ся) *impf*, опроки́нуть(ся) *pf*.
capsule *n* ка́псула.
captain *n* капита́н; *vt* быть капита́ном +*gen*.
caption *n* по́дпись; (*cin*) титр.
captious *adj* приди́рчивый.
captivate *vt* пленя́ть *impf*, плени́ть *pf*. **captivating** *adj* плени́тельный. **captive** *adj* & *n* плённый. **captivity** *n* нево́ля; (*esp mil*) плен. **capture** *n* взя́тие, захва́т, пои́мка; *vt* (*person*) брать *impf*, взять *pf* в плен; (*seize*) захва́тывать

impf, захвати́ть *pf*.
car *n* маши́на; автомоби́ль *m*; ~ **park** стоя́нка.
carafe *n* графи́н.
caramel(s) *n* караме́ль.
carat *n* кара́т.
caravan *n* фурго́н; (*convoy*) карава́н.
caraway (seeds) *n* тмин.
carbohydrate *n* углево́д. **carbon** *n* углеро́д; ~ **copy** ко́пия; ~ **dioxide** углекислота́; ~ **monoxide** о́кись углеро́да; ~ **paper** копирова́льная бума́га.
carburettor *n* карбюра́тор.
carcass *n* ту́ша.
card *n* (*stiff paper*) карто́н; (*visiting* ~) ка́рточка; (*playing* ~) ка́рта; (*greetings* ~) откры́тка; (*ticket*) биле́т. **cardboard** *n* карто́н; *adj* карто́нный.
cardiac *adj* серде́чный.
cardigan *n* кардига́н.
cardinal *adj* кардина́льный; ~ **number** коли́чественное числи́тельное *sb*; *n* кардина́л.
care *n* (*trouble*) забо́та; (*caution*) осторо́жность; (*tending*) ухо́д; **in the** ~ **of** на попече́нии *+gen*; **take** ~ осторо́жно!; смотри́(те)!; **take** ~ **of** забо́титься *impf*, по~ *pf* о+*prep*; *vi*: **I don't** ~ мне всё равно́; ~ **for** (*look after*) уха́живать *impf* за+*instr*; (*like*) нра́виться *impf*, по~ *pf impers* +*dat*.
career *n* карье́ра.
carefree *adj* беззабо́тный.
careful *adj* (*cautious*) осторо́жный; (*thorough*) тща́тельный. **careless** *adj* (*negligent*) небре́жный; (*incautious*) неосторо́жный.
caress *n* ла́ска; *vt* ласка́ть *impf*.
caretaker *n* смотри́тель *m*, ~ница; *attrib* вре́менный.
cargo *n* груз.
caricature *n* карикату́ра; *vt* изобража́ть *impf*, изобрази́ть *pf* в карикату́рном ви́де.
carnage *n* резня́.
carnal *adj* пло́тский.
carnation *n* гвозди́ка.
carnival *n* карнава́л.
carnivorous *adj* плотоя́дный.
carol *n* (рожде́ственский) гимн.
carouse *vi* кути́ть *impf*, кутну́ть *pf*.
carp[1] *n* карп.
carp[2] *vi* придира́ться *impf*, придра́ться *pf* (**at** к+*dat*).
carpenter *n* пло́тник. **carpentry** *n* пло́тничество.
carpet *n* ковёр; *vt* покрыва́ть *impf*, покры́ть *pf* ковро́м.
carping *adj* приди́рчивый.
carriage *n* (*vehicle*) каре́та; (*rly*) ваго́н; (*conveyance*) перево́зка; (*bearing*) оса́нка. **carriageway** *n* прое́зжая часть доро́ги. **carrier** *n* (*on bike*) бага́жник; (*firm*) тра́нспортная кампа́ния; (*med*) бацилloноси́тель *m*.
carrot *n* морко́вка; *pl* морко́вь (*collect*).
carry *vt* (*by hand*) носи́ть *indet*, нести́ *det*; переноси́ть *impf*, перенести́ *pf*; (*in vehicle*) вози́ть *indet*, везти́ *det*; (*sound*) передава́ть *impf*, переда́ть *pf*; *vi* (*sound*) быть слы́шен; **be carried away** увлека́ться *impf*, увле́чься *pf*; ~ **on** (*continue*) продолжа́ть *impf*; ~ **out** выполня́ть *impf*, вы́полнить *pf*; ~ **over** переноси́ть *impf*, перенести́ *pf*.

cart *n* теле́га; *vt* (*lug*) тащи́ть *impf*.

cartilage *n* хрящ.

carton *n* карто́нка

cartoon *n* карикату́ра; (*cin*) мультфи́льм. **cartoonist** *n* карикатури́ст, ~ка.

cartridge *n* патро́н; (*of record player*) звукоснима́тель *m*.

carve *vt* ре́зать *impf* по+*dat*; (*in wood*) выреза́ть *impf*, вы́резать *pf*; (*in stone*) высека́ть *impf*, вы́сечь; (*slice*) нареза́ть *impf*, наре́зать *pf*. **carving** *n* резьба́; ~ **knife** нож для нареза́ния мя́са.

cascade *n* каска́д; *vi* па́дать *impf*.

case[1] *n* (*instance*) слу́чай; (*law*) де́ло; (*med*) больно́й *sb*; (*gram*) паде́ж; **in** ~ (в слу́чае) е́сли; **in any** ~ во вся́ком слу́чае; **in no** ~ ни в ко́ем слу́чае; **just in** ~ на вся́кий слу́чай.

case[2] *n* (*box*) я́щик; (*suitcase*) чемода́н; (*small box*) футля́р; (*cover*) чехо́л; (*display* ~) витри́на.

cash *n* нали́чные *sb*; (*money*) де́ньги *pl*; ~ **on delivery** нало́женным платежо́м; ~ **desk, register** ка́сса; *vt*: ~ **a cheque** получа́ть *impf*, получи́ть *pf* де́ньги по че́ку. **cashier** *n* касси́р.

casing *n* (*tech*) кожу́х.

casino *n* казино́ *neut indecl*.

cask *n* бо́чка.

casket *n* шкату́лка.

casserole *n* (*pot*) ла́тка; (*stew*) рагу́ *neut indecl*.

cassette *n* кассе́та; ~ **recorder** кассе́тный магнитофо́н.

cassock *n* ря́са.

cast *vt* (*throw*) броса́ть *impf*, бро́сить *pf*; (*shed*) сбра́сывать *impf*, сбро́сить *pf*; (*theat*) распределя́ть *impf*, распредели́ть *pf* ро́ли +*dat*; (*found*) лить *impf*, с~ *pf*; ~ **off** (*knitting*) спуска́ть *impf*, спусти́ть *pf* пе́тли; (*naut*) отплыва́ть *impf*, отплы́ть *pf*; ~ **on** (*knitting*) набира́ть *impf*, набра́ть *pf* пе́тли; *n* (*of mind etc.*) склад; (*mould*) фо́рма; (*moulded object*) сле́пок; (*med*) ги́псовая повя́зка; (*theat*) де́йствующие ли́ца (-ц) *pl*. **castaway** *n* потерпе́вший *sb* кораблекруше́ние. **cast iron** *n* чугу́н. **cast-iron** *adj* чугу́нный. **cast-offs** *n pl* но́шеное пла́тье.

castanet *n* кастанье́та.

caste *n* ка́ста.

castigate *vt* бичева́ть *impf*.

castle *n* за́мок; (*chess*) ладья́.

castor *n* (*wheel*) ро́лик; ~ **sugar** са́харная пу́дра.

castrate *vt* кастри́ровать *impf* & *pf*. **castration** *n* кастра́ция.

casual *adj* (*chance*) случа́йный; (*offhand*) небре́жный; (*clothes*) обы́денный; (*unofficial*) неофициа́льный; (*informal*) лёгкий; (*labour*) подённый; ~ **labourer** подёнщик, -ица. **casualty** *n* (*wounded*) ра́неный *sb*; (*killed*) уби́тый *sb*; *pl* поте́ри (-рь) *pl*; ~ **ward** пала́та ско́рой по́мощи.

cat *n* ко́шка; (*tom*) кот; ~'**s-eye** (*on road*) (доро́жный) рефле́ктор.

catalogue *n* катало́г; (*price list*) прейскура́нт; *vt* каталогизи́ровать *impf* & *pf*.

catalyst *n* катализа́тор. **catalytic** *adj* каталити́ческий.

catapult *n* (*toy*) рога́тка; (*hist, aeron*) катапу́льта; *vt* & *i* катапультировать(ся) *impf* & *pf*.

cataract *n* (*med*) катара́кта.

catarrh *n* ката́р.

catastrophe *n* катастро́фа. **catastrophic** *adj* катастрофи́ческий.

catch *vt* (*ball, fish, thief*) лови́ть *impf*, пойма́ть *pf*; (*surprise*) застава́ть *impf*, заста́ть *pf*; (*disease*) заража́ться *impf*, зарази́ться *pf* +*instr*; (*be in time for*) успева́ть *impf*, успе́ть *pf* на+*acc*; *vt* & *i* (*snag*) зацепля́ть(ся) *impf*, зацепи́ть(ся) *pf* (**on** за+*acc*); ~ **on** (*become popular*) прививаться *impf*, приви́ться *pf*; ~ **up with** догоня́ть *impf*, догна́ть *pf*; *n* (*of fish*) уло́в; (*trick*) уло́вка; (*on door etc.*) защёлка. **catching** *adj* зара́зный. **catchy** *adj* прили́пчивый.

categorical *adj* категори́ческий. **category** *n* катего́рия.

cater *vi*: ~ **for** поставля́ть *impf*, поста́вить *pf* прови́зию для+*gen*; (*satisfy*) удовлетворя́ть *impf*, удовлетвори́ть *pf*. **caterer** *n* поставщи́к (прови́зии).

caterpillar *n* гу́сеница.

cathedral *n* собо́р.

catheter *n* кате́тер.

Catholic *adj* католи́ческий; *n* като́лик, -ичка. **Catholicism** *n* католи́чество.

cattle *n* скот.

Caucasus *n* Кавка́з.

cauldron *n* котёл.

cauliflower *n* цветна́я капу́ста.

cause *n* причи́на, по́вод; (*law etc.*) де́ло; *vt* причиня́ть *impf*, причини́ть *pf*; вызыва́ть *impf*, вы́звать *pf*; (*induce*) заставля́ть *impf*, заста́вить *pf*.

caustic *adj* е́дкий.

cauterize *vt* прижига́ть *impf*, приже́чь *pf*.

caution *n* осторо́жность; (*warning*) предостереже́ние; *vt* предостерега́ть *impf*, предостере́чь *pf*. **cautious** *adj* осторо́жный. **cautionary** *adj* предостерега́ющий.

cavalcade *n* кавалька́да. **cavalier** *adj* бесцеремо́нный.

cavalry *n* кавале́рия.

cave *n* пеще́ра; *vi*: ~ **in** обва́ливаться *impf*, обвали́ться *pf*; (*yield*) сдава́ться *impf*, сда́ться *pf*. **caveman** *n* пеще́рный челове́к. **cavern** *n* пеще́ра. **cavernous** *adj* пеще́ристый.

caviare *n* икра́.

cavity *n* впа́дина, по́лость; (*in tooth*) дупло́.

cavort *vi* скака́ть *impf*.

caw *vi* ка́ркать *impf*, ка́ркнуть *pf*.

CD *abbr* (*of* **compact disc**) компа́кт-ди́ск; ~ **player** проигрыватель *m* компа́кт-ди́сков; ~**-ROM** компа́кт-ди́ск ПЗУ.

cease *vt* & *i* прекраща́ть(ся) *impf*, прекрати́ть(ся) *pf*; *vt* перестава́ть *impf*, переста́ть *pf* (+*inf*); ~**-fire** прекраще́ние огня́. **ceaseless** *adj* непреста́нный.

cedar *n* кедр.

cede *vt* уступа́ть *impf*, уступи́ть *pf*.

ceiling *n* потоло́к; (*fig*) максима́льный у́ровень *m*.

celebrate *vt* & *i* пра́здновать *impf*, от~ *pf*; (*extol*) прославля́ть *impf*, просла́вить *pf*. **celebrated** *adj* знамени́тый. **celebration** *n* пра́зднование. **celebrity** *n* знамени́тость.

celery *n* сельдерéй.
celestial *adj* небéсный.
celibacy *n* безбрáчие. **celibate** *adj* холостóй; *n* холостя́к.
cell *n* (*prison*) кáмера; (*biol*) клéтка.
cellar *n* подвáл.
cello *n* виолончéль.
cellophane *n* целлофáн. **cellular** *adj* клéточный. **celluloid** *n* целлулóид.
Celt *n* кельт. **Celtic** *adj* кéльтский.
cement *n* цемéнт; *vt* цементи́ровать *impf*, за~ *pf*.
cemetery *n* клáдбище.
censor *n* цéнзор; *vt* подвергáть *impf*, подвéргнуть *pf* цензу́ре. **censorious** *adj* сверхкрити́ческий. **censorship** *n* цензу́ра. **censure** *n* порицáние; *vt* порицáть *impf*.
census *n* пéрепись.
cent *n* цент; **per** ~ процéнт.
centenary *n* столéтие. **centennial** *adj* столéтний. **centigrade** *adj*: **10°** ~ 10° по Цéльсию. **centimetre** *n* сантимéтр. **centipede** *n* сороконóжка.
central *adj* центрáльный; ~ **heating** центрáльное отоплéние. **centralization** *n* централизáция. **centralize** *vt* централизовáть *impf* & *pf*. **centre** *n* центр; середи́на; ~ **forward** центр нападéния; *vi* & *i*: ~ **on** сосредотóчивать(ся) *impf*, сосредотóчить(ся) *pf* на+*prep*. **centrifugal** *adj* центробéжный.
century *n* столéтие, век.
ceramic *adj* керами́ческий. **ceramics** *n pl* керáмика.
cereals *n pl* хлéбные злáки *m pl*; **breakfast** ~ зерновы́е хлóпья (-ев) *pl*.
cerebral *adj* мозговóй.
ceremonial *adj* церемониáльный; *n* церемониáл. **ceremonious** *adj* церемóнный.
ceremony *n* церемóния.
certain *adj* (*confident*) увéрен (-нна); (*undoubted*) несомнéнный; (*unspecified*) извéстный; (*inevitable*) вéрный; **for** ~ навернякá. **certainly** *adv* (*of course*) конéчно, безуслóвно; (*without doubt*) несомнéнно; ~ **not!** ни в кóем слу́чае. **certainty** *n* (*conviction*) увéренность; (*fact*) несомнéнный факт.
certificate *n* свидéтельство; сертификáт. **certify** *vt* удостоверя́ть *impf*, удостовéрить *pf*.
cervical *n* шéйный. **cervix** *n* шéйка мáтки.
cessation *n* прекращéние.
cf. *abbr* ср., сравни́.
CFCs *abbr* (*of* **chlorofluorocarbons**) хлори́рованные фторуглерóды *m pl*.
chafe *vt* (*rub*) терéть *impf*; (*rub sore*) натирáть *impf*, натерéть *pf*.
chaff *n* (*husks*) мяки́на; (*straw*) сéчка.
chaffinch *n* зя́блик.
chagrin *n* огорчéние.
chain *n* цепь; ~ **reaction** цепнáя реáкция; ~ **smoker** зая́длый кури́льщик.
chair *n* стул, (*armchair*) крéсло; (*univ*) кáфедра; *vt* (*preside*) председáтельствовать *impf* на+*prep*. **chairman, -woman** *n* председáтель *m*, ~ница.
chalice *n* чáша.
chalk *n* мел. **chalky** *adj* меловóй.
challenge *n* (*summons*, *fig*)

вы́зов; (*sentry's*) о́клик; (*law*) отво́д; *vt* вызыва́ть *impf*, вы́звать *pf*; (*sentry*) оклика́ть *impf*, окли́кнуть *pf*; (*law*) отводи́ть *impf*, отвести́ *pf*. **challenger** *n* претенде́нт. **challenging** *adj* интригу́ющий.

chamber *n* (*cavity*) ка́мера; (*hall*) зал; (*parl*) пала́та; *pl* (*law*) адвока́тская конто́ра, (*judge's*) кабине́т (судьи́); **~ music** ка́мерная му́зыка; **~ pot** ночно́й горшо́к. **chambermaid** *n* го́рничная *sb*.

chameleon *n* хамелео́н.

chamois *n* (*animal*) се́рна; (*~-leather*) за́мша.

champagne *n* шампа́нское *sb*.

champion *n* чемпио́н, ~ка; (*upholder*) побо́рник, -ица; *vt* боро́ться *impf* за *+acc*. **championship** *n* пе́рвенство, чемпиона́т.

chance *n* случа́йность; (*opportunity*) возмо́жность, (*favourable*) слу́чай; (*likelihood*) шанс (*usu pl*); **by ~** случа́йно; *adj* случа́йный; *vi*: **~ it** рискну́ть *pf*.

chancellery *n* канцеля́рия. **chancellor** *n* ка́нцлер; (*univ*) ре́ктор; **C~ of the Exchequer** ка́нцлер казначе́йства.

chancy *adj* риско́ванный.

chandelier *n* лю́стра.

change *n* переме́на; измене́ние; (*of clothes etc.*) сме́на; (*money*) сда́ча; (*of trains etc.*) переса́дка; **for a ~** для разнообра́зия; *vt & i* меня́ть(ся) *impf*; изменя́ть(ся) *impf*, измени́ть(ся) *pf*; *vi* (*one's clothes*) переодева́ться *impf*, переоде́ться *pf*; (*trains etc.*) переса́живаться *impf*, пересе́сть *pf*; *vt* (*a baby*) перепелёнывать *impf*, перепелена́ть *pf*; (*money*) обме́нивать *impf*, обменя́ть *pf*; (*give ~ for*) разме́нивать *impf*, разменя́ть *pf*; **~ into** превраща́ться *impf*, преврати́ться *pf* в+*acc*; **~ over to** переходи́ть *impf*, перейти́ *pf* на+*acc*. **changeable** *adj* изме́нчивый.

channel *n* (*water*) проли́в; (*also TV*) кана́л; (*fig*) путь *m*; **the (English) C~** Ла-Ма́нш; *vt* (*fig*) направля́ть *impf*.

chant *n* (*eccl*) песнопе́ние; *vt & i* петь *impf*; (*slogans*) сканди́ровать *impf & pf*.

chaos *n* хао́с. **chaotic** *adj* хаоти́чный.

chap *n* (*person*) па́рень *m*.

chapel *n* часо́вня; (*Catholic*) капе́лла.

chaperone *n* компаньо́нка.

chaplain *n* капелла́н.

chapped *adj* потреска́вшийся.

chapter *n* глава́.

char *vt & i* обу́гливать(ся) *impf*, обу́глить(ся) *pf*.

character *n* хара́ктер; (*theat*) де́йствующее лицо́; (*letter*) бу́ква; (*Chinese etc.*) иеро́глиф. **characteristic** *adj* характе́рный; *n* сво́йство; (*of person*) черта́ хара́ктера. **characterize** *vt* характеризова́ть *impf & pf*.

charade *n* шара́да.

charcoal *n* древе́сный у́голь *m*.

charge *n* (*for gun*; *electr*) заря́д; (*fee*) пла́та; (*person*) пито́мец, -мица; (*accusation*) обвине́ние; (*mil*) ата́ка; **be in ~ of** заве́довать *impf +instr*; **in the ~ of** на попече́нии *+gen*; *vt* (*gun*; *electr*) заряжа́ть *impf*, заряди́ть *pf*; (*accuse*) обвиня́ть *impf*, обвини́ть *pf* (**with** в+*prep*); (*mil*) атакова́ть *impf* & *pf*; *vi* броса́ться *impf*, бро́ситься *pf* в ата́ку; ~ **(for)** брать *impf*, взять *pf* (за+*acc*); ~ **to (the account of)** запи́сывать *impf*, записа́ть *pf* на счёт+*gen*.

chariot *n* колесни́ца.

charisma *n* обая́ние. **charismatic** *adj* обая́тельный.

charitable *adj* благотвори́тельный; (*kind, merciful*) милосе́рдный. **charity** *n* (*kindness*) милосе́рдие; (*organization*) благотвори́тельная организа́ция.

charlatan *n* шарлата́н.

charm *n* очарова́ние; пре́лесть; (*spell*) за́говор; *pl* ча́ры (чар) *pl*; (*amulet*) талисма́н; (*trinket*) брело́к; *vt* очаро́вывать *impf*, очарова́ть *pf*. **charming** *adj* очарова́тельный, преле́стный.

chart *n* (*naut*) морска́я ка́рта; (*table*) гра́фик; *vt* наноси́ть *impf*, нанести́ *pf* на гра́фик. **charter** *n* (*document*) ха́ртия; (*statutes*) уста́в; *vt* нанима́ть *impf*, наня́ть *pf*.

charwoman *n* приходя́щая убо́рщица.

chase *vt* гоня́ться *indet*, гна́ться *det* за+*instr*; *n* пого́ня; (*hunting*) охо́та.

chasm *n* (*abyss*) бе́здна.

chassis *n* шасси́ *neut indecl*.

chaste *adj* целому́дренный.

chastise *vt* кара́ть *impf*, по~ *pf*.

chastity *n* целому́дрие.

chat *n* бесе́да; *vi* бесе́довать *impf*; ~ **show** телевизио́нная бесе́да-интервью́ *f*.

chatter *n* болтовня́; *vi* болта́ть *impf*; (*teeth*) стуча́ть *impf*. **chatterbox** *n* болту́н. **chatty** *adj* разгово́рчивый.

chauffeur *n* шофёр.

chauvinism *n* шовини́зм. **chauvinist** *n* шовини́ст; *adj* шовинисти́ческий.

cheap *adj* дешёвый. **cheapen** *vt* (*fig*) опошля́ть *impf*, опошли́ть *pf*. **cheaply** *adv* дёшево.

cheat *vt* обма́нывать *impf*, обману́ть *pf*; *vi* плутова́ть *impf*, на~, с~ *pf*; *n* (*person*) обма́нщик, -ица; плут; (*act*) обма́н.

check[1] *n* контро́ль *m*, прове́рка; (*chess*) шах; **~mate** шах и мат; *vt* (*examine*) проверя́ть *impf*, прове́рить *pf*; контроли́ровать *impf*, про~ *pf*; (*restrain*) сде́рживать *impf*, сдержа́ть *pf*; ~ **in** регистри́роваться *impf*, за~ *pf*; ~ **out** выпи́сываться *impf*, вы́писаться *pf*; **~-out** ка́сса; **~-up** осмо́тр.

check[2] *n* (*pattern*) кле́тка. **check(ed)** *adj* кле́тчатый.

cheek *n* щека́; (*impertinence*) на́глость. **cheeky** *adj* на́глый.

cheep *vi* пища́ть *impf*, пи́скнуть *pf*.

cheer *n* ободря́ющий во́зглас; **~s!** за (ва́ше) здоро́вье!; *vt* (*applaud*) приве́тствовать *impf* & *pf*; ~ **up** ободря́ть(ся) *impf*, ободри́ть(ся) *pf*. **cheerful** *adj* весёлый. **cheerio** *int* пока́. **cheerless** *adj* уны́лый.

cheese *n* сыр; **~-cake** ватру́шка.

cheetah *n* гепа́рд.

chef *n* (шеф-)по́вар.

chemical *adj* хими́ческий; *n* химика́т. **chemist** *n* хи́мик; (*druggist*) апте́карь *m*; **~'s (shop)** апте́ка. **chemistry** *n* хи́мия.

cheque *n* чек; ~**-book** че́ковая кни́жка.
cherish *vt* (*foster*) леле́ять *impf*; (*hold dear*) дорожи́ть *impf* +*instr*; (*love*) не́жно люби́ть *impf*.
cherry *n* ви́шня; *adj* вишнёвый.
cherub *n* херуви́м.
chess *n* ша́хматы (-т) *pl*; ~**-board** ша́хматная доска́; ~**-men** *n* ша́хматы (-т) *pl*.
chest *n* сунду́к; (*anat*) грудь; ~ **of drawers** комо́д.
chestnut *n* кашта́н; (*horse*) гнеда́я *sb*.
chew *vt* жева́ть *impf*. **chewing-gum** *n* жева́тельная рези́нка.
chic *adj* элега́нтный.
chick *n* цыплёнок. **chicken** *n* ку́рица; цыплёнок; *adj* трусли́вый; ~ **out** тру́сить *impf*, с~ *pf*. **chicken-pox** *n* ветря́нка.
chicory *n* цико́рий.
chief *n* глава́ *m* & *f*; (*boss*) нача́льник; (*of tribe*) вождь *m*; *adj* гла́вный. **chiefly** *adv* гла́вным о́бразом. **chieftain** *n* вождь *m*.
chiffon *n* шифо́н.
child *n* ребёнок; ~**-birth** ро́ды (-дов) *pl*. **childhood** *n* де́тство. **childish** *adj* де́тский. **childless** *adj* безде́тный. **childlike** *adj* де́тский. **childrens'** *adj* де́тский.
chili *n* стручко́вый пе́рец.
chill *n* хо́лод; (*ailment*) просту́да; *vt* охлажда́ть *impf*, охлади́ть *pf*. **chilly** *adj* прохла́дный.
chime *n* (*set of bells*) набо́р колоколо́в; *pl* (*sound*) перезво́н; (*of clock*) бой; *vt* & *i* (*clock*) бить *impf*, про~ *pf*; *vi* (*bell*) звони́ть *impf*, по~ *pf*.
chimney *n* труба́; ~**-sweep** трубочи́ст.
chimpanzee *n* шимпанзе́ *m indecl*.
chin *n* подборо́док.
china *n* фарфо́р.
China *n* Кита́й. **Chinese** *n* кита́ец, -ая́нка; *adj* кита́йский.
chink[1] *n* (*sound*) звон; *vi* звене́ть *impf*, про~ *pf*.
chink[2] *n* (*crack*) щель.
chintz *n* си́тец.
chip *vt* & *i* отка́лывать(ся) *impf*, отколо́ть(ся) *pf*; *n* (*of wood*) ще́пка; (*in cup*) щерби́на; (*in games*) фи́шка; *pl* карто́фель-соло́мка (*collect*); (*electron*) чип, микросхе́ма.
chiropodist *n* челове́к, занима́ющийся педикю́ром. **chiropody** *n* педикю́р.
chirp *vi* чири́кать *impf*.
chisel *n* (*wood*) стаме́ска; (*masonry*) зуби́ло; *vt* высека́ть *impf*, вы́сечь *pf*.
chit *n* (*note*) запи́ска.
chivalrous *adj* ры́царский. **chivalry** *n* ры́царство.
chlorine *n* хлор. **chlorophyll** *n* хлорофи́лл.
chock-full *adj* битко́м наби́тый.
chocolate *n* шокола́д; (*sweet*) шокола́дная конфе́та; ~ **bar** шокола́дка.
choice *n* вы́бор; *adj* отбо́рный.
choir *n* хор *m*; ~**-boy** пе́вчий *sb*.
choke *n* (*valve*) дро́ссель *m*; *vi* дави́ться *impf*, по~ *pf*; (*with anger etc.*) задыха́ться *impf*, задохну́ться *pf* (**with** от+*gen*); *vt* (*suffocate*) души́ть *impf*, за~ *pf*; (*of plants*) заглуша́ть, глуши́ть *impf*, за-

глушить *pf.*
cholera *n* холе́ра.
cholesterol *n* холестери́н.
choose *vt* (*select*) выбира́ть *impf*, вы́брать *pf*; (*decide*) реша́ть *impf*, реши́ть *pf*. **choosy** *adj* разбо́рчивый.
chop *vt* (*also* ~ *down*) руби́ть *impf*, рубну́ть, рубану́ть *pf*; ~ **off** отруба́ть *impf*, отруби́ть *pf*; *n* (*cul*) отбивна́я котле́та.
chopper *n* топо́р. **choppy** *adj* бурли́вый.
chop-sticks *n* па́лочки *f pl* для еды́.
choral *adj* хорово́й. **chorale** *n* хора́л.
chord *n* (*mus*) акко́рд.
chore *n* обя́занность.
choreographer *n* хорео́граф. **choreography** *n* хореогра́фия.
chorister *n* пе́вчий *sb*.
chortle *vi* фы́ркать *impf*, фы́ркнуть *pf*.
chorus *n* хор; (*refrain*) припе́в.
christen *vt* крести́ть *impf* & *pf*. **Christian** *n* христиани́н, -а́нка; *adj* христиа́нский; ~ **name** и́мя *neut*. **Christianity** *n* христиа́нство. **Christmas** *n* Рождество́; ~ **Day** пе́рвый день Рождества́; ~ **Eve** соче́льник; ~ **tree** ёлка.
chromatic *adj* хромати́ческий. **chrome** *n* хром. **chromium** *n* хром. **chromosome** *n* хромосо́ма.
chronic *adj* хрони́ческий.
chronicle *n* хро́ника, ле́топись.
chronological *adj* хронологи́ческий.
chrysalis *n* ку́колка.
chrysanthemum *n* хризанте́ма.
chubby *adj* пу́хлый.
chuck *vt* броса́ть *impf*, бро́сить *pf*; ~ **out** вышиба́ть *impf*, вы́шибить *pf*.
chuckle *vi* посме́иваться *impf*.
chum *n* това́рищ.
chunk *n* ломо́ть *m*.
church *n* це́рковь. **churchyard** *n* кла́дбище.
churlish *adj* гру́бый.
churn *n* маслобо́йка; *vt* сбива́ть *impf*, сбить *pf*; *vi* (*foam*) пе́ниться *impf*, вс~ *pf*; (*stomach*) крути́ть *impf*; ~ **out** выпека́ть *impf*, вы́печь *pf*; ~ **up** взбить *pf*.
chute *n* жёлоб.
cider *n* сидр.
cigar *n* сига́ра. **cigarette** *n* сигаре́та; папиро́са; ~ **lighter** зажига́лка.
cinder *n* шлак; *pl* зола́.
cine-camera *n* киноаппара́т. **cinema** *n* кино́ *neut indecl*.
cinnamon *n* кори́ца.
cipher *n* нуль *m*; (*code*) шифр.
circle *n* круг; (*theatre*) я́рус; *vi* кружи́ться *impf*; *vt* (*walking*) обходи́ть *impf*, обойти́ *pf*; (*flying*) облета́ть *impf*, облете́ть *pf*. **circuit** *n* кругооборо́т; объе́зд, обхо́д; (*electron*) схе́ма; (*electr*) цепь. **circuitous** *adj* окружно́й. **circular** *adj* кру́глый; (*moving in a circle*) кругово́й; *n* циркуля́р. **circulate** *vi* циркули́ровать *impf*; *vt* распространя́ть *impf*, распространи́ть *pf*. **circulation** *n* (*air*) циркуля́ция; (*distribution*) распростране́ние; (*of newspaper*) тира́ж; (*med*) кровообраще́ние.
circumcise *vt* обреза́ть *impf*, обре́зать *pf*. **circumcision** *n* обреза́ние.

circumference *n* окру́жность. **circumspect** *adj* осмотри́тельный. **circumstance** *n* обстоя́тельство; **under the ~s** при да́нных обстоя́тельствах, в тако́м слу́чае; **under no ~s** ни при каки́х обстоя́тельствах, ни в ко́ем слу́чае. **circumvent** *vt* обходи́ть *impf*, обойти́ *pf*. **circus** *n* цирк. **cirrhosis** *n* цирро́з. **CIS** *abbr* (*of* **Commonwealth of Independent States**) СНГ. **cistern** *n* бачо́к. **citadel** *n* цитаде́ль. **cite** *vt* ссыла́ться *impf*, сосла́ться *pf* на+*acc*. **citizen** *n* граждани́н, -а́нка. **citizenship** *n* гражда́нство. **citrus** *n* ци́трус; *adj* ци́трусовый. **city** *n* го́род. **civic** *adj* гражда́нский. **civil** *adj* гражда́нский; (*polite*) ве́жливый; **~ engineer** гражда́нский инжене́р; **~ engineering** гражда́нское строи́тельство; **C~ Servant** госуда́рственный слу́жащий *sb*; чино́вник; **C~ Service** госуда́рственная слу́жба. **civilian** *n* шта́тский *sb*; *adj* шта́тский. **civility** *n* ве́жливость. **civilization** *n* цивилиза́ция. **civilize** *vt* цивилизова́ть *impf* & *pf*. **civilized** *adj* цивилизо́ванный. **clad** *adj* оде́тый. **claim** *n* (*demand*) тре́бование, притяза́ние; (*assertion*) утвержде́ние; *vt* (*demand*) тре́бовать *impf* +*gen*; (*assert*) утвержда́ть *impf*, утверди́ть *pf*. **claimant** *n* претенде́нт. **clairvoyant** *n* ясновидец, -дица; *adj* ясневи́дящий. **clam** *n* моллю́ск; *vi*: **~ up** отка́зываться *impf*, отказа́ться *pf* разгова́ривать. **clamber** *vi* кара́бкаться *impf*, вс~ *pf*. **clammy** *adj* вла́жный. **clamour** *n* шум; *vi*: **~ for** шу́мно тре́бовать *impf*, по~ *pf* +*gen*. **clamp** *n* зажи́м; *vt* скрепля́ть *impf*, скрепи́ть *pf*; **~ down on** прижа́ть *pf*. **clan** *n* клан. **clandestine** *adj* та́йный. **clang, clank** *n* лязг; *vt* & *i* ля́згать *impf*, ля́згнуть *pf* (+*instr*). **clap** *vt* & *i* хло́пать *impf*, хло́пнуть *pf* +*dat*; *n* хлопо́к; (*thunder*) уда́р. **claret** *n* бордо́ *neut indecl*. **clarification** *n* (*explanation*) разъясне́ние. **clarify** *vt* разъясня́ть *impf*, разъясни́ть *pf*. **clarinet** *n* кларне́т. **clarity** *n* я́сность. **clash** *n* (*conflict*) столкнове́ние; (*disharmony*) дисгармо́ния; *vi* ста́лкиваться *impf*, столкну́ться *pf*; (*coincide*) совпада́ть *impf*, совпа́сть *pf*; не гармони́ровать *impf*. **clasp** *n* застёжка; (*embrace*) объя́тие; *vt* обхва́тывать *impf*, обхвати́ть *pf*; **~ one's hands** сплести́ *pf* па́льцы рук. **class** *n* класс; **~-room** класс; *vt* классифици́ровать *impf* & *pf*. **classic** *adj* класси́ческий; *n* кла́ссик; *pl* (*literature*) кла́ссика; (*Latin and Greek*) класси́ческие языки́ *m pl*. **classical** *adj* класси́ческий. **classification** *n* классифика́-

ция. **classified** *adj* засекре́ченный. **classify** *vt* классифици́ровать *impf* & *pf*.

classy *adj* кла́ссный.

clatter *n* стук; *vi* стуча́ть *impf*, по~ *pf*.

clause *n* статья́; (*gram*) предложе́ние.

claustrophobia *n* клаустрофо́бия.

claw *n* ко́готь; *vt* цара́пать *impf* когтя́ми.

clay *n* гли́на; *adj* гли́няный.

clean *adj* чи́стый; *adv* (*fully*) соверше́нно; **~-shaven** гла́дко вы́бритый; *vt* чи́стить *impf*, вы́~, по~ *pf*. **cleaner** *n* убо́рщик, -ица. **cleaner's** *n* химчи́стка. **clean(li)ness** *n* чистота́. **cleanse** *vt* очища́ть *impf*, очи́стить *pf*.

clear *adj* я́сный; (*transparent*) прозра́чный; (*distinct*) отчётливый; (*free*) свобо́дный (**of** от+*gen*); (*pure*) чи́стый; *vt* & *i* очища́ть(ся) *impf*, очи́стить(ся) *pf*; *vt* (*jump over*) перепры́гивать *impf*, перепры́гнуть *pf*; (*acquit*) опра́вдывать *impf*, оправда́ть *pf*; **~ away** убира́ть *impf*, убра́ть *pf* со стола́; **~ off** (*go away*) убира́ться *impf*, убра́ться *pf*; **~ out** (*vt*) вычища́ть *impf*, вы́чистить *pf*; (*vi*) (*make off*) убира́ться *impf*, убра́ться *pf*; **~ up** (*tidy* (*away*)) убира́ть *impf*, убра́ть *pf*; (*weather*) проясня́ться *impf*, проясни́ться *pf*; (*explain*) выясня́ть *impf*, вы́яснить *pf*. **clearance** *n* расчи́стка; (*permission*) разреше́ние. **clearing** *n* (*glade*) поля́на. **clearly** *adv* я́сно.

cleavage *n* разре́з груди́.

clef *n* (*mus*) ключ.

cleft *n* тре́щина.

clemency *n* милосе́рдие.

clench *vt* (*fist*) сжима́ть *impf*, сжа́ть *pf*; (*teeth*) сти́скивать *impf*, сти́снуть *pf*.

clergy *n* духове́нство. **clergyman** *n* свяще́нник. **clerical** *adj* (*eccl*) духо́вный; (*of clerk*) канцеля́рский. **clerk** *n* конто́рский слу́жащий *sb*.

clever *adj* у́мный. **cleverness** *n* уме́ние.

cliche *n* клише́ *neut indecl*.

click *vt* щёлкать *impf*, щёлкнуть *pf* +*instr*.

client *n* клие́нт. **clientele** *n* клиенту́ра.

cliff *n* утёс.

climate *n* кли́мат. **climatic** *adj* климати́ческий.

climax *n* кульмина́ция.

climb *vt* & *i* ла́зить *indet*, лезть *det* на+*acc*; влеза́ть *impf*, влезть *pf* на+*acc*; поднима́ться *impf*, подня́ться *pf* на+*acc*; **~ down** (*tree*) слеза́ть *impf*, слезть *pf* (с+*gen*); (*mountain*) спуска́ться *impf*, спусти́ться *pf* (с+*gen*); (*give in*) отступа́ть *impf*, отступи́ть *pf*; *n* подъём. **climber** *n* альпини́ст, ~ка; (*plant*) вью́щееся расте́ние. **climbing** *n* альпини́зм.

clinch *vt*: **~ a deal** закрепи́ть *pf* сде́лку.

cling *vi* (*stick*) прилипа́ть *impf*, прили́пнуть *pf* (**to** к+*dat*); (*grasp*) цепля́ться *impf*, цепи́ться *pf* (**to** за+*acc*).

clinic *n* кли́ника. **clinical** *adj* клини́ческий.

clink *vt* & *i* звене́ть *impf*, про~ *pf* (+*instr*); **~ glasses** чо́каться *impf*, чо́кнуться *pf*; *n* звон.

clip[1] *n* скре́пка; зажи́м; *vt*

скрепля́ть *impf*, скрепи́ть *pf*. **clip**[2] *vt* (*cut*) подстрига́ть *impf*, подстри́чь *pf*. **clippers** *n pl* но́жницы *f pl*. **clipping** *n* (*extract*) вы́резка.
clique *n* кли́ка.
cloak *n* плащ. **cloakroom** *n* гардеро́б; (*toilet*) убо́рная *sb*.
clock *n* часы́ *m pl*; **~wise** по часово́й стре́лке; **~-work** часово́й механи́зм; *vi*: **~ in, out** отмеча́ться *impf*, отме́титься *pf* приходя́ на рабо́ту/уходя́ с рабо́ты.
clod *n* ком.
clog *vt*: **~ up** засоря́ть *impf*, засори́ть *pf*.
cloister *n* арка́да.
clone *n* клон.
close *adj* (*near*) бли́зкий; (*stuffy*) ду́шный; *vt & i* (*also* **~** *down*) закрыва́ть(ся) *impf*, закры́ть(ся) *pf*; (*conclude*) зака́нчивать *impf*, зако́нчить *pf*; *adv* бли́зко (**to** от+*gen*). **closed** *adj* закры́тый. **closeted** *adj*: **be ~ together** совеща́ться *impf* наедине́. **close-up** *n* фотогра́фия сня́тая кру́пным пла́ном. **closing** *n* закры́тие; *adj* заключи́тельный. **closure** *n* закры́тие.
clot *n* сгу́сток; *vi* сгуща́ться *impf*, сгусти́ться *pf*.
cloth *n* ткань; (*duster*) тря́пка; (*table-***~**) ска́терть.
clothe *vt* одева́ть *impf*, оде́ть (**in** +*instr*, в+*acc*) *pf*. **clothes** *n pl* оде́жда, пла́тье.
cloud *n* о́блако; (*rain* **~**) ту́ча; *vt* затемня́ть *impf*, затемни́ть *pf*; омрача́ть *impf*, омрачи́ть *pf*; **~ over** покрыва́ться *impf*, покры́ться *pf* облака́ми, ту́чами. **cloudy** *adj* о́блачный; (*liquid*) му́тный.
clout *vt* ударя́ть *impf*, уда́рить *pf*; *n* затре́щина; (*fig*) влия́ние.
clove *n* гвозди́ка; (*of garlic*) зубо́к.
cloven *adj* раздво́енный.
clover *n* кле́вер.
clown *n* кло́ун.
club *n* (*stick*) дуби́нка; *pl* (*cards*) тре́фы (треф) *pl*; (*association*) клуб; *vt* колоти́ть *impf*, по**~** *pf* дуби́нкой; *vi*: **~ together** скла́дываться *impf*, сложи́ться *pf*.
cluck *vi* куда́хтать *impf*.
clue *n* (*evidence*) ули́ка; (*to puzzle*) ключ; (*hint*) намёк.
clump *n* гру́ппа.
clumsiness *n* неуклю́жесть. **clumsy** *adj* неуклю́жий.
cluster *n* гру́ппа; *vi* собира́ться *impf*, собра́ться *pf* гру́ппами.
clutch *n* (*grasp*) хва́тка; ко́гти *m pl*; (*tech*) сцепле́ние; *vt* зажима́ть *impf*, зажа́ть *pf*; *vi*: **~ at** хвата́ться *impf*, хвати́ться *pf* за+*acc*.
clutter *n* беспоря́док; *vt* загроможда́ть *impf*, загромозди́ть *pf*.
c/o *abbr* (*of* **care of**) по а́дресу +*gen*; че́рез+*acc*.
coach *n* (*horse-drawn*) каре́та; (*rly*) ваго́н; (*bus*) авто́бус; (*tutor*) репети́тор; (*sport*) тре́нер; *vt* репети́ровать *impf*; тренирова́ть *impf*, на**~** *pf*.
coagulate *vi* сгуща́ться *impf*, сгусти́ться *pf*.
coal *n* у́голь *m*; **~mine** у́гольная ша́хта.
coalition *n* коали́ция.
coarse *adj* гру́бый.
coast *n* побере́жье, бе́рег; **~ guard** берегова́я охра́на; *vi* (*move without power*)

двúгаться *impf*, двúнуться *pf* по инéрции. **coastal** *adj* береговóй, прибрéжный.

coat *n* пальтó *neut indecl*; (*layer*) слой; (*animal*) шерсть, мех; ~ **of arms** герб; *vt* покрывáть *impf*, покрыть *pf*.

coax *vt* уговáривать *impf*, уговорúть *pf*.

cob *n* (*corn*-~) початок кукурýзы.

cobble *n* булыжник (*also collect*). **cobbled** *adj* булыжный.

cobbler *n* сапóжник.

cobweb *n* паутúна.

Coca-Cola *n* (*propr*) кóка-кóла.

cocaine *n* кокаúн.

cock *n* (*bird*) петýх; (*tap*) кран; (*of gun*) курóк; *vt* (*gun*) взводúть *impf*, взвестú *pf* курóк+*gen*.

cockerel *n* петушóк.

cockle *n* сердцевúдка.

cockpit *n* (*aeron*) кабúна.

cockroach *n* таракáн.

cocktail *n* коктéйль *m*.

cocky *adj* чвáнный.

cocoa *n* какáо *neut indecl*.

coco(a)nut *n* кокóс.

cocoon *n* кóкон.

cod *n* трескá.

code *n* (*of laws*) кóдекс; (*cipher*) код; *vt* шифровáть *impf*, за~ *pf*. **codify** *vt* кодифицúровать *impf* & *pf*.

co-education *n* совмéстное обучéние.

coefficient *n* коэффициéнт.

coerce *vt* принуждáть *impf*, принýдить *pf*. **coercion** *n* принуждéние.

coexist *vi* сосуществовáть *impf*. **coexistence** *n* сосуществовáние.

coffee *n* кóфе *m indecl*; ~-**mill** *n* кофéйница; ~-**pot** *n* кофéйник.

coffer *n pl* казнá.

coffin *n* гроб.

cog *n* зубéц. **cogwheel** *n* зубчáтое колесó.

cogent *adj* убедúтельный.

cohabit *vi* сожúтельствовать *impf*.

coherent *adj* свя́зный. **cohesion** *n* сплочённость. **cohesive** *adj* сплочённый.

coil *vt* & *i* свёртывать(ся) *impf*, свернýть(ся) *pf* кольцóм; *n* кольцó; (*electr*) катýшка.

coin *n* монéта; *vt* чекáнить *impf*, от~ *pf*.

coincide *vi* совпадáть *impf*, совпáсть *pf*. **coincidence** *n* совпадéние. **coincidental** *adj* случáйный.

coke *n* кокс.

colander *n* дуршлáг.

cold *n* хóлод; (*med*) простýда, нáсморк; *adj* холóдный; ~-**blooded** *adj* жестóкий; (*zool*) холоднокрóвный.

colic *n* кóлики *f pl*.

collaborate *vi* сотрýдничать *impf*. **collaboration** *n* сотрýдничество. **collaborator** *n* сотрýдник, -ица; (*traitor*) коллаборационúст, -úстка.

collapse *vi* рýхнуть *pf*; *n* падéние; крушéние.

collar *n* воротнúк; (*dog's*) ошéйник; ~-**bone** ключúца.

colleague *n* коллéга *m* & *f*.

collect *vt* собирáть *impf*, собрáть *pf*; (*as hobby*) коллекционúровать *impf*; (*fetch*) забирáть *impf*, забрáть *pf*. **collected** *adj* (*calm*) сóбранный; ~ **works** собрáние сочинéний. **collection** *n* (*stamps etc.*) коллéкция; (*church etc.*) сбор; (*post*) вы́емка. **collective** *n* коллектúв; *adj* коллекти́вный; ~ **farm** колхо́з; ~ **noun** собира́тельное существи́тельное *sb.* **collectivization** *n* коллективиза́ция. **collector** *n* сбо́рщик; коллекционе́р.

college *n* колле́дж, учи́лище.

collide *vi* ста́лкиваться *impf*, столкну́ться *pf.* **collision** *n* столкнове́ние.

colliery *n* каменноуго́льная ша́хта.

colloquial *adj* разгово́рный. **colloquialism** *n* разгово́рное выраже́ние.

collusion *n* та́йный сго́вор.

colon[1] *n* (*anat*) то́лстая кишка́.

colon[2] *n* (*gram*) двоето́чие.

colonel *n* полко́вник.

colonial *adj* колониа́льный. **colonialism** *n* колониали́зм. **colonize** *vt* колонизова́ть *impf* & *pf.* **colony** *n* коло́ния.

colossal *adj* колосса́льный.

colour *n* цвет, кра́ска; (*pl*) (*flag*) зна́мя *neut*; **~-blind** страда́ющий дальтони́змом; ~ **film** цветна́я плёнка; *vt* раскра́шивать *impf*, раскра́сить *pf*; *vi* красне́ть *impf*, по~ *pf.* **coloured** *adj* цветно́й. **colourful** *adj* я́ркий. **colourless** *adj* бесцве́тный.

colt *n* жеребёнок.

column *n* (*archit, mil*) коло́нна; (*of smoke etc.*) столб; (*of print*) столбе́ц. **columnist** *n* журнали́ст.

coma *n* ко́ма.

comb *n* гребёнка; *vt* причёсывать *impf*, причеса́ть *pf.*

combat *n* бой; *vt* боро́ться *impf* с+*instr*, про́тив+*gen*.

combination *n* сочета́ние; комбина́ция. **combine** *n* комбина́т; (~*-harvester*) комба́йн; *vt* & *i* совмеща́ть(ся) *impf*, совмести́ть(ся) *pf.* **combined** *adj* совме́стный.

combustion *n* горе́ние.

come *vi* (*on foot*) приходи́ть *impf*, прийти́ *pf*; (*by transport*) приезжа́ть *impf*, прие́хать *pf*; ~ **about** случа́ться *impf*, случи́ться *pf*; ~ **across** случа́йно ната́лкиваться *impf*, натолкну́ться *pf* на+*acc*; ~ **back** возвраща́ться *impf*, возврати́ться *pf*; ~ **in** входи́ть *impf*, войти́ *pf*; ~ **out** выходи́ть *impf*, вы́йти *pf*; ~ **round** (*revive*) приходи́ть *impf*, прийти́ *pf* в себя́; (*visit*) заходи́ть *impf*, зайти́ *pf*; (*agree*) соглаша́ться *impf*, согласи́ться *pf*; ~ **up to** (*approach*) подходи́ть *impf*, подойти́ *pf* к+*dat*; (*reach*) доходи́ть *impf*, дойти́ *pf* до+*gen*.

come-back *n* возвраще́ние.

come-down *n* униже́ние.

comedian *n* комедиа́нт. **comedy** *n* коме́дия.

comet *n* коме́та.

comfort *n* комфо́рт; (*convenience*) удо́бство; (*consolation*) утеше́ние; *vt* утеша́ть *impf*, уте́шить *pf.* **comfortable** *adj* удо́бный.

comic *adj* коми́ческий; *n* ко́мик; (*magazine*) ко́микс. **comical** *adj* смешно́й.

coming *adj* сле́дующий.

comma *n* запята́я *sb.*

command *n* (*order*) прика́з; (*order, authority*) кома́нда; **have** ~ **of** (*master*) владе́ть *impf* +*instr*; *vt* прика́зывать *impf*, приказа́ть *pf* +*dat*; (*mil*) кома́ндовать *impf*, с~ *pf* +*instr.* **commandant** *n* коменда́нт. **commandeer** *vt* реквизи́ровать *impf* & *pf.* **commander** *n* команди́р; **~-in-**

chief главнокома́ндующий *sb.* **commandment** *n* за́поведь. **commando** *n* деса́нтник.

commemorate *vt* ознамено́вывать *impf*, ознаменова́ть *pf*. **commemoration** *n* ознаменова́ние. **commemorative** *adj* па́мятный.

commence *vt* & *i* начина́ть(ся) *impf*, нача́ть(ся) *pf*. **commencement** *n* нача́ло.

commend *vt* хвали́ть *impf*, по~ *pf*; (*recommend*) рекомендова́ть *impf* & *pf*. **commendable** *adj* похва́льный. **commendation** *n* похвала́.

commensurate *adj* соразме́рный.

comment *n* замеча́ние; *vi* де́лать *impf*, с~ *pf* замеча́ния; ~ **on** комменти́ровать *impf* & *pf*, про~ *pf*. **commentary** *n* коммента́рий. **commentator** *n* коммента́тор.

commerce *n* комме́рция. **commercial** *adj* торго́вый; *n* рекла́ма.

commiserate *vi*: ~ **with** соболе́зновать *impf* +*dat*. **commiseration** *n* соболе́знование.

commission *n* (*order for work*) зака́з; (*agent's fee*) комиссио́нные *sb*; (*of inquiry etc.*) коми́ссия; (*mil*) офице́рское зва́ние; *vt* зака́зывать *impf*, заказа́ть *pf*. **commissionaire** *n* швейца́р. **commissioner** *n* комисса́р.

commit *vt* соверша́ть *impf*, соверши́ть *pf*; ~ **o.s.** обя́зываться *impf*, обяза́ться *pf*. **commitment** *n* обяза́тельство.

committee *n* комите́т.

commodity *n* това́р.

commodore *n* (*officer*) коммодо́р.

common *adj* о́бщий; (*ordinary*) просто́й; *n* общи́нная земля́; ~ **sense** здра́вый смысл. **commonly** *adv* обы́чно. **commonplace** *adj* бана́льный. **commonwealth** *n* содру́жество.

commotion *n* сумато́ха.

communal *adj* общи́нный, коммуна́льный. **commune** *n* комму́на; *vi* обща́ться *impf*.

communicate *vt* передава́ть *impf*, переда́ть *pf*; сообща́ть *impf*, сообщи́ть *pf*. **communication** *n* сообще́ние; связь. **communicative** *adj* разгово́рчивый.

communion *n* (*eccl*) прича́стие.

communiqué *n* коммюнике́ *neut indecl*.

Communism *n* коммуни́зм. **Communist** *n* коммуни́ст, ~ка; *adj* коммунисти́ческий.

community *n* общи́на.

commute *vt* заменя́ть *impf*, замени́ть *pf*; (*travel*) добира́ться *impf*, добра́ться *pf* тра́нспортом. **commuter** *n* регуля́рный пассажи́р.

compact[1] *n* (*agreement*) соглаше́ние.

compact[2] *adj* компа́ктный; ~ **disc** компа́кт-ди́ск; *n* пу́дреница.

companion *n* това́рищ; (*handbook*) спра́вочник. **companionable** *adj* общи́тельный. **companionship** *n* дру́жеское обще́ние. **company** *n* о́бщество, (*also firm*) компа́ния; (*theat*) тру́ппа; (*mil*) ро́та.

comparable *adj* сравни́мый. **comparative** *adj* сравнительный; *n* сравни́тельная сте́пень. **compare** *vt & i* сра́внивать(ся) *impf*, сравни́ть(ся) *pf* (**to, with** с+*instr*). **comparison** *n* сравне́ние.

compartment *n* отделе́ние; (*rly*) купе́ *neut indecl.*

compass *n* ко́мпас; *pl* ци́ркуль *m*.

compassion *n* сострада́ние. **compassionate** *adj* сострада́тельный.

compatibility *n* совмести́мость. **compatible** *adj* совмести́мый.

compatriot *n* сооте́чественник, -ица.

compel *vt* заставля́ть *impf*, заста́вить *pf*.

compensate *vt* компенси́ровать *impf & pf* (**for** за+*acc*). **compensation** *n* компенса́ция.

compete *vi* конкури́ровать *impf*; соревнова́ться *impf*.

competence *n* компете́нтность. **competent** *adj* компете́нтный.

competition *n* (*contest*) соревнова́ние, состяза́ние; (*rivalry*) конкуре́нция. **competitive** *adj* (*comm*) конкурентоспосо́бный. **competitor** *n* конкуре́нт, ~ка.

compilation *n* (*result*) компиля́ция; (*act*) составле́ние. **compile** *vt* составля́ть *impf*, соста́вить *pf*. **compiler** *n* состави́тель *m*, ~ница.

complacency *n* самодово́льство. **complacent** *adj* самодово́льный.

complain *vi* жа́ловаться *impf*, по~ *pf*. **complaint** *n* жа́лоба.

complement *n* дополне́ние; (*full number*) (ли́чный) соста́в; *vt* дополня́ть *impf*, допо́лнить *pf*. **complementary** *adj* дополни́тельный.

complete *vt* заверша́ть *impf*, заверши́ть *pf*; *adj* (*entire, thorough*) по́лный; (*finished*) зако́нченный. **completion** *n* заверше́ние.

complex *adj* сло́жный; *n* ко́мплекс. **complexity** *n* сло́жность.

complexion *n* цвет лица́.

compliance *n* усту́пчивость. **compliant** *adj* усту́пчивый.

complicate *vt* осложня́ть *impf*, осложни́ть *pf*. **complicated** *adj* сло́жный. **complication** *n* осложне́ние.

complicity *n* соуча́стие.

compliment *n* комплиме́нт; *pl* приве́т; *vt* говори́ть *impf* комплиме́нт(ы) +*dat*; хвали́ть *impf*, по~ *pf*. **complimentary** *adj* ле́стный; (*free*) беспла́тный.

comply *vi*: ~ **with** (*fulfil*) исполня́ть *impf*, испо́лнить *pf*; (*submit to*) подчиня́ться *impf*, подчини́ться *pf* +*dat*.

component *n* дета́ль; *adj* составно́й.

compose *vt* (*music etc.*) сочиня́ть *impf*, сочини́ть *pf*; (*draft; constitute*) составля́ть *impf*, соста́вить *pf*. **composed** *adj* споко́йный; **be** ~ **of** состоя́ть *impf* из+*gen*. **composer** *n* компози́тор. **composition** *n* сочине́ние; (*make-up*) соста́в.

compost *n* компо́ст.

composure *n* самооблада́ние.

compound[1] *n* (*chem*) соедине́ние; *adj* сло́жный.

compound[2] *n* (*enclosure*) огоро́женное ме́сто.

comprehend *vt* понима́ть *impf*,

поня́ть *pf*. **comprehensible** *adj* поня́тный. **comprehension** *n* понима́ние. **comprehensive** *adj* всеобъе́млющий; ~ **school** общеобразова́тельная шко́ла.

compress *vt* сжима́ть *impf*, сжать *pf*. **compressed** *adj* сжа́тый.

comprise *vt* состоя́ть *impf* из+*gen*.

compromise *n* компроми́сс; *vt* компромети́ровать *impf*, с~ *pf*; *vi* идти́ *impf*, пойти́ *pf* на компроми́сс.

compulsion *n* принужде́ние. **compulsory** *adj* обяза́тельный.

compunction *n* угрызе́ние со́вести.

computer *n* компью́тер; ~ **game** компью́терная игра́; ~ **science** электро́нно-вычисли́тельная нау́ка.

comrade *n* това́рищ. **comradeship** *n* това́рищество.

con[1] *see* **pro**[1]

con[2] *vt* надува́ть *impf*, наду́ть *pf*.

concave *adj* во́гнутый.

conceal *vt* скрыва́ть *impf*, скрыть *pf*.

concede *vt* уступа́ть *impf*, уступи́ть *pf*; (*admit*) признава́ть *impf*, призна́ть *pf*; (*goal*) пропуска́ть *impf*, пропусти́ть *pf*.

conceit *n* самомне́ние. **conceited** *adj* самовлюблённый.

conceivable *adj* мы́слимый. **conceive** *vt* (*plan, imagine*) заду́мывать *impf*, заду́мать *pf*; (*biol*) зачина́ть *impf* зача́ть *pf*; *vi* забере́менеть *pf*.

concentrate *vt* & *i* сосредото́чивать(ся) *impf*, сосредото́чить(ся) *pf* (**on** на+*prep*); *vt* (*also chem*) концентри́ровать *impf*, с~ *pf*. **concentration** *n* сосредото́ченность, концентра́ция.

concept *n* поня́тие. **conception** *n* поня́тие; (*biol*) зача́тие.

concern *n* (*worry*) забо́та; (*comm*) предприя́тие; *vt* каса́ться *impf* +*gen*; ~ **o.s. with** занима́ться *impf*, заня́ться *pf* +*instr*. **concerned** *adj* озабо́ченный; **as far as I'm** ~ что каса́ется меня́. **concerning** *prep* относи́тельно+*gen*.

concert *n* конце́рт. **concerted** *adj* согласо́ванный.

concertina *n* гармо́ника.

concession *n* усту́пка; (*econ*) конце́ссия. **concessionary** *adj* концессио́нный.

conciliation *n* примире́ние. **conciliatory** *adj* примири́тельный.

concise *adj* кра́ткий. **conciseness** *n* кра́ткость.

conclude *vt* заключа́ть *impf*, заключи́ть *pf*. **concluding** *adj* заключи́тельный. **conclusion** *n* заключе́ние; (*deduction*) вы́вод. **conclusive** *adj* реша́ющий.

concoct *vt* стря́пать *impf*, со~ *pf*. **concoction** *n* стряпня́.

concourse *n* зал.

concrete *n* бето́н; *adj* бето́нный; (*fig*) конкре́тный.

concur *vi* соглаша́ться *impf*, согласи́ться *pf*. **concurrent** *adj* одновре́ме́нный.

concussion *n* сотрясе́ние.

condemn *vt* осужда́ть *impf*, осуди́ть *pf*; (*as unfit for use*) бракова́ть *impf*, за~ *pf*. **condemnation** *n* осужде́ние.

condensation *n* конденса́ция.

condense *vt* (*liquid etc.*) конденси́ровать *impf* & *pf*; (*text etc.*) сокраща́ть *impf*, сократи́ть *pf*. **condensed** *adj* сжа́тый; (*milk*) сгущённый. **condenser** *n* конденса́тор.

condescend *vi* снисходи́ть *impf*, снизойти́ *pf*. **condescending** *adj* снисходи́тельный. **condescension** *n* снисхожде́ние.

condiment *n* припра́ва.

condition *n* усло́вие; (*state*) состоя́ние; *vt* (*determine*) обусло́вливать *impf*, обусло́вить *pf*; (*psych*) приуча́ть *impf*, приучи́ть *pf*. **conditional** *adj* усло́вный.

condolence *n*: *pl* соболе́знование.

condom *n* презервати́в.

condone *vt* закрыва́ть *impf*, закры́ть *pf* глаза́ на+*acc*.

conducive *adj* спосо́бствующий (**to** +*dat*).

conduct *n* (*behaviour*) поведе́ние; *vt* вести́ *impf*, по~, про~ *pf*; (*mus*) дирижи́ровать *impf* +*instr*; (*phys*) проводи́ть *impf*. **conduction** *n* проводи́мость. **conductor** *n* (*bus*) конду́ктор; (*phys*) проводни́к; (*mus*) дирижёр.

conduit *n* трубопрово́д.

cone *n* ко́нус; (*bot*) ши́шка.

confectioner *n* конди́тер; ~'**s** (*shop*) конди́терская *sb*. **confectionery** *n* конди́терские изде́лия *neut pl*.

confederation *n* конфедера́ция.

confer *vt* присужда́ть *impf*, присуди́ть (**on** +*dat*) *pf*; *vi* совеща́ться *impf*. **conference** *n* совеща́ние; конфере́нция.

confess *vt* & *i* (*acknowledge*) признава́ть(ся) *impf*, призна́ть(ся) *pf* (**to** в+*prep*); (*eccl*) испове́довать(ся) *impf* & *pf*. **confession** *n* призна́ние; и́споведь. **confessor** *n* духовни́к.

confidant(e) *n* бли́зкий собесе́дник. **confide** *vt* доверя́ть *impf*, дове́рить *pf*; ~ **in** дели́ться *impf*, по~ *pf* с+*instr*. **confidence** *n* (*trust*) дове́рие; (*certainty*) уве́ренность; (*self-*~) самоуве́ренность. **confident** *adj* уве́ренный. **confidential** *adj* секре́тный.

confine *vt* ограни́чивать *impf*, ограни́чить *pf*; (*shut in*) заключа́ть *impf*, заключи́ть *pf*. **confinement** *n* заключе́ние. **confines** *n pl* преде́лы *m pl*.

confirm *vt* подтвержда́ть *impf*, подтверди́ть *pf*. **confirmation** *n* подтвержде́ние; (*eccl*) конфирма́ция. **confirmed** *adj* закорене́лый.

confiscate *vt* конфискова́ть *impf* & *pf*. **confiscation** *n* конфиска́ция.

conflict *n* конфли́кт; противоре́чие; *vi*: ~ **with** противоре́чить *impf* +*dat*. **conflicting** *adj* противоречи́вый.

conform *vi*: ~ **to** подчиня́ться *impf*, подчини́ться *pf* +*dat*. **conformity** *n* соотве́тствие; (*compliance*) подчине́ние.

confound *vt* сбива́ть *impf*, сбить *pf* с то́лку. **confounded** *adj* прокля́тый.

confront *vt* стоя́ть *impf* лицо́м к лицу́ с+*instr*; ~ (*person*) **with** ста́вить *impf*, по~ *pf* лицо́м к лицу́ с+*instr*. **confrontation** *n* конфронта́ция.

confuse *vt* смуща́ть *impf*, смути́ть *pf*; (*also mix up*) пу́тать *impf*, за~, с~ *pf*. **confusion** *n* смуще́ние; пу́таница.

congeal *vt* густе́ть *impf*, за~ *pf*; (*blood*) свёртываться *impf*, сверну́ться *pf*.

congenial *adj* прия́тный.

congenital *adj* врождённый.

congested *adj* перепо́лненный. **congestion** *n* (*traffic*) зато́р.

congratulate *vt* поздравля́ть *impf*, поздра́вить *pf* (**on** с+*instr*). **congratulation** *n* поздравле́ние; **~s!** поздравля́ю!

congregate *vi* собира́ться *impf*, собра́ться *pf*. **congregation** *n* (*eccl*) прихожа́не (-н) *pl*.

congress *n* съезд. **Congressman** *n* конгрессме́н.

conic(al) *adj* кони́ческий.

conifer *n* хво́йное де́рево. **coniferous** *adj* хво́йный.

conjecture *n* дога́дка; *vt* гада́ть *impf*.

conjugal *adj* супру́жеский.

conjugate *vt* спряга́ть *impf*, про~ *pf*. **conjugation** *n* спряже́ние.

conjunction *n* (*gram*) сою́з; **in ~ with** совме́стно с+*instr*.

conjure *vi*: **~ up** (*in mind*) вызыва́ть *impf*, вы́звать *pf* в воображе́нии. **conjurer** *n* фо́кусник. **conjuring trick** *n* фо́кус.

connect *vt* & *i* свя́зывать(ся) *impf*, связа́ть(ся) *pf*; соединя́ть(ся) *impf*, соедини́ть(ся) *pf*. **connected** *adj* свя́занный. **connection, -exion** *n* связь; (*rly etc.*) переса́дка.

connivance *n* попусти́тельство. **connive** *vi*: **~ at** попусти́тельствовать *impf* +*dat*.

connoisseur *n* знато́к.

conquer *vt* (*country*) завоёвывать *impf*, завоева́ть *pf*; (*enemy*) побежда́ть *impf*, победи́ть *pf*; (*habit*) преодолева́ть *impf*, преодоле́ть *pf*. **conqueror** *n* завоева́тель *m*. **conquest** *n* завоева́ние.

conscience *n* со́вест. **conscientious** *adj* добросо́вестный. **conscious** *adj* созна́тельный; *predic* в созна́нии; **be ~ of** сознава́ть *impf* +*acc*. **consciousness** *n* созна́ние.

conscript *vt* призыва́ть *impf*, призва́ть *pf* на вое́нную слу́жбу; *n* призывни́к. **conscription** *n* во́инская пови́нность.

consecrate *vt* освяща́ть *impf*, освяти́ть *pf*. **consecration** *n* освяще́ние.

consecutive *adj* после́довательный.

consensus *n* согла́сие.

consent *vi* соглаша́ться *impf*, согласи́ться *pf* (**to** +*inf*, на+*acc*); *n* согла́сие.

consequence *n* после́дствие; **of great ~** большо́го значе́ния; **of some ~** дово́льно ва́жный. **consequent** *adj* вытека́ющий. **consequential** *adj* ва́жный. **consequently** *adv* сле́довательно.

conservation *n* сохране́ние; (*of nature*) охра́на приро́ды. **conservative** *adj* консервати́вный; *n* консерва́тор. **conservatory** *n* оранжере́я. **conserve** *vt* сохраня́ть *impf*, сохрани́ть *pf*.

consider *vt* (*think over*) обду́мывать *impf*, обду́мать *pf*; (*examine*) рассма́тривать *impf*, рассмотре́ть *pf*; (*regard* *as, be of opinion that*) считáть *impf*, счесть *pf* +*instr*, за+*acc*, что; (*take into account*) считáться *impf* c+*instr*. **considerable** *adj* значи́тельный. **considerate** *adj* внимáтельный. **consideration** *n* рассмотрéние; внимáние; (*factor*) фáктор; **take into ~** принимáть *impf*, приня́ть *pf* во внимáние. **considering** *prep* принимáя +*acc* во внимáние.

consign *vt* передавáть *impf*, передáть *pf*. **consignment** *n* (*goods*) пáртия; (*consigning*) отпрáвка товáров.

consist *vi*: **~ of** состоя́ть *impf* из+*gen*. **consistency** *n* послéдовательность; (*density*) консистéнция. **consistent** *adj* послéдовательный; **~ with** совмести́мый с+*instr*.

consolation *n* утешéние. **console**[1] *vt* утешáть *impf*, утéшить *pf*.

console[2] *n* (*control panel*) пульт управлéния.

consolidate *vt* укрепля́ть *impf*, укрепи́ть *pf*. **consolidation** *n* укреплéние.

consonant *n* соглáсный *sb*.

consort *n* супрýг, ~а.

conspicuous *adj* замéтный.

conspiracy *n* зáговор. **conspirator** *n* заговóрщик, -ица. **conspiratorial** *adj* заговóрщицкий. **conspire** *vi* устрáивать *impf*, устрóить *pf* зáговор.

constable *n* полицéйский *sb*.

constancy *n* постоя́нство. **constant** *adj* постоя́нный. **constantly** *adv* постоя́нно.

constellation *n* созвéздие.

consternation *n* тревóга.

constipation *n* запóр.

constituency *n* избирáтельный óкруг. **constituent** *n* (*component*) составнáя часть; (*voter*) избирáтель *m*; *adj* составнóй. **constitute** *vt* составля́ть *impf*, состáвить *pf*. **constitution** *n* (*polit, med*) конститýция; (*composition*) составлéние. **constitutional** *adj* (*polit*) конституциóнный.

constrain *vt* принуждáть *impf*, принýдить *pf*. **constrained** *adj* (*inhibited*) стеснённый. **constraint** *n* принуждéние; (*inhibition*) стеснéние.

constrict *vt* (*compress*) сжимáть *impf*, сжать *pf*; (*narrow*) сýживать *impf*, сýзить *pf*. **constriction** *n* сжáтие; сужéние.

construct *vt* стрóить *impf*, по~ *pf*. **construction** *n* строи́тельство; (*also gram*) констрýкция; (*interpretation*) истолковáние; **~ site** стрóйка. **constructive** *adj* конструкти́вный.

construe *vt* истолкóвывать *impf*, истолковáть *pf*.

consul *n* кóнсул. **consulate** *n* кóнсульство.

consult *vt* совéтоваться *impf*, по~ *pf* c+*instr*. **consultant** *n* консультáнт. **consultation** *n* консультáция.

consume *vt* потребля́ть *impf*, потреби́ть *pf*; (*eat or drink*) съедáть *impf*, съесть *pf*. **consumer** *n* потреби́тель *m*; **~ goods** товáры *m pl* ширóкого потреблéния.

consummate *vt* завершáть *impf*, заверши́ть *pf*; **~ a marriage** осуществля́ть *impf*, осуществи́ть *pf* брáчные отношéния. **consummation** *n* завершéние; (*of marriage*) осуществлéние.

consumption *n* потребле́ние.
contact *n* конта́кт; (*person*) связь; ~ **lens** конта́ктная ли́нза; *vt* свя́зываться *impf*, связа́ться *pf* с+*instr*.
contagious *adj* зара́зный.
contain *vt* содержа́ть *impf*; (*restrain*) сде́рживать *impf*, сдержа́ть *pf*. **container** *n* (*vessel*) сосу́д; (*transport*) конте́йнер.
contaminate *vt* загрязня́ть *impf*, загрязни́ть *pf*. **contamination** *n* загрязне́ние.
contemplate *vt* (*gaze*) созерца́ть *impf*; размышля́ть *impf*; (*consider*) предполага́ть *impf*, предположи́ть *pf*. **contemplation** *n* созерца́ние; размышле́ние. **contemplative** *adj* созерца́тельный.
contemporary *n* совреме́нник; *adj* совреме́нный.
contempt *n* презре́ние; ~ **of court** неуваже́ние к суду́; **hold in** ~ презира́ть *impf*. **contemptible** *adj* презре́нный. **contemptuous** *adj* презри́тельный.
contend *vi* (*compete*) состяза́ться *impf*; ~ **for** оспа́ривать *impf*; ~ **with** справля́ться *impf*, спра́виться *pf* с+*instr*; *vt* утвержда́ть *impf*. **contender** *n* претенде́нт.
content[1] *n* содержа́ние; *pl* содержи́мое *sb*; **(table of) ~s** содержа́ние.
content[2] *predic* дово́лен (-льна); *vt*: ~ **o.s. with** дово́льствоваться *impf*, у~ *pf* +*instr*. **contented** *adj* дово́льный.
contention *n* (*claim*) утвержде́ние. **contentious** *adj* спо́рный.
contest *n* состяза́ние; *vt* (*dispute*) оспа́ривать *impf*, оспо́рить *pf*. **contestant** *n* уча́стник, -ица, состяза́ния.
context *n* конте́кст.
continent *n* матери́к. **continental** *adj* материко́вый.
contingency *n* возмо́жный слу́чай; ~ **plan** вариа́нт пла́на. **contingent** *adj* случа́йный; *n* континге́нт.
continual *adj* непреста́нный. **continuation** *n* продолже́ние. **continue** *vt & i* продолжа́ть(ся) *impf*, продо́лжить(ся) *pf*. **continuous** *adj* непреры́вный.
contort *vt* искажа́ть *impf*, искази́ть *pf*. **contortion** *n* искаже́ние.
contour *n* ко́нтур; ~ **line** горизонта́ль.
contraband *n* контраба́нда.
contraception *n* предупрежде́ние зача́тия. **contraceptive** *n* противозача́точное сре́дство; *adj* противозача́точный.
contract *n* контра́кт, до́говор; *vi* (*make a* ~) заключа́ть *impf*, заключи́ть *pf* контра́кт; *vt & i* (*shorten, reduce*) сокраща́ть(ся) *impf*, сократи́ть(ся) *pf*; *vt* (*illness*) заболева́ть *impf*, заболе́ть *pf* +*instr*. **contraction** *n* сокраще́ние; *pl* (*med*) схва́тки *f pl*. **contractor** *n* подря́дчик.
contradict *vt* противоре́чить *impf* +*dat*. **contradiction** *n* противоре́чие. **contradictory** *adj* противоречи́вый.
contraflow *n* встре́чное движе́ние.
contralto *n* контра́льто (*voice*) *neut* & (*person*) *f indecl*.
contraption *n* приспособле́ние.
contrary *adj* (*opposite*) про-

тивополо́жный; (*perverse*) капри́зный; ~ **to** вопреки́ +*dat*; *n*: **on the** ~ наоборо́т. **contrast** *n* контра́ст, противополо́жность; *vt* противопоставля́ть *impf*, противопоста́вить *pf* (**with** +*dat*); *vi* контрасти́ровать *impf*.
contravene *vt* наруша́ть *impf*, нару́шить *pf*. **contravention** *n* наруше́ние.
contribute *vt* (*to fund etc.*) же́ртвовать *impf*, по~ *pf* (**to** в+*acc*); ~ **to** (*further*) соде́йствовать *impf* & *pf*, по~ *pf* +*dat*; (*write for*) сотру́дничать *impf* в+*prep*. **contribution** *n* (*money*) поже́ртвование; (*fig*) вклад. **contributor** *n* (*donor*) же́ртвователь *m*; (*writer*) сотру́дник.
contrite *adj* ка́ющийся.
contrivance *n* приспособле́ние. **contrive** *vt* ухитря́ться *impf*, ухитри́ться *pf* +*inf*.
control *n* (*mastery*) контро́ль *m*; (*operation*) управле́ние; *pl* управле́ния *pl*; *vt* (*dominate*; *verify*) контроли́ровать *impf*, про~ *pf*; (*regulate*) управля́ть *impf* +*instr*; ~ **o.s.** сде́рживаться *impf*, сдержа́ться *pf*.
controversial *adj* спо́рный. **controversy** *n* спор.
convalesce *vi* выздора́вливать *impf*. **convalescence** *n* выздоровле́ние.
convection *n* конве́кция. **convector** *n* конве́ктор.
convene *vt* созыва́ть *impf*, созва́ть *pf*.
convenience *n* удо́бство; (*public* ~) убо́рная *sb*. **convenient** *adj* удо́бный.
convent *n* же́нский монасты́рь *m*.
convention *n* (*assembly*) съезд; (*agreement*) конве́нция; (*custom*) обы́чай; (*conventionality*) усло́вность. **conventional** *adj* общепри́нятый; (*also mil*) обы́чный.
converge *vi* сходи́ться *impf*, сойти́сь *pf*. **convergence** *n* сходи́мость.
conversant *predic*: ~ **with** знако́м с+*instr*.
conversation *n* разгово́р. **conversational** *adj* разгово́рный. **converse**[1] *vi* разгова́ривать *impf*.
converse[2] *n* обра́тное *sb*. **conversely** *adv* наоборо́т. **conversion** *n* (*change*) превраще́ние; (*of faith*) обраще́ние; (*of building*) перестро́йка. **convert** *vt* (*change*) превраща́ть *impf*, преврати́ть *pf* (**into** в+*acc*); (*to faith*) обраща́ть *impf*, обрати́ть *pf* (**to** в+*acc*); (*a building*) перестра́ивать *impf*, перестро́ить *pf*. **convertible** *adj* обрати́мый; *n* автомоби́ль *m* со снима́ющейся кры́шей.
convex *adj* вы́пуклый.
convey *vt* (*transport*) перевози́ть *impf*, перевезти́ *pf*; (*communicate*) передава́ть *impf*, переда́ть *pf*. **conveyance** *n* перево́зка; переда́ча. **conveyancing** *n* нотариа́льная переда́ча. **conveyor belt** *n* транспортёрная ле́нта.
convict *n* осуждённый *sb*; *vt* осужда́ть *impf*, осуди́ть *pf*. **conviction** *n* (*law*) осужде́ние; (*belief*) убежде́ние. **convince** *vt* убежда́ть *impf*, убеди́ть *pf*. **convincing** *adj* убеди́тельный.
convivial *adj* весёлый.

convoluted *adj* изви́листый; (*fig*) запу́танный. **convoy** *n* конво́й.

convulse *vt*: **be ~d with** содрога́ться *impf*, содрогну́ться *pf* от+*gen*. **convulsion** *n* (*med*) конву́льсия.

cook *n* куха́рка, по́вар; *vt* гото́вить *impf*; *vi* вари́ться *impf*; с~ *pf*. **cooker** *n* плита́, печь. **cookery** *n* кулина́рия.

cool *adj* прохла́дный; (*calm*) хладнокро́вный; (*unfriendly*) холо́дный; *vt* охлажда́ть *impf*, охлади́ть *pf*; **~ down, off** остыва́ть *impf*, осты́(ну)ть *pf*. **coolness** *n* прохла́да; (*calm*) хладнокро́вие; (*manner*) холодо́к.

coop *n* куря́тник; *vt*: **~ up** держа́ть *impf* взаперти́.

cooperate *vi* сотру́дничать *impf*. **cooperation** *n* сотру́дничество. **cooperative** *n* кооперати́в; *adj* кооперати́вный; (*helpful*) услу́жливый.

co-opt *vt* коопти́ровать *impf* & *pf*.

coordinate *vt* координи́ровать *impf* & *pf*; *n* координа́та. **coordination** *n* координа́ция.

cope *vi*: **~ with** справля́ться *impf*, спра́виться *pf* с+*instr*.

copious *adj* оби́льный.

copper *n* (*metal*) медь; *adj* ме́дный.

coppice, copse *n* ро́щица.

copulate *vi* совокупля́ться *impf*, совокупи́ться *pf*.

copy *n* ко́пия; (*book*) экземпля́р; *vt* (*reproduce*) копи́ровать *impf*, с~ *pf*; (*transcribe*) переписывать *impf*, переписа́ть *pf*; (*imitate*) подража́ть *impf* +*dat*. **copyright** *n* а́вторское пра́во.

coral *n* кора́лл.

cord *n* (*string*) верёвка; (*electr*) шнур.

cordial *adj* серде́чный.

corduroy *n* ру́бчатый вельве́т.

core *n* сердцеви́на; (*fig*) суть.

cork *n* (*material*; *stopper*) про́бка; (*float*) поплаво́к. **corkscrew** *n* што́пор.

corn[1] *n* зерно́; (*wheat*) пшени́ца; (*maize*) кукуру́за. **cornflakes** *n pl* кукуру́зные хло́пья (-пьев) *pl*. **cornflour** *n* кукуру́зная мука́. **corny** *adj* (*coll*) бана́льный.

corn[2] *n* (*med*) мозо́ль.

cornea *n* рогова́я оболо́чка.

corner *n* у́гол; **~-stone** *n* краеуго́льный ка́мень *m*; *vt* загоня́ть *impf*, загна́ть *pf* в у́гол.

cornet *n* (*mus*) корне́т; (*ice-cream*) рожо́к.

cornice *n* карни́з.

coronary (thrombosis) *n* коронаротромбо́з. **coronation** *n* корона́ция. **coroner** *n* ме́дик суде́бной эксперти́зы.

corporal[1] *n* капра́л.

corporal[2] *adj* теле́сный; **~ punishment** теле́сное наказа́ние.

corporate *adj* корпорати́вный. **corporation** *n* корпора́ция.

corps *n* ко́рпус.

corpse *n* труп.

corpulent *adj* ту́чный.

corpuscle *n* кровяно́й ша́рик.

correct *adj* пра́вильный; (*conduct*) корре́ктный; *vt* исправля́ть *impf*, испра́вить *pf*. **correction** *n* исправле́ние.

correlation *n* соотноше́ние.

correspond *vi* соотве́тствовать *impf* (**to, with** +*dat*); (*by letter*) перепи́сываться *impf*.

correspondence *n* соотве́тствие; (*letters*) корреспонде́нция. **correspondent** *n* корреспонде́нт. **corresponding** *adj* соотве́тствующий (**to** +*dat*).
corridor *n* коридо́р.
corroborate *vt* подтвержда́ть *impf*, подтверди́ть *pf*.
corrode *vt* разъеда́ть *impf*, разъе́сть *pf*. **corrosion** *n* корро́зия. **corrosive** *adj* е́дкий.
corrugated iron *n* рифлёное желе́зо.
corrupt *adj* (*person*) развращённый; (*government*) прода́жный; *vt* развраща́ть *impf*, разврати́ть *pf*. **corruption** *n* развраще́ние; корру́пция.
corset *n* корсе́т.
cortège *n* корте́ж.
cortex *n* кора́.
corundum *n* кору́нд.
cosmetic *adj* космети́ческий. **cosmetics** *n pl* косме́тика.
cosmic *adj* косми́ческий. **cosmonaut** *n* космона́вт.
cosmopolitan *adj* космополити́ческий.
cosmos *n* ко́смос.
Cossack *n* каза́к, -а́чка.
cosset *vt* не́жить *impf*.
cost *n* сто́имость, цена́; *vt* сто́ить *impf*.
costly *adj* дорого́й.
costume *n* костю́м.
cosy *adj* ую́тный.
cot *n* де́тская крова́тка.
cottage *n* котте́дж; ~ **cheese** творо́г.
cotton *n* хло́пок; (*cloth*) хлопчатобума́жная ткань; (*thread*) ни́тка; ~ **wool** ва́та; *adj* хло́пковый; хлопчатобума́жный.
couch *n* дива́н.
couchette *n* спа́льное ме́сто.
cough *n* ка́шель *m*; *vi* ка́шлять *impf*.
council *n* сове́т; ~ **tax** ме́стный нало́г; ~ **house** жильё из обще́ственного фо́нда. **councillor** *n* член сове́та.
counsel *n* (*advice*) сове́т; (*lawyer*) адвока́т; *vt* сове́товать *impf*, по~ *pf* +*dat*.
count[1] *vt* счита́ть *impf*, со~, сче́сть *pf*; ~ **on** рассчи́тывать *impf* на+*acc*; *n* счёт. **countdown** *n* отсчёт вре́мени.
count[2] *n* (*title*) граф.
countenance *n* лицо́; *vt* одобря́ть *impf*, одо́брить *pf*.
counter *n* прила́вок; (*token*) фи́шка; *adv*: **run** ~ **to** идти́ *impf* вразре́з с+*instr*; *vt* пари́ровать *impf*, от~ *pf*. **counteract** *vt* противоде́йствовать *impf* +*dat*. **counterbalance** *n* противове́с; *vt* уравнове́шивать *impf*, уравнове́сить *pf*. **counterfeit** *adj* подде́льный. **counterpart** *n* соотве́тственная часть. **counterpoint** *n* контрапу́нкт. **counter-revolutionary** *n* контрреволюционе́р; *adj* контрреволюцио́нный. **countersign** *vt* ста́вить *impf*, по~ *pf* втору́ю по́дпись на+*prep*.
countess *n* графи́ня.
countless *adj* бесчи́сленный.
country *n* (*nation*) страна́; (*native land*) ро́дина; (*rural areas*) дере́вня; *adj* дереве́нский, се́льский. **countryman** *n* (*compatriot*) сооте́чественник; се́льский жи́тель *m*. **countryside** *n* приро́дный ландша́фт.
county *n* гра́фство.
coup *n* (*polit*) переворо́т.

couple *n* пáра; (*a few*) нéсколько *+gen*; *vt* сцеплять *impf*, сцепи́ть *pf*.
coupon *n* купóн; талóн; вáучер.
courage *n* хрáбрость. **courageous** *adj* хрáбрый.
courier *n* (*messenger*) курьéр; (*guide*) гид.
course *n* курс; (*process*) ход, течéние; (*of meal*) блю́до; **of ~** конéчно.
court *n* двор; (*sport*) корт, площáдка; (*law*) суд; **~ martial** воéнный суд; *vt* ухáживать *impf* за*+instr*. **courteous** *adj* вéжливый. **courtesy** *n* вéжливость. **courtier** *n* придвóрный *sb*. **courtyard** *n* двор.
cousin *n* двою́родный брат, -ная сестрá.
cove *n* бу́хточка.
covenant *n* договóр.
cover *n* (*covering*; *lid*) покры́шка; (*shelter*) укры́тие; (*chair ~*; *soft case*) чехóл; (*bed*) покрывáло; (*book*) переплёт, облóжка; **under separate ~** в отдéльном конвéрте; *vt* покрывáть *impf*, покры́ть *pf*; (*hide*, *protect*) закрывáть *impf*, закры́ть *pf*. **coverage** *n* освещéние. **covert** *adj* скры́тый.
covet *vt* пожелáть *pf +gen*.
cow[1] *n* корóва. **cowboy** *n* ковбóй. **cowshed** *n* хлев.
cow[2] *vt* запу́гивать *impf*, запугáть *pf*.
coward *n* трус. **cowardice** *n* тру́сость. **cowardly** *adj* трусли́вый.
cower *vi* съёживаться *impf*, съёжиться *pf*.
cox(swain) *n* рулевóй *m*.
coy *adj* жемáнно стыдли́вый.
crab *n* краб.
crack *n* (*in cup*, *ice*) трéщина; (*in wall*) щель; (*noise*) треск; *adj* первоклáссный; *vt* (*break*) колóть *impf*, рас~ *pf*; (*china*) дéлать *impf*, с~ *pf* трéщину в*+acc*; *vi* трéснуть *pf*. **crackle** *vi* потрéскивать *impf*.
cradle *n* колыбéль.
craft *n* (*trade*) ремеслó; (*boat*) су́дно. **craftiness** *n* хи́трость. **craftsman** *n* ремéсленник. **crafty** *adj* хи́трый.
crag *n* утёс. **craggy** *adj* скали́стый.
cram *vt* (*fill*) набивáть *impf*, наби́ть *pf*; (*stuff in*) впи́хивать *impf*, впихну́ть *pf*; *vi* (*study*) зубри́ть *impf*.
cramp[1] *n* (*med*) су́дорога.
cramp[2] *vt* стеснять *impf*, стесни́ть *pf*. **cramped** *adj* тéсный.
cranberry *n* клю́ква.
crane *n* (*bird*) журáвль *m*; (*machine*) кран; *vt* (*one's neck*) вытя́гивать *impf*, вы́тянуть *pf* (шéю).
crank[1] *n* заводнáя ру́чка; **~-shaft** колéнчатый вал; *vt* заводи́ть *impf*, завести́ *pf*.
crank[2] *n* (*eccentric*) чудáк. **cranky** *adj* чудáческий.
cranny *n* щель.
crash *n* (*noise*) грóхот, треск; (*accident*) авáрия; (*financial*) крах; **~ course** ускóренный курс; **~ helmet** защи́тный шлем; **~ landing** авари́йная посáдка; *vi* (**~ *into***) врезáться *impf*, врéзаться *pf* в*+acc*; (*aeron*) разбивáться *impf*, разби́ться *pf*; (*fall with ~*) грóхнуться *pf*; *vt* (*bang down*) грóхнуть *pf*.
crass *adj* гру́бый.
crate *n* я́щик.

crater *n* кра́тер.
crave *vi*: ~ **for** жа́ждать *impf* +*gen*. **craving** *n* стра́стное жела́ние.
crawl *vi* по́лзать *indet*, ползти́ *det*; ~ **with** кише́ть+*instr*; *n* (*sport*) кроль *m*.
crayon *n* цветно́й каранда́ш.
craze *n* ма́ния. **crazy** *adj* поме́шанный (**about** на+*prep*).
creak *n* скрип; *vi* скрипе́ть *impf*.
cream *n* сли́вки (-вок) *pl*; (*cosmetic*; *cul*) крем; ~ **cheese** сли́вочный сыр; **soured** ~ смета́на; *vt* сбива́ть *impf*, сбить *pf*; *adj* (*of cream*) сли́вочный; (*colour*) кре́мовый. **creamy** *adj* сли́вочный, кре́мовый.
crease *n* скла́дка; *vt* мять *impf*, из~, с~ *pf*. **creased** *adj* мя́тый.
create *vt* создава́ть *impf*, созда́ть *pf*. **creation** *n* созда́ние. **creative** *adj* тво́рческий. **creator** *n* созда́тель *m*.
creature *n* созда́ние.
crêche *n* (де́тские) я́сли (-лей) *pl*.
credence *n* ве́ра; **give** ~ ве́рить *impf* (**to** +*dat*). **credentials** *n pl* удостовере́ние; (*diplomacy*) вери́тельные гра́моты *f pl*. **credibility** *n* правдоподо́бие; (*of person*) спосо́бность вызыва́ть дове́рие. **credible** *adj* (*of thing*) правдоподо́бный; (*of person*) заслу́живающий дове́рия.
credit *n* дове́рие; (*comm*) креди́т; (*honour*) честь; **give** ~ кредитова́ть *impf* & *pf* +*acc*; отдава́ть *impf*, отда́ть *pf* до́лжное+*dat*; ~ **card** креди́тная ка́рточка; *vt*: ~ **with** припи́сывать *impf*, приписа́ть *pf* +*dat*. **creditable** *adj* похва́льный. **creditor** *n* кредито́р.
credulity *n* легкове́рие. **credulous** *adj* легкове́рный.
creed *n* убежде́ния *neut pl*; (*eccl*) вероисповеда́ние.
creep *vi* по́лзать *indet*, ползти́ *det*. **creeper** *n* (*plant*) ползу́чее расте́ние.
cremate *vt* креми́ровать *impf* & *pf*. **cremation** *n* крема́ция. **crematorium** *n* кремато́рий.
crêpe *n* креп.
crescendo *adv*, *adj*, & *n* креще́ндо *indecl*.
crescent *n* полуме́сяц.
crest *n* гре́бень *m*; (*heraldry*) герб.
crevasse, **crevice** *n* расще́лина, рассе́лина.
crew *n* брига́да; (*of ship*, *plane*) экипа́ж.
crib *n* (*bed*) де́тская крова́тка; *vi* спи́сывать *impf*, списа́ть *pf*.
crick *n* растяже́ние мышц.
cricket[1] *n* (*insect*) сверчо́к.
cricket[2] *n* (*sport*) кри́кет; ~ **bat** бита́.
crime *n* преступле́ние.
Crimea *n* Крым. **Crimean** *adj* кры́мский.
criminal *n* престу́пник; *adj* престу́пный; (*of crime*) уголо́вный.
crimson *adj* мали́новый.
cringe *vi* (*cower*) съёживаться *impf*, съёжиться *pf*.
crinkle *n* морщи́на; *vt* & *i* мо́рщить(ся) *impf*, на~, с~ *pf*.
cripple *n* кале́ка *m* & *f*; *vt* кале́чить *impf*, ис~ *pf*; (*fig*) расша́тывать *impf*, расшата́ть *pf*.

crisis *n* кри́зис.
crisp *adj* (*brittle*) хрустя́щий; (*fresh*) све́жий. **crisps** *n pl* хрустя́щий карто́фель *m*.
criss-cross *adv* крест-на́крест.
criterion *n* крите́рий.
critic *n* кри́тик. **critical** *adj* крити́ческий. **critically** *adv* (*ill*) тяжело́. **criticism** *n* кри́тика. **criticize** *vt* критикова́ть *impf*. **critique** *n* кри́тика.
croak *vi* ква́кать *impf*, ква́кнуть *pf*; хрипе́ть *impf*.
Croat *n* хорва́т, ~ка. **Croatia** *n* Хорва́тия. **Croatian** *adj* хорва́тский.
crochet *n* вяза́ние крючко́м; *vt* вяза́ть *impf*, с~ *pf* (крючко́м).
crockery *n* посу́да.
crocodile *n* крокоди́л.
crocus *n* кро́кус.
crony *n* закады́чный друг.
crook *n* (*staff*) по́сох; (*swindler*) моше́нник. **crooked** *adj* криво́й; (*dishonest*) нече́стный.
crop *n* (*yield*) урожа́й; *pl* культу́ры *f pl*; (*bird's*) зоб; *vt* (*cut*) подстрига́ть *impf*, подстри́чь *pf*; ~ **up** возника́ть *impf*, возни́кнуть *pf*.
croquet *n* кроке́т.
cross *n* крест; (*biol*) по́месь; *adj* (*angry*) злой; *vt* (*on foot*) переходи́ть *impf*, перейти́ *pf* (че́рез) +*acc*; (*by transport*) переезжа́ть *impf*, перее́хать *pf* (че́рез) +*acc*; (*biol*) скре́щивать *impf*, скрести́ть *pf*; ~ **off, out** вычёркивать *impf*, вы́черкнуть *pf*; ~ **o.s.** креститься *impf*, пере~ *pf*; ~ **over** переходи́ть *impf*, перейти́ *pf* (че́рез) +*acc*. ~**bar** попере́чина. ~**-breed** по́месь; ~**-country race** кросс; ~**-examination** перекрёстный допро́с; ~**-examine,** ~**-question** подверга́ть *impf*, подве́ргнуть *pf* перекрёстному допро́су; ~**-eyed** косогла́зый; ~**-legged: sit** ~ сиде́ть *impf* по-туре́цки; ~**-reference** перекрёстная ссы́лка; ~**road(s)** перекрёсток; ~**-section** перекрёстное сече́ние; ~**word (puzzle)** кроссво́рд. **crossing** *n* (*intersection*) перекрёсток; (*foot*) перехо́д; (*transport*; *rly*) перее́зд.
crotch *n* (*anat*) проме́жность.
crotchet *n* (*mus*) четвертна́я но́та.
crotchety *adj* раздражи́тельный.
crouch *vi* приседа́ть *impf*, присе́сть *pf*.
crow *n* воро́на; **as the** ~ **flies** по прямо́й ли́нии; *vi* кукаре́кать *impf*. **crowbar** *n* лом.
crowd *n* толпа́; *vi* тесни́ться *impf*, с~ *pf*; ~ **into** вти́скиваться *impf*, вти́снуться *pf*. **crowded** *adj* перепо́лненный.
crown *n* коро́на; (*tooth*) коро́нка; (*head*) те́ма; (*hat*) тулья́; *vt* коронова́ть *impf* & *pf*.
crucial *adj* (*important*) о́чень ва́жный; (*decisive*) реша́ющий; (*critical*) крити́ческий.
crucifix, crucifixion *n* распя́тие. **crucify** *vt* распина́ть *impf*, распя́ть *pf*.
crude *adj* (*rude*) гру́бый; (*raw*) сыро́й. **crudity** *n* гру́бость.
cruel *adj* жесто́кий. **cruelty** *n* жесто́кость.
cruise *n* круи́з; *vi* крейси́ровать *impf*. **cruiser** *n* кре́йсер.
crumb *n* кро́шка.
crumble *vt* кроши́ть *impf*, рас~ *pf*; *vi* обва́ливаться *impf*, обвали́ться *pf*. **crumbly** *adj* рассы́пчатый.

crumple *vt* мять *impf*, с~ *pf*; (*intentionally*) ко́мкать *impf*, с~ *pf*.

crunch *n* (*fig*) реша́ющий моме́нт; *vt* грызть *impf*, раз~ *pf*; *vi* хрусте́ть *impf*, хру́стнуть *pf*.

crusade *n* кресто́вый похо́д; (*fig*) кампа́ния. **crusader** *n* крестоно́сец; (*fig*) боре́ц (**for** за+*acc*).

crush *n* да́вка; (*infatuation*) си́льное увлече́ние; *vt* дави́ть *impf*, за~, раз~ *pf*; (*crease*) мять *impf*, с~ *pf*; (*fig*) подавля́ть *impf*, подави́ть *pf*.

crust *n* (*of earth*) кора́; (*bread etc.*) ко́рка.

crutch *n* косты́ль *m*.

crux *n*: ~ **of the matter** суть де́ла.

cry *n* крик; **a far ~ from** далеко́ от+*gen*; *vi* (*weep*) пла́кать *impf*; (*shout*) крича́ть *impf*, кри́кнуть *pf*.

crypt *n* склеп. **cryptic** *adj* зага́дочный.

crystal *n* криста́лл; (*glass*) хруста́ль *m*. **crystallize** *vt* & *i* кристаллизова́ть(ся) *impf* & *pf*.

cub *n* детёныш; **bear** ~ медвежо́нок; **fox** ~ лисёнок; **lion** ~ львёнок; **wolf** ~ волчо́нок.

cube *n* куб. **cubic** *adj* куби́ческий.

cubicle *n* каби́на.

cuckoo *n* куку́шка.

cucumber *n* огуре́ц.

cuddle *vt* обнима́ть *impf*, обня́ть *pf*; *vi* обнима́ться *impf*, обня́ться *pf*; ~ **up** прижима́ться *impf*, прижа́ться *pf* (**to** к+ *dat*).

cudgel *n* дуби́нка.

cue[1] *n* (*theat*) ре́плика.

cue[2] *n* (*billiards*) кий.

cuff[1] *n* манже́та; **off the ~** экспро́мтом; **~-link** за́понка.

cuff[2] *vt* (*hit*) шлёпать *impf*, шлёпнуть *pf*.

cul-de-sac *n* тупи́к.

culinary *adj* кулина́рный.

cull *vt* (*select*) отбира́ть *impf*, отобра́ть *pf*; (*slaughter*) бить *impf*.

culminate *vi* конча́ться *impf*, ко́нчиться *pf* (**in** +*instr*). **culmination** *n* кульминацио́нный пункт.

culpability *n* вино́вность. **culpable** *adj* вино́вный. **culprit** *n* вино́вник.

cult *n* культ.

cultivate *vt* (*land*) обраба́тывать *impf*, обрабо́тать *pf*; (*crops*) выра́щивать *impf*; вы́растить *impf*; (*develop*) развива́ть *impf*, разви́ть *pf*.

cultural *adj* культу́рный. **culture** *n* культу́ра. **cultured** *adj* культу́рный.

cumbersome *adj* громо́здкий.

cumulative *adj* кумуляти́вный.

cunning *n* хи́трость; *adj* хи́трый.

cup *n* ча́шка; (*prize*) ку́бок.

cupboard *n* шкаф.

cupola *n* ку́пол.

curable *adj* излечи́мый.

curative *adj* целе́бный.

curator храни́тель *m*.

curb *vt* обу́здывать *impf*, обузда́ть *pf*.

curd (*cheese*) *n* творо́г. **curdle** *vt* & *i* свёртывать(ся) *impf*, сверну́ть(ся) *pf*.

cure *n* сре́дство (**for** про́тив+*gen*); *vt* выле́чивать *impf*, вы́лечить *pf*; (*smoke*) копти́ть *impf*, за~ *pf*; (*salt*) соли́ть *impf*, по~ *pf*.

curfew *n* коменда́нтский час.

curiosity *n* любопы́тство.

curious *adj* любопы́тный.
curl *n* ло́кон; *vt* завива́ть *impf*, зави́ть *pf*; ~ **up** свёртываться *impf*, сверну́ться *pf*. **curly** *adj* кудря́вый.
currants *n pl* (*dried*) изю́м (*collect*).
currency *n* валю́та; (*prevalence*) хожде́ние. **current** *adj* теку́щий; *n* тече́ние; (*air*) струя́; (*water*; *electr*) ток.
curriculum *n* курс обуче́ния; ~ **vitae** автобиогра́фия.
curry¹ *n* кэ́рри *neut indecl*.
curry² *vt*: ~ **favour with** заи́скивать *impf* пе́ред+*instr*.
curse *n* прокля́тие; (*oath*) руга́тельство; *vt* проклина́ть *impf*, прокля́сть *pf*; *vi* руга́ться *impf*, по~ *pf*.
cursor *n* (*comput*) курсо́р.
cursory *adj* бе́глый.
curt *adj* ре́зкий.
curtail *vt* сокраща́ть *impf*, сократи́ть *pf*.
curtain *n* занаве́ска.
curts(e)y *n* ревера́нс; *vi* де́лать *impf*, с~ *pf* ревера́нс.
curve *n* изги́б; (*line*) крива́я *sb*; *vi* изгиба́ться *impf*, изогну́ться *pf*.
cushion *n* поду́шка; *vt* смягча́ть *impf*, смягчи́ть *pf*.
custard *n* сла́дкий заварно́й крем.
custodian *n* храни́тель *m*. **custody** *n* опе́ка; (*of police*) аре́ст; **to take into** ~ арестова́ть *pf*.
custom *n* обы́чай; (*comm*) клиенту́ра; *pl* (*duty*) тамо́женные по́шлины *f pl*; **go through** ~**s** проходи́ть *impf*, пройти́ *pf* тамо́женный осмо́тр; ~**-house** тамо́жня; ~ **officer** тамо́женник. **customary** *adj* обы́чный.
customer *n* клие́нт; покупа́тель *m*.
cut *vt* ре́зать *impf*, по~ *pf*; (*hair*) стричь *impf*, о~ *pf*; (*mow*) коси́ть *impf*, с~ *pf*; (*price*) снижа́ть *impf*, сни́зить *pf*; (*cards*) снима́ть *impf*, снять *pf* коло́ду; ~ **back** (*prune*) подреза́ть *impf*, подре́зать *pf*; (*reduce*) сокраща́ть *impf*, сократи́ть *pf*; ~ **down** сруба́ть *impf*, сруби́ть *pf*; ~ **off** отреза́ть *impf*, отре́зать *pf*; (*interrupt*) прерыва́ть *impf*, прерва́ть *pf*; (*disconnect*) отключа́ть *impf*, отключи́ть *pf*; ~ **out** выре́зывать *impf*, вы́резать *pf*; ~ **out for** со́зданный для+*gen*; ~ **up** разреза́ть *impf*, разре́зать *pf*; *n* (*gash*) поре́з; (*clothes*) покро́й; (*reduction*) сниже́ние; ~ **glass** хруста́ль *m*.
cute *adj* симпати́чный.
cutlery *n* ножи́, ви́лки и ло́жки *pl*.
cutlet *n* отбивна́я котле́та.
cutting *n* (*press*) вы́резка; (*plant*) черено́к; *adj* ре́зкий.
CV *abbr* (*of* **curriculum vitae**) автобиогра́фия.
cycle *n* цикл; (*bicycle*) велосипе́д; *vi* е́здить *impf* на велосипе́де. **cyclic(al)** *adj* цикли́ческий. **cyclist** *n* велосипеди́ст.
cylinder *n* цили́ндр. **cylindrical** *adj* цилиндри́ческий.
cymbals *n pl* таре́лки *f pl*.
cynic *n* ци́ник. **cynical** *adj* цини́чный. **cynicism** *n* цини́зм.
cypress *n* кипари́с.
Cyrillic *n* кири́ллица.
cyst *n* киста́.
Czech *n* чех, че́шка; *adj* че́шский; ~ **Republic** Че́шская Респу́блика.

D

dab *n* мазо́к; *vt* (*eyes etc.*) прикла́дывать *impf* плато́к к+*dat*; ~ **on** накла́дывать *impf*, наложи́ть *pf* мазка́ми.
dabble *vi*: ~ **in** пове́рхностно занима́ться *impf*, заня́ться *pf* +*instr*.
dachshund *n* та́кса.
dad, **daddy** *n* па́па; ~**-long-legs** *n* долгоно́жка.
daffodil *n* жёлтый нарци́сс.
daft *adj* глу́пый.
dagger *n* кинжа́л.
dahlia *n* георги́н.
daily *adv* ежедне́вно; *adj* ежедне́вный; *n* (*charwoman*) приходя́щая убо́рщица; (*newspaper*) ежедне́вная газе́та.
dainty *adj* изя́щный.
dairy *n* маслобо́йня; (*shop*) моло́чная *sb*; *adj* моло́чный.
dais *n* помо́ст.
daisy *n* маргари́тка.
dale *n* доли́на.
dally *vi* (*dawdle*) ме́шкать *impf*; (*toy*) игра́ть *impf* +*instr*; (*flirt*) флиртова́ть *impf*.
dam *n* (*barrier*) плоти́на; *vt* запру́живать *impf*, запруди́ть *pf*.
damage *n* поврежде́ние; *pl* убы́тки *m pl*; *vt* поврежда́ть *impf*, повреди́ть *pf*.
damn *vt* (*curse*) проклина́ть *impf*, прокля́сть *pf*; (*censure*) осужда́ть *impf*, осуди́ть *pf*; *int* чёрт возьми́!; **I don't give a** ~ мне наплева́ть. **damnation** *n* прокля́тие. **damned** *adj* прокля́тый.
damp *n* сы́рость; *adj* сыро́й; *vt* (*also* **dampen**) сма́чивать *impf*, смочи́ть *pf*; (*fig*) охлажда́ть *impf*, охлади́ть *pf*.
dance *vi* танцева́ть *impf*; *n* та́нец; (*party*) танцева́льный ве́чер. **dancer** *n* танцо́р, ~ка; (*ballet*) танцо́вщик, -ица; балери́на.
dandelion *n* одува́нчик.
dandruff *n* пе́рхоть.
Dane *n* датча́нин, -а́нка; **Great** ~ дог. **Danish** *adj* да́тский.
danger *n* опа́сность. **dangerous** *adj* опа́сный.
dangle *vt* &*i* пока́чивать(ся) *impf*.
dank *adj* промо́зглый.
dapper *adj* вы́холенный.
dare *vi* (*have courage*) осме́ливаться *impf*, осме́литься *pf*; (*have impudence*) сметь *impf*, по~ *pf*; *vt* вызыва́ть *impf*, вы́звать *pf*; *n* вы́зов. **daredevil** *n* лиха́ч; *adj* отча́янный. **daring** *n* отва́га; *adj* отча́янный.
dark *adj* тёмный; ~ **blue** тёмно-си́ний; *n* темнота́. **darken** *vt* затемня́ть *impf*, затемни́ть *pf*; *vi* темне́ть *impf*, по~ *pf*. **darkly** *adv* мра́чно. **darkness** *n* темнота́.
darling *n* дорого́й *sb*, ми́лый *sb*; *adj* дорого́й.
darn *vt* што́пать *impf*, за~ *pf*.
dart *n* стрела́; (*for game*) мета́тельная стрела́; (*tuck*) вы́тачка; *vi* бро́ситься *pf*.
dash *n* (*hyphen*) тире́ *neut indecl*; (*admixture*) при́месь; *vt* швыря́ть *impf*, швырну́ть *pf*; *vi* броса́ться *impf*, бро́ситься *pf*. **dashboard** *n* прибо́рная доска́. **dashing** *adj* лихо́й.
data *n pl* да́нные *sb pl*. **database** *n* ба́за да́нных.
date[1] *n* (*fruit*) фи́ник.
date[2] *n* число́, да́та; (*engage-*

ment) свида́ние; **out of ~** устаре́лый; **up to ~** совреме́нный; в ку́рсе де́ла; *vt* дати́ровать *impf* & *pf*; (*go out with*) встреча́ться *impf* с+*instr*; *vi* (*originate*) относи́ться *impf* (**from** к+*instr*).

dative *adj* (*n*) да́тельный (паде́ж).

daub *vt* ма́зать *impf*, на~ *pf* (**with** +*instr*).

daughter *n* дочь; **~-in-law** неве́стка (*in relation to mother*), сноха́ (*in relation to father*).

daunting *adj* угрожа́ющий.

dawdle *vi* ме́шкать *impf*.

dawn *n* рассве́т; (*also fig*) заря́; *vi* (*day*) рассвета́ть *impf*, рассвести́ *pf impers*; **~ (up)on** осеня́ть *impf*, осени́ть *pf*; **it ~ed on me** меня́ осени́ло.

day *n* день *m*; (*24 hours*) су́тки *pl*; *pl* (*period*) пери́од, вре́мя *neut*; **~ after ~** изо дня́ в де́нь; **the ~ after tomorrow** послеза́втра; **the ~ before** накану́не; **the ~ before yesterday** позавчера́; **the other ~** на днях; **by ~** днём; **every other ~** че́рез день; **~ off** выходно́й день *m*; **one ~** одна́жды; **these ~s** в на́ши дни. **daybreak** *n* рассве́т. **day-dreams** *n pl* мечты́ *f pl*. **daylight** *n* дневно́й свет; **in broad ~** средь бе́ла дня́. **daytime** *n*: **in the ~** днём.

daze *n*: **in a ~**, **dazed** *adj* оглушён (-ена́).

dazzle *vt* ослепля́ть *impf*, ослепи́ть *pf*.

deacon *n* дья́кон.

dead *adj* мёртвый; (*animals*) до́хлый; (*plants*) увя́дший; (*numb*) онеме́вший; *n*: **the ~** мёртвые *sb pl*; **at ~ of night** глубо́кой но́чью; *adv* соверше́нно; **~ end** тупи́к; **~ heat** одновре́ме́нный фи́ниш; **~line** преде́льный срок; **~lock** тупи́к.

deaden *vt* заглуша́ть *impf*, заглуши́ть *pf*.

deadly *adj* смерте́льный.

deaf *adj* глухо́й; **~ and dumb** глухонемо́й. **deafen** *vt* оглуша́ть *impf*, оглуши́ть *pf*. **deafness** *n* глухота́.

deal[1] *n*: **a great, good, ~** мно́го (+*gen*); (*with comp*) гора́здо.

deal[2] *n* (*bargain*) сде́лка; (*cards*) сда́ча; *vt* (*cards*) сдава́ть *impf*, сдать *pf*; (*blow*) наноси́ть *impf*, нанести́ *pf*; **~ in** торгова́ть *impf* +*instr*; **~ out** распределя́ть *impf*, распредели́ть *pf*; **~ with** (*take care of*) занима́ться *impf*, заня́ться *pf* +*instr*; (*handle a person*) поступа́ть *impf*, поступи́ть *pf* с+*instr*; (*treat a subject*) рассма́тривать *impf*, рассмотре́ть *pf*; (*cope with*) справля́ться *impf*, спра́виться *pf* с+*instr*. **dealer** *n* торго́вец (**in** +*instr*).

dean *n* дека́н.

dear *adj* дорого́й; (*also n*) ми́лый (*sb*).

dearth *n* недоста́ток.

death *n* смерть; **put to ~** казни́ть *impf* & *pf*; **~bed** *n* сме́ртное ло́же; **~ certificate** свиде́тельство о сме́рти; **~ penalty** сме́ртная казнь. **deathly** *adj* смерте́льный.

debar *vt*: **~ from** не допуска́ть *impf* до+*gen*.

debase *vt* унижа́ть *impf*, уни́зить *pf*; (*coinage*) понижа́ть *impf*, пони́зить *pf* ка́чество +*gen*.

debatable *adj* спо́рный. **debate** *n* пре́ния (-ий) *pl*; *vt* обсужда́ть *impf*, обсуди́ть *pf*. **debauched** *adj* развращённый. **debauchery** *n* развра́т. **debilitate** *vt* ослабля́ть; *impf*, осла́бить *pf*. **debility** *n* сла́бость.
debit *n* де́бет; *vt* дебетова́ть *impf* & *pf*.
debris *n* обло́мки *m pl*.
debt *n* долг. **debtor** *n* должни́к.
début *n* дебю́т; **make one's ~** дебюти́ровать *impf* & *pf*.
decade *n* десятиле́тие.
decadence *n* декаде́нтство. **decadent** *adj* декаде́нтский.
decaffeinated *adj* без кофеи́на.
decant *vt* перелива́ть *impf*, перели́ть *pf*. **decanter** *n* графи́н.
decapitate *vt* обезгла́вливать *impf*, обезла́вить *pf*.
decay *vi* гнить *impf*, с~ *pf*; (*tooth*) разруша́ться *impf*, разру́шиться *pf*; *n* гние́ние; (*tooth*) разруше́ние.
decease *n* кончи́на. **deceased** *adj* поко́йный; *n* поко́йник, -ица.
deceit *n* обма́н. **deceitful** *adj* лжи́вый. **deceive** *vt* обма́нывать *impf*, обману́ть *pf*.
deceleration *n* замедле́ние.
December *n* дека́брь *m*; *adj* дека́брьский.
decency *n* прили́чие. **decent** *adj* прили́чный.
decentralization *n* децентрализа́ция. **decentralize** *vt* децентрализова́ть *impf* & *pf*.
deception *n* обма́н. **deceptive** *adj* обма́нчивый.
decibel *n* децибе́л.
decide *vt* реша́ть *impf*, реши́ть *pf*. **decided** *adj* реши́тельный.
deciduous *adj* листопа́дный.
decimal *n* десяти́чная дробь; *adj* десяти́чный; **~ point** запята́я *sb*.
decimate *vt* (*fig*) коси́ть *impf*, с~ *pf*.
decipher *vt* расшифро́вывать *impf*, расшифрова́ть *pf*.
decision *n* реше́ние. **decisive** *adj* (*firm*) реши́тельный, (*deciding*) реша́ющий.
deck *n* па́луба; (*bus etc.*) эта́ж; **~-chair** *n* шезло́нг; *vt*: **~ out** украша́ть *impf*, укра́сить *pf*.
declaim *vt* деклами́ровать *impf*, про~ *pf*.
declaration *n* объявле́ние; (*document*) деклара́ция. **declare** *vt* (*proclaim*) объявля́ть *impf*, объяви́ть *pf*; (*assert*) заявля́ть *impf*, заяви́ть *pf*.
declension *n* склоне́ние. **decline** *n* упа́док; *vi* приходи́ть *impf*, прийти́ *pf* в упа́док; *vt* отклоня́ть *impf*, отклони́ть *pf*; (*gram*) склоня́ть *impf*, про~ *pf*.
decode *vt* расшифро́вывать *impf*, расшифрова́ть *pf*.
decompose *vi* разлага́ться *impf*, разложи́ться *pf*.
décor *n* эстети́ческое оформле́ние. **decorate** *vt* украша́ть *impf*, укра́сить *pf*; (*room*) ремонти́ровать *impf*, от~ *pf*; (*with medal etc.*) награжда́ть *impf*, награди́ть *pf*. **decoration** *n* украше́ние; (*medal*) о́рден. **decorative** *adj* декорати́вный. **decorator** *n* маля́р.
decorous *adj* прили́чный. **decorum** *n* прили́чие.
decoy *n* (*bait*) прима́нка; *vt* зама́нивать *impf*, замани́ть *pf*.

decrease *vt & i* уменьша́ть(ся) *impf*, уме́ньшить(ся) *pf*; *n* уменьше́ние.
decree *n* ука́з; *vt* постановля́ть *impf*, постанови́ть *pf*.
decrepit *adj* дря́хлый.
dedicate *vt* посвяща́ть *impf*, посвяти́ть *pf*. **dedication** *n* посвяще́ние.
deduce *vt* заключа́ть *impf*, заключи́ть *pf*.
deduct *vt* вычита́ть *impf*, вы́честь *pf*. **deduction** *n* (*subtraction*) вы́чет; (*inference*) вы́вод.
deed *n* посту́пок; (*heroic*) по́двиг; (*law*) акт.
deem *vt* счита́ть *impf*, счесть *pf +acc & instr*.
deep *adj* глубо́кий; (*colour*) тёмный; (*sound*) ни́зкий; ~ **freeze** морози́льник. **deepen** *vt & i* углубля́ть(ся) *impf*, углуби́ть(ся) *pf*.
deer *n* оле́нь *m*.
deface *vt* обезобра́живать *impf*, обезобра́зить *pf*.
defamation *n* диффама́ция. **defamatory** *adj* клеветни́ческий.
default *n* (*failure to pay*) неупла́та; (*failure to appear*) нея́вка; (*comput*) автомати́ческий вы́бор; *vi* не выполня́ть *impf* обяза́тельств.
defeat *n* пораже́ние; *vt* побежда́ть *impf*, победи́ть *pf*. **defeatism** *n* пораже́нчество. **defeatist** *n* пораже́нец; *adj* пораже́нческий.
defecate *vi* испражня́ться *impf*, испражни́ться *pf*.
defect *n* дефе́кт; *vi* перебега́ть *impf*, перебежа́ть *pf*. **defective** *adj* неиспра́вный. **defector** *n* перебе́жчик.
defence *n* защи́та. **defenceless** *adj* беззащи́тный. **defend** *vt* защища́ть *impf*, защити́ть *pf*. **defendant** *n* подсуди́мый *sb*. **defender** *n* защи́тник. **defensive** *adj* оборони́тельный.
defer[1] *vt* (*postpone*) отсро́чивать *impf*, отсро́чить *pf*.
defer[2] *vi*: ~ **to** подчиня́ться *impf +dat*. **deference** *n* уваже́ние. **deferential** *adj* почти́тельный.
defiance *n* неповинове́ние; **in** ~ **of** вопреки́+*dat*. **defiant** *adj* вызыва́ющий.
deficiency *n* недоста́ток. **deficient** *adj* недоста́точный.
deficit *n* дефици́т.
defile *vt* оскверня́ть *impf*, оскверни́ть *pf*.
define *vt* определя́ть *impf*, определи́ть *pf*. **definite** *adj* определённый **definitely** *adv* несомне́нно. **definition** *n* определе́ние. **definitive** *adj* оконча́тельный.
deflate *vt & i* спуска́ть *impf*, спусти́ть *pf*; *vt* (*person*) сбива́ть *impf*, сбить *pf* спесь с+*gen*. **deflation** *n* дефля́ция.
deflect *vt* отклоня́ть *impf*, отклони́ть *pf*.
deforestation *n* обезле́сение.
deformed *adj* уро́дливый. **deformity** *n* уро́дство.
defraud *vt* обма́нывать *impf*, обману́ть *pf*; ~ **of** выма́нивать *impf*, вы́манить *pf +acc* & у+*gen* (*of person*).
defray *vt* опла́чивать *impf*, оплати́ть *pf*.
defrost *vt* размора́живать *impf*, разморо́зить *pf*.
deft *adj* ло́вкий.
defunct *adj* бо́льше не существу́ющий.
defy *vt* (*challenge*) вызыва́ть

impf, вы́звать *pf*; (*disobey*) идти́ *impf*, по~ *pf* про́тив+*acc*; (*fig*) не поддава́ться *impf* +*dat*.

degenerate *vi* вырожда́ться *impf*, вы́родиться *pf*; *adj* вы́родившийся.

degradation *n* униже́ние. **degrade** *vt* унижа́ть *impf*, уни́зить *pf*. **degrading** *adj* унизи́тельный.

degree *n* сте́пень; (*math etc.*) гра́дус; (*univ*) учёная сте́пень.

dehydrate *vt* обезво́живать *impf*, обезво́дить *pf*. **dehydration** *n* обезво́живание.

deign *vi* снисходи́ть *impf*, снизойти́ *pf*.

deity *n* божество́.

dejected *adj* удручённый.

delay *n* заде́ржка; **without** ~ неме́дленно; *vt* заде́рживать *impf*, задержа́ть *pf*.

delegate *n* делега́т; *vt* делеги́ровать *impf* & *pf*. **delegation** *n* делега́ция.

delete *vt* вычёркивать *impf*, вы́черкнуть *pf*.

deliberate *adj* (*intentional*) преднаме́ренный; (*careful*) осторо́жный; *vt* & *i* размышля́ть *impf*, размы́слить *pf* (о+*prep*); (*discuss*) совеща́ться *impf* (о+*prep*). **deliberation** *n* размышле́ние; (*discussion*) совеща́ние.

delicacy *n* (*tact*) делика́тность; (*dainty*) ла́комство. **delicate** *adj* то́нкий; (*tactful, needing tact*) делика́тный; (*health*) боле́зненный.

delicatessen *n* гастроно́м.

delicious *adj* о́чень вку́сный.

delight *n* наслажде́ние; (*delightful thing*) пре́лесть. **delightful** *adj* преле́стный.

delinquency *n* престу́пность.

delinquent *n* правонаруши́тель *m*, ~ница; *adj* вино́вный.

delirious *adj*: **be** ~ бре́дить *impf*. **delirium** *n* бред.

deliver *vt* (*goods*) доставля́ть *impf*, доста́вить *pf*; (*save*) избавля́ть *impf*, изба́вить *pf* (**from** от+*gen*); (*lecture*) прочита́ть *impf*, проче́сть *pf*; (*letters*) разноси́ть *impf*, разнести́ *pf*; (*speech*) произноси́ть *impf*, произнести́ *pf*; (*blow*) наноси́ть *impf*, нанести́ *pf*. **deliverance** *n* избавле́ние. **delivery** *n* доста́вка.

delta *n* де́льта.

delude *vt* вводи́ть *impf*, ввести́ *pf* в заблужде́ние.

deluge *n* (*flood*) пото́п; (*rain*) ли́вень *m*; (*fig*) пото́к.

delusion *n* заблужде́ние; ~**s of grandeur** ма́ния вели́чия.

de luxe *adj* -люкс (*added to noun*).

delve *vi* углубля́ться *impf*, углуби́ться *pf* (**into** в+*acc*).

demand *n* тре́бование; (*econ*) спрос (**for** на+*acc*); *vt* тре́бовать *impf*, по~ *pf* +*gen*. **demanding** *adj* тре́бовательный.

demarcation *n* демарка́ция.

demean *vt*: ~ **o.s.** унижа́ться *impf*, уни́зиться *pf*.

demeanour *n* мане́ра вести́ себя́.

demented *adj* сумасше́дший. **dementia** *n* слабоу́мие.

demise *n* кончи́на.

demobilize *vt* демобилизова́ть *impf* & *pf*.

democracy *n* демокра́тия. **democrat** *n* демокра́т. **democratic** *adj* демократи́ческий. **democratization** *n* демократиза́ция.

demolish *vt* (*destroy*) разруша́ть *impf*, разру́шить *pf*; (*building*) сноси́ть *impf*, снести́ *pf*; (*refute*) опроверга́ть *impf*, опрове́ргнуть *pf*. **demolition** *n* разруше́ние; снос.

demon *n* де́мон.

demonstrable *adj* доказу́емый. **demonstrably** *adv* нагля́дно. **demonstrate** *vt* демонстри́ровать *impf* & *pf*; *vi* уча́ствовать *impf* в демонстра́ции. **demonstration** *n* демонстра́ция. **demonstrative** *adj* экспанси́вный; (*gram*) указа́тельный. **demonstrator** *n* демонстра́тор; (*polit*) демонстра́нт.

demoralize *vt* деморализова́ть *impf* & *pf*.

demote *vt* понижа́ть *impf*, пони́зить *pf* в до́лжности.

demure *adj* скро́мный.

den *n* берло́га.

denial *n* отрица́ние; (*refusal*) отка́з.

denigrate *vt* черни́ть *impf*, о~ *pf*.

denim *adj* джинсо́вый; *n* джинсо́вая ткань.

Denmark *n* Да́ния.

denomination *n* (*money*) досто́инство; (*relig*) вероисповеда́ние. **denominator** *n* знамена́тель *m*.

denote *vt* означа́ть *impf*, озна́чить *pf*.

denounce *vt* (*condemn*) осужда́ть *impf*, осуди́ть *pf*; (*inform on*) доноси́ть *impf*, донести́ *pf* на+*acc*.

dense *adj* густо́й; (*stupid*) тупо́й. **density** *n* пло́тность.

dent *n* вмя́тина; *vt* де́лать *impf*, с~ *pf* вмя́тину в+*prep*.

dental *adj* зубно́й. **dentist** *n* зубно́й врач. **dentures** *n pl* зубно́й проте́з.

denunciation *n* (*condemnation*) осужде́ние; (*informing*) доно́с.

deny *vt* отрица́ть *impf*; (*refuse*) отка́зывать *impf*, отказа́ть *pf* +*dat* (*person*) в+*prep*.

deodorant *n* дезодора́нт.

depart *vi* отбыва́ть *impf*, отбы́ть *pf*; (*deviate*) отклоня́ться *impf*, отклони́ться *pf* (**from** от+*gen*).

department *n* отде́л; (*univ*) ка́федра; ~ **store** универма́г.

departure *n* отбы́тие; (*deviation*) отклоне́ние.

depend *vi* зави́сеть *impf* (**on** от+*gen*); (*rely*) полага́ться *impf*, положи́ться *pf* (**on** на+*acc*). **dependable** *adj* надёжный. **dependant** *n* иждиве́нец. **dependence** *n* зави́симость. **dependent** *adj* зави́симый.

depict *vt* изобража́ть *impf*, изобрази́ть *pf*.

deplete *vt* истоща́ть *impf*, истощи́ть *pf*. **depleted** *adj* истощённый. **depletion** *n* истоще́ние.

deplorable *adj* плаче́вный. **deplore** *vt* сожале́ть *impf* о+*prep*.

deploy *vt* развёртывать *impf*, разверну́ть *pf*. **deployment** *n* развёртывание.

deport *vt* депорти́ровать *impf* & *pf*; высыла́ть *impf*, вы́слать *pf*. **deportation** *n* депорта́ция; вы́сылка.

deportment *n* оса́нка.

depose *vt* сверга́ть *impf*, све́ргнуть *pf*. **deposit** *n* (*econ*) вклад; (*advance*) зада́ток; (*sediment*) оса́док; (*coal etc.*) месторожде́ние; *vt* (*econ*) вноси́ть *impf*, внести́ *pf*.

depot *n* (*transport*) депо́ *neut*

indecl; (*store*) склад.
deprave *vt* развраща́ть *impf*, развратить *pf*. **depraved** *adj* развращённый. **depravity** *n* развра́т.
deprecate *vt* осужда́ть *impf*, осуди́ть *pf*.
depreciate *vt* & *i* (*econ*) обесце́нивать(ся) *impf*, обесце́нить(ся) *pf*. **depreciation** *n* обесце́нение.
depress *vt* (*dispirit*) удруча́ть *impf*, удручи́ть *pf*. **depressed** *adj* удручённый. **depressing** *adj* угнета́ющий. **depression** *n* (*hollow*) впа́дина; (*econ*, *med*, *meteorol*, *etc*.) депре́ссия.
deprivation *n* лише́ние. **deprive** *vt* лиша́ть *impf*, лиши́ть *pf* (**of** +*gen*)
depth *n* глубина́; **in the ~ of winter** в разга́ре зимы́.
deputation *n* депута́ция. **deputize** *vi* замеща́ть *impf*, замести́ть *pf* (**for** +*acc*). **deputy** *n* замести́тель *m*; (*parl*) депута́т.
derail *vt*: **be derailed** сходи́ть *impf*, сойти́ *pf* с ре́льсов. **derailment** *n* сход с ре́льсов.
deranged *adj* сумасше́дший.
derelict *adj* забро́шенный.
deride *vt* высме́ивать *impf*, вы́смеять *pf*. **derision** *n* высме́ивание. **derisive** *adj* (*mocking*) насме́шливый. **derisory** *adj* (*ridiculous*) смехотво́рный.
derivation *n* происхожде́ние. **derivative** *n* произво́дное *sb*; *adj* произво́дный. **derive** *vt* извлека́ть *impf*, извле́чь *pf*; *vi*: **~ from** происходи́ть *impf*, произойти́ *pf* от+*gen*.
derogatory *adj* отрица́тельный.
descend *vi* (& *t*) (*go down*) спуска́ться *impf*, спусти́ться *pf* (с+*gen*); **be descended from** происходи́ть *impf*, произойти́ *pf* из, от, +*gen*. **descendant** *n* пото́мок. **descent** *n* спуск; (*lineage*) происхожде́ние.
describe *vt* опи́сывать *impf*, описа́ть *pf*. **description** *n* описа́ние. **descriptive** *adj* описа́тельный.
desecrate *vt* оскверня́ть *impf*, оскверни́ть *pf*. **desecration** *n* оскверне́ние.
desert[1] *n* (*waste*) пусты́ня.
desert[2] *vt* покида́ть *impf*, поки́нуть *pf*; (*mil*) дезерти́ровать *impf* & *pf*. **deserter** *n* дезерти́р. **desertion** *n* дезерти́рство.
deserts *n pl* заслу́ги *f pl*. **deserve** *vt* заслу́живать *impf*, заслужи́ть *pf*. **deserving** *adj* досто́йный (**of** +*gen*).
design *n* (*pattern*) узо́р; (*of car etc*.) констру́кция, прое́кт; (*industrial*) диза́йн; (*aim*) у́мысел; *vt* проекти́ровать *impf*, с~ *pf*; (*intend*) предназнача́ть *impf*, предназна́чить *pf*.
designate *vt* (*indicate*) обознача́ть *impf*, обозна́чить *pf*; (*appoint*) назнача́ть *impf*, назна́чить *pf*.
designer *n* (*tech*) констру́ктор; (*industrial*) диза́йнер; (*of clothes*) моделье́р.
desirable *adj* жела́тельный.
desire *n* жела́ние; *vt* жела́ть *impf*, по~ *pf* +*gen*.
desist *vi* (*refrain*) возде́рживаться *impf*, воздержа́ться *pf* (**from** от+*gen*).
desk *n* пи́сьменный стол; (*school*) па́рта.
desolate *adj* забро́шенный.

desolation *n* забро́шенность.
despair *n* отча́яние; *vi* отча́иваться *impf*, отча́яться *pf*. **desperate** *adj* отча́янный. **desperation** *n* отча́яние.
despicable *adj* презре́нный. **despise** *vt* презира́ть *impf*, презре́ть *pf*.
despite *prep* несмотря́ на+*acc*.
despondency *n* уны́ние. **despondent** *adj* уны́лый.
despot *n* де́спот.
dessert *n* десе́рт.
destination *n* (*of goods*) ме́сто назначе́ния; (*of journey*) цель. **destiny** *n* судьба́.
destitute *adj* без вся́ких средств.
destroy *vt* разруша́ть *impf*, разру́шить *pf*. **destroyer** *n* (*naut*) эсми́нец. **destruction** *n* разруше́ние. **destructive** *adj* разруши́тельный.
detach *vt* отделя́ть *impf*, отдели́ть *pf*. **detached** *adj* отде́льный; (*objective*) беспристра́стный; ~ **house** особня́к. **detachment** *n* (*objectivity*) беспристра́стие; (*mil*) отря́д.
detail *n* дета́ль, подро́бность; **in detail** подро́бно; *vt* подро́бно расска́зывать *impf*, рассказа́ть *pf*. **detailed** *adj* подро́бный.
detain *vt* заде́рживать *impf*, задержа́ть *pf*. **detainee** *n* заде́ржанный *sb*.
detect *vt* обнару́живать *impf*, обнару́жить *pf*. **detection** *n* обнаруже́ние; (*crime*) рассле́дование. **detective** *n* детекти́в; ~ **film, story,** *etc.* детекти́в. **detector** *n* дете́ктор.
detention *n* задержа́ние; (*school*) заде́ржка в наказа́ние.
deter *vt* уде́рживать *impf*, удержа́ть *pf* (**from** от+*gen*).
detergent *n* мо́ющее сре́дство.
deteriorate *vi* ухудша́ться *impf*, уху́дшиться *pf*. **deterioration** *n* ухудше́ние.
determination *n* реши́мость. **determine** *vt* (*ascertain*) устана́вливать *impf*, установи́ть *pf*; (*be decisive factor*) определя́ть *impf*, определи́ть *pf*; (*decide*) реша́ть *impf*, реши́ть *pf*. **determined** *adj* реши́тельный.
deterrent *n* сре́дство устраше́ния.
detest *vt* ненави́деть *impf*. **detestable** *adj* отврати́тельный.
detonate *vt* & *i* взрыва́ть(ся) *impf*, взорва́ть(ся) *pf*. **detonator** *n* детона́тор.
detour *n* объе́зд.
detract *vi*: ~ **from** умаля́ть *impf*, умали́ть *pf* +*acc*.
detriment *n* уще́рб. **detrimental** *adj* вре́дный.
deuce *n* (*tennis*) ра́вный счёт.
devaluation *n* девальва́ция. **devalue** *vt* девальви́ровать *impf* & *pf*.
devastate *vt* опустоша́ть *impf*, опустоши́ть *pf*. **devastated** *adj* потрясённый. **devastating** *adj* уничтожа́ющий. **devastation** *n* опустоше́ние.
develop *vt* & *i* развива́ть(ся) *impf*, разви́ть(ся) *pf*; *vt* (*phot*) проявля́ть *impf*, прояви́ть *pf*. **developer** *n* (*of land etc.*) застро́йщик. **development** *n* разви́тие.
deviant *adj* ненорма́льный. **deviate** *vi* отклоня́ться *impf*, отклони́ться *pf* (**from** от+*gen*). **deviation** *n* отклоне́ние.
device *n* прибо́р.

devil *n* чёрт. **devilish** *adj* чертóвский.
devious *adj* (*circuitous*) окружнóй; (*person*) непоря́дочный.
devise *vt* приду́мывать *impf*, приду́мать *pf*.
devoid *adj* лишённый (**of** +*gen*).
devolution *n* передáча (влáсти).
devote *vt* посвящáть *impf*, посвяти́ть *pf*. **devoted** *adj* прéданный. **devotee** *n* поклóнник. **devotion** *n* прéданность.
devour *vt* пожирáть *impf*, пожрáть *pf*.
devout *adj* нáбожный.
dew *n* росá.
dexterity *n* лóвкость. **dext(e)rous** *adj* лóвкий.
diabetes *n* диабéт. **diabetic** *n* диабéтик; *adj* диабети́ческий.
diabolic(al) *adj* дья́вольский.
diagnose *vt* диагности́ровать *impf & pf*. **diagnosis** *n* диáгноз.
diagonal *n* диагонáль; *adj* диагонáльный. **diagonally** *adv* по диагонáли.
diagram *n* диагрáмма.
dial *n* (*clock*) цифербла́т; (*tech*) шкалá; *vt* набирáть *impf*, набрáть *pf*.
dialect *n* диалéкт.
dialogue *n* диалóг.
diameter *n* диáметр. **diametric(al)** *adj* диаметрáльный; **~ly opposed** диаметрáльно противополóжный.
diamond *n* алмáз; (*shape*) ромб; *pl* (*cards*) бу́бны (-бён, -бнáм) *pl*.
diaper *n* пелёнка.
diaphragm *n* диафрáгма.
diarrhoea *n* понóс.
diary *n* дневни́к.
dice *see* **die**[1]
dicey *adj* рискóванный.
dictate *vt* диктовáть *impf*, про~ *pf*. **dictation** *n* диктóвка. **dictator** *n* диктáтор. **dictatorial** *adj* диктáторский. **dictatorship** *n* диктату́ра.
diction *n* ди́кция.
dictionary *n* словáрь *m*.
didactic *adj* дидакти́ческий.
die[1] *n* (*pl* **dice**) игрáльная кость; (*pl* **dies**) (*stamp*) штамп.
die[2] *vi* (*person*) умирáть *impf*, умерéть *pf*; (*animal*) дóхнуть *impf*, из~, по~ *pf*; (*plant*) вя́нуть *impf*, за~ *pf*; **be dying to** óчень хотéть *impf*; **~ down** (*fire*, *sound*) угасáть *impf*, угáснуть *pf*; **~ out** вымирáть *impf*, вы́мереть *pf*.
diesel *n* (*engine*) ди́зель *m*; *attrib* ди́зельный.
diet *n* диéта; (*habitual food*) пи́ща; *vi* быть на диéте. **dietary** *adj* диети́ческий.
differ *vi* отличáться *impf*; различáться *impf*; (*disagree*) расходи́ться *impf*, разойти́сь *pf*. **difference** *n* рáзница; (*disagreement*) разноглáсие. **different** *adj* разли́чный, рáзный. **differential** *n* (*math*, *tech*) дифференциáл; (*difference*) рáзница. **differentiate** *vt* различáть *impf*, различи́ть *pf*.
difficult *adj* тру́дный. **difficulty** *n* тру́дность; (*difficult situation*) затруднéние; **without ~** без трудá.
diffidence *n* неувéренность в себé. **diffident** *adj* неувéренный в себé.

diffused *adj* рассе́янный.
dig *n* (*archaeol*) раско́пки *f pl*; (*poke*) тычо́к; (*gibe*) шпи́лька; *pl* (*lodgings*) кварти́ра; **give a ~ in the ribs** ткнуть *pf* ло́ктем под ребро́; *vt* копа́ть *impf*, вы́~ *pf*; рыть *impf*, вы́~ *pf*, **~ up** (*bone*) выка́пывать *impf*, вы́копать *pf*; (*land*) вска́пывать *impf*, вскопа́ть *pf*.
digest *vt* перева́ривать *impf*, перевари́ть *pf*. **digestible** *adj* удобовари́мый. **digestion** *n* пищеваре́ние.
digger *n* (*tech*) экскава́тор.
digit *n* (*math*) знак. **digital** *adj* цифрово́й.
dignified *adj* велича́вый. **dignitary** *n* сано́вник. **dignity** *n* досто́инство.
digress *vi* отклоня́ться *impf*, отклони́ться *pf*. **digression** *n* отклоне́ние.
dike *n* да́мба; (*ditch*) ров.
dilapidated *adj* ве́тхий.
dilate *vt* & *i* расширя́ть(ся) *impf*, расши́рить(ся) *pf*.
dilemma *n* диле́мма.
dilettante *n* дилета́нт.
diligence *n* прилежа́ние. **diligent** *adj* приле́жный.
dilute *vt* разбавля́ть *impf*, разба́вить *pf*.
dim *adj* (*not bright*) ту́склый; (*vague*) сму́тный; (*stupid*) тупо́й.
dimension *n* (*pl*) разме́ры *m pl*; (*math*) измере́ние. **-dimensional** *in comb* -ме́рный; **three-~** трёхме́рный.
diminish *vt* & *i* уменьша́ть(ся) *impf*, уме́ньшить(ся) *pf*. **diminutive** *adj* ма́ленький; *n* уменьши́тельное *sb*.
dimness *n* ту́склость.
dimple *n* я́мочка.
din *n* гро́хот; (*voices*) гам.
dine *vi* обе́дать *impf*, по~ *pf*. **diner** *n* обе́дающий *sb*.
dinghy *n* шлю́пка; (*rubber* ~) надувна́я ло́дка.
dingy *adj* (*drab*) ту́склый; (*dirty*) гря́зный.
dining-car *n* ваго́н-рестора́н. **dining-room** *n* столо́вая *sb*. **dinner** *n* обе́д; **~-jacket** смо́кинг.
dinosaur *n* диноза́вр.
diocese *n* епа́рхия.
dip *vt* (*immerse*) окуна́ть *impf*, окуну́ть *pf*; (*partially*) обма́кивать *impf*, обмакну́ть *pf*; *vi* (*slope*) понижа́ться *impf*, пони́зиться *pf*; *n* (*depression*) впа́дина; (*slope*) укло́н; **have a ~** (*bathe*) купа́ться *impf*, вы́~ *pf*.
diphtheria *n* дифтери́я.
diphthong *n* дифто́нг.
diploma *n* дипло́м. **diplomacy** *n* диплома́тия. **diplomat** *n* диплома́т. **diplomatic** *adj* дипломати́ческий.
dire *adj* стра́шный.
direct *adj* прямо́й; **~ current** постоя́нный ток; *vt* направля́ть *impf*, напра́вить *pf*; (*guide, manage*) руководи́ть *impf* +*instr*; (*film*) режисси́ровать *impf*. **direction** *n* направле́ние; (*guidance*) руково́дство; (*instruction*) указа́ние; (*film*) режиссу́ра; **stage ~** рема́рка. **directive** *n* директи́ва. **directly** *adv* пря́мо; (*at once*) сра́зу. **director** *n* дире́ктор; (*film etc.*) режиссёр(-постано́вщик). **directory** *n* спра́вочник, указа́тель *m*; (*tel*) телефо́нная кни́га.
dirt *n* грязь. **dirty** *adj* гря́зный; *vt* па́чкать *impf*, за~ *pf*.

disability *n* физи́ческий/психи́ческий недоста́ток; (*disablement*) инвали́дность. **disabled** *adj*: **he is ~** он инвали́д.
disadvantage *n* невы́годное положе́ние; (*defect*) недоста́ток. **disadvantageous** *adj* невы́годный.
disaffected *adj* недово́льный.
disagree *vi* не соглаша́ться *impf*, согласи́ться *pf*; (*not correspond*) не соотве́тствовать *impf* +*dat*. **disagreeable** *adj* неприя́тный. **disagreement** *n* разногла́сие; (*quarrel*) ссо́ра.
disappear *vi* исчеза́ть *impf*, исче́знуть *pf*. **disappearance** *n* исчезнове́ние.
disappoint *vt* разочаро́вывать *impf*, разочарова́ть *pf*. **disappointed** *adj* разочаро́ванный. **disappointing** *adj* разочаро́вывающий. **disappointment** *n* разочарова́ние.
disapproval *n* неодобре́ние. **disapprove** *vt* & *i* не одобря́ть *impf*.
disarm *vt* (*mil*) разоружа́ть *impf*., разоружи́ть *pf*; (*criminal*; *also fig*) обезору́живать *impf*, обезору́жить *pf*. **disarmament** *n* разоруже́ние.
disarray *n* беспоря́док.
disaster *n* бе́дствие. **disastrous** *adj* катастрофи́ческий.
disband *vt* распуска́ть *impf*, распусти́ть *pf*; *vi* расходи́ться *impf*, разойти́сь *pf*.
disbelief *n* неве́рие.
disc, **disk** *n* диск; **~ drive** дисково́д; **~ jockey** веду́щий *sb* переда́чу.
discard *vt* отбра́сывать *impf*, отбро́сить *pf*.
discern *vt* различа́ть *impf*, различи́ть *pf*. **discernible** *adj* различи́мый. **discerning** *adj* проница́тельный.
discharge *vt* (*ship etc.*) разгружа́ть *impf*, разгрузи́ть *pf* (*gun*; *electr*) разряжа́ть *impf*, разряди́ть *pf*; (*dismiss*) увольня́ть *impf*, уво́лить *pf*; (*prisoner*) освобожда́ть *impf*, освободи́ть *pf*; (*duty*) выполня́ть *impf*, вы́полнить *pf*; (*from hospital*) выпи́сывать *impf*, вы́писать *pf*; *n* разгру́зка; (*electr*) разря́д; увольне́ние; освобожде́ние; выполне́ние; (*med*) выделе́ния *neut pl*.
disciple *n* учени́к.
disciplinarian *n* сторо́нник дисципли́ны. **disciplinary** *adj* дисциплина́рный. **discipline** *n* дисципли́на; *vt* дисциплини́ровать *impf* & *pf*.
disclaim *vt* (*deny*) отрица́ть *impf*; **~ responsibility** слага́ть *impf*, сложи́ть *pf* с себя́ отве́тственность.
disclose *vt* обнару́живать *impf*, обнару́жить *pf*. **disclosure** *n* обнаруже́ние.
discoloured *adj* обесцве́ченный.
discomfit *vt* смуща́ть *impf*, смути́ть *pf*. **discomfiture** *n* смуще́ние.
discomfort *n* неудо́бство.
disconcert *vt* смуща́ть *impf*, смути́ть *pf*.
disconnect *vt* разъединя́ть *impf*, разъедини́ть *pf*; (*switch off*) выключа́ть *impf*, вы́ключить *pf*. **disconnected** *adj* (*incoherent*) бессвя́зный.
disconsolate *adj* неуте́шный.
discontent *n* недово́льство. **discontented** *adj* недово́льный.
discontinue *vt* прекраща́ть *impf*, прекрати́ть *pf*.

discord *n* разногла́сие; (*mus*) диссона́нс. **discordant** *adj* несогласу́ющийся; диссони́рующий.
discotheque *n* дискоте́ка.
discount *n* ски́дка; *vt* (*disregard*) не принима́ть *impf*, приня́ть *pf* в расчёт.
discourage *vt* обескура́живать *impf*, обескура́жить *pf*; (*dissuade*) отгова́ривать *impf*, отговори́ть *pf*.
discourse *n* речь.
discourteous *adj* неве́жливый.
discover *vt* открыва́ть *impf*, откры́ть *pf*; (*find out*) обнару́живать *impf*, обнару́жить *pf*. **discovery** *n* откры́тие.
discredit *n* позо́р; *vt* дискредити́ровать *impf* & *pf*.
discreet *adj* такти́чный. **discretion** *n* (*judgement*) усмотре́ние; (*prudence*) благоразу́мие; **at one's ~** по своему́ усмотре́нию.
discrepancy *n* несоотве́тствие.
discriminate *vt* различа́ть *impf*, различи́ть *pf*; **~ against** дискримини́ровать *impf* & *pf*. **discrimination** *n* (*taste*) разбо́рчивость; (*bias*) дискримина́ция.
discus *n* диск.
discuss *vt* обсужда́ть *impf*, обсуди́ть *pf*. **discussion** *n* обсужде́ние.
disdain *n* презре́ние. **disdainful** *adj* презри́тельный.
disease *n* боле́знь. **diseased** *adj* больно́й.
disembark *vi* выса́живаться *impf*, вы́садиться *pf*.
disenchantment *n* разочарова́ние.
disengage *vt* освобожда́ть *impf*, освободи́ть *pf*; (*clutch*) отпуска́ть *impf*, отпусти́ть *pf*.
disentangle *vt* распу́тывать *impf*, распу́тать *pf*.
disfavour *n* неми́лость.
disfigure *vt* уро́довать *impf*, из~ *pf*.
disgrace *n* позо́р; (*disfavour*) неми́лость; *vt* позо́рить *impf*, о~ *pf*. **disgraceful** *adj* позо́рный.
disgruntled *adj* недово́льный.
disguise *n* маскиро́вка; *vt* маскирова́ть *impf*, за~ *pf*; (*conceal*) скрыва́ть *impf*, скрыть *pf*. **disguised** *adj* замаскиро́ванный.
disgust *n* отвраще́ние; *vt* внуша́ть *impf*, внуши́ть *pf* отвраще́ние +*dat*. **disgusting** *adj* отврати́тельный.
dish *n* блю́до; *pl* посу́да *collect*; **~-washer** (посу́до)мо́ечная маши́на; *vt*: **~ up** подава́ть *impf*, пода́ть *pf*.
dishearten *vt* обескура́живать *impf*, обескура́жить *pf*.
dishevelled *adj* растрёпанный.
dishonest *adj* нече́стный. **dishonesty** *n* нече́стность. **dishonour** *n* бесче́стье; *vt* бесче́стить *impf*, о~ *pf*. **dishonourable** *adj* бесче́стный.
disillusion *vt* разочаро́вывать *impf*, разочарова́ть *pf*. **disillusionment** *n* разочаро́ванность.
disinclination *n* нескло́нность, неохо́та. **disinclined** *adj* **be ~** не хоте́ться *impers* +*dat*.
disinfect *vt* дезинфици́ровать *impf* & *pf*. **disinfectant** *n* дезинфици́рующее сре́дство.
disingenuous *adj* нейскренный.

disinherit *vt* лиша́ть *impf*, лиши́ть *pf* насле́дства.
disintegrate *vi* распада́ться *impf*, распа́сться *pf*. **disintegration** *n* распа́д.
disinterested *adj* бескоры́стный.
disjointed *adj* бессвя́зный.
disk *see* **disc**
dislike *n* нелюбо́вь (**for** к+*dat*); *vt* не люби́ть *impf*.
dislocate *vt* (*med*) вы́вихнуть *pf*.
dislodge *vt* смеща́ть *impf*, смести́ть *pf*.
disloyal *adj* нелоя́льный. **disloyalty** *n* нелоя́льность.
dismal *adj* мра́чный.
dismantle *vt* разбира́ть *impf*, разобра́ть *pf*.
dismay *vt* смуща́ть *impf*, смути́ть *pf*; *n* смуще́ние.
dismiss *vt* (*sack*) увольня́ть *impf*, уво́лить *pf*; (*disband*) распуска́ть *impf*, распусти́ть *pf*. **dismissal** *n* увольне́ние; ро́спуск.
dismount *vi* спе́шиваться *impf*, спе́шиться *pf*.
disobedience *n* непослуша́ние. **disobedient** *adj* непослу́шный. **disobey** *vt* не слу́шаться *impf* +*gen*.
disorder *n* беспоря́док. **disorderly** *adj* (*untidy*) беспоря́дочный; (*unruly*) бу́йный.
disorganized *adj* неорганизо́ванный.
disorientation *n* дезориента́ция. **disoriented** *adj*: **I am/was ~** я потеря́л(а) направле́ние.
disown *vt* отка́зываться *impf*, отказа́ться *pf* от+*gen*.
disparaging *adj* оскорби́тельный.
disparity *n* нера́венство.
dispassionate *adj* беспристра́стный.
dispatch *vt* (*send*) отправля́ть *impf*, отпра́вить *pf*; (*deal with*) расправля́ться *impf*, распра́виться *pf* с+*instr*; *n* отпра́вка; (*message*) донесе́ние; (*rapidity*) быстрота́; **~-rider** мотоцикли́ст свя́зи.
dispel *vt* рассе́ивать *impf*, рассе́ять *pf*.
dispensable *adj* необяза́тельный.
dispensary *n* апте́ка.
dispensation *n* (*exemption*) освобожде́ние (от обяза́тельства). **dispense** *vt* (*distribute*) раздава́ть *impf*, разда́ть *pf*; **~ with** обходи́ться *impf*, обойти́сь *pf* без+*gen*.
dispersal *n* распростране́ние. **disperse** *vt* (*drive away*) разгоня́ть *impf*, разогна́ть *pf*; (*scatter*) рассе́ивать *impf*, рассе́ять *pf*; *vi* расходи́ться *impf*, разойти́сь *pf*.
dispirited *adj* удручённый.
displaced *adj*: **~ persons** перемещённые ли́ца *neut pl*.
display *n* пока́з; *vt* пока́зывать *impf*, показа́ть *pf*.
displeased *predic* недово́лен (-льна). **displeasure** *n* недово́льство.
disposable *adj* однора́зовый. **disposal** *n* удале́ние; **at your ~** в ва́шем распоряже́нии. **dispose** *vi*: **~ of** избавля́ться *impf*, изба́виться *pf* от+*gen*. **disposed** *predic*: **~ to** располо́жен (-ена) к+*dat or* +*inf*. **disposition** *n* расположе́ние; (*temperament*) нрав.
disproportionate *adj* непропорциона́льный.
disprove *vt* опроверга́ть *impf*, опрове́ргнуть *pf*.

dispute *n* (*debate*) спор; (*quarrel*) ссóра; *vt* оспáривать *impf*, оспóрить *pf*.
disqualification *n* дисквалификáция. **disqualify** *vt* дисквалифицúровать *impf* & *pf*.
disquieting *adj* тревóжный.
disregard *n* пренебрежéние +*instr*; *vt* игнорúровать *impf* & *pf*; пренебрегáть *impf*, пренебрéчь *pf* +*instr*.
disrepair *n* неисправность.
disreputable *adj* пóльзующийся дурнóй слáвой. **disrepute** *n* дурнáя слáва.
disrespect *n* неуважéние. **disrespectful** *adj* непочтúтельный.
disrupt *vt* срывáть *impf*, сорвáть *pf*. **disruptive** *adj* подрывнóй.
dissatisfaction *n* недовóльство. **dissatisfied** *adj* недовóльный.
dissect *vt* разрезáть *impf*, разрéзать *pf*; (*med*) вскрывáть *impf*, вскрыть *pf*.
disseminate *vt* распространять *impf*, распространúть *pf*; **dissemination** *n* распространéние.
dissension *n* раздóр. **dissent** *n* расхождéние; (*eccl*) раскóл.
dissertation *n* диссертáция.
disservice *n* плохáя услýга.
dissident *n* диссидéнт.
dissimilar *adj* несхóдный.
dissipate *vt* (*dispel*) рассéивать *impf*, рассéять *pf*; (*squander*) промáтывать *impf*, промотáть *pf*. **dissipated** *adj* распýтный.
dissociate *vt*: ~ **o.s.** отмежёвываться *impf*, отмежевáться *pf* (**from** от+*gen*).
dissolute *adj* распýтный. **dissolution** *n* расторжéние; (*parl*) рóспуск. **dissolve** *vt* & *i* (*in liquid*) растворять(ся) *impf*, растворúть(ся) *pf*; *vt* (*annul*) расторгáть *impf*, растóргнуть *pf*; (*parl*) распускáть *impf*, распустúть *pf*.
dissonance *n* диссонáнс. **dissonant** *adj* диссонúрующий.
dissuade *vt* отговáривать *impf*, отговорúть *pf*.
distance *n* расстояние; **from a** ~ úздали; **in the** ~ вдалекé. **distant** *adj* далёкий, (*also of relative*) дáльний; (*reserved*) сдéржанный.
distaste *n* отвращéние. **distasteful** *adj* протúвный.
distended *adj* надýтый.
distil *vt* (*whisky*) перегонять *impf*, перегнáть *pf*; (*water*) дистиллúровать *impf* & *pf*.
distillation *n* перегóнка; дистилляция. **distillery** *n* перегóнный завóд.
distinct *adj* (*different*) отлúчный; (*clear*) отчётливый; (*evident*) замéтный. **distinction** *n* (*difference*; *excellence*) отлúчие; (*discrimination*) различие. **distinctive** *adj* отличúтельный. **distinctly** *adv* ясно.
distinguish *vt* различáть *impf*, различúть *pf*; ~ **o.s.** отличáться *impf*, отличúться *pf*.
distinguished *adj* выдающийся.
distort *vt* искажáть *impf*, исказúть *pf*; (*misrepresent*) извращáть *impf*, извратúть *pf*.
distortion *n* искажéние; извращéние.
distract *vt* отвлекáть *impf*, отвлéчь *pf*. **distraction** *n* (*amusement*) развлечéние; (*madness*) безýмие.
distraught *adj* обезýмевший.

distress *n* (*suffering*) огорчéние; (*danger*) бéдствие; *vt* огорчáть *impf*, огорчи́ть *pf*. **distribute** *vt* (*hand out*) раздавáть *impf*, раздáть *pf*; (*allocate*) распределя́ть *impf*, распредели́ть *pf*. **distribution** *n* распределéние. **distributor** *n* распредели́тель *m*.

district *n* рай́он.

distrust *n* недовéрие; *vt* не доверя́ть *impf*. **distrustful** *adj* недовéрчивый.

disturb *vt* беспокóить *impf*, о~ *pf*. **disturbance** *n* нарушéние покóя; *pl* (*polit etc.*) беспоря́дки *m pl*.

disuse *n* неупотреблéние; **fall into** ~ выходи́ть *impf*, вы́йти *pf* из употреблéния. **disused** *adj* заброшенный.

ditch *n* канáва, ров.

dither *vi* колебáться *impf*.

ditto *n* то же сáмое; *adv* так же.

divan *n* дивáн.

dive *vi* ныря́ть *impf*, нырнýть *pf*; (*aeron*) пики́ровать *impf* & *pf*; *n* нырóк, прыжóк в вóду. **diver** *n* водолáз.

diverge *vi* расходи́ться *impf*, разойти́сь *pf*. **divergent** *adj* расходя́щийся.

diverse *adj* разнообрáзный. **diversification** *n* расширéние ассортимéнта. **diversify** *vt* разнообрáзить *impf*. **diversion** *n* (*detour*) объéзд; (*amusement*) развлечéние. **diversity** *n* разнообрáзие. **divert** *vt* отклоня́ть *impf*, отклони́ть *pf*; (*amuse*) развлекáть *impf*, развлéчь *pf*. **diverting** *adj* забáвный.

divest *vt* (*deprive*) лишáть *impf*, лиши́ть *pf* (**of** +*gen*); ~ **o.s.** откáзываться *impf*, отказáться *pf* (**of** от+*gen*).

divide *vt* (*share*; *math*) дели́ть *impf*, по~ *pf*; (*separate*) разделя́ть *impf*, раздели́ть *pf*. **dividend** *n* дивидéнд.

divine *adj* божéственный.

diving *n* ныря́ние; ~**-board** трампли́н.

divinity *n* (*quality*) божéственность; (*deity*) божествó; (*theology*) богослóвие.

divisible *adj* дели́мый. **division** *n* (*dividing*) делéние, разделéние; (*section*) отдéл; (*mil*) диви́зия.

divorce *n* развóд; *vi* разводи́ться *impf*, развести́сь *pf*. **divorced** *adj* разведённый.

divulge *vt* разглашáть *impf*, разгласи́ть *pf*.

DIY *abbr* (*of* **do-it-yourself**): **he is good at** ~ у негó золоты́е рýки; ~ **shop** магази́н «сдéлай сам».

dizziness *n* головокружéние. **dizzy** *adj* (*causing dizziness*) головокружи́тельный; **I am** ~ у меня́ крýжится головá.

DNA *abbr* (*of* **deoxyribonucleic acid**) ДНК.

do *vt* дéлать *impf*, с~ *pf*; *vi* (*be suitable*) годи́ться *impf*; (*suffice*) быть достáточным; ~**-it-yourself** *see* **DIY**; **that will** ~! хвáтит!; **how** ~ **you** ~? здрáвствуйте!; как вы поживáете?; ~ **away with** (*abolish*) уничтожáть *impf*, уничтóжить *pf*; ~ **in** (*kill*) убивáть *impf*, уби́ть *pf*; ~ **up** (*restore*) ремонти́ровать *impf*, от~ *pf*; (*wrap up*) завёртывать *impf*, заверну́ть *pf*; (*fasten*) застёгивать *impf*, застегнýть *pf*; ~ **without** обходи́ться *impf*, обойти́сь *pf* без+*gen*.

docile *adj* покóрный. **docility** *n* покóрность.

dock[1] *n* (*naut*) док; *vt* стáвить *impf*, по~ *pf* в док; *vi* входи́ть *impf*, войти́ *pf* в док; *vi* (*spacecraft*) стыковáться *impf*, со~ *pf*. **docker** *n* дóкер. **dockyard** *n* верфь.

dock[2] *n* (*law*) скамья́ подсуди́мых.

docket *n* квитáнция; (*label*) ярлы́к.

doctor *n* врач; (*also univ*) дóктор; *vt* (*castrate*) кастри́ровать *impf* & *pf*; (*spay*) удаля́ть *impf*, удали́ть *pf* яи́чники у+*gen*; (*falsify*) фальсифици́ровать *impf* & *pf*. **doctorate** *n* стéпень дóктора.

doctrine *n* доктри́на.

document *n* докумéнт; *vt* документи́ровать *impf* & *pf*. **documentary** *n* документáльный фильм. **documentation** *n* документáция.

doddery *adj* дря́хлый.

dodge *n* увёртка; *vt* уклоня́ться *impf*, уклони́ться *pf* от+*gen*; (*jump to avoid*) отскáкивать *impf*, отскочи́ть *pf* (от+*gen*). **dodgy** *adj* кáверзный.

doe *n* сáмка.

dog *n* собáка, пёс; (*fig*) преслéдовать *impf*. **dog-eared** *adj* захвáтанный.

dogged *adj* упóрный.

dogma *n* дóгма. **dogmatic** *adj* догмати́ческий.

doings *n pl* делá *neut pl*.

doldrums *n*: **be in the ~** хандри́ть *impf*.

dole *n* пособие по безрабóтице; *vt* (~ *out*) выдавáть *impf*, вы́дать *pf*.

doleful *adj* скóрбный.

doll *n* кýкла.

dollar *n* дóллар.

dollop *n* соли́дная пóрция.

dolphin *n* дельфи́н.

domain *n* (*estate*) владéние; (*field*) óбласть.

dome *n* кýпол.

domestic *adj* (*of household*; *animals*) домáшний; (*of family*) семéйный; (*polit*) внýтренний; *n* прислýга. **domesticate** *vt* приручáть *impf*, приручи́ть *pf*. **domesticity** *n* домáшняя, семéйная, жизнь.

domicile *n* местожи́тельство.

dominance *n* госпóдство. **dominant** *adj* преобладáющий; госпóдствующий. **dominate** *vt* госпóдствовать *impf* над+*instr*. **domineering** *adj* влáстный.

dominion *n* влады́чество; (*realm*) владéние.

domino *n* кость доминó; *pl* (*game*) доминó *neut indecl*.

don *vt* надевáть *impf*, надéть *pf*.

donate *vt* жéртвовать *impf*, по~ *pf*. **donation** *n* пожéртвование.

donkey *n* осёл.

donor *n* жéртвователь *m*; (*med*) дóнор.

doom *n* (*ruin*) ги́бель; *vt* обрекáть *impf*, обрéчь *pf*.

door *n* дверь. **doorbell** *n* (двернóй) звонóк. **doorman** *n* швейцáр. **doormat** *n* полови́к. **doorstep** *n* порóг. **doorway** *n* дверной проём.

dope *n* (*drug*) наркóтик; *vt* дурмáнить *impf*, о~ *pf*.

dormant *adj* (*sleeping*) спя́щий; (*inactive*) бездéйствующий.

dormer window *n* слуховóе окнó.

dormitory *n* óбщая спáльня.

dormouse *n* со́ня.
dorsal *adj* спинно́й.
dosage *n* дозиро́вка. **dose** *n* до́за.
dossier *n* досье́ *neut indecl.*
dot *n* то́чка; *vt* ста́вить *impf*, по~ *pf* то́чки на+*acc*; (*scatter*) усе́ивать *impf*, усе́ять *pf* (**with** +*instr*); **~ted line** пункти́р.
dote *vi*: **~ on** обожа́ть *impf.*
double *adj* двойно́й; (*doubled*) удво́енный; **~-bass** контраба́с; **~ bed** двуспа́льная крова́ть; **~-breasted** двубо́ртный; **~-cross** обма́нывать *impf*, обману́ть *pf*; **~-dealing** двуру́шничество; **~-decker** двухэта́жный авто́бус; **~-edged** обоюдоо́стрый; **~-glazing** двойны́е ра́мы *f pl*; **~ room** ко́мната на двои́х; *adv* вдво́е; (*two together*) вдвоём; *n* двойно́е коли́чество; (*person's*) двойни́к; *pl* (*sport*) па́рная игра́; *vt & i* удва́ивать(ся) *impf*, удво́ить(ся) *pf*; **~ back** возвраща́ться *impf*, верну́ться *pf* наза́д; **~ up** (*in pain*) скрю́чиваться *impf*, скрю́читься *pf*; (*share a room*) помеща́ться *impf*, помести́ться *pf* вдвоём в одно́й ко́мнате; (**~** *up as*) рабо́тать *impf* + *instr* по совмести́тельству.
doubt *n* сомне́ние; *vt* сомнева́ться *impf* в+*prep*. **doubtful** *adj* сомни́тельный. **doubtless** *adv* несомне́нно.
dough *n* те́сто. **doughnut** *n* по́нчик.
douse *vt* (*drench*) залива́ть *impf*, зали́ть *pf.*
dove *n* го́лубь *m*. **dovetail** *n* ла́сточкин хвост.
dowdy *adj* неэлега́нтный.
down[1] *n* (*fluff*) пух.
down[2] *adv* (*motion*) вниз; (*position*) внизу́; **be ~ with** (*ill*) боле́ть *impf* +*instr*; *prep* вниз с+*gen*, по+*dat*; (*along*) (вдоль) по+*dat*; *vt*: (*gulp*) опроки́дывать *impf*, опроки́нуть *pf*; **~-and-out** бродя́га *m*; **~cast**, **~-hearted** уны́лый. **downfall** *n* ги́бель. **downhill** *adv* по́д гору. **download** *vt* (*comput*) загружа́ть *impf*, загрузи́ть *pf*. **downpour** *n* ли́вень *m*. **downright** *adj* я́вный; *adv* соверше́нно. **downstairs** *adv* (*motion*) вниз; (*position*) внизу́. **downstream** *adv* вниз по тече́нию. **down-to-earth** *adj* реалисти́ческий. **downtrodden** *adj* угнетё-нный.
dowry *n* прида́ное *sb.*
doze *vi* дрема́ть *impf.*
dozen *n* дю́жина.
drab *adj* бесцве́тный.
draft *n* (*outline*, *rough copy*) набро́сок; (*document*) прое́кт; (*econ*) тра́тта; *see also* **draught**; *vt* составля́ть *impf*, соста́вить *pf* план, прое́кт, +*gen*.
drag *vt* тащи́ть *impf*; (*river etc.*) драги́ровать *impf* & *pf*; **~ on** (*vi*) затя́гиваться *impf*, затяну́ться *pf*; *n* (*burden*) обу́за; (*on cigarette*) затя́жка; **in ~** в же́нской оде́жде.
dragon *n* драко́н. **dragonfly** *n* стрекоза́.
drain *n* водосто́к; (*leakage*; *fig*) уте́чка; *vt* осуша́ть *impf*, осуши́ть *pf*; *vi* спуска́ться *impf*, спусти́ться *pf*. **drainage** *n* дрена́ж; (*system*) канализа́ция.
drake *n* се́лезень *m*.
drama *n* дра́ма; (*quality*) драмати́зм. **dramatic** *adj*

драмати́ческий. **dramatist** *n* драмату́рг. **dramatize** *vt* драматизи́ровать *impf* & *pf*.
drape *vt* драпирова́ть *impf*, за~ *pf*; *n* драпиро́вка.
drastic *adj* радика́льный.
draught *n* (*air*) сквозня́к; (*traction*) тя́га; *pl* (*game*) ша́шки *f pl*; *see also* **draft**; **there is a ~** сквози́т; **~ beer** пи́во из бо́чки. **draughtsman** *n* чертёжник. **draughty** *adj*: **it is ~ here** здесь ду́ет.
draw *n* (*in lottery*) ро́зыгрыш; (*attraction*) прима́нка; (*drawn game*) ничья́; *vt* (*pull*) тяну́ть *impf*, по~ *pf*; таска́ть *indet*, тащи́ть *det*; (*curtains*) задёргивать *impf*, задёрнуть *pf* (занаве́ски); (*attract*) привлека́ть *impf*, привле́чь *pf*; (*pull out*) выта́скивать *impf*, вы́тащить *pf*; (*sword*) обнажа́ть *impf*, обнажи́ть *pf*; (*lots*) броса́ть *impf*, бро́сить *pf* (жре́бий); (*water*; *inspiration*) че́рпать *impf*, черпну́ть *pf*; (*evoke*) вызыва́ть *impf*, вы́звать *pf*; (*conclusion*) выводи́ть *impf*, вы́вести *pf* (заключе́ние); (*diagram*) черти́ть *impf*, на~ *pf*; (*picture*) рисова́ть *impf*, на~ *pf*; *vi* (*sport*) сыгра́ть *pf* вничью́; **~ aside** отводи́ть *impf*, отвести́ *pf* в сто́рону; **~ back** (*withdraw*) отступа́ть *impf*, отступи́ть *pf*; **~ in** втя́гивать *impf*, втяну́ть *pf*; (*train*) входи́ть *impf*, войти́ *pf* в ста́нцию; (*car*) подходи́ть *impf*, подойти́ *pf* (**to** к + *dat*); (*days*) стано́виться *impf* коро́че; **~ out** вытя́гивать *impf*, вы́тянуть *pf*; (*money*) выпи́сывать *impf*, вы́писать *pf*; (*train/car*) выходи́ть *impf*, вы́йти *pf* (со ста́нции/на доро́гу); **~ up** (*car*) подходи́ть *impf*, подойти́ *pf* (**to** к + *dat*); (*document*) составля́ть *impf*, соста́вить *pf*. **drawback** *n* недоста́ток. **drawbridge** *n* подъёмный мост. **drawer** *n* я́щик. **drawing** *n* (*action*) рисова́ние, черче́ние; (*object*) рису́нок, чертёж; **~-board** чертёжная доска́; **~-pin** кно́пка; **~-room** гости́ная *sb*.
drawl *n* протя́жное произноше́ние.
dread *n* страх; *vt* боя́ться *impf* +*gen*. **dreadful** *adj* ужа́сный.
dream *n* сон; (*fantasy*) мечта́; *vi* ви́деть *impf*, у~ *pf* сон; **~ of** ви́деть *impf*, у~ *pf* во сне́; (*fig*) мечта́ть *impf* о+*prep*.
dreary *adj* (*weather*) па́смурный; (*boring*) ску́чный.
dredge *vt* (*river etc.*) драги́ровать *impf* & *pf*. **dredger** *n* дра́га.
dregs *n pl* оса́дки (-ков) *pl*.
drench *vt* прома́чивать *impf*, промочи́ть *pf*; **get ~ed** промока́ть *impf*, промо́кнуть *pf*.
dress *n* пла́тье; (*apparel*) оде́жда; **~ circle** бельэта́ж; **~maker** портни́ха; **~ rehearsal** генера́льная репети́ция; *vt* & *i* одева́ть(ся) *impf*, оде́ть(ся) *pf*; *vt* (*cul*) приправля́ть *impf*, припра́вить *pf*; (*med*) перевя́зывать *impf*, перевяза́ть *pf*; **~ up** наряжа́ться *impf*, наряди́ться *pf* (**as** + *instr*).
dresser *n* ку́хонный шкаф.
dressing *n* (*cul*) припра́ва; (*med*) перевя́зка; **~-gown** хала́т; **~-room** убо́рная *sb*; **~-table** туале́тный сто́лик.
dribble *vi* (*person*) пуска́ть *impf*, пусти́ть *pf* слю́ни;

(*sport*) вести́ *impf* мяч.

dried *adj* сушёный. **drier** *n* суши́лка.

drift *n* (*meaning*) смысл; (*snow*) сугро́б; *vi* плыть *impf* по тече́нию; (*naut*) дрейфова́ть *impf*; (*snow etc.*) скопля́ться *impf*, скопи́ться *pf*; ~ **apart** расходи́ться *impf*, разойти́сь *pf*.

drill[1] *n* сверло́; (*dentist's*) бур; *vt* сверли́ть *impf*, про~ *pf*.

drill[2] *vt* (*mil*) обуча́ть *impf*, обучи́ть *pf* стро́ю; *vi* проходи́ть *impf*, пройти́ *pf* строеву́ю подгото́вку; *n* строева́я подгото́вка.

drink *n* напи́ток; *vt* пить *impf*, вы́~ *pf*; ~**-driving** вожде́ние в нетре́звом состоя́нии. **drinking-water** *n* питьева́я вода́.

drip *n* (*action*) ка́панье; (*drop*) ка́пля; *vi* ка́пать *impf*, ка́пнуть *pf*.

drive *n* (*journey*) езда́; (*excursion*) прогу́лка; (*campaign*) похо́д, кампа́ния; (*energy*) эне́ргия; (*tech*) приво́д; (*driveway*) подъездна́я доро́га; *vt* (*urge*; *chase*) гоня́ть *indet*, гнать *det*; (*vehicle*) води́ть *indet*, вести́ *det*; управля́ть *impf* +*instr*; (*convey*) вози́ть *indet*, везти́ *det*, по~ *pf*; *vi* (*travel*) е́здить *indet*, е́хать *det*, по~ *pf*; *vt* доводи́ть *impf*, довести́ *pf* (**to** до+*gen*); (*nail etc.*) вбива́ть *impf*, вбить *pf* (**into** в+*acc*); ~ **away** *vt* прогоня́ть *impf*, прогна́ть *pf*; *vi* уезжа́ть *impf*, уе́хать *pf*; ~ **up** подъезжа́ть *impf*, подъе́хать *pf* (**to** к+*dat*).

driver *n* (*of vehicle*) води́тель *m*, шофёр. **driving** *adj* (*force*) дви́жущий; (*rain*) проливно́й; ~**-licence** води́тельские права́ *neut pl*; ~**-test** экза́мен на получе́ние води́тельских прав; ~**-wheel** веду́щее колесо́.

drizzle *n* ме́лкий до́ждь *m*; *vi* мороси́ть *impf*.

drone *n* (*bee*; *idler*) тру́тень *m*; (*of voice*) жужжа́ние; (*of engine*) гул; *vi* (*buzz*) жужжа́ть *impf*; (~ *on*) бубни́ть *impf*.

drool *vi* пуска́ть *impf*, пусти́ть *pf* слю́ни.

droop *vi* поника́ть *impf*, пони́кнуть *pf*.

drop *n* (*of liquid*) ка́пля; (*fall*) паде́ние, пониже́ние; *vt & i* (*price*) снижа́ть(ся) *impf*, сни́зить(ся) *pf*; *vi* (*fall*) па́дать *impf*, упа́сть *pf*; *vt* (*let fall*) роня́ть *impf*, урони́ть *pf*; (*abandon*) броса́ть *impf*, бро́сить *pf*; ~ **behind** отстава́ть *impf*, отста́ть *pf*; ~ **in** заходи́ть *impf*, зайти́ *pf* (**on** к+*dat*); ~ **off** (*fall asleep*) засыпа́ть *impf*, засну́ть *pf*; (*from car*) выса́живать *impf*, вы́садить *pf*; ~ **out** выбыва́ть *impf*, вы́быть *pf* (**of** из +*gen*). **droppings** *n pl* помёт.

drought *n* за́суха.

droves *n pl*: **in** ~ то́лпами.

drown *vt* топи́ть *impf*, у~ *pf*; (*sound*) заглуша́ть *impf*, заглуши́ть *pf*; *vi* тону́ть *impf*, у~ *pf*.

drowsy *adj* сонли́вый.

drudgery *n* ну́дная рабо́та.

drug *n* медикаме́нт; (*narcotic*) нарко́тик; ~ **addict** наркома́н, ~ка; *vt* дава́ть *impf*, дать *pf* нарко́тик+*dat*.

drum *n* бараба́н; *vi* бить *impf* в бараба́н; бараба́нить *impf*; ~ **sth into s.o.** вда́лбливать *impf*, вдолби́ть *pf* + *dat of* *person* в го́лову. **drummer** *n* бараба́нщик.

drunk *adj* пья́ный. **drunkard** *n* пья́ница *m* & *f*. **drunken** *adj* пья́ный; ~ **driving** вожде́ние в нетре́звом состоя́нии. **drunkenness** *n* пья́нство.

dry *adj* сухо́й; ~ **land** су́ша; *vt* суши́ть *impf*, вы́~ *pf*; (*wipe dry*) вытира́ть *impf*, вы́тереть *pf*; *vi* со́хнуть *impf*, вы́~, про~ *pf*. **dry-cleaning** *n* химчи́стка. **dryness** *n* су́хость.

dual *adj* двойно́й; (*joint*) совме́стный; ~**-purpose** двойно́го назначе́ния.

dub[1] *vt* (*nickname*) прозыва́ть *impf*, прозва́ть *pf*.

dub[2] *vt* (*cin*) дубли́ровать *impf* & *pf*.

dubious *adj* сомни́тельный.

duchess *n* герцоги́ня. **duchy** *n* ге́рцогство.

duck[1] *n* (*bird*) у́тка.

duck[2] *vt* (*immerse*) окуна́ть *impf*, окуну́ть *pf*; (*one's head*) нагну́ть *pf*; (*evade*) увёртываться *impf*, уверну́ться *pf* от+*gen*; *vi* (~ *down*) наклоня́ться *impf*, наклони́ться *pf*.

duckling *n* утёнок.

duct *n* прохо́д; (*anat*) прото́к.

dud *n* (*forgery*) подде́лка; (*shell*) неразорва́вшийся снаря́д; *adj* подде́льный; (*worthless*) него́дный.

due *n* (*credit*) до́лжное *sb*; *pl* взно́сы *m pl*; *adj* (*proper*) до́лжный, надлежа́щий; *predic* (*expected*) до́лжен (-жна́); **in ~ course** со вре́менем; ~ **south** пря́мо на юг; ~ **to** благодаря́+*dat*.

duel *n* дуэ́ль.

duet *n* дуэ́т.

duke *n* ге́рцог.

dull *adj* (*tedious*) ску́чный; (*colour*) ту́склый, (*weather*) па́смурный; (*not sharp*; *stupid*) тупо́й; *vt* притупля́ть *impf*, притупи́ть *pf*.

duly *adv* надлежа́щим о́бразом; (*punctually*) своевре́менно.

dumb *adj* немо́й. **dumbfounded** *adj* ошара́шенный.

dummy *n* (*tailor's*) манеке́н; (*baby's*) со́ска; ~ **run** испыта́тельный рейс.

dump *n* сва́лка; *vt* сва́ливать *impf*, свали́ть *pf*.

dumpling *n* клёцка.

dumpy *adj* призе́мистый.

dune *n* дю́на.

dung *n* наво́з.

dungarees *n pl* комбинезо́н.

dungeon *n* темни́ца.

dunk *vt* мака́ть *impf*, макну́ть *pf*.

duo *n* па́ра; (*mus*) дуэ́т.

dupe *vt* надува́ть *impf*, наду́ть *pf*; *n* простофи́ля *m* & *f*.

duplicate *n* ко́пия; **in** ~ в двух экземпля́рах; *adj* (*double*) двойно́й; (*identical*) иденти́чный; *vt* размножа́ть *impf*, размно́жить *pf* **duplicity** *n* двули́чность.

durability *n* про́чность. **durable** *adj* про́чный. **duration** *n* продолжи́тельность.

duress *n* принужде́ние; **under** ~ под давле́нием.

during *prep* во вре́мя +*gen*; (*throughout*) в тече́ние +*gen*.

dusk *n* су́мерки (-рек) *pl*.

dust *n* пыль; ~**bin** му́сорный я́щик; ~**-jacket** суперобло́жка; ~**man** му́сорщик; ~**pan** сово́к; *vt* & *i* (*clean*) стира́ть *impf*, стере́ть *pf* пыль (с+*gen*); (*sprinkle*) посыпа́ть *impf*, посы́пать *pf sth* +*acc*, *with* +*instr*. **duster** *n* пы́льная тря́пка.

dusty *adj* пы́льный.
Dutch *adj* голла́ндский; *n*: **the** ~ голла́ндцы *m pl*. **Dutchman** *n* голла́ндец. **Dutchwoman** *n* голла́ндка.
dutiful *adj* послу́шный. **duty** *n* (*obligation*) долг; обя́занность; (*office*) дежу́рство; (*tax*) по́шлина; **be on** ~ дежу́рить *impf*; **~-free** *adj* беспо́шлинный.
duvet *n* стёганое одея́ло.
dwarf *n* ка́рлик; *vt* (*tower above*) возвыша́ться *impf*, возвы́ситься *pf* над+*instr*.
dwell *vi* обита́ть *impf*; ~ **upon** остана́вливаться *impf* на+*prep*. **dweller** *n* жи́тель *m*. **dwelling** *n* жили́ще.
dwindle *vi* убыва́ть *impf*, убы́ть *pf*.
dye *n* краси́тель *m*; *vt* окра́шивать *impf*, окра́сить *pf*.
dynamic *adj* динами́ческий. **dynamics** *n pl* дина́мика.
dynamite *n* динами́т.
dynamo *n* дина́мо *neut indecl*.
dynasty *n* дина́стия.
dysentery *n* дизентери́я.
dyslexia *n* дисле́ксия. **dyslexic** *adj*: **he is** ~ он дисле́ктик.

E

each *adj* & *pron* ка́ждый; ~ **other** друг дру́га (*dat* -гу, *etc*.).
eager *adj* (*pupil*) усе́рдный; **I am** ~ **to** мне не те́рпится +*inf*; о́чень жела́ю +*inf*. **eagerly** *adv* с нетерпе́нием; жа́дно. **eagerness** *n* си́льное жела́ние.
eagle *n* орёл.
ear[1] *n* (*corn*) ко́лос.
ear[2] *n* (*anat*) у́хо; (*sense*) слух; **~-ache** боль в у́хе; **~drum** бараба́нная перепо́нка; **~mark** (*assign*) предназнача́ть *impf*, предназна́чить *pf*; **~phone** нау́шник; **~ring** серьга́; (*clip-on*) клипс; **~shot**: **within/out of** ~ в преде́лах/вне преде́лов слы́шимости.
earl *n* граф.
early *adj* ра́нний; *adv* ра́но.
earn *vt* зараба́тывать *impf*, зарабо́тать *pf*; (*deserve*) заслу́живать *impf*, заслужи́ть *pf*. **earnings** *n pl* за́работок.
earnest *adj* серьёзный; *n*: **in** ~ всерьёз.
earth *n* земля́; (*soil*) по́чва; *vt* заземля́ть *impf*, заземли́ть *pf*. **earthenware** *adj* гли́няный. **earthly** *adj* земно́й. **earthquake** *n* землетрясе́ние. **earthy** *adj* земли́стый; (*coarse*) гру́бый.
earwig *n* уховёртка.
ease *n* (*facility*) лёгкость; (*unconstraint*) непринуждённость; **with** ~ легко́; *vt* облегча́ть *impf*, облегчи́ть *pf*; *vi* успока́иваться *impf*, успоко́иться *pf*.
easel *n* мольбе́рт.
east *n* восто́к; (*naut*) ост; *adj* восто́чный. **easterly** *adj* восто́чный. **eastern** *adj* восто́чный. **eastward(s)** *adv* на восто́к, к восто́ку.
Easter *n* Па́сха.
easy *adj* лёгкий; (*unconstrained*) непринуждённый; **~-going** ужи́вчивый.
eat *vt* есть *impf*, с~ *pf*; ку́шать *impf*, по~, с~ *pf*; ~ **away** разъеда́ть *impf*, разъе́сть *pf*; ~ **into** въеда́ться *impf*, въе́сться *pf* в+*acc*; ~ **up** доеда́ть *impf*, дое́сть *pf*. **eatable** *adj* съедо́бный.
eaves *n pl* стреха́. **eavesdrop**

vi подслу́шивать *impf.*
ebb *n* (*tide*) отли́в; (*fig*) упа́док.
ebony *n* чёрное де́рево.
ebullient *adj* кипу́чий.
EC *abbr* (*of* **European Community**) Европе́йское соо́бщество.
eccentric *n* чуда́к; *adj* эксцентри́чный.
ecclesiastical *adj* церко́вный.
echo *n* э́хо; *vi* (*resound*) отража́ться *impf*, отрази́ться *pf*; *vt* (*repeat*) повторя́ть *impf*, повтори́ть *pf.*
eclipse *n* затме́ние; *vt* затмева́ть *impf*, затми́ть *pf.*
ecological *adj* экологи́ческий. **ecology** *n* эколо́гия.
economic *adj* экономи́ческий. **economical** *adj* эконо́мный. **economist** *n* экономи́ст. **economize** *vt* & *i* эконо́мить *impf*, с~ *pf.* **economy** *n* эконо́мика; (*saving*) эконо́мия.
ecstasy *n* экста́з. **ecstatic** *adj* экстати́ческий.
eddy *n* водоворо́т.
edge *n* край; (*blade*) ле́звие; **on** ~ в не́рвном состоя́нии; **have the** ~ **on** име́ть *impf* преиму́щество над+*instr*; *vt* (*border*) окаймля́ть *impf*, окайми́ть *pf*; *vi* пробира́ться *impf*, пробра́ться *pf.* **edging** *n* кайма́. **edgy** *adj* раздражи́тельный.
edible *adj* съедо́бный.
edict *n* ука́з.
edifice *n* зда́ние. **edifying** *adj* назида́тельный.
edit *vt* редакти́ровать *impf*, от~ *pf*; (*cin*) монти́ровать *impf*, с~ *pf.* **edition** *n* изда́ние; (*number of copies*) тира́ж. **editor** *n* реда́ктор.
editorial *n* передова́я статья́; *adj* реда́кторский, редакцио́нный.
educate *vt* дава́ть *impf*, дать *pf* образова́ние +*dat*; **where was he educated?** где он получи́л образова́ние? **educated** *adj* образо́ванный. **education** *n* образова́ние. **educational** *adj* образова́тельный; (*instructive*) уче́бный.
eel *n* у́горь *m.*
eerie *adj* жу́ткий.
effect *n* (*result*) сле́дствие; (*validity*; *influence*) де́йствие; (*impression*; *theat*) эффе́кт; **in** ~ факти́чески; **take** ~ вступа́ть *impf*, вступи́ть *pf* в си́лу; (*medicine*) начина́ть *impf*, нача́ть *pf* де́йствовать; *vt* производи́ть *impf*, произвести́ *pf.* **effective** *adj* эффекти́вный; (*striking*) эффе́ктный; (*actual*) факти́ческий. **effectiveness** *n* эффекти́вность.
effeminate *adj* женоподо́бный.
effervesce *vi* пузы́риться *impf.* **effervescent** *adj* (*fig*) искря́щийся.
efficiency *n* эффекти́вность. **efficient** *adj* эффекти́вный; (*person*) организо́ванный.
effigy *n* изображе́ние.
effort *n* уси́лие.
effrontery *n* на́глость.
effusive *adj* экспанси́вный.
e.g. *abbr* напр.
egalitarian *adj* эгалита́рный.
egg[1] *n* яйцо́; ~**cup** рю́мка для яйца́; ~**shell** яи́чная скорлупа́.
egg[2] *vt*: ~ **on** подстрека́ть *impf*, подстрекну́ть *pf.*
ego *n* «Я». **egocentric** *adj*

эгоцентри́ческий. **egoism** *n* эгои́зм. **ego(t)ist** *n* эгои́ст, ~ка. **ego(t)istical** *adj* эгоцентри́ческий. **egotism** *n* эготи́зм.

Egypt *n* Еги́пет. **Egyptian** *n* египтя́нин, -я́нка; *adj* еги́петский.

elderdown *n* пухо́вое одея́ло.

eight *adj* & *n* во́семь; (*number 8*) восьмёрка. **eighteen** *adj* & *n* восемна́дцать. **eighteenth** *adj* & *n* восемна́дцатый. **eighth** *adj* & *n* восьмо́й; (*fraction*) восьма́я *sb*. **eightieth** *adj* & *n* восьмидеся́тый. **eighty** *adj* & *n* во́семьдесят; *pl* (*decade*) восьмидеся́тые го́ды (-до́в) *m pl*.

either *adj* & *pron* (*one of two*) оди́н из двух, тот и́ли друго́й; (*both*) и тот, и друго́й; о́ба; (*one or other*) любо́й; *adv* & *conj*: ~ ... **or** и́ли... и́ли, ли́бо... ли́бо.

eject *vt* выбра́сывать *impf*, вы́бросить *pf*; *vi* (*pilot*) катапульти́роваться *impf* & *pf*.

eke *vt*: ~ **out a living** перебива́ться *impf*, переби́ться *pf* ко́е-как.

elaborate *adj* (*ornate*) витиева́тый; (*detailed*) подро́бный; *vt* разраба́тывать *impf*, разрабо́тать *pf*; (*detail*) уточня́ть *impf*, уточни́ть *pf*.

elapse *vi* проходи́ть *impf*, пройти́ *pf*; (*expire*) истека́ть *impf*, истечь *pf*.

elastic *n* рези́нка; *adj* эласти́чный, ~ **band** рези́нка. **elasticity** *n* эласти́чность.

elated *adj* в восто́рге. **elation** *n* восто́рг.

elbow *n* ло́коть *m*; *vt*: ~ **(one's way) through** прота́лкиваться *impf*, протолкну́ться *pf* че́рез+*acc*.

elder[1] *n* (*tree*) бузина́.

elder[2] *n* (*person*) ста́рец; *pl* ста́ршие *sb*; *adj* ста́рший. **elderly** *adj* пожило́й. **eldest** *adj* ста́рший.

elect *adj* и́збранный; *vt* избира́ть *impf*, избра́ть *pf*. **election** *n* вы́боры *m pl*. **elector** *n* избира́тель *m*. **electoral** *adj* избира́тельный. **electorate** *n* избира́тели *m pl*.

electric(al) *adj* электри́ческий; ~ **shock** уда́р электри́ческим то́ком. **electrician** *n* эле́ктрик. **electricity** *n* электри́чество. **electrify** *vt* (*convert to electricity*) электрифици́ровать *impf* & *pf*; (*charge with electricity*; *fig*) электризова́ть *impf*, на~ *pf*.

electrode *n* электро́д. **electron** *n* электро́н. **electronic** *adj* электро́нный. **electronics** *n* электро́ника.

electrocute *vt* убива́ть *impf*, уби́ть *pf* электри́ческим то́ком; (*execute*) казни́ть *impf* & *pf* на электри́ческом сту́ле.

electrolysis *n* электро́лиз.

elegance *n* элега́нтность. **elegant** *adj* элега́нтный.

elegy *n* эле́гия.

element *n* элеме́нт; (*earth, wind, etc.*) стихи́я; **be in one's** ~ быть в свое́й стихи́и. **elemental** *adj* стихи́йный. **elementary** *adj* элемента́рный; (*school etc.*) нача́льный.

elephant *n* слон.

elevate *vt* поднима́ть *impf*, подня́ть *pf*. **elevated** *adj* возвы́шенный. **elevation** *n* (*height*) высота́. **elevator** *n* (*lift*) лифт.

eleven *adj* & *n* оди́ннадцать. **eleventh** *adj* & *n* оди́ннадцатый; **at the ~ hour** в после́днюю мину́ту.

elf *n* эльф.

elicit *vt* (*obtain*) выявля́ть *impf*, вы́явить *pf*; (*evoke*) вызыва́ть *impf*, вы́звать *pf*.

eligible *adj* име́ющий пра́во (**for** на+*acc*); (*bachelor*) подходя́щий.

eliminate *vt* устраня́ть *impf*, устрани́ть *pf*; (*rule out*) исключа́ть *impf*, исключи́ть *pf*.

élite *n* эли́та.

ellipse *n* э́ллипс. **elliptic(al)** *adj* эллипти́ческий.

elm *n* вяз.

elongate *vt* удлиня́ть *impf*, удлини́ть *pf*.

elope *vi* бежа́ть *det* (с возлю́бленным).

eloquence *n* красноре́чие. **eloquent** *adj* красноречи́вый.

else *adv* (*besides*) ещё; (*instead*) друго́й; (*with neg*) бо́льше; **nobody ~** никто́ бо́льше; **or ~** и́наче; а (не) то; и́ли же; **s.o. ~** кто-нибу́дь друго́й; **something ~?** ещё что́-нибудь? **elsewhere** *adv* (*place*) в друго́м ме́сте; (*direction*) в друго́е ме́сто.

elucidate *vt* разъясня́ть *impf*, разъясни́ть *pf*.

elude *vt* избега́ть *impf* +*gen*. **elusive** *adj* неулови́мый.

emaciated *adj* истощённый.

email *n* (*system, letters*) электро́нная по́чта; (*letter*) электро́нное письмо́; **~ address** электро́нный а́дрес.

emanate *vi* исходи́ть *impf* (**from** из, от, +*gen*).

emancipate *vt* эмансипи́ровать *impf* & *pf*. **emancipation** *n* эмансипа́ция.

embankment *n* (*river*) на́бережная *sb*; (*rly*) на́сыпь.

embargo *n* эмба́рго *neut indecl*.

embark *vi* сади́ться *impf*, сесть *pf* на кора́бль; **~ upon** предпринима́ть *impf*, предприня́ть *pf*. **embarkation** *n* поса́дка (на кора́бль).

embarrass *vt* смуща́ть *impf*, смути́ть *pf*; **be ~ed** чу́вствовать *impf* себя́ неудо́бно. **embarrassing** *adj* неудо́бный. **embarrassment** *n* смуще́ние.

embassy *n* посо́льство.

embedded *adj* вре́занный.

embellish *vt* (*adorn*) украша́ть *impf*, укра́сить *pf*; (*story*) прикра́шивать *impf*, прикра́сить *pf*. **embellishment** *n* украше́ние.

embers *n pl* тле́ющие уго́льки́ *m pl*.

embezzle *vt* растра́чивать *impf*, растра́тить *pf*. **embezzlement** *n* растра́та.

embittered *adj* озло́бленный.

emblem *n* эмбле́ма.

embodiment *n* воплоще́ние. **embody** *vt* воплоща́ть *impf*, воплоти́ть *pf*.

emboss *vt* чека́нить *impf*, вы́~, от~ *pf*.

embrace *n* объя́тие; *vi* обнима́ться *impf*, обня́ться *pf*; *vt* обнима́ть *impf*, обня́ть *pf*; (*accept*) принима́ть *impf*, приня́ть *pf*; (*include*) охва́тывать *impf*, охвати́ть *pf*.

embroider *vt* вышива́ть *impf*, вы́шить *pf*; (*story*) прикра́шивать *impf*, прикра́сить *pf*. **embroidery** *n* вы́шивка.

embroil *vt* впу́тывать *impf*, впу́тать *pf*.

embryo *n* эмбрио́н.

emerald *n* изумру́д.

emerge *vi* появля́ться *impf*, появи́ться *pf*. **emergence** *n*

появле́ние. **emergency** *n* кра́йняя необходи́мость; **state of ~** чрезвыча́йное положе́ние; **~ exit** запасно́й вы́ход.
emery paper *n* нажда́чная бума́га.
emigrant *n* эмигра́нт, ~ка. **emigrate** *vi* эмигри́ровать *impf* & *pf*. **emigration** *n* эмигра́ция.
eminence *n* (*fame*) знамени́тость. **eminent** *adj* выдаю́щийся. **eminently** *adv* чрезвыча́йно.
emission *n* испуска́ние. **emit** *vt* испуска́ть *impf*, испусти́ть *pf*; (*light*) излуча́ть *impf*, излучи́ть *pf*; (*sound*) издава́ть *impf*, изда́ть *pf*.
emotion *n* эмо́ция, чу́вство. **emotional** *adj* эмоциона́льный.
empathize *vt* сопережива́ть *impf*, сопережи́ть *pf*. **empathy** *n* эмпа́тия.
emperor *n* импера́тор.
emphasis *n* ударе́ние. **emphasize** *vt* подчёркивать *impf*, подчеркну́ть *pf*. **emphatic** *adj* вырази́тельный; категори́ческий.
empire *n* импе́рия.
empirical *adj* эмпири́ческий.
employ *vt* (*use*) по́льзоваться *impf* +*instr*; (*person*) нанима́ть *impf*, наня́ть *pf*. **employee** *n* сотру́дник, рабо́чий *sb*. **employer** *n* работода́тель *m*. **employment** *n* рабо́та, слу́жба; (*use*) испо́льзование.
empower *vt* уполномо́чивать *impf*, уполномо́чить *pf* (**to** на+*acc*).
empress *n* императри́ца.
emptiness *n* пустота́. **empty** *adj* пусто́й; **~-headed** пустоголо́вый; *vt* (*container*) опорожня́ть *impf*, опоро́жни́ть *pf*; (*solid*) высыпа́ть *impf*, вы́сыпать *pf*; (*liquid*) выливать *impf*, вы́лить *pf*; *vi* пусте́ть *impf*, о~ *pf*.
emulate *vt* достига́ть *impf*, дости́гнуть, дости́чь *pf* +*gen*; (*copy*) подража́ть *impf* +*dat*.
emulsion *n* эму́льсия.
enable *vt* дава́ть *impf*, дать *pf* возмо́жность +*dat* & *inf*.
enact *vt* (*law*) принима́ть *impf*, приня́ть *pf*; (*theat*) разы́грывать *impf*, разыгра́ть *pf*. **enactment** *n* (*law*) постановле́ние; (*theat*) игра́.
enamel *n* эма́ль; *adj* эма́левый; *vt* эмалирова́ть *impf* & *pf*.
encampment *n* ла́герь *m*.
enchant *vt* очаро́вывать *impf*, очарова́ть *pf*. **enchanting** *adj* очарова́тельный. **enchantment** *n* очарова́ние.
encircle *vt* окружа́ть *impf*, окружи́ть *pf*.
enclave *n* анкла́в.
enclose *vt* огора́живать *impf*, огороди́ть *pf*; (*in letter*) прикла́дывать *impf*, приложи́ть *pf*; **please find ~d** прилага́ется (-а́ются) +*nom*. **enclosure** *n* огоро́женное ме́сто; (*in letter*) приложе́ние.
encode *vt* шифрова́ть *impf*, за~ *pf*.
encompass *vt* (*encircle*) окружа́ть *impf*, окружи́ть *pf*; (*contain*) заключа́ть *impf*, заключи́ть *pf*.
encore *int* бис!; *n* вы́зов на бис.
encounter *n* встре́ча; (*in combat*) столкнове́ние; *vt*

встреча́ть *impf*, встре́тить *pf*; (*fig*) ста́лкиваться *impf*, столкну́ться *pf* с+*instr*.

encourage *vt* ободря́ть *impf*, ободри́ть *pf*. **encouragement** *n* ободре́ние. **encouraging** *adj* ободри́тельный.

encroach *vt* вторга́ться *impf*, вто́ргнуться *pf* (**on** в+*acc*). **encroachment** *n* вторже́ние.

encumber *vt* обременя́ть *impf*, обремени́ть *pf*. **encumbrance** *n* обу́за.

encyclopaedia *n* энциклопе́дия. **encyclopaedic** *adj* энциклопеди́ческий.

end *n* коне́ц; (*death*) смерть; (*purpose*) цель; **an ~ in itself** самоце́ль; **in the ~** в конце́ концо́в; **make ~s meet** своди́ть *impf*, свести́ *pf* концы́ с конца́ми; **no ~ of** ма́сса+*gen*; **on ~** (*upright*) стоймя́, ды́бом; (*continuously*) подря́д; **put an ~ to** класть *impf*, положи́ть *pf* коне́ц +*dat*; *vt* конча́ть *impf*, ко́нчить *pf*; (*halt*) прекраща́ть *impf*, прекрати́ть *pf*; *vi* конча́ться *impf*, ко́нчиться *pf*.

endanger *vt* подверга́ть *impf*, подве́ргнуть *pf* опа́сности.

endearing *adj* привлека́тельный. **endearment** *n* ла́ска.

endeavour *n* попы́тка; (*exertion*) уси́лие; (*undertaking*) де́ло; *vi* стара́ться *impf*, по~ *pf*.

endemic *adj* эндеми́ческий.

ending *n* оконча́ние. **endless** *adj* бесконе́чный.

endorse *vt* (*document*) подпи́сывать *impf*, подписа́ть *pf*; (*support*) подде́рживать *impf*, поддержа́ть *pf*. **endorsement** *n* по́дпись; подде́ржка; (*on driving licence*) проко́л.

endow *vt* обеспе́чивать *impf*, обеспе́чить *pf* постоя́нным дохо́дом; (*fig*) одаря́ть *impf*, одари́ть *pf*. **endowment** *n* поже́ртвование; (*talent*) дарова́ние.

endurance *n* (*of person*) выно́сливость; (*of object*) про́чность. **endure** *vt* выноси́ть *impf*, вы́нести *pf*; терпе́ть *impf*, по~ *pf*; *vi* продолжа́ться *impf*, продо́лжиться *pf*.

enemy *n* враг; *adj* вра́жеский.

energetic *adj* энерги́чный. **energy** *n* эне́ргия; *pl* си́лы *f pl*.

enforce *vt* (*law etc.*) следи́ть *impf* за выполне́нием +*gen*. **enforcement** *n* наблюде́ние за выполне́нием +*gen*.

engage *vt* (*hire*) нанима́ть *impf*, наня́ть *pf*; (*tech*) зацепля́ть *impf*, зацепи́ть *pf*. **engaged** *adj* (*occupied*) за́нятый; **be ~ in** занима́ться *impf*, заня́ться *pf* +*instr*; **become ~** обруча́ться *impf*, обручи́ться *pf* (**to** с+*instr*). **engagement** *n* (*appointment*) свида́ние; (*betrothal*) обруче́ние; (*battle*) бой; **~ ring** обруча́льное кольцо́. **engaging** *adj* привлека́тельный.

engender *vt* порожда́ть *impf*, породи́ть *pf*.

engine *n* дви́гатель *m*; (*rly*) локомоти́в; **~-driver** (*rly*) машини́ст. **engineer** *n* инжене́р; *vt* (*fig*) организова́ть *impf* & *pf*. **engineering** *n* инжене́рное де́ло, те́хника.

England *n* А́нглия. **English** *adj* англи́йский; *n*: **the ~** *pl* англича́не (-н) *pl*. **Englishman, -woman** *n* англича́нин, -а́нка.

engrave *vt* гравирова́ть *impf*, вы́~ *pf*; (*fig*) вреза́ть *impf*, вре́зать *pf*. **engraver** *n* граве́р. **engraving** *n* гравю́ра.

engross *vt* поглоща́ть *impf*, поглоти́ть *pf*; **be ~ed in** быть поглощённым +*instr*.

engulf *vt* поглоща́ть *impf*, поглоти́ть *pf*.

enhance *vt* увели́чивать *impf*, увели́чить *pf*.

enigma *n* зага́дка. **enigmatic** *adj* зага́дочный.

enjoy *vt* получа́ть *impf*, получи́ть *pf* удово́льствие от+*gen*; наслажда́ться *impf*, наслади́ться *pf* +*instr*; (*health etc.*) облада́ть *impf* +*instr*; **~ o.s.** хорошо́ проводи́ть *impf*, провести́ *pf* вре́мя. **enjoyable** *adj* прия́тный. **enjoyment** *n* удово́льствие.

enlarge *vt* увели́чивать *impf*, увели́чить *pf*; **~ upon** распространя́ться *impf*, распространи́ться *pf* о+*prep*. **enlargement** *n* увеличе́ние.

enlighten *vt* просвеща́ть *impf*, просвети́ть *pf*. **enlightenment** *n* просвеще́ние.

enlist *vi* поступа́ть *impf*, поступи́ть *pf* на вое́нную слу́жбу; *vt* (*mil*) вербова́ть *impf*, за~ *pf*; (*support etc.*) заруча́ться *impf*, заручи́ться *pf* +*instr*.

enliven *vt* оживля́ть *impf*, оживи́ть *pf*.

enmity *n* вражда́.

ennoble *vt* облагора́живать *impf*, облагоро́дить *pf*.

ennui *n* тоска́.

enormity *n* чудо́вищность. **enormous** *adj* огро́мный. **enormously** *adv* чрезвыча́йно.

enough *adj* доста́точно +*gen*; *adv* доста́точно, дово́льно; **be ~** хвата́ть *impf*, хвати́ть *pf impers+gen*.

enquire, enquiry *see* **inquire, inquiry**

enrage *vt* беси́ть *impf*, вз~ *pf*.

enrapture *vt* восхища́ть *impf*, восхити́ть *pf*.

enrich *vt* обогаща́ть *impf*, обогати́ть *pf*.

enrol *vt & i* запи́сывать(ся) *impf*, записа́ть(ся) *pf*. **enrolment** *n* за́пись.

en route *adv* по пути́ (**to, for** в+*acc*).

ensconce *vt*: **~ o.s.** заса́живаться *impf*, засе́сть *pf* (**with** за+*acc*).

ensemble *n* (*mus*) анса́мбль *m*.

enshrine *vt* (*fig*) охраня́ть *impf*, охрани́ть *pf*.

ensign *n* (*flag*) флаг.

enslave *vt* порабоща́ть *impf*, поработи́ть *pf*.

ensue *vi* сле́довать *impf*. **ensuing** *adj* после́дующий.

ensure *vt* обеспе́чивать *impf*, обеспе́чить *pf*.

entail *vt* (*necessitate*) влечь *impf* за собо́й.

entangle *vt* запу́тывать *impf*, запу́тать *pf*.

enter *vt & i* входи́ть *impf*, войти́ *pf* в+*acc*; (*by transport*) въезжа́ть *impf*, въе́хать *pf* в+*acc*; *vt* (*join*) поступа́ть *impf*, поступи́ть *pf* в, на, +*acc*; (*competition*) вступа́ть *impf*, вступи́ть *pf* в+*acc*; (*in list*) вноси́ть *impf*, внести́ *pf* в+*acc*.

enterprise *n* (*undertaking*) предприя́тие; (*initiative*) предприи́мчивость. **enterprising** *adj* предприи́мчивый.

entertain *vt* (*amuse*) развлека́ть *impf*, развле́чь *pf*;

(*guests*) принима́ть *impf*, приня́ть *pf*; угоща́ть *impf*, угости́ть *pf* (to +*instr*); (*hopes*) пита́ть *impf*. **entertaining** *adj* занима́тельный. **entertainment** *n* развлече́ние; (*show*) представле́ние.

enthral *vt* порабоща́ть *impf*, поработи́ть *pf*.

enthusiasm *n* энтузиа́зм. **enthusiast** *n* энтузиа́ст, ~ка. **enthusiastic** *adj* восто́рженный; по́лный энтузиа́зма.

entice *vt* зама́нивать *impf*, замани́ть *pf*. **enticement** *n* прима́нка. **enticing** *adj* зама́нчивый.

entire *adj* по́лный, це́лый, весь. **entirely** *adv* вполне́, соверше́нно; (*solely*) исключи́тельно. **entirety** *n*: **in its ~** по́лностью.

entitle *vt* (*authorize*) дава́ть *impf*, дать *pf* пра́во+*dat* (**to** на+*acc*); **be ~d** (*book*) называ́ться *impf*; **be ~d to** име́ть *impf* пра́во на+*acc*.

entity *n* объе́кт; феноме́н.

entomology *n* энтомоло́гия.

entourage *n* сви́та.

entrails *n pl* вну́тренности (-тей) *pl*.

entrance[1] *n* вход, въезд; (*theat*) вы́ход; **~ exam** вступи́тельный экза́мен; **~ hall** вестибю́ль *m*.

entrance[2] *vt* (*charm*) очаро́вывать *impf*, очарова́ть *pf*. **entrancing** *adj* очарова́тельный.

entrant *n* уча́стник (**for** +*gen*).

entreat *vt* умоля́ть *impf*, умоли́ть *pf*. **entreaty** *n* мольба́.

entrench *vt* **be, become ~ed** (*fig*) укореня́ться *impf*, укорени́ться *pf*.

entrepreneur *n* предпринима́тель *m*.

entrust *vt* (*secret*) вверя́ть *impf*, вве́рить *pf* (**to** +*dat*); (*object*; *person*) поруча́ть *impf*, поручи́ть *pf* (**to** +*dat*).

entry *n* вход, въезд; вступле́ние; (*theat*) вы́ход; (*note*) за́пись; (*in reference book*) статья́.

entwine *vt* (*interweave*) сплета́ть *impf*, сплести́ *pf*; (*wreathe*) обвива́ть *impf*, обви́ть *pf*.

enumerate *vt* перечисля́ть *impf*, перечи́слить *pf*.

enunciate *vt* (*express*) излага́ть *impf*, изложи́ть *pf*; (*pronounce*) произноси́ть *impf*, произнести́ *pf*. **enunciation** *n* изложе́ние; произноше́ние.

envelop *vt* оку́тывать *impf*, оку́тать *pf*. **envelope** *n* конве́рт.

enviable *adj* зави́дный. **envious** *adj* зави́стливый.

environment *n* среда́; (*the ~*) окружа́ющая среда́. **environs** *n pl* окре́стности *f pl*.

envisage *vt* предусма́тривать *impf*, предусмотре́ть *pf*.

envoy *n* посла́нник, аге́нт.

envy *n* за́висть; *vt* зави́довать *impf*, по~ *pf* +*dat*.

enzyme *n* энзи́м.

ephemeral *adj* эфеме́рный.

epic *n* эпопе́я; *adj* эпи́ческий.

epidemic *n* эпиде́мия.

epilepsy *n* эпиле́псия. **epileptic** *n* эпиле́птик; *adj* эпилепти́ческий.

epilogue *n* эпило́г.

episode *n* эпизо́д. **episodic** *adj* эпизоди́ческий.

epistle *n* посла́ние.

epitaph *n* эпита́фия.

epithet *n* эпи́тет.

epitome *n* воплоще́ние. **epitomize** *vt* воплоща́ть *impf*,

воплотить *pf.*
epoch *n* эпо́ха.
equal *adj* ра́вный, одина́ковый; (*capable of*) спосо́бный (**to** на+*acc*, +*inf*); *n* ра́вный *sb*; *vt* равня́ться *impf* +*dat*. **equality** *n* ра́венство. **equalize** *vt* ура́внивать *impf*, уравня́ть *pf*; *vi* (*sport*) равня́ть *impf*, с~ *pf* счёт. **equally** *adv* равно́, ра́вным о́бразом.
equanimity *n* хладнокро́вие.
equate *vt* прира́внивать *impf*, приравня́ть *pf* (**with** к+*dat*).
equation *n* (*math*) уравне́ние.
equator *n* эква́тор. **equatorial** *adj* экваториа́льный.
equestrian *adj* ко́нный.
equidistant *adj* равностоя́щий. **equilibrium** *n* равнове́сие.
equip *vt* обору́довать *impf* & *pf*; (*person*) снаряжа́ть *impf*, снаряди́ть *pf*; (*fig*) вооружа́ть *impf*, вооружи́ть *pf*. **equipment** *n* обору́дование, снаряже́ние.
equitable *adj* справедли́вый. **equity** *n* справедли́вость; *pl* (*econ*) обыкнове́нные а́кции *f pl*.
equivalent *adj* эквивале́нтный; *n* эквивале́нт.
equivocal *adj* двусмы́сленный.
era *n* э́ра.
eradicate *vt* искореня́ть *impf*, искорени́ть *pf*.
erase *vt* стира́ть *impf*, стере́ть *pf*; (*from memory*) вычёркивать *impf*, вы́черкнуть *pf* (из па́мяти). **eraser** *n* ла́стик.
erect *adj* прямо́й; *vt* сооружа́ть *impf*, сооруди́ть *pf*. **erection** *n* сооруже́ние; (*biol*) эре́кция.
erode *vt* разруша́ть *impf*, разру́шить *pf*. **erosion** *n* эро́зия; (*fig*) разруше́ние.
erotic *adj* эроти́ческий.
err *vi* ошиба́ться *impf*, ошиби́ться *pf*; (*sin*) греши́ть *impf*, со~ *pf*.
errand *n* поруче́ние; **run ~s** быть на посы́лках (**for** у+*gen*).
erratic *adj* неро́вный.
erroneous *adj* оши́бочный. **error** *n* оши́бка.
erudite *adj* учёный. **erudition** *n* эруди́ция.
erupt *vi* взрыва́ться *impf*, взорва́ться *pf*; (*volcano*) изверга́ться *impf*, изве́ргнуться *pf*. **eruption** *n* изверже́ние.
escalate *vi* возраста́ть *impf*, возрасти́ *pf*; *vt* интенсифици́ровать *impf* & *pf*.
escalator *n* эскала́тор.
escapade *n* вы́ходка. **escape** *n* (*from prison*) побе́г; (*from danger*) спасе́ние; (*leak*) уте́чка; **have a narrow ~** едва́ спасти́сь; *vi* (*flee*) бежа́ть *impf* & *pf*; убега́ть *impf*, убежа́ть *pf*; (*save o.s.*) спаса́ться *impf*, спасти́сь *pf*; (*leak*) утека́ть *impf*, уте́чь *pf*; *vt* избега́ть *impf*, избежа́ть *pf* +*gen*; (*groan*) вырыва́ться *impf*, вы́рваться *pf* из, у, +*gen*.
escort *n* (*mil*) эско́рт; (*of lady*) кавале́р; *vt* сопровожда́ть *impf*, сопроводи́ть *pf*; (*mil*) эскорти́ровать *impf* & *pf*.
Eskimo *n* эскимо́с, ~ка.
esoteric *adj* эзотери́ческий.
especially *adv* осо́бенно.
espionage *n* шпиона́ж.
espousal *n* подде́ржка. **espouse** *vt* (*fig*) подде́рживать

impf, поддержа́ть *pf.*
essay *n* о́черк; (*in school*) сочине́ние.
essence *n* (*philos*) су́щность; (*gist*) суть; (*extract*) эссе́нция. **essential** *adj* (*fundamental*) суще́ственный; (*necessary*) необходи́мый; *n pl* (*necessities*) необходи́мое *sb*; (*crux*) суть; (*fundamentals*) осно́вы *f pl.* **essentially** *adv* по существу́.
establish *vt* (*set up*) учрежда́ть *impf*, учреди́ть *pf*; (*fact etc.*) устана́вливать *impf*, установи́ть *pf.* **establishment** *n* (*action*) учрежде́ние, установле́ние; (*institution*) учрежде́ние.
estate *n* (*property*) име́ние; (*after death*) насле́дство; (*housing* ~) жило́й масси́в; ~ **agent** аге́нт по прода́же недви́жимости; ~ **car** автомоби́ль *m* с ку́зовом «универса́л».
esteem *n* уваже́ние; *vt* уважа́ть *impf.* **estimate** *n* (*of quality*) оце́нка; (*of cost*) сме́та; *vt* оце́нивать *impf*, оцени́ть *pf.* **estimation** *n* оце́нка, мне́ние.
Estonia *n* Эсто́ния. **Estonian** *n* эсто́нец, -нка; *adj* эсто́нский.
estranged *adj* отчуждённый.
estuary *n* у́стье.
etc. *abbr* и т.д. **etcetera** и так да́лее.
etch *vt* трави́ть *impf*, вы~ *pf.* **etching** *n* (*action*) травле́ние; (*object*) офо́рт.
eternal *adj* ве́чный. **eternity** *n* ве́чность.
ether *n* эфи́р. **ethereal** *adj* эфи́рный.
ethical *adj* эти́ческий, эти́чный. **ethics** *n* э́тика.
ethnic *adj* этни́ческий.
etiquette *n* этике́т.
etymology *n* этимоло́гия.
EU *abbr* (*of* **European Union**) ЕС.
eucalyptus *n* эвкали́пт.
Eucharist *n* прича́стие.
eulogy *n* похвала́.
euphemism *n* эвфеми́зм. **euphemistic** *adj* эвфемисти́ческий.
euro *n* е́вро *neut indecl.*
Europe *n* Евро́па. **European** *n* европе́ец; *adj* европе́йский; ~ **Community** Европе́йское соо́бщество; ~ **Union** Европе́йский сою́з.
evacuate *vt* (*person, place*) эвакуи́ровать *impf* & *pf.* **evacuation** *n* эвакуа́ция.
evade *vt* уклоня́ться *impf*, уклони́ться *pf* от+*gen.*
evaluate *vt* оце́нивать *impf*, оцени́ть *pf.* **evaluation** *n* оце́нка.
evangelical *adj* ева́нгельский. **evangelist** *n* евангели́ст.
evaporate *vt* & *i* испаря́ть(ся) *impf*, испари́ть(ся) *pf.* **evaporation** *n* испаре́ние.
evasion *n* уклоне́ние (**of** от+*gen*). **evasive** *adj* уклó́нчивый.
eve *n* кану́н; **on the** ~ накану́не.
even *adj* ро́вный; (*number*) чётный; **get** ~ расквита́ться *pf* (**with** с+*instr*); *adv* да́же; (*just*) как раз; (*with comp*) ещё; ~ **if** да́же е́сли; ~ **though** хотя́; ~ **so** всё-таки; **not** ~ да́же не; *vt* выра́внивать *impf*, вы́ровнять *pf.*
evening *n* ве́чер; *adj* вече́рний; ~ **class** вече́рние ку́рсы *m pl.*
evenly *adv* по́ровну, ро́вно.

evenness *n* ро́вность.

event *n* собы́тие, происше́ствие; **in the ~ of** в слу́чае+*gen*; **in any ~** во вся́ком слу́чае; **in the ~** в коне́чном счёте. **eventful** *adj* по́лный собы́тий. **eventual** *adj* коне́чный. **eventuality** *n* возмо́жность. **eventually** *adv* в конце́ концо́в.

ever *adv* (*at any time*) когда́-либо, когда́-нибудь; (*always*) всегда́; (*emph*) же; **~ since** с тех пор (как); **~ so** о́чень; **for ~** навсегда́; **hardly ~** почти́ никогда́. **evergreen** *adj* вечнозелёный; *n* вечнозелёное расте́ние. **everlasting** *adj* ве́чный. **evermore** *adv*: **for ~** навсегда́.

every *adj* ка́ждый, вся́кий, все (*pl*); **~ now and then** вре́мя от вре́мени; **~ other** ка́ждый второ́й; **~ other day** че́рез день. **everybody, everyone** *pron* ка́ждый, все (*pl*). **everyday** *adj* (*daily*) ежедне́вный; (*commonplace*) повседне́вный. **everything** *pron* всё. **everywhere** *adv* всю́ду, везде́.

evict *vt* выселя́ть *impf*, вы́селить *pf*. **eviction** *n* выселе́ние.

evidence *n* свиде́тельство, доказа́тельство; **give ~** свиде́тельствовать *impf* (о+*prep*; +*acc*; +что). **evident** *adj* очеви́дный.

evil *n* зло; *adj* злой.

evoke *vt* вызыва́ть *impf*, вы́звать *pf*.

evolution *n* эволю́ция. **evolutionary** *adj* эволюцио́нный. **evolve** *vt* & *i* развива́ть(ся) *impf*, разви́ть(ся) *pf*.

ewe *n* овца́.

ex- *in comb* бы́вший.

exacerbate *vt* обостря́ть *impf*, обостри́ть *pf*.

exact *adj* то́чный; *vt* взы́скивать *impf*, взыска́ть *pf* (**from, of** с+*gen*). **exacting** *adj* тре́бовательный. **exactitude, exactness** *n* то́чность. **exactly** *adv* то́чно; (*just*) как раз; (*precisely*) и́менно.

exaggerate *vt* преувели́чивать *impf*, преувели́чить *pf*. **exaggeration** *n* преувеличе́ние.

exalt *vt* возвыша́ть *impf*, возвы́сить *pf*; (*extol*) превозноси́ть *impf*, превознести́ *pf*.

examination *n* (*inspection*) осмо́тр; (*exam*) экза́мен; (*law*) допро́с. **examine** *vt* (*inspect*) осма́тривать *impf*, осмотре́ть *pf*; (*test*) экзаменова́ть *impf*, про~ *pf*; (*law*) допра́шивать *impf*, допроси́ть *pf*. **examiner** *n* экзамена́тор.

example *n* приме́р; **for ~** наприме́р.

exasperate *vt* раздража́ть *impf*, раздражи́ть *pf*. **exasperation** *n* раздраже́ние.

excavate *vt* раска́пывать *impf*, раскопа́ть *pf*. **excavations** *n pl* раско́пки *f pl*. **excavator** *n* экскава́тор.

exceed *vt* превыша́ть *impf*, превы́сить *pf*. **exceedingly** *adv* чрезвыча́йно.

excel *vt* превосходи́ть *impf*, превзойти́ *pf*; *vi* отлича́ться *impf*, отличи́ться *pf* (**at, in** в+*prep*). **excellence** *n* превосхо́дство. **excellency** *n* превосходи́тельство. **excellent** *adj* отли́чный.

except *vt* исключа́ть *impf*, исключи́ть *pf*; *prep* кро́ме+*gen*. **exception** *n* исключе́ние; **take ~ to** возража́ть *impf*, возрази́ть *pf* про́тив+*gen*. **exceptional** *adj* исключи́тельный.

excerpt *n* отры́вок.

excess *n* избы́ток. **excessive** *adj* чрезме́рный.

exchange *n* обме́н (**of** +*instr*); (*of currency*) разме́н; (*building*) би́ржа; (*telephone*) центра́льная телефо́нная ста́нция; ~ **rate** курс; *vt* обме́нивать *impf*, обменя́ть *pf* (**for** на+*acc*); обме́ниваться *impf*, обменя́ться *pf* +*instr*.

excise[1] *n* (*duty*) акци́з(ный сбор).

excise[2] *vt* (*cut out*) выреза́ть *impf*, вы́резать *pf*.

excitable *adj* возбуди́мый. **excite** *vt* (*cause*, *arouse*) возбужда́ть *impf*, возбуди́ть *pf*; (*thrill*, *agitate*) волнова́ть *impf*, вз~ *pf*. **excitement** *n* возбужде́ние; волне́ние.

exclaim *vi* восклица́ть *impf*, воскли́кнуть *pf*. **exclamation** *n* восклица́ние; ~ **mark** восклица́тельный знак.

exclude *vt* исключа́ть *impf*, исключи́ть *pf*. **exclusion** *n* исключе́ние. **exclusive** *adj* исключи́тельный; (*high-class*) эксклюзи́вный.

excommunicate *vt* отлуча́ть *impf*, отлучи́ть *pf* (от це́ркви).

excrement *n* экскреме́нты (-тов) *pl*.

excrete *vt* выделя́ть *impf*, вы́делить *pf*. **excretion** *n* выделе́ние.

excruciating *adj* мучи́тельный.

excursion *n* экску́рсия.

excusable *adj* прости́тельный. **excuse** *n* оправда́ние; (*pretext*) отгово́рка; *vt* (*forgive*) извиня́ть *impf*, извини́ть *pf*; (*justify*) опра́вдывать *impf*, оправда́ть *pf*; (*release*) освобожда́ть *impf*, освободи́ть *pf* (**from** от+*gen*); ~ **me!** извини́те!; прости́те!

execute *vt* исполня́ть *impf*, испо́лнить *pf*; (*criminal*) казни́ть *impf* & *pf*. **execution** *n* исполне́ние; казнь. **executioner** *n* пала́ч. **executive** *n* исполни́тельный о́рган; (*person*) руководи́тель *m*; *adj* исполни́тельный.

exemplary *adj* приме́рный. **exemplify** *vt* (*illustrate by example*) приводи́ть *impf*, привести́ *pf* приме́р +*gen*; (*serve as example*) служи́ть *impf*, по~ *pf* приме́ром +*gen*.

exempt *adj* освобождённый; *vt* освобожда́ть *impf*, освободи́ть *pf* (**from** от+*gen*). **exemption** *n* освобожде́ние.

exercise *n* (*use*) примене́ние; (*physical* ~; *task*) упражне́ние; **take** ~ упражня́ться *impf*; ~ **book** тетра́дь; *vt* (*use*) применя́ть *impf*, примени́ть *pf*; (*dog*) прогу́ливать *impf*; (*train*) упражня́ть *impf*.

exert *vt* ока́зывать *impf*, оказа́ть *pf*; ~ **o.s.** стара́ться *impf*, по~ *pf*. **exertion** *n* напряже́ние.

exhale *vt* выдыха́ть *impf*, вы́дохнуть *pf*.

exhaust *n* вы́хлоп; ~ **fumes** выхлопны́е га́зы *m pl*; ~ **pipe** выхлопна́я труба́; *vt* (*use up*) истоща́ть *impf*, истощи́ть *pf*; (*person*) изнуря́ть *impf*, изнури́ть *pf*; (*subject*) исчерпывать *impf*, исче́рпать *pf*. **exhausted** *adj*: **be** ~ (*person*) быть измождённым. **exhausting** *adj* изнури́тельный.

exhaustion *n* изнуре́ние; (*depletion*) истоще́ние. **exhaustive** *adj* исче́рпывающий.

exhibit *n* экспона́т; (*law*) веще́ственное доказа́тельство; *vt* (*manifest*) проявля́ть *impf*, прояви́ть *pf*; (*publicly*) выставля́ть *impf*, вы́ставить *pf*. **exhibition** *n* вы́ставка. **exhibitor** *n* экспоне́нт.

exhilarated *adj* в припо́днятом настрое́нии. **exhilarating** *adj* возбужда́ющий. **exhilaration** *n* возбужде́ние.

exhort *vt* увещева́ть *impf*. **exhortation** *n* увещева́ние.

exhume *vt* выка́пывать *impf*, вы́копать *pf*.

exile *n* изгна́ние; (*person*) изгна́нник; *vt* изгоня́ть *impf*, изгна́ть *pf*.

exist *vi* существова́ть *impf*. **existence** *n* существова́ние. **existing** *adj* существу́ющий.

exit *n* вы́ход; (*for vehicles*) вы́езд; (*theat*) ухо́д (со сце́ны); ~ **visa** выездна́я ви́за; *vi* уходи́ть *impf*, уйти́ *pf*.

exonerate *vt* опра́вдывать *impf*, оправда́ть *pf*.

exorbitant *adj* непоме́рный.

exorcize *vt* (*spirits*) изгоня́ть *impf*, изгна́ть *pf*.

exotic *adj* экзоти́ческий.

expand *vt* & *i* расширя́ть(ся) *impf*, расши́рить(ся) *pf*; ~ **on** распространя́ться *impf*, распространи́ться *pf* о+*prep*. **expanse** *n* простра́нство. **expansion** *n* расшире́ние. **expansive** *adj* экспанси́вный.

expatriate *n* экспатриа́нт, ~ка.

expect *vt* (*await*) ожида́ть *impf* +*gen*; ждать *impf* +*gen*, что; (*suppose*) полага́ть *impf*; (*require*) тре́бовать *impf* +*gen*, что́бы. **expectant** *adj* выжида́тельный; ~ **mother** бере́менная же́нщина. **expectation** *n* ожида́ние.

expediency *n* целесообра́зность. **expedient** *n* приём; *adj* целесообра́зный. **expedite** *vt* ускоря́ть *impf*, уско́рить *pf*. **expedition** *n* экспеди́ция. **expeditionary** *adj* экспедицио́нный.

expel *vt* (*drive out*) выгоня́ть *impf*, вы́гнать *pf*; (*from school etc.*) исключа́ть *impf*, исключи́ть *pf*; (*from country etc.*) изгоня́ть *impf*, изгна́ть *pf*.

expend *vt* тра́тить *impf*, ис~, по~ *pf*. **expendable** *adj* необяза́тельный. **expenditure** *n* расхо́д. **expense** *n* расхо́д; *pl* расхо́ды *m pl*, **at the ~ of** за счёт+*gen*; (*fig*) цено́ю+*gen*. **expensive** *adj* дорого́й.

experience *n* о́пыт; (*incident*) пережива́ние; *vt* испы́тывать *impf*, испыта́ть *pf*; (*undergo*) пережива́ть *impf*, пережи́ть *pf*. **experienced** *adj* о́пытный.

experiment *n* экспериме́нт; *vi* эксперименти́ровать *impf* (**on, with** над, с+*instr*). **experimental** экспериме́нта́льный.

expert *n* экспе́рт; *adj* о́пытный. **expertise** *n* специа́льные зна́ния *neut pl*.

expire *vi* (*period*) истека́ть *impf*, исте́чь *pf*. **expiry** *n* истече́ние.

explain *vt* объясня́ть *impf*, объясни́ть *pf*. **explanation** *n* объясне́ние. **explanatory** *adj* объясни́тельный.

expletive *n* (*oath*) бра́нное сло́во.

explicit *adj* я́вный; (*of person*) прямо́й.

explode *vt & i* взрыва́ть(ся) *impf*, взорва́ть(ся) *pf*; *vt* (*discredit*) опроверга́ть *impf*, опрове́ргнуть *pf*; *vi* (*with anger etc.*) разража́ться *impf*, разрази́ться *pf*.

exploit *n* по́двиг; *vt* эксплуати́ровать *impf*; (*use to advantage*) испо́льзовать *impf & pf*. **exploitation** *n* эксплуата́ция. **exploiter** *n* эксплуата́тор.

exploration *n* иссле́дование. **exploratory** *adj* иссле́довательский. **explore** *vt* иссле́довать *impf & pf*. **explorer** *n* иссле́дователь *m*.

explosion *n* взрыв. **explosive** *n* взры́вчатое вещество́; *adj* взрывчатый; (*fig*) взрывно́й.

exponent *n* (*interpreter*) истолкова́тель *m*; (*advocate*) сторо́нник.

export *n* вы́воз, э́кспорт; *vt* вывози́ть *impf*, вы́везти *pf*; экспорти́ровать *impf & pf*. **exporter** *n* экспортёр.

expose *vt* (*bare*) раскрыва́ть *impf*, раскры́ть *pf*; (*subject*) подверга́ть *impf*, подве́ргнуть *pf* (to +*dat*); (*discredit*) разоблача́ть *impf*, разоблачи́ть *pf*; (*phot*) экспони́ровать *impf & pf*.

exposition *n* изложе́ние.

exposure *n* подверга́ние (to +*dat*); (*phot*) вы́держка; (*unmasking*) разоблаче́ние; (*med*) хо́лод.

expound *vt* излага́ть *impf*, изложи́ть *pf*.

express *n* (*train*) экспре́сс; *adj* (*clear*) то́чный; (*purpose*) специа́льный; (*urgent*) сро́чный; *vt* выража́ть *impf*, вы́разить *pf*. **expression** *n* выраже́ние; (*expressiveness*) вырази́тельность. **expressive** *adj* вырази́тельный. **expressly** *adv* (*clearly*) я́сно; (*specifically*) специа́льно.

expropriate *vt* экспроприи́ровать *impf & pf*. **expropriation** *n* экспроприа́ция.

expulsion *n* (*from school etc.*) исключе́ние; (*from country etc.*) изгна́ние.

exquisite *adj* утончённый.

extant *adj* сохрани́вшийся.

extempore *adv* экспро́мптом. **extemporize** *vt & i* импровизи́ровать *impf*, сымпровизи́ровать *pf*.

extend *vt* (*stretch out*) протя́гивать *impf*, протяну́ть *pf*; (*enlarge*) расширя́ть *impf*, расши́рить *pf*; (*prolong*) продлева́ть *impf*, продли́ть *pf*; *vi* простира́ться *impf*, простере́ться *pf*. **extension** *n* (*enlarging*) расшире́ние; (*time*) продле́ние; (*to house*) пристро́йка; (*tel*) доба́вочный. **extensive** *adj* обши́рный. **extent** *n* (*degree*) сте́пень.

extenuating *adj*: ~ **circumstances** смягча́ющие вину́ обстоя́тельства *neut pl*.

exterior *n* вне́шность; *adj* вне́шний.

exterminate *vt* истребля́ть *impf*, истреби́ть *pf*. **extermination** *n* истребле́ние.

external *adj* вне́шний.

extinct *adj* (*volcano*) поту́хший; (*species*) вы́мерший; **become** ~ вымира́ть *impf*, вы́мереть *pf*. **extinction** *n* вымира́ние.

extinguish *vt* гаси́ть *impf*, по~ *pf*. **extinguisher** *n* огнетуши́тель *m*.

extol *vt* превозноси́ть *impf*,

превознести́ *pf.*
extort *vt* вымога́ть *impf* (**from** у+*gen*). **extortion** *n* вымога́тельство. **extortionate** *adj* вымога́тельский.
extra *n* (*theat*) стати́ст, ~ка; (*payment*) припла́та; *adj* дополни́тельный; (*special*) осо́бый; *adv* осо́бенно.
extract *n* экстра́кт; (*from book etc.*) вы́держка; *vt* извлека́ть *impf*, извле́чь *pf.* **extraction** *n* извлече́ние; (*origin*) происхожде́ние. **extradite** *vt* выдава́ть *impf*, вы́дать *pf.* **extradition** *n* вы́дача.
extramarital *adj* внебра́чный.
extraneous *adj* посторо́нний.
extraordinary *adj* чрезвыча́йный.
extrapolate *vt* & *i* экстраполи́ровать *impf* & *pf.*
extravagance *n* расточи́тельность. **extravagant** *adj* расточи́тельный; (*fantastic*) сумасбро́дный.
extreme *n* кра́йность; *adj* кра́йний. **extremity** *n* (*end*) край; (*adversity*) кра́йность; *pl* (*hands & feet*) коне́чности *f pl.*
extricate *vt* выпу́тывать *impf*, вы́путать *pf.*
exuberance *n* жизнера́достность. **exuberant** *adj* жизнера́достный.
exude *vt* & *i* выделя́ть(ся) *impf*, вы́делить(ся) *pf*; (*fig*) излуча́ть(ся) *impf*, излучи́ть(ся) *pf.*
exult *vi* ликова́ть *impf.* **exultant** *adj* лику́ющий. **exultation** *n* ликова́ние.
eye *n* глаз; (*needle etc.*) ушко́; *vt* разгля́дывать *impf*, разгляде́ть *pf.* **eyeball** *n* глазно́е я́блоко. **eyebrow** *n* бровь. **eyelash** *n* ресни́ца. **eyelid** *n* ве́ко. **eyeshadow** *n* те́ни *f pl* для век. **eyesight** *n* зре́ние. **eyewitness** *n* очеви́дец.

F

fable *n* ба́сня.
fabric *n* (*structure*) структу́ра; (*cloth*) ткань. **fabricate** *vt* (*invent*) выду́мывать *impf*, вы́думать *pf.* **fabrication** *n* вы́думка.
fabulous *adj* ска́зочный.
façade *n* фаса́д.
face *n* лицо́; (*expression*) выраже́ние; (*grimace*) грима́са; (*side*) сторона́; (*surface*) пове́рхность; (*clock etc.*) цифербла́т; **make ~s** ко́рчить *impf* ро́жи; **~ down** лицо́м вниз; **~ to ~** лицо́м к лицу́; **in the ~ of** пе́ред лицо́м+*gen*, вопреки́+*dat*; **on the ~ of it** на пе́рвый взгляд; *vt* (*be turned towards*) быть обращённым к+*dat*; (*of person*) стоя́ть *impf* лицо́м к+*dat*; (*meet firmly*) смотре́ть *impf* в лицо́+*dat*; (*cover*) облицо́вывать *impf*, облицева́ть *pf*; **I can't ~ it** я да́же ду́мать об э́том не могу́. **faceless** *adj* безли́чный.
facet *n* грань; (*fig*) аспе́кт.
facetious *adj* шутли́вый.
facial *adj* лицево́й.
facile *adj* пове́рхностный. **facilitate** *vt* облегча́ть *impf*, облегчи́ть *pf.* **facility** *n* (*ease*) лёгкость; (*ability*) спосо́бность; *pl* (*conveniences*) удо́бства *neut pl*, (*opportunities*) возмо́жности *f pl.*
facing *n* облицо́вка; (*of garment*) отде́лка.

facsimile *n* факси́миле *neut indecl.*

fact *n* факт; **the ~ is that** ... де́ло в том, что...; **as a matter of ~** со́бственно говоря́; **in ~** на са́мом де́ле.

faction *n* фра́кция.

factor *n* фа́ктор.

factory *n* фа́брика, заво́д.

factual *adj* факти́ческий.

faculty *n* спосо́бность; (*univ*) факульте́т.

fade *vi* (*wither*) вя́нуть *impf*, за~ *pf*; (*colour*) выцвета́ть *impf*, вы́цвести *pf*; (*sound*) замира́ть *impf*, замере́ть *pf*.

faeces *n pl* кал.

fag *n* (*cigarette*) сигаре́тка.

fail *n*: **without ~** обяза́тельно; *vi* (*weaken*) слабе́ть *impf*; (*break down*) отка́зывать *impf*, отказа́ть *pf*; (*not succeed*) терпе́ть *impf*, по~ *pf* неуда́чу; не удава́ться *impf*, уда́ться *pf impers+dat*; *vt & i* (*exam*) прова́ливать(ся) *impf*, провали́ть(ся) *pf.*; *vt* (*disappoint*) подводи́ть *impf*, подвести́ *pf.* **failing** *n* недоста́ток; *prep* за неиме́нием *+gen.* **failure** *n* неуда́ча; (*person*) неуда́чник, -ица.

faint *n* о́бморок; *adj* (*weak*) сла́бый; (*pale*) бле́дный; **I feel ~** мне ду́рно; **~-hearted** малоду́шный; *vi* па́дать *impf*, упа́сть *pf* в о́бморок.

fair[1] *n* я́рмарка.

fair[2] *adj* (*hair, skin*) све́тлый; (*weather*) я́сный; (*just*) справедли́вый; (*average*) сно́сный; **a ~ amount** дово́льно мно́го *+gen.* **fairly** *adv* дово́льно.

fairy *n* фе́я; **~-tale** ска́зка.

faith *n* ве́ра; (*trust*) дове́рие. **faithful** *adj* ве́рный; **yours ~ly** с уваже́нием.

fake *n* подде́лка; *vt* подде́лывать *impf*, подде́лать *pf.*

falcon *n* со́кол.

fall *n* паде́ние; *vi* па́дать *impf*, (у)па́сть *pf*; **~ apart** распада́ться *impf*, распа́сться *pf*; **~ asleep** засыпа́ть *impf*, засну́ть *pf*; **~ back on** прибега́ть *impf*, прибе́гнуть *pf* к*+dat*; **~ down** упа́сть *pf*; (*building*) разва́ливаться *impf*, развали́ться *pf*; **~ in** ру́хнуть *pf*; **~ in love with** влюбля́ться *impf*, влюби́ться *pf* в*+acc*; **~ off** отпада́ть *impf*, отпа́сть *pf*; **~ out** выпа́дать *impf*, вы́пасть *pf*; (*quarrel*) поссо́риться *pf*; **~ over** опроки́дываться *impf*, опроки́нуться *pf*; **~ through** прова́ливаться *impf*, провали́ться *pf*; **~-out** радиоакти́вные оса́дки (-ков) *pl.*

fallacy *n* оши́бка.

fallible *adj* подве́рженный оши́бкам.

fallow *n*: **lie ~** лежа́ть *impf* под па́ром.

false *adj* ло́жный; (*teeth*) иску́сственный; **~ start** неве́рный старт. **falsehood** *n* ложь. **falsification** *n* фальсифика́ция. **falsify** *vt* фальцифици́ровать *impf & pf.* **falsity** *n* ло́жность.

falter *vi* спотыка́ться *impf*, споткну́ться *pf*; (*stammer*) запина́ться *impf*, запну́ться *pf.*

fame *n* сла́ва. **famed** *adj* изве́стный.

familiar *adj* (*well known*) знако́мый; (*usual*) обы́чный; (*informal*) фамилья́рный. **familiarity** *n* знако́мство; фамилья́рность. **familiarize** *vt* ознакомля́ть *impf*, ознако́мить *pf* (**with** с*+instr*).

family *n* семья́; *attrib* семе́йный; ~ **tree** родосло́вная *sb.* **famine** *n* го́лод. **famished** *adj*: **be** ~ голода́ть *impf.*

famous *adj* знамени́тый.

fan[1] *n* ве́ер; (*ventilator*) вентиля́тор; ~**-belt** реме́нь *m* вентиля́тора; *vt* обма́хивать *impf*, обмахну́ть *pf*; (*flame*) раздува́ть *impf*, разду́ть *pf.*

fan[2] *n* покло́нник, -ица; (*sport*) боле́льщик. **fanatic** *n* фана́тик. **fanatical** *adj* фанати́ческий.

fanciful *adj* причу́дливый. **fancy** *n* фанта́зия; (*whim*) причу́да; **take a** ~ **to** увлека́ться *impf*, увле́чься *pf* +*instr*; *adj* витиева́тый; *vt* (*imagine*) представля́ть *impf*, предста́вить *pf* себе́; (*suppose*) полага́ть *impf*; (*like*) нра́виться *impf*, по~ *pf impers*+*dat*; ~ **dress** маскара́дный костю́м; ~**-dress** костюми́рованный.

fanfare *n* фанфа́ра.

fang *n* клык; (*serpent's*) ядови́тый зуб.

fantasize *vi* фантази́ровать *impf.* **fantastic** *adj* фантасти́ческий. **fantasy** *n* фанта́зия.

far *adj* да́льний; **Russia is** ~ **away** Росси́я о́чень далеко́; *adv* далёко́; (*fig*) намно́го; **as** ~ **as** (*prep*) до+*gen*; (*conj*) поско́льку; **by** ~ намно́го; **(in) so** ~ **as** поско́льку; **so** ~ до сих пор; ~**-fetched** притя́нутый за́ волосы; ~**-reaching** далеко́ иду́щий; ~**-sighted** дальнови́дный.

farce *n* фарс. **farcical** *adj* смехотво́рный.

fare *n* (*price*) проездна́я пла́та; (*food*) пи́ща; *vi* пожива́ть *impf.* **farewell** *int* проща́й(те)!; *n* проща́ние; *attrib* проща́льный; **bid** ~ проща́ться *impf*, прости́ться *pf* (**to** с+*instr*).

farm *n* фе́рма. **farmer** *n* фе́рмер. **farming** *n* се́льское хозя́йство.

fart (*vulg*) *n* пу́кание; *vi* пу́кать *impf*, пу́кнуть *pf.*

farther *see* **further. farthest** *see* **furthest.**

fascinate *vt* очаро́вывать *impf*, очарова́ть *pf.* **fascinating** *adj* очарова́тельный. **fascination** *n* очарова́ние.

Fascism *n* фаши́зм. **Fascist** *n* фаши́ст, ~ка; *adj* фаши́стский.

fashion *n* мо́да; (*manner*) мане́ра; **after a** ~ не́которым о́бразом; *vt* придава́ть *impf*, прида́ть *pf* фо́рму +*dat.* **fashionable** *adj* мо́дный.

fast[1] *n* пост; *vi* пости́ться *impf.*

fast[2] *adj* (*rapid*) ско́рый, бы́стрый; (*colour*) сто́йкий; (*shut*) пло́тно закры́тый; **be** ~ (*timepiece*) спеши́ть *impf.*

fasten *vt* (*attach*) прикрепля́ть *impf*, прикрепи́ть *pf* (**to** к+*dat*); (*tie*) привя́зывать *impf*, привяза́ть *pf* (**to** к+*dat*); (*garment*) застёгивать *impf*, застегну́ть *pf.* **fastener, fastening** *n* запо́р, задви́жка; (*on garment*) застёжка.

fastidious *adj* брезгли́вый.

fat *n* жир; *adj* (*greasy*) жи́рный; (*plump*) то́лстый; **get** ~ толсте́ть *impf*, по~ *pf.*

fatal *adj* рокобо́й; (*deadly*) смерте́льный. **fatalism** *n* фатали́зм. **fatality** *n* (*death*) смерте́льный слу́чай. **fate** *n* судьба́. **fateful** *adj* рокобо́й.

father *n* оте́ц; ~**-in-law** (*husband's* ~) свёкор; (*wife's* ~) тесть *m.* **fatherhood** *n* отцо́вство. **fatherland** *n* оте́чество. **fatherly** *adj* оте́ческий.

fathom *n* морска́я са́жень; *vt* (*fig*) понима́ть *impf*, поня́ть *pf*.

fatigue *n* утомле́ние; *vt* утомля́ть *impf*, утоми́ть *pf*.

fatten *vt* отка́рмливать *impf*, откорми́ть *pf*; *vi* толсте́ть *impf*, по~ *pf*. **fatty** *adj* жи́рный.

fatuous *adj* глу́пый.

fault *n* недоста́ток; (*blame*) вина́; (*geol*) сброс. **faultless** *adj* безупре́чный. **faulty** *adj* дефе́ктный.

fauna *n* фа́уна.

favour *n* (*kind act*) любе́зность; (*goodwill*) благоскло́нность; **in (s.o.'s) ~** в по́льзу +*gen*; **be in ~ of** быть за+*acc*; *vt* (*support*) благоприя́тствовать *impf* +*dat*; (*treat with partiality*) ока́зывать *impf*, оказа́ть *pf* предпочте́ние +*dat*. **favourable** *adj* (*propitious*) благоприя́тный; (*approving*) благоскло́нный. **favourite** *n* люби́мец, -мица; (*also sport*) фаво́рит, ~ка; *adj* люби́мый.

fawn[1] *n* оленёнок; *adj* желтова́то-кори́чневый.

fawn[2] *vi* подли́зываться *impf*, подлиза́ться *pf* (**on** к+*dat*).

fax *n* факс; *vt* посыла́ть *impf*, посла́ть *pf* по фа́ксу.

fear *n* страх, боя́знь, опасе́ние; *vt & i* боя́ться *impf* +*gen*; опаса́ться *impf* +*gen*. **fearful** *adj* (*terrible*) стра́шный; (*timid*) пугли́вый. **fearless** *adj* бесстра́шный. **fearsome** *adj* гро́зный.

feasibility *n* осуществи́мость. **feasible** *adj* осуществи́мый.

feast *n* (*meal*) пир; (*festival*) пра́здник; *vi* пирова́ть *impf*.

feat *n* по́двиг.

feather *n* перо́.

feature *n* черта́; (*newspaper*) (темати́ческая) статья́; **~ film** худо́жественный фильм; *vt* помеща́ть *impf*, помести́ть *pf* на ви́дном ме́сте; (*in film*) пока́зывать *impf*, показа́ть *pf*; *vi* игра́ть *impf* сыгра́ть *pf* роль.

February *n* февра́ль *m*; *adj* февра́льский.

feckless *adj* безала́берный.

federal *adj* федера́льный. **federation** *n* федера́ция.

fee *n* гонора́р; (*entrance ~ etc.*) взнос; *pl* (*regular payment, school, etc.*) пла́та.

feeble *adj* сла́бый.

feed *n* корм; *vt* корми́ть *impf*, на~, по~ *pf*; *vi* корми́ться *impf*, по~ *pf*; **~ up** отка́рмливать *impf*, откорми́ть *pf*; **I am fed up with** мне надое́л (-а, -о; -и) +*nom*. **feedback** *n* обра́тная связь.

feel *vt* чу́вствовать *impf*, по~ *pf*; (*think*) счита́ть *impf*, счесть *pf*; *vi* (*~ bad etc.*) чу́вствовать *impf*, по~ *pf* себя́ +*adv*, +*instr*; **~ like** хоте́ться *impf impers*+*dat*. **feeling** *n* (*sense*) ощуще́ние; (*emotion*) чу́вство; (*impression*) впечатле́ние; (*mood*) настрое́ние.

feign *vt* притворя́ться *impf*, притвори́ться *pf* +*instr*. **feigned** *adj* притво́рный.

feline *adj* коша́чий.

fell *vt* (*tree*) сруба́ть *impf*, сруби́ть *pf*; (*person*) сбива́ть *impf*, сбить *pf* с ног.

fellow *n* па́рень *m*; (*of society etc.*) член; **~ countryman** сооте́чественник. **fellowship** *n* това́рищество.

felt *n* фетр; *adj* фе́тровый; **~-tip pen** флома́стер.

female *n* (*animal*) са́мка; (*person*) же́нщина; *adj* же́нский. **feminine** *adj* же́нский, же́нственный; (*gram*) же́нского ро́да. **femininity** *n* же́нственность. **feminism** *n* фемини́зм. **feminist** *n* фемини́ст, ~ка; *adj* фемини́стский.

fence *n* забо́р; *vt*: **~ in** огора́живать *impf*, огороди́ть *pf*; **~ off** отгора́живать *impf*, отгороди́ть *pf*; *vi* (*sport*) фехтова́ть *impf*. **fencer** *n* фехтова́льщик, -ица. **fencing** *n* (*enclosure*) забо́р; (*sport*) фехтова́ние.

fend *vt*: **~ off** отража́ть *impf*, отрази́ть *pf*; *vi*: **~ for o.s.** забо́титься *impf*, по~ *pf* о себе́. **fender** *n* решётка.

fennel *n* фе́нхель *m*.

ferment *n* броже́ние; *vi* броди́ть *impf*; *vt* ква́сить *impf*, за~ *pf*; (*excite*) возбужда́ть *impf*, возбуди́ть *pf*. **fermentation** *n* броже́ние; (*excitement*) возбужде́ние.

fern *n* па́поротник.

ferocious *adj* свире́пый. **ferocity** *n* свире́пость.

ferret *n* хорёк; *vt*: **~ out** (*search out*) разню́хивать *impf*, разню́хать *pf*; *vi*: **~ about** (*rummage*) ры́ться *impf*.

ferry *n* паро́м; *vt* перевози́ть *impf*, перевезти́ *pf*.

fertile *adj* плодоро́дный. **fertility** *n* плодоро́дие. **fertilize** *vt* (*soil*) удобря́ть *impf*, удо́брить *pf*; (*egg*) оплодотворя́ть *impf*, оплодотвори́ть *pf*. **fertilizer** *n* удобре́ние.

fervent *adj* горя́чий. **fervour** *n* жар.

fester *vi* гнои́ться *impf*.

festival *n* пра́здник, (*music etc.*) фестива́ль *m*. **festive** *adj* пра́здничный. **festivities** *n pl* торжества́ *neut pl*.

festoon *vt* украша́ть *impf*, укра́сить *pf*.

fetch *vt* (*carrying*) приноси́ть *impf*, принести́ *pf*; (*leading*) приводи́ть *impf*, привести́ *pf*; (*go and come back with*) (*on foot*) идти́ *impf*, по~ *pf* за+*instr*; (*by vehicle*) заезжа́ть *impf*, зае́хать *pf* за+*instr*; (*price*) выруча́ть *impf*, вы́ручить *pf*. **fetching** *adj* привлека́тельный.

fetid *adj* злово́нный.

fetish *n* фети́ш.

fetter *vt* ско́вывать *impf*, скова́ть *pf*; *n*: *pl* кандалы́ (-ло́в) *pl*; (*fig*) око́вы (-в) *pl*.

fettle *n* состоя́ние.

feud *n* кро́вная месть.

feudal *adj* феода́льный. **feudalism** *n* феодали́зм.

fever *n* лихора́дка. **feverish** *adj* лихора́дочный.

few *adj & pron* немно́гие *pl*; ма́ло+*gen*; **a ~** не́сколько +*gen*; **quite a ~** нема́ло +*gen*.

fiancé *n* жени́х. **fiancée** *n* неве́ста.

fiasco *n* прова́л.

fib *n* враньё; *vi* привира́ть *impf*, привра́ть *pf*.

fibre *n* волокно́. **fibreglass** *n* стекловолокно́. **fibrous** *adj* волокни́стый.

fickle *adj* непостоя́нный.

fiction *n* худо́жественная литерату́ра; (*invention*) вы́думка. **fictional** *adj* беллетристи́ческий. **fictitious** *adj* вы́мышленный.

fiddle *n* (*violin*) скри́пка; (*swindle*) обма́н; *vi*: **~ about**

безде́льничать *impf*; ~ **with** верте́ть *impf*; *vt* (*falsify*) подде́лывать *impf*, подде́лать *pf*; (*cheat*) жи́лить *impf*, у~ *pf*.

fidelity *n* ве́рность.

fidget *n* непосе́да *m* & *f*; *vi* ёрзать *impf*; не́рвничать *impf*. **fidgety** *adj* непосе́дливый.

field *n* по́ле; (*sport*) площа́дка; (*sphere*) о́бласть; **~-glasses** полево́й бино́кль *m*. **~work** полевы́е рабо́ты *f pl*.

fiend *n* дья́вол. **fiendish** *adj* дья́вольский.

fierce *adj* свире́пый; (*strong*) си́льный.

fiery *adj* о́гненный.

fifteen *adj* & *n* пятна́дцать. **fifteenth** *adj* & *n* пятна́дцатый. **fifth** *adj* & *n* пя́тый; (*fraction*) пя́тая *sb*. **fiftieth** *adj* & *n* пятидеся́тый. **fifty** *adj* & *n* пятьдеся́т; *pl* (*decade*) пятидеся́тые го́ды (-до́в) *m pl*.

fig *n* инжи́р.

fight *n* дра́ка; (*battle*) бой; (*fig*) борьба́; *vt* боро́ться *impf* с+*instr*; *vi* дра́ться *impf*; *vt* & *i* (*wage war*) воева́ть *impf* с+*instr*. **fighter** *n* бое́ц; (*aeron*) истреби́тель *m*. **fighting** *n* бои́ *m pl*.

figment *n* плод воображе́ния.

figurative *adj* перено́сный. **figure** *n* (*form, body, person*) фигу́ра; (*number*) ци́фра; (*diagram*) рису́нок; (*image*) изображе́ние; (*of speech*) оборо́т ре́чи; **~-head** (*naut*) носово́е украше́ние; (*person*) номина́льная глава́; *vt* (*think*) полага́ть *impf*; *vi* фигури́ровать *impf*; ~ **out** вычисля́ть *impf*, вы́числить *pf*.

filament *n* волокно́; (*electr*) нить.

file[1] *n* (*tool*) напи́льник; *vt* подпи́ливать *impf*, подпили́ть *pf*.

file[2] *n* (*folder*) па́пка; (*comput*) файл; *vt* подшива́ть *impf*, подши́ть *pf*; (*complaint*) подава́ть *impf*, пода́ть *pf*.

file[3] *n* (*row*) ряд; **in (single)** ~ гусько́м.

filigree *adj* филигра́нный.

fill *vt* & *i* (*also* ~ **up**) наполня́ть(ся) *impf*, напо́лнить(ся) *pf*; *vt* заполня́ть *impf*, запо́лнить *pf*; (*tooth*) пломбирова́ть *impf*, за~ *pf*; (*occupy*) занима́ть *impf*, заня́ть *pf*; (*satiate*) насыща́ть *impf*, насы́тить *pf*; ~ **in** (*vt*) заполня́ть *impf*, запо́лнить *pf*; (*vi*) замеща́ть *impf*, замести́ть *pf*.

fillet *n* (*cul*) филе́ *neut indecl*.

filling *n* (*tooth*) пло́мба; (*cul*) начи́нка.

filly *n* кобы́лка.

film *n* (*layer*; *phot*) плёнка; (*cin*) фильм; ~ **star** кинозвезда́; *vt* снима́ть *impf*, снять *pf*.

filter *n* фильтр; *vt* фильтрова́ть *impf*, про~ *pf*; ~ **through, out** проса́чиваться *impf*, просочи́ться *pf*.

filth *n* грязь. **filthy** *adj* гря́зный.

fin *n* плавни́к.

final *n* фина́л; *pl* выпускны́е экза́мены *m pl*; *adj* после́дний; (*decisive*) оконча́тельный. **finale** *n* фина́л. **finalist** *n* финали́ст. **finality** *n* зако́нченность. **finalize** *vt* (*complete*) заверша́ть *impf*, заверши́ть *pf*; (*settle*) ула́живать *impf*, ула́дить *pf*. **finally** *adv* (*at last*) наконе́ц; (*in the end*) в конце́ концо́в.

finance *n* фина́нсы (-сов) *pl*; *vt* финанси́ровать *impf* & *pf*. **financial** *adj* фина́нсовый.

financier *n* финанси́ст.
finch *n see comb, e.g.* **bullfinch**
find *n* нахо́дка; *vt* находи́ть *impf*, найти́ *pf*; (*person*) застава́ть *impf*, заста́ть *pf*; ~ **out** узнава́ть *impf*, узна́ть *pf*; ~ **fault with** придира́ться *impf*, придра́ться *pf* к+*dat.* **finding** *n pl* (*of inquiry*) вы́воды *m pl.*
fine[1] *n* (*penalty*) штраф; *vt* штрафова́ть *impf*, о~ *pf.*
fine[2] *adj* (*weather*) я́сный; (*excellent*) прекра́сный; (*delicate*) то́нкий; (*of sand etc.*) ме́лкий; ~ **arts** изобрази́тельные иску́сства *neut pl*; *adv* хорошо́. **finery** *n* наря́д. **finesse** *n* то́нкость.
finger *n* па́лец; ~**-nail** но́готь; ~**-print** отпеча́ток па́льца; ~**-tip** ко́нчик па́льца; **have at (one's)** ~**s** знать *impf* как свой пять па́льцев; *vt* щу́пать *impf*, по~ *pf.*
finish *n* коне́ц; (*polish*) отде́лка; (*sport*) фи́ниш; *vt & i* конча́ть(ся) *impf*, ко́нчить(ся) *pf*; *vt* ока́нчивать *impf*, око́нчить *pf.*
finite *adj* коне́чный.
Finland *n* Финля́ндия. **Finn** *n* финн, фи́нка. **Finnish** *adj* фи́нский.
fir *n* ель, пи́хта.
fire *vt* (*bake*) обжига́ть *impf*, обже́чь *pf*; (*excite*) воспламеня́ть *impf*, воспламени́ть *pf*; (*gun*) стреля́ть *impf* из+*gen* (**at** в+*acc*, по+*dat*); (*dismiss*) увольня́ть *impf*, уво́лить *pf*; *n* ого́нь *m*; (*grate*) ками́н; (*conflagration*) пожа́р; (*bonfire*) костёр; (*fervour*) пыл; **be on** ~ горе́ть *impf*; **catch** ~ загора́ться *impf*, загоре́ться *pf*; **set** ~ **to, set on** ~ поджига́ть *impf*, подже́чь *pf*; ~**-alarm** пожа́рная трево́га; ~**arm(s)** огнестре́льное ору́жие; ~ **brigade** пожа́рная кома́нда; ~**-engine** пожа́рная маши́на; ~**-escape** пожа́рная ле́стница; ~ **extinguisher** огнетуши́тель *m*; ~**-guard** ками́нная решётка; ~**man** пожа́рный *sb*; ~ **place** ками́н; ~**side** ме́сто у ками́на; ~ **station** пожа́рное депо́ *neut indecl*; ~**wood** дрова́ (-в) *pl*; ~**work** фейерве́рк. **firing** *n* (*shooting*) стрельба́.
firm[1] *n* (*business*) фи́рма.
firm[2] *adj* твёрдый. **firmness** *n* твёрдость.
first *adj* пе́рвый; *n* пе́рвый *sb*; *adv* сперва́, снача́ла; (*for the* ~ *time*) впервы́е; **in the** ~ **place** во-пе́рвых; ~ **of all** пре́жде всего́; **at** ~ **sight** на пе́рвый взгляд; ~ **aid** пе́рвая по́мощь; ~**-class** первокла́ссный; ~**-hand** из пе́рвых рук; ~**-rate** первокла́ссный. **firstly** *adv* во-пе́рвых.
fiscal *adj* фина́нсовый.
fish *n* ры́ба; *adj* ры́бный; *vi* лови́ть *impf* ры́бу; ~ **out** выта́скивать *impf*, вы́таскать *pf.* **fisherman** *n* рыба́к. **fishery** *n* ры́бный про́мысел. **fishing** *n* ры́бная ло́вля; ~ **boat** рыболо́вное су́дно; ~ **line** ле́са́; ~ **rod** у́дочка. **fishmonger** *n* торго́вец ры́бой. **fishmonger's** *n* ры́бный магази́н. **fishy** *adj* ры́бный; (*dubious*) подозри́тельный.
fissure *n* тре́щина.
fist *n* кула́к.
fit[1] *n*: **be a good** ~ хорошо́ сиде́ть *impf*; *adj* (*suitable*) подходя́щий, го́дный; (*healthy*)

здоро́вый; *vt* (*be suitable*) годи́ться *impf* +*dat*, на+*acc*, для+*gen*; *vt* & *i* (*be the right size* (*for*)) подходи́ть *impf*, подойти́ *pf* (+*dat*); (*adjust*) прила́живать *impf*, прила́дить *pf* (**to** к+*dat*); (*be small enough for*) входи́ть *impf*, войти́ *pf* в+*acc*; **~ out** снабжа́ть *impf*, снабди́ть *pf*.

fit[2] *n* (*attack*) припа́док; (*fig*) поры́в. **fitful** *adj* поры́вистый.

fitter *n* монтёр. **fitting** *n* (*of clothes*) приме́рка; *pl* армату́ра; *adj* подходя́щий.

five *adj* & *n* пять; (*number 5*) пятёрка; **~-year plan** пятиле́тка.

fix *n* (*dilemma*) переде́лка; (*drugs*) уко́л; *vt* (*repair*) чини́ть *impf*, по~ *pf*; (*settle*) назнача́ть *impf*, назна́чить *pf*; (*fasten*) укрепля́ть *impf*, укрепи́ть *pf*; **~ up** (*organize*) организова́ть *impf* & *pf*; (*install*) устана́вливать *impf*, установи́ть *pf*. **fixation** *n* фикса́ция. **fixed** *adj* устано́вленный. **fixture** *n* (*sport*) предстоя́щее спорти́вное мероприя́тие; (*fitting*) приспособле́ние.

fizz, fizzle *vi* шипе́ть *impf*; **fizzle out** выдыха́ться *impf*, вы́дохнуться *pf*. **fizzy** *adj* шипу́чий.

flabbergasted *adj* ошеломлённый.

flabby *adj* дря́блый.

flag[1] *n* флаг, зна́мя *neut*; *vt*: **~ down** остана́вливать *impf*, останови́ть *pf*.

flag[2] *vi* (*weaken*) ослабева́ть *impf*, ослабе́ть *pf*.

flagon *n* кувши́н.

flagrant *adj* вопию́щий.

flagship *n* фла́гман.

flagstone *n* плита́.

flair *n* чутьё.

flake *n* слой; *pl* хло́пья (-ьев) *pl*; *vi* шелуши́ться *impf*. **flaky** *adj* слои́стый.

flamboyant *adj* цвети́стый.

flame *n* пла́мя *neut*, ого́нь *m*; *vi* пыла́ть *impf*.

flange *n* фла́нец.

flank *n* (*of body*) бок; (*mil*) фланг; *vt* быть сбо́ку +*gen*.

flannel *n* флане́ль; (*for face*) моча́лка для лица́.

flap *n* (*board*) откидна́я доска́; (*pocket, tent* ~) кла́пан; (*panic*) па́ника; *vt* взма́хивать *impf*, взмахну́ть *pf* +*instr*; *vi* развева́ться *impf*.

flare *n* вспы́шка; (*signal*) сигна́льная раке́та; *vi* вспы́хивать *impf*, вспы́хнуть *pf*; **~ up** (*fire*) возгора́ться *impf*, возгоре́ться *pf*; (*fig*) вспыли́ть *pf*.

flash *n* вспы́шка; **in a ~** ми́гом; *vi* сверка́ть *impf*, сверкну́ть *pf*. **flashback** *n* ретроспе́кция. **flashy** *adj* показно́й.

flask *n* фля́жка.

flat[1] *n* (*dwelling*) кварти́ра.

flat[2] *n* (*mus*) бемо́ль *m*; (*tyre*) спу́щенная ши́на; **on the ~** на пло́скости; *adj* пло́ский; **~-fish** ка́мбала. **flatly** *adv* наотре́з. **flatten** *vt* & *i* выра́внивать(ся) *impf*, вы́ровнять(ся) *pf*.

flatmate *n* сосе́д, ~ка по кварти́ре.

flatter *vt* льстить *impf*, по~ *pf* +*dat*. **flattering** *adj* льсти́вый. **flattery** *n* лесть.

flaunt *vt* щеголя́ть *impf*, щегольну́ть *pf* +*instr*.

flautist *n* флейти́ст.

flavour *n* вкус; (*fig*) при́вкус; *vt* приправля́ть *impf*, припра́вить *pf*.
flaw *n* изъя́н.
flax *n* лён. **flaxen** *adj* (*colour*) соло́менный.
flea *n* блоха́; ~ **market** бара-хо́лка.
fleck *n* кра́пинка.
flee *vi* бежа́ть *impf* & *pf* (**from** от+*gen*); *vt* бежа́ть *impf* из+*gen*.
fleece *n* руно́; *vt* (*fig*) обдира́ть *impf*, ободра́ть *pf*. **fleecy** *adj* шерсти́стый.
fleet *n* флот; (*vehicles*) парк.
fleeting *adj* мимолётный.
flesh *n* (*as opposed to mind*) плоть; (*meat*) мя́со; **in the ~** во плоти́. **fleshy** *adj* мяси́-стый.
flex *n* шну́р; *vt* сгиба́ть *impf*, согну́ть *pf*. **flexibility** *adj* ги́б-кость. **flexible** *adj* ги́бкий.
flick *vt* & *i* щёлкать *impf*, щёлкнуть *pf* (+*instr*); ~ **through** пролиста́ть *pf*.
flicker *n* мерца́ние; *vi* мер-ца́ть *impf*.
flier *see* **flyer**
flight[1] *n* (*fleeing*) бе́гство; **put (take) to ~** обраща́ть(ся) *impf*, обрати́ть(ся) *pf* в бе́гство.
flight[2] *n* (*flying*) полёт; (*trip*) рейс; ~ **of stairs** ле́стничный марш. **flighty** *adj* ве́треный.
flimsy *adj* (*fragile*) непро́ч-ный; (*dress*) лёгкий; (*excuse*) сла́бый.
flinch *vi* (*recoil*) отпря́дывать *impf*, отпря́нуть *pf*; (*fig*) уклоня́ться *impf*, уклони́ть-ся *pf* (**from** от+*gen*).
fling *vt* швыря́ть *impf*, швыр-ну́ть *pf*; *vi* (*also* ~ *o.s.*) бро-са́ться *impf*, бро́ситься *pf*.
flint *n* креме́нь *m*.
flip *vt* щёлкать *impf*, щёлк-нуть *pf* +*instr*.
flippant *adj* легкомы́сленный.
flipper *n* ласт.
flirt *n* коке́тка; *vi* флиртова́ть *impf* (**with** с+*instr*). **flirtation** *n* флирт.
flit *vi* порха́ть *impf*, порхну́ть *pf*.
float *n* поплаво́к; *vi* пла́вать *indet*, плыть *det*; *vt* (*company*) пуска́ть *impf*, пусти́ть *pf* в ход.
flock *n* (*animals*) ста́до; (*birds*) стая́; *vi* стека́ться *impf*, сте́чься *pf*.
flog *vt* сечь *impf*, вы́~ *pf*.
flood *n* наводне́ние; (*bibl*) пото́п; (*fig*) пото́к; *vi* (*river etc.*) выступа́ть *impf*, высту-пить *pf* из берего́в; *vt* за-топля́ть *impf*, затопи́ть *pf*. **floodgate** *n* шлюз. **flood-light** *n* проже́ктор.
floor *n* пол; (*storey*) эта́ж; ~**board** полови́ца; *vt* (*con-found*) ста́вить *impf*, по~ *pf* в тупи́к.
flop *vi* (*fall*) плю́хаться *impf*, плю́хнуться *pf*; (*fail*) прова́-ливаться *impf*, провали́ться *pf*.
flora *n* фло́ра. **floral** *adj* цве-то́чный.
florid *adj* цвети́стый; (*ruddy*) румя́ный. **florist** *n* торго́вец цвета́ми.
flounce[1] *vi* броса́ться *impf*, бро́ситься *pf*.
flounce[2] *n* (*of skirt*) обо́рка.
flounder[1] *n* (*fish*) ка́мбала.
flounder[2] *vi* бара́хтаться *impf*.
flour *n* мука́.
flourish *n* (*movement*) разма́-хивание (+*instr*); (*of pen*) ро́с-черк; *vi* (*thrive*) процвета́ть

impf; *vt* (*wave*) размáхивать *impf*, размахнýть *pf* +*instr*.
flout *vt* попирáть *impf*, попрáть *pf*.
flow *vi* течь *impf*; ли́ться *impf*; *n* течéние.
flower *n* цветóк; ~-**bed** клýмба; ~**pot** цветóчный горшóк; *vi* цвести́ *impf*. **flowery** *adj* цвети́стый.
flu *n* грипп.
fluctuate *vi* колебáться *impf*, по~ *pf*. **fluctuation** *n* колебáние.
flue *n* дымохóд.
fluent *adj* бéглый. **fluently** *adv* свобóдно.
fluff *n* пух. **fluffy** *adj* пуши́стый.
fluid *n* жи́дкость; *adj* жи́дкий.
fluke *n* случáйная удáча.
fluorescent *adj* флюоресцéнтный.
fluoride *n* фтори́д.
flurry *n* (*squall*) шквал; (*fig*) волнá.
flush *n* (*redness*) румя́нец; *vi* (*redden*) краснéть *impf*, по~ *pf*; *vt* спускáть *impf*, спусти́ть *pf* вóду в+*acc*.
flustered *adj* сконфýженный.
flute *n* флéйта.
flutter *vi* (*flit*) порхáть *impf*, порхнýть *pf*; (*wave*) развевáться *impf*.
flux *n*: **in a state of** ~ в состоя́нии изменéния.
fly[1] *n* (*insect*) мýха.
fly[2] *vi* летáть *indet*, летéть *det*, по~ *pf*; (*flag*) развевáться *impf*; (*hasten*) нести́сь *impf*, по~ *pf*; *vt* (*aircraft*) управля́ть *impf* +*instr*; (*transport*) перевози́ть *impf*, перевезти́ *pf* (самолётом); (*flag*) поднимáть *impf*, подня́ть *pf*. **flyer, flier** *n* лётчик. **flying** *n* полёт.
foal *n* (*horse*) жеребёнок.
foam *n* пéна; ~ **plastic** пенопл́аст; ~ **rubber** пенорези́на; *vi* пéниться *impf*, вс~ *pf*. **foamy** *adj* пéнистый.
focal *adj* фóкусный. **focus** *n* фóкус; (*fig*) центр; *vt* фокуси́ровать *impf*, с~ *pf*; (*concentrate*) сосредотóчивать *impf*, сосредотóчить *pf*.
fodder *n* корм.
foe *n* враг.
foetus *n* зарóдыш.
fog *n* тумáн. **foggy** *adj* тумáнный.
foible *n* слáбость.
foil[1] *n* (*metal*) фольгá; (*contrast*) контрáст.
foil[2] *vt* (*thwart*) расстрáивать *impf*, расстрóить *pf*.
foil[3] *n* (*sword*) рапи́ра.
foist *vt* навя́зывать *impf*, навязáть *pf* (**on** +*dat*).
fold[1] *n* (*sheep-*~) овчáрня.
fold[2] *n* склáдка, сгиб; *vt* склáдывать *impf*, сложи́ть *pf*. **folder** *n* пáпка. **folding** *adj* складнóй.
foliage *n* листвá.
folk *n* нарóд, лю́ди *pl*; *pl* (*relatives*) родня́ *collect*; *attrib* нарóдный. **folklore** *n* фольклóр.
follow *vt* слéдовать *impf*, по~ *pf* +*dat*, за+*instr*; (*walk behind*) идти́ *det* за+*instr*; (*fig*) следи́ть *impf* за+*instr*. **follower** *n* послéдователь *m*. **following** *adj* слéдующий.
folly *n* глýпость.
fond *adj* нéжный; **be** ~ **of** люби́ть *impf* +*acc*.
fondle *vt* ласкáть *impf*.
fondness *n* любóвь.
font *n* (*eccl*) купéль.
food *n* пи́ща, едá. **foodstuff** *n* пищевóй продýкт.
fool *n* дурáк, дýра; *vt* дурáчить

impf, о~ *pf*; *vi*: ~ **about** дура́читься *impf*. **foolhardy** *adj* безрассу́дно хра́брый. **foolish** *adj* глу́пый. **foolishness** *n* глу́пость. **foolproof** *adj* абсолю́тно надёжный.

foot *n* нога́; (*measure*) фут; (*of hill etc.*) подно́жие; **on** ~ пешко́м; **put one's** ~ **in it** сесть *pf* в лу́жу. **foot-and-mouth (disease)** *n* я́щур. **football** *n* футбо́л; *attrib* футбо́льный. **footballer** *n* футболи́ст. **foothills** *n pl* предго́рье. **footing** *n* (*fig*) ба́зис; **lose one's** ~ оступи́ться *pf*; **on an equal** ~ на ра́вной ноге́. **footlights** *n pl* ра́мпа. **footman** *n* лаке́й. **footnote** *n* сно́ска. **footpath** *n* тропи́нка; (*pavement*) тротуа́р. **footprint** *n* след. **footstep** *n* (sound) шаг; (*footprint*) след. **footwear** *n* о́бувь.

for *prep* (*of time*) в тече́ние +*gen*, на+*acc*; (*of purpose*) для+*gen*, за+*acc*, +*instr*; (*price*) за+*acc*; (*on account of*) из-за +*gen*; (*in place of*) вме́сто+*gen*; ~ **the sake of** ра́ди+*gen*; **as** ~ что каса́ется+*gen*; *conj* так как.

forage *n* фура́ж; *vi*: ~ **for** разы́скивать *impf*.

foray *n* набе́г.

forbearance *n* возде́ржанность.

forbid *vt* запреща́ть *impf*, запрети́ть *pf* (+*dat* (*person*) & *acc* (*thing*)). **forbidding** *adj* гро́зный.

force *n* си́ла; *pl* (*armed* ~) вооружённые си́лы *f pl*; **by** ~ си́лой; *vt* (*compel*) заставля́ть *impf*, заста́вить *pf*; (*lock etc.*) взла́мывать *impf*, взлома́ть *pf*. **forceful** *adj* си́льный; (*speech*) убеди́тельный. **forcible** *adj* наси́льственный.

forceps *n* щипцы́ (-цо́в) *pl*.

ford *n* брод; *vt* переходи́ть *impf*, перейти́ *pf* вброд+*acc*.

fore *n*: **come to the** ~ выдвига́ться *impf*, вы́двинуться *pf* на пере́дний пла́н.

forearm *n* предплéчье. **foreboding** *n* предчу́вствие. **forecast** *n* предсказа́ние; (*of weather*) прогно́з; *vt* предска́зывать *impf*, предсказа́ть *pf*. **forecourt** *n* пере́дний двор. **forefather** *n* пре́док. **forefinger** *n* указа́тельный па́лец. **forefront** *n* (*foreground*) пере́дний план; (*leading position*) аванга́рд. **foregone** *adj*: ~ **conclusion** предрешённый исхо́д. **foreground** *n* пере́дний план. **forehead** *n* лоб.

foreign *adj* (*from abroad*) иностра́нный; (*alien*) чу́ждый; (*external*) вне́шний; ~ **body** иноро́дное те́ло; ~ **currency** валю́та. **foreigner** *n* иностра́нец, -нка.

foreman *n* ма́стер.

foremost *adj* выдаю́щийся; **first and** ~ пре́жде всего́.

forename *n* и́мя.

forensic *adj* суде́бный.

forerunner *n* предве́стник. **foresee** *vt* предви́деть *impf*. **foreshadow** *vt* предвеща́ть *impf*. **foresight** *n* предви́дение; (*caution*) предусмотри́тельность.

forest *n* лес.

forestall *vt* предупрежда́ть *impf*, предупреди́ть *pf*.

forester *n* лесни́чий *sb*. **forestry** *n* лесово́дство.

foretaste *n* предвкуше́ние; *vt* предвкуша́ть *impf*,

предвкуси́ть *pf.* **foretell** *vt* предска́зывать *impf*, предсказа́ть *pf.* **forethought** *n* предусмотри́тельность. **forewarn** *vt* предостерега́ть *impf*, предостере́чь *pf.* **foreword** *n* предисло́вие.

forfeit *n* (*in game*) фант; *vt* лиша́ться *impf*, лиши́ться *pf* +*gen*.

forge[1] *n* (*smithy*) ку́зница; (*furnace*) горн; *vt* кова́ть *impf*, вы́~ *pf*; (*fabricate*) подде́лывать *impf*, подде́лать *pf.*

forge[2] *vi*: ~ **ahead** продвига́ться *impf*, продви́нуться *pf* вперёд.

forger *n* фальшивомоне́тчик. **forgery** *n* подде́лка.

forget *vt* забыва́ть *impf*, забы́ть *pf.* **forgetful** *adj* забы́вчивый.

forgive *vt* проща́ть *impf*, прости́ть *pf.* **forgiveness** *n* проще́ние.

forgo *vt* возде́рживаться *impf*, воздержа́ться *pf* от+*gen*.

fork *n* (*eating*) ви́лка; (*digging*) ви́лы (-л) *pl*; (*in road*) разветвле́ние; *vi* (*road*) разветвля́ться *impf*, разветви́ться *pf.*

forlorn *adj* жа́лкий.

form *n* (*shape*; *kind*) фо́рма; (*class*) класс; (*document*) анке́та; *vt* (*make*, *create*) образо́вывать *impf*, образова́ть *pf*; (*develop*; *make up*) составля́ть *impf*, соста́вить *pf*; *vi* образо́вываться *impf*, образова́ться *pf.* **formal** *adj* форма́льный; (*official*) официа́льный. **formality** *n* форма́льность. **format** *n* форма́т. **formation** *n* образова́ние. **formative** *adj*: ~ **years** молоды́е го́ды (-до́в) *m pl.*

former *adj* (*earlier*) пре́жний; (*ex*) бы́вший; **the** ~ (*of two*) пе́рвый. **formerly** *adv* пре́жде.

formidable *adj* (*dread*) гро́зный; (*arduous*) тру́дный.

formless *adj* бесфо́рменный.

formula *n* фо́рмула. **formulate** *vt* формули́ровать *impf*, с~ *pf.* **formulation** *n* формулиро́вка.

forsake *vt* (*desert*) покида́ть *impf*, поки́нуть *pf*; (*renounce*) отка́зываться *impf*, отказа́ться *pf* от+*gen*.

fort *n* форт.

forth *adv* вперёд, да́льше; **back and** ~ взад и вперёд; **and so** ~ и так да́лее. **forthcoming** *adj* предстоя́щий; **be** ~ (*available*) поступа́ть *impf*, поступи́ть *pf.* **forthwith** *adv* неме́дленно.

fortieth *adj* & *n* сороково́й.

fortification *n* укрепле́ние. **fortify** *vt* укрепля́ть *impf*, укрепи́ть *pf*; (*fig*) подкрепля́ть *impf*, подкрепи́ть *pf.* **fortitude** *n* сто́йкость.

fortnight *n* две неде́ли *f pl.* **fortnightly** *adj* двухнеде́льный; *adv* раз в две неде́ли.

fortress *n* кре́пость.

fortuitous *adj* случа́йный.

fortunate *adj* счастли́вый. **fortunately** *adv* к сча́стью. **fortune** *n* (*destiny*) судьба́; (*good* ~) сча́стье; (*wealth*) состоя́ние.

forty *adj* & *n* со́рок; *pl* (*decade*) сороковы́е го́ды (-до́в) *m pl.*

forward *adj* пере́дний; (*presumptuous*) развя́зный; *n* (*sport*) напада́ющий *sb*; *adv* вперёд; *vt* (*letter*) пересыла́ть *impf*, пересла́ть *pf.*

fossil *n* ископа́емое *sb*; *adj*

ископа́емый. **fossilized** *adj* ископа́емый.

foster *vt* (*child*) приюти́ть *pf*; (*idea*) вына́шивать *impf*, вы́носить *pf*; (*create*) создава́ть *impf*, созда́ть *pf*; (*cherish*) леле́ять *impf*; **~-child** приёмыш.

foul *adj* (*dirty*) гря́зный; (*repulsive*) отврати́тельный; (*obscene*) непристо́йный; *n* (*sport*) наруше́ние пра́вил; *vt* (*dirty*) па́чкать *impf*, за~, ис~ *pf*; (*entangle*) запу́тывать *impf*, запу́тать *pf*.

found *vt* осно́вывать *impf*, основа́ть *pf*.

foundation *n* (*of building*) фунда́мент; (*basis*) осно́ва; (*institution*) учрежде́ние; (*fund*) фонд. **founder**[1] *n* основа́тель *m*.

founder[2] *vi* (*naut, fig*) тону́ть *impf*, по~ *pf*.

foundry *n* лите́йная *sb*.

fountain *n* фонта́н; **~-pen** автору́чка.

four *adj* & *n* четы́ре; (*number 4*) четвёрка; **on all ~s** на четвере́ньках. **fourteen** *adj* & *n* четы́рнадцать. **fourteenth** *adj* & *n* четы́рнадцатый. **fourth** *adj* & *n* четвёртый; (*quarter*) че́тверть.

fowl *n* (*domestic*) дома́шняя пти́ца; (*wild*) дичь *collect*.

fox *n* лиса́, лиси́ца; *vt* озада́чивать *impf*, озада́чить *pf*.

foyer *n* фойе́ *neut indecl*.

fraction *n* (*math*) дробь; (*portion*) части́ца.

fractious *adj* раздражи́тельный.

fracture *n* перело́м; *vt* & *i* лома́ть(ся) *impf*, с~ *pf*.

fragile *adj* ло́мкий.

fragment *n* обло́мок; (*of conversation*) отры́вок; (*of writing*) фрагме́нт. **fragmentary** *adj* отры́вочный.

fragrance *n* арома́т. **fragrant** *adj* арома́тный, души́стый.

frail *adj* хру́пкий.

frame *n* о́стов; (*build*) телосложе́ние; (*picture*) ра́ма; (*cin*) кадр; **~ of mind** настрое́ние; *vt* (*devise*) создава́ть *impf*, созда́ть *pf*; (*formulate*) формули́ровать *impf*, с~ *pf*; (*picture*) вставля́ть *impf*, вста́вить *pf* в ра́му; (*incriminate*) фабрикова́ть *impf*, с~ *pf* обвине́ние про́тив+*gen*. **framework** *n* о́стов; (*fig*) ра́мки *f pl*.

franc *n* франк.

France *n* Фра́нция.

franchise *n* (*comm*) привиле́гия; (*polit*) пра́во го́лоса.

frank[1] *adj* открове́нный.

frank[2] *vt* (*letter*) франки́ровать *impf* & *pf*.

frantic *adj* неи́стовый.

fraternal *adj* бра́тский. **fraternity** *n* бра́тство.

fraud *n* обма́н; (*person*) обма́нщик. **fraudulent** *adj* обма́нный.

fraught *adj*: **~ with** чрева́тый +*instr*.

fray[1] *vt* & *i* обтрёпывать(ся) *impf*, обтрепа́ть(ся) *pf*.

fray[2] *n* бой.

freak *n* уро́д; *attrib* необы́чный.

freckle *n* весну́шка. **freckled** *adj* весну́шчатый.

free *adj* свобо́дный; (*gratis*) беспла́тный; **~ kick** штрафно́й уда́р; **~ speech** свобо́да сло́ва; *vt* освобожда́ть *impf*, освободи́ть *pf*. **freedom** *n* свобо́да. **freehold** *n* неограни́ченное пра́во со́бственности на недви́жимость.

freelance *adj* внешта́тный. **Freemason** *n* франкмасо́н. **freeze** *vi* замерза́ть *impf*, мёрзнуть *impf*, замёрзнуть *pf*; *vt* замора́живать *impf*, заморо́зить *pf*. **freezer** *n* морози́льник; (*compartment*) морози́лка. **freezing** *adj* моро́зный; **below ~** ни́же нуля́.
freight *n* фрахт. **freighter** *n* (*ship*) грузово́е су́дно.
French *adj* францу́зский; **~ bean** фасо́ль; **~ horn** валто́рна; **~ windows** двуство́рчатое окно́ до по́ла. **Frenchman** *n* францу́з. **Frenchwoman** *n* францу́женка.
frenetic *adj* нейстовый.
frenzied *adj* нейстовый. **frenzy** *n* нейстовство.
frequency *n* частота́. **frequent** *adj* ча́стый; *vt* ча́сто посеща́ть *impf*.
fresco *n* фре́ска.
fresh *adj* све́жий; (*new*) но́вый; **~ water** пре́сная вода́. **freshen** *vt* освежа́ть *impf*, освежи́ть *pf*; *vi* свеже́ть *impf*, по~ *pf*. **freshly** *adv* свежо́; (*recently*) неда́вно. **freshness** *n* све́жесть. **freshwater** *adj* пресново́дный.
fret[1] *vi* му́читься *impf*. **fretful** *adj* раздражи́тельный.
fret[2] *n* (*mus*) лад.
fretsaw *n* ло́бзик.
friar *n* мона́х.
friction *n* тре́ние; (*fig*) тре́ния *neut pl*.
Friday *n* пя́тница.
fridge *n* холоди́льник.
fried *adj*: **~ egg** яи́чница.
friend *n* друг, подру́га; прия́тель *m*, ~ница. **friendly** *adj* дру́жеский. **friendship** *n* дру́жба.
frieze *n* фриз.
frigate *n* фрега́т.
fright *n* испу́г. **frighten** *vt* пуга́ть *impf*, ис~, на~ *pf*. **frightful** *adj* стра́шный.
frigid *adj* холо́дный.
frill *n* обо́рка.
fringe *n* бахрома́; (*of hair*) чёлка; (*edge*) край.
frisk *vi* (*frolic*) резви́ться *impf*; *vt* (*search*) шмона́ть *impf*. **frisky** *adj* ре́звый.
fritter *vt*: **~ away** растра́чивать *impf*, растра́тить *pf*.
frivolity *n* легкомы́сленность. **frivolous** *adj* легкомы́сленный.
fro *adv*: **to and ~** взад и вперёд.
frock *n* пла́тье.
frog *n* лягу́шка.
frolic *vi* резви́ться *impf*.
from *prep* от+*gen*; (*~ off, down ~; in time*) с+*gen*; (*out of*) из+*gen*; (*according to*) по+*dat*; (*because of*) из-за+*gen*; **~ above** све́рху; **~ abroad** из-за грани́цы; **~ afar** и́здали; **~ among** из числа́+*gen*; **~ behind** из-за+*gen*; **~ day to day** изо дня́ в день; **~ everywhere** отовсю́ду; **~ here** отсю́да; **~ memory** по па́мяти; **~ now on** отны́не; **~ there** отту́да; **~ time to time** вре́мя от вре́мени; **~ under** из-под+*gen*.
front *n* фаса́д, пере́дняя сторона́; (*mil*) фронт; **in ~ of** впереди́+*gen*, пе́ред+*instr*; *adj* пере́дний; (*first*) пе́рвый.
frontier *n* грани́ца.
frost *n* моро́з; **~-bite** отмороже́ние; **~-bitten** отморо́женный. **frosted** *adj*: **~ glass** ма́товое стекло́. **frosty** *adj* моро́зный; (*fig*) ледяно́й.
froth *n* пе́на; *vi* пе́ниться *impf*,

вс~ *pf.* **frothy** *adj* пéнистый.

frown *n* хмýрый взгляд; *vi* хмýриться *impf*, на~ *pf.*

frugal *adj* (*careful*) бережли́вый; (*scanty*) скýдный.

fruit *n* плод; *collect* фрýкты *m pl*; *adj* фруктóвый. **fruitful** *adj* плодотвóрный. **fruition** *n*: **come to** ~ осуществи́ться *pf.* **fruitless** *adj* бесплóдный.

frustrate *vt* фрустри́ровать *impf* & *pf.* **frustrating** *adj* фрустри́рующий. **frustration** *n* фрустрáция.

fry[1] *n*: **small** ~ мелюзгá.

fry[2] *vt* & *i* жáрить(ся) *impf*, за~, из~ *pf.* **frying-pan** *n* сковородá.

fuel *n* тóпливо.

fugitive *n* беглéц.

fulcrum *n* тóчка опóры.

fulfil *vt* (*perform*) выполня́ть *impf*, вы́полнить *pf*; (*dreams*) осуществля́ть *impf*, осуществи́ть *pf.* **fulfilling** *adj* удовлетворя́ющий. **fulfilment** *n* выполнéние; осуществлéние; удовлетворéние.

full *adj* пóлный (**of** +*gen*, *instr*); (*replete*) сы́тый; ~ **stop** тóчка; ~ **time: I work** ~ **time** я рабóтаю на пóлную стáвку; *n*: **in** ~ пóлностью; **to the** ~ в пóлной мéре. **fullness** *n* полнотá. **fully** *adv* вполнé.

fulsome *adj* чрезмéрный.

fumble *vi*: ~ **for** нащýпывать *impf* +*acc*; ~ **with** вози́ться *impf* с+*instr*.

fume *vi* (*with anger*) кипéть *impf*, вс~ *pf* гнéвом. **fumes** *n pl* испарéния *neut pl.* **fumigate** *vt* окýривать *impf*, окури́ть *pf.*

fun *n* забáва; **it was** ~ бы́ло забáвно; **have** ~ забавля́ться *impf*; **make** ~ **of** смея́ться *impf*, по~ *pf* над+*instr*.

function *n* фýнкция; (*event*) вéчер; *vi* функциони́ровать *impf*; дéйствовать *impf.* **functional** *adj* функционáльный. **functionary** *n* чинóвник.

fund *n* фонд; (*store*) запáс.

fundamental *adj* основнóй; *n*: *pl* оснóвы *f pl.*

funeral *n* пóхороны (-óн, -онáм) *pl.*

fungus *n* гриб.

funnel *n* ворóнка; (*chimney*) дымовáя трубá.

funny *adj* смешнóй; (*odd*) стрáнный.

fur *n* мех; ~ **coat** шýба.

furious *adj* бéшеный.

furnace *n* горн, печь.

furnish *vt* (*provide*) снабжáть *impf*, снабди́ть *pf* (**with** с+*instr*); (*house*) обставля́ть *impf*, обстáвить *pf.* **furniture** *n* мéбель.

furrow *n* боруздá.

furry *adj* пуши́стый.

further, farther *comp adj* дальнéйший; *adv* дáльше; *vt* продвигáть *impf*, продви́нуть *pf.* **furthermore** *adv* к томý же. **furthest, farthest** *superl adj* сáмый дáльний.

furtive *adj* скры́тый, тáйный.

fury *n* я́рость.

fuse[1] *vt* & *i* (*of metal*) сплавля́ть(ся) *impf*, сплáвить(ся) *pf.*

fuse[2] *n* (*in bomb*) запáл; (*detonating device*) взрывáтель *m.*

fuse[3] *n* (*electr*) прóбка; *vi* перегорáть *impf*, перегорéть *pf.*

fuselage *n* фюзеля́ж.

fusion *n* плáвка, слия́ние.

fuss *n* сует́а; *vi* суети́ться

impf. **fussy** *adj* суетли́вый; (*fastidious*) разбо́рчивый.
futile *adj* тще́тный. **futility** *n* тще́тность.
future *n* бу́дущее *sb*; (*gram*) бу́дущее вре́мя *neut*; *adj* бу́дущий. **futuristic** *adj* футуристи́ческий.
fuzzy *adj* (*hair*) пуши́стый; (*blurred*) расплы́вчатый.

G

gabble *vi* тарато́рить *impf.*
gable *n* щипе́ц.
gad *vi*: ~ **about** шата́ться *impf.*
gadget *n* приспособле́ние.
gaffe *n* оплошность.
gag *n* кляп; *vt* засо́вывать *impf*, засу́нуть *pf* кляп в рот+*dat.*
gaiety *n* весёлость. **gaily** *adv* ве́село.
gain *n* при́быль; *pl* дохо́ды *m pl*; (*increase*) приро́ст; *vt* (*acquire*) получа́ть *impf*, получи́ть *pf*; ~ **on** нагоня́ть *impf*, нагна́ть *pf.*
gait *n* похо́дка.
gala *n* пра́зднество; *adj* пра́здничный.
galaxy *n* гала́ктика; (*fig*) плея́да.
gale *n* бу́ря, шторм.
gall[1] *n* (*bile*) жёлчь; (*cheek*) на́глость; **~-bladder** жёлчный пузы́рь *m.*
gall[2] *vt* (*vex*) раздража́ть *impf*, раздражи́ть *pf.*
gallant *adj* (*brave*) хра́брый; (*courtly*) гала́нтный. **gallantry** *n* хра́брость; гала́нтность.
gallery *n* галере́я.
galley *n* (*ship*) гале́ра; (*kitchen*) ка́мбуз.
gallon *n* галло́н.
gallop *n* гало́п; *vi* галопи́ровать *impf.*
gallows *n pl* ви́селица.
gallstone *n* жёлчный ка́мень *m.*
galore *adv* в изоби́лии.
galvanize *vt* гальванизи́ровать *impf* & *pf.*
gambit *n* гамби́т.
gamble *n* (*undertaking*) риско́ванное предприя́тие; *vi* игра́ть *impf* в аза́ртные и́гры; (*fig*) рискова́ть *impf* (**with** +*instr*); ~ **away** проигрывать *impf*, проигра́ть *pf.* **gambler** *n* игро́к. **gambling** *n* аза́ртные и́гры *f pl.*
game *n* игра́; (*single* ~) па́ртия; (*collect, animals*) дичь; *adj* (*ready*) гото́вый. **gamekeeper** *n* лесни́к.
gammon *n* о́корок.
gamut *n* га́мма.
gang *n* ба́нда; (*workmen*) брига́да.
gangrene *n* гангре́на.
gangster *n* га́нгстер.
gangway *n* (*passage*) прохо́д; (*naut*) схо́дни (-ней) *pl.*
gaol *n* тюрьма́; *vt* заключа́ть *impf*, заключи́ть *pf* в тюрьму́. **gaoler** *n* тюре́мщик.
gap *n* (*empty space; deficiency*) пробе́л; (*in wall etc.*) брешь; (*fig*) разры́в.
gape *vi* (*person*) зева́ть *impf* (*at* на+*acc*); (*chasm*) зия́ть *impf.*
garage *n* гара́ж.
garb *n* одея́ние.
garbage *n* му́сор.
garbled *adj* искажённый.
garden *n* сад; *attrib* садо́вый. **gardener** *n* садо́вник. **gardening** *n* садово́дство.
gargle *vi* полоска́ть *impf*,

про~ *pf* горло.
gargoyle *n* горгу́лья.
garish *adj* крича́щий.
garland *n* гирля́нда.
garlic *n* чесно́к.
garment *n* предме́т оде́жды.
garnish *n* гарни́р; *vt* гарни́ровать *impf* & *pf*.
garret *n* манса́рда.
garrison *n* гарнизо́н.
garrulous *adj* болтли́вый.
gas *n* газ; *attrib* га́зовый; *vt* отравля́ть *impf*, отрави́ть *pf* га́зом. **gaseous** *adj* газообра́зный.
gash *n* поре́з; *vt* поре́зать *pf*.
gasket *n* прокла́дка.
gasp *vi* задыха́ться *impf*, задохну́ться *pf*.
gastric *adj* желу́дочный.
gate *n* (*large*) воро́та (-т) *pl*; (*small*) кали́тка. **gateway** *n* (*gate*) воро́та (-т) *pl*; (*entrance*) вход.
gather *vt* & *i* собира́ть(ся) *impf*, собра́ть(ся) *pf*; *vt* заключа́ть *impf*, заключи́ть *pf*. **gathering** *n* (*assembly*) собра́ние.
gaudy *adj* крича́щий.
gauge *n* (*measure*) ме́ра; (*instrument*) кали́бр, измери́тельный прибо́р; (*rly*) колея́; (*criterion*) крите́рий; *vt* измеря́ть *impf*, изме́рить *pf*; (*estimate*) оце́нивать *impf*, оцени́ть *pf*.
gaunt *adj* то́щий.
gauntlet *n* рукави́ца.
gauze *n* ма́рля.
gay *adj* весёлый; (*bright*) пёстрый; (*homosexual*) гомосексуа́льный.
gaze *n* при́стальный взгляд; *vt* при́стально гляде́ть *impf* (**at** на+*acc*).
gazelle *n* газе́ль.
GCSE *abbr* (*of* **General Certificate of Secondary Education**) аттеста́т о сре́днем образова́нии.
gear *n* (*equipment*) принадле́жности *f pl*; (*in car*) ско́рость; ~ **lever** рыча́г; *vt* приспосабля́ть *impf*, приспосо́бить *pf* (**to** к+*dat*). **gearbox** *n* коро́бка переда́ч.
gel *n* космети́ческое желе́ *neut indecl*. **gelatine** *n* желати́н.
gelding *n* ме́рин.
gelignite *n* гелигни́т.
gem *n* драгоце́нный ка́мень *m*.
Gemini *n* Близнецы́ *m pl*.
gender *n* род.
gene *n* ген.
genealogy *n* генеало́гия.
general *n* генера́л; *adj* о́бщий; (*nationwide*) всео́бщий; **in** ~ вообще́. **generalization** *n* обобще́ние. **generalize** *vi* обобща́ть *impf*, обобщи́ть *pf*. **generally** *adv* (*usually*) обы́чно; (*in general*) вообще́.
generate *vt* порожда́ть *impf*, породи́ть *pf*. **generation** *n* (*in descent*) поколе́ние. **generator** *n* генера́тор.
generic *adj* родово́й; (*general*) о́бщий.
generosity *n* (*magnanimity*) великоду́шие; (*munificence*) ще́дрость. **generous** *adj* великоду́шный; ще́дрый.
genesis *n* происхожде́ние; (**G**~) Кни́га Бытия́.
genetic *adj* генети́ческий. **genetics** *n* гене́тика.
genial *adj* (*of person*) доброду́шный.
genital *adj* полово́й. **genitals** *n pl* половы́е о́рганы *m pl*.
genitive *adj* (*n*) роди́тельный (паде́ж).

genius *n* (*person*) ге́ний; (*ability*) гениа́льность.
genocide *n* геноци́д.
genome *n* гено́м.
genre *n* жанр.
genteel *adj* благовоспи́танный.
gentile *n* нееврé́й, ~ка.
gentility *n* благовоспи́танность.
gentle *adj* (*mild*) мя́гкий; (*quiet*) ти́хий; (*light*) лёгкий. **gentleman** *n* джентльме́н. **gentleness** *n* мя́гкость. **gents** *n pl* мужска́я убо́рная *sb*.
genuine *adj* (*authentic*) по́длинный; (*sincere*) и́скренний.
genus *n* род.
geographical *adj* географи́ческий. **geography** *n* геогра́фия. **geological** *adj* геологи́ческий. **geologist** *n* гео́лог. **geology** *n* геоло́гия. **geometric(al)** *adj* геометри́ческий. **geometry** *n* геоме́трия.
Georgia *n* Гру́зия. **Georgian** *n* грузи́н, ~ка; *adj* грузи́нский.
geranium *n* гера́нь.
geriatric *adj* гериатри́ческий.
germ *m* микро́б.
German *n* не́мец, не́мка; *adj* неме́цкий; ~ **measles** красну́ха.
germane *adj* уме́стный.
Germanic *adj* герма́нский.
Germany *n* Герма́ния.
germinate *vi* прораста́ть *impf*, прорасти́ *pf*.
gesticulate *vi* жестикули́ровать *impf*. **gesture** *n* жест.
get *vt* (*obtain*) достава́ть *impf*, доста́ть *pf*; (*receive*) получа́ть *impf*, получи́ть *pf*; (*understand*) понима́ть *impf*, поня́ть *pf*; (*disease*) заража́ться *impf*, зарази́ться *pf* +*instr*; (*induce*) угова́ривать *impf*, уговори́ть *pf* (**to do** +*inf*); (*fetch*) приноси́ть *impf*, принести́ *pf*; *vi* (*become*) станови́ться *impf*, стать *pf* +*instr*; **have got** (*have*) име́ть *impf*; **have got to** быть до́лжен (-жна́) +*inf*; ~ **about** (*spread*) распространя́ться *impf*, распространи́ться *pf*; (*move around*) передвига́ться *impf*; (*travel*) разъезжа́ть *impf*; ~ **at** (*mean*) хоте́ть *impf* сказа́ть; ~ **away** (*slip off*) ускольза́ть *impf*, ускользну́ть *pf*; (*escape*) убега́ть *impf*, убежа́ть *pf*; (*leave*) уезжа́ть *impf*, уе́хать *pf*; ~ **away with** избега́ть *impf*, избежа́ть *pf* отве́тственности за+*acc*; ~ **back** (*recover*) получа́ть *impf*, получи́ть *pf* обра́тно; (*return*) возвраща́ться *impf*, верну́ться *pf*; ~ **by** (*manage*) справля́ться *impf*, спра́виться *pf*; ~ **down** сходи́ть *impf*, сойти́ *pf*; ~ **down to** принима́ться *impf*, приня́ться *pf* за+*acc*; ~ **off** слеза́ть *impf*, слезть *pf* с+*gen*; ~ **on** сади́ться *impf*, сесть *pf* в, на, +*acc*; (*prosper*) преуспева́ть *impf*, преуспе́ть *pf*; ~ **on with** (*person*) ужива́ться *impf*, ужи́ться *pf* с+*instr*; ~ **out of** (*avoid*) избавля́ться *impf*, изба́виться *pf* от+*gen*; (*car*) выходи́ть *impf*, вы́йти *pf* из+*gen*; ~ **round to** успева́ть *impf*, успе́ть *pf*; ~ **to** (*reach*) достига́ть *impf*, дости́гнуть & дости́чь *pf* +*gen*; ~ **up** (*from bed*) встава́ть *impf*, встать *pf*.
geyser *n* (*spring*) ге́йзер; (*water-heater*) коло́нка.
ghastly *adj* ужа́сный.

gherkin *n* огуре́ц.
ghetto *n* ге́тто *neut indecl.*
ghost *n* привиде́ние. **ghostly** *adj* при́зрачный.
giant *n* гига́нт; *adj* гига́нтский.
gibberish *n* тараба́рщина.
gibbet *n* ви́селица.
gibe *n* насме́шка; *vi* насмеха́ться *impf* (**at** над+*instr*).
giblets *n pl* потроха́ (-хо́в) *pl.*
giddiness *n* головокруже́ние. **giddy** *predic*: **I feel ~** у меня́ кру́жится голова́.
gift *n* (*present*) пода́рок; (*donation*; *ability*) дар. **gifted** *adj* одарённый.
gig *n* (*theat*) выступле́ние.
gigantic *adj* гига́нтский.
giggle *n* хихи́канье; *vi* хихи́кать *impf*, хихи́кнуть *pf.*
gild *vt* золоти́ть *impf*, вы́~, по~ *pf.*
gill *n* (*of fish*) жа́бра.
gilt *n* позоло́та; *adj* золочённый.
gimmick *n* трюк.
gin *n* (*spirit*) джин.
ginger *n* имби́рь *m*; *adj* (*colour*) ры́жий.
gingerly *adv* осторо́жно.
gipsy *n* цыга́н, ~ка.
giraffe *n* жира́ф.
girder *n* ба́лка. **girdle** *n* по́яс.
girl *n* (*child*) де́вочка; (*young woman*) де́вушка. **girlfriend** *n* подру́га. **girlish** *adj* де́вичий.
girth *n* обхва́т; (*on saddle*) подпру́га.
gist *n* суть.
give *vt* дава́ть *impf*, дать *pf*; **~ away** выдава́ть *impf*, вы́дать *pf*; **~ back** возвраща́ть *impf*, возврати́ть *pf*; **~ in** (*yield*, *vi*) уступа́ть *impf*, уступи́ть *pf* (**to** +*dat*); (*hand in*, *vt*) вруча́ть *impf*, вручи́ть *pf*; **~ out** (*emit*) издава́ть *impf*, изда́ть *pf*; (*distribute*) раздава́ть *impf*, разда́ть *pf*; **~ up** отка́зываться *impf*, отказа́ться *pf* от+*gen*; (*habit etc.*) броса́ть *impf*, бро́сить *pf*; **~ o.s. up** сдава́ться *impf*, сда́ться *pf*. **given** *predic* (*inclined*) скло́нен (-онна́, -о́нно) (**to** к+*dat*).
glacier *n* ледни́к.
glad *adj* ра́достный; *predic* рад. **gladden** *vt* ра́довать *impf*, об~ *pf.*
glade *n* поля́на.
gladly *adv* охо́тно.
glamorous *adj* я́ркий; (*attractive*) привлека́тельный.
glamour *n* я́ркость; привлека́тельность.
glance *n* (*look*) бе́глый взгляд; *vi*: **~ at** взгля́дывать *impf*, взгляну́ть *pf* на+*acc.*
gland *n* железа́. **glandular** *adj* желе́зистый.
glare *n* (*light*) ослепи́тельный блеск; (*look*) свире́пый взгляд; *vi* свире́по смотре́ть *impf* (**at** на+*acc*). **glaring** *adj* (*dazzling*) ослепи́тельный; (*mistake*) гру́бый.
glasnost *n* гла́сность.
glass *n* (*substance*) стекло́; (*drinking vessel*) стака́н; (*wine ~*) рю́мка; (*mirror*) зе́ркало; *pl* (*spectacles*) очки́ (-ко́в) *pl*; *attrib* стекля́нный. **glassy** *adj* (*look*) ту́склый.
glaze *n* глазу́рь; *vt* (*with glass*) застекля́ть *impf*, застекли́ть *pf*; (*pottery*) глазурова́ть *impf* & *pf*; (*cul*) глази́ровать *impf* & *pf*. **glazier** *n* стеко́льщик.
gleam *n* про́блеск; *vi* свети́ться *impf.*
glean *vt* собира́ть *impf*, собра́ть *pf* по крупи́цам.

glee *n* весе́лье. **gleeful** *adj* лику́ющий.
glib *adj* бо́йкий.
glide *vi* скользи́ть *impf*; (*aeron*) плани́ровать *impf*, с~ *pf*. **glider** *n* планёр.
glimmer *n* мерца́ние; *vi* мерца́ть *impf*.
glimpse *vt* мельќом ви́деть *impf*, у~ *pf*.
glint *n* блеск; *vi* блесте́ть *impf*.
glisten, glitter *vi* блесте́ть *impf*.
gloat *vi* злора́дствовать *impf*.
global *adj* (*world-wide*) глоба́льный; (*total*) всео́бщий. **globe** *n* (*sphere*) шар; (*the earth*) земно́й шар; (*chart*) гло́бус. **globule** *n* ша́рик.
gloom *n* мрак. **gloomy** *adj* мра́чный.
glorify *vt* прославля́ть *impf*, просла́вить *pf*. **glorious** *adj* сла́вный; (*splendid*) великоле́пный. **glory** *n* сла́ва; *vi* торжествова́ть *impf*.
gloss *n* лоск; *vi*: ~ **over** зама́зывать *impf*, зама́зать *pf*.
glossary *n* глосса́рий.
glove *n* перча́тка.
glow *n* за́рево; (*of cheeks*) румя́нец; *vi* (*incandesce*) накаля́ться *impf*, накали́ться *pf*; (*shine*) сия́ть *impf*.
glucose *n* глюко́за.
glue *n* клей; *vt* прикле́ивать *impf*, прикле́ить *pf* (**to** к+*dat*).
glum *adj* угрю́мый.
glut *n* избы́ток.
glutton *n* обжо́ра *m* & *f*. **gluttonous** *adj* обжо́рливый. **gluttony** *n* обжо́рство.
gnarled *adj* (*hands*) шишкова́тый; (*tree*) сучкова́тый.
gnash *vt* скрежета́ть *impf* +*instr*.
gnat *n* кома́р.
gnaw *vt* грызть *impf*.
gnome *n* гном.
go *n* (*try*) попы́тка; **be on the** ~ быть в движе́нии; **have a** ~ пыта́ться *impf*, по~ *pf*; *vi* (*on foot*) ходи́ть *indet*, идти́ *det*, пойти́ *pf*; (*by transport*) е́здить *indet*, е́хать *det*, по~ *pf*; (*work*) рабо́тать *impf*; (*become*) станови́ться *impf*, стать *pf* +*instr*; (*belong*) идти́ *impf*; **be** ~**ing** (*to do*) собира́ться *impf*, собра́ться *pf* (+*inf*); ~ **about** (*set to work at*) бра́ться *impf*, взя́ться *pf* за+*acc*; (*wander*) броди́ть *indet*; ~ **away** (*on foot*) уходи́ть *impf*, уйти́ *pf*; (*by transport*) уезжа́ть *impf*, уе́хать *pf*; ~ **down** спуска́ться *impf*, спусти́ться *pf* (с+*gen*); ~ **in(to)** (*enter*) входи́ть *impf*, войти́ *pf* (в+*acc*); (*investigate*) рассле́довать *impf* & *pf*; ~ **off** (*go away*) уходи́ть *impf*, уйти́ *pf*; (*deteriorate*) по́ртиться *impf*, ис~ *pf*; ~ **on** (*continue*) продолжа́ть(ся) *impf*, продо́лжить(ся) *pf*; ~ **out** выходи́ть *impf*, вы́йти *pf*; (*flame etc.*) га́снуть *impf*, по~ *pf*; ~ **over** (*inspect*) пересма́тривать *impf*, пересмотре́ть *pf*; (*rehearse*) повторя́ть *impf*, повтори́ть *pf*; (*change allegiance etc.*) переходи́ть *impf*, перейти́ *pf* (**to** в, на, +*acc*, к+*dat*); ~ **through** (*scrutinize*) разбира́ть *impf*, разобра́ть *pf*; ~ **through with** доводи́ть *impf*, довести́ *pf* до конца́; ~ **without** обходи́ться *impf*, обойти́сь *pf* без+*gen*; ~**-ahead** предприи́мчивый; ~**-between** посре́дник.

goad *vt* (*instigate*) подстрека́ть *impf*, подстрекну́ть *pf* (**into** к+*dat*); (*taunt*) раздража́ть *impf*.

goal *n* (*aim*) цель; (*sport*) воро́та (-т) *pl*; (*point won*) гол. **goalkeeper** *n* врата́рь *m*.

goat *n* коза́; (*male*) козёл.

gobble *vt* (*eat*) жрать *impf*; ~ **up** пожира́ть *impf*, пожра́ть *pf*.

goblet *n* бока́л, ку́бок.

god *n* бог; (**G**~) Бог. **godchild** *n* кре́стник, -ица. **goddaughter** *n* кре́стница. **goddess** *n* боги́ня. **godfather** *n* крёстный *sb*. **God-fearing** *adj* богобоя́зненный. **godless** *adj* безбо́жный. **godly** *adj* на́божный. **godmother** *n* крёстная *sb*. **godparent** *n* крёстный *sb*. **godsend** *n* бо́жий дар. **godson** *n* кре́стник.

goggle *vi* тара́щить *impf* глаза́ (**at** на+*acc*); *n*: *pl* защи́тные очки́ (-ко́в) *pl*.

going *adj* де́йствующий. **goings-on** *n pl* дела́ *neut pl*.

gold *n* зо́лото; *adj* золото́й; ~**-plated** накладно́го зо́лота; ~**-smith** золоты́х дел ма́стер. **golden** *adj* золото́й; ~ **eagle** бе́ркут. **goldfish** *n* золота́я ры́бка.

golf *n* гольф; ~ **club** (*implement*) клю́шка; ~ **course** площа́дка для го́льфа. **golfer** *n* игро́к в гольф.

gondola *n* гондо́ла.

gong *n* гонг.

gonorrhoea *n* три́ппер.

good *n* добро́; *pl* (*wares*) това́р(ы); **do** ~ (*benefit*) идти́ *impf*, пойти́ *pf* на по́льзу +*dat*; *adj* хоро́ший, до́брый; ~**-humoured** доброду́шный; ~**-looking** краси́вый; ~ **morning** до́брое у́тро!; ~ **night** споко́йной но́чи! **goodbye** *int* проща́й(те)!; до свида́ния! **goodness** *n* доброта́.

goose *n* гусь *m*; ~**-flesh** гуси́ная ко́жа.

gooseberry *n* крыжо́вник.

gore[1] *n* (*blood*) запёкшаяся кровь.

gore[2] *vt* (*pierce*) бода́ть *impf*, за~ *pf*.

gorge *n* (*geog*) уще́лье; *vi* & *t* объеда́ться *impf*, объе́сться *pf* (**on** +*instr*).

gorgeous *adj* великоле́пный.

gorilla *n* гори́лла.

gorse *n* утёсник.

gory *adj* крова́вый.

gosh *int* бо́же мой!

Gospel *n* Ева́нгелие.

gossip *n* спле́тня; (*person*) спле́тник, -ица; *vi* спле́тничать *impf*, на~ *pf*.

Gothic готи́ческий.

gouge *vt*: ~ **out** выда́лбливать *impf*, вы́долбить *pf*; (*eyes*) выка́лывать *impf*, вы́колоть *pf*.

goulash *n* гуля́ш.

gourmet *n* гурма́н.

gout *n* пода́гра.

govern *vt* пра́вить *impf* +*instr*; (*determine*) определя́ть *impf*, определи́ть *pf*. **governess** *n* гуверна́нтка. **government** *n* прави́тельство. **governmental** *adj* прави́тельственный. **governor** *n* губерна́тор; (*of school etc.*) член правле́ния.

gown *n* пла́тье; (*official's*) ма́нтия.

grab *vt* хвата́ть *impf*, схвати́ть *pf*.

grace *n* (*gracefulness*) гра́ция; (*refinement*) изя́щество; (*favour*) ми́лость; (*at meal*) моли́тва; **have the** ~ **to** быть насто́лько такти́чен, что; **with bad** ~ нелюбе́зно; **with good** ~ с досто́инством; *vt* (*adorn*) украша́ть *impf*, укра́сить *pf*; (*favour*) удоста́ивать *impf*, удосто́ить *pf* (**with** +*gen*). **graceful** *adj* грацио́зный.

gracious *adj* ми́лостивый.

gradation *n* града́ция.

grade *n* (*level*) сте́пень; (*quality*) сорт; *vt* сортирова́ть *impf*, рас~ *pf*.

gradient *n* укло́н.

gradual *adj* постепе́нный.

graduate *n* око́нчивший *sb* университе́т, вуз; *vi* конча́ть *impf*, око́нчить *pf* (университе́т, вуз); *vt* градуи́ровать *impf* & *pf*.

graffiti *n* на́дписи *f pl*.

graft *n* (*bot*) черено́к; (*med*) переса́дка (живо́й тка́ни); *vt* (*bot*) привива́ть *impf*, приви́ть *pf* (**to** +*dat*); (*med*) переса́живать *impf*, пересади́ть *pf*.

grain *n* (*seed*; *collect*) зерно́; (*particle*) крупи́нка; (*of sand*) песчи́нка; (*of wood*) (древе́сное) волокно́; **against the** ~ не по нутру́.

gram(me) *n* грамм.

grammar *n* грамма́тика; ~ **school** гимна́зия. **grammatical** *adj* граммати́ческий.

gramophone *n* проигрыва́тель *m*; ~ **record** грампласти́нка.

granary *n* амба́р.

grand *adj* великоле́пный; ~ **piano** роя́ль *m*. **grandchild** *n* внук, вну́чка. **granddaughter** *n* вну́чка. **grandfather** *n* де́душка *m*. **grandmother** *n* ба́бушка. **grandparents** *n* ба́бушка и де́душка. **grandson** *n* внук. **grandstand** *n* трибу́на.

grandeur *n* вели́чие.

grandiose *adj* грандио́зный.

granite *n* грани́т.

granny *n* ба́бушка.

grant *n* (*financial*) дота́ция; (*univ*) стипе́ндия; *vt* дарова́ть *impf* & *pf*; (*concede*) допуска́ть *impf*, допусти́ть *pf*; **take for** ~**ed** (*assume*) счита́ть *impf*, счесть *pf* само́ собо́й разуме́ющимся; (*not appreciate*) принима́ть *impf* как до́лжное.

granular *adj* зерни́стый.

granulated *adj*: ~ **sugar** са́харный песо́к.

granule *n* зёрнышко.

grape *n* (*single grape*) виногра́дина; *collect* виногра́д.

grapefruit *n* гре́йпфрут.

graph *n* гра́фик.

graphic *adj* графи́ческий; (*vivid*) я́ркий.

graphite *n* графи́т.

grapple *vi* (*struggle*) боро́ться *impf* (**with** с+*instr*).

grasp *n* (*grip*) хва́тка; (*comprehension*) понима́ние; *vt* (*clutch*) хвата́ть *impf*, схвати́ть *pf*; (*comprehend*) понима́ть *impf*, поня́ть *pf*. **grasping** *adj* жа́дный.

grass *n* трава́. **grasshopper** *n* кузне́чик. **grassy** *adj* трави́стый.

grate[1] *n* (*fireplace*) решётка.

grate[2] *vt* (*rub*) тере́ть *impf*, на~ *pf*; *vi* (*sound*) скрипе́ть *impf*; ~ **(up)on** (*irritate*) раздража́ть *impf*, раздражи́ть *pf*.

grateful *n* благода́рный.

grater *n* тёрка.

gratify *vt* удовлетворя́ть *impf*, удовлетвори́ть *pf*.

grating *n* решётка.

gratis *adv* беспла́тно.

gratitude *n* благода́рность. **gratuitous** *adj* (*free*) даро́вый; (*motiveless*) беспричи́нный. **gratuity** *n* (*tip*) чаевы́е *sb pl.*
grave[1] *n* моги́ла. **gravedigger** *n* моги́льщик. **gravestone** *n* надгро́бный ка́мень *m.* **graveyard** *n* кла́дбище.
grave[2] *adj* серьёзный.
gravel *n* гра́вий.
gravitate *vi* тяготе́ть *impf* (**towards** к+*dat*). **gravitational** *adj* гравитацио́нный. **gravity** *n* (*seriousness*) серьёзность; (*force*) тя́жесть.
gravy *n* (мясна́я) подли́вка.
graze[1] *vi* (*feed*) пасти́сь *impf.*
graze[2] *n* (*abrasion*) цара́пина; *vt* (*touch*) задева́ть *impf*, заде́ть *pf*; (*abrade*) цара́пать *impf*, о~ *pf.*
grease *n* жир; (*lubricant*) сма́зка; **~-paint** грим; *vt* сма́зывать *impf*, сма́зать *pf.* **greasy** *adj* жи́рный.
great *adj* (*large*) большо́й; (*eminent*) вели́кий; (*splendid*) замеча́тельный; **to a ~ extent** в большо́й сте́пени; **a ~ deal** мно́го (+*gen*); **a ~ many** мно́гие; **~-aunt** двою́родная ба́бушка; **~-granddaughter** пра́внучка; **~-grandfather** пра́дед; **~-grandmother** праба́бка; **~-grandson** пра́внук; **~-uncle** двою́родный де́душка *m.* **greatly** *adv* о́чень.
Great Britain *n* Великобрита́ния.
Greece *n* Гре́ция.
greed *n* жа́дность (**for** к+*dat*). **greedy** *adj* жа́дный (**for** к+*dat*).
Greek *n* грек, греча́нка; *adj* гре́ческий.
green *n* (*colour*) зелёный цвет; (*grassy area*) лужа́йка; *pl* зе́лень *collect*; *adj* зелёный. **greenery** *n* зе́лень. **greenfly** *n* тля. **greengrocer** *n* зеленщи́к. **greengrocer's** *n* овощно́й магази́н. **greenhouse** *n* тепли́ца; **~ effect** парнико́вый эффе́кт.
greet *vt* здоро́ваться *impf*, по~ *pf* с+*instr*; (*meet*) встреча́ть *impf*, встре́тить *pf.* **greeting** *n* приве́т(ствие).
gregarious *adj* общи́тельный.
grenade *n* грана́та.
grey *adj* се́рый; (*hair*) седо́й.
greyhound *n* борза́я *sb.*
grid *n* (*grating*) решётка; (*electr*) сеть; (*map*) координа́тная се́тка.
grief *n* го́ре; **come to ~** терпе́ть *impf*, по~ *pf* неуда́чу.
grievance *n* жа́лоба, оби́да.
grieve *vt* огорча́ть *impf*, огорчи́ть *pf*; *vi* горева́ть *impf* (**for** о+*prep*).
grievous *adj* тя́жкий.
grill *n* ра́шпер; *vt* (*cook*) жа́рить *impf*, за~, из~ *pf* (на ра́шпере); (*question*) допра́шивать *impf*, допроси́ть *pf.*
grille *n* (*grating*) решётка.
grim *adj* (*stern*) суро́вый; (*unpleasant*) неприя́тный.
grimace *n* грима́са; *vi* грима́сничать *impf.*
grime *n* грязь. **grimy** *adj* гря́зный.
grin *n* усме́шка; *vi* усмеха́ться *impf*, усмехну́ться *pf.*
grind *vt* (*flour etc.*) моло́ть *impf*, с~ *pf*; (*axe*) точи́ть *impf*, на~ *pf*; **~ one's teeth** скрежета́ть *impf* зуба́ми.
grip *n* хва́тка; *vt* схва́тывать *impf*, схвати́ть *pf.*
gripe *vi* ворча́ть *impf.*
gripping *adj* захва́тывающий.

grisly *adj* жу́ткий.

gristle *n* хрящ.

grit *n* песо́к; (*for building*) гра́вий; (*firmness*) вы́держка.

grizzle *vi* хны́кать *impf*.

groan *n* стон; *vi* стона́ть *impf*.

grocer *n* бакале́йщик; **~'s (shop)** бакале́йная ла́вка, гастроно́м. **groceries** *n pl* бакале́я *collect*.

groggy *adj* разби́тый.

groin *n* (*anat*) пах.

groom *n* ко́нюх; (*bridegroom*) жени́х; *vt* (*horse*) чи́стить *impf*, по~ *pf*; (*prepare*) гото́вить *impf*, под~ *pf* (**for** к+*dat*); **well-groomed** хорошо́ вы́глядящий.

groove *n* желобо́к.

grope *vi* нащу́пывать *impf* (**for, after** +*acc*).

gross[1] *n* (*12 dozen*) гросс.

gross[2] *adj* (*fat*) ту́чный; (*coarse*) гру́бый; (*total*) валово́й; **~ weight** вес бру́тто.

grotesque *adj* гроте́скный.

grotto *n* грот.

ground *n* земля́; (*earth*) по́чва; *pl* (*dregs*) гу́ща; (*sport*) площа́дка; *pl* (*of house*) парк; (*reason*) основа́ние; **~ floor** пе́рвый эта́ж; *vt* (*instruct*) обуча́ть *impf*, обучи́ть *pf* осно́вам (**in** +*gen*); (*aeron*) запреща́ть *impf*, запрети́ть *pf* полёты +*gen*; *vi* (*naut*) сади́ться *impf*, сесть *pf* на мель. **groundless** *adj* необосно́ванный. **groundwork** *n* фунда́мент.

group *n* гру́ппа; *vt* & *i* группирова́ть(ся) *impf*, с~ *pf*.

grouse[1] *n* шотла́ндская куропа́тка.

grouse[2] *vi* (*grumble*) ворча́ть *impf*.

grove *n* ро́ща.

grovel *vi* пресмыка́ться *impf* (**before** пе́ред+*instr*).

grow *vi* расти́ *impf*; (*become*) станови́ться *impf*, стать *pf* +*instr*; *vt* (*cultivate*) выра́щивать *impf*, вы́растить *pf*; (*hair*) отра́щивать *impf*, отрасти́ть *pf*; **~ up** (*person*) выраста́ть *impf*, вы́расти *pf*; (*custom*) возника́ть *impf*, возни́кнуть *pf*.

growl *n* ворча́ние; *vi* ворча́ть *impf* (**at** на+*acc*).

grown-up *adj* взро́слый *sb*.

growth *n* рост; (*med*) о́пухоль.

grub *n* (*larva*) личи́нка; (*food*) жратва́; *vi*: **~ about** ры́ться *impf*. **grubby** *adj* запа́чканный.

grudge *n* зло́ба; **have a ~ against** име́ть *impf* зуб про́тив+*gen*; *vt* жале́ть *impf*, по~ *pf* +*acc*, +*gen*. **grudgingly** *adv* неохо́тно.

gruelling *adj* изнури́тельный.

gruesome *adj* жу́ткий.

gruff *adj* (*surly*) грубова́тый; (*voice*) хри́плый.

grumble *vi* ворча́ть *impf* (**at** на+*acc*).

grumpy *adj* брюзгли́вый.

grunt *n* хрю́канье; *vi* хрю́кать *impf*, хрю́кнуть *pf*.

guarantee *n* гара́нтия; *vt* гаранти́ровать *impf* & *pf* (**against** от+*gen*). **guarantor** *n* поручи́тель *m*.

guard *n* (*device*) предохрани́тель; (*watch; soldiers*) карау́л; (*sentry*) часово́й *sb*; (*watchman*) сто́рож; (*rly*) конду́ктор; *pl* (*prison*) надзира́тель *m*; *vt* охраня́ть *impf*, охрани́ть *pf*; *vi*: **~ against** остерега́ться *impf*, остере́чься *pf* +*gen*, *inf*.

guardian *n* храни́тель *m*;

(*law*) опеку́н.
guer(r)illa *n* партиза́н; **~ warfare** партиза́нская война́.
guess *n* дога́дка; *vt* & *i* дога́дываться *impf*, догада́ться *pf* (о+*prep*); *vt* (**~** *correctly*) уга́дывать *impf*, угада́ть *pf*. **guesswork** *n* дога́дки *f pl*.
guest *n* гость *m*; **~ house** ма́ленькая гости́ница.
guffaw *n* хо́хот; *vi* хохота́ть *impf*.
guidance *n* руково́дство. **guide** *n* проводни́к, гид; (*guidebook*) путеводи́тель *m*; *vt* води́ть *indet*, вести́ *det*; (*direct*) руководи́ть *impf* +*instr*; **~ed missile** управля́емая раке́та. **guidelines** *n pl* инстру́кции *f pl*; (*advice*) сове́т.
guild *n* ги́льдия, цех.
guile *n* кова́рство. **guileless** *adj* простоду́шный.
guillotine *n* гильоти́на.
guilt *n* вина́; (*guiltiness*) вино́вность. **guilty** *adj* (*of crime*) вино́вный (**of** в+*prep*); (*of wrong*) винова́тый.
guinea-pig *n* морска́я сви́нка; (*fig*) подо́пытный кро́лик.
guise *n*: **under the ~ of** под ви́дом+*gen*.
guitar *n* гита́ра. **guitarist** *n* гитари́ст.
gulf *n* (*geog*) зали́в; (*chasm*) про́пасть.
gull *n* ча́йка.
gullet *n* (*oesophagus*) пищево́д; (*throat*) го́рло.
gullible *adj* легкове́рный.
gully *n* (*ravine*) овра́г.
gulp *n* глото́к; *vt* жа́дно глота́ть *impf*.
gum[1] *n* (*anat*) десна́.
gum[2] *n* каме́дь; (*glue*) клей; *vt* скле́ивать *impf*, скле́ить *pf*.
gumption *n* инициати́ва.
gun *n* (*piece of ordnance*) ору́дие, пу́шка; (*rifle etc.*) ружьё; (*pistol*) пистоле́т; *vt*: **~ down** расстре́ливать *impf*, расстреля́ть *pf*. **gunner** *n* артиллери́ст. **gunpowder** *n* по́рох.
gurgle *vi* бу́лькать *impf*.
gush *vi* хлы́нуть *pf*.
gusset *n* клин.
gust *n* поры́в. **gusty** *adj* поры́вистый.
gusto *n* смак.
gut *n* кишка́; *pl* (*entrails*) кишки́ *f pl*; *pl* (*bravery*) му́жество; *vt* потроши́ть *impf*, вы́**~** *pf*; (*devastate*) опустоша́ть *impf*, опустоши́ть *pf*.
gutter *n* (*of roof*) (водосто́чный) жёлоб; (*of road*) сто́чная кана́ва.
guttural *adj* горта́нный.
guy[1] *n* (*rope*) оття́жка.
guy[2] *n* (*fellow*) па́рень *m*.
guzzle *vt* (*food*) пожира́ть *impf*, пожра́ть *pf*; (*liquid*) хлеба́ть *impf*, хлебну́ть *pf*.
gym *n* (*gymnasium*) гимнасти́ческий зал; (*gymnastics*) гимна́стика. **gymnasium** *n* гимнасти́ческий зал. **gymnast** *n* гимна́ст. **gymnastic** *adj* гимнасти́ческий. **gymnastics** *n* гимна́стика.
gynaecologist *n* гинеко́лог. **gynaecology** *n* гинеколо́гия.
gyrate *vi* враща́ться *impf*.

H

haberdashery *n* галантере́я; (*shop*) галантере́йный магази́н.
habit *n* привы́чка; (*monk's*) ря́са.
habitable *adj* приго́дный для

жилья́. **habitat** *n* есте́ственная среда́. **habitation** *n*: **unfit for ~** неприго́дный для жилья́.
habitual *adj* привы́чный.
hack[1] *vt* руби́ть *impf*; **~saw** ножо́вка.
hack[2] *n* (*hired horse*) наёмная ло́шадь; (*writer*) халту́рщик. **hackneyed** *adj* изби́тый.
haddock *n* пи́кша.
haemophilia *n* гемофили́я. **haemorrhage** *n* кровотече́ние. **haemorrhoids** *n pl* геморро́й *collect*.
hag *n* карга́.
haggard *adj* измождённый.
haggle *vi* торгова́ться *impf*, с~ *pf*.
hail[1] *n* град; *vi* **it is ~ing** идет град. **hailstone** *n* гра́дина.
hail[2] *vt* (*greet*) приве́тствовать *impf* (& *pf in past*); (*taxi*) подзыва́ть *impf*, подозва́ть *pf*.
hair *n* (*single ~*) во́лос; *collect* (*human*) во́лосы (-о́с, -оса́м) *pl*; (*animal*) шерсть. **hairbrush** *n* щётка для воло́с. **haircut** *n* стри́жка; **have a ~** постри́чься *pf*. **hair-do** *n* причёска. **hairdresser** *n* парикма́хер. **hairdresser's** *n* парикма́херская *sb*. **hair-dryer** *n* фен. **hairstyle** *n* причёска. **hairy** *adj* волоса́тый.
hale *adj*: **~ and hearty** здоро́вый и бо́дрый.
half *n* полови́на; (*sport*) тайм; *adj* полови́нный; **in ~** попола́м; **one and a ~** полтора́; **~ past** (*one etc.*) полови́на (второ́го и т.д.); **~-hearted** равноду́шный; **~ an hour** полчаса́; **~-time** переры́в ме́жду та́ймами; **~way** на полпути́; **~-witted** слабоу́мный.
hall *n* (*large room*) зал; (*entrance ~*) холл, вестибю́ль *m*; (*~ of residence*) общежи́тие. **hallmark** *n* проби́рное клеймо́; (*fig*) при́знак.
hallo *int* здра́вствуй(те), приве́т; (*on telephone*) алло́.
hallucination *n* галлюцина́ция.
halo *n* (*around Saint*) нимб; (*fig*) орео́л.
halt *n* остано́вка; *vt* & *i* остана́вливать(ся) *impf*, останови́ть(ся) *pf*; *int* (*mil*) стой(те)! **halting** *adj* запина́ющий.
halve *vt* дели́ть *impf*, раз~ *pf* попола́м.
ham *n* (*cul*) ветчина́.
hamlet *n* дереву́шка.
hammer *n* молото́к; *vt* бить *impf* молотко́м.
hammock *n* гама́к.
hamper[1] *n* (*basket*) корзи́на с кры́шкой.
hamper[2] *vt* (*hinder*) меша́ть *impf*, по~ *pf* +*dat*.
hamster *n* хомя́к.
hand *n* рука́; (*worker*) рабо́чий *sb*; (*writing*) по́черк; (*clock ~*) стре́лка; **at ~** под руко́й; **on ~s and knees** на четвере́ньках; *vt* передава́ть *impf*, переда́ть *pf*; **~ in** подава́ть *impf*, пода́ть *pf*; **~ out** раздава́ть *impf*, разда́ть *pf*. **handbag** *n* су́мка. **handbook** *n* руково́дство. **handcuffs** *n pl* нару́чники *m pl*. **handful** *n* горсть.
handicap *n* (*sport*) гандика́п; (*hindrance*) поме́ха. **handicapped** *adj*: **~ person** инвали́д.
handicraft *n* ремесло́.
handiwork *n* ручна́я рабо́та.
handkerchief *n* носово́й плато́к.

handle *n* ру́чка, рукоя́тка; *vt* (*people*) обраща́ться *impf* с+*instr*; (*situations*) справля́ться *impf*, спра́виться *pf* с+*instr*; (*touch*) тро́гать *impf*, тро́нуть *pf* руко́й, рука́ми. **handlebar(s)** *n* руль *m*.

handmade *adj* ручно́й рабо́ты.

handout *n* пода́чка; (*document*) лифле́т.

handrail *n* пери́ла (-л) *pl*.

handshake *n* рукопожа́тие.

handsome *adj* краси́вый; (*generous*) ще́дрый.

handwriting *n* по́черк.

handy *adj* (*convenient*) удо́бный; (*skilful*) ло́вкий; **come in ~** пригоди́ться *pf*.

hang *vt* ве́шать *impf*, пове́сить *pf*; *vi* висе́ть *impf*; **~ about** слоня́ться *impf*; **~ on** (*cling*) держа́ться *impf*; (*tel*) не ве́шать *impf* тру́бку; (*persist*) упо́рствовать *impf*; **~ out** выве́шивать *impf*, вы́весить *pf*; (*spend time*) болта́ться *impf*; **~ up** ве́шать *impf*, пове́сить *pf*; (*tel*) ве́шать *impf*, пове́сить *pf* тру́бку. **hanger** *n* ве́шалка. **hanger-on** *n* прилипа́ла *m* & *f*. **hangman** *n* пала́ч.

hangar *n* анга́р.

hangover *n* похме́лье.

hang-up *n* ко́мплекс.

hanker *vi*: **~ after** мечта́ть *impf* о+*prep*.

haphazard *adj* случа́йный.

happen *vi* (*occur*) случа́ться *impf*, случи́ться *pf*; происходи́ть *impf*, произойти́ *pf*; **~ upon** ната́лкиваться *impf*, натолкну́ться *pf* на+*acc*.

happiness *n* сча́стье. **happy** *adj* счастли́вый; **~-go-lucky** беззабо́тный.

harass *vt* (*pester*) дёргать *impf*; (*persecute*) пресле́довать *impf*. **harassment** *n* тра́вля; пресле́дование.

harbinger *n* предве́стник.

harbour *n* га́вань, порт; *vt* (*person*) укрыва́ть *impf*, укры́ть *pf*; (*thoughts*) зата́ивать *impf*, затаи́ть *pf*.

hard *adj* твёрдый; (*difficult*) тру́дный; (*difficult to bear*) тяжёлый; (*severe*) суро́вый; *adv* (*work*) мно́го; (*hit*) си́льно; (*try*) о́чень; **~-boiled egg** яйцо́ вкруту́ю; **~-headed** практи́чный; **~-hearted** жестокосе́рдный; **~-up** стеснённый в сре́дствах; **~-working** трудолюби́вый. **hardboard** *n* строи́тельный карто́н.

harden *vi* затвердева́ть *impf*, затверде́ть *pf*; (*fig*) ожесточа́ться *impf*, ожесточи́ться *pf*.

hardly *adv* едва́ (ли).

hardship *n* (*privation*) нужда́.

hardware *n* скобяны́е изде́лия *neut pl*; (*comput*) аппарату́ра.

hardy *adj* (*robust*) выно́сливый; (*plant*) морозосто́йкий.

hare *n* за́яц.

hark *vi*: **~ back to** возвраща́ться *impf*, верну́ться *pf* к+*dat*; *int* слу́шай(те)!

harm *n* вред; *vt* вреди́ть *impf*, по~ *pf* +*dat*. **harmful** *adj* вре́дный. **harmless** *adj* безвре́дный.

harmonic *adj* гармони́ческий. **harmonica** *n* губна́я гармо́ника. **harmonious** *adj* гармони́чный. **harmonize** *vi* гармони́ровать *impf* (**with** с+*instr*). **harmony** *n* гармо́ния.

harness *n* у́пряжь; *vt* запряга́ть *impf*, запря́чь *pf*; (*fig*) испо́льзовать *impf* & *pf*.

harp *n* а́рфа; *vi*: ~ **on** тверди́ть *impf* о+*prep*.

harpoon *n* гарпу́н.

harpsichord *n* клавеси́н.

harrow *n* борона́. **harrowing** *adj* душераздира́ющий.

harsh *adj* (*sound, colour*) ре́зкий; (*cruel*) суро́вый.

harvest *n* жа́тва, сбор (плодо́в); (*yield*) урожа́й; (*fig*) плоды́ *m pl*; *vt* & *abs* собира́ть *impf*, собра́ть *pf* (урожа́й).

hash *n*: **make a ~ of** напу́тать *pf* +*acc*, в+*prep*.

hashish *n* гаши́ш.

hassle *n* беспоко́йство.

hassock *n* поду́шечка.

haste *n* спе́шка. **hasten** *vi* спеши́ть *impf*, по~ *pf*; *vt* & *i* торопи́ть(ся) *impf*, по~ *pf*; *vt* ускоря́ть *impf*, уско́рить *pf*. **hasty** *adj* (*hurried*) поспе́шный; (*quick-tempered*) вспы́льчивый.

hat *n* ша́пка; (*stylish*) шля́па.

hatch[1] *n* люк; **~-back** маши́на-пика́п.

hatch[2] *vi* вылу́пливаться, вылупля́ться *impf*, вы́лупиться *pf*.

hatchet *n* топо́рик.

hate *n* не́нависть; *vt* ненави́деть *impf*. **hateful** *adj* ненави́стный. **hatred** *n* не́нависть.

haughty *adj* надме́нный.

haul *n* (*fish*) уло́в; (*loot*) добы́ча; (*distance*) езда́; *vt* (*drag*) тяну́ть *impf*; таска́ть *indet*, тащи́ть *det*. **haulage** *n* перево́зка.

haunt *n* люби́мое ме́сто; *vt* (*ghost*) обита́ть *impf*; (*memory*) пресле́довать *impf*. **haunted** *adj*: ~ **house** дом с привиде́ниями. **haunting** *adj* навя́зчивый.

have *vt* име́ть *impf*; **I ~** (*possess*) у меня́ (есть; был, -а́, -о) +*nom*; **I ~ not** у меня́ нет (*past* не́ было) +*gen*; **I ~ (got) to** я до́лжен +*inf*; **you had better** вам лу́чше бы +*inf*; ~ **on** (*wear*) быть оде́тым в +*prep*; (*be engaged in*) быть за́нятым +*instr*.

haven *n* (*refuge*) убе́жище.

haversack *n* рюкза́к.

havoc *n* (*devastation*) опустоше́ние; (*disorder*) беспоря́док.

hawk[1] *n* (*bird*) я́стреб.

hawk[2] *vt* (*trade*) торгова́ть *impf* вразно́с+*instr*. **hawker** *n* разно́счик.

hawser *n* трос.

hawthorn *n* боя́рышник.

hay *n* се́но; **make ~** коси́ть *impf*, с~ *pf* се́но; ~ **fever** се́нная лихора́дка. **haystack** *n* стог.

hazard *n* риск; *vt* рискова́ть *impf* +*instr*. **hazardous** *adj* риско́ванный.

haze *n* ды́мка.

hazel *n* лещи́на. **hazelnut** *n* лесно́й оре́х.

hazy *adj* тума́нный; (*vague*) сму́тный.

he *pron* он.

head *n* голова́; (*mind*) ум; (~ *of coin*) лицева́я сторона́ моне́ты; **~s or tails?** орёл и́ли ре́шка?; (*chief*) глава́ *m*, нача́льник; *attrib* гла́вный; *vt* (*lead*) возглавля́ть *impf*, возгла́вить *pf*; (*ball*) забива́ть *impf*, заби́ть *pf* голово́й; *vi*: ~ **for** направля́ться *impf*, напра́виться *pf* в, на, +*acc*, к+*dat*. **headache** *n* головна́я боль. **head-dress**

n головно́й убо́р. **header** *n* уда́р голово́й. **heading** *n* (*title*) загола́вок. **headland** *n* мыс. **headlight** *n* фа́ра. **headline** *n* заголо́вок. **headlong** *adv* стремгла́в. **headmaster, -mistress** *n* дире́ктор шко́лы. **head-on** *adj* головно́й; *adv* в лоб. **headphone** *n* нау́шник. **headquarters** *n* штаб-кварти́ра. **headscarf** *n* косы́нка. **headstone** *n* надгро́бный ка́мень *m*. **headstrong** *adj* своево́льный. **headway** *n* движе́ние вперёд. **heady** *adj* опьяня́ющий.

heal *vt* излечи́вать *impf*, излечи́ть *pf*; *vi* зажива́ть *impf*, зажи́ть *pf*. **healing** *adj* целе́бный.

health *n* здоро́вье; ~ **care** здравохране́ние. **healthy** *adj* здоро́вый; (*beneficial*) поле́зный.

heap *n* ку́ча; *vt* нагроможда́ть *impf*, нагромозди́ть *pf*.

hear *vt* слы́шать *impf*, у~ *pf*; (*listen to*) слу́шать *impf*, по~ *pf*; ~ **out** выслу́шивать *impf*, вы́слушать *pf*. **hearing** *n* слух; (*law*) слу́шание. **hearsay** *n* слух.

hearse *n* катафа́лк.

heart *n* се́рдце; (*essence*) суть; *pl* (*cards*) че́рви (-ве́й) *pl*; **by** ~ наизу́сть; ~ **attack** серде́чный при́ступ. **heartburn** *n* изжо́га. **hearten** *vt* ободря́ть *impf*, ободри́ть *pf*. **heartfelt** *adj* серде́чный. **heartless** *adj* бессерде́чный. **heart-rending** *adj* душераздира́ющий. **hearty** *adj* (*cordial*) серде́чный; (*vigorous*) здоро́вый.

hearth *n* оча́г.

heat *n* жара́; (*phys*) теплота́; (*of feeling*) пыл; (*sport*) забе́г, зае́зд; *vt* & *i* (*heat up*) нагрева́ть(ся) *impf*, нагре́ть(ся) *pf*; *vt* (*house*) топи́ть *impf*. **heater** *n* нагрева́тель *m*. **heating** *n* отопле́ние.

heath *n* пу́стошь.

heathen *n* язы́чник; *adj* язы́ческий.

heather *n* ве́реск.

heave *vt* (*lift*) поднима́ть *impf*, подня́ть *pf*; (*pull*) тяну́ть *impf*, по~ *pf*.

heaven *n* (*sky*) не́бо; (*paradise*) рай; *pl* небеса́ *neut pl*. **heavenly** *adj* небе́сный; (*divine*) боже́ственный.

heavy *adj* тяжёлый; (*strong, intense*) си́льный. **heavyweight** *n* тяжелове́с.

Hebrew *adj* (древне)евре́йский.

heckle *vt* препека́ться *impf* с+*instr*.

hectic *adj* лихора́дочный.

hedge *n* жива́я и́згородь. **hedgerow** *n* шпале́ра.

hedgehog *n* ёж.

heed *vt* обраща́ть *impf*, обрати́ть *pf* внима́ние на+*acc*. **heedless** *adj* небре́жный.

heel[1] *n* (*of foot*) пята́; (*of foot, sock*) пя́тка; (*of shoe*) каблу́к.

heel[2] *vi* крени́ться *impf*, на~ *pf*.

hefty *adj* дю́жий.

heifer *n* тёлка.

height *n* высота́; (*of person*) рост. **heighten** *vt* (*strengthen*) уси́ливать *impf*, уси́лить *pf*.

heinous *adj* гну́сный.

heir *n* насле́дник. **heiress** *n* насле́дница. **heirloom** *n* фами́льная вещь.

helicopter *n* вертолёт.

helium *n* ге́лий.

hell *n* ад. **hellish** *adj* áдский.
hello *see* **hallo**
helm *n* руль.
helmet *n* шлем.
help *n* пóмощь; *vt* помогáть *impf*, помóчь *pf* +*dat*; (*can't* ~) не мочь *impf* не +*inf*; ~ **o.s.** брать *impf*, взять *pf* себé; ~ **yourself!** берите! **helpful** *adj* полéзный; (*obliging*) услýжливый. **helping** *n* (*of food*) пóрция. **helpless** *adj* беспóмощный.
helter-skelter *adv* как попáло.
hem *n* рубéц; *vt* подрубáть *impf*, подрубить *pf*; ~ **in** окружáть *impf*, окружить *pf*.
hemisphere *n* полушáрие.
hemp *n* (*plant*) коноплЯ; (*fibre*) пенькá.
hen *n* (*female bird*) сáмка; (*domestic fowl*) кýрица.
hence *adv* (*from here*) отсЮда; (*as a result*) слéдовательно; **3 years** ~ чéрез три гóда. **henceforth** *adv* отнЫне.
henchman *n* приспéшник.
henna *n* хна.
hepatitis *n* гепатит.
her *poss pron* её; свой.
herald *n* вéстник; *vt* возвещáть *impf*, возвестить *pf*.
herb *n* травá. **herbaceous** *adj* травянóй; ~ **border** цветóчный бордЮр. **herbal** *adj* травянóй.
herd *n* стáдо; (*people*) толпиться *impf*, с~ *pf*; *vt* (*tend*) пасти *impf*; (*drive*) загонЯть *impf*, загнáть *pf* в стáдо.
here *adv* (*position*) здесь, тут; (*direction*) сюдá; ~ **is ...** вот (+*nom*); ~ **and there** там и сям; ~ **you are!** пожáлуйста. **hereabout(s)** *adv* поблизóсти. **hereafter** *adv* в бýдущем. **hereby** *adv* этим. **hereupon** *adv* (*in consequence*) вслéдствие этого; (*after*) пóсле этого. **herewith** *adv* при сём.
hereditary *adj* наслéдственный. **heredity** *n* наслéдственность.
heresy *n* éресь. **heretic** *n* еретик. **heretical** *adj* еретический.
heritage *n* наслéдие.
hermetic *adj* герметический.
hermit *n* отшéльник.
hernia *n* грЫжа.
hero *n* герóй. **heroic** *adj* героический.
heroin *n* героин.
heroine *n* героиня. **heroism** *n* героизм.
heron *n* цáпля.
herpes *n* лишáй.
herring *n* сельдь; (*food*) селёдка.
hers *poss pron* её; свой.
herself *pron* (*emph*) (онá) самá; (*refl*) себЯ.
hertz *n* герц.
hesitant *adj* нерешительный. **hesitate** *vi* колебáться *impf*, по~ *pf*; (*in speech*) запинáться *impf*, запнýться *pf*. **hesitation** *n* колебáние.
hessian *n* мешковина.
heterogeneous *adj* разнорóдный.
heterosexual *adj* гетеросексуáльный.
hew *vt* рубить *impf*.
hexagon *n* шестиугóльник.
hey *int* эй!
heyday *n* расцвéт.
hi *int* привéт!
hiatus *n* пробéл.
hibernate *vi* быть *impf* в спЯчке; впадáть *impf*, впасть *pf* в спЯчку. **hibernation** *n* спЯчка.

hiccup *vi* икáть *impf*, икнýть *pf*; *n*: *pl* икóта.
hide[1] *n* (*skin*) шкýра.
hide[2] *vt* & *i* (*conceal*) прятать(ся) *impf*, с~ *pf*; скрывáть(ся) *impf*, скрыть(ся) *pf*.
hideous *adj* отвратительный.
hideout *n* укрытие.
hiding *n* (*flogging*) пóрка.
hierarchy *n* иерáрхия.
hieroglyphics *n pl* иерóглифы *m pl*.
hi-fi *n* проигрыватель *m* с высококáчественным воспроизведéнием звýка зáписи.
higgledy-piggledy *adv* как придётся.
high *adj* высóкий; (*wind*) сильный; (*on drugs*) в наркотическом дурмáне; **~er education** высшее образовáние; **~-handed** своевóльный; **~-heeled** на высóких каблукáх; **~ jump** прыжóк в высотý; **~-minded** благорóдный; идéйный; **~-pitched** высóкий; **~-rise** высóтный. **highbrow** *adj* интеллектуáльный. **highland(s)** *n* гóрная странá. **highlight** *n* (*fig*) высшая тóчка; *vt* обращáть *impf*, обратить *pf* внимáние на+*acc*. **highly** *adv* весьмá; **~-strung** легкó возбуждáемый. **highness** *n* (*title*) высóчество. **highstreet** *n* глáвная ýлица. **highway** *n* магистрáль.
hijack *vt* похищáть *impf*, похитить *pf*. **hijacker** *n* похититель *m*.
hike *n* похóд.
hilarious *adj* уморительный. **hilarity** *n* весéлье.
hill *n* холм. **hillock** *n* хóлмик. **hillside** *n* склон холмá. **hilly** *adj* холмистый.
hilt *n* рукоятка.
himself *pron* (*emph*) (он) сам; (*refl*) себя.
hind *adj* (*rear*) зáдний.
hinder *vt* мешáть *impf*, по~ *pf* +*dat*. **hindrance** *n* помéха.
Hindu *n* индýс; *adj* индýсский.
hinge *n* шарнир; *vi* (*fig*) зависеть *impf* от+*gen*.
hint *n* намёк; *vi* намекáть *impf*, намекнýть *pf* (**at** на+*acc*).
hip *n* (*anat*) бедрó.
hippie *n* хиппи *neut indecl*.
hippopotamus *n* гиппопотáм.
hire *n* наём, прокáт; **~-purchase** покýпка в рассрóчку; *vt* нанимáть *impf*, нанять *pf*; **~ out** сдавáть *impf*, сдать *pf* напрокáт.
his *poss pron* егó; свой.
hiss *n* шипéние; *vi* шипéть *impf*; *vt* (*performer*) освистывать *impf*, освистáть *pf*.
historian *n* истóрик. **historic(al)** *adj* исторический. **history** *n* истóрия.
histrionic *adj* театрáльный.
hit *n* (*blow*) удáр; (*on target*) попадáние (в цель); (*success*) успéх; *vt* (*strike*) ударять *impf*, удáрить *pf*; (*target*) попадáть *impf*, попáсть *pf* (в цель); **~ (up)on** находить *impf*, найти *pf*.
hitch *n* (*stoppage*) задéржка; *vt* (*fasten*) привязывать *impf*, привязáть *pf*; **~ up** подтягивать *impf*, подтянýть *pf*; **~-hike** éздить *indet*, éхать *det*, по~ *pf* автостóпом.
hither *adv* сюдá. **hitherto** *adv* до сих пор.
HIV *abbr* (*of* **human immunodeficiency virus**) ВИЧ.
hive *n* ýлей.
hoard *n* запáс; *vt* скáпливать *impf*, скопить *pf*.
hoarding *n* реклáмный щит.

hoarse *adj* хри́плый.
hoax *n* надува́тельство.
hobble *vi* ковыля́ть *impf.*
hobby *n* хо́бби *neut indecl.*
hock *n* (*wine*) рейнве́йн.
hockey *n* хокке́й.
hoe *n* моты́га; *vt* моты́жить *impf.*
hog *n* бо́ров.
hoist *n* подъёмник; *vt* поднима́ть *impf*, подня́ть *pf.*
hold[1] *n* (*naut*) трюм.
hold[2] *n* (*grasp*) захва́т; (*influence*) влия́ние (**on** на+*acc*); **catch ~ of** ухвати́ться *pf* за+*acc*; *vt* (*grasp*) держа́ть *impf*; (*contain*) вмеща́ть *impf*, вмести́ть *pf*; (*possess*) владе́ть *impf* +*instr*; (*conduct*) проводи́ть *impf*, провести́ *pf*; (*consider*) счита́ть *impf*, счесть *pf* (+*acc* & *instr*, за+*acc*); *vi* держа́ться *impf*; (*weather*) продержа́ться *impf*, продержа́ться *pf*; **~ back** сде́рживать(ся) *impf*, сдержа́ть(ся) *pf*; **~ forth** разглаго́льствовать *impf*; **~ on** (*wait*) подожда́ть *pf*; (*tel*) не ве́шать *impf* тру́бку; (*grip*) держа́ться *impf* (**to** за+*acc*); **~ out** (*stretch out*) протя́гивать *impf*, протяну́ть *pf*; (*resist*) не сдава́ться *impf*; **~ up** (*support*) подде́рживать *impf*, поддержа́ть *pf*; (*impede*) заде́рживать *impf*, задержа́ть *pf.* **holdall** *n* су́мка. **hold-up** *n* (*robbery*) налёт; (*delay*) заде́ржка.
hole *n* дыра́; (*animal's*) нора́; (*golf*) лу́нка.
holiday *n* (*day off*) выходно́й день; (*festival*) пра́здник; (*annual leave*) о́тпуск; *pl* (*school*) кани́кулы (-л) *pl*; **~-maker** тури́ст; **on ~** в о́тпуске.
holiness *n* свя́тость.
Holland *n* Голла́ндия.
hollow *n* впа́дина; (*valley*) лощи́на; *adj* пусто́й; (*sunken*) впа́лый; (*sound*) глухо́й; *vt* (**~ out**) выда́лбливать *impf*, вы́долбить *pf.*
holly *n* остроли́ст.
holocaust *n* ма́ссовое уничтоже́ние.
holster *n* кобура́.
holy *adj* свято́й, свяще́нный.
homage *n* почте́ние; **pay ~ to** преклоня́ться *impf*, преклони́ться *pf* пе́ред+*instr.*
home *n* дом; (*native land*) ро́дина; **at ~** до́ма; **feel at ~** чу́вствовать *impf* себя́ как до́ма; *adj* дома́шний; (*native*) родно́й; **H~ Affairs** вну́тренние дела́ *neut pl*; *adv* (*direction*) домо́й; (*position*) до́ма. **homeland** *n* ро́дина. **homeless** *adj* бездо́мный. **home-made** *adj* (*food*) дома́шний; (*object*) самоде́льный. **homesick** *adj*: **be ~** скуча́ть *impf* по до́му. **homewards** *adv* домо́й, восвоя́си.
homely *adj* просто́й.
homicide *n* (*action*) уби́йство.
homogeneous *adj* однoро́дный.
homosexual *n* гомосексуали́ст; *adj* гомосексуа́льный.
honest *n* че́стный. **honesty** *n* че́стность.
honey *n* мёд. **honeymoon** *n* медо́вый ме́сяц. **honeysuckle** *n* жи́молость.
honk *vi* гуде́ть *impf.*
honorary *adj* почётный.
honour *n* честь; *vt* (*respect*) почита́ть *impf*; (*confer*) удоста́ивать *impf*, удосто́ить *pf* (**with** +*gen*); (*fulfil*) выполня́ть *impf*, вы́полнить *pf.*

honourable *adj* че́стный.
hood *n* капюшо́н; (*tech*) капо́т.
hoodwink *vt* обма́нывать *impf*, обману́ть *pf*.
hoof *n* копы́то.
hook *n* крючо́к; *vt* (*hitch*) зацепля́ть *impf*, зацепи́ть *pf*; (*fasten*) застёгивать *impf*, застегну́ть *pf*.
hooligan *n* хулига́н.
hoop *n* о́бруч.
hoot *vi* (*owl*) у́хать *impf*, у́хнуть *pf*; (*horn*) гуде́ть *impf*. **hooter** *n* гудо́к.
hop[1] *n* (*plant*; *collect*) хмель *m*.
hop[2] *n* (*jump*) прыжо́к; *vi* пры́гать *impf*, пры́гнуть *pf* (на одно́й ноге́).
hope *n* наде́жда; *vi* наде́яться *impf*, по~ *pf* (**for** на+*acc*). **hopeful** *adj* (*promising*) обнадёживающий; **I am** ~ я наде́юсь. **hopefully** *adv* с наде́ждой; (*it is hoped*) надо наде́яться. **hopeless** *adj* безнадёжный.
horde *n* (*hist*; *fig*) орда́.
horizon *n* горизо́нт. **horizontal** *adj* горизонта́льный.
hormone *n* гормо́н.
horn *n* рог; (*French horn*) валто́рна; (*car*) гудо́к.
hornet *n* ше́ршень *m*.
horny *adj* (*calloused*) мозо́листый.
horoscope *n* гороско́п.
horrible, horrid *adj* ужа́сный. **horrify** *vt* ужаса́ть *impf*, ужасну́ть *pf*. **horror** *n* у́жас.
hors-d'oeuvre *n* заку́ска.
horse *n* ло́шадь. **horsechestnut** *n* ко́нский кашта́н. **horseman, -woman** *n* вса́дник, -ица. **horseplay** *n* возня́. **horsepower** *n* лошади́ная си́ла. **horse-racing** *n* ска́чки (-чек) *pl*. **horse-radish** *n* хрен. **horseshoe** *n* подко́ва.
horticulture *n* садово́дство.
hose *n* (~-*pipe*) шланг.
hosiery *n* чуло́чные изде́лия *neut pl*.
hospitable *adj* гостеприи́мный.
hospital *n* больни́ца.
hospitality *n* гостеприи́мство.
host[1] *n* (*multitude*) мно́жество.
host[2] *n* (*entertaining*) хозя́ин.
hostage *n* зало́жник.
hostel *n* общежи́тие.
hostess *n* хозя́йка; (*air* ~) стюарде́сса.
hostile *adj* вражде́бный. **hostility** *n* вражде́бность; *pl* вое́нные де́йствия *neut pl*.
hot *adj* горя́чий, жа́ркий; (*pungent*) о́стрый; **~-headed** вспы́льчивый; **~-water bottle** гре́лка. **hotbed** *n* (*fig*) оча́г. **hothouse** *n* тепли́ца. **hotplate** *n* пли́тка.
hotel *n* гости́ница.
hound *n* охо́тничья соба́ка; *vt* трави́ть *impf*, за~ *pf*.
hour *n* час. **hourly** *adj* ежеча́сный.
house *n* дом; (*parl*) пала́та; *attrib* дома́шний; *vt* помеща́ть *impf*, помести́ть *pf*. **household** *n* семья́; *adj* хозя́йственный; дома́шний. **housekeeper** *n* эконо́мка. **housewarming** *n* новосе́лье. **housewife** *n* хозя́йка. **housework** *n* дома́шняя рабо́та. **housing** *n* (*accommodation*) жильё; (*casing*) кожу́х; ~ **estate** жило́й масси́в.
hovel *n* лачу́га.
hover *vi* (*bird*) пари́ть *impf*; (*helicopter*) висе́ть *impf*; (*person*) мая́чить *impf*. **hovercraft** *n* су́дно на возду́шной поду́шке, СВП.

how *adv* как, каки́м о́бразом; ~ **do you do?** здра́вствуйте!; ~ **many,** ~ **much** ско́лько (*+gen*). **however** *adv* как бы ни (*+past*); *conj* одна́ко, тем не ме́нее; ~ **much** ско́лько бы ни (*+gen & past*).

howl *n* вой; *vi* выть *impf*. **howler** *n* грубе́йшая оши́бка.

hub *n* (*of wheel*) ступи́ца; (*fig*) центр, средото́чие.

hubbub *n* шум, гам.

huddle *vi*: ~ **together** прижима́ться *impf*, прижа́ться *pf* друг к дру́гу.

hue *n* (*tint*) отте́нок.

huff *n*: **in a** ~ оскорблённый.

hug *n* объя́тие; *vt* (*embrace*) обнима́ть *impf*, обня́ть *pf*.

huge *adj* огро́мный.

hulk *n* ко́рпус (корабля́). **hulking** *adj* (*bulky*) грома́дный; (*clumsy*) неуклю́жий.

hull *n* (*of ship*) ко́рпус.

hum *n* жужжа́ние; *vi* (*buzz*) жужжа́ть *impf*; *vt & i* (*person*) напева́ть *impf*.

human *adj* челове́ческий, людско́й; *n* челове́к. **humane, humanitarian** *adj* челове́чный. **humanity** *n* (*human race*) челове́чество; (*humaneness*) гума́нность; **the Humanities** гуманита́рные нау́ки *f pl*.

humble *adj* (*person*) смире́нный; (*abode*) скро́мный; *vt* унижа́ть *impf*, уни́зить *pf*.

humdrum *adj* однообра́зный.

humid *adj* вла́жный. **humidity** *n* вла́жность.

humiliate *vt* унижа́ть *impf*, уни́зить *pf*. **humiliation** *n* униже́ние.

humility *n* смире́ние.

humorous *adj* юмористи́ческий. **humour** *n* ю́мор; (*mood*) настрое́ние; *vt* потака́ть *impf* *+dat*.

hump *n* горб; (*of earth*) буго́р.

humus *n* перегно́й.

hunch *n* (*idea*) предчу́вствие; *vt* го́рбить *impf*, с~ *pf*. **hunchback** *n* (*person*) горбу́н, ~ья. **hunchbacked** *adj* горба́тый.

hundred *adj & n* сто; ~**s of** со́тни *f pl* *+gen*; **two** ~ две́сти; **three** ~ три́ста; **four** ~ четы́реста; **five** ~ пятьсо́т. **hundredth** *adj & n* со́тый.

Hungarian *n* венгр, венге́рка; *adj* венге́рский. **Hungary** *n* Ве́нгрия.

hunger *n* го́лод; (*fig*) жа́жда (**for** *+gen*); ~ **strike** голодо́вка; *vi* голода́ть *impf*; ~ **for** жа́ждать *impf* *+gen*. **hungry** *adj* голо́дный.

hunk *n* ломо́ть *m*.

hunt *n* охо́та; (*fig*) по́иски *m pl* (**for** *+gen*); *vt* охо́титься *impf* на*+acc*, за*+instr*; (*persecute*) трави́ть *impf*, за~ *pf*; ~ **down** вы́следить *pf*; ~ **for** иска́ть *impf* *+acc or gen*; ~ **out** отыска́ть *pf*. **hunter** *n* охо́тник. **hunting** *n* охо́та.

hurdle *n* (*sport*; *fig*) барье́р. **hurdler** *n* барьери́ст. **hurdles** *n pl* (*sport*) барье́рный бег.

hurl *vt* швыря́ть *impf*, швырну́ть *pf*.

hurly-burly *n* сумато́ха.

hurrah, hurray *int* ура́!

hurricane *n* урага́н.

hurried *adj* торопли́вый. **hurry** *n* спе́шка; **be in a** ~ спеши́ть *impf*; *vt & i* торопи́ть(ся) *impf*, по~ *pf*; *vi* спеши́ть *impf*, по~ *pf*.

hurt *n* уще́рб; *vi* боле́ть *impf*; *vt* поврежда́ть *impf*, повреди́ть *pf*; (*offend*) обижа́ть *impf*, оби́деть *pf*.

hurtle *vi* нестись *impf*, по~ *pf*.
husband *n* муж.
hush *n* тишина́; *vt*: ~ **up** замина́ть *impf*, замя́ть *pf*; *int* ти́ше!
husk *n* шелуха́.
husky *adj* (*voice*) хри́плый.
hustle *n* толкотня́; *vt* (*push*) затолка́ть *impf*, затолкну́ть *pf*; (*herd people*) загоня́ть *impf*, загна́ть *pf*; *vt* & *i* (*hurry*) торопи́ть(ся) *impf*, по~ *pf*.
hut *n* хи́жина.
hutch *n* кле́тка.
hyacinth *n* гиаци́нт.
hybrid *n* гибри́д; *adj* гибри́дный.
hydrangea *n* горте́нзия.
hydrant *n* гидра́нт.
hydraulic *adj* гидравли́ческий.
hydrochloric acid *n* соляна́я кислота́. **hydroelectric** *adj* гидроэлектри́ческий; ~ **power station** гидроэлектроста́нция, ГЭС *f indecl.* **hydrofoil** *n* су́дно на подво́дных кры́льях, СПК.
hydrogen *n* водоро́д.
hyena *n* гие́на.
hygiene *n* гигие́на. **hygienic** *adj* гигиени́ческий.
hymn *n* гимн.
hyperbole *n* гипе́рбола.
hyphen *n* дефи́с. **hyphen(ate)** *vt* писа́ть *impf*, на~ *pf* че́рез дефи́с.
hypnosis *n* гипно́з. **hypnotic** *adj* гипноти́ческий. **hypnotism** *n* гипноти́зм. **hypnotist** *n* гипнотизёр. **hypnotize** *vt* гипнотизи́ровать *impf*, за~ *pf*.
hypochondria *n* ипохо́ндрия. **hypochondriac** *n* ипохо́ндрик.
hypocrisy *n* лицеме́рие. **hypocrite** *n* лицеме́р. **hypocritical** *adj* лицеме́рный.
hypodermic *adj* подко́жный.
hypothesis *n* гипо́теза. **hypothesize** *vi* стро́ить *impf*, по~ *pf* гипоте́зу. **hypothetical** *adj* гипотети́ческий.
hysterectomy *n* гистерэктоми́я, удале́ние ма́тки.
hysteria *n* истери́я. **hysterical** *adj* истери́ческий. **hysterics** *n pl* исте́рика.

I

I *pron* я.
ibid(em) *adv* там же.
ice *n* лёд; **~-age** леднико́вый пери́од; **~-axe** ледору́б; **~-cream** моро́женое *sb*; ~ **hockey** хокке́й (с ша́йбой); ~ **rink** като́к; ~ **skate** конёк; *vi* ката́ться *impf* на конька́х; *vt* (*chill*) замора́живать *impf*, заморо́зить *pf*; (*cul*) глазирова́ть *impf* & *pf*; *vi*: ~ **over, up** обледенева́ть *impf*, обледене́ть *pf*. **iceberg** *n* а́йсберг. **icicle** *n* сосу́лька. **icing** *n* (*cul*) глазу́рь. **icy** *adj* ледяно́й.
icon *n* ико́на.
ID *abbr* (*of* **identification**) удостовере́ние ли́чности.
idea *n* иде́я, мысль; (*conception*) поня́тие.
ideal *n* идеа́л; *adj* идеа́льный. **idealism** *n* идеали́зм. **idealist** *n* идеали́ст. **idealize** *vt* идеализи́ровать *impf* & *pf*.
identical *adj* тожде́ственный, одина́ковый. **identification** *n* (*recognition*) опозна́ние; (*of person*) установле́ние ли́чности. **identify** *vt* опознава́ть *impf*, опозна́ть *pf*. **identity** *n*

(*of person*) ли́чность; ~ **card** удостовере́ние ли́чности.
ideological *adj* идеологи́ческий. **ideology** *n* идеоло́гия.
idiom *n* идио́ма. **idiomatic** *adj* идиомати́ческий.
idiosyncrasy *n* идиосинкразия.
idiot *n* идио́т. **idiotic** *adj* идио́тский.
idle *adj* (*unoccupied*; *lazy*; *purposeless*) пра́здный; (*vain*) тще́тный; (*empty*) пусто́й; (*machine*) неде́йствующий; *vi* безде́льничать *impf*; (*engine*) рабо́тать *impf* вхолосту́ю; *vt*: ~ **away** пра́здно проводи́ть *impf*, провести́ *pf*. **idleness** *n* пра́здность.
idol *n* и́дол. **idolatry** *n* идолопокло́нство; (*fig*) обожа́ние. **idolize** *vt* боготвори́ть *impf*.
idyll *n* иди́ллия. **idyllic** *adj* идилли́ческий.
i.e. *abbr* т.е., то есть.
if *conj* е́сли, е́сли бы; (*whether*) ли; **as** ~ как бу́дто; **even** ~ да́же е́сли; ~ **only** е́сли бы то́лько.
ignite *vt* зажига́ть *impf*, заже́чь *pf*; *vi* загора́ться *impf*, загоре́ться *pf*. **ignition** *n* зажига́ние.
ignoble *adj* ни́зкий.
ignominious *adj* позо́рный.
ignoramus *n* неве́жда *m*. **ignorance** *n* неве́жество, (*of certain facts*) неве́дение. **ignorant** *adj* неве́жественный; (*uninformed*) несве́дущий (**of** в+*prep*).
ignore *vt* не обраща́ть *impf* внима́ния на+*acc*; игнори́ровать *impf* & *pf*.
ilk *n*: **of that** ~ тако́го ро́да.
ill *n* (*evil*) зло; (*harm*) вред; *pl* (*misfortunes*) несча́стья (-тий) *pl*; *adj* (*sick*) больно́й; (*bad*) дурно́й; *adv* пло́хо, ду́рно; **fall** ~ заболева́ть *impf*, заболе́ть *pf*; ~**-advised** неблагоразу́мный; ~**-mannered** неве́жливый; ~**-treat** *vt* пло́хо обраща́ться *impf* с+*instr*.
illegal *adj* нелега́льный. **illegality** *n* незако́нность, нелега́льность.
illegible *adj* неразбо́рчивый.
illegitimacy *n* незако́нность; (*of child*) незаконнорождённость. **illegitimate** *adj* незако́нный; незаконнорождённый.
illicit *adj* незако́нный, недозво́ленный.
illiteracy *n* негра́мотность. **illiterate** *adj* негра́мотный.
illness *n* боле́знь.
illogical *adj* нелоги́чный.
illuminate *vt* освеща́ть *impf*, освети́ть *pf*. **illumination** *n* освеще́ние.
illusion *n* иллю́зия. **illusory** *adj* иллюзо́рный.
illustrate *vt* иллюстри́ровать *impf* & *pf*, про~ *pf*. **illustration** *n* иллюстра́ция. **illustrative** *adj* иллюстрати́вный.
illustrious *adj* знамени́тый.
image *n* (*phys*; *statue etc.*) изображе́ние; (*optical* ~) отраже́ние; (*likeness*) ко́пия; (*metaphor*; *conception*) о́браз; (*reputation*) репута́ция. **imagery** *n* о́бразность.
imaginable *adj* вообрази́мый. **imaginary** *adj* вообража́емый. **imagination** *n* воображе́ние. **imagine** *vt* вообража́ть *impf*, вообрази́ть *pf*; (*conceive*) представля́ть *impf*, предста́вить *pf* себе́.
imbecile *n* слабоу́мный *sb*; (*fool*) глупе́ц.

imbibe *vt* (*absorb*) впи́тывать *impf*, впита́ть *pf*.
imbue *vt* внуша́ть *impf*, внуши́ть *pf* +*dat* (**with** +*acc*).
imitate *vt* подража́ть *impf* +*dat*. **imitation** *n* подража́ние (**of** +*dat*); *attrib* иску́сственный. **imitative** *adj* подража́тельный.
immaculate *adj* безупре́чный.
immaterial *adj* (*unimportant*) несуще́ственный.
immature *adj* незре́лый.
immeasurable *adj* неизмери́мый.
immediate *adj* (*direct*) непосре́дственный; (*swift*) неме́дленный. **immediately** *adv* то́тчас, сра́зу.
immemorial *adj*: **from time ~** с незапа́мятных времён.
immense *adj* огро́мный.
immerse *vt* погружа́ть *impf*, погрузи́ть *pf*. **immersion** *n* погруже́ние.
immigrant *n* иммигра́нт, ~ка. **immigration** *n* иммигра́ция.
imminent *adj* надвига́ющийся; (*danger*) грозя́щий.
immobile *adj* неподви́жный. **immobilize** *vt* парализова́ть *impf* & *pf*.
immoderate *adj* неуме́ренный.
immodest *adj* нескро́мный.
immoral *adj* безнра́вственный. **immorality** *n* безнра́вственность.
immortal *adj* бессме́ртный. **immortality** *n* бессме́ртие. **immortalize** *vt* обессме́ртить *pf*.
immovable *adj* неподви́жный; (*fig*) непоколеби́мый.
immune *adj* (*to illness*) невосприи́мчивый (**to** к+*dat*); (*free from*) свобо́дный (**from** от+*gen*). **immunity** *n* иммуните́т (**from** к+*dat*); освобожде́ние (**from** от+*gen*). **immunize** *vt* иммунизи́ровать *impf* & *pf*.
immutable *adj* неизме́нный.
imp *n* бесёнок.
impact *n* уда́р; (*fig*) влия́ние.
impair *vt* вреди́ть *impf*, по~ *pf*.
impale *vt* протыка́ть *impf*, проткну́ть *pf*.
impart *vt* дели́ться *impf*, по~ *pf* +*instr* (**to** с+*instr*).
impartial *adj* беспристра́стный.
impassable *adj* непроходи́мый; (*for vehicles*) непрое́зжий.
impasse *n* тупи́к.
impassioned *adj* стра́стный.
impassive *adj* бесстра́стный.
impatience *n* нетерпе́ние. **impatient** *adj* нетерпели́вый.
impeach *vt* обвиня́ть *impf*, обвини́ть *pf* (**for** в+*prep*).
impeccable *adj* безупре́чный.
impecunious *adj* безде́нежный.
impedance *n* по́лное сопротивле́ние. **impede** *vt* препя́тствовать *impf*, вос~ *pf* +*dat*. **impediment** *n* препя́тствие; (*in speech*) заика́ние.
impel *vt* побужда́ть *impf*, побуди́ть *pf* (**to** +*inf*, к+*dat*).
impending *adj* предстоя́щий.
impenetrable *adj* непроница́емый.
imperative *adj* необходи́мый; *n* (*gram*) повели́тельное наклоне́ние.
imperceptible *adj* незаме́тный.
imperfect *n* имперфе́кт; *adj* несоверше́нный. **imperfection** *n* несоверше́нство; (*fault*) недоста́ток. **imperfective** *adj* (*n*) несоверше́нный (вид).
imperial *adj* импе́рский.

imperialism *n* империали́зм. **imperialist** *n* империали́ст; *attrib* империалисти́ческий.
imperil *vt* подверга́ть *impf*, подве́ргнуть *pf* опа́сности.
imperious *adj* вла́стный.
impersonal *adj* безли́чный.
impersonate *vt* (*imitate*) подража́ть *impf*; (*pretend to be*) выдава́ть *impf*, вы́дать *pf* себя́ за+*acc*. **impersonation** *n* подража́ние.
impertinence *n* де́рзость. **impertinent** *adj* де́рзкий.
imperturbable *adj* невозмути́мый.
impervious *adj* (*fig*) глухо́й (**to** к+*dat*).
impetuous *adj* стреми́тельный.
impetus *n* дви́жущая си́ла.
impinge *vi*: ~ **(up)on** ока́зывать *impf*, оказа́ть *pf* (отрица́тельный) эффе́кт на+*acc*.
implacable *adj* неумоли́мый.
implant *vt* вводи́ть *impf*, ввести́ *pf*; (*fig*) се́ять *impf*, по~ *pf*.
implement[1] *n* ору́дие, инструме́нт.
implement[2] *vt* (*fulfil*) выполня́ть *impf*, вы́полнить *pf*.
implicate *vt* впу́тывать *impf*, впу́тать *pf*. **implication** *n* (*inference*) намёк; *pl* значе́ние.
implicit *adj* подразумева́емый; (*absolute*) безогово́рочный.
implore *vt* умоля́ть *impf*.
imply *vt* подразумева́ть *impf*.
impolite *adj* неве́жливый.
imponderable *adj* неопределённый.
import *n* (*meaning*) значе́ние; (*of goods*) и́мпорт; *vt* импорти́ровать *impf* & *pf*. **importer** *n* импортёр.
importance *n* ва́жность. **important** *adj* ва́жный.
impose *vt* (*tax*) облага́ть *impf*, обложи́ть *pf* +*instr* (**on** +*acc*); (*obligation*) налага́ть *impf*, наложи́ть *pf* (**on** на+*acc*); ~ **(o.s.) on** налега́ть *impf* на+*acc*. **imposing** *adj* внуши́тельный. **imposition** *n* обложе́ние, наложе́ние.
impossibility *n* невозмо́жность. **impossible** *adj* невозмо́жный.
impostor *n* самозва́нец.
impotence *n* бесси́лие; (*med*) импоте́нция. **impotent** *adj* бесси́льный; (*med*) импоте́нтный.
impound *vt* (*confiscate*) конфискова́ть *impf* & *pf*.
impoverished *adj* обедне́вший.
impracticable *adj* невыполни́мый.
imprecise *n* нето́чный.
impregnable *adj* непристу́пный.
impregnate *vt* (*fertilize*) оплодотворя́ть *impf*, оплодотвори́ть *pf*; (*saturate*) пропи́тывать *impf*, пропита́ть *pf*.
impresario *n* аге́нт.
impress *vt* производи́ть *impf*, произвести́ *pf* (како́е-либо) впечатле́ние на+*acc*; ~ **upon (s.o.)** внуша́ть *impf*, внуши́ть *pf* (+*dat*). **impression** *n* впечатле́ние; (*imprint*) отпеча́ток; (*reprint*) (стереоти́пное) изда́ние.
impressionism *n* импрессиони́зм. **impressionist** *n* импрессиони́ст.
impressive *adj* впечатля́ющий.
imprint *n* отпеча́ток; *vt* отпеча́тывать *impf*, отпеча́тать *pf*; (*on memory*) запечатле-

ва́ть *impf*, запечатле́ть *pf*.
imprison *vt* заключа́ть *impf*, заключи́ть *pf* (в тюрьму́). **imprisonment** *n* тюре́мное заключе́ние.
improbable *adj* невероя́тный.
impromptu *adj* импровизи́рованный; *adv* без подгото́вки, экспро́мтом.
improper *adj* (*incorrect*) непра́вильный; (*indecent*) неприли́чный. **impropriety** *n* неуме́стность.
improve *vt* & *i* улучша́ть(ся) *impf*, улу́чшить(ся) *pf*. **improvement** *n* улучше́ние.
improvisation *n* импровиза́ция. **improvise** *vt* импровизи́ровать *impf*, сымпровизи́ровать *pf*.
imprudent *adj* неосторо́жный.
impudence *n* на́глость. **impudent** *adj* на́глый.
impulse *n* толчо́к, и́мпульс; (*sudden tendency*) поры́в. **impulsive** *adj* импульси́вный.
impunity *n*: **with ~** безнака́занно.
impure *adj* нечи́стый.
impute *vt* припи́сывать *impf*, приписа́ть *pf* (**to** +*dat*).
in *prep* (*place*) в+*prep*, на+*prep*; (*into*) в+*acc*, на+*acc*; (*point in time*) в+*prep*, на+*prep*; **in the morning** (*etc*.) у́тром (*instr*); **in spring** (*etc*.) весно́й (*instr*); (*at some stage in*; *throughout*) во вре́мя +*gen*; (*duration*) за+*acc*; (*after interval of*) че́рез+*acc*; (*during course of*) в тече́ние+*gen*; (*circumstance*) в+*prep*, при+*prep*; *adv* (*place*) внутри́; (*motion*) внутрь; (*at home*) до́ма; (*in fashion*) в мо́де; **in here, there** (*place*) здесь, там; (*motion*) сюда́, туда́; *adj* вну́тренний; (*fashionable*) мо́дный; *n*: **the ins and outs** все ходы́ и вы́ходы.
inability *n* неспосо́бность.
inaccessible *adj* недосту́пный.
inaccurate *adj* нето́чный.
inaction *n* безде́йствие. **inactive** *adj* безде́йственный. **inactivity** *n* безде́йственность.
inadequate *adj* недоста́точный.
inadmissible *adj* недопусти́мый.
inadvertent *adj* неча́янный.
inalienable *adj* неотъе́млемый.
inane *adj* глу́пый.
inanimate *adj* неодушевлённый.
inappropriate *adj* неуме́стный.
inarticulate *adj* (*person*) косноязы́чный; (*indistinct*) невня́тный.
inasmuch *adv*: **~ as** так как; ввиду́ того́, что.
inattentive *adj* невнима́тельный.
inaudible *adj* неслы́шный.
inaugural *adj* вступи́тельный. **inaugurate** *vt* (*admit to office*) торже́ственно вводи́ть *impf*, ввести́ *pf* в до́лжность; (*open*) открыва́ть *impf*, откры́ть *pf*; (*introduce*) вводи́ть *impf*, ввести́ *pf*. **inauguration** *n* введе́ние в до́лжность; откры́тие; нача́ло.
inauspicious *adj* неблагоприя́тный.
inborn, inbred *adj* врождённый.
incalculable *adj* неисчисли́мый.
incandescent *adj* накалённый.
incantation *n* заклина́ние.
incapability *n* неспосо́бность. **incapable** *adj* неспосо́бный (**of** к+*dat*, на+*acc*).

incapacitate *vt* дéлать *impf*, с~ *pf* неспосóбным. **incapacity** *n* неспосóбность.
incarcerate *vt* заключáть *impf*, заключи́ть *pf* (в тюрьмý). **incarceration** *n* заключéние (в тюрьмý).
incarnate *adj* воплощённый. **incarnation** *n* воплощéние.
incendiary *adj* зажигáтельный.
incense[1] *n* фимиáм, лáдан.
incense[2] *vt* разгневáть *pf*.
incentive *n* побуждéние.
inception *n* начáло.
incessant *adj* непрестáнный.
incest *n* кровосмешéние.
inch *n* дюйм; ~ **by** ~ мáло-помáлу; *vi* ползти́ *impf*.
incidence *n* (*phys*) падéние; (*prevalence*) распространéние. **incident** *n* слýчай, инцидéнт. **incidental** *adj* (*casual*) случáйный; (*inessential*) несущéственный. **incidentally** *adv* мéжду прóчим.
incinerate *vt* испепеля́ть *impf*, испепели́ть *pf*. **incinerator** *n* мусоросжигáтельная печь.
incipient *adj* начинáющийся.
incision *n* надрéз (**in** на+*acc*). **incisive** *adj* (*fig*) óстрый. **incisor** *n* резéц.
incite *vt* подстрекáть *impf*, подстрекнýть *pf* (**to** к+*dat*). **incitement** *n* подстрекáтельство.
inclement *adj* сурóвый.
inclination *n* (*slope*) наклóн; (*propensity*) склóнность (**for, to** к+*dat*). **incline** *n* наклóн; *vt & i* склоня́ть(ся) *impf*, склони́ть(ся) *pf*. **inclined** *predic* (*disposed*) склóнен (-оннá, -óнно) (**to** к+*dat*).
include *vt* включáть *impf*, включи́ть *pf* (**in** в+*acc*); (*contain*) заключáть *impf*, заключи́ть *pf* в себé. **including** *prep* включáя+*acc*. **inclusion** *n* включéние. **inclusive** *adj* включáющий (в себé); *adv* включи́тельно.
incognito *adv* инкóгнито.
incoherent *adj* бессвя́зный.
income *n* дохóд; ~ **tax** подохóдный налóг.
incommensurate *adj* несоразмéрный.
incomparable *adj* несравни́мый (**to, with** с+*instr*); (*matchless*) несравнéнный.
incompatible *adj* несовмести́мый.
incompetence *n* некомпетéнтность. **incompetent** *adj* некомпетéнтный.
incomplete *adj* непóлный, незакóнченный.
incomprehensible *adj* непоня́тный.
inconceivable *adj* невообрази́мый.
inconclusive *adj* (*evidence*) недостáточный; (*results*) неопределённый.
incongruity *n* несоотвéтствие. **incongruous** *adj* несоотвéтствующий.
inconsequential *adj* незначи́тельный.
inconsiderable *adj* незначи́тельный.
inconsiderate *adj* невнимáтельный.
inconsistency *n* непослéдовательность. **inconsistent** *adj* непослéдовательный.
inconsolable *adj* безутéшный.
inconspicuous *adj* незамéтный.
incontinence *n* (*med*) недержáние. **incontinent** *adj*: **be** ~ страдáть *impf* недержáнием.

incontrovertible *adj* неопровержи́мый.
inconvenience *n* неудо́бство; *vt* затрудня́ть *impf*, затрудни́ть *pf*. **inconvenient** *adj* неудо́бный.
incorporate *vt* (*include*) включа́ть *impf*, включи́ть *pf*; (*unite*) объединя́ть *impf*, объедини́ть *pf*.
incorrect *adj* непра́вильный.
incorrigible *adj* неисправи́мый.
incorruptible *adj* неподку́пный.
increase *n* рост, увеличе́ние; (*in pay etc.*) приба́вка; *vt* & *i* увели́чивать(ся) *impf*, увели́чить(ся) *pf*.
incredible *adj* невероя́тный.
incredulous *adj* недове́рчивый.
increment *n* приба́вка.
incriminate *vt* изоблича́ть *impf*, изобличи́ть *pf*.
incubate *vt* (*eggs*) выводи́ть *impf*, вы́вести *pf* (в инкуба́торе). **incubator** *n* инкуба́тор.
inculcate *vt* внедря́ть *impf*, внедри́ть *pf*.
incumbent *adj* (*in office*) стоя́щий у вла́сти; **it is ~ (up)on you** вы обя́заны.
incur *vt* навлека́ть *impf*, навле́чь *pf* на себя́.
incurable *adj* неизлечи́мый.
incursion *n* (*invasion*) вторже́ние; (*attack*) набе́г.
indebted *predic* в долгу́ (**to** у+*gen*).
indecency *n* неприли́чие. **indecent** *adj* неприли́чный.
indecision *n* нереши́тельность. **indecisive** *adj* нереши́тельный.
indeclinable *adj* несклоня́емый.
indeed *adv* в са́мом де́ле, действи́тельно; (*interrog*) неуже́ли?
indefatigable *adj* неутоми́мый.
indefensible *adj* не име́ющий оправда́ния.
indefinable *adj* неопредели́мый. **indefinite** *adj* неопределённый.
indelible *adj* несмыва́емый.
indemnify *vt*: **~ against** страхова́ть *impf*, за~ *pf* от+*gen*; **~ for** (*compensate*) компенси́ровать *impf* & *pf*. **indemnity** *n* (*against loss*) гара́нтия от убы́тков; (*compensation*) компенса́ция.
indent *vt* (*printing*) писа́ть *impf*, с~ *pf* с о́тступом. **indentation** *n* (*notch*) зубе́ц; (*printing*) о́тступ.
independence *n* незави́симость, самостоя́тельность. **independent** *adj* незави́симый, самостоя́тельный.
indescribable *adj* неопису́емый.
indestructible *adj* неразруши́мый.
indeterminate *adj* неопределённый.
index *n* (*alphabetical*) указа́тель *m*; (*econ*) и́ндекс; (*pointer*) стре́лка; **~ finger** указа́тельный па́лец.
India *n* И́ндия. **Indian** *n* инди́ец, индиа́нка; (*American*) инде́ец, индиа́нка; *adj* инди́йский; (*American*) инде́йский; **~ summer** ба́бье ле́то.
indicate *vt* ука́зывать *impf*, указа́ть *pf*; (*be a sign of*) свиде́тельствовать *impf* о+*prep*. **indication** *n* указа́ние; (*sign*) при́знак. **indicative** *adj* ука́зывающий; (*gram*)

изъяви́тельный; *n* изъяви́тельное наклоне́ние. **indicator** *n* указа́тель *m*.

indict *vt* обвиня́ть *impf*, обвини́ть *pf* (**for** в+*prep*).

indifference *n* равноду́шие. **indifferent** *adj* равноду́шный; (*mediocre*) посре́дственный.

indigenous *adj* тузе́мный.

indigestible *adj* неудобовари́мый. **indigestion** *n* несваре́ние желу́дка.

indignant *adj* негоду́ющий; **be ~** негодова́ть *impf* (**with** на+*acc*). **indignation** *n* негодова́ние.

indignity *n* оскорбле́ние.

indirect *adj* непрямо́й; (*econ*; *gram*) ко́свенный.

indiscreet *adj* нескро́мный. **indiscretion** *n* нескро́мность.

indiscriminate *adj* неразбо́рчивый. **indiscriminately** *adv* без разбо́ра.

indispensible *adj* необходи́мый.

indisposed *predic* (*unwell*) нездоро́в.

indisputable *adj* бесспо́рный.

indistinct *adj* нея́сный.

indistinguishable *adj* неразличи́мый.

individual *n* ли́чность; *adj* индивидуа́льный. **individualism** *n* индивидуали́зм. **individualist** *n* индивидуали́ст. **individualistic** *adj* индивидуалисти́ческий. **individuality** *n* индивидуа́льность.

indivisible *adj* недели́мый.

indoctrinate *vt* внуша́ть *impf*, внуши́ть *pf* +*dat* (**with** +*acc*).

indolence *n* ле́ность. **indolent** *adj* лени́вый.

indomitable *adj* неукроти́мый.

Indonesia *n* Индоне́зия.

indoor *adj* ко́мнатный. **indoors** *adv* (*position*) в до́ме; (*motion*) в дом.

induce *vt* (*prevail on*) убежда́ть *impf*, убеди́ть *pf*; (*bring about*) вызыва́ть *impf*, вы́звать *pf*. **inducement** *n* побужде́ние.

induction *n* (*logic*, *electr*) инду́кция; (*in post*) введе́ние в до́лжность.

indulge *vt* потво́рствовать *impf* +*dat*; *vi* предава́ться *impf*, преда́ться *pf* (**in** +*dat*). **indulgence** *n* потво́рство; (*tolerance*) снисходи́тельность. **indulgent** *adj* снисходи́тельный.

industrial *adj* промы́шленный. **industrialist** *n* промы́шленник. **industrious** *adj* трудолюби́вый. **industry** *n* промы́шленность; (*zeal*) трудолю́бие.

inebriated *adj* пья́ный.

inedible *adj* несъедо́бный.

ineffective, ineffectual *adj* безрезульта́тный; (*person*) неспосо́бный.

inefficiency *n* неэффекти́вность. **inefficient** *adj* неэффекти́вный.

ineligible *adj* не име́ющий пра́во (**for** на+*acc*).

inept *adj* неуме́лый.

inequality *n* нера́венство.

inert *adj* ине́ртный. **inertia** *n* (*phys*) ине́рция; (*sluggishness*) ине́ртность.

inescapable *adj* неизбе́жный.

inevitability *n* неизбе́жность. **inevitable** *adj* неизбе́жный.

inexact *adj* нето́чный.

inexcusable *adj* непрости́тельный.

inexhaustible *adj* неистощи́мый.

inexorable *adj* неумоли́мый. **inexpensive** *adj* недорого́й. **inexperience** *n* нео́пытность. **inexperienced** *adj* нео́пытный.
inexplicable *adj* необъясни́мый.
infallible *adj* непогреши́мый.
infamous *adj* позо́рный. **infamy** *n* позо́р.
infancy *n* младе́нчество. **infant** *n* младе́нец. **infantile** *adj* де́тский.
infantry *n* пехо́та.
infatuate *vt* вскружи́ть *pf* го́лову +*dat*. **infatuation** *n* увлече́ние.
infect *vt* заража́ть *impf*, зарази́ть *pf* (**with** +*instr*). **infection** *n* зара́за, инфе́кция. **infectious** *adj* зара́зный; (*fig*) зарази́тельный.
infer *vt* заключа́ть *impf*, заключи́ть *pf*. **inference** *n* заключе́ние.
inferior *adj* (*in rank*) ни́зший; (*in quality*) ху́дший, плохо́й; *n* подчинённый *sb*. **inferiority** *n* бо́лее ни́зкое ка́чество; ~ **complex** ко́мплекс неполноце́нности.
infernal *adj* а́дский. **inferno** *n* ад.
infertile *adj* неплодоро́дный.
infested *adj*: **be** ~ **with** кише́ть *impf* +*instr*.
infidelity *n* неве́рность.
infiltrate *vt* постепе́нно проника́ть *impf*, прони́кнуть *pf* в+*acc*.
infinite *adj* бесконе́чный. **infinitesimal** *adj* бесконе́чно ма́лый. **infinitive** *n* инфинити́в. **infinity** *n* бесконе́чность.
infirm *adj* не́мощный. **infirmary** *n* больни́ца. **infirmity** *n* не́мощь.
inflame *vt* & *i* (*excite*) возбужда́ть(ся) *impf*, возбуди́ть(ся) *pf*; (*med*) воспаля́ть(ся) *impf*, воспали́ть(ся) *pf*. **inflammable** *adj* огнеопа́сный. **inflammation** *n* воспале́ние. **inflammatory** *adj* подстрека́тельский.
inflate *vt* надува́ть *impf*, наду́ть *pf*. **inflation** *n* (*econ*) инфля́ция.
inflection *n* (*gram*) фле́ксия.
inflexible *adj* неги́бкий; (*fig*) непреклонный.
inflict *vt* (*blow*) наноси́ть *impf*, нанести́ *pf* ((**up)on** +*dat*); (*suffering*) причиня́ть *impf*, причини́ть *pf* ((**up)on** +*dat*); (*penalty*) налага́ть *impf*, наложи́ть *pf* ((**up)on** на+*acc*); ~ **o.s. (up)on** навя́зываться *impf*, навяза́ться *pf* +*dat*.
inflow *n* втека́ние, прито́к.
influence *n* влия́ние; *vt* влия́ть *impf*, по~ *pf* на+*acc*. **influential** *adj* влия́тельный.
influenza *n* грипп.
influx *n* (*fig*) наплы́в.
inform *vt* сообща́ть *impf*, сообщи́ть *pf* +*dat* (**of, about** +*acc*, о+*prep*); *vi* доноси́ть *impf*, донести́ *pf* (**against** на+*acc*).
informal *adj* (*unofficial*) неофициа́льный; (*casual*) обы́денный.
informant *n* осведоми́тель *m*. **information** *n* информа́ция. **informative** *adj* поучи́тельный. **informer** *n* доно́счик.
infra-red *adj* инфракра́сный.
infrequent *adj* ре́дкий.
infringe *vt* (*violate*) наруша́ть *impf*, нару́шить *pf*; *vi*: ~ **(up)on** посяга́ть *impf*, посягну́ть *pf* на+*acc*. **infringement** *n* наруше́ние; посяга́тельство.

infuriate *vt* разъяря́ть *impf*, разъяри́ть *pf*.

infuse *vt* (*fig*) внуша́ть *impf*, внуши́ть *pf* (**into** +*dat*). **infusion** *n* (*fig*) внуше́ние; (*herbs etc*) насто́й.

ingenious *adj* изобрета́тельный. **ingenuity** *n* изобрета́тельность.

ingenuous *adj* бесхи́тростный.

ingot *n* сли́ток.

ingrained *adj* закорене́лый.

ingratiate *vt* ~ **o.s.** вкра́дываться *impf*, вкра́сться *pf* в ми́лость (**with** +*dat*).

ingratitude *n* неблагода́рность.

ingredient *n* ингредие́нт, составля́ющее *sb*.

inhabit *vt* жить *impf* в, на, +*prep*; обита́ть *impf* в, на, +*prep*. **inhabitant** *n* жи́тель *m*, ~ница.

inhalation *n* вдыха́ние. **inhale** *vt* вдыха́ть *impf*, вдохну́ть *pf*.

inherent *adj* прису́щий (**in** +*dat*).

inherit *vt* насле́довать *impf* & *pf*, у~ *pf*. **inheritance** *n* насле́дство.

inhibit *vt* стесня́ть *impf*, стесни́ть *pf*. **inhibited** *adj* стесни́тельный. **inhibition** *n* стесне́ние.

inhospitable *adj* негостеприи́мный; (*fig*) недружелю́бный.

inhuman(e) *adj* бесчелове́чный.

inimical *adj* вражде́бный; (*harmful*) вре́дный.

inimitable *adj* неподража́емый.

iniquity *n* несправедли́вость.

initial *adj* (перво)нача́льный; *n* нача́льная бу́ква; *pl* инициа́лы *m pl*; *vt* ста́вить *impf*, по~ *pf* инициа́лы на+*acc*. **initially** *adv* в нача́ле.

initiate *vt* вводи́ть *impf*, ввести́ *pf* (**into** в+*acc*). **initiation** *n* введе́ние.

initiative *n* инициати́ва.

inject *vt* вводи́ть *impf*, ввести́ *pf* (*person* +*dat*, *substance* +*acc*). **injection** *n* уко́л; (*fig*) инъе́кция.

injunction *n* (*law*) суде́бный запре́т.

injure *vt* поврежда́ть *impf*, повреди́ть *pf*. **injury** *n* ра́на.

injustice *n* несправедли́вость.

ink *n* черни́ла (-л).

inkling *n* представле́ние.

inland *adj* вну́тренний; *adv* (*motion*) внутрь страны́; (*place*) внутри́ страны́; **I~ Revenue** управле́ние нало́говых сбо́ров.

in-laws *n pl* ро́дственники *m pl* супру́га, -ги.

inlay *n* инкруста́ция; *vt* инкрусти́ровать *impf* & *pf*.

inlet *n* (*of sea*) у́зкий зали́в.

inmate *n* (*prison*) заключённый *sb*; (*hospital*) больно́й *sb*.

inn *n* гости́ница.

innate *adj* врождённый.

inner *adj* вну́тренний. **innermost** *adj* глубоча́йший; (*fig*) сокрове́ннейший.

innocence *n* неви́нность; (*guiltlessness*) невино́вность. **innocent** *adj* неви́нный; (*not guilty*) невино́вный (**of** в+*prep*).

innocuous *adj* безвре́дный.

innovate *vi* вводи́ть *impf*, ввести́ *pf* но́вшества. **innovation** *n* нововведе́ние. **innovative** *adj* нова́торский. **innovator** *n* нова́тор.

innuendo *n* намёк, инсинуа́ция.
innumerable *adj* бесчи́сленный.
inoculate *vt* привива́ть *impf*, приви́ть *pf* +*dat* (**against** +*acc*). **inoculation** *n* приви́вка.
inoffensive *adj* безоби́дный.
inopportune *adj* несвоевре́менный.
inordinate *adj* чрезме́рный.
inorganic *adj* неоргани́ческий.
in-patient *n* стациона́рный больно́й *sb*.
input *n* ввод.
inquest *n* суде́бное сле́дствие, дозна́ние.
inquire *vt* спра́шивать *impf*, спроси́ть *pf*; *vi* справля́ться *impf*, спра́виться *pf* (**about** о+*prep*); рассле́довать *impf* & *pf* (**into** +*acc*). **inquiry** *n* вопро́с, спра́вка; (*investigation*) рассле́дование.
inquisition *n* инквизи́ция. **inquisitive** *adj* пытли́вый, любозна́тельный.
inroad *n* (*attack*) набе́г; (*fig*) посяга́тельство (**on, into** на+*acc*).
insane *adj* безу́мный. **insanity** *n* безу́мие.
insatiable *adj* ненасы́тный.
inscribe *vt* надпи́сывать *impf*, надписа́ть *pf*; (*engrave*) выреза́ть *impf*, вы́резать *pf*. **inscription** *n* на́дпись.
inscrutable *adj* непостижи́мый, непроница́емый.
insect *n* насеко́мое *sb*. **insecticide** *n* инсектици́д.
insecure *adj* (*unsafe*) небезопа́сный; (*not confident*) неуве́ренный (в себе́).
insemination *n* оплодотворе́ние.
insensible *adj* (*unconscious*) потеря́вший созна́ние.
insensitive *adj* нечувстви́тельный.
inseparable *adj* неотдели́мый; (*people*) неразлу́чный.
insert *vt* вставля́ть *impf*, вста́вить *pf*; вкла́дывать *impf*, вложи́ть *pf*; (*coin*) опуска́ть *impf*, опусти́ть *pf*. **insertion** *n* (*inserting*) вставле́ние, вкла́дывание; (*thing inserted*) вста́вка.
inshore *adj* прибре́жный; *adv* бли́зко к бе́регу.
inside *n* вну́тренняя часть; *pl* (*anat*) вну́тренности *f pl*; **turn ~ out** вывёртывать *impf*, вы́вернуть *pf* наизна́нку; *adj* вну́тренний; *adv* (*place*) внутри́; (*motion*) внутрь; *prep* (*place*) внутри́+*gen*, в+*prep*; (*motion*) внутрь+*gen*, в+*acc*.
insidious *adj* кова́рный.
insight *n* проница́тельность.
insignia *n* зна́ки *m pl* разли́чия.
insignificant *adj* незначи́тельный.
insincere *adj* нейскренний.
insinuate *vt* (*hint*) намека́ть *impf*, намекну́ть *pf* на+*acc*. **insinuation** *n* инсинуа́ция.
insipid *adj* пре́сный.
insist *vt* & *i* наста́ивать *impf*, настоя́ть *pf* (**on** на+*prep*). **insistence** *n* насто́йчивость. **insistent** *adj* насто́йчивый.
insolence *n* на́глость. **insolent** *adj* на́глый.
insoluble *adj* (*problem*) неразреши́мый; (*in liquid*) нераствори́мый.
insolvent *adj* несостоя́тельный.
insomnia *n* бессо́нница.
inspect *vt* инспекти́ровать *impf*, про~ *pf*. **inspection** *n*

инспе́кция. **inspector** *n* инспе́ктор; (*ticket* ~) контролёр.

inspiration *n* вдохнове́ние. **inspire** *vt* вдохновля́ть *impf*, вдохнови́ть *pf*; внуша́ть *impf*, внуши́ть *pf* +*dat* (**with** +*acc*).

instability *n* неусто́йчивость; (*of character*) неуравнове́шенность.

install *vt* (*person in office*) вводи́ть *impf*, ввести́ *pf* в до́лжность; (*apparatus*) устана́вливать *impf*, установи́ть *pf*. **installation** *n* введе́ние в до́лжность; устано́вка; *pl* сооруже́ния *neut pl*.

instalment *n* (*comm*) взнос; (*publication*) вы́пуск; часть; **by ~s** в рассро́чку.

instance *n* (*example*) приме́р; (*case*) слу́чай; **for ~** наприме́р.

instant *n* мгнове́ние, моме́нт; *adj* неме́дленный; (*coffee etc.*) раствори́мый. **instantaneous** *adj* мгнове́нный. **instantly** *adv* неме́дленно, то́тчас.

instead *adv* вме́сто (**of** +*gen*); **~ of going** вме́сто того́, что́бы пойти́.

instep *n* подъём.

instigate *vt* подстрека́ть *impf*, подстрекну́ть *pf* (**to** к+*dat*). **instigation** *n* подстрека́тельство. **instigator** *n* подстрека́тель *m*, ~ница.

instil *vt* (*ideas etc.*) внуша́ть *impf*, внуши́ть *pf* (**into** +*dat*).

instinct *n* инсти́нкт. **instinctive** *adj* инстинкти́вный.

institute *n* институ́т; *vt* (*establish*) устана́вливать *impf*, установи́ть *pf*; (*introduce*) вводи́ть *impf*, ввести́ *pf*; (*reforms*) проводи́ть *impf*, провести́ *pf*. **institution** *n* учрежде́ние.

instruct *vt* (*teach*) обуча́ть *impf*, обучи́ть *pf* (**in** +*dat*); (*inform*) сообща́ть *impf*, сообщи́ть *pf* +*dat*; (*command*) прика́зывать *impf*, приказа́ть *pf* +*dat*. **instruction** *n* (*in pl*) инстру́кция; (*teaching*) обуче́ние. **instructive** *adj* поучи́тельный. **instructor** *n* инстру́ктор.

instrument *n* ору́дие, инструме́нт. **instrumental** *adj* (*mus*) инструмента́льный; (*gram*) твори́тельный; **be ~ in** спосо́бствовать *impf*, по~ *pf* +*dat*; *n* (*gram*) твори́тельный паде́ж. **instrumentation** *n* (*mus*) инструменто́вка.

insubordinate *adj* неподчиня́ющийся.

insufferable *adj* невыноси́мый.

insular *adj* (*fig*) ограни́ченный.

insulate *vt* изоли́ровать *impf* & *pf*. **insulation** *n* изоля́ция. **insulator** *n* изоля́тор.

insulin *n* инсули́н.

insult *n* оскорбле́ние; *vt* оскорбля́ть *impf*, оскорби́ть *pf*. **insulting** *adj* оскорби́тельный.

insuperable *adj* непреодоли́мый.

insurance *n* страхова́ние; *attrib* страхово́й. **insure** *vt* страхова́ть *impf*, за~ *pf* (**against** от+*gen*).

insurgent *n* повста́нец.

insurmountable *adj* непреодоли́мый.

insurrection *n* восста́ние.

intact *adj* це́лый.

intake *n* (*of persons*) набо́р; (*consumption*) потребле́ние.

intangible *adj* неосяза́емый.

integral *adj* неотъе́млемый. **integrate** *vt* & *i* интегри́роваться *impf* & *pf*. **integration** *n* интегра́ция.

integrity *n* (*honesty*) че́стность.

intellect *n* интелле́кт. **intellectual** *n* интеллиге́нт; *adj* интеллектуа́льный.

intelligence *n* (*intellect*) ум; (*information*) све́дения *neut pl*; (~ *service*) разве́дка. **intelligent** *adj* у́мный.

intelligentsia *n* интеллиге́нция.

intelligible *adj* поня́тный.

intemperate *adj* невозде́ржанный.

intend *vt* собира́ться *impf*, собра́ться *pf*; (*design*) предназнача́ть *impf*, предназна́чить *pf* (**for** для+*gen*, на+*acc*).

intense *adj* си́льный. **intensify** *vt* & *i* уси́ливать(ся) *impf*, уси́лить(ся) *pf*. **intensity** *n* интенси́вность, си́ла. **intensive** *adj* интенси́вный.

intent *n* наме́рение; *adj* (*resolved*) стремя́щийся (**on** к+*dat*); (*occupied*) погружённый (**on** в+*acc*); (*earnest*) внима́тельный. **intention** *n* наме́рение. **intentional** *adj* наме́ренный.

inter *vt* хорони́ть *impf*, по~ *pf*.

interact *vi* взаимоде́йствовать *impf*. **interaction** *n* взаимоде́йствие. **interactive** *adj* (*comput*) интеракти́вный.

intercede *vi* хода́тайствовать *impf*, по~ *pf* (**for** за+*acc*; **with** пе́ред+*instr*).

intercept *vt* перехва́тывать *impf*, перехвати́ть *pf*. **interception** *n* перехва́т.

interchange *n* обме́н (**of** +*instr*); (*junction*) тра́нспортная развя́зка; *vt* обме́ниваться *impf*, обменя́ться *pf* +*instr*. **interchangeable** *adj* взаимозаменя́емый.

inter-city *adj* междугоро́дный.

intercom *n* селе́ктор; (*to get into house*) домофо́н.

interconnected *adj* взаимосвя́занный.

intercourse *n* (*social*) обще́ние; (*trade*; *sexual*) сноше́ния *neut pl*.

interdisciplinary *adj* межотраслево́й.

interest *n* интере́с (**in** к+*dat*); (*econ*) проце́нты *m pl*; *vt* интересова́ть *impf*; (~ *person in*) заинтересо́вывать *impf*, заинтересова́ть *pf* (**in** +*instr*); **be ~ed in** интересова́ться *impf* +*instr*. **interesting** *adj* интере́сный.

interfere *vi* вме́шиваться *impf*, вмеша́ться *pf* (**in** в+*acc*). **interference** *n* вмеша́тельство; (*radio*) поме́хи *f pl*.

interim *n*: **in the ~** тем вре́менем; *adj* промежу́точный; (*temporary*) вре́менный.

interior *n* (*of building*) интерье́р; (*of object*) вну́тренность; *adj* вну́тренний.

interjection *n* восклица́ние; (*gram*) междоме́тие.

interlock *vt* & *i* сцепля́ть(ся) *impf*, сцепи́ть(ся) *pf*.

interloper *n* незва́ный гость *m*.

interlude *n* (*theat*) антра́кт; (*mus*, *fig*) интерлю́дия.

intermediary *n* посре́дник.

intermediate *adj* промежу́точный.

interminable *adj* бесконе́чный.

intermission *n* (*theat*) антра́кт.

intermittent *adj* преры́вистый.

intern *vt* интерни́ровать *impf* & *pf*.
internal *adj* вну́тренний; ~ **combustion engine** дви́гатель *m* вну́треннего сгора́ния.
international *adj* междунаро́дный; *n* (*contest*) междунаро́дные состяза́ния *neut pl*.
Internet *n* Интерне́т; **on the** ~ в Интерне́те.
internment *n* интерни́рование.
interplay *n* взаимоде́йствие.
interpret *vt* (*explain*) толкова́ть *impf*; (*understand*) истолко́вывать *impf*, истолкова́ть *pf*; *vi* переводи́ть *impf*, перевести́ *pf*. **interpretation** *n* толкова́ние. **interpreter** *n* перево́дчик, -ица.
interrelated *adj* взаимосвя́занный.
interrogate *vt* допра́шивать *impf*, допроси́ть *pf*. **interrogation** *n* допро́с. **interrogative** *adj* вопроси́тельный.
interrupt *vt* прерыва́ть *impf*, прерва́ть *pf*. **interruption** *n* переры́в.
intersect *vt* & *i* пересека́ть(ся) *impf*, пересе́чь(ся) *pf*. **intersection** *n* пересече́ние.
intersperse *vt* (*scatter*) рассыпа́ть *impf*, рассы́пать *pf* (**between, among** ме́жду+*instr*, среди́+*gen*).
intertwine *vt* & *i* переплета́ть(ся) *impf*, переплести́(сь) *pf*.
interval *n* интерва́л; (*theat*) антра́кт.
intervene *vi* (*occur*) происходи́ть *impf*, произойти́ *pf*; ~ **in** вме́шиваться *impf*, вмеша́ться *pf* в+*acc*. **intervention** *n* вмеша́тельство; (*polit*) интерве́нция.
interview *n* интервью́ *neut indecl*; *vt* интервью́ировать *impf* & *pf*, про~ *pf*. **interviewer** *n* интервьюе́р.
intestate *adj* без завеща́ния.
intestine *n* кишка́; *pl* кише́чник.
intimacy *n* инти́мность. **intimate**[1] *adj* инти́мный.
intimate[2] *vt* (*hint*) намека́ть *impf*, намекну́ть *pf* на+*acc*. **intimation** *n* намёк.
intimidate *vt* запу́гивать *impf*, запуга́ть *pf*.
into *prep* в, во+*acc*, на+*acc*.
intolerable *adj* невыноси́мый.
intolerance *n* нетерпи́мость.
intolerant *adj* нетерпи́мый.
intonation *n* интона́ция.
intoxicated *adj* пья́ный. **intoxication** *n* опьяне́ние.
intractable *adj* неподáтливый.
intransigent *adj* непримири́мый.
intransitive *adj* неперехо́дный.
intrepid *adj* неустраши́мый.
intricacy *n* запу́танность. **intricate** *adj* запу́танный.
intrigue *n* интри́га; *vi* интригова́ть *impf*; *vt* интригова́ть *impf*, за~ *pf*.
intrinsic *adj* прису́щий; (*value*) вну́тренний.
introduce *vt* вводи́ть *impf*, ввести́ *pf*; (*person*) представля́ть *impf*, предста́вить *pf*. **introduction** *n* введе́ние; представле́ние; (*to book*) предисло́вие. **introductory** *adj* вступи́тельный.
introspection *n* интроспе́кция.
intrude *vi* вторга́ться *impf*, вто́ргнуться *pf* (**into** в+*acc*); (*disturb*) меша́ть *impf*, по~ *pf*. **intruder** *n* (*burglar*) граби́тель *m*. **intrusion** *n* вторже́ние.

intuition *n* интуи́ция. **intuitive** *adj* интуити́вный.
inundate *vt* наводня́ть *impf*, наводни́ть *pf*. **inundation** *n* наводне́ние.
invade *vt* вторга́ться *impf*, вто́ргнуться *pf* в+*acc*. **invader** *n* захва́тчик.
invalid[1] *n* (*person*) инвали́д.
invalid[2] *adj* недействи́тельный. **invalidate** *vt* де́лать *impf*, с~ *pf* недействи́тельным.
invaluable *adj* неоцени́мый.
invariable *adj* неизме́нный.
invasion *n* вторже́ние.
invective *n* брань.
invent *vt* изобрета́ть *impf*, изобрести́ *pf*; (*think up*) выду́мывать *impf*, вы́думать *pf*. **invention** *n* изобрете́ние; вы́думка. **inventive** *adj* изобрета́тельный. **inventor** *n* изобрета́тель *m*.
inventory *n* инвента́рь *m*.
inverse *adj* обра́тный; *n* противополо́жность. **invert** *vt* перевора́чивать *impf*, переверну́ть *pf*. **inverted commas** *n pl* кавы́чки *f pl*.
invest *vt* & *i* (*econ*) вкла́дывать *impf*, вложи́ть *pf* (де́ньги) (**in** в+*acc*).
investigate *vt* иссле́довать *impf* & *pf*; (*law*) рассле́довать *impf* & *pf*. **investigation** *n* иссле́дование; рассле́дование.
investment *n* инвести́ция, вклад. **investor** *n* вкла́дчик.
inveterate *adj* закорене́лый.
invidious *adj* оскорби́тельный.
invigorate *vt* оживля́ть *impf*, оживи́ть *pf*.
invincible *adj* непобеди́мый.
inviolable *adj* неруши́мый.
invisible *adj* неви́димый.
invitation *n* приглаше́ние. **invite** *vt* приглаша́ть *impf*, пригласи́ть *pf*. **inviting** *adj* привлека́тельный.
invoice *n* факту́ра.
invoke *vt* обраща́ться *impf*, обрати́ться *pf* к+*dat*.
involuntary *adj* нево́льный.
involve *vt* (*entangle*) вовлека́ть *impf*, вовле́чь *pf*; (*entail*) влечь *impf* за собо́й. **involved** *adj* сло́жный.
invulnerable *adj* неуязви́мый.
inward *adj* вну́тренний. **inwardly** *adv* внутри́. **inwards** *adv* внутрь.
iodine *n* йод.
iota *n*: **not an** ~ ни на йо́ту.
IOU *n* долгова́я распи́ска.
Iran *n* Ира́н. **Iranian** *n* ира́нец, -нка; *adj* ира́нский.
Iraq *n* Ира́к. **Iraqi** *n* ира́кец; жи́тель *m*, ~ница Ира́ка; *adj* ира́кский.
irascible *adj* раздражи́тельный.
irate *adj* гне́вный.
Ireland *n* Ирла́ндия.
iris *n* (*anat*) ра́дужная оболо́чка; (*bot*) каса́тик.
Irish *adj* ирла́ндский. **Irishman** *n* ирла́ндец. **Irishwoman** *n* ирла́ндка.
irk *vt* раздража́ть *impf*, раздражи́ть *pf* +*dat*. **irksome** *adj* раздражи́тельный.
iron *n* желе́зо; (*for clothes*) утю́г; *adj* желе́зный; *vt* гла́дить *impf*, вы́~ *pf*.
ironic(al) *adj* ирони́ческий.
irony *n* иро́ния.
irradiate *vt* (*subject to radiation*) облуча́ть *impf*, облучи́ть *pf*. **irradiation** *n* облуче́ние.
irrational *adj* неразу́мный.

irreconcilable *adj* непримири́мый.
irrefutable *adj* неопровержи́мый.
irregular *adj* нерегуля́рный; (*gram*) непра́вильный; (*not even*) неро́вный.
irrelevant *adj* неуме́стный.
irreparable *adj* непоправи́мый.
irreplaceable *adj* незамени́мый.
irrepressible *adj* неудержи́мый.
irreproachable *adj* безупре́чный.
irresistible *adj* неотрази́мый.
irresolute *adj* нереши́тельный.
irrespective *adj*: ~ **of** несмотря́ на+*acc*.
irresponsible *adj* безотве́тственный.
irretrievable *adj* непоправи́мый.
irreverent *adj* непочти́тельный.
irreversible *adj* необрати́мый.
irrevocable *adj* неотменя́емый.
irrigate *vt* ороша́ть *impf*, ороси́ть *pf*. **irrigation** *n* ороше́ние.
irritable *adj* раздражи́тельный. **irritate** *vt* раздража́ть *impf*, раздражи́ть *pf*. **irritation** *n* раздраже́ние.
Islam *n* исла́м. **Islamic** *adj* мусульма́нский.
island, isle *n* о́стров. **islander** *n* островитя́нин, -я́нка.
isolate *vt* изоли́ровать *impf* & *pf*. **isolation** *n* изоля́ция.
Israel *n* Изра́иль *m*. **Israeli** *n* израильтя́нин, -я́нка; *adj* изра́ильский.
issue *n* (*question*) (спо́рный) вопро́с; (*of bonds etc.*) вы́пуск; (*of magazine*) но́мер; *vi* выходи́ть *impf*, вы́йти *pf*; (*flow*) вытека́ть *impf*, вы́течь *pf*; *vt* выпуска́ть *impf*, вы́пустить *pf*; (*give out*) выдава́ть *impf*, вы́дать *pf*.
isthmus *n* перешеек.
IT *abbr* (*of* **information technology**) информа́тика.
it *pron* он, она́, оно́; *demonstrative* э́то.
Italian *n* италья́нец, -нка; *adj* италья́нский.
italics *n pl* курси́в; **in** ~ курси́вом.
Italy *n* Ита́лия.
ITAR-Tass *abbr* ИТАР-ТА́СС.
itch *n* зуд; *vi* чеса́ться *impf*.
item *n* (*on list*) предме́т; (*in account*) статья́; (*on agenda*) пункт; (*in programme*) но́мер. **itemize** *vt* перечисля́ть *impf*, перечи́слить *pf*.
itinerant *adj* стра́нствующий.
itinerary *n* маршру́т.
its *poss pron* его́, её; свой.
itself *pron* (*emph*) (он(о́)) сам(о́), (она́) сама́; (*refl*) себя́; -ся (*suffixed to vt*).
ivory *n* слоно́вая кость.
ivy *n* плющ.

J

jab *n* толчо́к; (*injection*) уко́л; *vt* ты́кать *impf*, ткнуть *pf*.
jack *n* (*cards*) вале́т; (*lifting device*) домкра́т; *vt* (~ *up*) поднима́ть *impf*, подня́ть *pf* домкра́том.
jackdaw *n* га́лка.
jacket *n* (*tailored*) пиджа́к; (*anorak*) ку́ртка; (*on book*) (супер)обло́жка.
jackpot *n* банк.

jade *n* (*mineral*) нефри́т.
jaded *adj* утомлённый.
jagged *adj* зазу́бренный.
jaguar *n* ягуа́р.
jail *see* **gaol**
jam[1] *n* (*crush*) да́вка; (*in traffic*) про́бка; *vt* (*thrust*) впи́хивать *impf*, впихну́ть *pf* (**into** в+*acc*); (*wedge open*; *block*) закли́нивать *impf*, заклини́ть *pf*; (*radio*) заглуша́ть *impf*, заглуши́ть *pf*; *vi* (*machine*) закли́нивать *impf*, заклини́ть *pf impers+acc*.
jam[2] *n* (*conserve*) варе́нье, джем.
jangle *vi* (& *t*) звя́кать (+*instr*).
janitor *n* приврáтник.
January *n* янва́рь; *adj* янва́рский.
Japan *n* Япо́ния. **Japanese** *n* япо́нец, -нка; *adj* япо́нский.
jar[1] *n* (*container*) ба́нка.
jar[2] *vi* (*irritate*) раздража́ть *impf*, раздражи́ть *pf* (**upon** +*acc*).
jargon *n* жарго́н.
jasmin(e) *n* жасми́н.
jaundice *n* желту́ха. **jaundiced** *adj* (*fig*) цини́чный.
jaunt *n* прогу́лка.
jaunty *adj* бо́дрый.
javelin *n* копьё.
jaw *n* че́люсть; *pl* пасть, рот.
jay *n* со́йка.
jazz *n* джаз; *adj* джа́зовый.
jealous *adj* ревни́вый; (*envious*) зави́стливый; **be ~ of** (*person*) ревнова́ть *impf*; (*thing*) зави́довать *impf*, по~ *pf* +*dat*; (*rights*) ревни́во оберега́ть *impf*, обере́чь *pf*. **jealousy** *n* ре́вность; за́висть.
jeans *n pl* джи́нсы (-сов) *pl*.
jeer *n* насме́шка; *vt* & *i* насмеха́ться *impf* (**at** над+*instr*).
jelly *n* (*sweet*) желе́ *neut indecl*; (*aspic*) сту́день *m*. **jellyfish** *n* меду́за.
jeopardize *vt* подверга́ть *impf*, подве́ргнуть *pf* опа́сности.
jeopardy *n* опа́сность.
jerk *n* рыво́к; *vt* дёргать *impf* +*instr*; *vi* (*twitch*) дёргаться *impf*, дёрнуться *pf*. **jerky** *adj* неро́вный.
jersey *n* (*garment*) дже́мпер; (*fabric*) джёрси́ *neut indecl*.
jest *n* шу́тка; **in ~** в шу́тку; *vi* шути́ть *impf*, по~ *pf*.
jester *n* шут.
jet[1] *n* (*stream*) струя́; (*nozzle*) со́пло́; **~ engine** реакти́вный дви́гатель *m*; **~ plane** реакти́вный самолёт.
jet[2] *n* (*mineralogy*) гага́т; **~-black** чёрный как смоль.
jettison *vt* выбра́сывать *impf*, вы́бросить *pf* за́ борт.
jetty *n* при́стань.
Jew *n* евре́й, евре́йка. **Jewish** *adj* евре́йский.
jewel *n* драгоце́нность, драгоце́нный ка́мень *m*. **jeweller** *n* ювели́р. **jewellery** *n* драгоце́нности *f pl*.
jib *n* (*naut*) кли́вер; *vi*: **~ at** уклоня́ться *impf* от+*gen*.
jigsaw *n* (*puzzle*) моза́ика.
jingle *n* звя́канье; *vi* (& *t*) звя́кать *impf*, звя́кнуть *pf* (+*instr*).
job *n* (*work*) рабо́та; (*task*) зада́ние; (*position*) ме́сто. **jobless** *adj* безрабо́тный.
jockey *n* жоке́й; *vi* оттира́ть *impf* друг дру́га.
jocular *adj* шутли́вый.
jog *n* (*push*) толчо́к; *vt* подта́лкивать *impf*, подтолкну́ть *pf*; *vi* бе́гать *impf* трусцо́й. **jogger** *n* занима́ющийся оздорови́тельным бе́гом. **jogging** *n* оздорови́тельный бег.

join *vt & i* соединя́ть(ся) *impf*, соедини́ть(ся) *pf*; *vt* (*a group of people*) присоединя́ться *impf*, присоедини́ться *pf* к+*dat*; (*as member*) вступа́ть *impf*, вступи́ть *pf* в+*acc*; *vi*: ~ **in** принима́ть *impf*, приня́ть *pf* уча́стие (в+*prep*); ~ **up** вступа́ть *impf*, вступи́ть *pf* в а́рмию.

joiner *n* столя́р.

joint *n* соедине́ние; (*anat*) суста́в; (*meat*) кусо́к; *adj* совме́стный; (*common*) о́бщий.

joist *n* перекла́дина.

joke *n* шу́тка; *vi* шути́ть *impf*, по~ *pf*. **joker** *n* шутни́к; (*cards*) джо́кер.

jollity *n* весе́лье. **jolly** *adj* весёлый; *adv* о́чень.

jolt *n* толчо́к; *vt & i* трясти́(сь) *impf*.

jostle *vt & i* толка́ть(ся) *impf*, толкну́ть(ся) *pf*.

jot *n* йо́та; **not a** ~ ни на йо́ту; *vt* (~ *down*) запи́сывать *impf*, записа́ть *pf*.

journal *n* журна́л; (*diary*) дневни́к. **journalese** *n* газе́тный язы́к. **journalism** *n* журнали́стика. **journalist** *n* журнали́ст.

journey *n* путеше́ствие; *vi* путеше́ствовать *impf*.

jovial *adj* весёлый.

joy *n* ра́дость. **joyful, joyous** *adj* ра́достный. **joyless** *adj* безра́достный. **joystick** *n* рыча́г управле́ния; (*comput*) джо́йстик.

jubilant *adj* лику́ющий; **be** ~ ликова́ть *impf*. **jubilation** *n* ликова́ние.

jubilee *n* юбиле́й.

Judaism *n* иудаи́зм.

judge *n* судья́ *m*; (*connoisseur*) цени́тель *m*; *vt & i* суди́ть *impf*. **judgement** *n* (*legal decision*) реше́ние; (*opinion*) мне́ние; (*discernment*) рассуди́тельность.

judicial *adj* суде́бный. **judiciary** *n* судьи́ *m pl*. **judicious** *adj* здравомы́слящий.

judo *n* дзюдо́ *neut indecl*.

jug *n* кувши́н.

juggernaut *n* (*lorry*) многото́нный грузови́к; (*fig*) неумоли́мая си́ла.

juggle *vi* жонгли́ровать *impf*. **juggler** *n* жонглёр.

jugular *n* яре́мная ве́на.

juice *n* сок. **juicy** *adj* со́чный.

July *n* ию́ль *m*; *adj* ию́льский.

jumble *n* (*disorder*) беспоря́док; (*articles*) барахло́; *vt* перепу́тывать *impf*, перепу́тать *pf*.

jump *n* прыжо́к, скачо́к; *vi* пры́гать *impf*, пры́гнуть *pf*; скака́ть *impf*; (*from shock*) вздра́гивать *impf*, вздро́гнуть *pf*; *vt* (~ *over*) перепры́гивать *impf*, перепры́гнуть *pf*; ~ **at** (*offer*) ухва́тываться *impf*, ухвати́ться *pf* за+*acc*; ~ **up** вска́кивать *impf*, вскочи́ть *pf*.

jumper *n* дже́мпер.

jumpy *adj* не́рвный.

junction *n* (*rly*) у́зел; (*roads*) перекрёсток.

juncture *n*: **at this** ~ в э́тот моме́нт.

June *n* ию́нь *m*; *adj* ию́ньский.

jungle *n* джу́нгли (-лей) *pl*.

junior *adj* мла́дший; ~ **school** нача́льная шко́ла.

juniper *n* можжеве́льник.

junk *n* (*rubbish*) барахло́.

jurisdiction *n* юрисди́кция.

jurisprudence *n* юриспруде́нция.

juror *n* прися́жный *sb*. **jury** *n*

присяжные *sb*; (*in competition*) жюри *neut indecl.*

just *adj* (*fair*) справедливый; (*deserved*) заслуженный; *adv* (*exactly*) как раз, именно; (*simply*) просто; (*barely*) едва; (*very recently*) только что; ~ **in case** на всякий случай.

justice *n* (*proceedings*) правосудие; (*fairness*) справедливость; **do ~ to** отдавать *impf*, отдать *pf* должное *+dat.*

justify *vt* оправдывать *impf*, оправдать *pf*. **justification** *n* оправдание.

jut *vi* (~ *out*) выдаваться *impf*; выступать *impf*.

juvenile *n* & *adj* несовершеннолетний *sb* & *adj*.

juxtapose *vt* помещать *impf*, поместить *pf* рядом; (*for comparison*) сопоставлять *impf*, сопоставить *pf* (**with** с*+instr*).

K

kaleidoscope *n* калейдоскоп.

kangaroo *n* кенгуру *m indecl.*

Kazakhstan *n* Казахстан.

keel *n* киль *m*; *vi*: ~ **over** опрокидываться *impf*, опрокинуться *pf*.

keen *adj* (*enthusiastic*) полный энтузиазма; (*sharp*) острый; (*strong*) сильный; **be ~ on** увлекаться *impf*, увлечься *pf +instr*; (*want to do*) очень хотеть *impf +inf.*

keep[1] *n* (*tower*) главная башня; (*maintenance*) содержание.

keep[2] *vt* (*possess, maintain*) держать *impf*; хранить *impf*; (*observe*) соблюдать *impf*, соблюсти *pf* (*the law*); сдерживать *impf*, сдержать *pf* (*one's word*); (*family*) содержать *impf*; (*diary*) вести *impf*; (*detain*) задерживать *impf*, задержать *pf*; (*retain, reserve*) сохранять *impf*, сохранить *pf*; *vi* (*remain*) оставаться *impf*, остаться *pf*; (*of food*) не портиться *impf*; ~ **back** (*vt*) (*hold back*) удерживать *impf*, удержать *pf*; (*vi*) держаться *impf* сзади; ~ **doing sth** всё *+verb*: **she ~s giggling** она всё хихикает; ~ **from** удерживаться *impf*, удержаться *pf* от*+gen*; ~ **on** продолжать *impf*, продолжить *pf* (*+inf*); ~ **up (with)** (*vi*) не отставать *impf* (от*+gen*).

keepsake *n* подарок на память.

keg *n* бочонок.

kennel *n* конура.

kerb *n* край тротуара.

kernel *n* (*nut*) ядро; (*grain*) зерно; (*fig*) суть.

kerosene *n* керосин.

kettle *n* чайник.

key *n* ключ; (*piano, typewriter*) клавиш(а); (*mus*) тональность; *attrib* ведущий, ключевой. **keyboard** *n* клавиатура. **keyhole** *n* замочная скважина.

KGB *abbr* КГБ.

khaki *n* & *adj* хаки *neut, adj indecl.*

kick *n* удар ногой, пинок; *vt* ударять *impf*, ударить *pf* ногой; пинать *impf*, пнуть *pf*; *vi* (*of horse etc.*) лягаться *impf*. **kick-off** *n* начало (игры).

kid[1] *n* (*goat*) козлёнок; (*child*) малыш.

kid[2] *vt* (*deceive*) обманывать *impf*, обмануть *pf*; *vi* (*joke*) шутить *impf*, по~ *pf*.

kidnap *vt* похища́ть *impf*, похи́тить *pf*.
kidney *n* по́чка.
kill *vt* убива́ть *impf*, уби́ть *pf*. **killer** *n* уби́йца *m* & *f*. **killing** *n* уби́йство; *adj* (*murderous, fig*) уби́йственный; (*amusing*) умори́тельный.
kiln *n* о́бжиговая печь.
kilo *n* кило́ *neut indecl*. **kilohertz** *n* килоге́рц. **kilogram(me)** *n* килогра́мм. **kilometre** *n* киломе́тр. **kilowatt** *n* килова́тт.
kilt *n* шотла́ндская ю́бка.
kimono *n* кимоно́ *neut indecl*.
kin *n* (*family*) семья́; (*collect, relatives*) родня́.
kind[1] *n* сорт, род; **a ~ of** что́-то вро́де+*gen*; **this ~ of** тако́й; **what ~ of** что (э́то, он, *etc*.) за +*nom*; **~ of** (*adv*) как бу́дто, ка́к-то.
kind[2] *adj* до́брый.
kindergarten *n* де́тский сад.
kindle *vt* зажига́ть *impf*, заже́чь *pf*. **kindling** *n* расто́пка.
kindly *adj* до́брый; *adv* любе́зно; (*with imper*) (*request*) бу́дьте добры́, +*imper*. **kindness** *n* доброта́.
kindred *adj*: **~ spirit** родна́я душа́.
kinetic *adj* кинети́ческий.
king *n* коро́ль *m* (*also chess, cards, fig*); (*draughts*) да́мка. **kingdom** *n* короле́вство; (*fig*) ца́рство. **kingfisher** *n* зиморо́док.
kink *n* переги́б.
kinship *n* родство́; (*similarity*) схо́дство. **kinsman, -woman** *n* ро́дственник, -ица.
kiosk *n* кио́ск; (*telephone*) бу́дка.
kip *n* сон; *vi* дры́хнуть *impf*.
kipper *n* копчёная селёдка.
Kirghizia *n* Кирги́зия.
kiss *n* поцелу́й; *vt* & *i* целова́ть(ся) *impf*, по~ *pf*.
kit *n* (*clothing*) снаряже́ние; (*tools*) набо́р, компле́кт; *vt*: **~ out** снаряжа́ть *impf*, снаряди́ть *pf*. **kitbag** *n* вещево́й мешо́к.
kitchen *n* ку́хня; *attrib* ку́хонный; **~ garden** огоро́д.
kite *n* (*toy*) змей.
kitsch *n* дешёвка.
kitten *n* котёнок.
knack *n* сноро́вка.
knapsack *n* рюкза́к.
knead *vt* меси́ть *impf*, с~ *pf*.
knee *n* коле́но. **kneecap** *n* коле́нная ча́шка.
kneel *vi* стоя́ть *impf* на коле́нях; (**~** *down*) станови́ться *impf*, стать *pf* на коле́ни.
knickers *n pl* тру́сики (-ов) *pl*.
knick-knack *n* безделу́шка.
knife *n* нож; *vt* коло́ть *impf*, за~ *pf* ножо́м.
knight *n* (*hist*) ры́царь *m*; (*holder of order*) кавале́р; (*chess*) конь *m*. **knighthood** *n* ры́царское зва́ние.
knit *vt* (*garment*) вяза́ть *impf*, с~ *pf*; *vi* (*bones*) сраста́ться *impf*, срасти́сь *pf*; **~ one's brows** хму́рить *impf*, на~ *pf* бро́ви. **knitting** *n* (*action*) вяза́ние; (*object*) вяза́нье; **~-needle** спи́ца. **knitwear** *n* трикота́ж.
knob *n* ши́шка, кно́пка; (*door handle*) ру́чка. **knobb(l)y** *adj* шишкова́тый.
knock *n* (*noise*) стук; (*blow*) уда́р; *vt* & *i* (*strike*) ударя́ть *impf*, уда́рить *pf*; (*strike door etc*.) стуча́ть *impf*, по~ *pf* (**at** в+*acc*); **~ about** (*treat roughly*) колоти́ть *impf*, по~ *pf*;

(*wander*) шата́ться *impf*; ~ **down** (*person*) сбива́ть *impf*, сбить *pf* с ног; (*building*) сноси́ть *impf*, снести́ *pf*; ~ **off** сбива́ть *impf*, сбить *pf*; (*stop work*) шаба́шить *impf* (рабо́ту); (*deduct*) сбавля́ть *impf*, сба́вить *pf*; ~ **out** выбива́ть *impf*, вы́бить *pf*; (*sport*) нокаути́ровать *impf* & *pf*; ~**-out** нока́ут; ~ **over** опроки́дывать *impf*, опроки́нуть *impf*. **knocker** *n* дверно́й молото́к.

knoll *n* бугóр.

knot *n* ýзел; *vt* завя́зывать *impf*, завяза́ть *pf* узло́м. **knotty** *adj* (*fig*) запу́танный.

know *vt* знать *impf*; (~ *how to*) уме́ть *impf*, с~ *pf* +*inf*; ~**-how** уме́ние. **knowing** *adj* многозначи́тельный. **knowingly** *adv* созна́тельно. **knowledge** *n* зна́ние; **to my** ~ наско́лько мне изве́стно.

knuckle *n* суста́в па́льца; *vi*: ~ **down to** впряга́ться *impf*, впря́чься *pf* в+*acc*; ~ **under** уступа́ть *impf*, уступи́ть *pf* (**to** +*dat*).

Korea *n* Коре́я.

ko(w)tow *vi* (*fig*) раболе́пствовать *impf* (**to** пе́ред+*instr*).

Kremlin *n* Кремль *m*.

kudos *n* сла́ва.

L

label *n* этике́тка, ярлы́к; *vt* приклéивать *impf*, прикле́ить *pf* ярлы́к к+*dat*.

laboratory *n* лаборато́рия.

laborious *adj* кропотли́вый.

labour *n* труд; (*med*) ро́ды (-дов) *pl*; *attrib* трудово́й; ~ **force** рабо́чая си́ла; ~**-intensive** трудоёмкий; **L~ Party** лейбори́стская па́ртия; *vi* труди́ться *impf*; *vt*: ~ **a point** входи́ть *impf*, войти́ *pf* в изли́шние подро́бности. **laboured** *adj* затруднённый; (*style*) вы́мученный. **labourer** *n* чернорабо́чий *sb*. **labourite** *n* лейбори́ст.

labyrinth *n* лабири́нт.

lace *n* (*fabric*) кру́жево; (*cord*) шнуро́к; *vt* (~ *up*) шнурова́ть *impf*, за~ *pf*.

lacerate *vt* (*also fig*) терза́ть *impf*, ис~ *pf*. **laceration** *n* (*wound*) рва́ная ра́на.

lack *n* недоста́ток (**of** +*gen*, в+*prep*), отсу́тствие; *vt* & *i* не хвата́ть *impf*, хвати́ть *pf impers* +*dat* (*person*), +*gen* (*object*).

lackadaisical *adj* то́мный.

laconic *adj* лакони́чный.

lacquer *n* лак; *vt* лакирова́ть *impf*, от~ *pf*.

lad *n* па́рень *m*.

ladder *n* ле́стница.

laden *adj* нагружённый.

ladle *n* (*spoon*) поло́вник; *vt* че́рпать *impf*, черпну́ть *pf*.

lady *n* да́ма, ле́ди *f indecl*.

ladybird *n* бо́жья коро́вка.

lag[1] *vi*: ~ **behind** отстава́ть *impf*, отста́ть *pf* (от+*gen*).

lag[2] *vt* (*insulate*) изоли́ровать *impf* & *pf*.

lagoon *n* лагу́на.

lair *n* ло́говище.

laity *n* (*in religion*) миря́не (-н) *pl*.

lake *n* о́зеро.

lamb *n* ягнёнок; (*meat*) бара́нина.

lame *adj* хромо́й; **be** ~ хрома́ть *impf*; **go** ~ хроме́ть *impf*, о~ *pf*; *vt* кале́чить *impf*, о~ *pf*.

lament *n* плач; *vt* сожале́ть

impf о+*prep*. **lamentable** *adj* прискóрбный.
laminated *adj* слои́стый.
lamp *n* лáмпа; (*in street*) фонáрь *m*. **lamp-post** *n* фонáрный столб. **lampshade** *n* абажýр.
lance *n* пи́ка; *vt* (*med*) вскрывáть *impf*, вскрыть *pf* (ланцéтом).
land *n* земля́; (*dry* ~) сýша; (*country*) странá; *vi* (*naut*) причáливать *impf*, причáлить *pf*; *vt* & *i* (*aeron*) приземля́ть(ся) *impf*, приземли́ть(ся) *pf*; (*find o.s.*) попадáть *impf*, попáсть *pf*. **landing** *n* (*aeron*) посáдка; (*on stairs*) площáдка; **~-stage** при́стань. **landlady** *n* хозя́йка. **landlord** *n* хозя́ин. **landmark** *n* (*conspicuous object*) ориенти́р; (*fig*) вéха. **landowner** *n* землевладéлец. **landscape** *n* ландшáфт; (*also picture*) пейзáж. **landslide** *n* óползень *m*.
lane *n* (*in country*) дорóжка; (*street*) переýлок; (*passage*) прохóд; (*on road*) ряд; (*in race*) дорóжка.
language *n* язы́к; (*style, speech*) речь.
languid *adj* тóмный.
languish *vi* томи́ться *impf*.
languor *n* тóмность.
lank *adj* (*hair*) глáдкий. **lanky** *adj* долговя́зый.
lantern *n* фонáрь *m*.
lap[1] *n* (*of person*) колéни (-ней) *pl*; (*sport*) круг. **laptop** *n* (*comput*) портати́вный компьютер.
lap[2] *vt* (*drink*) лакáть *impf*, вы́~ *pf*; *vi* (*water*) плескáться *impf*.
lapel *n* отворóт.
lapse *n* (*mistake*) оши́бка; (*interval*) промежýток; (*expiry*) истечéние; *vi* впадáть *impf*, впасть *pf* (**into** в+*acc*); (*expire*) истекáть *impf*, истéчь *pf*.
lapwing *n* чи́бис.
larch *n* ли́ственница.
lard *n* свинóе сáло.
larder *n* кладовáя *sb*.
large *adj* большóй; *n*: **at** ~ (*free*) на свобóде; **by and** ~ вообщé говоря́. **largely** *adj* в значи́тельной стéпени.
largesse *n* щéдрость.
lark[1] *n* (*bird*) жáворонок.
lark[2] *n* прокáза; *vi* (~ *about*) резви́ться *impf*.
larva *n* личи́нка.
laryngitis *n* ларинги́т. **larynx** *n* гортáнь.
lascivious *adj* похотли́вый.
laser *n* лáзер.
lash *n* (*blow*) удáр плéтью; (*eyelash*) ресни́ца; *vt* (*beat*) хлестáть *impf*, хлестнýть *pf*; (*tie*) привя́зывать *impf*, привязáть *pf* (**to** к+*dat*).
last[1] *adj* (*final*) послéдний; (*most recent*) прóшлый; **the year** (*etc.*) **before** ~ позапрóшлый год (и т.д.); ~ **but one** предпослéдний; ~ **night** вчерá вéчером; **at** ~ наконéц; *adv* (*after all others*) пóсле всех; (*on the last occasion*) в послéдний раз; (*lastly*) наконéц.
last[2] *vi* (*go on*) продолжáться *impf*, продóлжиться *pf*; дли́ться *impf*, про~ *pf*; (*be preserved*) сохраня́ться *impf*, сохрани́ться *pf*; (*suffice*) хватáть *impf*, хвати́ть *pf*. **lasting** *adj* (*permanent*) постоя́нный; (*durable*) прóчный.
lastly *adv* в заключéние; наконéц.

latch *n* щеко́лда.
late *adj* по́здний; (*recent*) неда́вний; (*dead*) поко́йный; **be ~ for** опа́здывать *impf*, опозда́ть *pf* на+*acc*; *adv* по́здно. **lately** *adv* в после́днее вре́мя. **later** *adv* (*after vv*) по́зже; **a year ~** год спустя́; **see you ~!** пока́!
latent *adj* скры́тый.
lateral *adj* боково́й.
lath *n* ре́йка.
lathe *n* тока́рный стано́к.
lather *n* (мы́льная) пе́на; *vt* & *i* мы́лить(ся) *impf*, на~ *pf*.
Latin *adj* лати́нский; *n* лати́нский язы́к; **~-American** латиноамерика́нский.
latitude *n* свобо́да; (*geog*) широта́.
latter *adj* после́дний; **~-day** совреме́нный. **latterly** *adv* в после́днее вре́мя.
lattice *n* решётка.
Latvia *n* Ла́твия. **Latvian** *n* латви́ец, -и́йка; латы́ш, ~ка; *adj* латви́йский, латы́шский.
laud *vt* хвали́ть *impf*, по~ *pf*. **laudable** *adj* похва́льный.
laugh *n* смех; *vi* смея́ться *impf* (**at** над+*instr*); **~ it off** отшу́чиваться *impf*, отшути́ться *pf*; **~ing-stock** посме́шище. **laughable** *adj* смешно́й. **laughter** *n* смех.
launch[1] *vt* (*ship*) спуска́ть *impf*, спусти́ть *pf* на́ воду; (*rocket*) запуска́ть *impf*, запусти́ть *pf*; (*undertake*) начина́ть *impf*, нача́ть *pf*; *n* спуск на́ воду; за́пуск. **launcher** *n* (*for rocket*) пускова́я устано́вка. **launching pad** *n* пускова́я площа́дка.
launch[2] *n* (*naut*) ка́тер.
launder *vt* стира́ть *impf*, вы́~ *pf*. **laund(e)rette** *n* пра́чечная *sb* самообслу́живания.
laundry *n* (*place*) пра́чечная *sb*; (*articles*) бельё.
laurel *n* ла́вр(овое де́рево).
lava *n* ла́ва.
lavatory *n* убо́рная *sb*.
lavender *n* лава́нда.
lavish *adj* ще́дрый; (*abundant*) оби́льный; *vt* расточа́ть *impf* (**upon** +*dat*).
law *n* зако́н; (*system*) пра́во; **~ and order** правопоря́док. **law-court** *n* суд. **lawful** *adj* зако́нный. **lawless** *adj* беззако́нный.
lawn *n* газо́н; **~-mower** газонокоси́лка.
lawsuit *n* проце́сс.
lawyer *n* адвока́т, юри́ст.
lax *adj* сла́бый. **laxative** *n* слаби́тельное *sb*. **laxity** *n* сла́бость.
lay[1] *adj* (*non-clerical*) све́тский.
lay[2] *vt* (*place*) класть *impf*, положи́ть *pf*; (*cable, pipes*) прокла́дывать *impf*, проложи́ть *pf*; (*carpet*) стлать *impf*, по~ *pf*; (*trap etc.*) устра́ивать *impf*, устро́ить *pf*; (*eggs*) класть *impf*, положи́ть *pf*; *v abs* (*lay eggs*) нести́сь *impf*, с~ *pf*; **~ aside** откла́дывать *impf*, отложи́ть *pf*; **~ bare** раскрыва́ть *impf*, раскры́ть *pf*; **~ a bet** держа́ть *impf* пари́ (**on** на+*acc*); **~ down** (*relinquish*) отка́зываться *impf*, отказа́ться *pf* от+*gen*; (*rule etc.*) устана́вливать *impf*, установи́ть *pf*; **~ off** (*workmen*) увольня́ть *impf*, уво́лить *pf*; **~ out** (*spread*) выкла́дывать *impf*, вы́ложить *pf*; (*garden*) разбива́ть *impf*, разби́ть *pf*; **~ the table** накрыва́ть *impf*, накры́ть *pf* стол (**for** (*meal*)

к+*dat*); ~ **up** запаса́ть *impf*, запасти́ *pf* +*acc*, +*gen*; **be laid up** быть прико́ванным к посте́ли. **layabout** *n* безде́льник.

layer *n* слой, пласт.

layman *n* миря́нин; (*non-expert*) неспециали́ст.

laze *vi* безде́льничать *impf*. **laziness** *n* лень. **lazy** *adj* лени́вый; ~**-bones** лентя́й, ~ка.

lead[1] *n* (*example*) приме́р; (*leadership*) руково́дство; (*position*) пе́рвое ме́сто; (*theat*) гла́вная роль; (*electr*) про́вод; (*dog's*) поводо́к; *vt* води́ть *indet*, вести́ *det*; (*be in charge of*) руководи́ть *impf* +*instr*; (*induce*) побужда́ть *impf*, побуди́ть *pf*; *vt* & *i* (*cards*) ходи́ть *impf* (с+*gen*); *vi* (*sport*) занима́ть *impf*, заня́ть *pf* пе́рвое ме́сто; ~ **away** уводи́ть *impf*, увести́ *pf*; ~ **to** (*result in*) приводи́ть *impf*, привести́ *pf* к+*dat*.

lead[2] *n* (*metal*) свине́ц. **leaden** *adj* свинцо́вый.

leader *n* руководи́тель *m*, ~ница, ли́дер; (*mus*) пе́рвая скри́пка; (*editorial*) передова́я статья́. **leadership** *n* руково́дство.

leading *adj* веду́щий, выдаю́щийся; ~ **article** передова́я статья́.

leaf *n* лист; (*of table*) откидна́я доска́; *vi*: ~ **through** перели́стывать *impf*, перелиста́ть *pf*. **leaflet** *n* листо́вка.

league *n* ли́га; **in** ~ **with** в сою́зе с +*instr*.

leak *n* течь, уте́чка; *vi* (*escape*) течь *impf*; (*allow water to* ~) пропуска́ть *impf* во́ду; ~ **out** проса́чиваться *impf*, просочи́ться *pf*.

lean[1] *adj* (*thin*) худо́й; (*meat*) по́стный.

lean[2] *vt* & *i* прислоня́ть(ся) *impf*, прислони́ть(ся) *pf* (**against** к+*dat*); (*be inclined*) быть скло́нным (**to(wards)** к+*dat*); ~ **back** отки́дываться *impf*, отки́нуться *pf*; ~ **out of** высо́вываться *impf*, вы́сунуться *pf* в +*acc*. **leaning** *n* скло́нность.

leap *n* прыжо́к, скачо́к; *vi* пры́гать *impf*, пры́гнуть *pf*; скака́ть *impf*; ~ **year** високо́сный год.

learn *vt* (*a subject*) учи́ть *impf*, вы́~ *pf*; (*to do sth*) учи́ться *impf*, на~ *pf* +*inf*; (*find out*) узнава́ть *impf*, узна́ть *pf*. **learned** *adj* учёный. **learner** *n* учени́к, -и́ца. **learning** *n* (*studies*) уче́ние; (*erudition*) учёность.

lease *n* аре́нда; *vt* (*of owner*) сдава́ть *impf*, сдать *pf* в аре́нду; (*of tenant*) брать *impf*, взять *pf* в аре́нду. **leaseholder** *n* арендa̗тор.

leash *n* при́вязь.

least *adj* наиме́ньший, мале́йший; *adv* ме́нее всего́; **at** ~ по кра́йней ме́ре; **not in the** ~ ничу́ть.

leather *n* ко́жа; *attrib* ко́жаный.

leave[1] *n* (*permission*) разреше́ние; (*holiday*) о́тпуск; **on** ~ в о́тпуске; **take (one's)** ~ проща́ться *impf*, прости́ться *pf* (**of** с+*instr*).

leave[2] *vt* & *i* оставля́ть *impf*, оста́вить *pf*; (*abandon*) покида́ть *impf*, поки́нуть *pf*; (*go away*) уходи́ть *impf*, уйти́ *pf* (**from** от+*gen*); уезжа́ть *impf*, уе́хать *pf* (**from** от+*gen*);

(*go out of*) выходи́ть *impf*, вы́йти *pf* из+*gen*; (*entrust*) предоставля́ть *impf*, предоста́вить *pf* (**to** +*dat*); ~ **out** пропуска́ть *impf*, пропусти́ть *pf*.
lecherous *adj* развра́тный.
lectern *n* анало́й; (*in lecture room*) пюпи́тр.
lecture *n* (*discourse*) ле́кция; (*reproof*) нота́ция; *vi* (*deliver* ~(*s*)) чита́ть *impf*, про~ *pf* ле́кцию (-ии) (**on** по+*dat*); *vt* (*admonish*) чита́ть *impf*, про~ *pf* нота́цию+*dat*; ~ **room** аудито́рия. **lecturer** *n* ле́ктор; (*univ*) преподава́тель *m*, ~ница.
ledge *n* вы́ступ; (*shelf*) по́лочка.
ledger *n* гла́вная кни́га.
lee *n* защи́та; *adj* подве́тренный.
leech *n* (*worm*) пия́вка.
leek *n* лук-поре́й.
leer *vi* криви́ться *impf*, с~ *pf*.
leeward *n* подве́тренная сторона́; *adj* подве́тренный.
leeway *n* (*fig*) свобо́да де́йствий.
left *n* ле́вая сторона́; (**the L**~; *polit*) ле́вые *sb pl*; *adj* ле́вый; *adv* нале́во, сле́ва (**of** от+*gen*); ~**-hander** левша́ *m* & *f*; ~**-wing** ле́вый.
left-luggage office *n* ка́мера хране́ния.
leftovers *n pl* оста́тки *m pl*; (*food*) объе́дки (-ков) *pl*.
leg *n* нога́; (*of furniture etc.*) но́жка; (*of journey etc.*) эта́п.
legacy *n* насле́дство.
legal *adj* (*of the law*) правово́й; (*lawful*) лега́льный. **legality** *n* лега́льность. **legalize** *vt* легализи́ровать *impf* & *pf*.
legend *n* леге́нда. **legendary** *adj* легенда́рный.
leggings *n pl* вя́заные рейту́зы (-з) *pl*.
legible *adj* разбо́рчивый.
legion *n* легио́н.
legislate *vi* издава́ть *impf*, изда́ть *pf* зако́ны. **legislation** *n* законода́тельство. **legislative** *adj* законода́тельный.
legislator *n* законода́тель *m*.
legislature *n* законода́тельные учрежде́ния *neut pl*.
legitimacy *n* зако́нность; (*of child*) законнорождённость.
legitimate *adj* зако́нный; (*child*) законнорождённый.
legitimize *vt* узако́нивать *impf*, узако́нить *pf*.
leisure *n* свобо́дное вре́мя, досу́г; **at** ~ на досу́ге. **leisurely** *adj* нетороп́ливый.
lemon *n* лимо́н. **lemonade** *n* лимона́д.
lend *vt* дава́ть *impf*, дать *pf* взаймы́ (**to** +*dat*); ода́лживать *impf*, одолжи́ть *pf* (**to** +*dat*).
length *n* длина́; (*of time*) продолжи́тельность; (*of cloth*) отре́з; **at** ~ подро́бно. **lengthen** *vt* & *i* удлиня́ть(ся) *impf*, удлини́ть(ся) *pf*. **lengthways** *adv* в длину́, вдоль. **lengthy** *adj* дли́нный.
leniency *n* снисходи́тельность. **lenient** *adj* снисходи́тельный.
lens *n* ли́нза; (*phot*) объекти́в; (*anat*) хруста́лик.
Lent *n* вели́кий пост.
lentil *n* чечеви́ца.
Leo *n* Лев.
leopard *n* леопа́рд.
leotard *n* трико́ *neut indecl*.
leper *n* прокажённый *sb*. **leprosy** *n* прока́за.

lesbian *n* лесбиянка; *adj* лесбийский.
lesion *n* повреждение.
less *adj* меньший; *adv* меньше, менее; *prep* за вычетом *+gen*.
lessee *n* арендатор.
lessen *vt & i* уменьшать(ся) *impf*, уменьшить(ся) *pf*.
lesser *adj* меньший.
lesson *n* урок.
lest *conj* (*in order that not*) чтобы не; (*that*) как бы не.
let *n* (*lease*) сдача в наём; *vt* (*allow*) позволять *impf*, позволить *pf +dat*; разрешать *impf*, разрешить *pf +dat*; (*rent out*) сдавать *impf*, сдать *pf* внаём (**to** *+dat*); *v aux* (*imperative*) (*1st person*) давай(те); (*3rd person*) пусть; ~ **alone** не говоря уже о*+prep*; ~ **down** (*lower*) опускать *impf*, опустить *pf*; (*fail*) подводить *impf*, подвести *pf*; (*disappoint*) разочаровывать *impf*, разочаровать *pf*; ~ **go** выпускать *impf*, выпустить *pf*; **~'s go** пойдёмте!; пошли!; поехали!; ~ **in(to)** (*admit*) впускать *impf*, впустить *pf* в*+acc*; (*into secret*) посвящать *impf*, посвятить *pf* в*+acc*; ~ **know** давать *impf*, дать *pf* знать *+dat*; ~ **off** (*gun*) выстрелить *pf* из*+gen*; (*not punish*) отпускать *impf*, отпустить *pf* без наказания; ~ **out** (*release, loosen*) выпускать *impf*, выпустить *pf*; ~ **through** пропускать *impf*, пропустить *pf*; ~ **up** затихать *impf*, затихнуть *pf*.
lethal *adj* (*fatal*) смертельный; (*weapon*) смертоносный.
lethargic *adj* летаргический.
lethargy *n* летаргия.
letter *n* письмо; (*symbol*) буква; (*printing*) литера; **~-box** почтовый ящик. **lettering** *n* шрифт.
lettuce *n* салат.
leukaemia *n* лейкемия.
level *n* уровень; *adj* ровный; ~ **crossing** (железнодорожный) переезд; **~-headed** уравновешенный; *vt* (*make* ~) выравнивать *impf*, выровнять *pf*; (*sport*) сравнивать *impf*, сравнять *pf*; (*gun*) наводить *impf*, навести *pf* (**at** в, на, *+acc*); (*criticism*) направлять *impf*, направить *pf* (**at** против*+gen*).
lever *n* рычаг. **leverage** *n* действие рычага; (*influence*) влияние.
levity *n* легкомыслие.
levy *n* (*tax*) сбор; *vt* (*tax*) взимать *impf* (**from** с*+gen*).
lewd *adj* (*lascivious*) похотливый; (*indecent*) сальный.
lexicon *n* словарь *m*.
liability *n* (*responsibility*) ответственность (**for** за*+acc*); (*burden*) обуза. **liable** *adj* ответственный (**for** за*+acc*); (*susceptible*) подверженный (**to** *+dat*).
liaise *vi* поддерживать *impf* связь (с*+instr*). **liaison** *n* связь; (*affair*) любовная связь.
liar *n* лгун, ~ья.
libel *n* клевета; *vt* клеветать *impf*, на~ *pf* на*+acc*. **libellous** *adj* клеветнический.
liberal *n* либерал; *adj* либеральный; (*generous*) щедрый.
liberate *vt* освобождать *impf*, освободить *pf*. **liberation** *n* освобождение. **liberator** *n* освободитель *m*.
libertine *n* распутник.
liberty *n* свобода; **at** ~ на

свобо́де.

Libra *n* Весы́ (-со́в) *pl.*

librarian *n* библиоте́карь *m.* **library** *n* библиоте́ка.

libretto *n* либре́тто *neut indecl.*

licence[1] *n* (*permission, permit*) разреше́ние, лице́нзия; (*liberty*) (изли́шняя) во́льность. **license, -ce**[2] *vt* (*allow*) разреша́ть *impf*, разреши́ть *pf* +*dat*; дава́ть *impf*, дать *pf* пра́во +*dat*.

licentious *adj* распу́щенный.

lichen *n* лиша́йник.

lick *n* лиза́ние; *vt* лиза́ть *impf*, лизну́ть *pf*.

lid *n* кры́шка; (*eyelid*) ве́ко.

lie[1] *n* (*untruth*) ложь; *vi* лгать *impf*, со~ *pf*.

lie[2] *n*: ~ **of the land** (*fig*) положе́ние веще́й; *vi* лежа́ть *impf*; (*be situated*) находи́ться *impf*; ~ **down** ложи́ться *impf*, лечь *pf*; ~ **in** остава́ться *impf* в посте́ли.

lieu *n*: **in ~ of** вме́сто+*gen*.

lieutenant *n* лейтена́нт.

life *n* жизнь; (*way of* ~) о́браз жи́зни; (*energy*) живость. **lifebelt** *n* спаса́тельный по́яс. **lifeboat** *n* спаса́тельная ло́дка. **lifebuoy** *n* спаса́тельный круг. **lifeguard** *n* спаса́тель *m*, -ница. **life-jacket** *n* спаса́тельный жиле́т. **lifeless** *adj* безжи́зненный. **lifelike** *adj* реалисти́чный. **lifeline** *n* спаса́тельный коне́ц. **lifelong** *adj* пожи́зненный. **life-size(d)** *adj* в натура́льную величину́. **lifetime** *n* жизнь.

lift *n* (*machine*) лифт, подъёмник; (*force*) подъёмная си́ла; **give s.o. a ~** подвози́ть *impf*, подвезти́ *pf*; *vt* & *i* поднима́ть(ся) *impf*, подня́ть(ся) *pf*.

ligament *n* свя́зка.

light[1] *n* свет, освеще́ние; (*source of* ~) ого́нь *m*, ла́мпа, фона́рь *m*; *pl* (*traffic* ~) светофо́р; **can I have a ~?** мо́жно прикури́ть?; **~-bulb** ла́мпочка; *adj* (*bright*) све́тлый; (*pale*) бле́дный; *vt* & *i* (*ignite*) зажига́ть(ся) *impf*, заже́чь(ся) *pf*; *vt* (*illuminate*) освеща́ть *impf*, освети́ть *pf*; **~ up** освеща́ть(ся) *impf*, освети́ть(ся) *pf*; (*begin to smoke*) закури́ть *pf*.

light[2] *adj* (*not heavy*) лёгкий; **~-hearted** беззабо́тный.

lighten[1] *vt* (*make lighter*) облегча́ть *impf*, облегчи́ть *pf*; (*mitigate*) смягча́ть *impf*, смягчи́ть *pf*.

lighten[2] *vt* (*illuminate*) освеща́ть *impf*, освети́ть *pf*; *vi* (*grow bright*) светле́ть *impf*, по~ *pf*.

lighter *n* зажига́лка.

lighthouse *n* мая́к.

lighting *n* освеще́ние.

lightning *n* мо́лния.

lightweight *n* (*sport*) легкове́с; *adj* легкове́сный.

like[1] *adj* (*similar*) похо́жий (на+*acc*); **what is he ~?** что он за челове́к?

like[2] *vt* нра́виться *impf*, по~ *pf impers+dat*: **I ~ him** он мне нра́вится; люби́ть *impf*; *vi* (*wish*) хоте́ть *impf*; **if you ~** е́сли хоти́те; **I should ~** я хоте́л бы; мне хоте́лось бы. **likeable** *adj* симпати́чный.

likelihood *n* вероя́тность. **likely** *adj* (*probable*) вероя́тный; (*suitable*) подходя́щий.

liken *vt* уподобля́ть *impf*, уподо́бить *pf* (**to** +*dat*).

likeness *n* (*resemblance*) схо́дство; (*portrait*) портре́т.

likewise *adv* (*similarly*) подо́бно; (*also*) то́же, та́кже.
liking *n* вкус (**for** к+*dat*).
lilac *n* сире́нь; *adj* сире́невый.
lily *n* ли́лия; ~ **of the valley** ла́ндыш.
limb *n* член.
limber *vi*: ~ **up** размина́ться *impf*, размя́ться *pf*.
limbo *n* (*fig*) состоя́ние неопределённости.
lime[1] *n* (*mineralogy*) и́звесть. **limelight** *n*: **in the** ~ (*fig*) в це́нтре внима́ния. **limestone** *n* известня́к.
lime[2] *n* (*fruit*) лайм.
lime[3] *n* (~-*tree*) ли́па.
limit *n* грани́ца, преде́л; *vt* ограни́чивать *impf*, ограни́чить *pf*. **limitation** *n* ограниче́ние. **limitless** *adj* безграни́чный.
limousine *n* лимузи́н.
limp[1] *n* хромота́; *vi* хрома́ть *impf*.
limp[2] *adj* мя́гкий; (*fig*) вя́лый.
limpid *adj* прозра́чный.
linchpin *n* чека́.
line[1] *n* (*long mark*) ли́ния, черта́; (*transport, tel*) ли́ния; (*cord*) верёвка; (*wrinkle*) морщи́на; (*limit*) грани́ца; (*row*) ряд; (*of words*) строка́; (*of verse*) стих; *vt* (*paper*) линова́ть *impf*, раз~ *pf*; *vt* & *i* (~ *up*) выстра́ивать(ся) *impf*, вы́строить(ся) *pf* в ряд.
line[2] *vt* (*clothes*) класть *impf*, положи́ть *pf* на подкла́дку.
lineage *n* происхожде́ние.
linear *adj* лине́йный.
lined[1] *adj* (*paper*) лино́ванный; (*face*) морщи́нистый.
lined[2] *adj* (*garment*) на подкла́дке.
linen *n* полотно́; *collect* бельё.
liner *n* ла́йнер.
linesman *n* боково́й судья́ *m*.
linger *vi* задéрживаться *impf*, задержа́ться *pf*.
lingerie *n* да́мское бельё.
lingering *adj* (*illness*) затяжно́й.
lingo *n* жарго́н.
linguist *n* лингви́ст. **linguistic** *adj* лингвисти́ческий. **linguistics** *n* лингви́стика.
lining *n* (*clothing etc.*) подкла́дка; (*tech*) облицо́вка.
link *n* (*of chain*) звено́; (*connection*) связь; *vt* соединя́ть *impf*, соедини́ть *pf*; свя́зывать *impf*, связа́ть *pf*.
lino(leum) *n* лино́леум.
lintel *n* перемы́чка.
lion *n* лев. **lioness** *n* льви́ца.
lip *n* губа́; (*of vessel*) край. **lipstick** *n* губна́я пома́да.
liquefy *vt* & *i* превраща́ть(ся) *impf*, преврати́ть(ся) *pf* в жи́дкое состоя́ние.
liqueur *n* ликёр.
liquid *n* жи́дкость; *adj* жи́дкий.
liquidate *vt* ликвиди́ровать *impf* & *pf*. **liquidation** *n* ликвида́ция; **go into** ~ ликвиди́роваться *impf* & *pf*.
liquor *n* (спиртно́й) напи́ток.
liquorice *n* лакри́ца.
list[1] *n* спи́сок; *vt* составля́ть *impf*, соста́вить *pf* спи́сок +*gen*; (*enumerate*) перечисля́ть *impf*, перечи́слить *pf*.
list[2] *vi* (*naut*) накреня́ться *impf*, крени́ться *impf*, накрени́ться *pf*.
listen *vi* слу́шать *impf*, по~ *pf* (**to** +*acc*). **listener** *n* слу́шатель *m*.
listless *adj* апати́чный.
litany *n* лита́ния.
literacy *n* гра́мотность.
literal *adj* буква́льный.

literary *adj* литерату́рный.
literate *adj* гра́мотный.
literature *n* литерату́ра.
lithe *adj* ги́бкий.
lithograph *n* литогра́фия.
Lithuania *n* Литва́. **Lithuanian** *n* лито́вец, -вка; *adj* лито́вский.
litigation *n* тя́жба.
litre *n* литр.
litter *n* (*rubbish*) сор; (*brood*) помёт; *vt* (*make untidy*) сори́ть *impf*, на~ *pf* (**with** *+instr*).
little *n* немно́гое; **~ by ~** ма́ло-пома́лу; **a ~** немно́го *+gen*; *adj* ма́ленький, небольшо́й; (*in height*) небольшо́го ро́ста; (*in distance, time*) коро́ткий; *adv* ма́ло, немно́го.
liturgy *n* литурги́я.
live[1] *adj* живо́й; (*coals*) горя́щий; (*mil*) боево́й; (*electr*) под напряже́нием; (*broadcast*) прямо́й.
live[2] *vi* жить *impf*; **~ down** загла́живать *impf*, загла́дить *pf*; **~ on** (*feed on*) пита́ться *impf +instr*; **~ through** пережива́ть *impf*, пережи́ть *pf*; **~ until, to see** дожива́ть *impf*, дожи́ть *pf* до*+gen*; **~ up to** жить *impf* согла́сно *+dat*.
livelihood *n* сре́дства *neut pl* к жи́зни.
lively *adj* живо́й.
liven (up) *vt & i* оживля́ть(ся) *impf*, оживи́ть(ся) *pf*.
liver *n* пе́чень; (*cul*) печёнка.
livery *n* ливре́я.
livestock *n* скот.
livid *adj* (*angry*) взбешённый.
living *n* сре́дства *neut pl* к жи́зни; **earn a ~** зараба́тывать *impf*, зарабо́тать *pf* на жизнь; *adj* живо́й; **~-room** гости́ная *sb*.
lizard *n* я́щерица.
load *n* груз; (*also fig*) бре́мя *neut*; (*electr*) нагру́зка; *pl* (*lots*) ку́ча; *vt* (*goods*) грузи́ть *impf*, по~ *pf*; (*vehicle*) грузи́ть *impf*, на~ *pf*; (*fig*) обременя́ть *impf*, обремени́ть *pf*; (*gun, camera*) заряжа́ть *impf*, заряди́ть *pf*.
loaf[1] *n* буха́нка.
loaf[2] *vi* безде́льничать *impf*.
loafer *n* безде́льник.
loan *n* заём; *vt* дава́ть *impf*, дать *pf* взаймы́.
loath, loth *predic*: **be ~ to** не хоте́ть *impf +inf*.
loathe *vt* ненави́деть *impf*.
loathing *n* отвраще́ние.
loathsome *adj* отврати́тельный.
lob *vt* высоко́ подбра́сывать *impf*, подбро́сить *pf*.
lobby *n* вестибю́ль *m*; (*parl*) кулуа́ры (-ров) *pl*.
lobe *n* (*of ear*) мо́чка.
lobster *n* ома́р.
local *adj* ме́стный.
locality *n* ме́стность.
localized *adj* локализо́ванный.
locate *vt* (*place*) помеща́ть *impf*, помести́ть *pf*; (*find*) находи́ть *impf*, найти́ *pf*; **be ~d** находи́ться *impf*.
location *n* (*position*) местонахожде́ние; **on ~** (*cin*) на нату́ре.
locative *adj* (*n*) ме́стный (паде́ж).
lock[1] *n* (*of hair*) ло́кон; *pl* во́лосы (-о́с, -оса́м) *pl*.
lock[2] *n* замо́к; (*canal*) шлюз; *vt & i* запира́ть(ся) *impf*, запере́ть(ся) *pf*; **~ out** не впуска́ть *impf*; **~ up** (*imprison*) сажа́ть *impf*, посади́ть *pf*; (*close*) закрыва́ть(ся) *impf*, закры́ть(ся) *pf*.

locker *n* шка́фчик.
locket *n* медальо́н.
locksmith *n* сле́сарь *m*.
locomotion *n* передвиже́ние. **locomotive** *n* локомоти́в.
lodge *n* (*hunting*) (охо́тничий) до́мик; (*porter's*) сторо́жка; (*Masonic*) ло́жа; *vt* (*complaint*) подава́ть *impf*, пода́ть *pf*; *vi* (*reside*) жить *impf* (**with** у+*gen*); (*stick*) заса́живать *impf*, засе́сть *pf*. **lodger** *n* жиле́ц, жили́ца. **lodging** *n* (*also pl*) кварти́ра, (снима́емая) ко́мната.
loft *n* (*attic*) черда́к.
lofty *adj* о́чень высо́кий; (*elevated*) возвы́шенный.
log *n* бревно́; (*for fire*) поле́но; **~-book** (*naut*) ва́хтенный журна́л; *v.i.*: **~ on** (*comput*) входи́ть *impf*, войти́ *pf* в систе́му; **~ off** (*comput*) выходи́ть *impf*, вы́йти *pf* из систе́мы.
logarithm *n* логари́фм.
loggerhead *n*: **be at ~s** быть в ссо́ре.
logic *n* ло́гика. **logical** *adj* (*of logic*) логи́ческий; (*consistent*) логи́чный.
logistics *n pl* (*fig*) пробле́мы *f pl* организа́ции.
logo *n* эмбле́ма.
loin *n* (*pl*) поясни́ца; (*cul*) филе́йная часть.
loiter *vi* слоня́ться *impf*.
lone, **lonely** *adj* одино́кий. **loneliness** *n* одино́чество.
long[1] *vi* (*want*) стра́стно жела́ть *impf*, по~ *pf* (**for** +*gen*); (*miss*) тоскова́ть *impf* (**for** по+*dat*).
long[2] *adj* (*space*) дли́нный; (*time*) до́лгий; (*in measurements*) длино́й в+*acc*; **in the ~ run** в коне́чном счёте; **~-sighted** дальнозо́ркий; **~-suffering** долготерпели́вый; **~-term** долгосро́чный; **~-winded** многоречи́вый; *adv* до́лго; **~ ago** (уже́) давно́; **as ~ as** пока́; **~ before** задо́лго до+*gen*.
longevity *n* долгове́чность.
longing *n* стра́стное жела́ние (**for** +*gen*); тоска́ (**for** по+*dat*); *adj* тоску́ющий.
longitude *n* долгота́.
longways *adv* в длину́.
look *n* (*glance*) взгляд; (*appearance*) вид; (*expression*) выраже́ние; *vi* смотре́ть *impf*, по~ *pf* (**at** на, в, +*acc*); (*appear*) вы́глядеть *impf* +*instr*; (*face*) выходи́ть *impf* (**towards, onto** на+*acc*); **~ about** осма́триваться *impf*, осмотре́ться *pf*; **~ after** (*attend to*) присма́тривать *impf*, присмотре́ть *pf* за+*instr*; **~ down on** презира́ть *impf*; **~ for** иска́ть *impf* +*acc*, +*gen*; **~ forward to** предвкуша́ть *impf*, предвкуси́ть *pf*; **~ in on** загля́дывать *impf*, загляну́ть *pf* к+*dat*; **~ into** (*investigate*) рассма́тривать *impf*, рассмотре́ть *pf*; **~ like** быть похо́жим на+*acc*; **it ~s like rain** похо́же на (то, что бу́дет) дождь; **~ on** (*regard*) счита́ть *impf*, счесть *pf* (**as** +*instr*, за+*instr*); **~ out** выгля́дывать *impf*, вы́глянуть *pf* (в окно́); быть настороже́; *imper* осторо́жно!; **~ over, through** просма́тривать *impf*, просмотре́ть *pf*; **~ round** (*inspect*) осма́тривать *impf*, осмотре́ть *pf*; **~ up** (*raise eyes*) поднима́ть *impf*, подня́ть *pf* глаза́; (*in dictionary etc.*) иска́ть *impf*; (*improve*) улучша́ться *impf*,

улу́чшиться *pf*; ~ **up to** уважа́ть *impf*.

loom[1] *n* тка́цкий стано́к.

loom[2] *vi* вырисо́вываться *impf*, вы́рисоваться; (*fig*) надвига́ться *impf*.

loop *n* пе́тля; *vi* образо́вывать *impf*, образова́ть *pf* пе́тлю; (*fasten with loop*) закрепля́ть *impf*, закрепи́ть *pf* пе́тлей; (*wind*) обма́тывать *impf*, обмота́ть *pf* (**around** вокру́г+*gen*).

loophole *n* бойни́ца; (*fig*) лазе́йка.

loose *adj* (*free*; *not tight*) свобо́дный; (*not fixed*) неприкреплённый; (*connection*, *screw*) сла́бый; (*lax*) распу́щенный; **at a ~ end** без де́ла. **loosen** *vt* & *i* ослабля́ть(ся) *impf*, осла́бить(ся) *pf*.

loot *n* добы́ча; *vt* гра́бить *impf*, о~ *pf*.

lop *vt* (*tree*) подреза́ть *impf*, подре́зать *pf*; (~ *off*) отруба́ть *impf*, отруби́ть *pf*.

lope *vi* бе́гать *indet*, бежа́ть *det* вприпры́жку.

lopsided *adj* кривобо́кий.

loquacious *adj* болтли́вый.

lord *n* (*master*) господи́н; (*eccl*) Госпо́дь; (*peer*; *title*) лорд; *vt*: ~ **it over** помыка́ть *impf* +*instr*. **lordship** *n* (*title*) све́тлость.

lore *n* зна́ния *neut pl*.

lorry *n* грузови́к.

lose *vt* теря́ть *impf*, по~ *pf*; *vt* & *i* (*game etc.*) прои́грывать *impf*, проигра́ть *pf*; *vi* (*clock*) отстава́ть *impf*, отста́ть *pf*. **loss** *n* поте́ря; (*monetary*) убы́ток; (*in game*) про́игрыш.

lot *n* жре́бий; (*destiny*) у́часть; (*of goods*) па́ртия; **a ~, ~s** мно́го; **the ~** всё, все *pl*.

loth *see* **loath**

lotion *n* лосьо́н.

lottery *n* лотере́я.

loud *adj* (*sound*) гро́мкий; (*noisy*) шу́мный; (*colour*) крича́щий; **out ~** вслух. **loudspeaker** *n* громкоговори́тель *m*.

lounge *n* гости́ная *sb*; *vi* сиде́ть *impf* развaля́сь; (*idle*) безде́льничать *impf*.

louse *n* вошь. **lousy** *adj* (*coll*) парши́вый.

lout *n* балбе́с, у́валень *m*.

lovable *adj* ми́лый. **love** *n* любо́вь (**of, for** к+*dat*); **in ~ with** влюблённый в+*acc*; *vt* люби́ть *impf*. **lovely** *adj* прекра́сный; (*delightful*) преле́стный. **lover** *n* любо́вник, -ица.

low *adj* ни́зкий, невысо́кий; (*quiet*) ти́хий.

lower[1] *vt* опуска́ть *impf*, опусти́ть *pf*; (*price*, *voice*, *standard*) понижа́ть *impf*, пони́зить *pf*.

lower[2] *adj* ни́жний.

lowland *n* ни́зменность.

lowly *adj* скро́мный.

loyal *adj* ве́рный. **loyalty** *n* ве́рность.

LP *abbr* (*of* **long-playing record**) долгоигра́ющая пласти́нка.

Ltd. *abbr* (*of* **Limited**) с ограни́ченной отве́тственностью.

lubricant *n* сма́зка. **lubricate** *vt* сма́зывать *impf*, сма́зать *pf*. **lubrication** *n* сма́зка.

lucid *adj* я́сный. **lucidity** *n* я́сность.

luck *n* (*chance*) слу́чай; (*good ~*) сча́стье, уда́ча; (*bad ~*) неуда́ча. **luckily** *adv* к сча́стью. **lucky** *adj* счастли́вый; **be ~** везти́ *imp*, по~ *pf impers* +*dat*: **I was ~** мне повезло́.

lucrative *adj* прибыльный.
ludicrous *adj* смехотворный.
lug *vt* (*drag*) таскать *indet*, тащить *det*.
luggage *n* багаж.
lugubrious *adj* печальный.
lukewarm *adj* тепловатый; (*fig*) прохладный.
lull *n* (*in storm*) затишье; (*interval*) перерыв; *vt* (*to sleep*) убаюкивать *impf*, убаюкать *pf*; (*suspicions*) усыплять *impf*, усыпить *pf*.
lullaby *n* колыбельная песня.
lumbar *adj* поясничный.
lumber[1] *vi* (*move*) брести *impf*.
lumber[2] *n* (*domestic*) рухлядь; *vt* обременять *impf*, обременить *pf*. **lumberjack** *n* лесоруб.
luminary *n* светило.
luminous *adj* светящийся.
lump *n* ком; (*swelling*) опухоль; *vt*: ~ **together** смешивать *impf*, смешать *pf* (в одно).
lunacy *n* безумие.
lunar *adj* лунный.
lunatic *adj* (*n*) сумасшедший (*sb*).
lunch *n* обед; **~-hour, ~-time** обеденный перерыв; *vi* обедать *impf*, по~ *pf*.
lung *n* лёгкое *sb*.
lunge *vi* делать *impf*, с~ *pf* выпад (**at** против+*gen*).
lurch[1] *n*: **leave in the ~** покидать *impf*, покинуть *pf* в беде.
lurch[2] *vi* (*stagger*) ходить *indet*, идти *det* шатаясь.
lure *n* приманка; *vt* приманивать *impf*, приманить *pf*.
lurid *adj* (*gaudy*) кричащий; (*details*) жуткий.
lurk *vi* затаиваться *impf*, затаиться *pf*.
luscious *adj* сочный.
lush *adj* пышный, сочный.
lust *n* похоть (**of, for** к+*dat*); *vi* страстно желать *impf*, по~ *pf* (**for** +*gen*). **lustful** *adj* похотливый.
lustre *n* глянец. **lustrous** *adj* глянцевитый.
lusty *adj* (*healthy*) здоровый; (*lively*) живой.
lute *n* (*mus*) лютня.
luxuriant *adj* пышный.
luxuriate *vi* наслаждаться *impf*, насладиться *pf* (**in** +*instr*).
luxurious *adj* роскошный.
luxury *n* роскошь.
lymph *attrib* лимфатический.
lynch *vt* линчевать *impf* & *pf*.
lyric *n* лирика; *pl* слова *neut pl* песни. **lyrical** *adj* лирический.

M

MA *abbr* (*of* **Master of Arts**) магистр гуманитарных наук.
macabre *adj* жуткий.
macaroni *n* макароны (-н) *pl*.
mace *n* (*of office*) жезл.
machination *n* махинация.
machine *n* машина; (*state* ~) аппарат; *attrib* машинный; **~-gun** пулемёт; ~ **tool** станок; *vt* обрабатывать *impf*, обработать *pf* на станке; (*sew*) шить *impf*, с~ *pf* (на машине). **machinery** *n* (*machines*) машины *f pl*; (*of state*) аппарат. **machinist** *n* машинист; (*sewing*) швейник, -ица, швея.
mackerel *n* скумбрия, макрель.
mackintosh *n* плащ.
mad *adj* сумасшедший. **mad-**

den *vt* бесить *impf*, вз~ *pf*. **madhouse** *n* сумасше́дший дом. **madly** *adv* безу́мно. **madman** *n* сумасше́дший *sb*. **madness** *n* сумасше́ствие. **madwoman** *n* сумасше́дшая *sb*.

madrigal *n* мадрига́л.

maestro *n* маэ́стро *m indecl*.

Mafia *n* ма́фия.

magazine *n* журна́л; (*of gun*) магази́н.

maggot *n* личи́нка.

magic *n* ма́гия, волшебство́; *adj* (*also* **magical**) волше́бный. **magician** *n* волше́бник; (*conjurer*) фо́кусник.

magisterial *adj* авторите́тный.

magistrate *n* судья́ *m*.

magnanimity *n* великоду́шие. **magnanimous** *adj* великоду́шный.

magnate *n* магна́т.

magnesium *n* ма́гний.

magnet *n* магни́т. **magnetic** *adj* магни́тный; (*attractive*) притяга́тельный. **magnetism** *n* магнети́зм; притяга́тельность. **magnetize** *vt* намагни́чивать *impf*, намагни́тить *pf*.

magnification *n* увеличе́ние.

magnificence *n* великоле́пие. **magnificent** *adj* великоле́пный.

magnify *vt* увели́чивать *impf*, увели́чить *pf*; (*exaggerate*) преувели́чивать *impf*, преувели́чить *pf*. **magnifying glass** *n* увеличи́тельное стекло́.

magnitude *n* величина́; (*importance*) ва́жность.

magpie *n* соро́ка.

mahogany *n* кра́сное де́рево.

maid *n* прислу́га. **maiden** *adj* (*aunt etc.*) незаму́жняя; (*first*) пе́рвый; ~ **name** де́ви́чья фами́лия.

mail *n* (*letters*) по́чта; ~ **order** почто́вый зака́з; *vt* посыла́ть *impf*, посла́ть *pf* по по́чте.

maim *vt* кале́чить *impf*, ис~ *pf*.

main *n* (*gas* ~; *pl*) магистра́ль; **in the** ~ в основно́м; *adj* основно́й, гла́вный; (*road*) магистра́льный. **mainland** *n* матери́к. **mainly** *adv* в основно́м. **mainstay** *n* (*fig*) гла́вная опо́ра.

maintain *vt* (*keep up*) подде́рживать *impf*, поддержа́ть *pf*; (*family*) содержа́ть *impf*; (*machine*) обслу́живать *impf*, обслужи́ть *pf*; (*assert*) утвержда́ть *impf*. **maintenance** *n* подде́ржка; содержа́ние; обслу́живание.

maize *n* кукуру́за.

majestic *adj* вели́чественный. **majesty** *n* вели́чественность; (*title*) вели́чество.

major[1] *n* (*mil*) майо́р.

major[2] *adj* (*greater*) бо́льший; (*more important*) бо́лее ва́жный; (*main*) гла́вный; (*mus*) мажо́рный; *n* (*mus*) мажо́р. **majority** *n* большинство́; (*full age*) совершенноле́тие.

make *vt* де́лать *impf*, с~ *pf*; (*produce*) производи́ть *impf*, произвести́ *pf*; (*prepare*) гото́вить *impf*, при~ *pf*; (*amount to*) равня́ться *impf* +*dat*; (*earn*) зараба́тывать *impf*, зарабо́тать *pf*; (*compel*) заставля́ть *impf*, заста́вить *pf*; (*reach*) добира́ться *impf*, добра́ться *pf* до+*gen*; (*be in time for*) успева́ть *impf*, успе́ть *pf* на+*acc*; **be made of** состоя́ть *impf* из+*gen*;

~ as if, though де́лать *impf*, с~ *pf* вид, что; **~ a bed** стели́ть *impf*, по~ *pf* посте́ль; **~ believe** притворя́ться *impf*, притвори́ться *pf*; **~-believe** притво́рство; **~ do with** дово́льствоваться *impf*, у~ *pf* +*instr*; **~ off** удира́ть *impf*, удра́ть *pf*; **~ out** (*cheque*) выпи́сывать *impf*, вы́писать *pf*; (*assert*) утвержда́ть *impf*, утверди́ть *pf*; (*understand*) разбира́ть *impf*, разобра́ть *pf*; **~ over** передава́ть *impf*, переда́ть *pf*; **~ up** (*form, compose, complete*) составля́ть *impf*, соста́вить *pf*; (*invent*) выду́мывать *impf*, вы́думать *pf*; (*theat*) гримирова́ть(ся) *impf*, за~ *pf*; **~-up** (*theat*) грим; (*cosmetics*) косме́тика; (*composition*) соста́в; **~ it up** мири́ться *impf*, по~ *pf* (**with** с+*instr*); **~ up for** возмеща́ть *impf*, возмести́ть *pf*; **~ up one's mind** реша́ться *impf*, реши́ться *pf*. **make** *n* ма́рка. **makeshift** *adj* вре́менный.

malady *n* боле́знь.

malaise *n* (*fig*) беспоко́йство.

malaria *n* маляри́я.

male *n* (*animal*) саме́ц; (*person*) мужчи́на *m*; *adj* мужско́й.

malevolence *n* недоброжела́тельность. **malevolent** *adj* недоброжела́тельный.

malice *n* зло́ба. **malicious** *adj* зло́бный.

malign *vt* клевета́ть *impf*, на~ *pf* на+*acc*. **malignant** *adj* (*harmful*) зловре́дный; (*malicious*) зло́бный; (*med*) злока́чественный.

malinger *vi* притворя́ться *impf*, притвори́ться *pf* больны́м.

malingerer *n* симуля́нт.

mallard *n* кря́ква.

malleable *adj* ко́вкий; (*fig*) пода́тливый.

mallet *n* (деревя́нный) молото́к.

malnutrition *n* недоеда́ние.

malpractice *n* престу́пная небре́жность.

malt *n* со́лод.

maltreat *vt* пло́хо обраща́ться *impf* с+*instr*.

mammal *n* млекопита́ющее *sb*.

mammoth *adj* грома́дный.

man *n* (*human, person*) челове́к; (*human race*) челове́чество; (*male*) мужчи́на *m*; (*labourer*) рабо́чий *sb*; *pl* (*soldiers*) солда́ты *m pl*; *vt* (*furnish with men*) укомплекто́вывать *impf*, укомплектова́ть *pf* ли́чным соста́вом; ста́вить *impf*, по~ *pf* люде́й к+*dat*; (*stall etc.*) обслу́живать *impf*, обслужи́ть *pf*; (*gate, checkpoint*) стоя́ть *impf* на+*prep*.

manacle *n* нару́чник; *vt* надева́ть *impf*, наде́ть *pf* нару́чники на+*acc*.

manage *vt* (*control*) управля́ть *impf* +*instr*; *vi*(&*t*) (*cope*) справля́ться *impf*, спра́виться *pf* (с+*instr*); (*succeed*) суме́ть *pf*. **management** *n* управле́ние (**of** +*instr*); (*the* ~) администра́ция. **manager** *n* управля́ющий *sb* (**of** +*instr*); ме́неджер. **managerial** *adj* администрати́вный. **managing director** *n* дире́ктор-распоряди́тель *m*.

mandarin *n* мандари́н.

mandate *n* манда́т. **mandated** *adj* подманда́тный. **mandatory** *adj* обяза́тельный.

mane *n* грива.
manful *adj* мужественный.
manganese *n* марганец.
manger *n* ясли (-лей) *pl*; **dog in the ~** собака на сене.
mangle *vt* (*mutilate*) калечить *impf*, ис~ *pf*.
mango *n* манго *neut indecl*.
manhandle *vt* грубо обращаться *impf* с+*instr*.
manhole *n* смотровой колодец.
manhood *n* возмужалость.
mania *n* мания. **maniac** *n* маньяк, -ячка. **manic** *adj* маниакальный.
manicure *n* маникюр; *vt* делать *impf*, с~ *pf* маникюр +*dat*. **manicurist** *n* маникюрша.
manifest *adj* очевидный; *vt* (*display*) проявлять *impf*, проявить *pf*; *n* манифест. **manifestation** *n* проявление. **manifesto** *n* манифест.
manifold *adj* разнообразный.
manipulate *vt* манипулировать *impf* +*instr*. **manipulation** *n* манипуляция.
manly *adj* мужественный.
mankind *n* человечество.
manner *n* (*way*) образ; (*behaviour*) манера; *pl* манеры *f pl*. **mannerism** *n* манера.
mannish *adj* мужеподобный.
manoeuvrable *adj* манёвренный. **manoeuvre** *n* манёвр; *vt & i* маневрировать *impf*.
manor *n* поместье; (*house*) помещичий дом.
manpower *n* человеческие ресурсы *m pl*.
manservant *n* слуга *m*.
mansion *n* особняк.
manslaughter *n* непредумышленное убийство.
mantelpiece *n* каминная доска.
manual *adj* ручной; *n* руководство. **manually** *adv* вручную.
manufacture *n* производство; *vt* производить *impf*, произвести *pf*. **manufacturer** *n* фабрикант.
manure *n* навоз.
manuscript *n* рукопись.
many *adj* & *n* много +*gen*, многие *pl*; **how ~** сколько +*gen*.
map *n* карта; (*of town*) план; *vt*: **~ out** намечать *impf*, наметить *pf*.
maple *n* клён.
mar *vt* портить *impf*, ис~ *pf*.
marathon *n* марафон.
marauder *n* мародёр. **marauding** *adj* мародёрский.
marble *n* мрамор; (*toy*) шарик; *attrib* мраморный.
March *n* март; *adj* мартовский.
march *vi* маршировать *impf*, про~ *pf*; *n* марш.
mare *n* кобыла.
margarine *n* маргарин.
margin *n* (*on page*) поле; (*edge*) край; **profit ~** прибыль; **safety ~** запас прочности.
marigold *n* ноготки (-ков) *pl*.
marijuana *n* марихуана.
marina *n* марина.
marinade *n* маринад; *vt* мариновать *impf*, за~ *pf*.
marine *adj* морской; *n* (*soldier*) солдат морской пехоты; *pl* морская пехота. **mariner** *n* моряк.
marionette *n* марионетка.
marital *adj* супружеский, брачный.
maritime *adj* морской; (*near sea*) приморский.
mark[1] *n* (*coin*) марка.
mark[2] *n* (*for distinguishing*)

ме́тка; (*sign*) знак; (*school*) отме́тка; (*trace*) след; **on your ~s** на старт!; *vt* (*indicate*; *celebrate*) отмеча́ть *impf*, отме́тить *pf*; (*school etc.*) проверя́ть *impf*, прове́рить *pf*; (*stain*) па́чкать *impf*, за~ *pf*; (*sport*) закрыва́ть *impf*, закры́ть *pf*; **~ my words** по́мни(те) мои́ слова́!; **~ out** размеча́ть *impf*, разме́тить *pf*. **marker** *n* знак; (*in book*) закла́дка.

market *n* ры́нок; **~ garden** огоро́д; **~-place** база́рная пло́щадь; *vt* продава́ть *impf*, прода́ть *pf*. **marketing** *n* ма́ркетинг.

marksman *n* стрело́к.

marmalade *n* апельси́новый джем.

maroon[1] *adj* (*n*) (*colour*) тёмно-бордо́вый (цвет).

maroon[2] *vt* выса́живать *impf*, вы́садить *pf* (на необита́емый о́стров); (*cut off*) отреза́ть *impf*, отре́зать *pf*.

marquee *n* тэнт.

marquis *n* марки́з.

marriage *n* брак; (*wedding*) сва́дьба; *attrib* бра́чный. **marriageable** *adj*: **~ age** бра́чный во́зраст. **married** *adj* (*man*) жена́тый; (*woman*) заму́жняя, за́мужем; (*to each other*) жена́ты; (*of ~ persons*) супру́жеский.

marrow *n* ко́стный мозг; (*vegetable*) кабачо́к.

marry *vt* (*of man*) жени́ться *impf* & *pf* на *+prep*; (*of woman*) выходи́ть *impf*, вы́йти *pf* за́муж за *+acc*; *vi* (*of couple*) пожени́ться *pf*.

marsh *n* боло́то. **marshy** *adj* боло́тистый.

marshal *n* ма́ршал; *vt* выстра́ивать *impf*, вы́строить *pf*; (*fig*) собира́ть *impf*, собра́ть *pf*.

marsupial *n* су́мчатое живо́тное *sb*.

martial *adj* вое́нный; **~ law** вое́нное положе́ние.

martyr *n* му́ченик, -ица; *vt* му́чить *impf*, за~ *pf*. **martyrdom** *n* му́ченичество.

marvel *n* чу́до; *vi* изумля́ться *impf*, изуми́ться *pf*. **marvellous** *adj* чуде́сный.

Marxist *n* маркси́ст; *adj* маркси́стский. **Marxism** *n* маркси́зм.

marzipan *n* марципа́н.

mascara *n* тушь.

mascot *n* талисма́н.

masculine *adj* мужско́й; (*gram*) мужско́го ро́да; (*of woman*) мужеподо́бный.

mash *n* карто́фельное пюре́ *neut indecl*; *vt* размина́ть *impf*, размя́ть *pf*.

mask *n* ма́ска; *vt* маскирова́ть *impf*, за~ *pf*.

masochism *n* мазохи́зм. **masochist** *n* мазохи́ст. **masochistic** *adj* мазохи́стский.

mason *n* ка́менщик; (**M~**) масо́н. **Masonic** *adj* масо́нский. **masonry** *n* ка́менная кла́дка.

masquerade *n* маскара́д; *vi*: **~ as** выдава́ть *impf*, вы́дать *pf* себя́ за*+acc*.

Mass *n* (*eccl*) ме́сса.

mass *n* ма́сса; (*majority*) большинство́; *attrib* ма́ссовый; **~ media** сре́дства *neut pl* ма́ссовой информа́ции; **~-produced** ма́ссового произво́дства; **~ production** ма́ссовое произво́дство; *vt* масси́ровать *impf* & *pf*.

massacre *n* резня́; *vt* выреза́ть *impf*, вы́резать *pf*.

massage *n* масса́ж; *vt* масси́ровать *impf* & *pf*. **masseur, -euse** *n* массажи́ст, ~ка.
massive *adj* масси́вный; (*huge*) огро́мный.
mast *n* ма́чта.
master *n* (*owner*) хозя́ин; (*of ship*) капита́н; (*teacher*) учи́тель *m*; (**M**~, *univ*) маги́стр; (*workman*; *artist*) ма́стер; (*original*) по́длинник, оригина́л; **be ~ of** владе́ть *impf* +*instr*; **~-key** отмы́чка; *vt* (*overcome*) преодолева́ть *impf*, преодоле́ть *pf*; справля́ться *impf*, спра́виться *pf* с+*instr*; (*a subject*) овладева́ть *impf*, овладе́ть *pf* +*instr*. **masterful** *adj* вла́стный. **masterly** *adj* мастерско́й. **masterpiece** *n* шеде́вр. **mastery** *n* (*of a subject*) владе́ние (**of** +*instr*).
masturbate *vi* мастурби́ровать *impf*.
mat *n* ко́врик, (*at door*) полови́к; (*on table*) подста́вка.
match[1] *n* спи́чка. **matchbox** *n* спи́чечная коро́бка.
match[2] *n* (*equal*) ро́вня *m* & *f*; (*contest*) матч, состяза́ние; (*marriage*) па́ртия; *vi* & *t* (*go well* (*with*)) гармони́ровать *impf* (с+*instr*); подходи́ть *impf*, подойти́ *pf* (к+*dat*).
mate[1] *n* (*chess*) мат.
mate[2] *n* (*one of pair*) саме́ц, са́мка; (*fellow worker*) това́рищ; (*naut*) помо́щник капита́на; *vi* (*of animals*) спа́риваться *impf*, спа́риться *pf*.
material *n* материа́л; (*cloth*) мате́рия; *pl* (*necessary articles*) принадле́жности *f pl*. **materialism** *n* материали́зм. **materialistic** *adj* материалисти́ческий. **materialize** *vi* осуществля́ться *impf*, осуществи́ться *pf*.
maternal *adj* матери́нский; **~ grandfather** де́душка с матери́нской стороны́. **maternity** *n* матери́нство; **~ leave** декре́тный о́тпуск; **~ ward** роди́льное отделе́ние.
mathematical *adj* математи́ческий. **mathematician** *n* матема́тик. **mathematics, maths** *n* матема́тика.
matinée *n* дневно́й спекта́кль *m*.
matriarchal *adj* матриарха́льный. **matriarchy** *n* матриарха́т.
matriculate *vi* быть при́нятым в вуз. **matriculation** *n* зачисле́ние в вуз.
matrimonial *adj* супру́жеский. **matrimony** *n* брак.
matrix *n* ма́трица.
matron *n* ста́ршая сестра́.
matt *adj* ма́товый.
matted *adj* спу́танный.
matter *n* (*affair*) де́ло; (*question*) вопро́с; (*substance*) вещество́; (*philos*; *med*) мате́рия; (*printed*) материа́л; **a ~ of life and death** вопро́с жи́зни и сме́рти; **a ~ of opinion** спо́рное де́ло; **a ~ of taste** де́ло вку́са; **as a ~ of fact** факти́чески; со́бственно говоря́; **what's the ~?** в чём де́ло?; **what's the ~ with him?** что с ним?; **~-of-fact** прозаи́чный; *vi* име́ть *impf* значе́ние; **it doesn't ~** э́то не име́ет значе́ния; **it ~s a lot to me** для меня́ э́то о́чень ва́жно.
matting *n* рого́жа.
mattress *n* матра́с.
mature *adj* зре́лый; *vi* зреть *impf*, со~ *pf*. **maturity** *n* зре́лость.

maul *vt* терзáть *impf.*
mausoleum *n* мавзолéй.
mauve *adj* (*n*) розовáто-лилóвый (цвет).
maxim *n* сентéнция.
maximum *n* мáксимум; *adj* максимáльный.
may *v aux* (*possibility, permission*) мочь *impf*, с~ *pf*; (*possibility*) возмóжно, что *+indicative*; (*wish*) пусть *+indicative.*
May *n* (*month*) май; *adj* мáйский ~ **Day** Пéрвое *sb* мáя.
maybe *adv* мóжет быть.
mayonnaise *n* майонéз.
mayor *n* мэр. **mayoress** *n* женá мэ́ра; жéнщина-мэр.
maze *n* лабири́нт.
meadow *n* луг.
meagre *adj* скýдный.
meal[1] *n* едá; **at ~times** во врéмя еды́.
meal[2] *n* (*grain*) мукá. **mealy** *adj*: **~-mouthed** сладкоречи́вый.
mean[1] *adj* (*average*) срéдний; *n* (*middle point*) середи́на; *pl* (*method*) срéдство, спóсоб; *pl* (*resources*) срéдства *neut pl*; **by all ~s** конéчно, пожáлуйста; **by ~s of** при пóмощи *+gen*, посрéдством *+gen*; **by no ~s** совсéм не; **~s test** провéрка нуждáемости.
mean[2] *adj* (*ignoble*) пóдлый; (*miserly*) скупóй; (*poor*) убóгий.
mean[3] *vt* (*have in mind*) имéть *impf* в видý; (*intend*) намеревáться *impf +inf*; (*signify*) знáчить *impf.*
meander *vi* (*stream*) извивáться *impf*; (*person*) броди́ть *impf.* **meandering** *adj* изви́листый.
meaning *n* значéние. **meaningful** *adj* (много)значи́тельный. **meaningless** *adj* бессмы́сленный.
meantime, meanwhile *adv* мéжду тем.
measles *n* корь. **measly** *adj* ничтóжный.
measurable *adj* измери́мый.
measure *n* мéра; **made to ~** сши́тый по мéрке; сдéланный на закáз; *vt* измеря́ть *impf*, измéрить *pf*; (*for clothes*) снимáть *impf*, снять *pf* мéрку с*+gen*; *vi* имéть *impf +acc*: **the room ~s 30 feet in length** кóмната имéет три́дцать фýтов в длинý; **~ off, out** отмеря́ть *impf*, отмéрить *pf*; **~ up to** соотвéтствовать *impf +dat.* **measured** *adj* (*rhythmical*) мéрный. **measurement** *n* (*action*) измерéние; *pl* (*dimensions*) размéры *m pl.*
meat *n* мя́со. **meatball** *n* котлéта. **meaty** *adj* мяси́стый; (*fig*) содержáтельный.
mechanic *n* механик. **mechanical** *adj* механи́ческий; (*fig; automatic*) машинáльный; **~ engineer** инженéр-механик; **~ engineering** машиностроéние. **mechanics** *n* механика. **mechanism** *n* механи́зм. **mechanization** *n* механизáция. **mechanize** *vt* механизи́ровать *impf & pf.*
medal *n* медáль. **medallion** *n* медальóн. **medallist** *n* медали́ст.
meddle *vi* вмéшиваться *impf*, вмешáться *pf* (**in, with** в*+acc*).
media *pl of* **medium**
mediate *vi* посрéдничать *impf.* **mediation** *n* посрéдничество. **mediator** *n* посрéдник.
medical *adj* медици́нский; **~ student** мéдик, -и́чка. **med-**

icated *adj* (*impregnated*) пропи́танный лека́рством. **medicinal** *adj* (*of medicine*) лека́рственный; (*healing*) целе́бный. **medicine** *n* медици́на; (*substance*) лека́рство.

medieval *adj* средневеко́вый.

mediocre *adj* посре́дственный. **mediocrity** *n* посре́дственность.

meditate *vi* размышля́ть *impf*. **meditation** *n* размышле́ние. **meditative** *adj* заду́мчивый.

Mediterranean *adj* средизе́мномо́рский; *n* Средизе́мное мо́ре.

medium *n* (*means*) сре́дство; (*phys*) среда́; (*person*) ме́диум; *pl* (*mass media*) сре́дства *neut pl* ма́ссовой информа́ции; *adj* сре́дний; **happy ~** золота́я середи́на.

medley *n* смесь; (*mus*) попурри́ *neut indecl*.

meek *adj* кро́ткий.

meet *vt* & *i* встреча́ть(ся) *impf*, встре́тить(ся) *pf*; *vt* (*make acquaintance*) знако́миться *impf*, по~ *pf* c+*instr*; *vi* (*assemble*) собира́ться *impf*, собра́ться *pf*. **meeting** *n* встре́ча; (*of committee*) заседа́ние, ми́тинг.

megalomania *n* мегалома́ния.

megaphone *n* мегафо́н.

melancholic *adj* меланхоли́ческий. **melancholy** *n* грусть; *adj* уны́лый, гру́стный.

mellow *adj* (*colour, sound*) со́чный; (*person*) доброду́шный; *vi* смягча́ться *impf*, смягчи́ться *pf*.

melodic *adj* мелоди́ческий. **melodious** *adj* мелоди́чный. **melody** *n* мело́дия.

melodrama *n* мелодра́ма. **melodramatic** *adj* мелодрамати́ческий.

melon *n* ды́ня; (*water-~*) арбу́з.

melt *vt* & *i* растапливать(ся) *impf*, растопи́ть(ся) *pf*; (*smelt*) пла́вить(ся) *impf*, рас~ *pf*; (*dissolve*) растворя́ть(ся) *impf*, раствори́ть(ся) *pf*; *vi* (*thaw*) та́ять *impf*, рас~ *pf*; **~ing point** то́чка плавле́ния.

member *n* член. **membership** *n* чле́нство; (*number of ~*) коли́чество чле́нов; *attrib* чле́нский.

membrane *n* перепо́нка.

memento *n* сувени́р. **memoir** *n pl* мемуа́ры (-ров) *pl*; воспомина́ния *neut pl*. **memorable** *adj* достопа́мятный. **memorandum** *n* запи́ска. **memorial** *adj* мемориа́льный; *n* па́мятник. **memorize** *vt* запомина́ть *impf*, запо́мнить *pf*. **memory** *n* па́мять; (*recollection*) воспомина́ние.

menace *n* угро́за; *vt* угрожа́ть *impf* +*dat*. **menacing** *adj* угрожа́ющий.

menagerie *n* звери́нец.

mend *vt* чини́ть *impf*, по~ *pf*; (*clothes*) што́пать *impf*, за~ *pf*; **~ one's ways** исправля́ться *impf*, испра́виться *pf*.

menial *adj* ни́зкий, чёрный.

meningitis *n* менинги́т.

menopause *n* кли́макс.

menstrual *adj* менструа́льный. **menstruation** *n* менструа́ция.

mental *adj* у́мственный; (*of ~ illness*) психи́ческий; **~ arithmetic** счёт в уме́. **mentality** *n* ум; (*character*) склад ума́.

mention *vt* упомина́ть *impf*, упомяну́ть *pf*; **don't ~ it** не́ за что!; **not to ~** не говоря́ уже́ о+*prep*.

menu *n* меню́ *neut indecl.*
mercantile *adj* торго́вый.
mercenary *adj* коры́стный; (*hired*) наёмный; *n* наёмник.
merchandise *n* това́ры *m pl.* **merchant** *n* купе́ц; торго́вец; ~ **navy** торго́вый флот.
merciful *adj* милосе́рдный. **mercifully** *adv* к сча́стью. **merciless** *adj* беспоща́дный.
mercurial *adj* (*person*) изме́нчивый. **mercury** *n* ртуть.
mercy *n* милосе́рдие; **at the** ~ **of** во вла́сти *+gen.*
mere *adj* просто́й; **a** ~ **£40** всего́ лишь со́рок фу́нтов. **merely** *adv* то́лько, про́сто.
merge *vt & i* слива́ть(ся) *impf*, сли́ть(ся) *pf.* **merger** *n* объедине́ние.
meridian *n* меридиа́н.
meringue *n* мере́нга.
merit *n* заслу́га, досто́инство; *vt* заслу́живать *impf*, заслужи́ть *pf +gen.*
mermaid *n* руса́лка.
merrily *adv* ве́село. **merriment** *n* весе́лье. **merry** *adj* весёлый; ~**-go-round** карусе́ль; ~**-making** весе́лье.
mesh *n* сеть; *vi* сцепля́ться *impf*, сцепи́ться *pf.*
mesmerize *vt* гипнотизи́ровать *impf*, за~ *pf.*
mess *n* (*disorder*) беспоря́док; (*trouble*) беда́; (*eating-place*) столо́вая *sb*; *vi*: ~ **about** вози́ться *impf*; ~ **up** по́ртить *impf*, ис~ *pf.*
message *n* сообще́ние. **messenger** *n* курье́р.
Messiah *n* месси́я *m.* **Messianic** *adj* мессиа́нский.
Messrs *abbr* господа́ (*gen* -д) *m pl.*
messy *adj* (*untidy*) беспоря́дочный; (*dirty*) гря́зный.
metabolism *n* обме́н веще́ств.
metal *n* мета́лл; *adj* металли́ческий. **metallic** *adj* металли́ческий. **metallurgy** *n* металлу́ргия.
metamorphosis *n* метаморфо́за.
metaphor *n* мета́фора. **metaphorical** *adj* метафори́ческий.
metaphysical *adj* метафизи́ческий. **metaphysics** *n* метафи́зика.
meteor *n* метео́р. **meteoric** *adj* метеори́ческий. **meteorite** *n* метеори́т. **meteorological** *adj* метеорологи́ческий. **meteorology** *n* метеороло́гия.
meter *n* счётчик; *vt* измеря́ть *impf*, изме́рить *pf.*
methane *n* мета́н.
method *n* ме́тод. **methodical** *adj* методи́чный.
Methodist *n* методи́ст; *adj* методи́стский.
methodology *n* методоло́гия.
methylated *adj*: ~ **spirit(s)** денатура́т.
meticulous *adj* тща́тельный.
metre *n* ме́тр. **metric(al)** *adj* метри́ческий.
metronome *n* метроно́м.
metropolis *n* столи́ца. **metropolitan** *adj* столи́чный; *n* (*eccl*) митрополи́т.
mettle *n* хара́ктер.
Mexican *adj* мексика́нский; *n* мексика́нец, -а́нка. **Mexico** *n* Ме́ксика.
mezzanine *n* антресо́ли *f pl.*
miaow *int* мя́у; *n* мя́уканье; *vi* мя́укать *impf*, мя́укнуть *pf.*
mica *n* слюда́.
microbe *n* микро́б. **microchip** *n* чип, микросхе́ма. **microcomputer** *n* микрокомпью́тер. **microcosm** *n* микро-

ко́см. **microfilm** *n* микрофи́льм. **micro-organism** *n* микроорганизм. **microphone** *n* микрофо́н. **microscope** *n* микроско́п. **microscopic** *adj* микроскопи́ческий. **microwave** *n* микроволна́; **~ oven** микрово́лновая печь.

mid *adj*: **~ May** середи́на ма́я. **midday** *n* по́лдень *m*; *attrib* полу́денный. **middle** *n* середи́на; *adj* сре́дний; **~-aged** сре́дних лет; **M~ Ages** сре́дние века́ *m pl*; **~-class** буржуа́зный; **~man** посре́дник; **~-sized** сре́днего разме́ра. **middleweight** *n* сре́дний вес.

midge *n* мо́шка.

midget *n* ка́рлик, -ица.

midnight *n* по́лночь; *attrib* полу́но́чный. **midriff** *n* диафра́гма. **midst** *n* середи́на. **midsummer** *n* середи́на ле́та. **midway** *adv* на полпути́. **midweek** *n* середи́на неде́ли. **midwinter** *n* середи́на зимы́.

midwife *n* акуше́рка. **midwifery** *n* акуше́рство.

might *n* мощь; **with all one's ~** изо всех сил. **mighty** *adj* мо́щный.

migraine *n* мигре́нь.

migrant *adj* кочу́ющий; (*bird*) перелётный; *n* (*person*) переселе́нец; (*bird*) перелётная пти́ца. **migrate** *vi* мигри́ровать *impf* & *pf*. **migration** *n* мигра́ция. **migratory** *adj* кочу́ющий; (*bird*) перелётный.

mike *n* микрофо́н.

mild *adj* мя́гкий.

mildew *n* пле́сень.

mile *n* ми́ля. **mileage** *n* расстоя́ние в ми́лях; (*of car*) пробе́г. **milestone** *n* верстово́й столб; (*fig*) ве́ха.

militancy *n* войнственность. **militant** *adj* войнствующий; *n* активи́ст. **military** *adj* вое́нный; *n* вое́нные *sb pl*. **militate** *vi*: **~ against** говори́ть *impf* про́тив+*gen*. **militia** *n* мили́ция. **militiaman** *n* милиционе́р.

milk *n* молоко́; *attrib* моло́чный; *vt* дои́ть *impf*, по~ *pf*. **milkman** *n* продаве́ц молока́. **milky** *adj* моло́чный; **M~ Way** Мле́чный Путь *m*.

mill *n* ме́льница; (*factory*) фа́брика; *vt* (*grain etc.*) моло́ть *impf*, с~ *pf*; (*metal*) фрезерова́ть *impf*, от~ *pf*; (*coin*) гурти́ть *impf*; *vi*: **~ around** толпи́ться *impf*. **miller** *n* ме́льник.

millennium *n* тысячеле́тие.

millet *n* (*plant*) про́со; (*grain*) пшено́.

milligram(me) *n* миллигра́мм. **millimetre** *n* миллиме́тр.

million *n* миллио́н. **millionaire** *n* миллионе́р. **millionth** *adj* миллио́нный.

millstone *n* жёрнов; (*fig*) ка́мень *m* на ше́е.

mime *n* мим; (*dumb-show*) пантоми́ма; *vt* изобража́ть *impf*, изобрази́ть *pf* мими́чески. **mimic** *n* мими́ст; *vt* передра́знивать *impf*, передразни́ть *pf*. **mimicry** *n* имита́ция.

minaret *n* минаре́т.

mince *n* (*meat*) фарш; *vt* руби́ть *impf*; (*in machine*) пропуска́ть *impf*, пропусти́ть *pf* че́рез мясору́бку; *vi* (*walk*) семени́ть *impf*; **not ~ matters** говори́ть *impf* без обиняко́в. **mincemeat** *n* начи́нка из изю́ма, миндаля́ и т.п.

mind *n* ум; **bear in ~** име́ть *impf* в виду́; **change one's ~**

передумывать *impf*, передумать *pf*; **make up one's ~** решаться *impf*, решиться *pf*; **you're out of your ~** вы с ума сошли; *vt* (*give heed to*) обращать *impf*, обратить *pf* внимание на+*acc*; (*look after*) присматривать *impf*, присмотреть *pf* за+*instr*; **I don't ~** я ничего не имею против; **don't ~ me** не обращай(те) внимания на меня!; **~ you don't forget** смотри не забудь!; **~ your own business** не вмешивайтесь в чужие дела!; **never ~** ничего! **mindful** *adj* помнящий. **mindless** *adj* бессмысленный.

mine[1] *poss pron* мой; свой.

mine[2] *n* шахта, рудник; (*fig*) источник; (*mil*) мина; *vt* (*obtain from ~*) добывать *impf*, добыть *pf*; (*mil*) минировать *impf* & *pf*. **minefield** *n* минное поле. **miner** *n* шахтёр.

mineral *n* минерал; *adj* минеральный; **~ water** минеральная вода. **mineralogy** *n* минералогия.

mingle *vt* & *i* смешивать(ся) *impf*, смешать(ся) *pf*.

miniature *n* миниатюра; *adj* миниатюрный.

minibus *n* микроавтобус.

minidisc *n* минидиск.

minim *n* (*mus*) половинная нота. **minimal** *adj* минимальный. **minimize** *vt* (*reduce*) доводить *impf*, довести *pf* до минимума. **minimum** *n* минимум; *adj* минимальный.

mining *n* горное дело.

minister *n* министр; (*eccl*) священник. **ministerial** *adj* министерский. **ministration** *n* помощь. **ministry** *n* (*polit*) министерство; (*eccl*) духовенство.

mink *n* норка; *attrib* норковый.

minor *adj* (*unimportant*) незначительный; (*less important*) второстепенный; (*mus*) минорный; *n* (*person under age*) несовершеннолетний *n*; (*mus*) минор. **minority** *n* меньшинство.

minstrel *n* менестрель *m*.

mint[1] *n* (*plant*) мята; (*peppermint*) перечная мята.

mint[2] *n* (*econ*) монетный двор; **in ~ condition** новенький; *vt* чеканить *impf*, от~, вы~ *pf*.

minuet *n* менуэт.

minus *prep* минус+*acc*; без+*gen*; *n* минус.

minuscule *adj* малюсенький.

minute[1] *n* минута; *pl* протокол.

minute[2] *adj* мелкий. **minutiae** *n pl* мелочи (-чей) *f pl*.

miracle *n* чудо. **miraculous** *adj* чудесный.

mirage *n* мираж.

mire *n* (*mud*) грязь; (*swamp*) болото.

mirror *n* зеркало; *vt* отражать *impf*, отразить *pf*.

mirth *n* веселье.

misadventure *n* несчастный случай.

misapprehension *n* недопонимание. **misappropriate** *vt* незаконно присваивать *impf*, присвоить *pf*. **misbehave** *vi* дурно вести *impf* себя. **misbehaviour** *n* дурное поведение.

miscalculate *vt* неправильно рассчитывать *impf*, рассчитать *pf*; (*fig, abs*) просчитываться *impf*, просчитаться *pf*. **miscalculation** *n* просчёт. **miscarriage** *n* (*med*) выкидыш; **~ of justice** су-

де́бная оши́бка. **miscarry** *vi* (*med*) име́ть *impf* вы́кидыш. **miscellaneous** *adj* ра́зный, разнообра́зный. **miscellany** *n* смесь.
mischief *n* (*harm*) вред; (*naughtiness*) озорство́. **mischievous** *adj* озорно́й. **misconception** *n* непра́вильное представле́ние. **misconduct** *n* дурно́е поведе́ние. **misconstrue** *vt* непра́вильно истолко́вывать *impf*, истолкова́ть *pf*.
misdeed, misdemeanour *n* просту́пок. **misdirect** *vt* непра́вильно направля́ть *impf*, напра́вить *pf*; (*letter*) непра́вильно адресова́ть *impf* & *pf*.
miser *n* скупе́ц. **miserable** *adj* (*unhappy*, *wretched*) несча́стный, жа́лкий; (*weather*) скве́рный. **miserly** *adj* скупо́й. **misery** *n* страда́ние.
misfire *vi* дава́ть *impf*, дать *pf* осе́чку. **misfit** *n* (*person*) неуда́чник. **misfortune** *n* несча́стье. **misgiving** *n* опасе́ние. **misguided** *adj* обма́нутый.
mishap *n* неприя́тность. **misinform** *vt* непра́вильно информи́ровать *impf* & *pf*. **misinterpret** *vt* неве́рно истолко́вывать *impf*, истолкова́ть *pf*. **misjudge** *vt* неве́рно оце́нивать *impf*, оцени́ть *pf*. **misjudgement** *n* неве́рная оце́нка. **mislay** *vt* затеря́ть *pf*. **mislead** *vt* вводи́ть *impf*, ввести́ *pf* в заблужде́ние. **mismanage** *vt* пло́хо управля́ть *impf* +*instr*. **mismanagement** *n* плохо́е управле́ние. **misnomer** *n* непра́вильное назва́ние.
misogynist *n* женоненави́стник. **misogyny** *n* женоненави́стничество.
misplaced *adj* неуме́стный.
misprint *n* опеча́тка. **misquote** *vt* непра́вильно цити́ровать *impf*, про~ *pf*. **misread** *vt* (*fig*) непра́вильно истолко́вывать *impf*, истолкова́ть *pf*. **misrepresent** *vt* искажа́ть *impf*, искази́ть *pf*. **misrepresentation** *n* искаже́ние.
Miss *n* (*title*) мисс.
miss *n* про́мах; *vi* прома́хиваться *impf*, промахну́ться *pf*; *vt* (*fail to hit*, *see*, *hear*) пропуска́ть *impf*, пропусти́ть *pf*; (*train*) опа́здывать *impf*, опозда́ть *pf* на+*acc*; (*regret absence of*) скуча́ть *impf* по+*dat*; ~ **out** пропуска́ть *impf*, пропусти́ть *pf*; ~ **the point** не понима́ть *impf*, поня́ть *pf* су́ти.
misshapen *adj* уро́дливый.
missile *n* снаря́д, раке́та.
missing *adj* отсу́тствующий, недостаю́щий; (*person*) пропа́вший бе́з ве́сти.
mission *n* ми́ссия; команди-ро́вка. **missionary** *n* миссионе́р. **missive** *n* посла́ние.
misspell *vt* непра́вильно писа́ть *impf*, на~ *pf*. **misspelling** *n* непра́вильное написа́ние.
mist *n* тума́н; *vt* & *i* затума́нивать(ся) *impf*, затума́нить(ся) *pf*.
mistake *vt* непра́вильно понима́ть *impf*, поня́ть *pf*; ~ **for** принима́ть *impf*, приня́ть *pf* за+*acc*; *n* оши́бка; **make a** ~ ошиба́ться *impf*, ошиби́ться *pf*. **mistaken** *adj* оши́бочный; **be** ~ ошиба́ться *impf*, ошиби́ться *pf*.

mister *n* ми́стер, господи́н. **mistletoe** *n* оме́ла. **mistress** *n* хозя́йка; (*teacher*) учи́тельница; (*lover*) любо́вница. **mistrust** *vt* не доверя́ть *impf* +*dat*; *n* недове́рие. **mistrustful** *adj* недове́рчивый. **misty** *adj* тума́нный. **misunderstand** *vt* непра́вильно понима́ть *impf*, поня́ть *pf*. **misunderstanding** *n* недоразуме́ние. **misuse** *vt* непра́вильно употребля́ть *impf*, употреби́ть *pf*; (*ill treat*) ду́рно обраща́ться *impf* с+*instr*; *n* непра́вильное употребле́ние. **mite** *n* (*insect*) клещ. **mitigate** *vt* смягча́ть *impf*, смягчи́ть *pf*. **mitigation** *n* смягче́ние. **mitre** *n* ми́тра. **mitten** *n* рукави́ца. **mix** *vt* меша́ть *impf*, с~ *pf*; *vi* сме́шиваться *impf*, смеша́ться *pf*; (*associate*) обща́ться *impf*; ~ **up** (*confuse*) пу́тать *impf*, с~ *pf*; **get ~ed up in** заме́шиваться *impf*, замеша́ться *pf* в+*acc*; *n* смесь. **mixer** *n* смеси́тель *m*; (*cul*) ми́ксер. **mixture** *n* смесь; (*medicine*) миксту́ра. **moan** *n* стон; *vi* стона́ть *impf*, про~ *pf*. **moat** *n* (крепостно́й) ров. **mob** *n* толпа́; *vt* (*attack*) напада́ть *impf*, напа́сть *pf* толпо́й на+*acc*. **mobster** *n* банди́т. **mobile** *adj* подвижно́й, передвижно́й; ~ **phone** портати́вный телефо́н. **mobility** *n* подви́жность. **mobilize** *vt* & *i* мобилизова́ть(ся) *impf* & *pf*. **moccasin** *n* мокаси́н (*gen pl* -н).

mock *vt* & *i* издева́ться *impf* над+*instr*; *adj* (*sham*) подде́льный; (*pretended*) мни́мый; ~**-up** *n* маке́т. **mockery** *n* издева́тельство; (*travesty*) паро́дия. **mode** *n* (*manner*) о́браз; (*method*) ме́тод. **model** *n* (*representation*) моде́ль; (*pattern, ideal*) образе́ц; (*artist's*) нату́рщик, -ица; (*fashion*) манеке́нщик, -ица; (*make*) моде́ль; *adj* образцо́вый; *vt* лепи́ть *impf*, вы́~, с~ *pf*; (*clothes*) демонстри́ровать *impf* & *pf*; *vi* (*act as* ~) быть нату́рщиком, -ицей; быть манеке́нщиком, -ицей; ~ **after, on** создава́ть *impf*, созда́ть *pf* по образцу́ +*gen*. **modem** *n* мо́де́м. **moderate** *adj* (*various senses*; *polit*) уме́ренный; (*medium*) сре́дний; *vt* умеря́ть *impf*, уме́рить *pf*; *vi* стиха́ть *impf*, сти́хнуть *pf*. **moderation** *n* уме́ренность; **in** ~ уме́ренно. **modern** *adj* совреме́нный; (*language, history*) но́вый. **modernization** *n* модерниза́ция. **modernize** *vt* модернизи́ровать *impf* & *pf*. **modest** *adj* скро́мный. **modesty** *n* скро́мность. **modification** *n* модифика́ция. **modify** *vt* модифици́ровать *impf* & *pf*. **modish** *adj* мо́дный. **modular** *adj* мо́дульный. **modulate** *vt* модули́ровать *impf*. **modulation** *n* модуля́ция. **module** *n* мо́дуль *m*. **mohair** *n* мохе́р. **moist** *adj* вла́жный. **moisten** *vt* & *i* увлажня́ть(ся) *impf*, увлажни́ть(ся) *pf*. **moisture** *n* вла́га.

molar *n* (*tooth*) коренно́й зуб. **mole**[1] *n* (*on skin*) ро́динка. **mole**[2] *n* (*animal*; *agent*) крот. **molecular** *adj* молекуля́рный. **molecule** *n* моле́кула. **molest** *vt* пристава́ть *impf*, приста́ть *pf* к+*dat*. **mollify** *vt* смягча́ть *impf*, смягчи́ть *pf*. **mollusc** *n* моллю́ск. **molten** *adj* распла́вленный. **moment** *n* моме́нт, миг; **at the ~** сейча́с; **at the last ~** в после́днюю мину́ту; **just a ~** сейча́с! **momentarily** *adv* на мгнове́ние. **momentary** *adj* мгнове́нный. **momentous** *adj* ва́жный. **momentum** *n* коли́чество движе́ния; (*impetus*) дви́жущая си́ла; **gather ~** набира́ть *impf*, набра́ть *pf* ско́рость.

monarch *n* мона́рх. **monarchy** *n* мона́рхия.

monastery *n* монасты́рь *m*. **monastic** *adj* мона́шеский.

Monday *n* понеде́льник.

monetary *adj* де́нежный. **money** *n* де́ньги (-нег, -ньга́м) *pl*; **~-lender** ростовщи́к.

mongrel *n* дворня́жка.

monitor *n* (*naut*; *TV*) монито́р; *vt* проверя́ть *impf*, прове́рить *pf*.

monk *n* мона́х.

monkey *n* обезья́на.

mono *n* мо́но *neut indecl*. **monochrome** *adj* одноцве́тный. **monogamous** *adj* единобра́чный. **monogamy** *n* единобра́чие. **monogram** *n* моногра́мма. **monograph** *n* моногра́фия. **monolith** *n* моноли́т. **monolithic** *adj* моноли́тный. **monologue** *n* моноло́г. **monopolize** *vt* монополизи́ровать *impf* & *pf*. **monopoly** *n* монопо́лия. **monosyllabic** *adj* односло́жный. **monosyllable** *n* односло́жное сло́во. **monotone** *n* моното́нность; **in a ~** моното́нно. **monotonous** *adj* моното́нный. **monotony** *n* моното́нность.

monsoon *n* (*wind*) муссо́н; (*rainy season*) дождли́вый сезо́н.

monster *n* чудо́вище. **monstrosity** *n* чудо́вище. **monstrous** *adj* чудо́вищный; (*huge*) грома́дный.

montage *n* монта́ж.

month *n* ме́сяц. **monthly** *adj* ме́сячный; *n* ежеме́сячник; *adv* ежеме́сячно.

monument *n* па́мятник. **monumental** *adj* монумента́льный.

moo *vi* мыча́ть *impf*.

mood[1] *n* (*gram*) наклоне́ние.

mood[2] *n* настрое́ние. **moody** *adj* капри́зный.

moon *n* луна́. **moonlight** *n* лу́нный свет; *vi* халту́рить *impf*. **moonlit** *adj* лу́нный.

moor[1] *n* ме́стность, поро́сшая ве́реском. **moorland** *n* ве́ресковая пу́стошь.

moor[2] *vt* & *i* швартова́ть(ся) *impf*, при~ *pf*. **mooring** *n* (*place*) прича́л; *pl* (*cables*) шварто́вы *m pl*.

Moorish *adj* маврита́нский.

moose *n* америка́нский лось *m*.

moot *adj* спо́рный.

mop *n* шва́бра; *vt* протира́ть *impf*, протере́ть *pf* (шва́брой); **~ one's brow** вытира́ть *impf*, вы́тереть *pf* лоб; **~ up** вытира́ть *impf*, вы́тереть *pf*.

mope *vi* хандри́ть *impf*.

moped *n* мопе́д.

moraine *n* море́на.

moral *adj* мора́льный; *n* мора́ль; *pl* нра́вы *m pl*. **morale** *n* мора́льное состоя́ние. **morality** *n* нра́вственность, мора́ль. **moralize** *vi* морализи́ровать *impf*.

morass *n* боло́то.

moratorium *n* морато́рий.

morbid *adj* боле́зненный.

more *adj* (*greater quantity*) бо́льше +*gen*; (*additional*) ещё; *adv* бо́льше; (*forming comp*) бо́лее; **and what is ~** и бо́льше того́; **~ or less** бо́лее или ме́нее; **once ~** ещё раз. **moreover** *adv* сверх того́; кро́ме того́.

morgue *n* морг.

moribund *adj* умира́ющий.

morning *n* у́тро; **in the ~** у́тром; **in the ~s** по утра́м; *attrib* у́тренний.

moron *n* слабоу́мный *sb*.

morose *adj* угрю́мый.

morphine *n* мо́рфий.

Morse (code) *n* а́збука Мо́рзе.

morsel *n* кусо́чек.

mortal *adj* сме́ртный; (*fatal*) смерте́льный; *n* сме́ртный *sb*. **mortality** *n* сме́ртность.

mortar *n* (*vessel*) сту́п(к)а; (*cannon*) миномёт; (*cement*) (известко́вый) раство́р.

mortgage *n* ссу́да на поку́пку до́ма; *vt* закла́дывать *impf*, заложи́ть *pf*.

mortify *vt* унижа́ть *impf*, унизить *pf*.

mortuary *n* морг.

mosaic *n* моза́ика; *adj* моза́ичный.

mosque *n* мече́ть.

mosquito *n* кома́р.

moss *n* мох. **mossy** *adj* мши́стый.

most *adj* наибо́льший; *n* наибо́льшее коли́чество; *adj* & *n* (*majority*) большинство́ +*gen*; бо́льшая часть +*gen*; *adv* бо́льше всего́, наибо́лее; (*forming superl*) са́мый. **mostly** *adv* гла́вным о́бразом.

MOT (test) *n* техосмо́тр.

motel *n* моте́ль *m*.

moth *n* мотылёк; (*clothes-~*) моль.

mother *n* мать; *vt* относи́ться *impf* по-матери́нски к +*dat*; **~-in-law** (*wife's ~*) тёща; (*husband's ~*) свекро́вь; **~-of-pearl** перламу́тр; *adj* перламу́тровый; **~ tongue** родно́й язы́к. **motherhood** *n* матери́нство. **motherland** *n* ро́дина. **motherly** *adj* матери́нский.

motif *n* моти́в.

motion *n* движе́ние; (*gesture*) жест; (*proposal*) предложе́ние; *vt* пока́зывать *impf*, показа́ть *pf* +*dat* же́стом, что́бы +*past*. **motionless** *adj* неподви́жный. **motivate** *vt* побужда́ть *impf*, побуди́ть *pf*. **motivation** *n* побужде́ние. **motive** *n* моти́в; *adj* дви́жущий.

motley *adj* пёстрый.

motor *n* дви́гатель *m*, мото́р; **~ bike** мотоци́кл; **~ boat** мото́рная ло́дка; **~ car** автомоби́ль *m*; **~ cycle** мотоци́кл; **~-cyclist** мотоцикли́ст; **~ racing** автомоби́льные го́нки *f pl*; **~ scooter** моторо́ллер; **~ vehicle** автомаши́на. **motoring** *n* автомобили́зм. **motorist** *n* автомобили́ст, **~**ка. **motorize** *vt* моторизова́ть *impf* & *pf*. **motorway** *n* автостра́да.

mottled *adj* кра́пчатый.

motto *n* деви́з.
mould[1] *n* (*shape*) фо́рма, фо́рмочка; *vt* формова́ть *impf*, с~ *pf*. **moulding** *n* (*archit*) лепно́е украше́ние.
mould[2] *n* (*fungi*) пле́сень. **mouldy** *adj* заплесневе́лый.
moulder *vi* разлага́ться *impf*, разложи́ться *pf*.
moult *vi* линя́ть *impf*, вы́~ *pf*.
mound *n* холм; (*heap*) на́сыпь.
Mount *n* (*in names*) гора́.
mount *vt* (*ascend*) поднима́ться *impf*, подня́ться *pf* на+*acc*; (~ *a horse etc.*) сади́ться *impf*, сесть *pf* на+*acc*; (*picture*) накле́ивать *impf*, накле́ить *pf* на карто́н; (*gun*) устана́вливать *impf*, установи́ть *pf*; ~ **up** (*accumulate*) нака́пливаться *impf*, накопи́ться *pf*; *n* (*for picture*) карто́н; (*horse*) верхова́я ло́шадь.
mountain *n* гора́; *attrib* го́рный. **mountaineer** *n* альпини́ст, ~ка. **mountaineering** *n* альпини́зм. **mountainous** *adj* гори́стый.
mourn *vt* опла́кивать *impf*, опла́кать *pf*; *vi* скорбе́ть *impf* (**over** о+*prep*). **mournful** *adj* ско́рбный. **mourning** *n* тра́ур.
mouse *n* мышь.
mousse *n* мусс.
moustache *n* усы́ (усо́в) *pl*.
mousy *adj* мыши́ный; (*timid*) ро́бкий.
mouth *n* рот; (*poetical*) уста́ (-т) *pl*; (*entrance*) вход; (*of river*) у́стье; *vt* говори́ть *impf*, сказа́ть *pf* одни́ми губа́ми. **mouthful** *n* глото́к. **mouth-organ** *n* губна́я гармо́ника. **mouthpiece** *n* мундшту́к; (*person*) ру́пор.
movable *adj* подвижно́й.
move *n* (*in game*) ход; (*change of residence*) переéзд; (*movement*) движе́ние; (*step*) шаг; *vt* & *i* дви́гать(ся) *impf*, дви́нуться *pf*; *vt* (*affect*) тро́гать *impf*, тро́нуть *pf*; (*propose*) вноси́ть *impf*, внести́ *pf*; *vi* (*develop*) развива́ться *impf*, разви́ться *pf*; (~ *house*) переезжа́ть *impf*, перее́хать *pf*; ~ **away** (*vt* & *i*) удаля́ть(ся) *impf*, удали́ть(ся) *pf*; (*vi*) уезжа́ть *impf*, уе́хать *pf*; ~ **in** въезжа́ть *impf*, въе́хать *pf*; ~ **on** идти́ *impf*, пойти́ *pf* да́льше; ~ **out** съезжа́ть *impf*, съе́хать *pf* (**of** с+*gen*). **movement** *n* движе́ние; (*mus*) часть. **moving** *n* дви́жущийся; (*touching*) тро́гательный.
mow *vt* (*also* ~ *down*) коси́ть *impf*, с~ *pf*. **mower** *n* коси́лка.
MP *abbr* (*of* **Member of Parliament**) чле́н парла́мента.
Mr *abbr* ми́стер, господи́н. **Mrs** *abbr* ми́ссис *f indecl*, госпожа́.
Ms *n* миз, госпожа́.
much *adj* & *n* мно́го +*gen*; мно́гое *sb*; *adv* о́чень; (*with comp adj*) гора́здо.
muck *n* (*dung*) наво́з; (*dirt*) грязь; ~ **about** вози́ться *impf*; ~ **out** чи́стить *impf*, вы́~ *pf*; ~ **up** изга́живать *impf*, изга́дить *pf*.
mucous *adj* сли́зистый. **mucus** *n* слизь.
mud *n* грязь. **mudguard** *n* крыло́.
muddle *vt* пу́тать *impf*, с~ *pf*; *vi*: ~ **through** ко́е-ка́к справля́ться *impf*, спра́виться *pf*; *n* беспоря́док.
muddy *adj* гря́зный; *vt* обрызгивать *impf*, обры́згать *pf* гря́зью.

muff *n* му́фта.

muffle *vt* (*for warmth*) заку́тывать *impf*, заку́тать *pf*; (*sound*) глуши́ть *impf*, за~ *pf*.

mug *n* (*vessel*) кру́жка; (*face*) мо́рда.

muggy *adj* сыро́й и тёплый.

mulch *n* му́льча; *vt* мульчи́ровать *impf* & *pf*.

mule *n* мул.

mull *vt*: ~ **over** обду́мывать *impf*, обду́мать *pf*. **mulled** *adj*: ~ **wine** глинтве́йн.

mullet *n* (*grey* ~) кефа́ль; (*red* ~) барабу́лька.

multicoloured *adj* многокра́сочный. **multifarious** *adj* разнообра́зный. **multilateral** *adj* многосторо́нний. **multimillionaire** *n* мультимиллионе́р. **multinational** *adj* многонациона́льный.

multiple *adj* составно́й; (*numerous*) многочи́сленный; ~ **sclerosis** рассе́янный склеро́з; *n* кра́тное число́; **least common** ~ о́бщее наиме́ньшее кра́тное *sb*. **multiplication** *n* умноже́ние. **multiplicity** *n* многочи́сленность.

multiply *vt* (*math*) умножа́ть *impf*, умно́жить *pf*; *vi* размножа́ться *impf*, размно́житься *pf*.

multi-storey *adj* многоэта́жный.

multitude *n* мно́жество; (*crowd*) толпа́.

mum[1] *adj*: **keep** ~ молча́ть *impf*.

mum[2] *n* (*mother*) ма́ма.

mumble *vt* & *i* бормота́ть *impf*, про~ *pf*.

mummy[1] *n* (*archaeol*) му́мия.

mummy[2] *n* (*mother*) ма́ма, ма́мочка.

mumps *n* сви́нка.

munch *vt* жева́ть *impf*.

mundane *adj* земно́й.

municipal *adj* муниципа́льный. **municipality** *n* муниципалите́т.

munitions *n pl* вое́нное иму́щество.

mural *n* стенна́я ро́спись.

murder *n* уби́йство; *vt* убива́ть *impf*, уби́ть *pf*; (*language*) ковéркать *impf*, ис~ *pf*. **murderer, murderess** *n* уби́йца *m* & *f*. **murderous** *adj* уби́йственный.

murky *adj* тёмный, мра́чный.

murmur *n* шёпот; *vt* & *i* шепта́ть *impf*, шепну́ть *pf*.

muscle *n* му́скул. **muscular** *adj* мы́шечный; (*person*) мускули́стый.

Muscovite *n* москви́ч, ~ка.

muse *vi* размышля́ть *impf*.

museum *n* музе́й.

mush *n* ка́ша.

mushroom *n* гриб.

music *n* му́зыка; (*sheet* ~) но́ты *f pl*; ~**-hall** мю́зик-хо́лл; ~ **stand** пюпи́тр. **musical** *adj* музыка́льный; *n* опере́тта.

musician *n* музыка́нт.

musk *n* му́скус.

musket *n* мушке́т.

Muslim *n* мусульма́нин, -а́нка; *adj* мусульма́нский.

muslin *n* мусли́н.

mussel *n* ми́дия.

must *v aux* (*obligation*) до́лжен (-жна́) *predic+inf*; на́до *impers+dat* & *inf*; (*necessity*) ну́жно *impers+dat* & *inf*; ~ **not** (*prohibition*) нельзя́ *impers+dat* & *inf*.

mustard *n* горчи́ца.

muster *vt* собира́ть *impf*, собра́ть *pf*; (*courage etc.*) собира́ться *impf*, собра́ться *pf* с+*instr*.

musty *adj* за́тхлый.
mutation *n* мута́ция.
mute *adj* немо́й; *n* немо́й *sb*; (*mus*) сурди́нка. **muted** *adj* приглушённый.
mutilate *vt* уве́чить *impf*, из~ *pf*. **mutilation** *n* уве́чье.
mutineer *n* мяте́жник. **mutinous** *adj* мяте́жный. **mutiny** *n* мяте́ж; *vi* бунтова́ть *impf*, взбунтова́ться *pf*.
mutter *vi* бормота́ть *impf*; *impf*; *n* бормота́ние.
mutton *n* бара́нина.
mutual *adj* взаи́мный; (*common*) о́бщий.
muzzle *n* (*animal's*) мо́рда; (*on animal*) намо́рдник; (*of gun*) ду́ло; *vt* надева́ть *impf*, наде́ть *pf* намо́рдник на+*acc*; (*fig*) заставля́ть *impf*, заста́вить *pf* молча́ть.
my *poss pron* мой; свой.
myopia *n* близору́кость. **myopic** *adj* близору́кий.
myriad *n* мириа́ды (-д) *pl*; *adj* бесчи́сленный.
myrtle *n* мирт; *attrib* ми́ртовый.
myself *pron* (*emph*) (я) сам, сама́; (*refl*) себя́; -ся (*suffixed to vt*).
mysterious *adj* таи́нственный. **mystery** *n* та́йна.
mystic(al) *adj* мисти́ческий; *n* ми́стик. **mysticism** *n* мистици́зм. **mystification** *n* озада́ченность. **mystify** *vt* озада́чивать *impf*, озада́чить *pf*.
myth *n* миф. **mythical** *adj* мифи́ческий. **mythological** *adj* мифологи́ческий. **mythology** *n* мифоло́гия.

N

nag[1] *n* (*horse*) ло́шадь.
nag[2] *vt* (*also* ~ *at*) пили́ть *impf* +*acc*; *vi* (*of pain*) ныть *impf*.
nail *n* (*finger-*, *toe-*~) но́готь *m*; (*metal spike*) гвоздь *m*; ~ **varnish** лак для ногте́й; *vt* прибива́ть *impf*, приби́ть *pf* (гвоздя́ми).
naive *adj* наи́вный. **naivety** *n* наи́вность.
naked *adj* го́лый; ~ **eye** невооружённый глаз. **nakedness** *n* нагота́.
name *n* назва́ние; (*forename*) и́мя *neut*; (*surname*) фами́лия; (*reputation*) репута́ция; **what is his ~?** как его́ зову́т?; **~-plate** доще́чка с фами́лией; **~sake** тёзка *m* & *f*; *vt* называ́ть *impf*, назва́ть *pf*; (*appoint*) назнача́ть *impf*, назна́чить *pf*. **nameless** *adj* безымя́нный. **namely** *adv* (а) и́менно; то есть.
nanny *n* ня́ня.
nap *n* коро́ткий сон; *vi* вздремну́ть *pf*.
nape *n* загри́вок.
napkin *n* салфе́тка.
nappy *n* пелёнка.
narcissus *n* нарци́сс.
narcotic *adj* наркоти́ческий; *n* нарко́тик.
narrate *vt* расска́зывать *impf*, рассказа́ть *pf*. **narration** *n* расска́з. **narrative** *n* расска́з; *adj* повествова́тельный. **narrator** *n* расска́зчик.
narrow *adj* у́зкий; *vt* & *i* сужива́ть(ся) *impf*, су́зить(ся) *pf*. **narrowly** *adv* (*hardly*) чуть, е́ле-е́ле; **he ~ escaped drown-**

ing он чуть не утону́л. **narrow-minded** *adj* ограни́ченный. **narrowness** *n* у́зость.

nasal *adj* носово́й; (*voice*) гнуса́вый.

nasturtium *n* насту́рция.

nasty *adj* неприя́тный, проти́вный; (*person*) злой.

nation *n* (*people*) наро́д; (*country*) страна́. **national** *adj* национа́льный, наро́дный; (*of the state*) госуда́рственный; *n* по́дданный *sb*. **nationalism** *n* национали́зм. **nationalist** *n* национали́ст, ~ка. **nationalistic** *adj* националисти́ческий. **nationality** *n* национа́льность; (*citizenship*) гражда́нство, по́дданство. **nationalization** *n* национализа́ция. **nationalize** *vt* национализи́ровать *impf* & *pf*.

native *n* (~ *of*) уроже́нец, -нка (+*gen*); (*aborigine*) тузе́мец, -мка; *adj* (*innate*) приро́дный; (*of one's birth*) родно́й; (*indigenous*) тузе́мный; ~ **land** ро́дина; ~ **language** родно́й язы́к; ~ **speaker** носи́тель *m* языка́.

nativity *n* Рождество́ (Христо́во).

natter *vi* болта́ть *impf*.

natural *adj* есте́ственный, приро́дный; ~ **resources** приро́дные бога́тства *neut pl*; ~ **selection** есте́ственный отбо́р; *n* (*mus*) бека́р. **naturalism** *n* натурали́зм. **naturalist** *n* натурали́ст. **naturalistic** *adj* натуралисти́ческий. **naturalization** *n* натурализа́ция. **naturalize** *vt* натурализи́ровать *impf* & *pf*. **naturally** *adv* есте́ственно. **nature** *n* приро́да; (*character*) хара́ктер; **by** ~ по приро́де.

naught *n*: **come to** ~ своди́ться *impf*, свести́сь *pf* к нулю́.

naughty *adj* шаловли́вый.

nausea *n* тошнота́. **nauseate** *vt* тошни́ть *impf impers* от +*gen*. **nauseating** *adj* тошнотво́рный. **nauseous** *adj*: **I feel** ~ меня́ тошни́т.

nautical *n* морско́й.

naval *adj* (вое́нно-)морско́й.

nave *n* неф.

navel *n* пупо́к.

navigable *adj* судохо́дный. **navigate** *vt* (*ship*) вести́ *impf*; (*sea*) пла́вать *impf* по+*dat*. **navigation** *n* навига́ция. **navigator** *n* шту́рман.

navvy *n* землеко́п.

navy *n* вое́нно-морско́й флот; ~ **blue** тёмно-си́ний.

Nazi *n* наци́ст, ~ка; *adj* наци́стский. **Nazism** *n* наци́зм.

NB *abbr* нотабе́не.

near *adv* бли́зко; ~ **at hand** под руко́й; ~ **by** ря́дом; *prep* во́зле+*gen*, о́коло+*gen*, у+*gen*; *adj* бли́зкий; ~**-sighted** близору́кий; *vt* & *i* приближа́ться *impf*, прибли́зиться *pf* к+*dat*. **nearly** *adv* почти́.

neat *adj* (*tidy*) опря́тный, аккура́тный; (*clear*) чёткий; (*undiluted*) неразба́вленный.

nebulous *adj* нея́сный.

necessarily *adv* обяза́тельно. **necessary** *adj* необходи́мый; (*inevitable*) неизбе́жный. **necessitate** *vt* де́лать *impf*, с~ *pf* необходи́мым. **necessity** *n* необходи́мость; неизбе́жность; (*object*) предме́т пе́рвой необходи́мости.

neck *n* ше́я; (*of garment*) вы́рез; ~ **and** ~ голова́ в го́ло-

ву. **necklace** *n* ожере́лье. **neckline** *n* вы́рез.
nectar *n* некта́р.
née *adj* урождённая.
need *n* нужда́; *vt* нужда́ться *impf* в+*prep*; I (*etc*.) ~ мне (*dat*) ну́жен (-жна́, -жно, -жны́) +*nom*; **I ~ five roubles** мне ну́жно пять рубле́й.
needle *n* игла́, иго́лка; (*knitting*) спи́ца; (*pointer*) стре́лка; *vt* придира́ться *impf*, придра́ться *pf* к+*dat*.
needless *adj* нену́жный; ~ **to say** разуме́ется. **needy** *adj* нужда́ющийся.
negation *n* отрица́ние. **negative** *adj* отрица́тельный; *n* отрица́ние; (*phot*) негати́в.
neglect *vt* пренебрега́ть *impf*, пренебре́чь *pf* +*instr*; не забо́титься *impf* о+*prep*; *n* пренебреже́ние; (*condition*) забро́шенность. **neglectful** *adj* небре́жный, невнима́тельный (**of** к+*dat*). **negligence** *n* небре́жность. **negligent** *adj* небре́жный. **negligible** *adj* незначи́тельный.
negotiate *vi* вести́ *impf* перегово́ры; *vt* (*arrange*) заключа́ть *impf*, заключи́ть *pf*; (*overcome*) преодолева́ть *impf*, преодоле́ть *pf*. **negotiation** *n* (*discussion*) перегово́ры *m pl*.
Negro *n* негр; *adj* негритя́нский.
neigh *n* ржа́ние; *vi* ржать *impf*.
neighbour *n* сосе́д, ~ка. **neighbourhood** *n* ме́стность; **in the ~ of** о́коло+*gen*. **neighbouring** *adj* сосе́дний. **neighbourly** *adj* добрососе́дский.
neither *adv* та́кже не, то́же не; *pron* ни тот, ни друго́й; ~ ... **nor** ни… ни.
neon *n* нео́н; *attrib* нео́новый.
nephew *n* племя́нник.
nepotism *n* кумовство́.
nerve *n* нерв; (*courage*) сме́лость; (*impudence*) на́глость; **get on the ~s of** де́йствовать *impf*, по~ *pf* +*dat* на не́рвы. **nervous** *adj* не́рвный; ~ **breakdown** не́рвное расстро́йство. **nervy** *adj* нерво́зный.
nest *n* гнездо́; ~ **egg** сбереже́ния *neut pl*; *vi* гнезди́ться *impf*. **nestle** *vi* льнуть *impf*, при~ *pf*.
net[1] *n* сеть, се́тка; *vt* (*catch*) лови́ть *impf*, пойма́ть *pf* сетя́ми.
net[2], **nett** *adj* чи́стый; *vt* получа́ть *impf*, получи́ть *pf* … чи́стого дохо́да.
Netherlands *n* Нидерла́нды (-ов) *pl*.
nettle *n* крапи́ва.
network *n* сеть.
neurologist *n* невро́лог. **neurology** *n* невроло́гия. **neurosis** *n* невро́з. **neurotic** *adj* невроти́ческий.
neuter *adj* сре́дний, сре́днего ро́да; *n* сре́дний род; *vt* кастри́ровать *impf* & *pf*. **neutral** *adj* нейтра́льный; *n* (*gear*) нейтра́льная ско́рость. **neutrality** *n* нейтралите́т. **neutralize** *vt* нейтрализова́ть *impf* & *pf*. **neutron** *n* нейтро́н.
never *adv* никогда́; ~ **again** никогда́ бо́льше; ~ **mind** ничего́!; всё равно́!; ~ **once** ни ра́зу. **nevertheless** *conj*, *adv* тем не ме́нее.
new *adj* но́вый; (*moon*, *potatoes*) молодо́й. **new-born** *adj* новорождённый. **newcomer** *n* прише́лец. **newfangled** *adj* новомо́дный. **newly** *adv* то́лько что, неда́вно. **newness** *n* новизна́.

news *n* нóвость, -ти *pl*, извéстие, -ия *pl*. **newsagent** *n* продавéц газéт. **newsletter** *n* информациóнный бюллетéнь *m*. **newspaper** *n* газéта. **newsprint** *n* газéтная бумáга. **newsreel** *n* кинохрóника.
newt *n* тритóн.
New Zealand *n* Нóвая Зелáндия; *adj* новозелáндский.
next *adj* слéдующий, бýдущий; *adv* (~ *time*) в слéдующий раз; (*then*) потóм, затéм; ~ **door** (*house*) в сосéднем дóме; (*flat*) в сосéдней квартúре; ~ **of kin** ближáйший рóдственник; ~ **to** рядом с+*instr*; (*fig*) почтú. **next-door** *adj* сосéдний; ~ **neighbour** ближáйший сосéд.
nib *n* перó.
nibble *vt* & *i* грызть *impf*; *vt* обгрызáть *impf*, обгрызть *pf*; (*grass*) щипáть *impf*; (*fish*) клевáть *impf*.
nice *adj* (*pleasant*) приятный, хорóший; (*person*) мúлый. **nicety** *n* тóнкость.
niche *n* нúша; (*fig*) своё мéсто.
nick *n* (*scratch*) царáпина; (*notch*) зарýбка; **in the** ~ **of time** в сáмый послéдний момéнт; *vt* (*scratch*) царáпать *impf*, о~ *pf*; (*steal*) стибрить *pf*.
nickel *n* нúкель *m*.
nickname *n* прóзвище; *vt* прозывáть *impf*, прозвáть *pf*.
nicotine *n* никотúн.
niece *n* племянница.
niggardly *adj* скупóй.
niggling *adj* мéлочный.
night *n* ночь; (*evening*) вéчер; **at** ~ нóчью; **last** ~ вчерá вéчером; *attrib* ночнóй; ~**club** ночнóй клуб. **nightcap** *n* ночнóй колпáк; (*drink*) стакáнчик спиртнóго нá ночь. **nightdress** *n* ночнáя рубáшка. **nightfall** *n* наступлéние нóчи. **nightingale** *n* соловéй. **nightly** *adj* еженóщный; *adv* еженóщно. **nightmare** *n* кошмáр. **nightmarish** *adj* кошмáрный.
nil *n* нуль *m*.
nimble *adj* провóрный.
nine *adj* & *n* дéвять; (*number 9*) девятка. **nineteen** *adj* & *n* девятнáдцать. **nineteenth** *adj* & *n* девятнáдцатый. **ninetieth** *adj* & *n* девянóстый. **ninety** *adj* & *n* девянóсто; *pl* (*decade*) девянóстые гóды (-дóв) *m pl*. **ninth** *adj* & *n* девятый.
nip *vt* (*pinch*) щипáть *impf*, щипнýть *pf*; (*bite*) кусáть *impf*, укусúть *pf*; ~ **in the bud** пресекáть *impf*, пресéчь *pf* в зарóдыше; *n* щипóк; укýс; **there's a** ~ **in the air** вóздух пáхнет морóзцем.
nipple *n* сосóк.
nirvana *n* нирвáна.
nit *n* гнúда.
nitrate *n* нитрáт. **nitrogen** *n* азóт.
no *adj* (*not any*) никакóй, не одúн; (*not a* (*fool etc.*)) (совсéм) не; *adv* нет; (нискóлько) не+*comp*; *n* отрицáние, откáз; (*in vote*) гóлос „прóтив"; ~ **doubt** конéчно, несомнéнно; ~ **longer** ужé не, бóльше не; **no one** никтó; ~ **wonder** не удивúтельно.
Noah's ark *n* Нóев ковчéг.
nobility *n* (*class*) дворянство; (*quality*) благорóдство. **noble** *adj* дворянский; благорóдный. **nobleman** *n* дворянúн.
nobody *pron* никтó; *n* ничтóжество.

nocturnal *adj* ночно́й.
nod *vi* кива́ть *impf*, кивну́ть *pf* голово́й; *n* киво́к.
nodule *n* узело́к.
noise *n* шум. **noiseless** *adj* бесшу́мный. **noisy** *adj* шу́мный.
nomad *n* коче́вник. **nomadic** *adj* кочево́й.
nomenclature *n* номенклату́ра. **nominal** *adj* номина́льный. **nominate** *vt* (*propose*) выдвига́ть *impf*, вы́двинуть *pf*; (*appoint*) назнача́ть *impf*, назна́чить *pf*. **nomination** *n* выдвиже́ние; назначе́ние. **nominative** *adj* (*n*) имени́тельный (паде́ж). **nominee** *n* кандида́т.
non-alcoholic *adj* безалкого́льный. **non-aligned** *adj* неприсоедини́вшийся.
nonchalance *n* беззабо́тность. **nonchalant** *n* беззабо́тный.
non-commissioned *adj*: ~ **officer** у́нтер-офице́р. **noncommittal** *adj* уклóнчивый.
non-conformist *n* нонконформи́ст; *adj* нонконформи́стский.
nondescript *adj* неопределённый.
none *pron* (*no one*) никто́; (*nothing*) ничто́; (*not one*) не оди́н; *adv* ниско́лько не; ~ **the less** тем не ме́нее.
nonentity *n* ничто́жество.
non-existent *adj* несуществу́ющий. **non-fiction** *adj* документа́льный. **non-intervention** *n* невмеша́тельство. **non-party** *adj* беспарти́йный. **non-payment** *n* неплатёж.
nonplus *vt* ста́вить *impf*, по~ *pf* в тупи́к.
non-productive *adj* непроизводи́тельный. **non-resident** *adj* не прожива́ющий (где́-нибудь).
nonsense *n* ерунда́. **nonsensical** *adj* бессмы́сленный.
non-smoker *n* (*person*) некуря́щий *sb*; (*compartment*) купе́ *neut indecl*, для некуря́щих. **non-stop** *adj* безостано́вочный; (*flight*) беспоса́дочный; *adv* без остано́вок; без поса́док. **non-violent** *adj* ненаси́льственный.
noodles *n pl* лапша́.
nook *n* уголо́к.
noon *n* по́лдень *m*.
no one *see* **no**
noose *n* пе́тля.
nor *conj* и не; то́же; **neither ... ~** ни... ни.
norm *n* но́рма. **normal** *adj* норма́льный. **normality** *n* норма́льность. **normalize** *vt* нормализова́ть *impf* & *pf*.
north *n* се́вер; (*naut*) норд; *adj* се́верный; *adv* к се́веру, на се́вер; **~-east** се́веро-восто́к; **~-easterly, -eastern** се́веро-восто́чный; **~-west** се́веро-за́пад; **~-westerly, -western** се́веро-за́падный. **northerly** *adj* се́верный. **northern** *adj* се́верный. **northerner** *n* северя́нин, -я́нка. **northward(s)** *adv* на се́вер, к се́веру.
Norway *n* Норве́гия. **Norwegian** *adj* норве́жский; *n* норве́жец, -жка.
nose *n* нос; *vt*: ~ **about, out** разню́хивать *impf*, разню́хать *pf*. **nosebleed** *n* кровотече́ние и́з носу. **nosedive** *n* пике́ *neut indecl*.
nostalgia *n* ностальги́я. **nostalgic** *adj* ностальги́ческий.
nostril *n* ноздря́.
not *adv* не; нет; ни; ~ **at all** ниско́лько, ничу́ть; (*reply to*

thanks) не сто́ит (благода́рности); ~ **once** ни ра́зу; ~ **that** не то, что́бы; ~ **too** дово́льно +*neg*; ~ **to say** что́бы не сказа́ть; ~ **to speak of** не говоря́ уже́ о+*prep*.
notable *adj* заме́тный; (*remarkable*) замеча́тельный.
notably *adv* (*especially*) осо́бенно; (*perceptibly*) заме́тно.
notary (public) *n* нота́риус.
notation *n* нота́ция; (*mus*) но́тное письмо́.
notch *n* зару́бка; *vt*: ~ **up** вы́игрывать *impf*, вы́играть *pf*.
note *n* (*record*) заме́тка, за́пись; (*annotation*) примеча́ние; (*letter*) запи́ска; (*banknote*) банкно́т; (*mus*) но́та; (*tone*) тон; (*attention*) внима́ние; *vt* отмеча́ть *impf*, отме́тить *pf*; ~ **down** запи́сывать *impf*, записа́ть *pf*. **notebook** *n* записна́я кни́жка. **noted** *adj* знамени́тый; изве́стный (**for** +*instr*). **notepaper** *n* почто́вая бума́га. **noteworthy** *adj* досто́йный внима́ния.
nothing *n* ничто́, ничего́; ~ **but** ничего́ кро́ме+*gen*, то́лько; ~ **of the kind** ничего́ подо́бного; **come to** ~ конча́ться *impf*, ко́нчиться *pf* ниче́м; **for** ~ (*free*) да́ром; (*in vain*) зря, напра́сно; **have** ~ **to do with** не име́ть *impf* никако́го отноше́ния к+*dat*; **there is (was)** ~ **for it (but to)** ничего́ друго́го не остаётся (остава́лось) (как); **to say** ~ **of** не говоря́ уже́ о+*prep*.
notice *n* (*sign*) объявле́ние; (*warning*) предупрежде́ние; (*attention*) внима́ние; (*review*) о́тзыв; **give (in) one's** ~ подава́ть *impf*, пода́ть *pf* заявле́ние об ухо́де с рабо́ты; **give s.o.** ~ предупрежда́ть *impf*, предупреди́ть *pf* об увольне́нии; **take** ~ **of** обраща́ть *impf*, обрати́ть *pf* внима́ния на+*acc*; ~**-board** доска́ для объявле́ний; *vt* замеча́ть *impf*, заме́тить *pf*. **noticeable** *adj* заме́тный.
notification *n* извеще́ние.
notify *vt* извеща́ть *impf*, извести́ть *pf* (**of** о+*prep*).
notion *n* поня́тие.
notoriety *n* дурна́я сла́ва. **notorious** *adj* преслову́тый.
notwithstanding *prep* несмотря́ на+*acc*; *adv* те́м не ме́нее.
nought *n* (*nothing*) *see* **naught;** (*zero*) нуль *m*; (*figure 0*) ноль *m*.
noun *n* (имя *neut*) существи́тельное *sb*.
nourish *vt* пита́ть *impf*, на~ *pf*. **nourishing** *adj* пита́тельный. **nourishment** *n* пита́ние.
novel *adj* но́вый; (*unusual*) необыкнове́нный; *n* рома́н. **novelist** *n* романи́ст. **novelty** *n* (*newness*) новизна́; (*new thing*) нови́нка.
November *n* ноя́брь *m*; *adj* ноя́брьский.
novice *n* (*eccl*) по́слушник, -ица; (*beginner*) новичо́к.
now *adv* тепе́рь, сейча́с; (*immediately*) то́тчас же; (*next*) тогда́; *conj*: ~ **(that)** раз, когда́; **(every)** ~ **and again, then** вре́мя от вре́мени; **by** ~ уже́; **from** ~ **on** впредь.
nowadays *adv* в на́ше вре́мя.
nowhere *adv* (*place*) нигде́; (*direction*) никуда́; *pron*: **I have** ~ **to go** мне не́куда пойти́.
noxious *adj* вре́дный.
nozzle *n* со́пло́.
nuance *n* нюа́нс.

nuclear *adj* я́дерный. **nucleus** *n* ядро́.
nude *adj* обнажённый, наго́й; *n* обнажённая фигу́ра.
nudge *vt* подта́лкивать *impf*, подтолкну́ть *pf* ло́ктем; *n* толчо́к ло́ктем.
nudity *n* нагота́.
nugget *n* саморо́док.
nuisance *n* доса́да; (*person*) раздража́ющий челове́к.
null *adj*: ~ **and void** недействи́тельный. **nullify** *vt* аннули́ровать *impf* & *pf*. **nullity** *n* недействи́тельность.
numb *adj* онеме́лый; (*from cold*) окочене́лый; **go** ~ онеме́ть *pf*; (*from cold*) окочене́ть *pf*.
number *n* (*total*) коли́чество; (*total*; *symbol*; *math*; *gram*) число́; (*identifying numeral*; *item*) но́мер; **~-plate** номерна́я доще́чка; *vt* (*assign* ~ *to*) нумерова́ть *impf*, за~, про~ *pf*; (*contain*) насчи́тывать *impf*; ~ **among** причисля́ть *impf*, причи́слить *pf* к+*dat*; **his days are ~ed** его́ дни сочтены́.
numeral *n* ци́фра; (*gram*) (и́мя *neut*) числи́тельное *sb*. **numerical** *adj* числово́й. **numerous** *adj* многочи́сленный; (*many*) мно́го +*gen pl*.
nun *n* мона́хиня. **nunnery** *n* (же́нский) монасты́рь *m*.
nuptial *adj* сва́дебный; *n*: *pl* сва́дьба.
nurse *n* (*child's*) ня́ня; (*medical*) медсестра́; *vt* (*suckle*) корми́ть *impf*, на~, по~ *pf*; (*tend sick*) уха́живать *impf* за+*instr*; **nursing home** санато́рий; дом престаре́лых.
nursery *n* (*room*) де́тская *sb*; (*day* ~) я́сли (-лей) *pl*; (*for plants*) пито́мник; ~ **rhyme** де́тские прибау́тки *f pl*; ~ **school** де́тский сад.
nut *n* оре́х; (*for bolt etc.*) га́йка. **nutshell** *n*: **in a** ~ в двух слова́х.
nutmeg *n* муска́тный оре́х.
nutrient *n* пита́тельное вещество́. **nutrition** *n* пита́ние. **nutritious** *adj* пита́тельный.
nylon *n* нейло́н; *pl* нейло́новые чулки́ (-ло́к) *pl*.
nymph *n* ни́мфа.

O *int* о!; ах!
oaf *n* неуклю́жий челове́к.
oak *n* дуб; *attrib* дубо́вый.
oar *n* весло́. **oarsman** *n* гребе́ц.
oasis *n* оа́зис.
oath *n* прися́га; (*expletive*) руга́тельство.
oatmeal *n* овся́нка. **oats** *n pl* овёс (овса́) *collect*.
obdurate *adj* упря́мый.
obedience *n* послуша́ние. **obedient** *adj* послу́шный.
obese *n* ту́чный. **obesity** *n* ту́чность.
obey *vt* слу́шаться *impf*, по~ *pf* +*gen*; (*law*, *order*) подчиня́ться *impf*, подчини́ться *pf* +*dat*.
obituary *n* некроло́г.
object *n* (*thing*) предме́т; (*aim*) цель; (*gram*) дополне́ние; *vi* возража́ть *impf*, возрази́ть *pf* (**to** про́тив+*gen*); **I don't** ~ я не про́тив. **objection** *n* возраже́ние; **I have no** ~ я не возража́ю. **objectionable** *adj* неприя́тный. **objective** *adj* объекти́вный; *n* цель. **objectivity** *n* объекти́вность.

objector *n* возража́ющий *sb.*
obligation *n* обяза́тельство; **I am under an ~** я обя́зан(а).
obligatory *adj* обяза́тельный.
oblige *vt* обя́зывать *impf*, обяза́ть *pf*; **be ~d to** (*grateful*) быть обя́занным+*dat.*
obliging *adj* услу́жливый.
oblique *adj* косо́й; (*fig*; *gram*) ко́свенный.
obliterate *vt* (*efface*) стира́ть *impf*, стере́ть *pf*; (*destroy*) уничтожа́ть *impf*, уничто́жить *pf.* **obliteration** *n* стира́ние; уничтоже́ние.
oblivion *n* забве́ние. **oblivious** *adj* (*forgetful*) забы́вчивый; **to be ~ of** не замеча́ть *impf* +*gen.*
oblong *adj* продолгова́тый.
obnoxious *adj* проти́вный.
oboe *n* гобо́й.
obscene *adj* непристо́йный.
obscenity *n* непристо́йность.
obscure *adj* (*unclear*) нея́сный; (*little known*) малоизве́стный; *vt* затемня́ть *impf*, затемни́ть *pf*; де́лать *impf*, с~ *pf* нея́сным. **obscurity** *n* нея́сность; неизве́стность.
obsequious *adj* подобостра́стный.
observance *n* соблюде́ние; (*rite*) обря́д. **observant** *adj* наблюда́тельный. **observation** *n* наблюде́ние; (*remark*) замеча́ние. **observatory** *n* обсервато́рия. **observe** *vt* (*law etc.*) соблюда́ть *impf*, соблюсти́ *pf*; (*watch*) наблюда́ть *impf*; (*remark*) замеча́ть *impf*, заме́тить *pf.* **observer** *n* наблюда́тель *m.*
obsess *vt* пресле́довать *impf*; **obsessed by** одержи́мый +*instr.* **obsession** *n* одержи́мость; (*idea*) навя́зчивая иде́я. **obsessive** *adj* навя́зчивый.
obsolete *adj* устаре́лый, вы́шедший из употребле́ния.
obstacle *n* препя́тствие.
obstetrician *n* акуше́р. **obstetrics** *n* акуше́рство.
obstinacy *n* упря́мство. **obstinate** *adj* упря́мый.
obstreperous *adj* бу́йный.
obstruct *vt* загражда́ть *impf*, загради́ть *pf*; (*hinder*) препя́тствовать *impf*, вос~ *pf* +*dat.* **obstruction** *n* загражде́ние; (*obstacle*) препя́тствие. **obstructive** *adj* загражда́ющий; препя́тствующий.
obtain *vt* получа́ть *impf*, получи́ть *pf*; достава́ть *impf*, доста́ть *pf.*
obtrusive *adj* навя́зчивый; (*thing*) броса́ющийся в глаза́.
obtuse *adj* тупо́й.
obviate *vt* устраня́ть *impf*, устрани́ть *pf.*
obvious *adj* очеви́дный.
occasion *n* слу́чай; (*cause*) по́вод; (*occurrence*) собы́тие; *vt* причиня́ть *impf*, причини́ть *pf.* **occasional** *adj* ре́дкий. **occasionally** *adv* иногда́, вре́мя от вре́мени.
occult *adj* окку́льтный; *n*: **the ~** окку́льт.
occupancy *n* заня́тие. **occupant** *n* жи́тель *m*, ~ница. **occupation** *n* заня́тие; (*military ~*) оккупа́ция; (*profession*) профе́ссия. **occupational** *adj* профессиона́льный; **~ therapy** трудотерапи́я. **occupy** *vt* занима́ть *impf*, заня́ть *pf*; (*mil*) оккупи́ровать *impf & pf.*
occur *vi* (*happen*) случа́ться *impf*, случи́ться *pf*; (*be found*) встреча́ться *impf*; ~

to приходи́ть *impf*, прийти́ *pf* в го́лову+*dat*. **occurrence** *n* слу́чай, происше́ствие.

ocean *n* океа́н. **oceanic** *adj* океа́нский.

o'clock *adv*: **(at) six ~** (в) шесть часо́в.

octagonal *adj* восьмиуго́льный.

octave *n* (*mus*) окта́ва.

October *n* октя́брь *m*; *adj* октя́брьский.

octopus *n* осьмино́г.

odd *adj* (*strange*) стра́нный; (*not in a set*) разро́зненный; (*number*) нечётный; (*not paired*) непа́рный; (*casual*) случа́йный; **five hundred ~** пятьсо́т с ли́шним; **~ job** случа́йная рабо́та. **oddity** *n* стра́нность; (*person*) чуда́к, -а́чка. **oddly** *adv* стра́нно; **~ enough** как э́то ни стра́нно. **oddment** *n* оста́ток. **odds** *n pl* ша́нсы *m pl*; **be at ~ with** (*person*) не ла́дить с+*instr*; (*things*) не соотве́тствовать *impf* +*dat*; **long (short) ~** нера́вные (почти́ ра́вные) ша́нсы *m pl*; **the ~ are that** вероя́тнее всего́, что; **~ and ends** обры́вки *m pl*.

ode *n* о́да.

odious *adj* ненави́стный.

odour *n* за́пах.

oesophagus *n* пищево́д.

of *prep expressing* **1.** *origin*: из+*gen*: **he comes ~ a working-class family** он из рабо́чей семьи́; **2.** *cause*: от+*gen*: **he died ~ hunger** он у́мер от го́лода; **3.** *authorship*: *gen*: **the works ~ Pushkin** сочине́ния Пу́шкина; **4.** *material*: из+*gen*: **made ~ wood** сде́ланный из де́рева; **5.** *reference*: о+*prep*: **he talked ~ Lenin** он говори́л о Ле́нине; **6.** *partition*: *gen* (*often in* -у́(-ю)): **a glass ~ milk, tea** стака́н молока́, ча́ю; из+*gen*: **one ~ them** оди́н из них; **7.** *belonging*: *gen*: **the capital ~ England** столи́ца А́нглии.

off *adv*: *in phrasal vv, see v, e.g.* **clear ~** убира́ться; *prep* (*from surface of*) с+*gen*; (*away from*) от+*gen*; **~ and on** вре́мя от вре́мени; **~-white** не совсе́м бе́лый.

offal *n* требуха́.

offence *n* (*insult*) оби́да; (*against law*) просту́пок, преступле́ние; **take ~** обижа́ться *impf*, оби́деться *pf* (**at** на+*acc*). **offend** *vt* обижа́ть *impf*, оби́деть *pf*; **~ against** наруша́ть *impf*, нару́шить *pf*. **offender** *n* правонаруши́тель *m*, **~**ница. **offensive** *adj* (*attacking*) наступа́тельный; (*insulting*) оскорби́тельный; (*repulsive*) проти́вный; *n* нападе́ние.

offer *vt* предлага́ть *impf*, предложи́ть *pf*; *n* предложе́ние; **on ~** в прода́же.

offhand *adj* бесцеремо́нный.

office *n* (*position*) до́лжность; (*place, room etc.*) бюро́ *neut indecl*, конто́ра, канцеля́рия. **officer** *n* должностно́е лицо́; (*mil*) офице́р. **official** *adj* служе́бный; (*authorized*) официа́льный; *n* должностно́е лицо́. **officiate** *vi* (*eccl*) соверша́ть *impf*, соверши́ть *pf* богослуже́ние. **officious** *adj* (*intrusive*) навя́зчивый.

offing *n*: **be in the ~** предстоя́ть *impf*.

off-licence *n* ви́нный магази́н. **off-load** *vt* разгружа́ть *impf*, разгрузи́ть *pf*. **off-**

putting *adj* отта́лкивающий. **offset** *vt* возмеща́ть *impf*, возмести́ть *pf*. **offshoot** *n* о́тпрыск. **offshore** *adj* прибре́жный. **offside** *adv* вне игры́. **offspring** *n* пото́мок; (*collect*) пото́мки *m pl*.

often *adv* ча́сто.

ogle *vt & i* смотре́ть *impf* с вожделе́нием на+*acc*.

ogre *n* велика́н-людое́д.

oh *int* о!; ах!

ohm *n* ом.

oil *n* ма́сло; (*petroleum*) нефть; (*paint*) ма́сло, ма́сляные кра́ски *f pl*; *vt* сма́зывать *impf*, сма́зать *pf*; **~-painting** карти́на, напи́санная ма́сляными кра́сками; **~ rig** нефтяна́я вы́шка; **~-tanker** танке́р; **~-well** нефтяна́я сква́жина. **oilfield** *n* месторожде́ние не́фти. **oilskin** *n* клеёнка; *pl* непромока́емый костю́м. **oily** *adj* маслянистый.

ointment *n* мазь.

OK *adv & adj* хорошо́, норма́льно; *int* ла́дно!; *vt* одобря́ть *impf*, одо́брить *pf*.

old *adj* ста́рый; (*ancient*; *of long standing*) стари́нный; (*former*) бы́вший; **how ~ are you?** ско́лько тебе́, вам, (*dat*) лет?; **~ age** ста́рость; **~-age pension** пе́нсия по ста́рости; **old-fashioned** старомо́дный; **~ maid** ста́рая де́ва; **~ man** (*also father, husband*) стари́к; **~-time** стари́нный; **~ woman** стару́ха; (*coll*) стару́шка.

olive *n* (*fruit*) оли́вка; (*colour*) оли́вковый цвет; *adj* оли́вковый; **~ oil** оли́вковое ма́сло.

Olympic *adj* олимпи́йский; **~ games** Олимпи́йские и́гры *f pl*.

omelette *n* омле́т.

omen *n* предзнаменова́ние.

ominous *adj* злове́щий.

omission *n* про́пуск; (*neglect*) упуще́ние. **omit** *vt* (*leave out*) пропуска́ть *impf*, пропусти́ть *pf*; (*neglect*) упуска́ть *impf*, упусти́ть *pf*.

omnibus *n* (*bus*) авто́бус; (*collection*) колле́кция.

omnipotence *n* всемогу́щество. **omnipotent** *adj* всемогу́щий. **omnipresent** *adj* вездесу́щий. **omniscient** *adj* всеве́дущий.

on *prep* (*position*) на+*prep*; (*direction*) на+*acc*; (*time*) в+*acc*; **~ the next day** на сле́дующий день; **~ Mondays** (*repeated action*) по понеде́льникам (*dat pl*); **~ the first of June** пе́рвого ию́ня (*gen*); (*concerning*) по+*prep*, о+*prep*, на+*acc*; *adv* да́льше, вперёд; *in phrasal vv, see vv, e.g.* **move ~** идти́ да́льше; **and so ~** и так да́лее, и т.д.; **be ~** (*film etc.*) идти́ *impf*; **further ~** да́льше; **later ~** по́зже.

once *adv* (оди́н) раз; (*on past occasion*) одна́жды; (*formerly*) не́когда; **all at ~** неожи́данно; **at ~** сра́зу, неме́дленно; (*if, when*) **~** как то́лько; **~ again, more** ещё раз; **~ and for all** раз и навсегда́; **~ or twice** не́сколько раз; **~ upon a time there lived ...** жил-бы́л... .

oncoming *adj*: **~ traffic** встре́чное движе́ние.

one *adj* оди́н (одна́, -но́); (*only, single*) еди́нственный; *n* оди́н; *pron*: *not usu trans-*

lated; v translated in 2nd pers sg or by impers construction: ~ **never knows** никогда́ не зна́ешь; **where can ~ buy this book?** где мо́жно купи́ть э́ту кни́гу?; ~ **after another** оди́н за други́м; ~ **and all** все до одного́; все как оди́н; ~ **and only** еди́нственный; ~ **and the same** оди́н и тот же; ~ **another** друг дру́га (*dat* -гу, *etc.*); ~ **fine day** в оди́н прекра́сный день; ~ **o'clock** час; ~**-parent family** семья́ с одни́м роди́телем; ~**-sided, -track, -way** односторо́нний; ~**-time** бы́вший; ~**-way street** у́лица односторо́ннего движе́ния.

onerous *adj* тя́гостный.

oneself *pron* себя́; -ся (*suffixed to vt*).

onion *n* (*plant*; *pl collect*) лук; (*single* ~) лу́ковица.

onlooker *n* наблюда́тель *m*.

only *adj* еди́нственный; *adv* то́лько; **if** ~ е́сли бы то́лько; ~ **just** то́лько что; *conj* но.

onset *n* нача́ло.

onslaught *n* на́тиск.

onus *n* отве́тственность.

onward(s) *adv* вперёд.

ooze *vt* & *i* сочи́ться *impf.*

opal *n* опа́л.

opaque *adj* непрозра́чный.

open *adj* откры́тый; (*frank*) открове́нный; **in the ~ air** на откры́том во́здухе; ~**-minded** *adj* непредупреждённый; *vt* & *i* открыва́ть(ся) *impf*, откры́ть(ся) *pf*; *vi* (*begin*) начина́ться *impf*, нача́ться *pf*; (*flowers*) распуска́ться *impf*, распусти́ться *pf*. **opening** *n* откры́тие; (*aperture*) отве́рстие; (*beginning*) нача́ло; *adj* нача́льный, пе́рвый; (*introductory*) вступи́тельный.

opera *n* о́пера; *attrib* о́перный; ~**-house** о́перный теа́тр.

operate *vi* де́йствовать *impf* (**upon** на+*acc*); (*med*) опери́ровать *impf* & *pf* (**on** +*acc*); *vt* управля́ть *impf* +*instr.*

operatic *adj* о́перный.

operating-theatre *n* операцио́нная *sb.* **operation** *n* де́йствие; (*med*; *mil*) опера́ция. **operational** *adj* (*in use*) де́йствующий; (*mil*) операти́вный. **operative** *adj* де́йствующий. **operator** *n* опера́тор; (*telephone* ~) телефони́ст, ~ка.

operetta *n* опере́тта.

ophthalmic *adj* глазно́й.

opinion *n* мне́ние; **in my** ~ по-мо́ему; ~ **poll** опро́с обще́ственного мне́ния. **opinionated** *adj* догмати́чный.

opium *n* о́пиум.

opponent *n* проти́вник.

opportune *adj* своевре́менный. **opportunism** *n* оппортуни́зм. **opportunist** *n* оппортуни́ст. **opportunistic** *n* оппортунисти́ческий. **opportunity** *n* слу́чай, возмо́жность.

oppose *vt* (*resist*) проти́виться *impf*, вос~ *pf* +*dat*; (*speak etc. against*) выступа́ть *impf*, вы́ступить *pf* про́тив+*gen*. **opposed** *adj* про́тив (**to** +*gen*); **as ~ to** в противополо́жность+*dat.* **opposing** *adj* проти́вный; (*opposite*) противополо́жный. **opposite** *adj* противополо́жный; (*reverse*) обра́тный; *n* противополо́жность; **just the ~** как раз наоборо́т; *adv* напро́тив; *prep* (на)про́тив+*gen*. **opposition**

n (*resistance*) сопротивлéние; (*polit*) оппозúция.

oppress *vt* угнетáть *impf*. **oppression** *n* угнетéние. **oppressive** *adj* угнетáющий. **oppressor** *n* угнетáтель *m*.

opt *vi* выбирáть *impf*, вы́брать *pf* (**for** +*acc*); ~ **out** не принимáть *impf* учáстия (**of** в+*prep*).

optic *adj* зрúтельный. **optical** *adj* оптúческий. **optician** *n* óптик. **optics** *n* óптика.

optimism *n* оптимúзм. **optimist** *n* оптимúст. **optimistic** *adj* оптимистúческий. **optimum** *adj* оптимáльный.

option *n* вы́бор. **optional** *adj* необязáтельный.

opulence *n* богáтство. **opulent** *adj* богáтый.

opus *n* óпус.

or *conj* úли; ~ **else** инáче; ~ **so** приблизúтельно.

oracle *n* орáкул.

oral *adj* ýстный; *n* ýстный экзáмен.

orange *n* (*fruit*) апельсúн; (*colour*) орáнжевый цвет; *attrib* апельсúновый; *adj* орáнжевый.

oration *n* речь. **orator** *n* орáтор.

oratorio *n* оратóрия.

oratory *n* (*speech*) красноречие.

orbit *n* орбúта; *vt* вращáться *impf* по орбúте вокрýг+*gen*. **orbital** *adj* орбитáльный.

orchard *n* фруктóвый сад.

orchestra *n* оркéстр. **orchestral** *adj* оркестрóвый. **orchestrate** *vt* оркестровáть *impf* & *pf*. **orchestration** *n* оркестрóвка.

orchid *n* орхидéя.

ordain *vt* предпúсывать *impf*, предписáть *pf*; (*eccl*) посвящáть *impf*, посвятúть *pf* (в духóвный сан).

ordeal *n* тяжёлое испытáние.

order *n* порядок; (*command*) прикáз; (*for goods*) закáз; (*insignia, medal; fraternity*) óрден; (*archit*) óрдер; *pl* (*holy* ~) духóвный сан; **in** ~ **to** (для тогó) чтóбы +*inf*; *vt* (*command*) прикáзывать *impf*, приказáть *pf* +*dat*; (*goods etc.*) закáзывать *impf*, заказáть *pf*. **orderly** *adj* аккурáтный; (*quiet*) тúхий; *n* (*med*) санитáр; (*mil*) ординáрец.

ordinance *n* декрéт.

ordinary *adj* обыкновéнный, обы́чный.

ordination *n* посвящéние.

ore *n* рудá.

organ *n* óрган; (*mus*) оргáн. **organic** *adj* органúческий. **organism** *n* органúзм. **organist** *n* органúст. **organization** *n* организáция. **organize** *vt* организóвывать *impf* (*pres not used*), организовáть *impf* (*in pres*) & *pf*; устрáивать *impf*, устрóить *pf*. **organizer** *n* организáтор.

orgy *n* óргия.

Orient *n* Востóк. **oriental** *adj* востóчный.

orient, orientate *vt* ориентúровать *impf* &*pf* (**o.s.** -ся). **orientation** *n* ориентáция.

orifice *n* отвéрстие.

origin *n* происхождéние, начáло. **original** *adj* оригинáльный; (*initial*) первоначáльный; (*genuine*) пóдлинный; *n* оригинáл. **originality** *n* оригинáльность. **originate** *vt* порождáть *impf*, породúть *pf*; *vi* брать *impf*, взять *pf* начáло (**from, in** в+*prep*, от+*gen*); (*arise*) возникáть

impf, возни́кнуть *pf*. **originator** *n* а́втор, инициа́тор.
ornament *n* украше́ние; *vt* украша́ть *impf*, укра́сить *pf*. **ornamental** *adj* декорати́вный.
ornate *adj* витиева́тый.
ornithologist *n* орнито́лог. **ornithology** *n* орнитоло́гия.
orphan *n* сирота́ *m & f*; *vt*: **be ~ed** сироте́ть *impf*, о~ *pf*. **orphanage** *n* сиро́тский дом. **orphaned** *adj* осироте́лый.
orthodox *adj* ортодокса́льный; (*eccl*, **O~**) правосла́вный. **orthodoxy** *n* ортодо́ксия; (**O~**) правосла́вие.
orthopaedic *adj* ортопеди́ческий.
oscillate *vi* колеба́ться *impf*, по~ *pf*. **oscillation** *n* колеба́ние.
osmosis *n* о́смос.
ostensible *adj* мни́мый. **ostensibly** *adv* я́кобы.
ostentation *n* выставле́ние напока́з. **ostentatious** *adj* показно́й.
osteopath *n* остеопа́т. **osteopathy** *n* остеопа́тия.
ostracize *vt* подверга́ть *impf*, подве́ргнуть *pf* остраки́зму.
ostrich *n* стра́ус.
other *adj* друго́й, ино́й; тот; **every ~** ка́ждый второ́й; **every ~ day** че́рез день; **on the ~ hand** с друго́й стороны́; **on the ~ side** на той стороне́, по ту сто́рону; **one or the ~** тот и́ли ино́й; **the ~ day** на дня́х, неда́вно; **the ~ way round** наоборо́т; **the ~s** остальны́е *sb pl*. **otherwise** *adv & conj* и́наче, а то.
otter *n* вы́дра.
ouch *int* ой!, ай!
ought *v aux* до́лжен (-жна́) (бы) *+inf*.
ounce *n* у́нция.
our, ours *poss pron* наш; свой. **ourselves** *pron* (*emph*) (мы) са́ми; (*refl*) себя́; -ся (*suffixed to vt*).
oust *vt* вытесня́ть *impf*, вы́теснить *pf*.
out *adv* **1.** *in phrasal vv often rendered by pref* вы-; **2.: to be ~** *in various senses*: **he is ~** (*not at home*) его́ нет до́ма; (*not in office etc.*) он вы́шел; (*sport*) выходи́ть *impf*, вы́йти *pf* из игры́; (*of fashion*) вы́йти *pf* из мо́ды; (*be published*) вы́йти *pf* из печа́ти; (*of candle etc.*) поту́хнуть *pf*; (*of flower*) распусти́ться *pf*; (*be unconscious*) потеря́ть *pf* созна́ние; **3.: ~-and-~** отъя́вленный; **4.: ~ of** из*+gen*, вне*+gen*; **~ of date** устаре́лый, старомо́дный; **~ of doors** на откры́том во́здухе; **~ of work** безрабо́тный.
outbid *vt* предлага́ть *impf*, предложи́ть *pf* бо́лее высо́кую це́ну, чем*+nom*. **outboard** *adj*: **~ motor** подвесно́й мото́р *m*. **outbreak** *n* (*of anger, disease*) вспы́шка; (*of war*) нача́ло. **outbuilding** *n* надво́рная постро́йка. **outburst** *n* взрыв. **outcast** *n* изгна́нник. **outcome** *n* результа́т. **outcry** *n* (шу́мные) проте́сты *m pl*. **outdated** *adj* устаре́лый. **outdo** *vt* превосходи́ть *impf*, превзойти́ *pf*.
outdoor *adj*, **outdoors** *adv* на откры́том во́здухе, на у́лице.
outer *adj* (*external*) вне́шний, нару́жный; (*far from centre*) да́льний. **outermost** *adj* са́мый да́льний.

outfit *n* (*equipment*) снаряже́ние; (*set of things*) набо́р; (*clothes*) наря́д. **outgoing** *adj* уходя́щий; (*sociable*) общи́тельный. **outgoings** *n pl* изде́ржки *f pl*. **outgrow** *vt* выраста́ть *impf*, вы́расти *pf* из+*gen*. **outhouse** *n* надво́рная постро́йка.

outing *n* прогу́лка, экску́рсия.

outlandish *adj* дико́винный. **outlaw** *n* лицо́ вне зако́на; банди́т; *vt* объявля́ть *impf*, объяви́ть *pf* вне зако́на. **outlay** *n* изде́ржки *f pl*. **outlet** *n* выходно́е отве́рстие; (*fig*) вы́ход; (*market*) ры́нок; (*shop*) торго́вая то́чка. **outline** *n* очерта́ние, ко́нтур; (*sketch*, *summary*) набро́сок; *vt* оче́рчивать *impf*, очерти́ть *pf*; (*plans etc.*) набра́сывать *impf*, наброса́ть *pf*. **outlive** *vt* пережи́ть *pf*. **outlook** *n* перспекти́вы *f pl*; (*attitude*) кругозо́р. **outlying** *adj* периферийный. **outmoded** *adj* старомо́дный. **outnumber** *vt* чи́сленно превосходи́ть *impf*, превзойти́ *pf*. **out-patient** *n* амбулато́рный больно́й *sb*. **outpost** *n* форпо́ст. **output** *n* вы́пуск, проду́кция.

outrage *n* безобра́зие; (*indignation*) возмуще́ние; *vt* оскорбля́ть *impf*, оскорби́ть *pf*. **outrageous** *adj* возмути́тельный.

outright *adv* (*entirely*) вполне́; (*once for all*) раз (и) навсегда́; (*openly*) откры́то; *adj* прямо́й. **outset** *n* нача́ло; **at the ~** внача́ле; **from the ~** с са́мого нача́ла.

outside *n* нару́жная сторона́; **at the ~** са́мое бо́льшее; **from the ~** извне́; **on the ~** снару́жи; *adj* нару́жный, вне́шний; (*sport*) кра́йний; *adv* (*on the ~*) снару́жи; (*to the ~*) нару́жу; (*out of doors*) на откры́том во́здухе, на у́лице; *prep* вне+*gen*; за преде́лами+*gen*. **outsider** *n* посторо́нний *sb*; (*sport*) аутса́йдер.

outsize *adj* бо́льше станда́ртного разме́ра. **outskirts** *n pl* окра́ина. **outspoken** *adj* прямо́й. **outstanding** *adj* (*remarkable*) выдаю́щийся; (*unpaid*) неупла́ченный. **outstay** *vt*: **~ one's welcome** засиживаться *impf*, засиде́ться *pf*. **outstretched** *adj* распростёртый. **outstrip** *vt* обгоня́ть *impf*, обогна́ть *pf*.

outward *adj* (*external*) вне́шний, нару́жный. **outwardly** *adv* вне́шне, на вид. **outwards** *adv* нару́жу.

outweigh *vt* переве́шивать *impf*, переве́сить *pf*. **outwit** *vt* перехитри́ть *pf*.

oval *adj* ова́льный; *n* ова́л.

ovary *n* яи́чник.

ovation *n* ова́ция.

oven *n* (*industrial*) печь; (*domestic*) духо́вка.

over *adv & prep with vv*: *see vv*; *prep* (*above*) над+*instr*; (*through*; *covering*) по+*dat*; (*concerning*) о+*prep*; (*across*) че́рез+*acc*; (*on the other side of*) по ту сто́рону+*gen*; (*more than*) свы́ше+*gen*; бо́лее+*gen*; (*with age*) за+*acc*; **all ~** (*finished*) всё ко́нчено; (*everywhere*) повсю́ду; **all ~ the country** по всей стране́; **~ again** ещё раз; **~ against** по сравне́нию с+*instr*; **~ and**

above не говоря́ уже́ о+*prep*; ~ **the telephone** по телефо́ну; ~ **there** вон там.

overall *n* хала́т; *pl* комбинезо́н; *adj* о́бщий. **overawe** *vt* внуша́ть *impf*, внуши́ть *pf* благогове́йный страх+*dat*. **overbalance** *vi* теря́ть *impf*, по~ *pf* равнове́сие. **overbearing** *adj* вла́стный. **overboard** *adv* (*motion*) за́ борт; (*position*) за бо́ртом. **overcast** *adj* о́блачный. **overcoat** *n* пальто́ *neut indecl*. **overcome** *vt* преодолева́ть *impf*, преодоле́ть *pf*; *adj* охва́ченный. **overcrowded** *adj* перепо́лненный. **overcrowding** *n* переполне́ние. **overdo** *vt* (*cook*) пережа́ривать *impf*, пережа́рить *pf*; ~ **it, things** (*work too hard*) переутомля́ться *impf*, переутоми́ться *pf*; (*go too far*) переба́рщивать *impf*, переборщи́ть *pf*.

overdose *n* чрезме́рная до́за. **overdraft** *n* превыше́ние креди́та; (*amount*) долг ба́нку. **overdraw** *vi* превыша́ть *impf*, превы́сить *pf* креди́т (в ба́нке). **overdue** *adj* просро́ченный; **be** ~ (*late*) запа́здывать *impf*, запозда́ть *pf*. **overestimate** *vt* переоце́нивать *impf*, переоцени́ть *pf*. **overflow** *vi* перелива́ться *impf*, перели́ться *pf*; (*river etc.*) разлива́ться *impf*, разли́ться *pf*; (*outlet*) перели́в. **overgrown** *adj* заро́сший. **overhang** *vt* & *i* выступа́ть *impf* над+*instr*; *n* свес, вы́ступ.

overhaul *vt* ремонти́ровать *impf* & *pf*; *n*: ремо́нт. **overhead** *adv* наверху́, над голово́й; *adj* возду́шный, подвесно́й; *n*: *pl* накладны́е расхо́ды *m pl*. **overhear** *vt* нечáянно слы́шать *impf*, у~ *pf*. **overheat** *vt* & *i* перегрева́ть(ся) *impf*, перегре́ть(ся) *pf*. **overjoyed** *adj* в восто́рге (**at** от+*gen*). **overland** *adj* сухопу́тный; *adv* по су́ше. **overlap** *vt* части́чно покрыва́ть *impf*, покры́ть *pf*; *vi* части́чно совпада́ть *impf*, совпа́сть *pf*.

overleaf *adv* на оборо́те. **overload** *vt* перегружа́ть *impf*, перегрузи́ть *pf*. **overlook** *vt* (*look down on*) смотре́ть *impf* све́рху на+*acc*; (*of window*) выходи́ть *impf* на, в, +*acc*; (*not notice*) не замеча́ть *impf*, заме́тить *pf* +*gen*; (~ *offence etc.*) проща́ть *impf*, прости́ть *pf*.

overly *adv* сли́шком.

overnight *adv* (*during the night*) за́ ночь; (*suddenly*) неожи́данно; **stay** ~ ночева́ть *impf*, пере~ *pf*; *adj* ночно́й. **overpay** *vt* перепла́чивать *impf*, переплати́ть *pf*.

over-populated *adj* перенаселённый. **over-population** *n* перенаселённость. **overpower** *vt* одолева́ть *impf*, одоле́ть *pf*. **overpriced** *adj* завы́шенный в цене́. **overproduction** *n* перепроизво́дство. **overrate** *vt* переоце́нивать *impf*, переоцени́ть *pf*. **override** *vt* (*fig*) отверга́ть *impf*, отве́ргнуть *pf*. **overriding** *adj* гла́вный, реша́ющий. **overrule** *vt* отверга́ть *impf*, отве́ргнуть *pf*. **overrun** *vt* (*conquer*) завоёвывать *impf*, завоева́ть *pf*; **be** ~ **with** кише́ть *impf* +*instr*.

overseas *adv* за мо́рем,

через мо́ре; *adj* замо́рский. **oversee** *vt* надзира́ть *impf* за+*instr*. **overseer** *n* надзира́тель *m*, ~ница. **overshadow** *vt* затмева́ть *impf*, затми́ть *pf*. **overshoot** *vi* переходи́ть *impf*, перейти́ *pf* грани́цу. **oversight** *n* случа́йный недосмо́тр. **oversleep** *vi* просыпа́ть *impf*, проспа́ть *pf*. **overspend** *vi* тра́тить *impf* сли́шком мно́го. **overstate** *vt* преувели́чивать *impf*, преувели́чить *pf*. **overstep** *vt* переступа́ть *impf*, переступи́ть *pf* +*acc*, че́рез+*acc*.

overt *adj* я́вный, откры́тый.

overtake *vt* обгоня́ть *impf*, обогна́ть *pf*. **overthrow** *vt* сверга́ть *impf*, све́ргнуть *pf*.

overtime *n* (*work*) сверхуро́чная рабо́та; (*payment*) сверхуро́чное *sb*; *adv* сверхуро́чно.

overtone *n* скры́тый намёк.

overture *n* предложе́ние; (*mus*) увертю́ра.

overturn *vt* & *i* опроки́дывать(ся) *impf*, опроки́нуть(ся) *pf*. **overwhelm** *vt* подавля́ть *impf*, подави́ть *pf*. **overwhelming** *adj* подавля́ющий. **overwork** *vt* & *i* переутомля́ть(ся) *impf*, переутоми́ть(ся) *pf*; *n* переутомле́ние.

owe *vt* (~ *money*) быть до́лжным +*acc* & *dat*; (*be indebted*) быть обя́занным +*instr* & *dat*; **he, she, ~s me three roubles** он до́лжен, она́ должна́, мне три рубля́; **she ~s him her life** она́ обя́зана ему́ жи́знью. **owing** *adj*: **be ~** причита́ться *impf* (**to** +*dat*); **~ to** из-за+*gen*, по причи́не+*gen*.

owl *n* сова́.

own *adj* свой; (свой) со́бственный; **on one's ~** самостоя́тельно; (*alone*) оди́н; *vt* (*possess*) владе́ть *impf* +*instr*; (*admit*) признава́ть *impf*, призна́ть *pf*; **~ up** признава́ться *impf*, призна́ться *pf*. **owner** *n* владе́лец. **ownership** *n* владе́ние (**of** +*instr*), со́бственность.

ox *n* вол.

oxidation *n* окисле́ние. **oxide** *n* о́кись. **oxidize** *vt* & *i* окисля́ть(ся) *impf*, оки́слить(ся) *pf*. **oxygen** *n* кислоро́д.

oyster *n* у́стрица.

ozone *n* озо́н.

P

pace *n* шаг; (*fig*) темп; **keep ~ with** идти́ *impf* в но́гу с+*instr*; **set the ~** задава́ть *impf*, зада́ть *pf* темп; *vi*: **~ up and down** ходи́ть *indet* взад и вперёд. **pacemaker** *n* (*med*) электро́нный стимуля́тор.

pacifism *n* пацифи́зм. **pacifist** *n* пацифи́ст. **pacify** *vt* усмиря́ть *impf*, усмири́ть *pf*.

pack *n* у́зел, вьюк; (*soldier's*) ра́нец; (*hounds*) свора́; (*wolves*) ста́я; (*cards*) коло́да; *vt* (& *i*) упако́вывать(ся) *impf*, упакова́ть(ся) *pf*; (*cram*) набива́ть *impf*, наби́ть *pf*. **package** *n* посы́лка, паке́т; **~ holiday** организо́ванная туристи́ческая пое́здка. **packaging** *n* упако́вка. **packet** *n* паке́т; па́чка; (*large sum of money*) ку́ча де́нег. **packing-case** *n* я́щик.

pact *n* пакт.

pad *n* (*cushion*) поду́шечка; (*shin ~ etc.*) щито́к; (*of paper*)

блокно́т; *vt* подбива́ть *impf*, подби́ть *pf*. **padding** *n* наби́вка.
paddle[1] *n* (*oar*) весло́; *vi* (*row*) грести́ *impf*.
paddle[2] *vi* (*wade*) ходи́ть *indet*, идти́ *det*, пойти́ *pf* босико́м по воде́.
paddock *n* вы́гон.
padlock *n* вися́чий замо́к; *vt* запира́ть *impf*, запере́ть *pf* на вися́чий замо́к.
paediatric *adj* педиатри́ческий. **paediatrician** *n* педиа́тор.
pagan *n* язы́чник, -ица; *adj* язы́ческий. **paganism** *n* язы́чество.
page[1] *n* (~*-boy*) паж; *vt* (*summon*) вызыва́ть *impf*, вы́звать *pf*.
page[2] *n* (*of book*) страни́ца.
pageant *n* пы́шная проце́ссия. **pageantry** *n* пы́шность.
pail *n* ведро́.
pain *n* бо́ль; *pl* (*efforts*) уси́лия *neut pl*; **~-killer** болеутоля́ющее сре́дство; *vt* (*fig*) огорча́ть *impf*, огорчи́ть *pf*. **painful** *adj* боле́зненный; **be ~** (*part of body*) боле́ть *impf*. **painless** *adj* безболе́зненный. **painstaking** *adj* стара́тельный.
paint *n* кра́ска; *vt* кра́сить *impf*, по~ *pf*; (*portray*) писа́ть *impf*, на~ *pf* кра́сками. **paintbrush** *n* кисть. **painter** *n* (*artist*) худо́жник, -ица; (*decorator*) маля́р. **painting** *n* (*art*) жи́вопись; (*picture*) карти́на.
pair *n* па́ра; *often not translated with nn denoting a single object, e.g.* **a ~ of scissors** но́жницы (-ц) *pl*; **a ~ of trousers** па́ра брюк; *vt* спа́ривать *impf*, спа́рить *pf*; **~ off** разделя́ться *impf*, раздели́ться *pf* по па́рам.
Pakistan *n* Пакиста́н. **Pakistani** *n* пакиста́нец, -а́нка; *adj* пакиста́нский.
pal *n* прия́тель *m*, ~ница.
palace *n* дворе́ц.
palatable *adj* вку́сный; (*fig*) прия́тный. **palate** *n* нёбо; (*fig*) вкус.
palatial *adj* великоле́пный.
palaver *n* (*trouble*) беспоко́йство; (*nonsense*) чепуха́.
pale[1] *n* (*stake*) кол; **beyond the ~** невообрази́мый.
pale[2] *adj* бле́дный; *vi* бледне́ть *impf*, по~ *pf*.
palette *n* пали́тра.
pall[1] *n* покро́в.
pall[2] *vi*: **~ on** надоеда́ть *impf*, надое́сть *pf* +*dat*.
palliative *adj* паллиати́вный; *n* паллиати́в.
pallid *adj* бле́дный. **pallor** *n* бле́дность.
palm[1] *n* (*tree*) па́льма; **P~ Sunday** Ве́рбное воскресе́нье.
palm[2] *n* (*of hand*) ладо́нь; *vt*: **~ off** всу́чивать *impf*, всучи́ть *pf* (**on** +*dat*).
palpable *adj* осяза́емый.
palpitations *n pl* сердцебие́ние.
paltry *adj* ничто́жный.
pamper *vt* балова́ть *impf*, из~ *pf*.
pamphlet *n* брошю́ра.
pan[1] *n* (*saucepan*) кастрю́ля; (*frying-~*) сковорода́; (*of scales*) ча́шка; *vt*: **~ out** промыва́ть *impf*, промы́ть *pf*; (*fig*) выходи́ть *impf*, вы́йти *pf*.
pan[2] *vi* (*cin*) панорами́ровать *impf* & *pf*.
panacea *n* панаце́я.
panache *n* рисо́вка.

pancake *n* блин.
pancreas *n* поджелу́дочная железа́.
panda *n* па́нда.
pandemonium *n* гвалт.
pander *vi*: **~ to** потво́рствовать *impf +dat.*
pane *n* око́нное стекло́.
panel *n* пане́ль; (*control-~*) щит управле́ния; (*of experts*) гру́ппа специали́стов; (*of judges*) жюри́ *neut indecl.* **panelling** *n* пане́льная обши́вка.
pang *n pl* му́ки (-к) *pl.*
panic *n* па́ника; **~-stricken** охва́ченный па́никой; *vi* впада́ть *impf*, впасть *pf* в па́нику. **panicky** *adj* пани́ческий.
pannier *n* корзи́нка.
panorama *n* панора́ма. **panoramic** *adj* панора́мный.
pansy *n* аню́тины гла́зки (-зок) *pl.*
pant *vi* дыша́ть *impf* с оды́шкой.
panther *n* пантера.
panties *n pl* тру́сики (-ков) *pl.*
pantomime *n* рожде́ственское представле́ние; (*dumb show*) пантоми́ма.
pantry *n* кладова́я *sb.*
pants *n pl* трусы́ (-со́в) *pl*; (*trousers*) брю́ки (-к) *pl.*
papal *adj* па́пский.
paper *n* бума́га; *pl* докуме́нты *m pl*; (*newspaper*) газе́та; (*wallpaper*) обо́и (-о́ев) *pl*; (*treatise*) докла́д; *adj* бума́жный; *vt* окле́ивать *impf*, окле́ить *pf* обо́ями. **paperback** *n* кни́га в бума́жной обло́жке. **paperclip** *n* скре́пка. **paperwork** *n* канцеля́рская рабо́та.
par *n*: **feel below ~** чу́вствовать *impf* себя́ нева́жно; **on a ~ with** наравне́ с+*instr.*
parable *n* при́тча.
parabola *n* пара́бола.
parachute *n* парашю́т; *vi* спуска́ться *impf*, спусти́ться *pf* с парашю́том. **parachutist** *n* парашюти́ст.
parade *n* пара́д; *vi* шествова́ть *impf*; *vt* (*show off*) выставля́ть *impf*, вы́ставить *pf* напока́з.
paradigm *n* паради́гма.
paradise *n* рай.
paradox *n* парадо́кс. **paradoxical** *adj* парадокса́льный.
paraffin *n* (*~ oil*) кероси́н.
paragon *n* образе́ц.
paragraph *n* абза́ц.
parallel *adj* паралле́льный; *n* паралле́ль; *vt* соответствова́ть *impf +dat.*
paralyse *vt* парализова́ть *impf* & *pf.* **paralysis** *n* парали́ч.
parameter *n* пара́метр.
paramilitary *adj* полувое́нный.
paramount *adj* первостепе́нный.
paranoia *n* парано́йя. **paranoid** *adj*: **he is ~** он парано́ик.
parapet *n* (*mil*) бру́ствер.
paraphernalia *n* принадле́жности *f pl.*
paraphrase *n* переска́з; *vt* переска́зывать *impf*, пересказа́ть *pf.*
parasite *n* парази́т. **parasitic** *adj* паразити́ческий.
parasol *n* зо́нтик.
paratrooper *n* парашюти́ст-деса́нтник.
parcel *n* паке́т, посы́лка.
parch *vt* иссуша́ть *impf*, иссуши́ть *pf*; **become ~ed** пересыха́ть *impf*, пересо́хнуть *pf.*
parchment *n* перга́мент.
pardon *n* проще́ние; (*law*) поми́лование; *vt* проща́ть

impf, прости́ть *pf*; (*law*) поми́ловать *pf*.

pare *vt* (*fruit*) чи́стить *impf*, о~ *pf*; ~ **away, down** уре́зывать *impf*, уре́зать *pf*.

parent *n* роди́тель *m*, ~ница. **parentage** *n* происхожде́ние. **parental** *adj* роди́тельский.

parentheses *n pl* (*brackets*) ско́бки *f pl*.

parish *n* прихо́д. **parishioner** *n* прихожа́нин, -а́нка.

parity *n* ра́венство.

park *n* парк; (*for cars etc.*) стоя́нка; *vt* & *abs* ста́вить *impf*, по~ *pf* (маши́ну). **parking** *n* стоя́нка.

parliament *n* парла́мент. **parliamentarian** *n* парламента́рий. **parliamentary** *adj* парла́ментский.

parlour *n* гости́ная *sb*.

parochial *adj* прихо́дский; (*fig*) ограни́ченный. **parochialism** *n* ограни́ченность.

parody *n* паро́дия; *vt* пароди́ровать *impf* & *pf*.

parole *n* че́стное сло́во; **on** ~ освобождённый под че́стное сло́во.

paroxysm *n* пароксизм.

parquet *n* парке́т; *attrib* парке́тный.

parrot *n* попуга́й.

parry *vt* пари́ровать *impf* & *pf*, от~ *pf*.

parsimonious *adj* скупо́й.

parsley *n* петру́шка.

parsnip *n* пастерна́к.

parson *n* свяще́нник.

part *n* часть; (*in play*) роль; (*mus*) па́ртия; **for the most** ~ бо́льшей ча́стью; **in** ~ ча́стью; **for my** ~ что каса́ется меня́; **take** ~ **in** уча́ствовать *impf* в+*prep*; ~**-time** (за́нятый) непо́лный рабо́чий день; *vt* & *i* (*divide*) разделя́ть(ся) *impf*, раздели́ть(ся) *pf*; *vi* (*leave*) расстава́ться *impf*, расста́ться *pf* (**from, with** с+*instr*); ~ **one's hair** де́лать *impf*, с~ *pf* себе́ пробо́р.

partake *vi* принима́ть *impf*, приня́ть *pf* уча́стие (**in, of** в+*prep*); (*eat*) есть *impf*, съ~ *pf* (**of** +*acc*).

partial *adj* части́чный; (*biased*) пристра́стный; ~ **to** неравноду́шный к+*dat*. **partiality** *n* (*bias*) пристра́стность. **partially** *adv* части́чно.

participant *n* уча́стник, -ица (**in** +*gen*). **participate** *vi* уча́ствовать *impf* (**in** в+*prep*). **participation** *n* уча́стие.

participle *n* прича́стие.

particle *n* части́ца.

particular *adj* осо́бый, осо́бенный; (*fussy*) разбо́рчивый; *n* подро́бность; **in** ~ в ча́стности.

parting *n* (*leave-taking*) проща́ние; (*of hair*) пробо́р.

partisan *n* (*adherent*) сторо́нник; (*mil*) партиза́н; *attrib* (*biased*) пристра́стный; партиза́нский.

partition *n* (*wall*) перегоро́дка; (*polit*) разде́л; *vt* разделя́ть *impf*, раздели́ть *pf*; ~ **off** отгора́живать *impf*, отгороди́ть *pf*.

partly *adv* части́чно.

partner *n* (*in business*) компаньо́н; (*in dance, game*) партнёр, ~ша. **partnership** *n* това́рищество.

partridge *n* куропа́тка.

party *n* (*polit*) па́ртия; (*group*) гру́ппа; (*social gathering*) вечери́нка; (*law*) сторона́; **be a** ~ **to** принима́ть *impf*, приня́ть *pf* уча́стие в+*prep*; *attrib* парти́йный; ~ **line** (*polit*) ли́ния па́ртии; (*telephone*) о́бщий телефо́нный про́вод; ~ **wall** о́бщая стена́.

pass *vt* & *i* (*go past*; *of time*) проходи́ть *impf*, пройти́ *pf* (**by** ми́мо+*gen*); (*travel past*) проезжа́ть *impf*, прое́хать *pf* (**by** ми́мо+*gen*); (~ *examination*) сдать *pf* (экза́мен); *vt* (*sport*) пасова́ть *impf*, пасну́ть *pf*; (*overtake*) обгоня́ть *impf*, обогна́ть *pf*; (*time*) проводи́ть *impf*, провести́ *pf*; (*hand on*) передава́ть *impf*, переда́ть *pf*; (*law*, *resolution*) утвержда́ть *impf*, утверди́ть *pf*; (*sentence*) выноси́ть *impf*, вы́нести *pf* (**upon** +*dat*); ~ **as, for** слыть *impf*, про~ *pf* +*instr*, за+*acc*; ~ **away** (*die*) сконча́ться *pf*; ~ **o.s. off as** выдава́ть *impf*, вы́дать *pf* себя́ за+*acc*; ~ **out** теря́ть *impf*, по~ *pf* созна́ние; ~ **over** (*in silence*) обходи́ть *impf*, обойти́ *pf* молча́нием; ~ **round** передава́ть *impf*, переда́ть *pf*; ~ **up** подава́ть *impf*, пода́ть *pf*; (*miss*) пропуска́ть *impf*, пропусти́ть *pf*; *n* (*permit*) про́пуск; (*sport*) пас; (*geog*) перева́л; **come to** ~ случа́ться *impf*, случи́ться *pf*; **make a** ~ **at** пристава́ть *impf*, приста́ть *pf* к+*dat*.

passable *adj* проходи́мый, прое́зжий; (*not bad*) неплохо́й.

passage *n* прохо́д; (*of time*) тече́ние; (*sea trip*) рейс; (*in house*) коридо́р; (*in book*) отры́вок; (*mus*) пасса́ж.

passenger *n* пассажи́р.

passer-by *n* прохо́жий *sb*.

passing *adj* (*transient*) мимолётный; *n*: **in** ~ мимохо́дом.

passion *n* страсть (**for** к+*dat*). **passionate** *adj* стра́стный.

passive *adj* пасси́вный; (*gram*) страда́тельный; *n* страда́тельный зало́г. **passivity** *n* пасси́вность.

Passover *n* евре́йская Па́сха.

passport *n* па́спорт.

password *n* паро́ль *m*.

past *adj* про́шлый; (*gram*) проше́дший; *n* про́шлое *sb*; (*gram*) проше́дшее вре́мя *neut*; *prep* ми́мо+*gen*; (*beyond*) за+*instr*; *adv* ми́мо.

pasta *n* макаро́нные изде́лия *neut pl*.

paste *n* (*of flour*) те́сто; (*creamy mixture*) па́ста; (*glue*) кле́й; (*jewellery*) страз; *vt* накле́ивать *impf*, накле́ить *pf*.

pastel *n* (*crayon*) пасте́ль; (*drawing*) рису́нок пасте́лью; *attrib* пасте́льный.

pasteurize *vt* пастеризова́ть *impf* & *pf*.

pastime *n* времяпрепровожде́ние.

pastor *n* па́стор. **pastoral** *adj* (*bucolic*) пастора́льный; (*of pastor*) па́сторский.

pastry *n* (*dough*) те́сто; (*cake*) пиро́жное *sb*.

pasture *n* (*land*) па́стбище.

pasty[1] *n* пирожо́к.

pasty[2] *adj* (~*-faced*) бле́дный.

pat *n* шлепо́к; (*of butter etc.*) кусо́к; *vt* хлопа́ть *impf*, по~ *pf*.

patch *n* запла́та; (*over eye*) повя́зка (на глазу́); (*spot*) пятно́; (*of land*) уча́сток земли́; *vt* ста́вить *impf*, по~ *pf* запла́ту на+*acc*; ~ **up** (*fig*) ула́живать *impf*, ула́дить *pf*.

patchwork *n* лоску́тная рабо́та. **patchy** *adj* неро́вный.
pâté *n* паште́т.
patent *adj* я́вный; ~ **leather** лакиро́ванная ко́жа; *n* пате́нт; *vt* патентова́ть *impf*, за~ *pf*.
paternal *adj* отцо́вский. **paternity** *n* отцо́вство.
path *n* тропи́нка, тропа́; (*way*) путь *m*.
pathetic *adj* жа́лкий.
pathological *adj* патологи́ческий. **pathologist** *n* пато́лог.
pathos *n* па́фос.
pathway *n* тропи́нка, тропа́.
patience *n* терпе́ние; (*cards*) пасья́нс. **patient** *adj* терпели́вый; *n* больно́й *sb*, пацие́нт, ~ка.
patio *n* терра́са.
patriarch *n* патриа́рх. **patriarchal** *adj* патриарха́льный.
patriot *n* патрио́т, ~ка. **patriotic** *adj* патриоти́ческий. **patriotism** *n* патриоти́зм.
patrol *n* патру́ль *m*; **on** ~ на дозо́ре; *vt* & *i* патрули́ровать *impf*.
patron *n* покрови́тель *m*; (*of shop*) клие́нт. **patronage** *n* покрови́тельство. **patroness** *n* покрови́тельница. **patronize** *vt* (*treat condescendingly*) снисходи́тельно относи́ться *impf*, к+*dat*. **patronizing** *adj* покрови́тельственный.
patronymic *n* о́тчество.
patter *vi* (*sound*) бараба́нить *impf*; *n* посту́кивание.
pattern *n* (*design*) узо́р; (*model*) образе́ц; (*sewing*) вы́кройка.
paunch *n* брюшко́.
pauper *n* бедня́к.
pause *n* па́уза, переры́в; (*mus*) ферма́та; *vi* остана́вливаться *impf*, останови́ться *pf*.
pave *vt* мости́ть *impf*, вы́~ *pf*; ~ **the way** подготовля́ть *impf*, подгото́вить *pf* по́чву (**for** для+*gen*). **pavement** *n* тротуа́р.
pavilion *n* павильо́н.
paw *n* ла́па; *vt* тро́гать *impf* ла́пой; (*horse*) бить *impf* копы́том.
pawn[1] *n* (*chess*) пе́шка.
pawn[2] *n*: **in** ~ в закла́де; *vt* закла́дывать *impf*, заложи́ть *pf*. **pawnbroker** *n* ростовщи́к. **pawnshop** *n* ломба́рд.
pay *vt* плати́ть *impf*, за~, у~ *pf* (**for** за+*acc*); (*bill etc.*) опла́чивать *impf*, оплати́ть *pf*; *vi* (*be profitable*) окупа́ться *impf*, окупи́ться *pf*; *n* жа́лованье, зарпла́та; ~ **packet** полу́чка; ~**-roll** платёжная ве́домость. **payable** *adj* подлежа́щий упла́те. **payee** *n* получа́тель *m*. **payload** *n* поле́зная нагру́зка. **payment** *n* упла́та, платёж.
PC *abbr* (*of* **personal computer**) ПК; (*of* **politically correct**) полити́чески корре́ктный.
pea *n* (*also pl*, *collect*) горо́х.
peace *n* мир; **in** ~ в поко́е; ~ **and quiet** мир и тишина́. **peaceable, peaceful** *adj* ми́рный.
peach *n* пе́рсик.
peacock *n* павли́н.
peak *n* (*of cap*) козырёк; (*summit*; *fig*) верши́на; ~ **hour** часы́ *m pl* пик.
peal *n* (*sound*) звон, трезво́н; (*of laughter*) взрыв.
peanut *n* ара́хис.
pear *n* гру́ша.
pearl *n* (*also fig*) жемчу́жина; *pl* (*collect*) же́мчуг.
peasant *n* крестья́нин, -я́нка; *attrib* крестья́нский.

peat *n* торф.
pebble *n* га́лька.
peck *vt & i* клева́ть *impf*, клю́нуть *pf*; *n* клево́к.
pectoral *adj* грудно́й.
peculiar *adj* (*distinctive*) своеобра́зный; (*strange*) стра́нный; ~ **to** сво́йственный +*dat*. **peculiarity** *n* осо́бенность; стра́нность.
pecuniary *adj* де́нежный.
pedagogical *adj* педагоги́ческий.
pedal *n* педа́ль; *vi* нажима́ть *impf*, нажа́ть *pf* педа́ль; (*ride bicycle*) е́хать *impf*, по~ *pf* на велосипе́де.
pedant *n* педа́нт. **pedantic** *adj* педанти́чный.
peddle *vt* торгова́ть *impf* вразно́с+*instr*.
pedestal *n* пьедеста́л.
pedestrian *adj* пешехо́дный; (*prosaic*) прозаи́ческий; *n* пешехо́д; ~ **crossing** перехо́д.
pedigree *n* родосло́вная *sb*; *adj* поро́дистый.
pedlar *n* разно́счик.
pee *n* пи-пи́ *neut indecl*; *vi* мочи́ться *impf*, по~ *pf*.
peek *vi* (~ *in*) загля́дывать *impf*, загляну́ть *pf*; (~ *out*) выгля́дывать *impf*, вы́глянуть *pf*.
peel *n* кожура́; *vt* очища́ть *impf*, очи́стить *pf*; *vi* (*skin*) шелуши́ться *impf*; (*paint*, ~ *off*) сходи́ть *impf*, сойти́ *pf*. **peelings** *n pl* очи́стки (-ков) *pl*.
peep *vi* (~ *in*) загля́дывать *impf*, загляну́ть *pf*; (~ *out*) выгля́дывать *impf*, вы́глянуть *pf*; *n* (*glance*) бы́стрый взгляд; ~**-hole** глазо́к.
peer[1] *vi* всма́триваться *impf*, всмотре́ться *pf* (**at** в+*acc*).
peer[2] *n* (*noble*) пэр; (*person one's age*) све́рстник.
peeved *adj* раздражённый. **peevish** *adj* раздражи́тельный.
peg *n* ко́лышек; (*clothes* ~) крючо́к; (*for hat etc.*) ве́шалка; **off the** ~ гото́вый; *vt* прикрепля́ть *impf*, прикрепи́ть *pf* ко́лышком, -ками.
pejorative *adj* уничижи́тельный.
pelican *n* пелика́н.
pellet *n* ша́рик; (*shot*) дроби́на.
pelt[1] *n* (*skin*) шку́ра.
pelt[2] *vt* забра́сывать *impf*, заброса́ть *pf*; *vi* (*rain*) бараба́нить *impf*.
pelvis *n* таз.
pen[1] *n* (*for writing*) ру́чка; ~**-friend** друг по перепи́ске.
pen[2] *n* (*enclosure*) заго́н.
penal *adj* уголо́вный. **penalize** *vt* штрафова́ть *impf*, о~ *pf*. **penalty** *n* наказа́ние; (*sport*) штраф; ~ **area** штрафна́я площа́дка; ~ **kick** штрафно́й уда́р. **penance** *n* епитимья́.
penchant *n* скло́нность (**for** к+*dat*).
pencil *n* каранда́ш; ~**-sharpener** точи́лка.
pendant *n* подве́ска.
pending *adj* (*awaiting decision*) ожида́ющий реше́ния; *prep* (*until*) в ожида́нии +*gen*, до+*gen*.
pendulum *n* ма́ятник.
penetrate *vt* проника́ть *impf*, прони́кнуть *pf* в+*acc*. **penetrating** *adj* проница́тельный; (*sound*) пронзи́тельный. **penetration** *n* проникнове́ние; (*insight*) проница́тельность.

penguin *n* пингви́н.
penicillin *n* пеницилли́н.
peninsula *n* полуо́стров.
penis *n* пе́нис.
penitence *n* раска́яние. **penitent** *adj* раска́ивающийся; *n* ка́ющийся гре́шник.
penknife *n* перочи́нный нож.
pennant *n* вы́мпел.
penniless *adj* без гроша́.
penny *n* пе́нни *neut indecl*, пенс.
pension *n* пе́нсия; *vt*: ~ **off** увольня́ть *impf*, уво́лить *pf* на пе́нсию. **pensionable** *adj* (*age*) пенсио́нный. **pensioner** *n* пенсионе́р, ~ка.
pensive *adj* заду́мчивый.
pentagon *n* пятиуго́льник; **the P~** Пентаго́н.
Pentecost *n* Пятидеся́тница.
penthouse *n* шика́рная кварти́ра на ве́рхнем этаже́.
pent-up *adj* (*anger etc.*) сдёрживаемый.
penultimate *adj* предпосле́дний.
penury *n* нужда́.
peony *n* пио́н.
people *n pl* (*persons*) лю́ди *pl*; *sg* (*nation*) наро́д; *vt* населя́ть *impf*, насели́ть *pf*.
pepper *n* пе́рец; *vt* пе́рчить *impf*, на~, по~ *pf*. **peppercorn** *n* перчи́нка.
peppermint *n* пе́речная мя́та; (*sweet*) мя́тная конфе́та.
per *prep* (*for each*) (*person*) на+*acc*; **as** ~ согла́сно+*dat*; ~ **annum** в год; ~ **capita** на челове́ка; ~ **hour** в час; ~ **se** сам по себе́.
perceive *vt* воспринима́ть *impf*, восприня́ть *pf*.
per cent *adv* & *n* проце́нт. **percentage** *n* проце́нт; (*part*) часть.
perceptible *adj* заме́тный. **perception** *n* восприя́тие; (*quality*) понима́ние. **perceptive** *adj* то́нкий.
perch[1] *n* (*fish*) о́кунь *m*.
perch[2] *n* (*roost*) насе́ст; *vi* сади́ться *impf*, сесть *pf*. **perched** *adj* высоко́ сидя́щий, располо́женный.
percussion *n* (~ *instruments*) уда́рные инструме́нты *m pl*.
peremptory *adj* повели́тельный.
perennial *adj* (*enduring*) ве́чный; *n* (*bot*) многоле́тнее расте́ние.
perestroika *n* перестро́йка.
perfect *adj* соверше́нный; (*gram*) перфе́ктный; *n* перфе́кт; *vt* соверше́нствовать *impf*, у~ *pf*. **perfection** *n* соверше́нство. **perfective** *adj* (*n*) соверше́нный (вид).
perforate *vt* перфори́ровать *impf* & *pf*. **perforation** *n* перфора́ция.
perform *vt* (*carry out*) исполня́ть *impf*, испо́лнить *pf*; (*theat*, *mus*) игра́ть *impf*, сыгра́ть *pf*; *vi* выступа́ть *impf*, вы́ступить *pf*; (*function*) рабо́тать *impf*. **performance** *n* исполне́ние; (*of person*, *device*) де́йствие; (*of play etc.*) представле́ние, спекта́кль *m*; (*of engine etc.*) эксплуатацио́нные ка́чества *neut pl*. **performer** *n* исполни́тель *m*.
perfume *n* духи́ (-хо́в) *pl*; (*smell*) арома́т.
perfunctory *adj* пове́рхностный.
perhaps *adv* мо́жет быть.
peril *n* опа́сность, риск. **perilous** *adj* опа́сный, риско́ванный.

perimeter *n* вне́шняя грани́ца; (*geom*) пери́метр.

period *n* пери́од; (*epoch*) эпо́ха; (*menstrual*) ме́сячные *sb pl*. **periodic** *adj* периоди́ческий. **periodical** *adj* периоди́ческий; *n* периоди́ческое изда́ние.

peripheral *adj* перифери́йный. **periphery** *n* перифери́я.

periscope *n* периско́п.

perish *vi* погиба́ть *impf*, поги́бнуть *pf*; (*spoil*) по́ртиться *impf*, ис~ *pf*. **perishable** *adj* скоропо́ртящийся.

perjure *v*: ~ **o.s.** наруша́ть *impf*, нару́шить *pf* кля́тву. **perjury** *n* лжесвиде́тельство.

perk[1] *n* льго́та.

perk[2] *vi*: ~ **up** оживля́ться *impf*, оживи́ться *pf*. **perky** *adj* бо́йкий.

perm *n* перманéнт. **permanence** *n* постоя́нство. **permanent** *adj* постоя́нный.

permeable *adj* проница́емый. **permeate** *vt* проника́ть *impf*, прони́кнуть *pf* в+*acc*.

permissible *adj* допусти́мый. **permission** *n* разреше́ние. **permissive** *adj* (сли́шком) либера́льный; ~ **society** о́бщество вседозво́ленности. **permissiveness** *n* вседозво́ленность. **permit** *vt* разреша́ть *impf*, разреши́ть *pf* +*dat*; *n* про́пуск.

permutation *n* перестано́вка.

pernicious *adj* па́губный.

perpendicular *adj* перпендикуля́рный; *n* перпендикуля́р.

perpetrate *vt* соверша́ть *impf*, соверши́ть *pf*. **perpetrator** *n* вино́вник.

perpetual *adj* ве́чный. **perpetuate** *vt* увекове́чивать *impf*, увекове́чить *pf*. **perpetuity** *n* ве́чность; **in** ~ навсегда́, наве́чно.

perplex *vt* озада́чивать *impf*, озада́чить *pf*. **perplexity** *n* озада́ченность.

persecute *vt* пресле́довать *impf*. **persecution** *n* пресле́дование.

perseverance *n* насто́йчивость. **persevere** *vi* насто́йчиво, продолжа́ть *impf* (**in, at** *etc.* +*acc*, *inf*).

Persian *n* перс, ~ия́нка; *adj* перси́дский.

persist *vi* упо́рствовать *impf* (**in** в+*prep*); насто́йчиво продолжа́ть *impf* (**in** +*acc*, *inf*). **persistence** *n* упо́рство. **persistent** *adj* упо́рный.

person *n* челове́к; (*in play*; *gram*) лицо́; **in** ~ ли́чно. **personable** *adj* привлека́тельный. **personage** *n* ли́чность. **personal** *adj* ли́чный. **personality** *n* ли́чность. **personally** *adv* ли́чно. **personification** *n* олицетворе́ние. **personify** *vt* олицетворя́ть *impf*, олицетвори́ть *pf*.

personnel *n* ка́дры (-ров) *pl*, персона́л; ~ **department** отде́л ка́дров.

perspective *n* перспекти́ва.

perspiration *n* пот. **perspire** *vi* поте́ть *impf*, вс~ *pf*.

persuade *vt* (*convince*) убежда́ть *impf*, убеди́ть *pf* (**of** в+*prep*); (*induce*) угова́ривать *impf*, уговори́ть *pf*. **persuasion** *n* убежде́ние. **persuasive** *adj* убеди́тельный.

pertain *vi*: ~ **to** относи́ться *impf* отнести́сь *pf* к+*dat*.

pertinent *adj* уме́стный.

perturb *vt* трево́жить *impf*, вс~ *pf*.

peruse *vt* (*read*) внима́тельно чита́ть *impf*, про~ *pf*; (*fig*) рассма́тривать *impf*, рассмотре́ть *pf*.

pervade *vt* наполня́ть *impf*. **pervasive** *adj* распространённый.

perverse *adj* капри́зный. **perversion** *n* извраще́ние. **pervert** *vt* извраща́ть *impf*, изврати́ть *pf*; *n* извращённый челове́к.

pessimism *n* пессими́зм. **pessimist** *n* пессими́ст. **pessimistic** *adj* пессимисти́ческий.

pest *n* вреди́тель *m*; (*fig*) зану́да. **pester** *vt* пристава́ть *impf*, приста́ть *pf* к+*dat*. **pesticide** *n* пестици́д.

pet *n* (*animal*) дома́шнее живо́тное *sb*; (*favourite*) люби́мец, -мица; ~ **shop** зоомагази́н; *vt* ласка́ть *impf*.

petal *n* лепесто́к.

peter *vi*: ~ **out** (*road*) исчеза́ть *impf*, исче́знуть *pf*; (*stream*; *enthusiasm*) иссяка́ть *impf*, исся́кнуть *pf*.

petite *adj* ма́ленькая.

petition *n* пети́ция; *vt* подава́ть *impf*, пода́ть *pf* проше́ние +*dat*. **petitioner** *n* проси́тель *m*.

petrified *adj* окамене́лый; **be** ~ (*fig*) оцепене́ть *pf* (**with** от+*gen*).

petrol *n* бензи́н; ~ **pump** бензоколо́нка; ~ **station** бензозапра́вочная ста́нция; ~ **tank** бензоба́к. **petroleum** *n* нефть.

petticoat *n* ни́жняя ю́бка.

petty *adj* ме́лкий; ~ **cash** де́ньги (де́нег, -ньга́м) *pl* на ме́лкие расхо́ды.

petulant *adj* раздражи́тельный.

pew *n* (церко́вная) скамья́.

phallic *adj* фалли́ческий. **phallus** *n* фа́ллос.

phantom *n* фанто́м.

pharmaceutical *adj* фармацевти́ческий. **pharmacist** *n* фармаце́вт. **pharmacy** *n* фармаци́я; (*shop*) апте́ка.

phase *n* фа́за; *vt*: ~ **in, out** постепе́нно вводи́ть *impf*, упраздня́ть *impf*.

Ph.D. *abbr* (*of* **Doctor of Philosophy**) кандида́т нау́к.

pheasant *n* фаза́н.

phenomenal *adj* феномена́льный. **phenomenon** *n* фено́мен.

phial *n* пузырёк.

philanderer *n* волоки́та *m*.

philanthropic *adj* филантропи́ческий. **philanthropist** *n* филантро́п. **philanthropy** *n* филантро́пия.

philately *n* филатели́я.

philharmonic *adj* филармони́ческий.

Philistine *n* (*fig*) фили́стер.

philosopher *n* фило́соф. **philosophical** *adj* филосо́фский. **philosophize** *vi* филосо́фствовать *impf*. **philosophy** *n* филосо́фия.

phlegm *n* мокрота́. **phlegmatic** *adj* флегмати́ческий.

phobia *n* фо́бия.

phone *n* телефо́н; *vt* & *i* звони́ть *impf*, по~ *pf* +*dat*. *See also* **telephone**

phonetic *adj* фонети́ческий. **phonetics** *n* фоне́тика.

phoney *n* подде́льный.

phosphorus *n* фо́сфор.

photo *n* фо́то *neut indecl*. **photocopier** *n* копирова́льная маши́на. **photocopy** *n* фотоко́пия; *vt* де́лать *impf*, с~ *pf* фотоко́пию +*gen*. **photogenic** *adj* фотогени́чный.

photograph *n* фотогра́фия; *vt* фотографи́ровать *impf*, с~ *pf*. **photographer** *n* фото́граф. **photographic** *adj* фотографи́ческий. **photography** *n* фотогра́фия.

phrase *n* фра́за; *vt* формули́ровать *impf*, с~ *pf*.

physical *adj* физи́ческий; ~ **education** физкульту́ра; ~ **exercises** заря́дка. **physician** *n* врач. **physicist** *n* фи́зик. **physics** *n* фи́зика.

physiological *n* физиологи́ческий. **physiologist** *n* физио́лог. **physiology** *n* физиоло́гия. **physiotherapist** *n* физиотерапе́вт. **physiotherapy** *n* физиотерапи́я.

physique *n* телосложе́ние.

pianist *n* пиани́ст, ~ка. **piano** *n* фортепья́но *neut indecl*; (*grand*) роя́ль *m*; (*upright*) пиани́но *neut indecl*.

pick[1] *vt* (*flower*) срыва́ть *impf*, сорва́ть *pf*; (*gather*) собира́ть *impf*, собра́ть *pf*; (*select*) выбира́ть *impf*, вы́брать *pf*; ~ **one's nose, teeth** ковыря́ть *impf*, ковырну́ть *pf* в носу́, в зуба́х; ~ **a quarrel** иска́ть *impf* ссо́ры (**with** с+*instr*); ~ **one's way** выбира́ть *impf*, вы́брать *pf* доро́гу; ~ **on** (*nag*) придира́ться *impf* к+*dat*; ~ **out** отбира́ть *impf*, отобра́ть *pf*; ~ **up** (*lift*) поднима́ть *impf*, подня́ть *pf*; (*acquire*) приобрета́ть *impf*, приобрести́ *pf*; (*fetch*) (*on foot*) заходи́ть *impf*, зайти́ *pf* за+*instr*; (*in vehicle*) заезжа́ть *impf*, зае́хать *pf* за+*instr*; (*a cold*; *a girl*) подцепля́ть *impf*, подцепи́ть *pf*; ~ **o.s. up** подниматься *impf*, подня́ться *pf*; ~**-up** (*truck*) пика́п; (*electron*) звукоснима́тель *m*.

pick[2] *n* вы́бор; (*best part*) лу́чшая часть; **take your** ~ выбира́й(те)!

pick[3], **pickaxe** *n* кирка́.

picket *n* (*person*) пике́тчик, -ица; (*collect*) пике́т; *vt* пикети́ровать *impf*.

pickle *n* соле́нье; *vt* соли́ть *impf*, по~ *pf*. **pickled** *adj* солёный.

pickpocket *n* карма́нник.

picnic *n* пикни́к.

pictorial *adj* изобрази́тельный; (*illustrated*) иллюстри́рованный. **picture** *n* карти́на; (*of health etc.*) воплоще́ние; (*film*) фильм; **the** ~**s** кино́ *neut indecl*; *vt* (*to o.s.*) представля́ть *impf*, предста́вить *pf* себе́. **picturesque** *adj* живопи́сный.

pie *n* пиро́г.

piece *n* кусо́к, часть; (*one of set*) шту́ка; (*of paper*) листо́к; (*mus, literature*) произведе́ние; (*chess*) фигу́ра; (*coin*) моне́та; **take to** ~**s** разбира́ть *impf*, разобра́ть *pf* (на ча́сти); ~ **of advice** сове́т; ~ **of information** све́дение; ~ **of news** но́вость; ~**-work** сде́льщина; ~**-worker** сде́льщик; *vt*: ~ **together** воссоздава́ть *impf*, воссозда́ть *pf* карти́ну +*gen*. **piecemeal** *adv* по частя́м.

pier *n* (*mole*) мол; (*projecting into sea*) пирс; (*of bridge*) бык; (*between windows etc.*) просте́нок.

pierce *vt* пронза́ть *impf*, пронзи́ть *pf*; (*ears*) прока́лывать *impf*, проколо́ть *pf*. **piercing** *adj* пронзи́тельный.

piety *n* на́божность.

pig *n* свинья́. **pigheaded** *adj* упря́мый. **piglet** *n* поросёнок. **pigsty** *n* свина́рник. **pigtail** *n* коси́чка.

pigeon *n* го́лубь; **~-hole** отделе́ние для бума́г.

pigment *n* пигме́нт. **pigmentation** *n* пигмента́ция.

pike *n* (*fish*) щу́ка.

pilchard *n* сарди́н(к)а.

pile[1] *n* (*heap*) ку́ча, ки́па; *vt*: **~ up** сва́ливать *impf*, свали́ть *pf* в ку́чу; (*load*) нагружа́ть *impf*, нагрузи́ть *pf* (**with** +*instr*); *vi*: **~ in(to), on** забира́ться *impf*, забра́ться *pf* в+*acc*; **~ up** накопля́ться, нака́пливаться *impf*, накопи́ться *pf*.

pile[2] *n* (*on cloth etc.*) ворс.

piles *n pl* геморро́й *collect*.

pilfer *vt* ворова́ть *impf*.

pilgrim *n* пилигри́м. **pilgrimage** *n* пало́мничество.

pill *n* пилю́ля; **the ~** противозача́точная пилю́ля.

pillage *vt* гра́бить *impf*, о~ *pf*; *v abs* мародёрствовать *impf*.

pillar *n* столб; **~-box** стоя́чий почто́вый я́щик.

pillion *n* за́днее сиде́нье (мотоци́кла).

pillory *n* позо́рный столб; *vt* (*fig*) пригвожда́ть *impf*, пригвозди́ть *pf* к позо́рному столбу́.

pillow *n* поду́шка. **pillowcase** *n* на́волочка.

pilot *n* (*naut*) ло́цман; (*aeron*) пило́т; *adj* о́пытный, про́бный; *vt* пилоти́ровать *impf*.

pimp *n* сво́дник.

pimple *n* прыщ.

pin *n* була́вка; (*peg*) па́лец; **~-point** то́чно определя́ть *impf*, определи́ть *pf*; **~-stripe** то́нкая поло́ска; *vt* прика́лывать *impf*, приколо́ть *pf*; (*press*) прижима́ть *impf*, прижа́ть *pf* (**against** к+*dat*).

pinafore *n* пере́дник.

pincers *n pl* (*tool*) кле́щи (-щей) *pl*, пинце́т; (*claw*) клешни́ *f pl*.

pinch *vt* щипа́ть *impf*, (у)щипну́ть *pf*; (*finger in door etc.*) прищемля́ть *impf*, прищеми́ть *pf*; (*of shoe*) жать *impf*; (*steal*) стяну́ть *pf*; *n* щипо́к; (*of salt*) щепо́тка; **at a ~** в кра́йнем слу́чае.

pine[1] *vi* томи́ться *impf*; **~ for** тоскова́ть *impf* по+*dat*, *prep*.

pine[2] *n* (*tree*) сосна́.

pineapple *n* анана́с.

ping-pong *n* пинг-по́нг.

pink *n* (*colour*) ро́зовый цвет; *adj* ро́зовый.

pinnacle *n* верши́на.

pint *n* пи́нта.

pioneer *n* пионе́р, **~**ка; *vt* прокла́дывать *impf*, проложи́ть *pf* путь к+*dat*.

pious *adj* на́божный.

pip[1] *n* (*seed*) зёрнышко.

pip[2] *n* (*sound*) бип.

pipe *n* труба́; (*mus*) ду́дка; (*for smoking*) тру́бка; **~-dream** пуста́я мечта́; *vt* пуска́ть *impf*, пусти́ть *pf* по труба́м; *vi* **~ down** затиха́ть *impf*, зати́хнуть *pf*. **pipeline** *n* трубопрово́д; (*oil* **~**) нефтепрово́д. **piper** *n* волы́нщик. **piping** *adj*: **~ hot** с пы́лу.

piquant *adj* пика́нтный.

pique *n*: **in a fit of ~** в поры́ве раздраже́ния.

pirate *n* пира́т.

pirouette *n* пируэ́т; *vi* де́лать *impf*, с~ *pf* пируэ́т(ы).

Pisces *n* Ры́бы *f pl*.

pistol *n* пистоле́т.

piston *n* по́ршень *m*.

pit *n* я́ма; (*mine*) ша́хта; (*orchestra* ~) орке́стр; (*motor-racing*) запра́вочно-ремо́нтный пункт; *vt*: ~ **against** выставля́ть *impf*, вы́ставить *pf* про́тив+*gen*.

pitch[1] *n* (*resin*) смола́; **~-black** чёрный как смоль; **~-dark** о́чень тёмный.

pitch[2] *vt* (*camp, tent*) разбива́ть *impf*, разби́ть *pf*; (*throw*) броса́ть *impf*, бро́сить *pf*; *vi* (*fall*) па́дать *impf*, (у)па́сть *pf*; (*ship*) кача́ть *impf*, *n* (*football* ~ *etc.*) по́ле; (*degree*) у́ровень *m*; (*mus*) высота́; (*slope*) укло́н.

pitcher *n* (*vessel*) кувши́н.

pitchfork *n* ви́лы (-л) *pl*.

piteous *adj* жа́лкий.

pitfall *n* западня́.

pith *n* сердцеви́на; (*essence*) суть. **pithy** *adj* (*fig*) содержа́тельный.

pitiful *adj* жа́лкий. **pitiless** *adj* безжа́лостный.

pittance *n* жа́лкие гроши́ (-ше́й) *pl*.

pity *n* жа́лость; **it's a** ~ жа́лко, жаль; **take** ~ **on** сжа́литься *pf* над+*instr*; **what a** ~ как жа́лко!; *vt* жале́ть *impf*, по~ *pf*; **I** ~ **you** мне жаль тебя́.

pivot *n* сте́ржень *m*; (*fig*) центр; *vi* враща́ться *impf*.

pixie *n* эльф.

pizza *n* пи́цца.

placard *n* афи́ша, плака́т.

placate *vt* умиротворя́ть *impf*, умиротвори́ть *pf*.

place *n* ме́сто; **in** ~ **of** вме́сто+*gen*; **in the first, second,** ~ во-пе́рвых, во-вторы́х; **out of** ~ не на ме́сте; (*unsuitable*) неуме́стный; **take** ~ случа́ться *impf*, случи́ться *pf*; (*pre-arranged event*) состоя́ться *pf*; **take the** ~ **of** заменя́ть *impf*, замени́ть *pf*; *vt* (*stand*) ста́вить *impf*, по~ *pf*; (*lay*) класть *impf*, положи́ть *pf*; (*an order etc.*) помеща́ть *impf*, помести́ть *pf*.

placenta *n* плаце́нта.

placid *adj* споко́йный.

plagiarism *n* плагиа́т. **plagiarize** *vt* заи́мствовать *impf* & *pf*.

plague *n* чума́; *vt* му́чить *impf*, за~, из~ *pf*.

plaice *n* ка́мбала.

plain *n* равни́на; *adj* (*clear*) я́сный; (*simple*) просто́й; (*ugly*) некраси́вый; **~-clothes policeman** переоде́тый полице́йский *sb*.

plaintiff *n* исте́ц, исти́ца.

plaintive *adj* жа́лобный.

plait *n* коса́; *vt* плести́ *impf*, с~ *pf*.

plan *n* план; *vt* плани́ровать *impf*, за~, с~ *pf*; (*intend*) намерева́ться *impf* +*inf*.

plane[1] *n* (*tree*) плата́н.

plane[2] *n* (*tool*) руба́нок; *vt* строга́ть *impf*, вы~ *pf*.

plane[3] *n* (*surface*) пло́скость; (*level*) у́ровень *m*; (*aeroplane*) самолёт.

planet *n* плане́та.

plank *n* доска́.

plant *n* расте́ние; (*factory*) заво́д; *vt* сажа́ть *impf*, посади́ть *pf*; (*fix firmly*) про́чно ста́вить *impf*, по~ *pf*; (*garden etc.*) заса́живать *impf*, засади́ть *pf* (**with** +*instr*).

plantation *n* (*of trees*) (лесо)насажде́ние; (*of cotton etc.*) планта́ция.

plaque *n* доще́чка.

plasma *n* пла́зма.

plaster *n* пла́стырь *m*; (*for walls etc.*) штукату́рка; (*of Paris*) гипс; *vt* (*wall*) штукату́рить *impf*, от~, о~ *pf*; (*cover*) облепля́ть *impf*, облепи́ть *pf*. **plasterboard** *n* суха́я штукату́рка. **plasterer** *n* штукату́р.

plastic *n* пластма́сса; *adj* (*malleable*) пласти́чный; (*made of* ~) пластма́ссовый; ~ **surgery** пласти́ческая хирурги́я.

plate *n* таре́лка; (*metal sheet*) лист; (*in book*) (вкладна́я) иллюстра́ция; (*name ~ etc.*) доще́чка.

plateau *n* плато́ *neut indecl*.

platform *n* платфо́рма; (*rly*) перро́н.

platinum *n* пла́тина.

platitude *n* бана́льность.

platoon *n* взвод.

plausible *adj* правдоподо́бный.

play *vt* & *i* игра́ть *impf*, сыгра́ть *pf* (*game*) в+*acc*, (*instrument*) на+*prep*, (*record*) ста́вить *impf*, по~ *pf*; ~ **down** преуменьша́ть *impf*, преуме́ньшить *pf*; ~ **a joke, trick, on** подшу́чивать *impf*, подшути́ть *pf* над+*instr*; ~ **off** игра́ть *impf*, сыгра́ть *pf* реша́ющую па́ртию; ~**-off** реша́ющая встре́ча; ~ **safe** де́йствовать *impf* наверняка́; *n* игра́; (*theat*) пье́са. **player** *n* игро́к; (*actor*) актёр, актри́са; (*musician*) музыка́нт. **playful** *adj* игри́вый. **playground** *n* площа́дка для игр. **playgroup, playschool** *n* де́тский сад. **playing** *n*: ~**-card** игра́льная ка́рта; ~**-field** игрова́я площа́дка. **playmate** *n* друг де́тства. **plaything** *n* игру́шка. **playwright** *n* драмату́рг.

plea *n* (*entreaty*) мольба́; (*law*) заявле́ние. **plead** *vi* умоля́ть *impf* (**with** +*acc*; **for** о+*prep*); *vt* (*offer as excuse*) ссыла́ться *impf*, сосла́ться *pf* на+*acc*; ~ **(not) guilty** (не) признава́ть *impf*, призна́ть *pf* себя́ вино́вным.

pleasant *adj* прия́тный. **pleasantry** *n* любе́зность. **please** *vt* нра́виться *impf*, по~ *pf* +*dat*; *imper* пожа́луйста; бу́дьте добры́. **pleased** *adj* дово́льный; *predic* рад. **pleasing, pleasurable** *adj* прия́тный. **pleasure** *n* удово́льствие.

pleat *n* скла́дка; *vt* плиссирова́ть *impf*.

plebiscite *n* плебисци́т.

plectrum *n* плектр.

pledge *n* (*security*) зало́г; (*promise*) заро́к, обеща́ние; *vt* отдава́ть *impf*, отда́ть *pf* в зало́г; ~ **o.s.** обя́зываться *impf*, обяза́ться *pf*; ~ **one's word** дава́ть *impf*, дать *pf* сло́во.

plentiful *adj* оби́льный. **plenty** *n* изоби́лие; ~ **of** мно́го+*gen*.

plethora *n* (*fig*) изоби́лие.

pleurisy *n* плеври́т.

pliable *adj* ги́бкий.

pliers *n pl* плоскогу́бцы (-цев) *pl*.

plight *n* незави́дное положе́ние.

plimsolls *n pl* спорти́вные та́почки *f pl*.

plinth *n* пли́нтус.

plod *vi* тащи́ться *impf*.

plonk *vt* плю́хнуть *pf*.

plot *n* (*of land*) уча́сток; (*of book etc.*) фа́була; (*conspiracy*) за́говор; *vt* (*on graph, map,* *etc.*) нанося́ть *impf*, нанести́ на гра́фик, на ка́рту; *v abs* (*conspire*) составля́ть *impf*, соста́вить *pf* за́говор.

plough *n* плуг; *vt* паха́ть *impf*, вс~ *pf*; *vi*: ~ **through** пробива́ться *impf*, проби́ться *pf* сквозь+*acc*.

ploy *n* уло́вка.

pluck *n* (*courage*) сме́лость; *vt* (*chicken*) щипа́ть *impf*, об~ *pf*; (*mus*) щипа́ть *impf*; (*flower*) срыва́ть *impf*, сорва́ть *pf*; ~ **up courage** собира́ться *impf*, собра́ться *pf* с ду́хом; *vi*: ~ **at** дёргать *impf*, дёрнуть *pf*. **plucky** *adj* сме́лый.

plug *n* (*stopper*) про́бка; (*electr*) ви́лка; (*electr socket*) розе́тка; *vt* (~ *up*) затыка́ть *impf*, заткну́ть *pf*; ~ **in** включа́ть *impf*, включи́ть *pf*.

plum *n* сли́ва.

plumage *n* опере́ние.

plumb *n* лот; *adv* вертика́льно; (*fig*) то́чно; *vt* измеря́ть *impf*, изме́рить *pf* глубину́+*gen*; (*fig*) проника́ть *impf*, прони́кнуть *pf* в+*acc*; ~ **in** подключа́ть *impf*, подключи́ть *pf*.

plumber *n* водопрово́дчик. **plumbing** *n* водопрово́д.

plume *n* (*feather*) перо́; (*on hat etc.*) султа́н.

plummet *vi* па́дать *impf*, (у)па́сть *pf*.

plump[1] *adj* пу́хлый.

plump[2] *vi*: ~ **for** выбира́ть *impf*, вы́брать *pf*.

plunder *vt* гра́бить *impf*, о~ *pf*; *n* добы́ча.

plunge *vt* & *i* (*immerse*) погружа́ть(ся) *impf*, погрузи́ть(ся) *pf* (**into** в+*acc*); *vi* (*dive*) ныря́ть *impf*, нырну́ть *pf*; (*rush*) броса́ться *impf*, бро́ситься *pf*. **plunger** *n* плу́нжер.

pluperfect *n* давнопроше́дшее вре́мя *neut*.

plural *n* мно́жественное число́. **pluralism** *n* плюрали́зм. **pluralistic** *adj* плюралисти́ческий.

plus *prep* плюс+*acc*; *n* (знак) плюс.

plushy *adj* шика́рный.

plutonium *n* плуто́ний.

ply *vt* (*tool*) рабо́тать *impf* +*instr*; (*task*) занима́ться *impf* +*instr*; (*keep supplied*) по́тчевать *impf* (**with** +*instr*); ~ **with questions** засыпа́ть *impf*, засы́пать *pf* вопро́сами.

plywood *n* фане́ра.

p.m. *adv* по́сле полу́дня.

pneumatic *adj* пневмати́ческий; ~ **drill** отбо́йный молото́к.

pneumonia *n* воспале́ние лёгких.

poach[1] *vt* (*cook*) вари́ть *impf*; ~**ed egg** яйцо́-пашо́т.

poach[2] *vi* браконье́рствовать *impf*. **poacher** *n* браконье́р.

pocket *n* карма́н; **out of** ~ в убы́тке; ~ **money** карма́нные де́ньги (-нег, -ньга́м) *pl*; *vt* класть *impf*, положи́ть *pf*. в карма́н.

pock-marked *adj* рябо́й.

pod *n* стручо́к.

podgy *adj* то́лстенький.

podium *n* трибу́на; (*conductor's*) пульт.

poem *n* стихотворе́ние; (*longer* ~) поэ́ма. **poet** *n* поэ́т. **poetess** *n* поэте́сса. **poetic(al)** *adj* поэти́ческий. **poetry** *n* поэ́зия, стихи́ *m pl*.

pogrom *n* погро́м.

poignancy *n* острота́. **poignant** *adj* о́стрый.

point[1] *n* то́чка; (*place*; *in list*) пункт; (*in score*) очко́; (*in time*) моме́нт; (*in space*) ме́сто; (*essence*) суть; (*sense*) смысл; (*sharp* ~) остриё; (*tip*) ко́нчик; (*power* ~) ште́псель *m*; *pl* (*rly*) стре́лка; **be on the ~ of** (*doing*) собира́ться *impf*, собра́ться *pf* +*inf*; **beside, off, the ~** некста́ти; **that is the ~** в э́том и де́ло; **the ~ is that** де́ло в том, что; **there is no ~** (*in doing*) не име́ет смы́сла (+*inf*); **to the ~** кста́ти; **~-blank** прямо́й; **~ of view** то́чка зре́ния.

point[2] *vt* (*wall*) расшива́ть *impf*, расши́ть *pf* швы+*gen*; (*gun etc.*) наводи́ть *impf*, навести́ *pf* (**at** на+*acc*); *vi* по-, у-, ка́зывать *impf*, по-, у-, каза́ть *pf* (**at, to** на+*acc*). **pointed** *adj* (*sharp*) о́стрый. **pointer** *n* указа́тель *m*, стре́лка. **pointless** *adj* бессмы́сленный.

poise *n* уравнове́шенность. **poised** *adj* (*composed*) уравнове́шенный; (*ready*) гото́вый (**to** к+*dat*).

poison *n* яд; *vt* отравля́ть *impf*, отрави́ть *pf*. **poisonous** *adj* ядови́тый.

poke *vt* (*prod*) ты́кать *impf*, ткнуть *pf*; **~ fun at** подшу́чивать *impf*, подшути́ть *pf* над+*instr*; (*thrust*) сова́ть *impf*, су́нуть *pf*; **~ the fire** меша́ть *impf*, по~ *pf* у́гли в ками́не; *n* тычо́к. **poker**[1] *n* (*rod*) кочерга́.

poker[2] *n* (*cards*) по́кер.

poky *adj* те́сный.

Poland *n* По́льша.

polar *adj* поля́рный; **~ bear** бе́лый медве́дь *m*. **polarity** *n* поля́рность. **polarize** *vt* поляризова́ть *impf & pf*.

pole[1] *n* (*geog*; *phys*) по́люс; **~-star** Поля́рная звезда́.

pole[2] *n* (*rod*) столб, шест; **~-vaulting** прыжо́к с шесто́м.

Pole *n* поля́к, по́лька.

polecat *n* хорёк.

polemic *adj* полеми́ческий; *n* поле́мика.

police *n* поли́ция; (*as pl*) полице́йские *sb*; (*in Russia*) мили́ция; **~ station** полице́йский уча́сток. **policeman** *n* полице́йский *sb*, полисме́н; (*in Russia*) милиционе́р. **policewoman** *n* же́нщина-полице́йский *sb*; (*in Russia*) же́нщина-милиционе́р.

policy[1] *n* поли́тика.

policy[2] *n* (*insurance*) по́лис.

polio *n* полиомиели́т.

Polish *adj* по́льский.

polish *n* (*gloss, process*) полиро́вка; (*substance*) политу́ра; (*fig*) лоск; *vt* полирова́ть *impf*, от~ *pf*; **~ off** расправля́ться *impf*, распра́виться *pf* с+*instr*. **polished** *adj* отто́ченный.

polite *adj* ве́жливый. **politeness** *n* ве́жливость.

politic *adj* полити́чный. **political** *adj* полити́ческий; **~ economy** политэконо́мика; **~ prisoner** политзаключённый *sb*. **politician** *n* поли́тик. **politics** *n* поли́тика.

poll *n* (*voting*) голосова́ние; (*opinion* ~) опро́с; **go to the ~s** голосова́ть *impf*, про~ *pf*; *vt* получа́ть *impf*, получи́ть *pf*.

pollen *n* пыльца́. **pollinate** *vt* опыля́ть *impf*, опыли́ть *pf*.

polling *attrib*: **~ booth** каби́на

для голосова́ния; ~ **station** избира́тельный уча́сток.

pollutant *n* загрязни́тель *m*. **pollute** *vt* загрязня́ть *impf*, загрязни́ть *pf*. **pollution** *n* загрязне́ние.

polo *n* по́ло *neut indecl*; ~-**neck sweater** водола́зка.

polyester *n* полиэфи́р. **polyethylene** *n* полиэтиле́н. **polyglot** *n* полигло́т; *adj* многоязы́чный. **polygon** *n* многоуго́льник. **polymer** *n* полиме́р. **polystyrene** *n* полистиро́л. **polytechnic** *n* техни́ческий вуз. **polythene** *n* полиэтиле́н. **polyunsaturated** *adj*: ~ **fats** полиненасы́щенные жиры́ *m pl*. **polyurethane** *n* полиурета́н.

pomp *n* пы́шность. **pomposity** *n* напы́щенность. **pompous** *adj* напы́щенный.

pond *n* пруд.

ponder *vt* обду́мывать *impf*, обду́мать *pf*; *vi* размышля́ть *impf*, размы́слить *pf*.

ponderous *adj* тяжелове́сный.

pony *n* по́ни *m indecl*.

poodle *n* пу́дель *m*.

pool[1] *n* (*of water*) прудо́к; (*puddle*) лу́жа; (*swimming* ~) бассе́йн.

pool[2] *n* (*collective stakes*) совоку́пность ста́вок; (*common fund*) о́бщий фонд; *vt* объединя́ть *impf*, объедини́ть *pf*.

poor *adj* бе́дный; (*bad*) плохо́й; *n*: **the** ~ бедняки́ *m pl*. **poorly** *predic* нездоро́в.

pop[1] *vi* хло́пать *impf*, хло́пнуть *pf*; *vt* (*put*) бы́стро всу́нуть *pf* (**into** в+*acc*); ~ **in on** забега́ть *impf*, забежа́ть *pf* к+*dat*; *n* хлопо́к.

pop[2] *adj* поп-; ~ **concert** поп-конце́рт; ~ **music** поп-му́зыка.

pope *n* Па́па *m*.

poplar *n* то́поль *m*.

poppy *n* мак.

populace *n* просто́й наро́д. **popular** *adj* наро́дный; (*liked*) популя́рный. **popularity** *n* популя́рность. **popularize** *vt* популяризи́ровать *impf* & *pf*. **populate** *vt* населя́ть *impf*, насели́ть *pf*. **population** *n* населе́ние. **populous** *adj* (много)лю́дный.

porcelain *n* фарфо́р.

porch *n* крыльцо́.

porcupine *n* дикобра́з.

pore[1] *n* по́ра.

pore[2] *vi*: ~ **over** погружа́ться *impf*, погрузи́ться *pf* в+*acc*.

pork *n* свини́на.

pornographic *adj* порнографи́ческий. **pornography** *n* порногра́фия.

porous *adj* по́ристый.

porpoise *n* морска́я свинья́.

porridge *n* овся́ная ка́ша.

port[1] *n* (*harbour*) порт; (*town*) порто́вый го́род.

port[2] *n* (*naut*) ле́вый борт.

port[3] *n* (*wine*) портве́йн.

portable *adj* портати́вный.

portend *vt* предвеща́ть *impf*. **portent** *n* предзнаменова́ние. **portentous** *adj* злове́щий.

porter[1] *n* (*at door*) швейца́р.

porter[2] *n* (*carrier*)носи́льщик.

portfolio *n* портфе́ль *m*; (*artist's*) па́пка.

porthole *n* иллюмина́тор.

portion *n* часть, до́ля; (*of food*) по́рция.

portly *adj* доро́дный.

portrait *n* портре́т. **portray** *vt* изобража́ть *impf*, изобрази́ть *pf*. **portrayal** *n* изображе́ние.

Portugal *n* Португáлия. **Portuguese** *n* португáлец, -лка; *adj* португáльский.

pose *n* пóза; *vt* (*question*) стáвить *impf*, по~ *pf*; (*a problem*) представля́ть *impf*, предстáвить *pf*; *vi* позúровать *impf*; ~ **as** выдавáть *impf*, вы́дать *pf* себя́ за+*acc*.

posh *adj* шикáрный.

posit *vt* постулúровать *impf* & *pf*.

position *n* положéние, позúция; **in a ~ to** в состоя́нии +*inf*; *vt* стáвить *impf*, по~ *pf*.

positive *adj* положúтельный; (*convinced*) увéренный; (*proof*) несомнéнный; *n* (*phot*) позитúв.

possess *vt* обладáть *impf* +*instr*; владéть *impf* +*instr*; (*of feeling etc.*) овладевáть *impf*, овладéть *pf* +*instr*. **possessed** *adj* одержúмый. **possession** *n* владéние (**of** +*instr*); *pl* сóбственность. **possessive** *adj* сóбственнический. **possessor** *n* обладáтель *m*.

possibility *n* возмóжность. **possible** *adj* возмóжный; **as much as ~** скóлько возмóжно; **as soon as ~** как мóжно скорée. **possibly** *adv* возмóжно, мóжет (быть).

post[1] *n* (*pole*) столб; *vt* (~ *up*) вывéшивать *impf*, вы́весить *pf*.

post[2] *n* (*station*) пост; (*job*) дóлжность; *vt* (*station*) расставля́ть *impf*, расстáвить *pf*; (*appoint*) назначáть *impf*, назнáчить *pf*.

post[3] *n* (*letters*, ~ *office*) пóчта; **by ~** пóчтой; *attrib* почтóвый; **~-box** почтóвый я́щик; **~-code** почтóвый úндекс; **~ office** пóчта; *vt* (*send by ~*) отправля́ть *impf*, отпрáвить *pf* по пóчте; (*put in ~-box*) опускáть *impf*, опустúть *pf* в почтóвый я́щик. **postage** *n* почтóвый сбор, почтóвые расхóды *m pl*; **~ stamp** почтóвая мáрка. **postal** *adj* почтóвый; **~-order** почтóвый перевóд. **postcard** *n* откры́тка.

poster *n* афúша, плакáт.

poste restante *n* до востребования.

posterior *adj* зáдний; *n* зад.

posterity *n* потóмство.

post-graduate *n* аспирáнт.

posthumous *adj* посмéртный.

postman *n* почтальóн. **postmark** *n* почтóвый штéмпель *m*.

post-mortem *n* вскры́тие трýпа.

postpone *vt* отсрóчивать *impf*, отсрóчить *pf*. **postponement** *n* отсрóчка.

postscript *n* постскрúптум.

postulate *vt* постулúровать *impf* & *pf*.

posture *n* пóза, положéние.

post-war *adj* послевоéнный.

posy *n* букéтик.

pot *n* горшóк; (*cooking ~*) кастрю́ля; **~-shot** вы́стрел наугáд; *vt* (*food*) консервúровать *impf*, за~ *pf*; (*plant*) сажáть *impf*, посадúть *pf* в горшóк; (*billiards*) загоня́ть *impf*, загнáть *pf* в лýзу.

potash *n* потáш. **potassium** *n* кáлий.

potato *n* (*also collect*) картóшка (*no pl*); (*plant*; *also collect*) картóфель *m* (*no pl*).

potency *n* сúла. **potent** *adj* сúльный.

potential *adj* потенциа́льный; *n* потенциа́л. **potentiality** *n* потенциа́льность.

pot-hole *n* (*in road*) вы́боина.

potion *n* зе́лье.

potter[1] *vi*: ~ **about** вози́ться *impf*.

potter[2] *n* гонча́р. **pottery** *n* (*goods*) гонча́рные изде́лия *neut pl*; (*place*) гонча́рная *sb*.

potty[1] *adj* (*crazy*) поме́шанный (**about** на+*prep*).

potty[2] *n* ночно́й горшо́к.

pouch *n* су́мка.

poultry *n* дома́шняя пти́ца.

pounce *vi*: ~ **(up)on** набра́сываться *impf*, набро́ситься *pf* на+*acc*.

pound[1] *n* (*measure*) фунт; ~ **sterling** фунт сте́рлингов.

pound[2] *vt* (*strike*) колоти́ть *impf*, по~ *pf* по+*dat*, в+*acc*; *vi* (*heart*) колоти́ться *impf*; ~ **along** (*run*) мча́ться *impf* с гро́хотом.

pour *vt* лить *impf*; ~ **out** налива́ть *impf*, нали́ть *pf*; *vi* ли́ться *impf*; **it is ~ing (with rain)** дождь льёт как из ведра́.

pout *vi* ду́ть(ся) *impf*, на~ *pf*.

poverty *n* бе́дность; **~-stricken** убо́гий.

POW *abbr* военнопле́нный *sb*.

powder *n* порошо́к; (*cosmetic*) пу́дра; *vt* пу́дрить *impf*, на~ *pf*. **powdery** *adj* порошкообра́зный.

power *n* (*vigour*) си́ла; (*might*) могу́щество; (*ability*) спосо́бность; (*control*) власть; (*authorization*) полномо́чие; (*State*) держа́ва; ~ **cut** переры́в электропита́ния; ~ **point** розе́тка; ~ **station** электроста́нция. **powerful** *adj* си́льный. **powerless** *adj* бесси́льный.

practicable *adj* осуществи́мый. **practical** *adj* (*help, activities*) практи́ческий; (*person, object*) практи́чный. **practically** *adv* практи́чески.

practice *n* пра́ктика; (*custom*) обы́чай; (*mus*) заня́тия *neut pl*; **in** ~ на пра́ктике; **put into** ~ осуществля́ть *impf*, осуществи́ть *pf*. **practise** *vt* (*also abs of doctor etc.*) практикова́ть *impf*; упражня́ться *impf* в+*prep*; (*mus*) занима́ться *impf*, заня́ться *pf* на+*prep*. **practised** *adj* о́пытный. **practitioner** *n* (*doctor*) практику́ющий врач; **general** ~ врач о́бщей пра́ктики.

pragmatic *adj* прагмати́ческий. **pragmatism** *n* прагмати́зм. **pragmatist** *n* прагма́тик.

prairie *n* пре́рия.

praise *vt* хвали́ть *impf*, по~ *pf*; *n* похвала́. **praiseworthy** *adj* похва́льный.

pram *n* де́тская коля́ска.

prance *vi* гарцева́ть *impf*.

prank *n* вы́ходка.

prattle *vi* лепета́ть; *n* ле́пет.

prawn *n* креве́тка.

pray *vi* моли́ться *impf*, по~ *pf* (**to** +*dat*; **for** о+*prep*). **prayer** *n* моли́тва.

preach *vt* & *i* пропове́дывать *impf*. **preacher** *n* пропове́дник.

preamble *n* преа́мбула.

pre-arrange *vt* зара́нее организо́вывать *impf*, организова́ть *pf*.

precarious *adj* опа́сный.

precaution *n* предосторо́жность. **precautionary** *adj*: ~ **measures** ме́ры предосторо́жности.

precede *vt* предше́ствовать *impf* +*dat*. **precedence** *n* предпочте́ние. **precedent** *n* прецеде́нт. **preceding** *adj* предыду́щий.

precept *n* наставле́ние.

precinct *n* двор; *pl* окре́стности *f pl*. **pedestrian ~** уча́сток для пешехо́дов; **shopping ~** торго́вый пасса́ж.

precious *adj* драгоце́нный; (*style*) мане́рный; *adv* о́чень.

precipice *n* обры́в. **precipitate** *adj* (*person*) опроме́тчивый; *vt* (*throw down*) низверга́ть *impf*, низве́ргнуть *pf*; (*hurry*) ускоря́ть *impf*, уско́рить *pf*. **precipitation** *n* (*meteorol*) оса́дки *m pl*. **precipitous** *adj* обры́вистый.

précis *n* конспе́кт.

precise *adj* то́чный. **precisely** *adv* то́чно; (*in answer*) и́менно. **precision** *n* то́чность.

preclude *vt* предотвраща́ть *impf*, предотврати́ть *pf*.

precocious *adj* ра́но разви́вшийся.

preconceived *adj* предвзя́тый. **preconception** *n* предвзя́тое мне́ние.

pre-condition *n* предпосы́лка.

precursor *n* предше́ственник.

predator *n* хи́щник. **predatory** *adj* хи́щный.

predecessor *n* предше́ственник.

predestination *n* предопределе́ние.

predetermine *vt* предреша́ть *impf*, предреши́ть *pf*.

predicament *n* затрудни́тельное положе́ние.

predicate *n* (*gram*) сказу́емое *sb*. **predicative** *adj* предикати́вный.

predict *vt* предска́зывать *impf*, предсказа́ть *pf*. **predictable** *adj* предсказу́емый. **prediction** *n* предсказа́ние.

predilection *n* пристра́стие (**for** к+*dat*).

predispose *vt* предрасполага́ть *impf*, предрасположи́ть *pf* (**to** к+*dat*). **predisposition** *n* предрасположе́ние (**to** к+*dat*).

predominance *n* преоблада́ние. **predominant** *adj* преоблада́ющий. **predominate** *vi* преоблада́ть *impf*.

pre-eminence *n* превосхо́дство. **pre-eminent** *adj* выдаю́щийся.

pre-empt *vt* (*fig*) завладева́ть *impf*, завладе́ть *pf* +*instr* пре́жде други́х. **pre-emptive** *adj* (*mil*) упрежда́ющий.

preen *vt* (*of bird*) чи́стить *impf*, по~ *pf* клю́вом; **~ o.s.** (*be proud*) горди́ться *impf* собо́й.

pre-fab *n* сбо́рный дом. **prefabricated** *adj* сбо́рный.

preface *n* предисло́вие.

prefect *n* префе́кт; (*school*) ста́роста *m*.

prefer *vt* предпочита́ть *impf*, предпоче́сть *pf*. **preferable** *adj* предпочти́тельный. **preference** *n* предпочте́ние. **preferential** *adj* предпочти́тельный.

prefix *n* приста́вка.

pregnancy *n* бере́менность. **pregnant** *adj* бере́менная.

prehistoric *adj* доистори́ческий.

prejudice *n* предубежде́ние; (*detriment*) уще́рб; *vt* наноси́ть *impf*, нанести́ *pf* уще́рб+*dat*; **~ against** предубежда́ть *impf*, предубеди́ть *pf* про́тив+*gen*; **be ~d against** име́ть *impf*

предубеждение против *+gen.*
preliminary *adj* предварительный.
prelude *n* прелюдия.
premarital *adj* добрачный.
premature *adj* преждевременный.
premeditated *adj* преднамеренный.
premier *adj* первый; *n* премьер-министр. **première** *n* премьера.
premise, premiss *n* (*logic*) (пред)посылка. **premises** *n pl* помещение.
premium *n* премия.
premonition *n* предчувствие.
preoccupation *n* озабоченность; (*absorbing subject*) забота. **preoccupied** *adj* озабоченный. **preoccupy** *vt* поглощать *impf*, поглотить *pf*.
preparation *n* приготовление; *pl* подготовка (**for** к*+dat*); (*substance*) препарат. **preparatory** *adj* подготовительный. **prepare** *vt* & *i* при-, под-, готавливать(ся) *impf*, при-, под-, готовить(ся) *pf* (**for** к*+dat*). **prepared** *adj* готовый.
preponderance *n* перевес.
preposition *n* предлог.
prepossessing *adj* привлекательный.
preposterous *adj* нелепый.
prerequisite *n* предпосылка.
prerogative *n* прерогатива.
presage *vt* предвещать *impf*.
Presbyterian *n* пресвитерианин, -анка; *adj* пресвитерианский.
prescribe *vt* предписывать *impf*, предписать *pf*; (*med*) прописывать *impf*, прописать *pf*. **prescription** *n* (*med*) рецепт.
presence *n* присутствие; **~ of mind** присутствие духа.
present *adj* присутствующий; (*being dealt with*) данный; (*existing now*) нынешний; (*also gram*) настоящий; *predic* налицо; **be ~** присутствовать *impf* (**at** на*+prep*); **~-day** нынешний; *n*: **the ~** настоящее *sb*; (*gram*) настоящее время *neut*; (*gift*) подарок; **at ~** в настоящее время *neut*; **for the ~** пока; *vt* (*introduce*) представлять *impf*, представить *pf* (**to** *+dat*); (*award*) вручать *impf*, вручить *pf*; (*a play*) ставить *impf*, по~ *pf*; (*a gift*) преподносить *impf*, преподнести *pf +dat* (**with** *+acc*); **~ o.s.** являться *impf*, явиться *pf*. **presentable** *adj* приличный. **presentation** *n* (*introducing*) представление; (*awarding*) подношение.
presentiment *n* предчувствие.
presently *adv* вскоре.
preservation *n* сохранение. **preservative** *n* консервант. **preserve** *vt* (*keep safe*) сохранять *impf*, сохранить *pf*; (*maintain*) хранить *impf*; (*food*) консервировать *impf*, за~ *pf*; *n* (*for game etc*) заповедник; (*jam*) варенье.
preside *vi* председательствовать *impf* (**at** на*+prep*). **presidency** *n* президентство. **president** *n* президент. **presidential** *adj* президентский. **presidium** *n* президиум.
press *n* (*machine*) пресс; (*printing firm*) типография; (*publishing house*) издательство; (*the* ~) пресса, печать; **~ conference** пресс-кон-

ферéнция; *vt* (*button etc*) нажимáть *impf*, нажáть *pf*; (*clasp*) прижимáть *impf*, прижáть *pf* (**to** к+*dat*); (*iron*) глáдить *impf*, вы́~ *pf*; (*insist on*) настáивать *impf*, настоя́ть *pf* на+*prep*; (*urge*) уговáривать *impf*; ~ **on** (*make haste*) поторáпливаться *impf*.

pressing *adj* неотлóжный. **pressure** *n* давлéние; **~-cooker** скоровáрка; ~ **group** инициати́вная грýппа. **pressurize** *vt* (*fig*) окáзывать *impf*, оказáть *pf* давлéние на+*acc*. **pressurized** *adj* гермети́ческий.

prestige *n* прести́ж. **prestigious** *adj* прести́жный.

presumably *adv* предположи́тельно. **presume** *vt* полагáть *impf*; (*venture*) позволя́ть *impf*, позвóлить *pf* себé. **presumption** *n* предположéние; (*arrogance*) самонадéянность. **presumptuous** *adj* самонадéянный.

presuppose *vt* предполагáть *impf*.

pretence *n* притвóрство. **pretend** *vt* притворя́ться *impf*, притвори́ться *pf* (**to be** +*instr*); дéлать *impf*, с~ *pf* вид (что); *vi*: ~ **to** претендовáть *impf* на+*acc*. **pretender** *n* претендéнт. **pretension** *n* претéнзия. **pretentious** *adj* претенциóзный.

pretext *n* предлóг.

prettiness *n* милови́дность. **pretty** *adj* хорóшенький; *adv* довóльно.

prevail *vi* (*predominate*) преобладáть *impf*; ~ **(up)on** уговáривать *impf*, уговори́ть *pf*. **prevalence** *n* распространéние. **prevalent** *adj* распространённый.

prevaricate *vi* уви́ливать *impf* увильнýть *pf*.

prevent *vt* (*stop from happening*) предупреждáть *impf*, предупреди́ть *pf*; (*stop from doing*) мешáть *impf*, по~ *pf* +*dat*. **prevention** *n* предупреждéние. **preventive** *adj* предупреди́тельный.

preview *n* предвари́тельный просмóтр.

previous *adj* предыдýщий; *adv*: ~ **to** до+*gen*; прéжде чем +*inf*. **previously** *adv* рáньше.

pre-war *adj* довоéнный.

prey *n* (*animal*) добы́ча; (*victim*) жéртва (**to** +*gen*); **bird of** ~ хи́щная пти́ца; *vi*: ~ **(up)on** (*emotion etc.*) мýчить *impf*.

price *n* ценá; **~-list** прейскурáнт; *vt* назначáть *impf*, назнáчить *pf* цéну +*gen*. **priceless** *adj* бесцéнный.

prick *vt* колóть *impf*, у~ *pf*; (*conscience*) мýчить *impf*; ~ **up one's ears** навостри́ть *pf* ýши; *n* укóл. **prickle** *n* (*thorn*) колю́чка; (*spine*) иглá. **prickly** *adj* колю́чий.

pride *n* гóрдость; ~ **o.s. on** горди́ться *impf* +*instr*.

priest *n* свящéнник; (*non-Christian*) жрец.

prig *n* педáнт.

prim *adj* чóпорный.

primarily *adv* первоначáльно; (*above all*) прéжде всегó. **primary** *adj* основнóй; ~ **school** начáльная шкóла. **prime** *n*: **in one's** ~ в расцвéте сил; *adj* (*chief*) глáвный; ~ **minister** премьéр-мини́стр; *vt* (*engine*) заправля́ть *impf*, запрáвить *pf*;

(*bomb*) активизи́ровать *impf* & *pf*; (*with facts*) инструкти́ровать *impf* & *pf*; (*with paint etc.*) грунтова́ть *impf*, за~ *pf*. **primer** *n* (*paint etc.*) грунт. **prim(a)eval** *adj* первобы́тный. **primitive** *adj* первобы́тный; (*crude*) примити́вный. **primordial** *adj* иско́нный.

primrose *n* первоцве́т; (*colour*) бле́дно-жёлтый цвет.

prince *n* принц; (*in Russia*) князь. **princely** *adj* кня́жеский; (*sum*) огро́мный. **princess** *n* принце́сса; (*wife*) княги́ня; (*daughter*) княжна́.

principal *n* гла́вный; *n* дире́ктор. **principality** *n* кня́жество. **principally** *adv* гла́вным о́бразом.

principle *n* при́нцип; **in ~** в при́нципе; **on ~** принципиа́льно. **principled** *adj* принципиа́льный.

print *n* (*mark*) след; (*also phot*) отпеча́ток; (*printing*) печа́ть; (*picture*) о́ттиск; **in ~** в прода́же; **out of ~** распро́данный; *vt* (*impress*) запечатлева́ть *impf*, запечатле́ть *pf*; (*book etc.*) печа́тать *impf*, на~ *pf*; (*write*) писа́ть *impf*, на~ *pf* печа́тными бу́квами; (*phot*; **~** *out, off*) отпеча́тывать *impf*, отпеча́тать *pf*; **~ out** (*of computer etc.*) распеча́тывать *impf*, распеча́тать *pf*; **~-out** распеча́тка. **printer** *n* (*person*) печа́тник, типо́гаф; (*of computer*) при́нтер. **printing** *n* печа́тание; **~-press** печа́тный стано́к.

prior *adj* пре́жний; *adv*: **~ to** до+*gen*. **priority** *n* приорите́т. **priory** *n* монасты́рь *m*.

prise *vt*: **~ open** взла́мывать *impf*, взлома́ть *pf*.

prism *n* при́зма.

prison *n* тюрьма́; *attrib* тюре́мный; **~ camp** ла́герь *m*. **prisoner** *n* заключённый *sb*; (*~ of war*) (военно)пле́нный *sb*.

pristine *adj* нетро́нутый.

privacy *n* уедине́ние; (*private life*) ча́стная жизнь. **private** *adj* (*personal*) ча́стный, ли́чный; (*confidential*) конфиденциа́льный; **in ~** наедине́; в ча́стной жи́зни; *n* рядово́й *sb*.

privation *n* лише́ние.

privilege *n* привиле́гия. **privileged** *adj* привелигиро́ванный.

privy *adj*: **~ to** посвящённый в+*acc*.

prize *n* пре́мия, приз; **~-winner** призёр; *vt* высоко́ цени́ть *impf*.

pro[1] *n*: **~s and cons** до́воды *m pl* за и про́тив.

pro[2] *n* (*professional*) профессиона́л.

probability *n* вероя́тность. **probable** *adj* вероя́тный. **probably** *adv* вероя́тно.

probate *n* утвержде́ние завеща́ния.

probation *n* испыта́тельный срок; (*law*) усло́вный пригово́р; **got two years ~** получи́л два го́да усло́вно. **probationary** *adj* испыта́тельный.

probe *n* (*med*) зонд; (*fig*) рассле́дование; *vt* зонди́ровать *impf*; (*fig*) рассле́довать *impf* & *pf*.

probity *n* че́стность.

problem *n* пробле́ма, вопро́с; (*math*) зада́ча. **problematic** *adj* проблемати́чный.

procedural *adj* процеду́рный. **procedure** *n* процеду́ра. **proceed** *vi* (*go further*) идти́ *impf*, пойти́ *pf* да́льше; (*act*) поступа́ть *impf*, поступи́ть *pf*; (*abs*, ~ *to say*; *continue*) продолжа́ть *impf*, продо́лжить *pf*; (*of action*) продолжа́ться *impf*, продо́лжиться *pf*; ~ **from** исходи́ть *impf*. из, от+*gen*; ~ **to** (*begin to*) принима́ться *impf*, приня́ться *pf* +*inf*. **proceedings** *n pl* (*activity*) де́ятельность; (*legal* ~) судопроизво́дство; (*published report*) труды́ *m pl*, запи́ски *f pl*. **proceeds** *n pl* вы́ручка. **process** *n* проце́сс; *vt* обраба́тывать *impf*, обрабо́тать *pf*. **procession** *n* проце́ссия, ше́ствие.

proclaim *vt* провозглаша́ть *impf*, провозгласи́ть *pf*. **proclamation** *n* провозглаше́ние.

procure *vt* достава́ть *impf*, доста́ть *pf*.

prod *vt* ты́кать *impf*, ткнуть *pf*; *n* тычо́к.

prodigal *adj* расточи́тельный.

prodigious *adj* огро́мный. **prodigy** *n*: **child** ~ вундерки́нд.

produce *vt* (*evidence etc.*) представля́ть *impf*, предста́вить *pf*; (*ticket etc.*) предъявля́ть *impf*, предъяви́ть *pf*; (*play etc.*) ста́вить *impf*, по~ *pf*; (*manufacture*; *cause*) производи́ть *impf*, произвести́ *pf*; *n* (*collect*) проду́кты *m pl*. **producer** *n* (*econ*) производи́тель *m*; (*of play etc.*) режиссёр. **product** *n* проду́кт; (*result*) результа́т. **production** *n* произво́дство; (*of play etc.*) постано́вка. **productive** *adj* продукти́вный; (*fruitful*) плодотво́рный. **productivity** *n* производи́тельность.

profane *adj* све́тский; (*blasphemous*) богоху́льный. **profanity** *n* богоху́льство.

profess *vt* (*pretend*) притворя́ться *impf*, притвори́ться *pf* (**to be** +*instr*); (*declare*) заявля́ть *impf*, заяви́ть *pf*; (*faith*) испове́довать *impf*. **profession** *n* (*job*) профе́ссия. **professional** *adj* профессиона́льный; *n* профессиона́л. **professor** *n* профе́ссор.

proffer *vt* предлага́ть *impf*, предложи́ть *pf*.

proficiency *n* уме́ние. **proficient** *adj* уме́лый.

profile *n* про́филь *m*.

profit *n* (*benefit*) по́льза; (*monetary*) при́быль; *vt* приноси́ть *impf*, принести́ *pf* по́льзу +*dat*; *vi*: ~ **from** по́льзоваться *impf*, вос~ *pf* +*instr*; (*financially*) получа́ть *impf*, получи́ть *pf* при́быль на +*prep*. **profitable** *adj* (*lucrative*) при́быльный; (*beneficial*) поле́зный. **profiteering** *n* спекуля́ция.

profligate *adj* распу́тный.

profound *adj* глубо́кий.

profuse *adj* оби́льный. **profusion** *n* изоби́лие.

progeny *n* пото́мство.

prognosis *n* прогно́з.

program(m)e *n* програ́мма; *vt* программи́ровать *impf*, за~ *pf*. **programmer** *n* программи́ст.

progress *n* прогре́сс; (*success*) успе́хи *m pl*; **make** ~ де́лать *impf*, с~ *pf* успе́хи; *vi* продвига́ться *impf*, продви́нуться *pf* вперёд. **progression** *n* продвиже́ние.

progressive *adj* прогресси́вный.
prohibit *vt* запреща́ть *impf*, запрети́ть *pf*. **prohibition** *n* запреще́ние; (*on alcohol*) сухо́й зако́н. **prohibitive** *adj* запрети́тельный; (*price*) недосту́пный.
project *vt* (*plan*) проекти́ровать *impf*, с~ *pf*; (*a film*) демонстри́ровать *impf*, про~ *pf*; *vi* (*jut out*) выступа́ть *impf*; *n* прое́кт. **projectile** *n* снаря́д. **projection** *n* (*cin*) прое́кция; (*protrusion*) вы́ступ; (*forecast*) прогно́з. **projector** *n* прое́ктор.
proletarian *adj* пролета́рский. **proletariat** *n* пролетариа́т.
proliferate *vi* распространя́ться *impf*, распространи́ться *pf*. **proliferation** *n* распростране́ние.
prolific *adj* плодови́тый.
prologue *n* проло́г.
prolong *vt* продлева́ть *impf*, продли́ть *pf*.
promenade *n* ме́сто для гуля́нья; (*at seaside*) на́бережная *sb*; *vi* прогу́ливаться *impf*, прогуля́ться *pf*.
prominence *n* изве́стность. **prominent** *adj* выступа́ющий; (*distinguished*) выдаю́щийся.
promiscuity *n* лёгкое поведе́ние. **promiscuous** *adj* лёгкого поведе́ния.
promise *n* обеща́ние; *vt* обеща́ть *impf* & *pf*. **promising** *adj* многообеща́ющий.
promontory *n* мыс.
promote *vt* (*in rank*) продвига́ть *impf*, продви́нуть *pf*; (*assist*) спосо́бствовать *impf* & *pf* +*dat*; (*publicize*) реклами́ровать *impf*. **promoter** *n* (*of event etc.*) аге́нт. **promotion** *n* (*in rank*) продвиже́ние; (*comm*) рекла́ма.
prompt *adj* бы́стрый, неме́дленный; *adv* ро́вно; *vt* (*incite*) побужда́ть *impf*, побуди́ть *pf* (**to** к+*dat*; +*inf*); (*speaker*; *also fig*) подска́зывать *impf*, подсказа́ть *pf* +*dat*; (*theat*) суфли́ровать *impf* +*dat*; *n* подска́зка. **prompter** *n* суфлёр.
prone *adj* (лежа́щий) ничко́м; *predic*: ~ **to** скло́нен (-онна́, -о́нно) к+*dat*.
prong *n* зубе́ц.
pronoun *n* местоиме́ние.
pronounce *vt* (*declare*) объявля́ть *impf*, объяви́ть *pf*; (*articulate*) произноси́ть *impf*, произнести́ *pf*. **pronounced** *adj* я́вный; заме́тный. **pronouncement** *n* заявле́ние. **pronunciation** *n* произноше́ние.
proof *n* доказа́тельство; (*printing*) корректу́ра; **~-reader** корре́ктор; *adj* (*impenetrable*) непроница́емый (**against** для+*gen*); (*not yielding*) неподдаю́щийся (**against** +*dat*).
prop[1] *n* (*support*) подпо́рка; (*fig*) опо́ра; *vt* (~ *open*, *up*) подпира́ть *impf*, подпере́ть *pf*; (*fig*) подде́рживать *impf*, поддержа́ть *pf*.
prop[2] *n* (*theat*) *see* **props**
propaganda *n* пропага́нда.
propagate *vt* & *i* размножа́ть(ся) *impf*, размно́жить(ся) *pf*; (*disseminate*) распространя́ть(ся) *impf*, распространи́ть(ся) *pf*. **propagation** *n* размноже́ние; распростране́ние.
propel *vt* приводи́ть *impf*, привести́ *pf* в движе́ние. **propeller** *n* винт.

propensity *n* накло́нность (**to** к+*dat*; +*inf*).
proper *adj* (*correct*) пра́вильный; (*suitable*) подходя́щий; (*decent*) присто́йный; ~ **noun** и́мя со́бственное. **properly** *adv* как сле́дует.
property *n* (*possessions*) со́бственность, иму́щество; (*attribute*) сво́йство; *pl* (*theat*) реквизи́т.
prophecy *n* проро́чество. **prophesy** *vt* проро́чить *impf*, на~ *pf*. **prophet** *n* проро́к. **prophetic** *adj* проро́ческий.
propitious *adj* благоприя́тный.
proponent *n* сторо́нник.
proportion *n* пропо́рция; (*due relation*) соразме́рность; *pl* разме́ры *m pl*. **proportional** *adj* пропорциона́льный. **proportionate** *adj* соразме́рный (**to** +*dat*; с+*instr*).
proposal *n* предложе́ние. **propose** *vt* предлага́ть *impf*, предложи́ть *pf*; (*intend*) предполага́ть *impf*; *vi* (~ *marriage*) де́лать *impf*, с~ *pf* предложе́ние (**to** +*dat*). **proposition** *n* предложе́ние.
propound *vt* предлага́ть *impf*, предложи́ть *pf* на обсужде́ние.
proprietor *n* со́бственник, хозя́ин.
propriety *n* прили́чие.
props *n pl* (*theat*) реквизи́т.
propulsion *n* движе́ние вперёд.
prosaic *adj* прозаи́ческий.
proscribe *vt* (*forbid*) запреща́ть *impf*, запрети́ть *pf*.
prose *n* про́за.
prosecute *vt* пресле́довать *impf*. **prosecution** *n* суде́бное пресле́дование; (*prosecuting party*) обвине́ние. **prosecutor** *n* обвини́тель *m*.
prospect *n* вид; (*fig*) перспекти́ва; *vi*: ~ **for** иска́ть *impf*. **prospective** *adj* бу́дущий. **prospector** *n* разве́дчик. **prospectus** *n* проспе́кт.
prosper *vi* процвета́ть *impf*. **prosperity** *n* процвета́ние. **prosperous** *adj* процвета́ющий; (*wealthy*) зажи́точный.
prostate (gland) *n* проста́та.
prostitute *n* проститу́тка. **prostitution** *n* проститу́ция.
prostrate *adj* распростёртый, (лежа́щий) ничко́м; (*exhausted*) обесси́ленный; (*with grief*) уби́тый (**with** +*instr*).
protagonist *n* гла́вный геро́й; (*in contest*) протагони́ст.
protect *vt* защища́ть *impf*, защити́ть. **protection** *n* защи́та. **protective** *adj* защи́тный. **protector** *n* защи́тник.
protégé(e) *n* протеже́ *m* & *f indecl*.
protein *n* бело́к.
protest *n* проте́ст; *vi* протестова́ть *impf*; *vt* (*affirm*) утвержда́ть *impf*.
Protestant *n* протеста́нт, ~ка; *adj* протеста́нтский.
protestation *n* (торже́ственное) заявле́ние (о+*prep*; что); (*protest*) проте́ст.
protocol *n* протоко́л.
proton *n* прото́н.
prototype *n* прототи́п.
protract *vt* тяну́ть *impf*. **protracted** *adj* дли́тельный.
protrude *vi* выдава́ться *impf*, вы́даться *pf*.
proud *adj* го́рдый; **be ~ of** горди́ться *impf* +*instr*.
prove *vt* дока́зывать *impf*, доказа́ть *pf*; *vi* ока́зываться

impf, оказа́ться *pf* (**to be** +*instr*). **proven** *adj* дока́занный.

provenance *n* происхожде́ние.

proverb *n* посло́вица. **proverbial** *adj* воше́дший в погово́рку; (*well-known*) общеизве́стный.

provide *vt* (*supply person*) снабжа́ть *impf*, снабди́ть *pf* (**with** +*instr*); (*supply thing*) предоставля́ть *impf*, предоста́вить *pf* (**to, for** +*dat*); дава́ть *impf*, дать *pf* (**to, for** +*dat*); *vi*: ~ **for** предусма́тривать *impf*, предусмотре́ть *pf* +*acc*; (~ *for family etc.*) содержа́ть *impf* +*acc*. **provided (that)** *conj* при усло́вии, что; е́сли то́лько. **providence** *n* провиде́ние; (*foresight*) предусмотри́тельность. **provident** *adj* предусмотри́тельный. **providential** *adj* счастли́вый. **providing** *see* **provided (that)**

province *n* о́бласть; *pl* (*the* ~) прови́нция. **provincial** *adj* провинциа́льный.

provision *n* снабже́ние; *pl* (*food*) прови́зия; (*in agreement etc.*) положе́ние; **make** ~ **against** принима́ть *impf*, приня́ть *pf* ме́ры про́тив+*gen*. **provisional** *adj* вре́менный. **proviso** *n* усло́вие.

provocation *n* провока́ция. **provocative** *adj* провокацио́нный. **provoke** *vt* провоци́ровать *impf*, с~ *pf*; (*call forth, cause*) вызыва́ть *impf*, вы́звать *pf*.

prow *n* нос.

prowess *n* уме́ние.

prowl *vi* ры́скать *impf*.

proximity *n* бли́зость.

proxy *n* полномо́чие; (*person*) уполномо́ченный *sb*, замести́тель *m*; **by** ~ по дове́ренности; **stand** ~ **for** быть *impf* замести́телем +*gen*.

prudence *n* благоразу́мие. **prudent** *adj* благоразу́мный.

prudery *n* притво́рная стыдли́вость. **prudish** *adj* ни в ме́ру стыдли́вый.

prune[1] *n* (*plum*) черносли́в.

prune[2] *vt* (*trim*) об-, под-, реза́ть *impf*, об-, под-, ре́зать *pf*.

pry *vi* сова́ть *impf* нос (**into** в+*acc*).

PS *abbr* (*of* **postscript**) постскри́птум.

psalm *n* псало́м.

pseudonym *n* псевдони́м.

psyche *n* пси́хика. **psychiatric** *adj* психиатри́ческий. **psychiatrist** *n* психиа́тр. **psychiatry** *n* психиатри́я. **psychic** *adj* ясновидя́щий. **psychoanalysis** *n* психоана́лиз. **psychoanalyst** *n* психоанали́тик. **psychoanalytic(al)** *adj* психоаналити́ческий. **psychological** *adj* психологи́ческий. **psychologist** *n* психо́лог. **psychology** *n* психоло́гия. **psychopath** *n* психопа́т. **psychopathic** *adj* психопати́ческий. **psychosis** *n* психо́з. **psychotherapy** *n* психотерапи́я.

PTO *abbr* (*of* **please turn over**) см. на об., смотри́ на оборо́те.

pub *n* пивна́я *sb*.

puberty *n* полова́я зре́лость.

public *adj* обще́ственный; (*open*) публи́чный, откры́тый; ~ **school** ча́стная сре́дняя шко́ла; *n* пу́блика, обще́ственность; **in** ~ откры́то, публи́чно. **publication** *n* изда́ние. **publicity** *n* рекла́ма. **publicize** *vt* реклами́ровать *impf* & *pf*. **publicly** *adv* публи́чно, откры́то. **publish** *vt* публикова́ть *impf*, о~ *pf*; (*book*) издава́ть *impf*, изда́ть *pf*. **publisher** *n* изда́тель *m*. **publishing** *n* (*business*) изда́тельское де́ло; ~ **house** изда́тельство.

pucker *vt* & *i* мо́рщить(ся) *impf*, с~ *pf*.

pudding *n* пу́динг, запека́нка; (*dessert*) сла́дкое *sb*.

puddle *n* лу́жа.

puff *n* (*of wind*) поры́в; (*of smoke*) дымо́к; ~ **pastry** слоёное те́сто; *vi* пыхте́ть *impf*; ~ **at** (*pipe etc.*) попы́хивать *impf* +*instr*; *vt*: ~ **up, out** (*inflate*) надува́ть *impf*, наду́ть *pf*.

pugnacious *adj* драчли́вый.

puke *vi* рвать *impf*, вы́~ *pf* *impers*+*acc*.

pull *vt* тяну́ть *impf*, по~ *pf*; таска́ть *indet*, тащи́ть *det*, по~ *pf*; (*a muscle*) растя́гивать *impf*, растяну́ть *pf*; *vt* & *i* дёргать *impf*, дёрнуть *pf* (**at** (за)+*acc*); ~ **s.o's leg** разы́грывать *impf*, разыгра́ть *pf*; ~ **the trigger** спуска́ть *impf*, спусти́ть *pf* куро́к; ~ **apart, to pieces** разрыва́ть *impf*, разорва́ть *pf*; (*fig*) раскритикова́ть *pf*; ~ **down** (*demolish*) сноси́ть *impf*, снести́ *pf*; ~ **in** (*of train*) прибыва́ть *impf*, прибы́ть *pf*; (*of vehicle*) подъезжа́ть *impf*, подъе́хать *pf* к обо́чине (доро́ги); ~ **off** (*garment*) стя́гивать *impf*, стяну́ть *pf*; (*achieve*) успе́шно заверша́ть *impf*, заверши́ть *pf*; ~ **on** (*garment*) натя́гивать *impf*, натяну́ть *pf*; ~ **out** (*vt*) (*remove*) выта́скивать *impf*, вы́тащить *pf*; (*vi*) (*withdraw*) отка́зываться *impf*, отказа́ться *pf* от уча́стия (**of** в+*prep*); (*of vehicle*) отъезжа́ть *impf*, отъе́хать *pf* от обо́чины (доро́ги); (*of train*) отходи́ть *impf*, отойти́ *pf* (от ста́нции); ~ **through** выжива́ть *impf*, вы́жить *pf*; ~ **o.s. together** брать *impf*, взять *pf* себя́ в ру́ки; ~ **up** (*vt*) подтя́гивать *impf*, подтяну́ть *pf*; (*vt* & *i*) (*stop*) остана́вливать(ся) *impf*, останови́ть(ся) *pf*; *n* тя́га; (*fig*) блат.

pulley *n* блок.

pullover *n* пуло́вер.

pulp *n* пу́льпа.

pulpit *n* ка́федра.

pulsate *vi* пульси́ровать *impf*.

pulse *n* пульс.

pulses *n pl* (*food*) бобо́вые *sb*.

pulverize *vt* размельча́ть *impf*, размельчи́ть *pf*.

pummel *vt* колоти́ть *impf*, по~ *pf*.

pump *n* насо́с; *vt* кача́ть *impf*; ~ **in(to)** вка́чивать *impf*, вкача́ть *pf*; ~ **out** выка́чивать *impf*, вы́качать *pf*; ~ **up** нака́чивать *impf*, накача́ть *pf*.

pumpkin *n* ты́ква.

pun *n* каламбу́р.

punch[1] *vt* (*with fist*) ударя́ть *impf*, уда́рить *pf* кулако́м; (*hole*) пробива́ть *impf*, проби́ть *pf*; (*a ticket*) компости́ровать *impf*, про~ *pf*; ~-**up** дра́ка; *n* (*blow*) уда́р кулако́м; (*for tickets*) компо́стер; (*for piercing*) перфора́тор.

punch[2] *n* (*drink*) пунш.

punctilious *adj* щепети́льный.

punctual *adj* пунктуа́льный. **punctuality** *n* пунктуа́льность.

punctuate *vt* ста́вить *impf*, по~ *pf* зна́ки препина́ния в+*acc*; (*fig*) прерыва́ть *impf*, прерва́ть *pf*. **punctuation** *n* пунктуа́ция; ~ **marks** зна́ки *m pl* препина́ния.

puncture *n* проко́л; *vt* прока́лывать *impf*, проколо́ть *pf*.

pundit *n* (*fig*) знато́к.

pungent *adj* е́дкий.

punish *vt* нака́зывать *impf*, наказа́ть *pf*. **punishable** *adj* наказу́емый. **punishment** *n* наказа́ние. **punitive** *adj* кара́тельный.

punter *n* (*gambler*) игро́к; (*client*) клие́нт.

puny *adj* хи́лый.

pupil *n* учени́к, -и́ца; (*of eye*) зрачо́к.

puppet *n* марионе́тка, ку́кла.

puppy *n* щено́к.

purchase *n* поку́пка; (*leverage*) то́чка опо́ры; *vt* покупа́ть *impf*, купи́ть *pf*. **purchaser** *n* покупа́тель *m*.

pure *adj* чи́стый.

purée *n* пюре́ *neut indecl*.

purely *adv* чи́сто.

purgatory *n* чисти́лище; (*fig*) ад. **purge** *vt* очища́ть *impf*, очи́стить *pf*; *n* очище́ние; (*polit*) чи́стка.

purification *n* очи́стка. **purify** *vt* очища́ть *impf*, очи́стить *pf*.

purist *n* пури́ст.

puritan, P., *n* пурита́нин, -а́нка. **puritanical** *adj* пурита́нский.

purity *n* чистота́.

purple *adj* (*n*) пу́рпу́рный, фиоле́товый (цвет).

purport *vt* претендова́ть *impf*.

purpose *n* цель, наме́рение; **on** ~ наро́чно; **to no** ~ напра́сно. **purposeful** *adj* целеустремлённый. **purposeless** *adj* бесце́льный. **purposely** *adv* наро́чно.

purr *vi* мурлы́кать *impf*.

purse *n* кошелёк; *vt* поджима́ть *impf*, поджа́ть *pf*.

pursue *vt* пресле́довать *impf*. **pursuit** *n* пресле́дование; (*pastime*) заня́тие.

purveyor *n* поставщи́к.

pus *n* гной.

push *vt* толка́ть *impf*, толкну́ть *pf*; (*press*) нажима́ть *impf*, нажа́ть *pf*; (*urge*) подта́лкивать *impf*, подтолкну́ть *pf*; *vi* толка́ться *impf*; **be ~ed for** име́ть *impf* ма́ло+*gen*; **he is ~ing fifty** ему́ ско́ро сту́кнет пятьдеся́т; ~ **one's way** прота́лкиваться *impf*, протолкну́ться *pf*; ~ **around** (*person*) помыка́ть *impf* +*instr*; ~ **aside** (*also fig*) отстраня́ть *impf*, отстрани́ть *pf*; ~ **away** отта́лкивать *impf*, оттолкну́ть *pf*; ~ **off** (*vi*) (*in boat*) отта́лкиваться *impf*, оттолкну́ться *pf* (от бе́рега); (*go away*) убира́ться *impf*, убра́ться *pf*; ~ **on** (*vi*) продолжа́ть *impf* путь; *n* толчо́к; (*energy*) эне́ргия. **pushchair** *n* коля́ска. **pusher** *n* (*drugs*) продаве́ц нарко́тиков. **pushy** *adj* напо́ристый.

puss, pussy(-cat) *n* ки́ска.

put *vt* класть *impf*, положи́ть *pf*; (*upright*) ста́вить *impf*, по~ *pf*; помеща́ть *impf*, помести́ть *pf*; (*into specified state*) приводи́ть *impf*, привести́ *pf*; (*express*) выража́ть *impf*, вы́разить *pf*; (*a question*) задава́ть *impf*, зада́ть *pf*; ~ **an end, a stop, to**

класть *impf*, положи́ть *pf* коне́ц *+dat*; **~ o.s. in another's place** ста́вить *impf*, по~ *pf* себя́ на ме́сто *+gen*; **~ about** (*rumour etc.*) распространя́ть *impf*, распространи́ть *pf*; **~ away** (*tidy*) убира́ть *impf*, убра́ть *pf*; (*save*) откла́дывать *impf*, отложи́ть *pf*; **~ back** (*in place*) ста́вить *impf*, по~ *pf* на ме́сто; (*clock*) переводи́ть *impf*, перевести́ *pf* наза́д; **~ by** (*money*) откла́дывать *impf*, отложи́ть *pf*; **~ down** класть *impf*, положи́ть *pf*; (*suppress*) подавля́ть *impf*, подави́ть *pf*; (*write down*) запи́сывать *impf*, записа́ть *pf*; (*passengers*) выса́живать *impf*, вы́садить *pf*; (*attribute*) припи́сывать *impf*, приписа́ть *pf* (**to** *+dat*); **~ forward** (*proposal*) предлага́ть *impf*, предложи́ть *pf*; (*clock*) переводи́ть *impf*, перевести́ *pf* вперёд; **~ in** (*install*) устана́вливать *impf*, установи́ть *pf*; (*a claim*) предъявля́ть *impf*, предъяви́ть *pf*; (*interpose*) вставля́ть *impf*, вста́вить *pf*; **~ in an appearance** появля́ться *impf*, появи́ться *pf*; **~ off** (*postpone*) откла́дывать *impf*, отложи́ть *pf*; (*repel*) отта́лкивать *impf*, оттолкну́ть *pf*; (*dissuade*) отгова́ривать *impf*, отговори́ть *pf* от*+gen*, *+inf*; **~ on** (*clothes*) надева́ть *impf*, наде́ть *pf*; (*kettle, a record, a play*) ста́вить *impf*, по~ *pf*; (*turn on*) включа́ть *impf*, включи́ть *pf*; (*add to*) прибавля́ть *impf*, приба́вить *pf*; **~ on airs** ва́жничать *impf*; **~ on weight** толсте́ть *impf*, по~ *pf*; **~ out** (*vex*) обижа́ть *impf*, оби́деть *pf*; (*inconvenience*) затрудня́ть *impf*, затрудни́ть *pf*; (*a fire etc.*) туши́ть *impf*, по~ *pf*; **~ through** (*tel*) соединя́ть *impf*, соедини́ть *pf* по телефо́ну; **~ up** (*building*) стро́ить *impf*, по~ *pf*; (*hang up*) ве́шать *impf*, пове́сить *pf*; (*price*) повыша́ть *impf*, повы́сить *pf*; (*a guest*) дава́ть *impf*, дать *pf* ночле́г *+dat*; (*as guest*) ночева́ть *impf*, пере~ *pf*; **~ up to** (*instigate*) подбива́ть *impf*, подби́ть *pf* на*+acc*; **~ up with** терпе́ть *impf*.

putative *adj* предполага́емый.

putrefy *vi* гнить *impf*, с~ *pf*.

putrid *adj* гнило́й.

putty *n* зама́зка.

puzzle *n* (*enigma*) зага́дка; (*toy etc.*) головоло́мка; (*jigsaw*) моза́ика; *vt* озада́чивать *impf*, озада́чить *pf*; **~ out** разгада́ть *pf*; *vi*: **~ over** лома́ть *impf* себе́ го́лову над*+instr*.

pygmy *n* пигме́й.

pyjamas *n pl* пижа́ма.

pylon *n* пило́н.

pyramid *n* пирами́да.

pyre *n* погреба́льный костёр.

python *n* пито́н.

Q

quack[1] *n* (*sound*) кря́канье; *vi* кря́кать *impf*, кря́кнуть *pf*.

quack[2] *n* шарлата́н.

quad *n* (*court*) четырёхуго́льный двор; *pl* (*quadruplets*) че́тверо близнецо́в. **quadrangle** *n* (*figure*) четырёхуго́льник; (*court*) четырёхуго́льный двор. **quadrant** *n* квадра́нт.

quadruped *n* четвероно́гое живо́тное *sb*. **quadruple** *adj* четверно́й; *vt* & *i* учетверя́ть(ся) *impf*, учетвери́ть(ся) *pf*. **quadruplets** *n pl* че́тверо близнецо́в.

quagmire *n* боло́то.

quail *n* (*bird*) пе́репел.

quaint *adj* причу́дливый.

quake *vi* дрожа́ть *impf* (**with** от+*gen*).

Quaker *n* ква́кер, ~ка.

qualification *n* (*for post etc.*) квалифика́ция; (*reservation*) огово́рка. **qualified** *adj* компете́нтный; (*limited*) ограни́ченный. **qualify** *vt* & *i* (*prepare for job*) гото́вить(ся) *impf* (**for** к+*dat*; +*inf*); *vt* (*render fit*) де́лать *impf*, с~ *pf* приго́дным; (*entitle*) дава́ть *impf*, дать *pf* пра́во +*dat* (**to** на+*acc*); (*limit*): ~ **what one says** сде́лать *pf* огово́рку; *vi* получа́ть *impf*, получи́ть *pf* дипло́м; ~ **for** (*be entitled to*) име́ть *impf* пра́во на+*acc*.

qualitative *adj* ка́чественный. **quality** *n* ка́чество.

qualm *n* сомне́ние; (*of conscience*) угрызе́ние со́вести.

quandary *n* затрудни́тельное положе́ние.

quantify *vt* определя́ть *impf*, определи́ть *pf* коли́чество +*gen*. **quantitative** *adj* коли́чественный. **quantity** *n* коли́чество.

quarantine *n* каранти́н.

quarrel *n* ссо́ра; *vi* ссо́риться *impf*, по~ *pf* (**with** с+*instr*; **about, for** из-за+*gen*). **quarrelsome** *adj* вздо́рный.

quarry[1] *n* (*for stone etc.*) каменоло́мня; *vt* добыва́ть *impf*, добы́ть *pf*.

quarry[2] *n* (*prey*) добы́ча.

quart *n* ква́рта. **quarter** *n* че́тверть; (*of year*; *of town*) кварта́л; *pl* кварти́ры *f pl*; **a ~ to one** без че́тверти час; **~-final** четверть-фина́л; *vt* (*divide*) дели́ть *impf*, раз~ *pf* на четы́ре ча́сти; (*lodge*) расквартиро́вывать *impf*, расквартирова́ть *pf*. **quarterly** *adj* кварта́льный; *adv* раз в кварта́л. **quartet** *n* кварте́т.

quartz *n* кварц.

quash *vt* (*annul*) аннули́ровать *impf* & *pf*; (*crush*) подавля́ть *impf*, подави́ть *pf*.

quasi- *in comb* квази-.

quaver *vi* дрожа́ть *impf*; *n* (*mus*) восьма́я *sb* но́ты.

quay *n* на́бережная *sb*.

queasy *adj*: **I feel ~** меня́ тошни́т.

queen *n* короле́ва; (*cards*) да́ма; (*chess*) ферзь *m*.

queer *adj* стра́нный.

quell *vt* подавля́ть *impf*, подави́ть *pf*.

quench *vt* (*thirst*) утоля́ть *impf*, утоли́ть *pf*; (*fire, desire*) туши́ть *impf*, по~ *pf*.

query *n* вопро́с; *vt* (*express doubt*) выража́ть *impf* вы́разить *pf* сомне́ние в+*prep*. **quest** *n* по́иски *m pl*; **in ~ of** в по́исках+*gen*. **question** *n* вопро́с; **beyond ~** вне сомне́ния; **it is a ~ of** э́то вопро́с+*gen*; **it is out of the ~** об э́том не мо́жет быть и ре́чи; **the person in ~** челове́к, о кото́ром идёт речь; **the ~ is this** де́ло в э́том; **~ mark** вопроси́тельный знак; *vt* расспра́шивать *impf*, расспроси́ть *pf*; (*interrogate*) допра́шивать *impf* допроси́ть *pf*; (*doubt*) сомнева́ться *impf* в+*prep*. **questionable** *adj*

сомни́тельный. **questionnaire** *n* вопро́сник.
queue *n* о́чередь; *vi* стоя́ть *impf* в о́череди.
quibble *n* софи́зм; (*minor criticism*) приди́рка; *vi* придира́ться *impf*; (*argue*) спо́рить *impf*.
quick *adj* ско́рый, бы́стрый; **~-tempered** вспы́льчивый; **~-witted** нахо́дчивый; *n*: **to the ~** за живо́е; *adv* ско́ро, бы́стро; *as imper* скоре́е!
quicken *vt & i* ускоря́ть(ся) *impf*, уско́рить(ся) *pf*. **quickness** *n* быстрота́. **quicksand** *n* зыбу́чий песо́к. **quicksilver** *n* ртуть.
quid *n* фунт.
quiet *n* (*silence*) тишина́; (*calm*) споко́йствие; *adj* ти́хий; споко́йный; *int* ти́ше!; *vt & i* успока́ивать(ся) *impf*, успоко́ить(ся) *pf*.
quill *n* перо́; (*spine*) игла́.
quilt *n* (стёганое) одея́ло; *vt* стега́ть *impf*, вы́~ *pf*. **quilted** *adj* стёганый.
quintessential *adj* наибо́лее суще́ственный.
quintet *n* квинте́т. **quins, quintuplets** *n pl* пять близнецо́в.
quip *n* острота́; остри́ть *impf*, с~ *pf*.
quirk *n* причу́да. **quirky** *adj* с причу́дами.
quit *vt* (*leave*) покида́ть *impf*, поки́нуть *pf*; (*stop*) перестава́ть *impf*, переста́ть *pf*; (*give up*) броса́ть *impf*, бро́сить *pf*; (*resign*) уходи́ть *impf*, уйти́ *pf* с+*gen*.
quite *adv* (*wholly*) совсе́м; (*rather*) дово́льно; **~ a few** дово́льно мно́го.
quits *predic*: **we are ~** мы с тобо́й кви́ты; **I am ~ with him** я расквита́лся (*past*) с ним.
quiver *vi* (*tremble*) трепета́ть *impf*; *n* тре́пет.
quiz *n* виктори́на. **quizzical** *adj* насме́шливый.
quorum *n* кво́рум.
quota *n* но́рма.
quotation *n* цита́та; (*of price*) цена́; **~ marks** кавы́чки (-чек) *pl*. **quote** *vt* цити́ровать *impf*, про~ *pf*; ссыла́ться *impf*, сосла́ться *pf* на+*acc*; (*price*) назнача́ть *impf*, назна́чить *pf*.

R

rabbi *n* равви́н.
rabbit *n* кро́лик.
rabble *n* сброд.
rabid *adj* бе́шеный. **rabies** *n* бе́шенство.
race[1] *n* (*ethnic* ~) ра́са; род.
race[2] *n* (*contest*) (*on foot*) бег; (*of cars etc.*; *fig*) го́нка, го́нки *f pl*; (*of horses*) ска́чки *f pl*; **~-track** трек; (*for horse* ~) скакова́я доро́жка; *vi* (*compete*) состяза́ться *impf* в ско́рости; (*rush*) мча́ться *impf*; *vt* бежа́ть *impf* наперегонки́ с+*instr*. **racecourse** *n* ипподро́м. **racehorse** *n* скакова́я ло́шадь.
racial *adj* ра́совый. **rac(ial)ism** *n* раси́зм. **rac(ial)ist** *n* раси́ст, ~ка; *adj* раси́стский.
racing *n* (*horses*) ска́чки *f pl*; (*cars*) го́нки *f pl*; **~ car** го́ночный автомоби́ль *m*; **~ driver** го́нщик.
rack *n* (*for hats etc.*) ве́шалка; (*for plates etc.*) стелла́ж; (*in train etc.*) се́тка; *vt*: **~ one's brains** лома́ть *impf* себе́ го́лову.
racket[1] *n* (*bat*) раке́тка.

racket[2] *n* (*uproar*) шум; (*illegal activity*) рэ́кет. **racketeer** *n* рэкети́р.
racy *adj* колори́тный.
radar *n* (*system*) радиолока́ция; (*apparatus*) радиолока́тор, рада́р; *attrib* рада́рный.
radiance *n* сия́ние. **radiant** *adj* сия́ющий. **radiate** *vt* & *i* излуча́ть(ся) *impf*, излучи́ть-ся *pf*. **radiation** *n* излуче́ние. **radiator** *n* батаре́я; (*in car*) радиа́тор.
radical *adj* радика́льный; *n* радика́л.
radio *n* ра́дио *neut indecl*; (*set*) радиоприёмник; *vt* ради́ровать *impf* & *pf* +*dat*.
radioactive *adj* радиоакти́вный. **radioactivity** *n* радиоакти́вность. **radiologist** *n* радио́лог; рентгено́лог. **radiotherapy** *n* радиотерапи́я.
radish *n* реди́ска.
radius *n* ра́диус.
raffle *n* лотере́я; *vt* разы́грывать *impf*, разыгра́ть *pf* в лотере́е.
raft *n* плот.
rafter *n* (*beam*) стропи́ло.
rag *n* тря́пка; *pl* (*clothes*) лохмо́тья (-ьев) *pl*.
rage *n* я́рость; **all the ~** после́дний крик мо́ды; *vi* беси́ться *impf*; (*storm etc.*) бушева́ть *impf*.
ragged *adj* (*jagged*) зазу́бренный; (*of clothes*) рва́ный.
raid *n* налёт; (*by police*) обла́ва; *vt* де́лать *impf*, с~ *pf* налёт на+*acc*.
rail *n* пери́ла (-л) *pl*; (*rly*) рельс; **by ~** по́ездом. **railing** *n* пери́ла (-л) *pl*.
railway *n* желе́зная доро́га; *attrib* железнодоро́жный. **railwayman** *n* железнодоро́жник.
rain *n* дождь *m*; *v impers*: **it is (was) ~ing** идёт (шёл) дождь; *vt* осыпа́ть *impf*, осы́пать *pf* +*instr* (**upon** +*acc*); *vi* осыпа́ться *impf*, осы́паться *pf*. **rainbow** *n* ра́дуга. **raincoat** *n* плащ. **raindrop** *n* дождева́я ка́пля. **rainfall** *n* (*amount of rain*) коли́чество оса́дков. **rainy** *adj* дождли́вый; **~ day** чёрный день *m*.
raise *vt* (*lift*) поднима́ть *impf*, подня́ть *pf*; (*heighten*) повыша́ть *impf*, повы́сить *pf*; (*provoke*) вызыва́ть *impf*, вы́звать *pf*; (*money*) собира́ть *impf*, собра́ть *pf*; (*children*) расти́ть *impf*.
raisin *n* изю́минка; *pl* (*collect*) изю́м.
rake *n* (*tool*) гра́бли (-бель & -бле́й) *pl*; *vt* грести́ *impf*; (**~** *together*, *up*) сгреба́ть *impf*, сгрести́ *pf*.
rally *vt* & *i* спла́чивать(ся) *impf*, сплоти́ть(ся) *pf*; *vi* (*after illness etc.*) оправля́ться *impf*, опра́виться *pf*; *n* (*meeting*) слёт; ми́тинг; (*motoring* **~**) (авто)ра́лли *neut indecl*; (*tennis*) обме́н уда́рами.
ram *n* (*sheep*) бара́н; *vt* (*beat down*) трамбова́ть *impf*, у~ *pf*; (*drive in*) вбива́ть *impf*, вбить *pf*.
ramble *vi* (*walk*) прогу́ливаться *impf*, прогуля́ться *pf*; (*speak*) бубни́ть *impf*; *n* прогу́лка. **rambling** *adj* (*incoherent*) бессвя́зный.
ramification *n* (*fig*) после́дствие.
ramp *n* скат.
rampage *vi* бу́йствовать *impf*.
rampant *adj* (*plant*) бу́йный; (*unchecked*) безу́держный.
rampart *n* вал.

ramshackle *adj* ве́тхий.
ranch *n* ра́нчо *neut indecl.*
rancid *adj* прого́рклый.
rancour *n* зло́ба.
random *adj* случа́йный; **at ~** наудачу.
range *n* (*of mountains*) цепь; (*artillery* ~) полиго́н; (*of voice*) диапазо́н; (*scope*) круг, преде́лы *m pl*; (*operating distance*) да́льность; *vi* (*vary*) колеба́ться *impf*, по~ *pf*; (*wander*) броди́ть *impf*; **~ over** (*include*) охва́тывать *impf*, охвати́ть *pf*.
rank[1] *n* (*row*) ряд; (*taxi* ~) стоя́нка такси́; (*grade*) зва́ние, чин, ранг; *vt* (*classify*) классифици́ровать *impf* & *pf*; (*consider*) счита́ть *impf* (**as** +*instr*); *vi*: **~ with** быть в числе́+*gen*.
rank[2] *adj* (*luxuriant*) бу́йный; (*in smell*) зловóнный; (*gross*) я́вный.
rankle *vi* боле́ть *impf*.
ransack *vt* (*search*) обша́ривать *impf*, обша́рить *pf*; (*plunder*) гра́бить *impf*, о~ *pf*.
ransom *n* вы́куп; *vt* выкупа́ть *impf*, вы́купить *pf*.
rant *vi* вопи́ть *impf*.
rap *n* стук; *vt* (ре́зко) ударя́ть *impf*, уда́рить *pf*; *vi* стуча́ть *impf*, сту́кнуть *pf*.
rape[1] *vt* наси́ловать *impf*, из~ *pf*; *n* изнаси́лование.
rape[2] *n* (*plant*) рапс.
rapid *adj* бы́стрый; *n*: *pl* поро́г, быстрина́. **rapidity** *n* быстрота́.
rapt *adj* восхищённый; (*absorbed*) поглощённый. **rapture** *n* восто́рг. **rapturous** *adj* восто́рженный.
rare[1] *adj* (*of meat*) недожа́ренный.
rare[2] *adj* ре́дкий. **rarity** *n* ре́дкость.
rascal *n* плут.
rash[1] *n* сыпь.
rash[2] *adj* опроме́тчивый.
rasher *n* ло́мтик (беко́на).
rasp *n* (*file*) ра́шпиль *m*; (*sound*) скре́жет; *vt*: **~ out** га́ркнуть *pf*.
raspberry *n* мали́на (*no pl*; *usu collect*).
rasping *adj* (*sound*) скрипу́чий.
rat *n* кры́са; **~ race** го́нка за успе́хом.
ratchet *n* храпови́к.
rate *n* но́рма, ста́вка; (*speed*) ско́рость; *pl* ме́стные нало́ги *m pl*; **at any ~** во вся́ком слу́чае; *vt* оце́нивать *impf*, оцени́ть *pf*; (*consider*) счита́ть *impf*; *vi* счита́ться *impf* (**as** +*instr*).
rather *adv* скоре́е; (*somewhat*) дово́льно; **he (she) had (would) ~** он (она́) предпочёл (-чла́) бы+*inf*.
ratification *n* ратифика́ция. **ratify** *vt* ратифици́ровать *impf* & *pf*.
rating *n* оце́нка.
ratio *n* пропо́рция.
ration *n* паёк, рацио́н; *vt* норми́ровать *impf* & *pf*; **be ~ed** выдава́ться *impf*, вы́даться *pf* по ка́рточкам.
rational *adj* разу́мный. **rationalism** *n* рационали́зм. **rationality** *n* разу́мность. **rationalize** *vt* обосно́вывать *impf*, обоснова́ть *pf*; (*industry etc.*) рационализи́ровать *impf* & *pf*.
rattle *vi* & *t* (*sound*) греме́ть *impf* (+*instr*); **~ along** (*move*) грохота́ть *impf*; **~ off** (*utter*) отбараба́нить *pf*; *n* (*sound*)

треск, гро́хот; (*toy*) погре́мушка. **rattlesnake** *n* гремучая змея́.

raucous *adj* ре́зкий.

ravage *vt* опустоша́ть *impf*, опустоши́ть *pf*; *n*: *pl* разруши́тельное де́йствие.

rave *vi* бре́дить *impf*; ~ **about** быть в восто́рге от+*gen*.

raven *n* во́рон.

ravenous *adj* голо́дный как волк.

ravine *n* уще́лье.

ravishing *adj* восхити́тельный.

raw *adj* сыро́й; (*inexperienced*) нео́пытный; ~ **material(s)** сырьё (*no pl*).

ray *n* луч.

raze *vt*: ~ **to the ground** ровня́ть *impf*, с~ *pf* с землёй.

razor *n* бри́тва; ~**-blade** ле́звие.

reach *vt* (*attain*, *extend to*, *arrive at*) достига́ть *impf*, дости́чь & дости́гнуть *pf* +*gen*, до+*gen*; доходи́ть *impf*, дойти́ *pf* до+*gen*; (*with hand*) дотя́гиваться *impf*, дотяну́ться *pf* до+*gen*; *vi* (*extend*) простира́ться *impf*; *n* досяга́емость; (*pl*, *of river*) тече́ние.

react *vi* реаги́ровать *impf*, от~, про~ *pf* (**to** на+*acc*). **reaction** *n* реа́кция. **reactionary** *adj* реакцио́нный; *n* реакционе́р. **reactor** *n* реа́ктор.

read *vt* чита́ть *impf*, про~, проче́сть *pf*; (*mus*) разбира́ть *impf*, разобра́ть *pf*; (~ *a meter etc.*) снима́ть *impf*, снять *pf* показа́ния +*gen*; (*univ*) изуча́ть *impf*; (*interpret*) толкова́ть *impf*. **readable** *adj* интере́сный. **reader** *n* чита́тель *m*, ~ница; (*book*) хрестома́тия.

readily *adv* (*willingly*) охо́тно; (*easily*) легко́. **readiness** *n* гото́вность.

reading *n* чте́ние; (*on meter*) показа́ние.

ready *adj* гото́вый (**for** к+*dat*, на+*acc*); **get** ~ гото́виться *impf*; ~**-made** гото́вый; ~ **money** нали́чные де́ньги (-нег, -ньга́м) *pl*.

real *adj* настоя́щий, реа́льный; ~ **estate** недви́жимость. **realism** *n* реали́зм. **realist** *n* реали́ст. **realistic** *adj* реалисти́чный, -и́ческий. **reality** *n* действи́тельность; **in** ~ действи́тельно. **realization** *n* (*of plan etc.*) осуществле́ние; (*of assets*) реализа́ция; (*understanding*) осозна́ние. **realize** *vt* (*plan etc.*) осуществля́ть *impf*, осуществи́ть *pf*; (*assets*) реализова́ть *impf* & *pf*; (*apprehend*) осознава́ть *impf*, осозна́ть *pf*.

really *adv* действи́тельно, в са́мом де́ле.

realm *n* (*kingdom*) короле́вство; (*sphere*) о́бласть.

reap *vt* жать *impf*, сжать *pf*; (*fig*) пожина́ть *impf*, пожа́ть *pf*.

rear[1] *vt* (*lift*) поднима́ть *impf*, подня́ть *pf*; (*children*) воспи́тывать *impf*, воспита́ть *pf*; *vi* (*of horse*) станови́ться *impf*, стать *pf* на дыбы́.

rear[2] *n* за́дняя часть; (*mil*) тыл; **bring up the** ~ замыка́ть *impf*, замкну́ть *pf* ше́ствие; *adj* за́дний; (*also mil*) ты́льный. **rearguard** *n* арьерга́рд; ~ **action** арьерга́рдный бой.

rearmament *n* перевооруже́ние.

rearrange *vt* меня́ть *impf*.

reason *n* (*cause*) причи́на, основа́ние; (*intellect*) ра́зум, рассу́док; *vi* рассужда́ть *impf*; ~ **with** (*person*) угова́ривать *impf* +*acc*. **reasonable** *adj* разу́мный; (*inexpensive*) недорого́й.
reassurance *n* успока́ивание. **reassure** *vt* успока́ивать *impf*, успоко́ить *pf*.
rebate *n* ски́дка.
rebel *n* повста́нец; *vi* восстава́ть *impf*, восста́ть *pf*. **rebellion** *n* восста́ние. **rebellious** *adj* мяте́жный.
rebound *vi* отска́кивать *impf*, отскочи́ть *pf*; *n* рикоше́т.
rebuff *n* отпо́р; *vt* дава́ть *impf*, дать *pf* +*dat* отпо́р.
rebuild *vt* перестра́ивать *impf*, перестро́ить *pf*.
rebuke *vt* упрека́ть *impf*, упрекну́ть *pf*; *n* упрёк.
rebuttal *n* опроверже́ние.
recalcitrant *adj* непоко́рный.
recall *vt* (*an official*) отзыва́ть *impf*, отозва́ть *pf*; (*remember*) вспомина́ть *impf*, вспо́мнить *pf*; *n* о́тзыв; (*memory*) па́мять.
recant *vi* отрека́ться *impf*, отре́чься *pf*.
recapitulate *vt* резюми́ровать *impf* & *pf*.
recast *vt* переде́лывать *impf*, переде́лать *pf*.
recede *vi* отходи́ть *impf*, отойти́ *pf*.
receipt *n* (*receiving*) получе́ние; *pl* (*amount*) вы́ручка; (*written* ~) квита́нция; (*from till*) чек. **receive** *vt* (*admit, entertain*) принима́ть *impf*, приня́ть *pf*; (*get, be given*) получа́ть *impf*, получи́ть *pf*. **receiver** *n* (*radio, television*) приёмник; (*tel*) тру́бка.
recent *adj* неда́вний; (*new*) но́вый. **recently** *adv* неда́вно.
receptacle *n* вмести́лище. **reception** *n* приём; ~ **room** приёмная *sb*. **receptionist** *n* секрета́рь *m*, -рша, в приёмной. **receptive** *adj* восприи́мчивый.
recess *n* (*parl*) кани́кулы (-л) *pl*; (*niche*) ни́ша. **recession** *n* спад.
recipe *n* реце́пт.
recipient *n* получа́тель *m*.
reciprocal *adj* взаи́мный. **reciprocate** *vt* отвеча́ть *impf* (взаи́мностью) на+*acc*.
recital *n* (со́льный) конце́рт. **recitation** *n* публи́чное чте́ние. **recite** *vt* деклами́ровать *impf*, про~ *pf*; (*list*) перечисля́ть *impf*, перечи́слить *pf*.
reckless *adj* (*rash*) опроме́тчивый; (*careless*) неосторо́жный.
reckon *vt* подсчи́тывать *impf*, подсчита́ть *pf*; (*also regard as*) счита́ть *impf*, счесть *pf* (**to be** +*instr*); *vi*: ~ **on** рассчи́тывать *impf*, рассчита́ть *pf* на+*acc*; ~ **with** счита́ться *impf* с+*instr*. **reckoning** *n* счёт; **day of** ~ час распла́ты.
reclaim *vt* тре́бовать *impf*, по~ *pf* обра́тно; (*land*) осва́ивать *impf*, осво́ить *pf*.
recline *vi* полулежа́ть *impf*.
recluse *n* затво́рник.
recognition *n* узнава́ние; (*acknowledgement*) призна́ние. **recognize** *vt* узнава́ть *impf*, узна́ть *pf*; (*acknowledge*) признава́ть *impf*, призна́ть *pf*.
recoil *vi* отпря́дывать *impf*, отпря́нуть *pf*.
recollect *vt* вспомина́ть *impf*, вспо́мнить *pf*. **recollection** *n* воспомина́ние.

recommend *vt* рекомендова́ть *impf & pf*. **recommendation** *n* рекоменда́ция.

recompense *n* вознагражде́ние; *vt* вознагражда́ть *impf*, вознагради́ть *pf*.

reconcile *vt* примиря́ть *impf*, примири́ть *pf*; **~ o.s.** примиря́ться *impf*, примири́ться *pf* (**to** с+*instr*). **reconciliation** *n* примире́ние.

reconnaissance *n* разве́дка. **reconnoitre** *vt* разве́дывать *impf*, разве́дать *pf*.

reconstruct *vt* перестра́ивать *impf*, перестро́ить *pf*. **reconstruction** *n* перестро́йка.

record *vt* запи́сывать *impf*, записа́ть *pf*; *n* за́пись; (*minutes*) протоко́л; (*gramophone* ~) грампласти́нка; (*sport etc.*) реко́рд; **off the ~** неофициа́льно; *adj* реко́рдный; **~-breaker, -holder** рекордсме́н, ~ка; **~-player** прои́грыватель *m*. **recorder** *n* (*mus*) блок-фле́йта. **recording** *n* за́пись.

recount[1] *vt* (*narrate*) переска́зывать *impf*, пересказа́ть *pf*.

re-count[2] *vt* (*count again*) пересчи́тывать *impf*, пересчита́ть *pf*; *n* пересчёт.

recoup *vt* возвраща́ть *impf*, верну́ть *pf* (**losses** потерянное).

recourse *n*: **have ~ to** прибега́ть *impf*, прибе́гнуть *pf* к+*dat*.

recover *vt* (*regain possession*) получа́ть *impf*, получи́ть *pf* обра́тно; возвраща́ть *impf*, верну́ть *pf*; *vi* (*~ health*) поправля́ться *impf*, попра́виться *pf* (**from** по́сле+*gen*). **recovery** *n* возвраще́ние; выздоровле́ние.

recreate *vt* воссоздава́ть *impf*, воссозда́ть *pf*.

recreation *n* развлече́ние, о́тдых.

recrimination *n* взаи́мное обвине́ние.

recruit *n* новобра́нец; *vt* вербова́ть *impf*, за~ *pf*. **recruitment** *n* вербо́вка.

rectangle *n* прямоуго́льник. **rectangular** *adj* прямоуго́льный.

rectify *vt* исправля́ть *impf*, испра́вить *pf*.

rector *n* (*priest*) прихо́дский свяще́нник; (*univ*) ре́ктор. **rectory** *n* дом прихо́дского свяще́нника.

rectum *n* пряма́я кишка́.

recuperate *vi* поправля́ться *impf*, попра́виться *pf*. **recuperation** *n* выздоровле́ние.

recur *vi* повторя́ться *impf*, повтори́ться *pf*. **recurrence** *n* повторе́ние. **recurrent** *adj* повторя́ющийся.

recycle *vt* перераба́тывать *impf*, перерабо́тать *pf*.

red *adj* кра́сный; (*of hair*) ры́жий; *n* кра́сный цвет; (*polit*) кра́сный *sb*; **in the ~** в долгу́; **~-handed** с поли́чным; **~ herring** ло́жный след; **~-hot** раскалённый до́красна́; **R~ Indian** инде́ец, индиа́нка; **~ tape** волоки́та. **redcurrant** *n* кра́сная сморо́дина (*no pl*; *usu collect*). **redden** *vt* окра́шивать *impf*, окра́сить *pf* в кра́сный цвет; *vi* красне́ть *impf*, по~ *pf*. **reddish** *adj* красноватый; (*hair*) рыжева́тый.

redecorate *vt* отде́лывать *impf*, отде́лать *pf*.

redeem *vt* (*buy back*) выкупа́ть *impf*, вы́купить *pf*;

(*from sin*) искупа́ть *impf*, искупи́ть *pf*. **redeemer** *n* искупи́тель *m*. **redemption** *n* вы́куп; искупле́ние.

redeploy *vt* передислоци́ровать *impf* & *pf*.

redo *vt* переде́лывать *impf*, переде́лать *pf*.

redouble *vt* удва́ивать *impf*, удво́ить *pf*.

redress *vt* исправля́ть *impf*, испра́вить *pf*; ~ **the balance** восстана́вливать *impf*, восстанови́ть *pf* равнове́сие; *n* возмеще́ние.

reduce *vt* (*decrease*) уменьша́ть *impf*, уме́ньшить *pf*; (*lower*) снижа́ть *impf*, сни́зить *pf*; (*shorten*) сокраща́ть *impf*, сократи́ть *pf*; (*bring to*) доводи́ть *impf*, довести́ *pf* (**to** в+*acc*). **reduction** *n* уменьше́ние, сниже́ние, сокраще́ние; (*discount*) ски́дка.

redundancy *n* (*dismissal*) увольне́ние. **redundant** *adj* изли́шний; **make** ~ увольня́ть *impf*, уво́лить *pf*.

reed *n* (*plant*) тростни́к; (*in oboe etc.*) язычо́к.

reef *n* риф.

reek *n* вонь; *vi*: ~ **(of)** воня́ть *impf* (+*instr*).

reel[1] *n* кату́шка; *vt*: ~ **off** (*story etc.*) отбараба́нить *pf*.

reel[2] *vi* (*stagger*) поша́тываться *impf*, пошатну́ться *pf*.

refectory *n* (*monastery*) тра́пезная *sb*; (*univ*) столо́вая *sb*.

refer *vt* (*direct*) отсыла́ть *impf*, отосла́ть *pf* (**to** к+*dat*); *vi*: ~ **to** (*cite*) ссыла́ться *impf*, сосла́ться *pf* на+*acc*; (*mention*) упомина́ть *impf*, упомяну́ть *pf* +*acc*. **referee** *n* судья́ *m*; *vt* суди́ть *impf*. **reference** *n* (*to book etc.*) ссы́лка; (*mention*) упомина́ние; (*testimonial*) характери́стика; ~ **book** спра́вочник. **referendum** *n* рефере́ндум.

refine *vt* очища́ть *impf*, очи́стить *pf*. **refined** *adj* (*in style etc.*) утончённый; (*in manners*) культу́рный. **refinement** *n* утончённость. **refinery** *n* (*oil* ~) нефтеочисти́тельный заво́д.

refit *vt* переобору́довать *impf* & *pf*.

reflect *vt* отража́ть *impf*, отрази́ть *pf*; *vi* размышля́ть *impf*, размы́слить *pf* (**on** о+*prep*). **reflection** *n* отраже́ние; размышле́ние; **on** ~ поду́мав. **reflective** *adj* (*thoughtful*) серьёзный. **reflector** *n* рефле́ктор. **reflex** *n* рефле́кс; *adj* рефле́кторный. **reflexive** *adj* (*gram*) возвра́тный.

reform *vt* реформи́ровать *impf* & *pf*; *vt* & *i* (*of people*) исправля́ть(ся) *impf*, испра́вить(ся) *pf*; *n* рефо́рма; исправле́ние. **Reformation** *n* Реформа́ция.

refract *vt* преломля́ть *impf*, преломи́ть *pf*.

refrain[1] *n* припе́в.

refrain[2] *vi* возде́рживаться *impf*, воздержа́ться *pf* (**from** от+*gen*).

refresh *vt* освежа́ть *impf*, освежи́ть *pf*. **refreshments** *n pl* напи́тки *m pl*.

refrigerate *vt* охлажда́ть *impf*, охлади́ть *pf*. **refrigeration** *n* охлажде́ние. **refrigerator** *n* холоди́льник.

refuge *n* убе́жище; **take** ~ находи́ть *impf*, найти́ *pf* убе́жище. **refugee** *n* бе́женец, -нка.

refund *vt* возвращáть *impf*, возвратúть *pf*; (*expenses*) возмещáть *impf*, возместúть *pf*; *n* возвращéние (дéнег); возмещéние.
refusal *n* откáз. **refuse**[1] *vt* (*decline to accept*) откáзываться *impf*, отказáться *pf* от+*gen*; (*decline to do sth*) откáзываться *impf*, отказáться *pf* +*inf*; (*deny s.o. sth*) откáзывать *impf*, отказáть *pf* +*dat*+в+*prep*.
refuse[2] *n* мýсор.
refute *vt* опровергáть *impf*, опровéргнуть *pf*.
regain *vt* возвращáть *impf*, вернýть *pf*.
regal *adj* королéвский.
regalia *n pl* регáлии *f pl*.
regard *vt* смотрéть *impf*, по~ *pf* на+*acc*; (*take into account*) считáться *impf* с+*instr*; ~ **as** считáть *impf* +*instr*, за+*instr*; **as ~s** что касáется+*gen*; *n* (*esteem*) уважéние; *pl* привéт. **regarding** *prep* относúтельно +*gen*. **regardless** *adv* не обращáя внимáния; ~ **of** не считáясь с+*instr*.
regatta *n* регáта.
regenerate *vt* перерождáть *impf*, переродúть *pf*.
regent *n* рéгент.
régime *n* режúм.
regiment *n* полк. **regimental** *adj* полковóй. **regimentation** *n* регламентáция.
region *n* региóн. **regional** *adj* регионáльный.
register *n* реéстр; (*also mus*) регúстр; *vt* регистрúровать *impf*, за~ *pf*; (*a letter*) отправлять *impf*, отпрáвить *pf* заказнЫм. **registered** *adj* (*letter*) заказнóй. **registrar** *n* регистрáтор. **registration** *n* регистрáция; ~ **number** нóмер машúны. **registry** *n* регистратýра; ~ **office** загс.
regret *vt* сожалéть *impf* о+*prep*; *n* сожалéние. **regretful** *adj* пóлный сожалéния. **regrettable** *adj* прискóрбный. **regrettably** *adv* к сожалéнию.
regular *adj* регулярный; (*also gram*) прáвильный; *n* (*coll*) завсегдáтай. **regularity** *n* регулярность. **regulate** *vt* регулúровать *impf*, у~ *pf*. **regulation** *n* регулúрование; *pl* прáвила *neut pl*.
rehabilitate *vt* реабилитúровать *impf* & *pf*. **rehabilitation** *n* реабилитáция.
rehearsal *n* репетúция. **rehearse** *vt* репетúровать *impf*, от~ *pf*.
reign *n* цáрствование; *vi* цáрствовать *impf*; (*fig*) царúть *impf*.
reimburse *vt* возмещáть *impf*, возместúть *pf* (+*dat of person*). **reimbursement** *n* возмещéние.
rein *n* пóвод.
reincarnation *n* перевоплощéние.
reindeer *n* сéверный олéнь *m*.
reinforce *vt* подкреплять *impf*, подкрепúть *pf*. **reinforcement** *n* (*also pl*) подкреплéние.
reinstate *vt* восстанáвливать *impf*, восстановúть *pf*. **reinstatement** *n* восстановлéние.
reiterate *vt* повторять *impf*, повторúть *pf*.
reject *vt* отвергáть *impf*, отвéргнуть *pf*; (*as defective*) браковáть *impf*, за~ *pf*; *n* брак. **rejection** *n* откáз (**of** от+*gen*).

rejoice *vi* ра́доваться *impf*, об~ *pf* (**in, at** *+dat*). **rejoicing** *n* ра́дость.
rejoin *vt* (вновь) присоединя́ться *impf*, присоедини́ться *pf* к+*dat*.
rejuvenate *vt* омола́живать *impf*, омолоди́ть *pf*.
relapse *n* рециди́в; *vi* сно́ва впада́ть *impf*, впасть *pf* (**into** в+*acc*); (*into illness*) сно́ва заболева́ть *impf*, заболе́ть *pf*.
relate *vt* (*tell*) расска́зывать *impf*, рассказа́ть *pf*; (*connect*) свя́зывать *impf*, связа́ть *pf*; *vi* относи́ться *impf* (**to** к+*dat*). **related** *adj* ро́дственный. **relation** *n* отноше́ние; (*person*) ро́дственник, -ица. **relationship** *n* (*connection*; *liaison*) связь; (*kinship*) родство́. **relative** *adj* относи́тельный; *n* ро́дственник, -ица. **relativity** *n* относи́тельность.
relax *vt* ослабля́ть *impf*, осла́бить *pf*; *vi* (*rest*) расслабля́ться *impf*, рассла́биться *pf*. **relaxation** *n* ослабле́ние; (*rest*) о́тдых.
relay *n* (*shift*) сме́на; (*sport*) эстафе́та; (*electr*) реле́ *neut indecl*; *vt* передава́ть *impf*, переда́ть *pf*.
release *vt* (*set free*) освобожда́ть *impf*, освободи́ть *pf*; (*unfasten*, *let go*) отпуска́ть *impf*, отпусти́ть *pf*; (*film etc.*) выпуска́ть *impf*, вы́пустить *pf*; *n* освобожде́ние; вы́пуск.
relegate *vt* переводи́ть *impf*, перевести́ *pf* (в ни́зшую гру́ппу). **relegation** *n* перево́д (в ни́зшую гру́ппу).
relent *vi* смягча́ться *impf*, смягчи́ться *pf*. **relentless** *adj* непреста́нный.
relevance *n* уме́стность. **relevant** *adj* относя́щийся к де́лу; уме́стный.
reliability *n* надёжность. **reliable** *adj* надёжный. **reliance** *n* дове́рие. **reliant** *adj*: **be ~ upon** зави́сеть *impf* от+*gen*.
relic *n* оста́ток, рели́квия.
relief[1] *n* (*art*, *geol*) релье́ф.
relief[2] *n* (*alleviation*) облегче́ние; (*assistance*) по́мощь; (*in duty*) сме́на. **relieve** *vt* (*alleviate*) облегча́ть *impf*, облегчи́ть *pf*; (*replace*) сменя́ть *impf*, смени́ть *pf*; (*unburden*) освобожда́ть *impf*, освободи́ть *pf* (**of** от+*gen*).
religion *n* рели́гия. **religious** *adj* религио́зный.
relinquish *vt* оставля́ть *impf*, оста́вить *pf*; (*right etc.*) отка́зываться *impf*, отказа́ться *pf* от+*gen*.
relish *n* (*enjoyment*) смак; (*cul*) припра́ва; *vt* смакова́ть *impf*.
relocate *vt* & *i* перемеща́ть(ся) *impf*, перемести́ть(ся) *pf*.
reluctance *n* неохо́та. **reluctant** *adj* неохо́тный; **be ~ to** не жела́ть *impf* +*inf*.
rely *vi* полага́ться *impf*, положи́ться *pf* (**on** на+*acc*).
remain *vi* остава́ться *impf*, оста́ться *pf*. **remainder** *n* оста́ток. **remains** *n pl* оста́тки *m pl*; (*human* ~) оста́нки (-ков) *pl*.
remand *vt* содержа́ть *impf* под стра́жей; **be on ~** содержа́ться *impf* под стра́жей.
remark *vt* замеча́ть *impf*, заме́тить *pf*; *n* замеча́ние. **remarkable** *adj* замеча́тельный.
remarry *vi* вступа́ть *impf*, вступи́ть *pf* в но́вый брак.

remedial *adj* лечéбный. **remedy** *n* срéдство (**for** от, прóтив+*gen*); *vt* исправля́ть *impf*, испрáвить *pf*.

remember *vt* пóмнить *impf*, вспоминáть *impf*, вспóмнить *pf*; (*greet*) передавáть *impf*, передáть *pf* привéт от+*gen* (**to** +*dat*). **remembrance** *n* пáмять.

remind *vt* напоминáть *impf*, напóмнить *pf* +*dat* (**of** +*acc*, о+*prep*). **reminder** *n* напоминáние.

reminiscence *n* воспоминáние. **reminiscent** *adj* напоминáющий.

remiss *predic* небрéжный. **remission** *n* (*pardon*) отпущéние; (*med*) ремúссия. **remit** *vt* пересылáть *impf*, переслáть *pf*. **remittance** *n* перевóд дéнег; (*money*) дéнежный перевóд.

remnant *n* остáток.

remonstrate *vi*: ~ **with** увещевáть *impf* +*acc*.

remorse *n* угрызéния *neut pl* сóвести. **remorseful** *adj* пóлный раскáяния. **remorseless** *adj* безжáлостный.

remote *adj* отдалённый; ~ **control** дистанциóнное управлéние.

removal *n* (*taking away*) удалéние; (*of obstacles*) устранéние. **remove** *vt* (*take away*) убирáть *impf*, убрáть *pf*; (*get rid of*) устраня́ть *impf*, устранúть *pf*.

remuneration *n* вознаграждéние. **remunerative** *adj* вы́годный.

renaissance *n* возрождéние; **the R**~ Возрождéние.

render *vt* воздавáть *impf*, воздáть *pf*; (*help etc.*) окáзывать *impf*, оказáть *pf*; (*role etc.*) исполня́ть *impf*, испóлнить *pf*; (*stone*) штукатýрить *impf*, о~, от~ *pf*. **rendering** *n* исполнéние.

rendezvous *n* (*meeting*) свидáние.

renegade *n* ренегáт, ~ка.

renew *vt* (*extend*; *continue*) возобновля́ть *impf*, возобновúть *pf*; (*replace*) обновля́ть *impf*, обновúть *pf*. **renewal** *n* (воз)обновлéние.

renounce *vt* отвергáть *impf*, отвéргнуть *pf*; (*claim*) откáзываться *impf*, отказáться *pf* от+*gen*.

renovate *vt* ремонтúровать *impf*, от~ *pf*. **renovation** *n* ремóнт.

renown *n* слáва. **renowned** *adj* извéстный; **be** ~ **for** слáвиться *impf* +*instr*.

rent *n* (*for home*) квартплáта; (*for premises*) (арéндная) плáта; *vt* (*of tenant*) арендовáть *impf* & *pf*; (*of owner*) сдавáть *impf*, сдать *pf*.

renunciation *n* (*repudiation*) отрицáние; (*of claim*) откáз.

rep *n* (*comm*) агéнт.

repair *vt* ремонтúровать *impf*, от~ *pf*; *n* (*also pl*) ремóнт (*only sg*); почúнка; **in good/bad** ~ в хорóшем/плохóм состоя́нии.

reparations *n pl* репарáции *f pl*.

repatriate *vt* репатриúровать *impf* & *pf*. **repatriation** *n* репатриáция.

repay *vt* отплáчивать *impf*, отплатúть *pf* (*person* +*dat*). **repayment** *n* отплáта.

repeal *vt* отменя́ть *impf*, отменúть *pf*; *n* отмéна.

repeat *vt* & *i* повторя́ть(ся)

impf, повтори́ть(ся) *pf*; *n* повторе́ние. **repeatedly** *adv* неоднокра́тно.
repel *vt* отта́лкивать *impf*, оттолкну́ть *pf*; (*enemy*) отража́ть *impf*, отрази́ть *pf*.
repent *vi* раска́иваться *impf*, раска́яться *pf*. **repentance** *n* раска́яние. **repentant** *adj* раска́ивающийся.
repercussion *n* после́дствие.
repertoire *n* репертуа́р. **repertory** *n* (*store*) запа́с; (*repertoire*) репертуа́р; ~ **company** постоя́нная тру́ппа.
repetition *n* повторе́ние. **repetitious, repetitive** *adj* повторя́ющийся.
replace *vt* (*put back*) класть *impf*, положи́ть *pf* обра́тно; (*substitute*) заменя́ть *impf*, замени́ть *pf* (**by** +*instr*). **replacement** *n* заме́на.
replay *n* переигро́вка.
replenish *vt* пополня́ть *impf*, попо́лнить *pf*.
replete *adj* насы́щенный; (*sated*) сы́тый.
replica *n* ко́пия.
reply *vt* & *i* отвеча́ть *impf*, отве́тить *pf* (**to** на+*acc*); *n* отве́т.
report *vt* сообща́ть *impf*, сообщи́ть *pf*; *vi* докла́дывать *impf*, доложи́ть *pf*; (*present o.s.*) явля́ться *impf*, яви́ться *pf*; *n* сообще́ние; докла́д; (*school*) та́бель *m*; (*sound*) звук взры́ва, вы́стрела. **reporter** *n* корреспонде́нт.
repose *n* (*rest*) о́тдых; (*peace*) поко́й.
repository *n* храни́лище.
repossess *vt* изыма́ть *impf*, изъя́ть *pf* за неплатёж.
reprehensible *adj* предосуди́тельный.
represent *vt* представля́ть *impf*; (*portray*) изобража́ть *impf*, изобрази́ть *pf*. **representation** *n* (*being represented*) представи́тельство; (*statement of case*) представле́ние; (*portrayal*) изображе́ние. **representative** *adj* изобража́ющий (**of** +*acc*); (*typical*) типи́чный; *n* представи́тель *m*.
repress *vt* подавля́ть *impf*, подави́ть *pf*. **repression** *n* подавле́ние, репре́ссия. **repressive** *adj* репресси́вный.
reprieve *vt* отсро́чивать *impf*, отсро́чить *pf* +*dat* приведе́ние в исполне́ние (сме́ртного) пригово́ра; *n* отсро́чка приведе́ния в исполне́ние (сме́ртного) пригово́ра; (*fig*) переды́шка.
reprimand *n* вы́говор; *vt* де́лать *impf*, с~ *pf* вы́говор +*dat*.
reprint *vt* переиздава́ть *impf*, переизда́ть *pf*; *n* переизда́ние.
reprisal *n* отве́тная ме́ра.
reproach *vt* упрека́ть *impf*, упрекну́ть *pf* (**with** в+*prep*). **reproachful** *adj* укори́зненный.
reproduce *vt* воспроизводи́ть *impf*, воспроизвести́ *pf*; *vi* размножа́ться *impf*, размно́житься *pf*. **reproduction** *n* (*action*) воспроизведе́ние; (*object*) репроду́кция; (*of offspring*) размноже́ние. **reproductive** *adj* воспроизводи́тельный.
reproof *n* вы́говор. **reprove** *vt* де́лать *impf* с~ *pf* вы́говор +*dat*.
reptile *n* пресмыка́ющееся *sb*.
republic *n* респу́блика. **republican** *adj* республика́нский; *n* республика́нец, -нка.

repudiate *vt* (*renounce*) отка́зываться *impf*, отказа́ться *pf* от+*gen*; (*reject*) отверга́ть *impf*, отве́ргнуть *pf*. **repudiation** *n* отка́з (**of** от+*gen*).

repugnance *n* отвраще́ние. **repugnant** *adj* проти́вный.

repulse *vt* отража́ть *impf*, отрази́ть *pf*. **repulsion** *n* отвраще́ние. **repulsive** *adj* отврати́тельный.

reputable *adj* по́льзующийся хоро́шей репута́цией. **reputation, repute** *n* репута́ция. **reputed** *adj* предполага́емый. **reputedly** *adv* по о́бщему мне́нию.

request *n* про́сьба; **by, on, ~** по про́сьбе; *vt* проси́ть *impf*, по~ *pf* +*acc*, +*gen* (*person* +*acc*).

requiem *n* ре́квием.

require *vt* (*demand*; *need*) тре́бовать *impf*, по~ *pf* +*gen*; (*need*) нужда́ться *impf* в+*prep*. **requirement** *n* тре́бование; (*necessity*) потре́бность. **requisite** *adj* необходи́мый; *n* необходи́мая вещь. **requisition** *n* реквизи́ция; *vt* реквизи́ровать *impf* & *pf*.

resale *n* перепрода́жа.

rescind *vt* отменя́ть *impf*, отмени́ть *pf*.

rescue *vt* спаса́ть *impf*, спасти́ *pf*; *n* спасе́ние. **rescuer** *n* спаси́тель *m*.

research *n* иссле́дование (+*gen*); (*occupation*) иссле́довательская рабо́та; *vi*: **~ into** иссле́довать *impf* & *pf* +*acc*. **researcher** *n* иссле́дователь *m*.

resemblance *n* схо́дство. **resemble** *vt* походи́ть *impf* на+*acc*.

resent *vt* возмуща́ться *impf*, возмути́ться *pf*. **resentful** *adj* возмущённый. **resentment** *n* возмуще́ние.

reservation *n* (*doubt*) огово́рка; (*booking*) предвари́тельный зака́з; (*land*) резерва́ция. **reserve** *vt* (*keep*) резерви́ровать *impf* & *pf*; (*book*) зака́зывать *impf*, заказа́ть *pf*; *n* (*stock*; *mil*) запа́с, резе́рв; (*sport*) запасно́й игро́к; (*nature* ~ *etc.*) запове́дник; (*proviso*) огово́рка; (*self-restraint*) сде́ржанность; *attrib* запасно́й. **reserved** *adj* (*person*) сде́ржанный. **reservist** *n* резерви́ст. **reservoir** *n* (*for water*) водохрани́лище; (*for other fluids*) резервуа́р.

resettle *vt* переселя́ть *impf*, пересели́ть *pf*. **resettlement** *n* переселе́ние.

reshape *vt* видоизменя́ть *impf*, видоизмени́ть *pf*.

reshuffle *n* перестано́вка.

reside *vi* прожива́ть *impf*. **residence** *n* (*residing*) прожива́ние; (*abode*) местожи́тельство; (*official* ~ *etc.*) резиде́нция. **resident** *n* (постоя́нный) жи́тель *m*, ~ница; *adj* прожива́ющий; (*population*) постоя́нный. **residential** *adj* жило́й.

residual *adj* оста́точный. **residue** *n* оста́ток.

resign *vt* отка́зываться *impf*, отказа́ться *pf* от+*gen*; *vi* уходи́ть *impf*, уйти́ *pf* в отста́вку; **~ o.s. to** покоря́ться *impf*, покори́ться *pf* +*dat*. **resignation** *n* отста́вка, заявле́ние об отста́вке; (*being resigned*) поко́рность. **resigned** *adj* поко́рный.

resilient *adj* выно́сливый.

resin *n* смола́.

resist *vt* сопротивля́ться *impf* +*dat*; (*temptation*) устоя́ть *pf* пе́ред+*instr*. **resistance** *n* сопротивле́ние. **resistant** *adj* сто́йкий.

resolute *adj* реши́тельный. **resolution** *n* (*character*) реши́тельность; (*vow*) заро́к; (*at meeting etc.*) резолю́ция; (*of problem*) разреше́ние. **resolve** *vt* (*decide*) реша́ть *impf*, реши́ть *pf*; (*settle*) разреша́ть *impf*, разреши́ть *pf*; *n* реши́тельность; (*decision*) реше́ние.

resonance *n* резона́нс. **resonant** *adj* зву́чный.

resort *vi*: ~ **to** прибега́ть *impf*, прибе́гнуть *pf* к+*dat*; *n* (*place*) куро́рт; **in the last** ~ в кра́йнем слу́чае.

resound *vi* (*of sound etc.*) раздава́ться *impf*, разда́ться *pf*; (*of place*) оглаша́ться *impf*, огласи́ться *pf* (**with** +*instr*).

resource *n* (*usu pl*) ресу́рс. **resourceful** *adj* нахо́дчивый.

respect *n* (*relation*) отноше́ние; (*esteem*) уваже́ние; **with** ~ **to** что каса́ется+*gen*; *vt* уважа́ть *impf*. **respectability** *n* респекта́бельность. **respectable** *adj* прили́чный. **respectful** *adj* почти́тельный. **respective** *adj* свой. **respectively** *adv* соотве́тственно.

respiration *n* дыха́ние. **respirator** *n* респира́тор. **respiratory** *adj* дыха́тельный.

respite *n* передышка.

resplendent *adj* блиста́тельный.

respond *vi*: ~ **to** отвеча́ть *impf*, отве́тить *pf* на+*acc*; (*react*) реаги́ровать *impf*, про~, от~ *pf* на+*acc*. **response** *n* отве́т; (*reaction*) о́тклик. **responsibility** *n* отве́тственность; (*duty*) обя́занность. **responsible** *adj* отве́тственный (**to** пе́ред+*instr*; **for** за+*acc*); (*reliable*) надёжный. **responsive** *adj* отзы́вчивый.

rest[1] *vi* отдыха́ть *impf*, отдохну́ть *pf*; *vt* (*place*) класть *impf*, положи́ть *pf*; (*allow to* ~) дава́ть *impf*, дать *pf* о́тдых+*dat*; *n* (*repose*) о́тдых; (*peace*) поко́й; (*mus*) па́уза; (*support*) опо́ра.

rest[2] *n* (*remainder*) оста́ток; (*the others*) остальны́е *sb pl*.

restaurant *n* рестора́н.

restful *adj* успока́ивающий.

restitution *n* возвраще́ние.

restive *adj* беспоко́йный.

restless *adj* беспоко́йный.

restoration *n* реставра́ция; (*return*) восстановле́ние. **restore** *vt* реставри́ровать *impf* & *pf*; (*return*) восстана́вливать *impf*, восстанови́ть *pf*.

restrain *vt* уде́рживать *impf*, удержа́ть *pf* (**from** от+*gen*). **restraint** *n* сде́ржанность.

restrict *vt* ограни́чивать *impf*, ограни́чить *pf*. **restriction** *n* ограниче́ние. **restrictive** *adj* ограничи́тельный.

result *vi* сле́довать *impf*; происходи́ть *impf* (**from** из+*gen*); ~ **in** конча́ться *impf*, ко́нчиться *pf* +*instr*; *n* результа́т; **as a** ~ в результа́те (**of** +*gen*).

resume *vt* & *i* возобновля́ть(ся) *impf*, возобнови́ть(ся) *pf*. **résumé** *n* резюме́ *neut indecl*. **resumption** *n* возобновле́ние.

resurrect *vt* (*fig*) воскреша́ть *impf*, воскреси́ть *pf*. **resurrection** *n* (*of the dead*) воскресе́ние; (*fig*) воскреше́ние.

resuscitate *vt* приводи́ть *impf*, привести́ *pf* в созна́ние.

retail *n* ро́зничная прода́жа; *attrib* ро́зничный; *adv* в ро́зницу; *vt* продава́ть *impf*, прода́ть *pf* в ро́зницу; *vi* продава́ться *impf* в ро́зницу. **retailer** *n* ро́зничный торго́вец.

retain *vt* уде́рживать *impf*, удержа́ть *pf*.

retaliate *vi* отпла́чивать *impf*, отплати́ть *pf* тем же. **retaliation** *n* отпла́та, возме́здие.

retard *vt* замедля́ть *impf*, заме́длить *pf*. **retarded** *adj* отста́лый.

retention *n* удержа́ние. **retentive** *adj* (*memory*) хоро́ший.

reticence *n* сде́ржанность. **reticent** *adj* сде́ржанный.

retina *n* сетча́тка.

retinue *n* сви́та.

retire *vi* (*withdraw*) удаля́ться *impf*, удали́ться *pf*; (*from office etc.*) уходи́ть *impf*, уйти́ *pf* в отста́вку. **retired** *adj* в отста́вке. **retirement** *n* отста́вка. **retiring** *adj* скро́мный.

retort[1] *vt* отвеча́ть *impf*, отве́тить *pf* ре́зко; *n* возраже́ние.

retort[2] *n* (*vessel*) рето́рта.

retrace *vt*: **~ one's steps** возвраща́ться *impf*, возврати́ться *pf*.

retract *vt* (*draw in*) втя́гивать *impf*, втяну́ть *pf*; (*take back*) брать *impf*, взять *pf* наза́д.

retreat *vi* отступа́ть *impf*, отступи́ть *pf*; *n* отступле́ние; (*withdrawal*) уедине́ние; (*place*) убе́жище.

retrenchment *n* сокраще́ние расхо́дов.

retrial *n* повто́рное слу́шание де́ла.

retribution *n* возме́здие.

retrieval *n* возвраще́ние; (*comput*) по́иск (информа́ции); *vt* брать *impf*, взять *pf* обра́тно.

retrograde *adj* (*fig*) реакцио́нный. **retrospect** *n*: **in ~** ретроспекти́вно. **retrospective** *adj* (*law*) име́ющий обра́тную си́лу.

return *vt* & *i* (*give back*; *come back*) возвраща́ть(ся) *impf*, возврати́ть(ся) *impf*, верну́ть(ся) *pf*; *vt* (*elect*) избира́ть *impf*, избра́ть *pf*; *n* возвраще́ние; возвра́т; (*profit*) при́быль; **by ~** обра́тной по́чтой; **in ~** взаме́н (**for** +*gen*); **many happy ~s!** с днём рожде́ния!, **~ match** отве́тный матч; **~ ticket** обра́тный биле́т.

reunion *n* встре́ча (друзе́й и т. п.); **family ~** сбор всей семьи́. **reunite** *vt* воссоединя́ть *impf*, воссоедини́ть *pf*.

reuse *vt* сно́ва испо́льзовать *impf* & *pf*.

rev *n* оборо́т; *vt* & *i*: **~ up** рвану́ть(ся) *pf*.

reveal *vt* обнару́живать *impf*, обнару́жить *pf*. **revealing** *adj* показа́тельный.

revel *vi* пирова́ть *impf*; **~ in** наслажда́ться *impf* +*instr*.

revelation *n* открове́ние.

revenge *vt*: **~ o.s.** мстить *impf*, ото~ *pf* (**for** за+*acc*; **on** +*dat*); *n* месть.

revenue *n* дохо́д.

reverberate *vi* отража́ться *impf*. **reverberation** *n* отраже́ние; (*fig*) о́тзвук.

revere *vt* почита́ть *impf*. **reverence** *n* почте́ние. **Reverend** *adj* (*in title*) (его́) преподо́бие. **reverent(ial)** *adj*

почти́тельный.
reverie *n* мечта́ние.
reversal *n* (*change*) измене́ние; (*of decision*) отме́на. **reverse** *adj* обра́тный; ~ **gear** за́дний ход; *vt* (*change*) изменя́ть *impf*, измени́ть *pf*; (*decision*) отменя́ть *impf*, отмени́ть *pf*; *vi* дава́ть *impf*, дать *pf* за́дний ход; *n* (*the* ~) обра́тное *sb*, противополо́жное *sb*; (~ *gear*) за́дний ход; (~ *side*) обра́тная сторона́. **reversible** *adj* обрати́мый; (*cloth*) двусторо́нний. **reversion** *n* возвраще́ние. **revert** *vi* возвраща́ться *impf* (**to** в+*acc*, к+*dat*); (*law*) переходи́ть *impf*, перейти́ *pf* (**to** к+*dat*).
review *n* (*re-examination*) пересмо́тр; (*mil*) пара́д; (*survey*) обзо́р; (*criticism*) реце́нзия; *vt* (*re-examine*) пересма́тривать *impf*, пересмотре́ть *pf*; (*survey*) обозрева́ть *impf*, обозре́ть *pf*; (*troops etc.*) принима́ть *impf*, приня́ть *pf* пара́д+*gen*; (*book etc.*) рецензи́ровать *impf*, про~ *pf*. **reviewer** *n* рецензе́нт.
revise *vt* пересма́тривать *impf*, пересмотре́ть *pf*; исправля́ть *impf*, испра́вить *pf*; *vi* (*for exam*) гото́виться *impf* (**for** к+*dat*). **revision** *n* пересмо́тр, исправле́ние.
revival *n* возрожде́ние; (*to life etc.*) оживле́ние. **revive** *vt* возрожда́ть *impf*, возроди́ть *pf*; (*resuscitate*) оживля́ть *impf*, оживи́ть *pf*; *vi* ожива́ть *impf*, ожи́ть *pf*.
revoke *vt* отменя́ть *impf*, отмени́ть *pf*.
revolt *n* бунт; *vt* вызыва́ть *impf*, вы́звать *pf* отвраще́ние у+*gen*; *vi* бунтова́ть *impf*, взбунтова́ться *pf*. **revolting** *adj* отврати́тельный.
revolution *n* (*single turn*) оборо́т; (*polit*) револю́ция. **revolutionary** *adj* революцио́нный; *n* революционе́р. **revolutionize** *vt* революционизи́ровать *impf* & *pf*. **revolve** *vt* & *i* враща́ть(ся) *impf*. **revolver** *n* револьве́р.
revue *n* ревю́ *neut indecl*.
revulsion *n* отвраще́ние.
reward *n* вознагражде́ние; *vt* (воз)награжда́ть *impf*, (воз)награди́ть *pf*.
rewrite *vt* перепи́сывать *impf*, переписа́ть *pf*; (*recast*) переде́лывать *impf*, переде́лать *pf*.
rhapsody *n* рапсо́дия.
rhetoric *n* рито́рика. **rhetorical** *adj* ритори́ческий.
rheumatic *adj* ревмати́ческий.
rheumatism *n* ревмати́зм.
rhinoceros *n* носоро́г.
rhododendron *n* рододе́ндрон.
rhubarb *n* реве́нь *m*.
rhyme *n* ри́фма; *pl* (*verse*) стихи́ *m pl*; *vt* & *i* рифмова́ть(ся) *impf*.
rhythm *n* ритм. **rhythmic(al)** *adj* ритми́ческий, -чный.
rib *n* ребро́.
ribald *adj* непристо́йный.
ribbon *n* ле́нта.
rice *n* рис.
rich *adj* бога́тый; (*soil*) ту́чный; (*food*) жи́рный. **riches** *n pl* бога́тство. **richly** *adv* (*fully*) вполне́.
rickety *adj* (*shaky*) расша́танный.
ricochet *vi* рикошети́ровать *impf* & *pf*.
rid *vt* освобожда́ть *impf*, освободи́ть *pf* (**of** от+*gen*);

get ~ of избавля́ться *impf*, изба́виться *pf* от+*gen*. **riddance** *n*: **good ~!** ска́тертью доро́га!

riddle *n* (*enigma*) зага́дка.

riddled *adj*: **~ with** изрешечённый; (*fig*) прони́занный.

ride *vi* е́здить *indet*, е́хать *det*, по~ *pf* (**on horseback** верхо́м); *vt* е́здить *indet*, е́хать *det*, по~ *pf* в, на+*prep*; *n* пое́здка, езда́. **rider** *n* вса́дник, -ица; (*clause*) дополне́ние.

ridge *n* хребе́т; (*on cloth*) ру́бчик; (*of roof*) конёк.

ridicule *n* насме́шка; *vt* осме́ивать *impf*, осмея́ть *pf*. **ridiculous** *adj* смешно́й.

riding *n* (*horse ~*) (верхова́я) езда́.

rife *predic* распространённый.

riff-raff *n* подо́нки (-ков) *pl*.

rifle *n* винто́вка; *vt* (*search*) обы́скивать *impf*, обыска́ть *pf*.

rift *n* тре́щина (*also fig*).

rig *vt* оснаща́ть *impf*, оснасти́ть *pf*; **~ out** наряжа́ть *impf*, наряди́ть *pf*; **~ up** скола́чивать *impf*, сколоти́ть *pf*; *n* бурова́я устано́вка. **rigging** *n* такела́ж.

right *adj* (*position*; *justified*; *polit*) пра́вый; (*correct*) пра́вильный; (*the one wanted*) тот; (*suitable*) подходя́щий; **~ angle** прямо́й у́гол; *vt* исправля́ть *impf*, испра́вить *pf*; *n* пра́во; (*what is just*) справедли́вость; (**~** *side*) пра́вая сторона́; (**the R~**; *polit*) пра́вые *sb pl*; **be in the ~** быть пра́вым; **by ~s** по пра́ву; **~ of way** пра́во прохо́да, прое́зда; *adv* (*straight*) пря́мо; (*exactly*) то́чно, как раз; (*to the full*) соверше́нно; (*correctly*) пра́вильно; как сле́дует; (*on the ~*) спра́во (**of** от+*gen*); (*to the ~*) напра́во; **~ away** сейча́с.

righteous *adj* (*person*) пра́ведный; (*action*) справедли́вый.

rightful *adj* зако́нный.

rigid *adj* жёсткий; (*strict*) стро́гий. **rigidity** *n* жёсткость; стро́гость.

rigmarole *n* каните́ль.

rigorous *adj* стро́гий. **rigour** *n* стро́гость.

rim *n* (*of wheel*) о́бод; (*spectacles*) опра́ва. **rimless** *adj* без опра́вы.

rind *n* кожура́.

ring[1] *n* кольцо́; (*circle*) круг; (*boxing*) ринг; (*circus*) (цирково́й) аре́на; **~ road** кольцева́я доро́га; *vt* (*encircle*) окружа́ть *impf*, окружи́ть *pf*.

ring[2] *vi* (*sound*) звони́ть *impf*, по~ *pf*; (*ring out, of shot etc.*) раздава́ться *impf*, разда́ться *pf*; (*of place*) оглаша́ться *impf*, огласи́ться *pf* (**with** +*instr*); *vt* звони́ть *impf*, по~ *pf* в+*acc*; **~ back** перезва́нивать *impf*, перезвони́ть *pf*; **~ off** пове́сить *pf* тру́бку; **~ up** звони́ть *impf*, по~ *pf* +*dat*; *n* звон, звоно́к.

ringleader *n* глава́рь *m*.

rink *n* като́к.

rinse *vt* полоска́ть *impf*, вы́~ *pf*; *n* полоска́ние.

riot *n* бунт; **run ~** бу́йствовать *impf*; (*of plants*) бу́йно разраста́ться *impf*, разрасти́сь *pf*; *vi* бунтова́ть *impf*, взбунтова́ться *pf*. **riotous** *adj* бу́йный.

rip *vt* & *i* рва́ть(ся) *impf*; разо~ *pf*; **~ up** разрыва́ть *impf*, разорвáть *pf*; *n* прорéха, разрéз.

ripe *adj* зрéлый, спéлый. **ripen** *vt* дéлать *impf*, с~ *pf* зрéлым; *vi* созревáть *impf*, созрéть *pf*. **ripeness** *n* зрéлость.

ripple *n* рябь; *vt* & *i* покрывáть(ся) *impf*, покры́ть(ся) *pf* ря́бью.

rise *vi* поднимáться *impf*, подня́ться *pf*; повышáться *impf*, повы́ситься *pf*; (*get up*) вставáть *impf*, встать *pf*; (*rebel*) восставáть *impf*, восстáть *pf*; (*sun etc.*) в(о)сходи́ть *impf*, взойти́; *n* подъём, возвышéние; (*in pay*) прибáвка; (*of sun etc.*) восхóд. **riser** *n*: **he is an early** ~ он рáно встаёт. **rising** *n* (*revolt*) восстáние.

risk *n* риск; *vt* рисковáть *impf*, рискнýть *pf* +*instr*. **risky** *adj* рискóванный.

risqué *adj* непристóйный.

rite *n* обря́д. **ritual** *n* ритуáл; *adj* ритуáльный.

rival *n* сопéрник, -ица; *adj* сопéрничающий; *vt* сопéрничать *impf* с+*instr*. **rivalry** *n* сопéрничество.

river *n* рекá. **riverside** *attrib* прибрéжный.

rivet *n* заклёпка; *vt* заклёпывать *impf*, заклепáть *pf*; (*fig*) прикóвывать *impf*, приковáть *pf* (**on** к+*dat*).

road *n* дорóга; (*street*) ýлица; **~-block** заграждéние на дорóге; **~-map** (дорóжная) кáрта; **~ sign** дорóжный знак. **roadside** *n* обóчина; *attrib* придорóжный. **roadway** *n* мостовáя *sb*.

roam *vt* & *i* броди́ть *impf* (по+*dat*).

roar *n* (*animal's*) рёв; *vi* ревéть *impf*.

roast *vt* & *i* жáрить(ся) *impf*, за~, из~ *pf*; *adj* жáреный; **~ beef** рóстбиф; *n* жаркóе *sb*.

rob *vt* грáбить *impf*, о~ *pf*; красть *impf*, у~ *pf* у+*gen* (**of** +*acc*); (*deprive*) лишáть *impf*, лиши́ть *pf* (**of** +*gen*). **robber** *n* граби́тель *m*. **robbery** *n* грабёж.

robe *n* (*also pl*) мáнтия.

robin *n* мали́новка.

robot *n* рóбот.

robust *adj* крéпкий.

rock[1] *n* (*geol*) (гóрная) порóда; (*cliff etc.*) скалá; (*large stone*) большóй кáмень *m*; **on the ~s** (*in difficulty*) на мели́; (*drink*) со льдом.

rock[2] *vt* & *i* качáть(ся) *impf*, качнýть(ся) *pf*; *n* (*mus*) рок; **~ing-chair** качáлка; **~ and roll** рок-н-рóлл.

rockery *n* альпинáрий.

rocket *n* ракéта; *vi* подскáкивать *impf*, подскочи́ть *pf*.

rocky *adj* скали́стый; (*shaky*) шáткий.

rod *n* (*stick*) прут; (*bar*) стéржень *m*; (*fishing-~*) ýдочка.

rodent *n* грызýн.

roe[1] *n* икрá; (*soft*) молóки (-óк) *pl*.

roe[2] **(-deer)** *n* косýля.

rogue *n* плут.

role *n* роль.

roll[1] *n* (*cylinder*) рулóн; (*register*) реéстр; (*bread*) бýлочка; **~-call** перекли́чка.

roll[2] *vt* & *i* катáть(ся) *indet*, кати́ть(ся) *det*, по~ *pf*; (~ *up*) свёртывать(ся) *impf*, свернýть(ся) *pf*; *vt* (~ *out*) (*dough*) раскáтывать *impf*, раскатáть *pf*; *vi* (*sound*) гремéть *impf*; **~ over**

перевора́чиваться *impf*, переверну́ться *pf*; *n* (*of drums*) бараба́нная дробь; (*of thunder*) раска́т.

roller *n* (*small*) ро́лик; (*large*) като́к; (*for hair*) бигуди́ *neut indecl*; **~-skates** коньки́ *m pl* на ро́ликах.

rolling *adj* (*of land*) холми́стый; **~-pin** ска́лка. **~-stock** подвижно́й соста́в.

Roman *n* ри́млянин, -янка; *adj* ри́мский; **~ Catholic** (*n*) като́лик, -и́чка; (*adj*) ри́мско-католи́ческий.

romance *n* (*tale*; *love affair*) рома́н; (*quality*) рома́нтика.

Romanesque *adj* рома́нский.

Romania *n* Румы́ния. **Romanian** *n* румы́н, -ка; *adj* румы́нский.

romantic *adj* романти́чный, -ческий. **romanticism** *n* романти́зм.

romp *vi* вози́ться *impf*.

roof *n* кры́ша; **~ of the mouth** нёбо; *vt* крыть *impf*, покры́ть *pf*.

rook[1] *n* (*chess*) ладья́.

rook[2] *n* (*bird*) грач.

room *n* ко́мната; (*in hotel*) но́мер; (*space*) ме́сто. **roomy** *adj* просто́рный.

roost *n* насе́ст.

root[1] *n* ко́рень *m*; **take ~** укореня́ться *impf*, укорени́ться *pf*; *vi* пуска́ть *impf*, пусти́ть *pf* ко́рни; **~ out** вырыва́ть *impf*, вы́рвать *pf* с ко́рнем; **rooted to the spot** прико́ванный к ме́сту.

root[2] *vi* (*rummage*) ры́ться *impf*; **~ for** боле́ть *impf* за *+acc*.

rope *n* верёвка; **~-ladder** верёвочная ле́стница; *vt*: **~ in** (*enlist*) втя́гивать *impf*, втя́нуть *pf*; **~ off** о(т)гора́живать *impf*, о(т)городи́ть *pf* верёвкой.

rosary *n* чётки (-ток) *pl*.

rose *n* ро́за; (*nozzle*) се́тка.

rosemary *n* розмари́н.

rosette *n* розе́тка.

rosewood *n* ро́зовое де́рево.

roster *n* расписа́ние дежу́рств.

rostrum *n* трибу́на.

rosy *adj* ро́зовый; (*cheeks*) румя́ный.

rot *n* гниль; (*nonsense*) вздор; *vi* гнить *impf*, с~ *pf*; *vt* гнои́ть *impf*, с~ *pf*.

rota *n* расписа́ние дежу́рств.

rotary *adj* враща́тельный, ротацио́нный. **rotate** *vt* & *i* враща́ть(ся) *impf*. **rotation** *n* враще́ние; **in ~** по о́череди.

rote *n*: **by ~** наизу́сть.

rotten *adj* гнило́й; (*fig*) отврати́тельный.

rotund *adj* (*round*) кру́глый; (*plump*) по́лный.

rouble *n* рубль *m*.

rough *adj* (*uneven*) неро́вный; (*coarse*) гру́бый; (*sea*) бу́рный; (*approximate*) приблизи́тельный; **~ copy** чернови́к; *n*: **the ~** тру́дности *f pl*; *vt*: **~ it** жить *impf* без удо́бств. **roughage** *n* гру́бая пи́ща. **roughly** *adv* гру́бо; (*approximately*) приблизи́тельно.

roulette *n* руле́тка.

round *adj* кру́глый; **~-shouldered** суту́лый; *n* (**~** *object*) круг; (*circuit*; *also pl*) обхо́д; (*sport*) тур, ра́унд; (*series*) ряд; (*ammunition*) патро́н; (*of applause*) взрыв; *adv* вокру́г; (*in a circle*) по кру́гу; **all ~** круго́м; **all the year ~** кру́глый год; *prep* вокру́г*+gen*; круго́м*+gen*; по*+dat*; **~ the**

corner (*motion*) за́ угол, (*position*) за угло́м; *vt* (*go* ~) огиба́ть *impf*, обогну́ть *pf*; ~ **off** (*complete*) заверша́ть *impf*, заверши́ть *pf*; ~ **up** сгоня́ть *impf*, согна́ть *pf*; ~-**up** заго́н; (*raid*) обла́ва. **roundabout** *n* (*merry-go-round*) карусе́ль; (*road junction*) кольцева́я тра́нспортная развя́зка; *adj* око́льный.
rouse *vt* буди́ть *impf*, раз~ *pf*; (*to action etc.*) побужда́ть *impf*, побуди́ть *pf* (**to** к+*dat*). **rousing** *adj* восто́рженный.
rout *n* (*defeat*) разгро́м.
route *n* маршру́т, путь *m*.
routine *n* заведённый поря́док, режи́м; *adj* устано́вленный; очередно́й.
rove *vi* скита́ться *impf*.
row[1] *n* (*line*) ряд.
row[2] *vi* (*in boat*) грести́ *impf*.
row[3] *n* (*dispute*) ссо́ра; (*noise*) шум; *vi* ссо́риться *impf*, по~ *pf*.
rowdy *adj* бу́йный.
royal *adj* короле́вский; (*majestic*) великоле́пный. **royalist** *n* рояли́ст; *adj* рояли́стский. **royalty** *n* член, чле́ны *pl*, короле́вской семьи́; (*fee*) а́вторский гонора́р.
rub *vt* & *i* тере́ть(ся) *impf*; *vt* (*polish*; *chafe*) натира́ть *impf*, натере́ть *pf*; (~ *dry*) вытира́ть *impf*, вы́тереть *pf*; ~ **in, on** втира́ть *impf*, втере́ть *pf*; ~ **out** стира́ть *impf*, стере́ть *pf*; ~ **it in** растравля́ть *impf*, растрави́ть *pf* ра́ну.
rubber *n* рези́на; (*eraser*, *also* ~ *band*) рези́нка; *attrib* рези́новый; ~-**stamp** (*fig*) штампова́ть *impf*.
rubbish *n* му́сор; (*nonsense*) чепуха́.
rubble *n* щéбень *m*.
rubella *n* красну́ха.
ruby *n* руби́н.
ruck *vt* (~ *up*) мять *impf*, из~, с~ *pf*.
rucksack *n* рюкза́к.
rudder *n* руль *m*.
ruddy *adj* (*face*) румя́ный; (*damned*) прокля́тый.
rude *adj* гру́бый. **rudeness** *n* гру́бость.
rudimentary *adj* рудимента́рный. **rudiments** *n pl* осно́вы *f pl*.
rueful *adj* печа́льный.
ruff *n* (*frill*) бры́жи (-жей) *pl*; (*of feathers*, *hair*) кольцо́ (пе́рьев, ше́рсти) вокру́г шéи.
ruffian *n* хулига́н.
ruffle *n* обо́рка; *vt* (*hair*) еро́шить *impf*, взъ~ *pf*; (*water*) ряби́ть *impf*; (*person*) смуща́ть *impf*, смути́ть *pf*.
rug *n* (*mat*) ковёр; (*wrap*) плед.
rugby *n* ре́гби *neut indecl*.
rugged *adj* (*rocky*) скали́стый.
ruin *n* (*downfall*) ги́бель; (*building*, *ruins*) разва́лины *f pl*, руи́ны *f pl*; *vt* губи́ть *impf*, по~ *pf*. **ruinous** *adj* губи́тельный.
rule *n* пра́вило; (*for measuring*) лине́йка; (*government*) правле́ние; **as a** ~ как пра́вило; *vt* & *i* пра́вить *impf* (+*instr*); (*decree*) постановля́ть *impf*, постанови́ть *pf*; ~ **out** исключа́ть *impf*, исключи́ть *pf*. **ruled** *adj* лино́ванный. **ruler** *n* (*person*) прави́тель *m*, ~ница; (*object*) лине́йка. **ruling** *n* (*of court etc.*) постановле́ние.
rum *n* (*drink*) ром.

Rumania(n) *see* **Romania(n)**

rumble *vi* громыха́ть *impf*; *n* громыха́ние.

ruminant *n* жва́чное (живо́тное) *sb*. **ruminate** *vi* (*fig*) размышля́ть *impf* (**over, on** о+*prep*).

rummage *vi* ры́ться *impf*.

rumour *n* слух; *vt*: **it is ~ed that** хо́дят слу́хи (*pl*), что.

rump *n* кресте́ц; **~ steak** ромште́кс.

rumple *vt* мять *impf*, из~, с~ *pf*; (*hair*) еро́шить *impf*, взъ~ *pf*.

run *vi* бе́гать *indet*, бежа́ть *det*, по~ *pf*; (*work, of machines*) рабо́тать *impf*; (*ply, of bus etc.*) ходи́ть *indet*, идти́ *det*, (*seek election*) выставля́ть *impf*, вы́ставить *pf* свою́ кандидату́ру; (*of play etc.*) идти́ *impf*; (*of ink, dye*) расплыва́ться *impf*, расплы́ться *pf*; (*flow*) течь *impf*; (*of document*) гласи́ть *impf*; *vt* (*manage; operate*) управля́ть *impf* +*instr*; (*a business etc.*) вести́ *impf*; **~ dry, low** иссяка́ть *impf*, исся́кнуть *pf*; **~ risks** рискова́ть *impf*; **~ across, into** (*meet*) встреча́ться *impf*, встре́титься *pf* с+*instr*; **~ away** (*flee*) убега́ть *impf*, убежа́ть *pf*; **~ down** (*knock down*) задави́ть *pf*; (*disparage*) принижа́ть *impf*, прини́зить *pf*; **be ~ down** (*of person*) переутоми́ться *pf* (*in past tense*); **~-down** (*decayed*) запу́щенный; **~ in** (*engine*) обка́тывать *impf*, обката́ть *pf*; **~ into** *see* **~ across; ~ out** конча́ться *impf*, ко́нчиться *pf*; **~ out of** истоща́ть *impf*, истощи́ть *pf* свой запа́с +*gen*; **~ over** (*glance over*) бе́гло просма́тривать *impf*, просмотре́ть *pf*; (*injure*) задави́ть *pf*; **~ through** (*pierce*) прока́лывать *impf*, проколо́ть *pf*; (*money*) прома́тывать *impf*, промота́ть *pf*; (*review*) повторя́ть *impf*, повтори́ть *pf*; **~ to** (*reach*) (*of money*) хвата́ть *impf*, хвати́ть *pf impers*+*gen* на+*acc*; **the money won't ~ to a car** э́тих де́нег не хва́тит на маши́ну; **~ up against** ната́лкиваться *impf*, натолкну́ться *pf* на+*acc*; *n* бег; (*sport*) перебе́жка; (*journey*) пое́здка; (*period*) полоса́; **at a ~** бего́м; **on the ~** в бега́х; **~ on** большо́й спрос на+*acc*; **in the long ~** в конце́ концо́в.

rung *n* ступе́нька.

runner *n* (*also tech*) бегу́н; (*of sledge*) по́лоз; (*bot*) побе́г; **~ bean** фасо́ль; **~-up** уча́стник, заня́вший второ́е ме́сто. **running** *n* бег; (*management*) управле́ние (**of** +*instr*); **be in the ~** име́ть *impf* ша́нсы; *adj* бегу́щий; (*of ~*) бегово́й; (*after pl n, in succession*) подря́д; **~ commentary** репорта́ж; **~ water** водопрово́д. **runway** *n* взлётно-поса́дочная полоса́.

rupee *n* ру́пия.

rupture *n* разры́в; *vt & i* прорыва́ть(ся) *impf*, прорва́ть(ся) *pf*.

rural *adj* се́льский.

ruse *n* уло́вка.

rush[1] *n* (*bot*) тростни́к.

rush[2] *vt & i* (*hurry*) торопи́ть(ся) *impf*, по~ *pf*; *vi* (*dash*) броса́ться *impf*, бро́ситься *pf*; (*of water*) нести́сь *impf*; по~ *pf*; *vt* (*to hospital etc.*) умча́ть *pf*; *n* (*of blood etc.*) прили́в; (*hurry*) спе́шка; **be**

in a ~ торопи́ться *impf*; ~-**hour(s)** часы́ *m pl* пик.

Russia *n* Росси́я. **Russian** *n* ру́сский *sb*; *adj* (*of ~ nationality, culture*) ру́сский; (*of ~ State*) росси́йский.

rust *n* ржа́вчина; *vi* ржаве́ть *impf*, за~, по~ *pf*.

rustic *adj* дереве́нский.

rustle *n* ше́лест, шо́рох, шурша́ние; *vi* & *t* шелесте́ть *impf* (+*instr*); ~ **up** раздобыва́ть *impf*; раздобы́ть *pf*.

rusty *adj* ржа́вый.

rut *n* колея́.

ruthless *adj* безжа́лостный.

rye *n* рожь; *attrib* ржано́й.

S

Sabbath *n* (*Jewish*) суббо́та; (*Christian*) воскресе́нье. **sabbatical** *n* годи́чный о́тпуск.

sable *n* со́боль.

sabotage *n* диве́рсия; *vt* саботи́ровать *impf* & *pf*. **saboteur** *n* диверса́нт.

sabre *n* са́бля.

sachet *n* упако́вка.

sack[1] *vt* (*plunder*) разгра́бить *pf*.

sack[2] *n* мешо́к; (*dismissal*): **get the** ~ быть уво́ленным; *vt* увольня́ть *impf*, уво́лить *pf*. **sacking** *n* (*hessian*) мешкови́на.

sacrament *n* та́инство; (*Eucharist*) прича́стие. **sacred** *adj* свяще́нный, свято́й. **sacrifice** *n* же́ртва; *vt* же́ртвовать *impf*, по~ *pf* +*instr*. **sacrilege** *n* святота́тство. **sacrosanct** *adj* свяще́нный.

sad *adj* печа́льный, гру́стный. **sadden** *vt* печа́лить *impf*, о~ *pf*.

saddle *n* седло́; *vt* седла́ть *impf*, о~ *pf*; (*burden*) обременя́ть *impf*, обремени́ть *pf* (**with** +*instr*).

sadism *n* сади́зм. **sadist** *n* сади́ст. **sadistic** *adj* сади́стский.

sadness *n* печа́ль, грусть.

safe *n* сейф; *adj* (*unharmed*) невреди́мый; (*out of danger*) в безопа́сности; (*secure*) безопа́сный; (*reliable*) надёжный; ~ **and sound** цел и невреди́м. **safeguard** *n* предохрани́тельная ме́ра; *vt* предохраня́ть *impf*, предохрани́ть *pf*. **safety** *n* безопа́сность; ~-**belt** реме́нь *m* безопа́сности; ~ **pin** англи́йская була́вка; ~-**valve** предохрани́тельный кла́пан.

sag *vi* (*of rope, curtain*) провиса́ть *impf*, прови́снуть *pf*; (*of ceiling*) прогиба́ться *impf*, прогну́ться *pf*.

saga *n* са́га.

sage[1] *n* (*herb*) шалфе́й.

sage[2] *n* (*person*) мудре́ц; *adj* му́дрый.

Sagittarius *n* Стреле́ц.

sail *n* па́рус; *vt* (*a ship*) управля́ть *impf* +*instr*; *vi* пла́вать *indet*, плыть *det*; (*depart*) отплыва́ть *impf*, отплы́ть *pf*. **sailing** *n* (*sport*) па́русный спорт; ~-**ship** па́русное су́дно. **sailor** *n* матро́с, моря́к.

saint *n* свято́й *sb*. **saintly** *adj* свято́й.

sake *n*: **for the** ~ **of** ра́ди+*gen*.

salad *n* сала́т; ~-**dressing** припра́ва к сала́ту.

salami *n* саля́ми *f indecl*.

salary *n* жа́лованье.

sale *n* прода́жа; (*also amount sold*) сбыт (*no pl*); (*with reduced prices*) распрода́жа; **be**

for ~ продава́ться *impf*. **saleable** *adj* хо́дкий. **salesman** *n* продаве́ц. **saleswoman** *n* продавщи́ца.
salient *adj* основно́й.
saliva *n* слюна́.
sallow *adj* желтова́тый.
salmon *n* ло́со́сь *m*.
salon *n* сало́н. **saloon** *n* (*on ship*) сало́н; (*car*) седа́н; (*bar*) бар.
salt *n* соль; **~-cellar** соло́нка; **~ water** морска́я вода́; **~-water** морско́й; *adj* солёный; *vt* соли́ть *impf*, по~ *pf*. **salty** *adj* солёный.
salutary *adj* благотво́рный.
salute *n* отда́ча че́сти; (*with guns*) салю́т; *vt* & *i* отдава́ть *impf*, отда́ть *pf* честь (+*dat*).
salvage *n* спасе́ние; *vt* спаса́ть *impf*, спасти́ *pf*.
salvation *n* спасе́ние; **S~ Army** А́рмия спасе́ния.
salve *n* мазь; *vt*: **~ one's conscience** успока́ивать *impf*, успоко́ить *pf* со́весть.
salvo *n* залп.
same *adj*: **the ~** тот же (са́мый); (*applying to both or all*) оди́н; (*identical*) одина́ковый; *pron*: **the ~** одно́ и то́ же, то же са́мое; *adv*: **the ~** таки́м же о́бразом, так же; **all the ~** всё-таки, тем не ме́нее. **sameness** *n* однообра́зие.
samovar *n* самова́р.
sample *n* образе́ц; *vt* про́бовать *impf*, по~ *pf*.
sanatorium *n* санато́рий.
sanctify *vt* освяща́ть *impf*, освяти́ть *pf*. **sanctimonious** *adj* ха́нжеский. **sanction** *n* са́нкция; *vt* санкциони́ровать *impf* & *pf*. **sanctity** *n* (*holiness*) свя́тость; (*sacredness*) свяще́нность. **sanctuary** *n* святи́лище; (*refuge*) убе́жище; (*for wild life*) запове́дник.
sand *n* песо́к; *vt* (**~ down**) шку́рить *impf*, по~ *pf*; **~-dune** дю́на.
sandal *n* санда́лия.
sandalwood *n* санда́ловое де́рево.
sandbank *n* о́тмель.
sandpaper *n* шку́рка; *vt* шлифова́ть *impf*, от~ *pf* шку́ркой.
sandstone *n* песча́ник.
sandwich *n* бутербро́д; *vt*: **~ between** вти́скивать *impf*, вти́снуть *pf* ме́жду+*instr*.
sandy *adj* (*of sand*) песча́ный; (*like sand*) песо́чный; (*hair*) рыжева́тый.
sane *adj* норма́льный; (*sensible*) разу́мный.
sang-froid *n* самооблада́ние.
sanguine *adj* оптимисти́ческий.
sanitary *adj* санита́рный; гигиени́ческий; **~ towel** гигиени́ческая поду́шка. **sanitation** *n* (*conditions*) санита́рные усло́вия *neut pl*; (*system*) водопрово́д и канализа́ция. **sanity** *n* психи́ческое здоро́вье; (*good sense*) здра́вый смысл.
sap *n* (*bot*) сок; *vt* (*exhaust*) истоща́ть *impf*, истощи́ть *pf*.
sapling *n* са́женец.
sapphire *n* сапфи́р.
sarcasm *n* сарка́зм. **sarcastic** *adj* саркасти́ческий.
sardine *n* сарди́на.
sardonic *adj* сардони́ческий.
sash[1] *n* (*scarf*) куша́к.
sash[2] *n* (*frame*) скользя́щая ра́ма; **~-window** подъёмное окно́.

satanic *adj* сатани́нский.
satchel *n* ра́нец, су́мка.
satellite *n* спу́тник, сателли́т (*also fig*); ~ **dish** параболи́ческая анте́нна; таре́лка (*coll*); ~ **TV** спу́тниковое телеви́дение.
satiate *vt* насыща́ть *impf*, насы́тить *pf*.
satin *n* атла́с.
satire *n* сати́ра. **satirical** *adj* сатири́ческий. **satirist** *n* сати́рик. **satirize** *vt* высме́ивать *impf*, вы́смеять *pf*.
satisfaction *n* удовлетворе́ние. **satisfactory** *adj* удовлетвори́тельный. **satisfy** *vt* удовлетворя́ть *impf*, удовлетвори́ть *pf*; (*hunger, curiosity*) утоля́ть *impf*, утоли́ть *pf*.
saturate *vt* насыща́ть *impf*, насы́тить *pf*; **I got ~d** (*by rain*) я промо́к до ни́тки. **saturation** *n* насыще́ние.
Saturday *n* суббо́та.
sauce *n* со́ус; (*cheek*) на́глость. **saucepan** *n* кастрю́ля. **saucer** *n* блю́дце. **saucy** *adj* на́глый.
Saudi *n* сау́довец, -вка; *adj* сау́довский. **Saudi Arabia** *n* Сау́довская Ара́вия.
sauna *n* фи́нская ба́ня.
saunter *vi* прогу́ливаться *impf*.
sausage *n* соси́ска; (*salami-type*) колбаса́.
savage *adj* ди́кий; (*fierce*) свире́пый; (*cruel*) жесто́кий; *n* дика́рь *m*; *vt* искуса́ть *pf*. **savagery** *n* ди́кость; жесто́кость.
save *vt* (*rescue*) спаса́ть *impf*, спасти́ *pf*; (*money*) копи́ть *impf*, на~ *pf*; (*put aside, keep*) бере́чь *impf*; (*avoid using*) эконо́мить *impf*, с~ *pf*; *vi*: ~ **up** копи́ть *impf*, на~ *pf* де́ньги. **savings** *n pl* сбереже́ния *neut pl*; ~ **bank** сберега́тельная ка́сса. **saviour** *n* спаси́тель *m*.
savour *vt* смакова́ть *impf*.
savoury *adj* пика́нтный; (*fig*) поря́дочный.
saw *n* пила́; *vt* пили́ть *impf*; ~ **up** распи́ливать *impf*, распили́ть *pf*. **sawdust** *n* опи́лки (-лок) *pl*.
saxophone *n* саксофо́н.
say *vt* говори́ть *impf*, сказа́ть *pf*; **to ~ nothing of** не говоря́ уже́ о+*prep*; **that is to ~** то есть; (*let us*) ~ ска́жем; **it is said (that)** говоря́т (что); *n* (*opinion*) мне́ние; (*influence*) влия́ние; **have one's ~** вы́сказаться *pf*. **saying** *n* погово́рка.
scab *n* (*on wound*) струп; (*polit*) штрейкбре́хер.
scabbard *n* но́жны (*gen* -жен) *pl*.
scaffold *n* эшафо́т. **scaffolding** *n* леса́ (-со́в) *pl*.
scald *vt* обва́ривать *impf*, обвари́ть *pf*.
scale *n* (*ratio*) масшта́б; (*grading*) шкала́; (*mus*) га́мма; *vt* (*climb*) взбира́ться *impf*, взобра́ться *pf* на+*acc*; ~ **down** понижа́ть *impf*, пони́зить *pf*.
scales[1] *n pl* (*of fish*) чешуя́ (*collect*).
scales[2] *n pl* весы́ (-со́в) *pl*.
scallop *n* гребешо́к; (*decoration*) фесто́н.
scalp *n* ко́жа головы́.
scalpel *n* ска́льпель *m*.
scaly *adj* чешу́йчатый; (*of boiler etc.*) покры́тый на́кипью.
scamper *vi* бы́стро бе́гать *impf*; (*frolic*) резви́ться *impf*.

scan *vt* (*intently*) рассма́тривать *impf*; (*quickly*) просма́тривать *impf*, просмотре́ть *pf*; (*med*) просве́чивать *impf*, просвети́ть *pf*; *n* просве́чивание.

scandal *n* сканда́л; (*gossip*) сплéтни (-тен) *pl*. **scandalize** *vt* шоки́ровать *impf* & *pf*. **scandalous** *adj* сканда́льный.

Scandinavia *n* Скандина́вия. **Scandinavian** *adj* скандина́вский.

scanner *n* (*comput, med*) ска́нер.

scanty *adj* ску́дный.

scapegoat *n* козёл отпуще́ния.

scar *n* шрам; *vt* оставля́ть *impf*, оста́вить *pf* шрам на+*prep*.

scarce *adj* дефици́тный; (*rare*) ре́дкий. **scarcely** *adv* едва́. **scarcity** *n* дефици́т; ре́дкость.

scare *vt* пуга́ть *impf*, ис~, на~ *pf*; ~ **away, off** отпу́гивать *impf*, отпугну́ть *pf*; *n* па́ника. **scarecrow** *n* пу́гало.

scarf *n* шарф.

scarlet *adj* (*n*) а́лый (цвет).

scathing *adj* уничтожа́ющий.

scatter *vt* & *i* рассыпа́ть(ся) *impf*, рассы́пать(ся) *pf*; (*disperse*) рассе́ивать(ся) *impf*, рассе́ять(ся) *pf*; ~**-brained** ве́треный. **scattered** *adj* разбро́санный; (*sporadic*) отде́льный.

scavenge *vi* ры́ться *impf* в отбро́сах. **scavenger** *n* (*person*) му́сорщик; (*animal*) живо́тное *sb*, пита́ющееся па́далью.

scenario *n* сцена́рий. **scene** *n* (*place of disaster etc.*) ме́сто; (*place of action*) ме́сто де́йствия; (*view*) вид, пейза́ж; (*picture*) карти́на; (*theat*) сце́на, явле́ние; (*incident*) сце́на; **behind the ~s** за кули́сами; **make a ~** устра́ивать *impf*, устро́ить *pf* сце́ну. **scenery** *n* (*theat*) декора́ция; (*landscape*) пейза́ж. **scenic** *adj* живопи́сный.

scent *n* (*smell*) арома́т; (*perfume*) духи́ (-хо́в) *pl*; (*trail*) след. **scented** *adj* души́стый.

sceptic *n* ске́птик. **sceptical** *adj* скепти́ческий. **scepticism** *n* скептици́зм.

schedule *n* (*timetable*) расписа́ние; *vt* составля́ть *impf*, соста́вить *pf* расписа́ние +*gen*.

schematic *adj* схемати́ческий. **scheme** *n* (*plan*) прое́кт; (*intrigue*) махина́ция; *vi* интригова́ть *impf*.

schism *n* раско́л.

schizophrenia *n* шизофрени́я. **schizophrenic** *adj* шизофрени́ческий; *n* шизофре́ник.

scholar *n* учёный *sb*: **scholarly** *adj* учёный. **scholarship** *n* учёность; (*payment*) стипе́ндия.

school *n* шко́ла; *attrib* шко́льный; *vt* (*train*) приуча́ть *impf*, приучи́ть *pf* (**to** к+*dat*, +*inf*). **school-book** *n* уче́бник. **schoolboy** *n* шко́льник. **schoolgirl** *n* шко́льница. **schooling** *n* обуче́ние. **school-leaver** *n* выпускни́к, -и́ца. **school teacher** *n* учи́тель *m*, ~ница.

schooner *n* шху́на.

sciatica *n* и́шиас.

science *n* нау́ка; ~ **fiction** нау́чная фанта́стика. **scientific** *adj* нау́чный. **scientist**

n учёный *sb*.

scintillating *adj* блистáтельный.

scissors *n pl* нóжницы (-ц) *pl*.

scoff *vi* (*mock*) смеяться *impf* (**at** над+*instr*).

scold *vt* бранить *impf*, вы́~ *pf*.

scoop *n* (*large*) черпáк; (*ice-cream* ~) лóжка для морóженого; *vt* (~ *out*, *up*) вычéрпывать *impf*, вы́черпать *pf*.

scooter *n* (*motor* ~) моторóллер.

scope *n* (*range*) предéлы *m pl*; (*chance*) возмóжность.

scorch *vt* (*fingers*) обжигáть *impf*, обжéчь *pf*; (*clothes*) сжигáть *impf*, сжечь *pf*.

score *n* (*of points etc.*) счёт; (*mus*) партитýра; *pl* (*great numbers*) мнóжество; *vt* (*notch*) дéлать *impf*, с~ *pf* зарýбки на+*prep*; (*points etc.*) получáть *impf*, получи́ть *pf*; (*mus*) оркестровáть *impf* & *pf*; *vi* (*keep* ~) вести́ *impf*, с~ *pf* счёт. **scorer** *n* счётчик.

scorn *n* презрéние; *vt* презирáть *impf* презрéть *pf*. **scornful** *adj* презри́тельный.

Scorpio *n* Скорпиóн.

scorpion *n* скорпиóн.

Scot *n* шотлáндец, -дка. **Scotch** *n* (*whisky*) шотлáндское ви́ски *neut indecl*. **Scotland** *n* Шотлáндия. **Scots, Scottish** *adj* шотлáндский.

scoundrel *n* подлéц.

scour[1] *vt* (*cleanse*) отчищáть *impf*, отчи́стить *pf*.

scour[2] *vt* & *i* (*rove*) ры́скать *impf* (по+*dat*).

scourge *n* бич.

scout *n* развéдчик; (**S**~) бойскáут; *vi*: ~ **about** разы́скивать *impf* (**for** +*acc*).

scowl *vi* хмýриться *impf*, на~ *pf*; *n* хмýрый взгляд.

scrabble *vi*: ~ **about** ры́ться *impf*.

scramble *vi* карáбкаться *impf*, вс~ *pf*; (*struggle*) дрáться *impf* (**for** за+*acc*); ~**d eggs** яи́чница-болтýнья.

scrap[1] *n* (*fragment etc.*) кусóчек; *pl* остáтки *m pl*; *pl* (*of food*) объéдки (-ков) *pl*; ~ **metal** металлолóм; *vt* сдавáть *impf*, сдать *pf* в ути́ль.

scrap[2] *n* (*fight*) дрáка; *vi* дрáться *impf*.

scrape *vt* скрести́ *impf*; (*graze*) царáпать *impf*, о~ *pf*; ~ **off** отскребáть *impf*, отскрести́ *pf*; ~ **through** (*exam*) с трудóм вы́держивать *impf*, вы́держать *pf*; ~ **together** наскребáть *impf*, наскрести́ *pf*.

scratch *vt* царáпать *impf*, о~ *pf*; *vt* & *i* (*when itching*) чесáть(ся) *impf*, по~ *pf*; *n* царáпина.

scrawl *n* карáкули *f pl*; *vt* писáть *impf*, на~ *pf* карáкулями.

scrawny *adj* сухопáрый.

scream *n* крик; *vi* кричáть *impf*, кри́кнуть *pf*.

screech *n* визг; *vi* визжáть *impf*.

screen *n* ши́рма; (*cin*, *TV*) экрáн; ~**-play** сценáрий; *vt* (*protect*) защищáть *impf*, защити́ть *pf*; (*hide*) укрывáть *impf*, укры́ть *pf*; (*show film etc.*) демонстри́ровать *impf* & *pf*; (*check on*) проверя́ть *impf*, провéрить *pf*; ~ **off** отгорáживать *impf*, отгороди́ть *pf* ши́рмой.

screw *n* винт; *vt* (~ *on*) привинчивать *impf*, привинтить *pf*; (~ *up*) завинчивать *impf*, завинтить *pf*; (*crumple*) комкать *impf*, с~ *pf*; ~ **up one's eyes** щуриться *impf*, со~ *pf*. **screwdriver** *n* отвёртка.

scribble *vt* строчить *impf*, на~ *pf*; *n* каракули *f pl*.

script *n* (*of film etc.*) сценарий; (*of speech etc.*) текст; (*writing system*) письмо; ~-**writer** сценарист.

Scripture *n* священное писание.

scroll *n* свиток; (*design*) завиток.

scrounge *vt* (*cadge*) стрелять *impf*, стрельнуть *pf*; *vi* попрошайничать *impf*.

scrub[1] *n* (*brushwood*) кустарник; (*area*) заросли *f pl*.

scrub[2] *vt* мыть *impf*, вы~ *pf* щёткой.

scruff *n*: **by the ~ of the neck** за шиворот.

scruffy *adj* ободранный.

scrum *n* схватка вокруг мяча.

scruple *n* (*also pl*) колебания *neut pl*; угрызения *neut pl* совести. **scrupulous** *adj* скрупулёзный.

scrutinize *vt* рассматривать *impf*. **scrutiny** *n* рассмотрение.

scuffed *adj* поцарапанный.

scuffle *n* потасовка.

sculpt *vt* ваять *impf*, из~ *pf*. **sculptor** *n* скульптор. **sculpture** *n* скульптура.

scum *n* накипь.

scurrilous *adj* непристойный.

scurry *vi* поспешно бегать *indet*, бежать *det*.

scuttle[1] *n* (*coal* ~) ведёрко для угля.

scuttle[2] *vi* (*run away*) удирать *impf*, удрать *pf*.

scythe *n* коса.

sea *n* море; *attrib* морской; ~ **front** набережная *sb*; ~-**gull** чайка; ~-**level** уровень *m* моря; ~-**lion** морской лев; ~-**shore** побережье. **seaboard** *n* побережье. **seafood** *n* продукты *m pl* моря.

seal[1] *n* (*on document etc.*) печать; *vt* скреплять *impf*, скрепить *pf* печатью; (*close*) запечатывать *impf*, запечатать *pf*; ~ **up** заделывать *impf*, заделать *pf*

seal[2] *n* (*zool*) тюлень *m*; (*fur-*~) котик.

seam *n* шов; (*geol*) пласт.

seaman *n* моряк, матрос.

seamless *adj* без шва.

seamstress *n* швея.

seance *n* спиритический сеанс.

seaplane *n* гидросамолёт.

searing *adj* палящий.

search *vt* обыскивать *impf*, обыскать *pf*; *vi* искать *impf* (**for** +*acc*); *n* поиски *m pl*; обыск; ~-**party** поисковая группа. **searching** *adj* (*look*) испытующий. **searchlight** *n* прожектор.

seasick *adj*: **I was ~** меня укачало. **seaside** *n* берег моря.

season *n* сезон; (*one of four*) время *neut* года; ~ **ticket** сезонный билет; *vt* (*flavour*) приправлять *impf*, приправить *pf*. **seasonable** *adj* по сезону; (*timely*) своевременный. **seasonal** *adj* сезонный. **seasoning** *n* приправа.

seat *n* (*place*) место; (*of chair*) сиденье; (*chair*) стул; (*bench*) скамейка; (*of trousers*) зад; ~ **belt** привязной ремень *m*;

vt сажа́ть *impf*, посади́ть *pf*; (*of room etc.*) вмеща́ть *impf*, вмести́ть *pf*; **be ~ed** сади́ться *impf*, сесть *pf*.

seaweed *n* морска́я во́доросль.

secateurs *n pl* сека́тор.

secede *vi* отка́лываться *impf*, отколо́ться *pf*. **secession** *n* отко́л.

secluded *adj* укро́мный. **seclusion** *n* укро́мность.

second[1] *adj* второ́й; **~-class** второкла́ссный; **~-hand** подержа́нный; (*of information*) из вторы́х рук; **~-rate** второразря́дный; **~ sight** ясновидение; **on ~ thoughts** взве́сив всё ещё раз; **have ~ thoughts** переду́мывать *impf*, переду́мать *pf* (**about** +*acc*); *n* второ́й *sb*; (*date*) второ́е (число́) *sb*; (*time*) секу́нда; *pl* (*comm*) това́р второ́го со́рта; **~ hand** (*of clock*) секу́ндная стре́лка; *vt* (*support*) подде́рживать *impf*, поддержа́ть *pf*; (*transfer*) откомандиро́вывать *impf* откомандирова́ть *pf*. **secondary** *adj* втори́чный, второстепе́нный; (*education*) сре́дний. **secondly** *adv* во-вторы́х.

secrecy *n* секре́тность. **secret** *n* та́йна, секре́т; *adj* та́йный, секре́тный; (*hidden*) потайно́й.

secretarial *adj* секрета́рский. **secretariat** *n* секретариа́т. **secretary** *n* секрета́рь *m*, -рша; (*minister*) мини́стр.

secrete *vt* (*conceal*) укрыва́ть *impf*, укры́ть *pf*; (*med*) выделя́ть *impf*, вы́делить *pf*. **secretion** *n* укрыва́ние; (*med*) выделе́ние.

secretive *adj* скры́тный.

sect *n* се́кта. **sectarian** *adj* секта́нтский.

section *n* се́кция; (*of book*) разде́л; (*geom*) сече́ние. **sector** *n* се́ктор.

secular *adj* све́тский. **secularization** *n* секуляриза́ция.

secure *adj* (*safe*) безопа́сный; (*firm*) надёжный; (*emotionally*) уве́ренный; *vt* (*fasten*) закрепля́ть *impf*, закрепи́ть *pf*; (*guarantee*) обеспе́чивать *impf*, обеспе́чить *pf*; (*obtain*) достава́ть *impf*, доста́ть *pf*. **security** *n* безопа́сность; (*guarantee*) зало́г; *pl* це́нные бума́ги *f pl*.

sedate *adj* степе́нный.

sedation *n* успокое́ние. **sedative** *n* успока́ивающее сре́дство.

sedentary *adj* сидя́чий.

sediment *n* оса́док.

seduce *vt* соблазня́ть *impf*, соблазни́ть *pf*. **seduction** *n* обольще́ние. **seductive** *adj* соблазни́тельный.

see *vt & i* ви́деть *impf*, у~ *pf*; *vt* (*watch, look*) смотре́ть *impf*, по~ *pf*; (*find out*) узнава́ть *impf*, узна́ть *pf*; (*understand*) понима́ть *impf*, поня́ть *pf*; (*meet*) ви́деться *impf*, у~ *pf* с+*instr*; (*imagine*) представля́ть *impf*, предста́вить *pf* себе́; (*escort, ~ off*) провожа́ть *impf*, проводи́ть *pf*; **~ about** (*attend to*) забо́титься *impf*, по~ *pf* о+*prep*; **~ through** (*fig*) ви́деть *impf*, наскво́зь+*acc*.

seed *n* се́мя *neut*. **seedling** *n* се́янец; *pl* расса́да. **seedy** *adj* (*shabby*) потрёпанный.

seeing (that) *conj* ввиду́ того́, что.

seek *vt* иска́ть *impf* +*acc*, *gen*.

seem *vi* каза́ться *impf*, по~ *pf* (*+instr*). **seemingly** *adv* по-ви́димому.

seemly *adj* прили́чный.

seep *vi* проса́чиваться *impf*, просочи́ться *pf*.

seethe *vi* кипе́ть *impf*, вс~ *pf*.

segment *n* отре́зок; (*of orange etc.*) до́лька; (*geom*) сегме́нт.

segregate *vt* отделя́ть *impf*, отдели́ть *pf*. **segregation** *n* сегрега́ция.

seismic *adj* сейсми́ческий.

seize *vt* хвата́ть *impf*, схвати́ть *pf*; *vi*: ~ **up** заеда́ть *impf*, зае́сть *pf impers+acc*; ~ **upon** ухва́тываться *impf*, ухвати́ться *pf* за+*acc*. **seizure** *n* захва́т; (*med*) припа́док.

seldom *adv* ре́дко.

select *adj* и́збранный; *vt* отбира́ть *impf*, отобра́ть *pf*. **selection** *n* (*choice*) вы́бор. **selective** *adj* разбо́рчивый.

self *n* со́бственное «я» *neut indecl*.

self- *in comb* само-; ~**-absorbed** эгоцентри́чный; ~**-assured** самоуве́ренный; ~**-catering (accommodation)** жильё с ку́хней; ~**-centred** эгоцентри́чный; ~**-confessed** открове́нный; ~**-confidence** самоуве́ренность; ~**-confident** самоуве́ренный; ~**-conscious** засте́нчивый; ~**-contained** (*person*) незави́симый; (*flat etc.*) отде́льный; ~**-control** самооблада́ние; ~**-defence** самозащи́та; ~**-denial** самоотрече́ние; ~**-determination** самоопределе́ние; ~**-effacing** скро́мный; ~**-employed person** незави́симый предпринима́тель *m*; ~**-esteem** самоуваже́ние; ~**-evident** очеви́дный; ~**-governing** самоуправля́ющий; ~**-help** самопо́мощь; ~**-importance** самомне́ние; ~**-imposed** доброво́льный; ~**-indulgent** изба́лованный; ~**-interest** со́бственный интере́с; ~**-pity** жа́лость к себе́; ~**-portrait** автопортре́т; ~**-preservation** самосохране́ние; ~**-reliance** самостоя́тельность; ~**-respect** самоуваже́ние; ~**-righteous** *adj* ха́нжеский; ~**-sacrifice** самопоже́ртвование; ~**-satisfied** самодово́льный; ~**-service** самообслу́живание (*attrib*: *in gen after n*); ~**-styled** самозва́нный; ~**-sufficient** самостоя́тельный.

selfish *adj* эгоисти́чный. **selfless** *adj* самоотве́рженный.

sell *vt & i* продава́ть(ся) *impf*, прода́ть(ся) *pf*; *vt* (*deal in*) торгова́ть *impf +instr*; ~ **out** of распродава́ть *impf*, распрода́ть *pf*. **seller** *n* продаве́ц. **selling** *n* прода́жа. **sell-out** *n*: **the play was a** ~ пье́са прошла́ с аншла́гом.

Sellotape *n* (*propr*) ли́пкая ле́нта.

semantic *adj* семанти́ческий. **semantics** *n* сема́нтика.

semblance *n* ви́димость.

semen *n* се́мя *neut*.

semi- *in comb* полу-; ~**-detached house** дом, разделённый о́бщей стено́й. **semibreve** *n* це́лая но́та. **semicircle** *n* полукру́г. **semicircular** *adj* полукру́глый. **semicolon** *n* то́чка с запято́й. **semiconductor** *n* полупроводни́к. **semifinal** *n* полуфина́л.

seminar *n* семина́р. **seminary**

n семина́рия.
semiquaver *n* шестна́дцатая но́та.
semitone *n* полуто́н.
senate *n* сена́т; (*univ*) сове́т. **senator** *n* сена́тор.
send *vt* посыла́ть *impf*, посла́ть *pf* (**for** за+*instr*); ~ **off** отправля́ть *impf*, отпра́вить *pf*; ~-**off** про́воды (-дов) *pl*. **sender** *n* отправи́тель *m*.
senile *adj* ста́рческий. **senility** *n* ста́рческое слабоу́мие.
senior *adj* (*n*) ста́рший (*sb*); ~ **citizen** стари́к, стару́ха. **seniority** *n* старшинство́.
sensation *n* сенса́ция; (*feeling*) ощуще́ние. **sensational** *adj* сенсацио́нный.
sense *n* чу́вство; (*good* ~) здра́вый смысл; (*meaning*) смысл; *pl* (*sanity*) ум; *vt* чу́вствовать *impf*. **senseless** *adj* бессмы́сленный.
sensibility *n* чувстви́тельность; *pl* самолю́бие. **sensible** *adj* благоразу́мный.
sensitive *adj* чувстви́тельный; (*touchy*) оби́дчивый. **sensitivity** *n* чувстви́тельность.
sensory *adj* чувстви́тельный.
sensual, sensuous *adj* чу́вственный.
sentence *n* (*gram*) предложе́ние; (*law*) пригово́р; *vt* пригова́ривать *impf*, приговори́ть *pf* (**to** к+*dat*).
sentiment *n* (*feeling*) чу́вство; (*opinion*) мне́ние. **sentimental** *adj* сентимента́льный. **sentimentality** *n* сентимента́льность.
sentry *n* часово́й *sb*.
separable *adj* отдели́мый. **separate** *adj* отде́льный; *vt* & *i* отделя́ть(ся) *impf*, отдели́ть(ся) *pf*. **separation** *n* отделе́ние. **separatism** *n* сепарати́зм. **separatist** *n* сепарати́ст.
September *n* сентя́брь *m*; *adj* сентя́брьский.
septic *adj* септи́ческий.
sepulchre *n* моги́ла.
sequel *n* (*result*) после́дствие; (*continuation*) продолже́ние. **sequence** *n* после́довательность; ~ **of events** ход собы́тий.
sequester *vt* секвестрова́ть *impf* & *pf*.
sequin *n* блёстка.
Serb(ian) *adj* се́рбский; *n* серб, ~ка. **Serbia** *n* Се́рбия. **Serbo-Croat(ian)** *adj* сербскохорва́тский.
serenade *n* серена́да.
serene *adj* споко́йный. **serenity** *n* споко́йствие.
serf *n* крепостно́й *sb*. **serfdom** *n* крепостно́е пра́во.
sergeant *n* сержа́нт.
serial *adj*: ~ **number** сери́йный но́мер; *n* (*story*) рома́н с продолже́нием; (*broadcast*) сери́йная постано́вка. **serialize** *vt* ста́вить *impf*, по~ *pf* в не́скольких частя́х.
series *n* (*succession*) ряд; (*broadcast*) се́рия переда́ч.
serious *adj* серьёзный. **seriousness** *n* серьёзность.
sermon *n* про́поведь.
serpent *n* змея́.
serrated *adj* зазу́бренный.
serum *n* сы́воротка.
servant *n* слуга́ *m*, служа́нка.
serve *vt* служи́ть *impf*, по~ *pf* +*dat* (**as, for** +*instr*); (*attend to*) обслу́живать *impf*, обслужи́ть *pf*; (*food; ball*) подава́ть *impf*, пода́ть *pf*; (*sentence*) отбыва́ть *impf*, отбы́ть *pf*;

(*writ etc.*) вруча́ть *impf*, вручи́ть *pf* (**on** +*dat*); *vi* (*be suitable*) годи́ться (**for** на +*acc*, для+*gen*); (*sport*) подава́ть *impf*, пода́ть *pf* мяч; **it ~s him right** поделóм емý (*dat*). **server** *n* (*comput*) се́рвер. **service** *n* (*act of serving*; *branch of public work*; *eccl*) слу́жба; (*quality of* ~) обслу́живание; (*of car etc.*) техобслу́живание; (*set of dishes*) серви́з; (*sport*) пода́ча; (*transport*) сообще́ние; **at your ~** к ва́шим услу́гам; *vt* (*car*) проводи́ть *impf*, провести́ *pf* техобслу́живание + *gen*; **~ charge** пла́та за обслу́живание; **~ station** ста́нция обслу́живания. **serviceable** *n* (*useful*) поле́зный; (*durable*) про́чный. **serviceman** *n* военнослу́жащий *sb*.

serviette *n* салфе́тка.

servile *adj* раболе́пный.

session *n* заседа́ние, се́ссия.

set[1] *vt* (*put*; ~ *clock*, *trap*) ста́вить *impf*, по- *pf*; (*table*) накрыва́ть *impf*, накры́ть *pf*; (*bone*) вправля́ть *impf*, впра́вить *pf*; (*hair*) укла́дывать *impf*, уложи́ть *pf*; (*gem*) оправля́ть *impf*, опра́вить *pf*; (*bring into state*) приводи́ть *impf*, привести́ *pf* (**in, to** в+*acc*); (*example*) подава́ть *impf*, пода́ть *pf*; (*task*) задава́ть *impf*, зада́ть *pf*; *vi* (*solidify*) тверде́ть *impf*, за~ *pf*; застыва́ть *impf*, засты́(ну)ть *pf*; (*sun etc.*) заходи́ть *impf*, зайти́ *pf*; сади́ться *impf*, сесть *pf*; **~ about** (*begin*) начина́ть *impf*, нача́ть *pf*; (*attack*) напада́ть *impf*, напа́сть *pf* на+*acc*; **~ back** (*impede*) препя́тствовать *impf*, вос~ *pf* +*dat*; **~-back** неуда́ча; **~ in** наступа́ть *impf*, наступи́ть *pf*; **~ off** (*on journey*) отправля́ться *impf*, отпра́виться *pf*; (*enhance*) оттеня́ть *impf*, оттени́ть *pf*; **~ out** (*state*) излага́ть *impf*, изложи́ть *pf*; (*on journey*) *see* **~ off**; **~ up** (*business*) оснóвывать *impf*, основа́ть *pf*.

set[2] *n* набóр, компле́кт; (*of dishes*) серви́з; (*radio*) приёмник; (*television*) телеви́зор; (*tennis*) сет; (*theat*) декора́ция; (*cin*) съёмочная площа́дка.

set[3] *adj* (*established*) установ́ленный.

settee *n* дива́н.

setting *n* (*frame*) опра́ва; (*surroundings*) обстано́вка; (*of mechanism etc.*) установ́ка; (*of sun etc.*) захóд.

settle *vt* (*decide*) реша́ть *impf*, реши́ть *pf*; (*reconcile*) ула́живать *impf*, ула́дить *pf*; (*a bill etc.*) опла́чивать *impf*, оплати́ть *pf*; (*calm*) успока́ивать *impf*, успокóить *pf*; *vi* поселя́ться *impf*, посели́ться *pf*; (*subside*) оседа́ть *impf*, осе́сть *pf*; **~ down** уса́живаться *impf*, усе́сться *pf* (**to** за+*acc*). **settlement** *n* поселе́ние; (*agreement*) соглаше́ние; (*payment*) упла́та. **settler** *n* поселе́нец.

seven *adj* & *n* семь; (*number 7*) семёрка. **seventeen** *adj* & *n* семна́дцать. **seventeenth** *adj* & *n* семна́дцатый. **seventh** *adj* & *n* седьмóй; (*fraction*) седьма́я *sb*. **seventieth** *adj* & *n* семидеся́тый. **seventy** *adj* & *n* се́мьдесят; *pl* (*decade*) семидеся́тые гóды (-дóв) *m pl*.

sever *vt* (*cut off*) отреза́ть

impf, отрéзать *pf*; (*relations*) разрывáть *impf*, разорвáть *pf*.

several *pron* (*adj*) нéсколько (+*gen*).

severance *n* разры́в; ~ **pay** выходнóе посóбие.

severe *adj* стрóгий, сурóвый; (*pain, frost*) си́льный; (*illness*) тяжёлый. **severity** *n* стрóгость, сурóвость.

sew *vt* шить *impf*, с~ *pf*; ~ **on** пришивáть *impf*, приши́ть *pf*; ~ **up** зашивáть *impf*, заши́ть *pf*.

sewage *n* стóчные вóды *f pl*; ~**-farm** поля́ *neut pl* орошéния. **sewer** *n* стóчная трубá. **sewerage** *n* канализáция.

sewing *n* шитьё; ~**-machine** швéйная маши́на.

sex *n* (*gender*) пол; (*sexual activity*) секс; **have** ~ имéть *impf* сношéние. **sexual** *adj* половóй, сексуáльный; ~ **intercourse** половóе сношéние. **sexuality** *n* сексуáльность. **sexy** *adj* эроти́ческий.

sh *int* ти́ше!; тсс!

shabby *adj* вéтхий.

shack *n* лачýга.

shackles *n pl* окóвы (-в) *pl*.

shade *n* тень; (*of colour, meaning*) оттéнок; (*lamp*-~) абажýр; **a** ~ чуть-чýть; *vt* затеня́ть *impf*, затени́ть *pf*; (*eyes etc.*) заслоня́ть *impf* заслони́ть *pf*; (*drawing*) тушевáть *impf*, за~ *pf*. **shadow** *n* тень; *vt* (*follow*) тáйно следи́ть *impf* за+*instr*. **shadowy** *adj* тёмный. **shady** *adj* тени́стый; (*suspicious*) подозри́тельный.

shaft *n* (*of spear*) дрéвко; (*arrow; fig*) стрелá; (*of light*) луч; (*of cart*) оглóбля; (*axle*) вал; (*mine, lift*) шáхта.

shaggy *adj* лохмáтый.

shake *vt* & *i* трясти́(сь) *impf*; *vi* (*tremble*) дрожáть *impf*; *vt* (*weaken*) колебáть *impf*, по~ *pf*; (*shock*) потрясáть *impf* потрясти́ *pf*; ~ **hands** пожимáть *impf*, пожáть *pf* рýку (**with** +*dat*); ~ **one's head** покачáть *pf* головóй; ~ **off** стря́хивать *impf*, стряхнýть *pf*; (*fig*) избавля́ться *impf*, избáвиться *pf* от+*gen*.

shaky *adj* шáткий.

shallow *adj* мéлкий; (*fig*) повéрхностный.

sham *vt* & *i* притворя́ться *impf*, притвори́ться *pf* +*instr*; *n* притвóрство; (*person*) притвóрщик, -ица; *adj* притвóрный.

shambles *n* хаóс.

shame *n* (*guilt*) стыд; (*disgrace*) позóр; **what a** ~**!** как жаль!; *vt* стыди́ть *impf*, при~ *pf*. **shameful** *adj* позóрный. **shameless** *adj* бессты́дный.

shampoo *n* шампýнь *m*.

shanty[1] *n* (*hut*) хибáрка; ~ **town** трущóба.

shanty[2] *n* (*song*) матрóсская пéсня.

shape *n* фóрма; *vt* придавáть *impf*, придáть *pf* фóрму+*dat*; *vi*: ~ **up** склáдываться *impf*, сложи́ться *pf*. **shapeless** *adj* бесфóрменный. **shapely** *adj* строй́ный.

share *n* дóля; (*econ*) áкция; *vt* дели́ть *impf*, по~ *pf*; (*opinion etc.*; ~ *out*) разделя́ть *impf*, раздели́ть *pf*. **shareholder** *n* акционéр.

shark *n* акýла.

sharp *adj* óстрый; (*steep*) крутóй; (*sudden; harsh*) рéзкий; *n* (*mus*) диéз; *adv* (*with time*)

ро́вно; (*of angle*) кру́то.
sharpen *vt* точи́ть *impf*, на~ *pf*.
shatter *vt* & *i* разбива́ть(ся) *impf*, разби́ть(ся) *pf* вдре́безги; *vt* (*hopes etc.*) разруша́ть *impf*, разру́шить *pf*.
shave *vt* & *i* бри́ть(ся) *impf*, по~ *pf*; *n* бритьё. **shaver** *n* электри́ческая бри́тва.
shawl *n* шаль.
she *pron* она́.
sheaf *n* сноп; (*of papers*) свя́зка.
shear *vt* стричь *impf*, о~ *pf*. **shears** *n pl* но́жницы (-ц) *pl*.
sheath *n* но́жны (*gen* -жен) *pl*.
shed[1] *n* сара́й.
shed[2] *vt* (*tears, blood, light*) пролива́ть *impf*, проли́ть *pf*; (*skin, clothes*) сбра́сывать *impf*, сбро́сить *pf*.
sheen *n* блеск.
sheep *n* овца́. **sheepish** *adj* сконфу́женный. **sheepskin** *n* овчи́на; ~ **coat** дублёнка.
sheer *adj* (*utter*) су́щий; (*textile*) прозра́чный; (*rock etc.*) отве́сный.
sheet *n* (*on bed*) простыня́; (*of glass, paper, etc.*) лист.
sheikh *n* шейх.
shelf *n* по́лка.
shell *n* (*of mollusc*) ра́ковина; (*seashell*) раку́шка; (*of tortoise*) щит; (*of egg, nut*) скорлупа́; (*of building*) осто́в; (*explosive* ~) снаря́д; *vt* (*peas etc.*) лущи́ть *impf*, об~ *pf*; (*bombard*) обстре́ливать *impf*, обстреля́ть *pf*.
shellfish *n* (*mollusc*) моллю́ск; (*crustacean*) ракообра́зное *sb*.
shelter *n* убе́жище; *vt* (*provide with refuge*) приюти́ть *pf*; *vt* & *i* укрыва́ть(ся) *impf*, укры́ть(ся) *pf*.
shelve[1] *vt* (*defer*) откла́дывать *impf*, отложи́ть *pf*.
shelve[2] *vi* (*slope*) отло́го спуска́ться *impf*.
shelving *n* (*shelves*) стелла́ж.
shepherd *n* пасту́х; *vt* проводи́ть *impf*, провести́ *pf*.
sherry *n* хе́рес.
shield *n* щит; *vt* защища́ть *impf*, защити́ть *pf*.
shift *vt* & *i* (*change position*) перемеща́ть(ся) *impf*, перемести́ть(ся) *pf*; (*change*) меня́ть(ся) *impf*; *n* перемеще́ние; переме́на; (*of workers*) сме́на; ~ **work** сме́нная рабо́та. **shifty** *adj* ско́льзкий.
shimmer *vi* мерца́ть *impf*; *n* мерца́ние.
shin *n* го́лень.
shine *vi* свети́ть(ся) *impf*; (*glitter*) блесте́ть *impf*; (*excel*) блиста́ть *impf*; (*sun, eyes*) сия́ть *impf*; *vt* (*a light*) освеща́ть *impf*, освети́ть *pf* фонарём (**on** +*acc*); *n* гля́нец.
shingle *n* (*pebbles*) га́лька.
shingles *n* опоя́сывающий лиша́й.
shiny *adj* блестя́щий.
ship *n* кора́бль *m*; су́дно; *vt* (*transport*) перевози́ть *impf*, перевезти́ *pf*; (*dispatch*) отправля́ть *impf*, отпра́вить *pf*. **shipbuilding** *n* судострое́ние. **shipment** *n* (*dispatch*) отпра́вка; (*goods*) па́ртия. **shipping** *n* суда́ (-до́в) *pl*. **shipshape** *adv* в по́лном поря́дке. **shipwreck** *n* кораблекруше́ние; **be** ~**ed** терпе́ть *impf*, по~ *pf* кораблекруше́ние. **shipyard** *n* верфь.
shirk *vt* увиливать *impf*, увильну́ть *pf* от+*gen*.
shirt *n* руба́шка.

shit (*vulg*) *n* говно́; *vi* срать *impf*, по~ *pf*.
shiver *vi* (*tremble*) дрожа́ть *impf*; *n* дрожь.
shoal *n* (*of fish*) ста́я.
shock *n* (*emotional*) потрясе́ние; (*impact*) уда́р, толчо́к; (*electr*) уда́р то́ком; (*med*) шок; *vt* шоки́ровать *impf*. **shocking** *adj* (*outrageous*) сканда́льный; (*awful*) ужа́сный.
shoddy *adj* халту́рный.
shoe *n* ту́фля; *vt* подко́вывать *impf*, подкова́ть *pf*. **shoe-lace** *n* шнуро́к. **shoemaker** *n* сапо́жник. **shoestring** *n*: **on a ~** с небольши́ми сре́дствами.
shoo *int* кш!; *vt* прогоня́ть *impf*, прогна́ть *pf*.
shoot *vt* & *i* стреля́ть *impf*, вы́стрелить *pf* (*a gun* из +*gen*; **at** в+*acc*); (*arrow*) пуска́ть *impf*, пусти́ть *pf*; (*kill*) застрели́ть *pf*; (*execute*) расстре́ливать *impf*, расстреля́ть *pf*; (*hunt*) охо́титься *impf* на+*acc*; (*football*) бить *impf* (по воро́там); (*cin*) снима́ть *impf*, снять *pf* (фильм); *vi* (*go swiftly*) пронoси́ться *impf*, пронести́сь *pf*; **~ down** (*aircraft*) сбива́ть *impf*, сбить *pf*; **~ up** (*grow*) бы́стро расти́ *impf*, по~ *pf*; (*prices*) подска́кивать *impf*, подскочи́ть *pf*; *n* (*branch*) росто́к, побе́г; (*hunt*) охо́та. **shooting** *n* стрельба́; (*hunting*) охо́та; **~-gallery** тир.
shop *n* магази́н; (*workshop*) мастерска́я *sb*, цех; **~ assistant** продаве́ц, -вщи́ца; **~-lifter** магази́нный вор; **~-lifting** воровство́ в магази́нах; **~ steward** цехово́й ста́роста *m*; **~-window** витри́на; *vi* де́лать *impf*, с~ *pf* поку́пки (*f pl*). **shopkeeper** *n* ла́вочник. **shopper** *n* покупа́тель *m*, ~ница. **shopping** *n* поку́пки *f pl*; **go, do one's ~** де́лать *impf*, с~ *pf* поку́пки; **~ centre** торго́вый центр.
shore[1] *n* бе́рег.
shore[2] *vt*: **~ up** подпира́ть *impf*, подпере́ть *pf*.
short *adj* коро́ткий; (*not tall*) ни́зкого ро́ста; (*deficient*) недоста́точный; **be ~ of** испы́тывать *impf*, испыта́ть *pf* недоста́ток в+*prep*; (*curt*) ре́зкий; **in ~** одни́м сло́вом; **~-change** обсчи́тывать *impf*, обсчита́ть *pf*; **~ circuit** коро́ткое замыка́ние; **~ cut** коро́ткий путь *m*; **~ list** оконча́тельный спи́сок; **~-list** включа́ть *impf*, включи́ть *pf* в оконча́тельный спи́сок; **~-lived** недолгове́чный; **~-sighted** близору́кий; (*fig*) недальнови́дный; **~ story** расска́з; **in ~ supply** дефици́тный; **~-tempered** вспы́льчивый; **~-term** краткосро́чный; **~-wave** коротково́лно́вый. **shortage** *n* недоста́ток. **shortcoming** *n* недоста́ток. **shorten** *vt* & *i* укора́чивать(ся) *impf*, укороти́ть(ся) *pf*. **shortfall** *n* дефици́т. **shorthand** *n* стеногра́фия; **~ typist** машини́стка-стенографи́стка. **shortly** *adv*: **~ after** вско́ре (по́сле+*gen*); **~ before** незадо́лго (до+*gen*). **shorts** *n pl* шо́рты (-т) *pl*.
shot *n* (*discharge of gun*) вы́стрел; (*pellets*) дробь; (*person*) стрело́к; (*attempt*) попы́тка; (*phot*) сни́мок; (*cin*)

кадр; (*sport*) (*stroke*) уда́р; (*throw*) бросо́к; **like a ~** неме́дленно; **~-gun** дробови́к.

should *v aux* (*ought*) до́лжен (бы) +*inf*: **you ~ know that** вы должны́ э́то знать; **he ~ be here soon** он до́лжен бы быть тут ско́ро; (*conditional*) бы +*past*: **I ~ say** я бы сказа́л(а); **I ~ like** я бы хоте́л(а).

shoulder *n* плечо́; **~-blade** лопа́тка; **~-strap** брете́лька; взва́ливать *impf*, взвали́ть *pf* на пле́чи; (*fig*) брать *impf*, взять *pf* на себя́.

shout *n* крик; *vi* крича́ть *impf*, кри́кнуть *pf*; **~ down** перекри́кивать *impf*, перекрича́ть *pf*.

shove *n* толчо́к; *vt & i* толка́ть(ся) *impf*, толкну́ть *pf*; **~ off** (*coll*) убира́ться *impf*, убра́ться *pf*.

shovel *n* лопа́та; *vt* (**~** *up*) сгреба́ть *impf*, сгрести́ *pf*.

show *vt* пока́зывать *impf*, показа́ть *pf*; (*exhibit*) выставля́ть *impf*, вы́ставить *pf*; (*film etc.*) демонстри́ровать *impf*, про~ *pf*; *vi* (*also* **~** *up*) быть ви́дным, заме́тным; **~ off** (*vi*) привлека́ть *impf*; привле́чь *pf* к себе́ внима́ние; **~ up** *see vi*; (*appear*) появля́ться *impf*; появи́ться *pf*; *n* (*exhibition*) вы́ставка, шо́у *neut indecl*; (*theat*) спекта́кль *m*, шо́у *neut indecl*; (*effect*) ви́димость; **~ of hands** голосова́ние лоднятием руки́; **~ business** шо́у-би́знес; **~-case** витри́на; **~-jumping** соревнова́ние по ска́чкам; **~-room** сало́н. **showdown** *n* развя́зка.

shower *n* (*rain*) до́ждик; (*hail*; *fig*) град; (**~**-*bath*) душ; *vt* осыпа́ть *impf*, осы́пать *pf* +*instr* (**on** +*acc*); *vi* принима́ть *impf*, приня́ть *pf* душ. **showery** *adj* дождли́вый.

showpiece *n* образе́ц. **showy** *adj* показно́й.

shrapnel *n* шрапне́ль.

shred *n* клочо́к; **not a ~** ни ка́пли; *vt* мельчи́ть *impf*, из~ *pf*.

shrewd *adj* проница́тельный.

shriek *vi* визжа́ть *impf*; взви́гнуть *pf*.

shrill *adj* пронзи́тельный.

shrimp *n* креве́тка.

shrine *n* святы́ня.

shrink *vi* сади́ться *impf*, сесть *pf*; (*recoil*) отпря́нуть *pf*; *vt* вызыва́ть *impf*, вы́звать *pf* уса́дку +*gen*; **~ from** избега́ть *impf* +*gen*.

shrivel *vi* смо́рщиваться *impf*, смо́рщиться *pf*.

shroud *n* са́ван; *vt* (*fig*) оку́тывать *impf*, оку́тать *pf* (**in** +*instr*).

Shrove Tuesday вто́рник на ма́сленой неде́ле.

shrub *n* куст. **shrubbery** *n* куста́рник.

shrug *vt & i* пожима́ть *impf*, пожа́ть *pf* (плеча́ми).

shudder *n* содрога́ние; *vi* содрога́ться *impf*, содрогну́ться *pf*.

shuffle *vt & i* (*one's feet*) ша́ркать *impf* (нога́ми); *vt* (*cards*) тасова́ть *impf*, с~ *pf*.

shun *vt* избега́ть *impf* +*gen*.

shunt *vi* (*rly*) маневри́ровать *impf*, с~ *pf*; *vt* (*rly*) переводи́ть *impf*, перевести́ *pf* на запасно́й путь.

shut *vt & i* (*also* **~** *down*) закрыва́ть(ся) *impf*, закры́ть(ся) *pf*; **~ out** (*exclude*) исключа́ть *impf*, исключи́ть *pf*; (*fence off*) загора́живать *impf*, загороди́ть *pf*; (*keep out*) не пуска́ть *impf*, пусти́ть *pf*; ~ **up** (*vi*) замолча́ть *pf*; (*imper*) заткни́сь!

shutter *n* ста́вень *m*; (*phot*) затво́р.

shuttle *n* челно́к.

shy¹ *adj* засте́нчивый.

shy² *vi* (*in alarm*) отпря́дывать *impf*, отпря́нуть *pf*.

Siberia *n* Сиби́рь. **Siberian** *adj* сиби́рский; *n* сибиря́к, -я́чка.

sick *adj* больно́й; **be** ~ (*vomit*) рвать *impf*, вы́~ *pf impers* +*acc*: **he was** ~ его́ вы́рвало; **feel** ~ тошни́ть *impf impers* +*acc*; **be** ~ **of** надоеда́ть *impf*, надое́сть *pf* +*nom* (*object*) & *dat* (*subject*): **I'm** ~ **of her** она́ мне надое́ла; ~**-leave** о́тпуск по боле́зни. **sicken** *vt* вызыва́ть *impf*, вы́звать *pf* тошноту́, (*disgust*) отвраще́ние, у+*gen*; *vi* заболева́ть *impf*, заболе́ть *pf*. **sickening** *adj* отврати́тельный.

sickle *n* серп.

sickly *adj* боле́зненный; (*nauseating*) тошнотво́рный. **sickness** *n* боле́знь; (*vomiting*) тошнота́.

side *n* сторона́; (*of body*) бок; ~ **by** ~ ря́дом (**with** с+*instr*); **on the** ~ на стороне́; *vi*: ~ **with** встава́ть *impf*, встать *pf* на сто́рону+*gen*; ~**-effect** побо́чное де́йствие; ~**-step** (*fig*) уклоня́ться *impf*, уклони́ться *pf* от+*gen*; ~**-track** (*distract*) отвлека́ть *impf*, отвле́чь *pf*. **sideboard** *n* буфе́т; *pl* ба́ки (-к) *pl*. **sidelight** *n* боково́й фона́рь *m*. **sideline** *n* (*work*) побо́чная рабо́та.

sidelong *adj* (*glance*) косо́й.

sideways *adv* бо́ком.

siding *n* запасно́й путь *m*.

sidle *vi*: ~ **up to** подходи́ть *impf*, подойти́ *pf* к (+*dat*) бочко́м.

siege *n* оса́да; **lay** ~ **to** осажда́ть *impf*, осади́ть *pf*; **raise the** ~ **of** снима́ть *impf*, снять *pf* оса́ду с+*gen*.

sieve *n* си́то; *vt* просе́ивать *impf*, просе́ять *pf*.

sift *vt* просе́ивать *impf*, просе́ять *pf*; (*fig*) тща́тельно рассма́тривать *impf*, рассмотре́ть *pf*.

sigh *vi* вздыха́ть *impf*, вздохну́ть *pf*; *n* вздох.

sight *n* (*faculty*) зре́ние; (*view*) вид; (*spectacle*) зре́лище; *pl* достопримеча́тельности *f pl*; (*on gun*) прице́л; **at first** ~ с пе́рвого взгля́да; **catch** ~ **of** уви́деть *pf*; **know by** ~ знать *impf* в лицо́; **lose** ~ **of** теря́ть *impf*, по~ *pf* из ви́ду; (*fig*) упуска́ть *impf*, упусти́ть *pf* из ви́ду.

sign *n* знак; (*indication*) при́знак; (~*board*) вы́веска; *vt* & *abs* подпи́сывать(ся) *impf*, подписа́ть(ся) *pf*; *vi* (*give* ~) подава́ть *impf*, пода́ть *pf* знак; ~ **on** (*as unemployed*) запи́сываться *impf*, записа́ться *pf* в спи́ски безрабо́тных; (~ *up*) нанима́ться *impf*, наня́ться *pf*.

signal *n* сигна́л; *vt* & *i* сигнализи́ровать *impf* & *pf*. **signal-box** *n* сигна́льная бу́дка. **signalman** *n* сигна́льщик.

signatory *n* подписа́вший *sb*; (*of treaty*) сторона́, подписа́вшая догово́р.

signature *n* по́дпись.

significance *n* значе́ние. **significant** *adj* значи́тельный.

signify *vt* означа́ть *impf.*
signpost *n* указа́тельный столб.
silage *n* си́лос.
silence *n* молча́ние, тишина́; *vt* заста́вить *pf* замолча́ть. **silencer** *n* глуши́тель *m.* **silent** *adj* (*not speaking*) безмо́лвный; (*of film*) немо́й; (*without noise*) ти́хий; **be ~** молча́ть *impf.*
silhouette *n* силуэ́т; *vt*: **be ~d** вырисо́вываться *impf*, вы́рисоваться *pf* (**against** на фо́не+*gen*).
silicon *n* кре́мний. **silicone** *n* силико́н.
silk *n* шёлк; *attrib* шёлковый. **silky** *adj* шелкови́стый.
sill *n* подоко́нник.
silly *adj* глу́пый.
silo *n* си́лос.
silt *n* ил.
silver *n* серебро́; (*cutlery*) столо́вое серебро́; *adj* (*of ~*) сере́бряный; (*silvery*) серебри́стый; **~-plated** посеребрённый. **silversmith** *n* сере́бряных дел ма́стер. **silverware** *n* столо́вое серебро́. **silvery** *adj* серебри́стый.
similar *adj* подо́бный (**to** +*dat*). **similarity** *n* схо́дство. **similarly** *adv* подо́бным о́бразом.
simile *n* сравне́ние.
simmer *vt* кипяти́ть *impf* на ме́дленном огне́; *vi* кипе́ть *impf* на ме́дленном огне́; **~ down** успока́иваться *impf*, успоко́иться *pf.*
simper *vi* жема́нно улыба́ться *impf*, улыбну́ться *pf.*
simple *adj* просто́й; **~-minded** тупова́тый. **simplicity** *n* простота́. **simplify** *vt* упроща́ть *impf*, упрости́ть *pf.* **simply** *adv* про́сто.
simulate *vt* притворя́ться *impf*, притвори́ться *pf* +*instr*; (*conditions etc.*) модели́ровать *impf* & *pf.* **simulated** *adj* (*pearls etc.*) иску́сственный.
simultaneous *adj* одновре́ме́нный.
sin *n* грех; *vi* греши́ть *impf*, со~ *pf.*
since *adv* с тех пор; *prep* с+*gen*; *conj* с тех пор как; (*reason*) так как.
sincere *adj* и́скренний. **sincerely** *adv* и́скренне; **yours ~** и́скренне Ваш. **sincerity** *n* и́скренность.
sinew *n* сухожи́лие.
sinful *adj* гре́шный.
sing *vt* & *i* петь *impf*, про~, с~ *pf.*
singe *vt* пали́ть *impf*, о~ *pf.*
singer *n* певе́ц, -ви́ца.
single *adj* оди́н; (*unmarried*) (*of man*) нежена́тый; (*of woman*) незаму́жняя; (*bed*) односпа́льный; **~-handed** без посторо́нней по́мощи; **~-minded** целеустремлённый; **~ parent** мать/оте́ц-одино́чка; **~ room** ко́мната на одного́; *n* (*ticket*) биле́т в оди́н коне́ц; *pl* (*tennis etc.*) одино́чная игра́ *vt*: **~ out** выделя́ть *impf*, вы́делить *pf.* **singly** *adv* по-одному́.
singular *n* еди́нственное число́; *adj* еди́нственный; (*unusual*) необыча́йный. **singularly** *adv* необыча́йно.
sinister *adj* злове́щий.
sink *vi* (*descend slowly*) опуска́ться *impf*, опусти́ться *pf*; (*in mud etc.*) погружа́ться *impf*, погрузи́ться *pf*; (*in water*) тону́ть *impf*, по~ *pf*; *vt* (*ship*) топи́ть *impf*, по~ *pf*;

(*pipe, post*) вка́пывать *impf*, вкопа́ть *pf*; *n* ра́ковина.
sinner *n* гре́шник, -ица.
sinus *n* па́зуха.
sip *vt* пить *impf*, ма́ленькими глотка́ми; *n* мале́нький глото́к.
siphon *n* сифо́н; ~ **off** (*also fig*) перека́чивать *impf*, перекача́ть *pf*.
sir *n* сэр.
siren *n* сире́на.
sister *n* сестра́; ~**-in-law** (*husband's sister*) золо́вка; (*wife's sister*) своя́ченица; (*brother's wife*) неве́стка.
sit *vi* (*be sitting*) сиде́ть *impf*; (~ *down*) сади́ться *impf*, сесть *pf*; (*parl, law*) заседа́ть *impf*; *vt* уса́живать *impf*, усади́ть *pf*; (*exam*) сдава́ть *impf*; ~ **back** отки́дываться *impf*, отки́нуться *pf*; ~ **down** сади́ться *impf*, сесть *pf*; ~ **up** приподнима́ться *impf*, приподня́ться *pf*; (*not go to bed*) не ложи́ться *impf* спать.
site *n* (*where a thing takes place*) ме́сто; (*where a thing is*) местоположе́ние.
sitting *n* (*parl etc.*) заседа́ние; (*for meal*) сме́на; ~**-room** гости́ная *sb*.
situated *adj*: **be** ~ находи́ться *impf*. **situation** *n* местоположе́ние; (*circumstances*) положе́ние; (*job*) ме́сто.
six *adj* & *n* шесть; (*number 6*) шестёрка. **sixteen** *adj* & *n* шестна́дцать. **sixteenth** *adj* & *n* шестна́дцатый. **sixth** *adj* & *n* шесто́й; (*fraction*) шеста́я *sb*. **sixtieth** *adj* & *n* шестидеся́тый. **sixty** *adj* & *n* шестьдеся́т; *pl* (*decade*) шестидеся́тые го́ды (-до́в) *m pl*.
size *n* разме́р; *vt*: ~ **up** оце́нивать *impf*, оцени́ть *pf*. **sizeable** *adj* значи́тельный.
sizzle *vi* шипе́ть *impf*.
skate[1] *n* (*fish*) скат.
skate[2] *n* (*ice-*~) конёк; (*roller-*~) конёк на ро́ликах; *vi* ката́ться *impf* на конька́х; **skating-rink** като́к.
skeleton *n* скеле́т.
sketch *n* зарисо́вка; (*theat*) скетч; *vt* & *i* зарисо́вывать *impf*, зарисова́ть *pf*. **sketchy** *adj* схемати́ческий; (*superficial*) пове́рхностный.
skew *adj* косо́й; **on the** ~ ко́со.
skewer *n* ве́ртел.
ski *n* лы́жа; ~**-jump** трампли́н; *vi* ходи́ть *impf* на лы́жах.
skid *n* зано́с; *vi* заноси́ть *impf*, занести́ *pf impers+acc*.
skier *n* лы́жник. **skiing** *n* лы́жный спорт.
skilful *adj* иску́сный. **skill** *n* мастерство́; (*countable*) поле́зный на́вык. **skilled** *adj* иску́сный; (*trained*) квалифици́рованный.
skim *vt* снима́ть *impf*, снять *pf* (*cream* сли́вки *pl*, *scum* на́кипь) с+*gen*; *vi* скользи́ть *impf* (**over, along** по+*dat*); ~ **through** бе́гло просма́тривать *impf*, просмотре́ть *pf*; *adj*: ~ **milk** снято́е молоко́.
skimp *vt* & *i* скупи́ться *impf* (на+*acc*). **skimpy** *adj* ску́дный.
skin *n* ко́жа; (*hide*) шку́ра; (*of fruit etc.*) кожура́; (*on milk*) пе́нка; *vt* сдира́ть *impf*, содра́ть *pf* ко́жу, шку́ру, с+*gen*; (*fruit*) снима́ть *impf*, снять *pf* кожуру́ с+*gen*. **skinny** *adj* то́щий.
skip[1] *vi* скака́ть *impf*; (*with rope*) пры́гать *impf* че́рез

скака́лку; *vt* (*omit*) пропуска́ть *impf*, пропусти́ть *pf*.
skip[2] *n* (*container*) скип.
skipper *n* (*naut*) шки́пер.
skirmish *n* схва́тка.
skirt *n* ю́бка; *vt* обходи́ть *impf*, обойти́ *pf* стороно́й; **~ing-board** пли́нтус.
skittle *n* ке́гля; *pl* ке́гли *f pl*.
skulk *vi* (*hide*) скрыва́ться *impf*; (*creep*) кра́сться *impf*.
skull *n* че́реп.
skunk *n* скунс.
sky *n* не́бо. **skylark** *n* жа́воронок. **skylight** *n* окно́ в кры́ше. **skyline** *n* горизо́нт. **skyscraper** *n* небоскрёб.
slab *n* плита́; (*of cake etc.*) кусо́к.
slack *adj* (*loose*) сла́бый; (*sluggish*) вя́лый; (*negligent*) небре́жный; *n* (*of rope*) слабина́; *pl* брю́ки (-к) *pl*. **slacken** *vt* ослабля́ть *impf*, осла́бить *pf*; *vt & i* (*slow down*) замедля́ть(ся) *impf*, заме́длить(ся) *pf*; *vi* ослабева́ть *impf*, ослабе́ть *pf*.
slag *n* шлак.
slam *vt & i* захло́пывать(ся) *impf*, захло́пнуть(ся) *pf*.
slander *n* клевета́; *vt* клевета́ть *impf*, на~ *pf* на+*acc*. **slanderous** *adj* клеветни́ческий.
slang *n* жарго́н. **slangy** *adj* жарго́нный.
slant *vt & i* наклоня́ть(ся) *impf*, наклони́ть(ся) *pf*; *n* укло́н. **slanting** *adj* косо́й.
slap *vt* шлёпать *impf*, шлёпнуть *pf*; *n* шлепо́к; *adv* пря́мо. **slapdash** *adj* небре́жный. **slapstick** *n* фарс.
slash *vt* (*cut*) поро́ть *impf*, рас~ *pf*; (*fig*) уре́зывать *impf*, уре́зать *pf*; *n* разре́з; (*sign*) дробь.
slat *n* пла́нка.
slate[1] *n* сла́нец; (*for roofing*) (кро́вельная) пли́тка.
slate[2] *vt* (*criticize*) разноси́ть *impf*, разнести́ *pf*.
slaughter *n* (*of animals*) убо́й; (*massacre*) резня́; *vt* (*animals*) ре́зать *impf*, за~ *pf*; (*people*) убива́ть *impf*, уби́ть *pf*. **slaughterhouse** *n* бо́йня.
Slav *n* славяни́н, -я́нка; *adj* славя́нский.
slave *n* раб, рабы́ня; *vi* рабо́тать *impf* как раб. **slavery** *n* ра́бство.
Slavic *adj* славя́нский.
slavish *adj* ра́бский.
Slavonic *adj* славя́нский.
slay *vt* убива́ть *impf*, уби́ть *pf*.
sleazy *adj* убо́гий.
sledge *n* са́ни (-не́й) *pl*.
sledge-hammer *n* кува́лда.
sleek *adj* гла́дкий.
sleep *n* сон; **go to ~** засыпа́ть *impf*, засну́ть *pf*; *vi* спать *impf*; (*spend the night*) ночева́ть *impf*, пере~ *pf*. **sleeper** *n* спя́щий *sb*; (*on track*) шпа́ла; (*sleeping-car*) спа́льный ваго́н. **sleeping** *adj* спя́щий; **~-bag** спа́льный мешо́к; **~-car** спа́льный ваго́н; **~-pill** снотво́рная табле́тка. **sleepless** *adj* бессо́нный. **sleepy** *adj* со́нный.
sleet *n* мо́крый снег.
sleeve *n* рука́в; (*of record*) конве́рт.
sleigh *n* са́ни (-не́й) *pl*.
sleight-of-hand *n* ло́вкость рук.
slender *adj* (*slim*) то́нкий; (*meagre*) ску́дный; (*of hope etc.*) сла́бый.
sleuth *n* сы́щик.

slice *n* кусóк; *vt* (~ *up*) нарезáть *impf*, нарéзать *pf*.
slick *adj* (*dextrous*) лóвкий; (*crafty*) хи́трый; *n* нефтянáя плёнка.
slide *vi* скользи́ть *impf*; *vt* (*drawer etc.*) задвигáть *impf*, задви́нуть *pf*; *n* (*children's* ~) гóрка; (*microscope* ~) предмéтное стеклó; (*phot*) диапозити́в, слайд; (*for hair*) закóлка. **sliding** *adj* (*door*) задвижнóй.
slight[1] *adj* (*slender*) тóнкий; (*inconsiderable*) небольшóй; (*light*) лёгкий; **not the ~est** ни малéйшего, -шей (*gen*); **not in the ~est** ничýть.
slight[2] *vt* пренебрегáть *impf*, пренебрéчь *pf* +*instr*; *n* оби́да.
slightly *adv* слегкá, немнóго.
slim *adj* тóнкий; (*chance etc.*) слáбый; *vi* худéть *impf*, по~ *pf*.
slime *n* слизь. **slimy** *adj* сли́зистый; (*person*) скóльзкий.
sling *vt* (*throw*) швыря́ть *impf*, швырнýть *pf*; (*suspend*) подвéшивать *impf*, подвéсить *pf*; *n* (*med*) пéревязь.
slink *vi* крáсться *impf*.
slip *n* (*mistake*) оши́бка; (*garment*) комбинáция; (*pillowcase*) нáволочка; (*paper*) листóчек; ~ **of the tongue** обмóлвка; **give the** ~ ускользнýть *pf* от+*gen*; *vi* скользи́ть *impf*, скользнýть *pf*; (*fall over*) поскользнýться *pf*; (*from hands etc.*) выскáльзывать *impf*, вы́скользнуть *pf*; *vt* (*insert*) совáть *impf*, сýнуть *pf*; ~ **off** (*depart*) ускользáть *impf*, ускользнýть *pf*; ~ **up** (*make mistake*) ошибáться *impf*, ошиби́ться *pf*. **slipper** *n* тáпка. **slippery** *adj* скóльзкий.
slit *vt* разрезáть *impf*, разрéзать *pf*; (*throat*) перерéзать *pf*; *n* щель; (*cut*) разрéз.
slither *vi* скользи́ть *impf*.
sliver *n* щéпка.
slob *n* неря́ха *m* & *f*.
slobber *vi* пускáть *impf*, пусти́ть *pf* слю́ни.
slog *vt* (*hit*) си́льно ударя́ть *impf*, удáрить *pf*; (*work*) упóрно рабóтать *impf*.
slogan *n* лóзунг.
slop *n*: *pl* помóи (-óев) *pl*; *vt* & *i* выплёскивать(ся) *impf*, вы́плескать(ся) *pf*.
slope *n* (*artificial*) наклóн; (*geog*) склон; *vi* имéть *impf* наклóн. **sloping** *adj* наклóнный.
sloppy *adj* (*work*) неря́шливый; (*sentimental*) сентиментáльный.
slot *n* отвéрстие; **~-machine** автомáт; *vt*: ~ **in** вставля́ть *impf*, встáвить *pf*.
sloth *n* лень.
slouch *vi* (*stoop*) сутýлиться *impf*.
slovenly *adj* неря́шливый.
slow *adj* мéдленный; (*tardy*) медли́тельный; (*stupid*) тупóй; (*business*) вя́лый; **be** ~ (*clock*) отставáть *impf*, отстáть *pf*; *adv* мéдленно; *vt* & *i* (~ *down*, *up*) замедля́ть(ся) *impf*, замéдлить(ся) *pf*.
sludge *n* (*mud*) грязь; (*sediment*) отстóй.
slug *n* (*zool*) слизня́к.
sluggish *adj* вя́лый.
sluice *n* шлюз.
slum *n* трущóба.
slumber *n* сон; *vi* спать *impf*.
slump *n* спад; *vi* рéзко пáдать *impf*, (у)пáсть *pf*; (*of person*) свáливаться *impf*, свали́ться *pf*.

slur *vt* говорить *impf* невнятно; *n* (*stigma*) пятно́.
slush *n* слякоть.
slut *n* (*sloven*) неряха; (*trollop*) потаскуха.
sly *adj* хитрый; **on the** ~ тайко́м.
smack[1] *vi*: ~ **of** пахнуть *impf* +*instr*.
smack[2] *n* (*slap*) шлепо́к; *vt* шлёпать *impf*, шлёпнуть *pf*.
small *adj* маленький, небольшо́й, малый; (*of agent, particles; petty*) ме́лкий; ~ **change** ме́лочь; ~**-scale** мелкомасштабный; ~ **talk** светская бесе́да.
smart[1] *vi* саднить *impf impers*.
smart[2] *adj* элегантный; (*brisk*) быстрый; (*cunning*) ловкий; (*sharp*) смекалистый (*coll*).
smash *vt* & *i* разбивать(ся) *impf*, разбить(ся) *pf*; *vi*: ~ **into** врезаться *impf*, вре́заться *pf* в+*acc*; *n* (*crash*) гро́хот; (*collision*) столкнове́ние; (*blow*) сильный уда́р.
smattering *n* пове́рхностное знание.
smear *vt* смазывать *impf*, смазать *pf*; (*dirty*) пачкать *impf*, за~, ис~ *pf*; (*discredit*) поро́чить *impf*, о~ *pf*; *n* (*spot*) пятно́; (*slander*) клевета́; (*med*) мазо́к.
smell *n* (*sense*) обоняние; (*odour*) запах; *vt* чувствовать *impf* запах+*gen*; (*sniff*) нюхать *impf*, по~ *pf*; *vi*: ~ **of** пахнуть *impf* +*instr*. **smelly** *adj* вонючий.
smelt *vt* (*ore*) плавить *impf*; (*metal*) выплавлять *impf*, выплавить *pf*.
smile *vi* улыбаться *impf*, улыбну́ться *pf*; *n* улыбка.
smirk *vi* ухмыляться *impf*, ухмыльну́ться *pf*; *n* ухмылка.
smith *n* кузне́ц.
smithereens *n*: **(in)to** ~ вдре́безги.
smithy *n* кузница.
smock *n* блуза.
smog *n* туман (с дымом).
smoke *n* дым; ~**-screen** дымовая заве́са; *vt* & *i* (*cigarette etc.*) курить *impf*, по~ *pf*; *vt* (*cure; colour*) коптить *impf*, за~ *pf*; *vi* (*abnormally*) дымить *impf*; (*of fire*) дымиться *impf*. **smoker** *n* курильщик, -ица, курящий *sb*. **smoky** *adj* дымный.
smooth *adj* (*surface etc.*) гладкий; (*movement etc.*) плавный; *vt* приглаживать *impf*, пригладить *pf*; ~ **over** сглаживать *impf*, сгладить *pf*.
smother *vt* (*stifle, also fig*) душить *impf*, за~ *pf*; (*cover*) покрывать *impf*, покрыть *pf*.
smoulder *vi* тлеть *impf*.
smudge *n* пятно́; *vt* смазывать *impf*, смазать *pf*.
smug *adj* самодово́льный.
smuggle *vt* провозить *impf*, провезти *pf* контрабандой; (*convey secretly*) проносить *impf*, пронести *pf*. **smuggler** *n* контрабандист. **smuggling** *n* контрабанда.
smut *n* сажа; (*indecency*) непристо́йность. **smutty** *adj* грязный; непристо́йный.
snack *n* закуска; ~ **bar** закусочная *sb*, (*within institution*) буфе́т.
snag *n* (*fig*) загво́здка; *vt* зацеплять *impf*, зацепить *pf*.
snail *n* улитка.
snake *n* змея́.
snap *vi* (*of dog or person*)

огрыза́ться *impf*, огрызну́ться *pf* (**at** на+*acc*); *vt* & *i* (*break*) обрыва́ть(ся) *impf*, оборва́ть(ся) *pf*; *vt* (*make sound*) щёлкать *impf*, щёлкнуть *pf* +*instr*; ~ **up** (*buy*) расхва́тывать *impf*, расхвата́ть *pf*; *n* (*sound*) щёлк; (*photo*) сни́мок; *adj* (*decision*) скоропали́тельный. **snappy** *adj* (*brisk*) живо́й; (*stylish*) шика́рный. **snapshot** *n* сни́мок.

snare *n* лову́шка.

snarl *vi* рыча́ть *impf*, за~ *pf*; *n* рыча́ние.

snatch *vt* хвата́ть *impf*, (с)хвати́ть *pf*; *vi*: ~ **at** хвата́ться *impf*, (с)хвати́ться *pf* за+*acc*; *n* (*fragment*) обры́вок.

sneak *vi* (*slink*) кра́сться *impf*; *vt* (*steal*) стащи́ть *pf*; *n* я́бедник, -ица (*coll*). **sneaking** *adj* та́йный. **sneaky** *adj* лука́вый.

sneer *vi* насмеха́ться *impf* (**at** над+*instr*).

sneeze *vi* чиха́ть *impf*, чихну́ть *pf*; *n* чиха́нье.

snide *adj* ехи́дный.

sniff *vi* шмы́гать *impf*, шмыгну́ть *pf* но́сом; *vt* ню́хать *impf*, по~ *pf*.

snigger *vi* хихи́кать *impf*, хихи́кнуть *pf*; *n* хихи́канье.

snip *vt* ре́зать *impf* (но́жницами); ~ **off** среза́ть *impf*, сре́зать *pf*.

snipe *vi* стреля́ть *impf* из укры́тия (**at** в+*acc*); (*fig*) напада́ть *impf*, напа́сть *pf* на+*acc*. **sniper** *n* сна́йпер.

snippet *n* отре́зок; *pl* (*of news etc.*) обры́вки *m pl*.

snivel *vi* (*run at nose*) распуска́ть *impf*, распусти́ть *pf* со́пли; (*whimper*) хны́кать *impf*.

snob *n* сноб. **snobbery** *n* сноби́зм. **snobbish** *adj* снобистский.

snoop *vi* шпио́нить *impf*; ~ **about** разню́хивать *impf*, разню́хать *pf*.

snooty *adj* чва́нный.

snooze *vi* вздремну́ть *pf*; *n* коро́ткий сон.

snore *vi* храпе́ть *impf*.

snorkel *n* шно́ркель *m*.

snort *vi* фы́ркать *impf*, фы́ркнуть *pf*.

snot *n* со́пли (-ле́й) *pl*.

snout *n* ры́ло, мо́рда.

snow *n* снег; ~**-white** белосне́жный; *vi*: **it is ~ing, it snows** идёт снег; ~**ed under** зава́ленный рабо́той; **we were ~ed up, in** нас занесло́ сне́гом. **snowball** *n* снежо́к. **snowdrop** *n* подсне́жник. **snowflake** *n* снежи́нка. **snowman** *n* сне́жная ба́ба. **snowstorm** *n* мете́ль. **snowy** *adj* сне́жный; (*snow-white*) белосне́жный.

snub *vt* игнори́ровать *impf* & *pf*.

snuff[1] *n* (*tobacco*) ню́хательный таба́к.

snuff[2] *vt*: ~ **out** туши́ть *impf*, по~ *pf*.

snuffle *vi* сопе́ть *impf*.

snug *adj* ую́тный.

snuggle *vi*: ~ **up to** прижима́ться *impf*, прижа́ться *pf* к+*dat*.

so *adv* так; (*in this way*) так; (*thus, at beginning of sentence*) ита́к; (*also*) та́кже, то́же; *conj* (*therefore*) так что, поэ́тому; **and ~ on** и так да́лее; **if ~** в тако́м слу́чае; **~ ... as** так(о́й)... как; **~ as to** с тем что́бы; **~-called** так называ́емый; **(in) ~ far as** насто́лько; ~

long! пока́!; ~ **long as** поско́льку; ~ **much** насто́лько; ~ **much** ~ до тако́й сте́пени; ~ **much the better** тем лу́чше; ~ **that** что́бы; ~... **that** так... что; ~ **to say, speak** так сказа́ть; ~ **what?** ну и что?

soak *vt* мочи́ть *impf*, на~ *pf*; (*drench*) прома́чивать *impf*, промочи́ть *pf*; ~ **up** впи́тывать *impf*, впита́ть *pf*; *vi*: ~ **through** проса́чиваться *impf*, просочи́ться *pf*; **get** ~**ed** промока́ть *impf*, промо́кнуть *pf*.

soap *n* мы́ло; *vt* мы́лить *impf*, на~ *pf*; ~ **opera** многосери́йная переда́ча; ~ **powder** стира́льный порошо́к. **soapy** *adj* мы́льный.

soar *vi* пари́ть *impf*; (*prices*) подска́кивать *impf*, подскочи́ть *pf*.

sob *vi* рыда́ть *impf*; *n* рыда́ние.

sober *adj* тре́звый; *vt* & *i*: ~ **up** отрезвля́ть(ся) *impf*, отрезви́ть(ся) *pf*. **sobriety** *n* тре́звость.

soccer *n* футбо́л.

sociable *adj* общи́тельный. **social** *adj* обще́ственный, социа́льный; **S**~ **Democrat** социа́л-демокра́т; ~ **sciences** обще́ственные нау́ки *f pl*; ~ **security** социа́льное обеспе́чение. **socialism** *n* социали́зм. **socialist** *n* социали́ст; *adj* социалисти́ческий. **socialize** *vt* обща́ться *impf*. **society** *n* о́бщество. **sociological** *adj* социологи́ческий. **sociologist** *n* социо́лог. **sociology** *n* социоло́гия.

sock *n* носо́к.

socket *n* (*eye*) впа́дина; (*electr*) ште́псель *m*; (*for bulb*) патро́н.

soda *n* со́да; ~**-water** со́довая вода́.

sodden *adj* промо́кший.

sodium *n* на́трий.

sodomy *n* педера́стия.

sofa *n* дива́н.

soft *adj* мя́гкий; (*sound*) ти́хий; (*colour*) нея́ркий; (*malleable*) ко́вкий; (*tender*) не́жный; ~ **drink** безалкого́льный напи́ток. **soften** *vt* & *i* смягча́ть(ся) *impf*, смягчи́ть(ся) *pf*. **softness** *n* мя́гкость. **software** *n* програ́ммное обеспе́чение.

soggy *adj* сыро́й.

soil[1] *n* по́чва.

soil[2] *vt* па́чкать *impf*, за~, ис~ *pf*.

solace *n* утеше́ние.

solar *adj* со́лнечный.

solder *n* припо́й; *vt* пая́ть *impf*; (~ *together*) спа́ивать *impf*, спая́ть *pf*. **soldering iron** *n* пая́льник.

soldier *n* солда́т.

sole[1] *n* (*of foot, shoe*) подо́шва.

sole[2] *n* (*fish*) морско́й язы́к.

sole[3] *adj* еди́нственный.

solemn *adj* торже́ственный. **solemnity** *n* торже́ственность.

solicit *vt* проси́ть *impf*, по~ *pf* +*acc*, *gen*, о+*prep*; *vi* (*of prostitute*) пристава́ть *impf* к мужчи́нам. **solicitor** *n* адвока́т. **solicitous** *adj* забо́тливый.

solid *adj* (*not liquid*) твёрдый; (*not hollow; continuous*) сплошно́й; (*firm*) про́чный; (*pure*) чи́стый; *n* твёрдое те́ло; *pl* твёрдая пи́ща. **solidarity** *n* солида́рность. **solidify** *vi* затвердева́ть *impf*, затверде́ть *pf.* **solidity** *n* твёрдость; прочность.

soliloquy *n* моноло́г.

solitary *adj* одино́кий, уединённый; ~ **confinement** одино́чное заключе́ние. **solitude** *n* одино́чество, уедине́ние.

solo *n* со́ло *neut indecl*; *adj* со́льный; *adv* со́ло. **soloist** *n* соли́ст, ~ка.

solstice *n* солнцестоя́ние.

soluble *adj* раствори́мый. **solution** *n* раство́р; (*of puzzle etc.*) реше́ние. **solve** *vt* реша́ть *impf*, реши́ть *pf*. **solvent** *adj* растворя́ющий; (*financially*) платёжеспосо́бный; *n* раствори́тель *m*.

sombre *adj* мра́чный.

some *adj* & *pron* (*any*) како́й-нибудь; (*a certain*) како́й-то; (*a certain amount or number of*) не́который, *or often expressed by noun in* (*partitive*) *gen*; (*several*) не́сколько+*gen*; (~ *people, things*) не́которые *pl*; ~ **day** когда́-нибудь; ~ **more** ещё; ~ ... **others** одни́... други́е. **somebody, someone** *n*, *pron* (*def*) кто́-то; (*indef*) кто́-нибудь. **somehow** *adv* ка́к-то; ка́к-нибудь; (*for some reason*) почему́-то; ~ **or other** так и́ли ина́че.

somersault *n* са́льто *neut indecl*; *vi* кувырка́ться *impf*, кувыр(к)ну́ться *pf*.

something *n* & *pron* (*def*) что́-то; (*indef*) что́-нибудь; ~ **like** (*approximately*) приблизи́тельно; (*a thing like*) что́-то вро́де+*gen*. **sometime** *adv* не́когда; *adj* бы́вший. **sometimes** *adv* иногда́. **somewhat** *adv* не́сколько, дово́льно. **somewhere** *adv* (*position*) (*def*) где́-то; (*indef*) где́-нибудь; (*motion*) куда́-то; куда́-нибудь.

son *n* сын; ~-**in-law** зять *m*.

sonata *n* сона́та.

song *n* пе́сня.

sonic *adj* звуково́й.

sonnet *n* соне́т.

soon *adv* ско́ро; (*early*) ра́но; **as ~ as** как то́лько; **as ~ as possible** как мо́жно скоре́е; ~**er or later** ра́но и́ли по́здно; **the ~er the better** чем ра́ньше, тем лу́чше.

soot *n* са́жа, ко́поть.

soothe *vt* успока́ивать *impf*, успоко́ить *pf*; (*pain*) облегча́ть *impf*, облегчи́ть *pf*.

sophisticated *adj* (*person*) искушённый; (*equipment*) сло́жный.

soporific *adj* снотво́рный.

soprano *n* сопра́но (*voice*) *neut* & (*person*) *f indecl*.

sorcerer *n* колду́н. **sorcery** *n* колдовство́.

sordid *adj* гря́зный.

sore *n* боля́чка; *adj* больно́й; **my throat is** ~ у меня́ боли́т го́рло.

sorrow *n* печа́ль. **sorrowful** *adj* печа́льный. **sorry** *adj* жа́лкий; *predic*: **be** ~ жале́ть *impf* (**about** о+*prep*); жаль *impers*+*dat* (**for** +*gen*); ~! извини́(те)!

sort *n* род, вид, сорт; *vt* (*also* ~ *out*) сортирова́ть *impf*, рас~ *pf*; (*also fig*) разбира́ть *impf*, разобра́ть *pf*.

sortie *n* вы́лазка.

SOS *n* (радио)сигна́л бе́дствия.

soul *n* душа́.

sound[1] *adj* (*healthy, thorough*) здоро́вый; (*in good condition*) испра́вный; (*logical*)

здра́вый, разу́мный; (*of sleep*) кре́пкий.
sound[2] *n* (*noise*) звук, шум; *attrib* звуково́й; ~ **effects** звуковы́е эффе́кты *m pl*; *vi* звуча́ть *impf*, про~ *pf*.
sound[3] *vt* (*naut*) измеря́ть *impf*, изме́рить *pf* глубину́ +*gen*; ~ **out** (*fig*) зонди́ровать *impf*, по~ *pf*; *n* зонд.
sound[4] *n* (*strait*) проли́в.
soup *n* суп; *vt*: ~**ed up** форси́рованный.
sour *adj* ки́слый; ~ **cream** смета́на; *vt* & *i* (*fig*) озлобля́ть(ся) *impf*, озло́бить(ся) *pf*.
source *n* исто́чник; (*of river*) исто́к.
south *n* юг; (*naut*) зюйд; *adj* ю́жный; *adv* к ю́гу, на юг; ~**-east** ю́го-восто́к; ~**-west** ю́го-за́пад. **southerly** *adj* ю́жный. **southern** *adj* ю́жный. **southerner** *n* южа́нин, -а́нка. **southward(s)** *adv* на юг, к ю́гу.
souvenir *n* сувени́р.
sovereign *adj* сувере́нный; *n* мона́рх. **sovereignty** *n* суверените́т.
soviet *n* сове́т; **S~ Union** Сове́тский Сою́з; *adj* (**S~**) сове́тский.
sow[1] *n* свинья́.
sow[2] *vt* (*seed*) се́ять *impf*, по~ *pf*; (*field*) засе́ивать *impf*, засе́ять *pf*.
soya *n*: ~ **bean** со́евый боб.
spa *n* куро́рт.
space *n* (*place*, *room*) ме́сто; (*expanse*) простра́нство; (*interval*) промежу́ток; (*outer* ~) ко́смос; *attrib* косми́ческий; *vt* расставля́ть *impf*, расста́вить *pf* с промежу́тками. **spacecraft, -ship** *n* косми́ческий кора́бль *m*.
spacious *adj* просто́рный.
spade *n* (*tool*) лопа́та; *pl* (*cards*) пи́ки (пик) *pl*.
spaghetti *n* спаге́тти *neut indecl*.
Spain *n* Испа́ния.
span *n* (*of bridge*) пролёт; (*aeron*) разма́х; *vt* (*of bridge*) соединя́ть *impf*, соедини́ть *pf* сто́роны +*gen*, (*river*) берега́ +*gen*; (*fig*) охва́тывать *impf*, охвати́ть *pf*.
Spaniard *n* испа́нец, -нка.
Spanish *adj* испа́нский.
spank *vt* шлёпать *impf*, шлёпнуть *pf*.
spanner *n* га́ечный ключ.
spar[1] *n* (*aeron*) лонжеро́н.
spar[2] *vi* бокси́ровать *impf*; (*fig*) препира́ться *impf*.
spare *adj* (*in reserve*) запасно́й; (*extra*, *to* ~) ли́шний; (*of seat*, *time*) свобо́дный; ~ **parts** запасны́е ча́сти *f pl*; ~ **room** ко́мната для госте́й; *n*: *pl* запча́сти *f pl*; *vt* (*grudge*) жале́ть *impf*, по~ *pf* +*acc*, *gen*; **he ~d no pains** он не жале́л трудо́в; (*do without*) обходи́ться *impf*, обойти́сь *pf* без+*gen*; (*time*) уделя́ть *impf*, удели́ть *pf*; (*show mercy towards*) щади́ть *impf*, по~ *pf*; (*save from*) избавля́ть *impf*, изба́вить *pf* от+*gen*: ~ **me the details** изба́вьте меня́ от подро́бностей.
spark *n* и́скра; ~**-plug** запа́льная свеча́; *vt* (~ *off*) вызыва́ть *impf*, вы́звать *pf*.
sparkle *vi* сверка́ть *impf*.
sparrow *n* воробе́й.
sparse *adj* ре́дкий.
Spartan *adj* спарта́нский.
spasm *n* спазм. **spasmodic** *adj* спазмоди́ческий.

spastic *n* паралитик.
spate *n* разли́в; (*fig*) пото́к.
spatial *adj* простра́нственный.
spatter, splatter *vt* (*liquid*) бры́згать *impf* +*instr*; (*person etc.*) забры́згивать *impf*, забры́згать *pf* (**with** +*instr*); *vi* плеска́ть(ся) *impf*, плесну́ть *pf*.
spatula *n* шпа́тель *m*.
spawn *vt* & *i* мета́ть *impf* (икру́); *vt* (*fig*) порожда́ть *impf*, породи́ть *pf*.
speak *vt* & *i* говори́ть *impf*, сказа́ть *pf*; *vi* (*make speech*) выступа́ть *impf*, вы́ступить *pf* (с ре́чью); (~ *out*) выска́зываться *impf*, вы́сказаться *pf* (**for** за+*acc*; **against** про́тив+*gen*). **speaker** *n* говоря́щий *sb*; (*giving speech*) выступа́ющий *sb*; (*orator*) ора́тор; (**S**~, *parl*) спи́кер; (*loud*-~) громкоговори́тель *m*.
spear *n* копьё; *vt* пронза́ть *impf*, пронзи́ть *pf* копьём. **spearhead** *vt* возглавля́ть *impf*, возгла́вить *pf*.
special *adj* осо́бый, специа́льный. **specialist** *n* специали́ст, ~ка. **speciality** *n* (*dish*) фи́рменное блю́до; (*subject*) специа́льность. **specialization** *n* специализа́ция. **specialize** *vt* & *i* специализи́ровать(ся) *impf* & *pf*. **specially** *adv* осо́бенно.
species *n* вид.
specific *adj* осо́бенный. **specification(s)** *n* специфика́ция. **specify** *vt* уточня́ть *impf*, уточни́ть *pf*.
specimen *n* образе́ц, экземпля́р.
speck *n* кра́пинка, пя́тнышко. **speckled** *adj* кра́пчатый.
spectacle *n* зре́лище; *pl* очки́ (-ко́в) *pl*.
spectacular *adj* эффе́ктный; (*amazing*) потряса́ющий.
spectator *n* зри́тель *m*.
spectre *n* при́зрак.
spectrum *n* спектр.
speculate *vi* (*meditate*) размышля́ть *impf*, размы́слить *pf* (**on** о+*prep*); (*conjecture*) гада́ть *impf*; (*comm*) спекули́ровать *impf*. **speculation** *n* (*conjecture*) дога́дка; (*comm*) спекуля́ция. **speculative** *adj* гипотети́ческий; спекуляти́вный. **speculator** *n* спекуля́нт.
speech *n* речь. **speechless** *adj* (*fig*) онеме́вший.
speed *n* ско́рость; *vi* мча́ться *impf*, про~ *pf*; (*illegally*) превыша́ть *impf*, превы́сить *pf* ско́рость; ~ **up** ускоря́ть(ся *impf*, уско́рить(ся *pf*. **speedboat** *n* быстрохо́дный ка́тер. **speedometer** *n* спидо́метр. **speedy** *adj* бы́стрый.
spell[1] *n* (*charm*) загово́р.
spell[2] *vt* (*say*) произноси́ть *impf*, произнести́ *pf* по бу́квам; (*write*) пра́вильно писа́ть *impf*, на~ *pf*; **how do you ~ that word?** как пи́шется э́то сло́во?
spell[3] *n* (*period*) пери́од.
spellbound *adj* зачаро́ванный.
spelling *n* правописа́ние.
spend *vt* (*money*; *effort*) тра́тить *impf*, ис~, по~ *pf*; (*time*) проводи́ть *impf*, провести́ *pf*.
sperm *n* спе́рма.
sphere *n* сфе́ра; (*ball*) шар. **spherical** *adj* сфери́ческий.
spice *n* пря́ность; *vt* приправля́ть *impf*, припра́вить *pf*.

spicy *adj* пря́ный; (*fig*) пика́нтный.
spider *n* пау́к.
spike *n* (*point*) остриё; (*on fence*) зубе́ц; (*on shoes*) шип.
spill *vt & i* (*liquid*) пролива́ть(ся) *impf*, проли́ть(ся) *pf*; (*dry substance*) рассыпа́ть(ся) *impf*, рассы́пать(ся) *pf*.
spin *vt* (*thread etc.*) прясть *impf*, с~ *pf*; (*coin*) подбра́сывать *impf*, подбро́сить *pf*; *vt & i* (*turn*) кружи́ть(ся) *impf*; ~ **out** (*prolong*) затя́гивать *impf*, затяну́ть *pf*.
spinach *n* шпина́т.
spinal *adj* спинно́й; ~ **column** спинно́й хребе́т; ~ **cord** спинно́й мозг.
spindle *n* ось *m*. **spindly** *adj* дли́нный и то́нкий.
spine *n* (*anat*) позвоно́чник, хребе́т; (*prickle*) игла́; (*of book*) корешо́к. **spineless** *adj* (*fig*) бесхара́ктерный.
spinning *n* пряде́ние; ~-**wheel** пря́лка.
spinster *n* незаму́жняя же́нщина.
spiral *adj* спира́льный; (*staircase*) винтово́й; *n* спира́ль; *vi* (*rise sharply*) ре́зко возраста́ть *impf*, возрасти́ *pf*.
spire *n* шпиль *m*.
spirit *n* дух, душа́; *pl* (*mood*) настрое́ние; *pl* (*drinks*) спиртно́е *sb*; ~-**level** ватерпа́с; *vt*: ~ **away** та́йно уноси́ть *impf*, унести́ *pf*. **spirited** *adj* живо́й. **spiritual** *adj* духо́вный. **spiritualism** *n* спирити́зм. **spiritualist** *n* спири́т.
spit[1] *n* (*skewer*) ве́ртел.
spit[2] *vi* плева́ть *impf*, плю́нуть *pf*; (*of rain*) мороси́ть *impf*; (*of fire*) разбры́згивать *impf*, разбры́згать *pf* и́скры; (*sizzle*) шипе́ть *impf*; *vt*: ~ **out** выплёвывать *impf*, вы́плюнуть *pf*; ~**ing image** то́чная ко́пия; *n* слюна́.
spite *n* зло́ба; **in** ~ **of** несмотря́ на+*acc*. **spiteful** *adj* зло́бный.
spittle *n* слюна́.
splash *vt* (*person*) забры́згивать *impf*, забры́згать *pf* (**with** +*instr*); (~ *liquid*) бры́згать *impf* +*instr*; *vi* плеска́ть(ся) *impf*, плесну́ть *pf*; (*move*) шлёпать *impf*, шлёпнуть *pf* (**through** по+*dat*); *n* (*act, sound*) плеск; (*mark made*) пятно́.
splatter *see* **spatter**
spleen *n* селезёнка
splendid *adj* великоле́пный. **splendour** *n* великоле́пие.
splice *vt* (*ropes etc.*) сра́щивать *impf*, срасти́ть *pf*; (*film, tape*) скле́ивать *impf*, скле́ить *pf* концы́+*gen*.
splint *n* ши́на.
splinter *n* оско́лок; (*in skin*) зано́за; *vt & i* расщепля́ть(ся) *impf*, расщепи́ть(ся) *pf*.
split *n* расще́лина, расще́п; (*schism*) раско́л; *pl* шпага́т; *vt & i* расщепля́ть(ся) *impf*, расщепи́ть(ся) *pf*; раска́лывать(ся) *impf*, расколо́ть(ся) *pf*; *vt* (*divide*) дели́ть *impf*, раз~ *pf*; ~ **second** мгнове́ние о́ка; ~ **up** (*part company*) расходи́ться *impf*, разойти́сь *pf*.
splutter *vi* бры́згать *impf* слюно́й; *vt* (*utter*) говори́ть *impf* захлёбываясь.
spoil *n* (*booty*) добы́ча; *vt & i* (*damage*; *decay*) по́ртить(ся) *impf*, ис~ *pf*; *vt* (*indulge*) балова́ть *impf*, из~ *pf*.
spoke *n* спи́ца.

spokesman, -woman *n* представи́тель *m*, ~ница.
sponge *n* гу́бка; ~ **cake** бискви́т; *vt* (*wash*) мыть *impf*, вы́~, по~ *pf* гу́бкой; *vi*: ~ **on** жить *impf* на счёт+*gen*. **sponger** *n* приживи́льщик. **spongy** *adj* гу́бчатый.
sponsor *n* спо́нсор; *vt* финанси́ровать *impf* & *pf*.
spontaneity *n* спонта́нность. **spontaneous** *adj* спонта́нный.
spoof *n* паро́дия.
spooky *adj* жу́ткий.
spool *n* кату́шка.
spoon *n* ло́жка; *vt* че́рпать *impf*, черпну́ть *pf* ло́жкой. **spoonful** *n* ло́жка.
sporadic *adj* споради́ческий.
sport *n* спорт; ~**s car** спорти́вный автомоби́ль *m*; *vt* щеголя́ть *impf*, щегольну́ть *pf* +*instr*. **sportsman** *n* спортсме́н. **sporty** *adj* спорти́вный.
spot *n* (*place*) ме́сто; (*mark*) пятно́; (*pimple*) пры́щик; **on the** ~ на ме́сте; (*at once*) сра́зу; ~ **check** вы́борочная прове́рка; *vt* (*notice*) замеча́ть *impf*, заме́тить *pf*. **spotless** *adj* абсолю́тно чи́стый. **spotlight** *n* прожéктор; (*fig*) внима́ние. **spotty** *adj* прыщева́тый.
spouse *n* супру́г, ~а.
spout *vi* бить *impf* струёй; хлы́нуть *pf*; (*pontificate*) ора́торствовать *impf*; *vt* изверга́ть *impf*, изве́ргнуть *pf*; (*verses etc.*) деклами́ровать *impf*, про~ *pf*; *n* (*tube*) но́сик; (*jet*) струя́.
sprain *vt* растя́гивать *impf*, растяну́ть *pf*; *n* растяже́ние.
sprawl *vi* (*of person*) развали́ваться *impf*, развали́ться *pf*; (*of town*) раски́дываться *impf*, раски́нуться *pf*.
spray[1] *n* (*flowers*) ве́т(оч)ка.
spray[2] *n* бры́зги (-г) *pl*; (*atomizer*) пульвериза́тор; *vt* опры́скивать *impf*, опры́скать *pf* (**with** +*instr*); (*cause to scatter*) распыля́ть *impf*, распыли́ть *pf*.
spread *vt* & *i* (*news, disease, etc.*) распространя́ть(ся) *impf*, распространи́ть(ся) *pf*; *vt* (~ *out*) расстила́ть *impf*, разостла́ть *pf*; (*unfurl, unroll*) развёртывать *impf*, разверну́ть *pf*; (*bread etc. +acc*; *butter etc. +instr*) нама́зывать *impf*, нама́зать *pf*; *n* (*expansion*) распростране́ние; (*span*) разма́х; (*feast*) пир; (*paste*) па́ста.
spree *n* кутёж; **go on a** ~ кути́ть *impf*, кутну́ть *pf*.
sprig *n* ве́точка.
sprightly *adj* бо́дрый.
spring *vi* (*jump*) пры́гать *impf*, пры́гнуть *pf*; *vt* (*tell unexpectedly*) неожи́данно сообща́ть *impf*, сообщи́ть *pf* (**on** +*dat*); ~ **a leak** дава́ть *impf*, дать *pf* течь; ~ **from** (*originate*) происходи́ть *impf*, произойти́ *pf* из+*gen*; *n* (*jump*) прыжо́к; (*season*) весна́, *attrib* весе́нний; (*water*) исто́чник; (*elasticity*) упру́гость; (*coil*) пружи́на; ~**-clean** генера́льная убо́рка. **springboard** *n* трампли́н.
sprinkle *vt* (*with liquid*) опры́скивать *impf*, опры́скать *pf* (**with** +*instr*); (*with solid*) посыпа́ть *impf*, посы́пать *pf* (**with** +*instr*). **sprinkler** *n* разбры́згиватель *m*.
sprint *vi* бежа́ть *impf* на

коро́ткую диста́нцию; (*rush*) рвану́ться *pf*; *n* спринт. **sprinter** *n* спри́нтер.

sprout *vi* пуска́ть *impf*, пусти́ть *pf* ростки́; *n* росто́к; *pl* брюссе́льская капу́ста.

spruce[1] *adj* наря́дный, элега́нтный; *vt*: ~ **o.s. up** приводи́ть *impf*, привести́ *pf* себя́ в поря́док.

spruce[2] *n* ель.

spur *n* шпо́ра; (*fig*) сти́мул; **on the ~ of the moment** под влия́нием мину́ты; *vt*: ~ **on** подхлёстывать *impf*, подхлестну́ть *pf*.

spurious *adj* подде́льный.

spurn *vt* отверга́ть *impf*, отве́ргнуть *pf*.

spurt *n* (*jet*) струя́; (*effort*) рыво́к; *vi* бить *impf* струёй; (*make an effort*) де́лать *impf*, с~ *pf* рыво́к.

spy *n* шпио́н; *vi* шпио́нить *impf* (**on** за+*instr*). **spying** *n* шпиона́ж.

squabble *n* перебра́нка; *vi* вздо́рить *impf*, по~ *pf*.

squad *n* кома́нда, гру́ппа.

squadron *n* (*mil*) эскадро́н; (*naut*) эска́дра; (*aeron*) эскадри́лья.

squalid *adj* убо́гий.

squall *n* шквал.

squalor *n* убо́жество.

squander *vt* растра́чивать *impf*, растра́тить *pf*.

square *n* (*shape*) квадра́т; (*in town*) пло́щадь; (*on paper, material*) кле́тка; (*instrument*) науго́льник; *adj* квадра́тный; (*meal*) пло́тный; ~ **root** квадра́тный ко́рень *m*; *vt* (*accounts*) своди́ть *impf*, свести́ *pf*; (*math*) возводи́ть *impf*, возвести́ *pf* в квадра́т; *vi* (*correspond*) соотве́тствовать *impf* (**with** +*dat*).

squash *n* (*crowd*) толку́чка; (*drink*) сок; *vt* разда́вливать *impf*, раздави́ть *pf*; (*suppress*) подавля́ть *impf*, подави́ть *pf*; *vi* вти́скиваться *impf*, вти́снуться *pf*.

squat *adj* призе́мистый; *vi* сиде́ть *impf* на ко́рточках; ~ **down** сади́ться *impf*, сесть *pf* на ко́рточки.

squatter *n* незако́нный жиле́ц.

squawk *n* клёкот; *vi* клекота́ть *impf*.

squeak *n* писк; (*of object*) скрип; *vi* пища́ть *impf*, пи́скнуть *pf*; (*of object*) скрипе́ть *impf*, скри́пнуть *pf*. **squeaky** *adj* пискли́вый, скрипу́чий.

squeal *n* визг; *vi* визжа́ть *impf*, ви́згнуть *pf*.

squeamish *adj* брезгли́вый.

squeeze *n* (*crush*) да́вка; (*pressure*) сжа́тие; (*hand*) пожа́тие; *vt* дави́ть *impf*; сжима́ть *impf*, сжать *pf*; ~ **in** впи́хивать(ся) *impf*, впихну́ть(ся) *pf*; вти́скивать(ся) *impf*, вти́снуть(ся) *pf*; ~ **out** выжима́ть *impf*, вы́жать *pf*; ~ **through** проти́скивать(ся) *impf*, проти́снуть(ся) *pf*.

squelch *vi* хлю́пать *impf*, хлю́пнуть *pf*.

squid *n* кальма́р.

squint *n* косогла́зие; *vi* коси́ть *impf*; (*screw up eyes*) щу́риться *impf*.

squire *n* сквайр, поме́щик.

squirm *vi* (*wriggle*) извива́ться *impf*, изви́ться *pf*.

squirrel *n* бе́лка.

squirt *n* струя́; *vi* бить *impf* струёй; *vt* пуска́ть *impf*, пусти́ть *pf* струю́ (*substance* +*gen*; **at** на+*acc*).

St. *abbr* (*of* **Street**) ул., у́лица;

(*of* **Saint**) св., Свято́й, -а́я.

stab *n* уда́р (ножо́м *etc.*); (*pain*) внеза́пная о́страя боль; *vt* наноси́ть *impf*, нанести́ *pf* уда́р (ножо́м *etc.*) (*person* +*dat*).

stability *n* усто́йчивость, стаби́льность. **stabilize** *vt* стабилизи́ровать *impf* & *pf*.

stable *adj* усто́йчивый, стаби́льный; (*psych*) уравнове́шенный; *n* коню́шня.

staccato *n* стакка́то *neut indecl*; *adv* стакка́то; *adj* отры́вистый.

stack *n* ку́ча; *vt* скла́дывать *impf*, сложи́ть *pf* в ку́чу.

stadium *n* стадио́н.

staff *n* (*personnel*) штат, сотру́дники *m pl*; (*stick*) посо́х, жезл; *adj* шта́тный; (*mil*) штабно́й.

stag *n* саме́ц-оле́нь *m*.

stage *n* (*theat*) сце́на; (*period*) ста́дия; *vt* (*theat*) ста́вить *impf*, по~ *pf*; (*organize*) организова́ть *impf* & *pf*; **~-manager** режиссёр.

stagger *vi* шата́ться *impf*, шатну́ться *pf*; *vt* (*hours of work etc.*) распределя́ть *impf*, распредели́ть *pf*. **be staggered** *vi* поража́ться *impf*, порази́ться *pf*. **staggering** *adj* потряса́ющий.

stagnant *adj* (*water*) стоя́чий; (*fig*) засто́йный. **stagnate** *vi* заста́иваться *impf*, застоя́ться *pf*; (*fig*) косне́ть *impf*, за~ *pf*.

staid *adj* степе́нный.

stain *n* пятно́; (*dye*) кра́ска; *vt* па́чкать *impf*, за~, ис~ *pf*; (*dye*) окра́шивать *impf*, окра́сить *pf*; **~ed glass** цветно́е стекло́. **stainless** *adj*: **~ steel** нержаве́ющая сталь.

stair *n* ступе́нька. **staircase, stairs** *n pl* ле́стница.

stake *n* (*stick*) кол; (*bet*) ста́вка; (*comm*) до́ля; **be at ~** быть поста́вленным на ка́рту; *vt* (*mark out*) огора́живать *impf*, огороди́ть *pf* ко́льями; (*support*) укрепля́ть *impf*, укрепи́ть *pf* коло́м; (*risk*) ста́вить *impf*, по~ *pf* на ка́рту.

stale *adj* несве́жий; (*musty, damp*) за́тхлый; (*hackneyed*) изби́тый.

stalemate *n* пат; (*fig*) тупи́к.

stalk *n* сте́бель *m*; *vt* высле́живать *impf*; *vi* (& *t*) (*stride*) ше́ствовать *impf* (по+*dat*).

stall *n* сто́йло; (*booth*) ларёк; *pl* (*theat*) парте́р; *vi* (*of engine*) гло́хнуть *impf*, за~ *pf*; (*play for time*) оття́гивать *impf*, оття́нуть *pf* вре́мя; *vt* (*engine*) неча́янно заглуша́ть *impf*, заглуши́ть *pf*.

stallion *n* жеребе́ц.

stalwart *adj* сто́йкий; *n* сто́йкий приве́рженец.

stamina *n* выно́сливость.

stammer *vi* заика́ться *impf*; *n* заика́ние.

stamp *n* печа́ть; (*postage*) (почто́вая) ма́рка; *vt* штампова́ть *impf*; *vi* то́пать *impf*, то́пнуть *pf* (нога́ми); **~ out** поборо́ть *pf*.

stampede *n* пани́ческое бе́гство; *vi* обраща́ться *impf* в пани́ческое бе́гство.

stance *n* пози́ция.

stand *n* (*hat, coat*) ве́шалка; (*music*) пюпи́тр; (*umbrella, support*) подста́вка; (*booth*) ларёк; (*taxi*) стоя́нка; (*at stadium*) трибу́на; (*position*) пози́ция; (*resistance*) сопротивле́ние; *vi* стоя́ть *impf*; (**~** *up*) встава́ть *impf*, встать *pf*; (*remain in force*) остава́ться *impf*, оста́ться в си́ле; *vt* (*put*) ста́вить *impf*, по~ *pf*; (*endure*) терпе́ть *impf*, по~ *pf*; ~ **back** отходи́ть *impf*, отойти́ *pf* (**from** от+*gen*); (*not go forward*) держа́ться *impf* позади́; ~ **by** (*vi*) (*not interfere*) не вме́шиваться *impf*, вмеша́ться *pf*; (*be ready*) быть *impf* на гото́ве; (*vt*) (*support*) подде́рживать *impf*, поддержа́ть *pf*; (*stick to*) приде́рживаться *impf* +*gen*; ~ **down** (*resign*) уходи́ть *impf*, уйти́ *pf* с по́ста (**as** +*gen*); ~ **for** (*signify*) означа́ть *impf*; (*tolerate*): **I shall not ~ for it** я не потерплю́; **~-in** замести́тель *m*; ~ **in** (*for*) замеща́ть *impf*, замести́ть *pf*; ~ **out** выделя́ться *impf*, вы́делиться *pf*; ~ **up** встава́ть *impf*, встать *pf*; ~ **up for** (*defend*) отста́ивать *impf*, отстоя́ть *pf*; ~ **up to** (*endure*) выде́рживать *impf*, вы́держать *pf*; (*not give in to*) противостоя́ть *impf* +*dat*.

standard *n* (*norm*) станда́рт, норм; (*flag*) зна́мя *neut*; ~ **of living** жи́зненный у́ровень *m*; *adj* норма́льный, станда́ртный. **standardization** *n* нормализа́ция, стандартиза́ция. **standardize** *vt* стандартизи́ровать *impf* & *pf*; нормализова́ть *impf* & *pf*.

standing *n* положе́ние; *adj* (*upright*) стоя́чий; (*permanent*) постоя́нный.

standpoint *n* то́чка зре́ния.

standstill *n* остано́вка, засто́й, па́уза; **be at a ~** стоя́ть *impf* на мёртвой то́чке; **bring (come) to a ~** остана́вливать(ся) *impf*, останови́ть(ся) *pf*.

stanza *n* строфа́.

staple[1] *n* (*metal bar*) скоба́; (*for paper*) скре́пка; *vt* скрепля́ть *impf*, скрепи́ть *pf*.

staple[2] *n* (*product*) гла́вный проду́кт; *adj* основно́й.

star *n* звезда́; (*asterisk*) звёздочка; *vi* игра́ть *impf*, сыгра́ть *pf* гла́вную роль. **starfish** *n* морска́я звезда́.

starboard *n* пра́вый борт.

starch *n* крахма́л; *vt* крахма́лить *impf*, на~ *pf*. **starchy** *adj* крахма́листый; (*prim*) чо́порный.

stare *n* при́стальный взгляд; *vi* при́стально смотре́ть *impf* (**at** на+*acc*).

stark *adj* (*bare*) го́лый; (*desolate*) пусты́нный; (*sharp*) ре́зкий; *adv* соверше́нно.

starling *n* скворе́ц.

starry *adj* звёздный.

start *n* нача́ло; (*sport*) старт; *vi* начина́ться *impf*, нача́ться *pf*; (*engine*) заводи́ться *impf*, завести́сь *pf*; (*set out*) отправля́ться *impf*, отпра́виться *pf*; (*shudder*) вздра́гивать *impf*, вздро́гнуть *pf*; (*sport*) стартова́ть *impf* & *pf*; *vt* начина́ть *impf*, нача́ть *pf* (*gerund*, *inf*, +*inf*; *by*, +*gerund* с того́, что...; **with** +*instr*, с+*gen*); (*car*, *engine*) заводи́ть *impf*, завести́ *pf*; (*fire*, *rumour*) пуска́ть *impf*, пусти́ть *pf*; (*found*) осно́вывать *impf*, основа́ть *pf*. **starter** *n* (*tech*) ста́ртёр; (*cul*) заку́ска. **starting-point** *n* отправно́й пункт.

startle *vt* испуга́ть *pf*.

starvation *n* го́лод. **starve** *vi* голода́ть *impf*; (*to death*) умира́ть *impf*, умере́ть с го́лоду; *vt* мори́ть *impf*, по~, у~ *pf* го́лодом. **starving** *adj* голода́ющий; (*hungry*) о́чень голо́дный.

state *n* (*condition*) состоя́ние; (*polit*) госуда́рство, штат; *adj* (*ceremonial*) торже́ственный; пара́дный; (*polit*) госуда́рственный; *vt* (*announce*) заявля́ть *impf*, заяви́ть *pf*; (*expound*) излага́ть *impf*, изложи́ть *pf*. **stateless** *adj* не име́ющий гражда́нства. **stately** *adj* вели́чественный. **statement** *n* заявле́ние; (*comm*) отчёт. **statesman** *n* госуда́рственный де́ятель *m*.

static *adj* неподви́жный.

station *n* (*rly*) вокза́л, ста́нция; (*social*) обще́ственное положе́ние; (*meteorological, hydro-electric power, radio etc.*) ста́нция; (*post*) пост; *vt* размеща́ть *impf*, размести́ть *pf*.

stationary *adj* неподви́жный.

stationery *n* канцеля́рские принадле́жности *f pl*; (*writing-paper*) почто́вая бума́га; ~ **shop** канцеля́рский магази́н.

statistic *n* статисти́ческое да́нное. **statistical** *adj* статисти́ческий. **statistician** *n* стати́стик. **statistics** *n* стати́стика.

statue *n* ста́туя. **statuette** *n* статуэ́тка.

stature *n* рост; (*merit*) кали́бр.

status *n* ста́тус. **status quo** *n* ста́тус-кво́ *neut indecl*.

statute *n* стату́т. **statutory** *adj* устано́вленный зако́ном.

staunch *adj* ве́рный.

stave *vt*: ~ **off** предотвраща́ть *impf*, предотврати́ть *pf*.

stay *n* (*time spent*) пребыва́ние; *vi* (*remain*) остава́ться *impf*, оста́ться *pf* (**to dinner** обе́дать); (*put up*) остана́вливаться *impf*, останови́ться *pf* (**at** (*place*) в+*prep*; **at** (*friends' etc.*) у+*gen*); (*live*) жить; ~ **behind** остава́ться *impf*, оста́ться *pf*; ~ **in** остава́ться *impf*, оста́ться *pf* до́ма; ~ **up** не ложи́ться *impf* спать; (*trousers*) держа́ться *impf*. **staying-power** *n* выно́сливость.

stead *n*: **stand s.o. in good** ~ ока́зываться *impf*, оказа́ться *pf* поле́зным кому́-л.

steadfast *adj* сто́йкий, непоколеби́мый.

steady *adj* (*firm*) усто́йчивый; (*continuous*) непреры́вный; (*wind, temperature*) ро́вный; (*speed*) постоя́нный; (*unshakeable*) непоколеби́мый; *vt* (*boat etc.*) приводи́ть *impf*, привести́ *pf* в равнове́сие.

steak *n* бифште́кс.

steal *vt & abs* ворова́ть *impf*, с~ *pf*; красть *impf*, у~ *pf*; *vi* (*creep*) кра́сться *impf*; подкра́дываться *impf*, подкра́сться *pf*. **stealth** *n*: **by** ~ укра́дкой. **stealthy** *adj* ворова́тый, та́йный, скры́тый.

steam *n* пар; **at full** ~ на всех пара́х; **let off** ~ (*fig*) дава́ть *impf*, дать *pf* вы́ход свои́м чу́вствам; *vt* па́рить *impf*; *vi* па́риться *impf*, по~ *pf*; (*vessel*) ходи́ть *indet*, идти́ *det* на пара́х; ~ **up** (*mist over*) запотева́ть *impf*, запоте́ть *pf*; поте́ть *impf*, за~, от~ *pf*; ~ **engine** парова́я маши́на. **steamer, steamship** *n* парохо́д. **steamy** *adj* напо́лненный па́ром; (*passionate*) горя́чий.

steed *n* конь *m*.
steel *n* сталь; *adj* стальной; *vt*: ~ **o.s.** ожесточаться *impf*, ожесточиться *pf*; ~ **works** сталелитейный завод. **steely** *adj* стальной.
steep[1] *adj* крутой; (*excessive*) чрезмерный.
steep[2] *vt* (*immerse*) погружать *impf*, погрузить *pf* (**in** в+*acc*); (*saturate*) пропитывать *impf*, пропитать *pf* (**in** +*instr*).
steeple *n* шпиль *m*. **steeplechase** *n* скачки *f pl* с препятствиями.
steer *vt* управлять *impf*, править *impf* +*instr*; *v abs* рулить *impf*; ~ **clear of** избегать *impf*, избежать *pf* +*gen*. **steering-wheel** *n* руль *m*.
stem[1] *n* стебель *m*; (*of wineglass*) ножка; (*ling*) основа; *vi*: ~ **from** происходить *impf*, произойти *pf* от+*gen*.
stem[2] *vt* (*stop*) останавливать *impf*, остановить *pf*.
stench *n* зловоние.
stencil *n* трафарет; (*tech*) шаблон; *vt* наносить *impf*, нанести *pf* по трафарету. **stencilled** *adj* трафаретный.
step *n* (*pace*, *action*) шаг; (*dance*) па *neut indecl*; (*of stairs*, *ladder*) ступень; ~ **by** ~ шаг за шагом; **in** ~ в ногу; **out of** ~ не в ногу; **take** ~**s** принимать *impf*, принять *pf* меры *vi* шагать *impf*, шагнуть *pf*; ступать *impf*, ступить *pf*; ~ **aside** сторониться *impf*, по~ *pf*; ~ **back** отступать *impf*, отступить *pf*; ~ **down** (*resign*) уходить *impf*, уйти *pf* в отставку; ~ **forward** выступать *impf*, выступить *pf*; ~ **in** (*intervene*) вмешиваться *impf*, вмешаться *pf*; ~ **on** наступать *impf*, наступить *pf* на+*acc* (**s.o.'s foot** кому-л. на ногу); ~ **over** перешагивать *impf*, перешагнуть *pf* +*acc*, через+*acc*; ~ **up** (*increase*) повышать *impf*, повысить *pf*. **step-ladder** *n* стремянка. **stepping-stone** *n* камень *m* для перехода; (*fig*) средство. **steps** *n pl* лестница.
stepbrother *n* сводный брат. **stepdaughter** *n* падчерица. **stepfather** *n* отчим. **stepmother** *n* мачеха. **stepsister** *n* сводная сестра. **stepson** *n* пасынок.
steppe *n* степь.
stereo *n* (*system*) стереофоническая система; (*stereophony*) стереофония; *adj* (*recorded in* ~) стерео *indecl*. **stereophonic** *adj* стереофонический. **stereotype** *n* стереотип. **stereotyped** *adj* стереотипный.
sterile *adj* стерильный. **sterility** *n* стерильность. **sterilization** *n* стерилизация. **sterilize** *vt* стерилизовать *impf* & *pf*.
sterling *n* стерлинг; **pound** ~ фунт стерлингов; *adj* стерлинговый.
stern[1] *n* корма.
stern[2] *adj* суровый, строгий.
stethoscope *n* стетоскоп.
stew *n* (*cul*) мясо тушёное вместе с овощами; *vt* & *i* (*cul*) тушить(ся) *impf*, с~ *pf*; (*fig*) томить(ся) *impf*.
steward *n* бортпроводник. **stewardess** *n* стюардесса.
stick[1] *n* палка; (*of chalk etc.*) палочка; (*hockey*) клюшка.
stick[2] *vt* (*spear*) закалывать

impf, заколо́ть *pf*; (*make adhere*) прикле́ивать *impf*, прикле́ить *pf* (**to** к+*dat*); (*coll*) (*put*) ста́вить *impf*, по~ *pf*; (*lay*) класть *impf*, положи́ть *pf*; (*endure*) терпе́ть *impf*, вы́~ *pf*; *vi* (*adhere*) ли́пнуть *impf* (**to** к+*dat*); прилипа́ть *impf*, прили́пнуть *pf* (**to** к+*dat*); ~ **in** (*thrust in*) втыка́ть *impf*, воткну́ть *pf*; (*into opening*) всо́вывать *impf*, всу́нуть *pf*; ~ **on** (*glue on*) накле́ивать *impf*, накле́ить *pf*; ~ **out** (*thrust out*) высо́вывать *impf*, вы́сунуть *pf* (**from** из+*gen*); (*project*) торча́ть *impf*; ~ **to** (*keep to*) приде́рживаться *impf*, придержа́ться *pf* +*gen*; (*remain at*) не отвлека́ться *impf* от+*gen*; ~ **together** держа́ться *impf* вме́сте; ~ **up for** защища́ть *impf*, защити́ть *pf*; **be, get, stuck** застрева́ть *impf*, застря́ть *pf*. **sticker** *n* накле́йка.

sticky *adj* ли́пкий.

stiff *adj* жёсткий, неги́бкий; (*prim*) чо́порный; (*difficult*) тру́дный; (*penalty*) суро́вый; **be** ~ (*ache*) боле́ть *impf*. **stiffen** *vt* де́лать *impf*, с~ *pf* жёстким; *vi* станови́ться *impf*, стать *pf* жёстким. **stiffness** *n* жёсткость; (*primness*) чо́порность.

stifle *vt* души́ть *impf*, за~ *pf*; (*suppress*) подавля́ть *impf*, подави́ть *pf*; (*sound*) заглуша́ть *impf*, заглуши́ть *pf*; *vi* задыха́ться *impf*, задохну́ться *pf*. **stifling** *adj* уду́шливый.

stigma *n* клеймо́.

stile *n* перела́з (*coll*).

stilettos *n pl* ту́фли *f pl* на шпи́льках.

still *adv* (всё) ещё; (*nevertheless*) тем не ме́нее; (*motionless*) неподви́жно; **stand** ~ не дви́гаться *impf*, дви́нуться *pf*; *n* (*quiet*) тишина́; *adj* ти́хий; (*immobile*) неподви́жный. **still-born** *adj* мертворождённый. **still life** *n* натюрмо́рт. **stillness** *n* тишина́.

stilted *adj* ходу́льный.

stimulant *n* возбужда́ющее сре́дство. **stimulate** *vt* возбужда́ть *impf*, возбуди́ть *pf*. **stimulating** *adj* возбуди́тельный. **stimulation** *n* возбужде́ние. **stimulus** *n* сти́мул.

sting *n* (*wound*) уку́с; (*stinger*; *fig*) жа́ло; *vt* жа́лить *impf*, у~ *pf*; *vi* (*burn*) жечь *impf*. **stinging** *adj* (*caustic*) язви́тельный.

stingy *adj* скупо́й.

stink *n* вонь; *vi* воня́ть *impf* (**of** +*instr*). **stinking** *adj* воню́чий.

stint *n* срок; *vi*: ~**on** скупи́ться *impf*, по~ *pf* на+*acc*.

stipend *n* (*salary*) жа́лование; (*grant*) стипе́ндия.

stipulate *vt* обусло́вливать *impf*, обусло́вить *pf*. **stipulation** *n* усло́вие.

stir *n* (*commotion*) шум; *vt* (*mix*) меша́ть *impf*, по~ *pf*; (*excite*) волнова́ть *impf*, вз~ *pf*; *vi* (*move*) шевели́ться *impf*, шевельну́ться *pf*; ~ **up** возбужда́ть *impf*, возбуди́ть *pf*. **stirring** *adj* волну́ющий.

stirrup *n* стре́мя *neut*.

stitch *n* стежо́к; (*knitting*) петля́; (*med*) шов; (*pain*) ко́лики *f pl*; *vt* (*embroider, make line of ~es*) строчи́ть *impf*, про~ *pf*; (*join by sewing, make, suture*) сшива́ть *impf*, сшить *pf*; ~ **up** зашива́ть *impf*, заши́ть *pf*. **stitching** *n* (*stitches*) стро́чка.

stoat *n* горноста́й.

stock *n* (*store*) запа́с; (*of shop*) ассортиме́нт; (*live*~) скот; (*cul*) бульо́н; (*lineage*) семья́; (*fin*) а́кции *f pl*; **in** ~ в нали́чии; **out of** ~ распро́дан; **take** ~ **of** крити́чески оце́нивать *impf*, оцени́ть *pf*; *adj* станда́ртный; *vt* име́ть в нали́чии; ~ **up** запаса́ться *impf*, запасти́сь *pf* (**with** +*instr*). **stockbroker** *n* биржево́й ма́клер. **stock-exchange** *n* би́ржа. **stockpile** *n* запа́с; *vt* нака́пливать *impf*, накопи́ть *pf*. **stock-taking** *n* переучёт.

stocking *n* чуло́к.

stocky *adj* призе́мистый.

stodgy *adj* тяжёлый.

stoic(al) *adj* стои́ческий. **stoicism** *n* стоици́зм.

stoke *vt* топи́ть *impf*.

stolid *adj* флегмати́чный.

stomach *n* желу́док, (*also surface of body*) живо́т; *vt* терпе́ть *impf*, по~ *pf*. **stomach ache** *n* боль в животе́.

stone *n* ка́мень *m*; (*of fruit*) ко́сточка; *adj* ка́менный; *vt* побива́ть *impf*, поби́ть *pf* камня́ми; (*fruit*) вынима́ть *impf*, вы́нуть *pf* ко́сточки из+*gen*. **Stone Age** *n* ка́менный век. **stone-deaf** *adj* соверше́нно глухо́й. **stone-mason** *n* ка́менщик. **stonily** *adv* с ка́менным выраже́нием, хо́лодно. **stony** *adj* камени́стый; (*fig*) ка́менный.

stool *n* табуре́т, табуре́тка.

stoop *n* суту́лость; *vt & i* суту́лить(ся) *impf*, с~ *pf*; (*bend (down)*) наклоня́ть(ся) *impf*, наклони́ть(ся) *pf*; ~ **to** (*abase o.s.*) унижа́ться *impf*, уни́зиться *pf* до+*gen*; (*condescend*) снисходи́ть *impf*, снизойти́ *pf* до+*gen*. **stooped, stooping** *adj* суту́лый.

stop *n* остано́вка; **put a ~ to** положи́ть *pf* коне́ц +*dat*; *vt* остана́вливать *impf*, останови́ть *pf*; (*discontinue*) прекраща́ть *impf*, прекрати́ть *pf*; (*restrain*) уде́рживать *impf*, удержа́ть *pf* (**from** от+*gen*); *vi* остана́вливаться *impf*, останови́ться *pf*; (*discontinue*) прекраща́ться *impf*, прекрати́ться *pf*; (*cease*) перестава́ть *impf*, переста́ть *pf* (+*inf*); ~ **up** *vt* затыка́ть *impf*, заткну́ть *pf*. **stoppage** *n* остано́вка; (*strike*) забасто́вка. **stopper** *n* про́бка. **stop-press** *n* э́кстренное сообще́ние в газе́те. **stopwatch** *n* секундоме́р.

storage *n* хране́ние. **store** *n* запа́с; (*storehouse*) склад; (*shop*) магази́н; **set ~ by** цени́ть *impf*; **what is in ~ for me?** что ждёт меня́ впереди́?; *vt* запаса́ть *impf*, запасти́ *pf*; (*put into storage*) сдава́ть *impf*, сдать *pf* на хране́ние. **storehouse** *n* склад. **store-room** кладова́я *sb*.

storey *n* эта́ж.

stork *n* а́ист.

storm *n* бу́ря, (*thunder* ~) гроза́; *vt* (*mil*) штурмова́ть *impf*; *vi* бушева́ть *impf*. **stormy** *adj* бу́рный.

story *n* расска́з, по́весть; (*anecdote*) анекдо́т; (*plot*) фа́була; ~**-teller** расска́зчик.

stout *adj* (*strong*) кре́пкий; (*staunch*) сто́йкий; (*portly*) доро́дный.

stove *n* (*with fire inside*) печь;

(*cooker*) плита́.

stow *vt* укла́дывать *impf*, уложи́ть *pf*. **stowaway** *n* безбиле́тный пассажи́р.

straddle *vt* (*sit astride*) сиде́ть *impf* верхо́м на+*prep*; (*stand astride*) стоя́ть *impf*, расста́вив но́ги над+*instr*.

straggle *vi* отстава́ть *impf*, отста́ть *pf*. **straggler** *n* отста́вший *sb*. **straggling** *adj* разбро́санный. **straggly** *adj* растрёпанный.

straight *adj* прямо́й; (*undiluted*) неразба́вленный; *predic* (*in order*) в поря́дке; *adv* пря́мо; ~ **away** сра́зу. **straighten** *vt & i* выпрямля́ть(ся) *impf*, вы́прямить(ся) *pf*; *vt* (*put in order*) поправля́ть *impf*, попра́вить *pf*. **straightforward** *adj* прямо́й; (*simple*) просто́й.

strain[1] *n* (*tension*) натяже́ние; (*sprain*) растяже́ние; (*effort*, *exertion*) напряже́ние; (*tendency*) скло́нность; (*sound*) звук; *vt* (*stretch*) натя́гивать *impf*, натяну́ть *pf*; (*sprain*) растя́гивать *impf*, растяну́ть *pf*; (*exert*) напряга́ть *impf*, напря́чь *pf*; (*filter*) проце́живать *impf*, процеди́ть *pf*; *vi* (*also exert o.s.*) напряга́ться *impf*, напря́чься *pf*. **strained** *adj* натя́нутый. **strainer** *n* (*tea* ~) си́течко; (*sieve*) си́то.

strain[2] *n* (*breed*) поро́да.

strait(s) *n* (*geog*) проли́в. **strait-jacket** *n* смири́тельная руба́шка. **straits** *n pl* (*difficulties*) затрудни́тельное положе́ние.

strand[1] *n* (*hair*, *rope*) прядь; (*thread*, *also fig*) нить.

strand[2] *vt* сажа́ть *impf*, посади́ть *pf* на мель. **stranded** *adj* на мели́.

strange *adj* стра́нный; (*unfamiliar*) незнако́мый; (*alien*) чужо́й. **strangely** *adv* стра́нно. **strangeness** *n* стра́нность. **stranger** *n* незнако́мец.

strangle *vt* души́ть *impf*, за~ *pf*. **stranglehold** *n* мёртвая хва́тка. **strangulation** *n* удуше́ние.

strap *n* реме́нь *m*; *vt* (*tie up*) стя́гивать *impf*, стяну́ть *pf* ремнём. **strapping** *adj* ро́слый.

stratagem *n* хи́трость. **strategic** *adj* стратеги́ческий. **strategist** *n* страте́г. **strategy** *n* страте́гия.

stratum *n* слой.

straw *n* соло́ма; (*drinking*) соло́минка; **the last** ~ после́дняя ка́пля; *adj* соло́менный.

strawberry *n* клубни́ка (*no pl*; *usu collect*); (*wild* ~) земляни́ка (*no pl*; *usu collect*).

stray *vi* сбива́ться *impf*, сби́ться *pf*; (*digress*) отклоня́ться *impf*, отклони́ться *pf*; *adj* (*lost*) заблуди́вшийся; (*homeless*) бездо́мный; *n* (*from flock*) отби́вшееся от ста́да живо́тное *sb*; ~ **bullet** шальна́я пу́ля.

streak *n* полоса́ (**of luck** везе́ния); (*tendency*) жи́лка; *vi* (*rush*) проноси́ться *impf*, пронести́сь *pf*. **streaked** *adj* с полоса́ми (**with** +*gen*). **streaky** *adj* полоса́тый; (*meat*) с просло́йками жи́ра.

stream *n* (*brook*, *tears*) ручей; (*brook*, *flood*, *tears*, *people etc.*) пото́к; (*current*) тече́ние; **up/down** ~ вверх/вниз по тече́нию; *vi* течь *impf*; струи́ться *impf*; (*rush*) проноси́ться *impf*, пронести́сь

pf; (*blow*) развева́ться *impf*. **streamer** *n* вы́мпел. **streamlined** *adj* обтека́емый; (*fig*) хорошо́ нала́женный.
street *n* у́лица; *adj* у́личный; ~ **lamp** у́личный фона́рь *m*.
strength *n* си́ла; (*numbers*) чи́сленность; **on the ~ of** в си́лу+*gen*. **strengthen** *vt* уси́ливать *impf*, уси́лить *pf*.
strenuous *adj* (*work*) тру́дный; (*effort*) напряжённый.
stress *n* напряже́ние; (*mental*) стресс; (*emphasis*) ударе́ние; *vt* (*accent*) ста́вить *impf*, по~ *pf* ударе́ние на+*acc*; (*emphasize*) подчёркивать *impf* подчеркну́ть *pf*. **stressful** *adj* стре́ссовый.
stretch *n* (*expanse*) отре́зок; **at a ~** (*in succession*) подря́д; *vt* & *i* (*widen, spread out*) растя́гивать(ся) *impf*, растяну́ть(ся) *pf*; (*in length*, ~ *out limbs*) вытя́гивать(ся) *impf*, вы́тянуть(ся) *pf*; (*tauten*) натя́гивать(ся) *impf*, натяну́ть(ся) *pf*; (*extend, e.g. rope*, ~ *forth limbs*) протя́гивать(ся) *impf*, протяну́ть(ся) *pf*; *vi* (*material, land*) тяну́ться *impf*; ~ **one's legs** (*coll*) размина́ть *impf*, размя́ть *pf* но́ги. **stretcher** *n* носи́лки (-лок) *pl*.
strew *vt* разбра́сывать *impf*, разброса́ть *pf*; ~ **with** посыпа́ть *impf*, посы́пать *pf* +*instr*.
stricken *adj* поражённый.
strict *adj* стро́гий. **stricture(s)** *n* (стро́гая) кри́тика.
stride *n* (большо́й) шаг; *pl* (*fig*) успе́хи *m pl*; **to take sth in one's ~** преодолева́ть *impf*, преодоле́ть *pf* что-л. без уси́лий; *vi* шага́ть *impf*.
strident *adj* ре́зкий.
strife *n* раздо́р.
strike *n* (*refusal to work*) забасто́вка; (*mil*) уда́р; *vi* (*be on* ~) бастова́ть *impf*; (*go on* ~) забастова́ть *pf*; (*attack*) ударя́ть *impf*, уда́рить *pf*; (*the hour*) бить *impf*, про~ *pf*; *vt* (*hit*) ударя́ть *impf*, уда́рить *pf*; (*impress*) поража́ть *impf*, порази́ть *pf*; (*discover*) открыва́ть *impf*, откры́ть *pf*; (*match*) зажига́ть *impf*, заже́чь *pf*; (*the hour*) бить *impf*, про~ *pf*; (*occur to*) приходи́ть *impf*, прийти́ *pf* в го́лову+*dat*; ~ **off** вычёркивать *impf*, вы́черкнуть *pf*; ~ **up** начина́ть *impf*, нача́ть *pf*. **striker** *n* забасто́вщик. **striking** *adj* порази́тельный.
string *n* бечёвка; (*mus*) струна́; (*series*) ряд; *pl* (*mus*) стру́нные инструме́нты *m pl*; ~ **bag**, ~ **vest** се́тка; *vt* (*thread*)низа́ть *impf*, на~ *pf*; ~ **along** (*coll*) води́ть *impf* за нос; ~ **out** (*prolong*) растя́гивать *impf*, растяну́ть *pf*; **strung up** (*tense*) напряжённый. **stringed** *adj* стру́нный. **stringy** *adj* (*fibrous*) волокни́стый; (*meat*) жи́листый.
stringent *adj* стро́гий.
strip[1] *n* полоса́, поло́ска.
strip[2] *vt* (*undress*) раздева́ть *impf*, разде́ть *pf*; (*deprive*) лиша́ть *impf*, лиши́ть *pf* (**of** +*gen*); ~ **off** (*tear off*) сдира́ть *impf*, содра́ть *pf*; *vi* раздева́ться *impf*, разде́ться *pf*.
strip-tease *n* стрипти́з.
stripe *n* полоса́. **striped** *adj* полоса́тый.
strive *vi* (*endeavour*) стреми́ться *impf* (**for** к+*dat*); (*struggle*) боро́ться *impf* (**for** за+*acc*; **against** про́тив+*gen*).

stroke *n* (*blow*, *med*) уда́р; (*of oar*) взмах; (*swimming*) стиль *m*; (*of pen etc.*) штрих; (*piston*) ход; *vt* гла́дить *impf*, по~ *pf*.
stroll *n* прогу́лка; *vi* прогу́ливаться *impf*, прогуля́ться *pf*.
strong *adj* си́льный; (*stout*; *of drinks*) кре́пкий; (*healthy*) здоро́вый; (*opinion etc.*) твёрдый. **stronghold** *n* кре́пость. **strong-minded, strong-willed** *adj* реши́тельный.
structural *adj* структу́рный. **structure** *n* структу́ра; (*building*) сооруже́ние; *vt* организова́ть *impf* & *pf*.
struggle *n* борьба́; *vi* боро́ться *impf* (**for** за+*acc*; **against** про́тив+*gen*); (*writhe*, ~ *with* (*fig*)) би́ться (**with** над+*instr*).
strum *vi* бренча́ть *impf* (**on** на+*prep*).
strut[1] *n* (*vertical*) сто́йка; (*horizontal*) распо́рка.
strut[2] *vi* ходи́ть *indet*, идти́ *det* го́голем.
stub *n* огры́зок; (*cigarette*) оку́рок; (*counterfoil*) корешо́к; *vt*: ~ **one's toe** ударя́ться *impf*, уда́риться *pf* ного́й (**on** на+*acc*); ~ **out** гаси́ть *impf*, по~ *pf*.
stubble *n* жнивьё; (*hair*) щети́на.
stubborn *adj* упря́мый. **stubbornness** *n* упря́мство.
stucco *n* штукату́рка.
stud[1] *n* (*collar*, *cuff*) за́понка; (*nail*) гвоздь *m* с большо́й шля́пкой; *vt* (*bestrew*) усе́ивать *impf*, усе́ять *pf* (**with** +*instr*).
stud[2] *n* (*horses*) ко́нный заво́д.
student *n* студе́нт, ~ка.
studied *adj* напускно́й.
studio *n* сту́дия.
studious *adj* лю́бящий нау́ку; (*diligent*) стара́тельный.
study *n* изуче́ние; *pl* заня́тия *neut pl*; (*investigation*) иссле́дование; (*art*, *mus*) этю́д; (*room*) кабине́т; *vt* изуча́ть *impf*, изучи́ть *pf*; учи́ться *impf*, об~ *pf* +*dat*; (*scrutinize*) рассма́тривать *impf*, рассмотре́ть *pf*; *vi* (*take lessons*) учи́ться *impf*, об~ *pf*; (*do one's studies*) занима́ться *impf*.
stuff *n* (*material*) материа́л; (*things*) ве́щи *f pl*; *vt* набива́ть *impf*, наби́ть *pf*; (*cul*) начиня́ть *impf*, начини́ть *pf*; (*cram into*) запи́хивать *impf*, запиха́ть *pf* (**into** в+*acc*); (*shove into*) сова́ть *impf*, су́нуть *pf* (**into** в+*acc*); *vi* (*overeat*) объеда́ться *impf*, объе́сться *pf*. **stuffiness** *n* духота́. **stuffing** *n* наби́вка; (*cul*) начи́нка. **stuffy** *adj* ду́шный.
stumble *vi* (*also fig*) спотыка́ться *impf*, споткну́ться *pf* (**over** о+*acc*); ~ **upon** натыка́ться *impf*, наткну́ться *pf* на+*acc*. **stumbling-block** *n* ка́мень *m* преткнове́ния.
stump *n* (*tree*) пень *m*; (*pencil*) огры́зок; (*limb*) культя́; *vt* (*perplex*) ста́вить *impf*, по~ *pf* в тупи́к.
stun *vt* (*also fig*) оглуша́ть *impf*, оглуши́ть *pf*. **stunning** *adj* потряса́ющий.
stunt[1] *n* трюк.
stunt[2] *vt* заде́рживать *impf*, задержа́ть *pf* рост+*gen*. **stunted** *adj* низкоро́слый.
stupefy *vt* оглуша́ть *impf*, оглуши́ть *pf*. **stupendous** *adj* колосса́льный. **stupid** *adj* глу́пый. **stupidity** *n* глу́пость. **stupor** *n* оцепене́ние.

sturdy *adj* крéпкий.
stutter *n* заикáние; *vi* заикáться *impf*.
sty[1] *n* (*pig*~) свинáрник.
sty[2] *n* (*on eye*) ячмéнь *m*.
style *n* стиль *m*; (*taste*) вкус; (*fashion*) мóда; (*sort*) род; (*of hair*) причёска. **stylish** *adj* мóдный. **stylist** *n* (*of hair*) парикмáхер. **stylistic** *adj* стилистúческий. **stylize** *vt* стилизовáть *impf* & *pf*.
stylus *n* иглá звукоснимáтеля.
suave *adj* обходúтельный.
subconscious *adj* подсознáтельный; *n* подсознáние. **subcontract** *vt* давáть *impf*, дать *pf* подря́дчику. **subcontractor** *n* подря́дчик. **subdivide** *vt* подразделя́ть *impf*, подразделúть *pf*. **subdivision** *n* подразделéние. **subdue** *vt* покоря́ть *impf*, покорúть *pf*. **subdued** *adj* (*suppressed, dispirited*) подáвленный; (*soft*) мя́гкий; (*indistinct*) приглушённый. **sub-editor** *n* помóщник редáктора.
subject *n* (*theme*) тéма; (*discipline, theme*) предмéт; (*question*) вопрóс; (*thing on to which action is directed*) объéкт; (*gram*) подлежáщее *sb*; (*national*) пóдданный *sb*; *adj*: ~ **to** (*susceptible to*) подвéрженный+*dat*; (*on condition that*) при услóвии, что...; éсли; **be** ~ **to** (*change etc.*) подлежáть *impf* +*dat*; *vt*: ~ **to** подвергáть *impf*, подвéргнуть *pf* +*dat*. **subjection** *n* подчинéние. **subjective** *adj* субъектúвный. **subjectivity** *n* субъектúвность. **subject-matter** *n* (*of book, lecture*) содержáние, тéма; (*of discussion*) предмéт.
subjugate *vt* покоря́ть *impf*, покорúть *pf*. **subjugation** *n* покорéние.
subjunctive (mood) *n* сослагáтельное наклонéние.
sublet *vt* передавáть *impf*, передáть *pf* в субарéнду.
sublimate *vt* сублимúровать *impf* & *pf*. **sublimation** *n* сублимáция. **sublime** *adj* возвы́шенный.
subliminal *adj* подсознáтельный. **sub-machine-gun** *n* автомáт. **submarine** *n* подвóдная лóдка. **submerge** *vt* погружáть *impf*, погрузúть *pf*. **submission** *n* подчинéние; (*for inspection*) представлéние. **submissive** *adj* покóрный. **submit** *vi* подчиня́ться *impf*, подчинúться *pf* (**to** +*dat*); *vt* представля́ть *impf*, предстáвить *pf*. **subordinate** *n* подчинённый *sb*; *adj* подчинённый; (*secondary*) второстепéнный; (*gram*) придáточный; *vt* подчиня́ть *impf*, подчинúть *pf*. **subscribe** *vi* подпúсываться *impf*, подписáться *pf* (**to** на+*acc*); ~ **to** (*opinion*) присоединя́ться *impf*, присоединúться *pf* к+*dat*. **subscriber** *n* подпúсчик; абонéнт. **subscription** *n* подпúска, абонемéнт; (*fee*) взнос. **subsection** *n* подраздéл. **subsequent** *adj* послéдующий. **subsequently** *adv* впослéдствии. **subservient** *adj* раболéпный. **subside** *vi* убывáть *impf*, убы́ть *pf*; (*soil*) оседáть *impf*, осéсть *pf*. **subsidence** *n* (*soil*) оседáние. **subsidiary** *adj* вспомогáтельный; (*secondary*) второстепéнный; *n* филиáл. **subsidize** *vt* субсидúровать

impf & *pf*. **subsidy** *n* субсидия. **subsist** *vi* (*live*) жить *impf* (**on** +*instr*). **substance** *n* веществó; (*essence*) сýщность, суть; (*content*) содержáние. **substantial** *adj* (*durable*) прóчный; (*considerable*) значи́тельный; (*food*) плóтный. **substantially** *adv* (*basically*) в основнóм; (*considerably*) значи́тельно. **substantiate** *vt* обоснóвывать *impf*, обосновáть *pf*. **substitute** *n* (*person*) замести́тель *m*; (*thing*) замéна; *vt* заменя́ть *impf*, замени́ть *pf* +*instr* (**for** +*acc*); **I ~ water for milk** заменя́ю молокó водóй. **substitution** *n* замéна. **subsume** *vt* относи́ть *impf*, отнести́ *pf* к какóй-л. категóрии. **subterfuge** *n* увёртка. **subterranean** *adj* подзéмный. **subtitle** *n* подзаголóвок; (*cin*) субти́тр.

subtle *adj* тóнкий. **subtlety** *n* тóнкость.

subtract *vt* вычитáть *impf*, вы́честь *pf*. **subtraction** *n* вычитáние. **suburb** *n* при́город. **suburban** *adj* пригорóдный. **subversion** *n* подрывнáя дéятельность. **subversive** *adj* подрывнóй. **subway** *n* подзéмный перехóд.

succeed *vi* удавáться *impf*, удáться *pf*; **the plan will ~** план удáстся; **he ~ed in buying the book** емý удалóсь купи́ть кни́гу; (*be successful*) преуспевáть *impf*, преуспéть *pf* (**in** в+*prep*); (*follow*) сменя́ть *impf*, смени́ть *pf*; (*be heir*) наслéдовать *impf* & *pf* (**to** +*dat*). **succeeding** *adj* послéдующий. **success** *n* успéх. **successful** *adj* успéшный.

succession *n* (*series*) ряд; (*to throne*) престолонаслéдие; **right of ~** прáво наслéдования; **in ~** подря́д, оди́н за други́м. **successive** *adj* (*consecutive*) последовáтельный. **successor** *n* преéмник.

succinct *adj* сжáтый.

succulent *adj* сóчный.

succumb *vi* (*to pressure*) уступáть *impf*, уступи́ть *pf* (**to** +*dat*); (*to temptation*) поддавáться *impf*, поддáться *pf* (**to** +*dat*).

such *adj* такóй; **~ people** таки́е лю́ди; **~ as** (*for example*) так напримéр; (*of ~ a kind as*) такóй как; **~ beauty as yours** такáя красотá как вáша; (*that which*) тот, котóрый; **I shall read ~ books as I like** я бýду читáть те кни́ги, котóрые мне нрáвятся; **~ as to** такóй, чтóбы; **his illness was not ~ as to cause anxiety** егó болéзнь былá не такóй (серьёзной), чтóбы вы́звать беспокóйство; **~ and ~** такóй-то; *pron* такóв; **~ was his character** такóв был егó харáктер; **as ~** сам по себé; **~ is not the case** э́то не так. **suchlike** *pron* (*inanimate*) томý подóбное; (*people*) такие лю́ди *pl*.

suck *vt* сосáть *impf*; **~ in** всáсывать *impf*, всосáть *pf*; (*engulf*) засáсывать *impf*, засосáть *pf*; **~ out** высáсывать *impf*, вы́сосать *pf*; **~ up to** (*coll*) подли́зываться *impf*, подлизáться *pf* к+*dat*. **sucker** *n* (*biol*, *rubber device*) присóска; (*bot*) корневóй побéг. **suckle** *vt* корми́ть *impf*, на~ *pf* грýдью. **suction** *n* всáсывание.

sudden *adj* внеза́пный. **suddenly** *adv* вдруг. **suddenness** *n* внеза́пность.

sue *vt & i* подава́ть *impf*, пода́ть *pf* в суд (на+*acc*); **~ s.o. for damages** предъявля́ть *impf*, предъяви́ть *pf* (к) кому́-л. иск о возмеще́нии уще́рба.

suede *n* за́мша; *adj* за́мшевый.

suet *n* нутряно́е са́ло.

suffer *vt* страда́ть *impf*, по~ *pf* +*instr*, от+*gen*; (*loss, defeat*) терпе́ть *impf*, по~ *pf*; (*tolerate*) терпе́ть *impf*; *vi* страда́ть *impf*, по~ *pf* (**from** +*instr*, от+*gen*). **sufferance** *n*: **he is here on ~** его́ здесь те́рпят. **suffering** *n* страда́ние.

suffice *vi & t* быть доста́точным (для+*gen*); хвата́ть *impf*, хвати́ть *pf impers*+*gen* (+*dat*). **sufficient** *adj* доста́точный.

suffix *n* су́ффикс.

suffocate *vt* удуша́ть *impf*, удуши́ть *pf*; *vi* задыха́ться *impf*, задохну́ться *pf*. **suffocating** *adj* уду́шливый. **suffocation** *n* удуше́ние.

suffrage *n* избира́тельное пра́во.

suffuse *vt* залива́ть *impf*, зали́ть *pf* (**with** +*instr*).

sugar *n* са́хар; *adj* са́харный; *vt* подсла́щивать *impf*, подсласти́ть *pf*; **~ basin** са́харница; **~ beet** са́харная свёкла; **~ cane** са́харный тро́стник. **sugary** *adj* са́харный; (*fig*) слаща́вый.

suggest *vt* предлага́ть *impf*, предложи́ть *pf*; (*evoke*) напомина́ть *impf*, напо́мнить *pf*; (*imply*) намека́ть *impf*, намекну́ть *pf* на+*acc*; (*indicate*) говори́ть *impf* о+*prep*. **suggestion** *n* предложе́ние; (*psych*) внуше́ние. **suggestive** *adj* вызыва́ющий мы́сли (**of** о+*prep*); (*indecent*) соблазни́тельный.

suicidal *adj* самоуби́йственный; (*fig*) губи́тельный. **suicide** *n* самоуби́йство; **commit ~** соверша́ть *impf*, соверши́ть *pf* самоуби́йство.

suit *n* (*clothing*) костю́м; (*law*) иск; (*cards*) масть; **follow ~** (*fig*) сле́довать *impf*, по~ *pf* приме́ру; *vt* (*be convenient for*) устра́ивать *impf*, устро́ить *pf*; (*adapt*) приспоса́бливать *impf*, приспосо́бить *pf*; (*be ~able for, match*) подходи́ть *impf*, подойти́ *pf* (+*dat*); (*look attractive on*) идти́ *impf* +*dat*. **suitability** *n* приго́дность. **suitable** *adj* (*fitting*) подходя́щий; (*convenient*) удо́бный. **suitably** *adv* соотве́тственно. **suitcase** *n* чемода́н.

suite *n* (*retinue*) сви́та; (*furniture*) гарниту́р; (*rooms*) апарта́менты *m pl*; (*mus*) сюи́та.

suitor *n* покло́нник.

sulk *vi* ду́ться *impf*. **sulky** *adj* наду́тый.

sullen *adj* угрю́мый.

sully *vt* пятна́ть *impf*, за~ *pf*.

sulphur *n* се́ра. **sulphuric** *adj*: **~ acid** се́рная кислота́.

sultana *n* (*raisin*) изю́минка; *pl* кишми́ш (*collect*).

sultry *adj* зно́йный.

sum *n* су́мма; (*arithmetical problem*) арифмети́ческая зада́ча; *pl* арифме́тика; *v*: **~ up** *vi & t* (*summarize*) подводи́ть *impf*, подвести́ *pf* ито́ги (+*gen*); *vt* (*appraise*) оце́нивать *impf*,

оцени́ть *pf.*
summarize *vt* сумми́ровать *impf* & *pf.* **summary** *n* резюме́ *neut indecl*, сво́дка; *adj* сумма́рный; (*dismissal*) бесцеремо́нный.
summer *n* ле́то; *attrib* ле́тний. **summer-house** *n* бесе́дка.
summit *n* верши́на; ~ **meeting** встре́ча на верха́х.
summon *vt* вызыва́ть *impf*, вы́звать *pf*; ~ **up one's courage** собира́ться *impf*, собра́ться *pf* с ду́хом. **summons** *n* вы́зов; (*law*) пове́стка в суд; *vt* вызыва́ть *impf*, вы́звать *pf* в суд.
sumptuous *adj* роско́шный.
sun *n* со́лнце; **in the** ~ на со́лнце. **sunbathe** *vi* загора́ть *impf.* **sunbeam** *n* со́лнечный луч. **sunburn** *n* зага́р; (*inflammation*) со́лнечный ожо́г. **sunburnt** *adj* загоре́лый; **become** ~ загора́ть *impf*, загоре́ть *pf.*
Sunday *n* воскресе́нье.
sundry *adj* ра́зный; **all and** ~ всё и вся.
sunflower *n* подсо́лнечник. **sun-glasses** *n pl* очки́ (-ко́в) *pl* от со́лнца.
sunken *adj* (*cheeks, eyes*) впа́лый; (*submerged*) погружённый; (*ship*) зато́пленный; (*below certain level*) ни́же (како́го-л. у́ровня).
sunlight *n* со́лнечный свет. **sunny** *adj* со́лнечный. **sunrise** *n* восхо́д со́лнца. **sunset** *n* зака́т. **sunshade** *n* (*parasol*) зо́нтик; (*awning*) наве́с. **sunshine** *n* со́лнечный свет. **sunstroke** *n* со́лнечный уда́р. **suntan** *n* зага́р. **sun-tanned** *adj* загоре́лый.
super *adj* замеча́тельный. **superb** *adj* превосхо́дный. **supercilious** *adj* высокоме́рный. **superficial** *adj* пове́рхностный. **superficiality** *n* пове́рхностность. **superfluous** *adj* ли́шний. **superhuman** *adj* сверхчелове́ческий. **superintendent** *n* заве́дующий *sb* (**of** +*instr*); (*police*) ста́рший полице́йский офице́р. **superior** *n* ста́рший *sb*; *adj* (*better*) превосхо́дный; (*in rank*) ста́рший; (*haughty*) высокоме́рный. **superiority** *n* превосхо́дство. **superlative** *adj* превосхо́дный; *n* (*gram*) превосхо́дная сте́пень. **superman** *n* сверхчелове́к. **supermarket** *n* универса́м. **supernatural** *adj* сверхъесте́ственный. **superpower** *n* сверхдержа́ва. **supersede** *vt* заменя́ть *impf*, замени́ть *pf.* **supersonic** *adj* сверхзвуково́й. **superstition** *n* суеве́рие. **superstitious** *adj* суеве́рный. **superstructure** *n* надстро́йка. **supervise** *vt* наблюда́ть *impf* за+*instr.* **supervision** *n* надзо́р. **supervisor** *n* нача́льник; (*of studies*) руководи́тель *m.*
supper *n* у́жин; **have** ~ у́жинать *impf*, по~ *pf.*
supple *adj* ги́бкий. **suppleness** *n* ги́бкость.
supplement *n* (*to book*) дополне́ние; (*to periodical*) приложе́ние; *vt* дополня́ть *impf*, допо́лнить *pf.* **supplementary** *adj* дополни́тельный.
supplier *n* поставщи́к. **supply** *n* (*stock*) запа́с; (*econ*) предложе́ние; *pl* (*mil*) припа́сы (-ов) *pl*, *vt* снабжа́ть *impf*, снабди́ть *pf* (**with** +*instr*).

support *n* поддéржка; *vt* поддéрживать *impf*, поддержáть *pf*; (*family*) содержáть *impf*. **supporter** *n* сторóнник; (*sport*) болéльщик. **supportive** *adj* учáстливый.

suppose *vt* (*think*) полагáть *impf*; (*presuppose*) предполагáть *impf*, предположи́ть *pf*; (*assume*) допускáть *impf*, допусти́ть *pf*. **supposed** *adj* (*assumed*) предполагáемый. **supposition** *n* предположéние.

suppress *vt* подавля́ть *impf*, подави́ть *pf*. **suppression** *n* подавлéние.

supremacy *n* госпóдство. **supreme** *adj* верхóвный.

surcharge *n* нацéнка.

sure *adj* увéренный (of в+*prep*; **that** что); (*reliable*) вéрный; **~ enough** действи́тельно; **he is ~ to come** он обязáтельно придёт; **make ~ of** (*convince o.s.*) убеждáться *impf*, убеди́ться *pf* в+*prep*; **make ~ that** (*check up*) проверя́ть *impf*, провéрить *pf* что. **surely** *adv* навернякá. **surety** *n* порýка; **stand ~ for** ручáться *impf*, поручи́ться *pf* за+*acc*.

surf *n* прибóй; *vi* занимáться *impf*, заня́ться *pf* сéрфингом.

surface *n* повéрхность; (*exterior*) внéшность; **on the ~** (*fig*) внéшне; **under the ~** (*fig*) по существý; *adj* повéрхностный; *vi* всплывáть *impf*, всплыть *pf*.

surfeit *n* (*surplus*) изли́шек.

surge *n* волнá; *vi* (*rise, heave*) вздымáться *impf*; (*emotions*) нахлы́нуть *pf*; **~ forward** ри́нуться *pf* вперёд.

surgeon *n* хирýрг. **surgery** *n* (*treatment*) хирурги́я; (*place*) кабинéт; (**~** *hours*) приёмные часы́ *m pl* (врачá). **surgical** *adj* хирурги́ческий.

surly *adj* (*morose*) угрю́мый; (*rude*) грýбый.

surmise *vt & i* предполагáть *impf*, предположи́ть *pf*.

surmount *vt* преодолевáть *impf*, преодолéть *pf*.

surname *n* фами́лия.

surpass *vt* превосходи́ть *impf*, превзойти́ *pf*.

surplus *n* изли́шек; *adj* изли́шний.

surprise *n* (*astonishment*) удивлéние; (*surprising thing*) сюрпри́з; *vt* удивля́ть *impf*, удиви́ть *pf*; (*come upon suddenly*) заставáть *impf*, застáть *pf* врасплóх; **be ~d** (*at*) удивля́ться *impf*, удиви́ться *pf* (+*dat*). **surprising** *adj* удиви́тельный.

surreal *adj* сюрреалисти́ческий. **surrealism** *n* сюрреали́зм. **surrealist** *n* сюрреали́ст; *adj* сюрреалисти́ческий.

surrender *n* сдáча; (*renunciation*) откáз; *vt* сдавáть *impf*, сдать *pf*; (*give up*) откáзываться *impf*, отказáться *pf* от+*gen*; *vi* сдавáться *impf*, сдáться *pf*; **~ o.s. to** предавáться *impf*, предáться *pf* +*dat*.

surreptitious *adj* тáйный.

surrogate *n* замени́тель *m*.

surround *vt* окружáть *impf*, окружи́ть *pf* (**with** +*instr*). **surrounding** *adj* окружáющий. **surroundings** *n* (*environs*) окрéстности *f pl*; (*milieu*) средá.

surveillance *n* надзóр.

survey *n* (*review*) обзóр; (*inspection*) инспéкция; (*poll*) опрóс; *vt* (*review*) обозрева́ть *impf*, обозре́ть *pf*; (*inspect*) инспекти́ровать *impf*, про~ *pf*; (*poll*) опра́шивать *impf*, опроси́ть *pf*. **surveyor** *n* инспе́ктор.

survival *n* (*surviving*) выжива́ние; (*relic*) пережи́ток. **survive** *vt* пережива́ть *impf*, пережи́ть *pf*; *vi* выжива́ть *impf*, вы́жить *pf*. **survivor** *n* уцеле́вший *sb*; (*fig*) боре́ц.

susceptible *adj* подве́рженный (**to** влия́нию *+gen*); (*sensitive*) чувстви́тельный (**to** к*+dat*); (*impressionable*) впечатли́тельный.

suspect *n* подозрева́емый *sb*; *adj* подозри́тельный; *vt* подозрева́ть *impf* (**of** в*+prep*); (*assume*) полага́ть *impf*.

suspend *vt* (*hang*) подве́шивать *impf*, подве́сить *pf*; (*delay*) приостана́вливать *impf*, приостанови́ть *pf*; (*debar temporarily*) вре́менно отстраня́ть *impf*, отстрани́ть *pf*; **~ed sentence** усло́вный пригово́р. **suspender** *n* (*stocking*) подвя́зка. **suspense** *n* неизве́стность. **suspension** *n* (*halt*) приостано́вка; (*of car*) рессо́ры *f pl*; **~ bridge** вися́чий мост.

suspicion *n* подозре́ние; **on ~** по подозре́нию (**of** в*+loc*); (*trace*) отте́нок. **suspicious** *adj* подозри́тельный.

sustain *vt* (*support*) подде́рживать *impf*, поддержа́ть *pf*; (*suffer*) потерпе́ть *pf*. **sustained** *adj* непреры́вный. **sustenance** *n* пи́ща.

swab *n* (*mop*) шва́бра; (*med*) тампо́н; (*specimen*) мазо́к.

swagger *vi* расха́живать *impf* с ва́жным ви́дом.

swallow[1] *n* глото́к; *vt* прогла́тывать *impf*, проглоти́ть *pf*; **~ up** поглоща́ть *impf*, поглоти́ть *pf*.

swallow[2] *n* (*bird*) ла́сточка.

swamp *n* боло́та; *vt* залива́ть *impf*, зали́ть *pf*; (*fig*) зава́ливать *impf*, завали́ть *pf* (**with** *+instr*). **swampy** *adj* боло́тистый.

swan *n* ле́бедь *m*.

swap *n* обме́н; *vt* (*for different thing*) меня́ть *impf*, об~, по~ *pf* (**for** на*+acc*); (*for similar thing*) обме́ниваться *impf*, обменя́ться *pf +instr*.

swarm *n* рой; (*crowd*) толпа́; *vi* рои́ться *impf*; толпи́ться *impf*; (*teem*) кише́ть *impf* (**with** *+instr*).

swarthy *adj* сму́глый.

swastika *n* сва́стика.

swat *vt* прихло́пывать *impf*, прихло́пнуть *pf*.

swathe *n* (*expanse*) простра́нство; *vt* (*wrap*) заку́тывать *impf*, заку́тать *pf*.

sway *n* (*influence*) влия́ние; (*power*) власть *vt & i* кача́ть(ся) *impf*, качну́ть(ся) *pf*; *vt* (*influence*) име́ть *impf* влия́ние на*+acc*.

swear *vi* (*vow*) кля́сться *impf*, по~ *pf*; (*curse*) руга́ться *impf*, ругну́ться *pf*; **~-word** руга́тельство.

sweat *n* пот; *vi* поте́ть *impf*, вс~ *pf*. **sweater** *n* сви́тер. **sweatshirt** *n* тёплая футбо́лка с дли́нными рукава́ми. **sweaty** *adj* по́тный.

swede *n* брю́ква.

Swede *n* швед, ~дка. **Sweden** *n* Шве́ция. **Swedish** *adj* шве́дский.

sweep *n* (*span*) разма́х; (*chimney-~*) трубочи́ст; *vt* подмета́ть *impf*, подмести́ *pf*; *vi* (*go majestically*) ходи́ть *indet*, идти́ *det*, пойти́ *pf* велича́во; (*move swiftly*) мча́ться *impf*; ~ **away** смета́ть *impf*, смести́ *pf*. **sweeping** *adj* (*changes*) радика́льный; (*statement*) огу́льный.

sweet *n* (*sweetmeat*) конфе́та; (*dessert*) сла́дкое *sb*; *adj* сла́дкий; (*fragrant*) души́стый; (*dear*) ми́лый. **sweeten** *vt* подсла́щивать *impf*, подсласти́ть *pf*. **sweetheart** *n* возлю́бленный, -нная *sb*. **sweetness** *n* сла́дость.

swell *vi* (*up*) опуха́ть *impf*, опу́хнуть *pf*; *vt & i* (*a sail*) надува́ть(ся) *impf*, наду́ть(ся) *pf*; *vt* (*increase*) увели́чивать *impf*, увели́чить *pf*; *n* (*of sea*) зыбь. **swelling** *n* о́пухоль.

swelter *vi* изнемога́ть *impf* от жары́. **sweltering** *adj* зно́йный.

swerve *vi* ре́зко свёртывать, свора́чивать *impf*, сверну́ть *pf*.

swift *adj* бы́стрый.

swig *n* глото́к; *vt* хлеба́ть *impf*.

swill *n* по́йло; *vt* (*rinse*) полоска́ть *impf*, вы́~ *pf*.

swim *vi* пла́вать *indet*, плыть *det*; *vt* (*across*) переплыва́ть *impf*, переплы́ть *pf* +*acc*, че́рез+*acc*. **swimmer** *n* плове́ц, пловчи́ха. **swimming** *n* пла́вание. **swimming-pool** *n* бассе́йн для пла́вания. **swimsuit** *n* купа́льный костю́м.

swindle *vt* обма́нывать *impf*, обману́ть *pf*; *n* обма́н. **swindler** *n* моше́нник.

swine *n* свинья́.

swing *vi* кача́ться *impf*, качну́ться *pf*; *vt* кача́ть *impf*, качну́ть *pf* +*acc*, *instr*; (*arms*) разма́хивать *impf* +*instr*; *n* кача́ние; (*shift*) крен; (*seat*) каче́ли (-лей) *pl*; **in full** ~ в по́лном разга́ре.

swingeing *adj* (*huge*) грома́дный; (*forcible*) си́льный.

swipe *n* си́льный уда́р; *vt* с сило́й ударя́ть *impf*, уда́рить *pf*.

swirl *vi* крути́ться *impf*; *n* (*of snow*) вихрь *m*.

swish *vi* (*cut the air*) рассека́ть *impf*, рассе́чь *pf* во́здух со сви́стом; (*rustle*) шелесте́ть *impf*; *vt* (*tail*) взма́хивать *impf*, взмахну́ть *pf* +*instr*; (*brandish*) разма́хивать *impf* +*instr*; *n* (*of whip*) свист; (*rustle*) ше́лест.

Swiss *n* швейца́рец, -ца́рка, *adj* швейца́рский.

switch *n* (*electr*) выключа́тель *m*; (*change*) измене́ние; *vt & i* (*also* ~ **over**) переключа́ть(ся) *impf*, переключи́ть(ся) *pf*; *vt* (*swap*) меня́ться *impf*, об~, по~ *pf* +*instr*; ~ **off** выключа́ть *impf*, вы́ключить *pf*; ~ **on** включа́ть *impf*, включи́ть *pf*. **switchboard** *n* коммута́тор.

Switzerland *n* Швейца́рия.

swivel *vt & i* враща́ть(ся) *impf*.

swollen *adj* взду́тый.

swoon *n* о́бморок; *vi* па́дать *impf*, упа́сть *pf* в о́бморок.

swoop *vi*: ~ **down** налета́ть *impf*, налете́ть *pf* (**on** на+*acc*); *n* налёт; **at one fell** ~ одни́м уда́ром.

sword *n* меч.

sycophantic *adj* льсти́вый.

syllable *n* слог.

syllabus *n* програ́мма.

symbol *n* си́мвол. **symbolic(al)** *adj* символи́ческий. **symbolism** *n* символи́зм. **symbolize** *vt* символизи́ровать *impf*.

symmetrical *adj* симметри́ческий. **symmetry** *n* симметри́я.
sympathetic *adj* сочу́вственный. **sympathize** *vi* сочу́вствовать *impf* (**with** +*dat*). **sympathizer** *n* сторо́нник. **sympathy** *n* сочу́вствие.
symphony *n* симфо́ния.
symposium *n* симпо́зиум.
symptom *n* симпто́м. **symptomatic** *adj* симтомати́чный.
synagogue *n* синаго́га.
synchronization *n* синхрониза́ция. **synchronize** *vt* синхронизи́ровать *impf* & *pf*.
syndicate *n* синдика́т.
syndrome *n* синдро́м.
synonym *n* сино́ним. **synonymous** *adj* синоними́ческий.
synopsis *n* конспе́кт.
syntax *n* си́нтаксис.
synthesis *n* си́нтез. **synthetic** *adj* синтети́ческий.
syphilis *n* си́филис.
Syria *n* Си́рия. **Syrian** *n* сири́ец, сири́йка; *adj* сири́йский.
syringe *n* шприц; *vt* спринцева́ть *impf*.
syrup *n* сиро́п; (*treacle*) па́тока.
system *n* систе́ма; (*network*) сеть; (*organism*) органи́зм. **systematic** *adj* системати́ческий. **systematize** *vt* систематизи́ровать *impf* & *pf*.

T

tab *n* (*loop*) пе́телька; (*on uniform*) петли́ца; (*of boot*) ушко́; **keep ~s on** следи́ть *impf* за+*instr*.
table *n* стол; (*chart*) табли́ца; **~cloth** ска́терть; **~spoon** столо́вая ло́жка; **~ tennis** насто́льный те́ннис; *vt* (*for discussion*) предлага́ть *impf*, предложи́ть *pf* на обсужде́ние.
tableau *n* жива́я карти́на.
tablet *n* (*pill*) табле́тка; (*of stone*) плита́; (*memorial ~*) мемориа́льная доска́; (*name plate*) доще́чка.
tabloid *n* (*newspaper*) малоформа́тная газе́та; (*derog*) бульва́рная газе́та.
taboo *n* табу́ *neut indecl*; *adj* запрещённый.
tacit *adj* молчали́вый. **taciturn** *adj* неразгово́рчивый.
tack[1] *n* (*nail*) гво́здик; (*stitch*) намётка; (*naut*) галс; (*fig*) курс; *vt* (*fasten*) прикрепля́ть *impf*, прикрепи́ть *pf* гво́здиками; (*stitch*) смётывать *impf*, смета́ть *pf* на живу́ю ни́тку; (*fig*) добавля́ть *impf*, доба́вить *pf* (**(on)to** +*dat*); *vi* (*naut*; *fig*) лави́ровать *impf*.
tack[2] *n* (*riding*) сбру́я (*collect*).
tackle *n* (*requisites*) снасть (*collect*); (*sport*) блокиро́вка; *vt* (*problem*) бра́ться *impf*, взя́ться *pf* за+*acc*; (*sport*) блоки́ровать *impf* & *pf*.
tacky *adj* ли́пкий.
tact *n* такт(и́чность). **tactful** *adj* такти́чный.
tactical *adj* такти́ческий. **tactics** *n pl* та́ктика.
tactless *adj* беста́ктный.
tadpole *n* голова́стик.
Tadzhikistan *n* Таджикиста́н.
tag *n* (*label*) ярлы́к; (*of lace*) наконе́чник; *vt* (*label*) прикрепля́ть *impf*, прикрепи́ть *pf* ярлы́к на+*acc*; *vi*: **~ along** (*follow*) тащи́ться *impf* сзади́; **may I ~ along?** мо́жно с ва́ми?
tail *n* хвост; (*of shirt*) ни́жний

конéц; (*of coat*) фáлда; (*of coin*) обрáтная сторонá монéты; **heads or ~s?** орёл или рéшка?; *pl* (*coat*) фрак; *vt* (*shadow*) выслéживать *impf*; *vi*: **~ away, off** постепéнно уменьшáться *impf*; (*grow silent*, *abate*) затихáть *impf*. **tailback** *n* хвост. **tailcoat** *n* фрак.

tailor *n* портнóй *sb*; **~-made** сшúтый на закáз; (*fig*) сдéланный индивидуáльно.

taint *vt* пóртить *impf*, ис~ *pf*.

Taiwan *n* Тайвáнь *m*.

take *vt* (*various senses*) брать *impf*, взять *pf*; (*also seize*, *capture*) захвáтывать *impf*, захватúть *pf*; (*receive*, *accept*; **~** *breakfast*; **~** *medicine*, **~** *steps*) принимáть *impf*, принять *pf*; (*convey*, *escort*) провожáть *impf*, проводúть *pf*; (*public transport*) éздить *indet*, éхать *det*, по~ *pf* +*instr*, на+*prep*; (*photograph*) снимáть *impf*, снять *pf*; (*occupy*; **~** *time*) занимáть *impf*, занять *pf*; (*impers*) **how long does it ~?** скóлько врéмени нýжно?; (*size in clothing*) носúть *impf*; (*exam*) сдавáть *impf*; *vi* (*be successful*) имéть *impf* успéх (*of injection*) прививáться *impf*, привúться *pf*; **~ after** походúть *impf* на+*acc*; **~ away** (*remove*) убирáть *impf*, убрáть *pf*; (*subtract*) вычитáть *impf*, вы́честь *pf*; **~-away** магазúн, где продаю́т на вы́нос; **~ back** (*return*) возвращáть *impf*, возвратúть *pf*; (*retrieve*, *retract*) брать *impf*, взять *pf* назáд; **~ down** (*in writing*) запúсывать *impf*, записáть *pf*; (*remove*) снимáть *impf*, снять *pf*; **~ s.o., sth for, to be** принимáть *impf*, принять *pf* за+*acc*; **~ from** отнимáть *impf*, отнять *pf* у, от+*gen*; **~ in** (*carry in*) вносúть *impf*, внестú *pf*; (*lodgers*; *work*) брать *impf*, взять *pf*; (*clothing*) ушивáть *impf*, ушúть *pf*; (*understand*) понимáть *impf*, понять *pf*; (*deceive*) обмáнывать *impf*, обманýть *pf*; **~ off** (*clothing*) снимáть *impf*, снять *pf*; (*mimic*) передрáзнивать *impf*, передразнúть *pf*; (*aeroplane*) взлетáть *impf*, взлетéть *pf*; **~-off** (*imitation*) подражáние; (*aeron*) взлёт; **~ on** (*undertake*; *hire*) брать *impf*, взять *pf* на себя́; (*acquire*) приобретáть *impf*, приобрестú *pf*; (*at game*) сражáться *impf*, сразúться *pf* с+*instr* (**at** в+*acc*); **~ out** вынимáть *impf*, вы́нуть *pf*; (*dog*) выводúть *impf*, вывести *pf* (**for a walk** на прогýлку); (*to theatre*, *restaurant etc.*) приглашáть *impf*, пригласúть *pf* (**to** в+*acc*); **we took them out every night** мы приглашáли их кудá-нибудь кáждый вéчер; **~ it out on** срывáть *impf*, сорвáть *pf* всё на+*prep*; **~ over** принимáть *impf*, принять *pf* руковóдство +*instr*; **~ to** (*thing*) пристрастúться *pf* к+*dat*; (*person*) привя́зываться *impf*, привязáться *pf* к+*dat*; (*begin*) станóвиться *impf*, стать *pf* +*inf*; **~ up** (*interest oneself in*) занимáться *impf*, заняться *pf*; (*with an official etc.*) обращáться *impf*, обратúться *pf* с+*instr*, к+*dat*; (*challenge*) принимáть *impf*, принять *pf*; (*time*, *space*) за-

нима́ть *impf*, заня́ть *pf*; ~ **up with** (*person*) свя́зываться *impf*, связа́ться *pf* с+*instr*; *n* (*cin*) дубль *m*.
taking *adj* привлека́тельный.
takings *n pl* сбор.
talcum powder *n* тальк.
tale *n* расска́з.
talent *n* тала́нт. **talented** *adj* тала́нтливый.
talk *vi* разгова́ривать *impf* (**to, with** с+*instr*); (*gossip*) спле́тничать *impf*, на~ *pf*; *vt* & *i* говори́ть *impf*, по~ *pf*; ~ **down to** говори́ть *impf* свысока́ с+*instr*; ~ **into** угова́ривать *impf*, уговори́ть *pf* +*inf*; ~ **out of** отгова́ривать *impf*, отговори́ть *pf* +*inf*, от+*gen*; ~ **over** (*discuss*) обсужда́ть *impf*, обсуди́ть *pf*; ~ **round** (*persuade*) переубежда́ть *impf*, переубеди́ть *pf*; *n* (*conversation*) разгово́р; (*lecture*) бесе́да; *pl* перегово́ры (-ров) *pl*. **talkative** *adj* разгово́рчивый; (*derog*) болтли́вый. **talker** *n* говоря́щий *sb*; (*chatterer*) болту́н (*coll*); (*orator*) ора́тор. **talking-to** *n* (*coll*) вы́говор.
tall *adj* высо́кий; (*in measurements*) ро́стом в+*acc*.
tally *n* (*score*) счёт; *vi* соотве́тствовать (**with** +*dat*).
talon *n* ко́готь *m*.
tambourine *n* бу́бен.
tame *adj* ручно́й; (*insipid*) пре́сный; *vt* прируча́ть *impf*, приручи́ть *pf*. **tamer** *n* укроти́тель *m*.
tamper *vi*: ~ **with** (*meddle*) тро́гать *impf*, тро́нуть *pf*; (*forge*) подде́лывать *impf*, подде́лать *pf*.
tampon *n* тампо́н.
tan *n* (*sun*~) зага́р; *adj* желтова́то-кори́чневый; *vt* (*hide*) дуби́ть *impf*, вы́~ *pf*; (*beat*) (*coll*) дуба́сить *impf*, от~ *pf*; *vi* загора́ть *impf*, загоре́ть *pf*; (*of sun*): **tanned** загоре́лый.
tang *n* (*taste*) ре́зкий при́вкус; (*smell*) о́стрый за́пах.
tangent *n* (*math*) каса́тельная *sb*; (*trigonometry*) та́нгенс; **go off at a** ~ отклоня́ться *impf*, отклони́ться *pf* от те́мы.
tangerine *n* мандари́н.
tangible *adj* осяза́емый.
tangle *vt* & *i* запу́тывать(ся) *impf*, запу́таться *pf*; *n* пу́таница.
tango *n* та́нго *neut indecl*.
tangy *adj* о́стрый; ре́зкий.
tank *n* бак; (*mil*) танк.
tankard *n* кру́жка.
tanker *n* (*sea*) та́нкер; (*road*) автоцисте́рна.
tantalize *vt* дразни́ть *impf*.
tantamount *predic* равноси́лен (-льна) (**to** +*dat*).
tantrum *n* при́ступ раздраже́ния.
tap[1] *n* кран; *vt* (*resources*) испо́льзовать *impf* & *pf*; (*telephone conversation*) подслу́шивать *impf*.
tap[2] *n* (*knock*) стук; *vt* стуча́ть *impf*, по~ *pf* в+*acc*, по+*dat*; ~**-dance** (*vi*) отбива́ть *impf*, отби́ть *pf* чечётку; (*n*) чечётка; ~**-dancer** чечёточник, -ица.
tape *n* (*cotton strip*) тесьма́; (*adhesive, magnetic, measuring, etc.*) ле́нта; ~**-measure** руле́тка; ~ **recorder** магнитофо́н; ~ **recording** за́пись; *vt* (*seal*) закле́ивать *impf*, закле́ить *pf*; (*record*) запи́сывать *impf*, записа́ть *pf* на ле́нту.

taper *vt* & *i* сýживать(ся) *impf*, сýзить(ся) *pf*.
tapestry *n* гобелéн.
tar *n* дёготь *m*.
tardy *adj* (*slow*) медли́тельный; (*late*) запоздáлый.
target *n* мишéнь, цель.
tariff *n* тари́ф.
tarmac *n* (*material*) гудрóн; (*road*) гудрони́рованное шоссé *neut indecl*; (*runway*) бетони́рованная площáдка; *vt* гудрони́ровать *impf* & *pf*.
tarnish *vt* дéлать *impf*, с~ *pf* тýсклым; (*fig*) пятнáть *impf*, за~ *pf*; *vi* тускнéть *impf*, по~ *pf*.
tarpaulin *n* брезéнт.
tarragon *n* эстрагóн.
tart[1] *adj* (*taste*) кислый; (*fig*) кóлкий.
tart[2] *n* (*pie*) слáдкий пирóг.
tart[3] *n* (*prostitute*) шлю́ха.
tartan *n* шотлáндка.
tartar *n* ви́нный кáмень *m*.
task *n* задáча; **take to ~** дéлать *impf*, с~ *pf* вы́говор+*dat*; **~ force** операти́вная грýппа.
Tass *abbr* ТАСС, Телегрáфное агéнтство Совéтского Сою́за.
tassel *n* ки́сточка.
taste *n* (*also fig*) вкус; **take a ~ of** прóбовать *impf*, по~ *pf*; *vt* чýвствовать *impf*, по~ *pf* вкус+*gen*; (*sample*) прóбовать *impf*, по~ *pf*; (*fig*) вкушáть *impf*, вкуси́ть *pf*; (*wine etc.*) дегусти́ровать *impf* & *pf*; *vi* имéть *impf* вкус, при́вкус (**of** +*gen*). **tasteful** *adj* (сдéланный) со вкýсом. **tasteless** *adj* безвкýсный. **tasting** *n* дегустáция. **tasty** *adj* вкýсный.
tatter *n pl* лохмóтья (-ьев) *pl*. **tattered** *adj* обóрванный.
tattoo *n* (*design*) татуирóвка; *vt* татуи́ровать *impf* & *pf*.
taunt *n* насмéшка; *vt* насмехáться *impf* над+*instr*.
Taurus *n* Телéц.
taut *adj* тýго натя́нутый; тугóй.
tavern *n* тавéрна.
tawdry *adj* мишýрный.
tawny *adj* рыжевáто-кори́чневый.
tax *n* налóг; **~-free** освобождённый от налóга; *vt* облагáть *impf*, обложи́ть *pf* налóгом; (*strain*) напрягáть *impf*, напря́чь *pf*; (*patience*) испы́тывать *impf*, испытáть *pf*. **taxable** *adj* подлежáщий обложéнию налóгом. **taxation** *n* обложéние налóгом. **taxing** *adj* утоми́тельный. **taxpayer** *n* налогоплатéльщик.
taxi *n* такси́ *neut indecl*; **~-driver** води́тель *m* такси́; **~ rank** стоя́нка такси́; *vi* (*aeron*) рули́ть *impf*.
tea *n* чай; **~ bag** пакéтик с сухи́м чáем; **~ cloth, ~ towel** полотéнце для посýды; **~ cosy** чехóльщик (для чáйника); **~cup** чáйная чáшка; **~-leaf** чáйный лист; **~-pot** чáйник; **~spoon** чáйная лóжка; **~ strainer** чáйное си́течко.
teach *vt* учи́ть *impf*, на~ *pf* (*person* +*acc*; *subject* +*dat*, *inf*); преподавáть *impf* (*subject* +*acc*); (*coll*) проýчивать *impf*, проучи́ть *pf*. **teacher** *n* учи́тель *m*, ~ница; преподавáтель *m*, ~ница; **~-training college** педогоги́ческий институ́т. **teaching** *n* (*instruction*) обучéние; (*doctrine*) учéние.

teak *n* тик; *attrib* ти́ковый.
team *n* (*sport*) кома́нда; (*of people*) брига́да; (*of horses etc.*) упря́жка; **~-mate** член той же кома́нды; **~work** сотру́дничество; *vi* (**~** *up*) объединя́ться *impf*, объедини́ться *pf*.
tear[1] *n* (*rent*) проре́ха; *vt* (*also* **~** *up*) рвать *impf*; (*also* **~** *up*) разрыва́ть *impf*, разорва́ть *pf*; *vi* рва́ться *impf*; (*rush*) мча́ться *impf*; **~ down, off** срыва́ть *impf*, сорва́ть *pf*; **~ out** вырыва́ть *impf*, вы́рвать *pf*.
tear[2] *n* (**~**-*drop*) слеза́; **~-gas** слезоточи́вый газ. **tearful** *adj* слезли́вый.
tease *vt* дразни́ть *impf*.
teat *n* сосо́к.
technical *adj* техни́ческий; **~ college** техни́ческое учи́лище. **technicality** *n* форма́льность. **technically** *adv* (*strictly*) форма́льно. **technician** *n* те́хник. **technique** *n* те́хника; (*method*) ме́тод. **technology** *n* техноло́гия, те́хника. **technological** *adj* технологи́ческий. **technologist** *n* техно́лог.
teddy-bear *n* медвежо́нок.
tedious *adj* ску́чный. **tedium** *n* ску́ка.
teem[1] *vi* (*swarm*) кише́ть *impf* (**with** +*instr*).
teem[2] *vi*: **it is ~ing (with rain)** дождь льёт как из ведра́.
teenage *adj* ю́ношеский. **teenager** *n* подро́сток. **teens** *n pl* во́зраст от трина́дцати до девятна́дцати лет.
teeter *vi* кача́ться *impf*, качну́ться *pf*.
teethe *vi*: **the child is teething** у ребёнка проре́зываются зу́бы; **teething troubles** (*fig*) нача́льные пробле́мы *f pl*.
teetotal *adj* тре́звый. **teetotaller** *n* тре́звенник.
telecommunication(s) *n* да́льняя связь. **telegram** *n* телегра́мма. **telegraph** *n* телегра́ф; **~ pole** телегра́фный столб. **telepathic** *adj* телепати́ческий. **telepathy** *n* телепа́тия. **telephone** *n* телефо́н; *vt* (*message*) телефони́ровать *impf* & *pf* +*acc*, о+*prep*; (*person*) звони́ть *impf*, по~ *pf* (по телефо́ну) +*dat*; **~ box** телефо́нная бу́дка; **~ directory** телефо́нная кни́га; **~ exchange** телефо́нная ста́нция; **~ number** но́мер телефо́на. **telephonist** *n* телефони́ст, ~ка. **telephoto lens** *n* телеобъекти́в. **telescope** *n* телеско́п. **telescopic** *adj* телескопи́ческий. **televise** *vt* пока́зывать *impf*, показа́ть *pf* по телеви́дению. **television** *n* телеви́дение; (*set*) телеви́зор; *attrib* телевизио́нный. **telex** *n* те́лекс.
tell *vt* & *i* (*relate*) расска́зывать *impf*, рассказа́ть *pf* (*thing told* +*acc*, о+*prep*; *person told* +*dat*); *vt* (*utter, inform*) говори́ть *impf*, сказа́ть *pf* (*thing uttered* +*acc*; *thing informed about* о+*prep*; *person informed* +*dat*); (*order*) веле́ть *impf* & *pf* +*dat*; **~ one thing from another** отлича́ть *impf*, отличи́ть *pf* +*acc* от+*gen*; *vi* (*have an effect*) ска́зываться *impf*, сказа́ться *pf* (**on** на+*prep*); **~ off** отчи́тывать *impf*, отчита́ть *pf*; **~ on, ~ tales about** ябе́дничать *impf*, на~ *pf* на+*acc*.

teller *n* (*of story*) расска́зчик; (*of votes*) счётчик; (*in bank*) касси́р. **telling** *adj* (*effective*) эффекти́вный; (*significant*) многозначи́тельный. **telltale** *n* спле́тник; *adj* преда́тельский.

temerity *n* дёрзость.

temp *n* рабо́тающий *sb* вре́менно; *vi* рабо́тать *impf* вре́менно.

temper *n* (*character*) нрав; (*mood*) настрое́ние; (*anger*) гнев; **lose one's ~** выходи́ть *impf*, вы́йти *pf* из себя́; *vt* (*fig*) смягча́ть *impf*, смягчи́ть *pf*.

temperament *n* темпера́мент. **temperamental** *adj* темпера́ментный.

temperance *n* (*moderation*) уме́ренность; (*sobriety*) тре́звенность.

temperate *adj* уме́ренный.

temperature *n* температу́ра; (*high ~*) повы́шенная температу́ра; **take s.o.'s ~** измеря́ть *impf*, изме́рить *pf* температу́ру *+dat*.

tempest *n* бу́ря. **tempestuous** *adj* бу́рный.

template *n* шабло́н.

temple[1] *n* (*religion*) храм.

temple[2] *n* (*anat*) висо́к.

tempo *n* темп.

temporal *adj* (*of time*) временно́й; (*secular*) мирско́й.

temporary *adj* вре́менный.

tempt *vt* соблазня́ть *impf*, соблазни́ть *pf*; **~ fate** испы́тывать *impf*, испыта́ть *pf* судьбу́. **temptation** *n* собла́зн. **tempting** *adj* соблазни́тельный.

ten *adj* & *n* де́сять; (*number 10*) деся́тка. **tenth** *adj* & *n* деся́тый.

tenable *adj* (*logical*) разу́мный.

tenacious *adj* це́пкий. **tenacity** *n* це́пкость.

tenancy *n* (*renting*) наём помеще́ния; (*period*) срок аре́нды. **tenant** *n* аренда́тор.

tend[1] *vi* (*be apt*) име́ть скло́нность (**to** к*+dat*, *+inf*).

tend[2] *vt* (*look after*) уха́живать *impf* за*+instr*.

tendency *n* тенде́нция. **tendentious** *adj* тенденцио́зный.

tender[1] *vt* (*offer*) предлага́ть *impf*, предложи́ть *pf*; *vi* (*make ~ for*) подава́ть *impf*, пода́ть *pf* зая́вку (на торга́х); *n* предложе́ние; **legal ~** зако́нное платёжное сре́дство.

tender[2] *adj* (*delicate, affectionate*) не́жный. **tenderness** *n* не́жность.

tendon *n* сухожи́лие.

tendril *n* у́сик.

tenement *n* (*dwelling-house*) жило́й дом; **~-house** многокварти́рный дом.

tenet *n* до́гмат, при́нцип.

tennis *n* те́ннис.

tenor *n* (*direction*) направле́ние; (*purport*) смысл; (*mus*) те́нор.

tense[1] *n* вре́мя *neut*.

tense[2] *vt* напряга́ть *impf*, напря́чь *pf*; *adj* напряжённый. **tension** *n* напряже́ние.

tent *n* пала́тка.

tentacle *n* щу́пальце.

tentative *adj* (*experimental*) про́бный; (*preliminary*) предвари́тельный.

tenterhooks *n pl*: **be on ~** сиде́ть *impf* как на иго́лках.

tenth *see* **ten**

tenuous *adj* (*fig*) неубеди́тельный.

tenure *n* (*of property*) владе́ние; (*of office*) пребыва́ние в до́лжности; (*period*) срок; (*guaranteed employment*) несменя́емость.

tepid *adj* тепловáтый.

term *n* (*period*) срок; (*univ*) семе́стр; (*school*) че́тверть; (*technical word*) те́рмин; (*expression*) выраже́ние; *pl* (*conditions*) усло́вия *neut pl*; (*relations*) отноше́ния *neut pl*; **on good ~s** в хоро́ших отноше́ниях; **come to ~s with** (*resign o.s. to*) покоря́ться *impf*, покори́ться *pf* к+*dat*; *vt* называ́ть *impf*, назва́ть *pf*.

terminal *adj* коне́чный; (*med*) смерте́льный; *n* (*electr*) зажи́м; (*computer, aeron*) термина́л; (*terminus*) коне́чная остано́вка.

terminate *vt* & *i* конча́ть(ся) *impf*, ко́нчить(ся) *pf* (**in** +*instr*). **termination** *n* прекраще́ние.

terminology *n* терминоло́гия.

terminus *n* коне́чная остано́вка.

termite *n* терми́т.

terrace *n* терра́са; (*houses*) ряд домо́в.

terracotta *n* террако́та.

terrain *n* ме́стность.

terrestrial *adj* земно́й.

terrible *adj* ужа́сный. **terribly** *adv* ужа́сно.

terrier *n* терье́р.

terrific *adj* (*huge*) огро́мный; (*splendid*) потряса́ющий. **terrify** *vt* ужаса́ть *impf*, ужасну́ть *pf*.

territorial *adj* территориа́льный. **territory** *n* террито́рия.

terror *n* у́жас; (*person; polit*) терро́р. **terrorism** *n* террори́зм. **terrorist** *n* террори́ст, ~ка. **terrorize** *vt* терроризи́ровать *impf* & *pf*.

terse *adj* кра́ткий.

tertiary *adj* трети́чный; (*education*) вы́сший.

test *n* испыта́ние, про́ба; (*exam*) экза́мен; контро́льная рабо́та; (*analysis*) ана́лиз; **~-tube** проби́рка; *vt* (*try out*) испы́тывать *impf*, испыта́ть *pf*; (*check up on*) проверя́ть *impf*, прове́рить *pf*; (*give exam to*) экзаменова́ть *impf*, про~ *pf*.

testament *n* завеща́ние; **Old, New T~** Ве́тхий, Но́вый заве́т.

testicle *n* яи́чко.

testify *vi* свиде́тельствовать *impf* (**to** в по́льзу+*gen*; **against** про́тив+*gen*); *vt* (*declare*) заявля́ть *impf*, заяви́ть *pf*; (*be evidence of*) свиде́тельствовать о+*prep*.

testimonial *n* рекоменда́ция, характери́стика. **testimony** *n* свиде́тельство.

tetanus *n* столбня́к.

tetchy *adj* раздражи́тельный.

tête-à-tête *n* & *adv* тет-а-те́т.

tether *n*: **be at, come to the end of one's ~** дойти́ *pf* до то́чки; *vt* привя́зывать *impf*, привяза́ть *pf*.

text *n* текст. **textbook** *n* уче́бник.

textile *adj* тексти́льный; *n* ткань; *pl* тексти́ль *m* (*collect*).

textual *adj* текстово́й.

texture *n* тексту́ра.

than *conj* (*comparison*) чем; **other ~** (*except*) кро́ме+*gen*.

thank *vt* благодари́ть *impf*, по~ *pf* (**for** за+*acc*); **~ God** сла́ва Бо́гу; **~ you** спаси́бо; благодарю́ вас; *n pl* благода́рность; **~s to** (*good result*) благодаря́ *+dat*; (*bad result*) из-за*+gen*. **thankful** *adj* благода́рный. **thankless** *adj* неблагода́рный. **thanksgiving** *n* благодаре́ние.

that *demonstrative adj & pron* тот; ~ **which** тот кото́рый; *rel pron* кото́рый; *conj* что; (*purpose*) что́бы; *adv* так, до тако́й сте́пени.

thatched *adj* соло́менный.

thaw *vt* раста́пливать *impf*, растопи́ть *pf*; *vi* та́ять *impf*, рас~ *pf*; *n* о́ттепель.

the *def article, not translated*; *adv* тем; **the ... the ...** чем...тем; ~ **more** ~ **better** чем бо́льше, тем лу́чше.

theatre *n* теа́тр; (*lecture* ~) аудито́рия; (*operating* ~) операцио́нная *sb*; ~**-goer** театра́л. **theatrical** *adj* театра́льный.

theft *n* кра́жа.

their, theirs *poss pron* их; свой.

theme *n* те́ма.

themselves *pron* (*emph*) (они́) са́ми; (*refl*) себя́; -ся (*suffixed to vt*).

then *adv* (*at that time*) тогда́; (*after that*) пото́м; **now and** ~ вре́мя от вре́мени; *conj* в тако́м слу́чае, тогда́; *adj* тогда́шний; **by** ~ к тому́ вре́мени; **since** ~ с тех пор.

thence *adv* отту́да. **thenceforth, -forward** *adv* с того́/ э́того вре́мени.

theologian *n* тео́лог. **theological** *adj* теологи́ческий. **theology** *n* теоло́гия.

theorem *n* теоре́ма. **theoretical** *adj* теорети́ческий. **theorize** *vi* теоретизи́ровать *impf*. **theory** *n* тео́рия.

therapeutic *adj* терапевти́ческий. **therapist** *n* (*psychotherapist*) психотерапе́вт. **therapy** *n* терапи́я.

there *adv* (*place*) там; (*direction*) туда́; *int* вот!; ну!; ~ **is, are** есть, име́ется (-е́ются); ~ **you are** (*on giving sth*) пожа́луйста. **thereabouts** *adv* (*near*) побли́зости; (*approximately*) приблизи́тельно. **thereafter** *adv* по́сле э́того. **thereby** *adv* таки́м о́бразом. **therefore** *adv* поэ́тому. **therein** *adv* в э́том. **thereupon** *adv* зате́м.

thermal *adj* теплово́й, терми́ческий; (*underwear*) тёплый.

thermometer *n* термо́метр, гра́дусник. **thermos** *n* те́рмос. **thermostat** *n* термоста́т.

thesis *n* (*proposition*) те́зис; (*dissertation*) диссерта́ция.

they *pron* они́.

thick *adj* то́лстый, (*in measurements*) толщино́й в*+acc*; (*dense*) густо́й; (*stupid*) тупо́й; ~**-skinned** толстоко́жий. **thicken** *vt & i* утолща́ть(ся) *impf*, утолсти́ть(ся) *pf*; (*make, become denser*) сгуща́ть(ся) *impf*, сгусти́ть(ся) *pf*; *vi* (*become more intricate*) усложня́ться *impf*, усложни́ться *pf*. **thicket** *n* ча́ща. **thickness** *n* (*also dimension*) толщина́; (*density*) густота́; (*layer*) слой. **thickset** *adj* корена́стый.

thief *n* вор. **thieve** *vi* ворова́ть *impf*. **thievery** *n* воровство́.

thigh *n* бедро́.

thimble *n* напёрсток.

thin *adj* (*slender*; *not thick*) то́нкий; (*lean*) худо́й; (*too liquid*) жи́дкий; (*sparse*) ре́дкий; *vt* & *i* де́лать(ся) *impf*, с~ *pf* то́нким, жи́дким; *vi*: (*also* ~ *out*) реде́ть *impf*, по~ *pf*; *vt*: ~ **out** проре́живать *impf*, прореди́ть *pf*.

thing *n* вещь; (*object*) предме́т; (*matter*) де́ло.

think *vt* & *i* ду́мать *impf*, по~ *pf* (**about, of** о+*prep*); (*consider*) счита́ть *impf*, счесть *pf* (**to be** +*instr*, за+*acc*; **that** что); *vi* (*reflect, reason*) мы́слить *impf*; (*intend*) намерева́ться *impf* (*of doing* +*inf*); ~ **out** проду́мывать *impf*, проду́мать *pf*; ~ **over** обду́мывать *impf*, обду́мать *pf*; ~ **up, of** приду́мывать *impf*, приду́мать *pf*. **thinker** *n* мысли́тель *m*. **thinking** *adj* мы́слящий; *n* (*reflection*) размышле́ние; **to my way of** ~ по моему́ мне́нию.

third *adj* & *n* тре́тий; (*fraction*) треть; **T~ World** стра́ны *f pl* тре́тьего ми́ра.

thirst *n* жа́жда (**for** +*gen* (*fig*)); *vi* (*fig*) жа́ждать *impf* (**for** +*gen*). **thirsty** *adj*: **be** ~ хоте́ть *impf* пить.

thirteen *adj* & *n* трина́дцать. **thirteenth** *adj* & *n* трина́дцатый.

thirtieth *adj* & *n* тридца́тый. **thirty** *adj* & *n* три́дцать; *pl* (*decade*) тридца́тые го́ды (-до́в) *m pl*.

this *demonstrative adj* & *pron* э́тот; **like** ~ вот так; ~ **morning** сего́дня у́тром.

thistle *n* чертополо́х.

thither *adv* туда́.

thorn *n* шип. **thorny** *adj* колю́чий; (*fig*) терни́стый.

thorough *adj* основа́тельный; (*complete*) соверше́нный. **thoroughbred** *adj* чистокро́вный. **thoroughfare** *n* прое́зд; (*walking*) прохо́д. **thoroughgoing** *adj* радика́льный. **thoroughly** *adv* (*completely*) соверше́нно. **thoroughness** *n* основа́тельность.

though *conj* хотя́; несмотря́ на то, что; **as** ~ как бу́дто; *adv* одна́ко.

thought *n* мысль; (*meditation*) размышле́ние; (*intention*) наме́рение; *pl* (*opinion*) мне́ние. **thoughtful** *adj* заду́мчивый; (*considerate*) внима́тельный. **thoughtless** *adj* необду́манный; (*inconsiderate*) невнима́тельный.

thousand *adj* & *n* ты́сяча. **thousandth** *adj* & *n* ты́сячный.

thrash *vt* бить *impf*, по~ *pf*; ~ **out** (*discuss*) обстоя́тельно обсужда́ть *impf*, обсуди́ть *pf*; *vi*: ~ **about** мета́ться *impf*. **thrashing** *n* (*beating*) взбу́чка (*coll*).

thread *n* ни́тка, нить (*also fig*); (*of screw etc.*) резьба́; *vt* (*needle*) продева́ть *impf*, проде́ть *pf* ни́тку в+*acc*; (*beads*) нани́зывать *impf*, наниза́ть *pf*; ~ **one's way** пробира́ться *impf*, пробра́ться *pf* (**through** че́рез+*acc*). **threadbare** *adj* потёртый.

threat *n* угро́за. **threaten** *vt* угрожа́ть *impf*, грози́ть *impf*, при~ *pf* (*person* +*dat*; **with** +*instr*; *to do* +*inf*).

three *adj* & *n* три; (*number 3*) тро́йка; ~**-dimensional** трёхме́рный; ~**-quarters** три че́тверти. **threefold** *adj* тройно́й; *adv* втройне́. **threesome** *n* тро́йка.

thresh *vt* молоти́ть *impf*.

threshold *n* поро́г.
thrice *adv* три́жды.
thrift *n* бережли́вость. **thrifty** *adj* бережли́вый.
thrill *n* тре́пет; *vt* восхища́ть *impf*, восхити́ть *pf*; **be thrilled** быть в восто́рге. **thriller** *n* приключе́нческий, детекти́вный (*novel*) рома́н, (*film*) фильм. **thrilling** *adj* захва́тывающий.
thrive *vi* процвета́ть *impf*.
throat *n* го́рло.
throb *vi* (*heart*) си́льно би́ться *impf*; пульси́ровать *impf*; *n* бие́ние; пульса́ция.
throes *n pl*: **in the ~** в мучи́тельных попы́тках.
thrombosis *n* тромбо́з.
throne *n* трон, престо́л; **come to the ~** вступа́ть *impf*, вступи́ть *pf* на престо́л.
throng *n* толпа́; *vi* толпи́ться *impf*; *vt* заполня́ть *impf*, запо́лнить *pf*.
throttle *n* (*tech*) дро́ссель *m*; *vt* (*strangle*) души́ть *impf*, за~ *pf*; (*tech*) дроссели́ровать *impf* & *pf*; **~ down** сбавля́ть *impf*, сба́вить *pf* газ.
through *prep* (*across, via, ~ opening*) че́рез+*acc*; (*esp ~ thick of*) сквозь+*acc*; (*air, streets etc.*) по+*dat*; (*agency*) посре́дством+*gen*; (*reason*) из-за+*gen*; *adv* насквозь; (*from beginning to end*) до конца́; **be ~ with** (*sth*) ока́нчивать *impf*, око́нчить *pf*; (*s.o.*) порыва́ть *impf*, порва́ть *pf* с+*instr*; **put ~** (*on telephone*) соединя́ть *impf*, соедини́ть *pf*; **~ and ~** соверше́нно; *adj* (*train*) прямо́й; (*traffic*) сквозно́й. **throughout** *adv* повсю́ду, во всех отноше́ниях; *prep* по всему́ (всей, всему́; *pl* всем)+*dat*; (*from beginning to end*) с нача́ла до конца́+*gen*.
throw *n* бросо́к; *vt* броса́ть *impf*, бро́сить *pf*; (*confuse*) смуща́ть *impf*, смути́ть *pf*; (*rider*) сбра́сывать *impf*, сбро́сить *pf*; (*party*) устра́ивать *impf*, устро́ить *pf*; **~ o.s. into** броса́ться *impf*, бро́ситься *pf* в+*acc*; **~ away, out** выбра́сывать *impf*, вы́бросить *pf*; **~ down** сбра́сывать *impf*, сбро́сить *pf*; **~ in** (*add*) добавля́ть *impf*, доба́вить *pf*; (*sport*) вбра́сывать *impf*, вбро́сить *pf*; **~-in** вбра́сывание мяча́; **~ off** сбра́сывать *impf*, сбро́сить *pf*; **~ open** распа́хивать *impf*, распахну́ть *pf*; **~ out** (*see also* **~** *away*) (*expel*) выгоня́ть *impf*, вы́гнать *pf*; (*reject*) отверга́ть *impf*, отве́ргнуть *pf*; **~ over, ~ up** (*abandon*) броса́ть *impf*, бро́сить *pf*; **~ up** подбра́сывать *impf*, подбро́сить *pf*; (*vomit*) рвать *impf*, вы́~ *pf impers*; **he threw up** его́ вы́рвало.
thrush *n* (*bird*) дрозд.
thrust *n* (*shove*) толчо́к; (*tech*) тя́га; *vt* (*shove*) толка́ть *impf*, толкну́ть *pf*; (**~** *into, out of; give quickly, carelessly*) сова́ть *impf*, су́нуть *pf*.
thud *n* глухо́й звук; *vi* па́дать *impf*, *pf* с глухи́м сту́ком.
thug *n* головоре́з (*coll*).
thumb *n* большо́й па́лец; **under the ~ of** под башмако́м у+*gen*; *vt*: **~ through** перели́стывать *impf*, перелиста́ть *pf*; **~ a lift** голосова́ть *impf*, про~ *pf*.
thump *n* (*blow*) тяжёлый

уда́р; (*thud*) глухо́й звук, стук; *vt* колоти́ть *impf*, по~ *pf* в+*acc*, по+*dat*; *vi* колоти́ться *impf*.

thunder *n* гром; *vi* греме́ть *impf*; **it thunders** гром греми́т. **thunderbolt** *n* уда́р мо́лнии. **thunderous** *adj* громово́й. **thunderstorm** *n* гроза́. **thundery** *adj* грозово́й.

Thursday *n* четве́рг.

thus *adv* так, таки́м о́бразом.

thwart *vt* меша́ть *impf*, по~ *pf* +*dat*; (*plans*) расстра́ивать *impf*, расстро́ить *pf*.

thyme *n* тимья́н.

thyroid *n* (~ *gland*) щитови́дная железа́.

tiara *n* тиа́ра.

tick *n* (*noise*) ти́канье; (*mark*) пти́чка; *vi* ти́кать *impf*, ти́кнуть *pf*; *vt* отмеча́ть *impf*, отме́тить *pf* пти́чкой; ~ **off** (*scold*) отде́лывать *impf*, отде́лать *pf*.

ticket *n* биле́т; (*label*) ярлы́к; (*season* ~) ка́рточка; (*cloakroom* ~) номеро́к; (*receipt*) квита́нция; ~ **collector** контролёр; ~ **office** (биле́тная) ка́сса.

tickle *n* щеко́тка; *vt* щекота́ть *impf*, по~ *pf*; (*amuse*) весели́ть *impf*, по~, раз~ *pf*; *vi* щекота́ть *impf*, по~ *pf* *impers*; **my throat ~s** у меня́ щеко́чет в го́рле. **ticklish** *adj* (*fig*) щекотли́вый; **to be ~** боя́ться *impf* щеко́тки.

tidal *adj* прили́во-отли́вный; ~ **wave** прили́вная волна́.

tide *n* прили́в и отли́в; **high ~** прили́в; **low ~** отли́в; (*current*, *tendency*) тече́ние; **the ~ turns** (*fig*) собы́тия принима́ют друго́й оборо́т; *vt*: ~ **over** помога́ть *impf*, помо́чь *pf* +*dat of person* спра́виться (*difficulty* с+*instr*); **will this money ~ you over?** вы протя́нете с э́тими деньга́ми?

tidiness *n* аккура́тность. **tidy** *adj* аккура́тный; (*considerable*) поря́дочный; *vt* убира́ть *impf*, убра́ть *pf*; приводи́ть *impf*, привести́ *pf* в поря́док.

tie *n* (*garment*) га́лстук; (*cord*) завя́зка; (*link*; *tech*) связь; (*equal points etc.*) ра́вный счёт; **end in a ~** зака́нчиваться *impf*, зако́нчиться *pf* вничью́; (*burden*) обу́за; *pl* (*bonds*) у́зы (уз) *pl*; *vt* свя́зывать *impf*, связа́ть *pf* (*also fig*); (~ *up*) завя́зывать *impf*, завяза́ть *pf*; (*restrict*) ограни́чивать *impf*, ограни́чить *pf*; ~ **down** (*fasten*) привя́зывать *impf*, привяза́ть *pf*; ~ **up** (*tether*) привя́зывать *impf*, привяза́ть *pf*; (*parcel*) перевя́зывать *impf*, перевяза́ть *pf*; *vi* (*be ~d*) завя́зываться *impf*, завяза́ться *pf*; (*sport*) сыгра́ть *pf* вничью́; ~ **in, up, with** совпада́ть *impf*, совпа́сть *pf* с+*instr*.

tier *n* ряд, я́рус.

tiff *n* размо́лвка.

tiger *n* тигр.

tight *adj* (*cramped*) те́сный; у́зкий; (*strict*) стро́гий; (*taut*) туго́й; ~ **corner** (*fig*) тру́дное положе́ние. **tighten** *vt & i* натя́гиваться *impf*, натяну́ться *pf*; (*clench*, *contract*) сжима́ть(ся) *impf*, сжа́ться *pf*; ~ **one's belt** поту́же затя́гивать *impf*, затяну́ть *pf* по́яс (*also fig*); ~ **up** (*discipline etc.*) подтя́гивать *impf*, подтяну́ть *pf* (*coll*). **tightly** *adv* (*strongly*) прóчно; (*closely, cramped*) тéсно. **tightrope** *n* натя́нутый канáт. **tights** *n pl* колгóтки (-ток) *pl.*

tile *n* (*roof*) черепи́ца (*also collect*); (*decorative*) кáфель *m* (*also collect*); *vt* крыть *impf*, по~ *pf* черепи́цей, кáфелем. **tiled** *adj* (*roof*) черепи́чный; (*floor*) кáфельный.

till[1] *prep* до+*gen*; **not** ~ тóлько (**Friday** в пя́тницу; **the next day** на слéдующий день); *conj* покá не; **not** ~ тóлько когдá.

till[2] *n* кáсса.

till[3] *vt* возделывать *impf*, воздéлать *pf.*

tiller *n* (*naut*) рýмпель *m.*

tilt *n* наклóн; **at full** ~ пóлным хóдом; *vt* & *i* наклоня́ть(ся) *impf*, наклони́ть(ся) *pf*; (*heel* (*over*)) крени́ть(ся) *impf*, на~ *pf.*

timber *n* лесоматериáл.

time *n* врéмя *neut*; (*occasion*) раз; (*mus*) такт; (*sport*) тайм; *pl* (*period*) временá *pl*; (*in comparison*) раз; **five** ~**s as big** в пять раз бóльше; (*multiplication*) **four** ~**s four** четы́режды четы́ре; ~ **and** ~ **again,** ~ **after** ~ не раз, ты́сячу раз; **at a** ~ рáзом, одноврéмéнно; **at the** ~ в э́то врéмя; **at** ~**s** временáми; **at the same** ~ в то же врéмя; **before my** ~ до меня́; **for a long** ~ дóлго; (*up to now*) давнó; **for the** ~ **being** покá; **from** ~ **to** ~ врéмя от врéмени; **in** ~ (*early enough*) вó-время; (*with* ~) со врéменем; **in good** ~ заблаговрéменно; **in** ~ **with** в такт +*dat*; **in no** ~ моментáльно; **on** ~ вó-время; **one at a** ~ по одномý; **be in** ~ успевáть *impf*, успéть *pf* (**for** к+*dat*, на+*acc*); **have** ~ **to** (*manage*) успевáть *impf*, успéть *pf* +*inf*; **have a good** ~ хорошó проводи́ть *impf*, провести́ *pf* врéмя; **it is** ~ порá (**to** +*inf*); **what is the** ~? котóрый час?; ~ **bomb** бóмба замéдленного дéйствия; ~**-consuming** отнимáющий мнóго врéмени; ~ **difference** рáзница во врéмени; ~**-lag** отставáние во врéмени; ~ **zone** часовóй пóяс; *vt* (*choose* ~) выбирáть *impf*, вы́брать *pf* врéмя +*gen*; (*ascertain* ~ *of*) измеря́ть *impf*, измéрить *pf* врéмя +*gen*. **timeless** *adj* вéчный. **timely** *adj* своеврéменный. **timetable** *n* расписáние; грáфик.

timid *adj* рóбкий.

tin *n* (*metal*) óлово; (*container*) бáнка; (*cake*-~) фóрма; (*baking* ~) прóтивень *m*; ~ **foil** оловя́нная фольгá; ~**-opener** консéрвный нож; ~**ned food** консéрвы (-вов) *pl.*

tinge *n* оттéнок; *vt* (*also fig*) слегкá окрáшивать *impf*, окрáсить *pf.*

tingle *vi* (*sting*) колóть *impf impers*; **my fingers** ~ у меня́ кóлет пáльцы; **his nose** ~**d with the cold** морóз пощи́пывал емý нос; (*burn*) горéть *impf.*

tinker *vi*: ~ **with** вози́ться *impf* с+*instr.*

tinkle *n* звон, звя́канье; *vi* (& *t*) звенéть *impf* (+*instr*).

tinsel *n* мишурá.

tint *n* оттéнок; *vt* подкрáшивать *impf*, подкрáсить *pf.*

tiny *adj* крóшечный.

tip[1] *n* (*end*) кóнчик.

tip[2] *n* (*money*) чаевы́е (-ы́х) *pl*; (*advice*) сове́т; (*dump*) сва́лка; *vt* & *i* (*tilt*) наклоня́ть(ся) *impf*, наклони́ть(ся) *pf*; (*give* ~) дава́ть *impf*, дать *pf* (*person* +*dat*; *money* де́ньги на чай, *information* ча́стную информа́цию); ~ **out** выва́ливать *impf*, вы́валить *pf*; ~ **over, up** (*vt* & *i*) опроки́дывать(ся) *impf*, опроки́нуть(ся) *pf*.
Tippex *n* (*propr*) бели́ла.
tipple *n* напи́ток.
tipsy *adj* подвы́пивший.
tiptoe *n*: **on** ~ на цы́почках.
tip-top *adj* превосхо́дный.
tirade *n* тира́да.
tire *vt* (*weary*) утомля́ть *impf*, утоми́ть *pf*; *vi* утомля́ться *impf*, утоми́ться *pf*. **tired** *adj* уста́лый; **be** ~ **of**: **I am** ~ **of him** он мне надое́л; **I am** ~ **of playing** мне надое́ло игра́ть; ~ **out** изму́ченный. **tiredness** *n* уста́лость. **tireless** *adj* неутоми́мый. **tiresome** *adj* надое́дливый. **tiring** *adj* утоми́тельный.
tissue *n* ткань; (*handkerchief*) бума́жная салфе́тка. **tissue-paper** *n* папиро́сная бума́га.
tit[1] *n* (*bird*) сини́ца.
tit[2] *n*: ~ **for tat** зуб за́ зуб.
titbit *n* ла́комый кусо́к; (*news*) пика́нтная но́вость.
titillate *vt* щекота́ть *impf*, по~ *pf*.
title *n* (*of book etc.*) загла́вие; (*rank*) зва́ние; (*sport*) зва́ние чемпио́на; ~**-holder** чемпио́н; ~**-page** ти́тульный лист; ~ **role** загла́вная роль. **titled** *adj* титуло́ванный.
titter *n* хихи́канье; *vi* хихи́кать *impf*, хихи́кнуть *pf*.
to *prep* (*town, a country, theatre, school, etc.*) в+*acc*; (*the sea, the moon, the ground, post-office, meeting, concert, north, etc.*) на+*acc*; (*the doctor; towards, up* ~; ~ *one's surprise etc.*) к+*dat*; (*with accompaniment of*) под+*acc*; (*in toast*) за+*acc*; (*time*): **ten minutes** ~ **three** без десяти́ три; (*compared with*) в сравне́нии с+*instr*; **it is ten** ~ **one that** де́вять из десяти́ за то, что; ~ **the left (right)** нале́во (напра́во); (*in order to*) что́бы +*inf*; *adv*: **shut the door** ~ закро́йте дверь; **come** ~ приходи́ть *impf*, прийти́ *pf* в созна́ние; ~ **and fro** взад и вперёд.
toad *n* жа́ба. **toadstool** *n* пога́нка.
toast *n* (*bread*) поджа́ренный хлеб; (*drink*) тост; *vt* (*bread*) поджа́ривать *impf*, поджа́рить *pf*; (*drink*) пить *impf*, вы́~ *pf* за здоро́вье +*gen*. **toaster** *n* то́стер.
tobacco *n* таба́к. **tobacconist's** *n* (*shop*) таба́чный магази́н.
toboggan *n* са́ни (-не́й) *pl*; *vi* ката́ться *impf* на саня́х.
today *adv* сего́дня; (*nowadays*) в на́ши дни; *n* сего́дняшний день *m*; ~**'s newspaper** сего́дняшняя газе́та.
toddler *n* малы́ш.
toe *n* па́лец ноги́; (*of sock etc.*) носо́к; *vt*: ~ **the line** (*fig*) ходи́ть *indet* по стру́нке.
toffee *n* (*substance*) ири́с; (*a single* ~) ири́ска.
together *adv* вме́сте; (*simultaneously*) одновре́ме́нно.
toil *n* тяжёлый труд; *vi* труди́ться *impf*.
toilet *n* туале́т; ~ **paper** туале́тная бума́га. **toiletries** *n*

pl туалéтные принадлéжности *f pl*.

token *n* (*sign*) знак; (*coin substitute*) жетóн; **as a ~ of** в знак +*gen*; *attrib* символи́ческий.

tolerable *adj* терпи́мый; (*satisfactory*) удовлетвори́тельный. **tolerance** *n* терпи́мость. **tolerant** *adj* терпи́мый. **tolerate** *vt* терпéть *impf*, по~ *pf*; (*allow*) допускáть *impf*, допусти́ть *pf*. **toleration** *n* терпи́мость.

toll[1] *n* (*duty*) пóшлина; **take its ~** скáзываться *impf*, сказáться *pf* (**on** на+*prep*).

toll[2] *vi* звони́ть *impf*, по~ *pf*.

tom(-cat) *n* кот.

tomato *n* помидóр; *attrib* томáтный.

tomb *n* моги́ла. **tombstone** *n* надгрóбный кáмень *m*.

tomboy *n* сорванéц.

tome *n* том.

tomorrow *adv* зáвтра; *n* зáвтрашний день *m*; **~ morning** зáвтра ýтром; **the day after ~** послезáвтра; **see you ~** до зáвтра.

ton *n* тóнна; (*pl*, *lots*) мáсса.

tone *n* тон; *vt*: **~ down** смягчáть *impf*, смягчи́ть *pf*; **~ up** тонизи́ровать *impf* & *pf*.

tongs *n* щипцы́ (-цóв) *pl*.

tongue *n* язы́к; **~-in-cheek** с насмéшкой, ирони́чески; **~-tied** косноязы́чный; **~-twister** скороговóрка.

tonic *n* (*med*) тонизи́рующее срéдство; (*mus*) тóника; (*drink*) напи́ток «тóник».

tonight *adv* сегóдня вéчером.

tonnage *n* тоннáж.

tonsil *n* минда́лина. **tonsillitis** *n* тонзилли́т.

too *adv* сли́шком; (*also*) тáкже, тóже; (*very*) óчень; (*moreover*) к томý же; **none ~** не сли́шком.

tool *n* инструмéнт; (*fig*) орýдие.

toot *n* гудóк; *vi* гудéть *impf*.

tooth *n* зуб; (*tech*) зубéц; *attrib* зубнóй; **~-brush** зубнáя щётка. **toothache** *n* зубнáя боль. **toothless** *adj* беззýбый. **toothpaste** *n* зубнáя пáста. **toothpick** *n* зубочи́стка. **toothy** *adj* зубáстый (*coll*).

top[1] *n* (*toy*) волчóк.

top[2] *n* (*of object*; *fig*) верх; (*of hill etc.*) верши́на; (*of tree*) верхýшка; (*of head*) макýшка; (*lid*) кры́шка; (*upper part*) вéрхняя часть; **~ hat** цили́ндр; **~-heavy** перевéшивающий в своéй вéрхней чáсти; **~-secret** совершéнно секрéтный; **on ~ of** (*position*) на+*prep*, сверх+*gen*; (*on to*) на+*acc*; **on ~ of everything** сверх всегó; **from ~ to bottom** свéрху дóнизу; **at the ~ of one's voice** во весь гóлос; **at ~ speed** во весь опóр; *adj* вéрхний, вы́сший, сáмый высóкий; (*foremost*) пéрвый; *vt* (*cover*) покрывáть *impf*, покры́ть *pf*; (*exceed*) превосходи́ть *impf*, превзойти́ *pf*; (*cut ~ off*) обрезáть *impf*, обрéзать *pf* верхýшку +*gen*; **~ up** (*with liquid*) доливáть *impf*, доли́ть *pf*.

topic *n* тéма, предмéт. **topical** *adj* актуáльный.

topless *adj* с обнажённой грýдью.

topmost *adj* сáмый вéрхний; сáмый вáжный.

topographical *adj* топографи́ческий. **topography** *n* топогра́фия.

topple *vt* & *i* опроки́дывать(ся) *impf*, опроки́нуть(ся) *pf*.

topsy-turvy *adj* повёрнутый вверх дном; (*disorderly*) беспоря́дочный; *adv* вверх дном.

torch *n* электри́ческий фона́рь *m*; (*flaming*) фа́кел.

torment *n* муче́ние, му́ка; *vt* му́чить *impf*, за~, из~ *pf*.

tornado *n* торна́до *neut indecl*.

torpedo *n* торпе́да; *vt* торпеди́ровать *impf* & *pf*.

torrent *n* пото́к. **torrential** *adj* (*rain*) проливно́й.

torso *n* ту́ловище; (*art*) торс.

tortoise *n* черепа́ха. **tortoiseshell** *n* черепа́ха.

tortuous *adj* изви́листый.

torture *n* пы́тка; (*fig*) му́ка; *vt* пыта́ть *impf*; (*torment*) му́чить *impf*, за~, из~ *pf*.

toss *n* бросо́к; **win (lose) the ~** (не) выпада́ть *impf*, вы́пасть *pf* жре́бий *impers* (**I won the ~** мне вы́пал жре́бий); *vt* броса́ть *impf*, бро́сить *pf*; (*coin*) подбра́сывать *impf*, подбро́сить *pf*; (*head*) вски́дывать *impf*, вски́нуть *pf*; (*salad*) переме́шивать *impf*, перемеша́ть *pf*; *vi* (*in bed*) мета́ться *impf*; **~ aside, away** отбра́сывать *impf*, отбро́сить *pf*; **~ up** броса́ть *impf*, бро́сить *pf* жре́бий.

tot[1] *n* (*child*) малы́ш; (*of liquor*) глото́к.

tot[2]: **~ up** (*vt*) скла́дывать *impf*, сложи́ть *pf*; (*vi*) равня́ться *impf* (**to** +*dat*).

total *n* ито́г, су́мма; *adj* о́бщий; (*complete*) по́лный; **in ~** в це́лом, вме́сте; *vt* подсчи́тывать *impf*, подсчита́ть *pf*; *vi* равня́ться *impf* +*dat*.

totalitarian *adj* тоталита́рный. **totality** *n* вся су́мма целико́м; **the ~ of** весь. **totally** *adv* соверше́нно.

totter *vi* шата́ться *impf*.

touch *n* прикоснове́ние; (*sense*) осяза́ние; (*shade*) отте́нок; (*taste*) при́вкус; (*small amount*) чу́точка; (*of illness*) лёгкий при́ступ; **get in ~ with** свя́зываться *impf*, связа́ться *pf* с+*instr*; **keep in (lose) ~ with** подде́рживать *impf*, поддержа́ть *pf* (теря́ть *impf*, по~ *pf*) связь, конта́кт с+*instr*; **put the finishing ~es to** отде́лывать *impf*, отде́лать *pf*; *vt* (*lightly*) прикаса́ться *impf*, прикосну́ться *pf* к+*dat*; каса́ться *impf*, косну́ться *pf* +*gen*; (*also disturb*; *affect*) тро́гать *impf*, тро́нуть *pf*; (*be comparable with*) идти́ *impf* в сравне́нии с+*instr*; *vi* (*be contiguous*; *come into contact*) соприкаса́ться *impf*, соприкосну́ться *pf*; **~ down** приземля́ться *impf*, приземли́ться *pf*; **~down** поса́дка; **~ (up)on** (*fig*) каса́ться *impf*, косну́ться *pf* +*gen*; **~ up** поправля́ть *impf*, попра́вить *pf*. **touched** *adj* тро́нутый. **touchiness** *n* оби́дчивость. **touching** *adj* тро́гательный. **touchstone** *n* про́бный ка́мень *m*. **touchy** *adj* оби́дчивый.

tough *adj* жёсткий; (*durable*) про́чный; (*difficult*) тру́дный; (*hardy*) выно́сливый. **toughen** *vt* & *i* де́лать(ся) *impf*, с~ *pf* жёстким.

tour *n* (*journey*) путеше́ствие, пое́здка; (*excursion*) экску́рсия; (*of artistes*) гастро́ли *f pl*; (*of duty*) объе́зд; *vi* (& *t*) путешéствовать *impf* (по +*dat*); (*theat*) гастроли́ровать *impf*. **tourism** *n* тури́зм. **tourist** *n* тури́ст, ~ка.

tournament *n* турни́р.

tousle *vt* взъеро́шивать *impf*, взъеро́шить *pf* (*coll*).

tout *n* зазывáла *m*; (*ticket* ~) жучóк.

tow *vt* букси́ровать *impf*; *n*: **on** ~ на букси́ре.

towards *prep* к+*dat*.

towel *n* полотéнце.

tower *n* бáшня; *vi* вы́ситься *impf*, возвышáться *impf* (**above** над+*instr*).

town *n* гóрод; *attrib* городскóй; ~ **hall** рáтуша. **townsman** *n* горожáнин.

toxic *adj* токси́ческий

toy *n* игру́шка; *vi*: ~ **with** (*sth in hands*) вертéть *impf* в рукáх; (*trifle with*) игрáть *impf* (с)+*instr*.

trace *n* след; *vt* (*track* (*down*)) выслéживать *impf*, вы́следить *pf*; (*copy*) кальки́ровать *impf*, с~ *pf*; ~ **out** (*plan*) набрáсывать *impf*, набросáть *pf*; (*map, diagram*) черти́ть *impf*, на~ *pf*.

tracing-paper *n* кáлька.

track *n* (*path*) дорóжка; (*mark*) след; (*rly*) путь *m*, (*sport, on tape*) дорóжка; (*on record*) зáпись; ~ **suit** тренирóвочный костю́м; **off the beaten** ~ в глуши́; **go off the** ~ (*fig*) отклоня́ться *impf*, отклони́ться *pf* от тéмы; **keep** ~ **of** следи́ть *impf* за+*instr*; **lose** ~ **of** теря́ть *impf*, по~ *pf* след+*gen*; *vt* прослéживать *impf*, проследи́ть *pf*; ~ **down** выслéживать *impf*, вы́следить *pf*.

tract[1] *n* (*land*) пространство.

tract[2] *n* (*pamphlet*) брошю́ра.

tractor *n* трáктор.

trade *n* торгóвля; (*occupation*) профéссия, ремеслó; ~ **mark** фабри́чная мáрка; ~ **union** профсою́з; ~-**unionist** член профсою́за; *vi* торговáть *impf* (**in** +*instr*); *vt* (*swap like things*) обмéниваться *impf*, обменя́ться *pf* +*instr*; (~ *for sth different*) обмéнивать *impf*, обменя́ть *pf* (**for** на+*acc*); ~ **in** сдавáть *impf*, сдать *pf* в счёт поку́пки нóвого. **trader, tradesman** *n* торгóвец. **trading** *n* торгóвля.

tradition *n* тради́ция. **traditional** *adj* традициóнный. **traditionally** *adv* по тради́ции.

traffic *n* движéние; (*trade*) торгóвля; ~ **jam** прóбка; *vi* торговáть *impf* (**in** +*instr*). **trafficker** *n* торгóвец (**in** +*instr*). **traffic-lights** *n pl* светофóр.

tragedy *n* трагéдия. **tragic** *adj* траги́ческий.

trail *n* (*trace, track*) след; (*path*) тропи́нка; *vt* (*track*) выслéживать *impf*, вы́следить *pf*; *vt* & *i* (*drag*) таскáть(ся) *indet*, тащи́ть(ся) *det*. **trailer** *n* (*on vehicle*) прицéп; (*cin*) (кино)рóлик.

train *n* пóезд; (*of dress*) шлейф; *vt* (*instruct*) обучáть *impf*, обучи́ть *pf* (**in** +*dat*); (*prepare*) готóвить *impf* (**for** к+*dat*); (*sport*) тренировáть *impf*, на~ *pf*; (*animals*) дрессировáть *impf*, вы́~ *pf*; (*aim*) наводи́ть *impf*, навести́ *pf*; (*plant*) направля́ть *impf*, напрáвить *pf* рост+*gen*; *vi* приготáвливаться *impf*,

пригото́виться *pf* (**for** к+*dat*); (*sport*) тренирова́ться *impf*, на~ *pf*. **trainee** *n* стажёр, практика́нт. **trainer** *n* (*sport*) тре́нер; (*of animals*) дресси-ро́вщик; (*shoe*) кроссо́вка. **training** *n* обуче́ние; (*sport*) трениро́вка; (*of animals*) дрес-сиро́вка; **~-college** (*teachers'*) педагоги́ческий институ́т.
traipse *vi* таска́ться *indet*, тащи́ться *det*.
trait *n* черта́.
traitor *n* преда́тель *m*, ~ница.
trajectory *n* траекто́рия.
tram *n* трамва́й.
tramp *n* (*vagrant*) бродя́га *m*; *vi* (*walk heavily*) то́пать *impf*. **trample** *vt* топта́ть *impf*, по~, ис~ *pf*; ~ **down** выта́птывать *impf*, вы́топтать *pf*; ~ **on** (*fig*) попира́ть *impf*, попра́ть *pf*.
trampoline *n* бату́т.
trance *n* транс.
tranquil *adj* споко́йный. **tranquillity** *n* споко́йствие. **tranquillize** *vt* успока́ивать *impf*, успоко́ить *pf*. **tranquillizer** *n* транквилиза́тор.
transact *vt* (*business*) вести́ *impf*; (*a deal*) заключа́ть *impf*, заключи́ть *pf*. **transaction** *n* де́ло, сде́лка; *pl* (*publications*) труды́ *m pl*.
transatlantic *adj* трансатланти́ческий.
transcend *vt* превосходи́ть *impf*, превзойти́ *pf*. **transcendental** *adj* (*philos.*) трансцендента́льный.
transcribe *vt* (*copy out*) перепи́сывать *impf*, переписа́ть *pf*. **transcript** *n* ко́пия. **transcription** *n* (*copy*) ко́пия.
transfer *n* (*of objects*) перено́с, перемеще́ние; (*of money*; *of people*) перево́д; (*of property*) переда́ча; (*design*) переводна́я карти́нка; *vt* (*objects*) переноси́ть *impf*, перенести́ *pf*; перемеща́ть *impf*, перемести́ть *pf*; (*money*; *people*; *design*) переводи́ть *impf*, перевести́ *pf*; (*property*) передава́ть *impf*, переда́ть *pf*; *vi* (*to different job*) переходи́ть *impf*, перейти́ *pf*; (*change trains etc.*) переса́живаться *impf*, пересе́сть *pf*. **transferable** *adj* допуска́ющий переда́чу.
transfix *vt* (*fig*) прико́вывать *impf*, прикова́ть *pf* к ме́сту.
transform *vt* & *i* преобразо́вывать(ся) *impf*, преобразова́ть(ся) *pf*; ~ **into** *vt* (*i*) превраща́ть(ся) *impf*, преврати́ть(ся) *pf* в+*acc*. **transformation** *n* преобразова́ние; превраще́ние. **transformer** *n* трансформа́тор.
transfusion *n* перелива́ние (кро́ви).
transgress *vt* наруша́ть *impf*, нару́шить *pf*; *vi* (*sin*) греши́ть *impf*, за~ *pf*. **transgression** *n* наруше́ние; (*sin*) грех.
transience *n* мимолётность. **transient** *adj* мимолётный.
transistor *n* транзи́стор; ~ **radio** транзи́сторный приёмник.
transit *n* транзи́т; **in** ~ (*goods*) при перево́зке; (*person*) по пути́; ~ **camp** транзи́тный ла́герь *m*. **transition** *n* перехо́д. **transitional** *adj* перехо́дный. **transitive** *adj* перехо́дный. **transitory** *adj* мимолётный.
translate *vt* переводи́ть *impf*, перевести́ *pf*. **translation** *n*

перево́д. **translator** *n* перево́дчик.

translucent *adj* полупрозра́чный.

transmission *n* переда́ча. **transmit** *vt* передава́ть *impf*, переда́ть *pf*. **transmitter** *n* (радио)переда́тчик.

transparency *n* (*phot*) диапозити́в. **transparent** *adj* прозра́чный.

transpire *vi* (*become known*) обнару́живаться *impf*, обнару́житься *pf*; (*occur*) случа́ться *impf*, случи́ться *pf*.

transplant *vt* переса́живать *impf*, пересади́ть *pf*; (*med*) де́лать *impf*, с~ *pf* переса́дку+*gen*; *n* (*med*) переса́дка.

transport *n* (*various senses*) тра́нспорт; (*conveyance*) перево́зка; *attrib* тра́нспортный; *vt* перевози́ть *impf*, перевезти́ *pf*. **transportation** *n* тра́нспорт, перево́зка.

transpose *vt* переставля́ть *impf*, переста́вить *pf*; (*mus*) транспони́ровать *impf* & *pf*. **transposition** *n* перестано́вка; (*mus*) транспониро́вка.

transverse *adj* попере́чный.

transvestite *n* трансвести́т.

trap *n* лову́шка (*also fig*), западня́; *vt* (*catch*) лови́ть *impf*, пойма́ть *pf* (в лову́шку); (*jam*) защемля́ть *impf*, защеми́ть *pf*. **trapdoor** *n* люк.

trapeze *n* трапе́ция.

trapper *n* звероло́в.

trappings *n pl* (*fig*) (*exterior attributes*) вне́шние атрибу́ты *m pl*; (*adornments*) украше́ния *neut pl*.

trash *n* дрянь (*coll*). **trashy** *adj* дрянно́й.

trauma *n* тра́вма. **traumatic** *adj* травмати́ческий.

travel *n* путеше́ствие; ~ **agency** бюро́ *neut indecl* путеше́ствий; ~ **sick: be ~-sick** ука́чивать *impf*, ука-ча́ть *pf impers +acc*; **I am ~-sick in cars** меня́ в маши́не ука́чивает; *vi* путеше́ствовать *impf*; *vt* объезжа́ть *impf*, объе́хать *pf*. **traveller** *n* путеше́ственник; (*salesman*) коммивояжёр; **~'s cheque** тури́стский чек.

traverse *vt* пересека́ть *impf*, пересе́чь *pf*.

travesty *n* паро́дия.

trawler *n* тра́улер.

tray *n* подно́с; **in- (out-)~** корзи́нка для входя́щих (исходя́щих) бума́г.

treacherous *adj* преда́тельский; (*unsafe*) ненадёжный. **treachery** *n* преда́тельство.

treacle *n* па́тока.

tread *n* похо́дка; (*stair*) ступе́нька; (*of tyre*) проте́ктор; *vi* ступа́ть *impf*, ступи́ть *pf*; ~ **on** наступа́ть *impf*, наступи́ть *pf* на+*acc*; *vt* топта́ть *impf*.

treason *n* изме́на.

treasure *n* сокро́вище; *vt* высоко́ цени́ть *impf*. **treasurer** *n* казначе́й. **treasury** *n* (*also fig*) сокро́вищница; **the T~** госуда́рственное казначе́йство.

treat *n* (*pleasure*) удово́льствие; (*entertainment*) угоще́ние; *vt* (*have as guest*) угоща́ть *impf*, угости́ть *pf* (**to** +*instr*); (*med*) лечи́ть *impf* (**for** от+*gen*; **with** +*instr*); (*behave towards*) обраща́ться *impf* с+*instr*; (*process*) обраба́тывать *impf*, обрабо́тать *pf* (**with** +*instr*); (*discuss*) трактова́ть *impf* о+*prep*; (*regard*) относи́ться *impf*, отнести́сь *pf* к+*dat* (**as** как к+*dat*). **treatise** *n* тракта́т. **treatment** *n* (*behaviour*) обраще́ние; (*med*) лече́ние; (*processing*) обрабо́тка; (*discussion*) тракто́вка. **treaty** *n* догово́р.

treble *adj* тройно́й; (*trebled*) утро́енный; *adv* втро́е; *n* (*mus*) диска́нт; *vt* & *i* утра́ивать(ся) *impf*, утро́ить(ся) *pf*.

tree *n* де́рево.

trek *n* (*migration*) переселе́ние; (*journey*) путеше́ствие; *vi* (*migrate*) переселя́ться *impf*, пересели́ться *pf*; (*journey*) путеше́ствовать *impf*.

trellis *n* шпале́ра; (*for creepers*) решётка.

tremble *vi* дрожа́ть *impf* (**with** от+*gen*). **trembling** *n* дрожь; **in fear and ~** трепеща́.

tremendous *adj* (*huge*) огро́мный; (*excellent*) потряса́ющий.

tremor *n* дрожь; (*earthquake*) толчо́к. **tremulous** *adj* дрожа́щий.

trench *n* кана́ва, ров; (*mil*) око́п.

trend *n* направле́ние, тенде́нция. **trendy** *adj* мо́дный.

trepidation *n* тре́пет.

trespass *n* (*on property*) наруше́ние грани́ц; *vi* наруша́ть *impf*, нару́шить *pf* грани́цу (**on** +*gen*); (*fig*) вторга́ться *impf*, вто́ргнуться *pf* (**on** в+*acc*). **trespasser** *n* наруши́тель *m*.

trestle *n* ко́злы (-зел, -злам) *pl*; **~ table** стол на ко́злах.

trial *n* (*test*) испыта́ние (*also ordeal*), про́ба; (*law*) проце́сс, суд; (*sport*) попы́тка; **on ~** (*probation*) на испыта́нии; (*of objects*) взя́тый на про́бу; (*law*) под судо́м; **~ and error** ме́тод проб и оши́бок.

triangle *n* треуго́льник. **triangular** *adj* треуго́льный.

tribal *adj* племенно́й. **tribe** *n* пле́мя *neut*.

tribulation *n* го́ре, несча́стье.

tribunal *n* трибуна́л.

tributary *n* прито́к. **tribute** *n* дань; **pay ~** (*fig*) отдава́ть *impf*, отда́ть *pf* дань (уваже́ния) (**to** +*dat*).

trice *n*: **in a ~** мгнове́нно.

trick *n* (*ruse*) хи́трость; (*deception*) обма́н; (*conjuring ~*) фо́кус; (*stunt*) трюк; (*joke*) шу́тка; (*habit*) привы́чка; (*cards*) взя́тка; **play a ~ on** игра́ть *impf*, сыгра́ть *pf* шу́тку с+*instr*; *vt* обма́нывать *impf*, обману́ть *pf*. **trickery** *n* обма́н.

trickle *vi* сочи́ться *impf*.

trickster *n* обма́нщик. **tricky** *adj* сло́жный.

tricycle *n* трёхколёсный велосипе́д.

trifle *n* пустя́к; **a ~** (*adv*) немно́го +*gen*; *vi* шути́ть *impf*, по~ *pf* (**with** с+*instr*). **trifling** *adj* пустяко́вый.

trigger *n* (*of gun*) куро́к; *vt*: **~ off** вызыва́ть *impf*, вы́звать *pf*.

trill *n* трель.

trilogy *n* трило́гия.

trim *n* поря́док, гото́вность; **in fighting ~** в боево́й гото́вности; **in good ~** (*sport*) в хоро́шей фо́рме; (*haircut*) подстри́жка; *adj* опря́тный; *vt* (*cut, clip, cut off*) подреза́ть *impf*, подре́зать *pf*; (*hair*) подстрига́ть *impf*, подстри́чь *pf*; (*a dress etc.*) отде́лывать *impf*, отде́лать *pf*. **trimming** *n* (*on dress*) отде́лка; (*to food*) гарни́р.

Trinity *n* Тро́ица.

trinket *n* безделу́шка.

trio *n* три́о *neut indecl*; (*of people*) тро́йка.

trip *n* пое́здка, путеше́ствие, экску́рсия; (*business* ~) командиро́вка; *vi* (*stumble*) спотыка́ться *impf*, споткну́ться *pf* (**over** о+*acc*); *vt* (*also* ~ *up*) подставля́ть *impf*, подста́вить *pf* но́жку +*dat* (*also fig*); (*confuse*) запу́тывать *impf*, запу́тать *pf*.

triple *adj* тройно́й; (*tripled*) утро́енный; *vt* & *i* утра́ивать(ся) *impf*, утро́ить(ся) *pf*. **triplet** *n* (*mus*) трио́ль; (*one of* ~*s*) близне́ц (из тро́йни); *pl* тро́йня.

tripod *n* трено́жник.

trite *adj* бана́льный.

triumph *n* торжество́, побе́да; *vi* торжествова́ть *impf*, вос~ *pf* (**over** над+*instr*). **triumphal** *adj* триумфа́льный. **triumphant** *adj* (*exultant*) торжеству́ющий; (*victorious*) победоно́сный.

trivia *n pl* ме́лочи (-че́й) *pl*. **trivial** *adj* незначи́тельный. **triviality** *n* тривиа́льность. **trivialize** *vt* опошля́ть *impf*, опо́шлить *pf*.

trolley *n* теле́жка; (*table on wheels*) сто́лик на колёсиках. **trolley-bus** *n* тролле́йбус.

trombone *n* тромбо́н.

troop *n* гру́ппа, отря́д; *pl* (*mil*) войска́ *neut pl*; *vi* идти́ *impf*, по~ *pf* стро́ем.

trophy *n* трофе́й; (*prize*) приз.

tropic *n* тро́пик. **tropical** *adj* тропи́ческий.

trot *n* рысь; *vi* рыси́ть *impf*; (*rider*) е́здить *indet*, е́хать *det*, по~ *pf* ры́сью; (*horse*) ходи́ть *indet*, идти́ *det*, пойти́ *pf* ры́сью.

trouble *n* (*worry*) беспоко́йство, трево́га; (*misfortune*) беда́; (*unpleasantness*) неприя́тности *f pl*; (*effort, pains*) труд; (*care*) забо́та; (*disrepair*) неиспра́вность (**with** в+*prep*); (*illness*) боле́знь; **heart** ~ больно́е се́рдце; ~-**maker** наруши́тель *m*, ~ница споко́йствия; **ask for** ~ напра́шиваться *impf*, напроси́ться *pf* на неприя́тности; **be in** ~ име́ть *impf* неприя́тности; **get into** ~ попа́сть *pf* в беду́; **take** ~ стара́ться *impf*, по~ *pf*; **take the** ~ труди́ться *impf*, по~ *pf* (**to** +*inf*); **the** ~ **is (that)** беда́ в том, что; *vt* (*make anxious, disturb, give pain*) беспоко́ить *impf*; **may I** ~ **you for ...?** мо́жно попроси́ть у вас +*acc*?; *vi* (*take the* ~) труди́ться *impf*. **troubled** *adj* беспоко́йный. **troublesome** *adj* (*restless, fidgety*) беспоко́йный; (*capricious*) капри́зный; (*difficult*) тру́дный.

trough *n* (*for food*) корму́шка.

trounce *vt* (*beat*) поро́ть *impf*, вы́~ *pf*; (*defeat*) разбива́ть *impf*, разби́ть *pf*.

troupe *n* тру́ппа.

trouser-leg *n* штани́на (*coll*). **trousers** *n pl* брю́ки (-к) *pl*, штаны́ (-но́в) *pl*.

trout *n* форе́ль.

trowel *n* (*for building*) мастеро́к; (*garden* ~) садо́вый сово́к.

truancy *n* прогу́л. **truant** *n*

прогу́льщик; **play ~** прогу́ливать *impf*, прогуля́ть *pf*.
truce *n* переми́рие.
truck[1] *n*: **have no ~ with** не име́ть никаки́х дел с+*instr*.
truck[2] *n* (*lorry*) грузови́к; (*rly*) ваго́н-платфо́рма.
truculent *adj* свире́пый.
trudge *vi* уста́ло тащи́ться *impf*.
true *adj* (*faithful, correct*) ве́рный; (*correct*) пра́вильный; (*story*) правди́вый; (*real*) настоя́щий; **come ~** сбыва́ться *impf*, сбы́ться *pf*.
truism *n* трюи́зм. **truly** *adv* (*sincerely*) и́скренне; (*really, indeed*) действи́тельно; **yours ~** пре́данный Вам.
trump *n* ко́зырь *m*; *vt* бить *impf*, по~ *pf* ко́зырем; **~ up** фабрикова́ть *impf*, с~ *pf*.
trumpet *n* труба́; *vt* (*proclaim*) труби́ть *impf* о+*prep*. **trumpeter** *n* труба́ч.
truncate *vt* усека́ть *impf*, усе́чь *pf*.
truncheon *n* дуби́нка.
trundle *vt & i* ката́ть(ся) *indet*, кати́ть(ся) *det*, по~ *pf*.
trunk *n* (*stem*) ствол; (*anat*) ту́ловище; (*elephant's*) хо́бот; (*box*) сунду́к; *pl* (*swimming*) пла́вки (-вок) *pl*; (*boxing etc.*) трусы́ (-со́в) *pl*; **~ call** вы́зов по междугоро́дному телефо́ну; **~ road** магистра́льная доро́га.
truss *n* (*girder*) фе́рма; (*med*) грыжево́й банда́ж; *vt* (*tie* (*up*), *bird*) свя́зывать *impf*, связа́ть *pf*; (*reinforce*) укрепля́ть *impf*, укрепи́ть *pf*.
trust *n* дове́рие; (*body of trustees*) опе́ка; (*property held in* ~) довери́тельная со́бственность; (*econ*) трест; **take on ~** принима́ть *impf*, приня́ть *pf* на ве́ру; *vt* доверя́ть *impf*, дове́рить *pf* +*dat* (**with** +*acc*; **to** +*inf*); *vi* (*hope*) наде́яться *impf*, по~ *pf*. **trustee** *n* опеку́н. **trustful, trusting** *adj* дове́рчивый. **trustworthy, trusty** *adj* надёжный, ве́рный.
truth *n* пра́вда; **tell the ~** говори́ть *impf*, сказа́ть *pf* пра́вду; **to tell you the ~** по пра́вде говоря́. **truthful** *adj* правди́вый.
try *n* (*attempt*) попы́тка; (*test, trial*) испыта́ние, про́ба; *vt* (*taste; sample*) про́бовать *impf*, по~ *pf*; (*patience*) испы́тывать *impf*, испыта́ть *pf*; (*law*) суди́ть *impf* (**for** за+*acc*); *vi* (*endeavour*) стара́ться *impf*, по~ *pf*; **~ on** (*clothes*) примеря́ть *impf*, приме́рить *pf*. **trying** *adj* тру́дный.
tsar *n* царь *m*. **tsarina** *n* цари́ца.
T-shirt *n* футбо́лка.
tub *n* ка́дка; (*bath*) ва́нна; (*of margarine etc.*) упако́вка.
tubby *adj* то́лстенький.
tube *n* тру́бка, труба́; (*toothpaste etc.*) тю́бик; (*underground*) метро́ *neut indecl*.
tuber *n* клу́бень *m*. **tuberculosis** *n* туберкулёз.
tubing *n* тру́бы *m pl*. **tubular** *adj* тру́бчатый.
tuck *n* (*in garment*) скла́дка; *vt* (*thrust into*, ~ *away*) засо́вывать *impf*, засу́нуть *pf*; (*hide away*) пря́тать *impf*, с~ *pf*; **~ in** (*shirt etc.*) заправля́ть *impf*, запра́вить *pf*; **~ in, up** (*blanket, skirt*) подтыка́ть *impf*, подоткну́ть *pf*; **~ up** (*sleeves*) засу́чивать *impf*, засучи́ть *pf*; (*in bed*) укрыва́ть *impf*, укры́ть *pf*.

Tuesday *n* вто́рник.
tuft *n* пучо́к.
tug *vt* тяну́ть *impf*, по~ *pf*; *vi* (*sharply*) дёргать *impf*, дёрнуть *pf* (**at** за+*acc*); *n* рыво́к; (*tugboat*) букси́р.
tuition *n* обуче́ние (**in** +*dat*).
tulip *n* тюльпа́н.
tumble *vi* (*fall*) па́дать *impf*, (у)па́сть *pf*; *n* паде́ние. **tumbledown** *adj* полуразру́шенный. **tumbler** *n* стака́н.
tumour *n* о́пухоль.
tumult *n* (*uproar*) сумато́ха; (*agitation*) волне́ние. **tumultuous** *adj* шу́мный.
tuna *n* туне́ц.
tundra *n* ту́ндра.
tune *n* мело́дия; **in** ~ в тон, (*of instrument*) настро́енный; **out of** ~ не в тон, фальши́вый, (*of instrument*) расстро́енный; **change one's** ~ (пере)меня́ть *impf*, перемени́ть *pf* тон; *vt* (*instrument*; *radio*) настра́ивать *impf*, настро́ить *pf*; (*engine etc.*) регули́ровать *impf*, от~ *pf*; ~ **in** настра́ивать *impf*, настро́ить (*radio*) ра́дио (**to** на+*acc*); *vi*: ~ **up** настра́ивать *impf*, настро́ить *pf* инструме́нт(ы). **tuneful** *adj* мелоди́чный. **tuner** *n* (*mus*) настро́йщик; (*receiver*) приёмник.
tunic *n* туни́ка; (*of uniform*) ки́тель *m*.
tuning *n* настро́йка; (*of engine*) регулиро́вка; **~-fork** камерто́н.
tunnel *n* тунне́ль *m*; *vi* прокла́дывать *impf*, проложи́ть *pf* тунне́ль *m*.
turban *n* тюрба́н.
turbine *n* турби́на.
turbulence *n* бу́рность; (*aeron*) турбуле́нтность. **turbulent** *adj* бу́рный.
tureen *n* су́пник.
turf *n* дёрн.
turgid *adj* (*pompous*) напы́щенный.
Turk *n* ту́рок, турча́нка. **Turkey** *n* Ту́рция.
turkey *n* индю́к, *f* инде́йка; (*dish*) индю́шка.
Turkish *adj* туре́цкий. **Turkmenistan** *n* Туркменииста́н.
turmoil *n* (*disorder*) беспоря́док; (*uproar*) сумато́ха.
turn *n* (*change of direction*) поворо́т; (*revolution*) оборо́т; (*service*) услу́га; (*change*) измене́ние; (*one's* ~ *to do sth*) о́чередь; (*theat*) но́мер; ~ **of phrase** оборо́т ре́чи; **at every** ~ на ка́ждом шагу́; **by, in turn(s)** по о́череди; *vt* (*handle, key, car around, etc.*) повора́чивать *impf*, поверну́ть *pf*; (*revolve, rotate*) враща́ть *impf*; (*page*; *on its face*) перевёртывать *impf*, переверну́ть *pf*; (*direct*) направля́ть *impf*, напра́вить *pf*; (*cause to become*) де́лать *impf*, с~ *pf* +*instr*; (*on lathe*) точи́ть *impf*; *vi* (*change direction*) повора́чивать *impf*, поверну́ть *pf*; (*rotate*) враща́ться *impf*; (~ *round*) повора́чиваться *impf*, поверну́ться *pf*; (*become*) станови́ться *impf*, стать *pf* +*instr*; ~ **against** ополча́ться *impf*, ополчи́ться *pf* на+*acc*, про́тив+*gen*; ~ **around** *see* ~ **round**; ~ **away** (*vt & i*) отвора́чивать(ся) *impf*, отверну́ть(ся) *pf*; (*refuse admittance*) прогоня́ть *impf*, прогна́ть *pf*; ~ **back** (*vi*) повора́чивать *impf*, поверну́ть *pf* наза́д; (*vt*) (*bend*

back) отгибáть *impf*, отогнýть *pf*; ~ **down** (*refuse*) отклонять *impf*, отклонить *pf*; (*collar*) отгибáть *impf*, отогнýть *pf*; (*make quieter*) дéлать *impf*, с~ *pf* тише; ~ **grey** (*vi*) седéть *impf*, по~ *pf*; ~ **in** (*so as to face inwards*) поворáчивать *impf*, повернýть *pf* вовнýтрь; ~ **inside out** выворáчивать *impf*, вы́вернуть *pf* наизнáнку; ~ **into** (*change into*) (*vt* & *i*) превращáть(ся) *impf*, превратить(ся) *pf* в+*acc*; (*street*) сворáчивать *impf*, свернýть *pf* на+*acc*; ~ **off** (*light, radio etc.*) выключáть *impf*, вы́ключить *pf*; (*tap*) закрывáть *impf*, закры́ть *pf*; (*vi*) (*branch off*) сворáчивать *impf*, свернýть *pf*; ~ **on** (*light, radio etc.*) включáть *impf*, включи́ть *pf*; (*tap*) открывáть *impf*, откры́ть *pf*; (*attack*) нападáть *impf*, напáсть *pf* на+*acc*; ~ **out** (*light etc.*): *see* ~ **off**; (*prove to be*) окáзываться *impf*, оказáться *pf* (**to be** +*instr*); (*drive out*) выгонять *impf*, вы́гнать *pf*; (*pockets*) вывёртывать *impf*, вы́вернуть *pf*; (*be present*) приходи́ть *impf*, прийти *pf*; (*product*) выпускáть *impf*, вы́пустить *pf*; ~ **over** (*page, on its face, roll over*) (*vt* & *i*) перевёртывать(ся) *impf*, перевернýть(ся) *pf*; (*hand over*) передавáть *impf*, передáть *pf*; (*think about*) обдýмывать *impf*, обдýмать *pf*; (*overturn*) (*vt* & *i*) опроки́дывать(ся) *impf*, опроки́нуть(ся) *pf*; ~ **pale** бледнéть *impf*, по~ *pf*; ~ **red** краснéть *impf*, по~ *pf*; ~ **round** (*vi*) (*rotate*; ~ *one's back*; ~ *to face sth*) повёртываться *impf*, повернýться *pf*; (~ *to face*) оборáчиваться *impf*, обернýться *pf*; (*vt*) повёртывать *impf*, повернýть *pf*; ~ **sour** скисáть *impf*, ски́снуть *pf*; ~ **to** обращáться *impf*, обрати́ться *pf* к+*dat* (**for** за+*instr*); ~ **up** (*appear*) появляться *impf*, появи́ться *pf*; (*be found*) находи́ться *impf*, найти́сь *pf*; (*shorten garment*) подшивáть *impf*, подши́ть *pf*; (*crop up*) подвёртываться *impf*, подвернýться *pf*; (*bend up*; *stick up*) (*vt* & *i*) загибáть(ся) *impf*, загнýть(ся) *pf*; (*make louder*) дéлать *impf*, с~ *pf* грóмче; ~ **up one's nose** вороти́ть *impf* нос (**at** от+*gen*) (*coll*); ~ **upside down** перевoрáчивать *impf*, перевернýть *pf* вверх дном. **turn-out** *n* коли́чество приходя́щих. **turn-up** *n* (*on trousers*) обшлáг.

turner *n* тóкарь *m*.

turning *n* (*road*) поворóт. **turning-point** *n* поворóтный пункт.

turnip *n* рéпа.

turnover *n* (*econ*) оборóт; (*of staff*) текýчесть рабóчей си́лы.

turnpike *n* дорóжная застáва.

turnstile *n* турникéт.

turntable *n* (*rly*) поворóтный круг; (*gramophone*) диск.

turpentine *n* скипидáр.

turquoise *n* (*material, stone*) бирюзá; *adj* бирюзóвый.

turret *n* бáшенка.

turtle *n* черепáха.

turtle-dove *n* гóрлица.

tusk *n* би́вень *m*, клык.

tussle *n* дрáка; *vi* дрáться *impf* (**for** за+*acc*).

tutor *n* (*private teacher*) ча́стный дома́шний учи́тель *m*, ~ница; (*univ*) преподава́тель *m*, ~ница; (*primer*) учёбник; *vt* (*instruct*) обуча́ть *impf*, обучи́ть *pf* (**in** +*dat*); (*give lessons to*) дава́ть *impf*, дать *pf* уро́ки+*dat*; (*guide*) руководи́ть *impf* +*instr*. **tutorial** *n* консульта́ция.

tutu *n* (*ballet*) па́чка.

TV *abbr* (*of* **television**) ТВ, телеви́дение; (*set*) телеви́зор.

twang *n* (*of string*) ре́зкий звук (натя́нутой струны́); (*voice*) гнуса́вый го́лос.

tweak *n* щипо́к; *vt* щипа́ть *impf*, (у)щипну́ть *pf*.

tweed *n* твид.

tweezers *n pl* пинце́т.

twelfth *adj* & *n* двена́дцатый. **twelve** *adj* & *n* двена́дцать.

twentieth *adj* & *n* двадца́тый. **twenty** *adj* & *n* два́дцать; *pl* (*decade*) двадца́тые го́ды (-до́в) *m pl*.

twice *adv* два́жды; ~ **as** вдво́е, в два ра́за +*comp*.

twiddle *vt* (*turn*) верте́ть *impf* +*acc*, *instr*; (*toy with*) игра́ть *impf* +*instr*; ~ **one's thumbs** (*fig*) безде́льничать *impf*.

twig *n* ве́точка, прут.

twilight *n* су́мерки (-рек) *pl*.

twin *n* близне́ц; *pl* (*Gemini*) Близнецы́ *m pl*; ~ **beds** па́ра односпа́льных крова́тей; ~ **brother** брат-близне́ц; ~ **town** го́род-побрати́м.

twine *n* бечёвка, шпага́т; *vt* (*twist*, *weave*) вить *impf*, с~ *pf*; *vt* & *i* (~ *round*) обвива́ть(ся) *impf*, обви́ть(ся) *pf*.

twinge *n* при́ступ (бо́ли); (*of conscience*) угрызе́ние.

twinkle *n* мерца́ние; (*of eyes*) огонёк; *vi* мерца́ть *impf*, сверка́ть *impf*. **twinkling** *n* мерца́ние; **in the ~ of an eye** в мгнове́ние о́ка.

twirl *vt* & *i* (*twist*, *turn*) верте́ть(ся) *impf*; (*whirl*, *spin*) кружи́ть(ся) *impf*.

twist *n* (*bend*) изги́б, поворо́т; (~*ing*) круче́ние; (*in story*) поворо́т фа́булы; *vt* скру́чивать *impf*, крути́ть *impf*, с~ *pf*; (*distort*) искажа́ть *impf*, искази́ть *pf*; (*sprain*) подвёртывать *impf*, подверну́ть *pf*; *vi* (*climb*, *meander*, *twine*) ви́ться *impf*. **twisted** *adj* искривлённый (*also fig*).

twit *n* дура́к.

twitch *n* подёргивание; *vt* & *i* дёргать(ся) *impf*, дёрнуть(ся) *pf* (**at** за+*acc*).

twitter *n* щёбет; *vi* щебета́ть *impf*, чири́кать *impf*.

two *adj* & *n* два, две (*f*); (*collect*; *2 pairs*) дво́е; (*number 2*) дво́йка; **in** ~ (*in half*) на́двое, попола́м; ~**-seater** двухме́стный (автомоби́ль); ~**-way** двусторо́нний. **twofold** *adj* двойно́й; *adv* вдвойне́. **twosome** *n* па́ра.

tycoon *n* магна́т.

type *n* тип, род; (*printing*) шрифт; *vt* писа́ть *impf*, на~ *pf* на маши́нке. **typescript** *n* маши́нопись. **typewriter** *n* пи́шущая маши́нка. **typewritten** *adj* машинопи́сный.

typhoid *n* брюшно́й тиф.

typical *adj* типи́чный. **typify** *vt* служи́ть *impf*, по~ *pf* типи́чным приме́ром +*gen*.

typist *n* машини́стка.

typography *n* книгопеча́тание; (*style*) оформле́ние.

tyrannical *adj* тирани́ческий. **tyrant** *n* тира́н.

tyre *n* ши́на.

U

ubiquitous *adj* вездесу́щий. **udder** *n* вы́мя *neut*.
UFO *abbr* (*of* **unidentified flying object**) НЛО, неопо́знанный лета́ющий объе́кт.
ugh *int* тьфу!
ugliness *n* уро́дство. **ugly** *adj* некраси́вый, уро́дливый; (*unpleasant*) неприя́тный.
UK *abbr* (*of* **United Kingdom**) Соединённое Короле́вство.
Ukraine *n* Украи́на. **Ukrainian** *n* украи́нец, -нка; *adj* украи́нский.
ulcer *n* я́зва.
ulterior *adj* скры́тый.
ultimate *adj* (*final*) после́дний, оконча́тельный; (*purpose*) коне́чный. **ultimately** *adv* в коне́чном счёте, в конце́ концо́в. **ultimatum** *n* ультима́тум.
ultrasound *n* ультразву́к. **ultra-violet** *adj* ультрафиоле́товый.
umbilical *adj*: **~ cord** пупови́на.
umbrella *n* зо́нтик, зонт.
umpire *n* судья́ *m*; *vt & i* суди́ть *impf*.
umpteenth *adj*: **for the ~ time** в кото́рый раз.
unabashed *adj* без вся́кого смуще́ния. **unabated** *adj* неосла́бленный. **unable** *adj*: **be ~ to** не мочь *impf*, с~ *pf*; быть не в состоя́нии; (*not know how to*) не уме́ть *impf*, с~ *pf*. **unabridged** *adj* несокращённый. **unaccompanied** *adj* без сопровожде́ния; (*mus*) без аккомпанеме́нта. **unaccountable** *adj* необъясни́мый. **unaccustomed** *adj* (*not accustomed*) непривы́кший (**to** к+*dat*); (*unusual*) непривы́чный. **unadulterated** *adj* настоя́щий; (*utter*) чисте́йший. **unaffected** *adj* непринуждённый. **unaided** *adj* без по́мощи, самостоя́тельный. **unambiguous** *adj* недвусмы́сленный. **unanimity** *n* единоду́шие. **unanimous** *adj* единоду́шный. **unanswerable** *adj* (*irrefutable*) неопровержи́мый. **unarmed** *adj* невооружённый. **unashamed** *adj* бессо́вестный. **unassailable** *adj* непристу́пный; (*irrefutable*) неопровержи́мый. **unassuming** *adj* скро́мный. **unattainable** *adj* недосяга́емый. **unattended** *adj* без присмо́тра. **unattractive** *adj* непривлека́тельный. **unauthorized** *adj* неразрешённый. **unavailable** *adj* не име́ющийся в нали́чии, недосту́пный. **unavoidable** *adj* неизбе́жный. **unaware** *predic*: **be ~ of** не сознава́ть *impf* +*acc*; не знать *impf* о+*prep*. **unawares** *adv* врасплóх.
unbalanced *adj* (*psych*) неуравнове́шенный. **unbearable** *adj* невыноси́мый. **unbeatable** *adj* (*unsurpassable*) не могу́щий быть превзойдённым; (*invincible*) непобеди́мый. **unbeaten** *adj* (*undefeated*) непокорённый; (*unsurpassed*) непревзойдённый. **unbelief** *n* неве́рие. **unbelievable** *adj* невероя́тный. **unbeliever** *n* неве́рующий *sb*. **unbiased** *adj* беспристра́стный. **unblemished** *adj* незапя́тнанный. **unblock** *vt*

прочища́ть *impf*, прочи́стить *pf*. **unbolt** *vt* отпира́ть *impf*, отпере́ть *pf*. **unborn** *adj* ещё не рождённый. **unbounded** *adj* неограни́ченный. **unbreakable** *adj* небью́щийся. **unbridled** *adj* разну́зданный. **unbroken** *adj* (*intact*) неразби́тый, це́лый; (*continuous*) непреры́вный; (*unsurpassed*) непоби́тый; (*horse*) необъе́зженный. **unbuckle** *vt* расстёгивать *impf*, расстегну́ть *pf*. **unburden** *vt*: ~ **o.s.** отводи́ть *impf*, отвести́ *pf* ду́шу. **unbutton** *vt* расстёгивать *impf*, расстегну́ть *pf*.

uncalled-for *adj* неуме́стный. **uncanny** *adj* жу́ткий, сверхъесте́ственный. **unceasing** *adj* непреры́вный. **unceremonious** *adj* бесцеремо́нный. **uncertain** *adj* (*not sure, hesitating*) неуве́ренный; (*indeterminate*) неопределённый, нея́сный; **be** ~ (*not know for certain*) то́чно не знать *impf*; **in no** ~ **terms** недвусмы́сленно. **uncertainty** *n* неизве́стность; неопределённость. **unchallenged** *adj* не вызыва́ющий возраже́ний. **unchanged** *adj* неизмени́вшийся. **unchanging** *adj* неизменя́ющийся. **uncharacteristic** *adj* нетипи́чный. **uncharitable** *adj* немилосе́рдный, жесто́кий. **uncharted** *adj* неиссле́дованный. **unchecked** *adj* (*unrestrained*) необу́зданный. **uncivilized** *adj* нецивилизо́ванный. **unclaimed** *adj* невостре́бованный.

uncle *n* дя́дя *m*.

unclean *adj* нечи́стый. **unclear** *adj* нея́сный. **uncomfortable** *adj* неудо́бный. **uncommon** *adj* необыкнове́нный; (*rare*) ре́дкий. **uncommunicative** *adj* неразгово́рчивый, сде́ржанный. **uncomplaining** *adj* безро́потный. **uncomplicated** *adj* несло́жный. **uncompromising** *adj* бескомпроми́ссный. **unconcealed** *adj* нескрыва́емый. **unconcerned** *adj* (*unworried*) беззабо́тный; (*indifferent*) равноду́шный. **unconditional** *adj* безогово́рочный, безусло́вный. **unconfirmed** *adj* неподтверждённый. **unconnected** *adj* ~ **with** не свя́занный с+*instr*. **unconscious** *adj* (*also unintentional*) бессозна́тельный; (*predic*) без созна́ния; **be** ~ **of** не сознава́ть *impf* +*gen*; *n* подсозна́тельное *sb*. **unconsciousness** *n* бессозна́тельное состоя́ние. **unconstitutional** *adj* неконституцио́нный. **uncontrollable** *adj* неудержи́мый. **uncontrolled** *adj* бесконтро́льный. **unconventional** *adj* необы́чный; оригина́льный. **unconvincing** *adj* неубеди́тельный. **uncooked** *adj* сыро́й. **uncooperative** *adj* неотзы́вчивый. **uncouth** *adj* гру́бый. **uncover** *vt* раскрыва́ть *impf*, раскры́ть *pf*. **uncritical** *adj* некрити́чный.

unctuous *adj* еле́йный.

uncut *adj* неразре́занный; (*unabridged*) несокращённый.

undamaged *adj* неповреждённый. **undaunted** *adj* бесстра́шный. **undecided** *adj* (*not settled*) нерешённый; (*irresolute*) нереши́тельный.

undefeated *adj* непокорённый. **undemanding** *adj* нетребовательный. **undemocratic** *adj* недемократический. **undeniable** *adj* неоспоримый.

under *prep* (*position*) под+*instr*; (*direction*) под+*acc*; (*fig*) под +*instr*; (*less than*) меньше+*gen*; (*in view of, in the reign, time of*) при+*prep*; **~-age** несовершеннолетний; **~ way** на ходу; *adv* (*position*) внизу; (*direction*) вниз; (*less*) меньше.

undercarriage *n* шасси *neut indecl.* **underclothes** *n pl* нижнее бельё. **undercoat** *n* (*of paint*) грунтовка. **undercover** *adj* тайный. **undercurrent** *n* подводное течение; (*fig*) скрытая тенденция. **undercut** *vt* (*price*) назначать *impf*, назначить *pf* более низкую цену чем+*nom.* **underdeveloped** *adj* слаборазвитый. **underdog** *n* неудачник.

underdone *adj* недожаренный. **underemployment** *n* неполная занятость. **underestimate** *vt* недооценивать *impf*, недооценить *pf*; *n* недооценка. **underfoot** *adv* под ногами.

undergo *vt* подвергаться *impf*, подвергнуться *pf* +*dat*; (*endure*) переносить *impf*, перенести *pf.* **undergraduate** *n* студент, ~ка. **underground** *n* (*rly*) метро *neut indecl*; (*fig*) подполье; *adj* подземный; (*fig*) подпольный; *adv* под землёй; (*fig*) подпольно. **undergrowth** *n* подлесок. **underhand** *adj* закулисный. **underlie** *vt* (*fig*) лежать *impf* в основе +*gen.* **underline** *vt* подчёркивать *impf*, подчеркнуть *pf.* **underlying** *adj* лежащий в основе. **underling** *n* подчинённый *sb.*

undermine *vt* (*authority*) подрывать *impf*, подорвать *pf*; (*health*) разрушать *impf*, разрушить *pf.*

underneath *adv* (*position*) внизу; (*direction*) вниз; *prep* (*position*) под+*instr*; (*direction*) под+*acc*; *n* нижняя часть; *adj* нижний.

undernourished *adj* исхудалый; **be ~** недоедать *impf.*

underpaid *adj* низкооплачиваемый. **underpants** *n pl* трусы (-сов) *pl.* **underpass** *n* проезд под полотном дороги; тоннель *m.* **underpin** *vt* подводить *impf*, подвести *pf* фундамент под+*acc*; (*fig*) поддерживать *impf*, поддержать *pf.* **underprivileged** *adj* обделённый; (*poor*) бедный. **underrate** *vt* недооценивать *impf*, недооценить *pf.*

underscore *vt* подчёркивать *impf*, подчеркнуть *pf.* **under-secretary** *n* заместитель *m* министра. **underside** *n* нижняя сторона, низ. **undersized** *adj* малорослый. **understaffed** *adj* неукомплектованный.

understand *vt* понимать *impf*, понять *pf*; (*have heard say*) слышать *impf.* **understandable** *adj* понятный. **understanding** *n* понимание; (*agreement*) соглашение; *adj* (*sympathetic*) отзывчивый.

understate *vt* преуменьшать *impf*, преуменьшить *pf.* **understatement** *n* преуменьшение.

understudy *n* дублёр.

undertake *vt* (*enter upon*)

предпринимáть *impf*, предпринять *pf*; (*responsibility*) брать *impf*, взять *pf* на себя́; (+*inf*) обя́зываться *impf*, обязáться *pf*. **undertaker** *n* гробовщи́к. **undertaking** *n* предприя́тие; (*pledge*) гарáнтия.

undertone *n* (*fig*) подтéкст; **in an ~** вполго́лоса. **underwater** *adj* подво́дный. **underwear** *n* ни́жнее бельё. **underweight** *adj* исхудáлый. **underworld** *n* (*mythology*) преиспо́дняя *sb*; (*criminals*) престу́пный мир. **underwrite** *vt* (*guarantee*) гаранти́ровать *impf* & *pf*. **underwriter** *n* страхо́вщик.

undeserved *adj* незаслу́женный. **undesirable** *adj* нежелáтельный; *n* нежелáтельное лицó. **undeveloped** *adj* нерáзвитый; (*land*) незастро́енный. **undignified** *adj* недосто́йный. **undiluted** *adj* неразбáвленный. **undisciplined** *adj* недисциплини́рованный. **undiscovered** *adj* неоткры́тый. **undisguised** *adj* я́вный. **undisputed** *adj* бесспо́рный. **undistinguished** *adj* зауря́дный. **undisturbed** *adj* (*untouched*) нетро́нутый; (*peaceful*) споко́йный. **undivided** *adj*: **~ attention** по́лное внимáние **undo** *vt* (*open*) открывáть *impf*, откры́ть *pf*; (*untie*) развя́зывать *impf*, развязáть *pf*; (*unbutton, unhook, unbuckle*) расстёгивать *impf*, расстегну́ть *pf*; (*destroy, cancel*) уничтожáть *impf*, уничто́жить *pf*. **undoubted** *adj* несомнéнный. **undoubtedly** *adv* несомнéнно. **undress** *vt* & *i* раздевáть(ся) *impf*, раздéть(ся) *pf*. **undue** *adj* чрезмéрный. **unduly** *adv* чрезмéрно. **undulating** *adj* волни́стый; (*landscape*) холми́стый. **undying** *adj* (*eternal*) вéчный. **unearth** *vt* (*dig up*) выкáпывать *impf*, вы́копать *pf* из земли́; (*fig*) раскáпывать *impf*, раскопáть *pf*. **uneasiness** *n* (*anxiety*) беспоко́йство; (*awkwardness*) нело́вкость. **uneasy** *adj* беспоко́йный; нело́вкий. **uneconomic** *adj* нерентáбельный. **uneconomical** *adj* (*car etc.*) неэкономи́чный; (*person*) неэконо́мный. **uneducated** *adj* необразо́ванный. **unemployed** *adj* безрабо́тный. **unemployment** *n* безрабо́тица; **~ benefit** посо́бие по безрабо́тице. **unending** *adj* бесконéчный. **unenviable** *adj* незави́дный. **unequal** *adj* нерáвный. **unequalled** *adj* непревзойдённый. **unequivocal** *adj* недвусмы́сленный. **unerring** *adj* безоши́бочный.

uneven *adj* неро́вный. **uneventful** *adj* непримечáтельный. **unexceptional** *adj* обы́чный. **unexpected** *adj* неожи́данный. **unexplored** *adj* неисслéдованный.

unfailing *adj* неизмéнный; (*inexhaustible*) неисчерпáемый. **unfair** *adj* несправедли́вый. **unfaithful** *adj* невéрный. **unfamiliar** *adj* незнако́мый; (*unknown*) невéдомый. **unfashionable** *adj* немо́дный. **unfasten** *vt* (*detach, untie*) открепля́ть *impf*, открепи́ть *pf*; (*undo, unbutton, unhook*) расстёгивать *impf*, расстегну́ть *pf*; (*open*) открывáть *impf*, откры́ть *pf*. **unfavour-**

able *adj* неблагоприя́тный. **unfeeling** *adj* бесчу́вственный. **unfinished** *adj* незако́нченный. **unfit** *adj* негóдный; (*unhealthy*) нездорóвый. **unflagging** *adj* неослабева́ющий. **unflattering** *adj* нелéстный. **unflinching** *adj* непоколеби́мый. **unfold** *vt & i* развёртывать(ся) *impf*, развернýть(ся) *pf*; *vi* (*fig*) раскрыва́ться *impf*, раскры́ться *pf*. **unforeseen** *adj* непредви́денный. **unforgettable** *adj* незабыва́емый. **unforgivable** *adj* непрости́тельный. **unforgiving** *adj* непроща́ющий. **unfortunate** *adj* несча́стный; (*regrettable*) неуда́чный; *n* неуда́чник. **unfortunately** *adv* к сожалéнию. **unfounded** *adj* необоснóванный. **unfriendly** *adj* недружелю́бный. **unfulfilled** *adj* (*hopes etc.*) неосуществлённый; (*person*) неудовлетворённый. **unfurl** *vt & i* развёртывать(ся) *impf*, развернýть(ся) *pf*. **unfurnished** *adj* немеблирóванный.

ungainly *adj* неуклю́жий. **ungovernable** *adj* неуправля́емый. **ungracious** *adj* нелюбéзный. **ungrateful** *adj* неблагода́рный. **unguarded** *adj* (*incautious*) неосторóжный.

unhappiness *n* несча́стье. **unhappy** *adj* несчастли́вый. **unharmed** *adj* невреди́мый. **unhealthy** *adj* нездорóвый; (*harmful*) врéдный. **unheard-of** *adj* неслы́ханный. **unheeded** *adj* незамéченный. **unheeding** *adj* невнима́тельный. **unhelpful** *adj* бесполéзный; (*person*) неотзы́вчивый. **unhesitating** *adj* реши́тельный. **unhesitatingly** *adv* без колеба́ния. **unhindered** *adj* беспрепя́тственный. **unhinge** *vt* (*fig*) расстра́ивать *impf*, расстрóить *pf*. **unholy** *adj* (*impious*) нечести́вый; (*awful*) ужа́сный. **unhook** *vt* (*undo hooks of*) расстёгивать *impf*, расстегнýть *pf*; (*uncouple*) расцепля́ть *impf*, расцепи́ть *pf*. **unhurt** *adj* невреди́мый.

unicorn *n* единорóг.

unification *n* объединéние.

uniform *n* фóрма; *adj* единообра́зный; (*unchanging*) постоя́нный. **uniformity** *n* единообра́зие.

unify *vt* объединя́ть *impf*, объедини́ть *pf*.

unilateral *adj* односторóнний.

unimaginable *adj* невообрази́мый. **unimaginative** *adj* лишённый воображéния, прозаи́чный. **unimportant** *adj* нева́жный. **uninformed** *adj* (*ignorant*) несвéдущий (**about** в+*prep*); (*ill-informed*) неосведомлённый. **uninhabited** *adj* необита́емый. **uninhibited** *adj* нестеснённый. **uninspired** *adj* бана́льный. **unintelligible** *adj* непоня́тный. **unintentional** *adj* нечая́нный. **unintentionally** *adv* нечая́нно. **uninterested** *adj* незаинтересóванный. **uninteresting** *adj* неинтерéсный. **uninterrupted** *adj* непреры́вный.

union *n* (*alliance*) сою́з; (*joining together, alliance*) объединéние; (*trade* ~) профсою́з. **unionist** *n* член профсою́за; (*polit*) униони́ст.

unique *adj* уника́льный.

unison *n*: **in** ~ (*mus*) в уни́сон; (*fig*) в согла́сии.

unit *n* едини́ца; (*mil*) часть.

unite *vt* & *i* соединя́ть(ся) *impf*, соедини́ть(ся) *pf*; объединя́ть(ся) *impf*, объедини́ть(ся) *pf*. **united** *adj* соединённый, объединённый; **U~ Kingdom** Соединённое Короле́вство; **U~ Nations** Организа́ция Объединённых На́ций; **U~ States** Соединённые Шта́ты *m pl* Аме́рики. **unity** *n* еди́нство.

universal *adj* всео́бщий; (*many-sided*) универса́льный. **universe** *n* вселённая *sb*; (*world*) мир.

university *n* университе́т; *attrib* университе́тский.

unjust *adj* несправедли́вый. **unjustifiable** *adj* непрости́тельный. **unjustified** *adj* неопра́вданный.

unkempt *adj* нечёсаный. **unkind** *adj* недо́брый, злой. **unknown** *adj* неизве́стный.

unlawful *adj* незако́нный. **unleaded** *adj* неэтили́рованный. **unleash** *vt* (*also fig*) развя́зывать *impf*, развяза́ть *pf*.

unless *conj* е́сли… не.

unlike *adj* непохо́жий (на+*acc*); (*in contradistinction to*) в отли́чие от+*gen*. **unlikely** *adj* маловероя́тный; **it is ~ that** вряд ли. **unlimited** *adj* неограни́ченный. **unlit** *adj* неосвещённый. **unload** *vt* (*vehicle etc.*) разгружа́ть *impf*, разгрузи́ть *pf*; (*goods etc.*) выгружа́ть *impf*, вы́грузить *pf*. **unlock** *vt* отпира́ть *impf*, отпере́ть *pf*; открыва́ть *impf*, откры́ть *pf*. **unlucky** *adj* (*number etc.*) несчастли́вый; (*unsuccessful*) неуда́чный.

unmanageable *adj* тру́дный, непоко́рный. **unmanned** *adj* автомати́ческий. **unmarried** *adj* холосто́й; (*of man*) неженáтый; (*of woman*) незаму́жняя. **unmask** *vt* (*fig*) разоблача́ть *impf*, разоблачи́ть *pf*. **unmentionable** *adj* неупомина́емый. **unmistakable** *adj* несомне́нный, я́сный. **unmitigated** *adj* (*thorough*) отъя́вленный. **unmoved** *adj*: **be ~** остава́ться *impf*, оста́ться *pf* равноду́шен, -шна.

unnatural *adj* неесте́ственный. **unnecessary** *adj* нену́жный. **unnerve** *vt* лиша́ть *impf*, лиши́ть *pf* му́жества; (*upset*) расстра́ивать *impf*, расстро́ить *pf*. **unnoticed** *adj* незаме́ченный **unobserved** *adj* незаме́ченный. **unobtainable** *adj* недосту́пный. **unobtrusive** *adj* скро́мный, ненавя́зчивый. **unoccupied** *adj* неза́нятый, свобо́дный; (*house*) пусто́й. **unofficial** *adj* неофициа́льный. **unopposed** *adj* не встре́тивший сопротивле́ния. **unorthodox** *adj* неортодокса́льный.

unpack *vt* распако́вывать *impf*, распакова́ть *pf*. **unpaid** *adj* (*bill*) неупла́ченный; (*person*) не получа́ющий пла́ты; (*work*) беспла́тный. **unpalatable** *adj* невку́сный; (*unpleasant*) неприя́тный. **unparalleled** *adj* несравни́мый. **unpleasant** *adj* неприя́тный. **unpleasantness** *n* неприя́тность. **unpopular** *adj* непопуля́рный. **unprecedented** *adj* беспреце́дентный. **unpredictable** *adj* непредсказу́емый. **unprejudiced** *adj* беспристра́стный. **unprepared** *adj* неподгото́вленный, негото́вый. **unprepossessing** *adj* непривлека́тельный. **unpretentious** *adj* просто́й, без прете́нзий. **unprincipled** *adj* беспринци́пный. **unproductive** *adj* непродукти́вный. **unprofitable** *adj* невы́годный. **unpromising** *adj* малообеща́ющий. **unprotected** *adj* незащищённый. **unproven** *adj* недока́занный. **unprovoked** *adj* непровоци́рованный. **unpublished** *adj* неопублико́ванный, неи́зданный. **unpunished** *adj* безнака́занный.

unqualified *adj* неквалифици́рованный; (*unconditional*) безогово́рочный. **unquestionable** *adj* несомне́нный, неоспори́мый. **unquestionably** *adv* несомне́нно, бесспо́рно.

unravel *vt & i* распу́тывать(ся) *impf*, распу́тать(ся) *pf*; *vt* (*solve*) разга́дывать *impf*, разгада́ть *pf*. **unread** *adj* (*book etc.*) непрочи́танный. **unreadable** *adj* (*illegible*) неразбо́рчивый; (*boring*) неудобочита́емый. **unreal** *adj* нереа́льный. **unrealistic** *adj* нереа́льный. **unreasonable** *adj* (*person*) неразу́мный; (*behaviour, demand, price*) необосно́ванный. **unrecognizable** *adj* неузнава́емый. **unrecognized** *adj* непри́знанный. **unrefined** *adj* неочи́щенный; (*manners etc.*) гру́бый. **unrelated** *adj* не име́ющий отноше́ния (**to** к+*dat*), несвя́занный (**to** с+*instr*); **we are ~** мы не ро́дственники. **unrelenting** *adj* (*ruthless*) безжа́лостный; (*unremitting*) несла́бный. **unreliable** *adj* ненадёжный. **unremarkable** *adj* невыдаю́щийся. **unremitting** *adj* несла́бный; (*incessant*) беспреста́нный. **unrepentant** *adj* нераска́явшийся. **unrepresentative** *adj* нетипи́чный. **unrequited** *adj*: **~ love** неразделённая любо́вь. **unreserved** *adj* (*full*) по́лный; (*open*) открове́нный; (*unconditional*) безогово́рочный; (*seat*) незаброни́рованный. **unresolved** *adj* нерешённый. **unrest** *n* беспоко́йство; (*polit*) волне́ния *neut pl*. **unrestrained** *adj* несде́ржанный. **unrestricted** *adj* неограни́ченный. **unripe** *adj* незре́лый. **unrivalled** *adj* беспо́добный. **unroll** *vt & i* развёртывать(ся) *impf*, разверну́ть(ся) *pf*. **unruffled** *adj* (*smooth*) гла́дкий; (*calm*) споко́йный. **unruly** *adj* непоко́рный.

unsafe *adj* опа́сный; (*insecure*) ненадёжный. **unsaid** *adj*: **leave ~** молча́ть *impf* о+*prep*. **unsaleable** *adj* нехо́дкий. **unsalted** *adj* несолёный. **unsatisfactory** *adj* неудовлетвори́тельный. **unsatisfied** *adj* неудовлетворённый. **unsavoury** *adj* (*unpleasant*) неприя́тный; (*disreputable*) сомни́тельный. **unscathed** *adj* невреди́мый; (*predic*) цел и невреди́м. **unscheduled** *adj* (*transport*) внеочередно́й; (*event*) незаплани́рованный. **unscientific** *adj* ненау́чный. **unscrew** *vt & i* отви́нчивать(ся) *impf*, отвинти́ть(ся) *pf*. **unscrupulous** *adj* беспринци́пный. **unseat** *vt* (*of horse*) сбра́сывать *impf*, сбро́сить *pf* с седла́; (*parl*) лиша́ть *impf*, лиши́ть *pf* парла́ментского манда́та.

unseemly *adj* неподоба́ющий. **unseen** *adj* неви́данный. **unselfconscious** *adj* непосре́дственный. **unselfish** *adj* бескоры́стный. **unsettle** *vt* выбива́ть *impf*, вы́бить *pf* из коле́и; (*upset*) расстра́ивать *impf*, расстро́ить *pf*. **unsettled** *adj* (*weather*) неусто́йчивый; (*unresolved*) нерешённый. **unsettling** *adj* волну́ющий. **unshakeable** *adj* непоколеби́мый. **unshaven** *adj* небри́тый. **unsightly** *adj* непригля́дный, уро́дливый. **unsigned** *adj* неподпи́санный. **unskilful** *adj* неуме́лый. **unskilled** *adj* неквалифици́рованный. **unsociable** *adj* необщи́тельный. **unsold** *adj* непро́данный. **unsolicited** *adj* непро́шеный. **unsolved** *adj* нерешённый. **unsophisticated** *adj* просто́й. **unsound** *adj* (*unhealthy*, *unwholesome*) нездоро́вый; (*not solid*) непро́чный; (*unfounded*) необосно́ванный; **of ~ mind** душевнобольно́й. **unspeakable** *adj* (*inexpressible*) невырази́мый; (*very bad*) отврати́тельный. **unspecified** *adj* то́чно не ука́занный, неопределённый. **unspoilt** *adj* неиспо́рченный. **unspoken** *adj* невы́сказанный. **unstable** *adj* неусто́йчивый; (*mentally*) неуравнове́шенный. **unsteady** *adj* неусто́йчивый. **unstuck** *adj*: **come ~** откле́иваться *impf*, откле́иться *pf*; (*fig*) прова́ливаться *impf*, провали́ться *pf*. **unsuccessful** *adj* неуда́чный, безуспе́шный. **unsuitable** *adj* неподходя́щий. **unsuited** *adj* неприго́дный. **unsung** *adj* невоспе́тый. **unsupported** *adj* неподде́ржанный. **unsure** *adj* неуве́ренный (**of o.s.** в себе́). **unsurpassed** *adj* непревзойдённый. **unsurprising** *adj* неудиви́тельный. **unsuspected** *adj* (*unforeseen*) непредви́денный. **unsuspecting** *adj* неподозрева́ющий. **unsweetened** *adj* неподсла́щенный. **unswerving** *adj* непоколеби́мый. **unsympathetic** *adj* несочу́вствующий. **unsystematic** *adj* несистемати́чный.

untainted *adj* неиспо́рченный.

untangle *vt* распу́тывать *impf*, распу́тать *pf*. **untapped** *adj*: **~ resources** неиспо́льзованные ресу́рсы *m pl*. **untenable** *adj* несостоя́тельный. **untested** *adj* неиспы́танный. **unthinkable** *adj* невообрази́мый. **unthinking** *adj* безду́мный. **untidiness** *n* неопря́тность; (*disorder*) беспоря́док. **untidy** *adj* неопря́тный; (*in disorder*) в беспоря́дке. **untie** *vt* развя́зывать *impf*, развяза́ть *pf*; (*set free*) освобожда́ть *impf*, освободи́ть *pf*.

until *prep* до+*gen*; **not ~** не ра́ньше+*gen*; **~ then** до тех пор; *conj* пока́, пока́... не; **not ~** то́лько когда́.

untimely *adj* (*premature*) безвре́менный; (*inappropriate*) неуме́стный. **untiring** *adj* неутоми́мый. **untold** *adj* (*incalculable*) бессчётный, несме́тный; (*inexpressible*) невырази́мый. **untouched** *adj* нетро́нутый; (*indifferent*) равноду́шный. **untoward** *adj* неблагоприя́тный. **untrained** *adj* необу́ченный. **untried** *adj* неиспы́танный. **untroubled** *adj* споко́йный. **untrue** *adj* неве́рный. **untrustworthy** *adj* ненадёжный. **untruth** *n* непра́вда, ложь. **untruthful** *adj* лжи́вый.

unusable *adj* неприго́дный.

unused *adj* неиспо́льзованный; (*unaccustomed*) непривы́кший (**to** к+*dat*); **I am ~ to this** я к э́тому не привы́к.

unusual *adj* необыкнове́нный, необы́чный. **unusually** *adv* необыкнове́нно. **unutterable** *adj* невырази́мый.

unveil *vt* (*statue*) торже́ственно открыва́ть *impf*, откры́ть *pf*; (*disclose*) обнаро́довать *impf* & *pf*.

unwanted *adj* нежела́нный.

unwarranted *adj* неопра́вданный. **unwary** *adj* неосторо́жный. **unwavering** *adj* непоколеби́мый. **unwelcome** *adj* нежела́тельный; (*unpleasant*) неприя́тный. **unwell** *adj* нездоро́вый. **unwieldy** *adj* громо́здкий. **unwilling** *adj* несклó нный; **be ~** не хоте́ть *impf*, за~ *pf* (**to** +*inf*). **unwillingly** *adv* неохо́тно. **unwillingness** *n* неохо́та. **unwind** *vt* & *i* разма́тывать(ся) *impf*, размота́ть(ся) *pf*; (*rest*) отдыха́ть *impf*, отдохну́ть *pf*. **unwise** *adj* не(благо)разу́мный. **unwitting** *adj* нево́льный. **unwittingly** *adv* нево́льно. **unworkable** *adj* неприменимый. **unworldly** *adj* не от ми́ра сего́. **unworthy** *adj* недосто́йный. **unwrap** *vt* развёртывать *impf*, разверну́ть *pf*. **unwritten** *adj*: **~ law** непи́саный зако́н.

unyielding *adj* упо́рный, неподáтливый.

unzip *vt* расстёгивать *impf*, расстегну́ть *pf* (мо́лнию+*gen*).

up *adv* (*motion*) наве́рх, вверх; (*position*) наверху́, вверху́; **~ and down** вверх и вниз; (*back and forth*) взад и вперёд; **~ to** (*towards*) к+*dat*; (*as far as, until*) до+*gen*; **~ to now** до сих пор; **be ~ against** име́ть *impf* де́ло с+*instr*; **it is ~ to you**+*inf*, э́то вам+*inf*, вы должны́+*inf*; **what's ~?** что случи́лось?; в чём де́ло?; **your time is ~** ва́ше вре́мя истекло́; **~ and about** на нога́х; **he isn't ~ yet** он ещё не встал; **he isn't ~ to this job** он не годи́тся для э́той рабо́ты; *prep* вверх по+*dat*; (*along*) (вдоль) по+*dat*; *vt* повыша́ть *impf*, повы́сить; *vi* (*leap up*) взять *pf*; *adj*: **~-to-date** совреме́нный; (*fashionable*) мо́дный; **~-and-coming** многообеща́ющий; *n*: **~s and downs** (*fig*) превра́тности *f pl* судьбы́.

upbringing *n* воспита́ние.

update *vt* модернизи́ровать *impf* & *pf*; (*a book etc.*) дополня́ть *impf*, допо́лнить *pf*.

upgrade *vt* повыша́ть *impf*, повы́сить *pf* (по слу́жбе).

upheaval *n* потрясе́ние.

uphill *adj* (*fig*) тяжёлый; *adv* в го́ру.

uphold *vt* подде́рживать *impf*, поддержа́ть *pf*.

upholster *vt* обива́ть *impf*, оби́ть *pf*. **upholsterer** *n* обо́йщик. **upholstery** *n* оби́вка.

upkeep *n* содержа́ние.

upland *n* гори́стая часть страны́; *adj* наго́рный.

uplift *vt* поднима́ть *impf*, подня́ть *pf*.
up-market *adj* дорого́й.
upon *prep* (*position*) на+*prep*, (*motion*) на+*acc*; *see* **on**
upper *adj* ве́рхний; (*socially, in rank*) вы́сший; **gain the ~ hand** одéрживать *impf*, одержа́ть *pf* верх (**over** над+*instr*); *n* передо́к. **uppermost** *adj* са́мый ве́рхний, вы́сший; **be ~ in person's mind** бо́льше всего́ занима́ть *impf*, заня́ть *pf* мы́сли кого́-л.
upright *n* сто́йка; *adj* вертика́льный; (*honest*) че́стный; **~ piano** пиани́но *neut indecl*.
uprising *n* восста́ние.
uproar *n* шум, гам.
uproot *vt* вырыва́ть *impf*, вы́рвать *pf* с ко́рнем; (*people*) выселя́ть *impf*, вы́селить *pf*.
upset *n* расстро́йство; *vt* расстра́ивать *impf*, расстро́ить *pf*; (*overturn*) опроки́дывать *impf*, опроки́нуть *pf*; *adj* (*miserable*) расстро́енный; **~ stomach** расстро́йство желу́дка.
upshot *n* развя́зка, результа́т.
upside-down *adj* перевёрнутый вверх дном; *adv* вверх дном; (*in disorder*) в беспоря́дке.
upstairs *adv* (*position*) наверху́; (*motion*) наве́рх; *n* ве́рхний эта́ж; *adj* находя́щийся в ве́рхнем этаже́.
upstart *n* вы́скочка *m & f*.
upstream *adv* про́тив тече́ния; (*situation*) вверх по тече́нию.
upsurge *n* подъём, волна́.
uptake *n*: **be quick on the ~** бы́стро сообража́ть *impf*, сообрази́ть *pf*.
upturn *n* (*fig*) улучше́ние. **upturned** *adj* (*face etc.*) по́днятый кве́рху; (*inverted*) перевёрнутый.
upward *adj* напра́вленный вверх. **upwards** *adv* вверх; **~ of** свы́ше+*gen*.
uranium *n* ура́н.
urban *adj* городско́й.
urbane *adj* ве́жливый.
urchin *n* мальчи́шка *m*.
urge *n* (*incitement*) побужде́ние; (*desire*) жела́ние; *vt* (*impel*, **~ on**) подгоня́ть *impf*, подогна́ть *pf*; (*warn*) предупрежда́ть *impf*, предупреди́ть *pf*; (*try to persuade*) убежда́ть *impf*. **urgency** *n* сро́чность, ва́жность; **a matter of great ~** сро́чное де́ло. **urgent** *adj* сро́чный; (*insistent*) настоя́тельный. **urgently** *adv* сро́чно.
urinate *vi* мочи́ться *impf*, по~ *pf*. **urine** *n* моча́.
urn *n* у́рна.
US(A) *abbr* (*of* **United States of America**) США, Соединённые Шта́ты Аме́рики.
usable *adj* го́дный к употребле́нию. **usage** *n* употребле́ние; (*treatment*) обраще́ние.
use *n* (*utilization*) употребле́ние, по́льзование; (*benefit*) по́льза; (*application*) примене́ние; **it is no ~ (-ing)** бесполе́зно (+*inf*); **make ~ of** испо́льзовать *impf & pf*; по́льзоваться *impf* +*instr*; *vt* употребля́ть *impf*, употреби́ть *pf*; по́льзоваться *impf* +*instr*; (*apply*) применя́ть *impf*, примени́ть *pf*; (*treat*) обраща́ться *impf* с+*instr*; **I ~d to see him often** я ча́сто его́ встреча́л; **be, get ~d to** привыка́ть *impf*, привы́кнуть *pf* (**to** к+*dat*); **~ up** рас-

хо́довать *impf*, из~ *pf*. **used** *adj* (*second-hand*) ста́рый. **useful** *adj* поле́зный; **come in ~, prove ~** пригоди́ться *pf* (**to** +*dat*). **useless** *adj* бесполе́зный. **user** *n* потреби́тель *m*.

usher *n* (*theat*) билетёр; *vt* (*lead in*) вводи́ть *impf*, ввести́ *pf*; (*proclaim*, ~ *in*) возвеща́ть *impf*, возвести́ть *pf*. **usherette** *n* билетёрша.

USSR *abbr* (*of* **Union of Soviet Socialist Republics**) СССР, Сою́з Сове́тских Социалисти́ческих Респу́блик.

usual *adj* обыкнове́нный, обы́чный; **as ~** как обы́чно. **usually** *adv* обыкнове́нно, обы́чно.

usurp *vt* узурпи́ровать *impf* & *pf*. **usurper** *n* узурпа́тор.

usury *n* ростовщи́чество.

utensil *n* инструме́нт; *pl* у́тварь, посу́да.

uterus *n* ма́тка.

utilitarian *adj* утилита́рный. **utilitarianism** *n* утилитари́зм. **utility** *n* поле́зность; *pl*: **public utilities** коммуна́льные услу́ги *f pl*. **utilize** *vt* испо́льзовать *impf* & *pf*.

utmost *adj* (*extreme*) кра́йний; **this is of the ~ importance to me** э́то для меня́ кра́йне ва́жно; *n*: **do one's ~** де́лать *impf*, с~ *pf* всё возмо́жное.

Utopia *n* уто́пия. **utopian** *adj* утопи́ческий.

utter *attrib* по́лный, абсолю́тный; (*out-and-out*) отъя́вленный (*coll*); *vt* произноси́ть *impf*, произнести́ *pf*; (*let out*) издава́ть *impf*, изда́ть *pf*. **utterance** *n* (*uttering*) произнесе́ние; (*pronouncement*) выска́зывание. **utterly** *adv* соверше́нно.

Uzbek *n* узбе́к, -е́чка. **Uzbekistan** *n* Узбекиста́н.

V

vacancy *n* (*for job*) вака́нсия, свобо́дное ме́сто; (*at hotel*) свобо́дный но́мер. **vacant** *adj* (*post*) вака́нтный; (*post; not engaged, free*) свобо́дный; (*empty*) пусто́й; (*look*) отсу́тствующий. **vacate** *vt* освобожда́ть *impf*, освободи́ть *pf*. **vacation** *n* кани́кулы (-л) *pl*; (*leave*) о́тпуск.

vaccinate *vt* вакцини́ровать *impf* & *pf*. **vaccination** *n* приви́вка (**against** от, про́тив +*gen*). **vaccine** *n* вакци́на.

vacillate *vi* колеба́ться *impf*. **vacillation** *n* колеба́ние.

vacuous *adj* пусто́й. **vacuum** *n* ва́куум; (*fig*) пустота́; *vt* пылесо́сить *impf*, про~ *pf*; **~ cleaner** пылесо́с; **~ flask** те́рмос.

vagabond *n* бродя́га *m*.

vagary *n* капри́з.

vagina *n* влага́лище.

vagrant *n* бродя́га *m*.

vague *adj* (*indeterminate, uncertain*) неопределённый; (*unclear*) нея́сный; (*dim*) сму́тный; (*absent-minded*) рассе́янный. **vagueness** *n* неопределённость, нея́сность; (*absent-mindedness*) рассе́янность.

vain *adj* (*futile*) тще́тный, напра́сный; (*empty*) пусто́й; (*conceited*) тщесла́вный; **in ~** напра́сно.

vale *n* дол, доли́на.

valentine *n* (*card*) поздрави́тельная ка́рточка с днём свято́го Валенти́на.

valet *n* камерди́нер.

valiant *adj* хра́брый.

valid *adj* действи́тельный; (*weighty*) ве́ский. **validate** *vt* (*ratify*) утвержда́ть *impf*, утверди́ть *pf*. **validity** *n* действи́тельность; (*weightiness*) ве́скость.

valley *n* доли́на.

valour *n* до́блесть.

valuable *adj* це́нный; *n pl* це́нности *f pl*. **valuation** *n* оце́нка. **value** *n* це́нность; (*math*) величина́; *pl* це́нности *f pl*; **~-added tax** нало́г на доба́вленную сто́имость; **~ judgement** субъекти́вная оце́нка; *vt* (*estimate*) оце́нивать *impf*, оцени́ть *pf*; (*hold dear*) цени́ть *impf*.

valve *n* (*tech*, *med*, *mus*) кла́пан; (*tech*) ве́нтиль *m*; (*radio*) электро́нная ла́мпа.

vampire *n* вампи́р.

van *n* фурго́н.

vandal *n*ванда́л. **vandalism** *n* вандали́зм. **vandalize** *vt* разруша́ть *impf*, разру́шить *pf*.

vanguard *n* аванга́рд.

vanilla *n* вани́ль.

vanish *vi* исчеза́ть *impf*, исче́знуть *pf*.

vanity *n* (*futility*) тщета́; (*conceit*) тщесла́вие.

vanquish *vt* побежда́ть *impf*, победи́ть *pf*.

vantage-point *n* (*mil*) наблюда́тельный пункт; (*fig*) вы́годная пози́ция.

vapour *n* пар.

variable *adj* изме́нчивый; (*weather*) неусто́йчивый, переме́нный; *n* (*math*) переме́нная (величина́). **variance** *n*: **be at ~ with** (*contradict*) противоре́чить *impf* +*dat*; (*disagree*) расходи́ться *impf*, разойти́сь *pf* во мне́ниях с+*instr*.

variant *n* вариа́нт. **variation** *n* (*varying*) измене́ние; (*variant*) вариа́нт; (*variety*) разнови́дность; (*mus*) вариа́ция.

varicose *adj*: **~ veins** расшире́ние вен.

varied *adj* разнообра́зный. **variegated** *adj* разноцве́тный. **variety** *n* разнообра́зие; (*sort*) разнови́дность; (*a number*) ряд; **~ show** варьете́ *neut indecl*. **various** *adj* ра́зный.

varnish *n* лак; *vt* лакирова́ть *impf*, от~ *pf*.

vary *vt* разнообра́зить *impf*, меня́ть *impf*; *vi* (*change*) меня́ться *impf*; (*differ*) разни́ться *impf*.

vase *n* ва́за.

Vaseline *n* (*propr*) вазели́н.

vast *adj* грома́дный. **vastly** *adv* значи́тельно.

VAT *abbr* (*of* **value-added tax**) нало́г на доба́вленную сто́имость.

vat *n* чан, бак.

vaudeville *n* водеви́ль *m*.

vault[1] *n* (*leap*) прыжо́к; *vt* перепры́гивать *impf*, перепры́гнуть *pf*; *vi* пры́гать *impf*, пры́гнуть *pf*.

vault[2] *n* (*arch*, *covering*) свод; (*cellar*) по́греб; (*tomb*) склеп. **vaulted** *adj* сво́дчатый.

VDU *abbr* (*of* **visual display unit**) монито́р.

veal *n* теля́тина.

vector *n* (*math*) ве́ктор.

veer *vi* (*change direction*) изменя́ть *impf*, измени́ть *pf* направле́ние; (*turn*) повора́чивать *impf*, повороти́ть *pf*.

vegetable *n* о́вощ; *adj* овощно́й. **vegetarian** *n* вегетариа́нец, -нка; *attrib* вегетариа́нский. **vegetate** *vi* (*fig*) прозяба́ть *impf.* **vegetation** *n* расти́тельность.

vehemence *n* (*force*) си́ла; (*passion*) стра́стность. **vehement** *adj* (*forceful*) си́льный; (*passionate*) стра́стный.

vehicle *n* тра́нспортное сре́дство; (*motor* ~) автомоби́ль *m*; (*medium*) сре́дство.

veil *n* вуа́ль; (*fig*) заве́са. **veiled** *adj* скры́тый.

vein *n* ве́на; (*of leaf*; *streak*) жи́лка; **in the same** ~ в том же ду́хе.

velocity *n* ско́рость.

velvet *n* ба́рхат; *adj* ба́рхатный. **velvety** *adj* бархати́стый.

vending-machine *n* торго́вый автома́т. **vendor** *n* продаве́ц, -вщи́ца.

vendetta *n* венде́тта.

veneer *n* фане́ра; (*fig*) лоск.

venerable *adj* почте́нный. **venerate** *vt* благогове́ть *impf* пе́ред+*instr.* **veneration** *n* благогове́ние.

venereal *adj* венери́ческий.

venetian blind *n* жалюзи́ *neut indecl.*

vengeance *n* месть; **take** ~ мстить *impf*, ото~ *pf* (**on** +*dat*; **for** за+*acc*); **with a** ~ вовсю́. **vengeful** *adj* мсти́тельный.

venison *n* олени́на.

venom *n* яд. **venomous** *adj* ядови́тый.

vent[1] *n* (*opening*) вы́ход (*also fig*), отве́рстие; *vt* (*feelings*) дава́ть *impf*, дать *pf* вы́ход+*dat*; излива́ть *impf*, изли́ть *pf* (**on** на+*acc*).

vent[2] *n* (*slit*) разре́з.

ventilate *vt* прове́тривать *impf*, прове́трить *pf.* **ventilation** *n* вентиля́ция. **ventilator** *n* вентиля́тор.

ventriloquist *n* чревовеща́тель *m.*

venture *n* предприя́тие; *vi* (*dare*) осме́ливаться *impf*, осме́литься *pf*; *vt* (*risk*) рискова́ть *impf* +*instr.*

venue *n* ме́сто.

veranda *n* вера́нда.

verb *n* глаго́л. **verbal** *adj* (*oral*) у́стный; (*relating to words*) слове́сный; (*gram*) отглаго́льный. **verbatim** *adj* досло́вный; *adv* досло́вно. **verbose** *adj* многосло́вный.

verdict *n* пригово́р.

verge *n* (*also fig*) край; (*of road*) обо́чина; (*fig*) грань; **on the** ~ **of** на гра́ни+*gen*; **he was on the** ~ **of telling all** он чуть не рассказа́л всё; *vi*: ~ **on** грани́чить *impf* с+*instr*.

verification *n* прове́рка; (*confirmation*) подтвержде́ние. **verify** *vt* проверя́ть *impf*, прове́рить *pf*; (*confirm*) подтвержда́ть *impf*, подтверди́ть *pf.*

vermin *n* вреди́тели *m pl.*

vernacular *n* родно́й язы́к; ме́стный диале́кт; (*homely language*) разгово́рный язы́к.

versatile *adj* многосторо́нний.

verse *n* (*also bibl*) стих; (*stanza*) строфа́; (*poetry*) стихи́ *m pl.* **versed** *adj* о́пытный, све́дущий (**in** в+*prep*).

version *n* (*variant*) вариа́нт; (*interpretation*) ве́рсия; (*text*) текст.

versus *prep* про́тив+*gen.*

vertebra *n* позвоно́к; *pl* позвоно́чник. **vertebrate** *n* позвоно́чное живо́тное *sb.*

vertical *adj* вертика́льный; *n*

вертика́ль.
vertigo *n* головокруже́ние.
verve *n* жи́вость, энтузиа́зм.
very *adj* (*that* ~ *same*) тот са́мый; (*this* ~ *same*) э́тот са́мый; **at that ~ moment** в тот са́мый моме́нт; (*precisely*) как раз; **you are the ~ person I was looking for** как раз вас я иска́л; **the ~** (*even the*) да́же, оди́н; **the ~ thought frightens me** одна́, да́же, мысль об э́том меня́ пуга́ет; (*the extreme*) са́мый; **at the ~ end** в са́мом конце́; *adv* о́чень; **~ much** о́чень; **~ much** +*comp* гора́здо +*comp*; ~+*superl*, *superl*; **~ first** са́мый пе́рвый; **~ well** (*agreement*) хорошо́, ла́дно; **not ~** не о́чень, дово́льно +*neg*.
vessel *n* сосу́д; (*ship*) су́дно.
vest[1] *n* ма́йка; (*waistcoat*) жиле́т.
vest[2] *vt* (*with power*) облека́ть *impf*, обле́чь *pf* (**with** +*instr*). **vested** *adj*: **~ interest** ли́чная заинтересо́ванность; **~ interests** (*entrepreneurs*) кру́пные предпринима́тели *m pl*.
vestibule *n* вестибю́ль *m*.
vestige *n* (*trace*) след; (*sign*) при́знак.
vestments *n pl* (*eccl*) облаче́ние. **vestry** *n* ри́зница.
vet *n* ветерина́р; *vt* (*fig*) проверя́ть *impf*, прове́рить *pf*.
veteran *n* ветера́н; *adj* ста́рый.
veterinary *adj* ветерина́рный; *n* ветерина́р.
veto *n* ве́то *neut indecl*; *vt* налага́ть *impf*, наложи́ть *pf* ве́то на+*acc*.
vex *vt* досажда́ть *impf*, досади́ть *pf* +*dat*. **vexation** *n* доса́да. **vexed** *adj* (*annoyed*) серди́тый; (*question*) спо́рный. **vexatious, vexing** *adj* доса́дный.
via *prep* че́рез+*acc*.
viable *adj* (*able to survive*) жизнеспосо́бный; (*feasible*) осуществи́мый.
viaduct *n* виаду́к.
vibrant *adj* (*lively*) живо́й. **vibrate** *vi* вибри́ровать *impf*; *vt* (*make* ~) заставля́ть *impf*, заста́вить *pf* вибри́ровать. **vibration** *n* вибра́ция. **vibrato** *n* вибра́то *neut indecl*.
vicar *n* прихо́дский свяще́нник. **vicarage** *n* дом свяще́нника.
vicarious *adj* чужо́й.
vice[1] *n* (*evil*) поро́к.
vice[2] *n* (*tech*) тиски́ (-ко́в) *pl*.
vice- *in comb* вице-, замести́тель *m*; **~-chairman** замести́тель *m* председа́теля; **~-chancellor** (*univ*) прор́ектор; **~-president** вице-президе́нт. **viceroy** *n* вице-коро́ль *m*.
vice versa *adv* наоборо́т.
vicinity *n* окре́стность; **in the ~** поблизо́сти (**of** от+*gen*).
vicious *adj* зло́бный; **~ circle** поро́чный круг.
vicissitude *n* превра́тность.
victim *n* же́ртва; (*of accident*) пострада́вший *sb*. **victimization** *n* пресле́дование. **victimize** *vt* пресле́довать *impf*.
victor *n* победи́тель *m*, ~ница.
Victorian *adj* викториа́нский.
victorious *adj* победоно́сный. **victory** *n* побе́да.
video *n* (~ *recorder*, ~ *cassette*, ~ *film*) ви́део *neut indecl*; **~ camera** видеока́мера; **~ cassette** видеокассе́та; **~ (cassette) recorder** видеомагнитофо́н; **~ game** видеоигра́; *vt* запи́сывать *impf*,

записа́ть *pf* на ви́део.

vie *vi* сопе́рничать *impf* (**with** c+*instr*; **for** в+*prep*).

Vietnam *n* Вьетна́м. **Vietnamese** *n* вьетна́мец, -мка; *adj* вьетна́мский.

view *n* (*prospect*, *picture*) вид; (*opinion*) взгляд; (*viewing*) просмо́тр; (*inspection*) осмо́тр; **in ~ of** ввиду́+*gen*; **on ~** вы́ставленный для обозре́ния; **with a ~ to** с це́лью+*gen*, +*inf*; *vt* (*pictures etc.*) рассма́тривать *impf*; (*inspect*) осма́тривать *impf*, осмотре́ть *pf*; (*mentally*) смотре́ть *impf* на+*acc*. **viewer** *n* зри́тель *m*, ~ница. **viewfinder** *n* видоиска́тель *m*. **viewpoint** *n* то́чка зре́ния.

vigil *n* бде́ние; **keep ~** дежу́рить *impf*. **vigilance** *n* бди́тельность. **vigilant** *adj* бди́тельный. **vigilante** *n* дружи́нник.

vigorous *adj* си́льный, энерги́чный. **vigour** *n* си́ла, эне́ргия.

vile *adj* гну́сный. **vilify** *vt* черни́ть *impf*, о~ *pf*.

villa *n* ви́лла.

village *n* дере́вня; *attrib* дереве́нский. **villager** *n* жи́тель *m* дере́вни.

villain *n* злоде́й.

vinaigrette *n* припра́ва из у́ксуса и оли́вкового ма́сла.

vindicate *vt* опра́вдывать *impf*, оправда́ть *pf*. **vindication** *n* оправда́ние.

vindictive *adj* мсти́тельный.

vine *n* виногра́дная лоза́.

vinegar *n* у́ксус.

vineyard *n* виногра́дник.

vintage *n* (*year*) год; (*fig*) вы́пуск; *attrib* (*wine*) ма́рочный; (*car*) архаи́ческий.

viola *n* (*mus*) альт.

violate *vt* (*treaty*, *privacy*) наруша́ть *impf*, нару́шить *pf*; (*grave*) оскверня́ть *impf*, оскверни́ть *pf*. **violation** *n* наруше́ние; оскверне́ние.

violence *n* (*physical coercion*, *force*) наси́лие; (*strength*, *force*) си́ла. **violent** *adj* (*person*, *storm*, *argument*) свире́пый; (*pain*) си́льный; (*death*) наси́льственный. **violently** *adv* си́льно, о́чень.

violet *n* (*bot*) фиа́лка; (*colour*) фиоле́товый цвет; *adj* фиоле́товый.

violin *n* скри́пка. **violinist** *n* скрипа́ч, ~ка.

VIP *abbr* (*of* **very important person**) о́чень ва́жное лицо́.

viper *n* гадю́ка.

virgin *n* де́вственница, (*male*) де́вственник; **V~ Mary** де́ва Мари́я. **virginal** *adj* де́вственный. **virginity** *n* де́вственность. **Virgo** *n* Де́ва.

virile *adj* му́жественный. **virility** *n* му́жество.

virtual *adj* факти́ческий; (*comput*) виртуа́льный. **virtually** *adv* факти́чески. **virtue** *n* (*excellence*) доброд-е́тель; (*merit*) досто́инство;

by ~ of на основа́нии+*gen*. **virtuosity** *n* виртуо́зность. **virtuoso** *n* виртуо́з. **virtuous** *adj* доброде́тельный.

virulent *adj* (*med*) вируле́нтный; (*fig*) зло́бный.

virus *n* ви́рус.

visa *n* ви́за.

vis-à-vis *prep* (*with regard to*) по отноше́нию к+*dat*.

viscount *n* вико́нт. **viscountess** *n* виконте́сса.

viscous *adj* вя́зкий.

visibility *n* ви́димость. **visible**

adj ви́димый. **visibly** *adv* я́вно, заме́тно.
vision *n* (*sense*) зре́ние; (*apparition*) виде́ние; (*dream*) мечта́; (*insight*) проница́тельность. **visionary** *adj* (*unreal*) при́зрачный; (*impracticable*) неосуществи́мый; (*insightful*) проница́тельный; *n* (*dreamer*) мечта́тель *m*.
visit *n* посеще́ние, визи́т; *vt* посеща́ть *impf*, посети́ть *pf*; (*call on*) заходи́ть *impf*, зайти́ *pf* к+*dat*. **visitation** *n* официа́льное посеще́ние. **visitor** *n* гость *m*, посети́тель *m*.
visor *n* (*of cap*) козырёк; (*in car*) солнцезащи́тный щито́к; (*of helmet*) забра́ло.
vista *n* перспекти́ва, вид.
visual *adj* (*of vision*) зри́тельный; (*graphic*) нагля́дный; ~ **aids** нагля́дные посо́бия *neut pl*. **visualize** *vt* представля́ть *impf*, предста́вить *pf* себе́.
vital *adj* абсолю́тно необходи́мый (**to, for** для+*gen*); (*essential to life*) жи́зненный; **of** ~ **importance** первостепе́нной ва́жности. **vitality** *n* (*liveliness*) эне́ргия. **vitally** *adv* жи́зненно.
vitamin *n* витами́н.
vitreous *adj* стекля́нный.
vitriolic *adj* (*fig*) е́дкий.
vivacious *adj* живо́й. **vivacity** *n* жи́вость.
viva (voce) *n* у́стный экза́мен.
vivid *adj* (*bright*) я́ркий; (*lively*) живо́й. **vividness** *n* я́ркость; жи́вость.
vivisection *n* вивисе́кция.
vixen *n* лиси́ца-са́мка.
viz. *adv* то есть, а и́менно.
vocabulary *n* (*range, list, of words*) слова́рь *m*; (*range of words*) запа́с слов; (*of a language*) слова́рный соста́в.
vocal *adj* голосово́й; (*mus*) вока́льный; (*noisy*) шу́мный; ~ **chord** голосова́я свя́зка. **vocalist** *n* певе́ц, -ви́ца.
vocation *n* призва́ние. **vocational** *adj* профессиона́льный.
vociferous *adj* шу́мный.
vodka *n* во́дка.
vogue *n* мо́да; **in** ~ в мо́де.
voice *n* го́лос; *vt* выража́ть *impf*, вы́разить *pf*.
void *n* пустота́; *adj* пусто́й; (*invalid*) недействи́тельный; ~ **of** лишённый +*gen*.
volatile *adj* (*chem*) лету́чий; (*person*) непостоя́нный, неусто́йчивый.
volcanic *adj* вулкани́ческий. **volcano** *n* вулка́н.
vole *n* (*zool*) полёвка.
volition *n* во́ля; **by one's own** ~ по свое́й во́ле.
volley *n* (*missiles*) залп; (*fig*) град; (*sport*) уда́р с лёта; *vt* (*sport*) ударя́ть *impf*, уда́рить *pf* с лёта. **volleyball** *n* волейбо́л.
volt *n* вольт. **voltage** *n* напряже́ние.
voluble *adj* говорли́вый.
volume *n* (*book*) том; (*capacity, size*) объём; (*loudness*) гро́мкость. **voluminous** *adj* обши́рный.
voluntary *adj* доброво́льный. **volunteer** *n* доброво́лец; *vt* предлага́ть *impf*, предложи́ть *pf*; *vi* (*offer*) вызыва́ться *impf*, вы́зваться *pf* (*inf*, +*inf*; **for** в+*acc*); (*mil*) идти́ *impf*, пойти́ *pf* доброво́льцем.
voluptuous *adj* сластолюби́вый.
vomit *n* рво́та; *vt* (& *i*) рвать

impf, вы́рвать *pf impers* (+*instr*); **he was ~ing blood** его́ рва́ло кро́вью.

voracious *adj* прожо́рливый; (*fig*) ненасы́тный.

vortex *n* (*also fig*) водоворо́т, вихрь *m*.

vote *n* (*poll*) голосова́ние; (*individual* ~) го́лос; **the** ~ (*suffrage*) пра́во го́лоса; (*resolution*) во́тум *no pl*; ~ **of no confidence** во́тум недове́рия (**in** +*dat*); ~ **of thanks** выраже́ние благода́рности; *vi* голосова́ть *impf*, про~ *pf* (**for** за+*acc*; **against** про́тив+*gen*); *vt* (*allocate by* ~) ассигнова́ть *impf* & *pf*; (*deem*) признава́ть *impf*, призна́ть *pf*; **the film was ~d a failure** фильм был при́знан неуда́чным; ~ **in** избира́ть *impf*, избра́ть *pf* голосова́нием. **voter** *n* избира́тель *m*.

vouch *vi*: ~ **for** руча́ться *impf*, поручи́ться *pf* за+*acc*. **voucher** *n* (*receipt*) распи́ска; (*coupon*) тало́н.

vow *n* обе́т; *vt* кля́сться *impf*, по~ *pf* в+*prep*.

vowel *n* гла́сный *sb*.

voyage *n* путеше́ствие.

vulgar *adj* вульга́рный, гру́бый, по́шлый. **vulgarity** *n* вульга́рность, по́шлость.

vulnerable *adj* уязви́мый.

vulture *n* гриф; (*fig*) хи́щник.

W

wad *n* комо́к; (*bundle*) па́чка. **wadding** ва́та; (*padding*) наби́вка.

waddle *vi* ходи́ть *indet*, идти́ *det*, пойти́ *pf* вперева́лку (*coll*).

wade *vt* & *i* (*river*) переходи́ть *impf*, перейти́ *pf* вброд; *vi*: ~ **through** (*mud etc.*) пробира́ться *impf*, пробра́ться *pf* по+*dat*; (*sth boring etc.*) одолева́ть *impf*, одоле́ть *pf*.

wafer *n* ва́фля.

waffle[1] *n* (*dish*) ва́фля.

waffle[2] *vi* трепа́ться *impf*.

waft *vt* & *i* нести́(сь) *impf*, по~ *pf*.

wag *vt* & *i* (*tail*) виля́ть *impf*, вильну́ть *pf* (+*instr*); *vt* (*finger*) грози́ть *impf*, по~ *pf* +*instr*.

wage[1] *n* (*pay*) *see* **wages**

wage[2] *vt*: ~ **war** вести́ *impf*, про~ *pf* войну́.

wager *n* пари́ *neut indecl*; *vi* держа́ть *impf* пари́ (**that** что); *vt* ста́вить *impf* по~ *pf*.

wages *n pl* за́работная пла́та.

waggle *vt* & *i* пома́хивать *impf*, помаха́ть *pf* (+*instr*).

wag(g)on *n* (*carriage*) пово́зка; (*cart*) теле́га; (*rly*) ваго́н-платфо́рма.

wail *n* вопль *m*; *vi* вопи́ть *impf*.

waist *n* та́лия; (*level of* ~) по́яс; **~-deep, high** (*adv*) по по́яс. **waistband** *n* по́яс. **waistcoat** *n* жиле́т.**waistline** *n* та́лия.

wait *n* ожида́ние; **lie in ~ (for)** подстерега́ть *impf*; подстере́чь *pf*; *vi* (& *t*) (*also* ~ *for*) ждать *impf* (+*gen*); *vi* (*be a waiter, waitress*) быть официа́нтом, -ткой; ~ **on** обслу́живать *impf*, обслужи́ть *pf*. **waiter** *n* официа́нт. **waiting** *n*: **~-list** спи́сок; **~-room** приёмная *sb*; (*rly*) зал ожида́ния. **waitress** *n* официа́нтка.

waive *vt* отка́зываться *impf*, отказа́ться *pf* от+*gen*.

wake[1] *n* (*at funeral*) поми́нки (-нок) *pl*.
wake[2] *n* (*naut*) кильва́тер; **in the ~ of** по сле́ду *+gen*, за*+instr*.
wake[3] *vt* (*also ~ up*) буди́ть *impf*, раз~ *pf*; *vi* (*also ~ up*) просыпа́ться *impf*, просну́ться *pf*.
Wales *n* Уэ́льс.
walk *n* (*walking*) ходьба́; (*gait*) похо́дка; (*stroll*) прогу́лка; (*path*) тропа́; **~-out** (*strike*) забасто́вка; (*as protest*) демонстрати́вный ухо́д; **~-over** лёгкая побе́да; **ten minutes' ~ from here** де́сять мину́т ходьбы́ отсю́да; **go for a ~** идти́ *impf*, пойти́ *pf* гуля́ть; **from all ~s of life** всех слоёв о́бщества; *vi* ходи́ть *indet*, идти́ *det*, пойти́ *pf*; гуля́ть *impf*, по~ *pf*; **~ away, off** уходи́ть *impf*, уйти́ *pf*; **~ in** входи́ть *impf*, войти́ *pf*; **~ out** выходи́ть *impf*, вы́йти *pf*; **~ out on** броса́ть *impf*, бро́сить *pf*; *vt* (*traverse*) обходи́ть *impf*, обойти́ *pf*; (*take for ~*) выводи́ть *impf*, вы́вести *pf* гуля́ть. **walker** *n* ходо́к. **walkie-talkie** *n* ра́ция. **walking** *n* ходьба́; **~-stick** трость.
Walkman *n* (*propr*) во́кмен.
wall *n* стена́; *vt* обноси́ть *impf*, обнести́ *pf* стено́й; **~ up** (*door, window*) заде́лывать *impf*, заде́лать *pf*; (*brick up*) замуро́вывать *impf*, замурова́ть *pf*.
wallet *n* бума́жник.
wallflower *n* желтофио́ль.
wallop *n* си́льный уда́р; *vt* си́льно ударя́ть *impf*, уда́рить *pf*.
wallow *vi* валя́ться *impf*; **~ in** (*give o.s. up to*) погружа́ться *impf*, погрузи́ться *pf* в*+acc*.
wallpaper *n* обо́и (обо́ев) *pl*.
walnut *n* гре́цкий оре́х; (*wood, tree*) оре́ховое де́рево, оре́х.
walrus *n* морж.
waltz *n* вальс; *vi* вальси́ровать *impf*.
wan *adj* бле́дный.
wand *n* па́лочка.
wander *vi* броди́ть *impf*; (*also of thoughts etc.*) блужда́ть *impf*; **~ from the point** отклоня́ться *impf*, отклони́ться *pf* от те́мы. **wanderer** *n* стра́нник.
wane *n*: **be on the ~** убыва́ть *impf*; *vi* убыва́ть *impf*, убы́ть *pf*; (*weaken*) ослабева́ть *impf*, ослабе́ть *pf*.
wangle *vt* заполуча́ть *impf*, заполучи́ть *pf*.
want *n* (*lack*) недоста́ток; (*requirement*) потре́бность; (*desire*) жела́ние; **for ~ of** за недоста́тком *+gen*; *vt* хоте́ть *impf*, за~ *pf +gen, acc*; (*need*) нужда́ться *impf* в*+prep*; **I ~ you to come at six** я хочу́, что́бы ты пришёл в шесть. **wanting** *adj*: **be ~** недостава́ть *impf* (*impers+gen*); **experience is ~** недостаёт о́пыта.
wanton *adj* (*licentious*) распу́тный; (*senseless*) бессмы́сленный.
war *n* война́; (*attrib*) вое́нный; **at ~** в состоя́нии войны́; **~ memorial** па́мятник па́вшим в войне́.
ward *n* (*hospital*) пала́та; (*child etc.*) подопе́чный *sb*; (*district*) райо́н; *vt*: **~ off** отража́ть *impf*, отрази́ть *pf*.
warden *n* (*prison*) нача́льник; (*college*) ре́ктор; (*hostel*)

коменда́нт.
warder *n* тюре́мщик.
wardrobe *n* платяно́й шкаф.
warehouse *n* склад. **wares** *n pl* изде́лия *neut pl*, това́ры *m pl*.
warfare *n* война́.
warhead *n* боева́я голо́вка.
warily *adv* осторо́жно.
warlike *adj* во́инственный.
warm *n* тепло́; *adj* (*also fig*) тёплый; **~-hearted** серде́чный; *vt* & *i* греть(ся) *impf*; согрева́ть(ся) *impf*, согре́ть(ся) *pf*; **~ up** (*food etc.*) подогрева́ть(ся) *impf*, подогре́ть(ся) *pf*; (*liven up*) оживля́ть(ся) *impf*, оживи́ть(ся) *pf*; (*sport*) размина́ться *impf*, размя́ться *pf*; (*mus*) разы́грываться *impf*, разыгра́ться *pf*. **warmth** *n* тепло́; (*cordiality*) серде́чность.
warn *vt* предупрежда́ть *impf*, предупреди́ть *pf* (**about** о+*prep*). **warning** *n* предупрежде́ние.
warp *vt* & *i* (*wood*) коро́бить(ся) *impf*, по~, с~ *pf*; *vt* (*pervert*) извраща́ть *impf*, изврати́ть *pf*.
warrant *n* (*for arrest etc.*) о́рдер; *vt* (*justify*) опра́вдывать *impf*, оправда́ть *pf*; (*guarantee*) гаранти́ровать *impf* & *pf*. **warranty** *n* гара́нтия.
warrior *n* во́ин.
warship *n* вое́нный кора́бль *m*.
wart *n* борода́вка.
wartime *n*: **in ~** во вре́мя войны́.
wary *adj* осторо́жный.
wash *n* мытьё; (*thin layer*) то́нкий слой; (*lotion*) приму́чка; (*surf*) прибо́й; (*backwash*) попу́тная волна́; **at the ~** в сти́рке; **have a ~** мы́ться *impf*, по~ *pf*; **~-basin** умыва́льник; **~-out** (*fiasco*) прова́л; **~-room** умыва́льная *sb*; *vt* & *i* мы́ть(ся) *impf*, вы́~, по~ *pf*; *vt* (*clothes*) стира́ть *impf*, вы́~ *pf*; (*of sea*) омыва́ть *impf*; **~ away, off, out** смыва́ть(ся) *impf*, смы́ть(ся) *pf*; (*carry away*) сноси́ть *impf*, снести́ *pf*; **~ out** (*rinse*) спола́скивать *impf*, сполосну́ть *pf*; **~ up** (*dishes*) мыть *impf*, вы́~, по~ *pf* (посу́ду); **~ one's hands (of it)** умыва́ть *impf*, умы́ть *pf* ру́ки. **washed-out** *adj* (*exhausted*) утомлённый. **washer** *n* (*tech*) ша́йба. **washing** *n* (*of clothes*) сти́рка; (*clothes*) бельё; **~-machine** стира́льная маши́на; **~-powder** стира́льный порошо́к; **~-up** (*action*) мытьё посу́ды; (*dishes*) гря́зная посу́да; **~-up liquid** жи́дкое мы́ло для мытья́ посу́ды.
wasp *n* оса́.
wastage *n* уте́чка. **waste** *n* (*desert*) пусты́ня; (*refuse*) отбро́сы *m pl*; (*of time, money, etc.*) тра́та; **go to ~** пропада́ть *impf*, пропа́сть *pf* да́ром; *adj* (*desert*) пусты́нный; (*superfluous*) нену́жный; (*uncultivated*) невозде́ланный; **lay ~** опустоша́ть *impf*, опустоши́ть *pf*; **~land** пусты́рь *m*; **~ paper** нену́жные бума́ги *f pl*; (*for recycling*) макулату́ра; **~ products** отхо́ды (-дов) *pl*; **~-paper basket** корзи́на для бума́ги; *vt* тра́тить *impf*, по~, ис~ *pf*; (*time*) теря́ть *impf*, по~ *pf*; *vi*: **~ away** ча́хнуть *impf*, за~ *pf*.

wasteful *adj* расточи́тельный.

watch *n* (*timepiece*) часы́ (-со́в) *pl*; (*duty*) дежу́рство; (*naut*) ва́хта; **keep ~ over** наблюда́ть *impf* за+*instr*; **~-dog** сторожево́й пёс; **~-tower** сторожева́я ба́шня; *vt* (*observe*) наблюда́ть *impf*; (*keep an eye on*) следи́ть *impf* за+*instr*; (*look after*) смотре́ть *impf*, по~ *pf* за+*instr*; **~ television, a film** смотре́ть *impf*, по~ *pf* телеви́зор, фильм; *vi* смотре́ть *impf*; **~ out** (*be careful*) бере́чься *impf* (**for** +*gen*); **~ out for** ждать *impf* +*gen*; **~ out!** осторо́жно! **watchful** *adj* бди́тельный. **watchman** *n* (ночно́й) сто́рож. **watchword** *n* ло́зунг.

water *n* вода́; **~-colour** акваре́ль; **~-heater** кипяти́льник; **~-main** водопрово́дная магистра́ль; **~ melon** арбу́з; **~-pipe** водопрово́дная труба́; **~-ski** (*n*) во́дная лы́жа; **~-skiing** водолы́жный спорт; **~-supply** водоснабже́ние; **~-way** во́дный путь *m*; *vt* (*flowers etc.*) полива́ть *impf*, поли́ть *pf*; (*animals*) пои́ть *impf*, на~ *pf*; (*irrigate*) ороша́ть *impf*, ороси́ть *pf*; *vi* (*eyes*) слези́ться *impf*; (*mouth*): **my mouth ~s** у меня́ слю́нки теку́т; **~ down** разбавля́ть *impf*, разба́вить *pf*. **watercourse** *n* ру́сло. **watercress** *n* кресс водяно́й. **waterfall** *n* водопа́д. **waterfront** *n* часть го́рода примыка́ющая к бе́регу. **watering-can** *n* ле́йка. **waterlogged** *adj* заболо́ченный. **watermark** *n* водяно́й знак. **waterproof** *adj* непромока́емый; *n* непромока́емый плащ. **watershed** *n* водоразде́л. **waterside** *n* бе́рег. **watertight** *adj* водонепроница́емый; (*fig*) неопровержи́мый. **waterworks** *n pl* водопрово́дные сооруже́ния *neut pl*. **watery** *adj* водяни́стый.

watt *n* ватт.

wave *vt* (*hand etc.*) маха́ть *impf*, махну́ть *pf* +*instr*; (*flag*) разма́хивать *impf* +*instr*; *vi* (~ *hand*) маха́ть *impf*, по~ *pf* (**at** +*dat*); (*flutter*) развева́ться *impf*; **~ aside** отма́хиваться *impf*, отмахну́ться *pf* от+*gen*; **~ down** остана́вливать *impf*, останови́ть *pf*; *n* (*in various senses*) волна́; (*of hand*) взмах; (*in hair*) зави́вка. **wavelength** *n* длина́ волны́. **waver** *vi* колеба́ться *impf*. **wavy** *adj* волни́стый.

wax *n* воск; (*in ear*) се́ра; *vt* вощи́ть *impf*, на~ *pf*. **waxwork** *n* воскова́я фигу́ра; *pl* музе́й восковы́х фигу́р.

way *n* (*road, path, route*; *fig*) доро́га, путь *m*; (*direction*) сторона́; (*manner*) о́браз; (*method*) спо́соб; (*respect*) отноше́ние; (*habit*) привы́чка; **by the ~** (*fig*) кста́ти, ме́жду про́чим; **on the ~** по доро́ге, по пути́; **this ~** (*direction*) сюда́; (*in this ~*) таки́м о́бразом; **the other ~ round** наоборо́т; **under ~** на ходу́; **be in the ~** меша́ть *impf*; **get out of the ~** уходи́ть *impf*, уйти́ *pf* с доро́ги; **give ~** (*yield*) поддава́ться *impf*, подда́ться *pf* (**to** +*dat*); (*collapse*) обру́шиваться *impf*, обру́шиться *pf*; **go out of one's ~ to** стара́ться *impf*, по~ *pf* изо всех сил *+inf*; **get, have, one's own** ~ добиваться *impf*, добиться *pf* своего́; **make** ~ уступа́ть *impf*, уступи́ть *pf* доро́гу (**for** *+dat*). **waylay** *vt* (*lie in wait for*) подстерега́ть *impf*, подстере́чь *pf*; (*stop*) перехва́тывать *impf*, перехвати́ть *pf* по пути́. **wayside** *adj* придоро́жный; *n*: **fall by the** ~ выбыва́ть *impf*, вы́быть *pf* из стро́я.

wayward *adj* своенра́вный.

WC *abbr* (*of* **water-closet**) убо́рная *sb*.

we *pron* мы.

weak *adj* сла́бый. **weaken** *vt* ослабля́ть *impf*, ослабить *pf*; *vi* слабе́ть *impf*, о~ *pf*. **weakling** *n* (*person*) сла́бый челове́к; (*plant*) сла́бое расте́ние. **weakness** *n* сла́бость.

weal *n* (*mark*) рубе́ц.

wealth *n* бога́тство; (*abundance*) изоби́лие. **wealthy** *adj* бога́тый.

wean *vt* отнима́ть *impf*, отня́ть *pf* от груди́; (*fig*) отуча́ть *impf*, отучи́ть *pf* (**of, from** от*+gen*).

weapon *n* ору́жие. **weaponry** *n* вооруже́ние.

wear *n* (*wearing*) но́ска; (*clothing*) оде́жда; (~ *and tear*) изно́с; *vt* носи́ть *impf*; быть в*+prep*; **what shall I** ~? что мне наде́ть?; *vi* носи́ться *impf*; ~ **off** (*pain, novelty*) проходи́ть *impf*, пройти́ *pf*; (*cease to have effect*) перестава́ть *impf*, переста́ть *pf* де́йствовать; ~ **out** (*clothes*) изна́шивать(ся) *impf*, износи́ть(ся) *pf*; (*exhaust*) измуч́ивать *impf*, изму́чить *pf*.

weariness *n* уста́лость. **wearing, wearisome** *adj* утоми́тельный. **weary** *adj* уста́лый; *vt & i* утомля́ть(ся) *impf*, утоми́ть(ся) *pf*.

weasel *n* ла́ска.

weather *n* пого́да; **be under the** ~ нева́жно себя́ чу́вствовать *impf*; ~**-beaten** обве́тренный; ~ **forecast** прогно́з пого́ды; *vt* (*storm etc.*) выде́рживать *impf*, вы́держать *pf*; (*wood*) подверга́ть *impf*, подве́ргнуть *pf* атмосфе́рным влия́ниям. **weather-cock, weathervane** *n* флю́гер. **weatherman** *n* метеоро́лог.

weave[1] *vt & i* (*fabric*) ткать *impf*, со~ *pf*; *vt* (*fig*; *also wreath etc.*) плести́ *impf*, с~ *pf*. **weaver** *n* ткач, ~и́ха.

weave[2] *vi* (*wind*) ви́ться *impf*.

web *n* (*cobweb*; *fig*) паути́на; (*fig*) сплете́ние; **the Web** (*comput*) веб, Интерне́т; **web page** страни́ца в Интерне́те; **web site** вебса́йт. **webbed** *adj* перепо́нчатый.

wed *vt* (*of man*) жени́ться *impf & pf* на*+prep*; (*of woman*) выходи́ть *impf*, вы́йти *pf* за́муж за*+acc*; (*unite*) сочета́ть *impf & pf*; *vi* пожени́ться *pf*. **wedded** *adj* супру́жеский; ~ **to** (*fig*) пре́данный *+dat*. **wedding** *n* сва́дьба, бракосочета́ние; ~**-cake** сва́дебный торт; ~**-day** день *m* сва́дьбы; ~**-dress** подвене́чное пла́тье; ~**-ring** обруча́льное кольцо́.

wedge *n* клин; *vt* (~ *open*) закли́нивать *impf*, закли́нить *pf*; *vt & i*: ~ **in(to)** вкли́нивать(ся) *impf*, вкли́нить(ся) *pf* (в*+acc*).

wedlock *n* брак; **born out of** ~ внебра́чный.

Wednesday *n* среда́.

weed *n* сорня́к; **~-killer** гербици́д; *vt* поло́ть *impf*, вы́~ *pf*; **~ out** удаля́ть *impf*, удали́ть *pf*. **weedy** *adj* (*person*) то́щий.

week *n* неде́ля; **~-end** суббо́та и воскресе́нье, выходны́е *sb pl*. **weekday** *n* бу́дний день *m*. **weekly** *adj* еженеде́льный; (*wage*) неде́льный; *adv* еженеде́льно; *n* еженеде́льник.

weep *vi* пла́кать *impf*. **weeping willow** *n* плаку́чая и́ва.

weigh *vt* (*also fig*) взве́шивать *impf*, взве́сить *pf*; (*consider*) обду́мывать *impf*, обду́мать *pf*; *vt & i* (*so much*) ве́сить *impf*; **~ down** отягоща́ть *impf*, отяготи́ть *pf*; **~ on** тяготи́ть *impf*; **~ out** отве́шивать *impf*, отве́сить *pf*; **~ up** (*appraise*) оце́нивать *impf*, оцени́ть *pf*. **weight** *n* (*also authority*) вес; (*load, also fig*) тя́жесть; (*sport*) шта́нга; (*influence*) влия́ние; **lose ~** худе́ть *impf*, по~ *pf*; **put on ~** толсте́ть *impf*, по~ *pf*; **~-lifter** штанги́ст; **~-lifting** подня́тие тя́жестей; *vt* (*make heavier*) утяжеля́ть *impf*, утяжели́ть *pf*. **weightless** *adj* невесо́мый. **weighty** *adj* ве́ский.

weir *n* плоти́на.

weird *adj* (*strange*) стра́нный.

welcome *n* приём; *adj* жела́нный; (*pleasant*) прия́тный; **you are ~** (*don't mention it*) пожа́луйста; **you are ~ to use my bicycle** мой велосипе́д к ва́шим услу́гам; **you are ~ to stay the night** вы мо́жете переночева́ть у меня́/нас; *vt* приве́тствовать *impf* (*& pf in past tense*); *int* добро́ пожа́ловать!

weld *vt* сва́ривать *impf*, свари́ть *pf*. **welder** *n* сва́рщик.

welfare *n* благососто́яние; **W~ State** госуда́рство всео́бщего благососто́яния.

well[1] *n* коло́дец; (*for stairs*) ле́стничная кле́тка.

well[2] *vi*: **~ up** (*anger etc.*) вскипа́ть *impf*, вскипе́ть *pf*; **tears ~ed up** глаза́ напо́лнились слеза́ми.

well[3] *adj* (*healthy*) здоро́вый; **feel ~** чу́вствовать *impf*, по~ *pf* себя́ хорошо́, здоро́вым; **get ~** поправля́ться *impf*, попра́виться *pf*; **look ~** хорошо́ вы́глядеть *impf*; **all is ~** всё в поря́дке; *int* ну(!); *adv* хорошо́; (*very much*) о́чень; **as ~** то́же; **as ~ as** (*in addition to*) кро́ме+*gen*; **it may ~ be true** вполне́ возмо́жно, что э́то так; **very ~!** хорошо́!; **~ done!** молоде́ц!; **~-balanced** уравнове́шенный; **~-behaved** (благо)воспи́танный; **~-being** благополу́чие; **~-bred** благовоспи́танный; **~-built** кре́пкий; **~-defined** чёткий; **~-disposed** благоскло́нный; **~ done** (*cooked*) (хорошо́) прожа́ренный; **~-fed** отко́рмленный; **~-founded** обосно́ванный; **~-groomed** (*person*) хо́леный; **~-heeled** состоя́тельный; **~-informed** (хорошо́) осведомлённый (**about** в+*prep*); **~-known** изве́стный; **~-meaning** де́йствующий из лу́чших побужде́ний; **~-nigh** почти́; **~-off** состоя́тельный; **~-paid** хорошо́ опла́чиваемый; **~-preserved** хорошо́ сохрани́вшийся; **~-to-do** состоя́тельный; **~-wisher** доброжела́тель *m*.

wellington (boot) *n* рези́новый сапо́г.

Welsh *adj* уэ́льский. **Welshman** *n* валли́ец. **Welshwoman** *n* валли́йка.

welter *n* пу́таница.

wend *vt*: ~ **one's way** держа́ть *impf* путь.

west *n* за́пад; (*naut*) вест; *adj* за́падный; *adv* на за́пад, к за́паду. **westerly** *adj* за́падный. **western** *adj* за́падный; *n* (*film*) ве́стерн. **westward(s)** *adv* на за́пад, к за́паду.

wet *adj* мо́крый; (*paint*) непросо́хший; (*rainy*) дождли́вый; ~ **through** промо́кший до ни́тки; *n* (*dampness*) вла́жность; (*rain*) дождь *m*; *vt* мочи́ть *impf*, на~ *pf*.

whack *n* (*blow*) уда́р; *vt* колоти́ть *impf*, по~ *pf*. **whacked** *adj* разби́тый.

whale *n* кит.

wharf *n* при́стань.

what *pron* (*interrog, int*) что; (*how much*) ско́лько; (*rel*) (то,) что; ~ **(...) for** заче́м; ~ **if** а что е́сли; ~ **is your name** как вас зову́т?; *adj* (*interrog, int*) како́й; ~ **kind of** како́й. **whatever, whatsoever** *pron* что бы ни+*past* (~ **you think** что бы вы ни ду́мали); всё, что (**take** ~ **you want** возьми́те всё, что хоти́те); *adj* како́й бы ни+*past* (~ **books he read(s)** каки́е бы кни́ги он ни прочита́л); (*at all*): **there is no chance** ~ нет никако́й возмо́жности; **is there any chance** ~? есть ли хоть кака́я-нибу́дь возмо́жность?

wheat *n* пшени́ца.

wheedle *vt* (*coax into doing*) угова́ривать *impf*, уговори́ть *pf* с по́мощью ле́сти; ~ **out of** выма́нивать *impf*, вы́манить *pf* у+*gen*.

wheel *n* колесо́; (*steering* ~, *helm*) руль *m*; (*potter's*) гонча́рный круг; *vt* (*push*) ката́ть *indet*, кати́ть *det*, по~ *pf*; *vt* & *i* (*turn*) повёртывать(ся) *impf*, поверну́ть(ся) *pf*; *vi* (*circle*) кружи́ться *impf*. **wheelbarrow** *n* та́чка. **wheelchair** *n* инвали́дное кре́сло.

wheeze *vi* сопе́ть *impf*.

when *adv* когда́; *conj* когда́, в то вре́мя как; (*whereas*) тогда́ как; (*if*) е́сли; (*although*) хотя́. **whence** *adv* отку́да. **whenever** *adv* когда́ же; *conj* (*every time*) вся́кий раз когда́; (*at any time*) когда́; (*no matter when*) когда́ бы ни+*past*; **we shall have dinner** ~ **you arrive** во ско́лько бы вы ни прие́хали, мы пообе́даем.

where *adv* & *conj* (*place*) где; (*whither*) куда́; **from** ~ отку́да. **whereabouts** *adv* где; *n* местонахожде́ние. **whereas** *conj* тогда́ как; хотя́. **whereby** *adv* & *conj* посре́дством чего́. **wherein** *adv* & *conj* в чём. **wherever** *adv* & *conj* (*place*) где бы ни+*past*; (*whither*) куда́ бы ни+*past*; ~ **he goes** куда́ бы он ни пошёл; ~ **you like** где/куда́ хоти́те. **wherewithal** *n* сре́дства *neut pl*.

whet *vt* точи́ть *impf*, на~ *pf*; (*fig*) возбужда́ть *impf*, возбуди́ть *pf*.

whether *conj* ли; **I don't know** ~ **he will come** я не зна́ю, придёт ли он; ~ **he comes or not** придёт (ли) он и́ли нет.

which *adj* (*interrog, rel*) како́й; *pron* (*interrog*) како́й; (*person*) кто; (*rel*) кото́рый; (*rel to whole statement*) что; **~ is ~?** (*persons*) кто из них кто?; (*things*) что-что? **whichever** *adj* & *pron* како́й бы ни+*past* (**~ book you choose** каку́ю бы кни́гу ты ни вы́брал); любо́й (**take ~ book you want** возьми́те любу́ю кни́гу).

whiff *n* за́пах.

while *n* вре́мя *neut*; **a little ~** недо́лго; **a long ~** до́лго; **for a long ~** (*up to now*) давно́; **for a ~** на вре́мя; **in a little ~** ско́ро; **it is worth ~** сто́ит э́то сде́лать; *vt*: **~ away** проводи́ть *impf*, провести́ *pf*; *conj* пока́; в то вре́мя как; (*although*) хотя́; (*contrast*) а; **we went to the cinema ~ they went to the theatre** мы ходи́ли в кино́, а они́ в теа́тр. **whilst** *see* **while**

whim *n* при́хоть, капри́з.

whimper *vi* хны́кать *impf*; (*dog*) скули́ть *impf*.

whimsical *adj* капри́зный; (*odd*) причу́дливый.

whine *n* (*wail*) вой; (*whimper*) хны́канье; *vi* (*dog*) скули́ть *impf*; (*wail*) выть; (*whimper*) хны́кать *impf*.

whinny *vi* ти́хо ржать *impf*.

whip *n* кнут, хлыст; *vt* (*lash*) хлеста́ть *impf*, хлестну́ть *pf*; (*cream*) сбива́ть *impf*, сбить *pf*; **~ off** ски́дывать *impf*, ски́нуть *pf*; **~ out** выхва́тывать *impf*, вы́хватить *pf*; **~ round** бы́стро повёртываться *impf*, поверну́ться *pf*; **~-round** сбор де́нег; **~ up** (*stir up*) разжига́ть *impf*, разже́чь *pf*.

whirl *n* круже́ние; (*of dust, fig*) вихрь *m*; (*turmoil*) сумато́ха; *vt* & *i* кружи́ть(ся) *impf*, за~ *pf*. **whirlpool** *n* водоворо́т. **whirlwind** *n* вихрь *m*.

whirr *vi* жужжа́ть *impf*.

whisk *n* (*of twigs etc.*) ве́ничек; (*utensil*) муто́вка; (*movement*) пома́хивание; *vt* (*cream etc.*) сбива́ть *impf*, сбить *pf*; **~ away, off** (*brush off*) сма́хивать *impf*, смахну́ть *pf*; (*take away*) бы́стро уноси́ть *impf*, унести́ *pf*.

whisker *n* (*human*) во́лос на лице́; (*animal*) ус; *pl* (*human*) бакенба́рды *f pl*.

whisky *n* ви́ски *neut indecl*.

whisper *n* шёпот; *vt* & *i* шепта́ть *impf*, шепну́ть *pf*.

whistle *n* (*sound*) свист; (*instrument*) свисто́к; *vi* свисте́ть *impf*, сви́стнуть *pf*; *vt* насви́стывать *impf*.

white *adj* бе́лый; (*hair*) седо́й; (*pale*) бле́дный; (*with milk*) с молоко́м; **paint ~** кра́сить *impf*, по~ *pf* в бе́лый свет; **~-collar worker** слу́жащий *sb*; **~ lie** неви́нная ложь; *n* (*colour*) бе́лый цвет; (*egg, eye*) бело́к; (**~** *person*) бе́лый *sb*. **whiten** *vt* бели́ть *impf*, на~, по~, вы́~ *pf*; *vi* беле́ть *impf*, по~ *pf*. **whiteness** *n* белизна́. **whitewash** *n* побе́лка; *vt* бели́ть *impf*, по~ *pf*; (*fig*) обеля́ть *impf*, обели́ть *pf*.

whither *adv* & *conj* куда́.

Whitsun *n* Тро́ица.

whittle *vt*: **~ down** уменьша́ть *impf*, уме́ньшить *pf*.

whiz(z) *vi*: **~ past** просвисте́ть *pf*.

who *pron* (*interrog*) кто; (*rel*) кото́рый.

whoever *pron* кто бы ни+*past*; (*he who*) тот, кто.

whole *adj* (*entire*) весь, це́лый; (*intact, of number*) це́лый; *n* (*thing complete*) це́лое *sb*; (*all there is*) весь *sb*; (*sum*) су́мма; **on the ~** в о́бщем. **whole-hearted** *adj* беззаве́тный. **whole-heartedly** *adv* от всего́ се́рдца. **wholemeal** *adj* из непросе́янной муки́. **wholesale** *adj* опто́вый; (*fig*) ма́ссовый; *adv* о́птом. **wholesaler** *n* опто́вый торго́вец. **wholesome** *adj* здоро́вый. **wholly** *adv* по́лностью.

whom *pron* (*interrog*) кого́ *etc.*; (*rel*) кото́рого *etc.*

whoop *n* крик; *vi* крича́ть *impf*, кри́кнуть *pf*; **~ it up** бу́рно весели́ться *impf*; **~ing cough** коклю́ш.

whore *n* проститу́тка.

whose *pron* (*interrog, rel*) чей; (*rel*) кото́рого.

why *adv* почему́; *int* да ведь!

wick *n* фити́ль *m*.

wicked *adj* ди́кий. **wickedness** *n* ди́кость.

wicker *attrib* плетёный.

wicket *n* (*cricket*) воро́тца.

wide *adj* широ́кий; (*extensive*) обши́рный; (*in measurements*) в+*acc* ширино́й; **~ awake** по́лный внима́ния; **~ open** широко́ откры́тый; *adv* (*off target*) ми́мо це́ли. **widely** *adv* широко́. **widen** *vt* & *i* расширя́ть(ся) *impf*, расши́рить(ся) *pf*. **widespread** *adj* распространённый.

widow *n* вдова́. **widowed** *adj* овдове́вший. **widower** *n* вдове́ц.

width *n* ширина́; (*fig*) широта́; (*of cloth*) поло́тнище.

wield *vt* (*brandish*) разма́хивать *impf* +*instr*; (*power*) по́льзоваться *impf* +*instr*.

wife *n* жена́.

wig *n* пари́к.

wiggle *vt* & *i* (*move*) шевели́ть(ся) *impf*, по~, шевельну́ть(ся) *pf* (+*instr*).

wigwam *n* вигва́м.

wild *adj* ди́кий; (*flower*) полево́й; (*uncultivated*) невозде́ланный; (*tempestuous*) бу́йный; (*furious*) нейстовый; (*ill-considered*) необду́манный; **be ~ about** быть без ума́ от+*gen*; **~-goose chase** сумасбро́дная зате́я; *n*: *pl* де́бри (-рей) *pl*. **wildcat** *adj* (*unofficial*) неофициа́льный. **wilderness** *n* пусты́ня. **wildfire** *n*: **spread like ~** распространя́ться *impf*, распространи́ться *pf* с молниено́сной быстрото́й. **wildlife** *n* жива́я приро́да. **wildness** *n* ди́кость.

wile *n* хи́трость.

wilful *adj* (*obstinate*) упря́мый; (*deliberate*) преднаме́ренный.

will *n* во́ля; (*~-power*) си́ла во́ли; (*at death*) завеща́ние; **against one's ~** про́тив во́ли; **of one's own free ~** доброво́льно; **with a ~** с энтузиа́змом; **good ~** до́брая во́ля; **make one's ~** писа́ть *impf*, на~ *pf* завеща́ние; *vt* (*want*) хоте́ть *impf*, за~ *pf* +*gen*, *acc*; *v aux*: **he ~ be president** он бу́дет президе́нтом; **he ~ return tomorrow** он вернётся за́втра; **~ you open the window?** откро́йте окно́, пожа́луйста.

willing *adj* гото́вый; (*eager*) стара́тельный. **willingly** *adv* охо́тно. **willingness** *n* гото́вность.

willow *n* и́ва.
willy-nilly *adv* во́лей-нево́лей.
wilt *vi* поника́ть *impf*, пони́кнуть *pf*.
wily *adj* хи́трый.
win *n* побе́да; *vt* & *i* выи́грывать *impf*, вы́играть *pf*; *vt* (*obtain*) добива́ться *impf*, доби́ться *pf* +*gen*; ~ **over** угова́ривать *impf*, уговори́ть *pf*; (*charm*) располага́ть *impf*, расположи́ть *pf* к себе́.
wince *vi* вздра́гивать *impf*, вздро́гнуть *pf*.
winch *n* лебёдка; поднима́ть *impf*, подня́ть *pf* с по́мощью лебёдки.
wind[1] *n* (*air*) ве́тер; (*breath*) дыха́ние; (*flatulence*) ве́тры *m pl*; ~ **instrument** духово́й инструме́нт; ~**-swept** откры́тый ветра́м; **get ~ of** проню́хивать *impf*, проню́хать *pf*; *vt* (*make gasp*) заставля́ть *impf*, заста́вить *pf* задохну́ться.
wind[2] *vi* (*meander*) ви́ться *impf*; извива́ться *impf*; *vt* (*coil*) нама́тывать *impf*, намота́ть *pf*; (*watch*) заводи́ть *impf*, завести́ *pf*; (*wrap*) уку́тывать *impf*, уку́тать *pf*; ~ **up** (*vt*) (*reel*) сма́тывать *impf*, смота́ть *pf*; (*watch*) *see* **wind**[2]; (*vt* & *i*) (*end*) конча́ть(ся) *impf*, ко́нчить(ся) *pf*. **winding** *adj* (*meandering*) изви́листый; (*staircase*) винтово́й.
windfall *n* па́далица; (*fig*) золото́й дождь.
windmill *n* ветряна́я ме́льница.
window *n* окно́; (*of shop*) витри́на; ~**-box** нару́жный я́щик для цвето́в; ~**-cleaner** мо́йщик о́кон; ~**-dressing** оформле́ние витри́н; (*fig*) показу́ха; ~**-frame** око́нная ра́ма; ~**-ledge** подоко́нник; ~**-pane** око́нное стекло́; ~**-shopping** рассма́тривание витри́н; ~**-sill** подоко́нник.
windpipe *n* дыха́тельное го́рло. **windscreen** *n* ветрово́е стекло́; ~ **wiper** дво́рник. **windsurfer** *n* виндсёрфинги́ст. **windsurfing** *n* виндсёрфинг. **windward** *adj* наве́тренный. **windy** *adj* ве́треный.
wine *n* вино́; ~ **bar** ви́нный погребо́к; ~ **bottle** ви́нная бyты́лка; ~ **list** ка́рта вин; ~**-tasting** дегуста́ция вин. **wineglass** *n* рю́мка. **winery** *n* ви́нный заво́д. **winy** *adj* ви́нный.
wing *n* (*also polit*) крыло́; (*archit*) фли́гель *m*; (*sport*) фланг; *pl* (*theat*) кули́сы *f pl*. **winged** *adj* крыла́тый.
wink *n* (*blink*) морга́ние; (*as sign*) подми́гивание; *vi* мига́ть *impf*, мигну́ть *pf*; ~ **at** подми́гивать *impf*, подмигну́ть *pf* +*dat*; (*fig*) смотре́ть *impf*, по~ *pf* сквозь па́льцы на+*acc*.
winkle *vt*: ~ **out** выковы́ривать *impf*, вы́ковырять *pf*.
winner *n* победи́тель *m*, ~ница. **winning** *adj* (*victorious*) вы́игравший; (*shot etc.*) реша́ющий; (*charming*) обая́тельный; *n*: *pl* вы́игрыш; ~**-post** фи́нишный столб.
winter *n* зима́; *attrib* зи́мний. **wintry** *adj* зи́мний; (*cold*) холо́дный.
wipe *vt* (*also ~ out inside of*) вытира́ть *impf*, вы́тереть *pf*; ~ **away, off** стира́ть *impf*, стере́ть *pf*; ~ **out** (*exterminate*) уничтожа́ть *impf*, уни-

чтóжить *pf*; (*cancel*) смывáть *impf*, смыть *pf*.

wire *n* прóволока; (*carrying current*) прóвод; ~ **netting** прóволочная сéтка. **wireless** *n* рáдио *neut indecl*. **wiring** *n* электропровóдка. **wiry** *adj* жи́листый.

wisdom *n* мýдрость; ~ **tooth** зуб мýдрости. **wise** *adj* мýдрый; (*prudent*) благоразýмный.

wish *n* желáние; **with best ~es** всегó хорóшего, с наилýчшими пожелáниями; *vt* хотéть *impf*, за~ *pf* (**I ~ I could see him** мне хотéлось бы егó ви́деть; **I ~ to go** я хочý пойти́; **I ~ you to come early** я хочý, чтóбы вы рáно пришли́; **I ~ the day were over** хорошó бы день ужé кóнчился); желáть *impf* +*gen* (**I ~ you luck** желáю вам удáчи); (*congratulate on*) поздравля́ть *impf*, поздрáвить *pf* (**I ~ you a happy birthday** поздравля́ю тебя́ с днём рождéния); *vi*: ~ **for** желáть *impf* +*gen*; мечтáть *impf* о+*prep*. **wishful** *adj*: ~ **thinking** самообольщéние; приня́тие желáемого за действи́тельное.

wisp *n* (*of straw*) пучóк; (*hair*) клочóк; (*smoke*) струйка.

wisteria *n* глици́ния.

wistful *adj* тосккли́вый.

wit *n* (*mind*) ум; (*wittiness*) остроýмие; (*person*) остря́к; **be at one's ~'s end** не знать *impf* что дéлать.

witch *n* вéдьма; **~-hunt** охóта за вéдьмами. **witchcraft** *n* колдовствó.

with *prep* (*in company of, together ~*) (вмéсте) с+*instr*; (*as a result of*) от+*gen*; (*at house of, in keeping of*) у+*gen*; (*by means of*) +*instr*; (*in spite of*) несмотря́ на+*acc*; (*including*) включáя+*acc*; ~ **each/one another** друг с дрýгом.

withdraw *vt* (*retract*) брать *impf*, взять *pf* назáд; (*hand*) отдёргивать *impf*, отдёрнуть *pf*; (*cancel*) снимáть *impf*, снять *pf*; (*mil*) выводи́ть *impf*, вы́вести *pf*; (*money from circulation*) изымáть *impf*, изъя́ть из обращéния; (*diplomat etc.*) отзывáть *impf*, отозвáть *pf*; (*from bank*) брать *impf*, взять *pf*; *vi* удаля́ться *impf*, удали́ться *pf*; (*drop out*) выбывáть *impf*, вы́быть *pf*; (*mil*) отходи́ть *impf*, отойти́ *pf*. **withdrawal** *n* (*retraction*) взя́тие назáд; (*cancellation*) сня́тие; (*mil*) отхóд; (*money from circulation*) изъя́тие; (*departure*) ухóд. **withdrawn** *adj* зáмкнутый.

wither *vi* вя́нуть *impf*, за~ *pf*. **withering** *adj* (*fig*) уничтожáющий.

withhold *vt* (*refuse to grant*) не давáть *impf*, дать *pf* +*gen*; (*payment*) удéрживать *impf*, удержáть *pf*; (*information*) утáивать *impf*, утаи́ть *pf*.

within *prep* (*inside*) внутри́+*gen*, в+*prep*; (~ *the limits of*) в предéлах +*gen*; (*time*) в течéние +*gen*; *adv* внутри́; **from ~** изнутри́.

without *prep* без+*gen*; ~ **saying good-bye** не прощáясь; **do ~** обходи́ться *impf*, обойти́сь *pf* без+*gen*.

withstand *vt* выдéрживать *impf*, вы́держать *pf*.

witness *n* (*person*) свидéтель *m*; (*eye-~*) очеви́дец; (*to sig-*

nature etc.) завери́тель *m*; **bear ~ to** свиде́тельствовать *impf*, за~ *pf*; **~-box** ме́сто для свиде́тельских показа́ний; *vt* быть свиде́телем+*gen*; (*document etc.*) заверя́ть *impf*, заве́рить *pf*.

witticism *n* остро́та. **witty** *adj* остроу́мный.

wizard *n* волше́бник, колду́н.

wizened *adj* морщи́нистый.

wobble *vt* & *i* шата́ть(ся) *impf*, шатну́ть(ся) *pf*; *vi* (*voice*) дрожа́ть *impf*. **wobbly** *adj* ша́ткий.

woe *n* го́ре; **~ is me!** го́ре мне! **woeful** *adj* жа́лкий.

wolf *n* волк; *vt* пожира́ть *impf*, пожра́ть *pf*.

woman *n* же́нщина. **womanizer** *n* волоки́та. **womanly** *adj* же́нственный.

womb *n* ма́тка.

wonder *n* чу́до; (*amazement*) изумле́ние; **(it's) no ~** неудиви́тельно; *vt* интересова́ться *impf* (**I ~ who will come** интере́сно, кто придёт); *vi*: **I shouldn't ~ if** неудиви́тельно бу́дет, е́сли; **I ~ if you could help me** не могли́ бы вы мне помо́чь?; **~ at** удивля́ться *impf*, удиви́ться *pf* +*dat*. **wonderful, wondrous** *adj* замеча́тельный.

wont *n*: **as is his ~** по своему́ обыкнове́нию; *predic*: **be ~ to** име́ть привы́чку+*inf*.

woo *vt* уха́живать *impf* за +*instr*.

wood *n* (*forest*) лес; (*material*) де́рево; (*firewood*) дрова́ *pl*. **woodcut** *n* гравю́ра на де́реве. **wooded** *adj* леси́стый. **wooden** *adj* (*also fig*) деревя́нный. **woodland** *n* леси́стая ме́стность; *attrib* лесно́й. **woodpecker** *n* дя́тел. **woodwind** *n* деревя́нные духовы́е инструме́нты *m pl*. **woodwork** *n* столя́рная рабо́та; (*wooden parts*) деревя́нные ча́сти (-те́й) *pl*. **woodworm** *n* жучо́к. **woody** *adj* (*plant etc.*) деревяни́стый; (*wooded*) леси́стый.

wool *n* шерсть. **woollen** *adj* шерстяно́й. **woolly** *adj* шерсти́стый; (*indistinct*) нея́сный.

word *n* сло́во; (*news*) изве́стие; **by ~ of mouth** у́стно; **have a ~ with** поговори́ть *pf* с+*instr*; **in a ~** одни́м сло́вом; **in other ~s** други́ми слова́ми; **~ for ~** сло́во в сло́во; **~ processor** компью́тер(-изда́тель) *m*; *vt* выража́ть *impf*, вы́разить *pf*; формули́ровать *impf*, с~ *pf*. **wording** *n* формулиро́вка.

work *n* рабо́та; (*labour*; *toil*; *scholarly ~*) труд; (*occupation*) заня́тие; (*studies*) заня́тия *neut pl*; (*of art*) произведе́ние; (*book*) сочине́ние; *pl* (*factory*) заво́д; (*mechanism*) механи́зм; **at ~** (*doing ~*) за рабо́той; (*at place of ~*) на рабо́те; **out of ~** безрабо́тный; **~-force** рабо́чая си́ла; **~-load** нагру́зка; *vi* (*also function*) рабо́тать *impf* (**at, on** над+*instr*); (*study*) занима́ться *impf*, заня́ться *pf*; (*also toil, labour*) труди́ться *impf*; (*have effect, function*) де́йствовать *impf*; (*succeed*) удава́ться *impf*, уда́ться *pf*; *vt* (*operate*) управля́ть *impf* +*instr*; обраща́ться *impf* с+*instr*; (*wonders*) твори́ть *impf*, со~ *pf*; (*soil*) обраба́тывать *impf*, обрабо́тать *pf*; (*compel to* ~) заставля́ть *impf*, заста́вить *pf* рабо́тать; ~ **in** вставля́ть *impf*, вста́вить *pf*; ~ **off** (*debt*) отраба́тывать *impf*, отрабо́тать *pf*; (*weight*) сгоня́ть *impf*, согна́ть *pf*; (*energy*) дава́ть *impf*, дать *pf* вы́ход +*dat*; ~ **out** (*solve*) находи́ть *impf*, найти́ *pf* реше́ние +*gen*; (*plans etc.*) разраба́тывать *impf*, разрабо́тать *pf*; (*sport*) трениро-ва́ться *impf*; **everything ~ed out well** всё ко́нчилось хорошо́; ~ **out at** (*amount to*) составля́ть *impf*, соста́вить *pf*; ~ **up** (*perfect*) выраба́тывать *impf*, вы́работать *pf*; (*excite*) возбужда́ть *impf*, возбуди́ть *pf*; (*appetite*) нагу́ливать *impf*, нагуля́ть *pf*. **workable** *adj* осуществи́мый, реа́льный. **workaday** *adj* бу́дничный. **workaholic** *n* тру́женик. **worker** *n* рабо́тник; (*manual*) рабо́чий *sb*. **working** *adj*: ~ **class** рабо́чий класс; ~ **hours** рабо́чее вре́мя *neut*; ~ **party** коми́ссия. **workman** *n* рабо́тник. **workmanlike** *adj* иску́сный. **workmanship** *n* иску́сство, мастерство́. **workshop** *n* мастерска́я *sb*.

world *n* мир, свет; *attrib* миро-во́й; ~**-famous** всеми́рно изве́стный; ~ **war** мирова́я война́; ~**-wide** всеми́рный. **worldly** *adj* мирско́й; (*person*) о́пытный.

worm *n* червь *m*; (*intestinal*) глист; *vt*: ~ **o.s. into** вкра́дываться *impf*, вкра́сться *pf* в+*acc*; ~ **out** выве́дывать *impf*, вы́ведать *pf* (**of** у+*gen*); ~ **one's way** пробира́ться *impf*, пробра́ться *pf*.

worry *n* (*anxiety*) беспоко́йство; (*care*) забо́та; *vt* беспоко́ить *impf*, о~ *pf*; *vi* беспоко́иться *impf*, о~ *pf* (**about** о+*prep*).

worse *adj* ху́дший; *adv* ху́же; *n*: **from bad to** ~ всё ху́же и ху́же. **worsen** *vt* & *i* ухудша́ть(ся) *impf*, уху́дшить(ся) *pf*.

worship *n* поклоне́ние (**of** +*dat*); (*service*) богослуже́ние; *vt* поклоня́ться *impf* +*dat*; (*adore*) обожа́ть *impf*. **worshipper** *n* покло́нник, -ица.

worst *adj* наиху́дший, са́мый плохо́й; *adv* ху́же всего́; *n* са́мое плохо́е.

worth *n* (*value*) цена́, це́нность; (*merit*) досто́инство; **give me a pound's ~ of petrol** да́йте мне бензи́на на фунт; *adj*: **be** ~ (*of equal value to*) сто́ить *impf* (**what is it ~?** ско́лько э́то сто́ит?); (*deserve*) сто́ить *impf* +*gen* (**is this film ~ seeing?** сто́ит посмотре́ть э́тот фильм?). **worthless** *adj* ничего́ не сто́ящий; (*useless*) бесполе́зный. **worthwhile** *adj* сто́ящий. **worthy** *adj* досто́йный.

would *v aux* (*conditional*): **he ~ be angry if he found out** он бы рассерди́лся, е́сли бы узна́л; (*expressing wish*) **she ~ like to know** она́ бы хоте́ла знать; **I ~ rather** я бы предпочёл; (*expressing indirect speech*): **he said he ~ be late** он сказа́л, что придёт по́здно.

would-be *adj*: ~ **actor** челове́к мечта́ющий стать актёром.

wound *n* ра́на; *vt* ра́нить *impf* & *pf*. **wounded** *adj* ра́неный.

wrangle *n* препира́ние; *vi* препира́ться *impf*.

wrap *n* (*shawl*) шаль; *vt* (*also* ~ *up*) завёртывать *impf*, заверну́ть *pf*; ~ **up** (*in wraps*) заку́тывать(ся) *impf*, заку́тать(ся) *pf*; **~ped up in** (*fig*) поглощённый *+instr*. **wrapper** *n* обёртка. **wrapping** *n* обёртка; ~ **paper** обёрточная бума́га.

wrath *n* гнев.

wreak *vt*: ~ **havoc on** разоря́ть *impf*, разори́ть *pf*.

wreath *n* вено́к.

wreck *n* (*ship*) оста́нки (-ов) корабля́; (*vehicle, person, building, etc.*) развали́на; *vt* (*destroy, also fig*) разруша́ть *impf*, разру́шить *pf*; **be ~ed** терпе́ть *impf*, по~ *pf* круше́ние; (*of plans etc.*) ру́хнуть *pf*. **wreckage** *n* обло́мки *m pl* круше́ния.

wren *n* крапи́вник.

wrench *n* (*jerk*) дёрганье; (*tech*) га́ечный ключ; (*fig*) боль; *vt* (*snatch, pull out*) вырыва́ть *impf*, вы́рвать *pf* (**from** у+*gen*); ~ **open** взла́мывать *impf*, взлома́ть *pf*.

wrest *vt* (*wrench*) вырыва́ть *impf*, вы́рвать *pf* (**from** у+*gen*).

wrestle *vi* боро́ться *impf*. **wrestler** *n* боре́ц. **wrestling** *n* борьба́.

wretch *n* несча́стный *sb*; (*scoundrel*) негодя́й. **wretched** *adj* жа́лкий; (*unpleasant*) скве́рный.

wriggle *vi* извива́ться *impf*, изви́ться *pf*; (*fidget*) ёрзать *impf*; ~ **out of** увиливать *impf*, увильну́ть от+*gen*.

wring *vt* (*also* ~ *out*) выжима́ть *impf*, вы́жать *pf*; (*extort*) исторга́ть *impf*, исто́ргнуть *pf* (**from** у+*gen*); (*neck*) свёртывать *impf*, сверну́ть *pf* (**of** +*dat*); ~ **one's hands** лома́ть *impf*, с~ *pf* ру́ки.

wrinkle *n* морщи́на; *vt* & *i* мо́рщить(ся) *impf*, с~ *pf*.

wrist *n* запя́стье; **~-watch** нару́чные часы́ (-со́в) *pl*.

writ *n* пове́стка.

write *vt* & *i* писа́ть *impf*, на~ *pf*; ~ **down** запи́сывать *impf*, записа́ть *pf*; ~ **off** (*cancel*) спи́сывать *impf*, списа́ть *pf*; **the car was a ~-off** маши́на была́ соверше́нно испо́рчена; ~ **out** выпи́сывать *impf*, вы́писать *pf* (**in full** по́лностью); ~ **up** (*account of*) подро́бно опи́сывать *impf*, описа́ть *pf*; (*notes*) перепи́сывать *impf*, переписа́ть *pf*; **~-up** (*report*) отчёт. **writer** *n* писа́тель *m*, ~ница.

writhe *vi* ко́рчиться *impf*, с~ *pf*.

writing *n* (*handwriting*) по́черк; (*work*) произведе́ние; **in** ~ в пи́сьменной фо́рме; **~-paper** почто́вая бума́га.

wrong *adj* (*incorrect*) непра́вильный, неве́рный; (*the wrong ...*) не тот (**I have bought the ~ book** я купи́л не ту кни́гу; **you've got the ~ number** (*tel*) вы не туда́ попа́ли); (*mistaken*) непра́вый (**you are ~** ты непра́в); (*unjust*) несправедли́вый; (*sinful*) дурно́й; (*out of order*) нела́дный; (*side of cloth*) ле́вый; ~ **side out** наизна́нку; ~ **way round** наоборо́т; *n* зло; (*injustice*) несправедли́вость; **be in the ~** быть непра́вым; **do ~** греши́ть

impf, со~ *pf*; *adv* непра́вильно, неве́рно; **go ~** не получа́ться *impf*, получи́ться *pf*; *vt* обижа́ть *impf*, оби́деть *pf*; (*be unjust to*) быть несправедли́вым к+*dat*. **wrongdoer** *n* престу́пник, гре́шник, -ица. **wrongful** *adj* несправедли́вый. **wrongly** *adv* непра́вильно; (*unjustly*) несправедли́во.
wrought *adj*: **~ iron** сва́рочное желе́зо.
wry *adj* (*smile*) криво́й; (*humour*) сухо́й, ирони́ческий.

X

xenophobia *n* ксенофо́бия.
X-ray *n* (*picture*) рентге́н(овский сни́мок); *pl* (*radiation*) рентге́новы лучи́ *m pl*; *vt* (*photograph*) де́лать *impf*, с~ *pf* рентге́н *+gen*.

Y

yacht *n* я́хта. **yachting** *n* па́русный спорт. **yachtsman** *n* яхтсме́н.
yank *vt* рвану́ть *pf*.
yap *vi* тя́вкать *impf*, тя́вкнуть *pf*.
yard[1] *n* (*piece of ground*) двор.
yard[2] *n* (*measure*) ярд. **yardstick** *n* (*fig*) мери́ло.
yarn *n* пря́жа; (*story*) расска́з.
yawn *n* зево́к; *vi* зева́ть *impf*, зевну́ть *pf*; (*chasm etc.*) зия́ть *impf*.
year *n* год; **~ in, ~ out** из го́да в год. **yearbook** *n* ежего́дник. **yearly** *adj* ежего́дный, годово́й; *adv* ежего́дно.
yearn *vi* тоскова́ть *impf* (**for** по+*dat*). **yearning** *n* тоска́ (**for** по+*dat*).
yeast *n* дро́жжи (-же́й) *pl*.
yell *n* крик; *vi* крича́ть *impf*, кри́кнуть *pf*.
yellow *adj* жёлтый; *n* жёлтый цвет. **yellowish** *adj* желтова́тый.
yelp *n* визг; *vi* визжа́ть *impf*, ви́згнуть *pf*.
yes *adv* да; *n* утвержде́ние, согла́сие; (*in vote*) го́лос «за».
yesterday *adv* вчера́; *n* вчера́шний день *m*; **~ morning** вчера́ у́тром; **the day before ~** позавчера́; **~'s newspaper** вчера́шняя газе́та.
yet *adv* (*still*) ещё; (*so far*) до сих пор; (*in questions*) уже́; (*nevertheless*) тем не ме́нее; **as ~** пока́, до сих пор; **not ~** ещё не; *conj* одна́ко, но.
yew *n* тис.
Yiddish *n* и́диш.
yield *n* (*harvest*) урожа́й; (*econ*) дохо́д; *vt* (*fruit, revenue, etc.*) приноси́ть *impf*, принести́ *pf*; дава́ть *impf*, дать *pf*; (*give up*) сдава́ть *impf*, сдать *pf*; *vi* (*give in*) (*to enemy etc.*) уступа́ть *impf*, уступи́ть *pf* (**to** *+dat*); (*give way*) поддава́ться *impf*, подда́ться *pf* (**to** *+dat*).
yoga *n* йо́га.
yoghurt *n* кефи́р.
yoke *n* (*also fig*) ярмо́; (*fig*) и́го; (*of dress*) коке́тка; *vt* впряга́ть *impf*, впрячь *pf* в ярмо́.
yolk *n* желто́к.
yonder *adv* вон там; *adj* вон тот.
you *pron* (*familiar sg*) ты; (*familiar pl, polite sg & pl*) вы; (*one*) *not usu translated*; *v translated in 2nd pers sg or by impers construction*: **~ never**

know никогда́ не зна́ешь.

young *adj* молодо́й; **the ~** молодёжь; *n* (*collect*) детёныши *m pl*. **youngster** *n* ма́льчик, де́вочка.

your(s) *poss pron* (*familiar sg*; *also in letter*) твой; (*familiar pl*, *polite sg & pl*; *also in letter*) ваш; свой. **yourself** *pron* (*emph*) (*familiar sg*) (ты) сам (*m*), сама́ (*f*); (*familiar pl*, *polite sg & pl*) (вы) са́ми; (*refl*) себя́; -ся (*suffixed to vt*); **by ~** (*independently*) самостоя́тельно, сам; (*alone*) оди́н.

youth *n* (*age*) мо́лодость; (*young man*) ю́ноша *m*; (*collect*, *as pl*) молодёжь; **~ club** молодёжный клуб; **~ hostel** молодёжная турба́за. **youthful** *adj* ю́ношеский.

Yugoslavia *n* Югосла́вия.

Z

zany *adj* смешно́й.

zeal *n* рве́ние, усе́рдие. **zealot** *n* фана́тик. **zealous** *adj* ре́вностный, усе́рдный.

zebra *n* зе́бра.

zenith *n* зени́т.

zero *n* нуль *m*, ноль *m*.

zest *n* (*piquancy*) пика́нтность; (*ardour*) энтузиа́зм; **~ for life** жизнера́достность.

zigzag *n* зигза́г; *adj* зигзагообра́зный; *vi* де́лать *impf*, с~ *pf* зигза́ги; идти́ *det* зигза́гами.

zinc *n* цинк.

Zionism *n* сиони́зм. **Zionist** *n* сиони́ст.

zip *n* (**~** *fastener*) (застёжка-) мо́лния; *vt & i*: **~ up** застёгивать(ся) *impf*, застегну́ть(ся) *pf* на мо́лнию.

zodiac *n* зодиа́к; **sign of the ~** знак зодиа́ка.

zombie *n* челове́к спя́щий на ходу́.

zone *n* зо́на; (*geog*) по́яс.

zoo *n* зоопа́рк. **zoological** *adj* зоологи́ческий; **~ garden(s)** зоологи́ческий сад. **zoologist** *n* зоо́лог. **zoology** *n* зооло́гия.

zoom *vi* (*rush*) мча́ться *impf*; **~ in** (*phot*) де́лать *impf*, с~ *pf* наплы́в; **~ lens** объекти́в с переме́нным фо́кусным расстоя́нием.

Zulu *adj* зулу́сский; *n* зулу́с, ~ка.

Appendix I **Spelling Rules**

It is assumed that the user is acquainted with the following spelling rules which affect Russian declension and conjugation.

1. **ы, ю,** and **я** do not follow **г, к, х, ж, ч, ш,** and **щ;** instead, **и, у,** and **а** are used, e.g. **ма́льчики, кричу́, лежа́т, ноча́ми;** similarly, **ю** and **я** do not follow **ц;** instead, **у** or **а** are used.

2. Unstressed **о** does not follow **ж, ц, ч, ш,** or **щ;** instead, **е** is used, e.g. **му́жем, ме́сяцев, хоро́шее.**

Appendix II **Declension of Russian Adjectives**

The following patterns are regarded as regular and are not shown in the dictionary entries.

Singular	nom	acc	gen	dat	instr	prep
Masculine	**тёпл|ый**	~ый	~ого	~ому	~ым	~ом
Feminine	**тёпл|ая**	~ую	~ой	~ой	~ой	~ой
Neuter	**тёпл|ое**	~ое	~ого	~ому	~ым	~ом

Plural	nom	acc	gen	dat	instr	prep
Masculine	**тёпл|ые**	~ые	~ых	~ым	~ыми	~ых
Feminine	**тёпл|ые**	~ые	~ых	~ым	~ыми	~ых
Neuter	**тёпл|ые**	~ые	~ых	~ым	~ыми	~ых

Appendix III **Declension of Russian Nouns**

The following patterns are regarded as regular and are not shown in the dictionary entries. Forms marked * should be particularly noted.

1 *Masculine*

Singular nom	acc	gen	dat	instr	prep
обе́д	~	~а	~у	~ом	~е
слу́ча|й	~й	~я	~ю	~ем	~е
марш	~	~а	~у	~ем	~е
каранда́ш	~	~а́	~у́	~о́м*	~е́
сцена́ри|й	~й	~я	~ю	~ем	~и*
портфе́л|ь	~ь	~я	~ю	~ем	~е

Plural nom	acc	gen	dat	instr	prep
обе́д|ы	~ы	~ов	~ам	~ами	~ах
слу́ча|и	~и	~ев	~ям	~ями	~ях
ма́рш|и	~и	~ей*	~ам	~ами	~ах
карандаш|и́	~и́	~е́й*	~а́м	~а́ми	~а́х
сцена́ри|и	~и	~ев*	~ям	~ями	~ях
портфе́л|и	~и	~ей*	~ям	~ями	~ях

2 *Feminine*

Singular nom	acc	gen	dat	instr	prep
газе́т|а	~у	~ы	~е	~ой	~е
ба́н|я	~ю	~и	~е	~ей	~е
ли́ни|я	~ю	~и	~и*	~ей	~и*
ста́ту|я	~ю	~и	~е*	~ей	~е*
бол|ь	~ь	~и	~и*	~ью*	~и*

Plural	nom	acc	gen	dat	instr	prep
	газе́т|ы	~ы	~	~ам	~ами	~ах
	ба́н|и	~и	~ь*	~ям	~ями	~ях
	ли́ни|и	~и	~й*	~ям	~ями	~ях
	ста́ту|и	~и	~й*	~ям	~ями	~ях
	бо́л|и	~и	~ей*	~ям	~ями	~ях

3 *Neuter*

Singular	nom	acc	gen	dat	instr	prep
	чу́вств|о	~о	~а	~у	~ом	~е
	учи́лищ|е	~е	~а	~у	~ем	~е
	зда́ни|е	~е	~я	~ю	~ем	~и*
	уще́л|ье	~ье	~ья	~ью	~ьем	~ье

Plural	nom	acc	gen	dat	instr	prep
	чу́вств|а	~а	~	~ам	~ами	~ах
	учи́лищ|а	~а	~	~ам	~ами	~ах
	зда́ни|я	~я	~й*	~ям	~ями	~ях
	уще́л|ья	~ья	~ий*	~ьям	~ьями	~ьях

Appendix IV **Conjugation of Russian Verbs**

The following patterns are regarded as regular and are not shown in the dictionary entries.

1. **-е-** conjugation

(a)	**чита́|ть**	~ю	~ешь	~ет	~ем	~ете	~ют
(b)	**сия́|ть**	~ю	~ешь	~ет	~ем	~ете	~ют
(c)	**про́б|овать**	~ую	~уешь	~ует	~уем	~уете	~уют
(d)	**рис|ова́ть**	~у́ю	~у́ешь	~у́ет	~у́ем	~у́ете	~у́ют

2. **-и-** conjugation

(a)	**говор|и́ть**	~ю́	~и́шь	~и́т	~и́м	~и́те	~я́т
(b)	**стро́|ить**	~ю	~ишь	~ит	~им	~ите	~ят

Notes

1. Also belonging to the **-е-** conjugation are:

i) most other verbs in **-ать** (but see Note 2(v) below), e.g. **жа́ждать** (жа́жду, -ждешь); **пря́тать** (пря́чу, -чешь), **колеба́ть** (коле́блю, -блешь).

ii) verbs in **-еть** for which the 1st pers sing **-ею** is given, e.g. **жале́ть.**

iii) verbs in **-нуть** for which the 1st pers sing **-ну** is given (e.g. **вя́нуть**), **ю** becoming **у** in the 1st pers sing and 3rd pers pl.

iv) verbs in **-ять** which drop the **я** in conjugation, e.g. **ла́ять** (ла́ю, ла́ешь); **се́ять** (се́ю, се́ешь).

2. Also belonging to the **-и-** conjugation are:

i) verbs in consonant + **-ить** which change the consonant in the first person singular, e.g. **досади́ть** (-ажу́, -ади́шь), or insert an **-л-**, e.g. **доба́вить** (доба́влю, -вишь).

ii) other verbs in vowel + **-ить**, e.g. **затаи́ть, кле́ить** (as 2b above).

iii) verbs in **-еть** for which the 1st pers sing is given as consonant + **ю** or **у**, e.g. **звене́ть** (-ню́, -ни́шь), **ви́деть** (ви́жу, ви́дишь).

iv) two verbs in **-ять (стоя́ть, боя́ться).**

v) verbs in **-ать** whose stem ends in **ч, ж, щ,** or **ш,** not changing between the infinitive and conjugation, e.g. **крича́ть** (-чу́, -чи́шь). Cf. Note 1(i).

Key to the Russian Alphabet

Capital	*Lower-case*	*Approx. English Sound*
А	а	a
Б	б	b
В	в	v
Г	г	g
Д	д	d
Е	е	ye
Ё	ё	yo
Ж	ж	zh (as in mea*s*ure)
З	з	z
И	и	i
Й	й	y
К	к	k
Л	л	l
М	м	m
Н	н	n
О	о	o
П	п	p
Р	р	r
С	с	s
Т	т	t
У	у	oo
Ф	ф	f
Х	х	kh (as in lo*ch*)
Ц	ц	ts
Ч	ч	ch
Ш	ш	sh
Щ	щ	shch
Ъ	ъ	″ ('hard sign'; not pronounced as separate sound)
Ы	ы	y
Ь	ь	′ ('soft sign'; not pronounced as separate sound)
Э	э	e
Ю	ю	yu
Я	я	ya